BRITAIN IN EUROPE

CAMBRIDGE
UNIVERSITY PRESS
LONDON: BENTLEY HOUSE
NEW YORK, TORONTO, BOMBAY
CALCUTTA, MADRAS: MACMILLAN
TOKIO: MARUZEN COMPANY LTD

BRITAIN IN EUROPE

1789–1914

A SURVEY OF FOREIGN POLICY

BY

R. W. SETON-WATSON

D.Litt., Ph.D., F.B.A.

*Masaryk Professor of Central European History
in the University of London*

*Men ought not to suffer from disenchantment: they ought
to know that ideals in politics are never realised.*
W. E. GLADSTONE (1891)

*It is not wise to believe that in so small a house as Europe
it is possible to have differing conceptions of right.*
ADOLF HITLER (7 March 1936)

CAMBRIDGE

AT THE UNIVERSITY PRESS

1938

First Edition 1937
Reprinted 1938

PRINTED IN GREAT BRITAIN

PREFACE

The present volume is essentially an experiment, and is laid before the public with some diffidence: it originated in its author's own need for a clear and connected survey of the main problems into which British policy resolved itself during the last century and a half. It lays no claim to originality, much less to finality: in order to qualify fully for the task here set, it would be necessary to spend thirty years digging in the Record Office and other mines of diplomatic lore. The most that can be said of it is that it is the first full and connected narrative, by a single writer, of British policy, as distinct from general European diplomacy; and that it takes fuller account of Continental sources than is usually the case in English historical writings.

No country can compete with our own in political biography, and there is practically no statesman, even of the second rank, in British public life during the last 100 years, who has not been made the subject of a two-volume "Life". But, with the very rarest exceptions, such books are based almost exclusively on the private papers of the individual in question, and degenerate, whenever he leaves office, into mere reminiscence or social gossip: and little or no attempt is made to collate these papers with similar collections either at home or abroad. And thus, incredible as it may seem, that invaluable enterprise, the *Cambridge History of British Foreign Policy*, when it appeared in 1920, was performing the functions of a pioneer, cutting his way through virgin forest. It would be most unfair to accuse earlier writers, such as Sir Spencer Walpole or Mr Herbert Paul, of neglecting foreign affairs: but what they had to say on the subject was almost always incidental, lacked any real documentary basis, and betrayed an essentially insular outlook. Professors Webster and Temperley set an altogether new standard by their monographs on Castlereagh and Canning, and the contrast between Professor H. C. F. Bell's recent life of Palmerston, and the amateur, though still enlightening, biographies of Bulwer and Ashley, is the measure of the progress achieved. But it seemed to me that the time was long overdue for a general survey, embodying the main results of recent scholarship over a longer period. It would, however, be more than ungracious on my part to miss this opportunity of acknowledging my debt to such recent writers as Mr E. L. Woodward, Mr Kingsley Martin, Mr Algernon Cecil and Miss Alicia Ramsay (to mention only a very few), whose merit consists not so much in filling in the gaps of documentary evidence as in providing a new perspective and a new interpretation.

The study of foreign policy has been transformed since the War by the publication of enormous masses of diplomatic material in most European countries: and though this has of course greatly increased the amount of the historian's reading, it has undoubtedly given him certain advantages as against any of his fellow-craftsmen in all previous eras, whilst the advance in bibliographical method has reduced the danger of his overlooking essential material.

It should be explained that this volume, as originally planned, was to have been limited to the period from 1822 to 1874—the Eastern crisis of the 'seventies being reserved for detailed treatment. In actual fact *Britain in Europe* had to be laid aside unfinished, while *Disraeli, Gladstone and the Eastern Question* (Macmillan, 1935) was being completed. But when the work was resumed, it soon became clear that my main object would be defeated unless both a prologue and an epilogue could be added—if only for the reason that some of the most essential threads of our policy during the Early and Mid-Victorian Era are closely interwoven with the period of Pitt and Castlereagh, and continue to form the pattern of the more democratic era which the Midlothian Campaign may be said to have ushered in. As author I am the last person qualified to decide whether the method employed is a sound one: but I would ask the reader to bear in mind that Prologue and Epilogue are deliberately planned on a smaller scale than the rest of the book.

R. W. SETON-WATSON

6 *April* 1937

CONTENTS

CONTENTS

England has saved herself by her exertions, and will, as I trust, save Europe by her example. WILLIAM PITT (1805)

Leur histoire est pleine de ces alternatives d'une indifférence qui fait croire à leur décadence, et d'un emportement qui déconcerte leurs ennemis. On les voit tour à tour abandonner l'Europe et la commander, négliger les plus grandes affaires du Continent et prétendre diriger jusqu'aux plus petites, passer de la paix quand'même à la guerre à outrance.

ALBERT SOREL, *L'Europe et la Révolution*

So long as the power and advice of England are felt in the councils of Europe, peace, I believe, will be maintained, and for a long period. Without their presence war...seems to me inevitable. DISRAELI at the Guildhall (1879)

PROLOGUE

THE GENESIS OF OUR FOREIGN POLICY

POLICY IN EMBRYO

One of our greatest Foreign Secretaries once admitted to one of our greatest ambassadors, that "logic is of no use in diplomacy": and Sir Edward Grey, the most transparently, disarmingly honest holder of that office, has committed himself, at the beginning of his memoirs, to the belief that "British Foreign Ministers have been guided by what seemed to them to be the immediate interest of this country, without making elaborate calculations for the future". By way of contrast, large sections of continental opinion are profoundly persuaded that "Perfide Albion" has for generations pursued a deep-laid and consistent policy of calculated interest and of sheer aggrandisement.

The first of these views is doubtless nearer to the truth than the second: yet it is undoubtedly possible to detect certain persistent tendencies in British foreign policy, dating at least as far back as Tudor days. It is already a commonplace to affirm that Wolsey, by his somewhat abrupt transfer of England's friendship, laid the foundations of that principle of the Balance of Power which was to form a main clue to European policy for four centuries, and which seems once more to be emerging from the eclipse which it had suffered after the Great War. Wolsey is often described as England's first great Foreign Minister: before him policy was predominantly dynastic rather than national. The final loss of England's continental possessions, the profound changes wrought by the Reformation, and the union of the English and Scottish crowns, gradually transformed the problem of national defence in these islands, and stimulated that movement of overseas expansion for which the Elizabethan seamen had prepared the way. It is of course true that yet other causes were at work. The decay of the Hansa power, from which England and Holland were to reap the main profit, was accelerated by the Turkish conquests and the consequent ruin of the medieval trade routes from Europe into Asia. The discovery of America, the Cape, and Cape Horn, opened up new worlds of fabulous wealth and opportunity in place of those which were being lost.

In the sixteenth century the fear inspired by the threatened world
dominion of the Habsburgs went hand in hand with a struggle of the
"new religion" against the Counter-Reformation, and with a challenge to the
economic exclusivism asserted by Spain in the New World. Under Mary
Tudor there was a violent movement of the tiller in favour of a Spanish
Alliance which might well have assured to Spain the hegemony of Europe,
and simultaneously in favour of a return to Catholicism. But this proved to be
a mere passing interlude of five years. Queen Elizabeth shook herself free
from both these entanglements, and in a reign of forty years steered her way
through the shoals of European policy by a rare combination of inaction,
prevarication, diplomatic skill and consummate espionage. She had gained
the necessary breathing-space for England, and though the foreign policy
of James I was weak and inglorious—involving subservience to Spain and
in effect, despite all verbal sympathy, a betrayal of the Protestant cause—
the real danger was already a thing of the past. It is not too much to say
that under James I and Charles I England sank to the level of a third-rate
Power in Europe: it could not even defend its coasts from Barbary corsairs.
While Richelieu played his pawns in the great game of war that for thirty
years devastated Europe, Charles was of no account in continental affairs,
and of course during the closing years of the German struggle England was
absorbed in its own civil strife. Not that English initiative had vanished
from the world. On the contrary, the first half of the seventeenth century
marks the beginnings of colonial settlement in America, and the development of commercial enterprise through the three great corporations, the
East India, the Levant and the Russia Companies. Out of the grudging and
prohibitionist outlook which still dominated foreign trade arose a succession
of quarrels with Holland, which made an unnatural breach in the forces of
northern Protestantism. Looked at from another aspect, the three Dutch
Wars, which two generations earlier might have proved suicidal, did less
damage than might have been expected, in that the disproportion between
the strength and resources of Spain and England diminished decade by
decade.

In foreign policy the Commonwealth was a brief interlude of glory between two periods of eclipse. To-day we can see clearly enough that
Cromwell attached an exaggerated value to Protestantism as an instrument
of policy; but if his various dealings with Sweden are open to criticism, he
was far more alive than most of his contemporaries to the folly of quarrelling
with Holland, though he did not foresee the events which were to drive the
two countries into alliance a generation later. His efforts to hold aloof from
the Franco-Spanish rivalry of his day proved in the end impossible—partly,
no doubt, for reasons which in another garb might well have appealed to

Palmerston. His conditions for co-operation with Spain were that British subjects should be free from the control of the Inquisition and free to sail to the West Indies: and here, in the words of the Spanish Ambassador, he was "asking for the King of Spain's two eyes". His alliance with France, with its romantic episode of Cromwellian Ironsides and the great Turenne fighting side by side at Dunkirk, was the first real forerunner of the periodic *Ententes Cordiales* of modern times: that it was afterwards abandoned was the inevitable result of Louis XIV's arrogant and soaring ambition. Another enduring result of the Cromwellian interlude was the appearance of the British fleet as a prime factor in the Mediterranean. In the words of Andrew Marvell, the Protector "once more joined us to the Continent". The greatness of the man emerges from the contrast between his own French policy and that of the Restoration period, in which Charles II became the dependant, and even the pensionary, of his cousin Louis. Of James II it will suffice to say that his outlook upon Europe was as disastrous as his attitude towards the British Constitution. But with the accession of William III a new era opened, in which for the first time our foreign policy was in the hands of a far-sighted statesman who possessed the continental outlook and was fully versed in all the rival currents in the Europe of his day. There is much to be said for the Whig theory, that foreign policy, in any modern sense of the term, begins with William III.

THE SETTLEMENT OF UTRECHT

As Spain and Habsburg declined, France and Bourbon grew mightily in strength, and at length it required the joint efforts of England and Holland, supported by the Emperor as male heir to the Spanish Habsburgs, to prevent the establishment of a French hegemony in Europe. Once again Britain turned the scale of war: yet no sooner was the danger averted than her policy swerved dangerously, and she resumed an attitude of reserve and isolation corresponding to her geographical position. This significant attitude—which was not merely assumed once in 1713, but repeated in varying forms in 1763, in 1802, in 1815, and last, but not least, in 1920 and in 1934–6—can hardly be explained by failure to grasp the issues involved, but may rather be due to some deep-lying instinct that opposes the supremacy of any one Power, but is acutely anxious to avoid substituting the supremacy of an ally.

There can be no question of analysing here the complicated issues of the War of Spanish Succession, in which Britain's position as a World Power of the first order is established no longer as a passing phenomenon, but as a permanent factor in the calculations of all Europe. The settlement reached

at Utrecht in 1713 has from that day to this been open to severe criticism
—at first because it was unfortunately, though perhaps inevitably, tied up
with the party feud between Whig and Tory, but also because with the
passage of time Britain's attitude on that occasion remained a test case on
the delicate problem of alliances, their duration and the limits of their
obligation. There were those who regarded the Treaty of Utrecht—concluded without the Emperor, on whose behalf and in close alliance with
whom the long war had been waged—as a signal revelation of the methods
of "Perfide Albion". To this the best, and indeed the only adequate,
rejoinder is that the terms eventually secured coincided in the main with
the aims originally laid down by the Grand Alliance. If the Balance of
Power had demanded that France and Spain should not have one and the
same monarch, it seemed to follow logically that a similar objection applied
to Charles VI uniting the Spanish and Austrian possessions of the House of
Habsburg.

Whatever may be the verdict on this vexed question, there can be no
doubt that the settlement of 1713 laid the necessary foundations for a new
era of British maritime expansion. The retention of Gibraltar and the temporary acquisition of Minorca secured Britain's access to the Mediterranean
and placed a definite handicap upon Spain: while the demolition of Dunkirk, the transfer of the Spanish Netherlands to the sovereignty of Vienna,
and the series of Barrier Treaties, relieved her of that menace to the independence of the Low Countries and to the freedom of the narrow seas
which had provided the motive power of her resistance to Louis XIV. For
a short time it seemed as though the Whigs were about to reconstitute the
Grand Alliance; but Stanhope's peace policy prevailed, and the understanding which he reached with Dubois and the French Regency—resting
no doubt as yet upon the will of a small group of statesmen rather than upon
any real popular sentiment—was perpetuated by Walpole and Fleury, and
secured to Britain a long period of recuperation and growth, during which
she could aspire to be the arbiter of Europe, and, with Nova Scotia and
Newfoundland added to her other American colonies, could husband her
resources for a later expansion. Meanwhile the accident of a foreign king,
ignorant of English, partly resident abroad, and inevitably dependent upon
his ministers, strengthened the tendency already noticeable under an
amiable but mediocre woman sovereign. The growth of Cabinet Government and the deliberate reliance of the Premier upon parliamentary support, and hence upon opinion in the country—already quite vocal, even if
more fitful, passionate and restricted in its range, than in the age of the
popular press—tended to limit the control of the Crown over foreign policy,
at any rate in actual practice. To-day no one would dare to challenge the

superlative merits of Stanhope and Walpole as formative forces in the whole domain of British foreign policy.*

Despite, however, the genuinely pacific tendencies of Walpole and Fleury, "the alliance had not sunk deeply into the soil": crude nationalist animosities inspired the bulk of the nation alike against France and Spain, and the incident of the corsair Jenkins and his ear illustrates the predatory sentiments and interests which at almost any moment during the eighteenth century might tear the delicate woof of policy and drive even the most conciliatory statesman into war.

The Seven Years' War

At the very moment when Walpole found himself forced, against his better judgement, into a resumption of the continental struggle—in the first instance through war with Spain—two dynastic changes occurred which proved to be the signal for an almost complete reorientation of European politics.[1] The Emperor Charles VI was succeeded by an only daughter, whose rights he had sought to secure by a long series of negotiations with the Powers: and the shameless manner in which most of them hastened to fling all obligations to the winds and scramble for the loot, is indeed worthy of a century whose diplomatic perfidy culminated in the Polish partitions. Meanwhile Frederick William I of Prussia was succeeded by a son whom he had long regarded with aversion and contempt, and who behind the screen of musical and literary dilettantism concealed an iron will and a ruthless ambition which, when opportunity presented itself, took all his contemporaries by surprise. Frederick the Great's seizure of Silesia inaugurated that long rivalry of Prussia and Austria for hegemony in the German lands, which was decided in 1866 by the latter's simultaneous exclusion from Germany and Italy. In the War of Austrian Succession British subsidies to Maria Theresa played their part, but there was already a marked cooling in the old alliance of Vienna and London, in proportion as it became obvious that the sort of ally whom Austria above all needed was one with a large land army, and that Britain not merely did not meet this requirement, but was herself mainly interested in continental operations as diverting her Western enemies from the colonial field. The Peace of Aix-la-Chapelle (1748), due on our side to Newcastle's failure to hold together the continental coalition, brought no very precise gains for England, but she had more than held her own on the sea, and Jacobite designs

* See the standard works of Prof. Vaucher on Walpole and of Prof. Basil Williams on Stanhope. The late Mr F. S. Oliver's study of Walpole—*The Endless Adventure*—is written with great charm and originality, but is highly contentious both as to its real subject and still more as to the modern conclusions to be drawn from it.

had received a blow from which they never recovered. Dettingen and Fontenoy represented, as it were, the least common factor between opposition to the Stuarts and the defence of the Electorate of Hanover.

Henceforward Prince Kaunitz continued to urge upon Maria Theresa the desirability of an understanding with France, and indeed spent some years as Ambassador in Paris, in order to prepare it. The breach between Vienna and Berlin was by now irreparable, and Kaunitz would certainly have endorsed the remark of Frederick, that the two could no more mingle than fire and water. And meanwhile there was a parallel growth of Anglo-French rivalry in the colonial sphere, and a never-ending series of incidents. On all sides there was almost equal insincerity, Austria finding no use for British help save as a means of recovering Silesia, while Britain once more calculated that Austria would keep the French involved in a formidable land war and thus handicap their efforts overseas. And so it came to the famous "Reversal of Alliances", in 1755–6, when the two protagonists on the Continent, like Hamlet and Laertes, changed weapons and fought on. Frederick on his part dropped the French for the British alliance, and in the negotiations leading to the Treaty of Westminster obtained more than he had at first hoped for. Austria, on the other hand, now finally convinced that British aid could not bring back Silesia, abandoned her traditional ally of three generations and leagued herself with France. The Seven Years' War, which was the immediate consequence, bore from the very first a double character, and indeed consisted of two quite distinct, though parallel, wars, with two sets of aims which had little or no relation to each other. Austria still pursued the fixed idea of recovering Silesia and reducing Prussia to her former insignificance, France was bent upon arresting British maritime and colonial expansion: *per contra*, Frederick, steeled by the prospect of Austro-Russian co-operation, was resolved to hold the plunder of his earlier wars, and to establish Prussia as the leading Power of northern Europe, while Britain, inspired by the commanding genius of the "Great Commoner", pursued a policy of undisguised aggression in every quarter of the globe—prompted, it is necessary to add, by a natural desire to forestall similar French designs of invasion and conquest. After "three years of almost uninterrupted victory", for which Lecky saw no parallel since the days of Henry V, Pitt had ended all prospect of French dominion over India, had conquered Canada and burst the strategic chain which France had established from the Mississipi to the Great Lakes, and so had opened up to the New England colonies a path of almost indefinite expansion westwards. Needless to say, this could not have been done without Pitt's parallel insistence upon Mediterranean sea power and continental subsidies. If ever there was a situation in which the European and overseas issues were linked together, it was that which arose during the Seven Years' War, and which prompted Pitt himself to declare that "Hanover ought to be as dear to us as Hampshire, and that he would conquer America in Germany". To-day some of those who are most intent upon the Imperial issue are blind to the lessons which the elder Pitt's experience supplies.

FROM THE ELDER TO THE YOUNGER PITT

The Peace of Paris will remain to all time as one of the most splendid results of the old system of aggression and conquest. That its terms were less vindictive than Pitt himself would have made them—that certain conquests which could have been retained were handed back, and that his extreme notions of commercial policy, such as a monopoly in the slave trade, or in sugar, were not put into practice—is interpreted, in our more sentimental age, as an extenuating circumstance. Unhappily there is a less creditable explanation: for the peace was forced through "by corruption and intimidation of the worst kind",[2] the attitude of George III and his subservient placemen towards Pitt, as the organiser of victory, being far more discreditable than that of Queen Anne's Tory Ministers towards Marlborough at the Peace of Utrecht. As Mr Trevelyan has pointed out, the appeal to patriotism—despite the high sentiment in the country—was not one by which the elder Pitt could maintain his hold upon Parliament, and he "had to make terms with the arch-corruptionist Newcastle before he was permitted to win the Seven Years' War for England".[3]

The enduring stain upon the settlement of 1763, as upon that of 1713, is that Britain concluded a separate peace without consulting the allies whom she was pledged to consult. That "circumstances alter cases", and that in this case the whole situation in Europe had been completely transformed by the death of the Empress Elizabeth and the consequent defection of Russia from the coalition against Frederick, is a fact which the casuist can cite, but which the moralist must dismiss as irrelevant.* It is, of course, notorious that Frederick's whole policy rested upon breaches of plighted faith and sudden acts of aggression, that he was now hoist with his own petard by the loss of his principal ally, and that the sudden accession of his devoted admirer Peter III was a stroke of good fortune which saved him from ruin. But this cannot alter the essential accuracy of Macaulay's view, stated, no doubt, with his usual overemphasis: "The policy then followed inspired Frederick with an unjust, but deep and bitter aversion to the English name.

* For instance, Sir A. Ward pleads "the complete change of the circumstances from those in which her (Britain's) alliance with him (Frederick) had been concluded" (*C.H.F.P.* 1, 126).

...To that policy it was owing that, some years later, England could not find on the whole Continent a single ally to stand by her, in her extreme need, against the House of Bourbon. To that policy it was owing that Frederick, alienated from England, was compelled to connect himself closely, during his later years, with Russia, and was induced to assist in that great crime, the fruitful parent of other great crimes, the first partition of Poland." If the latter phrase requires considerable qualification, it is certain that Britain's abandonment of Prussia confirmed the Continent in its belief in British inconstancy and perfidy, and the indignant protests which it aroused in many quarters, being in their turn savagely overstated by such men as Wilkes, only increased that other impression, so long rife upon the Continent and not yet extinguished, that the variable character of parliamentary government—in Pitt's day still determined by a narrow and factious oligarchy—rendered impossible a sustained and consistent foreign policy on the part of Britain. "The late frequent changes in England", wrote Sir Andrew Mitchell (our Minister to Prussia for most of the war and long after, and a man versed in all continental problems), "have created a degree of diffidence in foreign Powers, which renders all negotiations with them difficult and disagreeable."

These strictures cannot of course alter the decisive fact of Britain's assertion of naval and commercial supremacy, bringing in its train the conquest of India and the substitution of Anglo-Celtic for Latin rule in North America. But her triumphant efforts under the elder Pitt were followed by a period of humiliating decline, during which the perverse and obstinate King set himself to re-establish personal government at home, undermined the good relations between motherland and colonies which Pitt had built up, and left Britain without an ally on the European Continent. The quarrel with America culminated in open war, in which France and Spain aided and abetted the rebels, and Britain did not scruple to place wholesale orders in human flesh with the petty princes of Germany, that these slaves in uniform might impose upon America the despotism of which they were the victims in their own homes. Once more the interdependence of European and overseas development was strikingly illustrated: and despite the diversions caused in Europe by varying projects for the destruction of Poland and of Turkey, Britain found herself confronted by something not very far removed from a world coalition. The Bourbon "Family Compact" had united France and Spain against her, while Russia, Prussia, Holland and Scandinavia formed an "armed neutrality of the North", in self-defence against our attitude towards neutral trading on the high seas. The war ended quite inevitably in American independence: that for Britain the disaster was strictly limited to a single field of operations, was due to the greatness of her naval commanders and to the skill and endurance of those who directed on the spot the civil administration of India and Canada. Never has the importance of sea power been more signally demonstrated than in the years leading to the peace of 1782.

American independence is the end of an era, and to those who could not read the future it must have seemed to oppose a fatal obstacle to the "Expansion of England". But it is also the beginning of another era of still greater expansive energy, a transitional era which has been fitly named that of the Second British Empire, preparatory to the crowning experiment of the Third British Empire, transformed into a free commonwealth of nations, whose fate is still in the balance.

It is unnecessary to insist upon the role of George III in upholding and deepening the quarrel with the American colonies, and at the same time in keeping at arm's length the only statesman who might have proved capable of achieving a compromise. Chatham's memorable protest in the House of Lords only served to illuminate the hopelessness and folly of his opponents: it was the voice of the future, and the King's failure in foreign policy was the death-knell of the last experiment in personal government from which these realms have suffered. George III soon found it necessary, and even convenient, to accept the Great Commoner's son as Prime Minister of an administration that lasted longer, and concentrated more power in its head, than any of its successors.

Pitt's access to power had been preceded in 1782 by a rearrangement of the now unworkable system of three Secretaryships of State: and henceforth the Foreign Office more and more acquired that position which was essential if our relations with foreign Powers were to be placed upon a proper footing. It is true that at first the two new Secretaries of Foreign and of Home Affairs were at daggers drawn and sent each their plenipotentiary to Paris for the negotiation of peace.[4] But this was the last flicker of a dying regime, and henceforward the triple control of foreign affairs by Crown, Premier and Foreign Secretary becomes a reality.

ISOLATION AND NEUTRALITY

In the opening years of Pitt's administration Britain found herself again entirely isolated in Europe, and he followed a policy of wary reserve, avoiding all entanglements, while, in constant contrast to the *ancien régime* in France, he addressed himself to far-reaching financial reform and thus nourished the sinews of future naval war. While Lord Carmarthen* remained Foreign Secretary, the real direction of policy was much more in

* Afterwards Duke of Leeds.

the hands of Pitt himself, but our diplomatists abroad were to a singular degree kept without instructions, and the main tendency of their chief seems to have been to gain time and avoid commitments, to consider a problem not on its merits, but on purely opportunist grounds. And isolation had this merit, that it left Britain a quite unusual freedom of choice, though it is true that even the efforts of so able a diplomatist as Sir James Harris did not at first avail to reassert Britain's lost influence at The Hague, while neither the dying Frederick nor Joseph II, now at the zenith of his power, had any confidence whatsoever in British recovery. The re-establishment of closer relations between Britain and Prussia was retarded not only by the existence of an anti-British party, but also by a succession of fantastic projects of wholesale territorial readjustment propounded by her Foreign Minister Hertzberg. None the less, after the old King's death, it came in 1788 to an Anglo-Prussian alliance, with the defence of Holland as one of its main objects—Harris arguing that "if we lost the Netherlands, France will acquire what she has always considered as the climax of her power", and here success was in no small degree due to the blunders of French diplomacy. This coincided with a renewed effort on the part of Austria and Russia to partition the Turkish Empire: but not merely did the Turks display quite unsuspected powers of resistance, but Joseph found himself simultaneously exposed to dangerous discontent in Hungary, open rebellion in the Austrian Netherlands, and the massing of the Prussian army on his northern border. Thus Britain became for the moment the potential ally of Prussia against the House of Habsburg, and may perhaps be said to have indirectly contributed towards a shifting of forces in Europe which made of Poland rather than Turkey the principal victim. Certainly Pitt was definitely hostile to Russian designs against Turkey, but by his very insistence increased the disposition of Catherine to follow a line of lesser resistance, and to fall in with Prussia's unholy designs for a fresh Polish partition. Meanwhile he submitted to a somewhat effaced role during the troubles in Holland, and continued to play a waiting game. Peace, always a foremost British interest, he felt to be, in the circumstances of those days, a paramount necessity.

It was at a moment when all these sinister designs were ripening, that the whole European situation was transformed by the French Revolution and its external repercussions. There is no little irony in the fact that Pitt, in the first decade of his career, asked nothing better than a friendly *entente* with France, and in the belief that it would not merely benefit both nations, but ensure a general European peace, concluded in 1786 a commercial treaty of great liberality for that "mercantile" age. If he failed to foresee the true significance of what was happening in Paris, his failure was shared by all the most responsible statesmen of Europe, who in the year following the fall of the Bastille repeated in a variety of forms the phrase of William Eden, that France was "no longer an object of alarm", and assumed that the Revolution would effectually prevent her intervention in the main issues of continental policy. Pitt did not share Fox's unmeasured enthusiasm, and never committed himself to the invective of Burke, but even after the Bastille had fallen he assured the French Government of his desire "to cultivate and promote that friendship and harmony which so happily subsists between the two countries": and a year later in the House of Commons he foretold that "the present convulsions of France must sooner or later terminate in general harmony and regular order.... France will stand forth as one of the most brilliant Powers in Europe: she will enjoy just that kind of liberty which I venerate, and the valuable existence of which it is my duty, as an Englishman, peculiarly to cherish."[5] He was doubtless right as to the ultimate issue in France, just as he was right in denying "that any nation could be unalterably the enemy of another": but he did not foresee that the goal would only be reached through a sea of blood.

In the first instance, to the general surprise of the Continent, Britain did not take advantage of France's internal disorders to declare war: she was indeed the last of the Great Powers to intervene in a military sense, remaining a spectator to the last possible moment, and perhaps beyond. In other directions her whole weight was thrown into the scale of appeasement. When Joseph II died and his sagacious but unhappily short-lived brother Leopold II made immediate overtures for a renewal of the ancient friendship of Austria and Britain, Pitt set himself to hold back Prussia from an invasion of Habsburg territory, to which she was tempted by the acute unrest in Hungary, and by Joseph's reverses at the hands of the Turks. He also opposed Russia's territorial demands against Turkey, and thus the relatively unimportant question of the fortress of Ochakov may be said to have inaugurated a policy in the Near East, which eventually led to the full-blooded Russophobia of Palmerston and Disraeli. The result was that Britain faded out of the alliance with Prussia, and that the three Northern Courts acted more and more without her. The menacing turn which French affairs were now taking forced Austria and Prussia to suspend their rivalry and combine in defence of monarchical principles: but throughout all the complications that ensued they and their Russian ally were almost equally absorbed by the Polish crisis, and while calculating that intervention on behalf of Louis XVI might bring them advantages at the expense of France, were simultaneously bent on wrecking Poland's tardy efforts at reform and each securing the largest possible share of the booty. Thus the Second Partition of Poland was signed within a few days of the execution of Louis

—a fact far more sinister, but less emphasised, than the appeal of the French *émigrés* on the Rhine for foreign aid, which first revealed the full explosive force of the Revolution. To the last Pitt and his advisers assumed that a German army would occupy Paris, and held themselves in reserve for a mediatory role: unlike Burke, they do not seem to have foreseen the downfall of the monarchy, or the imminent danger to the Low Countries, whose absorption by France Pitt had unswervingly declared to be a *casus belli* for Britain.[6] How utterly mistaken Pitt was in the calculations on which his own financial and foreign policy rested is shown by his speech of 17 February 1792, when he declared that "unquestionably there never was a time in the history of this country when from the situation of Europe we might more reasonably expect fifteen years of peace, than we may at the present moment".

During 1792 the situation grew steadily worse, and the September Massacres reacted strongly upon public opinion in England: to the deep disillusionment among many who had at first welcomed the fall of the old regime in Paris was now added the fear of infection from the new ideas, and a tendency towards repressive measures which was to set back the cause of political reform for forty years. And meanwhile, across the Channel, the desperation of the ragged revolutionary armies before Valmy was replaced by elation and boundless self-confidence; and it was believed that the patriots of all countries were waiting to rise against their monarchs, and would combine with the new France to "give liberty to Europe and peace to the world". Even in this situation, while France, who in May had solemnly rejected "all ideas of aggrandisement", was overrunning Belgium and threatening Holland, Pitt and his cousin Grenville shrank from the arbitrament of war, and were ready not merely to negotiate with France, but to recognise the new form of government in return for the abandonment of recent conquests and for the "giving in some public and unequivocal manner a pledge of their intention no longer to foment troubles or to excite disturbances against other Governments". This condition, which has a strangely modern ring, never had the slightest prospect of being accepted by a Government which openly invited the English republicans to rise, and threatened "a descent on the island" and the planting of the sacred tree of liberty on English soil. Yet even George III was anxious to avoid war long after his fellow-sovereign had become a helpless prisoner: while Henry Dundas, the most powerful influence upon the two ruling ministers, steadily opposed war, arguing that "the strength of our cause consists in maintaining that we have nothing to do with the internal politics of foreign nations".[7] History knows no more cruel irony than the fact that Pitt was essentially a peace minister, forced against his will to give the lead in one of the greatest of all wars, and that despite all his courage, endurance and self-sacrifice, he had—in the words of our leading authority upon him and upon Napoleon— "no knowledge either of continental peoples or their policies".* What finally turned the scale of war was not the execution of King Louis—though that rallied the great mass of British opinion behind the Government—but the French conquest of the Low Countries, with its open threat of further aggression. But already on the day before the British Parliament protested against the execution of Louis XVI as "an outrage on religion, justice and humanity" and voted an increase of armaments, Danton had bidden the Convention "fling down the head of a King as gage of battle". A day later war was declared upon Britain and Holland, and we had no choice but to accept the challenge.

PITT AND THE REVOLUTION

We are not here concerned to give even the barest outline of the long struggle with revolutionary and Napoleonic France into which Britain now found herself plunged: but it was essential to stress the extreme forbearance, not to say reluctance, with which her statesmen entered the arena, following upon a period of unquestioned eagerness for peace and reconciliation with their old enemy. These events offer a key to British psychology which has in no way lost its value after the lapse of a century and a half. They show that a blend of hesitation, detachment and ignorance do not necessarily spell degeneracy, and that the very men who showed such extreme reluctance to take the fateful plunge could develop a stubborn staying power, an elasticity of resistance, such as outweighed countless blunders and miscalculations and simply refused to accept failure.

Once involved in war, Pitt used those financial resources which he had so jealously built up in the years of peace, to maintain or strengthen British naval supremacy and to organise the resistance of the continental Powers by a system of subsidies. The Convention, in its frenzy, denounced Pitt as an enemy of the human race, and the mob blamed him for the shortage of bread in France. Unhappily his war plans speedily resulted in a succession of failures: it was not Pitt, but Carnot, who won the title of "organiser of victory". The reactionary émigré leaders were a grave handicap to the common cause; the Toulon adventure had to be abandoned and only roused France to fresh exertions; while Pitt's West Indian expedition, modelled on the altogether different circumstances of the Seven Years' War, drained

---

* *C.H.F.P.* p. 219. Sorel's considered verdict on Pitt is that "no statesman was ever more exclusively English or showed less taste for continental affairs" (*L'Europe et la Révolution Française*, 1, 349).

away forces which might have been used in Europe with far greater effect. Austria under Thugut evacuated Belgium and sought an easy indemnity in Poland, calculating the while that at the final peace Britain would have to "buy back" Austria's lost provinces by the sacrifice of her own overseas conquests, as in 1748. Thus there was from the outset a dry-rot in the Grand Alliance, torn by divergent aims and dynastic appetites. Early in 1795, by the Treaty of Basel, France detached the ever unstable King of Prussia; Holland was overrun by French armies, and Britain, lacking the military force to prevent or undo the accomplished fact, had to reckon, for the rest of the war, with her deadliest enemy entrenched along the whole North Sea coast and controlling the mouths of the Rhine and Scheldt. Faced by the desertion of his allies, Pitt twice made overtures for peace during 1796, thereby again proving his pacific outlook, but only convincing the French that their enemies were finally on the run. Steering a middle course between the Jacobin sympathies of Charles James Fox and the thunderous eloquence of Burke's *Letters on a Regicide Peace*, he was not prepared to accept the only terms which the revolutionary government would have considered. "Wholly unprepared," writes Dr Holland Rose, "Great Britain was engaged in a struggle of unsuspected magnitude and duration. Her methods were therefore empirical, her warfare tentative, her blunders colossal. Trusting inevitably to her allies, she saw them falter or fall away, a prey to the jealousies necessarily aroused by her policy of limited largesse on land and unlimited acquisitions at sea. Critics from among his own supporters could, therefore, claim that his war policy was a failure when judged by his own standard."[8] By the winter of 1796 Britain had not only failed to save Holland, but was at war with Spain: she "stood on the defensive in Europe in order to guard and strengthen her colonial Empire. She abandoned Corsica and Elba: she withdrew her fleet from the Mediterranean, so that Ireland might be screened from attack."[9]

In 1797 there was less hope of peace than ever. Austria, brought to her knees by Bonaparte's sensational Italian victories, followed Prussia's example and allowed herself to be hectored and bought off at Campoformio by the substantial bribe of Venice and Dalmatia. Left alone, Pitt and Grenville were eager for peace, and did not reject offhand the fantastic idea of bribing the French Directory. The victory of Cape St Vincent reaffirmed British predominance at sea, but it was soon followed by the mutiny at Spithead, one of the most dangerous incidents in all our history, due to the inhumanity and corruption of the navy's civil administrators. Professor Trevelyan, while not attempting to conceal the blunders of Pitt's diplomacy, touches the heart of the whole matter when he affirms that "in this evil hour", when England's prestige was again very low and there seemed to be a real danger of the Continent uniting for her destruction, "she was saved by the high quality of Pitt's courage and by his instinct for naval affairs".[10] For the time being, however, everything combined to force upon Pitt a policy that was essentially negative: but if in his attitude to Europe he was still "fain to plod along in the old paths and use the nation's wealth, not its manhood",[11] he now did much for that urgent reform of the navy without which final victory could not have been attained. Meanwhile he reminded Parliament that the aim of revolutionary France was "the annihilation of British liberty and the obliteration of everything that has rendered you a great, a flourishing and a happy people".[12] He expressed his "impatience for the hour of peace", but insisted that "should peace be proclaimed without security, you may indeed have a peace that is nominal and delusive".[13]

The *coup d'état* of Fructidor (4 September 1797) marked a new stage in the struggle: for the Terror had already "devoured its children", and now the victor of Italy returned to France, resolved to concentrate all his efforts upon the destruction of Britain. But when his inspection of the Norman coast convinced him of the obstacles to a successful invasion, his wayward genius turned suddenly to a project in which he could at one and the same time indulge his hatred of England and his dreams of Oriental triumph. In May 1798, to the no small relief of the Directory, he organised an expedition against Egypt, reminding his troops before sailing that "You are one of the wings of the Army of England", and again, that by conquering Egypt, "You will deal at England the surest and most effective blow, while waiting to give it the death-blow." He had already hoisted the French flag at Ancona and Corfu, as stepping stones towards the East, and his seizure of Malta, on the way to Egypt, was a further bid for the mastery of the Mediterranean. But Nelson was already on his heels, and though Bonaparte soon overthrew the Mamelukes and invaded Syria, the decisive Battle of the Nile cut off the French retreat by sea and rendered the ultimate failure of the Eastern adventure inevitable. Nelson and Sidney Smith, following in the footsteps of Jervis and Duncan and many others, ensured the victory of British sea power and retrieved the many failures of British diplomacy. The exploits of Alexandria and Acre also mark a new era in the development of the Eastern Question, which had for the previous century been a sort of monopoly over the ever-suspicious but allied rivals Austria and Russia. Henceforth France and Britain take an equal and growing share in every aspect of the question, and the Concert of Powers is the logical result.

During 1798–9 Britain set herself to build up the Second Coalition, but its prospects were ruined by the premature and ill-judged action of Ferdinand of Naples, and by the rigid attitude of the Emperor Francis and his able but unscrupulous minister Baron Thugut. Ere long Britain's role on land was reduced to preventing an open quarrel between her Austrian and Russian colleagues: and in the end the French resisted all efforts for the liberation of Switzerland and overran northern Italy into the bargain, while the Duke of York was completely unsuccessful in Holland and was forced to withdraw, leaving the Dutch once more at the mercy of the French. Suvorov and his contingent of Russian troops felt themselves to be abandoned by Austria, and certainly could complain of gross incompetence and even indifference in Vienna: and Tsar Paul vented his fury by a withdrawal from the coalition. Britain still held firm, and Pitt told the House of Commons that "a common feeling of danger has produced a common spirit of exertion, and we have cheerfully come forward with a surrender of part of our property, not merely for recovering ourselves, but for the general recovery of mankind". Britain, he contended, had been able "to animate the public spirit of Europe, to revive its dismayed energy and to give a turn to the political aspect of the world favourable to the cause of humanity".[14]

Britain, then, concentrated her main efforts upon control of the Mediterranean and defence of the Ottoman Porte, compelling the French to evacuate Syria and assume the defensive in Egypt. Her capture of Malta from the French in 1800 was dictated by compelling reasons of strategy, which in the changed circumstances of modern warfare are to-day fast losing their efficacy. But though its immense value at that time speedily became apparent and amply explains the prominent part which it was to play in the ensuing negotiations, its capture completed the alienation of Russia, for the personal reason that Tsar Paul was keenly interested in the fate of the Knights of St John and was even fooled by Bonaparte into believing that the island might be ceded to him. The fluctuations of Paul, as madness strengthened its hold upon him, added to the complications of the time: and though he was himself removed by assassination in March 1801, the armed neutrality of the northern Powers, which he had initiated, remained as an embarrassing legacy to his son Alexander.

The *coup d'état* of Brumaire (10 November 1799) ended the life of the Directory and left Bonaparte all-powerful as First Consul, under a new constitution well suited to the development of dictatorial power. One of his first acts was to offer terms of peace to Francis II and George III, which the two sovereigns and their ministers agreed in regarding as a mere device for separating Britain and Austria. Pitt himself was not inclined to make the restoration of the French monarchy a condition of peace, but he found that the King, Grenville, Canning and Dundas all concurred in thinking that it was "the shortest road to peace".[15] The overture was therefore rejected, and on 3 February 1800 Pitt delivered a great philippic in Parliament, recapitulating French enormities since the beginning of the war, counting up the many perfidies of "the person who is now the absolute ruler of France" —alike towards Venice, Rome, Austria, Egypt, Turkey—and refusing "to believe that the present usurpation will be more permanent than any other military despotism which has been established by the same means and with the same defiance of public opinion".[16] He refused to declare that under no circumstances would he ever treat with Bonaparte—"this last adventurer in the lottery of revolutions". But he argued that "we ought to wait for experience and the evidence of facts, before we are convinced that such a treaty is admissible". "As a sincere lover of peace, I will not sacrifice it by grasping at the shadow, when reality is not substantially within my reach. Cur igitur pacem nolo? Quia infida est, quia periculosa, quia esse non posset." In answer to the criticism of the Opposition and in particular to Tierney's demand that he should define his war aims "without his ifs and buts and special pleading ambiguity", Pitt rejoined: "In one word I can tell him that it is *Security*—security against a danger the greatest that ever threatened the world.... against a danger which has been resisted by all the nations of Europe, and resisted by none with so much success as by this nation, because by none has it been resisted so uniformly and with so much energy."[17] History can endorse the indictment of Napoleon and his predecessors, and yet admit that this haughty rejection of the profferred hand was a blunder which brought many evils in its train. It is necessary to add that Pitt and Grenville, while denouncing Napoleon's seizure of Venice, were perfectly ready to hand over the sister Republic of Genoa to Austria, and indeed to do almost anything for the sake of "strengthening that barrier which the military means and resources of Vienna can alone oppose against the future enterprises of France".[18]

This speech was Pitt's last public utterance before his resignation on 14 March 1801. It lies quite outside my present purpose to consider the various motives of prejudice and impending madness which alienated the King from his great minister, or again the reasons which led Pitt on his side to give the fatal pledge to abandon Catholic emancipation and then to withdraw from office. Suffice it to say that the choice of the mediocre but correct Addington as his successor was made at Pitt's direct instance, and that "by far the weakest ministry of recent times"[19] was much more successful than anyone had a right to expect. Initial difficulties were smoothed over by the news, within three weeks of its taking office, of Nelson's victory off Copenhagen over the northern confederacy. This and the removal of the mad Tsar put an end to Bonaparte's hope of "rousing all nations against the tyrant of the seas".[20]

ABORTIVE PEACE AND RENEWED WAR

Peace was already in the air. Austria had made her terms with France by the Peace of Lunéville (9 February 1801); the Baltic states were only too ready to follow the new Tsar's example in concluding peace with England, and now that the failure of the French expedition to Egypt was only a matter of time, feelers were put out between London and Paris. The struggle of eight years "had ended in stalemate": for France was unassailable in western Europe, while Britain was "in command of every sea".[21] A continental coalition had twice failed ignominiously to restrain France within her former bounds, and it was felt on all sides that Britain alone could not reimpose the lost Balance of Power, and was therefore justified in attempting to reach some kind of compromise or *modus vivendi* with the victor on land. It was with Pitt's full approval that the new Foreign Secretary, Lord Hawkesbury, opened negotiations for peace. Unfortunately the preliminaries were unduly hurried on, and the British signature was obtained just before the news of the French surrender in Egypt arrived. In essence the Peace of Amiens was a compromise, Ceylon and Trinidad being retained, while Britain's other conquests—and notably the Cape—were restored to France, Spain and Holland, while France, as unchallengeable upon land as Britain upon sea, undertook to evacuate Naples, Rome and Egypt. Pitt freely admitted that his earlier hopes were not fulfilled, but that the surrender of Austria at Lunéville, and the dissolution of "the Confederacy of the states of Europe" had left Britain "the sole and unassisted mark for a hostile League". Sea power would secure immunity from attack and make it possible to husband our resources until such time as the Continent could again take up the struggle. "This country", Pitt told the House, "always was, and I trust always will be, able to check the ambitious projects of France and to give that degree of assistance to the rest of Europe which we have done on this occasion.... I am inclined to hope everything that is good. But I am bound to act as if I feared otherwise."[22] Meanwhile Hawkesbury privately assured the veteran Malmesbury that peace was unavoidable, because we "had been abandoned by everybody, allies and all", but that none the less it was "an experimental peace and nothing else".[23]

There was considerable insincerity on both sides. The game was drawn, and the rivals were merely planning a redistribution of forces. Britain, by "the unskilful, hasty and conceding way" (Pitt's own phrase) in which her concessions had been framed, had failed to insist on the independence of France's four vassals, the sham Batavian, Helvetic, Cisalpine and Ligurian Republics (names that concealed Holland, Switzerland, Lombardy-

Tuscany and Piedmont-Genoa). But under no circumstances was she ready to gratify the First Consul's desire to turn the Mediterranean into a French lake, or to afford him a fresh chance of aiming at the route to India or of disintegrating Turkey. Thus it was natural enough that the pivot of fresh disputes between London and Paris should have been Malta, which Britain was pledged to restore to the Knights of St John, but which they were obviously incapable of holding against French aggression. Sea power, and the control of the Mediterranean, was obviously the dominant issue.

Hawkesbury, then, sent Lord Whitworth to Paris, with instructions to protest, "with moderation and temper", against a series of Bonaparte's aggressions in Italy. He was ready to recognise the new Italian states, since Britain could not prevent their erection, but only on the condition that Britain should after all retain Malta, that Turkey should be immune, and that France should evacuate Holland and Switzerland. The First Consul not merely proved intractable on all points, but lost his temper and publicly insulted the ambassador during a famous reception at the Tuileries, talking "more like a captain of dragons than the head of one of the great states of Europe". In March 1803 it was thought necessary to withdraw Whitworth from Paris: but Addington had held back as long as he could, telling Malmesbury he was resolved to wait till France "had heaped wrong upon wrong, and made her arrogant designs so notorious, and her views of unceasing aggrandisement so demonstrable as to leave no doubt on the public mind, nor a possibility of mistake on the part of the most uninformed man".[24] While Addington adopted this attitude of tactical restraint, Hawkesbury, in his instructions to Whitworth, had stressed his Majesty's desire for peace, but also "his determination never to forego his right of interfering in the affairs of the Continent on every occasion in which the interests of his own dominions, or those of Europe in general, may appear to require it".[25] Both Ministers have often been criticised for their mismanagement of the situation, but it is difficult to see how war could have been avoided, in view of Napoleon's soaring ambition and utter disregard of every kind of treaty pledge. "So the two weary nations turned again to war." This time it was Britain who declared it, and Napoleon promptly retorted by the seizure of all British subjects within his reach, and by overrunning Hanover and blocking the Elbe in defiance of Prussian protests.

There was now a widespread demand for the recall of Pitt to power, as the only man capable of weathering such a storm. But he himself deprecated any such change in wartime, and though fully alive to the weakness of the Ministry, gave it his full backing in a speech which compared "the irresistible force and overwhelming progress of French ambition to those dreadful convulsions of nature by which provinces and kingdoms are consumed and buried in ruins". Arguing that we had "no option between the blessings of peace and the dangers of war", he ended on a somewhat self-satisfied note, showing "what abundant reason we have to be grateful to Providence for the distinction we enjoy over most of the countries of Europe, and for all the advantages and blessings which the national wisdom and virtue have hitherto protected".[26] In the meantime he led the demand for the prompt arming of the nation, and impressed upon ministers their duty to "rouse the spirit of the country" by revealing the magnitude of the danger and the enemy's true aims, and to "give that spirit a just and powerful direction.[27] By May 1804, however, Addington himself urged upon the King the advisability of recalling Pitt to office, and he accepted, though already enfeebled in health and weakened by the abstention of the Grenville group and the King's refusal to include Fox. The temporary breakdown of the party system tended towards a revival of the royal power, but the growing enfeeblement of George III's intellect—always obstinate rather than firm, personal rather than principled—served to check the danger, but in some ways increased the confusion. Incidentally, for the next eight years there was a constant series of changes at the Foreign Office, for which our history offers no parallel, and which was not conducive to the maintenance of a clear-cut foreign policy.*

Pitt's return to office coincided with Napoleon's proclamation as Emperor of the French, and soon the gathering of the army of Boulogne was an outward sign of the implacable nature of the feud between the principles for which these two men stood. From the first Pitt set himself to construct yet a Third Coalition and found a ready hearing at the Russian Court, which under the mutable but imaginative Alexander planned a Congress whose task it would be to establish a system of international law, as the basis of an European federation. But neither Prussia nor Austria were yet ready to play their due part. Francis II had countered Napoleon's imperial presumption by himself assuming the title of Emperor of Austria; but though incensed beyond words by Napoleon's coronation with the Iron Crown of Italy, he was exceedingly slow to move in a military sense, and his fraternal jealousy kept the Archduke Charles at arm's length till the last moment, left army reform in the hands of incompetent generals like Mack, and thus simply courted the disasters which in those days surely befell the laggard. The ambitious allied plan of campaign which slowly ripened by the autumn of 1805, rested upon bad generalship and lack of true co-operation or of a joint

* May 1804, Lord Harrowby; January 1805, Lord Mulgrave; February 1806, Charles James Fox; September 1806, Lord Howick (afterwards Grey); March 1807, George Canning; October 1809, Lord Bathurst; December 1809, Lord Wellesley. At last in March 1812, Lord Castlereagh came to the Foreign Office and remained for ten memorable years.

time-table, but above all upon an error of judgment which is even graver than inadequate preparations, namely belief in the unpreparedness of the enemy. In reality Napoleon was all the time maturing his own plans, and when he had once convinced himself that the French navy was not equal to the task of covering that decisive invasion of England of which he had so long dreamt, he was able with a minimum of delay to transfer his forces to the Danube, keep the Prussians in play, deal a deadly blow to Austrian prestige by the collapse of her army at Ulm, occupy Vienna unopposed, and then on 2 December 1805 win a smashing victory at Austerlitz over Austrians and Russians combined. The Third Coalition thus came to a still more catastrophic end than either of its predecessors. Austria was "cut off at once from Italy, from Switzerland and from the Rhine"; Venetia and the east Adriatic coast were incorporated with the new vassal kingdom of Italy, Tirol was handed to Bavaria as the price of treason to the German cause. The process of dynastic rearrangement among the lesser German states, which Napoleon had pursued for some years past, was crowned by the final liquidation of the Holy Roman Empire: and the royal, grand-ducal or electoral title was distributed as largesse by the Corsican usurper to those German dynasts whom he desired to rally against Prussia, and who preferred personal aggrandisement to national honour. As a supplement to these methods, Napoleon began to create thrones for members of his own family, some by the ejection of their rightful owners, some by the ruthless redrawing of existing frontiers, and so to build up a system of vassal states for the strategic protection of what he had conquered outright. In this situation Russia, though driven to retreat, still armed for a fresh struggle, but Prussia sought to buy immunity from attack by allying herself with the victor, and accepted the bribe of Hanover at his hands, failing to perceive that she herself would be the next object of Napoleon's onslaught.

For Europe these vast happenings seemed to spell final subjection: for Britain the situation was redeemed by the victory of Trafalgar, whose decisive character, as ensuring to her the unquestioned mastery of the seas, and so the weapon by which the tyranny of Napoleon was eventually to be worn down, must never be allowed to eclipse those earlier achievements of St Vincent, the Nile, Camperdown and Copenhagen. Nelson himself fell, but his work was done: Napoleon's hope of converting the Mediterranean into a French lake—"the principal aim of my policy", he once declared,[28] —was henceforth doomed, though never finally abandoned: Sicily, Corfu and the Dalmatian islands were, during the remainder of the war, used as strategic supplements to Gibraltar and Malta.

Austerlitz and Trafalgar imposed a final strain upon the health of Pitt, who died on 23 January 1806, unflinching but worn out with anxiety. At the Guildhall banquet in the preceding November he had been hailed by the Lord Mayor as "the Saviour of Europe", and had replied in the brief but memorable phrase, "I return you many thanks for the honour you have done me: but Europe is not to be saved by any single man. England has saved herself by her exertions, and will, as I trust, save Europe by her example."

Pitt, it has often been argued, was greater as a financial and naval reformer than in the diplomatic or military sphere, where he committed every imaginable blunder owing to lack of any real acquaintance with continental affairs and an altogether excessive reliance upon hidebound and reactionary allies. He can hardly be blamed for accepting the only material which lay ready to his hand, but even then his methods must be regarded as unduly opportunist and fluctuating. Peace, security, patriotism—no one will deny his unvarying attachment to these fundamental aims: but he was only too apt to generalise rather than to define. In home affairs he was only reluctantly and gradually driven into the paths of reaction, by the imminence of foreign menace and the panic this engendered in wide circles of public opinion: and no just estimate of his career can be formed which does not stress the supreme handicap represented by the King, who showed in later life towards Ireland, towards Reform, towards Catholic Emancipation, the same invincible perversity which had baffled the elder Pitt and lost us America. But above all Pitt's career must be considered in the light of one fact that dwarfed all others—the French Revolution. In Lord Rosebery's words, he "could only perceive the heavens darkened, and the sound of a mighty rushing wind that filled all Europe....Pitt faced the cataclysm, and made everything subservient to the task of averting it....There was no middle course, and the Revolution had to be accepted or repelled". To this task Pitt sacrificed every nerve and sinew of his being, and in the words of Wilberforce—who was both his friend and critic, and in the eyes of posterity is the highest expression of the political idealism of that age—"every other consideration was absorbed in one great ruling passion—love of his country". The second of the two periods which so sharply divide his political career ended in relative failure; but his example lived on, and he left behind him a band of disciples which after some years of kaleidoscopic adjustment became the solid phalanx which forced its way to victory.

PITT'S SUCCESSORS

A note of tragic pessimism surrounded the dying Minister, and even his most fervent followers felt that the ignominious collapse of Britain's three great allies rendered a continuance of the struggle on the old lines hopeless. An attempt was made to fill the void which Pitt left behind him by forming a coalition between Grenville and Fox, known, for no very obvious reason, as "the Ministry of All the Talents". Fox, who less than a year earlier had openly criticised Pitt's policy of "arousing Europe", now took the Foreign Office himself and lost no time in making overtures for peace. But Napoleon's appetite was far superior to Fox's pacifist desires. He was, it is true, ready to restore Hanover to King George, after forcing the King of Prussia to declare war upon the ally whose territory he had so recently grabbed. But Fox insisted that Russia must be included in the negotiations, and when Napoleon, still harping upon Mediterranean supremacy, demanded that Sicily should be relinquished, Fox saw through the manœuvre. "It is not Sicily", he told Lord Holland, "but the shuffling, insincere way in which they act, that shows me they are playing a false game: and in that case it would be very imprudent to make any concessions which by possibility would be thought inconsistent with our honour, or furnish our allies with a plausible pretence for suspecting, reproaching or deserting us."[29] Fox was already stiffening noticeably, and the hope of peace had vanished once more, when in mid-September he followed his old rival to a grave in the Abbey. Events had been too strong for him, and his successor rejected out of hand the terms which Napoleon offered as a cynical bribe for British passivity, while he was concentrating his armies for the overthrow of Prussia.

The next twelve months represent in many ways the nadir of continental resistance to Napoleon. Prussia, badly led and foolishly refusing to wait for Austrian and Russian reinforcements, was crushingly defeated at Jena and Auerstädt: and from her occupied capital Napoleon issued the famous Berlin Decree of commercial boycott against Britain and her colonies. He then wooed the Poles with promises of restoration, and marched eastwards against Russia: a first check at Eylau, in a February snowstorm, was more than made good by the victory of Friedland (14 June 1807). There followed the sudden decision of Tsar Alexander to make terms at Tilsit with the conqueror, in the belief that the two autocrats could divide the control of the Continent between them, and perhaps even conspire for the dominion of the East. In so acting he was undoubtedly influenced not only by the passivity into which Francis of Austria had sunk, but also by his rooted distrust of the successors of Pitt and of the parliamentary system, which seemed to him at once factious and chaotic. He certainly had good grounds for criticising the hesitations and inactivity of the Grenville administration, though posterity will ever judge it with leniency, in the light of its abolition of the slave trade, "under the spell of Wilberforce's persuasive eloquence".[30] The ill-considered forcing of the Dardanelles, followed by withdrawal and then by a hopelessly bungled expedition to Egypt, doubtless weighed still further with the Tsar, to whom nothing that affected the Turkish Empire could be indifferent.

The fall of the Whigs in March 1807 was mainly due to the personal prejudices of George III: but though this brought back the Tories to a prolonged period of office, their two principal leaders, the Duke of Portland and Spencer Perceval, were men of mediocre attainments and vision, interpreting the isolation which disaster had brought upon them as an excuse for non-intervention. The first sign of returning energy was the resolve of George Canning—who succeeded the Whig Lord Howick at the Foreign Office—under no circumstances to permit Napoleon, as a sequel to the Tilsit bargain, to secure the control of Scandinavian naval and commercial resources. On Canning's initiative a British expedition was sent to Denmark, whose resistance was overcome after a bombardment of Copenhagen. There can be no doubt that this drastic action forestalled a design of Napoleon to seize the Danish fleet for himself, but none the less the verdict of history has gone against its bold, if successful author, and the whole incident has left a stain upon the memory of Pitt's most brilliant pupil, now at the beginning of his somewhat chequered ministerial career. Canning's appointment as Foreign Secretary had aroused keen indignation on the Whig side: and Sydney Smith, who for all his versatile wit was often wrong on matters of policy, had expressed doubt whether "a nation is to be saved by schoolboy jokes and doggerel rhymes, by affronting petulance and by the tones and gestures of Mr Pitt. When he [Canning] is jocular, he is strong, when he is serious, he is Samson in a wig".[31] Apart from the indignation which for a time alienated the greater part of continental opinion from Britain, there were also weighty protests in Parliament, which were even embodied in a formal address to the Crown. But at least, after Copenhagen, no one could doubt Canning's vigour and his foresight, even if they might condemn his defiance of international law; and he was soon to avert an exactly similar danger from Portugal, this time by less objectionable methods. The full measure of Napoleon's unscrupulousness was revealed in his secret treaty with Charles IV for the partition of Portugal (October 1807) and Junot's prompt invasion of the little kingdom. All that Britain could do for the moment was to send a fleet to the Tagus, convey the royal family to an honourable exile in Brazil, and pluck away the Portuguese fleet from under the very eyes of its would-be captors.

Two months later this fresh act of aggression was followed by a French invasion of Spain. At first posing as the protector of King Charles, Napoleon terrorised him into abdication, staged an elaborate intrigue between Charles and his son Ferdinand, then wrung from both a surrender of their joint rights, and at last induced a packed assembly at Bayonne to elect his own brother Joseph Bonaparte to the vacant throne. Within less than three months, however, the Spanish nation was in full revolt against the invaders and had driven most of their forces either to capitulate or to withdraw to defensive positions. A new note had been struck in Europe: resistance to French domination was no longer the monopoly of selfish dynasts, looking askance at each other, but was henceforth, more and more, to be the work of whole peoples in arms. And to this Canning made immediate response, little foreseeing that he was inaugurating a new era of foreign policy, based upon national sentiment and an appeal to public opinion. On 15 June 1808 in the House of Commons Sheridan urged the Government to seize the greatest opportunity since 1789. "Hitherto Bonaparte has had to contend against princes without dignity and ministers without wisdom. He has fought against countries in which the population have been indifferent as to his success. He has yet to learn what it is to fight against a country in which the people are animated with one spirit to resist him." Canning at once declared Britain's official sympathy with the Spanish rising and her desire to provide material help. "We shall proceed upon the principle that any nation of Europe which starts up with a determination to oppose a Power which is the common enemy of all nations, becomes instantly our essential ally." Acting upon this principle—destined to act with such explosive force for a least a century to come—Canning, in close conjunction with Castlereagh, who as Secretary for War had done much to reorganise our army system, despatched Sir Arthur Wellesley to Spain, and set on foot the decisive Peninsular adventure. There was an unfortunate start, due to the restraint imposed by older and less efficient generals: the French army of occupation in Portugal was not forced to utter surrender, but repatriated to French ports on British vessels, and a period of inaction followed. But Spain's example and immunity echoed through Europe, and its effect upon German sentiment and even upon the fickle and now wavering Tsar was so great that Napoleon found it advisable himself to assume the Spanish command. The results of his campaign were to restore Madrid to his brother Joseph and to force Moore to his glorious retreat upon Corunna.

After the death of Moore there were acute disagreements at home as to a continuance of the Peninsular campaign. Canning was able to prevent the recall of Wellesley, but during 1809 most of his colleagues, and especially Castlereagh, held the view that our main military effort should be directed, not towards the Iberian Peninsula, but to the Low Countries, since this would be our most effective diversion in favour of Prussia and Austria. For during the previous winter national feeling had been steadily rising throughout the German lands, and in April 1809 the Emperor Francis, for the only time in his life carried away by such unwonted sentiments, issued a manifesto addressed "To the German Nation", and prepared to place himself at its head, thereby temporarily reducing Prussia to the second rank in the eyes of all true patriots. But though Tirol rose for the Habsburgs and expelled the Franco-Bavarian garrison, the Archduke Charles was not able to hold his own in Bavaria, and was soon driven to retreat before Napoleon's overwhelming forces and even to evacuate Vienna itself. The victory which Charles won at Aspern broke for the first time the spell of Napoleon's invincibility, and sent an electric thrill across Europe: but none the less Napoleon, by the supreme effort of Wagram (6 July), forced Austria to her knees once more, and after an interval of three months dictated a vindictive peace at Schönbrunn—cutting her off completely from the sea by the new "Illyrian Provinces", transferring Galicia to the artificial Grand Duchy of Warsaw, ceding Salzburg to Bavaria, and aggrandising the Kings of Saxony and Bavaria for their treason to the German cause.

Austria's acquiescence in this fourth, and most disastrous, defeat was in no small degree influenced by Britain's attitude—on the one hand by Wellesley's forced withdrawal after his success at Talavera, and on the other by the ignominious collapse of the long-planned Walcheren expedition.[32] It is impossible, in such a general survey as the present, to do more than indicate the main changes produced by Napoleon's conquest of Austria: but even a bare catalogue of his peace terms, which he may be said to have supplemented in the summer of 1809 by the annexation of the Papal states and a year later by the full incorporation of Holland within his Empire, and finally by the annexation of Valais with the western Swiss passes, and the whole North Sea coast of Germany—all this proved, beyond all possibility of doubt, the insatiable character of his ambitions and the hopelessness of any real peace with him, save on terms that would make a mockery of security.

The failure of Walcheren brought to a head the friction, based on personal jealousy, between Canning and Castlereagh, the former urging that the latter should be transferred from the War Office to some other post. The weak Premier, ill and evasive, concealed from each the remonstrances of the other, until a moment arrived when each was convinced of his rival's bad faith: Canning resigned in anger, and there followed the inevitable duel on Putney Heath. This incident, so scathingly and so justly criticised even in days when political duels were by no means uncommon, shook the Government to its core, and not many weeks after the Duke of Portland died. He was succeeded by the correct, but mediocre, Spencer Perceval, who assigned the Foreign Office first to Lord Bathurst, then to the Marquis Wellesley, one more inept and unsuccessful than the other. None the less the new Cabinet, despite financial stringency and continental disappointments, stood firm against the enemy: and in Lord Liverpool, who replaced Lord Castlereagh, the War Office found a far more competent chief, though one of much inferior intellectual calibre. But Castlereagh was ere long to find another office worthy of his genius, while Canning underwent a political eclipse of twelve years such as has no parallel in the history of our public men.

During 1810 and 1811 there was a pause of sullen exhaustion throughout the centre of the Continent, while the commercial blockade, aimed by Napoleon through his unwilling subjects against the staying power of Britain, slowly but surely crumbled, as the Tsar resented the injuries inflicted upon Russian trade and grew more sceptical of Napoleon's final success. During this lull all eyes were turned towards Spain, where Lord Wellington, as Wellesley became early in 1810, was organising his future offensive behind the lines of Torres Vedras. By the spring of 1811 he had won the second bout against Masséna and forced him to retreat: then, forced again on to the defensive by the furious assaults of Soult, he more than held his own, and after the capture of Ciudad Rodrigo in April 1812 was at last able to advance into Spanish territory. The steady pressure which Britain, thanks to her control of the sea routes, was able to exercise in the Peninsula served as a constant drain upon Napoleon's resources, a growing deterrent from new adventures, an encouragement to the three Eastern Courts to believe that the hour of his downfall and of their emancipation was no longer far off. "The Spanish ulcer destroyed me", Napoleon once said at St Helena: and this corresponds fairly exactly with the truth: for it was the cancer at his vitals that slowly undermined his strength for the decisive round against the grand coalition.

During 1811 relations between Napoleon and the Tsar steadily deteriorated, in proportion as the latter drew away from the continental blockade: if Russia could only be overthrown, the Continent would be finally at Napoleon's feet, the land route to the East would stand open to him, and Britain, completely isolated, might at last lose her nerve and accept the inevitable. With these unmeasured aims in view he imposed alliances, only varying in the degree of humiliation, upon Prussia and Austria in the early months of 1812, and compelled them to contribute contingents for the immense military expedition which he was now preparing. The Tsar hurriedly concluded his six years' war with the Porte—leaving the Serbs and Roumanians to their fate, indemnifying himself with the province of Bessarabia, and abandoning for the immediate future all hope of a drastic solution of the Eastern Question. He did this in order to concentrate all his forces upon the defence of Russia, and during the second half of 1812 his Fabian tactics, the Russian climate, its vast spaces and distances and their bearing upon the all-important problem of French transport, brought dire disaster upon the invader, who not merely lost 400,000 men, but returned across Germany with diminished prestige and the halo of his invincibility battered out of recognition. It is the merest commonplace to say that the debacle in Russia "created a new order of things in Europe", in which the French hegemony, at any rate in its original form, could no longer be upheld. Indeed the Russian retreat released an avalanche of national forces that had slowly been accumulating throughout the Continent: henceforward the monarchs of the three Eastern Powers set themselves, insincerely enough, to canalise these forces, for which they had little or no comprehension, still less sympathy, but which, they dimly perceived, could be enlisted to promote their own ultimate ends. Amid the spontaneous uprising of German sentiment Napoleon soon found himself on the defensive in Central Europe, and though he was still able during 1813 to organise a titanic resistance, the shadow of a new and this time successful encirclement was already upon him.

In the meantime Britain had steadily pursued her policy of blockade, as counter to Napoleon's "continental system", and being incapable of waging a land war on a grand scale in Central Europe, concentrated upon the liberation of Portugal and Spain from French control. At first definitely on the defensive, Wellington gradually evolved a system of glorified raids into Spain, each marked by a victorious battle, yet ending in temporary withdrawal westwards. But the madness with which Napoleon squandered his resources "in cannon fodder" and material upon adventures in eastern and central Europe, reacted all the time in favour of Wellington. Stage by stage he advanced towards his goal, building up his strategic position as he went, always handicapped by the intrigues of the despicable Ferdinand VII, and by the struggle between the Spanish Crown and the constitutional reformers, but on the other hand slowly overcoming the disproportion of forces between himself and the French commanders in Spain, and bracing himself for the final advance across the Pyrenees. If, then, successive British Governments, during the later stages of the great conflict, wisely concentrated their main efforts upon the Spanish Peninsula, they never lost interest in the Mediterranean, where sea power and economic pressure went hand in hand. Hoste, by his naval victory at Lissa in March 1811, drove the French from the Adriatic, and his just administration of the Dalmatian islands from then until the peace remains a vivid memory among the seafaring Jugoslav population and still assures the British fleet at all times of a hearty welcome. The British occupation of Sicily was also no more than a momentary political experiment, but the "English constitution" of 1812, due to the enlightened policy of Lord William Bentinck, remained, long after its abrogation by the perjured King of Naples, a signpost to the whole Italian Liberal movement.

It was while Napoleon was passing through Germany on his way to the Russian frontier that for the first and only time a British Premier fell at the hands of an assassin. Spencer Perceval, though he had never been more than an honest mediocrity, enjoyed great popularity in the country, and his sudden disappearance caused dismay and dissension in both parties, which for a certain time baffled the Prince Regent. When, however, Lord Wellesley's attempt to rally the Whigs in a comprehensive coalition had proved obviously unworkable, the Premiership was entrusted to Lord Liverpool, who had been Perceval's War Minister. Indeed it was in a large measure his resentment at the factious attitude of the Opposition towards the Peninsular campaign and his own firm resolve to support Wellington at all costs, that now made co-operation with such men as Grenville and even Wellesley impossible.

No one would claim Liverpool as a man of genius, but he had qualities of tact, firmness and endurance to which historians have rarely done full justice: and thus it came about that he held the office of Premier over a period more than twice as long as any other successor of Pitt, long after peace had been restored to Europe. One reason for his ascendancy was that he had an unrivalled insight into the whole machinery of government, having filled successively every Secretaryship of State, and tested the efficiency and mutual relations of politicians and officials alike. It is, moreover, to be remembered that he had a much wider acquaintance with foreign affairs than many who have held his high office. He had indeed made his mark by a speech in the House of Commons in 1791, devoted to the European situation: it aroused much attention at the time, and deserves to be recalled as one more proof how little even the shrewdest observer, with a great future before him, can foresee the development of the foreign situation. For on that occasion he assumed that no further danger need be apprehended from the side of France (*Gallos quoque in bellis floruisse audivimus*, he quoted): but he went on to argue that "A Power has succeeded to France, no less deserving of attention from its restless politics and ambitious views, namely Russia." If Russian designs upon Turkey should succeed, he argued, "the balance of Europe would be totally destroyed, to the manifest injury of every state in this quarter of the globe". He therefore advocated an alliance with the King of Prussia, as best qualified "to stem the torrent of Russian aggression"—somewhat oblivious of the ties which already linked the two powers together despite their rivalries. Britain, he concluded, was "constitutionally the foe of all wars of ambition and wanton aggression", and a stable peace was "equally her interest and inclination". After his notable maiden speech young Jenkinson, as he still was, travelled in Europe, visited the French emigrants in the army of Coblenz, protested against Fox's proposal to negotiate with the Revolution, and settled down, under the wise tutelage of his father (who in 1796 was made Earl of Liverpool), into a devoted follower of Pitt. In 1801, when Addington became Prime Minister, Hawkesbury succeeded Grenville at the Foreign Office, with the full approval and encouragement of his retiring chief. He was thus in charge of the very vital negotiations which led to the Peace of Amiens in 1802, and his policy was attacked and misunderstood in many quarters: but, as we already have seen, he again had the approval of Pitt, and in the end Parliament gave its consent without a division. It was he, too, who sent Lord Whitworth on his mission to Paris and recalled him when the First Consul's conduct became altogether too provocative. He firmly faced the renewal of hostilities, and, without showing genius, followed worthily in the steps of Grenville.

When Pitt again became Premier in 1804, Hawkesbury was transferred to the Home Office: he obviously did not like this and insisted upon its being made clear that he had consented "*solely* on the ground of *personal* accommodation".[33] But he none the less led the House of Lords, and his new office brought him into close contact with George III, over whom he steadily acquired influence. He succeeded to his father's earldom in 1809, and in the same year was made Secretary for War, contributing, by his foresight and persistence, to the defeat of a factious Opposition which foolishly clamoured for the head of Wellington. It may be that he became Prime Minister by a process of exclusion, but he was none the less the only obvious candidate for that office, and he soon had behind him "a Cabinet united as no Cabinet had been since the early days of the war".[34]

Liverpool, then, who attached a very special importance to the Foreign Office,* wished Canning to return to it, but met on his part a stubborn and altogether unreasoning refusal to "go into the House of Commons *under* Lord Castlereagh" (who was succeeding Perceval as Leader of the House). Castlereagh was generous to a fault, and in order to secure his former rival as a colleague, was ready to renounce the Foreign Office and take the Exchequer for himself, but the leadership he could not abandon without stultifying his whole career, and all were agreed that there was no serious alternative. Canning, said the Regent, "takes as much courting as a woman, and a great deal more than most",[35] and here he spoke as a true connoisseur. Canning ended by admitting that Castlereagh's offer was "perhaps the handsomest that was ever made to an individual": he owed it to his own obstinacy that the settlement of Europe fell into other hands. Never did a man of genius commit so rank a blunder.

* "The office of Foreign Secretary of State", he wrote, "will always give to the person who holds it a degree of consequence in Parliament and the country, which perhaps belongs to no other department" (Yonge, *op. cit.* p. 408).

The Grand Alliance

The disasters which had befallen the Grand Army had an immense repercussion among all Napoleon's unwilling subjects. The volcanic outburst of German popular feeling that followed may still be studied in the poetry of Körner and Arndt and in the sober prose of Fichte: but even more significant of the times was the act of General von Yorck in rejecting the King of Prussia's veto on his convention with the Russians, and in continuing the war on his own responsibility. It is easy to plead on behalf of Frederick William III that he was not a free agent, and was still under the spell of a ruthless conqueror: it is more profitable to remember that never was monarch of such mediocre capacity served by so many statesmen, soldiers and writers of high courage, initiative and resource, able to retrieve his blunders. Already in February 1813 Stein and Hardenberg had come to terms with Russia, not without considerable territorial sacrifice: and in March the War of Liberation began.

Of this new situation Castlereagh, enjoying the full confidence of the Prince Regent and of the Prime Minister, was eager to take the fullest possible advantage. Despite the financial strain of recent years and the added complication of the American War, the Government was determined to prosecute the war to a victorious issue: and the first essential was to secure co-operation between Russia and Prussia. At the height of the Napoleonic tyranny normal diplomatic relations had virtually broken down, but Lord Cathcart and Sir Charles Stewart were now sent to central Europe to re-establish contact, and to hold out the prospect of substantial subsidies. Castlereagh had every ground for distrust and uncertainty, and indeed the elaborate duplicity of Metternich led him to wonder whether Austria was contemplating the same policy of weak desertion as had been followed by Prussia in 1805–6. It was only at a later stage that he revealed his true motive, namely, to avoid the danger of Napoleon throwing his whole forces against Austria and crushing her before the Russians could arrive. If again he showed himself a supreme master in the art of dissembling —to the extent of misleading even Napoleon himself in a conversation of many hours at Dresden—it may doubtless be argued that with such a man as Napoleon the sole hope was to out-manœuvre him with his own weapons. Meanwhile Liverpool, who already after the Borodino had forecast the expulsion of the French from Spain, told Wellington that if Austria and Prussia "would really take advantage of the Russian successes, we might have hopes of effecting the deliverance of the Continent: but nothing can be more abject than the councils of Vienna at this time, and I fear that neutrality is all that can be expected from them".[36]

Prussia declared war on 17 March, and Blücher advanced across the Elbe: but Napoleon was swift to accept the challenge, and in May defeated the allies at Lützen and Bautzen and occupied Dresden. Then for once in his career, and some have called it his most fatal blunder, he refrained from striking home, and by granting an armistice in June gave the Allies time to organise fresh efforts. In August the titanic struggle was resumed in a long-drawn series of battles on Saxon soil: then, after another pause, the "Battle of the Nations" at Leipzig (18 October) at last turned the scale and compelled Napoleon to retreat to the French border, with the allied armies in pursuit, with King Jerome in flight from Westphalia, and with Napoleon's Rhenish vassals meanly leaving him in the lurch.

Throughout this period the British Government had used its whole influence to bring the three Eastern Powers together and to unite them, well in advance of the future peace negotiations, upon a plan for the rearrangement of Europe. It is true that, despite all the renewed subsidies, they could not make their weight as strongly felt in the scales as the vast armies of Alexander, Francis and Frederick William: but Wellington's steady progress in Spain, and especially the battle of Vittoria (21 June), undoubtedly impressed the Allies. The realist Castlereagh, then, concealed his suspicions of Metternich, and took the line that "the risk of treating with France is great, but the risk of losing our continental allies and the confidence of our own nation is greater. We must preserve our own faith inviolate to Spain, Portugal, Sicily and Sweden".[37] To the last moment before Leipzig he had grounds for fearing that one or other of the Powers which were bargaining for his subsidies might make a separate peace: and it was really the reckless intransigeance of Napoleon himself that averted the danger and drove Metternich into open war.

Castlereagh has been somewhat criticised for sending as his representative at allied headquarters in September 1813 the young and inexperienced Lord Aberdeen, who thus made his *début* in high politics. He was under thirty, spoke no French, and was both diffident and secretive: he seems to have owed his selection mainly to his high rank and to the fact that he had been the ward of Pitt and Dundas. He was soon enthralled by the personal charm of Metternich[38] but Castlereagh saw much further, and was already planning "a common alliance" which was to survive the war as "the only invigorating remedy" likely to check "the unbounded and faithless ambition of an individual".* The Cabinet grew more and more concerned as the winter drew in, and as negotiations with the continental Powers dragged

* Castlereagh wrote to Aberdeen, 13 November 1813: "After such a tide of success this nation is likely to view with disfavour any peace which does not confine France strictly within her ancient limits. Indeed, peace with Bonaparte on any terms will be far from popular" (*Castlereagh Correspondence*, IX, 76).

on interminably: and it very wisely concluded that someone possessed of real authority to speak and act in their name must proceed to headquarters. Thus in the last week of 1813 Castlereagh left England on a mission which was destined to last for sixteen months and is unique in the annals of our foreign policy. His instructions, which he himself of course helped to draft, laid the main stress upon detaching Antwerp, the Low Countries and as much territory west of the Rhine as possible from the hands of France, and if necessary to buy her off with colonial concessions. Malta, the Cape, Mauritius, Tobago and Guiana were to be treated as outside any bargaining, but all else, including the Dutch Indies, could be discussed. In Europe the restoration of the Pope and of Piedmont were specially stressed. He was to aim at the conversion of the Alliance into something permanent, surviving the war: and there was as yet no refusal to deal with Napoleon as Emperor.

Between January and May 1814 Castlereagh played his part in a long series of negotiations at Basel, at Langres and at Châtillon, finding himself between the two extremes of Metternich and Alexander, and eager, amid the fluctuations of the allied invasion of France, to maintain a united front. "Our policy", wrote Liverpool, "should be to keep the Alliance together and not to separate ourselves from it either in peace or in war. But we ought not to conceal from ourselves that any peace with Bonaparte will be only a state of preparation for renewed hostilities."[39] Steady British pressure was the main factor in securing, as a sequel to the Treaty of Chaumont, that restoration of the Bourbons which Pitt had already favoured in 1804 and 1805, and which, after the long exile of Louis XVIII in England, seemed most likely to promote good Anglo-French relations, subject always to French opinion manifesting itself. Two days before the allied sovereigns entered Paris on 30 March 1814, restoration became their definite policy: and Napoleon's appeal to the Emperor Francis on behalf of the little King of Rome came too late, though Parma was assigned to Marie Louise. It was the Tsar's folly which gave the fallen tyrant the sovereignty of Elba: and indeed he was only with difficulty restrained from putting forward Bernadotte as his candidate for the French throne.

Castlereagh spent six weeks in Paris negotiating the First Peace of Paris (30 May), and acting as the finger on the balance. It was, above all, the working agreement between Castlereagh and Metternich which was the determining factor. France in the end accepted a frontier more or less identical with that of 1792, and consented that Belgium should go to Holland. "I felt it of the last importance", Castlereagh wrote home, "not to go to a Congress without the most essential point acquiesced in by France."[40] Otherwise England showed great moderation, limiting her claims to Malta, the Cape, Mauritius and Tobago, and not pushing beyond a certain point for the abolition of the slave trade. The three Eastern Allies were, however, in profound disagreement, especially as to the fate of Poland and Saxony: and the European Congress was postponed till the autumn, while the sovereigns amused themselves in Paris and visited the Prince Regent at Windsor.

During these six months of delicate negotiation Castlereagh, by his personal contacts with continental statesmen and by his diplomatic skill in the management of men, became an international figure to a degree hitherto unknown in our history. Hence, after a brief interval in the House of Commons during the summer of 1814, it became obvious that he alone could worthily represent Britain at the Congress of Vienna and hold his own against such men as Metternich, Talleyrand, Hardenberg and Alexander. He played the role of mediator with consummate skill, and it was in large measure due to him that the thorny question of Saxony did not cause a fatal rupture between the Allies. His success resulted from the bold expedient of concluding a treaty of defensive alliance with Austria and France, and warning Hardenberg privately that Prussia's menaces would be resisted by Great Britain "with her whole power and resources, and that every man in Parliament, of whatever party, would support the Government in doing so".[41] The treaty, he told Liverpool, "may save Austria and consequently the Continent": and in the meantime his attitude made France increasingly dependent upon Britain in the still more vital questions of Belgium, of the so-called "natural frontiers", and also of Hanover, which dynastic reasons forced him to keep in the forefront of his calculations. According to Metternich's *Eminence grise*, Friedrich von Gentz, Castlereagh "worked night and day", and in "the Committee of Five", which owed its origin above all to him and Metternich, and in which the real settlement of Europe was effected, he played to the full that mediatory part which he and all our greatest Foreign Secretaries have held to be Britain's true function in continental affairs. Nor did he allow himself to be bounced into a premature return to England, and though the Cabinet, faced by a difficult parliamentary situation, clamoured for his presence in London, he insisted on not leaving Vienna until agreement on all essentials had been reached and his departure could no longer deflect the scales. Attempts have more than once been made to assign the whole credit, or discredit, for the settlement of Vienna to Castlereagh on the one hand or to Metternich on the other. The only just verdict is one which assigns it to their practical alliance, and to their joint skill in combining with the astute Talleyrand to defeat the rapacity of Russia and Prussia.*

---

* Prof. von Srbik's monumental biography of Metternich certainly does not do justice to Castlereagh, and even the admirably judicial Prof. Webster sometimes allows his enthusiasm for Castlereagh to be vented at the expense of Metternich.

Even more admirable was the calm, steadying influence exercised by Castlereagh both in Parliament and in the councils of the Allies, when Napoleon's return from Elba threatened to plunge Europe into fresh confusion. He again had to steer a middle course, helping Wellington to organise the resistance which triumphed at Waterloo, convincing British opinion that a renewal of the war was absolutely essential, and yet restraining it from concluding a vindictive peace. Hence Britain's was the only army which paid its way during the renewed occupation of French territory: and the Government's whole weight was once more thrown in favour of the restoration of the Bourbons—this time no longer on a basis of pure legitimacy, but with some pretence of an appeal to the popular will. The corollary of this was that, subject to minor changes, the frontiers of France should be respected. Castlereagh and Wellington were completely at one in wishing that France, enfeebled by twenty years of aggression, should not be unduly humiliated, and so tempted to renew the fatal experiment of military expansion.

GENERAL TENDENCIES

From the history of the two centuries which preceded Waterloo there emerge certain broad but unmistakable tendencies. First and foremost is Britain's instinctive opposition to any bid for world power, from whatever quarter, and her no less marked preference for a certain equilibrium of forces on the European Continent. The long struggles against Philip of Spain and Louis XIV were but rehearsals for the Seven Years' War and for the great war against the French Revolution in all its changing phases, when the continental alliance was four times overthrown and only a supreme effort of European coalition was finally successful. But in each case no sooner was victory assured than British statesmen set themselves to correct its exaggerations and to explore the possibilities of good neighbourly relations with the vanquished nation: and it was considerations of continental equilibrium, no less than of political doctrine, that gradually alienated them after 1815 from the closely allied Eastern Courts and produced the first of a succession of *ententes* between London and Paris. Thus it cannot reasonably be denied that the Balance of Power in Europe has for generations been a fundamental maxim of British policy, and that it asserted itself once more in the supreme crisis of the Great War—this time of course against Germany instead of France. After 1919 it seemed for a time as though we were entering a new phase, in which the Balance of Power in its original sense had been overthrown, thanks to the rapid shrinkage of the world, the merging of European and extra-European issues, and the growing international influence of Powers—notably America and Japan—which till the very turn of the century had held aloof from European affairs. But the latest developments in Central Europe suggest that the principle of the Balance of Power is not extinct after all: and it is still too soon to say whether it will prove more powerful than those ideas of international government which have their centre in Geneva.

Next to a sure instinct for discouraging the rise of any omnipotent rival, British policy may be said to have thrown its weight from time to time into the European scales in order to secure virtual immunity for her overseas designs. This was especially noticeable in the mid-eighteenth century, when Prussia saved her skin, but Britain secured Canada and India. But it was also true, in a much more creditable form, during and after the Napoleonic Wars, when colonial gains were sometimes regarded as "gages" by which to extract concessions in other fields, but peace was none the less never concluded without substantial additions being made to Britain's colonial empire. Far too little attention has been paid to the essential interaction of our continental and overseas policies, or it would not be possible for newspaper theorists of to-day to expound the doctrine of isolation, not merely as a possibility of the present, but as a fact of the past. It should be sufficiently obvious that scientific invention and improved communications by land, sea and air have broken down all the remaining barriers behind which a nation might still hope to live a life of isolation; but it should be no less obvious that save for a brief interval at the close of the nineteenth century Britain has never been able to pursue a policy of deliberate isolation—though her appetite for intervention has varied very considerably—and above all, that colonial issues of the first magnitude have repeatedly been decided in Europe. What, however, has scarcely ever varied is the importance attached to naval power, both as a bulwark against invasion, as a protection to British carrying trade, and as a screen behind which colonial expansion could be conducted. If trade does not necessarily follow the flag, the fate of the navy and of the merchant service have always been intimately linked together. From this it follows that certain strategic routes of empire have always been specially in the mind of British statesmen. On the one hand our attitude towards continental Powers has always been vitally affected by *their* attitude to the Low Countries, where trade and strategy play almost equal parts. Alike in the days of Elizabeth, of William III, of Napoleon, of William II, of the Third Reich, we could not, and cannot, view with indifference the control of Antwerp and Rotterdam, of the Dutch and Flemish coasts, by an alien Great Power: and thus the Barrier Treaties find their later parallels in the ephemeral arrangement of 1815–30, in the treaty guaranteeing Belgian neutrality, and in the British attitude towards Belgium in 1914 and since the Great War. On the other hand, for two centuries and a half Mediterranean interests have also bulked very largely—it may be said only less largely—in British calculations: and Gibraltar, Minorca, Sicily, Corfu, Cyprus, have all at one time or another served as strategic points of vantage, while no Power has taken so keen and persistent an interest in the question of the Straits.

Viewed realistically, British policy is the natural expression of the national character, with its defects and its qualities. It has too often shown a distrust of other countries, based upon ignorance or prejudice: but in the main it was a sound instinct to hold aloof from, or if need be to resist, Powers whose appetite for power was all too unrestrained. It is not surprising that foreign governments should have entirely failed, or should have simply refused, to distinguish between the daring and rapacity of individual adventurers and the settled policy of an inactive government at home, which in the end reaped many a harvest sown without its knowledge. None the less it remains absolutely true that no Empire was ever formed in a more casual and haphazard manner than the British—given the all-important factors of opportunity and private initiative. Perhaps the real secret of foreign misunderstanding is the hesitation which has time after time asserted itself and led to Britain's temporary withdrawal, thereby deranging every balance and every calculation—a hesitation probably due to the vague feeling that Britain is of Europe, and yet not of it. The desire for isolation, the knowledge that it is impossible—these are the two poles between which the needle of the British compass continues to waver.

CHAPTER I

INTRODUCTORY: CASTLEREAGH AND THE
HOLY ALLIANCE*

BRITAIN AFTER WATERLOO

Twenty years of war and convulsion had transformed Europe almost out of recognition, and therefore, before we pass on, it may not be amiss to subject it to a bird's-eye survey. In our own island there was a reaction of sentiment and opinion in almost every sphere, after the long strain of the revolutionary and Napoleonic wars—not merely Reaction with a big R, but a natural release of the pendulum. On the one hand there were acute agrarian and industrial difficulties, which led to ever-recurring minor disorders. The industrial revolution had entered on a new phase, the towns were growing rapidly, the old rural population was affected by the fall in corn prices, there were mill riots and outbreaks of so-called Luddism. On the other hand there was a widespread fear of revolution among the propertied classes, and a desire to prevent political agitation, even by such drastic measures as the suspension of the Habeas Corpus and the Seditious Meetings Bill. Both these tendencies were accentuated by the economic crisis which followed upon the first brief abnormal post-war prosperity: and this crisis culminated in the famous riot known as the "Massacre of Peterloo" and in the passing of the "Six Acts", which imposed drastic restrictions on the carrying of arms, the right of public meeting and liberty of the press. It is to be borne in mind that the soul of these restrictive measures, the man who actually steered them through the House of Commons, was no other than Castlereagh, and that this fact not unnaturally coloured the attitude of contemporaries and even of later generations towards his foreign policy also. There was, moreover, a certain icy aloofness in his bearing that antagonised all save the inner ring of those attached to him by political or personal ties.

Meanwhile Parliament was absorbed to a very large extent in financial

* If this chapter is still written in outline, it is because the reader has an authoritative and indispensable guide in the books of Prof. C. K. Webster, *The Foreign Policy of Castlereagh* 1812–15 (1931) and 1815–22 (1925); chapter IV in *C.H.F.P.* vol. I; *The Congress of Vienna* (1919); and *British Diplomacy* 1813–15 (selected Documents).

and economic questions and in such vital issues as the reform of the poor law administration.* At the outset there was a certain agitation for reform, led by such men as Sir Francis Burdett and Hunt, and then again by William Cobbett, who occupies a peculiar place of his own in English history, as a champion of the rural classes and of democratic institutions, and as the pioneer of a certain section of the modern press, but who spoiled his prospects by his diatribes and quarrelsome, not to say scurrilous, language. The revolutionary party could not in any case make much impression on the unreformed Parliament of those days: but it also rapidly lost ground in the country, because its leaders were either second-rate or irresponsible, and partly also because some of them saw fit to adopt a markedly irreligious tone, which antagonised almost all sections of opinion. The Whigs showed extreme caution, their party was still dominated by the great territorial magnates: and more than a decade passed before some of them are again to be observed actively leading the reform movement. In the Castlereagh period this movement may be regarded as virtually dormant.

In the intellectual sphere England also pursues a development of her own. It is the period when extreme formalism in the Church has produced the breach with Wesley and those secessions which to-day we are prone to think might well have been avoided. The Evangelical school of thought may be described as a first wave of religious revival inside the Establishment, to be followed in the 'forties by the Oxford movement. But till that movement gathers weight, Oxford and Cambridge show but few signs of their ancient vitality and remain little better than preserves of privilege. It is the Scottish Universities which in the preceding period have been the chief centres of academic culture, under Robertson, Adam Smith, Ferguson and the philosophers: and it is a detail worth noting that the young Palmerston was sent not only to Cambridge, but to Edinburgh University, where he actually lodged in the house of Dugald Stewart, as well as attending his lectures.

There is an epoch-making school of political thought in England too, but as yet divorced from academic life, though it is ere long to preside over the first germs of the future University of London. These are the Utilitarians, who in contrast to the prevailing pietism, are if not irreligious, at least emancipated from Christian teaching. They are disliked in some quarters as unduly open to foreign influence, but retort by claiming to be essentially English, and the spiritual descendants of Locke. In reality Benthamism has been quite fairly defined by M. Halévy as the adaptation of eighteenth-

---

* M. Halévy's great *History of England since* 1815 gives a very full account of this aspect, while Sir Spencer Walpole's *History of England* will always have a certain value, as a sane presentment of the moderate Whig point of view.

century French philosophy to an English milieu.[1] Its basis is individualism, private initiative, *laisser-faire*, and its pure theory has the most far-reaching effects in the material sphere, in social legislation and in the general outlook alike towards economic problems and towards the state. And side by side with Bentham and Mill, the economic teachings of Ricardo and Malthus are slowly penetrating the public mind.

As yet, however, the Utilitarians form a watertight compartment, and there are other currents in the life of the nation which have still deeper roots and provide one of the main explanations of our outlook upon the Continent. The one may be quite summarily described as the moral and philanthropic, and comprises such many-sided activities as the anti-slavery agitation, the demand for prison reform and the restriction of capital punishment, the wonderful outburst of missionary enterprise, the abolition of simony (as the existing abuses in the Church would have been roundly designated in a less squeamish age), and the long drawn-out agitation for justice to the Catholics and Dissenters and the removal of antiquated religious tests. The other, in literature—romanticism—is at its height, with Scott, Byron, Shelley, Keats, the Lake School, and such now faded favourites as Tom Moore and Southey. But it is instructive to note that their influence upon the Continent is infinitely greater than that of the Continent upon them: indeed, Byron alone of them can be really described as cosmopolitan, which is doubtless one reason why his fame has lingered longest outside his own country. Of the others, Scott was in the very marrow of his being a Tory, while Wordsworth and Coleridge turned away from democratic tendencies in later life. Speaking quite broadly, we are entitled to identify the romantic movement in this country with tradition and with the maintenance of authority in church and state, whereas on the Continent it assumed in the main a revolutionary or semi-revolutionary character.

Lastly, we may note the rise of the modern press and the growing reputation, independence and influence of journalists. *The Times*, the *Courier*, the *Morning Post*, and the *Morning Chronicle*, are already powers to be reckoned with: journals like the *Political Register* and the *Examiner*, now long since extinct, and the two great rivals, then recently founded, the *Edinburgh* and *Quarterly Reviews*, command attention to an extent which we can hardly grasp in these days of over-commercialised newspapers, jostling each other in their noisy insignificance. And though there are great restrictions on liberty of speech and writing, yet by comparison with her neighbours Britain is the very home and fortress of such freedom.

In a word, Britain after Waterloo formed very much a world of its own, self-contained and in every sense insular. In politics this expressed itself in a belief, if not in the absolute perfection, at any rate in the perfectibility, of British institutions, and in a tendency to look down upon those who did not possess such signal benefits and to frown on those who showed a due lack of appreciation.

CONTINENTAL CURRENTS

It is in no way the purpose of this volume to attempt a survey of the Europe in which Castlereagh lived: but none the less, as an introduction to the man and his policy, it is necessary to remind the reader, if only in a few sentences, of the main factors upon the Continent with which he had to reckon.

Exhaustion, even greater than ours, was common to every country, and with it went the jarred nerves which expressed themselves in the two conflicting tendencies that came to be loosely known as Legitimacy and the Revolution. The alarm and resentment aroused among the dynasties and the ruling classes of the Continent by the French Revolution and its effects, made it possible, when the great effort was over and peace had at last returned, to bolster up at all costs what could still be reconstructed of the old regime, and to identify quite deliberately the conceptions of "revolutionary" and "liberal"—in much the same way as in some countries of post-war Europe it has often been sought to discredit advanced Liberals or Radicals by identifying them with Communism.

Austria, for instance, which in the eighteenth century under Maria Theresa and Joseph II had been in the very van of enlightened, though of course paternal, reform, had become under Francis impervious to new ideas—the chief fortress of reaction and immobility, or "Stability", as Francis and Metternich preferred to call it. One result of the settlement of 1815 was to leave Austria not merely free to maintain this rigid system throughout her own dominions, but to exercise a predominant influence both in Germany and in Italy, and thus to retard the political and even intellectual development in both those countries. The German Confederation was a lifeless automat, well-nigh incapable of initiative, and Prussia, the only state within it that was seriously in a position to hold Austria in check, was during the critical period following the Congress of Vienna, thanks to the weak personality of Frederick William III, almost entirely under the spell of Metternich, and had been induced by him to repress all movements in favour of political change, to muzzle the universities and the academic youth, and to repudiate the solemn pledges of constitutional reform given by the King under the Federal Act of 1815. Only in Würtemberg, Baden and some of the petty Thuringian states was there any approach to political liberty.

Italy meanwhile was bent beneath the yoke. Lombardy and Venetia were integral parts of Austria. Scions of the House of Habsburg reigned in

Tuscany, Modena and Parma. The King of the Two Sicilies was the near kinsman of the Emperor and bound to him by a secret treaty. The Pope was scarcely less dependent upon Austrian bayonets. Sardinia was isolated and as yet barely conscious of its future mission. The whole Peninsula was riddled with disaffection, the secret societies were the constant preoccupation of the authorities, and liberal tendencies were everywhere sternly discouraged.

In Spain neither the enlightened rule of Charles III nor the long convulsions of the Peninsular War had availed to rouse the nation from its essentially medieval outlook and traditions. The Constitution of 1812, though it was to serve as a battle cry and an example for Liberals in other lands, had no very wide support at home, and the sinister Ferdinand VII, on his return from exile, had no difficulty in repudiating it, with the help of the Conservative nobility and above all the Church and the Orders, who kindled the fanaticism of the masses in favour of the old regime. Ferdinand was alike odious as a man and incompetent as a ruler, and from the first Spain was a prey to misgovernment and financial disorder, rendered more acute by the growing unrest in her South American colonies. Meanwhile, the course of events in Spain quite naturally reacted upon Portugal, which was for the next few decades to follow a curiously parallel development.

Turning to the east of Europe, we find that in Turkey there had been three palace revolutions, the central authority had lost control over the provinces, Egypt and the whole of northern Africa were independent in all but name. The Serbs, left to their fate by Russia in 1812, had for the moment been reconquered, but from 1815 onwards, under the more cautious leadership of Miloš Obrenović, were establishing piecemeal their autonomous position. Wallachia and Moldavia still groaned under the corrupt Phanariot regime, now tottering to its fall. The Congress of Vienna had shown itself somewhat indifferent to the Eastern Question, but among all the subject races the fire was smouldering, and in Greece especially was soon to burst into flame.

Russia under Alexander I offered the curious spectacle of an absolute monarchy, controlled by a sentimental mystic, dabbling in liberalism and posing as constitutional King of Poland, though not willing to extend political liberties to Russia itself. Behind the scenes lurked always the memory of the tragedy by which he came to the throne, and the military revolt which followed his death in 1825 was to prove that he had not been wrong in fearing sedition even in the army. It is also a material point that his peculiar personality, while giving the impulse to the Holy Alliance, felt specially drawn towards the Christians of the East, with the result that when the Greek Revolution produced international complications, he found himself torn between two conflicting motives—the repression of a subversive movement and the emancipation of his co-religionists of the Orthodox faith.

CASTLEREAGH AND THE PEACE

Such, in the barest possible outline, is the European framework in 1814. But of course the settlement in one sense rested upon the new regime imposed by the Allies upon France: and this was in a peculiar degree the achievement of Castlereagh. But for him it may be doubted whether Louis XVIII would have returned, even if Tsar Alexander's candidature of Bernadotte for the French throne had in any case been rejected.

Again, it was Castlereagh who insisted on Britain guarding the person of Napoleon, against the wishes of the Cabinet. This half-way position was perhaps typical of the man, just as it was typical of Blücher to announce that he would shoot Napoleon if he caught him. Castlereagh wrote to Liverpool: "After fighting him for twenty years, as a trophy he seems to belong to us." With his record in home politics alike in England and Ireland, he was naturally enough indifferent to the odium attaching to a gaoler; he was quite proof against Napoleon's appeal for generous treatment and was playing above all for safety, and the cold-blooded decision of transportation to St Helena was pre-eminently safe.

On the other hand, he was strongly opposed to a vindictive or humiliating peace. His Conservative principles led him to favour the lawful heir to the French throne, and brought him into line with strict legitimist doctrine. But only up to a point. For it is highly characteristic of Britain's and of Castlereagh's half-way position, that he had no sympathy for the "Ultras" who surrounded the King's brother, the future Charles X, and that he threw all his weight in favour of the Charter which Louis XVIII accepted as the basis of his restoration, and which was gall and wormwood to such unalloyed legitimists as Metternich and Francis. But he was more logical than Wellington—the most illogical or opportunist of men, when he left the battlefield for the council chamber—and he drew the necessary conclusions from the restoration of the Bourbons, thereby discovering common ground between himself and Metternich. Castlereagh's openly proclaimed aim was "to bring the world back to peaceful habits": and both he and Metternich realised that to restore the Bourbons and at the same time to strip France not merely of her ill-gotten gains, but also of all that she had acquired on her eastern frontier since the days of Louis XIV (as a large section of allied opinion wished), was to condemn the dynasty to a short reign and to pave the way for some fresh upheaval. The result was that

France was eventually left with the frontiers of 1792. Wellington joined Castlereagh in favouring leniency, just as later on he favoured the evacuation of the occupied territory at the earliest practicable date.

In pressing for leniency, Castlereagh, like Metternich, was thinking of Europe as a whole. His central aim, stated in theoretic outline, was to restore the old Balance of Power which had been disturbed by Napoleon's inordinate ambitions—"the just equilibrium", as he constantly called it. Stated in general terms, it was to render it impossible for any one Power to attack its neighbours with a real prospect of success: translated into practice, it was to prevent any repetition of such events as those of the previous decade, to give France a sober, unsensational Government and to keep her within just bounds. This purpose is visible from the first in Castlereagh's actions: it is the foundation of the Treaty of Chaumont of March 1814, which, though at that stage a temporary fighting alliance, was converted by his insistence into an alliance of twenty years and contains a special clause (§xvi) in favour of the Balance of Power. In this Treaty, which on 25 March 1815 becomes the Quadruple Alliance of the four Powers, Britain, Austria, Russia and Prussia, there is the germ of what Pitt had vaguely defined as "a general and comprehensive system of public law in Europe". Dovetailed into this by the exigencies of the moment at the Congress of Vienna, is the triple pact between Britain, Austria and France —the work of Metternich, Talleyrand and Castlereagh—which led to the admission of France into the inner counsels of the Congress, the Committee of Four thus becoming the Committee of Five.*

France, then, was to be brought back into the Concert of Europe without delay, and not to be treated as an outlaw. But she was to be carefully watched and kept within strict bounds. As regards frontiers, this meant (1) the line of 1792, not "the natural frontiers", as the Rhine had been called only a few short years earlier, even by the Rhinelander Metternich himself; (2) the strengthening of Sardinia by the annexation of Genoa; and (3) what concerned Britain most of all, the union of Belgium and Holland into a single Kingdom of the Netherlands under the House of Orange. To this end Austria gracefully renounced her Belgian provinces, which she had held from the Peace of Utrecht in 1713 till their conquest by the French in 1794. This emancipation of Belgium and the Scheldt from French control interested Britain very specially: it had indeed been the most steadfast note in all British policy since the days of Cromwell.

---

* It is most interesting and instructive to contrast the methods adopted in Vienna in 1815 with those of Paris in 1919—especially the different attitude towards the defeated Power. This may be studied in Prof. C. K. Webster's admirable little Foreign Office Handbook, *The Congress of Vienna* (written for the Peace Conference of 1919).

Apart from this point, on which the Cabinet particularly insisted, the general European plan was left very much to Castlereagh, and his main ideas were to keep Russia as far away from Europe as possible, to prevent her from linking up with France, and as a double precaution, to strengthen Central Europe and to maintain Turkish integrity. This meant strengthening Prussia in the north and west—Westphalia and the Lower Rhine—and Austria elsewhere, but at the same time to promote a sincere Austro-Prussian friendship (it was for this that he was at one time ready to sacrifice Saxony), and lastly to leave Italy as an Austrian province. This general conception was supplemented in north and south by the union of Norway and Sweden—designed to render Scandinavia as a whole immune from Russian influence—and by the restoration of the worthless Bourbon dynasty at Naples. From a slightly different angle Castlereagh shared Metternich's desire to protect the centre of the Continent against Russia no less than against France.

Whatever we may think of it to-day, this was a real European system, resting in the main upon the realities of the moment. Meanwhile British sea power was absolutely assured: the drastic maritime rights which we had exercised at sea during the war and which produced the second American war of 1812, had been successfully asserted: and the way was open to the gigantic colonial expansion of the nineteenth century. Not that either official or public opinion was specially keen or prescient about the colonies: indeed, as on earlier occasions, they were sometimes used as the small change to facilitate transactions in Europe. Martinique and Guadaloupe were restored to France, Java to the Dutch and everything to Denmark. What we retained were essentially strategic points to safeguard commercial rights—Gibraltar, Malta, Corfu, St Helena, Mauritius and so on. The colonies were not the result of deliberate home policy, but were engendered by the industrial revolution, and by the growth of a surplus population, inspired by an enterprising and adventurous spirit. None the less it was this system, to whose establishment Castlereagh contributed so materially, that made possible the rise of what is sometimes called the Second British Empire.

CASTLEREAGH AND NATIONALITY

The essentially weak spot in the system was that it took no account of that decisive new factor, Nationality, and still acted in the true spirit of the eighteenth century by treating the peoples as little better than chattels of the dynasties. Castlereagh was as blind to national feeling as was Metternich himself, and in arranging the transference of Genoa to Piedmont and of

Norway to Sweden, was quite undeterred by the fact that in each case it ran counter to the express wishes of the peoples concerned. This was still more true of Sicily, and indeed the whole Italian Peninsula was carved upon purely dynastic principles and assigned to the sphere of absolutist Austria. In the Near East Turkish territorial integrity was regarded as sacred, and Castlereagh declined no less than six times to receive the Serbian delegates who knocked so patiently at his door during the Congress of Vienna. In Germany again the wishes of the people were never consulted, when portions of Saxony and Westphalia were transferred to Prussia and when other territorial readjustments were made between the various reigning houses. Consequently many of the foundations of 1815 proved to have been laid upon sand, and their piecemeal undermining by the flowing tide of Nationality fills and directs the diplomatic history of Europe right through the century.

It is interesting that there should have been just one exception to Castlereagh's general indifference to national questions, namely, Poland. Early in 1815 he made a strong appeal to the three partitioning Powers, to consider "the habits and usages" of the Poles "as a people", and to treat them "as Poles", whatever political system might be adopted. He may have been influenced by personal sentiment, but his main motive was almost certainly political expediency and the belief that his advice, if adopted, would make for peace and consolidation in Eastern Europe. In any case it was largely due to Castlereagh that the Vienna settlement guaranteed special institutions to the Poles and provided at any rate a legal basis for the protests— futile enough, it is true—which the Western Powers were to raise against the methods of repression applied by Russia in Poland after the two risings of 1831 and 1863.

Castlereagh was not only in the main indifferent to Nationality, he was definitely hostile to "democratic principles": but as may be seen from his famous State Paper of 5 May 1820,[2] he did not make Metternich's mistake of trying to identify democracy and revolution. He was simply a strong Conservative, to whom the new political movements of the Continent, with their strongly middle-class tinge, were antipathetic. Like so many members of the unreformed House of Commons, from Burke downwards, he looked upon liberty through aristocratic spectacles. But none the less his outlook differed essentially from that of his continental colleagues, as was to become increasingly apparent in the seven years after Waterloo. He was responsible to a somewhat refractory Parliament, and was careful, in his dealings with foreign Powers, to stress the constitutional aspect and the need for even "the strongest Administration which ever served the Crown", to assure itself that it is supported by "the Voice of the Country" (written with a big V). This, moreover, was an aspect which he was able to impress upon the Prince Regent, who was keenly interested in foreign policy and constantly meddled with it.

"The Confederation of Europe"

After 1815, then, Europe rested on a triple basis: (1) the Quadruple Alliance of Austria, Russia, Prussia and Britain, to maintain the peace terms imposed upon France; (2) the Pentarchy of the five Great Powers, to maintain public order and stability; and (3) the Holy Alliance, signed by the rulers of Russia, Austria and Prussia in September 1815, which has given its name to the decade following Waterloo.

This last was due to the initiative of Tsar Alexander, in whom the mystical and romantic strain inculcated by his tutor Laharpe and further encouraged by Frau von Krüdener, had reached its height at the period of the Congress of Vienna. It proclaimed as its aim "to take for their sole guide the precepts of the Christian religion—justice, charity and peace", and invited all the other Powers to join. The three allied Powers, it declared, regarded themselves "as merely delegated by Providence to govern three branches of the One family—thus confessing that the Christian world of which they and their people form a part, has in reality no other sovereign but Him to whom alone power really belongs". It concluded by recommending their subjects to follow Christian principles.[3]

These unusual but seemingly unexceptionable phrases really appealed to none except the sentimental Alexander, and in a mild and hesitating way to Frederick William III of Prussia. The practical Francis of Austria disliked it but signed, on the advice of Metternich, who scoffed at it as "a loud-sounding nothing". Castlereagh himself regarded it as "a piece of sublime mysticism and nonsense", and told Liverpool that the Tsar was not quite right in the head and must be humoured. So while not allowing the Prince Regent to give his name to the document on constitutional grounds, he sent a personal letter of agreement which satisfied the Tsar. For obvious reasons neither the Pope nor the Sultan could sign, and devout reactionaries shook their heads over a manifesto of Christian doctrine, launched by an Orthodox, a Catholic and a Protestant.

From the outset it remained on paper, the mere expression of a pious wish. But owing to the fact that it originated from the three absolutist sovereigns of Eastern Europe, and assumed a mainly dynastic and also a distinctly didactic character, it very speedily won the repute of being directed against popular liberties and so became the bugbear of the progressive party in every country. As Professor Webster has pointed out, such a charge is quite false "so far as the original conception of the Holy Alliance was concerned. But when the real Treaty of Alliance of 20 November 1815 was diverted from its original objects, the gibe appeared to be fulfilled, and the Holy Alliance became the name applied not to the original instrument, but to the whole system of Diplomacy by Conference".[4] This was the line taken by the British Opposition in the House of Commons.

It is important to distinguish between the two instruments, the Quadruple Alliance and the Holy Alliance, if we are to do justice to Castlereagh's ideas. The latter he laughed at, and merely assumed an attitude of external civility, because he could not afford to quarrel with or offend the Tsar. But the former was essentially Castlereagh's own achievement, and he it was who prevented the Tsar from inserting a guarantee both of King Louis and of his newly granted Charter. As Castlereagh argued, this revealed "too strong and undisguised a complexion of interference on the part of the Allied Sovereigns in the internal affairs of France", and in the end the treaty did not go further in this direction than to rule out any possible Bonapartist restoration.

Its most original feature, however, is Article VI, which, drafted by Castlereagh himself and representing his most practical contribution to the European system of his day, deserves to be quoted in full, even in the present outline. "To facilitate and secure the execution of the present Treaty, and to consolidate the connexions which at the present so closely unite the Four Sovereigns for the happiness of the world, the High Contracting Parties have agreed to renew their meetings at fixed periods, either under the immediate auspices of the Sovereigns themselves, or by their respective Ministers, for the purpose of consulting upon their common interests, and for the consideration of the measures which at each of these periods shall be considered the most salutary for the repose and prosperity of Nations, and for the maintenance of the Peace of Europe."

This, it has not unfairly been argued, is the first germ of the League of Nations, considered as an instrument of international peace and reached by successive stages. There is a clear and obvious evolution from this agreement through the tentative experiments between 1818 and 1822, the last of which broke down owing to the incompatibility of the rulers and the immaturity and indifference of public opinion; the next stage is the Concert of Europe as it was evolved from the Eastern crisis of 1839–41, and as it again established itself after the violent interlude of the Crimean War; and a third stage may be detected in the growing habit of international congresses which characterised the close of the century, and in the system of constant inter-allied conference and personal contact which established itself during the Great War, owing to the pressing needs of the moment.

Castlereagh is the true pioneer of personal contact between the statesmen of Europe, as an instrument of conciliation and a practical means of transacting business, not as superseding ordinary diplomacy, but supplementing and humanising it. It is also essential to realise that thanks to him Britain became more closely identified with the Peace settlement as a whole, than on any occasion previous to 1815: he deliberately rejected isolation as an altogether impracticable policy, holding that the experience of his master Pitt, who had tried it for a time and signally failed, was proof to all time that this island is bound to the Continent and cannot hold aloof.

In this very brief survey Castlereagh has been treated as the dominant figure, so far as this country is concerned, and of this there can be no question. But it would be a complete mistake to draw the conclusion that his chief, Lord Liverpool, was a mere figurehead. It is true that during the critical period of 1813–15 Castlereagh more than once imposed his will upon the Prime Minister and the Cabinet, but this was not by any arbitrary disregard of their wishes or by simply "rushing" them into action: and indeed there is the greatest possible contrast between his methods and those of Palmerston in 1840–1, still more in 1849–51. As British representative he followed his instructions loyally on essential points, and his advocacy of the abolition of the slave trade is a notable example of this: where he differed, he carried his view by force of character and weighty argument; he was at once the man on the spot who was able to convey essential information to his colleagues at a distance, and the trusted delegate who knew himself to be indispensable at home, but also had formed a very shrewd estimate of the lengths to which he could hope to carry others with him.

LIVERPOOL AND CASTLEREAGH

Lord Liverpool, we have already seen, was far from being a mere cipher: indeed, this is sufficiently proved by the fact that he was Prime Minister for a longer consecutive period than any other man save Pitt and Walpole, and was successful in holding together many divergent characters. That, in spite of holding such decided views of his own on foreign policy, he none the less entrusted the Foreign Office to two men of such mark as Castlereagh and Canning, clearly shows that he was free from personal jealousies and was a sound judge of character. But he constantly took a stronger line than Castlereagh, and only reluctantly allowed himself to be dissuaded. When the French Restoration Government indulged in vindictive measures against some of Napoleon's foremost generals and ministers, Liverpool, so far from showing indignation, gave his encouragement. "One can never feel that the King is secure on his throne, until he had dared to spill traitors' blood", he wrote to Castlereagh; and the execution of Marshal Ney, whom his victorious opponent Wellington would gladly have spared, and whom the royalists would not have shot in defiance of an allied veto, has been laid by more than one historian at Liverpool's door. It is necessary to add that Castlereagh had the bad taste to attend Ney's court-martial, and that he showed a singular indifference to the brutality and bad faith of Ferdinand VII of Spain and Ferdinand IV of Naples in suppressing those Liberal movements in their dominions which the British Alliance had done so much to foster. Indeed he stands convicted of a conspiracy with Metternich and Ruffo to condone the suppression of Sicilian liberty and to mislead the British Parliament as to the facts.

On the other hand, on the fundamental question Castlereagh stood firm. In July 1815 the Prime Minister had written to him: "The more I consider the present internal state of France and the little chance there is of security to Europe from the character and strength of the French Government, the more I am satisfied that we must look for security on the frontier, and in really weakening the power of France": and he therefore disapproved of leaving France "as she was left by the Treaty of Paris, and even as she was before the Revolution".[5] But he was convinced by Castlereagh's reasoning, and in the end gave him full and loyal backing in the task of European appeasement.

During the three years that separate Vienna from Aachen, the main problem that faced Castlereagh was how to secure a return to normal conditions, first in France itself, where the excesses of the White Terror soon spent themselves, and where the so-called "Chambre Introuvable", with its curious affinities to the Restoration Parliament in England, slowly yielded to the soothing influences of the Duc de Richelieu, a statesman of moderation, clear views and personal charm, who has not always received his due from historians. It was the settled policy of Castlereagh and Wellington, whose whole-hearted co-operation was a decisive factor in the situation, to make things easy for Richelieu, and to extract from the moderates a toning down of the regime, in return for a gradual reduction of the army of occupation, and of the financial claims put forward by the Allies.

Meanwhile, inside the Alliance the dominant factor in both London and Vienna was nervous suspicion of Russia, whose agents were actively stirring up trouble in Spain and Italy, and of her strange, unbalanced, mystical Tsar. No other than Metternich himself once propounded a highly plausible theory of Alexander's character,[6] as compounded of manly virtues and feminine weaknesses, subject to a sort of periodicity of moods: and he argued that the Tsar was alternately, and for about five years at a time, swayed by a blend of Liberalism and religious revivalism, and by an equally strong revulsion to extreme political reaction. Certain it is that the former of these tendencies reached its height between 1812 and 1817, but declined very noticeably after the latter year, and that Castlereagh and Metternich were at one in regarding both moods with almost equal suspicion. It was the working alliance between these two men that really decided the trend of events in Europe, and one of their main points of contact was undoubtedly their vigilant reserve towards Russia. There has at times been a mistaken tendency to ascribe undue importance to one or the other, rather than to recognise the greatness of both and their frequent interdependence. Professor von Srbik, the latest and infinitely the most serious biographer of Metternich, assigns a quite disproportionate value to his own hero and allows him to dwarf the British statesman. Professor Webster, on the other hand, points out that "the praises which Metternich gave to Castlereagh, and in particular the contrast which he drew between him and Canning, have done more to injure his reputation than all the abuse of Byron and Cobbett".[7] But not content with denying that Castlereagh was ever "the dupe of Metternich", as the next generation was prone to believe, he goes too far in his turn, when he claims that "in the major problems of diplomacy Castlereagh led and Metternich followed". It may suffice to maintain that for the first critical years after the Congress of Vienna the good understanding between London and Vienna provides the main key.

THE CONGRESS OF AACHEN

The last four years of Castlereagh's tenure of office (1818–22) witnessed a series of meetings between the sovereigns and statesmen of the five Great Powers—the first experiment in the government of Europe by international conference. The scheme adopted in the present volume renders it unnecessary to treat this period in detail.[8]

Already in 1817 Metternich had proposed a Congress of the Great Powers, and Aachen (Aix-la-Chapelle) had been selected as its scene: the problem of the evacuation of French territory became increasingly urgent in proportion as domestic calm returned to France, and some such international discussions were felt to be necessary. Incidentally it was the first Congress of its kind, to be convoked amid profound peace, rather than for the liquidation of a general war.

The various problems connected with evacuation and war debts were settled with unexpected ease, to the satisfaction of France and of the Bourbon dynasty. The sustained moderation of Wellington played a vital part, but also the half-acknowledged fear that the new French regime was far from stable and might collapse, unless it were given active encouragement.

The Quadruple Alliance was still upheld, in case France should make some fresh bid for power, but as the result of a compromise she was invited to adhere to the so-called "diplomatic Concert of the Courts". The Russian Ambassador in Vienna had argued that "under Napoleon, Europe was despotic: if she is not to become democratic, she must be maintained by the four great Courts which are at the head of the European state-system, with the later addition of France".[9] But Castlereagh was averse to further extensions or definitions, and this not only because both he and Liverpool instinctively hesitated to commit themselves too far, but because Parliament was in an insular and restive mood, while even inside the Cabinet itself criticism found a focussing-point in George Canning. Already at this date Canning held the view that Britain's consent to hold regular conferences "with the great despotic monarchs...would really amount to a combination of governments against liberty".[10] He spoke in this sense in the House of Commons, and Liverpool himself reminded the British delegates at Aachen of the need for caution. "We must recollect in the whole of this business, and ought to make our Allies feel, that the general and European discussions of these questions will be in the British Parliament, and that we have a new Parliament to meet, which has not been tried, of a doubtful character, and certainly not accustomed to look at foreign questions as Parliaments were some years ago, when under the pressure or immediate recollection of great foreign danger."[11]

When once evacuation had been decided, the discussions at Aachen centred round the Tsar's proposal for a Universal League "of all the Powers of Europe, guaranteeing to each other [to quote the words of Castlereagh's confidential report to the Cabinet] the existing order of things in thrones as well as in territories, all being bound to march if requisite, against the first Power that offended either by her ambitions or by her revolutionary transgressions".[12]

Metternich was ready to accept, in the belief that such pledges would at least serve as a brake upon Russian aggression and Prussian militarism, while Frederick William III might have signed without a full perception of all that the document implied. But Castlereagh from the first firmly opposed a scheme which neither Cabinet nor public opinion could have been induced to accept. He pointed out to his Allies, that "the idea of an 'Alliance Solidaire', by which each state shall be bound to support the state of succession, government and possession within all other states from violence and attack, upon condition of receiving for itself a similar guarantee, must be understood as morally implying the previous establishment of such a system of general government as may secure and enforce upon all kings and nations an internal system of peace and justice. Till the mode of constructing such a system shall be devised, the consequence is inadmissible, as nothing would be more immoral or more prejudicial to the character of government generally, than the idea that their force was collectively to be prostituted to the support of established power without any consideration of the extent to which it was abused".[13]

Castlereagh did his best to explain to the Tsar the peculiar British mentality towards international commitments taken in advance, and "admitted that it was perhaps a misfortune in our system that we could not act upon precautionary principles so early or so easily as His Imperial Majesty, but that the only chance we had of making the nation feel the wisdom of such a course was to be free, at the moment, to urge the policy of so acting, *not because we had no choice, but as having a choice*".[14] Acting upon this principle, he and Wellington insisted on restricting future meetings of the sovereigns and their ministers "to those interests that grow out of the transactions in question": no further attempt was made to define the phrase "at fixed periods", or to give clearer shape to "the Areopagus of Europe". The Tsar seems to have shown considerable understanding for what has always been the fundamental dilemma of British policy (and never more so than in 1914 and in 1936).

On this, as on other occasions, Castlereagh occupied a middle position, fully in keeping with British sentiment: for while refusing the guarantee for which the Tsar had asked, he steadily defended towards the Cabinet his policy of maintaining the Congress system, within reasonable bounds. "I am quite convinced", he wrote home, "that past habits, common glory and these occasional meetings, displays and repledges are among the best securities Europe now has for a durable peace."[15] The opposite view was again voiced by Canning, who argued that "the system of periodical meetings" was "new and of very questionable policy, and that it will necessarily involve us deeply in all the politics of the Continent, whereas our true policy has always been not to interfere except in great emergencies and then with commanding force".[16] In actual fact the difference between the two statesmen was far more one of method and of temperament than of principle. Both recognised isolation to be an utterly unattainable aim for a country with such world-wide interests as Britain. If Castlereagh, thanks to the close personal contacts which he had established, still hoped to maintain the grand alliance as an effective instrument of peace and European co-operation, he was by no means blind to those dangers of entanglement which the more ardent Canning stressed: and indeed the events of the next three years were to force the two men slowly nearer to each other, until in the famous State Paper of 1820 a highest common factor may be said to have emerged. To the superficial contemporary, Canning in office may have seemed to be engaged in reversing Castlereagh's policy: but what killed the first tentative experiment in international government was the fundamental conflict of political ideas which, especially from 1819 onwards, tended to separate Europe into two spiritual camps, whose members could only co-operate spasmodically and for specific and transitory aims.

Castlereagh returned home from Aachen, well enough satisfied that the reins of government were being everywhere drawn tighter, subversive influences subjected to fuller control and the mutual jealousies and misunderstandings of statesmen allayed: and he received the special thanks of the British Cabinet for his exertions. Metternich for his part might rest content, for his position in Europe had never been stronger: a few months later he quoted with slightly fatuous approval Talleyrand's epigram: "Austria is Europe's House of Lords: so long as it is not dissolved, it will keep the Commons in check."* For the rest, he had to be content with the old all too complicated machinery—the Quadruple Alliance, to prevent any fresh French upheaval, the Concert of Five to maintain peace and discuss fresh problems as they arose, and as a wheel within wheels, a provisional Austro-British entente, acting not unlike a reinsurance policy, and directed not least of all towards keeping Russia and France apart.

Unrest and Reaction

There was, however, no permanent ground for satisfaction: for the situation throughout Europe very speedily deteriorated. The latent conflict between sovereigns and peoples could no longer be concealed, and nowhere was the disillusionment greater than in Germany, where the rising middle class, and especially the universities and the academic youth, were infected with liberal ideas, and not unnaturally indignant at the failure of Frederick William III to fulfil his constitutional pledges. The famous demonstrations of the Wartburg in October 1817—the tercentenary of Luther's theses— caused great alarm at the German Courts: and henceforth Metternich never lost an opportunity for poisoning the mind of Frederick William and convincing him that the introduction of a representative and elective system meant in effect "the dissolution of the Prussian State",[17] and that on the King's decision rested the failure or triumph of "the Revolution" in Europe as a whole. In particular, with a sure but perverted instinct, he laid stress on the efforts of the revolutionaries to capture the rising generation, and on the consequent need for drastic common action on the part of Austria and Prussia, to crush the student organisations and restrict freedom

---

* *Nachg. Papiere*, III, 298. He had told his wife, on the eve of Aachen, that he had come "like the Messiah to deliver sinners" (*ibid.* III, 111).

of the press. The murder of Kotzebue—the German poetaster turned Tsarist secret agent—by a crackbrained student of Erlangen (March 1819) and an attempt on the life of the Nassau statesman Ibell, seemed to justify Metternich's reiterated plea for repression. Following on the discovery of subversive plots inside the Russian army, it greatly hastened the Tsar's conversion to whole-hearted reaction: and Metternich wrote to Gentz that he intended "to make the utmost possible capital out of it" in Berlin. During the summer of 1819 Metternich had a personal interview with Frederick William, and reduced him to a state of thoroughgoing panic: and their deliberations soon resulted in the Karlsbad Decrees, which imposed restrictions upon the press, a new censorship, a central commission of inquisition into "treasonable practices", and special measures for the control of the German Universities. It is true that in the three chief South German states—Bavaria, Württemberg and Baden—at this very time certain mild measures of constitutional reform were introduced: but the agreement between Vienna and Berlin meant that the greater part of Germany was dominated by what the jubilant Gentz described as "the greatest retrograde movement in Europe for thirty years past". Modesty was never one of Metternich's failings: "we have had the courage", he assured the Prince Regent, "to take up the glove thrown down by the revolutionaries", and to his wife he did not hesitate to write, " I hope to beat the German Revolution, just as I conquered the conqueror of the world".[18]

Even in Britain there was considerable unrest, and acute alarm on the part of the propertied classes, though the grotesque disproportion between the name popularly given to the "Peterloo Massacre" and the actual facts of the case is in itself a proof that "Reaction" meant quite different things in Lancashire and Dorset, or in Spain, Lombardy and the Spielberg. Castlereagh privately assured Neumann, "We are always pleased to see evil germs destroyed, without the power to give our approbation openly": and to Metternich himself he penned the oft-quoted phrase, "The monster still lives and shows itself in new shapes: but we do not despair of crushing him with time and patience".[19] The essence of his view is contained in an earlier despatch, in which he refers to "the danger that the transition [to liberty] may be too sudden to ripen into anything likely to make the world better or happier", and held it to be better "to retard than accelerate the operation of this most hazardous principle which is abroad".[20] But he refused to associate the British Government with the policy of repression adopted at Karlsbad, and set himself to discourage Metternich's interventionist ardour. The utmost to which he was ready to assent was intervention to prevent infringements of the constitutional settlements embodied in the Treaty of Vienna and therefore endorsed by the Allied Powers. But this again reveals the essential difference of outlook between the conservative Castlereagh and his continental colleagues, who were incapable of drawing, or at least quite disinclined to draw, any distinction between revolution and anarchy on the one hand and those representative institutions or currents of constitutional and liberal reform which in the main derived from the British example and evoked a certain sympathy even from the most hidebound of British Tories. When early in 1820 the news of the murder of the Duke of Berri, heir to the French throne, first reached Metternich, he penned the revealing phrase, "Liberalism goes its ways, it rains murderers".[21] This perverse identification speaks volumes: and Castlereagh himself was already conscious of the gulf of ideas that separated the sovereigns and the peoples, and that was now in process of dividing Europe into two main camps.

A YEAR OF REVOLUTION

The year 1820 was like the breaking of a dam in Europe: no sooner had the Powers assured themselves that the revolution had been averted in France and in Germany, than the floods forced an opening in one Mediterranean country after another. The Spanish insurrection in January of that year had begun in the army, but spread with great rapidity and forced the perjured King to re-establish the suppressed Constitution of 1812 and to feign satisfaction, while secretly appealing for foreign aid. The example was infectious, and in July and August there were no less successful revolutions in Naples and in Portugal: events gave a fresh stimulus to the chronic resistance of the Spanish Colonies and made their independence a mere matter of time. The Cabinets of Europe were entirely taken by surprise, and their boasted unity was soon rent by deep fissures. The Tsar demanded intervention everywhere in defence of the existing order, and was perfectly ready to march armies across Europe to suppress the Spanish Revolution. Metternich agreed in principle, but so long as only Spain was in question, was content to leave the precedence to England, and feared any steps which might lead to a Russian hegemony, while France naturally had no desire to see foreign troops on her soil, even in a cause with which her reactionary Government might sympathise. When Naples followed Spain, Metternich's alarm increased, for Austrian prestige throughout Italy was at stake: he soon found himself on the horns of a dilemma, for which his secret treaty with Ferdinand of Naples gave him the excuse he needed, and while neither France nor Britain raised any objection to a purely Austrian intervention, as opposed to action in the name of the whole Alliance, it was just this latter alternative upon which the Tsar eagerly insisted.

The attitude of the British Government was partly determined by the curious domestic situation which followed the death of George III in January 1820. The scandalous brawl between the new King and his ill-used but quite impossible wife produced great political uncertainty: George IV was furious at the Cabinet's refusal to consent to his divorce, and for a time Castlereagh was the only minister who had any influence over him, so that to all his work at the Foreign Office and as Leader of the Commons was superadded the thankless task of mediating between King and Premier. His health was thus undermined, with fatal results two years later.

This somewhat precarious situation, in which George IV might perhaps revert to his earlier practice of alliance with the Whigs, rendered Castlereagh more than usually circumspect. He and his colleagues were shocked at the Spanish Revolution, but deprecated any general action and did all in their power to restrain Metternich. Great weight attached to Wellington's view that "there is no country in Europe, in the affairs of which foreigners can interfere with so little advantage as Spain":[22] and there was clearly much to be said for the claim that after her efforts from 1808 to 1814 Britain had special interest in, and comprehension of, Spanish and Portuguese affairs, and that they involved no direct danger for the rest of Europe. It was the Tsar's insistence upon joint action that led Castlereagh to define his attitude in a memorandum which was long ascribed erroneously to Canning, and which, since its full text was published in our own day, has rightly been regarded as one of the most important State Papers of its kind.*

THE CONGRESS OF TROPPAU

Metternich found himself between the two fires of St Petersburg and London, but yielded to the Tsar's insistence upon the summons of a fresh Conference, at the pleasant little health-resort of Troppau, in Austrian Silesia. But Castlereagh—once more influenced by the attitude of Parliament—flatly refused to regard Troppau as a full conference of the Five Powers, writing to his brother Lord Stewart, the Ambassador in Vienna, that "the more Russia wishes to transport us to the heights, the further we must descend into the plain", and warning Prince Esterházy that while ready for continued co-operation, Britain could not consent "to extend the Alliance so as to include all objects, present and future, foreseen and unforeseen".[23]

When, then, the Conference met in October 1820, Britain and France were only represented by Ambassadors, acting as little more than friendly observers: and the breach between the Eastern and Western Powers steadily widened. The three former were left to enunciate the principle of interven-

* See *infra* p. 73.

tion in a cruder form than ever before. "If in states belonging to the European Alliance changes of government are produced by a revolution, and if their consequences threaten other states, then they are excluded from the Alliance until their situation offers guarantees of legitimate order and permanence." And further, the Allies agreed "to refuse recognition to changes brought about by illegal methods", and laid down their right in case of danger— of which they themselves would of course be the judges—to bring back errant members to the fold of the Alliance, "first by friendly representations, then by measures of coercion, if the employment of such coercion is indispensable". In effect, this was a mutual guarantee of the three Eastern Powers against "Revolution". In Fyffe's words, "the Alexander who designed the Holy Alliance was the Alexander who had forced Louis XVIII to grant the Charta": but the Alexander of 1820 was an entirely different being, increasingly under the spell of Metternich.

The principles embodied in this Protocol were promptly denounced by Castlereagh as "so directly opposed to the political and constitutional system of Great Britain, that the latter must disavow and even protest against them.... If the King were to sanction them, he would be on the road to his own abdication".[24] Britain could not approve of any "attempt to reduce to an abstract rule of conduct possible cases of interference in the internal affairs of independent states". "The wide sweeping powers claimed for the Allies", so Castlereagh argued, "conflicted with the Alliance and were an unwarranted assumption of a sovereign power over the other States of Europe." Britain had an almost equal objection to secret societies and revolutions, and to the idea of the Allies becoming "the armed guardians of all thrones". And then, fully conscious of the latent opposition in the House of Commons, he went on, "The House of Hanover could not well maintain the principles upon which the House of Stuart forfeited the throne.... We cannot adhere to their [i.e. the three Powers'] doctrine, and if they will be theorists, we must act in separation upon matters not specifically provided for by Treaty". Europe had indeed reached a parting of the ways, when the arch-Tory statesman was reduced to quoting the doctrines of 1688 and 1713 against his legitimist colleagues in Vienna and St Petersburg. Even the French revolutionaries rejected the idea of "a new public law" which would entitle the three Eastern Powers "to put a ban upon any country in which in their opinion an internal change was introduced in an illegal manner".[25] Metternich, so long "divided between the fear of revolutions and the fear of Russia,[26] believed himself to be engaged in a life and death struggle between the old system and the new in Europe, and regretfully recognising that Castlereagh was escaping from his grasp, concentrated his efforts upon influencing Alexander and Frederick William. His memorandum to the

Tsar pleaded for "union between the monarchs", as the sole hope of political salvation: but let their Governments really *govern*, maintain existing institutions unimpaired, reform their finances and root out the secret societies which are like a gangrene in the body politic. He now proposed a fresh Conference at Laibach, at which the King of Two Sicilies and other Italian delegates should be invited to attend.

THE CONGRESS OF LAIBACH AND THE GREEK REVOLUTION

The Congress of Laibach represented the highest point of Metternich's influence in Europe. The Tsar was now as completely under his spell as he had been immune from it during the Congress of Vienna, and the Chancellor could write exultantly of him: "If ever anyone has turned from black to white, it is he." The Tsar and the King of Prussia speedily authorised the despatch of Austrian troops in aid of the King of Naples, and when a military revolt broke out in Piedmont in March 1821, Austria was again entrusted with the necessary measures for its suppression. On 3 April Metternich seemed triumphant all along the line: "I have one extinguished revolution and two budding ones on my hands", he wrote, "one monarch who wont budge an inch, and a second who wants to march double quick time." Austria's power in Italy seemed stronger than ever, and Russia was ready to help her with 100,000 men. "Let us save Europe", said Alexander, "for it is God's will."[27] The worthless Ferdinand was restored at Naples, and encouraged to repeat his habitual perjury. The King of Sardinia abdicated, and his brother Charles Felix, with the open backing of Austria, reasserted the absolutist position of the Crown, and incidentally ignored the hope of the British Government that Victor Emmanuel I would recall his abdication. Metternich rashly assumed "the diplomatic battle to be gained", and received from Emperor Francis the title of "State Chancellor" as a crowning honour.

More openly than ever Castlereagh was driven to withold co-operation from his former allies. The Circular which he addressed to all the Courts, in answer to the resolutions of Troppau, roundly declared that "the system of measures proposed...would be in direct repugnance to the fundamental laws of this country" (a typical instance of his clumsy English). In the special case of Naples a strong distinction was drawn between intervention by Austria, which was admitted, and intervention by the Allies, which could not "without the utmost danger...be incorporated into the ordinary diplomacy of states, or into the institutes of the law of nations".[28] This time the British Government had been driven to make known its special attitude to all the world: and there followed debates in Parliament which made it abundantly clear to the Eastern allies that it was useless to count upon British public opinion for the old co-operation. Castlereagh, it is true, said what he could for the Alliance on more abstract lines, resented Lord Holland's attack upon the Tsar and warned Mackintosh that "it was too much to be told that the British Government ought to dictate moral lessons to Europe". But he used an ominous, if obscure, phrase about the Allied Sovereigns, who with the best motives seemed to be unaware "how soon the blood of their own people might become the sacrifice of the revolutionary principles which were advocated throughout Europe".[29]

The increasing reserve shown by Castlereagh during 1821 was strengthened by developments at two opposite extremities of Europe. At home the scandal of Queen Caroline's trial kept opinion in a ferment, undermined the reputation of the Crown, caused acute friction between the King and his Ministers, and for a time threatened to upset the Cabinet and bring back the Whigs to power. Meanwhile, as if the troubles in Naples and Piedmont, following upon those of Spain and Portugal, had not been enough for allied nerves, the Congress of Laibach was still sitting when news came of the first mutterings of the Greek Revolution. It is true that Ypsilanti's famous invasion of Moldavia ended in swift fiasco, thanks to his own incompetence and to the well grounded suspicions of the native Roumanian population: and though Ypsilanti had long enjoyed the special favour of the Tsar, and though Alexander's own Foreign Minister, Capodistrias, was himself a Greek and naturally sympathetic to the cause of his compatriots, Metternich none the less found it comparatively easy to win over Alexander for a public disavowal of the rebels. He could indeed plead the unanswerable argument that to give his sanction to Ypsilanti's enterprise would explode the very foundations of the Holy Alliance. But there soon followed a much more serious rising among the Greeks of the Morea and the Archipelago, venting itself only too often in massacres of the Turkish landlords: and Sultan Mahmud, in addition to the usual reprisals, took a fearful vengeance by hanging the Greek Patriarch and three of his clergy in full canonicals before the gate of his own Cathedral (23 April). This changed the whole aspect of affairs, for Orthodox feeling was kindled in Russia, and henceforth Tsar Alexander himself, always so open to religious and semi-mystical motives, was torn in two opposite directions. Logically, the Greeks were of course no less rebels than the Neapolitans or Spaniards, and to recognise their right to resist Turkish conquest and misrule was a breach in the principles on which the Holy Alliance rested. "Beyond our Eastern frontiers, 300,000 or 400,000 hanged, strangled and impaled, do not count much," so wrote the cynical Metternich:[30] but his attempts to treat the Greek revolt solely as a challenge to social order and monarchical authority fell upon deaf ears. The twin forces of religion and nationality were already ranging themselves against him. Russia felt acutely the challenge to her position as protector of the Eastern Christians, and could not be indifferent to their fate, which was, moreover, bound up with the complex problem of her Imperialistic designs against Turkey, and of Russian access to the Mediterranean. In August 1821 the Russian Ambassador was withdrawn from Constantinople, and although Alexander allowed himself to be held back by the constant appeals of his Austrian and Prussian allies and by the fear of doing anything which might react unfavourably upon central or western Europe, a conflict between Russia and Turkey was henceforth really only a question of time, especially in view of the utter intransigeance of the Sultan and his Ministers.

Castlereagh had always been fully alive to the importance of the Eastern Question: it was doubtless in the nature of things that he should have laid the main stress upon the *status quo* and failed to take the Christian subjects of the Porte very seriously. "Barbarous as it is", he once assured the Tsar, "Turkey forms in the system of Europe a necessary evil."[31] But while constantly exhorting the Porte to moderation—a quality which even his very Turcophil Ambassador, Lord Strangford, was unable to detect at Constantinople—he also spared no effort to restrain the Tsar on his side. One of his principal despatches to Bagot in St Petersburg shows the extent to which he misjudged the Greek Revolution. "They form a branch of that organised spirit of insurrection which is systematically propagating itself throughout Europe, and which explodes wherever the hand of the governing Power from whatever cause is enfeebled. If its symptoms are more destructive in Turkey, it is because, in that unhappy country, it finds all those passions and prejudices, and above all those religious animosities, which give to civil commotions their most odious and afflicting colours."[32]

CASTLEREAGH AND METTERNICH

In the course of the summer the advantages of a direct exchange of views appear to have occurred almost simultaneously to Metternich and Castlereagh: and the latter took advantage of George IV's visit to Hanover in October, to transmit a cordial invitation to the Austrian Chancellor. This journey helped to soothe down the King, who was in a highly refractory mood, had refused for months past to have any dealings with Liverpool and most of his colleagues, and had virtually driven Canning out of the Cabinet, owing to the latter's espousal of Queen Caroline's cause. The meeting proved a great success: George, in his talks with Metternich, made "passionate outbursts" against the Tsar and Capodistrias, and also indulged in much indiscreet abuse of Liverpool and the whole Tory Cabinet. He made a solitary exception in favour of Castlereagh, who, he told Metternich, "understands you, and is your friend, and that says everything". On returning home, he spoke openly of Metternich as "the first statesman in Europe, and after him Londonderry: these statesmen understand each other so perfectly, and their agreement is so important in the present state of Europe, that this circumstance alone ought to outweigh all other considerations".[33] Metternich, on his side, was vain enough to take at their face value King George's extravagant compliments, and reported to Francis that Austria's "political standpoint would undoubtedly win by England taking a more energetic part in world affairs".[34] He and Lord Londonderry—for Castlereagh had recently succeeded his father as second Marquis—resumed their old cordiality, and applied themselves in earnest to the task of mediation between Tsar Alexander and the Turks. To the latter they put forward "Four Points", the essence of which were the protection of the Greek Orthodox faith and the evacuation of the Principalities: but their efforts shattered against the utter intractability of Mahmud, who had already disgraced a Grand Vizier on the express ground of his "humanity towards the Christians", and who now, in April 1822, horrified Europe by almost wiping out the defenceless population of Chios.

None the less they were surprisingly successful in holding back the Tsar, who allowed himself to be convinced of the connection between the Philike Hetairia (the Greek secret society) and the Carbonari, and to be frightened by the alleged "Solidarity of Revolution throughout Europe".[35] Castlereagh, in particular, had already made it clear to the Tsar that he could "not reconcile it to my sense of duty to embark in a scheme for new-modelling the position of the Greek population in those countries at the hazard of all the destructive confusion and disunion which such an attempt may lead to, not only within Turkey but in Europe": the Greeks, he vaguely argued, must rely upon "the hand of time and of Providence to achieve their aims".*

For the moment the Greek question had brought Britain and Austria together again, while the renewed trouble in Spain cast a passing shadow upon Franco-British relations. Castlereagh regarded the whole Eastern Question, "not as a theoretical, but as a practical, consideration of the highest moment".[36] But events were steadily forcing Britain to adopt a new attitude, both as regards the Spanish Colonies and the Greek Revolution, and in both cases fundamental principles were involved. Castlereagh was

---

* 28 October 1821, to Bagot and the Tsar—cit. Webster, pp. 376–8. Esterházy reported to Metternich from London; "The public here of course look on the question as one of liberalism, but they are not prepared to see the liberty of Greece bought at the price of Russian supremacy in the Mediterranean" (*ibid*. p. 362).

confronted by a European situation in which the principles of public law were being identified with the territorial *status quo*, the legitimacy of thrones and arbitrary government: and this was more than even so staunch a Tory could stomach, conscious as he was of English constitutional origins.

Meanwhile the quarrel between the Spanish clericals and progressives— "Exaltados" and "Serviles" were their significant nicknames—grew daily more acute and was steadily fomented by King Ferdinand. The British Government, with its long experience of that impossible monarch, leant slightly towards the constitutional party, but held aloof from all ideas of intervention, and of course viewed with extreme disapproval the rhetorical appeals of the Clericals to Louis XVIII, to save "the prisoners of Madrid" from a repetition of 1793. The Tsar went to the opposite extreme from England, and was ready to send 40,000 Russian troops to Spain, as his contingent to a "European army": but even Metternich, though he was glad of anything that might divert Alexander's attention from eastern Europe, realised very clearly that drastic action in Spain would speedily undo all the good effects of the Hanover meeting, and might fatally alienate Britain from the Alliance. In France the ultra-Royalist faction, including the Foreign Minister Montmorency, clamoured for an immediate march on Madrid, and were with difficulty restrained by the more statesmanlike Villèle.

Castlereagh's immediate policy was to allow the Spanish Revolution to run its course, and to use all his influence in order that the other Powers should do likewise. But it was obvious that a new situation had arisen in Europe, in which the front of the stage was no longer occupied by questions of only secondary interest to Britain, such as Naples or Piedmont, but by problems which vitally concerned her—the fate of Turkey and the Aegean on the one hand, of Spain and above all her rebellious colonies on the other. The question of British trade with the Levant and with Spanish America was interwoven with the general diplomatic and political situation. When, then, Metternich pressed for yet another Congress, this time at Verona, to complete the work of Laibach, Castlereagh felt that Britain must no longer be represented by a mere diplomatic observer, but by a statesman who knew the whole mind of the Cabinet and could commit them in case of need: and despite the strain of an unusually arduous parliamentary session and the additional task of "managing" the King, he eventually decided that he must be his own ambassador. He had the great advantage of being able to draw up his own instructions, which left him very considerable latitude and were to have been supplemented by personal conversations, on the way to Verona, with Villèle, King Louis and above all Metternich. The lines which he proposed to follow did not differ in essentials from the Memorandum of 5 May 1820, which was to form the point of departure for his successor's policy. The direction in which Castlereagh's mind was working is clearly shown by his insistence that *de facto* recognition must after a certain lapse of time inevitably be followed by full diplomatic recognition, and that the only practical question was "how long": and little as he sympathised with the Greeks, he felt that this applied to them no less than to the Spanish colonists.* In a very frank despatch to Madrid he argued that the King of Spain "must be aware that so large a portion of the world cannot, without fundamentally disturbing the intercourse of civilised society, long continue without some recognised and established relations; that the State which can neither by its councils nor by its arms effectually assert its own rights over its dependencies so as to enforce obedience and make itself responsible for maintaining their relations with other Powers, must sooner or later be prepared to see those relations established, from the overruling necessity of the case under some other form".[37] What Canning was eventually to carry out with so much *éclat* in Greece and in South America, can already be traced in embryo in Castlereagh's cumbrous enough phrases.

CASTLEREAGH AS STATESMAN

At this point high tragedy intervened, and Castlereagh's career came to an abrupt close. His health had been steadily breaking down under the strain of overwork and responsibility, he suffered from illusions which his doctor utterly failed to diagnose, and on 12 August 1822 he took his own life. No British statesman of modern times has ever been so misjudged by contemporaries, or exposed to such scurrilous libels: and the lofty contempt which was his answer served to perpetuate the widespread popular assumption, that he, and not their real author, the panic-stricken Sidmouth, was responsible for the repressive Six Acts, and at the same time the chief inspirer of Reaction on the Continent. When he died, party rancour went to such lengths that his coffin was hissed while it was being carried into the Abbey: and it speaks volumes for the period, that such obscene doggerel as Byron's quatrain upon Castlereagh's grave should have been thought fit for inclusion in the poet's collected works!† He had never cared about public opinion, and public opinion took an ample vengeance for the slight. Yet "as a manager of men, he had no equal", and though he remained inscrutable to his colleagues and had few intimate friends, he was unquestionably a great

---

* *Well. Desp.* 1, 284. Recognition of the Greeks as belligerents must, he held, "be done with caution and without ostentation, lest it should render the Turks wholly inaccessible to our remonstrances".

† See too the dedication to *Don Juan*. Shelley also showered abuse upon him:
  "I met Murder on the way:
  He had a mask like Castlereagh."

diplomatist, conciliatory, informed, courageous, adroit, patient, full of tact and consideration for others. In the words of Croker, "Like Mont Blanc he continues to gather all the sunshine upon his icy head....It is a splendid summit of bright and polished frost, which, like the travellers in Switzerland, we all admire: but no one can hope and few would wish to reach."[38]

Castlereagh was as secretive as any old-world diplomatist: for all his clear and original thinking, he expressed himself in dry, stilted and involved language, and in the end he left his papers in complete disorder. This, and the rancorous traditions of his own day, delayed the process of clearing his memory from many a myth and deliberate calumny.* But when at last the vindication came, it was thorough and impressive: and it is difficult to believe that the preliminary spadework of Alison Phillips, followed by the minute and scholarly, yet broadly balanced, research work of C. K. Webster, can ever again be superseded.[39] However much the verdict upon the settlement of Vienna may fluctuate—according as its omission to take due account of the new fermenting influence of Nationality be judged with greater or lesser severity, as being inevitable, or as sowing the seeds of all the worst troubles of the century—no one to-day will seriously deny that Castlereagh was one of the very greatest, and most constructive, of British Foreign Secretaries. It has been said with much truth that he was the most European and least insular of them all: and indeed he was one of the first to recognise the uncomfortable, but incontestable fact that Britain is an integral part of Europe and cannot with impunity neglect its problems. He has often been criticised for his attention to international, and not merely to narrowly British interests: but this is the feeblest of all gibes against him, for he who uses it proves himself to be incapable of realising that the fundamental task of true statesmanship is the due adjustment of international and national interests.

Castlereagh, then, was foremost in laying "the foundation for a new experiment in International Government": and though much that is most characteristic of post-war Geneva would doubtless have left him very cold, he is certainly to be regarded as one of its chief precursors: in particular, he was one of the first to apply the Genevan principle of close and constant personal contact between the statesmen of Europe. In one notable respect he was inferior to his successor, in his mistaken indifference to public opinion, and in his failure to present the main lines of his policy in an attractive and easily comprehended form. But this, like his excessive reliance upon the Great Powers, was probably inherent in the aristocratic

* Stapleton's *Life of Canning* and Greville's *Memoirs* contain many inaccurate statements about Castlereagh. The first serious estimate of him came from the pen of Lord Robert Cecil (afterwards the great Lord Salisbury) in 1862, in *Quarterly Review* (reprinted in *Biographical Essays*): but its inadequacy is a measure of the subsequent progress in research.

and insular traditions in which he had been reared. If he failed to solve the crucial problem of the relations of Great and Small Powers in Europe, it is but necessary to remember that this is still with us in 1936, in a more unsolved form than ever. But no one had a broader outlook upon European and world affairs than Castlereagh, and events were to justify the *cri de cœur* of his last conversation with George IV—"No one after me understands the affairs of the Continent".[40] For Canning, great as he was, must be admitted to have entered on a backward, not a forward path, when he proclaimed the facile catchword, "Every nation for itself, and God for us all", thus leaving the Devil to take the hindmost.

CHAPTER II

CANNING AND THE NEW DIPLOMACY

If Castlereagh stood for diplomacy by conference, Canning stood for diplomacy resting on an appeal to public opinion. As Dr Temperley has well said,* the principles were the same, but their application was utterly different. Hence, if Castlereagh's period of office marks an epoch because it coincides with the first real experiment in international government, Canning's period also marks an epoch, because it is the first serious attempt of a Foreign Secretary to interest public opinion in the details of policy, to get the nation solidly behind him and to cut his cloth according to their requirements, instead of supplying them with something ready-made. It would be ridiculous to suggest that Pitt was indifferent to the opinion of the country. But the appeal which Canning made was something quite new in British history and took account of factors which Pitt had either ignored or not found it necessary to consider.

REACTION IN ENGLAND

Before we consider the man and his policy, a thumbnail sketch of the situation at home and abroad is needed, in order to bring home to the reader the rapid transformation wrought in the seven years following upon Waterloo. The Industrial Revolution is now proceeding apace, the population growing by leaps and bounds, the old rural life breaking down, while new means of communication are revolutionising everything. There is already a network of canals, and it is the age of Macadam. Indeed we are already upon the threshold of the Railway Age, and our shipping trade is a greater factor in the national life than ever before. We are just ceasing to be exporters of agricultural produce: we have scarcely yet entered on the stage with which we are now painfully familiar, of not being self-supporting in food supplies. Economic and financial questions give Parliament great concern, and an outstanding part is played by Huskisson as President of the Board of Trade under Lord Liverpool. It is he who, as member of a Tory Cabinet, took the first steps towards Free Trade, by his reform of the

* See his authoritative study, *The Foreign Policy of Canning* (1925), his earlier *Life of George Canning* (1905), and not least his chapter on Canning in vol. II of *Cambridge History of British Foreign Policy*, 51–118.

Navigation Acts, the reduction of duties on manufactured goods and foreign imports, and the repeal of quarantine duties. He was also responsible for the Sinking Fund, a sliding scale for the Corn Duties, and the repeal of the most oppressive labour laws. His death in 1830, by a railway accident, was a serious loss to the country, though Peel and others were ready to take his place.

POPULAR FEELING AGAINST THE CROWN

Huskisson's legislation gave a more enlightened tone to the reactionary regime of Liverpool and Castlereagh, and combined with Canning's popular foreign policy, assured to the Cabinet a new lease of life. There can be no question that it had been intensely unpopular at the time of Castlereagh's death, partly because public opinion was resentful of the restrictive legislation which had culminated in the Six Acts, partly because of the abominable scandals of the Queen's trial, during which the Government found itself caught between two fires, on the one hand from a half-hysterical mob, and on the other from the King himself in his most uncompromising mood. So intense was the feeling against George IV that the dynasty was in real danger, and indeed its prospects of survival seemed far from good until the almost providential interposition of Queen Victoria. In 1819 Shelley could write of

An old, mad, blind, despised and dying King—
Princes, the dregs of their dull race, who flow
Through public scorn—mud from a muddy spring....

Indeed, the Royal Dukes by their blatancy and their scandalous morals had long been the butt of hostile opinion. Even the exemplary George III had been publicly insulted by the mob on his way to Parliament: in 1813 the Prince Regent—"Nobs Junior" or "Prinney", as he was familiarly called—was hooted loudly when going to Court;[1] the mob became more vocal than ever during the trial of Queen Caroline, and this time had many men of note upon its side: and even William IV soon after his accession judged it inadvisable to pay a state visit to the City. In 1818 the Duke of Wellington wrote thus of the Princes: "They are the damnedest millstone about the necks of any Government, that can be imagined. They have insulted—*personally* insulted—two-thirds of the gentlemen of England."[2] And though it would be unfair to accept this outburst as typifying the Duke's considered attitude, the fact that he of all men could have penned such lines at all is sufficiently significant.

The countless lampoons and broadsheets of the period exploited the shortcomings of the Royal House in very much the same manner as the Yellow Press of our own day revels in spiteful gossip about such Courts as Ruritania and Szimia. "Peter Pindar junior" may serve as the type of many lesser scribes. His *Three R——l Bloods, or a Lame R——t, a Darling Commander and a Love-Sick Admiral* went through nine editions in 1812 and boldly declared that

> The only point on which a doubt remains
> Is whether Royalty is born with brains.[3]

Byron, coarsely though not inaccurately, wrote of George IV as "Royal Stallion", and during the King's visit to Ireland produced the more than indifferent lines:

> Spread, spread for Vitellius the royal repast,
> 　Till the gluttonous despot be stuff'd to the gorge
> And the roar of the drunkards proclaim him at last
> 　The fourth of the fools and oppressors called "George".[4]

A year earlier, in *The Vision of Judgment*, he had written of George III,

> A better farmer ne'er brushed dew from lawn,
> A worse King never left a realm undone.

had declared George IV to share his father's qualities,

> Except that household virtue, most uncommon,
> Of constancy to a bad, ugly woman.

and had run on

> God save the King! It is a large economy
> In God to save the like.

GEORGE CANNING

Such was the atmosphere in England when Canning succeeded Londonderry as Foreign Secretary in September 1822.

George Canning, like his predecessor, came of a good Ulster Protestant family, but not one of sufficient eminence to achieve title or territorial power by the customary methods of the Ascendancy and Union period. Left an orphan in infancy by an improvident father, he spent his childhood with the none too savory associates of his actress mother, until her third husband, a Plymouth tradesman, saved them from privation and until at last his father's family took pity on the boy and sent him to Eton. These early associations weighed heavily upon him, and long afterwards were regarded by upholders of the narrow aristocratic tradition in politics as disqualifying him from the office of Prime Minister.*

* Lord Grey expressed this view, "in terms of the most violent and virulent contempt", to Sir Robert Wilson and Lord Lansdowne. See Sir R. Wilson, *Canning's Administration* (1872), p. 17.

Canning first entered Parliament in 1793, and in his early flights of eloquence was sneered at by the Whigs as "Apollo imitating Hercules".[5] But
his speech against the resumption of negotiations with France (1798) already
won him an assured place as one of the chief orators of the House of Commons. In the closing years of the century he was not only Pitt's lieutenant,
but one of his closest confidants, especially in the foreign correspondence
which he conducted behind the back of his colleagues in the Cabinet.
During this first stage of his political career Canning was one of the most
active, and certainly the most effective, contributors to the famous *Anti-
Jacobin*, whose often coarse and mordent satire played a part difficult for the
modern reader to comprehend, in alienating public sympathy from French
revolutionary doctrine. Canning was a true product of the eighteenth century, in that he was more eminent for his wit than for his humour, and all
but a few famous epigrams have long since been consigned to oblivion.
But his gift of facile verse made him a force in his day and once led Wilberforce to say that "his lash would have fetched the hide off a rhinoceros".[6]
It also made him many enemies—Addington, of whom he had written,
"As London to Paddington, so Pitt is to Addington", refused to serve in
the same Cabinet with him—and earned him an undue reputation for
levity, which it took long to live down. He was indignant at Pitt's resignation in 1800 and their relations were never again quite so cordial, but on his
former chief's death in 1806 he pronounced, as was most fitting, the eulogy
in the House of Commons. After refusing to take office in Fox's "Ministry
of all the Talents", he at last attained to full Cabinet rank under the Duke of
Portland and was Foreign Secretary from March 1807 till September 1809.
Napoleon was at this time plotting to redress his naval inferiority by laying
his hands upon the Danish and Portuguese fleets, and it was Canning who
forestalled him, firstly by the drastic step of bombarding Copenhagen and
seizing the Danish ships, and then in a more legitimate manner by concluding a treaty of mutual defence with Portugal and conveying the Regent
(afterwards John VI), to his Brazilian exile on a British man-of-war. He
openly proclaimed the policy that any nation which voluntarily resisted
Napoleon "becomes instantly our essential ally", and it was above all to his
initiative that the Peninsular expedition, and later on the appointment of
Wellesley as its commander, were due. Unhappily acute friction and divergence of opinion between him and Castlereagh, then at the War Office, culminated in a duel between colleagues and his resignation in September
1809. For twelve years he remained more or less under eclipse—either out
of office altogether or holding posts obviously inferior to his outstanding
merit, conscious of his ability, but also conscious that opinion in the House
was in the main hostile to him. Lord Liverpool, when in 1812 he succeeded

the murdered Perceval as Prime Minister, offered Canning the Foreign Office once more, and Castlereagh, more or less reconciled, declared himself willing to stand aside—in Canning's own words, "the handsomest offer ever yet made to an individual". But by a miscalculation such as would have finally wrecked any other career, Canning refused, only to witness the new administration, whose situation he had regarded as so precarious, speedily gaining in strength, thanks to Wellington's victories in Spain, which he himself had rendered possible. And thus it came about that Liverpool remained Prime Minister for a longer consecutive period than any British statesman save Walpole and Pitt, and that Castlereagh, not Canning, shaped the policy of Britain in the supreme crisis of the Napoleonic wars, at the Congress of Vienna and in the first seven years of peace.

After an interlude of two years as Ambassador at Lisbon, Canning returned to the Cabinet in 1816 as President of the Indian Board of Control, but he was gradually drifting into a backwater and found himself by no means in accord with the rigidly conservative outlook of the dominant party. The inevitable reaction from over twenty years of revolutionary clamour and the uncertainties of a gigantic struggle expressed itself in hostility to any change whatsoever, and in a pathetic belief that the British Constitution, in its unreformed state, was not merely perfect but impregnable. Canning, with all his hatred for revolution, felt the necessity for moving with the times, and adopted an attitude towards public opinion, and its chief mouthpiece the press, that was markedly different from that of Tory and Whig alike and was indeed an innovation in the political practice of his day. Added to this growing dissent from a policy of repression both at home and abroad, was his keen sympathy for Queen Caroline, who had befriended him in former years: and in 1820 he resigned office rather than endorse the Cabinet's stern measures against her, thereby naturally arousing the displeasure of the new King. In the summer of 1822 he was offered, and accepted, the Governor-Generalship of India, his Tory colleagues hoping thereby to rid themselves honourably of an irksome competitor, while he himself, seeing no prospect of occupying the front of the stage at home, was doubtless tempted by the compensations of Eastern splendour. But in the very moment when he was about to embark for India the situation was dramatically transformed by the tragic death of Castlereagh. Canning's qualifications for the vacant post were obvious, even to the most hostile, all the more so since in the preceding four years he had from the background increasingly pressed upon Castlereagh his views regarding foreign policy. Indeed he had great influence upon the drafting of the State Paper of May 1820, one of the most memorable statements of British policy on record,* and thus it came about that at one time its authorship was erroneously claimed for Canning. His withdrawal from the Cabinet a little later in the same year was sincerely regretted by Castlereagh, who wrote to assure him that they agreed on all questions of foreign policy.[7]

CANNING AT THE FOREIGN OFFICE

It was, however, natural enough that his appointment as Castlereagh's successor should have been strenuously opposed both by the King and by the right wing of the Cabinet, especially by the arch-reactionary Chancellor, Lord Eldon, who wished to see the Duke of Wellington at the Foreign Office. But though half the Cabinet was hostile, and indeed maintained a sort of passive resistance to his views for some considerable time to come, Canning had on his side the still all-powerful Prime Minister, Lord Liverpool, and two future Premiers besides—Robinson and William Lamb, better known as Lords Goderich and Melbourne. In the end the Duke of Wellington, whose Toryism, rigid as it was, was not impervious to political necessity, turned the scale in favour of Canning. George IV yielded with a fairly good grace,† and a couple of years later was able to remind the Duke and the Prime Minister that he had "consented to bury in oblivion all that had previously passed".‡ Canning, however, when he saw events turning in his favour, insisted upon "the whole heritage" of Castlereagh, and thus became not only Foreign Secretary but leader of the House of Commons, a task which even in those days imposed too great a strain upon any man and undoubtedly shortened his life.

When he took office, he was isolated. He attempted to appease the King by tactfully selecting as his Under-Secretary Lord Francis Conyngham, the son of George's mistress: but this only had a passing effect, and much of his energy had to be devoted to overcoming the King's hostility and active intrigues. But he soon won for himself an almost unassailable position, and by his foreign policy saved the Cabinet from disaster at home.

* As Prof. C. K. Webster points out in his *Foreign Policy of Castlereagh*, II, 246, Dr Temperley "was the first historian to realise the importance of this paper".

† Writing on 8 September 1822 to Liverpool, he said, "I have sacrificed my private feelings, as you and other members of the Cabinet have represented to me that it is what you consider to be for the good of the public service": Yonge, *Life of Lord Liverpool*, III, 199. "The King is aware that the brightest ornament of his Crown is the power of extending grace and favour to a subject who may have incurred his displeasure" (*ibid.* p. 200).

‡ 1 May 1824, King to Liverpool—Yonge, *op. cit.* III, 280; also *Wellington Despatches*, II, 251. The King also declares himself "quite satisfied that he has since acted with the most uniform condescending, conciliatory and confidential kindness towards Mr Canning".

THE STATE PAPER OF MAY 1820

The State Paper of 5 May 1820, drawn up by Castlereagh as a summary of his policy, and circulated to the leading European Governments, was published by Canning in 1823, though only in a very truncated form.[8] It is because Canning so definitely adopted it as embodying his own views, that he was so long credited with its authorship, and a selection from its contents is perhaps the best introduction to his period of office.

This noteworthy document aimed at a definition of policy in face of the conflicting attitude of the Powers towards the Spanish Revolution, and from the outset it opposes any idea of intervention and even "the interposition of good offices": and it quotes at an early stage the great authority of the Duke of Wellington and his knowledge of Spanish affairs, as to the imminent dangers which such intervention would provoke in so sensitive a nation as the Spanish. "The alliance", it declares, "was an union for the liberation of a great proportion of the Continent from the military dominion of France.... It never was, however, intended as an union for the government of the world or for the superintendence of the internal affairs of other states."[9] It definitely challenges the view that "any great political event", such as the Spanish Revolution, provides the Allies with an excuse for interference, and argues that this cannot be done "without seriously embarrassing the internal administration of their own affairs" and without rousing "public opinion". This is fundamental, and it is highly significant of the evolution since 1815 that Castlereagh and Canning should have been at one in reminding Metternich, even if in diplomatic language, of the fact that while two at least of the three Eastern Powers had no public opinion to consider owing to their methods of repression and censorship, it was necessary in the West to take it very seriously into account. In this connection it is pointed out that the Tsar has nothing to consider save the "physical or moral difficulties" in which a war might involve him abroad, whereas the King of Great Britain, "from the nature of our constitution, has on the contrary all his means to acquire through Parliament", and not even the strongest administration could advocate a war against "the Voice of the country" (written with a big V). It is further argued that at a time when the main energies of statesmen are absorbed "in defence of our existing institutions, and to put down the spirit of treason and disaffection", it would be deplorable if interference by the Allies led to discussions of continental home affairs in the British Parliament. "Identity of view can only be obtained by a proportionate degree of inaction in all the States." And having by this time warmed to his argument, the writer goes on to affirm quite plainly: "The fact is that we do not and cannot feel alike on all subjects. Our position, our institutions, the habits of thinking and the prejudice of our people, render us essentially different." And again, "The principle of one state interfering by force in the internal affairs of another, in order to enforce obedience to the governing authority, is always a question of the greatest possible moral as well as political delicacy.... No country having a Representative system of Government could act upon" the system now proposed, and "the sooner such a doctrine shall be distinctly abjured as forming in any degree the basis of our alliance, the better." The closing paragraphs reaffirm the desire for co-operation with the Allies, but hint that they were departing from the original purpose of the alliance, and that Britain's action would always depend not merely on "the expediency of the case, but on those maxims which a system of government strongly popular and national in its character, has irresistibly imposed upon us".

It is abundantly clear from these extracts that Castlereagh was already moving away from the Allies some time before his death, or—perhaps it would be fairer to assert—that Castlereagh considered *them* to be moving steadily away from *him*. In any case, Canning merely continued on a road already indicated by his predecessor. But everything depends upon the personality behind a policy: and Metternich in particular, though aware of Castlereagh's growing reserve, despite their cordial discussions at Hanover in 1821, had confidence in him as a man, and believed that agreement could be reached between the two of them, whereas Canning was utterly unsympathetic to him and indeed his very antithesis. In his dismay at Castlereagh's death, Metternich wrote: "The man is irreplaceable, especially for me. He is the only man in England who has foreign experience. He was devoted to me heart and soul, not only from personal inclination, but from conviction."[10] A few months later he is lamenting the effacement of England and calls Canning "merely the personification of that evil which fills every pulse of his country, an evil which has broken its energy and threatens to give over its weakened body to dissolution".[11]

To him the idea that a statesman, and especially a Foreign Minister, should appeal openly to public opinion was peculiarly distasteful: and during the last few years before taking office Canning had set a definite precedent in this direction. For instance, in 1818 he had expressed alarm at "the periodical meetings" of the Allies, which "will", he said, "necessarily involve us deeply in all politics of the Continent". And in 1821, in face of Troppau and Laibach, he demanded "neutrality in word and deed",[12] since Britain was not prepared to go to war for such matters as a constitutional regime in Naples. "Let us not", he said, "in the foolish spirit of romance, suppose that we alone could regenerate Europe."

But if not prepared to commit himself to the support of one particular regime rather than another, Canning was increasingly unwilling to see the other Powers upholding or bolstering up the particular regime which they themselves most favoured. He was thoroughly suspicious of what he called "the predominating Areopagitic spirit",[13] and this was at once reflected in his attitude to the Congress of Verona.

THE CONGRESS OF VERONA

A year earlier, at Laibach, it had been decided that a fresh Congress should meet at Verona in October 1822, and Metternich believed that he could again exercise a dominant influence not only upon Tsar Alexander, who had promised to attend in person, but upon the British and French representatives, Londonderry and the legitimist Montmorency. But all his calculations were upset by the death of Londonderry, and the preparatory discussions at Vienna had to be abandoned. When at length the Congress met, there could be no pretence at unity of programme, and Metternich's main efforts had to be directed towards holding back the Tsar, who wished to lead a crusading army against Spain, as the centre of Jacobin infection in Europe. Metternich found himself on the horns of a triple dilemma. He shared the determination of all the other Powers to prevent Russian troops from crossing Europe, yet he was afraid to postpone the repression of subversive forces in Spain; he felt that French intervention was a reasonable substitute, yet all too recent memories warned him against fresh encouragement to French military effort, and he realised that it might very easily provoke a conflict with Britain and finally alienate her from the alliance at a moment of uncertainty at the Foreign Office when he was especially anxious to humour her.

Lord Londonderry not long before his death had submitted for the Cabinet's approval a set of instructions for his own guidance as British delegate. The Duke of Wellington was now induced to take the vacant post, and Londonderry's instructions were handed to him unaltered. They, to an even greater extent than the State Paper of May 1820, show that their author had already been preparing a change in British policy: and indeed in the two documents it is already possible to trace the germ of Canning's action in several matters of capital importance. In the Eastern Question stress was laid upon the need of preserving peace between Russia and Turkey, but also upon the need for neutrality as between the Turks and the Greeks, and upon the possibility of a *de facto* Greek Government being eventually accorded "the ordinary privileges of a belligerent". As regards Spain, there was to be "a rigid abstinence from any interference in the internal affairs of that country". As regards the Spanish colonies, it was assumed that sooner or later their recognition would be inevitable, and the Conference was asked to consider the exact form which this should take— whether recognition *de facto* only, or actually *de jure*, or the intermediate method of sending diplomatic agents.

Londonderry, however cautiously, was already moving along the path which led to Navarino and to South American independence. But with the advent of Canning the peace was hastened, a louder note was struck, and within two months of taking office he assumed, in a memorandum to the Cabinet, that the recognition of the South American states cannot be indefinitely postponed. "We do not take her anarchy as an offence, but she must not plead it as a privilege."[14] This was already very different from Castlereagh.

There was no little irony in the fact that the Duke, whom Metternich had regarded as the only worthy successor of Castlereagh, should be the very man to act upon the latter's final instructions, and thereby to deal the first blow to the system of government by congress. On 27 September Canning, whose main immediate object was to prevent any form of *collective* intervention in Spain, in the calculation that he could deal with France singly later, sent supplementary instructions of a very explicit kind to the Duke. The culminating phrase bade him take any opportunity of declaring "frankly and peremptorily, that to any such interference, come what may, His Majesty will not be a party".[15]

At Verona the Tsar's eagerness to throw Russian troops into Spain was met by the tacit disapproval and obstruction of all his allies, and undoubtedly facilitated France's own design of separate action. But it was reserved for the Tory Wellington, in obstinate loyalty to his instructions, reinforced by his own Spanish memories, to express open disapproval of collective intervention and a blunt disbelief in the theory of "moral contagion".[16] Finally, when the three Eastern Powers proceeded to define the circumstances in which they would give their support to French action in Spain, Wellington flatly refused to sign the protocol, treated their attitude as calculated to irritate the Spanish Government, and after showing his disagreement in the questions of South American recognition and the slave trade also, withdrew from Verona in a thoroughly bad humour. Metternich, it is true, had carried his way in the Italian and Greek questions, and the Tsar had again been induced to sacrifice Russian and Orthodox sentiment in the Near East to the ideals of the Holy Alliance: but the alienation of London was already patent to the whole world, and the essential divergence of outlook between the Eastern and Western Powers was to become more and more obvious.

THE SPANISH REVOLUTION

The situation in Spain continued to be both obscure and dangerous. The perjured and tyrannous King, Ferdinand VII, who celebrated his return from exile by abolishing the Constitution of 1812, had proved quite incapable of establishing just and ordered government: and the summons of the extraordinary Cortes in June 1821 had, if possible, rendered still more acute the struggle of the rival factions of Exaltados and Serviles. The King, after an unsuccessful attempt to re-establish absolutism in the summer of 1822, set his hopes more and more upon foreign help, in the first instance upon the Tsar, but also, and with far better prospects, upon the French reactionaries, who since the Duc de Richelieu's death were strengthening their hold upon public affairs under the active influence of "Monsieur", Louis XVIII's brother and heir. France had considerable excuse for nervousness at the prolonged unrest on her south-western frontier, and every motive for forestalling Russian intervention, and with this was doubtless intermingled the desire to remind Europe of her own military revival. Canning, in endeavouring to detach her from the Eastern Powers, had of necessity given her an added incentive in this direction: it was a risk which he had foreseen, but none the less a risk which had unpleasant results. The watchword of the French Ultras was to liberate "the prisoner of Madrid" and save him from the fate of Louis XVI. The Premier, Count Villèle, exercised a moderating influence, but was not prepared to accept the British offer of mediation, made to him by Wellington on his way home from Verona. Chateaubriand, fresh from his colloquies with the Tsar, succeeded Montmorency as Foreign Minister at the turn of the year and worked ardently for intervention: and though Canning, relying on their former personal relations, had immediately after assuming the Foreign Office hastened to make friendly overtures to him, he in his turn, though affecting to believe that they would easily agree "as friends and statesmen",[17] worked behind Canning's back, instructing his Minister in Madrid to "put no trust in the English"[18] and assumed that "all the noise that is being made in London will pass".[19]

On 28 January 1823 Louis XVIII, in his Speech from the Throne, announced that 100,000 French troops were ready to march, under the orders of his nephew the Duke of Angoulême, in order "to preserve the Spanish throne for a descendant of Henry IV", and that Ferdinand VII "might be free to give to his peoples institutions which they could hold from him alone". The sensation in England was profound, the City and the press—which at this period was gaining in influence by leaps and bounds

—were almost unanimous in condemning a step which was interpreted as an assault upon constitutional government: and it was but natural that there should be wide interest in a country whose emancipation from foreign rule had been achieved by British arms less than a decade earlier. Brougham wittily denounced the intrigues of "the three gentlemen of Verona", who stood behind France, and the Spanish Ambassador in Paris, who withdrew to England after the rupture of Franco-Spanish relations, was carried in triumph by the London mob and greeted with demonstrative attention by Canning at Covent Garden. And here the fundamental difference in temperament between the ardent Canning and his cold-blooded predecessor became at once apparent: for he found himself in sympathy with public opinion and associated himself more and more openly with the prevalent dislike of absolutist principles. He told the French through diplomatic channels that King Louis had proclaimed "a principle which strikes at the root of the British constitution", and that we should not countenance any attempt to impose upon others constitutions that owed their existence to royal decree. He also wrote an earnest personal appeal to "Monsieur", assuring him that there was no parallel for "the tumultuous expression of feeling" in England, since the country had been roused to defend Spain against Napoleon in 1808. After this ominous comparison he did his best to discourage French intervention in Spain on so doubtful a basis as "the principle that nations can only receive freedom at the hands of their King, and such a King (the world will add, however irreverently) as Ferdinand has shown himself to be". With a persuasive daring, he reminded a Prince whose acquaintance with him dated from the darkest days of exile, that he of all men could hardly "be suspected of infection with Jacobin principles, having spent his public life in combating them". And yet he did not hesitate to prefer "the Sovereignty of the People" to the principles laid down by the King of France!*

On 14 April 1823 the question of French intervention was debated at considerable length, and with no little heat, in the House of Commons; and Canning, while declaring openly for neutrality and against war, employed language such as must have been most offensive to French ears. Referring to the French Speech from the Throne, he said that "of the construction to which its words were liable...there was not a man in the House who thought with more disgust and abhorrence" than himself, and that "not a day was lost" in telling the French that "the principle avowed was one which a British statesman could not acknowledge", since "it struck at the root of the

* 1 February 1823, *Canning Corresp.*, ed. E. J. Stapleton, I, 71–6. To this the Count of Artois somewhat inconsequently replied that France's only motive was to prevent Ferdinand VII from losing his throne.

British constitution", and that negotiation was impossible on such a basis. He added that "as Great Britain did not put forward her own political institutions as the model on which those of other states were to be framed, or as the only system from which national freedom and happiness could flow, so neither could she allow France to make her own example a rule for other nations, not less to force that example on Spain in virtue of the consanguinity of the reigning dynasties". His plain speech went still further when he referred to France's disavowal of "this obnoxious construction" and her adoption of "another, which, I am free to confess, the words were not altogether qualified to bear!" Then in precise and categorical language he assured the House that he had made it absolutely clear to Spain that Britain would be neutral in a Franco-Spanish war, and to France, that "any attack wantonly made on Portugal, would bring Britain into the field", and to both that Britain "would not tolerate for an instant any cession which Spain might make of colonies over which she did not exercise a direct and positive influence". But he declined to threaten France with war, for "the country which menaced war ought always to be ready to carry those menaces into execution", and the Government was not prepared to give "actual and efficient support" to Spain, though it "earnestly hoped and trusted she would come triumphantly out of the struggle!"[20] In the resumed debate he justified neutrality by an even more insulting phrase. "If one of the contending parties poisons the well-springs of national liberty and the other employs against its adversary the venomed weapons of political fanaticism", should Britain, he asked, associate with either?[21]

Language such as this took the wind out of the Opposition's sails. Mackintosh denounced French action as "an open and profligate attack on the liberties of mankind", while Lord Grey—always on the opposite side from Canning—spoke of "the foulest disgrace that had ever befallen this country". But the essential difference lay in the fact that Canning repudiated the warlike action which their policy would inevitably have involved, and the French Government, knowing exactly what to expect and how far it might go with impunity, presumably found it worth while to pocket the insult. None the less, it is impossible to justify such a tone in any statesman, however great, and it is not surprising that the King should have been furious and forced Liverpool and Peel to admit that their colleague had gone too far.

Canning, however, had from the first no intention of going to war with France, except under extreme provocation. Rather than that, he held, it would be better to risk the re-establishment of French influence in Madrid. There were, however, two things that could not be tolerated, namely, French or Spanish intervention in South America, or an attack upon

Portugal.[22] Meanwhile he had no answer to Wellington's contention that war must be avoided, since we should enter it "with a certainty of the loss of Hanover and Portugal and of the Dutch alliance", and also "of doing no service to Spain".[23] M. de Marcellus, the astute and brilliant young French royalist whom Chateaubriand left as Chargé d'Affaires in London during these critical months, was perhaps not so far wrong in representing Canning as "still irresolute" and "floating between the monarchical opinions which made his former reputation and the popular favour which opens to him the surest avenue to power".[24] Very acutely Marcellus assured Chateaubriand that he could rely upon British neutrality,[25] if only France acted rapidly and created accomplished facts in Spain: and to this he received the reply, "Let Canning be as annoyed as he pleases. He has lost his way: he had dreamt of war and cannot make it: that is the secret cause of his illhumour." And again a week later, "Give entertainments and reply firmly to Mr Canning."[26]

George IV and the Cottage Coterie

Marcellus was certainly right when he sought the key of Canning's hesitation "in his ministerial duties and in his parliamentary situation": for it was more than doubtful whether popular enthusiasm could carry him very far against the disapproval of his colleagues and the comparative coldness of the House. He was between two fires, for he soon quarrelled with the unbalanced Brougham, while his own outspoken language brought protests not merely from Eldon and Peel, but above all from the King. Here, indeed, lies the clue to Britain's inaction during the French expedition: for the Duke of Wellington expressed open delight at Chateaubriand's attitude towards the end of April, while George IV, during an audience which he accorded to Marcellus, wished all success to the Bourbon enterprise in Spain, and by a calculated indiscretion allowed his words to be repeated. He remained entirely unrepentant when *The Times* made one of its frontal attacks upon him for expressing a wish directly contrary to that of his Ministers and of the whole nation. In a word, the King was working behind Canning's back and actually encouraging the French to persist in their adventure. In March 1823 he went so far as to tell the Austrian Ambassador, Prince Esterházy, that he disapproved of Canning, but that it was not easy to dismiss him.[27]

The period from 1823 to 1825 represents the high-water mark of the so-called "Cottage Coterie", the clique of foreign diplomats who frequented the King in the Windsor cottage to which he and his mistress, Lady Conyngham, retreated. These were the Hanoverian agent Count Münster; the Austrian Ambassador Prince Paul Esterházy and his first secretary Baron Neumann, who, it is true was equally constant in his intrigues against his own chief; to a lesser degree their French colleague, Prince Polignac, who superseded Marcellus in July 1823; and above all the Russian Ambassador, Count Lieven, and his famous wife, *née* Benckendorff, who had already come to occupy an almost unique position in the diplomatic world of London. She had by this time had her passing love affair with Metternich at the Congress of Aachen: she had exercised great influence upon Castlereagh, she now contrived to win the ear of King George, and in time she was to captivate her present bugbear Canning, and the future Prime Minister, Lord Grey, and was to end her astonishing career as the Egeria of Guizot in Paris. Her influence was at this time exerted in favour of the Holy Alliance and its policy, and was therefore keenly hostile to Canning, whom she affected to regard as an upstart and a Jacobin. Later on, when George became reconciled, or resigned, to his brilliant Foreign Secretary, she was the great exponent of Russo-British friendship and played a salutary part in the later stages of the long Greek crisis.

Canning and George IV

At this earlier date George IV was a great danger, bent on interfering with foreign policy, which really interested him, and envious of his brother sovereigns, who could command and dismiss their Ministers as they pleased. In the words of Dr Temperley,[28] "A King who is both clever and perfidious is a dangerous opponent for any British Minister. For while he may overmatch his sovereign in cleverness, he cannot overmatch him in perfidy. For it is one thing to detect a King in a lie or an intrigue, quite another to tax him with it."

The tension between Canning and the King is best shown by a conversation recorded by M. de Marcellus, shortly after the French Speech from the Throne had kindled such excitement and indignation by its assertion that only King Ferdinand himself was qualified to grant his people free institutions. "A King free?" exclaimed Canning. "Do you know a King who deserves to be free in the implicit sense of the word? Can he ever be free, ought he even to be so? The only really free King is either a despot or an usurper—scourges of the world, terrifying comets which shine and are extinguished in blood. Our constitution and yours leave in appearance to the King the vain privilege of choosing his Ministers: but does he really exercise this privilege? Were the first Georges free to reject the Walpole Ministry? Could George III, with his clouded reason, make a choice around him? No, most happily for England. And George IV, do you think that I should be his Minister if he had been *free* to choose? Do you suppose he has forgotten that I invariably avoided the orgies of his youth, that I always opposed his tastes and his favourites? He hates me for my opposition, for my political attitude, and above all for the intimate recollections of his domestic life."[29] This passage, which may well have been embroidered in Marcellus' imagination, is reminiscent of the alleged remark of George IV, "I wish to God someone would assassinate Knighton" (his private physician, who knew all his secrets and was inside the magic ring of the Coterie).* But it must also be taken in conjunction with the essential fact that Lord Liverpool resolutely kept Canning in office, in the knowledge that as he himself steadily failed in health, the Ministry could hardly hope to survive if Canning were ejected.

Not the least curious feature of the situation was that Canning in the House of Commons alluded to himself as "a Liberal, yea, a Radical Minister", and therefore won the increasing support of the Whigs. By the spring of 1825 Canning was strong enough to stand up to the King and was confident that the intrigues of the Coterie had failed. Metternich, during a visit to Paris, had been busily engaged in poisoning French opinion against Canning, and Esterházy was sent across the Channel with a special invitation in King George's name to London,† where it was hoped that his presence might finally turn the scales against the obnoxious Foreign Secretary. But "some incredibly unadvised expressions" found their way to the ear of Canning, who wrote to Lord Granville roundly denouncing Metternich as "the greatest rogue and liar on the Continent, perhaps in the civilised world".[30] Not content with this outburst, he added that if the King's "intemperance or miscalculation" had not brought the intrigue "to a premature *dénouement*", he himself would have resigned on the Spanish-American question and declared openly in the House that he "was driven from office by the Holy Alliance", and further, that "the system which he found established, of personal communications between the sovereign and the foreign ministers, was one under which no English Minister could do his duty. If after such a denunciation and the debates which would have followed it the Lievens and Esterházy did not find London too hot for them, I know nothing of the present temper of the English nation". The Ambassador is to discourage Metternich from visiting Windsor:

---

* Lord Redesdale, writing to Lord Colchester (a former Speaker of the House of Commons, whose diary is full of intimate light upon contemporary history) says that "the King fancies he has acted with great dexterity, under the guidance of Lady Conyngham and Sir William Knighton, two intriguants who are looking only to themselves" (19 January 1828, Colchester, *Diaries*, III, 539). Lord Lyndhurst once spoke of Knighton to Disraeli, as "very able—the real King of the country—did everything, wrote all the King's letters" (Monypenny, *Disraeli*, I, 391).

† Prince Polignac reported to Count Villèle (6 April 1825) that the invitation came from the King alone, probably without Canning's knowledge (Villèle, *Mémoires*, III, 175).

"he would have come to triumph, I would not advise him to come to intrigue."

Metternich's sources of information were very good, and he was not the man to risk an open rebuff. On 17 March he reported to the Emperor Francis[31] that King George "thinks it would be easy for me in a few days to complete the moral education of Canning. Should he not come into line readily, one would have a reason, and would find the means, for sending him away". But on reflection he did not cross the Channel and merely sent the message, "how far the evil must have gone for it to have made impossible the appearance of an Austrian Minister in England".

THE FRENCH IN SPAIN

Relations between France and Spain were broken off in the middle of March 1823, and on 24 May the French army under the Duke of Angoulême entered Madrid virtually unopposed. The constitutional Government carried off the treacherous King Ferdinand with it, first to Seville, then to Cadiz, where a third Regency was formed in opposition to the two already existing. The British Minister, Sir William A'Court, had followed the Cortes and the reluctant Ferdinand, but finally took up the position of observer at Gibraltar. Canning announced British neutrality as early as 21 March, but in a communication to the French Government made it quite clear that this attitude would change if France attempted to make her military occupation permanent, to seize any of the Spanish colonies, or to infringe Portuguese independence. These conditions the French respected, but the course of events in Spain gave them but little satisfaction. Long before Cadiz surrendered and Ferdinand found himself a free man, the Duke of Angoulême was privately expressing to M. de Villèle his disgust at the excesses of the Royalist bands, and was under no illusions as to the King for whose sake he had invaded Spain. "Ferdinand", he wrote, "would make me a hundred promises, but would not keep them the moment I turned my back.... We might stay ten years in Spain, but at the end the parties would begin to massacre each other again." Ferdinand's first action was to repudiate all his promises, to annul all the acts of "the so-called constitutional" Government, and to indulge in reprisals so savage and vindictive that Angoulême refused a triumphal entry into Madrid and left Spain in disgust. Even Chateaubriand and Metternich were driven to remonstrate, but the King was incorrigible and continued to misgovern till his death. The Duke of Wellington's prophecy that French policy in Spain would end neither in complete success nor in complete failure,[32] was ful- filled to the letter, and while Chateaubriand had to confess that the Bourbon champion of legitimacy had speedily reduced his kingdom to "complete anarchy", France earned little or no gratitude from Ferdinand's fanatical adherents, to whom even the French Royalists were tainted with Liberal ideas. After long resistance Ferdinand granted an extremely inadequate amnesty, and at the instance of the Allies accepted the more moderate Zea as his Premier. But the influence of Zea was far more than counterbalanced by the King's reactionary entourage, and Ferdinand took the first safe opportunity of dismissing him, making it quite clear that the main reason was the very fact of his being acceptable to the Powers. Nor did French opinion, even among the "Ultras", obtain much satisfaction or increase of influence from the Spanish adventure, and the romantic Chateaubriand found in it the ruin of his political career.

CANNING AND THE SPANISH COLONIES

Meanwhile Canning adhered faithfully to his original policy of disapproval, but complete passivity, so long as the French kept clear of Portugal and Spanish America. In fact he was inclined to concentrate more and more upon the question of the Spanish colonies, and to assume that their recovery by the mother country was by now hopeless. He was one of the first to foresee their great possibilities and the value of commercial relations with them, when once they were free to develop on healthy lines. Indeed, he did not hesitate to urge on Wellington the view that "in the present state of the world the American questions are out of all proportion more important to us than the European, and that if we do not seize and turn them to our advantage in time, we shall rue the loss of an opportunity never to be recovered".[33] He disclaimed all idea of acquiring territory, but was also determined to prevent any of the colonies from falling into French hands, and set his face against any idea of establishing petty Bourbon thrones in South America. He declined to make "abstract principles"—in other words, the adoption of monarchical rather than republican forms—the basis of recognition. He insisted upon leaving the decision to the colonists them-selves, and this attitude contributed very materially to the final triumph of republicanism. In October 1823 he wrung from the French Ambassador, Prince Polignac, the assurance that his Government regarded the reconquest of Spanish America as "utterly hopeless" and had no territorial designs of its own in that continent: and by communicating this to the Powers in the form of a private memorandum, he achieved the double object of making it impossible for France to go back upon the pledge and of isolating her from the three Eastern allies.

He followed this up by a public speech at Plymouth,* which contains one of his most famous flights of eloquence. Referring to the men-of-war in the harbour, he exclaimed: "You well know how soon one of these stupendous masses, now reposing on their shadows in perfect stillness, would, upon any call of patriotism or of necessity, assume the likeness of an animated thing, instinct with life and motion: how soon it would ruffle, as it were, its swelling plumage, how quickly it would put forth all its beauty and its bravery, collect its scattered elements of strength and waken its dormant thunder...." "Such", he went on, "is England herself: while apparently passive and motionless, she silently concentrates the power to be put forth on an adequate occasion": and that occasion all England took to mean the day when France should interfere in South America.

An attitude such as this naturally brought him closer to the United States, and he made definite overtures to Washington for joint action to keep out the French. He even declared in another speech at Liverpool, that "the force of blood again prevails", and that "the mother and the daughter stand together against the world".[34] America was not uncordial, but also not without suspicion, and preferred to follow her own line: the joint declaration was never made. As early as March 1822 Congress had approved of recognition, the report submitted to it declaring that "to deny to the peoples of Spanish America their right to independence would be in fact to renounce our own independence". In December 1823 President Monroe proclaimed his famous "Doctrine" and culminated in the principle that "the American Continents...are henceforth not to be considered as subjects for colonisation by any European Powers", and that any such "interposition" would be regarded as an unfriendly act.

Canning did not altogether like this attitude, and it spurred him to action. "The effect of the ultra-liberalism of our Yankee cooperators", he wrote to Bagot, "or the utter despotism of the Aix-la-Chapelle Allies, gives me just the balance that I wanted."[35] Early in 1824 he declined the Congress on the affairs of Latin America, proposed by Ferdinand VII and advocated by Chateaubriand, and successfully maintained his opposition in the teeth of all the intrigues of Metternich, King George, and the Coterie. He was by now convinced of the futility of the congress system: "We protested at Laibach, we remonstrated at Verona; our protest was treated as waste paper, our remonstrances mingled with the air."[36] He told Polignac quite flat-footedly, that "conferences are useless or dangerous—useless if we are in agreement, dangerous if we are not". "There are real, fundamental, essential, irreconcilable differences of principle," he told Bagot, "and every attempt to represent them as trifling or fictitious we must steadily repel.

* Cf. *infra*, p. 93.

The times are too big for compromise of this sort." And he added, and repeated with the utmost emphasis, "This only is sure. Conference *there shall be none*, with us in it."[37] Backed, then, by the petitions of influential City merchants, he concluded a commercial treaty with Buenos Ayres (the germ of the future Argentine) and was already drawing a distinction between *de jure* and *de facto* recognition. During the autumn he gradually won over some of his dissentient colleagues by pressing the claims of British trade and the obvious drawbacks of allowing the Americans to be first in the field. It is, however, open to question whether he could have enforced his views but for the strong backing of Lord Liverpool himself, who in a lengthy memorandum argued the case for recognition, ascribed Spain's loss of her colonies to "the injustice and to the rigid and inflexible obstinacy of the Court and nation", stressed the risk of throwing the colonies into the arms of the United States, and contended that the friendship of the new states would not only bring great commercial advantages to Britain, but help her to establish "a fair counterpoise to the combined maritime power" of France and America.[38] The Prime Minister supported this policy so ardently that in December he actually threatened resignation, unless Canning were allowed to act upon it. Its chief opponents, Wellington and Eldon, angrily capitulated, and it was decided to recognise the independence of Buenos Ayres, Colombia and Mexico. A last desperate attempt to get the decision revoked was made by King George, who circulated a memorandum to individual members of the Cabinet, asking for an explicit answer to the question whether "the great principles of policy established in 1814, 1815 and 1818" were to be abandoned. "The Liberalism of late adopted" by the Government was, he argued, "a substantial part" of the French revolutionary creed, whose adoption had led him to abandon his early political friends. And "can the present Government suppose that the King will permit any individuals to force upon him at this time a line of policy of which he entirely disapproves and which is in direct opposition to those wise principles", in force for so many years?[39] But Liverpool, undismayed by the King's "strong prejudices",[40] induced the Cabinet to show a united front to the Crown: and its minute of reply pointed out that "the divergence of opinion" with the Allies had already begun in 1815, that it had become still more apparent at Aachen in 1818, and that Lord Londonderry had already found it necessary to draw attention to it in the Circular Note of 19 January 1821. As for the Spanish-American decision, it had not been taken "till after as long and as continued a deliberation as ever has been given to any great question of national policy"; and the Cabinet was unanimous in regarding it as irrevocable, and the faith and honour of the country as pledged. In the face of such firm language as this the King was obliged to give way with as good a grace as he could muster, the more so as

Wellington frightened him with the possibility of an exposure in Parliament and a *coup d'état* if he resisted further.* But he pled the gout rather than read the obnoxious announcement in the Speech from the Throne at the new parliamentary session: and thus by a refinement of irony it was given to the world by that arch-reactionary, Lord Chancellor Eldon.

As so often in his political career, it was the Duke of Wellington who really turned the scale in favour of a measure that was intensely distasteful to him. For some months previously his relations with Canning had been specially strained. In August 1824 Canning, in his desire to improve relations with France, decided to remove Sir Charles Stuart from the Paris Embassy† and replace him by Lord Granville: and he was therefore not a little annoyed to find that the King, who (so he told Liverpool) "had persecuted him for two years to recall him", now objected to the change. This incident, and the changes incidental to the death of Louis XVIII (16 September), gave Canning the idea of himself paying a visit to Paris and establishing direct personal contact with Villèle and his new master Charles X. When Wellington demurred to this, Canning pointed out that Lord Westmorland—at once the most reactionary and the most mediocre member of the Cabinet, who as Lord Privy Seal (Sceau Privé) was jocularly known as "Le Sot Privé"—had obtained an audience with Charles X, discussed foreign affairs in a sense contrary to Canning, and then reported direct to George IV without coming near the Foreign Secretary. The Duke answered that Westmorland denied the audience, but this naturally seemed to Canning an unworthy quibble, since Westmorland, though he only spoke to King Charles at a public reception, had had the opportunity of saying what he wanted. In the end Canning sent his correspondence with the Duke to Liverpool and complained that it was "not fair" of the Duke not to admit that King George himself "was privy to" the whole intrigue.[41] But he deferred to the Prime Minister's judgement and abandoned his visit to Paris, all the more reluctantly because he felt that a frank talk with Villèle might have cleared up many misunderstandings. The "absolute fatuity" of the new King's language, he told Granville,[42] "augurs very ill for the possibility of any reasonable good understanding between the two countries".

* In his reply he somewhat lamely expressed himself as satisfied "if the Cabinet acts on the earnest desire of maintaining the system of confidential and reciprocal communication with the Allies" (30 January 1824—Yonge, *Life of Liverpool*, III, 404; see also Temperley, *Foreign Policy*, p. 147).

† On 12 October 1824 Canning wrote to the Duke, "Polignac has told me over and over again that if I wished to be on a footing of confidence with Villèle, I must change our Ambassador" (*Canning Corresp.* I, 158). Meanwhile on 2 August Villèle had written to Polignac, "I am tired of my constant explanations to Sir Charles Stuart: la plupart du temps pour des fagots que je ne voudrais pas que mes enfants crûssent, si leur bonne les leur faisait" (Villèle, *Mémoires*, III, 107). Obviously it was time for a change.

RECOGNITION OF SPANISH AMERICA

British recognition of the three new states aroused paroxysms of fury and criticism from all the chief continental powers.* First Polignac, then the representatives of Russia, Austria, and Prussia, lodged their protests against this outrage upon monarchical principles. But Canning took a high line and told his cousin Stratford: "I mean to have it understood that no such language is to be held to us, by either of the persons of the Continental Trinity." To the Prussian Minister by way of a joke he invented a new French word, saying that he did not choose to be *lecturé*, and asked him how Prussia could object to this recognition and yet recognise Bernadotte as King of Sweden, while the heir of the Vasas was "wandering in exile and beggary through Europe".[43]

The legitimist Powers might storm and bluster, but in an extra-European question they were at a hopeless disadvantage towards England, and Canning only had to stand firm. The fact that the United States held similar views on the future of Latin America served to emphasise the hopelessness of any return to legitimacy: naturally enough they welcomed from the very first the revolt of the Spanish colonists, as tending to emancipate the whole American continent from European political influence and to increase its detachment and freedom of development. But it is hardly too much to assert that Canning's attitude rather than the Monroe Doctrine, was the decisive factor in "creating the New World": for the United States were admittedly not ready to go the length of war, whereas Canning quite definitely was, and Europe, realising it, was duly impressed.†

Not the least impressive feature of Canning's career was his capacity for not taking up any position which he was not either ready or able to defend in case of need. In a letter to the British Minister at Madrid, he declared that "a menace not intended to be executed is an engine which Great Britain could never condescend to employ"[44]—a phrase of which we shall be regretfully reminded when we come to the strong words and weak deeds of some of his successors at the Foreign Office in the middle of the century, in such questions as Poland and Schleswig-Holstein.

"For three years", writes M. Émile Bourgeois in a none too cordial estimate of Canning, "his policy of non-intervention preserved the peace of

---

* "It has set the Continent quite wild with rage and joy, hope and fear", wrote Sir Robert Wilson, the confidant of Bolivar, to Lord Grey, 1 February 1825 (cit. Temperley, *Life of Canning*, p. 189).

† The reader may be again reminded that the details of Anglo-American relations, even in this immensely important formative period, lie quite outside the scope of the present volume, which is in the main concerned with Europe.

Europe, by obliging France and Russia by threat and force to moderate the ardours kindled by the Spanish war. He had a further aim, and brought it about, that this peace, instead of serving Austria in Italy and in Germany, should serve the greatness of the English people and its interests in the world. And this was the end of the reign of Metternich".[45]

CANNING AND PORTUGAL

Having by his firm attitude paralysed intervention in the New World in favour of despotic government, Canning proceeded to turn the tables in favour of constitutional government by intervention in Portugal. The basis of his action was of course the traditional alliance with Portugal, which may not unfairly be described as the oldest and most constant factor in British foreign policy, and which included a pledge to defend Portugal's territorial integrity against attack.* The situation which Canning found in Portugal, when he succeeded to the Foreign Office in 1822, was the direct outcome of the events which had occurred during his first tenure of office and on which he himself had exercised a decisive influence. The French invasion had led to the flight of the Portuguese royal family to Brazil, and there the Regent remained throughout the Peninsular War and even after his accession to the throne in 1816 as John VI. The home Government was feeble and unpopular, quite unequal to remedying the agricultural and financial distress occasioned by the long wars: indeed, it owed its survival very largely to the backing of London and to Marshal Beresford, who had remained commander-in-chief of the army since the peace. Though friction with Spain was a permanent element in the situation, the outbreak of the Spanish Revolution had its immediate reactions in Portugal: and a revolutionary Junta established itself in Lisbon in September 1820. Henceforward events in the two neighbouring states developed on curiously parallel lines.

Only after prolonged pressure, culminating in a minor revolution at Rio itself, could King John be induced to return to Portugal, where he took the oath to the new constitution early in July 1821. The essential difference between the Spanish and Portuguese revolutions—apart from the personal contrast between the sluggish John VI, a reactionary more *in posse* than *in esse*, and the savagely uncompromising Ferdinand VII—was that in the latter case the Powers of the Holy Alliance, however reluctantly, admitted

* The earliest treaty of alliance was signed in 1373, and this was constantly renewed during the following century. The treaty of 1642 (after the recovery of Portuguese independence) reaffirmed former alliances, and that of 1661 confirmed all treaties since 1641 (including both one of the latter year and one concluded by Cromwell) and pledged Britain "to defend all colonies or conquests of Portugal". The new treaties of alliance were abrogated in 1815, but the earlier undertakings remained at least nominally in force, though it could be argued that they had long fallen into desuetude.

from the first Britain's prior claim to direct events. It is hardly necessary to say that this admission rested far more on geographical remoteness and the strength of the British fleet than upon any undue respect for treaties of guarantee. In any case Castlereagh's strong representations led the Allies to disclaim any application to Portugal of the principles of legitimist intervention enunciated at Laibach: but while making it clear to King John that Britain would not tolerate "a crusade for the re-establishment of the old system", he also declined to give an absolute guarantee either to the King or to the Liberals,[46] his main object being to promote a compromise between them. Canning, in a private letter to Bagot, gave a very frank opinion as to the Portuguese revolutionaries: they were "the scum of the earth and the Portuguese earth—fierce, rascally, thieving, ignorant ragamuffins, hating England and labouring with all their might and cunning to force or entrap us into war", and he was genuinely relieved at the coming into power of Palmella, "the very best of the Portuguese".[47]

Appeasement was rendered more difficult and the dynasty's prestige undermined by the secession of Brazil, which declared itself independent under the King's eldest son, Dom Pedro, as "constitutional Emperor", and also by the constant intrigues at Court, between liberals and reactionaries. Queen Carlotta, who shared the intolerant views of her brother Ferdinand of Spain, worked actively for a counter-revolution, in open league with the Eastern Powers and with the very able and energetic French Minister, Hyde de Neuville: and the Duke of Angoulême's expedition naturally encouraged her faction to seize the person of the King and prevent the Cortes from meeting. In April 1824 Dom Miguel, the King's younger son, was proclaimed dictator, a reign of terror prevailed in Lisbon, and the King fled on board the British flagship. From this point of vantage John VI was able to order his son's submission and in the end to send him into exile at Vienna. But the Portuguese situation still remained extremely obscure and unsettled and centred more and more round the rivalry of the French and British Ministers. Not to be outdone by Hyde de Neuville's offer of French troops, Thornton encouraged the Portuguese Government to ask for the despatch of a British force and warmly recommended the scheme to London. This drew down upon his head a sharp reprimand from Canning, and he was eventually recalled from Lisbon, but not until Canning, by playing with the compromise idea of sending a Hanoverian army, had frightened the French Government into disavowing Hyde de Neuville and abandoning the idea of active French interference (July 1824). Thornton had been unwise enough to attend conferences in which the allied ministers discussed measures for reducing the Portuguese Court to reason, and this Canning flatly repudiated as "wholly out of your province and entirely disapproved by your Court".[48] Thornton's successor, Sir William A'Court, was a man of different calibre, and speedily acquired the ascendant not only over his French rival, who was recalled in disgrace, but over the Francophil Premier Subserra, who was dismissed from office (21 January 1835). "We have undoubtedly struck the great blow," wrote A'Court to Canning.[49]

British influence being once more supreme at Lisbon, Canning attempted to regulate the position in Brazil by sending Sir Charles Stuart on a special mission to Rio, in the name of Britain, but also with the direct authorisation of John VI. Stuart's negotiations lasted through the summer of 1825, but on 29 August resulted in a treaty by which Portugal recognised the Brazilian Empire, while reserving to King John the barren right of himself assuming the Imperial title and thus not yielding precedence to his own son. Canning could well congratulate himself upon the result, for a peaceful separation of the two countries had been effected through British mediation, without the possibility of further interference from France or the Eastern Powers. The way had also been prepared for the suppression of the Brazilian slave trade,* which Canning, like Castlereagh, had much at heart: and this had the further advantage of checking any excessive influence of the United States, which was not to repudiate the principle of slavery within its own bounds till over a generation later.

The death of John VI on 10 March 1826 opened a new phase in Portuguese affairs. The Emperor Pedro, who automatically succeeded to the Portuguese throne, abdicated the latter in favour of his daughter Maria da Gloria, a child of eight, having three days previously promulgated a new constitution, on lines somewhat similar to the French *Charte*. His aim was to appease the Liberals and checkmate his brother Miguel, but as a compromise he proposed uniting the rival factions by the eventual marriage of uncle and niece—an odious experiment for which the Iberian Peninsula offered a number of precedents, one more disastrous than the other.†

---

* "The one great mart of legal slave trade is Brazil"—so Canning writes in a memorandum for the Cabinet, circulated 15 November 1822 (*Canning Corresp.* I, 61).

† Philip II of Spain had married as his fourth wife his niece and first cousin Anne, daughter of Maximilian II. Their son Philip III married Maria of Styria, who was his second cousin on his father's side, and first cousin once removed on her mother's side. Their son again, Philip IV, married his niece, daughter of Ferdinand III (his first and second cousin by three other descents): and from this marriage resulted two children—the degenerate Charles II, with whom the Spanish line ends, and Margaret, who married her maternal uncle Leopold I. Their only child married the Elector of Bavaria, and became the mother of the Electoral Prince, whose death in 1699 made the Spanish conflict inevitable. In other words, three marriages between uncle and niece in four generations, between two already closely related families.

In 1829 Ferdinand VII resumed the disastrous practice, and his fourth wife, who was his own niece, became mother of Isabella II.

In Portugal there was a similar precedent, in the marriage of Queen Maria I in 1777 to her uncle Pedro III, John VI being their son and Miguel their grandson.

Canning, though taken by surprise by these decisions, accepted them a little nervously, and disagreed with the Duke of Wellington, who held that liberty of the press and publicity of parliamentary debate ought, at least temporarily, to be suspended in Portugal. In a long memorandum addressed to the Liberal leader Palmella (at the time Portuguese Minister in London) he made clear the British official attitude—that the treaty of 1807 had been superseded by the alliance of 1810, and this in its turn cancelled by the Treaty of Vienna: that there was no British guarantee regarding the succession to the Portuguese throne, and that Britain was bound to prevent the designs of any foreign Power against the dynasty, but not to interfere in civil contests.[50]

Metternich regarded the charter as "an act of madness", and the Emperor Francis, though the young Queen Maria was his own grandchild, was equally furious and favoured Miguel's pretensions. But for once the reactionary Powers found themselves hoist with their own petard: for having denounced a series of constitutions in Italy and Spain for no other reason than that they were not put forward by legitimate sovereigns, they now had no excuse for condemning one which so manifestly fulfilled their own test.* France again for her part had no possible excuse for inter-ference, since Pedro's action was an almost exact imitation of Louis XVIII in proclaiming the Charte of 1814. Moreover, in the autumn of 1826 Canning visited Paris and was completely successful in dispelling the sus-picions of Villèle and counteracting Metternich's hostile influence. The great role played by Sir Charles Stuart at Lisbon and Rio had led the French to assume Canning's collusion in the abdication of Dom Pedro: but Canning, admitting these suspicions to be not unnatural, categorically declared that he had "never authorised", and now "regretted", "Stuart's agency in this affair".[51] Nor did he hesitate to repudiate the treaties of commerce which Stuart had negotiated at Rio, declaring that the minister had acted without instructions: and indeed in a letter to Lord Granville he credited Stuart with the motives of "thinking himself cleverer than all the rest of mankind and believing himself to be protected by the King against the responsible Minister under whom he is acting".[52] As a result of Canning's new *entente* with Villèle, the French representatives in Madrid and Lisbon were instructed to work hand in hand with their British colleagues.

But though Metternich had to submit to the new Portuguese constitution as an accomplished fact, and though even Miguel, in his Viennese exile, had found it expedient to take oath to it, the position of the Regent Isabella

---

* He reminded them that they had suppressed the Constitutions of Naples and Spain, "not on the ground of their intrinsic worthlessness, but simply and declaredly because they were not *octroyées* by the Sovereign".

Maria* and her Liberal supporters remained anything but secure. The Queen Dowager Carlotta† was in league with her brother Ferdinand of Spain, who, not content with welcoming deserters from the Portuguese army, tolerated and indeed encouraged the formation of irregular forces on Spanish soil, to raid Portugal and restore autocracy. Faced by this danger, the Palmella Cabinet on 3 December 1826 appealed to Canning for military assistance, under the terms of the treaty of guarantee: and rarely has there been a response so prompt and decided. The message reached London on a Friday, the Cabinet met on Saturday and accepted Canning's proposals, and on the following Tuesday he was able to announce to the House of Commons that British troops were already on their way to Portugal.

It was on this occasion that he delivered the most justly celebrated of all his speeches (12 December). After expatiating upon the ancient alliance with Portugal—"never seriously interrupted"—he claimed that quite apart from all treaties we had "a decided moral obligation to act as the effectual defender of Portugal". He bluntly admitted that "a vast majority of the Spanish nation entertain a decided attachment to arbitrary power", and painted "the natural antipathy of the two nations, the one prizing its recent freedom, the other hugging its traditional servitude". A few years earlier he had defined the British attitude as "one of neutrality, not only between contending nations, but between contending principles"—that neutrality by which alone "we could maintain that balance, the preservation of which I believed to be essential to the welfare of mankind. I feared the next war in Europe would be one, not so much of armies as of opinions", and after four years "behold my apprehension realised" in the war of opinion by Spain upon Portugal.

England's situation he defined in the words,

> Celsa sedet Aeolus arce,
> Sceptra tenens, mollitque animos et temperat iras.

But he feared that "this country could not in such case avoid seeing ranked under her banners all the restless and dissatisfied of any nation with which she might come in conflict", and he feared the giant strength of the new forces that were rising. In an eloquent peroration he exclaimed, "Let us fly to the aid of Portugal, by whomsoever attacked....We go to Portugal, not to rule, not to dictate, not to prescribe constitutions, but to defend and to preserve the independence of an ally. We go to plant the standard of England on the well-known heights of Lisbon. Where that standard is

* "La jeune folle qui règne en ce moment au jour le jour", wrote M. de Moustier to M. de Villèle, on 4 October 1826 (Villèle, *Mémoires*, IV, 235).

† Henri Martin, in his *Histoire de France depuis* 1789 goes the length of calling her "une vraie mégère, digne sœur de Ferdinand VII" (IV, 333).

planted, foreign dominion shall not come."[53] On the other hand, without British aid "Portugal will be trampled down, to your irretrievable disgrace, and then will come war in the train of national degradation."[54]

After speeches of no great weight by Sir Robert Wilson and others, Canning again rose to defend himself against charges of weakness. He pleaded "guilty to the charge of wishing to avoid war", in 1826 as in 1823: he claimed that the effects of the French occupation of Spain had been "infinitely exaggerated", that the presence of a French army was "now a protection to that very party which it was originally called in to put down", and that its withdrawal would "give full scope to the unbridled rage of a fanatical faction". He then passed to more general principles and asked, " Is the balance of power a fixed and unalterable standard? Or is it a standard perpetually varying, as civilisation advances and as new nations spring up.... To look to the policy of Europe in the times of William and Anne for the purpose of regulating the balance of power in Europe at the present day, is to disregard the progress of events and to confuse dates and facts." "It would be disingenuous not to admit that the French invasion of Spain...was in a certain sense a disparagement, a blow to the feelings of England." But "was there no other mode of resistance than by a direct attack upon France?...No. I looked another way, sought materials of compensation in another hemisphere. Contemplating Spain, such as our ancestors had known her, I resolved that if France had Spain, it should not be Spain 'with the Indies'. I called the New World into existence to redress the balance of the Old".

Canning's bold language was completely justified by events: the expedition to Portugal attained its immediate object without war, Spain was duly warned, and Spanish America went on its course with fresh courage. After the lapse of a century six Republics of the New World in celebrating the centenary of their greatest leader, Simon Bolivar, placed a wreath below the statue of Canning on Parliament Square. Some of his own colleagues resented the use of " I " in his crowning phrase: but posterity has accepted its truth and allowed it to become proverbial.

The speech, then, made a profound sensation both at home, where it caught the public imagination, and abroad, where it was received with rage and horror by the autocratic Governments and was greeted as a rallying cry by all the progressive elements. It was in a sense the echo of those twin forces of Liberalism and Nationalism which were soon to transform the face of Europe. It was a scarcely veiled warning to the Holy Alliance, and as such it was understood. Metternich expressed himself unable to understand how Canning could dare "to make the banner of an Empire the oriflame of destruction for the social order".[55] To sum up the situation in Dr Temperley's words, "Not only was the New World free, but the New World had endowed an European state with a constitution. This was bringing America into Europe with a vengeance."[56]

During 1827 the affairs of Portugal continued to exercise both Liverpool and Canning, the former holding that Britain must either evacuate at the earliest possible moment, or leave her army "till the whole business of Dom Miguel is settled", while the latter argued that "the imposition of Miguel on Portugal, not by his brother as Regent, but by foreign force or intrigue, as absolute King, would after all that has passed be a deadly disgrace as well as a lasting injury to England". To this Liverpool replied with the suggestion that British troops should be withdrawn, but subject to a clear pronouncement that Portugal must be left alone by other Powers also, and that "we will not suffer Spain, or any other country, to interfere in their internal concerns". The overthrow of the Charter and the restoration of absolutist power under Miguel would, he added, "be a triumph to Spain and the 'Apostolics' throughout Europe, and would for a time destroy British influence at Lisbon".[57] The Portuguese situation was still quite obscure and fluid, when first Liverpool, and then Canning died, and their immediate successors seem to have waited on events.*

CANNING AND METTERNICH

Nowhere was Canning's challenge felt so keenly as in Vienna, and indeed Metternich, who had so long regarded Castlereagh as his mainstay in Europe, now agreed, in conversation with Lord Hertford, that Canning was "a world-scourge".[58] For a long time he underestimated him, assuming that "l'intérêt du jour"[59] was the sole guide to Canning's policy, and that as long as he was in power, "we must renounce seeing British policy take a regular course: this is not in his character".[60] Eventually he had to admit that Canning was not a mere adventurer, of the same class as Pozzo di Borgo or Capodistrias, but he classed him with the Chateaubriands and the Steins as a type with which he could not get on any better.[61] His main antipathy was due to the Liberal and to the man who relied on public opinion: Canning's manifold contradictions—the fact that in home politics he took the Tory line of defending the Six Acts and opposing electoral reform and the relief of Dissenters—did not affect his attitude: it was the innovator in foreign policy with whom he was concerned. He admitted that England's insular position imposed on her a special political outlook, but he based his main criticism of Canning on his pet theory that "to attack the principle of the Alliance is to attack Society". "I admit", he said, "that Mr Canning

* See *infra*, p. 142.

belongs to the class of men who often try to strike out new paths or what are reputed as such, and attaches to certain clamours and certain votes more value than they merit." But though wrong in concluding that this would bring Canning to ruin, he saw clearly that "in the existing state of public feeling all that would tend to cement a special union between us and England, would infallibly destroy us".[62] In a word, a gulf had opened between the ruling methods and outlook of Vienna and London, and Metternich hated Liberals much more than Radicals. "The most honest revolutionaries", he wrote, "are after all the Radicals, and if I were to be converted to-day to the Revolution, I would preach to-morrow at Spitalfields."[63]

There was always a complete incompatibility of temper between the two men: and Metternich once wrote: "As Canning always does the contrary of what I should do, it is fair to admit that he also thinks the opposite of what I think."[64] His considered judgement on Canning, which throws valuable light on the two men and their systems, runs as follows: "There are in this world two kinds of spirits: one skims over everything, but never goes very deep: the other rests upon facts and masters them. Canning possesses to a high degree the former: I have much less than he, but I belong to the second category. Canning flies, I walk: he climbs to a region where men do not live, I keep to the level of human affairs. The result of this difference is that Canning will always have the romantics on his side, while I shall be reduced to the simple prose-writers. His role is brilliant as a flash of lightning, but also as passing: mine does not dazzle, but it preserves what the other consumes."[65] This is assuredly not the verdict of history, but it is a key to the conflict of the two men.*

The antipathy was mutual. In October 1825 Canning repeats to his chief Liverpool the confidences of the Russian Ambassador regarding Metternich's double game in the Greek question, and adds his own conviction: "I am quite clear that there is no honesty in Metternich, and that we cannot enter into joint counsel with him, without the certainty of being betrayed. It is not only his practice, but in our case it will be his pride and pleasure."[66]

With these opinions may be coupled the characteristic verdict passed by Chateaubriand upon Canning at a late stage in the Spanish crisis. "Wounded *amour-propre* never repents, never pardons, unless combated in a lofty soul by noble sentiments and a generous leaning towards sacrifice. Mr Canning has nothing of this. A man of talent, education and *esprit*, he has nothing great or sincere, and his ambition will always dominate his prin-

---

* An interesting indication of the animus with which Metternich regarded Canning throughout life, is provided by a phrase in one of his letters of a quarter of a century later. Writing on 1 August 1852 to Baron Koller, he refers to "M. Canning de néfaste mémoire" (*ibid.* VIII, 321).

ciples." [67] It is difficult to resist the conclusion that Chateaubriand was here reading into the mind of his quondam friend and present rival some of the prime motives which prompted his own actions.

Canning's Reconciliation with the Crown

The King's failure to prevent British recognition of the Spanish Colonies appears at last to have convinced him of the strength of Canning's position in the country and even in the Cabinet. Moreover, Canning, not content with opposing Metternich's proposed visit to London, used very outspoken language about the Coterie and frightened the King by talking of the leakage of state secrets to foreign Powers. This was a reference to the fact that George IV, as absolute sovereign of Hanover, had special channels of his own for receiving and transmitting direct communications with the statesmen of the Continent. Partly warned by Wellington, he decided that it was necessary to come to terms, and on 27 April 1825 sent his confidential agent, Sir William Knighton, to discuss matters with Canning. The latter was only too ready to build a golden bridge for his royal master's retreat, and during the summer a real reconciliation was effected. Henceforth the King showed Canning all his Hanover correspondence, thus virtually putting an end to the danger of duplicating policy: and Count Münster and other Hanoverian agents had the task of breaking discreetly to Vienna and other capitals the changed sentiments of Windsor. Early in 1826 Knighton confided to Lord Granville that the King was "of a forgiving temper" and regarded with pride the prestige which Canning had won for England: he also warned Granville against the intrigues of the Austrian and Russian Ambassadors, thereby indicating clearly enough that the Coterie was virtually dissolved.

With the usual resentment of the pot for the kettle, Metternich indignantly complained of King George's "double dealing", but his influence, already on the decline, received a serious blow from the death of Tsar Alexander in December 1825 and the inclination of Nicholas I to come to terms with London rather than Vienna. This explains the seeming *volte-face* of Count and Countess Lieven, who already by the spring of 1826 were making the most cordial overtures to Canning and eagerly trying to convince St Petersburg that he was not a Jacobin—as they had so often alleged in the past—but merely the enemy of Metternich:[68] nor was their attitude without its effect in bringing George closer to his Minister. So complete was the change of sentiment that by the time of Liverpool's withdrawal less than eighteen months later the King was ready to throw himself definitely on to the side of Canning against Wellington and the Tory Ultras.

S-W

7

CANNING AND THE LIBERATION OF GREECE

It remains to consider the decisive part played by Canning in the Eastern Question, and this is best treated as a connected whole, the more so as it was so intimately linked up with the final phase of Canning's Premiership.

At the moment of Castlereagh's death the Greek problem was already acting as a dissolvent upon the Holy Alliance. Tsar Alexander was torn between his hatred of revolution and his sympathies for the Orthodox Christians of the East, and though he preferred to disavow his former favourite Ypsilanti and to repudiate the Greeks rather than risk a breach in the Holy Alliance, the repressive savagery of the Turks put an intolerable strain upon Alexander's forbearance, and provoked a diplomatic rupture. Metternich, who was cynically indifferent to the fate of the Greeks, was above all concerned with the maintenance of his "system" in Europe: and Castlereagh agreed with him to the extent of assuring the Tsar that the Greeks "form a branch of that organised spirit of insurrection which is systematically propagating itself throughout Europe".[69] Britain was represented at the Porte by Lord Strangford, who carried his Turcophil enthusiasm to the length of finding excuses even for the execution of the Patriarch.[70] He was, however, horrified at the events of Chios and protested vigorously, even before his chief wrote that the Porte was making peace impossible and was leaving to friendly Powers no alternative save to withdraw their missions from a country that showed "such hateful barbarism". The Porte, however, was utterly intransigeant and refused to send a representative to the forthcoming Congress of Verona: for if Turkish affairs were to be discussed there, he would at once have to withdraw and would then be accused of a fresh rupture, when the real blame lay with Russia for withdrawing her Ambassador and thus encouraging the rising. The Reis Effendi concluded this inversion of chronology by the phrase—full of meaning, since it was uttered a bare two months after the massacre of Chios—"We know better than anyone how to treat our own subjects."[71] At a later interview he again rejected all idea of foreign intervention, adding "Let everyone mind his own business, and the world will be much better governed".[72]

Verona was the turning-point in Britain's attitude towards the Holy Alliance, and Wellington, as her principal delegate, carried out his instructions with a thoroughness which Metternich found incomprehensible in so staunch a Tory. But in one direction—namely, in the Eastern Question—Metternich was still able to carry Britain with him, mainly because the Duke himself was an inveterate Turcophil, while the second British delegate was Lord Strangford himself, who pursued the double policy of championing the Turkish cause and upholding the principles of the Holy Alliance.* Tsar Alexander, then, under the combined seductions of Metternich and Strangford, consented to remain inactive and allowed the Greek Question to be separated from the Russo-Turkish dispute, which neither Power had any special incentive to patch up, and which might drag on interminably, leaving the Greek rising, as Metternich hoped and calculated, to expire from exhaustion and lack of support. The Greek delegates, Metaxas and Jourdain, waited in vain at Ancona and were not even given a hearing by the Congress: and Metternich's *alter ego* Gentz was able to report in triumph that "not one voice was raised in their favour".[73] But the calculations of Vienna were thoroughly false, and while the rupture between St Petersburg and Constantinople continued, the war of independence also dragged on, and like the first ripple on a sluggish surface, drew ever widening circles in the European pond.

In 1823 the tide of popular feeling already began to turn in favour of the Greeks, both in England and in France. Lord Erskine had already addressed a memorial to the Prime Minister, demanding the overthrow of Turkish tyranny: and voluntary Philhellenic organisations now began to form, and not merely to hold public meetings, but to collect subscriptions and discuss the floating of a loan in favour of the insurgents. The death of the masterful Governor of the Ionian Islands, "King Tom" Maitland (17 January), was not without its importance: for his successor Adam no longer discouraged so sternly the sympathies of the islanders for their kinsmen on the mainland, and indeed Corfu soon came to be used as a convenient centre for all kinds of communication with the insurgents. Canning, though entirely opposed to the destruction of Turkey, grew more and more impatient of the dilatory and uncompromising tactics of the Porte, and finding that the warnings of urgency which he sent through Strangford were utterly disregarded, he took on 25 March a step which may not unfairly be described as the thin end of the wedge. His recognition of the Greeks as belligerents rested on the

---

* Metternich's correspondence reveals the extent to which he courted and relied upon Strangford. In a despatch to Count Lützow, his Inter-Nuncio in Constantinople (3 June 1822), he assumes joint action between him and Strangford, and appeals "au zèle éclairé, à l'énergie et aux talents" of the latter to continue the work already achieved, the aim of which has been to "faire évanouir" Russian influence at the Porte and prepare a new era for the Ottoman Empire. (Incidentally this is striking proof of Metternich's perfidy towards his ally the Tsar), Metternich, *Nachg. Papiere*, III, 558. In a personal letter to Strangford (31 July 1822) he refers to "l'ascendant que vous avez su acquérir sur l'esprit des ministres turcs" (*ibid.* p. 571) and goes on to urge the need for separating the Greek question from the Russo-Turkish dispute—a direction in which Austrian and British policy were in complete accord.

"I, the Turk *par excellence*", Strangford jokingly calls himself in a letter to Bagot, 4 February 1826 (Bagot, *Canning and his Friends*, II, 330).

contention that the sole alternative was to treat them as pirates and that this was incompatible with vital British commercial interests. Austria and Russia were of course unaware that this step had already been contemplated by Castlereagh and had been made optional in his instructions for Verona, and they therefore treated it as a fresh proof of Canning's revolutionary tendencies and protested loudly. But Canning retorted that "belligerency was not so much a principle as a fact",[74] and remained entirely unmoved. All through the spring and summer Strangford was tireless in his efforts to wring from the Porte concessions towards Russia, but they were from the outset foredoomed to failure and need not detain us.

The Greek Committee in London* was by now in full swing, led by such prominent Whigs as Lord Erskine, Sir James Mackintosh, Lord John Russell, Burdett and Hobhouse, with Jeremy Bentham as an ornamental figurehead, and John Bowring as its secretary. But it was the interposition of Byron which did more than anything else to kindle the enthusiasm of Europe: for in the words of Mr Harold Nicolson, it "lifted the cause from the muddied byways of party politics, and rendered it at once an enterprise, a novelty, an excitement and a very emotional romance". Byron had few illusions about the Greeks, who were by now quarrelling fiercely and squalidly among themselves: and before he had time to achieve anything, he fell ill and died at Missolonghi. But the magic of his name and of his verse, at the very height of the romantic era, was worth more than several battles. The spell survived his death, and Victor Hugo, Wilhelm Müller, and a host of minor writers sang the resurrection of Hellas. On the practical side, two loans were raised in England for the revolutionaries, both bearing interest at 5 per cent, but first quoted on the market at 59 and 55½ per cent respectively. The first was for £800,000, the second for £2,000,000, but both were badly administered, and the investors lost very heavily: commenting on the public report which was drawn up in 1826, *The Times* spoke of it as "a timid compromise between peculation, indolence and incapacity". It was doubtless the bad feeling generated by this which led to a marked cooling in public sentiment towards the Greeks in 1826: and the Committee seems not so much to have been wound up, as simply to have faded out of existence.[75]

Proofs now began to accumulate that Bagot had been a true prophet when he warned Canning against the illusion of Metternich and Strangford, that "since Verona" they had the Tsar "completely in hand". "Be assured", he declared, "that no man living has him in hand." In January 1824, then,

---

* Interesting details will be found in two articles on "Philhellenism in England (1821–7)", by Virginia Penn, in *Slavonic Review*, Nos. 41 and 42 (January and April 1936). Edward Blaquière was sent round the country to rouse opinion in the provinces and interest the local press.

the Tsar took the initiative in proposing a special Congress for the settlement of Greek affairs: he still hoped to be able to square the circle, and laid down the two conflicting principles that the Moslem yoke could not be reimposed upon a Christian population, but that full independence could not be conceded, since it might serve as point of departure for fresh revolutionary movements. He therefore suggested the creation of three vassal Principalities, of Eastern, Western and Southern Greece (consisting respectively of Thessaly and Attica, of Epirus, and of the Morea and Crete), paying a fixed tribute to the Turkish suzerain, but trading freely under their own flags, while the Archipelago would also be autonomous. This fantastic scheme, he hoped, would at one and the same time restore peace, convince the Turks of Russian friendship and perpetuate the principles of the Holy Alliance. Incidentally the main result would be that "six meagre and divided Balkan Principalities would revolve as satellites round the Russian sun".* By one of those diplomatic indiscretions which were to become more and more frequent as the century lengthened, the memorandum in which Nesselrode had embodied the Tsar's ideas was published in Paris on 31 May and created an immense sensation. For though the Greek Committee vigorously denounced its contents to Canning and the Greeks themselves declared that they would rather die than submit to Turkish suzerainty, it speedily became obvious that their cause was progressing if the Tsar could contemplate drawing such generous frontiers even for vassals of the Porte. And meanwhile, despite the scandalous dissensions within their own ranks and the still more unedifying scramble for the pickings from the loan negotiations in London, it was equally obvious that the Sultan was incapable of reimposing his authority upon Greece, without some external help.

STRATFORD CANNING'S MISSION

In June 1824 discussions were set on foot at St Petersburg between the Ambassadors of the Powers, on the basis of the memorandum: but Canning withdrew Sir Charles Bagot for attending,† and persisted in holding aloof from any action which might commit Britain in a Turcophobe sense. Throughout 1824, indeed, Canning played a lone hand in the Eastern Question, going farther than any Power in his recognition of the Greeks, but declining to co-operate with Russia even in the most moderate repre-

---

* See Temperley, *op. cit.* p. 330. "C'est un roman mal digéré", was Villèle's contemporary comment to Polignac, 17 March 1824 (Villèle, *Mémoires*, III, 168).

† To Bagot, with whom he was intimate, he wrote on 29 July 1824: "Sorry to have to snub or snouch you...I think of putting the Greek question into his (Stratford's) hands and sending him to St Petersburg on a special mission to treat it there" (Bagot, *Canning and his Friends*, II, 266). Bagot was moved to the Hague.

sentations to the Porte. Tiring of the incorrigible Turcophilism of Strangford, he transferred him from Constantinople to St Petersburg, where his
real knowledge of Turkish affairs might give him a strong hand in any game
with the sentimental and wavering Tsar: and in the latter's place he sent his
young cousin Stratford Canning, at this stage of his career an ardent
Philhellene. It is worth stopping to record that "the Great Eltchi" of a
later generation had written as early as September 1821 to George Canning:
"As a matter of humanity I wish with all my soul that the Greeks were put
in possession of their whole patrimony, and that the Sultan were driven,
bag and baggage, into the heart of Asia"[76]—words which over fifty years
later, in the mouth of Gladstone, were to serve as a fresh landmark in the
perennial Eastern Question.

On his way to his new post, Stratford Canning was to discuss the Greek
Question both in Vienna and in St Petersburg, and in his instructions British
policy was defined as follows: "To preserve the peace of the world is the
leading policy of England. For this purpose it is necessary in the first place
to prevent to the utmost of our power the breaking out of new quarrels: in
the second, to compose, where it can be done by friendly mediation, existing
differences; third, where that is hopeless, to narrow as much as possible
their range: and fourthly to maintain for ourselves an imperturbable
neutrality in all cases where nothing occurs to affect injuriously our interests or our honour."[77] As a theoretical statement of the policy of non-
intervention this could hardly be bettered: in actual fact, Canning at this
stage was running a certain risk of isolation, though his skilful steering may
be said to have amply justified it in the end.

Stratford has left an interesting record of his encounter with Metternich,
who greeted him after the first formalities with the not very encouraging
remark, "You have a bug on your sleeve". Yet the visitor was afterwards
able to report that "considering his belief that I was in habits of intimacy
with his bitterest enemy, to say nothing of an old grudge and the sin of
relationship with you, he has treated me with civility".[78] Metternich, who
assumed Canning to be in the hands of "the Liberal faction" and keeping
"his elbows free" for any contingency,* brought himself to express regret
that for the past three years he had looked around and found "no England
on the Continent".

A juster appreciation of the British attitude at this period is provided by
the private correspondence of Canning and Liverpool only a few weeks
earlier. On 18 October the Prime Minister conveyed to the Foreign

---

* 6 January 1825, *Nachg. Papiere*, IV, 199. And again, on 15 January to Lebzeltern,
"L'intérêt du jour étant désormais le seul guide que l'on soit en droit d'attribuer à la
politique de M. Canning" (*ibid.* p. 209).

Secretary his own personal impression "that the Turkish Empire in Europe
will fall to pieces sooner or later, and it would be highly inexpedient that
Russia, Austria and France should have a pretence to agree among themselves" as to what should replace it, without Great Britain also being represented.[79] A fortnight later he sums up as follows his attitude to the war
of independence: "The Greeks will be satisfied with nothing but independence. The Turks will be satisfied with nothing but submission. I am
not prepared to say that either party is *so wrong* as would warrant third
parties in interfering by force."[80] This view, which Canning unreservedly
endorsed,[81] meant that London was as yet resolved to balance between the
two rivals and did not realise as clearly as did Vienna, that the mere act of
treating Greek and Turk as two scales capable of being balanced against
each other was in the long run a deflection of the balance in favour of the
former. Meanwhile the Duke of Wellington, though naturally leaning more
towards Metternich, expressed to Canning the characteristic view, "*I believe
and fear* that no Power in Europe, except ourselves and France, can prevent
the establishment of Greek independence".[82] In a word, London was as
yet content to play a waiting game and assume that the natural operation of
time would favour the Greek cause no less than that of Spanish America.
His difficulties with the King and with some of his own colleagues rendered
Canning more cautious than he might otherwise have been.

When Stratford reached St Petersburg, he found that the Tsar, in his
annoyance at Canning's evasion of a Congress, had forbidden both Nesselrode at home and Lieven in London, to discuss the Greek Question with
any British representative. Stratford therefore had to wait till 19 March
1825 before he was admitted to an audience, and then was hard put to it to
smooth away the Tsar's irritation against England. There is a sentence in
his report of this audience which deserves special emphasis, as a foretaste of
his grasp of essentials: "In speaking of the war in Greece, he (Alexander I)
betrayed a mind divided between sympathy with a people of his own persuasion goaded into rebellion by their sufferings, and disapprobation of the
revolutionary principles which had been mixed up with the causes of their
struggle."[83] In no other contemporary writing is the fundamental dilemma
of the two Tsars, Alexander and Nicholas, summed up so clearly and
succinctly.

RUSSIAN OVERTURES

While, however, Stratford was still waiting for access to the Tsar, two
events occurred which speedily modified the general situation. Metternich,
indifferent as ever to the Greek cause, but increasingly alarmed at possible
reactions elsewhere in Europe and like everyone else concerned, losing

patience at the arrogance and tergiversations of the Porte, suddenly instructed his Ambassador in St Petersburg to propose, as the best issue from the deadlock, that the Powers should recognise the independence of the Morea and the islands.* Thus by an irony of fate the first to adopt the full programme of Greek independence was its most inveterate enemy, for reasons of the purest opportunism. But not merely was this rejected by Alexander and his faithful Nesselrode: it was the first step towards the rapid alienation of the Tsar from Metternich, a process which was completed when the latter, during his visit to Paris in March, indiscreetly boasted of his ascendancy over Alexander, and his words were promptly reported by Pozzo di Borgo to St Petersburg.† The result was to "irritate the Tsar's feelings, destroy all confidence in his allies and throw him back upon himself in a temper of gloomy abstraction".[84] By August the Tsar had moved so far as to inform his representatives abroad that he was no longer willing to work with Metternich, and he was ready to accept as the corollary of this attitude the necessity for collaboration with England. Countess Lieven was definitely entrusted by Alexander with the mission of winning Canning for action, in the belief that "the Turkish power is crumbling", and that the two Powers together could "establish in the East an order of things conformable to the interests of Europe and to the laws of religion and humanity".[85]

The summer of 1825, then, is a turning point alike in the affairs of Canning and of Greece. In February Count Lieven reported home that George IV and the Duke of Wellington were ready to disavow Canning, and a month later the Coterie intrigue against him reached its height in the King's attempt to bring Metternich across the Channel.‡ But Canning triumphant soon turned from breathing threats against the Lievens to private overtures of the most cordial kind, and they in turn were soon endeavouring to rid the Tsar of his suspicion that Canning was a Jacobin. The reconciliation of Canning and the King kept pace with the rupture between Metternich and Alexander, and the two processes were not unconnected with each other. Meanwhile Canning was steadily improving his relations with France, where Charles X was distinctly more reactionary than his brother, but happened to be a confirmed Philhellene and was already attracted by the idea of a French prince upon the throne of an independent Greece, while Villèle favoured Anglo-French friendship and regarded Metternich as

---

* "Non pas comme une reconnaissance de droit, mais comme une mesure de fait et de nécessité, dirigée en forme de menace contre une opposition autrement insurmontable", 15 January 1825 (*Nachg. Papiere*, IV, 204–5).

† It is but fair to add that the visit was clouded by the death of his second wife, and that Metternich may well have been unstrung.

‡ See *supra*, p. 83.

Machiavellian.[86] Each of these causes made it easier for Canning to show a firm hand, and sensitive as he always was to public opinion, the steady growth of Philhellenic sentiment and the pressure of new trade interests, outweighing the blind and selfish Turcophilism of the Levantine mono- polists—all forced him in the same direction.

The Greeks appeal to London

But the decisive factor was undoubtedly the intransigeance of the Porte. On the one hand it flatly rejected all foreign interference as incompatible with its dignity and its religious principles, while on the other it was un- willing to make the slightest concession to the rebels, yet in the disorganised state of the Turkish army and administration it lacked the power to enforce obedience. Under such circumstances the Sultan's only hope lay in securing an effective ally abroad, and this he found in Mehemet Ali, the Pasha of Egypt, who was already hostile to the Greeks owing to the depredations caused by their ships on Egyptian commerce, and who feared the advent of a Russian fleet in the Mediterranean. Mahmud therefore stooped to acclaim his powerful vassal as the champion of Islam and proclaimed his son Ibrahim as Vizier of the Morea, with command over the operations by sea and land. Already in the summer of 1824 Egyptian forces decided the capture of Kasos and Psara, two key positions of the Greeks in the Eastern Aegean, and helped the Turks in several indecisive naval actions: in the winter Ibrahim established himself in Crete, and in February 1825 began to disembark his army in Greece. By the end of March he was able to lay siege to Navarino, and ere long to establish himself on the sites rendered for ever famous by the narrative of Thucydides. The Greek cause, threatened by this succession of reverses, was also torn by violent internal dissensions: and it gradually be- gan to transpire that Mahmud and Ibrahim had agreed upon a systematic plan for exterminating or transplanting the Greek population of the Morea and replacing them by Egyptians. Whether overstated or not, this was widely believed, and roused the Philhellenes throughout Europe to fresh efforts: and it was not without its effect upon Canning. In the following year Thomas Gordon and that famous sailor adventurer Lord Cochrane went to Greece " with considerable funds with which to reinforce the Greek Navy ", while Sir Richard Church became commander-in-chief of their land forces and permanently linked his fortunes with the young state struggling to birth.[87]

American sympathy for the Greeks also began to show itself: President Monroe in the famous message ever since associated with his name, ex- pressed a firm belief in the ultimate victory of the Greeks, and added

mysteriously that facts in his possession convinced him that their enemy
had for ever lost his power over them. A few days later Daniel Webster
urged upon Congress the appointment of an American diplomatic agent in
Greece: and ere long an American squadron, under Admiral Rodgers,
made its appearance in the Aegean. The new French "Société Phil-
anthropique", was founded in March 1825, thanks to the initiative of men
like Chateaubriand, Benjamin Constant and Sebastiani, and its first
emissary in Greece, General Roche, lost no time in proposing a French
prince for the future throne. The names of the Duke of Orleans and of his
second son the Duke of Nemours, were openly mentioned. Unhappily
there was already considerable jealousy between the French and British
supporters of the Greeks, and in London mention was already made of a
rival candidate in the person of Leopold of Saxe-Coburg, who had at one
time seemed destined to become Prince Consort of England. But with the
Greeks themselves the scale was weighted in favour of Britain by the
memory of Byron, and by the influence of Commodore Hamilton, whose
appearance with a British frigate off Nauplia had deterred Ibrahim from
pushing home an attack upon the provisional seat of government. At the end of
July it was decided at Nauplia to place Greece under the exclusive protection
of Great Britain, and the "French party" was left almost without support.
While then Ibrahim held most of the Morea in his clutches and a new
Turkish army was slowly overcoming the heroic defence of Missolonghi,
three Greek delegates were despatched from Nauplia to London, to lay their
Government's appeal before Canning. Canning received them cordially,
but rejected the proposed protectorate, on the ground that it would be
regarded in many quarters as "territorial aggradisement" and "would break
up the present system of treaties" in Europe. He was evasive when they
mentioned Prince Leopold and the Duke of Sussex as possible candidates,
and when pressed for an opinion—since "they will certainly choose a King
during the winter"—he merely hinted that Leopold was not likely to accept
any such offer without the approval of King George. When they declared
that they must either be entirely independent or perish, he warned them
that Great Britain would reaffirm neutrality, but earnestly begged them not
to consider this as a hostile measure.[88] A few days later a proclamation of
neutrality was issued, and justified to the diplomatic corps by the argument
that belligerency is a question of fact, not of principle. From the despatch
in which he informs his Ambassador in Vienna of these happenings, it is
clear that Canning was still genuinely bent upon "adjusting the balance of
neutrality", but was influenced by the strength of Philhellenic feeling. At the
same time he complained that Metternich was "heart and soul" upon the
Turkish side, and that France was playing a double game—helping to create

the Egyptian army, yet encouraging Greek resistance and the idea of a French prince for the Greek throne.

Events were slowly pushing Canning along the road to recognition, yet the fresh instructions which he issued to his cousin Stratford on 12 October show quite clearly the reluctant slowness with which his mind was still moving—a mood very different from the revolutionary outlook ascribed to him by Metternich. The long delay in accrediting Stratford Canning as Lord Strangford's successor was, he writes, intended to prove that Britain was resolved not to take part in the conferences of St Petersburg. He recognises that this had given a start of sixteen months to the French Ambassador, General Guilleminot, but adds, "I cannot conceal from myself that we as well as France have something to explain and extenuate with the Porte", in view of the military activities of both French and British subjects on the Greek side. Stratford is to warn the Porte as to the fatal consequences of prolonging the struggle, and still more of war with Russia. "Every success of the Turkish army renders the Greeks more and more objects of sympathy and compassion, and every failure contributes to place Turkey in the light of a more tempting and easy prey." Moreover, "to suppose that Greece can ever be brought back...is vain": and Great Britain, though not "obtruding" her services, is ready to enquire, if desired, "with how much less than complete separation and independence Greece would be satisfied".[89] In a word, Canning saw that the Turks had not a moment to lose if they were to save some fragments from the wreck. But the Porte was not open to reason, and Mahmud II, then already plotting the wholesale massacre of the Janissaries, was not the man to yield to anything short of triumphant force.

Tsar Nicholas I

At this stage, however, the whole situation was radically transformed by the unexpected death of Tsar Alexander. The strange circumstances under which Nicholas I succeeded to the throne—after the renunciation of his brother Constantine and the suppression of the Decabrist military revolt— were to leave a permanent mark upon the new Tsar's character. Already a confirmed believer in autocratic government and its divine origin, but wholly untouched by the sentimental liberalism into which his brother had periodically lapsed, he regarded it as his mission in life to combat revolution in every form, and to him revolution was an elastic expression which included even the mildest attempt to impose further constitutional restraints upon a sovereign. Yet, by a strange perversity, Nicholas was deeply suspicious of

Metternich, the very pillar of the legitimist cause in Europe:* and several critical years were to pass before the two natural allies were to be reconciled. Hence the tendency, already noticeable under Alexander, for Russia to seek a rapprochement with England, was accelerated, and the confident phrase of Metternich about "the lawsuit (le procès) between the world and Mr Canning"[90] was falsified by events almost as soon as it was uttered.

A brief interval necessarily elapsed while Nicholas was absorbed in stabilising a dangerous situation at home: and this interval was employed by the Lievens in London to complete their reconciliation with Canning. Canning himself was all the more ready for this, for several reasons—because he was justly annoyed with Lord Strangford for exceeding his instructions at St Petersburg and therefore all the more disposed to make the Lievens his sole channel of communication with Russia: because he realised that Alexander in the last months of his life had been bent upon war with Turkey, and was therefore relieved at his removal and still hopeful of restraining the new Tsar: and finally because he was more suspicious of Metternich than ever and at last saw a chance of isolating him in Europe. The desirability of direct personal contacts was more obvious than ever, especially as Canning had lost all confidence in Strangford and reprimanded him with what seemed to the victim "unexampled severity",† but at the same time did not quite know how to get rid of him. Canning, then, hit upon a device which would at one and the same time establish contact, gratify and flatter Nicholas, eliminate Strangford, and perhaps also win a doubtful colleague at home. This was the appointment of the Duke of Wellington on a special mission to convey King George's congratulations to the new Tsar on his accession. The inner meaning of this was that Canning used the very man upon whom Metternich had most relied in England since Londonderry's death, to complete the process of detaching Russia from Austria. Countess Lieven undoubtedly went too far when she assumed that Canning wanted to "compromise" the Duke "and mock him at the same time—a double pleasure":‡ and it appears certain that the Duke "not only accepted, but *jumped at* the proposal".[91]

* The fact that Lebzeltern, the Austrian Ambassador at St Petersburg, was a brother-in-law of the Decabrist leader Trubetskoy, and that even Prince Felix Schwarzenberg, then a young attaché, had been closely associated with some of the conspirators, was a grave additional embarrassment for Metternich.

† Cit. Temperley, *op. cit.* p. 291. A despatch of Lieven to Nesselrode, of 5 October 1825 (quoted by Schiemann, *Gesch. Russlands*, I, 348), shows that the former believed Strangford to be accessible to bribes: "L'homme est à nous si nous le voulons. L'étonnement que j'ai éprouvé de cette découverte, ne m'a pas décontenancé; je l'ai assuré qu'il n'aurait pas à se plaindre de la cherté de Pétersbourg." And again on 30 October, "d'une probité équivoque...mais puisqu'il a été gagné, il peut donc l'être encore." There seems no escape from the conclusion.

‡ *Lieven Diary*, p. 111. Her husband also reported home (21 January and 11 February) that Canning wished, for reasons of home policy, to get the Duke out of the way (cit. Schiemann, II, 129).

It was indeed high time that Britain should no longer be represented at the Tsar's Court by so rabid a Turcophil as Lord Strangford, whose bias is sufficiently revealed in a phrase which he used to Bagot—at once exultant and inaccurate—"The young Nick does not care a straw for the virtuous and suffering Greeks."[91]

The Wellington Mission to Russia

It is clear that Canning, and even more so Wellington, still hoped to hold the Tsar back from war, whereas the French had already reached the conclusion that the Porte's obstinacy rendered a Russo-Turkish war inevitable, and that the wisest course would therefore be to make Russia "the instrument of the general alliance", that is, the mouthpiece of Europe's will. In that case the Sultan might be forced to make terms with the Greeks, the object of the war would be "limited and specific", and Russia could not dispute the right of the other Powers to be consulted as to the final peace, whereas if Russia acted entirely on her own initiative she would feel "at liberty to seek the aggrandisement which has always been the favourite object of the Russian army and people".[92] Even Wellington, whose political mind moved slowly, realised before he started the dilemma before the Powers—namely, that they could not raise objections to Russia making war if the Porte continued much longer to refuse all concessions. In that event, therefore, and if the design of depopulating the Morea should be proved, he was ready that Britain, jointly with Russia, should inform the Turks that they would not permit it, and that the British navy would be used to block communications between Egypt and Greece. In doing so the Duke significantly added, "we are aware that we shall in fact decide the result of the war".[93] In this phrase, whose importance has not been sufficiently stressed, we may already detect the germ of Navarino. But in home and in foreign politics the Duke more than once played the part of Balaam.

Canning's very full instructions to the Duke show that his main object is to prevent or postpone war, and that he regards "confidential concert between Russia and England" as the best means towards that end. He considers that "Strangford's proceedings at St Petersburg" have increased the chances of Stratford's failure at the Porte, and recognising the patience of the Tsar to be worn out, he would accept joint Russo-British, in place of purely British, mediation. He does not believe that a Conference would be "likely to settle the Turco-Greek dispute", and therefore enumerates so many conditions as the price of his consent as almost to block the way to that solution. In his view "no merely Russian quarrel" would be an excuse for war, but he sees only two ways of holding Russia back, first by co-operation with Austria and France, which he regards as hopeless, because of their "ulterior aims", and secondly by telling Russia that "we would not see the Turkish power destroyed", and this might involve a single-handed war against Russia, and therefore against the Greeks also—an enterprise to which Parliament would never consent. Britain must therefore pursue the parallel tactics of holding Russia back and forcing the Porte to concession, and must combine with the Tsar to secure a Turco-Greek settlement, which could then be placed under the joint guarantee of the five Powers.[94] Wellington before he left expressed to his high Tory friend Lord Bathurst the opinion that the country would not tolerate interference to save Turkey from Russia, still less to support Turkey against Greece, and this being his mood, he went to Russia with his hands tied.[95] Not the least significant point in Canning's instructions is his argument that war for any reason save the Greek Question "would be a war of ambition and conquest": in other words, for him war for the Greek cause already stands definitely in another category. The Duke himself gave a crudely naïve definition of his object—"to induce the Emperor of Russia to put himself in our hands".[96] But Canning's aim is clearly revealed in a phrase to Granville[97]: "I hope to save Greece through the agency of the Russian name upon the fears of Turkey, without a war."

Simultaneously, Canning instructed his cousin Stratford to press the Porte for a disavowal of the aims ascribed to Ibrahim, and even for definite orders to the Pasha to desist, and stated that without this Britain must intervene by sea, even at the risk of abandoning strict neutrality and deciding the issue.[98] With this we are reaching the final stage in Canning's evolution. For Stratford merely ran his head against a brick wall. The Reis Effendi took the uncompromising line that the Greeks were Rayahs, and no one had any business to interfere between them and their masters—a rebuff all the more marked because Stratford had recently met the Greek delegates, Mavrocordato and Zographos, off Hydra, in the hope of winning them for a compromise, and had actually extracted their consent to a tribute and an indemnity. About the same time the Reis assured the French dragoman, Desgranges, that Stratford would never get an answer to his enquiries and would have to get accustomed to this.[99] On 15 March Stratford argued for five hours with the Reis, without the slightest effect, and by 17 April had reached the categorical conclusion that "the Turkish Government is dead to every consideration but that of force".[100]

One motive of the Petersburg mission lay in the desire to penetrate the mind of its new ruler. Of Alexander, Canning had been "persuaded that though there were moments of enthusiasm and paroxysm of ambition, the fixed purpose of his mind was not so much to liberate Greece as to do that work as the blessed instrument of the Holy Alliance".[101] Nicholas, he believed, would be more Russian in outlook and policy, but he was admittedly in the dark about him and calculated that a man of Wellington's vast prestige and reputation might extract confidences which an autocrat would withhold from any ordinary envoy. And in actual fact the Tsar, when he received the Duke, spoke with much apparent frankness, disclaimed all desire for war, but showed keen irritation against the Turks and treated their recalcitrance as driving him towards a rupture. He was most emphatic as to his lack of interest in the Greeks, described them as "revolted subjects to whom he could not extend his protection", and though objecting to the Morean deportations, insisted that "his quarrel was not about the Greeks, but for his own just rights under the treaties which the Porte had violated". Nor was he shaken in this attitude when Wellington reminded him of the late Tsar's assertions that the pacification of Greece was a *sine qua non* of Russian reconciliation with the Turks. At the end of the audience he struck for one moment a new note, when he remarked that "he would willingly place himself at the head of a crusade to drive the Turks into Asia, but to that the other Powers would not agree", and he must therefore seek the next best solution.* It is probable that the Tsar was playing with the Duke, for in describing the conversation to his own brother Constantine he wrote: "I affected surprise, let him talk and then said, I could only regard what he proposed as something quite new."[102]

This early attitude of Nicholas towards the Greek "rebels" was not exactly insincere, though it suited his tactics to let England blow hot while Russia for once in a way blew cold: but he was from the very first torn in two opposite directions, for he could not withhold his sympathies from an Orthodox population struggling against the traditional enemy of the Slavs, and obviously well adapted to serve as pawns in the game which might eventually give Russia access to the Mediterranean, nor could he ever forget that Russia since the treaty of 1774 had an international status as protector of the Eastern Christians. Moreover, it was not a mere accident that his close confidant Speranski was an ardent Philhellene and that his attitude towards the disgraced Capodistrias was by no means one of disfavour. Canning, on receiving the Duke's report, expressed himself as puzzled by "the vehement and ostentatious manner" in which the Tsar "disclaimed any interest in the Greek cause", and remembered that the first information regarding Ibrahim's Morean designs came from the Russian Ambassador, with the avowed object of interesting the British Government more keenly in the fate of the Greeks.[103]

* Wellington to Canning, 5 and 16 March 1826 (*Wellington Desp.* IV, 149, 180). This phrase was taken up in London, and the Duke, after his return, wrote an explanatory letter to Canning, declaring that he had given a very erroneous representation of the Tsar's views, "if it is believed that he has the most distant intention of endeavouring to drive the Turks out of Europe", 20 April 1826 (*Wellington Desp.* III, 308).

Despite all personal friendliness—according to the perhaps jealous Strangford, the Duke was "treated like a Divinity"[104]—Nicholas showed no inclination to accept Wellington's suggestions of British mediation, and only a few days after the audience despatched an ultimatum to the Porte without informing his guest. It demanded the restoration of the Roumanian Principalities to the position before 1821: it demanded the enforcement, in favour of Serbia, of the Treaty of 1812: and it gave the Porte six weeks to send envoys to the frontier to negotiate all points of difference: the Greeks were not even mentioned. This step came somewhat as a shock to the Duke, but he was reassured when Nesselrode brought him the Tsar's assurances that if reluctantly driven to war, "he would have no views of conquest and territorial aggrandisement in Europe" and that he earnestly desired Russo-British co-operation.[105] In the end, with the help of Prince Lieven, who was summoned specially from London for the purpose, the Duke was induced —after what was in effect a rearguard action, ending in a sharp skirmish*— to sign the so-called Protocol of St Petersburg (4 April 1826). The essence of this agreement was that the Greeks should form a vassal state, paying an annual tribute, but enjoying entire freedom of administration, religion and commerce and the right to expropriate the Turkish estates; that Russia should support British mediation at the Porte; that both Russia and Britain should renounce alike territorial extension or commercial advantage, and that they should agree later as to the boundaries of the future "Greece". There can be no doubt that Wellington did not fully realise the full significance of his action.

The Protocol is the first international recognition of Greece, whose name figures for the first time in a diplomatic document. The first intention had been to communicate it confidentially to the other Powers: and to the Austrian Ambassador Nicholas professed to be acting in the interests of his continental allies. But in reality no more serious blow to the solidarity of that alliance could be imagined than separate action by the two Powers seemingly farthest apart in Europe: and as the secret was soon allowed to become public, and indeed was announced by *The Times* early in May,†

* "Count Nesselrode", he reported to Canning, "was very violent, as indeed was Count Lieven" (4 April, *Wellington Desp.* III, 2). The Duke does not always seem to have shown great tact. A Prussian report, based upon information given by the Prince of Orange to the Grand Duke Constantine, describes him as having asked Nicholas, "What were Your Majesty's sentiments during the day of 14 December?" (i.e. during the Decabrist revolt): to which the Tsar bluntly replied, "I suppose, those which you had at Waterloo before Marshal Blücher arrived" (cit. Schiemann, *Gesch. Russlands*, II, 139, who never misses a chance of quoting anything spiteful about England).

† The revelation, which caused much annoyance in England (see e.g. *Wellington Desp.* III, 323), ascribed by Canning to the Russians and by the Russians to King George. In reality it was due to a certain Christoph Wilhelm Hufeland, who wrote the facts to Paris, where a journalist got hold of them and gave them to *The Times* (see Schiemann, *op. cit.* II, 139).

Canning found himself committed more deeply than he had originally intended, but speedily seized upon the agreement as a powerful lever for no less an end than shattering the whole Congress system which the Holy Alliance had built up.* Nay more, he lost no opportunity of making it clear that such was his deliberate aim, and drew the attention of Prussia in particular to the fundamental difference between the policies embodied in the Protocol and in all previous projects. The Holy Alliance, he wrote gleefully to Stratford, "no longer marches *en corps*. I have resolved them into individuality, and having done so, I employ the *disjecta membra* each in its respective place and for its respective use, without scruple or hesitation".[106]

Metternich was furious, because he felt himself now isolated in Europe and his legitimist principles undermined by their natural champion: and his anger led him to assume that "British policy, instead of saving the Greeks, will have caused their massacre in detail and their final ruin"[107]—the wish being here obviously the father of the thought. He denounced Wellington's role as pitiable, and the Protocol as "an abortion".[108] He raged against the Philhellenes and claimed to be more humane and a better friend of the Greeks than Constant, Hobhouse, Cochrane or Chateaubriand. "Both Turks and Greeks", he said, "are barbarians, but there is more resource with the Christians than with the Moslems."[109] He professed complete willingness to consider the expulsion of the Turks from Europe, but argued that there was no possibility of replacing them by a great Christian state,[110] and that no one could wish "a republic of bandits or a monarchy organised by the scum of the revolutionaries of Europe".[111]

RUSSIA, BRITAIN AND FRANCE

The Protocol duly impressed the Porte: the Russian ultimatum was accepted on 12 May, the last Turkish troops were withdrawn from the Principalities, the Serbian deputies were released, and envoys were sent to negotiate at the border fortress of Akerman. This unwonted compliance on the part of Sultan Mahmud was soon to be explained by a grim domestic tragedy in Constantinople. Convinced of the extreme danger of war in the existing state of indiscipline, and hence of the absolute need for military reform, he issued an edict in May 1826 for the formation of a regular army, and on 15 June met the insubordination and mutiny of the famous Janissary corps by a savage and well-planned massacre and the dispersal or banishment of the survivors. By this drastic measure he removed one of the worst cankers of the Turkish state and rendered possible a re-organisation of its

---

* Prof. Temperley brings out very clearly "the diplomatic revolution" which this involved (*op. cit.* pp. 356–62).

defences on lines which were to bear fruit in the Crimea and at Plevna. In terms of the immediate situation, however, it meant that Admiral de Rigny was right in his diagnosis: "The Turks can exterminate, they cannot pacify, hence intervention is necessary."[112]

For the moment, however, this involved acceptance of the Russian demands, and the Turkish envoys, after the usual oriental haggling, gave way on every essential point and signed the Convention of Akerman on 6 October. Its special significance consists in reaffirming the many unfulfilled provisions of the Treaty of Bucarest (1812) and defining, in the most precise and minute terms, the future status both of the Danubian Principalities and of Serbia, for all of whom it marks an entirely new stage of autonomous development: and hence Schiemann is entitled to regard it as in a certain sense the real beginning of the Ottoman decline. No less striking, however, are its omissions: the Greek Question is passed over in complete silence.

If the Russo-British agreement at St Petersburg rendered the Porte more disposed to yield at Akerman, Russia's success in these negotiations convinced Canning that the moment had now come to win France also for his Eastern policy. The French Government had complained both in London and in St Petersburg at having been left out in the cold during the Duke's negotiations: and while the Tsar assured La Ferronays that he had struggled for eight days in vain to win over Wellington for France's inclusion, Canning told Polignac that it was Russia who had insisted on her exclusion.[113] In any case one of Canning's main objects in visiting Paris during the early autumn of 1826 was to reassure Villèle and Damas, to separate Paris from Vienna, and to win the former for closer naval co-operation, and if necessary for a withdrawal of ambassadors from Constantinople. On 22 November he formally communicated the Protocol to the Powers, and was only too pleased to find that while Prussia remained indifferent and Austria definitely unfavourable, France almost at once expressed her readiness to make it the basis of a treaty à trois.[114] In this the French Cabinet had the strong backing of Charles X, who, in Canning's own words, "appeared to enter into the question of pacifying Greece not only with the sound views of a politician, but with the enthusiasm of a Christian soldier".[115] The negotiations lasted several months, partly because Canning was not prepared to give any general guarantee of the Turkish Empire, such as Villèle began by proposing, but at most a strictly limited guarantee "of our own work in Greece",[116] which was as far as Lord Liverpool was prepared to go. But his ultimate success was now assured: and he himself was the highest common factor between France and Russia, between help for the Greeks and the maintenance of Turkish integrity.

Metternich might draw a spiteful comparison between Canning's exploitation of the Tsar and the attitude of "clever speculators towards young and inexperienced heirs to a fortune".[117] But Nicholas was well aware that his own prestige had been greatly strengthened at Constantinople and throughout the Balkans, and that his co-operation with Britain had contributed to his success at Akerman. In the words of Lieven to Canning,[118] the Tsar "now takes up the Greek question with the firm resolve to solve it". At the same time France was eager for co-operation, and Metternich was powerless to restrain either Paris or St Petersburg.

CANNING'S "HUNDRED DAYS"

While these negotiations were still pending, events occurred which radically transformed the internal situation in England. The death of the Duke of York (5 January 1827), whose accession to the throne had for some time past seemed an immediate possibility in view of George IV's wretched state of health, deprived the Tory highflyers of their most eminent supporter and greatly weakened their prospects, since the next heir, the Duke of Clarence, was at once less reactionary and less influential. But still more decisive was the sudden illness of Lord Liverpool (18 February) from which, though he was to linger on for a couple of years, he never even recovered sufficiently to be able to hand in his formal resignation. Though not a man of great eminence and though certainly lacking any very consistent or clear-cut policy, he had retained the Premiership for fifteen years—a feat which none of his successors has even remotely rivalled—and supplied the link between very discordant elements in the Tory party. With his removal the latent crisis inside the Cabinet came rapidly to a head and was prolonged for nearly two months, in the first instance because Canning was also seriously ill—too ill to attend the House till five weeks after his chief's seizure—but above all because of the acute issues involved in the question of Catholic emancipation. As staunch "political" Protestants, neither Wellington nor Peel were willing to serve under Canning, who on his side was ready to accept a compromise Premier, but only on condition that he himself possessed, and was known to possess, "the substantive power of First Minister". By 29 March his point of view was, "I will be head of the Government or nothing", while Peel refused to serve under him, but did not want the post for himself,[119] and again the Duke freely recognised that he would be mad to accept office without the help of Canning. The inevitable breach followed. When the King, on 10 April, asked Canning to form a Government, the Duke at once resigned, saying that he "could not bring his mind to the conviction" that such a Government "could be conducted on the principles of Lord Liverpool",[120] and that it was one thing to recommend Canning as

Foreign Secretary in 1822, but quite another thing to act under him as Premier in 1827.[121] Disapproval of Canning's foreign policy undoubtedly played its part: for the Duke felt that he had been duped, or at any rate led too far, at St Petersburg, as at Verona: he was incorrigibly Turcophil, he disliked the implications of the Greek affair, and told his friend Lord Bathurst that "we pass in Europe for a Jacobin Club".[122]

The King, for his part, declared that "the doubt and mistrust which he had felt for some of the first acts of Canning's foreign policy had given way to feelings of a directly opposite character".[123] But Wellington was by now furious, thought he had been duped by Canning, and insisted upon resigning the command of the army, in which he had succeeded the Duke of York only three months earlier. The breach between the two men was widened still further by incidents in Parliament, and less than two months before his death Canning wrote to Lord Granville the bitter words: "The Duke, I am afraid, has greatly lowered his high estimation by his trickery or dupery (I will not venture to pronounce which) on the Corn Bill."[124]

The secession of the Tory Ultras forced Canning into alliance with the Whigs: and though Lord Grey, who to the last maintained a "morbid irritation" against Canning,[125] held coldly aloof, Lansdowne, Holland, Brougham and William Lamb entered the Cabinet—the first but decisive step towards a shifting of the party balance. The inclusion of the Duke of Clarence, the King's heir, as Lord High Admiral, was at once a bid for the support of the Court and a counter to the Duke of Wellington's withdrawal from the army. Party feeling flared up fiercely, and both sides of the press were scurrilous to a degree which it is difficult for the present generation to conceive.

Canning found it necessary to relinquish the Foreign Office, but retained absolute control of policy till his death. His nominal successor, Lord Dudley, had enjoyed a high reputation in the Commons, but it seems to have been mainly for his social gifts and wide general culture, and the wits said of him that "ses affaires lui ont été toujours étrangères".[126] Palmerston, however, who had not expected much of him, thought four months later that he had "done incomparably well".[127] Princess Lieven in her diary calls Dudley "spirituel, very bizarre, very peevish, hypochondriacal, *médisant*, a little touched with folly, much sought after in the elegant world, and never having dreamt of entering into affairs".[128] If she is to be believed, Canning was influenced in his choice by the knowledge that Dudley and Metternich detested each other.

The Treaty of London

By February 1827 London had become the real centre of negotiations in the Greek Question, but the long Cabinet crisis and Canning's own illness delayed a decision, and Metternich nursed the illusion that the Tsar was turning towards Vienna.[129] But the course which Russia was now urging upon Canning—joint naval action to prevent either Egyptian or Turkish reinforcements from reaching the Morea or the Greek islands—aroused Metternich's protest, without for a moment deflecting either the Russian or French Government. Indeed, by May the impatience of the two Powers knew no bounds, but Canning was again delayed by his new duties as Prime Minister. The need for action had meanwhile become increasingly apparent, for despite the renewed activities of the Philhellenes throughout Europe, the appointment of Sir Richard Church and Lord Cochrane to the command of the Greek military and naval forces, the proclamation of a new constitution and the election of Count Capodistrias as first President of Greece—steps which were intended to bar every line of retreat—the cause of the Greeks did not prosper during 1827. Caught between the two fires of Ibrahim in the Morea and Reshid in Attica, they were driven from Athens in May, and by midsummer found themselves exhausted, desperate, and not very far from collapse.

Yet more than ever European policy seemed to revolve around the Greek Question, and indeed continued to do so until 1830. Metternich feigned readiness to co-operate, but secretly instructed Esterházy to work against agreement, and this, being discovered, heightened the Tsar's suspicions of Austria, whom he denounced to the King of Prussia as "un gouvernement fourbe".* But the prime factor in bringing the three Powers together was the utter intransigeance of the Porte, which laid the entire blame upon "the Byrons, the Cochranes, the Fabviers". "The Porte", said the Reis Effendi Said, "does not need foreign medicines. The sword will reply to the sword. There is no place for mediation."[130] His successor, Pertev Effendi, was even more categorical, assuring the representatives of the three Powers that "a madman knows his own house better than his cleverest neighbours can", and that for the Porte the Protocol of 4 April was merely "un papier blanc".[131] Reshid's successes rendered Pertev and his ferocious master the Sultan if possible more intractable than ever.

At last, on 6 July 1827, the momentous Treaty of London was signed by Britain, France, and Russia, with a view to "setting a term to the sanguinary

* 30 October 1827—These sentiments were increased when the correspondence of Gentz (Metternich's *alter ego*) with the Hospodar of Wallachia was betrayed to Russia and proved Metternich's disloyalty (see Schiemann, II, 210).

struggle which, while handing over the Greek provinces and islands to all the disorders of anarchy, brings each day fresh obstacles to the commerce of the European states". To this end they agree to offer the Porte their mediation in its quarrel with the Greeks, and to insist upon an immediate armistice. They propose that the Greeks shall pay a fixed annual tribute to the Sultan as their suzerain, that they shall be governed by authorities of their own choice, subject to the Porte's approval: that the Turkish proprietors on Greek soil shall be bought out with fair compensation: and that the frontiers shall be fixed by subsequent negotiation between the Powers and the two parties. The Powers renounce any exclusive territorial or commercial advantage, and undertake to guarantee the new settlement. By a secret additional clause they undertake to notify to the Porte their decision to enter upon consular relations with the Greeks, and if either side refuses to accept an armistice within the term of one month, to do all in their power to prevent any further collision between the two.

Only a week later, to Canning's acute annoyance, the treaty was published in *The Times*—the first notable example of those sensational diplomatic indiscretions in which the nineteenth and twentieth centuries were to be so rich. On the Continent his denials of complicity were disbelieved and incensed his enemies still further.

Fate was to leave Canning's Greek policy as a torso, and hence his exact intentions in a fluid situation will always remain to some extent a matter of conjecture. But it is impossible to suppose that he did not realise the direction in which events were moving and the certainty that hostilities in some form or other were bound to result from the treaty. He was certainly influenced on the one hand by the hopelessly arrogant and negative attitude of the Porte and on the other hand by the hope of holding Russia back from extremer courses if he worked in friendly co-operation with her: and a share must be assigned to his constant desire to checkmate Metternich, who on first learning the terms of the agreement, denounced it as "consummating the triumph of a new revolution in Europe".* He believed that British interests would be best served by preventing the revival of Moslem sea power in the Eastern Mediterranean, whether under the Sultan or the Pasha of Egypt: he felt that the emergence of a vassal but autonomous Greek state would be favourable to British trade and would probably leave Britain "in fact the masters of navigation" in the Mediterranean. He wished to preserve Turkey as long as possible, but he would in the end have resigned himself to very drastic curtailments, so long as Russia could be kept from

---

* 11 June, to Apponyi, *Nachg. Papiere*, IV, 368. This is the same idea which he expressed on 13 November 1826 to the Prince of Hesse: "We shall see whether Russia will agree with England to serve the cause of revolutions" (*ibid.* p. 349).

any territorial access to the Mediterranean. The negation and hesitation of his immediate successors would have been anathema to him.

Canning's own view of the true canons of foreign policy may be not inaptly tested by a comparison of two utterances early and late in his career. In the exuberance of his Anti-Jacobin period he wrote the following lines upon a type of Englishman whom we still have with us to-day:

> No narrow bigot he—his reason'd view
> Thy interests, England, ranks with thine, Peru!
> France at our doors, he sees no danger nigh,
> But heaves for Turkey's woes the impartial sigh,
> A steady patriot of the world alone,
> The friend of every country—but his own.

His maturer judgment is reflected in a passage from the famous Plymouth speech of 1823. "I hope that my heart beats as high for the general interests of humanity...as anyone who vaunts his philanthropy most highly: but I am contented to confess that in the conduct of political affairs the grand object of my contemplation is the interest of England. Not that the interest of England is an interest which stands isolated and alone. The situation which she holds forbids an exclusive selfishness....But intimately connected as we are with the system of Europe, it does not follow that we are therefore called upon to mix ourselves on every occasion, with a restless and meddling activity, in the concerns of the nations which surround us. It is upon a just balance of conflicting duties and of rival, but sometimes incompatible, advantages that a Government must judge when to put forth its strength and when to husband it for occasions yet to come. Our ultimate object must be the peace of the world."

CANNING AS STATESMAN

The Triple Alliance was Canning's last notable achievement. His health had already been seriously undermined by overwork, but to the general public his death on 8 August came as a thunderbolt from clear heavens. It is not easy to exaggerate the sensation in Europe: for the eyes of all fighters for liberty, nationality and progress had long been turned towards him, and the reactionaries were correspondingly elated. The dragoman of the Porte in all solemnity declared Canning's death to be "a miracle of Our Prophet". A Royalist correspondent of Countess Nesselrode wrote that Providence had considered the welfare of Britain and of all Europe, in cutting short the days of Canning.[132] In Vienna also Friedrich von Gentz spoke of "an act of God's grace", while Metternich himself called it "an immense event, for the man was a whole revolution in himself alone". "He has shaken everything and destroyed much," he wrote to Esterházy, "but he has built nothing:[133] and he compared Canning's career to "a meteor", whose disappearance is followed by "profound night". And again he assured Zichy that "Canning did not build, but merely tore down. His three months of office will take a place in history beside other notorious Hundred Days."[134] Well might Princess Lieven write to her brother: "*We* have just lost Canning. The mercantile class is in dismay, the people in tears, everybody who is not Metternichian is in despair."[135]

It is seldom that a contemporary comment can be more unreservedly endorsed after the lapse of a century, than that of Sir James Mackintosh, the Whig historian and politician on Canning. "His death was an event in the internal history of every country. From Lima to Athens every nation struggling for independence or existence was filled by it with sorrow and dismay. The Miguelites of Portugal, the Apostolicals of Spain, the Jesuit faction in France and the Divan of Constantinople raised a shout of joy at the fall of their dreaded enemy. He was regretted by all who, heated by no personal or party resentment, felt for genius struck down in the act of attempting to heal the revolutionary distemper...."[136]

CHAPTER III

INTERLUDE: WELLINGTON AND ABERDEEN

The Goderich Cabinet

The vacant Premiership was taken, but emphatically not filled, by Thomas Robinson, Lord Goderich (afterwards the first Lord Ripon), a friend of Canning who had frequently held office since 1809, had in 1813 assisted Castlereagh during his long negotiations on the Continent, and had in 1823 succeeded Vansittart as Chancellor of the Exchequer. He was the King's choice, amiable and businesslike, but entirely unfit for such a difficult task, and unable to keep together a Government resting upon an uneasy truce between the Canningites (or "Tory deserters", as their enemies called them) and the fraction of the Whigs controlled by Lansdowne and Holland. Cobbett's mordant nicknames for the new chief—"Prosperity Robinson" and "Goody Goderich"—represent the verdict of many contemporaries upon his rather smug ineptitude. A modern biographer is not going too far when he calls him "probably the weakest Prime Minister who ever held office in this country" and "the only one who never faced Parliament in that capacity".[1]

Goderich inherited as his Foreign Secretary Lord Dudley, whom Canning had selected as one who could be trusted to leave to his chief the actual control of foreign affairs, and who, though not without ability, left as little mark upon affairs under the phantom Goderich as under the great Canning himself. Indeed, during the five months for which this Government lasted, both Premier and Foreign Secretary were negligible quantities, and British policy in Europe was virtually under eclipse, while events took their course.

Navarino and After

Not long before his death Canning had sent Major Cradock on a secret mission to Egypt, in the hope of inducing Mehemet Ali to desist from helping the Sultan and not to oppose the fulfilment of the Treaty of London. On this occasion the Pasha made a dramatic bid for Britain's support: "Syria and Damascus are in fact at my disposition.... If your Government support and acknowledge me, when occasion comes, as an independent Prince, I shall be satisfied."[2] It is interesting to speculate what would have happened if this overture to London had been taken up. But in any case Cradock arrived just two days too late, and had nothing concrete to offer in return for the Pasha's suggestion of "a lasting league of commerce with England". On 5 August a large new Egyptian fleet had left Alexandria, carrying reinforcements and ammunition for Ibrahim's army. The danger of a collision thus became imminent: for the British and French squadrons under Admirals Codrington and de Rigny were already off the Greek coast and Russian ships were on their way from the Baltic to join them, actually reaching Portsmouth on the day of Canning's death. The Admirals, acting on instructions, communicated the decisions of the three allies to the Greek Government at Nauplia, which at once accepted the armistice. Very different was the attitude of the Porte, for when the three ambassadors sent their dragomans with a formal Note containing the decisions, Pertev Effendi refused even to take it out of their hands, and it was eventually left lying on a sofa! (16 August.) Five days later Pertev burst out to the French dragoman Desgranges: "The insurrection has lasted seven years, and if it were prolonged for forty, that would change nothing.... The Porte will never renounce its rights.... The Moslems fear no power on earth." After an interval of a fortnight the three dragomans returned, but Pertev, acting on the express orders of the Sultan, declared: "My reply positive, invariable, eternal, is that the Porte accepts no proposal concerning the Greeks and will persist till the Last Judgment."[3] The Note was again left on the sofa. The Sultan himself actually threatened to "slay every Greek in all our territories", and if the Armenians and other rayahs shared this fate, so much the worse for them. Thus those in power at Constantinople were deaf to all reason and reality, and quite disinclined to accept the last-hour warnings of the canny Pasha of Egypt.[4]

Codrington—who, in the words of Stratford Canning, "had sailed from England with the famous motto of 'Go it, Ned' in his thoughts, if not on his flag"*—had instructions "to prevent any Turkish or Egyptian help in men, arms, ships, or munitions arriving in Greece", but to use force only if the Turks "insist on forcing a passage".[5] Realising more and more the incompatibility of two such orders, he applied to the allied Ambassadors at Constantinople for guidance: and Stratford, with the approval of his two colleagues, Guilleminot and Ribeaupierre, gave the significant answer, "to avoid if possible anything that may bring on war, yet the prevention of supplies is ultimately to be enforced, if necessary, and when all other means are exhausted, by *cannon shot*".[6] This phrase was undoubtedly decisive. Codrington and de Rigny joined forces off Zante on 20 September, ob-

---

* A reference to the contemporary legend that the Duke of Clarence had written these words to Codrington.

tained an interview with Ibrahim Pasha and gave him fair warning of their purpose and the consequences of resistance: and the next month was spent in enforcing the blockade, protesting against Ibrahim's barbarous conduct in the interior and preventing a series of attempts at evasion, until the now inevitable incident was produced. Finally, five days after the arrival of the Russian ships under Heyden, the allied fleet entered the harbour of Navarino: a dispute arose about anchorage, the boats of the *Dartmouth* were fired upon by the Turks, the infection spread, and soon a general action was in progress, which ended in the complete destruction of the Turco-Egyptian fleet (20 October 1827). There will always be controversy as to the real responsibility for the collision. It is clear that Codrington was in some perplexity and relied upon Stratford's bold lead, while de Rigny is now known to have been secretly encouraged to action by Charles X and to have forewarned certain Frenchmen in the service of Egypt not to fight against the French flag.[7] It is but fair to point out that Mehemet Ali, unlike his son Ibrahim, realised the futility of resisting the allies, and had on 5 October urgently warned the Porte of the danger of losing fleet and army.[8]

Navarino produced a sensation throughout Europe even greater than that which followed the death of Canning. The Philhellenes might well rejoice, for the result of the battle was to make Ibrahim's position sooner or later untenable and to put an end to all hopes of Turkey reimposing her authority upon Greece: and this was from the first moment obvious to men like Victor Hugo in France or Baron Stein in Germany. To Metternich, on the other hand, it was "a terrible catastrophe", an event which "opens a new era for Europe", while the Emperor Francis regarded it as the act of an assassin and was more deeply affected than his Minister had seen him since Austerlitz. They therefore ordered complete passivity, based on the *mot d'ordre* that they no longer understood in the least what the three Courts were aiming at. Strangely enough, of the three allies by far the most enthusiastic was Russia: Nesselrode wrote of "this gigantic triumph", and the Tsar sent warm congratulations and his highest order to the three Admirals. In France, too, King, Cabinet and people were full of delight at the news. But in England it was received with mixed feelings. Clarence was too good a sailor not to be pleased, but his royal brother, when sending Codrington the Bath, said that it really ought to be a halter. The Whigs and the Philhellenes were jubilant, but the Cabinet, already divided over internal questions, was torn in two, could not even bring itself to celebrate the victory by a salute of guns and held an enquiry into the discretion of Codrington's behaviour.

While the weak Goderich Cabinet was in its death-throes, the allied representatives at Constantinople had to bear the brunt of Turkish fury and to congratulate themselves that the days were past when ambassadors were left to languish in the Seven Towers for far more trifling offences. A diplomatic rupture followed, and they had to leave without even extracting passports from the Porte. It is typical of Turkish methods that Pertev made an insidious attempt to separate Stratford from his colleagues, promising that "if H.M.G. would abstain from pressing the Greek question, the Porte was ready to enter into engagements most advantageous to Great Britain, and the Sultan would in that case even go the length of according a kind of constitution to his people".[9] A fortnight later the Sultan issued a high-sounding manifesto, proclaiming war, "at once religious and national", against the Infidels, denouncing Russia as the chief villain of the piece, and repudiating the Convention of Akerman as null and void. This of course simply tied the hands of Turkey's well-wishers and gave a perfect excuse for action to the Tsar, who at once asked London's approval for his occupation of the Principalities, and promised not to desist till the Treaty of London had been enforced: while France was ready to recognise Greece forthwith, block the Dardanelles and back up Russia's action. To calm British suspicions a Protocol was signed at London on 12 December, reaffirming the pledge against exclusive territorial or commercial advantages. It did not satisfy the Tsar, who towards the end of the month intimated that if the Allies would not let him "merge his special grievances in the general cause", he would act alone "selon ses convenances et intérêts"—a phrase which British statesmen reiterate in varying notes of alarm for months to come.[10] Metternich was left lamenting "au milieu d'un monde en démence".[11]

WELLINGTON AS PRIME MINISTER

By the close of the year the position of Lord Goderich had become untenable, and on 8 January 1828 the Duke of Wellington succeeded him as Prime Minister. Unhappily he seems to have imagined that the main function of his Cabinet, as of his staff in former days, was to listen to and execute his orders. He at first secured the support of Huskisson and the Canningites, and left Lord Dudley for the time being at the Foreign Office. In spite of all his great qualities he was a deplorable failure as Prime Minister, and though obsessed with the danger of revolution and honestly concerned to avert it, he found himself more than once carrying into effect the very measures to which he most objected. On this occasion he broke up the Tory party within three years, whereas Lord Liverpool, whom it is still the fashion to represent as illustrating the capital importance of mediocrity in British political history, had retained power and upheld unity for fifteen years on end. The great Duke lacked both tact and adaptability, and a critic once attributed to him "an intellectual contempt for his social equals, and a social contempt for his intellectual equals".[12] At home his attitude to the three great questions of Catholic emancipation, electoral reform, and the Corn Laws, clearly benefitted the country, but leaves a deplorable impression of his political judgement, consistency, and management: while in foreign policy also he more than once stayed to bless what he had come to curse and allowed himself to be outstripped or outmanœuvred by events. "Like a true military commander, he made no difficulties about sudden changes of front."[13] But as Hobhouse once said of him in the House of Commons, it was impossible to apply to him the Latin eulogy, "eodem animo scripsit quo bellavit". While in power he was very weak and only carried out a series of retreats with the skill of a good general: his best quality was his ability to manage the two Kings, though this, it is true, tasked all his powers.

"An Untoward Event"

Such being his general attitude, it is not surprising that his foreign policy was also very weak. Lord Dudley he had retained at the Foreign Office, mainly in order to conciliate the Canningite wing of the party, and Dudley, while accepting Canning's Eastern policy and regarding the Turks as "hateful barbarians",[14] was negative, irresolute and procrastinating, and "his slow and painful style of composition, both in writing and oratory, rendered him quite unable to keep abreast of the business of his office",[15] in which he welcomed more and more the assistance of Lord Aberdeen.

In the Eastern Question, which was the dominant issue when he took office, the Duke clung pathetically to his Turcophil views, and while the Porte was, not unnaturally, fulminating against the Christian Powers for their perfidy, he opposed any joint military action against the Turks, on the plea that it might lead to a general insurrection. In fact, he had never forgiven himself for his concessions at St Petersburg, frankly disliked the Treaty of London, and was now seeking an excuse for drawing back. At the opening of Parliament on 29 January 1828 the King's Speech referred to Navarino as "a collision wholly unexpected by His Majesty" and "an untoward event", while Lord Chichester, in moving the Address, spoke of our "ancient alliance" with the Porte and claimed that "whatever may be said of Turkish apathy and indifference, there is one thing to which that people have never been indifferent—a friendly connection with England". This view was at once challenged with crushing effect by Lord Holland, who reminded the House that he himself could remember the first treaty of alliance ever formed by Britain with Turkey,[16] with the simple object of keeping the French out of Egypt. A series of quotations from Chatham,

Frederick the Great and others culminated in the phrase of Burke: "What have these worse than savages to do with the Powers of Europe but to spread war, destruction and pestilence among them? The Ministers and the policy which shall give these people any weight in Europe, will deserve all the bans and curses of posterity."[17] He closed with the assertion that Navarino was "a great step towards the pacification of Europe".[18] Lord John Russell in the House of Commons also challenged the phrase "our ancient ally" as "a rather ludicrous mistake", and there were also loud protests from other Philhellene circles. On this, the Government hedged: both Palmerston and the Duke defended the phrase "untoward" on the ground that the collision was "unexpected" and "not desired", and were careful to avoid any criticism of Codrington. But the Duke adhered to the view that Turkey was an ally, and "its power an essential part of the Balance of Power in Europe". "Its preservation has been for a considerable number of years an object not only to this country, but to the whole of Europe", and, he added, seemingly as an afterthought, "to Russia also."

His motive is revealed in a letter addressed by Lord Dudley to Prince Lieven in March 1828 and apparently the joint composition of himself and the Duke: "The Ottoman Empire is not a country like some of those whose example we could cite within our own times, which after having been invaded, resume their domestic tranquillity and their political existence upon the retreat of the invaders; once broken up, its capital taken and its provinces in rebellion, the recomposition of it as an independent state would be a work scarcely within the reach of human integrity and human skill. A new order of things must arise in those countries of which it now consists. What that order would be it is vain to conjecture, but we may venture to foretell that a final adjustment would not take place till after a series of troubles and disasters, for which the greatest benefits that could be supposed to arise from it could not for many years afford a sufficient compensation."[19] He laid down as the general rule of our foreign policy that "no country had a right to interfere in the internal affairs of another nation, except where the law of necessity or great political interests rendered interference indispensable": the Turco-Greek conflict was such an exception and "justified the means resorted to", though they had not at first been intended.[20]

Wellington, indeed, still clung to the conception of Metternich and Castlereagh in the very different situation of 1821—that general European complications could best be avoided by keeping Russia's special grievances distinct from the Greek problem: and while assuring the French Ambassador that he would carry out the Treaty of London, he defined his aim as "the pacification of Greece without injury, or at least with as little injury as possible, to the power of the Porte".[21] Metternich strained every nerve to hold back his old friend the Duke, as a brand plucked from the burning, but even he had to admit that the intransigeance of the Porte rendered a peaceful issue wellnigh hopeless. Early in January 1828 he instructed the Internuncio at Constantinople to warn the Reis Effendi that his tactics were rendering the ruin of the Empire "wellnigh certain", and that by conceding the half of what was actually conceded a few months later at Akerman, Turkey might have avoided the Petersburg Protocol, the Treaty of London, the Triple Alliance and Navarino.[22] He was forced to admit[23] that "the Porte's errors, false calculations, the illusions of its pride, the aberrations of its despair" were obvious to "the most vulgar eyes", and that further obstinacy was bound to lead to European recognition of Greek independence, and that the Porte would be signing its own death sentence.

In such circumstances as these, Wellington's extreme reserve, so far from settling anything, left the initiative and perhaps the final decisions in the hands of Russia and France, the more so as the French were increasingly in favour of settling the Greek Question. In France Navarino was regarded not as an untoward event, but as "une occasion de gloire pour nos armes".[24] The Villèle Cabinet, defeated at the elections, fell in the same week as Lord Goderich, and Count de La Ferronays, who now became Foreign Minister, had been for six years Ambassador and *persona grata* at the Russian Court. Under him France was able to hold the balance between her two allies and thus exercise a decisive influence upon events. When he urged on Wellington the need for energetic measures against the Porte, the Duke replied by stressing the need for the Porte's survival in Europe: "We are not prepared for its destruction."* Dudley answered the appeals of Russia by opposing equally the occupation of the Principalities and a naval demonstration before Constantinople, and would at the most consent to the blockade of Alexandria, in order to force Ibrahim to evacuate Morea.[25] Russia saw that she must act alone: and Metternich's attempt, at the eleventh hour, to revive his insincere proposal of 1825 for the independence of Morea and the islands, was not listened to by anyone.

The Tsar seemed by now to have reverted to his earlier attitude of showing far less interest in the Greeks than in his own quarrels with the Porte. "I detest and abhor the Greeks, though they are my co-religionists. I still regard them as rebels: I do not want their liberation, they do not

---

* *Wellington Desp.* IV, 270. Typical of his confused thought and expression is the following sentence: "Even if the want of wisdom and moderation in the councils of the Divan should, notwithstanding all our precautions and efforts to maintain peace for the Allies, force war upon us, the previous attainment of the object of the Allies in Greece will enable them in some degree to control its consequences" (Wellington to La Ferronays, 26 February 1828—*ibid.* IV, 278). What a contrast to Canning.

deserve it", so he told the Austrian Ambassador.[26] Whether he was entirely disingenuous is at least open to question, in view of his personal encouragement to Capodistrias to accept the Presidency and of his readiness to finance the provisional Government. In any case, nothing could now hold him back, and he declared war upon Turkey, in the belief that it would be "the second Punic War" and would deal the death-blow to the Sultan's power.[27] This was highly distasteful to the British Cabinet, but its hands were tied by the attitude of France, which on 20 April declined Wellington's proposal that the two Powers should act without Russia in endeavouring to enforce the Treaty of London. The Tsar had already made a personal appeal to Charles X, in case of some such attempt, and the latter in his reply treated the declaration of war as fully justified by the conduct of the Porte, though insisting upon the maintenance of Turkey-in-Europe, as an interest of the first order for France and for Europe.[28] Meanwhile, Wellington was absorbed in home affairs and by no means sure of his colleagues. In the spring of 1828 the Duke's idea of a Greek settlement was a tributary state, consisting of "Morea and the adjacent islands only", with an executive subject to the sanction of the Porte, and without diplomatic relations with the outside world.[29] The evacuation of Morea was to be enforced by a blockade, and the settlement could then go on under the protection of the fleets : but he had to admit that only combined pressure of the Powers could induce the Porte to recognise even a solution so unfavourable to the Greeks as this, and on the other hand that "it is now impossible that the Porte can reconquer Greece". In a word, though he might refuse to make war "in a quarrel purely Russian",[30] he had manœuvred himself into a position of tactical negation, in which, as he and Aberdeen agreed, Britain and France were practically co-operating with Russia in the prosecution of her war with Turkey, and in which, if Russia should persist in including the settlement of Greece in her final terms of peace, "we are at the mercy of Russia"[31]—in other words, in which Britain had lost control of events, since she could not win France away from Russia and could not face the prospect of a single-handed war against Russia and against the Greeks. Moreover, quite apart from this French attitude, his case for adopting a stiff line towards Russia was extremely weak, since it was impossible to deny that Nicholas, and his brother before him, had allowed themselves to be held back for no less than six years and had shown great forbearance under the endless provocation of the Porte.

On 26 April 1828 Russia declared war upon Turkey, disclaiming at the same time any intention of retaining conquests or destroying the Ottoman Empire, but pointing out that if her allies held back, she must proceed alone to the enforcement of the Treaty of London. "That treaty had tied

Russia's hands and compelled her to march in concert with her allies: the folly of the Porte had given her not only an excuse but a justification for independent action."[32]

LORD ABERDEEN AT THE FOREIGN OFFICE

The weakness of the Duke's foreign policy was accentuated by the uncertainties of the situation at home. In England the political scene was dominated by the struggle for Catholic Emancipation, all the more so since the Test and Corporation Acts had been repealed in favour of the Dissenters: and Wellington was engrossed by the problem how best to effect a tactical retreat, embarrassed by the obstructive attitude of the King and confronted by disruptive tendencies inside his own party. Already in May 1828 the Canningite group, led by Huskisson—whom some of the Duke's friends suspected of intriguing for the Premiership[33]—withdrew from the Government, which thus became a high and dry Tory preserve. Not without reluctance, Dudley, who greatly relished the Foreign Office, though it was so obviously beyond his powers, felt bound to throw in his lot with Huskisson, Palmerston, William Lamb, and Grant: and on 27 May he was succeeded in office by his friend Lord Aberdeen. There had not been a Cabinet of such unadulterated Toryism since the days of Addington, or one so lacking in distinction for an almost indefinite period.

Though in a sense a new man, Aberdeen had very considerable experience of continental politics. He had travelled widely in his youth, and had, as we saw, been sent in 1813 by Castlereagh on a very important mission to win Austria for the Coalition: during the long campaign he had been intimately associated with Metternich and Schwarzenberg, had won to an amazing degree the confidence of the Emperor Francis, and had only less influence on the final settlement than Castlereagh and Wellington themselves. His reserved, austere nature had led him to hold aloof from public life and to prefer the role of a busy territorial magnate in days when clan loyalty still meant very much. By inclination he was a Philhellene, and had told Castlereagh in 1821 that "the attempt of any Government in Europe to support the Turkish power for the avowed purpose of riveting the chains of their unhappy Christian subjects", would "scarcely be tolerated".[34]

As Foreign Secretary he found his hands already somewhat tied, and as events steadily moved in the opposite direction from that favoured by himself and his chief, their joint policy could not fail to be negative and hesitating. Aberdeen's first act was to recall Codrington, but at the same time he consented to a resumption of the conference of the three Powers in London, at which he was to be led on from one concession to another. At the first meeting (15 June) it was decided that the Russian ships in the Aegean should not engage in war, and that the three ambassadors who had been withdrawn from Constantinople should go to Corfu and start discussions with the Greeks. On 19 July it was further agreed that a French expedition under General Maison should be sent to the Morea, to eject Ibrahim by force: and Britain, though refusing to send troops and affecting to regard the decision as directed solely against Mehemet Ali, not against the Porte, offered all naval facilities, and declared that so long as France and Britain went hand in hand, the peace of Europe could not be troubled.[35] Soon after, the Reis Effendi sent a special appeal to Wellington for the return of the British Ambassador, and referred to "the true friendship of Britain and the Porte".[36] But the Duke, while reciprocating these friendly feelings, reminded the Porte that the Treaty of London had been solely due to the Porte's persistent neglect of all warnings and remonstrances and to "the obnoxious spirit" in which it waged war, and that there could be no resumption of relations until Turkey accepted the stipulations of the Treaty.[37] Meanwhile, Codrington negotiated a convention with Mehemet Ali for the repatriation of the Egyptian troops, and as the French began to disembark at the end of August, as the Russians had already overrun Moldavia and the Dobrogea and were threatening Silistria and Shumla, and as Admiral Heyden proceeded to blockade the Dardanelles—under protest from Aberdeen, who treated this as a breach of engagement—Ibrahim, in his slow and tortuous way, came to terms with the allied Admirals, and at last on 2 October began to embark. For Greece the real danger was over, and the authority of her new President Capodistrias was rapidly consolidated. But Britain had weakly abdicated her leading position and left the initiative in other hands.

Early in September the three allied ambassadors—Stratford Canning, Guilleminot, and Ribeaupierre—installed themselves on the island of Poros and proceeded to explore the various solutions of the Greek Question. But the Porte absolutely refused to be represented, and Pertev Effendi told the neutral Netherlands Minister that the Greeks being "rayahs" and "a rebel country", the Sultan was graciously disposed to make certain concessions to them, but would never treat with them as he did with the Principalities or with Serbia.[38] The only effect of this attitude was that the envoys negotiated with the Greeks alone, and that the London Conference, incensed at the Porte, took another halting step along the path to independence. This time (16 November) it was decided to place Morea and the islands under the guarantee of the three Powers, and perhaps as a set-off to this, to resume negotiations at Constantinople—a step only reluctantly sanctioned by Russia, since she, being at war with the Porte, naturally could not participate and had perforce to leave France and Britain to act on her behalf. The three ambassadors had meanwhile reached agreement on much more ample lines and eventually submitted recommendations in favour of a monarchical form of government, an annual tribute of 1,500,000 piastres, the complete expropriation of the Turkish landowners, and the extension of the frontier to include Attica, Thessaly and Euboea (12 December). Moreover, when orders reached them from London to discontinue the blockade, they felt that this might enable the Turks to regain the upper hand, and "believing that the home authorities would never have issued their instructions if they had been in possession of the facts, they postponed their execution, and merely converted the blockade into a naval observation of the ports".[39] For this Stratford Canning incurred Lord Aberdeen's strong censure.*

The fact is that while the French had made up their minds in favour of as great a Greece as possible, Lord Aberdeen—partly from fear that such a state might become a vassal of Russia and serve to secure her a foothold in the Mediterranean, partly from fear of its influence upon Britain's protectorate of the Ionian Islands—wished to see the new frontiers drawn as narrowly as possible. His motive was certainly not affection for the Turks, of whose "barbarous rule" he spoke quite openly in the House of Lords. Yet even before the Poros Conference, he had his doubts as to the inclusion of Attica in a free Greece, for reasons which must be described as purely tactical and extremely shortsighted:[40] and as late as January 1829 he announced to Canning his intention "to use every exertion to limit the Greek State to the Morea and the islands".[41] Aberdeen's attitude was all the more regrettable, since Paris and St Petersburg fully endorsed the action of Guilleminot and Ribeaupierre at Poros.

Meanwhile Metternich was pulling every wire in order to win French support for a new Congress to settle the Eastern Question: but this was manfully countered by the arch-intriguer Pozzo di Borgo, and rejected by Charles X and La Ferronays. It only had the effect of incensing Nicholas still further against Austria and Metternich: "this man", he said to the Duke of Mortemart, "is working both among you and among us to throw everything into confusion."[42] Not even a special mission from the Emperor Francis could avail to pacify the Tsar, and Metternich found himself in the opening months of 1829 more isolated than ever, and felt Wellington and Aberdeen to be broken reeds.

This was amply demonstrated when on 22 March 1829 the Conference reached a new and important decision in the Greek Question. This time it

* A full and lucid account of the Poros Conference may be found in C. W. Crawley, *The Question of Greek Independence*, pp. 142-54. Mr Crawley is justified in treating it as an early classic example of "Stratford's manner of dealing with unwelcome orders from home".

was agreed, much against the will of Aberdeen, that the new frontier should run from Volo to Arta, that after four years of exemption an annual tribute of 1,500,000 piastres should be paid to the Porte, and that a vassal Christian Prince should be appointed, subject to the joint approval of the Porte and the three Powers, who would apply a self-denying ordinance to their own three dynasties. The outlines of the new structure are thus already visible.

Yet even now Aberdeen was not resigned to the inevitable, and only a week later he notified Stratford that though the British Government had accepted "the terms agreed to at Poros" as the basis of future negotiations of the ambassadors with the Porte, it none the less regarded these terms as "in the highest degree improper and unjust". "Obviously, therefore," he went on, "any objections made by the Porte will be admitted as valid by the British Government: but it would undoubtedly be too much to expect from you that you should labour with zeal to destroy at Constantinople what you had constructed with so much pains at Poros. Yet this will be the main object of the British Minister, so far as the question of limits is concerned." [43] Stratford Canning took this broadest of hints and did not attempt to resume his post at the Porte, to which Lord Aberdeen then appointed his own brother, Sir Robert Gordon. The Duke himself, when he saw Stratford Canning, confirmed this extraordinary attitude. The Government's view, he said, had always been that the Greek frontier should not extend "much, if at all, beyond Corinth", and it had only accepted the new basis at the instance of the other two Powers. As Stratford drew the very natural conclusion that the proposals "were not to be pressed *bona fide* on the Porte", the Duke wrote a special letter to assure him that "such is distinctly the fact".[44] In a word, Stratford was disavowed, yet his work could no longer be undone.

THE TREATY OF ADRIANOPLE

It is of course essential to realise the extent to which, during the opening months of 1829, the great internal crisis in England immobilised the British Government for any constructive action abroad. The fierce conflict of opinion upon Catholic Emancipation greatly weakened the Cabinet, absorbed its full attention and also alienated it from the King,* who in the months that followed was therefore more open to the unwearying intrigues of the Lievens to undermine Wellington's position. Princess Lieven, on the one hand, actually allied herself with the King's truculent and reactionary brother the

---

* Cf. Wellington's very enlightening letters of 18 and 26 June to Sir W. Knighton regarding his strained relations with the King ("The King wishes to get rid of us all") (*Wellington Desp.* v, 620).

Duke of Cumberland,* while on the other she established terms of close intimacy with the Whig leader Lord Grey and throughout this period exchanged letters with him almost every few days. The Duke himself declared that they had "knocked at every door—viz. the King, Lady Conyngham, and every description of faction and party"—not from personal dislike, "but because we are an *English* administration and have the discernment to know what they are about".† The Duke warned his Ambassador at St Petersburg of these intrigues, but refused to lodge any complaint or to demand their recall, being "perhaps vain enough to think that I am too strong for Prince and Princess Lieven".[45] In December 1829 Lord Aberdeen wrote to Lord Heytesbury on the same subject, stating it to be "impossible that anything like cordiality should exist" between Russia and Britain, if the former's representatives in London were "engaged in every intrigue which can possibly be set on foot to shake the King's ministers. Their hostility is open and avowed", especially towards the Duke.[46]

The lengths to which the estrangement from King George had gone may be gathered from the letter in which the Duke describes to Knighton "a very distressing scene" with the King. "If I had known in January 1828", he writes, "one tithe of what I do now...I should never have been the King's Minister and should have avoided loads of misery. However I trust that God Almighty will soon determine that I have been sufficiently punished for my sins and will relieve me from the unhappy lot which has befallen me. I believe there never was a man suffered so much, and for so little purpose."[47]

The utter futility of this requires no emphasis: for Wellington and Aberdeen had meanwhile lost all control of the Eastern situation, which continued to dominate the situation in Europe. The Russians, after capturing Varna in the middle of October 1828, had suspended hostilities for the winter. A new campaign was opened in April, and for some months Europe held its breath while awaiting the decision. On 11 June the Turks were defeated at Kulevcha, and only a week afterwards the French and British

* "Your friend the Duke of Cumberland" (Grey to Princess Lieven, 18 November 1829). "I see the Duke and Duchess of Cumberland daily, but beyond Windsor gossip they have nothing to tell me" (Princess to Grey, 21 November). "News however from that quarter will now begin to be very interesting. From all that I can observe and hear... intercourse between the King and his Minister does not improve in confidence and cordiality. For this the constant visits of the Duke of Cumberland at Windsor are sufficient to account. But...does he imagine that he has the means of forming an administration such as he would like?...Is his desire to gratify his revenge...to embarrass the Duke of Wellington? Surely you must have it in your power to afford me some light on these matters?" (Grey to Princess, 26 November—*Correspondence with Lord Grey*, 1, 358, 360, 364).

† 29 July 1829, Wellington to Aberdeen, *Wellington Desp.* VI, 58. "The Lievens have played an English party game instead of doing the business of their sovereign, since I have been in office" (24 August—*ibid.* p. 103).

Ambassadors returned to Constantinople, to be followed a little later by the Prussian General Müffling on an unpromising mission of mediation. But even now the Turks had not learnt their lesson, and on 9 July Pertev announced to the astounded diplomats the gracious resolve of his master the Sultan to amnesty those of his rayahs who showed their repentance, to appoint "a good governor, just, and a friend of the rayahs", and to sanction arrears of taxation. Of any real autonomy to the Greeks, even on the inadequate and uncertain basis enjoyed by Serbia, there could be no question, still less of the Poros proposals or the March Protocol. Such was the Porte's idea of concession, when the clock was almost striking twelve. But during the second half of July Diebitch effected the passage of the Balkans, and Thrace lay before the invader. On 5 August, in sudden panic, the Porte announced its readiness to grant to the Morea the status enjoyed by Wallachia and Moldavia, but insisted on retaining Turkish garrisons and keeping the islands separate. During the next week it formulated further concessions, then receded from them, and finally adhered to the Treaty of London (11 August). Gordon naïvely assumed this to settle the Greek Question, but the settlement of course now lay with Diebitch, whose armies pressed swiftly forward and occupied Adrianople on 20 August, while news came from Asia that Erzerum had fallen to the Russians and even Trebizond was threatened. The banner of the Prophet was displayed, without arousing popular enthusiasm, and the Sultan, at last faced by grim realities, sent envoys to negotiate. On 14 September the Treaty of Adrianople was concluded, before any of the Powers could make their opinions felt, much less impose their veto. Müffling with the amplest means of judging on the spot, described the Turkish army as "not only beaten, dispersed and in frightful disorder, but in full rebellion", and held that there was nothing to stop Diebitch from seizing the capital.[48] But Diebitch's own army was in an exhausted state, and he was above all influenced by the fear that his advance might provoke a revolution and drive the Sultan into flight, in which case there would be no one with whom to negotiate.

Meanwhile the Tsar and his advisers had reached the conclusion that the complete downfall of Turkey would after all be contrary to Russian interests, and that it would be far wiser to promote Russian predominance by more indirect means. A virtual protectorate could be established over the vassal Balkan states, and Turkey herself could be kept in a state of inanition, pending her collapse and death from natural causes. "The idea of driving the Turks out of Europe", wrote Nesselrode to Lieven, "and restoring the cult of the true God in Santa Sofia, is certainly very beautiful...but what would Russia gain by it? Undoubtedly glory, but at the same time loss of all the real advantages assured to her by the neighbourhood of a state weakened by many wars, and inevitable conflicts with the chief Powers of Europe."[49]

The terms of peace duly reflected these considerations. Territorially, Russia shows the greatest moderation and consents to restore the two Roumanian Principalities and all her Asiatic conquests—Kars and Erzerum—save a small strip on the Caucasian frontier. But she insists upon the re-affirmation and punctilious execution of her existing treaties with the Porte. She lays particular stress upon the unregulated position of Wallachia, Moldavia and Serbia, and two separate conventions are appended to the treaty, providing in such detail for the future self-government of the three provinces, as to make of them one of the most notable landmarks in the history of Roumanian and Serbian independence. The old restrictions upon Black Sea navigation are removed, a large indemnity is exacted, the evacuation of Roumania being made contingent upon its payment—the actual result being that the Russian occupation was prolonged till 1834 and was rendered memorable by the introduction of the first modern Roumanian constitution, the "Règlement Organique", by the military representative of the most autocratic of all Tsars. Finally, in the Greek Question the Porte was constrained to accept the Treaty of London and the Protocol of 22 March 1829 as the joint basis of immediate negotiations with the three Powers. In other words, Russia forced upon the Turks those very Poros conditions from which the London Cabinet was so anxious to recede. The net result of the treaty was to enhance Russian prestige enormously throughout the Moslem world, to reaffirm her moral authority over the Eastern Christians, and to leave Turkey in great military and financial embarrassment.

A Policy of Panic

While these great events were taking place, Wellington and Aberdeen were reduced to complete negation, receding at intervals from one position after another. On 19 July the latter, realising that they might be compelled "to go beyond the Morea", launched the preposterous idea of "making a northern state under a separate Government. This would be more agreeable to the Porte: it would be more in unison with the declamations of classical dreamers: but above all it would operate as a check upon the encroaching and restless spirit of Greek ambition, which we must expect to see in any state to be established, especially under one head."[50] Their correspondence reveals them as helplessly waiting for a decision that lay elsewhere, in utter doubt as to the Tsar's intentions and unable to control the French or even to hasten the withdrawal of their troops from Greece. "No one," wrote Wellington on 24 August, "can expect us to go to war single-handed to prevent Russia from taking possession of Constantinople, while all Europe look on and take no step": and again, "We are certainly in a bad way, and nobody can see a creditable way out of our difficulties. We have made the greatest sacrifices of opinions, principles and national pride and prejudice to our Allies. In return they have not fulfilled their promises."[51] To which all that Aberdeen could rejoin was, "We are at the mercy of the Emperor: he can insult us if he pleases."[52] Almost to the last Wellington disliked the idea of recognising Greek independence, "as a fresh act of hostility against the Porte":[53] yet the two colleagues are driven to discuss it, as a possible means of forestalling Diebitch.

By the second week of September this mood turns suddenly to panic. If once the Russians are in Constantinople, writes the Duke,[54] "there is an end to the Greek affair and to the Turkish Empire in Europe": the world must then be reconstructed, and Constantinople and the Straits should be in the same hands as the mouth of the Danube, but not in the same hands as the Crimea. "We must reconstruct a Greek Empire and give it to Prince Frederick of Orange or Prince Charles of Prussia." When the news of Adrianople came, he declared: "It would be absurd to think of bolstering up the Turkish Power in Europe: it is gone, in fact, and the tranquillity of the world along with it."[55] "There is no doubt that it would have been better for the world if the Treaty had not been signed, if the Russians had entered Constantinople, and if the Turkish Empire had been dissolved."[56] If this is characteristic enough of the man who so often ended by pressing through measures which he had spent many years in opposing, it says but little for his balance and discrimination.

Lord Aberdeen's pessimism was undoubtedly increased by the knowledge that France was in disagreement and that Austria, mainly for reasons of internal policy, was unable or entirely indisposed to oppose Russia in the field. It was to Metternich that he had addressed a memorandum in the previous winter, contrasting "the situation and character of the Ottoman dominions with those of any other European states. In ordinary cases peace heals all wounds. Governments may be changed, and dynasties overthrown or destroyed, without the general frame of society and the due exercise of lawful authority being materially affected. But if the Turkish power be once destroyed, its reconstruction is impossible."[57]

After Adrianople Metternich fully shared these alarms, and to Esterházy he ventured the opinion that "the mischief is done, the losses are irreparable and the existence of the Ottoman Empire has become problematical":[58] yet he had no programme of action to put forward, and Aberdeen seems to have resented somewhat his hints that greater firmness on the part of London might have averted disaster. Certainly he was fully justified in meeting

Metternich's reproaches by the reminder that Turkey's "blind obstinacy" had more than once rejected the Tsar's "pacific overtures", and that Russia had given the Powers "no excuse for intervention".[59] Meanwhile Gordon had written home an alarmist despatch, assuring his brother that the internal dangers threatening Turkey were even graver than the Russian menace, and that "total destruction" seemed imminent.[60]

What followed can only be described as an abrupt reversal of British policy in the Near East. On 10 November Aberdeen informed Sir Robert Gordon that Turkey's inability to resist Russia compels Britain to be ready for the fall of Turkey, whether through risings, invasion or agreed partition. After so long endeavouring to uphold Turkish integrity, it was necessary to prepare for the possibility "that independently of all foreign or hostile impulse, this clumsy fabric of barbarous power will speedily crumble to pieces from its own inherent causes of decay....We cannot be blind to the detestable character of Turkish tyranny. Every day renders more certain the impossibility of any European sympathy with a system founded upon ignorance and ferocity." Even a guarantee of Turkish integrity by the Powers could not, he very truly argued, offer any "real security against the causes of internal dissolution". The confirmed Turcophil of the 'fifties, if he had then been able to read this utterance of the Premier who reluctantly concluded the Turkish alliance against Russia, might have been tempted to resent it as hitting a man when he was down. But the real key to the feeble policy of 1829 is to be found by comparing Aberdeen's instructions with a *cri de cœur* uttered by the Duke of Wellington under the stress of events: "The Ottoman Empire stands not for the benefit of the Turks, but of Christian Europe."[61]

The direction in which Aberdeen's mind was working is revealed in another passage from a letter to his brother. "You know that to preserve the Porte substantially entire was my great wish. But the instant that the Russians had arrived at Adrianople and we saw of what the Turkish Empire was composed, I changed my views and determined to lay the foundation, if possible, of making something out of Greece....I now look to establish a solid power in Greece, with which we may form a natural connection."[62] When the question was raised by Lord Holland in the House of Lords early in the following year, the Foreign Secretary did not hesitate to declare publicly: "I do not regret the change from any love of the Turks or of the Turkish Government, God forbid! I have seen and know the effect of the barbarous rule existing there, and nobody can be more alive to the horrors with which it abounds. But the improvement of Turkey may be purchased at too dear a rate." And he met the strictures of Holland—who had described our policy towards Russia as "the acme of imbecility"—

by throwing the main blame upon "the obstinacy and infatuation of the Porte".[63] Yet Holland was not far wrong when he wrote to John Russell: "We have somehow or another exasperated the two greatest Powers on the Continent—the Cabinet of St Petersburg and the public opinion of France, and we have done so without serving ourselves, or our pretended Allies, and without ingratiating ourselves either with those we wished well to or those who are really benefitted by the transactions. Neither Turks nor Greeks have to thank us."[64]

THE POLIGNAC PROJECT

One factor of decisive influence upon Britain's negative policy was the equivocal attitude of France. Navarino had acted as a wild intoxicant upon French opinion, and the Morean expedition served to keep this mood alive. As a Russian victory over Turkey became increasingly probable, more than one Frenchman of note played with the idea of far-reaching French compensation for possible readjustments in the Near East. Chateaubriand boldly suggested informing the Tsar that if he wanted the partition of Turkey, "we want the line of the Rhine from Strasburg to Cologne". Sebastiani, with his long Turkish experience, held similar views, and a certain General Richemont published a pamphlet demanding Belgium and Luxemburg and advancing the thesis that what the Bosphorus is for Russia, the Rhine is for France. This talk at once became serious when Charles X, who had resisted the proposal to replace La Ferronays by Chateaubriand as Foreign Minister, dismissed the pseudo-Liberal Martignac Cabinet and called to power his personal favourite, the lively, but mediocre and ultra-reactionary Prince Polignac, for the last six years Ambassador in London (29 August 1829). "No one but a King as stupid as Charles X," said a witty Frenchman, "would have chosen as minister a man so stupid as Polignac."[65] One of Polignac's first acts was to lay before the King and Council of Ministers a fantastic project for the revision of the treaties of 1815 and the redistribution of Europe. When he began by claiming for France all Belgium to the Meuse and Scheldt, the Dauphin objected that Britain would never consent to see Antwerp in French hands, and therefore suggested working for the Rhine frontier instead. At a second sitting Polignac tried to prove that Belgium was more valuable than the Rhine provinces and that it was necessary to risk British enmity. But his further suggestions were intended to provide a sop for the British Cerberus. Russia would annex the Principalities, Armenia and as much of Asia Minor as she pleased, while Austria would take Bosnia and Serbia. The rest of European Turkey, with Constantinople, would become a Christian Kingdom under the King of Holland, while Syria and Arabia would be united with Egypt and the whole north African coast, under Mehemet Ali. The obnoxious Kingdom of the Netherlands would disappear from the map, Belgium with Luxemburg and the Saar going to France, Holland to Prussia and the Dutch colonies to Britain, as the price of acquiescence. Prussia would also annex Saxony, whose king would receive Rhenish Prussia in exchange.[66] In a word, the plan was not merely a defiance of the principles laid down in 1815, but ran roughshod over legitimate principles and the rights of the weaker states alike: in its quest after "gloire" it ignored every obstacle and took no account of reality.

All this was to be achieved by a secret bargain between Paris and St Petersburg, though it was admitted that it might lead to general war, with Britain and Austria pitted against Russia, France, Prussia and Bavaria. Incredible as it may seem, the King and his Cabinet approved the scheme, and it was sent in strictest confidence to the Duke of Mortemart at St Petersburg, with instructions to win over the Tsar. Unfortunately the despatch only arrived after the signature of peace with Turkey, when the Tsar was already in a complacently pacific mood and exclaiming that he could not imagine more convenient neighbours than the Turks. But what finally proved fatal was the absolute refusal of Frederick William III, when sounded, even to consider for one moment the cession of the Rhine frontier to France.* Polignac dropped the idea, and the events of 1830 transformed the problem of the Low Countries, on radical and unexpected lines: but such ambitions smouldered on, and made their appearance in a new form during the 'sixties.

The full facts remained a secret, but enough was known to cause real uneasiness both in London and Vienna. Palmerston, during a visit to Paris early in January 1829, found ideas of this kind prevalent among men of the first importance, for he records in his diary a conversation at Count Flahault's, with Sebastiani and Talleyrand—with both of whom he himself was to have constant official dealings less than two years later—the former declaring the Rhine frontier to be "essential and indispensable to France", and "cordial alliance" with England to be impossible until she withdrew her opposition to such a change on the map.[67] Thus nervousness as to French intentions served as an additional motive for the British Government pressing forward the settlement of Greece, and on 30 November the conferences at London were resumed. As late as September, Aberdeen, having only reluctantly conceded Attica to free Greece, still wished to leave Euboea and Crete in the hands of the Turks, so that they might "effectually control" the new state.[68] After Adrianople, Wellington still opposed con-

* On 3 January 1830 he informed St Petersburg and Paris that "his resolve was irrevocable". Cf. Bourgeois, *Manuel de Polit. Étrangère*, II, 781.

ceding Euboea to the Greeks,[69] and on New Year's Day 1830 was still arguing that to make Greece a sovereign and not a vassal state was a violation of the Treaty of London. He now regarded the suggestion of a Greek Empire as a mere passing aberration and reverted to his fixed idea of a Russian danger in Greece.* The more nimble Aberdeen had to remind his chief that the situation had greatly changed since they first took office and that "all Europe expects the independence of Greece".[70] He therefore took independence for granted and concentrated on the task of finding a suitable sovereign for the new state. The favourite candidate, Prince Frederick of Orange, refused to stand, and after a perfect bevy of obscure princelings had been considered and rejected, the choice fell upon Prince Leopold of Coburg, who, but for the death of the gifted Princess Charlotte, might ere long have become Prince Consort of England. But Leopold, with considerable Whig backing, held out for an extension of the Greek frontier, reckoning that to arrive with such a concession from the Powers in his hands would raise his prestige and ease the task of governing the new kingdom, whereas to come without it would almost foredoom him to failure. His failure to secure this concession left him free to accept the Belgian throne in the following year, with happy results for all Europe.

There is some picquancy in the fact that Wellington pushed his advocacy of Leopold to the length of threatening to resign unless George IV abandoned his obstruction. The double concession was made that Leopold should renounce his British pension and should bear the title of "Sovereign", not "King", of Greece. This incident illustrates Wellington's stiff attitude towards the Crown: as he once remarked to Lord Clarendon, "he had had to do with many sovereigns, and always found he could bring them to reason".[71]

The London Protocol of 3 February 1830 proclaimed the independence of Greece, within frontiers including Attica, Boeotia and Euboea, but only the merest strip north of the Gulf of Corinth: to this were added the Cyclades, but Crete and Samos were resolutely excluded. The new state was to enjoy the guarantee of Russia, France and Britain. The form of government was to be a hereditary monarch, but the Prince might not be chosen from the reigning families of the three protecting Powers. This decision had the defects common to all compromises. The British Government wished to create a new state, freed from Turkish interference, strong enough not to become a mere Russian outpost in the Mediterranean, and guarded by its new dynastic character against subversive and revolutionary influences from

* "I think we have seen enough of the objects of Russia in it (i.e. in Greece) to be very certain that the establishment of the Greek Power can never be otherwise than disadvantageous to this Country"—Wellington to Aberdeen, 31 August 1830, cit. Crawley, *Greek Independence*, p. 202.

Italy or Germany. But at the same time it was afraid to make it too strong, lest it should serve to attract the Ionian Islands into its orbit, or increase the temptations to Russia to secure a naval station. As a result, the Conference adopted frontiers so impossible that they had to be extended under the final Protocol of 21 July 1832 to the full Volo-Arta line: and even this left the seeds of infinite future trouble which might have been averted by a little more foresight and statesmanship at the outset. Thessaly came to Greece in 1881, after the Powers in Congress at Berlin had imposed another impracticable line. The exclusion of Crete caused periodical risings and even international complications, at intervals throughout the century: while Epirus, Salonica and the northern shores of the Aegean were the bait which brought Greece into the Balkan League of 1912 and sealed the doom of Turkey-in-Europe. The shortsighted outlook of British statesmen at the cradle of modern Greece is the beginning of that fixed idea which haunts their more eminent successors on both sides of politics for the next two generations—that the liberated Christians will inevitably be mere tools of their liberators or co-religionists—an illusion first shaken by Bulgaria's attitude towards Russia in the 'eighties, but not finally dispelled till the events of the present century. As so often in continental problems, Britain had allowed her first enthusiasms to fade, and after some really decisive contributions to the cause of Hellenic freedom, became in the final stages lukewarm and almost grudging. The feeble policy of Wellington and Aberdeen only serves to throw into stronger relief the daring and constructive ability of Canning: nor, it must be added, is there much trace in this first brief interlude of office of the sober, consistent and conciliatory policy pursued by Aberdeen in his later phase under Sir Robert Peel.

The idea of a joint guarantee of Turkish integrity by the Powers, favoured both by Wellington and Metternich, failed to find acceptance with Russia, who lost no time during the winter of 1829 in establishing her influence at the Porte, to the detriment alike of the weak Gordon and the experienced Guilleminot. Chosrev and Halil Pashas were definitely Russophil, and it was thanks above all to Russian influence—wisely enforced by the Tsar's promise to reduce the indemnity—that the Porte was induced on 23 April 1830 to endorse the decisions of the London Conference. In August of the same year the Sultan issued a Hatti-Sheriff which was to form the basis of Serbia's autonomous status for the next half century.

THE REVERSAL OF POLICY IN PORTUGAL

Canning's energetic action in the winter of 1826 had saved Portugal from Spanish interference and checked the triumph of autocracy. But though the troops of General Clinton maintained order, the constitutional cause struck but little root in the nation at large, and only a month before the death of Canning the Liberal ministry of Saldanha fell, and Dom Pedro nominated his brother Miguel as Regent, believing that only the advent of a strong man could save Portugal from civil discord. In this question, as in all else, Goderich and Dudley played an entirely effaced role, and the decisive negotiations took place in Vienna under the auspices of Metternich. Accordingly, Miguel authorised his sister to proclaim his allegiance to the constitution and went out of his way to pay special complimentary visits to Paris and London. Here his natural desire for a loan was favourably considered, and his position was further strengthened by the fact that the newly appointed British Minister, Sir Frederick Lamb, went to Lisbon in his suite. On arrival in February 1828, Miguel solemnly renewed his oath to the constitution, but immediately began to conspire against it with his mother, Queen Carlota. Lamb soon reported that "no party of any consequence appears to attach the least value to the Charter", but contemptuously treated "the riding whip" as the only means of bringing either side to reason:[72] and the withdrawal of the British forces on 5 April removed the last restraint upon Miguel's activities. A Liberal revolt at Oporto was easily suppressed, and on 26 June a carefully picked Parliament proclaimed Miguel as King, and abolished the constitution altogether. This was too much even for Metternich, who, little as he loved the new constitution, described the body which revoked it as "nothing but selected instruments and notorious accomplices of the usurper", and proposed that government should be carried on in the joint names of Miguel and Maria, until the latter was old enough to marry.

Aberdeen had but recently succeeded Dudley at the Foreign Office, and it was only natural that in Portuguese affairs the main decision should lie with the Duke of Wellington, in view of his previous connections with the Peninsula. Wellington disapproved from the first of the attitude of Lamb, who, he told Aberdeen, had "taken an erroneous view of the relative situation" of Britain and Portugal. "We are not the protectors of Portugal", he added: "Portugal is not a dependency either *de jure* or *de facto*."[73] This of course meant a withdrawal from the strong line taken by Canning: and there was corresponding embarrassment in London, when the little Queen, whom her father the Emperor Pedro had at last despatched to Europe, learned on her arrival at Gibraltar the news of her uncle's *coup* and was therefore diverted to England. Here she was received with all honour and welcomed by George IV at Windsor, but Wellington complained to Aberdeen that her coming was "the work of an intrigue, intended to give us trouble".[74] Aberdeen rejected Barbacena's appeal for renewed intervention and Lord Holland's advocacy of the same course in the House of Lords: indeed, he very plausibly contended that "there would be no end to interference if we were liable to be called on in every case of dispute between the members of the family [of Braganza] or between the King and his people".[75] He looked with equal disfavour upon the designs of the Portuguese Liberal exiles in England for a naval expedition to the Azores, which held out for Queen Maria: and when Saldanha and Palmella, disregarding all warnings, actually set sail from Plymouth on 6 January 1829, two British frigates were sent by Wellington's orders to prevent them from landing, and kept them under observation till they abandoned the scheme and returned to the Channel. The vigorous protests of Mackintosh, Brougham and Palmerston in the House of Commons were unavailing, and Miguel owed his impunity very largely to a reversal of Canning's policy. Already on this occasion Palmerston struck a note that was ere long to become familiar. "The civilised world," he declared, "rings with execrations upon Miguel, and yet this destroyer of constitutional freedom, this faithless usurper...is in the opinion of Europe mainly indebted for his success to a belief...that the Cabinet of England looks upon his usurpation with no unfriendly eye."[*]

During the second half of 1828 and throughout 1829 Portugal was subjected by the savage Miguel to a veritable reign of terror. The withdrawal of the diplomatic corps released him from an embarrassing foreign control, for which the recognition accorded by a kindred regime in Spain doubtless more than atoned in his eyes. He therefore continued to govern by wholesale deportation, confiscation and espionage: a number of prominent Liberals were executed, and the strangled victims in some cases publicly burnt. Queen Carlota encouraged her son in his worst excesses and pressed for the revival of the Inquisition. Her death in January 1830 weakened the fanatics, but Miguel's misgovernment continued unabated, and financial distress was superadded.

It would be absurd to credit the Wellington Cabinet with any sympathy for Dom Miguel, but it was increasingly disposed to assume that he was acceptable to the great majority of Portuguese, that opposition to him would merely injure British trade interests, and that it would be unwise to risk complications in the west while the situation remained so obscure in

---

[*] 1 June 1829, *Hansard*, XXI, 1643–70. He even went so far as to argue that by Miguel's actions "the personal honour of our sovereign has been insulted", *ibid.* p. 1659.

Eastern Europe. Wellington seems also to have been highly suspicious as to the possibility of union between the Azores and Brazil. The only consideration which deterred him and Aberdeen from accepting the new regime as final was the desire to secure an amnesty for the numerous exiled Liberals: and in February 1830 Aberdeen openly admitted in the House of Lords that he had "long considered recognition as a question of time only".[76] As Miguel was not willing to make even the very moderate concessions demanded by London, a deadlock had been reached in the relations of the two countries many months before the advent of the Whigs to power.

FRANCE AND ALGIERS

The Polignac Cabinet, frustrated in its dreams of European reconstruction, and sinking ever deeper in the quagmire of legitimist and personal government, sought to win back its vanished popularity with easy foreign laurels. One important item in Polignac's stillborn project had been the creation of a new Arab Empire out of the African and south Asiatic dominions of Turkey, his ulterior motive being to provide a useful counterweight to British sea power in the Mediterranean. His secret negotiations with Mehemet Ali gradually resolved themselves into a plan for joint military operations, in which France should annex Algiers and allow her ally to seize the Regencies of Tunis and Tripoli. The plan was distasteful to Polignac's colleagues in office and was in any case betrayed both to the British and to the Sultan,* who obliged his vassal to postpone his ambitions for a more favourable moment and sent an envoy to discuss African affairs with the French. But meanwhile a purely French expedition was being fitted up to enforce the demands pending since the rupture with the Dey of Algiers in 1827: and this caused great alarm and annoyance in London. Lord Stuart in Paris failed to extract any clear assurances from Polignac, while the Duke and Aberdeen were equally unsuccessful with the French Ambassador, the Duke of Laval. On 7 May 1830 it came to a long and acrimonious discussion at the Foreign Office, in which Wellington emphasised Britain's interest in preserving the Mediterranean *status quo* and Laval expressed the fear that such language "might tend to put an end to the intimate relations existing" between London and Paris.[77] The insistence upon written explanations which neither Charles X nor Polignac were ready to give, the "malaise inexprimable" and "expressions peu ménagées" of Aberdeen, as reported by Laval,[78] opened

* The British Consul-General Barker reported his French colleague Drovetti's dealings with the Pasha: the Divan communicated to Sir R. Gordon the information gleaned by its spies, and Metternich, having intercepted some of Guilleminot's despatches from Constantinople, sent copies to London through Lord Cowley. See Dodwell, *The Founder of Modern Egypt*, p. 101.

up dangerous possibilities of conflict. But Polignac was not to have or to hold, and on 25 May the expedition sailed from Marseilles. On 21 June Aberdeen congratulated Laval on the safe arrival of the fleet, but added that his congratulations on its return would be much more cordial![79] On 4 July Algiers fell, and a fortnight later Polignac, while still refusing any official explanation, assured Stuart that France had no idea of conquest and proposed negotiating with the Porte direct as to the new status of Algiers.[80] It is difficult to believe that he was sincere in these professions,* or to see how an open rupture could have been averted if he had remained in office. But within a week of this conversation with Stuart the issue of the illegal Ordinances, prompted by Opposition successes at the recent general elections, provoked a fresh outburst of popular feeling: the July Revolution was almost instantly successful, and while its effects reverberated across Europe, Charles X fled into exile across the Channel and his unpopular and incompetent ministers were consigned to a fortress. Nothing could bolster up again the elder Bourbon line, and after a brief period of uncertainty, what was then felt to be the only possible alternative to a Republic was adopted, and the Duke of Orleans was elected not as Regent for the youthful " Henry V ", but as " Louis Philippe, King of the French ", with the tricolor as substitute for the fleur-de-lis.

THE DEATH OF GEORGE IV

The extremely opportunist attitude adopted by the British Government was due in the first instance to its own somewhat precarious position at home, and this had been accentuated by the death of George IV, which occurred on 26 June 1830. It cannot be denied that George possessed great abilities, and even in middle life great charm: but to the title of "first gentleman in Europe", which he presumably owed to this charm, he gave the lie by a grossness of speech and manners which nothing can pardon. His word could not be relied upon, and his private life was simply disgusting. Though exceedingly well-informed on public affairs and well served by his entourage, he was lacking alike in judgement and in courage, and therefore was providentially incapable of standing up to his ministers as he often would have liked to do. For the last two years of his life the ill-health due to lifelong excesses steadily undermined his powers, and his unreasoning resistance to Catholic emancipation—so frantic and sustained as to cause doubts as to his sanity, yet at the final crisis so precipitately abandoned—was a clear

---

* Polignac, in his *Études historiques politiques et morales*, p. 227 (a sententious *apologia pro vita sua*, published in 1845), openly states that as Ambassador he had "long meditated on the importance of the conquest of Algiers for France, and the consequent advantages for European society", and that on coming to power he decided to realise this aim.

sign of his political impotence. By the beginning of 1830 he was partially blind, suffered from delusions, and was little better than a cipher.

Some idea of the hostility felt in the widest circles towards George IV may best be conveyed by an extract from a leading article published in *The Times* immediately after his funeral. Answering alternate charges of "sycophancy" and "malignity towards the defunct Prince", it declared: "The truth is—and it speaks volumes about the man—that there never was an individual less regretted by his fellow creatures than this deceased King. What eye has wept for him? What heart has heaved one throb of unmercenary sorrow? Was there at any time a gorgeous pageant on the stage more completely forgotten than he has been, even from the day on which the heralds proclaimed his successor? Has not that successor gained more upon the English tastes and prepossessions of his subjects, by the blunt and unaffected—even should it be the grotesque—cordiality of his demeanour, within a few short weeks, than George IV—that Leviathan of the *haut ton*— ever did during the 68 years of his existence."[81] It needs a considerable effort of imagination to transport ourselves into the atmosphere in which such sentiments could be uttered by a journal, not yet, it is true, at its very zenith, but already one of the mouthpieces of the rising Fourth Estate. A month after George's death the gossip Greville recorded in his diary: "Nobody thinks any more of the late King than if he had been dead for 50 years, unless it be to abuse him and to rake up all his vices and misdeeds."[*]

King George was succeeded by the "Sailor King", William IV, who, though much less brilliant and entirely lacking in dignity or real prestige, was not without a certain popularity of his own. Eccentric, but bluff and straightforward, he was much less prone to interfere in the policy of his ministers. Unlike his brother, he was on good terms with Wellington, nor did he, like his brother, bear a fierce grudge against Lord Grey for his attitude towards the affair of Queen Caroline. The new King enjoyed, without very good reason, it is true, the reputation of a Whig, and was certainly far more ready to resign himself to the changes and chances of a kaleidoscopic situation. M. Halévy's somewhat drastic verdict deserves to be quoted: "C'etait un vieux fou comme son frère...mais c'était un brave homme de fou, qui conquit les sympathies du grand public par la simplicité bourgeoise de ses manières"[82]—or in Charles Greville's phrase, "a plain vulgar hospitable gentleman".[83] The influence of the Crown upon foreign policy still continued, for even William IV was keenly interested in it. But it was henceforth a somewhat intermittent influence, and now finally lost its

---

[*] *Memoirs*, II, I. This passage was already written in 1932; in 1936 the universal and profound outburst of grief at the death of King George V has provided an overwhelming contrast such as will at once occur to every reader.

former character of secret intrigue and rancour. For the moment, however, the change of sovereign increased the tendency of a weak Government to wait upon events, instead of attempting to shape them to its will.

The cautious and temporising attitude adopted by the Duke's Government towards the new situation in France was partly due to the obscure and as yet unregulated relations in which it found itself towards the Crown. But above all it hoped that the new French Government would be less rash and adventurous than its predecessor and would liquidate the Algerian affair. It was moreover anxious to avoid any step which might give the slightest impulse to revolutionary feeling. While Pozzo di Borgo a year earlier had prophesied with amazing precision the exact course of events in France, Lord Stuart had been completely deceived and on the very eve of the *coup d'état* had strongly denied its possibility.* Yet Wellington, though not forewarned, seems not to have been greatly surprised, for he had come to regard Charles X as incorrigible and wept no tears for the dynasty which he himself had done so much to restore. At first he was prepared to discuss the idea of intervention, but soon allowed himself to be dissuaded by Aberdeen and agreed that anything was better than a quarrel with France. "There are some bitter pills to swallow", he wrote, "the cockade, the alterations of the Charter, the act of placing it under the *sauvegarde* of the National Guard, the tone assumed by La Fayette. However, the best chance of peace is to swallow them all."[84] It was pointed out that the treaties of 1815 and 1818 had been concluded with "the legitimate and constitutional monarch" of France, that Charles X had abdicated, and having violated the constitution by his ordinances, could in no case claim any right; that, if there should be a breach, "the Liberal party in every country" would have the protection of France, and a situation not unlike that after Valmy and Jemappes might arise: that the Duke of Orleans was the only authority to whom the four Powers could look with confidence if the choice lay with them, and that to declare against him would increase the danger of revolution in many quarters.[85] For all these reasons it was decided to recognise the new Government at an early date. The Tsar would have liked to take action, but Metternich, who had lost no friend in Charles X, and who knew that Austria dared not risk such an adventure, also thought it advisable to recognise the new regime. Austria, then, and with her Prussia, speedily followed Britain's example, but the Tsar remained violently hostile, and though in January 1831 he instructed Pozzo di Borgo to resume relations, his antipathy for Louis Philippe and his regime remained undiminished, and contributed very materially to that gradual regrouping of the Powers which dates from 1830.

* Princess Lieven wrote to Lord Grey on 29 August 1829 (*Corresp.* I, 283): "You have a very ill-informed Ambassador in Paris."

Louis Philippe on his side realised the value, and indeed the necessity, of British friendship, and his Premier, Count Molé, hastened to make overtures to London. It is difficult to read without a smile his assurance to the Tory Duke that "never did revolution better reveal the spirit of the age", and that "it was achieved without conspiracy, because the whole of France was its accomplice".[86] As a special sign of the importance which he attached to the English connection, Louis Philippe decided to send the veteran Talleyrand as his Ambassador to London, and though Aberdeen was at first puzzled and displeased by this, Wellington on the contrary welcomed the prospect of again dealing with one "with whose manner of doing business he was so intimately acquainted".[87]

The position of the Government was by now highly precarious, and the Duke's overtures—after the tragic death of Huskisson—to some of his former colleagues, were a proof of weakness and foredoomed to failure. Already in July he tried to win over Palmerston, but was not prepared to accept the latter's condition that Grey and Lansdowne should also be admitted to the Cabinet. A dissolution automatically followed the change upon the throne, and the Royal Speech with which Parliament was closed contained congratulations upon "the general tranquillity of Europe".[88] But the news of revolutions on the Continent speedily disproved this fatuous verdict, and agrarian unrest was again on the increase. Under this stimulus, the general elections greatly strengthened and encouraged the Whig Opposition, and stimulated the reform agitation throughout the country. Wellington's foreign policy, alike towards Greece, Portugal and France, was loudly criticised and could not be claimed as successful even by his most ardent followers: indeed it was very widely believed—quite unjustly, but with a certain passing plausibility—that he had given his backing and his sympathy to the reactionary Polignac. And now his hesitating attitude towards the Belgian Revolution increased the indignation of the Whigs against him, and convinced them that he was in league with all the reactionary forces of the Continent. His open declaration against any measure of franchise reform, soon after the opening of Parliament, alienated all save a mere handful. Palmerston declined, almost contemptuously, a second overture from the Duke, who by this time "could find room" for Melbourne and Grant also.[89] Panic and negation prevailed, and the new King, acting on official advice, actually abandoned his state visit to the City. On 15 November the Government was defeated in the House of Commons, and William IV sent for Lord Grey.

CHAPTER IV

THE RAPPROCHEMENT OF THE WESTERN POWERS (1830–39)

The year 1830 was a turning point for Europe and for England. It ushered in an era in which the whole outlook and trend of affairs was markedly different from that which followed Waterloo. The Great War had already become a distant memory—almost certainly more distant than that of a century later seemed to ourselves at the corresponding date of 1933. England and Europe are recovering economically, but there is much unrest and lawlessness, even in our own island, and the Industrial Revolution, with its pace hastened by improved communications in the early railway and steamship era, is rooting up ancient habits and traditions, transforming the countryside and creating those great urban agglomerations which are to be the chief problem of later generations. New classes are becoming vocal, and pressing for political power—the middle class with its two main upper and lower strata and many intermediate stages, but, it is well to remember, not identical in every point with the *grande* and *petite bourgeoisie* of the Continent, though the product of a somewhat similar process. It is this class that is on the whole identified with Liberalism, which most of the continental dynasts persist in regarding as identical with Revolution. In Britain also there is grave alarm as to the possibility of revolution, yet the danger, though quite real, is tempered by the remarkable elasticity of the British Constitution, which had shown itself capable of drastic repair and extension, and by the adaptability of the ruling class, which was never so rigid a caste as those of the Continent, and always preserved intimate connections with the classes below it. Moreover, the accidents of the Two-Party system, which had reached one of its periodical crises about 1830, automatically promoted an alliance between the old Whig aristocracy—the "Outs" of that day—and the new Liberal and Radical *bourgeoisie*, against the Tory "Ins".

This process was completed just at the moment when the reactionary group surrounding Charles X challenged all believers in constitutional and representative government in France by the illegal Ordinances of July 1830: and the immediate result was the overthrow of the elder Bourbon line and the establishment of the Bourgeois Monarchy. In actual practice the change was not perhaps as great as might have been expected: but its effect upon opinion throughout Europe was magical and overwhelming. In Britain also—despite the very decided isolation into which she had fallen since 1815 and especially since Castlereagh's death in 1822—the Revolution had a profound influence, not of course in inspiring ideas, for British constitutional development needed no help from outside, but in stimulating the movement for reform. Events moved with extreme rapidity. In 1827 Lord Grey, the Whig leader, admittedly had stood alone in the political world, and for another two years the country was absorbed in the struggle for Catholic emancipation. Yet by the close of 1830 he was at the head of a powerful and eager Coalition of Whigs and Canningites, pledged to reform, and the country was in the throes of intense political agitation, suddenly shaking off the lethargy and reaction into which it had fallen after the prolonged struggle against Napoleon. In this situation Lord Grey, a man of 68, a great territorial landlord who had dabbled in Jacobin views in his youth, but whose outlook was essentially aristocratic and who had the backing of other great Whig magnates such as Lansdowne and Holland, was very soon carried much farther than he could ever have foreseen, and made a lasting breach in the privileges of his own class. It is necessary to realise that not only the Duke of Wellington, whom he succeeded as Prime Minister, but many of the leading Tories of the day, believed that Grey was letting loose the red spectre and would be swept away by forces which he could not control. Indeed, the Duke gave it quite frankly as his opinion, "that a democracy once set going must sooner or later work itself out in anarchy, and that some sort of despotism must then come to restore society".[1] The disorders of 1831–2 seemed to many at the time to justify such a view.

In actual fact, the Reform Bill of 1832 proved all such fears to have been entirely false, and the advent of the Whigs to power—lasting, with one brief interlude of five months, for ten solid years—soon transformed and tranquillised the internal situation, though the rumblings of Luddism and Peterloo and the Reform riots were to echo on into the days of the Chartists and Fenians. The new regime soon found such absorbing interests as the Repeal agitation of O'Connell, the victory of the anti-slavery campaign, the reform of the Poor Law, the beginnings of popular education and factory supervision, and the many philanthropic measures associated with the name of Lord Shaftesbury. In a word, the period is to a special degree one of transition, or perhaps more accurately one in which, as in a dissolving view, the last faint outlines of the old are still visible through the very definite pattern of the new.

Meanwhile on the general European landscape the main features are still the struggle of Legitimacy against the twin forces of Liberalism and Nationality, which we saw marshalling themselves in the previous decade. The Romantic movement has split, and its influence is to be traced in such very different writers as Heine, Pushkin, Victor Hugo and Mazzini, and again in the modern schools of history, resting on a national basis, which are springing up in Germany and France and profoundly affecting the political aspirations of central and eastern no less than western Europe. The ideas of which Herder was a forerunner have by now struck root among the Slavs and serve as the stimulus to a whole series of national revivals, in which the historian, the philosopher and by no means least of all the philologist and grammarian, lay the foundations upon which the poet, the literary critic and the politician are soon to build.

The 'thirties, then, are a period of latent unrest on the Continent. The July Revolution is followed by other revolutions in Belgium and Poland, in Brunswick and Hesse, in the Papal States: and though all but the first of these are suppressed, the result has been to divide Europe quite definitely into two camps—the Eastern Powers, as the exponents of autocracy, led by Metternich, Tsar Nicholas and Frederick William III, and the Liberal West, resting on constitutional progress at home and eager, despite many mutual jealousies, to promote it in Spain and Portugal against the ferocious reaction of the Carlists and Dom Miguel.

In Prussia and Austria there is stagnation, and in Austria in particular the principle of "stability" has become a fetish with Metternich and the Emperor Francis. The all-pervading censorship and secret police strangle at birth all political activities and render any intellectual or literary movement wellnigh impossible: and after the death of Francis in 1835, his half-imbecile son is in the hands of a triumvirate of which the nominal head, Archduke Louis, is a mere cipher, while the other two, Metternich and Kolowrat, are in permanent conflict and neutralise each other. In Italy the situation is even worse, and Austria not only holds down her own provinces of Lombardy and Venice, but controls and supports the black reaction of Pope Gregory XVI and King "Bomba" of Naples. Young Italy and Young Poland are working abroad in many underground channels as heirs of the Carbonari. Young Germany is reduced to political impotence, but can at least write poetry: while economic processes are already at work which are ere long to culminate in the Zollverein and completely transform the internal German situation.

The immediate result of the Revolution in European politics was the reconciliation of Austria and Russia and an attempt to reconstruct the close accord of the three Eastern and Conservative Courts. For a time Metternich was able to reassert his old supremacy, for the prolonged strain of the

Polish revolt rendered Austrian friendship more valuable to the Tsar, and the rupture of the Franco-Russian entente became a permanence owing to the acute personal antipathy felt by Nicholas for Louis Philippe, while at the same time the Government of Berlin was seriously alarmed at the revolutionary outbreak in Belgium and drew nearer to Vienna. Yet Metternich, though well aware that Austria could not risk war and that the new regime must therefore be promptly recognised, was quick enough to realise its significance as "the breaking of a dam in Europe" and confided to Nesselrode, the Russian Foreign Minister, that "the old Europe is at the beginning of the end".[2]

THE GREY CABINET

It was characteristic of the difference of outlook in East and West, that to the Tsar the new Grey Cabinet seemed scarcely less subversive or objectionable than the Orleanist regime in France. For this very reason there is a certain picquancy in the fact that Lord Grey had for some years past been on terms of close intimacy with Princess Lieven, sometimes jocularly described as "second Russian Ambassador" in London, though indeed her role was really superior to that of her husband. Year in year out, at intervals of a few days, they exchanged letters on every topic of internal and foreign policy. A study of this voluminous correspondence[3] will show that the Prime Minister, while listening most attentively and cordially to her suggestions, constantly dissented from her views, but that the general effect was to avert many a chance of misunderstanding between London and St Petersburg. "People would have to be very clever", she once wrote, "ever to know whether I am Whig or Tory. I only display one colour— that is, yours. I am *Grey*, and I defy them to convict me of anything else."[4] Her avowed aim was to maintain good relations between the two Powers whom she rightly regarded, under the circumstances of the day, as the pivots of the Eastern and Western groups. Her perseverance, combined with much diplomatic skill and personal charm, was bound to have its effect, and a widespread rumour credited her with influencing the new Prime Minister in favour of his momentous appointment of Lord Palmerston as Foreign Secretary. The only direct evidence of this is the Princess's own assertion, in her diary, that Grey had hitherto "had little liking" for Palmerston, had thought him "frivolous and pushing", and had only seriously considered him when she warmly recommended him, partly at Palmerston's own instance.[5] The incredulous will note that in a letter which she addressed to Grey while he was actually forming his Cabinet, she docs not even allude to Palmerston, though she offers concrete advice on two other points.[6] It may well be that she spoke her word of praise and that the

Whig statesman listened in his courtly way. But the fact remains that the post was first offered to Lord Lansdowne, and next to Lord Holland, and that Lord Palmerston was only considered after both had refused and when no other obvious candidate was in sight.

LORD PALMERSTON

As Mr Guedalla has very rightly insisted, Palmerston was a real product of the eighteenth century, projected far into the nineteenth. In the late seventeenth century his family had already produced, in Sir William Temple, a diplomatist of very high quality: he himself was the fourth holder of an Irish viscounty, which gave him agreeable social rank without access to the British House of Lords, and therefore—what was far more important—without exclusion from the British House of Commons. He was a considerable Irish landlord, but resident in the south of England, a *beau* and a man of fashion when Beau Brummell was the intimate of the Prince Regent, a great rider, devoted to the turf, a genial sceptic entirely untouched either by the Evangelical or the Neo-Catholic schools of thought which bulked so large in the England of a century ago. He had been educated at Harrow and Cambridge, had sat at the feet of the philosopher Dugald Stewart at Edinburgh University, and had learned a great deal from the first Lord Malmesbury, the leading British diplomatist of the dying eighteenth century and the mentor of the great Pitt in foreign policy. He had travelled extensively in the *western* half of Europe and spoke admirable French and Italian. He had belonged to Canning's group, that is to say, to that section of the Tories which was least Conservative in home politics and increasingly Liberal in its outlook upon continental affairs. For almost twenty years, from 1809 till 1828, he had been War Minister (the first five years coinciding with Britain's Peninsular campaign), yet he had not made much mark either in Parliament or outside it, and was still regarded as rather a dark horse. He was an indifferent speaker, and *The Times* of this period caustically described him as "a flippant dandy" and "an exquisite".[7] From 1828, when he left the Duke of Wellington's Cabinet, in company with his future Prime Minister and future brother-in-law William Lamb, Lord Melbourne, Palmerston was "slowly drifting towards Whiggery", and in 1829 he was saying of the Tories, in spite of their overtures to him, that "to belong to people you do not think with cannot answer". In 1830, when the news of revolution came from Paris, he welcomed it with ecstasy in a letter to Lady Cowper. "We shall drink the cause of Liberalism all over the world. Let Spain and Austria look to themselves: this reaction can't end where it began, and Spain and Italy and parts of Germany will sooner or later be affected. This event is decisive of the ascendancy of Liberal principles throughout Europe: the evil spirit has been put down and will be trodden under foot. The reign of Metternich is over, and the days of the Duke's policy might be measured by algebra, if not by arithmetic."[8] As he was writing to the lady for whose sake he remained a bachelor till past fifty, we may suppose that this represented his real sentiments: and we need not be surprised at his refusal to consider the offer of a post in the tottering Tory Cabinet.

THE BELGIAN REVOLUTION

Palmerston first took office at a highly critical moment in the affairs of Europe. The July Revolution reverberated across the Continent and naturally caused alarm to such Conservative statesmen as Wellington and Aberdeen. They had none the less hastened to recognise Louis Philippe, whom they rightly regarded as a *juste milieu* between autocracy and revolution and as a guarantee against an all too adventurous foreign policy. It very speedily became apparent that despite many points of disagreement the two Western Powers now stood for liberal and constitutional government against the reactionary principles enforced by the three Eastern Courts. But the situation was greatly complicated by the Belgian crisis, and by the very obvious desire of Vienna and St Petersburg to use it as a means of sowing discord between London and Paris.

It is difficult to exaggerate the jubilation with which the July Revolution was greeted in popular circles throughout Europe, and it was only natural that the first sparks from the Paris conflagration should kindle the inflammable material which had been accumulating in Brussels for many years past. The union of Belgium and Holland as a "Kingdom of the Netherlands" had been one of the most notable decisions of the Allied Powers in 1815:[9] resting on similar motives to those which had prompted successive "barrier treaties" of the previous century and a half, it was designed to ensure to the new state the possibility of "upholding its independence by its own means", and it was intended to last "à toute perpetuité".* Unfortunately, it was an essentially artificial and dynastic solution, and took but little account of popular wishes. In the late Middle Ages the peoples of the Low Countries had developed on uniform lines and attained a prosperity and culture unequalled in Northern Europe: but the long and desperate struggle against Philip II and Alba resulted in a deep cleavage, spiritual no less than political and economic, between the provinces to which we now

---

* See text of secret article appended to the Treaty of Paris, 30 May 1814. The creation of the new kingdom rested on the Acts of 21 July 1814 and the Treaty of 31 May 1815, both of which were incorporated in the resolutions of the Congress of Vienna.

apply the names of "Holland" and "Belgium". While the former developed into a free community, renowned for its commercial and colonial enterprise, its seamanship and its zeal for the Protestant cause at home and abroad, the latter went its own way, first under Spanish, then under Austrian rule, and after the era of persecution had passed, maintained a fervent devotion to that Catholic creed which it had once vainly sought to discard. This divergence of outlook and tradition was accentuated still further by the linguistic distinction between Dutch and Walloon, and even the Flemish districts, despite natural affinities with their neighbours to the north, were permeated by French influences. If this was already true in the eighteenth century, it was much more so after twenty years of union with France, in a period so memorable as that which lay between the French Revolution and Waterloo: and it is remarkable that the southern provinces accepted without much demur the legislation imposed upon them by the French, but keenly resented by their Dutch fellow-victims, but that they none the less preserved their clericalism almost unalloyed.

The union between the two ill-assorted partners was from the outset unpopular in Belgium, firstly because it was imposed from outside, without their wishes being consulted, and secondly because many of its details were regarded as unduly favouring the north against the south. While the Dutch had long since become reconciled to the House of Nassau and regarded it as a national institution, the Belgians looked upon King William as alien by blood, religion and traditions, and were confirmed in their dislike by his tactlessness and obstinacy, his absolutist leanings and his Dutch preferences. Under the new constitution many high administrative and judicial posts were filled by strangers from the north, the absence of ministerial responsibility told in favour of the Dutch, and press freedom was virtually non-existent. Specially irreconcilable were the rival views as to parliamentary representation. The Belgians, who were as three to two of the total population, held out for a purely numerical basis, whereas the Dutch claimed exact equality between the two halves: the former plan would have placed the Dutch in an open minority at the outset, the latter would give them a veiled majority. The Dutch view carried the day, but only because after its rejection by the Belgian notables the King disallowed the votes of those who had given a qualified dissent and added to the ayes the votes of those who had abstained. Thus from the first all hope of a homogeneous Parliament was destroyed, and the latent friction was increased by financial, linguistic and educational disputes and above all by the hostility of the Catholic clergy. Though Belgium flourished exceedingly in the fifteen years following Waterloo, her moral alienation from the King and his whole regime grew year by year, and from 1828 onwards the Clerical and Liberal parties were closely linked together for its overthrow. The attempts of Potter and his friends to organise a Patriotic League led to their arrest and banishment in April 1830, and feelings were already at white heat when the news came from Paris. The performance of a revolutionary opera in Brussels on 25 August gave the first signal for trouble; during the next month the movement spread from town to town, and the Prince of Orange found little or no support for a well-meaning attempt to mediate between his father and the Belgian patriots. The troops despatched by King William against Brussels forced their way into the suburbs, but found it necessary to retire: on 26 September a provisional Government was formed, and already on 4 October decisions were taken in favour of Belgian independence and the summons of a National Congress.

Belgium's secession from Holland aroused no little concern in London, where it was regarded as the first breach in the system established in 1815, and it was feared that France might deliberately use the situation thus created as a lever by which to raise further issues. It was notorious that the movement was being encouraged from Paris, and that there existed a party which actually favoured union with France. Wellington, though at first anxious to preserve the unity of the Netherlands, very soon realised that the tide of revolution could no longer be stemmed, and thereupon concentrated his efforts upon holding back the French and saving the crown for the House of Nassau, though even this latter aim was speedily compromised by the divergent aims and tactics of King William and the Prince of Orange. Not even the most ardent friend of Holland could fail to regard King William as a fatal handicap to his own cause, while Wellington, who had been closely associated with the Prince during the Waterloo campaign, had almost as little confidence in him as in his father, and confessed to Aberdeen that there was in the Prince "a foundation of vanity, levity and thirst for vulgar popularity which makes me tremble for the success of everything he undertakes".[10] And indeed his bid for the favour of the Belgians only alienated him from the Dutch and from his own family, without in any way attaining its object.

King William early in September appealed for Prussian intervention, but Berlin refused to move without the approval of London, and this Wellington withheld, in the knowledge that French intervention would automatically follow—though he would have done anything to preserve the Kingdom of the Netherlands as a unit and inserted in the King's Speech an expression of regret that "the enlightened administration of the Dutch King had failed to avert a revolt".[11] For the same reason he declined the Dutch appeal for British troops. Every instinct drove him towards a compromise with France, and here Louis Philippe met him more than half-way. The veteran Talleyrand, who had successively served the Convention, the Directory, the Empire and the Restoration, and who now returned to the London Embassy at the age of seventy-six and after an absence of almost forty years, exercised, even at that distance, a far more effective control of foreign policy than the nominal Foreign Minister of the day: he was in constant correspondence with the King's sister and adviser, Madame Adelaide, he shared Louis Philippe's pacific temperament, and, like him, regarded peace as France's most vital need, "which alone can render stable our new dynasty".[12] They fully realised that many supporters of the new regime would have welcomed a policy of foreign expansion,* oblivious of the fact that this meant isolation in Europe and in all probability a new coalition of the Powers against her. The best way to avert such a coalition was to secure a working alliance, not necessarily in name, with one other Power, and England, the only one whom there was much hope of winning in the circumstances of the moment, was only to be won on a basis of the principle of non-intervention. Talleyrand accordingly preached on this text from the moment of his arrival in London, making it clear that the only means of holding back his countrymen from active interference in Belgian affairs, was to prevent Holland from re-asserting her lost authority, either alone or with foreign aid. It was in this sense that the French Premier, Molé, sounded by Wellington, replied that France desired nothing so much as peace, but would feel bound to repel any armed intervention in Belgium or dictation to its people—an attitude which he had already conveyed confidentially to the Prussian Government.

THE LONDON CONFERENCE

On this, Wellington suggested friendly discussions between the Powers responsible for the settlement of 1815 and insisted that London, not Paris, should be the place of meeting, in the first instance because the Conference of Ambassadors which had been dealing with Greek affairs was still in being and could turn its attention to the new crisis with a minimum of delay, but also because it was notorious that Russia at any rate, if not all the three Eastern Courts, would have declined to take part in negotiations at the revolutionary centre. The Tsar was indeed ready to send troops to the aid of King William, but reluctantly reached the conclusion that separate action would do more harm than good. King William complained of being "left in the lurch", when the Conference met on 4 November and insisted upon an armistice. For a fortnight there was a certain lull, during which the Welling-

---

* On 30 July Cavaignac had told Louis Philippe, "It is the sight of the tricolor that has roused the people, and it would certainly be easier to push from Paris to the Rhine than to St Cloud" [where Charles X still was at the moment] (cit. Bourgeois, *op. cit.* II, 784).

ton Cabinet fell: but between 18 and 24 November the new Belgian Congress successively declared its independence, adopted the principle of an hereditary monarchy, and by 161 votes to 28 definitely excluded the House of Nassau.

At this early stage both Paris and London still favoured the Prince of Orange as sovereign of a separate Belgian state, and he himself crossed the Channel to push his claim, somewhat to the embarrassment of the British Government. General Maison instructed Talleyrand in favour of Orange,[13] as the only candidate whom the Tsar would accept, and treated the idea of electing one of Louis Philippe's sons, which was already being broached, as one "which one must not even stop to consider". But Sebastiani, who succeeded Maison almost immediately after, still had lingering hopes of partition and sent Count Flahault over to London as a discreet sponsor of the scheme. Talleyrand, however, saw the danger of alienating the new Cabinet and so resolutely discouraged any such idea that Sebastiani was forced to abandon it out of hand.

Talleyrand and Palmerston speedily reached agreement on the main lines of settlement, and their firmness carried the other three Powers with them, and led to the unanimous recognition of Belgian independence (20 December). There is no doubt whatever that the compliance of the Tsar, who had at the first been ready to send 60,000 troops to enforce the treaties of 1815, was solely determined by the outbreak of revolution in Poland at the end of November: and the fact that the Poles maintained a desperate resistance till far on in 1831 and kept the Russians fully occupied, was not the least decisive factor in securing Belgian immunity. It reacted upon Metternich also, who was not ready to face a war without Russian help. He would have liked the Conference to be held in Vienna, and to concern itself with general European questions, but he could not arrest the natural trend of events.[14]

On 20 January 1831 the five Great Powers went a stage farther, by assigning to Holland the frontiers of 1790 and leaving everything else—with the special exception of Luxemburg—to Belgium, by renouncing for themselves all territorial ambitions at her expense and all "exclusive influence upon her policy", and by assuming a permanent guarantee of the neutrality of the new kingdom. Several highly delicate issues still remained—the selection of a sovereign, Dutch ratification, the border fortresses, and the fate of Luxemburg. When Palmerston suggested the union of Belgium and Luxemburg under the Prince of Orange, Talleyrand mooted the possibility of the latter falling to France, only to meet a very strong refusal. Indeed Palmerston wrote off to Lord Granville, now once more Ambassador in Paris, in a tone reminiscent of his most aggressive days, and bade him "hint, upon any fitting occasion, that though we are anxious...to be on terms of the most intimate friendship" with France, "yet it is only on the supposition that she contents herself with the finest territory in Europe and does not mean to open a new chapter of encroachment and conquest".[15] Talleyrand continued to hold out for Luxemburg—"fighting like a dragon", to use Palmerston's own words—and then attempted to bargain for Philippe-ville and Marienburg as compensation: but in the end he had to choose between signing the self-denying ordinance of 20 January or disproving his Government's professions of non-intervention. Palmerston's zeal far exceeded that of his chief Lord Grey, who had told Princess Lieven not long before, that in his opinion "the barrier of fortresses established at our expense" along the Belgian frontier was "one of the most absurd provisions" of the settlement of 1815.[16] But it was not to the French alone that Palmerston was very outspoken: for at the close of the year he sent a message to the King of the Netherlands, that by refusing to uphold the armistice he would expose himself to seeing the boundaries of his state fixed without him![17]

THE BELGIAN THRONE

Meanwhile various candidatures were put forward for the new throne. Prince Otto of Bavaria[18] was handicapped by his extreme youth. The name of Archduke Charles was promptly ruled out by his indignant brother Francis. The Duke of Leuchtenberg,[19] who would have been acceptable to Russia, was vetoed by the French Government owing to his Bonapartist connections. Little or no enthusiasm could be aroused for a Neapolitan Prince. Grey clung to the last to the Prince of Orange, and is said to have drafted the manifesto which the latter addressed to the Belgians early in January.[20] But the French party, losing all sense of realities, pressed for the election of Louis Philippe's son, the Duke of Nemours, and on 3 February this was carried by a bare majority in the Belgian Congress. This was keenly resented in London, as a sign that Paris was playing a double game, and some days before the election Palmerston had written to Granville, that the choice of Nemours would be "a proof that the policy of France is like an infection clinging to the walls of a dwelling and breaking out in every successive occupant who comes within their influence".[21] He even told Talleyrand to his face that Louis Philippe had but one course open to him, "without a violation of public faith!" The Cabinet confirmed this attitude, and Talleyrand reported to Paris that it had "agreed upon the necessity of an immediate war" if the election was confirmed by France. Sebastiani beat a hurried retreat, and on 17 February Louis Philippe declined the Belgian throne in his son's name.

French policy was at this time curiously hesitating and inconsequent. As early as 3 January Talleyrand had warned Madame Adelaide of the need for preventing Nemour's election, "if the King feels strong enough to maintain peace"—a highly significant phrase: and to this Sebastiani immediately replied, "We shall refuse without hesitation (*sans balancer*) both union with France and the Crown for Nemours", adding with lingering regret, "We thought that other arrangements would have been best, but will wait till the Powers accept this."[22] Some weeks later even Talleyrand himself wrote to Sebastiani that the reunion of Belgium with France would be of advantage to the latter, but that "aggrandisement on the Rhine would better satisfy my own views on French policy".[23] In a word, Paris was still weighing alternatives, but prompted by a very robust appetite.

There was, however, another candidate in the field, who gradually overshadowed all his rivals—namely, Prince Leopold of Coburg, who had so nearly become King of Greece in the previous year. At the very moment when the letters just quoted were being exchanged, the Belgian patriot Gendebien visited Paris in order to plead the cause of Leopold, and found Louis Philippe frankly prejudiced against the Prince.* But with Sebastiani Gendebien had a far more significant passage of arms, in which he argued that the proper course for Belgium was to urge upon London the election of Leopold and a French alliance, and to elect him even if Louis Philippe should oppose. When Sebastiani retorted, "If he puts his foot in Belgium, we shall fire on him", Gendebien countered, "And we shall ask England to reply to your cannon." "That will be universal war", said the French Minister. "So be it," was the answer, "we prefer war to restoration, to permanent humiliation." It may well be that this version is too highly coloured, but it corresponds entirely with what is known of Sebastiani's political tendencies.

PALMERSTON AND THE FRENCH

Meanwhile Palmerston continued to be alarmingly frank. Flahault again came to London, this time to sound him as to an offensive and defensive alliance between France and Britain: and to this Palmerston rejoined that such alliances were unpopular in England, and that though France, if "unjustly attacked", would certainly have British support, still "whichever side breaks the peace will find us against them".[24] On 15 February Granville was instructed to inform Sebastiani "that our desire for peace will never

* "Il y a un 'mais'—...des répugnances de famille, des préjugés peut-être"; see Gendebien's account of his conversations, in *Léopold I et Léopold II*, pp. 69–71 (originally published in *La Liberté*, 3rd year, No. 11).

lead us to submit to affront either in language or in act".[25] Two days later, Palmerston added—though it is to be presumed that the tactful Granville kept the phrase to himself—"Sebastiani must have the goodness to learn to keep his temper, or when it fails him, let him go to vent his ill-humour upon some other quarter and not bestow it upon England."[26] Certainly this is a very unwonted tone, poles apart from that of Aberdeen or Canning or Castlereagh. But it does not mean aggression. Britain is already absorbed in one of the great crises of her history, public opinion is uniformly pacific,* and Grey has no intention of embroiling himself with France. Meanwhile Russia is all too busy in Poland, and Austria is engaged with Italian affairs. Hence Palmerston was giving very sound advice when he urged the French to settle quickly, before the Eastern Powers could make their weight felt. To use his own all too drastic phrase: "I wish the French would make up their minds to act with good faith about Belgium, and we should settle the matter in three weeks."[27]

The advent of Casimir Périer to power in France (13 March) led to an early *détente*. Sebastiani retained the Foreign Office, but the real control lay in the hands of the King, the new Premier and Talleyrand: Périer was a confirmed believer in the Entente, while Palmerston in his delight at the change of Government told Granville to "cultivate him" and make it clear that London "considers his appointment as the strongest pledge and security for peace".[28] In the same breath he declared that "France cannot have Belgium without a war with the four Powers", and a little later, "union with France we cannot permit, because it would give to France an increase of power dangerous to our security. We know we should have to fight France after such an union, and we had better therefore do so before it."[29] In all these phrases there is an unmistakable ring of the future Palmerston, who was the terror of Windsor and of Europe. But at least it can be said that such explicit language served as a warning signal to the French, not to advance impossible demands.

The rejection of Nemours and the stubborn refusal of the Belgians to reconsider the Prince of Orange left Prince Leopold as the most obvious candidate. His name had been mentioned between Palmerston and Talleyrand as early as 14 December, and the latter on 30 January pretended that Leopold had always been his favourite.[30] In April a Belgian deputation waited upon Leopold in London, but he very wisely made his acceptance conditional upon the territorial and financial settlement obtaining the sanction of the Powers. For a time the Belgians tried to have their cake and

* Palmerston himself writes to his brother on 1 March: "We are all too busy with Reform to make it possible to give you instructions about Italy"; peace is the main interest Bulwer, *Life of Palmerston* 1, p. 48).

eat it, sheltering themselves behind the international guarantee on points which suited them better than the Dutch, but repudiating the decision of the Conference when it met the Dutch view by excluding Luxemburg and Limburg from the new Kingdom. In the end, Leopold was elected King by the National Congress on 4 June, but still made his acceptance conditional upon his future subjects accepting the terms laid down by the Conference.

A situation of no little danger now arose, owing to the intransigeance of the Belgians, Sebastiani's secret hope that they would throw over Leopold and hoist the tricolor at Brussels, and the now only too patent determination of King William to embroil the Powers and fish in troubled waters.[31] The shifty tactics of Talleyrand himself are shown by the fact that within ten days of proposing a special treaty of guarantee by France and Britain —which the British Cabinet declined—he was telling Sebastiani that it might after all come to "*my favourite idea*, of dividing up Belgium, in which case France would undoubtedly find the part which suited her best."[32]

At last on 26 June the Conference adopted eighteen articles, to be submitted separately to Belgium and Holland for their acceptance. The decision was hastened by the insistence of Lord Ponsonby—the British agent in Brussels and brother-in-law of the Prime Minister—upon the dangers of delay, and also by Louis Philippe's fear of a republican movement in Belgium. The Eastern Courts were influenced by these motives, but above all by the fear that France and Britain might act alone. The Austrian plenipotentiaries in particular, Prince Esterházy and Baron Wessenberg, were fully conscious that they might be criticised in Vienna for giving their sanction to the protocol; indeed they had only endorsed independence in December 1830, "in order to keep England in the alliance" and to avert a general war and the spread of Jacobinism which they assumed would follow.* But they could not help condemning the King of Holland's deliberate unreason, and Wessenberg, whom the Conference chose as its emissary to the Hague because of his own and his Government's good relations with King William, returned more disgusted than ever with the latter's *non possumus* attitude and his obvious desire to resort to force. Even William IV, who leant decidedly towards his Dutch namesake and was by no means partial to Leopold, was alienated by "the obstinacy of character of the King of Holland and the ungracious manner in which he concedes".[33]

The protocol of 26 June assigned to Holland the frontiers of 1790, left the possession of Maestricht in suspense, maintained the *status quo* in

---

* Arneth, *Johann Freiherr von Wessenberg*, II, 104: "We dared not risk the contrary", wrote Wessenberg, "in view of the fact that France is arming from head to feet and burning with impatience to cross the frontiers."

Luxemburg until negotiations could be concluded between Holland and the German Confederation (of which Luxemburg was a member), assured to Antwerp special rights upon the Scheldt, and definitely adopted the international guarantee of Belgian neutrality. The Conference had already, on 17 April, agreed upon the demolition of the fortresses of Mons, Charleroi and Marienbourg: and Palmerston had steadfastly opposed the various feelers in favour of ceding Bouillon or Landau to France—insisting that "the moment we give France a cabbage garden or a vineyard, we lose all our vantage ground of principle".[34]

This basis Leopold assumed, and on 9 July it was ratified by the Belgians, though not with a very good grace. But King William, on the contrary, infuriated by Leopold's inauguration at Brussels, not merely protested against the protocol, but denounced the armistice and threw his troops into Belgium. He thereby placed himself fatally in the wrong. Leopold appealed for help to London and Paris; Périer abandoned his intention of retiring from office and took up the challenge; the Conference authorised joint Franco-British intervention, and while the Dutch were still threatening Antwerp, a French army of 50,000 men hurried to the aid of the Belgians, and a British squadron was ordered to the Scheldt. This news brought King William to relative reason, and he recalled his troops after a brief campaign of ten days.* But he showed no disposition for a compromise and more and more obviously reckoned upon embroiling the Powers. No sooner was the French army in occupation of Belgium than there was a recrudescence of old hopes, and an attempt to obtain some kind of territorial compensation for France's withdrawal. Talleyrand again began to talk of partition, but Palmerston was more peremptory than ever. Spurred on by a crop of questions in Parliament, he demanded of Paris an explicit pledge of evacuation, warning Granville that neither the Cabinet nor British public opinion would give way, and that it was "a question of war or peace".† "One thing is certain", he wrote four days later, "the French must go out of Belgium, or we have a general war, and war in a given number of days.... Sebastiani and Soult apparently want to pick a quarrel with all their neighbours, or to compel everybody to submit to their insolence and aggressions."[35] By this time Palmerston, having convinced himself that Talleyrand was preaching to all and sundry "the necessity of partitioning Belgium and sending Leopold to Claremont",[36] was becoming entirely

---

* Sir Robert Adair, the new British Minister in Brussels, prevailed upon the Prince of Orange to accept a kind of armistice.

† 13 August, Bulwer, II, 105. To Adair he wrote on the same day, "We should be compelled either to go out, or go to war, and from the jealous feeling of the Cabinet upon the subject, I have little doubt that we should take the latter alternative" (Johnston Collection, cit. Bell, *Palmerston*, I, 132).

unconciliatory and impervious to the argument that the Périer Cabinet needed concessions to appease the French Chamber. "There is no reason why we should undergo humiliation to give him strength ",[37] he argued, and the British Cabinet had to think of its own parliamentary position. "We will never endure", he told Granville, "that France should dictate to us in this matter at the point of the bayonet.... The only value to us of Périer and his Cabinet is that we believe them to be lovers of peace and observers of treaties: but if they are to be merely puppets, put up to play the part cast for them by the violent party, what is it to us whether they stand or fall? "[38] Fortunately Talleyrand gauged the situation most accurately, and was insistent in his warnings, even telling Madame Adelaide that "if Grey is to stay, the troops must withdraw".[39] At last, then, in return for King Leopold's promise that Charleroi, Tournai and three other fortresses should be dismantled, Louis Philippe gave orders for the complete withdrawal of French troops from Belgium by the end of September.

It may well be that Palmerston really felt bound to stiffen his attitude, owing to the unmeasured criticism of the Opposition. The Duke of Wellington in the House of Lords argued that British policy for a century and a half had been concentrated on "keeping Belgium out of the possession of France ",[40] and in a special memorandum on Belgium committed himself to the view that King William of Holland was "one of the wisest and most beneficent sovereigns that ever reigned over a people":[41] while Lord Aberdeen protested against seeing "our ancient ally thus at the mercy of the navy of France".[42] It is true that these views were to some extent set off by the invective of O'Connell, who wildly declared that the King of Holland's "scaffolds had reeked with the blood of his subjects"[43], and that "there never was a more iniquitous and unjust union" than that between Holland and Belgium.[44]

To the last moment the Dutch King was eager for the French to remain, in the logical calculation that that would lead to the downfall of the Grey Cabinet, a general war and the eventual partition of Belgium, which he personally would have preferred to Belgian independence. When Louis Philippe yielded, William I continued to sulk in his corner, consoling himself with the barren sympathy of the Emperor Francis and never losing a chance of making further mischief. But henceforth the danger of international complications grew steadily less acute.

On 14 October the Conference drafted the final status of Belgium in 24 Articles, which were in some respects less favourable than the original 18 of the preliminary peace: Maestricht and the whole province of Limburg had to be abandoned, and Antwerp had to be content with the free navigation of the Scheldt, without territorial access to the river mouth.

Despite these defects, the articles assured full independence, the guarantee of the Powers, the position of the new dynasty and a reasonable division of the joint debt, and in a word gave Belgium her definite place within the commonwealth of nations. Talleyrand had no little difficulty in reconciling Paris to what was regarded as a patchwork settlement, but in the end the French yielded rather than risk the abdication of King Leopold and the throwing of the whole question back into the melting pot. Palmerston on his side made the most of the public criticism levelled against him in England, and reminded Paris that he was constantly being attacked in the House for letting his compatriots "stand by, passive spectators of hostilities committed by France on two ancient allies, Portugal and Holland."[45]

Leopold himself needed all the pressure of the sagacious Stockmar, who warned him that London regarded the Belgians as "too French", but at the same time begged him "always to assume the good faith of the French" and "to bombard Paris daily and hourly".[46]

On 15 November, then, the five Powers concluded with Belgium a formal treaty based upon the 24 Articles. At the last moment, however, the whole settlement was jeopardised by the Fortress Convention, which was provisionally agreed between the Belgian General Goblet and the three Eastern Powers with Great Britain, and then submitted to Paris in a form which differed materially from the earlier proposals, the chief fortresses designated for demolition being no longer Charleroi and Tournay, but Marienbourg and Philippeville, on which France was specially sensitive, as having been ceded by her in 1815. The discreet Baron Stockmar, passing to and fro as Leopold's confidential agent, reported Talleyrand as "spitting fire and flames" and accusing Belgium of a breach of contract towards Paris: but he gained the impression that a determined game of bluff was being played between Louis Philippe, Talleyrand and Sebastiani,* who was unquestionably ruffled and uncompromising. The publication of Talleyrand's private papers has, however, shown that he was all the time throwing cold water on the flames, calming Madame Adelaide and her brother, and assuring Périer that the whole question was really of "secondary importance". It is not uninteresting to note that while the Duke of Wellington laid all the stress of a military mind upon the fortresses, as a defence of the Balance of Power in Europe, the new King Leopold assured General Goblet and Le Hon that "you and your fortresses are making a lot of bad blood for me, and yet they hardly interest me, nor the country either".[47] This must have been a real douche of cold water for the General, coming only three days

---

* Bell, *Palmerston*, p. 213. This point is made very clear by Alfred Stern, *Gesch. Europas*, IV, 252, who therefore finally rejects the version of Hillebrand (*Gesch. Frankreichs*, I, 250), hitherto accepted by most historians.

after a strangely indiscreet letter of Palmerston, which contains the phrase:
"Prince Talleyrand and General Sebastiani must learn that they are no
longer the organs of the imperious will of a Napoleon, and Louis Philippe
must also know that the laurels of Valmy and Jemappes cannot serve as
scarecrow to all Europe."*

The main outlines of the new settlement had now been achieved, but
there were long delays in ratification, the Eastern Powers, and in particular
the Tsar, insisting upon the Dutch King's preliminary consent as a sop to
their legitimist feelings, and William I again trying to fish in troubled
waters. The Russian and Austrian representatives had only signed the protocol of 15 November because they thought it a lesser evil than the certain
alternative that France and Britain would act alone and thereby reveal to
Europe the impotence of the Eastern Powers to prevent a Western guarantee
of Belgium. But this motive did not weigh with Metternich, who reproved
Esterházy and Wessenberg for signing and persisted in waiting for the Tsar's
lead. Yet Wessenberg, who was at once a staunch Conservative and a special
friend of Holland, kept warning his chief that King William was incorrigible
and entirely to blame: "he is like a shipwrecked man who accuses his
rescuer for not restoring his belongings also, which the sea has swallowed".
William, he added pertinently, forgets the origin of his own House, when he
lays such stress upon legitimist principles. After long hesitations even the
Tsar realised that the King was unreasonable and sent Count Orlov to the
Hague, in a vain attempt to bring him to reason. Evidently Orlov soon came
to the same conclusion as Stockmar, namely that the Dutch were playing
for the fall of Grey, a general war and partition as their part of the spoils.

At last in April and early May the Eastern Powers ratified, Francis
grumbling over "this in my eyes disgraceful document"[48] and the Tsar
making his consent conditional upon a direct agreement between Belgium
and Holland. The King of Holland tried very hard to induce the Emperor
Francis to repudiate his signature, but though "the whole Belgian affair
was odious" to the latter, as "protection accorded to rebellion",[49] the more
sagacious Metternich was fully alive to the King's unscrupulous motives
and to the grave objections to a general war between the eastern and
western groups. He equally detested the French and British Cabinets, as
playing "le gros jeu des révolutions"—the former, as he said, "à la hausse"
and the latter "à la baisse".[50] But above all he knew that the Austrian army
was far from ready, and he was afraid of the internal consequences of war
both in Italy and Germany. Meanwhile the Tsar had been held back from
intervention by a double motive—on the one hand the unexpectedly pro-

* 22 December 1831—Bell, *op. cit.* p. 492. On 1 January 1832 Palmerston told Stockmar
that it was all "a piece of personal vanity" on the part of Louis Philippe, Sebastiani and
Talleyrand (Stockmar, *op. cit.* p. 216).

longed resistance of the Polish insurrection, and on the other the need for watching with the closest attention the new Eastern crisis which was by now rapidly developing out of the quarrel between the Sultan and his unruly Egyptian vassal. The net result of all these rival currents was that the Concert of the Powers covered the infant Belgium with its wings and left the initiative to Britain and France.

During the summer of 1832 the view ripened both in London and Paris, that only coercion would overcome Dutch obstruction of a settlement: and after Leopold's marriage in August to Princess Louise of Orléans his new father-in-law showed increased readiness for action, while Grey was highly incensed at William I. "I am aristocratic both by position and by nature," Grey pompously wrote to Princess Lieven, "and have with you a predilection for old institutions ": but while eager to do all that was possible for Holland, he considered its conduct as "marked throughout by chicanery and bad faith".* Already in July Palmerston warned the Dutch envoy that if necessary France and Britain would enforce their wishes without waiting for the other Powers.[51] The compromise which he put forward—often known as the "Thème de Lord Palmerston"—was accepted by Belgium on 20 September, but not even admitted for discussion by Holland: whereupon a concrete proposal of intervention was laid before the Conference on 1 October, and as the Eastern Powers temporised, France and Britain resolved to go their own way. On 22 October Palmerston and Talleyrand signed an agreement for joint enforcement of the Treaty of November 1831. Both parties were ordered to evacuate disputed territory, and when King William as usual proved recalcitrant, a French army under Marshal Gérard was sent to expel the Dutch from Antwerp, which was obliged to surrender on 23 December 1832. The Eastern Powers were furious, and the Tsar withdrew his representatives from the Conference: but neither he nor Frederick William III was ready to risk war for their intransigeant kinsman at the Hague. The French kept their promise of handing over Antwerp to the Belgians and withdrawing their troops: but a Franco-British blockade of the Scheldt had to be maintained, pending Dutch submission. On 21 May 1833 Palmerston and Talleyrand reached a provisional arrangement with the Dutch envoy, but after long and barren negotiations a fresh deadlock was reached in the questions of Luxemburg and Limburg, once more owing to the attitude of the King of Holland. So obstinate had he become that in September the Austrian and Russian Emperors, meeting at Münchengrätz, nominated Prince Felix Schwarzenberg as their joint delegate to the Dutch

* 10 September 1832—*Grey-Lieven Corresp.* 11, 392. That this was no passing mood on his part is shown by letters of 3 June 1831 and 14 September 1833: "As to the King of Holland, it is for the five Powers to determine how long they will allow him to set them at defiance and keep all Europe in a state of uneasiness" (*ibid.* p. 464).

Court. At the Hague Schwarzenberg soon had to admit the King's "obstinacy", but in his capacity as envoy sent a message to Palmerston urging a more conciliatory attitude towards Holland, and expressed keen indignation at receiving a "lecture" instead of an "answer".[52] This incident seems to have rankled, and may be noted as the first encounter in a personal conflict that was to flare up fiercely in 1848, when Schwarzenberg was Premier of autocratic Austria and Palmerston appeared to his distorted vision as the champion of subversive principles in Europe.

For our present purpose it is unnecessary to follow the dispute further. Thanks to the energy of the Western allies, and not least of Palmerston himself, the Belgian question was by now solved in all essentials: its unsolved details were, so to speak, put into cold storage, and when at last, after an interval of six more years, the remarkable progress of the new Belgian Kingdom was patent to all Europe and time was seen to be on its side, the final settlement (Treaty of London, 19 April 1839) was concluded without any great difficulty.

In this first great crisis of his career as Foreign Secretary the outlook, reasoning and methods with which Palmerston afterwards became identified, are all to be detected in embryo. But the need for Franco-British co-operation was so imperative as to overshadow all points of dispute between the two nations, and Belgian independence was an admirable compromise between the two extreme policies of bolstering up an artificial Kingdom of the Netherlands or partitioning Belgium between her neighbours—a spectre which was to raise its head periodically during the next half-century. It is not too much to say that Palmerston's services to Belgian independence constitute one of his most lasting titles to fame: and this sentiment was widely expressed by the Belgians themselves during their centenary celebrations.

Palmerston's attitude to Leopold illustrates at its best his sanity and breadth of view. He favoured Leopold for the admirable reason, justified tenfold by subsequent events, "because he will make a good *Belgian* King, neither French nor English".[53] Palmerston cannot, however, be given the sole credit for this sentiment, for it was openly avowed by Lord Grey himself in the House of Lords.[54] In this connection it is worth recording what the new King himself wrote to Prince Metternich a year later: "I have really come here to prevent Belgium from falling either wholly or partly into the hands of France."[55] Here is overstatement to soothe the ruffled susceptibilities of reactionary Austria: the central note of his policy was undoubtedly to balance Paris and London against each other and extract all the advantages he could from each, while exerting a personal influence wherever possible. It may be admitted that Palmerston was right in his view that "we shall never get on with the Belgians till the French are out of Belgium ",[56] and again in his calculation that Louis Philippe's Government could not possibly risk a quarrel with London and that the Eastern Powers would stop short of actual war. Yet it must equally be admitted that his general tactics put a quite unjustifiable strain upon relations with so sensitive a nation as the French. The fact that the rope held may be argued to have proved Palmerston right: but it encouraged him in a habit which grew upon him, of putting a maximum rather than a minimum of strain upon most ropes.

None the less it is abundantly clear that Palmerston, from the very outset of his long career as controller of British foreign policy, regarded good relations with Paris as its very axle. Already on 26 March 1832 he told the House of Commons with pardonable pride in his own recent achievements, that "there never was a period when England was more respected than at present in her foreign relations, in consequence of her good faith, moderation and firmness": and he went on to affirm that "the interest of England was the maintenance of general peace throughout Europe, and this object was, in the mind of H.M.G., most easily, most safely and most securely to be attained by the maintenance of a firm and strict alliance between France and this country".[57] In the following year he again told the House that he looked "with feelings of pride and satisfaction at the part which he had played in bringing about good understanding" between France and Britain.

PALMERSTON AND PORTUGAL

The savage intransigeance of Dom Miguel had been too much even for the complaisance of Wellington and Aberdeen, and by the middle of 1830 relations between London and Lisbon had reached a complete deadlock. The new Foreign Secretary was rightly looked upon as an enemy by the dominant Miguelite faction in Lisbon: as recently as June 1829 he had made a flaming speech in the House of Commons, denouncing Miguel as "the destroyer of constitutional freedom, this breaker of solemn oaths, this faithless usurper", and much more in the same strain.[58] In February and March of the following year acute friction was revived by a series of outrages upon British subjects in Portugal itself and by the seizure of certain British ships trading with the Azores. Palmerston at once threatened to send the British fleet to the Tagus, unless full satisfaction were accorded within ten days: and Miguel had the wisdom to climb down. But similar outrages were perpetrated upon French subjects at Lisbon: indeed one of them was publicly whipped through the streets. The French Consul withdrew, and on 15 May a French squadron cast anchor and demanded atonement. As Miguel obstinately held out, in disregard of very frank advice from London, Admiral Roussin imposed a blockade and on 11 July, after a sort of ultimatum, took possession of the Portuguese fleet. Palmerston, in view of the action which he himself had so recently ordered and of his parallel co-operation with the French in Belgium, could not reasonably oppose these measures. But public opinion in England grew nervous, and the Duke of Wellington went so far as to declare in the House of Lords that he blushed when he heard that the French flag was waving before the walls of Lisbon. Palmerston argued unanswerably that we had no exclusive right to satisfaction, and Mackintosh, in defending him, declared that the Anglo-Portuguese alliance was not "a league of robbers". Here too, as in Belgium, the solidarity of the Western Powers was maintained. Meanwhile it is not too much to maintain that both Governments, and especially the British, stretched their interpretation of neutrality beyond its farthest limits, allowing thousands of their subjects to be enlisted in the cause of Maria, and British naval officers to serve in the Queen's navy under assumed Portuguese names.[59]

During the summer of 1831 the Portuguese situation was modified by the advent of Dom Pedro, whom a revolution had forced to renounce the Brazilian throne, and who now wished to further the cause of his daughter Maria. During the winter of 1831, with the help of British and French financiers and the connivance of the two Governments, he rallied the Portuguese exiles and prepared an expedition against his treacherous brother. A manifesto was issued from his little island fastness of Terceira, and at last in July 1832 his troops were able to occupy and hold Oporto, the second city of the kingdom. For many months to come a deadlock ensued, complicated by the growth of a strangely analogous situation in Spain.

The Eastern Powers had watched this situation with growing anxiety. Metternich in particular regarded the cause of Dom Miguel as identified with the monarchical principle in the Peninsula, and the Emperor Francis openly frowned upon Pedro and Maria, though they were his own son-in-law and grandchild. But all the sympathies of the three autocratic courts for Miguel were promptly neutralised by Palmerston's blunt warning that he would regard any interference on the usurper's behalf as "a revival of the principles of the Holy Alliance".[60] Grey and Palmerston were prepared to accept a son of Archduke Charles as Queen Maria's consort in place of her hateful uncle, but apart from this concession British policy aimed quite definitely at eliminating alike the two warring brothers and the reactionary charter of 1826 and placing the young Queen in the hands of a moderate constitutional party. The idea of Vienna that Spain might be actively enlisted in favour of Miguel—due partly to the Zea Cabinet's sympathy with Miguel—had to be abandoned when it was seen to involve active British, and probably also French, intervention.

Late in 1832 Stratford Canning was sent to Madrid for the purpose of convincing the Spanish Government that Miguel's cause must be abandoned, and found a situation strangely similar to the Portuguese in process of development. In his old age the childless Ferdinand VII had taken as his fourth wife a young Neapolitan Princess, Maria Christina, who was at once his own and his first wife's niece! and round the cradle of their infant daughter Isabella an envenomed struggle was waged for and against the enforcement of the Salic Law. In September 1832, believing himself to be on his deathbed, Ferdinand revoked his daughter's rights, thus leaving the succession to his reactionary brother Don Carlos. But on his recovery two months later he solemnly revoked his revocation, and it soon became obvious that a disputed succession was imminent. In March 1833 Don Carlos withdrew to the Court of Dom Miguel, with whom he was linked by close ties of blood and by political affinities: and the lists were opened for the conflict between the two young queens and their ultra-reactionary uncles. Carlos circularised all the sovereigns of Europe in favour of his cause, while the Cortes were summoned to swear allegiance to the infant Isabella.

In June 1833 Wellington criticised the whole Portuguese policy very strongly in the House of Lords, and obtained something very like a vote of censure: but Palmerston was entirely unabashed and told the other House that "the principle of embarking in the contests of other countries had prevailed, and had been acted upon, in the brightest periods of our history".[61]

Soon after midsummer 1833, however, a sudden change occurred in the affairs of Portugal. Sartorius, the none too effective British officer to whom Pedro had entrusted the command of his fleet, was replaced by the brilliant and energetic Charles Napier, who on 5 July defeated and captured Miguel's entire naval forces. Within a few weeks Lisbon fell into the hands of Dom Pedro, and the prompt recognition of Queen Maria by the Western Powers deterred the Spanish Government from action and at last undermined the authority of Miguel.

PALMERSTON AND THE SPANISH CROWN

Only a week later King Ferdinand died at Madrid, and Spain found herself plunged almost at once into the throes of a peculiarly savage civil war. The forces of reaction, and in particular the Church, wholeheartedly espoused the cause of Don Carlos, while the Queen Regent Christina, whose sympathies were entirely in favour of strong monarchical rule, was forced into unwilling reliance upon the Liberal elements. Palmerston had at first been much more interested in Portugal than in Spain and before Ferdinand's death had been offering British recognition of Isabella as the price of Spanish help "in establishing Maria".[62] In a word, he had not merely reverted to Canning's Portuguese policy and continued it with vigour, he had not merely warned the Eastern Powers against interference, but he had in effect inverted his own principle of non-intervention by direct encouragement to the constitutional regime in Portugal. He was not long in reaching the conclusion that "the triumph of Maria and the accession of Isabella will be important events in Europe, and will give great strength to the Liberal party".[63] "In Spain Liberal measures must be pursued"—so he unburdened himself still more frankly to his brother—"which is saying in other words that the influence of England and France must take that of the three Northern Powers." Here we see the foundations upon which he was to build for twenty years to come.

THE ITALIAN QUESTION

During the winter of 1830–1 a general war had more than once seemed imminent. To the dangerous possibilities of the Belgian question were added fresh complications in Italy, where the election of an ignorant and reactionary friar as Pope Gregory XVI gave the signal for risings in the Romagna and along the Adriatic coast, while Marie Louise and the Duke of Parma—in other words, two out of the three Habsburg subdynasts in Italy—were temporarily driven into flight. While Metternich prepared for intervention in accordance with those Italian ambitions which Austria had steadfastly pursued since the days of Joseph II, the Laffitte Cabinet in France was only too disposed to become the champion of Italian liberalism and challenged Austria's right to interfere in the Papal States. Metternich rejoined that if the Pope appealed to him, Austrian troops would enter not merely Modena and Parma, but Bologna and Ancona also, and told his Ambassador in Paris that "if France wants war, let her declare it upon Europe and try to re-establish the revolution in places where we crush it by merely appearing at a distance".[64] Fortunately at the very moment when the Austrians invaded the Romagna, there was a change of Government in Paris, and the new Premier Casimir Périer, acting on the pacific instructions of Louis Philippe, made a conciliatory speech upholding the principle of non-intervention and repudiating any desire to encourage popular risings in other countries. Metternich was wise enough to meet Périer half-way, and no sooner had the Provisional Government collapsed and the Legate's authority been restored, than a gradual withdrawal of the invading forces was effected. Flysheets were circulated in Paris on the anniversary of the Bastille, denouncing the double betrayal of Poland and of Italy, but Louis Philippe was at least able to claim that evacuation was due to his insistence.

Metternich, it may be added, had been very hostile to Charles X, and unlike Nicholas I, he realised that Louis Philippe was much more conservative than the circumstances of his accession might at first suggest. He soon found common ground with General Maison, when sent as Ambassador to Vienna. He could not face war, with Russia virtually demobilised in Poland and with the further handicap of active hostility from the whole Italian population: but he continued to bluff by assuring Maison that it was "better to die of steel than of poison",[65] and by playing the card of Bonapartism against the Orleanist regime. France's proclamation of the principle of non-intervention had a magic effect in Italy, but this was very much toned down when Sebastiani publicly told La Fayette that "there is a great difference between not consenting and making war", and still more when Périer declared: "we do not recognise the right of any people to force us to fight for its cause: the blood of Frenchmen belongs to France alone" (18 March 1831).

Throughout this conflict the attitude of the Grey Cabinet was watchfully negative, but benevolent towards France, and indeed did not differ in any essentials from that assumed by Palmerston in the 'forties, as the Italian question began to enter a still more decisive stage. It formed part of Palmerston's tactics of establishing a block of the Western Powers against the three autocratic Courts.

THE EASTERN QUESTION: EGYPT AND THE PORTE

While the Belgian problem was still unsolved and the affairs of the Iberian Peninsula were attracting increased international attention, the Eastern Question entered upon a new and acute phase, owing to the trial of strength between Sultan Mahmud and his Egyptian vassal. Since the Treaty of Adrianople and the recognition of Greek independence the situation of the Porte had been distinctly precarious, and as at the beginning of the century, the control of Constantinople over the provinces weakened. But the risings which broke out in Albania and Bosnia, though serious enough, were mere petty local disturbances, compared with the trouble which radiated from Cairo. Twenty years had now passed since the tobacco farmer of Kavala had finally established his sway over Egypt by the massacre of the Mameluke chiefs, and in that period Mehemet Ali had successfully built up a strong army and a highly centralised state on French models, in which all was subordinated to his own personal rule, and which assured to him something very like a monopoly in the chief economic resources of the country. At the same time he had pursued an independent foreign policy of his own. The need for securing his eastern frontier involved him in a long struggle with the Wahabites, which ended in 1818 with the overthrow of their power in Arabia: and meanwhile he was steadily expanding his influence along the Red Sea and up the Valley of the Nile. The Greek Revolution strengthened his position still further by absorbing all the energies of the Porte elsewhere: and we have already seen how Sultan Mahmud was reduced to appealing for Egyptian help, how Ibrahim set himself to conquer Morea and was only thwarted by the disaster of Navarino, and how Crete was the price paid by Constantinople to the Pasha of Egypt. After 1830 Mehemet Ali watched with a certain anxiety the Sultan's persistent efforts to subdue local tyrants and restore the central authority. It is doubtful whether he ever seriously dreamt of seizing power at Constantinople: at most it was perhaps his aim to become a sort of Mayor of the Palace, controlling the policy of a phantom sovereign. But he did definitely aspire to the possession of Palestine, Syria and Arabia, alike for political and economic reasons: and from that moment a clash with Mahmud became sooner or later inevitable. British suspicion was also aroused, for "his military action affected three regions in which they were already interested—the Red Sea, the Persian Gulf and Abyssinia".[66] Yet he on his side made periodic bids for British friendship, being more than ever impressed by the lesson of sea power which Navarino had read him. "With the English for my friends, I can do anything: without their friendship I can do nothing.... Wherever I turn, she is there to baffle me"—so he told the British Consul-General at Alexandria in 1830.[67]

In the late autumn of 1831 Mehemet Ali picked a quarrel with Abdullah Pasha, who controlled the Lebanon and northern Syria, and sent his son Ibrahim to invest Acre by land and sea. The Porte tried to mediate, but Mehemet Ali demanded as the price of peace the administration of Acre and Damascus and remained unmoved when the Sultan proclaimed him as a rebel and sent an army against him under the command of Hussein, the destroyer of the Janissaries. Acre fell on 27 May, and at the beginning and end of July Ibrahim inflicted two crushing defeats upon the Turks, which placed all Syria at his feet and opened the road into Asia Minor. Mahmud, furious, arrogant, over-confident and encouraged in his obstinacy by more than one diplomatic representative at the Porte, bluntly refused his victorious vassal's offer, dismissed Hussein, and sent a fresh army under Reshid Pasha against the invader. On 21 December 1832 that army was in its turn utterly routed by Ibrahim at Konia, its general was taken prisoner, and there was nothing to prevent the Egyptians from overrunning Asia Minor and advancing to the Sea of Marmora.

The Sultan in his need turned to London, and in an autograph letter to William IV begged for British ships to defend him against Mehemet Ali. But at this juncture the Grey Cabinet was absorbed in the Reform struggle at home, and all its spare energies were concentrated upon Belgium and Portugal, where squadrons were already engaged in blockading the Scheldt and watching the Miguelists.* It therefore maintained extreme reserve towards the Porte, and was not to be moved by Talleyrand's advocacy of joint Franco-British armed intervention at both Constantinople and Alexandria. Metternich meanwhile declined under any circumstances to consider the idea of mediation between a sovereign and his rebellious vassal. But the inevitable result of this inactivity was that Mahmud, in his distress, turned to Russia for help, and at last, alarmed by Ibrahim's steady advance, formally begged the Tsar to send a fleet and army (3 February 1833). The French and British Chargés d'Affaires did all in their power to hold back the Porte, but met with the unanswerable retort of the Reis Effendi, that "a drowning man will clutch at a serpent".[68] Nicholas at once responded, and seventeen days later a Russian squadron cast anchor off the Golden Horn. Russia's action had the full approval of Vienna and Berlin, but was keenly resented both in Paris and in London. The new French Ambassador at the Porte, Admiral Roussin, gave full rein to his natural arrogance and threatened Turkey with a breach of diplomatic relations unless the Russians were requested to withdraw—at the same time pledging France to bring Mehemet Ali to reason. For a moment the anti-Russian party regained the upper hand and accepted Roussin's terms: and letters were written by him to the Pasha of Egypt, with the approval of the British Chargé d'Affaires, demanding the immediate withdrawal of Ibrahim. On this the Sultan himself requested the Russians to withdraw.

The French Government was much elated and Palmerston expressed

---

* Palmerston defended his inaction in the House of Commons, on 11 July 1831, *Hansard*, xx, 578–81. He declared that it was "of the utmost importance for the interest of England and the peace of Europe, that the Ottoman Empire should remain entire and be an independent state". The British Government "undoubtedly feel it to be their duty to resist any attempt of Russia to partition Turkey, and would equally have felt themselves at liberty to interfere and prevent the Pasha of Egypt from dismembering any portion of the dominions of the Sultan". But he "very much doubted" whether Russia had "any intention to partition". He repudiated the idea that England was "afraid to go to war" or was "afraid of Russia"—a taunt which was puerile, "for no country on the face of the globe was likely to suffer less than England from war". But the Government had "full confidence in the honour and good faith of Russia", and believed that her troops would soon be withdrawn.

Prof. Webster, however, has published a letter of Palmerston to Granville, of 3 June 1831, in which "with some complacency" he assumes that "Turkey is falling rapidly to pieces". (See Raleigh Lecture, already quoted, p. 133.)

satisfaction at seeing the Russian Admiral sent home "with a flea in his ear". But Roussin's triumph was short-lived, for Mehemet Ali and Ibrahim not merely refused to yield, but threatened a march on Constantinople unless their terms were accepted within five days. Automatically the Sultan was forced back into the arms of the Tsar, and this time Russian troops were sent to reinforce the fleet, and remained until a preliminary peace could be signed at Kutahiya on 6 May. By this, Mehemet Ali was left in control of all the country from the Nile to the Euphrates and the Taurus range, while by a quibble that deceived no one Adana was ceded not to him, but to Ibrahim. Towards the close of the negotiations Roussin had enjoyed the support of the new British Ambassador, Lord Ponsonby, who as the years passed was to become increasingly Turcophil and Russophobe: French and British squadrons were sent to Smyrna, the agents of the two Powers in Alexandria worked hand in hand, and for a time Talleyrand and Palmerston worked at the project of a quadruple agreement in favour of Turkish integrity.

But Roussin, for all his energy, had not the same means as Russia for enforcing his will, and indeed his master Louis Philippe was even less inclined for an Eastern adventure than for a war with Austria "pour les beaux yeux" of Young Italy. The Tsar sent one of his most trusted advisers, Count Orlov, on a special mission to the Porte, with instructions to win over Sultan Mahmud and thus legitimise Russian military aid in the eyes of Europe—to conciliate Austria, neutralise Britain and combat France to the utmost limits short of actual rupture, and to maintain fleet and army in position until Ibrahim had withdrawn south of the Taurus. An autograph letter of Nicholas assured Mahmud that "of all the sovereigns who have succeeded to the throne of Constantine, you are the first to place a noble confidence in the loyalty of Russian policy. I shall know how to justify this." Orlov combined conciliation with firmness, telling the Porte that if French and British forces should pass the Dardanelles he should feel obliged to defend Constantinople against them. The consequence was that the Sultan himself declined the French application for access to the Sea of Marmora, and Ponsonby restrained his colleague Roussin from a step which he saw would only be playing into the hands of Russia. The new French Foreign Minister, the Duke of Broglie, had been prepared to force the Straits, but Palmerston, despite his growing suspicions of Russia, shrank from such a drastic step, and the withdrawal of the Russian forces from Constantinople eased the situation.

This withdrawal, however, was preceded on 8 July 1833 by the conclusion at Unkiar Skelessi, of a treaty of mutual alliance and defence by land and sea, between Russia and the Porte. But while the Sultan was free to decide

the amount of help for which he might appeal, a secret clause released him
from the obligation of sending troops to Russia's aid and in return for this
pledged him to close the Dardanelles to all foreign warships. The underlying idea was both simple and ingenious: it was to make Russia inaccessible
to the Western Powers from the south, while leaving to her the possibility
of reaching the Mediterranean in the event of war. The principle of a *mare
clausum* between the Aegean and Black Sea *in both directions* was thus overthrown in Russia's favour. Yet it must be admitted that Russia showed no
little restraint—in marked contrast to her attitude twenty years later: for
there can be little doubt that she could have smashed Turkey at this
moment if she had chosen, and on the one hand could have defied the
Western Powers with impunity, and on the other could have squared
Austria by due emphasis on the legitimist order in Central Europe. But
Nicholas and Nesselrode preferred to leave Turkey in so weakened a state
that it could only exist under Russian protection and must submit to their
wishes: and meanwhile it would be their task to prevent any hostile Power
from establishing itself at Constantinople or even asserting undue influence
there. Already in the previous February he had given frank assurances to the
Austrian "Inter-Nuncio" Ficquelmont, that Russia would give the Sultan
all the support in her power against his rebellious vassal: but he added still
more frankly, that he had "no power to give life to the dead.... It will fall
a little earlier or a little later". In his view the essential aim must be for
Russia and Austria to agree beforehand, and thus avert the worst dangers
which dismemberment might conjure up.[69]

The news of the treaty soon leaked out and aroused no little excitement in
Paris and London—*The Times*, for instance, denouncing its provisions as
"barefaced and impudent".[70] The two Western Governments affected to
treat the decisions taken as null and void, their squadrons remained off
Tenedos, and Admiral Malcolm came to consult with the Ambassador. But
Palmerston's protest against the treaty, submitted to the Porte on 27 August,
could not avail to alter the accomplished fact or to open the Dardanelles to
their ships: while Metternich, so far from sharing their annoyance, was
highly satisfied with the Tsar's Eastern policy.[71]

When, then, in the summer a meeting between the Russian and Austrian
Emperors was suggested, Metternich was entirely reassured. Starting from
the assumption that the maintenance of Turkey and the Ottoman dynasty
was a common interest of Europe and "especially a political necessity for
Austria",[72] he welcomed the Tsar's abandonment of the idea of partition:
and this was the basis of the secret Austro-Russian agreement concluded at
Münchengrätz in the following September. The two Powers pledged themselves to maintain Turkish independence, especially against further en-

croachments of the Pasha of Egypt, and if despite all their efforts the existing order in Turkey should be overthrown, to work together for a settlement in conformity with the European balance of power. It is not too much to affirm that this agreement contributed very materially towards that *détente* which is so noticeable in the Eastern Question from 1833 to 1839. The further Russo-Turkish Convention concluded at St Petersburg on 29 January 1834 was a fresh proof of the Tsar's moderation, since it provided for the evacuation of the Danubian Principalities and cancelled 2,000,000 ducats of the Turkish war debt to Russia.

Throughout this period the Government's policy in the Near East was followed with mingled feelings by Parliament and foreign opinion. Early in 1834 the Duke of Wellington claimed that a plain veto by Britain upon Mehemet Ali carrying on his contest in Syria and Asia Minor would have put an end to war "without the risk of the Tsar sending fleet and army". Some weeks later Lord Stanley in the House of Commons affirmed that what stopped the progress of the Egyptian Pasha was the distinct declaration of France and Britain that they would not permit the occupation of Constantinople by his troops. And during the same debate Palmerston himself put forward the claim that the representations of Britain to the Pasha and his son Ibrahim "materially contributed" to the agreement of Kutahiya.[73]

Meanwhile, Palmerston's interest in Turkey was steadily growing. In March 1833 he told his brother that he looked upon the Turks as a better "occupier of the road to India" than the ruler of an independent Arab kingdom, and added, "We must try to help the Sultan in organising his army, navy and finances."[74] Colonel Campbell, the new British agent in Egypt, was instructed that H.M.G. aimed at preventing "not only a dissolution, but even a partial dismemberment of the Turkish Empire".[75] He made it clear that an Austro-Russian partition of Turkey, which he suspected Nicholas and Metternich of discussing at Münchengrätz, would be opposed by England and France "to the utmost of their means".[76] In December we find him writing as follows: "Russia is the only Power with which we are likely to come to a real quarrel, and even with her I trust we shall be able to keep the peace".[77] And early in 1834: "With Russia we are on a footing of civil civility. She is not ready to go to war for Turkey.... We shall therefore have no war this year: and a year gained is a great deal in such matters. Austria may open her eyes, and if she joins us *really* in resisting the schemes of Russia, we shall checkmate Nicholas."[78] And again: "With Russia we are just as we were, snarling at each other, but neither wishing for war...."[79]

THE POLISH QUESTION

We have seen that Palmerston's growing suspicion of Russia was in the main determined by his interest in Turkey. In the Polish question, on the other hand, he showed unusual reserve and declined a French proposal for joint mediation. Altogether, though Poland had a few fervent advocates in Britain, and though her cause was pleaded in the House of Commons by Joseph Hume, O'Connell and de Lacy Evans, there was never the slightest chance of Britain taking action. Palmerston expressed "the greatest admiration" for the Poles and heartily wished them success,[80] but he regarded them as doomed from the outset, and was only ready to help them "in any way consistent with our good faith towards Russia"—a diplomatic phrase very hard to decipher! He received Wielopolski and Walewski, the two envoys sent to London by the Polish revolutionary Government, but he told them quite plainly that "we must stand upon our treaties", and that though we should remonstrate if Russia tried to depart from the Treaty of Vienna, "we could not do so ourselves by helping to make Poland entirely independent".* "We cannot send an army to Poland," he told Czartoryski, 'and the burning of the Russian fleet would be about as effectual as the burning of Moscow."[81] Like most British statesmen before and since, he shrank from any step which might involve us in military action in the east of Europe. But he was only too alive to the importance of the Polish diversion in saving Belgium, deterring Austria and averting a general European war. Very different was the attitude of Sebastiani—it is true, an old comrade-in-arms of the Poles under Napoleon—who went so far as to warn Nesselrode that general peace depended in no small degree upon Russia's attitude to Poland. He even suggested to Palmerston some kind of joint action, but met with no response.

How little hope there was of anything beyond Platonic expressions of sympathy from this country, became apparent when her friends raised the question in Parliament on 7 September 1831. Sir Francis Burdett, in seconding de Lacy Evans's petition for the appointment of a British Resident in Warsaw—in itself an entirely impracticable suggestion—freely admitted that "it might be incompatible with the interests of this country to take an active part to reinstate the Poles in their rights and re-establish the independence of Poland: but this he would say, that no cause more just ever called forth the sympathy of nations".[82] O'Connell added that "the time

---

* 29 March 1831—Bulwer, *op. cit.* p. 61. In 1836 Palmerston still took the same line, telling Durham that "England only knows the Poland of the Vienna Congress and cannot encourage mad plans for the restoration of the Polish Kingdom" (Schiemann, *Gesch. Russlands*, III, 291).

has now arrived when all Europe should stand forth to secure the constitution of Poland which had been given to it by treaty, if it were only to protect the rest of Europe from the barbarism of her invader".[83] Here the matter was allowed to rest. The insurrection was mercilessly put down, Poland was held to have forfeited by rebellion all the rights conceded to her in 1815, and for 30 years the silence of the tomb descended upon her, while many of her greatest sons became political emigrants, and like Mickiewicz in Paris, sought to promote and keep alive the "Messianic" tradition of Poland the Crucified among the nations. A few British stalwarts continued to plead the Polish cause—notably David Urquhart and Lord Dudley Stuart—but long before resurrection became possible, the links between the two countries had been all but severed.

RELATIONS WITH RUSSIA

In view of subsequent developments it is worth dwelling upon Palmerston's early relations with Russia. In March 1832 Count Orlov, whom the Tsar had sent to the Hague, paid a visit to London also, and Grey seems to have suspected a foreign intrigue against the Whig Cabinet. Orlov, however, explained in the most disarming fashion, that there were probably not twenty persons in all Russia who knew the difference between Whig and Tory, and that the Tsar's will alone counted. Soon after, the Polish question was again raised in the House, and this led Grey and Palmerston to take a decision of no little boldness and originality. Lord Durham—in other words, the most radical and uncompromising member of the Grey Cabinet, but at the same time the Prime Minister's own son-in-law—was sent on a special mission to Tsar Nicholas, to clear up the various pending questions—Belgium, Poland, the Papal States, the progressive movement in Germany, and Russia's alleged designs on Khiva. He was to explain the principles of British policy and "to make them [i.e. Russia] understand, that *though friends to free institutions, we are not promoters of revolution*, and to moderate down to its proper and useful degree the apprehension entertained by the Russian Cabinet, that we are forming too close an alliance with France".[84] This was a really conciliatory step, for it was taken at the very time when Joseph Hume, one of Durham's chief Radical associates, was airing our relations with Russia in the House of Commons and denouncing the Tsar as not only a miscreant, but a monster in human form. In actual fact, the appointment was a great success, and Durham soon won golden opinions in St Petersburg.*

The first rift with Russia came in the following year, when Palmerston

---

* Princess Lieven had not been favourable and had written to her brother: "The man's vanity is proverbial: he is the haughtiest aristocrat....Here he is cordially and universally disliked" (29 June 1832—*Letters of Princess Lieven*, ed. Robinson, p. 328).

recalled our Ambassador at St Petersburg, Lord Heytesbury, and appointed Sir Stratford Canning in his place. This the Tsar absolutely refused to ratify, for reasons which have never been quite definitely ascertained, though there has been many a wild surmise. Canning's biographer contends (though without proof or even much plausibility, as the story of the two Durham missions amply shows) that "Russia thought fit to dictate to England what sort of Ambassador she should send to Petersburg, and that the sort she would accept must not be one who knew too much about her proceedings in the East". In view, however, of the well-known diplomatic rule that names should be submitted to a foreign Court before the final accrediting, it seems difficult to justify Palmerston's contention that the Tsar's conduct was "an outrageous piece of arrogance", still more his use of this violent and undiplomatic phrase to the Russian Ambassador.[85] The fact is that Palmerston was forewarned and having deliberately disregarded the warning, came up against an even stronger will in the autocratic Nicholas. Conclusive evidence for this view is to be found in Lord Durham's written account of the incident. "Lord Palmerston was told that there was only one man in England to whom the Emperor objected, namely Canning. This was communicated in the most friendly way to Lord Palmerston by Lieven and myself, and before Palmerston had even named Canning. In despite of this Palmerston appointed Canning and even gazetted him, without conveying any notice of his intention to Lord Grey. When remonstrated with by Lieven, he said, 'Canning is of my party, and I must provide for him'."* The fact is that Palmerston resented the interference of the Princess, and still more Durham's lobbying with his father-in-law the Prime Minister. In the end he had to give way, but retaliated most unwisely by leaving this important Embassy in the hands of a *chargé d'affaires* for over two years, and this despite all the dangers of an acute Eastern crisis. It is but fair to add that on 11 July 1833 Palmerston pointedly assured the House of Commons that he had "full confidence in the honour and good faith of Russia". A few days earlier he had won the assent of the House for the view that "it was wise not to involve Europe in a general war in the hope and expectation of ultimately rescuing Poland from the oppression under which it suffered".†

* The story of an alleged affront by Canning to Nicholas when Grand Duke appears to be quite imaginary, and was actually denied both by the Tsar and by Nesselrode to the British Minister *ad interim*, Mr Bligh (see Lane-Poole, *op. cit.* II, 20). "Don't let it be Canning", Nesselrode wrote to Princess Lieven, "he is soupçonneux, pointilleux, défiant" (16 February 1833—Greville, *Memoirs*, II, 365).

† 9 July—*Hansard*, XIX, 434. It was on this occasion that O'Connell declared that he "would as soon keep company with a thief who had been tried at the Old Bailey as with Nicholas", and spoke of "that outrageous public prostitute Catherine, the grandmother of this Emperor"—a woman "who should have been consigned to the treadmill or the ducking stool" (*ibid.* p. 442).

Petty though it is, this disagreement about Canning deserves to be stressed, for it had two important effects. As a direct consequence, the Lievens were recalled from London,* and the Princess's twenty years' reign—unique in the annals of the London diplomatic corps—came to a sudden end, though from 1837 onwards she was to hold a new salon in Paris and once more to exercise a vital influence upon politics through the enslaved Guizot. But even more momentous, though far less easy to estimate, was the permanent resentment which Stratford Canning seems to have borne towards Tsar Nicholas: twenty years later the two men were to become in a very real sense the two chief protagonists in the Crimean War.

Wellington, during his short-lived tenure of the Foreign Office in 1834 proposed appointing Lord Londonderry:[86] but Lord Stanley attacked him in the House of Commons as "the last person whom England ought to have sent to Russia to represent the feelings of the people of this country", and indeed as "the most unfit man in the Empire to represent those feelings".[87] Fortunately the Cabinet fell before the negotiations were concluded. Palmerston, when he returned to power, consented to the appointment of Lord Durham, who, it was known, would be acceptable to the Tsar: and there was the further motive that neither Melbourne nor Grey wished to have him in the Cabinet, but felt bound to offer him some good post. Durham remained at St Petersburg from October 1835 till the summer of 1837 and did much to improve Russo-British relations, ridiculing in his despatches "the hourly dread of Russia", but warning Nesselrode very frankly that "nothing would ever induce us to connive at her designs on Turkey" or to allow her seizure of Constantinople.[88]

THE QUADRUPLE ALLIANCE

During 1833, as the Belgian danger gradually subsided and as the Whig ascendancy became stabilised at home, Palmerston had kept an equally vigilant eye upon Russia and upon Austria. He was not the man to leave the renewed rapprochement of the three Eastern Powers to go unchallenged, especially when he found Metternich already trying hard to win over Louis Philippe to their side and only handicapped by the Tsar's personal antipathy to the usurper. Metternich indeed had already grasped the fact which was only to become generally apparent in the 'forties, that the July Monarchy

* "As to this producing the recall of the Lievens, *gioia, gioia*, if it does", wrote Planta to Canning, 23 July 1833 (Lane-Poole, *op. cit.* II, p. 22). Lady Cowper (afterwards Lady Palmerston) told Greville that Palmerston had been "provoked by Princess Lieven's interference" and "thought both *she* and her *Court* wanted to be taken down a peg". She appealed to Grey and Durham against Palmerston and thus made things worse. Her own diary contains the comment, "thus Palmerston rewarded the service I had done him" (*Diary*, p. 186).

despite its revolutionary origin was not merely conservative, but ultra-conservative in its inclinations.

None the less, the underlying differences of motive and outlook between London and Paris were as yet far outweighed by their common interests in the West of Europe. This had been especially marked in Belgium, and it now prompted Palmerston's initiative in April 1834, in converting his triangular understanding with Spain and Portugal into a Quadruple Alliance of the Western Powers, committing the two major partners actively to the cause of the two Queens. As he told his brother, it "was a capital hit and all my own doing".[89] "I carried it through the Cabinet by a *coup de main*, taking them by surprise and not leaving them time to make objections. I reckon this to be a great stroke. In the first place it will settle Portugal and go some way to settle Spain also. But what is of more permanent and extensive importance, it establishes a Quadruple Alliance among the constitutional states of the West, which will serve as a powerful counterpoise to the Holy Alliance of the East."[90] This, then, was Palmerston's idea of non-intervention. It was a direct challenge to Metternich, who regarded Isabella as "the revolution incarnate in its most dangerous form" and Carlos as "representative of the monarchical principle in conflict with the Revolution."[91] Palmerston, who very prematurely assumed that the case of Carlos was already "desperate",[92] was also by now frankly defiant of Metternich, of whom he said that his chief mistake since 1830 was not to realise that "the political system of England is settled and unchangeable, whether Governments are stable or tottering", and that he was always expecting to have "his dear Tories in power within six months".[93]

THE TORY INTERLUDE

This little outburst was written in July 1834, at the moment when Lord Grey resigned office, worn out by the stress of the long Reform agitation and discouraged by the transference of the almost indispensable Althorpe from the Commons to the Lords. To Princess Lieven Grey confided, "My life for the last eight months has been one of such unhappiness as nobody can imagine, and as far as I am personally concerned, I rejoice at having escaped from so painful and thankless a situation."[94]

The new Premier, Lord Melbourne, had only been in power for four months, when he became the victim of what is known as "the King's *coup d'état*". William IV was of course technically within his rights, but the trend of events was against him, and the incident is noticeable as the last occasion on which the Crown has not merely asserted but actually exercised its power to dismiss a whole Cabinet as opposed to an individual Minister, though it has on occasion vindicated its right to send for whom it pleases.

This time Sir Robert Peel became Prime Minister, and the Duke of Wellington went to the Foreign Office. But he was there barely six months, and in that time nothing occurred to modify the policy which he found there. It was a somewhat singular combination, which once surprised the bluff old soldier into the apologetic comment, " I have no small talk, and Peel has no manners ".[95] A letter which Palmerston wrote to his brother during what was for him a breathing space, gives a clue both to his own and to the Duke's attitude. " The Duke of Wellington," he says, " is, I suspect, if possible more hostile to Russia than I was—fully as much impressed with the necessity of checking her insatiable ambition and quite as determined to employ the means which England possesses to do so. The fact is that Russia is a great humbug, and that if England were fairly to go to work with her, we should throw her back half a century in one campaign. But Nicholas the proud and insolent knows this, and will always check his pride and moderate his insolence when he finds England is firmly determined and fully prepared to resist him."[96] Here in germ we have the aggressive Palmerston of a later date, and we can already see the dangers which threaten the future from such a temperament, pitted against so intolerably autocratic a will as that of Nicholas I. But this is in a private letter to his brother, when public opinion could not yet look over his shoulder. And so it came about that after his return to office no other than David Urquhart, the most redoubtable Turco-phil and Russophobe of his day, actually put forward the grotesque allegation that Palmerston was influenced by Russian gold. Meanwhile in actual fact the Duke cultivated better relations with Russia than his predecessor, and the Tsar was not without hope of winning him to the cause of legitimacy or of wheedling him as at St Petersburg in 1826.

The six brief months during which the Duke remained at the Foreign Office were not marked by any outstanding event or change of policy: and when Lord Melbourne resumed office in April 1835 there was no very obvious substitute for Palmerston, after Lord Grey's refusal. Yet Grey, Lansdowne and Holland each urged Melbourne to pass over Palmerston, and the Ambassadors of the three Eastern Powers went the length of expressing a hope in the same sense. But Palmerston himself was by now thoroughly bitten with the work, and told his chief, " distinctly, unequivocally, unalterably ", that without the Foreign Office he " had rather not engage in the administration at all ".[97] That his insistence proved successful, was probably due to two main causes, firstly his close friendship with Lord Melbourne himself—whose brother-in-law he was to become in 1839 by his marriage with the widowed Lady Cowper, for whom he had waited so long and so faithfully—and secondly because of his relatively cordial relations with William IV. "The King and the Court hate us and wish us all to the devil", Palmerston wrote to Durham: "I believe I am the only one of the ministers whom the King likes personally."[98] Besides his first term of office had proved him, despite many outbursts of temperament, to be a man of outstanding ability—to quote the words of Charles Grey, he was "firm and even bold: quite steady to his friends: indifferent to abuse, full of resources...not punctilious or vain, or standing upon trifles and personalities.... I highly disapprove his foreign meddling, but I speak of his general talents".[99]

Melbourne at this period still held Palmerston in leash and impressed upon him "the extreme danger of taking strong steps"[100]—a lesson which was certainly lost upon Palmerston, with his "healthy appetite for 'incidents'".[101] And indeed year by year the restraining influence grew noticeably weaker.

PALMERSTON'S ATTITUDE TO FRANCE AND RUSSIA

From 1835 to 1839 there is relative quiet in Europe, marked, so far as British policy is concerned, by a gradual alienation from France and a simultaneous growth of suspicion towards Russia. Once again it is highly instructive to study the reactions of Metternich towards both tendencies. Early in 1833 he had already convinced himself that Palmerston's character was made up of "presumption and naivety, audacity and gêne".[102] Two years later we find him again writing to his Ambassador in Paris, Count Apponyi, that "at Paris they are terrified at *la fougue anglaise*". Every day will prove that he is right in calling England "*la propagatrice du mal*" and France an extinct crater. "France is yesterday, England will be to-morrow: we and the states which are to-day, are *froissés* on every occasion by the elements which jostle us." To Sainte-Aulaire's remark that the English Ministers wanted war with Russia, Metternich agreed, but said that it would not go beyond "les limites d'une velléité" of Palmerston. If France could hold back England, he himself would undertake to keep Tsar Nicholas "dans ses dispositions toutes pacifiques".[103] This throws light on Metternich's egotism, but it also shows the impression that Palmerston was beginning to create in foreign diplomatic circles.

Palmerston on his side writes to Melbourne (1 March 1835) that "we must not look to Metternich for any co-operation in measures destined to hold

Russia in check".[104] Melbourne's own brother, Sir Frederick Lamb,* was now Ambassador in Vienna, and the Prime Minister enquires of him "how he finds the land lying at Vienna", and contrasts Metternich's ill-humour and "tone of haughtiness and imperiousness" with Russia's tone, which is "in the highest degree moderate and conciliatory".[105] But Palmerston, for all his forcible language, had accurately gauged the international situation, when he wrote to his chief: "The division of Europe into two camps (as Ancillon calls it), to which you so much object, is the result of events beyond our control, and is the consequence of the French Revolution of July.... The three (Powers) and the two"—that is, the Eastern and Western groups —"think differently, and therefore they act differently", whether in Belgium, in Portugal or in Spain. What Metternich and Ancillon really dislike, he pertinently adds, is not "the existence", but "the equality of the two camps".[106]

There is already an undercurrent of friction in the relations of Britain and Russia, which is accentuated by the attitude of our Embassy at the Porte. It is the first of a series of eventful rivalries between the British and Russian representatives in Constantinople. This time it was Lord Ponsonby, who had a fanatical hatred and distrust of Russia, and of whom his own cousin Lord Durham once declared: "If I were Minister, Ponsonby would not stay twenty-four hours at the Porte."† The easy-going and cynical Melbourne wrote of Ponsonby's "ridiculous Russophobia, which leads him to shut his eyes to everything else".[107] Ponsonby was a man of alternating moods, indolent, violent and not amenable to discipline, indeed often completely out of hand. His *Private Letters on the Eastern Question*, published in pamphlet form in 1854, insisting on force as the only possible solution and the only way to "get England out of the filth in which she is attempted to be smothered" (the grammar is his), suggest a very mediocre intelligence and judgment. Ponsonby never varied in his hatred of Russia, but after 1834 he came to abandon his original belief in Mehemet Ali as Britain's natural ally against Russia, and pressed on Palmerston the view that by supporting Mahmud against the Pasha of Egypt, Britain could draw the Sultan altogether within her sphere of influence.[108] At this earlier period he

* Afterwards Lord Beauvale, who, in Prof. Webster's words, "handled Metternich with so judicious a mixture of flattery and frankness, and kept in such close touch with the intricate machinery of the Austrian State, that he had more influence at Vienna than any other Ambassador"—*Palmerston, Metternich and the European System* (Raleigh Lecture), p. 129.

† Barante, *Souvenirs*, V, 381. Barante, writing to Thiers in May 1836, quotes this phrase as used by Durham to himself. Durham remonstrated with Palmerston against Ponsonby's intransigeance, but received the answer, "Ponsonby goes perhaps too far in his suspicions of Russia and certainly is too warlike in his own inclinations... but has great merits and has done us good service at Constantinople" (31 May 1836)—cit. Stuart Reid, *op. cit.* II, 43.

was reinforced at the Constantinople Embassy by David Urquhart as First Secretary. Urquhart, who had a remarkable knowledge of the Near East, had already written many books and pamphlets[109] and was an ardent Turcophil to whom Russia was a positive obsession. Indeed he had in 1835 in his review *The Portfolio* published a collection of Russian secret documents which had been seized in Warsaw during the Polish insurrection, and which contained various details highly embarrassing to Metternich also. His press campaign in England was conducted with the approval and even co-operation of Ponsonby.[110] Thanks to the private influence of William IV, Urquhart was in 1836 sent out to the Constantinople Embassy and there continued to work actively against Russia. He was recalled after the King's death and bore a lasting grudge against Palmerston, but what really spoilt his diplomatic career was his share in aggravating two delicate incidents of the year 1836.

The first was the case of an English merchant named Churchill, who having accidentally killed a Turkish child, was attacked by the mob and thrown into prison. Ponsonby went so far as to break off relations with the Porte until the Reis Effendi and Ahmed Pasha had been dismissed and Churchill indemnified. On this the Tsar wrote to the Sultan, exhorting him not to sacrifice his servants to the unjust demands of Lord Ponsonby. The Porte was even advised to ask London for the recall of Ponsonby, who on his side tried to convince his chief that the conflict could only be ended by the complete disgrace of Russia or of Britain.*

The second incident was still more serious. A London merchant named Bell—directly encouraged by Ponsonby and Urquhart behind the back of the Foreign Office—fitted out the sloop *Vixen* with a cargo of salt and ran the Russian blockade to the coast of Circassia. The Russians, alleging that the vessel contained gunpowder as well as salt, promptly confiscated her. There were indignant complaints in the London press, and Palmerston used very blunt language to Pozzo di Borgo about the Circassian struggle for liberty. In the end, however, he had to recognise the justice of the seizure: but quite apart from this he had "no wish to go to war with Russia", and moreover, if war was to prove inevitable, he wanted "some real and well-defined ground of quarrel, and not to begin fighting at the good will and bidding of Mr James Bell, the bankrupt of Bucarest".[111] Ponsonby urged Palmerston to send a fleet into the Black Sea, and if he had been

---

* See Bolsover, *op. cit.* p. 110, who charges Ponsonby with trying to embroil the two countries. Barante reported to Thiers that Ponsonby's two colleagues, Butenyev and Roussin, found him "si excessif et si peu raisonnable", that they could not share in his démarche. (Barante, *Souvenirs*, v, 414.) Admiral Roussin appears to have blamed Ponsonby very freely as "un fou", and this was repeated by Butenyev to the Internuncio. Barante, v, 441, 453.

listened to by the Foreign Secretary, it might very easily have come to war.

The incident was again raised during the debate of 1 March 1848, when Anstey, at Urquhart's instigation, accused Palmerston of subservience to Russia and of actual treason. Palmerston, in a reply that was very damaging for Urquhart, maintained that Bell had calculated upon the British Government being forced to send a fleet to the Baltic. "I have been accused frequently", he added, "of being too warlike, but I own my courage did not rise to that point": and Urquhart was therefore not allowed to return to Constantinople and envenom the situation still further.[112] By that time he had in any case quarrelled with the Ambassador.

In these activities Urquhart seems to have relied upon the interest of the "Sailor King" and of his secretary Sir Herbert Taylor, in the fortifications which Nicholas I was erecting both at Kronstadt and Sebastopol, and again upon William's personal antipathy for Nicholas. Urquhart certainly helped to implant in Ponsonby the fixed idea that the Tsar aimed at the possession of Constantinople, which as a distant ultimate goal was doubtless accurate enough.

There were other points of friction with Russia—the question of a steamer concession on the Euphrates, and in particular relations with Persia and their effect upon Afghanistan. Russia was already advancing slowly into Central Asia, and Palmerston could not be blamed for looking askance at this. But most of all he was afraid of what a generation later was to become the *cauchemar* of Germany—namely, an alliance between Russia and France: and it followed from this that as he became involved in friction with France owing to Western affairs, he was forced into more friendly accord with Russia in the crisis of 1839–41. Till then, however, his typical method is revealed in a phrase used to Lord John Russell (15 December 1838): "What Lord Howick says of the real weakness of Russia for aggressive war is quite true: but the knowledge of that fact ought rather to encourage us to make a stout stand against her systematic encroachment on Peace."[113]

SPANISH AFFAIRS

The Quadruple Alliance, due to the initiative of Palmerston and the cordial approval of Talleyrand, filled the Liberals of the West with joy, led the Eastern Powers to withdraw their ministers from Madrid and decided the weak Spanish Government to help Maria against her uncle Miguel. It speedily attained its first aim of checking the civil war in Portugal, and henceforth Maria, who was proclaimed of age in September 1834, was able to maintain herself peacefully on the throne, despite the death of her

father, the ex-Emperor. But in Spain the situation was much more precarious, and there can be little doubt that but for foreign backing to the two
Queens, the Carlist cause, with its roots in medieval clericalism, would
eventually have triumphed. In the summer of 1834 Don Carlos himself
found his way back to Spain, and had the advantage of financial help from
the Tsar, Frederick William III, Carlo Alberto and the French legitimists,
and the even greater advantage of a brilliant guerilla general in Zumala-
carregui.

The advent of a Tory Cabinet to power in England roused Carlist hopes,
but our Minister in Madrid, George Villiers—the future Lord Clarendon—
was able to hold back the Duke of Wellington from any definite action: and
all that was done was to despatch Lord Eliot and Colonel Wylde to the
Carlist headquarters, in the hope of imposing some check upon the mutual
savagery of the contending forces. Wellington was already out of office
before they had time to conclude the convention of 27 April 1835, and its
terms were soon to be set at open defiance.

Under the stress of Carlist successes, the Government of Madrid appealed
in May for French assistance, but this was refused by Louis Philippe, owing
to the reserved attitude of London. He did, however, lend to Spain the
French Foreign Legion and permit the recruiting of French volunteers,
while Palmerston, in defiance of Tory protests, authorised the raising of a
Spanish Legion of 10,000 men, under the command of Colonel De Lacy
Evans, a Peninsular veteran who had won Westminster for the Radical
cause.* The retort of Don Carlos was to declare foreign volunteers exempt
from the Eliot convention: no quarter was given, and the civil war assumed
an increasingly "bloody and ferocious character".[114]

The course of events now led inevitably towards increased friction between France and Britain, and especially between their representatives in
Madrid, Villiers and Rayneval. It is impossible to absolve the former from
all blame: for on his own responsibility he signed with the Mendizabal
Cabinet a convention securing a British loan to Spain, in return for a reduction in the duties upon British goods. The secret was at once betrayed
by Queen Christina to Rayneval and transmitted to Paris, so that Palmerston's repudiation of his zealous subordinate was robbed of much of its
virtue. The French grew exceedingly jealous of the open alliance between
Villiers and Mendizabal, and began to draw closer to the Eastern Powers,
refusing Palmerston's suggestions of joint intervention in favour of the
"Cristinos". The appearance of a British squadron under Lord John Hay
on the eastern coast of Spain only increased their nervousness. In Palmer-

* Of Evans Villiers had the poorest opinion—"a conceited, incapable coxcomb, with no
real merit beyond personal bravery" (Maxwell, *Life of Clarendon*, I, 147).

ston's view the British Government, "by assisting the Spanish people to establish a constitutional form of government, were assisting to secure the independence of Spain, and they had no doubt that the maintenance of that independence would be conducive to important British interests".[115] This only thinly veils his very definite aim of preventing French predominance in Spain. Moreover, it only fits in very imperfectly with the views of Villiers in Madrid, who at this period of his career showed a certain immature naivety. In writing home, he very frankly avowed the belief that "the mass of the nation" was Carlist and absolutist in its sympathies, and that Spain was "unfit for liberal institutions",[116] and yet continued to press for military intervention. He only too obviously enjoyed Madrid's atmosphere of adventure, crime and intrigue: "after all," he wrote, "here I am *somebody*, and in London *nobody* can be *anybody*".[117]

The fall of Mendizabal in May 1836 led to an improvement in the relations with France, but Spain's situation remained pitiable. Queen Christina seemed at the last gasp and thought seriously of flight to her brother's Court at Naples: and in the end she and her daughter were saved less by their own virtue than by the arrogant incompetence of Don Carlos and his entourage. The Carlist failure before Madrid in the autumn of 1837 marks the turning of the tide, and after two more years of dissension Don Carlos fled the country. But though the Progressist party seemed to hold the field, and the Queen Regent also had to withdraw from Spain, it was really to make way for the dictatorship of Espartero, and the effects of civil war lingered for many decades.

There can be little doubt that Spanish affairs contributed very materially towards loosening the ties between the two Western Powers, but the exact responsibility is difficult to determine. Palmerston genuinely desired co-operation between the two chief exponents of liberalism and could not conceal his chagrin at Louis Philippe's growing inclination towards a rapprochement with Austria. But it may fairly be asked whether his own cavalier attitude towards France did not drive her into the arms of Metternich, just as it unquestionably made London unbearable for the veteran Talleyrand, despite his devotion to a Franco-British entente—one of the few passions of his life. How intolerable Palmerston could already make himself may be seen from the instructions which he sent in September 1836 to Lord Granville in Paris. The Ambassador was to inform M. Molé, the French Premier, "that we look upon France as backing out of the alliance as fast as she can, that we are sorry for it, but wash our hands of the consequences". France "will lose her credit with the Liberal party in Europe, whom she is about to desert", and will become identified "with arbitrary power in Europe and with the enemies of free institutions", without, however, ever winning the trust or favour of the Holy Alliance, since she "could never assimilate her Government to their model".[118] This may or may not have been true, but it was not calculated to soothe the susceptibilities of the French.

Far more moderate, meanwhile, was the definition of policy given by Lord Melbourne to the King's secretary. This was "to hold aloof": England was "not to ally herself either with the spirit of general revolution or of arbitrary government", but also not "to take exception to any form of government, despotic or republican, which may be established".[119] William IV for his part was against intervention, but believed that "jealousy of the property and grandeur of this country is the dominant feeling of France and of every state on the Continent"*—an insular view which shows him to have reflected pretty faithfully the attitude of his average subject towards "damned foreigners". Of Melbourne it is not unfair to quote the considered verdict of Guizot in later life—remembering of course that he was not quite impartial after his experiences at the London Embassy—"the least Radical of the Whigs, a judicious epicurean, an agreeable egoist, gay without warmth and mingling a natural air of authority with a carelessness which he took delight in proclaiming".[120]

---

* Maxwell, *Life of Clarendon*, I, 358. In September 1833 he had been unwise enough in a public speech to refer to the French as "the natural enemies of England" (Brougham, *Life*, III, 306).

CHAPTER V

THE EASTERN QUESTION AND THE CRISIS
OF THE ENTENTE

We saw that the year 1833 brought a *détente* in the Eastern Question, the two Western Powers being too absorbed elsewhere to risk an armed conflict with Russia, and Sultan Mahmud resigning himself to a direct agreement with Tsar Nicholas, as his best, and indeed at the moment only effective, guarantee against the aggression of Mehemet Ali. We saw also that the Tsar, after the triumph of his policy at Unkiar Skelessi, showed singular moderation towards the Porte and was content to await a dissolution which he regarded as slow but inevitable, securing himself meanwhile against sudden unforeseen developments by his secret agreement with Austria at München-grätz. The lull that followed in Eastern affairs somewhat allayed Palmerston's suspicions of Russia, and he remained politely vigilant, save for the already recorded lapse into aggression in connection with Stratford Canning's nomination to the Petersburg Embassy.

THE ROUTE TO THE EAST

During the remainder of the 'thirties Palmerston's interest in the Near and Middle East grew steadily, for three almost equal reasons. British trade in the Levant was steadily increasing in volume, while the advent of the steamship was bringing India nearer to England and stimulating the search for alternatives to the old sailing route round the Cape of Good Hope. These alternatives could only be through Suez and the Red Sea, or across the Syrian desert to the Euphrates and the Persian Gulf. In both cases Turkey was a factor of prime importance: in the former Britain looked nervously upon the Russian penetration in Asia and her intrigues in Persia, while in the latter she feared French aspirations towards naval control of the Mediterranean and suspected Mehemet Ali as a mere tool of Paris. In this role, indeed, Mehemet Ali was doubly obnoxious, for his ambitions seemed to threaten equally the two new Indian routes and again to hamper British commerce by his cotton and coffee monopolies. France had retained her sympathy for Mehemet Ali since the days of Napoleon, provided him with many efficient officers and civil instructors, and regarded a strong Egypt under his rule as likely to strengthen her own position in the Mediterranean and to fit in with her designs upon North Africa. Britain, on the other hand, was in constant fear that a fresh attack by Mehemet Ali upon the Sultan might bring Russia into motion and so precipitate the collapse of Turkey: and again in 1834 she protested so vigorously against the Pasha's projected expedition across the Hedjaz towards Basra and Bagdad, that he found it wiser to abandon it altogether. In October of that year Palmerston warned Mehemet Ali against a declaration of independence, or any interference with the *status quo*, while at the same time discouraging the Porte from attacking its vassal. Already in December 1838 he had urged the Porte to "revert to its ancient policy" and look for aid to England, "instead of leaning upon a powerful and systematically encroaching neighbour": and in his instructions to our new Ambassador, Lord Ponsonby, he explained his desire "to preserve Turkish integrity and independence", to encourage financial reform and—here there showed a cloven hoof—to supply muskets for the Turkish army.[1]

In 1835 Colonel Chesney, by a special concession from the Porte, was allowed to transport two small steamboats in sections from the Orontes to the Euphrates, one of which was navigated successfully as far as the Persian Gulf. Nesselrode jealously protested against this concession, and nothing came of this ambitious project for an overland route to India. A year later Palmerston sent Colonel Considine and other British officers to study the Turkish army and promote military reforms, but this mission was undermined by intrigue and evasion, and at last in November 1837 the Porte decided to entrust the task to Prussian officers, notably Hellmuth von Moltke, who thus first made his reputation in Eastern lands.

With every year the importance of Suez and the Red Sea became more obvious: at first the monsoon was regarded as a fatal obstacle to steamships, but this soon proved to be a false alarm, and opinion concentrated on the difficulties of transhipment and the advantages of a canal. Britain's interest in the new route to India sharpened her eye for strategic points, and an outrage committed on a British crew near Aden led to the occupation of that outpost in January 1839.

The treaty concluded at Kutahiya in 1833 was in reality a mere truce. Sultan Mahmud's hatred of his victorious vassal knew no bounds, and his whole mind was dominated by the thought of future revenge, while Mehemet Ali spent on armaments most of the surplus income derived from his experiments in cotton. The fall of the latter's old enemy, Chosrev Pasha, in 1836 led to a certain *détente*, and in the following year the Porte was ready, in return for the surrender of Adana and the interior of Syria, to make

Egypt and the rest of Syria hereditary in the Pasha's family. But Mehemet Ali was then bent upon full independence and something very like an Arab Empire, bounded by the Taurus, the Euphrates and the Indian Ocean: in 1835 he sounded Marshal Marmont during a visit to Egypt, and in May 1838 told the Consuls very frankly that he meant to shake off the Sultan's rule and declare his independence, though British dissuasion held him back for the moment. Relations between Constantinople and Alexandria grew steadily worse: both sides began to arm. A Druse revolt in the Lebanon was encouraged by the Turks, and its suppression by Ibrahim increased the tension.

At this stage Palmerston proposed a Conference in London to discuss the Turco-Egyptian question, which he rightly foresaw was leading towards war. Russia, however, strongly demurred, not merely because she was not yet ready to share with other Powers the rights conferred on her at Unkiar Skelessi, but above all because she felt that her use of those rights would unite the Western Powers against her, whereas her main desire was to drive a wedge between London and Paris. Metternich at once endorsed the Russian view and condemned Palmerston's "disastrous idea".² But the British Cabinet was prepared "to give naval aid to the Sultan against Mehemet Ali" in case of need, and to send a fleet to Alexandria as an earnest of their intention.³

There were no half-tones in Palmerston's estimate of the Pasha. "For my own part", he wrote to Granville, "I hate Mehemet Ali, whom I consider as nothing but an ignorant barbarian, who by cunning and boldness and mother-wit has been successful in rebellion;...I look upon his boasted civilisation of Egypt as the arrantest humbug, and I believe that he is as great a tyrant and oppressor as ever made a people wretched."⁴ This fitted in with his general aims: "The maintenance of the Turkish Empire ought to be the basis of our policy....No ideas therefore of fairness towards Mehemet ought to stand in the way of such great and paramount interests."⁵ Nor did Palmerston hesitate to give the Pasha a fair and frank warning, that "if he should unfortunately proceed to execute his announced intentions" (of independence), "and if hostilities should break out thereupon between Sultan and Pasha, the Pasha must expect to find Great Britain taking part with the Sultan, in order to obtain redress for so flagrant a wrong done to the Sultan, and for the purpose of preventing the dismemberment of the Turkish Empire", and that Mehemet Ali would "fatally deceive himself" if he were to reckon upon "any jealousies among the Powers".⁶ The sense of this despatch was communicated to the Turks.

This attitude greatly facilitated the new Anglo-Turkish commercial treaty negotiated by Ponsonby and Bulwer in the summer of 1838. Its chief feature, the pledge to abolish all monopolies in the Turkish Empire, was directly aimed at Mehemet Ali: two birds were to be killed with one stone, Mehemet Ali's revenues and his powers of resistance to the suzerain being simultaneously diminished, and a chief obstacle to British trade in the Levant being removed.*

Sultan Mahmud, towards the close of his life, was fanatically bent upon war, and he was, if possible, encouraged still further by Lord Ponsonby, who displayed equal antipathy towards Mehemet Ali and towards the Tsar, only too often exceeded or neglected his official instructions,[7] used wild and unguarded language† and assumed war to be inevitable. It is a striking fact that in January 1839 the Tsar tried to induce Metternich, as more in favour with London, to work for Ponsonby's recall, on the ground that he was "a danger to the peace of Europe".[8] Metternich himself was on good terms with Ponsonby and was glad to see him some years later as Ambassador in Vienna, but at this time he declined to take Ponsonby's "bellicose forecasts" seriously.‡

PALMERSTON'S VIEWS ON TURKEY

Palmerston himself from the first took up a straight and logical position, whatever may be thought of its assumptions. "My opinion", he told Granville,[9] "is and has long been made up: it is that we ought to support the Sultan heartily and vigorously—with France, if France will act with us; without her, if she should decline." He already hoped that Unkiar Skelessi might be terminated, by "merging it in some more general compact of the same nature", in other words a joint guarantee of Turkey by the Powers. Meanwhile he had convinced himself of Turkey's reformability. "When people say that Turkey is rapidly falling to decay, one always replies, 'It will last our time, if we try to prop it up and not to pull it down'."[10] Not content with challenging the view that Turkey's decay was "inevitable and progressive", he told Bulwer, "I much question that there is any process of decay going on in the Turkish Empire."[11] And a year later he wrote to the same correspondent in even more categorical terms: "As to the Turkish

---

* Palmerston wrote to Bulwer, 13 September 1838: "the abolition of monopolies will increase in the end the resources of Egypt, as well as of Turkey, though it may for the moment paralyse Mehemet Ali's scheme of finance" (Bulwer, op. cit. II, 285).

† Königsmarck reported him to Frederick William III as talking wildly of the destruction of Odessa and Sebastopol by the British fleet—cit. Hasenclever, Die orientalische Frage in den Jahren 1839–41, p. 18. Cf. Thureau-Dangin, Histoire de la Monarchie de Juillet, IV, 8, who quotes from Sainte-Aulaire's memoirs a phrase used by Ponsonby to Bois-le-Comte in 1834.

‡ Sainte-Aulaire to Barante, 20 November 1838—Barante, Souvenirs, VI, 157. Cf. Metternich to Sainte-Aulaire, 21 May 1839, on Palmerston's "tolérance pour les errements les plus extravagants" of Ponsonby (Metternich, Nachg. Papiere, VI, 345).

Empire, if we can procure for it ten years of peace under the joint protection of the five Powers, and if those years are profitably employed in reorganising the internal system of the Empire, there is no reason whatever why it should not become again a respectable Power....All we hear about the decay of Turkey and its being a dead body or a sapless trunk...is pure and un-adulterated nonsense."[12] Here we see Palmerston already possessed by that *idée fixe* which was never to leave him, which was one of the main contributory causes of the Crimean War—the most unnecessary war waged by Britain during the past century—which was taken over twenty years later by Disraeli and the Conservative party and became mainly responsible for the disastrous Eastern crisis of the 'seventies, and which was not fully discarded until Lord Salisbury publicly admitted that in the Crimea "we had put our money on the wrong horse", and not fully atoned for until the Great War.

Early in 1839 Mahmud reappointed as Grand Vizier the veteran Chosrev Pasha, whom thirty-five years earlier Mehemet Ali had ejected from the viceroyalty of Egypt and who had been sent in 1833 to negotiate terms with the victorious Ibrahim—in other words, an irreconcilable opponent of the Egyptian Pasha, and in the words of Henry Bulwer, then at the Constantinople Embassy, "a shrewd, bold, illiterate barbarian,...ready to have every man in the Empire drowned, shot, poisoned or decapitated, if it was necessary to carry out the views of himself or his master".[13] The prevailing mentality at the Porte was revealed by Nuri Effendi's remark to Lord Ponsonby, that "no treaty would be of any use to the interests of the Porte, which had not for its object the destruction of Mehemet Ali".[14] The initiative was undoubtedly taken by the Sultan, who allowed Hafiz Pasha and his Prussian officers[15] to cross the Euphrates on 21 April. In May he told Ponsonby that he would sooner die or be the vassal of Russia than renounce the subjection of a rebellious vassal:[16] and indeed it was clear from the first that concessions from Mehemet Ali would merely have whetted the appetite of Mahmud, who was bent on recovering complete control not only of Syria but of Egypt also. It may indeed be said of Mahmud that he was a bloodthirsty tyrant, with passing gleams of enlightenment, feeling amid the ravages of delirium tremens the need for haste if death was not to snatch from him his revenge. Meanwhile Colonel Campbell, the British Agent in Alexandria, rightly acquitted Mehemet Ali of any intention of making the first move, but saw that only force would induce him to recall Ibrahim or evacuate Syria. He reported home the Pasha's talk of co-operation with England in the task of freeing Turkey and Persia from the Russian yoke, and was himself inclined to wonder whether an Arab Caliphate under Mehemet Ali would not be a more effective barrier against Russia than the decaying

Turkey ever could be.[17] Campbell enjoyed great personal influenc[e with] the Pasha and was sure that he could restrain him: but the violent Por[te] persuaded Palmerston to recall Campbell, and in December 1839 his [place] was taken by Colonel Hodges, whose Russophobe mission in Belgrade had just failed, and who "proved to be hot-tempered, blustering and quarrel-some".[18]

Meanwhile, there can be no doubt that Ponsonby definitely encouraged the warlike tendencies of the Turks: yet his own personal prejudices had brought him to the belief that the Russians and Prussians were inciting the Sultan to war, though he admitted that his Russian colleague Butenyev was peaceably disposed.* In reality the Tsar was in no warlike mood, and embarrassed by home finances: indeed the assurances which he bade Nessel-rode give to Clanricarde in respect of a Persian attack upon Herat—to the effect that Russia did not harbour designs upon India—had been accepted in December 1838 by Palmerston as entirely satisfactory.[19] At this time the main antipathies of Nicholas were concentrated upon France, as the em-bodiment of revolutionary and subversive principles,† and he still looked upon Turkey with the interested benevolence of one who hopes for an inheritance in the course of nature rather than one who seeks to wrest it prematurely from its present holder.

In France, meanwhile, Louis Philippe and his chief minister, Marshal Soult, were equally averse to war, and eager for an understanding with England, since without it they foresaw their abandonment by Metternich and France's isolation in the face of a hostile Russia. On the other hand, the mass of French public opinion was consistently, even ardently, sympathetic to Mehemet Ali, alike from memories of the Napoleonic era and as a prop for French Mediterranean ambitions. Meanwhile Palmerston saw clearly that as between Mahmud and Mehemet the question at stake was the very vital one of prestige in the Islamic world and the possession of the Holy Cities, and that the fate of Egypt and of Constantinople closely affected British commerce and our connections with India. To the Pasha he sent through Campbell the warning that Britain would not tolerate an Egyptian military and naval Power on the Persian Gulf, while Ponsonby was in-

* Ponsonby to Palmerston, 19 March and 6 April—cit. Guichen, op. cit. p. 38. Metter-nich on 14 July wrote of Ponsonby, that he was "un visionnaire whose fixed idea was the Tsar's design for the conquest of Constantinople" and who "considère depuis longtemps la guerre comme le meilleur moyen d'empêcher la réalisation de ce plan" (Nachg. Papiere, VI, 345).

† In April 1839 Ficquelmont wrote thus to Metternich: "Une guerre telle que l'Em-pereur Nicholas rêve, celle qui plaît à son courage et excite le plus vivement ses passions, c'est une guerre de principes contre la France. Or, cette guerre est impossible, tant que l'alliance de la France et de l'Angleterre subsiste: il faut donc les séparer et attirer à soi l'Angleterre. Tel est le but instinctif non moins que le calcul raisonné de l'Empereur dans sa conduite avec l'Angleterre" (Guichen, op. cit. p. 52).

structed to warn the Porte of the danger which might ensue if the Egyptians reached so far. His main idea at this early stage of the crisis was that the Syrian desert must be made a sort of barrier between the two rivals, as the only sure guarantee of peace.[20] Moreover, he feared that if Mehemet Ali once secured control of Bagdad and Diarbekr, he would inevitably ally with Russia: Turkey would then be doomed, Russia would then lie across all routes to the East, and a conflict with her would logically follow. In his view, then, it was better to risk war with the Pasha to-day than with the Tsar to-morrow. Campbell was therefore instructed to warn the Pasha that Britain "could not see with indifference" any movement on his part towards Bagdad or the Gulf.[21]

The events of the summer created an entirely new and complex situation. On 24 June Hafiz was utterly routed by Ibrahim at the battle of Nezib, and Egyptian rule was unchallenged south of the Taurus. Sultan Mahmud did not live to hear the disastrous news, but died on 30 June and was succeeded by his son Abdul Medjid, a mediocre and neurasthenic youth of sixteen, in the hands of Chosrev and the Russophil party at the Porte. Barely a week later the Kapitan Pasha Ahmed—partly for personal motives, and partly in the belief that a surrender to Russia was contemplated—went over to Mehemet Ali with the entire Turkish fleet, acting in this with the collusion of the French Admiral Lalande, who, it is true, afterwards received a severe reproof from his Government. Mehemet Ali made fulsome professions of loyalty to the Sultan, but declined to surrender the fleet unless Chosrev were dismissed from office and his own hereditary rule in both Egypt and Syria recognised.

INTERVENTION

Turkey was thus struck by paralysis, and but for the intervention of the Powers would have been even more at the mercy of Mehemet Ali than in 1833. The idea of a Conference at Vienna to settle the dispute had already been accepted by all the Powers, but to Metternich's intense disgust was rejected by the Tsar, in favour of a direct agreement between the two rivals. "Spain and Portugal", he told Ficquelmont, "are France's and England's concern, Italy is Austria's, Germany Austria's and Prussia's, *but Turkey is my affair.*" Nesselrode shortly before had urged Britain to warn the Pasha that so long as he merely repelled Turkish aggression and did not carry war beyond the boundaries of the Kutahiya agreement, no action would be taken against him, but that if he pressed on into the centre of Asia Minor Britain would regard this as action against herself. Palmerston greeted this proposal with suspicion and told Granville that "the interests of France, Austria and

England are so identical, so diametrically opposed to those of Russia", that they were bound to act in common.[22] But he treated the agreement of Kutahiyah as non-existent, on the ground that the parties were "a sovereign and a rebel" and that "no treaty can be made between such parties".[23]

As yet he retained his belief in the Franco-British alliance—despite all efforts to smash it, he told Granville:[24] and even a month later he wrote, "Soult is a jewel: nothing can be more satisfactory than his course with regard to us, and the union of England and France upon these Turkish affairs will embolden Metternich and save Europe".[25] Soult on his side told his representative in London, Baron Bourqueney, that he favoured "an intimate and sustained concert", and that there was "more reason than ever for our strict unanimity".[26]

For a brief moment the initiative lay with Metternich, and a collective Note was addressed to the Porte by the representatives of the five Powers, led by the Austrian Internuncio Stürmer, assuring it of their unanimity on the Eastern Question and requesting it "to suspend any definitive resolution without their concurrence". At first this step seemed reassuring to the Porte, but it soon became apparent that most of the ministers were not acting on instructions—indeed, the Russian, Butenyev, acted against his instructions, to the annoyance of Nesselrode—and had no clear programme. While Britain, Austria and Prussia favoured the restoration of Syria to the Porte, France and Russia opposed this: but when Ponsonby and Roussin announced their intention to summon the British and French fleets to the Golden Horn as soon as the Sultan was in danger, Butenyev flatly declared that he would leave Constantinople if any foreign ship entered the Dardanelles. The collective Note brought to a head the real divergence of views between Britain and France, which became more marked from day to day. Palmerston was thoroughly roused by the fact that Mehemet Ali had accepted the Turkish fleet only a few days after his promise to Colonel Campbell not to accept it if offered.[27] He now talked of a blockade of Alexandria and urged on Paris joint naval action against the Pasha: "means of pressure, gradually increasing in their stringency", was the formula sent to Admiral Stopford.[28] But Soult was not ready for such drastic action, or indeed for any real coercion: the most that he could be induced to do was to inform Mehemet Ali that France would not tolerate the overthrow of the Sultan or the dismemberment of Turkey.[29] To "make Mehemet withdraw into his original shell of Egypt", as Palmerston demanded,[30] would have been intolerable to French public opinion, with its exaggerated ideas of Egyptian power. Yet there were French diplomats who saw farther afield. The wise Barante warned Soult that the Tsar was bent on setting France and Britain by the ears, while even Sainte-Aulaire in Vienna wrote of Mehemet

Ali as "France's evil genius", who would ruin her relations with all her allies.[31] On 9 August Palmerston argued to Bourqueney that to grant to Mehemet Ali hereditary rule in Syria, led necessarily to independence, and so to the collapse of Turkey:[32] whereas Soult only a few days earlier took the line that "in ruining the Pasha of Egypt we shall bring about the destruction of the Ottoman Empire".[33] The disagreement was complete: and Palmerston told Metternich, "We can't agree with France, because she wants the contrary of what we must aim at."[34] The cause of Mehemet Ali was becoming identified with that of France.

THE BRUNNOV MISSION

Palmerston was not merely ready for action, but eager to force the pace: it was something to win over Metternich to his views, but an ally was indispensable, and Austria was not enough as an ally. More and more he found it necessary to choose between France and Russia: and this provided Tsar Nicholas with the very opportunity for which he had been waiting. In September Baron Brunnov, one of the astutest of Russian diplomatists, sometimes known as "the Russian Gentz",[35] arrived in London, bearing special proposals from the Tsar, of whom rumour described him as "la pensée intime".[36] It was suggested that the Western Powers should renounce any general guarantee of Turkey and not send ships to the Sea of Marmora, while Russia would not only work loyally with them to solve the Turco-Egyptian quarrel, but would undertake not to renew Unkiar Skelessi and to defend Constantinople in the name of Europe. The closing of the Straits would then be proclaimed as part of the public law of Europe. Finally—and this was the thin end of the wedge—he was ready to pursue these lines without waiting for France.

Palmerston did not accept the Russian overture outright: he had to reckon with certain Francophil elements in the British Cabinet and also with press suspicions of Russia. But Brunnov was able to take back to St Petersburg counter-proposals that formed a hopeful basis of negotiations. He insisted that if Russian ships entered the Bosphorus, French and British ships must be free to pass the Dardanelles, but he accepted the principle of closing the Straits and proposed a general guarantee of the Turkish Empire and its dynasty, and joint action to end the crisis, merely asking that in the event of Mehemet Ali resisting, Russian troops should not be used beyond the Taurus. The Tsar would naturally have preferred a complete acceptance of his own ideas, but he realised that Palmerston was moving towards him by great strides and watched with satisfaction the Foreign Secretary's rising irritation against Paris and the French press attacks upon "perfide Albion", while at the same time he increased his ascendancy over Metternich, with the help of the Russophil Ficquelmont. To Lord Clanricarde he openly abused the Orleans dynasty and declared that Mehemet Ali had the backing of France, simply because he was a rebel subject.[37] In the eyes of Palmerston the Russian readiness to renounce Unkiar Skelessi outweighed all else. He still had to walk circumspectly, because of his colleagues in the Cabinet, but by October the shadow of a Russo-British combination against France was already faintly visible upon the canvas.

Palmerston sent a very frank message to Soult, giving him "the substance" of his conversations with Brunnov and warning him that Britain would probably "proceed in conjunction with the three Powers, whether France joins or not, but that on every possible account we should deeply regret that France should not be a party".[38] He had however by now reached the conclusion that "the first object of France is the Pasha, not the Sultan".[39] As a maximum he was ready to concede to Mehemet Ali not only Egypt but also the pashalik of Acre—except the fortress, "which is the key of Syria"[40]— though at the back of his mind there was always the hope that Mehemet Ali might lose Egypt also. But he laid down as a condition that France must share in coercion, if the Pasha proved refractory: and this condition Soult definitely declined, adding that if the result was a Russo-British alliance, France "would lament it as the rupture of an alliance to which we attach much value—but would apprehend little from its immediate effects", since so unnatural a combination could not last.[41] On this Palmerston promptly withdrew the British offer with regard to Acre, and began to play his cards quite deliberately for the isolation of France, encouraging the Porte meanwhile to "remain firm, make no concessions to Mehemet Ali and rely on allied support".[42]

His influence may also be traced in the Hatti-Sheriff of Gülhane, the famous charter of reform issued on 3 November by the Sultan and his minister Reshid Pasha, without previous consultation of the Ambassadors. Reshid had spent the summer in London, trying in vain to negotiate an Anglo-Turkish alliance against the Pasha of Egypt, but had genuinely imbibed Western ideas of government and was at the same time fully alive to the tactical advantages of the Sultan out-trumping the Pasha as champion of progress in the Moslem world.[43] By one and the same stroke Turkey secured the sympathies of the Liberal West, which was too naïve or too ill-informed to foresee that reform was destined to remain very largely on paper.

In December Brunnov returned to London, bringing with him, as a special concession to Palmerston, the Tsar's consent to British and French ships entering the Straits in the event of Russian troops being sent through the Bosphorus for the defence of Constantinople, and also giving definite assurances with regard to Russian designs in Central Asia. In fact, Brunnov had virtually *carte blanche* to come to terms, and indeed could hardly risk the negotiations falling through, without a real loss of prestige for his master. Metternich was by now following the Tsar's lead, but sent Baron Neumann to London to maintain a certain friendly control over the activities of Brunnov and the Prussian envoy Bülow. Palmerston, whose recent marriage with the widowed Lady Cowper gave him a new lease of life, was increasingly eager for a settlement: and while Louis Philippe and his ministers remained convinced that Mehemet Ali could not be forced to evacuate Syria, the British Foreign Secretary confidently argued (and quoted military opinion in his support) that "an expedition of 5000 men from Bombay to Suez would suffice to overrun all Egypt, denuded of troops".[44] At the same time he assumed that the French, though they might "talk big, cannot make war for such a cause" as Mehemet Ali.[45] Soult on his side was much alarmed at the Brunnov mission and wrote to Sebastiani, assuming the object of these tactics to be that "they want to smash the Anglo-French alliance, to which Europe owes ten years of peace"[46]: but he did not yield an inch of his ground.

In February 1840 it was decided to recall Sebastiani from the London Embassy, and appoint M. Guizot, who to an established reputation as a political and educational leader added the prestige acquired by his historical studies, his profound interpretation of the great English revolution, his Protestantism and his known Anglophil sentiments. Guizot at once assumed a place of his own in the social life of London, but no effort on his part could avail to close the widening breach. The French Government was by now prepared that their protégé should renounce Crete, Arabia and Adana, but insisted upon hereditary rule in Egypt and Syria as far as the Taurus. This neither Britain nor Russia, the protagonists of the four Powers, would concede, and the latent friction between Paris and St Petersburg flared up again. But as Nesselrode reminded Brunnov, "we only play a secondary part: the quarrel is not between us and France, but between England and France": to which the wily Brunnov replied, "Leave them time to quarrel", but let Russia stand behind England.[47]

ANGLO-FRENCH RELATIONS. THE THIERS CABINET

On 1 March Marshal Soult was replaced as Premier by Adolphe Thiers, who had more than once pronounced publicly in favour of the Anglo-French alliance[48] and who shared the King's reluctance to break with London, but none the less played for time and waited for proposals from the other side.

For many reasons the dispute was allowed to drag on for the first six months of 1840, contributary causes being Brunnov's deliberate tactics,* Metternich's aversion to too cordial relations between London and St Petersburg, Prussia's negative attitude to the Eastern Question, the diversion created by Queen Victoria's wedding, the declining popularity of the Whig Cabinet, the Francophil leanings of many of its members—notably Russell, Clarendon and Holland—and the consequent need for unwonted caution and patience on the part of Palmerston. But undoubtedly the main cause of delay lay in the profound miscalculations of the French Cabinet. Thiers exaggerated the weakness of the Whigs and the deterrent effects of Anglo-American friction or of the Chinese opium war, but still more did he exaggerate Mehemet Ali's powers of resistance and the powerlessness of the four Powers against him. The Pasha himself was resolved not to surrender anything save Arabia, and Colonel Hodges reported that only a fleet before Alexandria would bring him to reason.[49]

Thiers during a debate in the Chamber on 24 March spoke of England as "in matter of principles our natural ally and in the East our necessary ally":[50] and Palmerston as late as 21 February had spoken in the House of Commons of "the union so happily existing" between France and Britain as "essential to the interests of the two nations and the peace of Europe". But it may be doubted whether this expressed his sincere conviction. Late in March he spoke to the Austrian, Baron Neumann, of French designs along the whole North African coast, to eliminate England from the Mediterranean.[51] By the middle of April he was writing to Granville of French "double-dealing" and the untrustworthy character of Louis Philippe,[52] and brushed away the Ambassador's assurances that "the King does not want to quarrel with us", with the slapdash phrase, "I can't enter into motives, I must look to acts. And if a reputed friend will not act as a friend, I must consider he is not one." Already in his first official talk with Guizot he complained of "a less friendly disposition" on the part of France since the fall of Molé, and he made it abundantly clear that England opposed "the foundation of new and independent states which might assume in the Mediterranean a role not easy to foresee", but preferred "to maintain a great state which we know, as a barrier against all ambitions". He stressed Russia's readiness to renounce the Unkiar Skelessi conditions, reaffirmed his belief in Turkish recovery and already talked of sending British and Austrian troops to Syria. Guizot "remained incredulous"[53] on this point, but warned his home Government that their policy of postponement might

---

* On 14 February he wrote home, "the best course for our plans is not to conclude, but to let negotiations drag on: the greater the delay, the more painful will be the relations between France and England" (cit. Hasenclever, p. 122).

in the end drive the British Cabinet into acting without France. To him there were only two alternatives—either to collaborate with England in the question of Constantinople, while obtaining from her concessions in Syria for Mehemet Ali, or to "withdraw from the affair, leave the four Powers to come to terms among themselves and hold aloof, waiting on events", and this latter course he regarded as most dangerous. But Thiers merely rejoined, "If Palmerston is bent on taking action against the Pasha with three continental Courts for lack of four, we can't help it" (*nous n'y pouvons rien*): and he continued to assume that Mehemet Ali could not be coerced and that Palmerston's policy was "one of blindness and ruin".[54] On 1 April Guizot informally sounded Palmerston as to a scheme for granting the heredity of Egypt and Syria, in return for the surrender of Crete, the Holy Places and Adana; and a month later Neumann proposed to Palmerston a compromise on the lines of a partition of Syria, pledging Austria, if Mehemet Ali should reject this, to join Britain in naval measures of coercion. But Thiers, after a month's delay, definitely rejected partition as "a practical compromise"[55] and told Guizot that the Cabinet was "little disposed towards concession", and that he must "postpone explanations".[56]

Two further incidents misled Thiers. Great Britain had become involved in acute conflict with the King of Naples over the Sicilian sulphur mines, the introduction of a royal monopoly having injured trade and violated the commercial treaty of 1816. On the initiative of Guizot, Thiers offered his mediation, and this was gratefully accepted by Palmerston, and less readily by King Ferdinand, and after some two months' dispute was happily solved (7 July). Moreover, Palmerston showed admirable feeling in facilitating the transfer of Napoleon's remains from St Helena to France, where they were interred with all due pomp at the Invalides. But Thiers was quite wrong in thinking that this meant any relaxation of Palmerston's standpoint in the Eastern Question, and indeed his acceptance of French good offices in Sicily was almost certainly due to a desire to release a British squadron for service off the coast of Syria.[57]

Matters had thus dragged on into June, when suddenly the Russophil Grand Vizier Chosrev Pasha was overthrown, largely owing to the influence of the French Ambassador, M. de Pontois, a zealous rival of Lord Ponsonby. Mehemet Ali, who had persistently disregarded the advice of all the Consuls —including even the French, M. Cochelet, who told him, on orders from Thiers, that "France will not sacrifice its alliance with England to the interests of the Pasha"[58]—was overjoyed at the news and at once decided to send Sami Bey to the Sultan, to offer back the fleet and to pull wires among the faction of the Sultan's mother. News of this step reached Paris on 30 June and was welcomed by Thiers, both as likely to promote direct understanding between Constantinople and Alexandria, and as "a powerful argument against any immediate decision" in the West.* But the news had exactly the opposite effect in London, where it was assumed that Mehemet Ali's success would mean the triumph of France both in Egypt and at the Porte. Palmerston was determined to prevent French intervention, and told Hodges that it would be "the business of the four Powers so to press Mehemet Ali as not to give France such an opportunity".[59] He therefore decided on prompt and energetic action and had a series of meetings with Brunnov, Neumann and Bülow without the knowledge of Guizot. At the same time he overcame the acute disagreement inside the Cabinet by a direct appeal to his easy-going chief, Lord Melbourne. It so happened that Bülow had prepared the way by urging the hesitating Prime Minister to vigorous action: on Melbourne's assurance that Britain had adequate naval forces in the Mediterranean, he advised the despatch of a fleet to Alexandria and troops to Beirut, and the conclusion of a treaty between the four Powers and Turkey. But above all "be quick and bold", before the Pasha or France could be ready.[60] On the very top of this came Palmerston's letter, with the blunt complaint that some of his own colleagues had hinted to "various ministers with whom he was negotiating", that he was "not the organ of the sentiments of the Government". Yet his policy, he said, rested on the expediency of maintaining Turkish independence and integrity. Having failed to secure the co-operation of France, he felt it to be of the utmost importance "for the interests of England, the preservation of the balance of power and the maintenance of peace in Europe", that the other four Powers should go on alone. To draw back now would be to place Britain "in leading strings" to France, and then Russia would again act alone and renew the Treaty of Unkiar Skelessi "under some still more objectionable form". The result would be "the practical division of Turkey into two separate states—one the dependency of France, and the other a satellite of Russia, in both of which our political influence will be annulled and our commercial interests sacrificed". His policy, he reminded the Prime Minister, had "twice been overruled by the Cabinet, first in 1833, when the Sultan appealed for British aid, and again in 1835 when France was ready to undertake a joint guarantee of Turkey. Rather than this should happen again, he declared himself ready to resign—a step which, he very well knew, would have brought down the Whig Government.[61]

Faced by so uncompromising an attitude, Melbourne capitulated. In his effort "to conciliate all parties in his rickety Government"† he could not

---

* Guizot, v, p. 208. Yet as late as 19 June Thiers had written to Guizot, "The Pasha's head is inflated and we are sure of nothing with him "—*ibid.* p. 204. Cf. Rodkey, *op. cit.* p. 152.

† This is the phrase used by Lord Cowper (the nephew of Lord Melbourne and Lady Palmerston) on p. xi of his preface to *The Melbourne Papers.*

risk the loss of his Foreign Secretary: and the very serious attempt of such influential Whigs as Russell, Holland and Ellice to get Palmerston replaced by Clarendon, failed. Palmerston was left triumphant—in the words of John Morley, "the ruling member of the weak Whig Government", and one who "made sensible men tremble".[62]

A day after the Cabinet's surrender he wrote to Beauvale: "We shall in all probability accomplish this [the coercion of Mehemet Ali] without any great exertion of force, for I am satisfied that the power of Mehemet Ali is a power built upon delusion and fancy, as much as upon injustice, a bubble which will burst as soon as it is strongly pressed.... If we had shrunk from pursuing a course separate from that of France, and if we had truckled to the French Government on this occasion, we should have been considered as a merely secondrate Power in Europe, held in leadingstrings by France, and incapable of any manly or independent course of action."[63] Here we obviously have his tone and innermost sentiments.

THE QUADRUPLE AGREEMENT OF 15 JULY 1840

On 15 July Palmerston, Brunnov, Neumann and Bülow signed a Quadruple Agreement behind the back of Guizot, with the deliberate object of imposing their own terms upon Mehemet Ali and if necessary helping the Sultan to enforce them against him. The Straits were only to be used as a last resort for the defence of Constantinople, and in future were to be closed in time of peace to foreign warships. The Sultan was to offer Mehemet Ali Egypt as an hereditary possession, and southern Syria, including the pashalik of Acre, for his life: but on condition that he surrendered northern Syria, Adana, Crete and Arabia. Only ten days were allowed for his acceptance of these terms, failing which he was to be deprived of Acre also, and if within a further period of ten days he had still not submitted, the Sultan would be at liberty to withdraw even the offer of hereditary rule in Egypt. To make this drastic decision irrevocable, Admiral Stopford, with his Austrian naval colleague, was instructed to act without waiting for ratification. One reason for this haste was undoubtedly the news of an insurrection in Syria against Ibrahim's rule.

Two days later Palmerston, in notifying the Convention to Guizot, expressed profound if insincere regret that all efforts to secure French cooperation had failed, and that the French should "maintain conditions which the four Powers regard as incompatible with the maintenance of Turkish independence and integrity and the future calm of Europe". They had no choice but to act without her, but hoped that her separation from them would be short, and that she would give her "moral support" to pressure upon Mehemet Ali. But these perfunctory professions of regret hardly fit in with Palmerston's outspoken language to Henry Bulwer: for he assumes with obvious satisfaction that Thiers will be "very angry" and "will probably at first swagger", and that "it is a great blow to France", and ends by saying that if French naval forces "should dare to meddle with ours, it is *war*", and France "would be made to pay dearly for war so brought on".[64] "We none of us", he wrote next day, superbly oblivious of his own reflection in the mirror, "intend that France shall domineer over the other Powers of Europe, or even over England alone. Of all mistakes, in public affairs as well as in private, the greatest is to truckle to swagger and bully, or even to unjustifiable violence."[65]

French opinion was not unnaturally indignant and excited, and Thiers complained bitterly to Bulwer: "I have been the partisan of the English alliance. Why do you now break it? For a little land more or less for the Pasha of Egypt."[66] To Guizot he treated such conduct "as difficult to explain" on the part of one who professed to be "our faithful ally since 1830".[67] Guizot in his turn reproached Palmerston for his secrecy, as an unfriendly act. "The alliance of France and England has given ten years of peace to Europe: the Whig Ministry was born under its flag and drew from it some of its strength": and now "a grave blow" had been dealt to the alliance. Thiers told Granville on his return to Paris that the whole French nation felt the affront, and Louis Philippe shared this nervousness. Meanwhile Brunnov reported home that Palmerston would never forgive Thiers and Guizot for rousing his own colleagues against him, while they would never forgive Palmerston for covering them with ridicule: and this appears to have encouraged the Tsar to assure Palmerston that in the event of a Franco-British War he would regard himself as also at war with France.[68] The liberal elements in the House of Commons were roused by Palmerston's tendency to move from France towards Russia, and on 6 August, in answer to Joseph Hume's criticisms, he found it advisable to deny categorically any idea of abandoning France or embarking on a new Holy Alliance. Meanwhile, he wrote to Bulwer, his confidant in Paris, "However inconsiderate the French nation may be, the French interests growing up every day will make them pause before they begin an unprovoked and aggressive war against the four Powers".[69]

In the House Palmerston denied all share in encouraging the Syrians to rise, but subsequently published correspondence shows quite clearly that Ponsonby had had his agents in the Lebanon since early in the year, and that his dragoman Mr Wood maintained "personal relations with most of the chiefs", especially the Emir Beshir.[70] So successful were these "relations", that he was appointed Vice-Consul at Beirut in September, and in December we find Palmerston himself telling Ponsonby that as the Syrians were induced to take up arms, it was a duty of the British Government to consult their interests in the final settlement.

At this moment feeling in Paris was fanned by the abortive landing of Louis Napoleon at Boulogne, which was widely ascribed—though quite unjustly, as both Guizot and Thiers acknowledged—to British machinations, and again by the omission of any allusion to French friendship in the Queen's speech on the prorogation of Parliament.

King Leopold, who was on a visit to England, worked hard on a scheme of mediation, the main idea being to merge the Convention of the four Powers in a wider Treaty of all the five, for a guarantee of Turkish independence and integrity. But this proved inacceptable to Louis Philippe and Thiers, unless Mehemet Ali were allowed to retain the boundaries laid down at Kutahiya, and unless mediation between Sultan and Pasha were left in French hands—an obviously preposterous demand. Moreover, Mehemet Ali remained intractable as ever, insisting upon all the territory he had occupied by force of arms and dreaming of a Holy War: and he found encouragement in the ominous instructions sent by Thiers to Cochelet on 29 July. The best means, he said, of annulling the convention was "the submission of Syria": the Pasha should be advised to put an army at the foot of the Taurus and to defend both Alexandria and Acre, but not to march upon Constantinople, since this would set the Russians in motion. At home Thiers and the King took advantage of the rising feeling to increase French armaments and above all to extend the hitherto neglected fortifications of Paris. Somewhat illogically, chauvinist opinion turned its eyes towards the eastern frontier and showed a disposition to challenge the boundaries established in 1815: this in its turn kindled patriotic fervour in Germany, of which the songs of Becker and Schneckenburger, on "the free German Rhine" and "Die Wacht am Rhein" were the outward expression. The defenceless plight of the German Federal forces caused real uneasiness both in Vienna and Berlin, military preparations were pushed forward, and the two major German courts drew closer together. The recent death of Frederick William III had placed on the Prussian throne a sovereign who combined a high romanticism alike in politics and religion with strongly Anglophil tendencies and a genuine zeal for European peace.

Not the least curious feature of the whole crisis is the rapidity with which the Rhine danger flared up and then died down again, and again the relative lack of attention devoted to it by British statesmen. It is this which absolves us from pursuing its details in a book devoted to British foreign policy, while emphasising the fact that the crisis left a fresh scar upon Franco-German relations which was to become visible on more than one future occasion.

OPERATIONS IN SYRIA AND THE WALEWSKI MISSION

Palmerston, having decided upon action, did not let the grass grow under his feet. Admiral Stopford was instructed to cut off all communications between Egypt and Syria, and weapons were placed at his disposal for distribution among the Syrian insurgents.[71] Commodore Charles Napier was sent early in August to Beirut, and patrolled the Syrian coast, issuing a proclamation inviting the inhabitants to throw off the Egyptian yoke. Almost at the same time Rifaat Pasha appeared in Alexandria, to demand Mehemet Ali's submission to the terms of the July Convention: yet the Pasha, defying the advice of all the Consuls, replied that what he had acquired by the sword he would only restore at the sword's point.[72] In the second half of August Count Walewski, the future French Premier and a natural son of the great Napoleon, arrived on a special misson from Thiers to Mehemet Ali and warned him that if he refused the latest French proposals—the heredity of Egypt and the possession of Syria for life only, with the possible but not certain retention of Crete and Adana—France would look on until Russia had seized Constantinople and Britain Alexandria. Then indeed she might go to war, but it would be on the Rhine![73] This was very foolish language, but none the less Walewski succeeded in inducing the Pasha, after some violent outbursts, to renounce Crete and Adana at once, and to promise the restoration of the fleet under certain conditions. There is no doubt that so far from encouraging the Pasha in further resistance, as Palmerston wrongly suspected, Walewski aimed above all at solving the crisis by a direct understanding between Sultan and vassal. But when he reached Constantinople and laid Mehemet Ali's proposals before the Porte, he found the ground already cut from under his feet by the violent counsels of Ponsonby and by the Turks' own reading of the European situation. So far from treating his vassal's concessions as serious, the Sultan was induced, on 14 September, to declare his deposition even from the viceroyalty of Egypt, Izzet Pasha being temporarily appointed in his place.

It has been established beyond all doubt that the main responsibility for this decision lay with Ponsonby, and though Palmerston afterwards admitted to Russell that the advice had been given "without instructions", he showed his own leanings by adding, "I am much inclined to think he is right in this".* The weak Melbourne characteristically confessed to no other

* 6 November—Spencer Walpole, *Life of Russell*, I, 360. Cf. also Russell to Melbourne, 8 October, *ibid.* p. 355, and Greville, *Memoirs*, IV, 329 ("There is no doubt that Palmerston and Ponsonby between them will do all they can to embroil matters and to make a transaction impossible"). On 2 October Melbourne reported to the Queen that the deposition of Mehemet Ali had been "by the advice of Lord Ponsonby" (Queen Victoria's *Letters*, I, 232).

than Guizot the fear lest Ponsonby, who was "not afraid of war", might encourage the Sultan in "every sort of violent measure",[74] but he shrank from the logical conclusion of recalling his Ambassador. Indeed, he agreed with Palmerston that Ponsonby's recall "would seem to disavow and retract the whole of our policy, past, present and future, and would cast a damp on the cause of the Sultan from which it would never recover."[75]

DISSENSIONS IN THE WHIG CABINET

At home, while Melbourne himself showed "a melancholy picture of indecision, weakness and pusillanimity",[76] the Francophil section of the Cabinet was roused to action. Lord John Russell, in particular, was resolved "to oppose Palmerston's headlong policy", even at the risk of a rupture inside the Government, and Holland and Clarendon threatened to resign. On 29 September it came to a lively debate inside the Cabinet, and Palmerston made "a violent philippic against France", exhibiting, in the words of Lord Holland, "all the violence of '93".[77] Lord John proposed conciliatory overtures towards France, and to this Palmerston consented, though apparently in the knowledge that nothing would come of the scheme owing to Russian opposition. Russell went so far as to advise the acceptance of Walewski's terms and to make his own resignation the alternative. When he learned that Ponsonby had definitely urged the Sultan to reject them, he condemned this as "highly criminal" and meriting disavowal: and he continued to press for Ponsonby's removal from his post as "the first preliminary to any arrangement".[78] But fate was against him. Melbourne appealed to him not merely in his own name, but in that of the Queen, who was very near her first confinement† and declared that she could not face a political crisis. The success of the Syrian operations greatly strengthened Palmerston's strategic position, and in the end Lord John yielded, though convinced that a violent article in the *Chronicle* had been inspired, or even written, by Palmerston, with the direct object of driving him out of office.[79] On 7 October Greville, then even more behind the scenes than usual, recorded in his journal, "the peace party in the Cabinet is silenced, Palmerston has triumphed and Lord John succumbed....Palmerston alone is resolute, entrenched in a strong position, with unity and determination of purpose" (thus far no one can fail to endorse his verdict), and added the more questionable phrase "quite unscrupulous, very artful and in possession of the Foreign Office".[80]

＊ The Princess Royal was born on 21 November 1840. The Queen wrote on 16 October to her uncle: "I think our child ought to have besides its other names those of *Turco Egypto*, as we think of nothing else" (*Letters*, I, 243).

The death of Lord Holland at this juncture was a blow to the French party in the Cabinet, and Thiers' public expression of regret led *The Times* to draw attention to the leakage of Cabinet secrets, in a way that was notoriously aimed at Holland House. Melbourne himself spoke of "the talking at Holland House" as "irremediable". "They cannot help it."[81]

It is important to dwell upon the coulisses of this struggle, and we are fortunate in possessing the testimony of so impartial and well-informed a critic as King Leopold, who was keenly interested in preventing a breach between London and Paris and had already written to Queen Victoria of Thiers as being "as reckless of consequences as your own Foreign Minister".[82] By September he was complaining that "the form towards France was, and still is, harsh and insulting".[83] He sent on to the British Prime Minister a letter which he had received from his father-in-law Louis Philippe, and this Melbourne frankly admitted to be "in the tone of a man much hurt and very sore, and also much puzzled, perplexed and annoyed with his situation".[84] On 2 October he forwarded another letter of Louis Philippe, alluding to "the rage (*fureur*) against England and the general conviction that Palmerston wants to reduce France to the level of a secondary Power, though the Entente is really the basis of world peace". And Leopold himself added, "I can't understand what has rendered Palmerston so extremely hostile to the King and Government of France. A little civility would have gone a long way. But Palmerston likes to put his foot on their necks".[85] In a letter to Bülow we find him assuming, with an obvious note of doubt in his voice, that "we have to do with Downing Street, and not with Bedlam!"[86]

PALMERSTON'S DUEL WITH THIERS

How little King Leopold exaggerated, may be seen from Palmerston's despatches to Henry Bulwer, who was then Chargé d'Affaires in Paris—Lord Granville having absented himself because the whole situation was so distasteful to him. Thiers had used somewhat menacing language to Bulwer during a private conversation at Auteuil :* and Palmerston, as soon as this was reported to him, told Bulwer that the next time Thiers used "the language of menace, however indistinctly and vaguely shadowed out", he must tell the Premier to his face that "if France throws down the gauntlet, we shall not refuse to pick it up: that if she begins a war, she will to a

---

* 18 September. If Palmerston would join in persuading Sultan and Powers to accept Walewski's scheme, "there is once more a cordial entente between us. If not, France must support Mehemet Ali. Vous comprenez la gravité de ce que je viens de vous dire" (though he at once qualified this by saying that he spoke as M. Thiers, not as French Premier) (Bulwer, *op. cit.* II, 324–5).

certainty lose her ships, colonies and commerce before she sees the end of it: that her army of Algiers will cease to give her anxiety, and that Mehemet Ali will just be chucked into the Nile".[87] It is to be presumed that Bulwer toned down this message in delivery, but it is small wonder that relations between the two countries did not improve, if such was the mentality of our Foreign Secretary. Moreover, Palmerston could never resist the temptation to be polemical, and on 31 August had addressed a long and argumentative Note to Thiers, affirming his desire for peace and French co-operation, but insisting on the re-establishment of Turkish power in Syria and underlining the consistency of Britain and the inconsistency of French policy throughout the crisis.[88] To this Thiers replied on 3 October in the same argumentative vein, claiming to have readily co-operated with Britain in the earlier stages of the dispute and to have always held back Mehemet Ali. He also claimed that the Pasha, having beaten the Turks without himself being the aggressor and having then desisted, deserved more consideration than the allies were showing him; that Crete, Adana and Arabia were a sufficient renunciation for a victor, that the use of force was extremely dangerous, and that the heredity of both Egypt *and* Syria was the proper solution. He reminded the four Powers that no attempt had been made to force back Wallachia, Moldavia, Greece or Serbia under Turkish rule: why then should this attempt be made in Syria or Egypt? It was impossible to argue that Turkish integrity was saved if Egypt and Acre were detached from the Empire, but destroyed if Damascus and Aleppo were also detached: and it was a singular way of saving Turkey, to wrest several provinces from the Pasha and "give them not to the Sultan but to anarchy".

The closing passages of the Note deserve special consideration, as illustrating how Palmerston's brutal tactics were driving a declared Anglophil into a blind alley of hostility to England. The alliance of France and Britain, Thiers argued, was a much surer basis of Turkish integrity than the Treaty of 15 July, but a new alliance had now been concluded without France's knowledge and to promote her isolation. It was being affirmed that the old alliance was not broken: "but when the four have pursued, without us and despite us, an aim bad in itself, or one which we at least believed and declared to be bad; when this aim has been pursued by an alliance all too like those coalitions which for fifty years have drenched Europe in blood, then to expect France to show no distrust or resentment at such a rebuff is to form an idea of her national pride such as she has never offered to the world."

On second thoughts Thiers went still further, and in a letter of 8 October bade Guizot announce that he regarded Mehemet Ali's rule in Egypt as "an essential and necessary part of the Ottoman Empire", and that his ejection would be "a blow to the general balance of power", such as France could not tolerate. He therefore insisted upon a *double guarantee* of Sultan and Pasha alike.[89] This Note has been somewhat unfairly described as a "*casus belli* Note": it did however show that the crisis was developing into a duel between two obstinate and tactless ministers.

Writing in cold blood after a lapse of years, Guizot admitted that French policy had attached an exaggerated importance to Egypt and yielded unduly to Mehemet Ali's Syrian ambitions, thus playing into the hands of the Tsar in his desire to isolate France. But he was fully justified in writing at the height of the crisis,[90] that "the real insult is the slight account which England has taken of the French alliance", which "she has risked and sacrificed for a very secondary interest, namely the immediate forfeiture of Syria by the Pasha". Here in a nutshell is the main indictment against Palmerston during the Eastern crisis—his utter indifference to the susceptibilities of other nations, even of his French allies. On the other hand Broglie's answer to Guizot shows very clearly the extent to which the French Cabinet on its side was bluffing and risking universal war for reasons of prestige. "Will Mehemet Ali yield everything?" the Duke asks. "M. Thiers is not afraid of this. Will he be able to hold the Syrian coast? That is our strong card— that on which we have staked our money in the lottery."[91] Yet, as Guizot pointed out, "the treatment of France is a reason for coldness, for isolation, for an entirely independent policy, but it is not a case for war".

After the news from Syria and the exchange of Notes the situation in Paris was undoubtedly grave, and a fresh attempt on the life of Louis Philippe increased the excitement. Even the calmest observers talked of a revolutionary atmosphere, such as they had noticed in 1831: the Duke of Orleans* and his brothers used warlike language, even the King spoke of "unmuzzling the tiger", and the Thiers Cabinet was obviously drifting towards war.

PALMERSTON'S INTRANSIGEANCE

Yet Palmerston remained at once unconciliatory and confident, and wrote wildly to Bulwer of "the menaces of France" and "a succession of aggressions and insults" against the four Powers.[92] He was so elated by the news of the first bombardment of Beirut, that he bade Granville "try to persuade the King and Thiers that they have lost the game and that it would be unwise now to make a brawl about it".[93] He also instructed Granville to warn the King "in the most friendly but earnest manner" against either an "Anconade"† or a public declaration of "what France will or will not permit", as likely to

---

* He would rather be killed in action on the Rhine than be shot in a street fight (Hall, *op. cit.* p. 294).

† A reference to the French expedition to Ancona in 1831.

produce either war or unfriendly relations.[94] And that he seriously reckoned with the possibility of war, is shown by his warning to Lord Granville, that "in the event of your coming away, you should bring all your archives away with you".[95] Yet a few days later he submitted letters to the Queen, to show that there was "never any real foundation for the alarm of war with France".[96] It is but fair to add that the Queen was not deceived, and used all her efforts, directly and also indirectly through Brussels, to soothe French irritation, showing herself specially gracious to Guizot and insisting that Palmerston should give a conciliatory turn to his messages.[97] Her anxiety was not diminished by the knowledge that, in the words of the Prime Minister himself, the two groups in the Cabinet "proceed upon principles, opinions and expectations which are entirely different from one another, and which therefore necessarily lead to a different course of action".[98] Melbourne's correspondence with Russell shows indeed that he had to choose between risking war with France or breaking up the Government, and had long felt that "the avoiding of war, if it can be done with honour and safety, would be well bought by a change of Government".[99]

Much of the credit for averting a rupture lies with the three Courts of Windsor, the Tuileries and Brussels. King Leopold wrote with growing asperity of "Palmerston rex and autocrat" and added a whole shower of adjectives—"irritable, violent, childish, malicious, excessively nonchalant, absolutely baseless, totally valueless".[100] Queen Victoria continued to argue with Palmerston and Melbourne against "driving France to extremities"[101] and to cultivate friendly personal relations with Louis Philippe, while he on his part set his face against the war mania, and knowing that he had the backing of the commercial classes and realising the blunder of counting on the Pasha's resistance and on the four Powers' fear of action, decided to part with the Thiers Cabinet before the meeting of the Chambers. "Unless they put a knife to my throat", he told Lord Granville, "I'll do all I can to avoid war."[102] A new Government was formed on 29 October by Marshal Soult, with Guizot at the Foreign Office, and secured a majority in Parliament for a more moderate policy. Thiers, as leader of the Opposition, put forward the criticism that "under the new Cabinet peace is certain", but Guizot neatly countered, that this was only half the truth, for under the old Cabinet *war* was certain.[103] The ceremonies surrounding Napoleon's reinterment at the Invalides served as a welcome diversion for French sentiment.

NAPIER AT ACRE AND ALEXANDRIA

Meanwhile events continued to move in the Near East. On 2 November the combined British, Austrian and Turkish forces appeared off Acre, and within two days Ibrahim himself had been defeated in the open field and the fortress so often regarded as impregnable had been forced to surrender. The hero of the hour, Commodore Napier, was then sent by his superior officer Admiral Stopford, with the Ambassador's approval, to demonstrate off Alexandria. Napier was a man after Palmerston's own heart,* and characteristically wrote off to the Foreign Secretary, suggesting that Mehemet Ali should be allowed to retain Egypt, in return for surrendering Syria and the Turkish fleet. "Try me as negotiator, with six sail-of-the-line.... I believe Egypt would be just as well governed by him as by one of the Turkish Pashas: he is an old man, and it is hardly worth while risking a European war to turn him out."[104] On reaching his destination, he was shown a despatch of Palmerston to Ponsonby, advising the Sultan to reinstate Mehemet Ali as hereditary Pasha of Egypt, in return for public submission, the surrender of the fleet and the evacuation of Syria, Crete and Arabia. Inspired by this, the impulsive Napier plunged into direct negotiations with Mehemet Ali, without a shadow of authority from anyone, but justifying himself on the ground that the situation in Syria was far more critical than might appear, and that Ibrahim might still rally his forces. After two days of negotiation the Pasha signed a convention following the lines of Palmerston's despatch, and Napier, in notifying it to the First Lord in London, Lord Minto, wrote with a magnificent simplicity, "I do not know whether I have done right in settling the Eastern Question", and at the same time told his wife, "I shall either be hung by the Government or made a bishop!"[105] Napier doubtless had before him the precedent of Sidney Smith's convention for the French evacuation of Egypt in 1801. He was at once repudiated and rebuked by Admiral Stopford, who sent Captain Fanshawe to Egypt to negotiate all over again with Mehemet Ali, and by Lord Ponsonby, who actually discussed the idea of burning the Turkish fleet in the harbour of Alexandria, in order to deprive the Pasha of his last trump of restoring it![106] The Porte, grown arrogant with its allies' success, was furious and clamoured for abject submission. But it now suited Palmerston to uphold the rash sailor, and to relieve Sir Charles Smith of his Syrian command, on grounds of "health": and both Austria and Prussia endorsed his view, Metternich instructing Stürmer to demand from Reshid the hereditary investiture of the Egyptian Pasha.

* "...like all his race", writes Prof. Temperley (*The Crimea*, p. 119), "distinguished for quarrelsomeness, for reckless daring and for vanity".

As late as 3 October Palmerston had expressed the wish that "Mehemet Ali could be got rid of altogether", but regarded this as "very improbable".[107] To him the Pasha was a tyrant, and "the people of Syria heart and soul for the Sultan". But the essential fact was that "he is a beaten man, and his political and physical existence are both at their last gasp",[108] so prompt submission will "save us the trouble of going through the whole process of forcible ejectment".[109] Palmerston indeed already regarded Mehemet Ali as something of a pricked bubble, and as his personal triumph seemed complete, he could afford to be generous. He had settled the Syrian question by force, while France had looked on inactive—a contrast well calculated to impress the Oriental mind. A certain lull in the crisis ensued, while the Turks fulminated against Mehemet Ali and Ponsonby encouraged their unreason.

On 11 January Mehemet Ali sent back the Turkish fleet, and still they remained unyielding. At last on 28 January Palmerston flatly declined to help them towards the expulsion of the Pasha, and next day the four Allies recommended the Porte to grant the heredity of Egypt. This was decisive, and on 13 February, three days after the Note reached Constantinople, the Sultan consented to issue the necessary firman. Yet even now the obstinacy of the Porte caused infinite delays: for the firman, when it reached Alexandria, was found to reserve the Sultan's right to select Mehemet Ali's successor inside the family, to nominate all the higher officers of the Egyptian army and to receive one-quarter of the Egyptian revenues as tribute. Guizot was almost certainly right in ascribing to Ponsonby much of the blame for this blocking attitude: indeed Palmerston, with the Queen's full approval, sent him (Ponsonby) a reprimand, to which he "truculently answered, 'I think I acted right'".[110] A change came with the fall of Reshid Pasha on 30 March, very largely at the instance of Metternich, and this was a serious blow to Ponsonby's influence: but even then it was not till 1 June that a new firman, dated 22 May, was despatched to Alexandria. In the teeth of Ponsonby's prophecy of rejection, this was accepted by the Pasha, with every pretence of loyalty and gratitude. The Porte thus recovered the territory lost at Kutahiya, and also the Holy Places, while Mehemet Ali was bound to send his whole army to the help of the Sultan in case of need. In reality, however, though he lost his dream of empire, he made his position in Egypt unassailable, save for the merest paper control: his army and administration became, what they already were to all intents and purposes, independent, and he was free to expand southwards if he chose.

PALMERSTON AND GUIZOT

The real danger of a further conflict in the Near East had been at an end since the Napier convention, though the Porte now developed the same dilatory and captious tactics as in the final stages of Greek independence. The French, much as they might resent the collapse of their *protégé*, could not be more Papal than the Pope, and withdrew into a sullen, watching attitude. Thus the main problem of 1841 was to build a golden bridge across which they might, without undue loss of dignity and prestige, resume their due place in the counsels of Europe. That this took so long, was unquestionably due to the utter intransigeance of Palmerston. As Henry Reeve wrote to his mother, "Lord Palmerston has now bowled everybody out, and the consequence is that the earth can scarcely *contain him*....Wolsey himself was not more formidable".[111] Even in the press voices of criticism were raised, *The Times* complaining of his "wilful opposition to every species of concession".

The substitution of Guizot for Thiers might have been accepted as in itself an earnest of better things, and many people, including our Ambassador in Paris, felt that concessions might be made to ease the admittedly difficult position of the new Premier, who had not merely taken a very moderate line, but had warned Thiers long beforehand. But Palmerston argued that "nothing is more unsound than the notion that anything is to be gained by trying to conciliate those who are trying to intimidate us....If we were to give way, the French nation would believe that we gave way to their menaces, and not to the entreaties of Louis Philippe....My opinion is that we shall not have war now with France, but that we ought to make our minds up to have it at any time....I do not blame the French for disliking us. Their vanity prompts them to be the first nation in the world: and yet at every turn they find that we are their equals. It is a misfortune to Europe that the national character of a great and powerful people, placed in the centre of Europe, should be such as it is: but it is the business of other nations not to shut their eyes to the truth and to shape their conduct by prudent precautions."[112] When Granville reported the wish of Paris "that the final settlement of the Eastern Question shall not appear to have been concluded without their concurrence", Palmerston at once replied, "But that is exactly what I now wish *should* appear."[113] "At an earlier date we had desired their help, but now they would come as protector of Mehemet Ali, not as friend of the Sultan." "France", he insisted, "acted from much deeper and more rational motives than vanity and *amour-propre*", and had had a systematic plan of aggrandisement in the Levant for fifty years past. But the essence of Palmerston's calculation was that a France in isolation could not risk war with the four other Great Powers, and that Louis Philippe was in any case "not a man to run amuck".[114]

The numerous extracts from Palmerston's correspondence sufficiently illustrate the habitual recklessness of his language. But special emphasis deserves to be placed on an answer sent to the Prime Minister on 25 October 1840, in which he treats a letter of King Leopold as a proof that French armaments were "a manœuvre..., in fact, a mere trick". It "brushes away at once the whole web of deception about imminent war, by which some people have endeavoured to blind our eyes". Louis Philippe, so he runs on, "gave Thiers permission to bully and swagger and threaten", and himself "played up to Thiers's acting...by hints and innuendoes": then, there is "a well arranged wind-up,...Thiers saves his consistency with the French people, and the King saves his pacific relations with Europe."[115] Surely a Minister who could write thus to his chief in an acute crisis must, despite all his admirable principles, be described as a very real danger to the peace of the world.

THE CONVENTION OF THE STRAITS

During the spring of 1841 Palmerston did nothing to make things easier for Guizot and Louis Philippe. The omission of any reference to France in the Queen's speech was regarded as a further slight, the press was encouraged to dwell upon French armaments and to discuss the idea of a defensive alliance of the four Powers to counter them. In Berlin there was a growing fear that Palmerston actually desired a breach, and Metternich also, who had long chafed at Palmerston's methods,[116] shared this uneasiness. The notorious fact that Russia showed no interest in bringing France and Britain together and had even gone so far as to propose a Russo-British alliance, based on spheres of influence in Asia—a proposal which the Cabinet declined from fear of public opinion[117]—increased the nervousness of Vienna and Berlin and led her representatives in London, behind Palmerston's back, to discuss with their French colleague Bourqueney a way out of the *impasse*. Meanwhile Palmerston played for time, torn between his need for a settlement before the Cabinet tottered to its fall and the need for greater caution imposed by the Chinese war, by the acute friction with America—over the right of search of slaving vessels and the Maine frontier[118] —and by very wide press resentment at the arrogant attitude of the Porte.

On 13 March 1841 the four Powers addressed a Note to the Turkish envoy, declaring the Eastern crisis to be at an end and the adjustment of outstanding details to be an internal matter between the Sultan and his vassal, and on this basis a definite convention was signed two days later. But there were still long delays. Palmerston, as the American danger died down, again began to talk of the complete ejection of Mehemet Ali; Louis Philippe felt his position stronger after the fortification projects had passed through the Senate and was waiting eagerly for the fall of the Whigs, while Ponsonby to the last incited the Turks to resistance and involved himself in a violent feud with Stürmer, the Austrian Internuncio at the Porte. During the renewed negotiations in London early in May Palmerston raised the question of again using force against Mehemet Ali, but was strongly opposed by Bülow: and when he at last entered into discussions with Bourqueney, there followed a long polemic as to what exactly had passed between them. While Guizot refused active co-operation with the four Powers until he had a public assurance that no further steps would be taken against Mehemet Ali, Palmerston obstinately refused any such assurance until Mehemet Ali's submission was an accomplished fact: indeed he held out until Esterházy and Bülow threatened to leave London, and he was ready to go on with Russia alone. It was thus early July before the news of Mehemet Ali's acceptance became known in London.

Meanwhile the Whig Government was in the last stages of decay. Failing to balance the budget, it decided upon a reduction of the corn and sugar duties, in the hope of promoting consumption, and as a result was defeated by 36 votes in the House of Commons (7 May 1841). Clinging, pathetically to office, it was again defeated on Peel's direct motion of no confidence, this time by a single vote. A dissolution could no longer be avoided, and the general election gave the Tories a majority of over 70. The new Parliament assembled in August, and this time the Government, being decisively defeated by 360 to 269, had to make way for a Tory Cabinet.

It was under circumstances such as these that the negotiations passed their final stage. The news of Mehemet Ali's submission removed the last obstacle, and a preliminary protocol was signed by the four Powers, announcing that the objects of their alliance had been fully attained, thus enabling France to abandon her isolation. Three days later, on 13 July 1841, the so-called Convention of the Straits followed. In form it was an agreement between the sovereigns of the five Great Powers and the Sultan, to affirm "their unanimous determination to conform to the ancient rule of the Ottoman Empire, by which the passage of the Straits must always be closed to foreign warships, so long as the Porte is at peace". The Sultan reserved the right to grant a special permit of entry to individual lesser ships of a friendly Power. The emphasis upon ancient custom doubtless had the double motive of flattering the susceptibilities of the Porte and covering up the essential fact that Russia's special privileged position, under the Treaty of

Unkiar Skelessi, had expired and was to be replaced by a collective guarantee of the five Powers in favour of the *status quo*. It marks the temporary entry of Turkey into the Concert of Europe, based upon the miscalculation that she is capable of such liberal reforms as will restore, at any rate in large measure, her former power and prestige. As regards Russia, it marks a continuation of the policy pursued by Tsar Nicholas for the previous decade, of leaving Turkey a breathing space, during which he, in contrast to his Allies, assumed that so far from strengthening herself through reforms, she would slowly succumb to a natural process of inanition and decay. Or if we approach the question from another angle, it may be said that Nicholas sacrificed a forward policy in the Near East in order to divide France and Britain and thus isolate what he persisted in regarding as the most subversive Power in Europe, while at the same time strengthening his prospects of remaining undisturbed when at long last the Turkish fruit was ripe for plucking.

Turkey on her side might seem to be restricted in her sovereignty by the new agreement, but in reality she gained enormously, recovering territories which her own strength could not have obtained and sheltering herself behind an ostensibly united Europe.

It may be thought that undue space has been devoted to this long and complicated struggle. But this has been done deliberately, in the belief that the events of 1839–41 were not merely of capital importance in themselves in their bearing upon Franco-British relations as one of the cardinal points of European development, but also in providing insight into British policy and British mentality in the Early Victorian period, and above all into the methods employed by Palmerston in his great days—methods which were to bring us into repeated collisions in the future and to win for Britain during the middle of the century a great but not altogether enviable reputation.

PALMERSTON'S TRIUMPH

By common consent the chief laurels of the long crisis fell to Palmerston. His calculations were proved to be right: the much vaunted Mehemet Ali was a broken reed, and France, despite her fulminations, was not prepared to risk universal war for the sake of Egypt or Syria. And yet, viewed in the perspective of nearly a century, the balance of his achievement remains doubtful. It is true that he checked the power of Mehemet Ali, frustrated his designs of a big Arab state, prevented Asiatic Turkey from splitting into two halves and made her, more than ever before, an international factor. It is also true that he induced Russia to renounce her exclusive protectorate and substituted the Concert of Europe. But on the other hand he did not thereby arrest the decay of Turkey, and nothing could destroy Russia's place in the hearts of almost all the Christians of the Near East. It has also been cogently argued that while intervention in Belgium and Portugal could be justified by treaty rights, by interests of a very direct kind and by such provocation as the outrages of Miguel, intervention in Syria was in no way based upon treaty obligations and at the very best replaced one inefficient and semi-tyrannous rule by another. Above all, success was dearly purchased by the humiliation of France and the encouragement given to chauvinist currents on both sides of the Channel. He professed throughout to desire French friendship, and even to value it as a pledge of European peace, yet he placed an intolerable strain upon it by methods and a tone such as his knowledge of French character should have warned him against using.

We have more than once quoted Metternich's verdicts on British statesmen, for even when most unfair, they are always instructive. On this occasion he would seem to have come nearer to the truth, when he wrote: "But what does Lord Palmerston then want? He wants to make France feel the power of England, by proving to her that the Egyptian affair will only finish as he may wish, and without France having any right to take a hand. He wants to prove to the two German Powers that he does not need them, that Russia's help suffices for England. He wants to keep Russia in check and drag her in his train by her permanent anxiety of seeing England draw near to France again. Thus the Powers are in his hand instruments to play with: he finds personal satisfaction in it, and England lets him do it because she sees in it a proof of his power."[119] Without endorsing the whole of this, it may be claimed that Palmerston sacrificed a major for a minor interest. Moreover, whatever may be thought of the tortuous aims and doctrinaire arguments of Thiers in the Eastern Question, there can be no doubt that he, no less than Soult, Guizot and Louis Philippe, genuinely desired friendship with England, that Palmerston goaded them into a state of permanent exasperation and distrust, and that *ménagement* instead of affront would have had very different effects.

To the very last Palmerston kept up his feud with the French. As late as 20 July Guizot, after scrupulously avoiding all argument with Palmerston, at last boiled over and requested Bourqueney to lay before him three personal grievances: (1) his despatch of 2 November 1840—written in answer to Thiers, yet inconsiderately delivered unaltered to Guizot on taking office; (2) the refusal of co-operation with France in the dispute between Buenos Aires and Montevideo, and (3) a passage in his electoral speech at Tiverton, contrasting the tactics of the French army towards the Algerian population with those of the British in Afghanistan.* Palmerston's reply was highly unsatisfactory. While regretting Guizot's annoyance and expressing "a great regard and esteem for him", he adhered to his words about the French army and ended with the hope that the French Government might find his successors "as anxious as we have been to maintain the closest possible union between France and England!"[120] This was a risk which all Paris was longing to take, and within a fortnight the French learned with immense relief that the Whigs had fallen and that Lord Aberdeen had succeeded Lord Palmerston as Foreign Secretary.

Palmerston's admirers argue with much force that he was a real peace Minister, because he was not ready for "peace at any price" and always made it abundantly clear how far he was prepared to go: while his critics have concentrated on the retort that his success was dearly bought at the expense of good relations with France, and that it took some years of effort on the part of Aberdeen and Peel, aided by the two Courts and King Leopold, to wipe out the lamentable impression.

It can hardly be denied that Palmerston showed his likes and dislikes to a degree very dangerous in a Foreign Minister. A recent biographer has defended him against the charge of flippancy and jauntiness: but if we substitute the words "nonchalant" and "irritable"—both also contemporary phrases—we shall not be guilty of excessive or unfair criticism, and certainly no one can deny his irritating effect upon most foreigners. Though never in his private outlook upon life a typical Englishman—he was too much of a sceptic, a latitudinarian, a dandy, for that—he none the less contrived in matters of foreign policy to typify to an extraordinary degree the assertiveness and assurance, the self-centred outlook, the incapacity to see with others' eyes, and therefore the lack of *nuances*, the inelasticity, which are such noticeable features of the early Victorian era. It is true, on the other hand, that he showed but few traces of smugness or snobbery—two consuming vices of contemporary England: but in most other ways he may stand for his epoch.

* "The French Army is tarnished by the character of their operations." It is worth quoting the passage in which Guizot introduced his complaint: "J'ai confiance dans sa parole. Sa manière de traiter, quoique un peu étroite et taquine, me convient: elle est nette, prompte, ferme. Je ne crois ni à sa haine pour la France et le roi, ni à ses perfidies." (*Mémoires* VI, 131.)

CHAPTER VI

ABERDEEN AND THE ENTENTE CORDIALE

That inimitable caricaturist, Mr Max Beerbohm, who may be earnestly commended to those foreigners desirous of penetrating the secret of British psychology, once produced a triple caricature of the older generation taking critical note of the younger, in three successive centuries. In the eighteenth an elderly beau, dressed in the height of fashion, inspects his son and finds him to be a less fashionable and more anaemic edition of himself, but on the whole not much changed. In the mid-nineteenth century a stout, self-assertive, self-satisfied City merchant inspects *his* son and finds him to be an exact replica of himself, but twice as stout, twice as prosperous and self-assertive and far more self-satisfied and self-centred, without a single doubt as to the duration of that order of which he fancies himself to be the centre. In the third decade of our own century a middle-aged survivor of the Great War, with nothing to distinguish him from thousands of his contemporaries, surveys a flat and level landscape and sees nothing whatever before him, save dense clouds on the horizon and against them a gigantic note of interrogation! This interpretation seems to me to go very deep. In any case the central figure should be much in our minds when we are considering the later period of Lord Palmerston. Nor is any apology needed for reminding the reader of the growing importance of caricature as an interpretation of British politics, both internal and foreign.

It is important to distinguish clearly between the two phases of Palmerston: and Mr Guedalla is perfectly right in warning us against the all too common habit of regarding him as the aged, rather flippant and blatant "Pam" of *Punch*'s cartoons in the 'fifties and 'sixties. It is certainly the earlier period, from 1830 to 1841, when he is at his best—outspoken, rather reckless, but frank, seeing consequences far ahead, never afraid to make his meaning clear and thus forewarning those who dealt with him. Moreover, if we consider the details of his policy and the results obtained, it is difficult to deny the soundness of his views—whether in Belgium or Spain, in Portugal or Egypt. It is in his methods that he is so open to criticism, and even in his earlier period we already see those tendencies towards bluster and hectoring which become so marked in his later phase, from 1846 to 1851, and still more from 1853 to 1865, and which were to earn him such widespread ill-will and distrust among Continental Governments.

In dealing with the long crisis which closed Palmerston's first and greatest period, it was natural enough to concentrate attention on the Foreign Secretary himself and on his chief, Lord Melbourne. But it is essential to turn without further delay to that other factor which had already begun to play a decisive part in the political situation, and not least of all in foreign policy—namely, the young Queen, and ere very long her husband also.

The Influence of the Crown

It requires a certain effort for our generation to realise the precarious position of the Royal family at the time of Queen Victoria's accession in 1837—the extent to which the Regent and some of his brothers had tarnished its reputation and undermined its prestige by a long series of scandals and bickerings, of which the most notorious and incredible were the trial of Queen Caroline, her exclusion from the coronation, and her open appeal to the sympathies of the London mob. George IV, that odious *roué* miscalled "the First Gentleman of Europe", had been followed by his brother William IV, a jovial and outspoken sailor, not renowned either for intellect or tact, and though not exactly unpopular, carrying but little weight, even though his position inevitably led him to play a big part in the Reform crisis, and though he was capable of initiative, as in the crisis of 1834. The memoirs of the Duke of Buckingham reveal something of the extraordinary relations between William IV and the Duke of Cumberland—the most objectionable and reactionary of George III's seven sons—who but for the fortunate accident that the Duke of Kent, after marrying late in life, had left a daughter behind him, would have inherited, and probably lost, the throne.

Providentially, the education of the Princess was left mainly in the hands of her mother the Duchess of Kent, who, having no aptitude for politics, was wise enough to keep her daughter away from the Court and to bring her up in strict seclusion and simplicity. In such a *milieu* the rapid development of her character is all the more remarkable. Her position as heiress to the Crown was concealed from her till she was twelve, but we have the testimony of her governess, Baroness Lehzen, that when it was revealed to her, she said, "I see I am nearer the throne than I thought", then, after some moments, "Now many a child would boast, but they don't know the difficulty. There is much splendour, but there is more responsibility." Then, giving Lehzen her little hand, she exclaimed, "I will be good. I will be good."* This at the age of twelve! But even this is as nothing compared

* Sir T. Martin, *Life of the Prince Consort*, I, 13. To this passage the Queen in later life added in her own hand, "I cried much on learning it and ever deplored this contingency."

with the little incident which followed her first public function as Queen— to my mind the most significant and enlightening in her whole career. "When, after her first Council", says Mr Lytton Strachey, "she crossed the ante-room and found her mother waiting for her, she said, 'And now, Mamma, am I really and truly Queen?' 'You see, my dear, that it is so.' 'Then, dear Mamma, I hope you will grant me the first request I make to you, as Queen. Let me be by myself for an hour.' For an hour she remained in solitude. Then she reappeared and gave a significant order: her bed was to be moved out of her mother's room."[1]

We, who are wise after the event, need not stop to wonder that with such a character at eighteen, she should speedily have made herself felt in her great position: and it has become a commonplace of history—though one which can never be emphasised too strongly—that long before she was forty she had wrought a complete transformation in the outlook of the nation, and especially of the new middle class, towards the throne. It is essential to an understanding of our foreign policy, to bear in mind this great change which is taking place in the background during the late 'thirties and the 'forties, and to realise that Queen Victoria was from her early days keenly interested in European politics. The chief influence to which she owed this was her maternal uncle, King Leopold of the Belgians, the widower of her cousin Charlotte of Wales, who in the most impressionable period of her life was her constant mentor and intimate adviser, and who even after she had come to think and act for herself, was always listened to and trusted right up to his death in 1865. All Leopold's tact and political experience and knowledge were placed at the disposal of his niece, for whom he had a real affection, that grew even stronger after he had helped to find a husband for her in one of his Coburg nephews.

It was his deliberate and systematic aim to fit her for her great position: and it is very enlightening to read one of his first letters to her after accession, recommending her to keep near her his own confidential friend Baron Stockmar, as "a living dictionary of all matters scientific and political that happened these thirty years, which to you is of the greatest importance, because you must study the political history of at least the last thirty-seven years more particularly", and in fact the whole reign of George III.[2]

He was the first to advise her to retain the Whigs in power and to act with them cordially, abandoning the negative attitude of William IV, who had only been forced to tolerate them since his *coup* with the Tories in 1834 had proved a failure. "For them [the Whigs] as well as for the Liberals at large", Leopold reminded her, "you are the only Sovereign that offers them *des chances d'existence et de durée*. Except the Duke of Sussex, there is no one in the family that offers them anything like what they can reasonably expect from you, and your immediate successor with the moustaches" (he means the dreadful uncle Ernest of Cumberland) "is enough to frighten them into the most violent attachment for you."[3]

In more than one letter she tells him, "you may depend on it, I shall profit by your excellent advice respecting Politics".[4] He on his side shows the impression left on the mind of one of the closest and acutest foreign students of British politics of that generation, when he writes in January 1838, begging her to speak to Lord Melbourne "on the subject of what ought to be done to keep for the Crown the little influence it may still possess.... You are too clever not to know that it is not the being *called* Queen or King which can be of the least consequence, when to the title there is not also annexed the power indispensable for the exercise of those functions. All trades must be learned, and nowadays the trade of a constitutional Sovereign, to do it well, is a very difficult one."[5]

The whole influence of Leopold was very naturally exerted in favour of Anglo-French friendship, not merely because he was Louis Philippe's son-in-law, but because a quarrel between the two countries could not fail to be a grave danger to Belgium. The Queen was already predisposed in favour of "my kind and dear friend Louis Philippe, whom I do so respect and for whom I have a great affection" (this already in July 1837), or "the dear French family" (25 April 1838). Throughout the crisis of 1840-1 the Queen, to use again her own words, "worked hard to bring about something conciliatory" (16 October 1840),[6] and messages passed between Windsor and the Tuileries through the medium of Brussels, which helped very materially to allay the danger. The Queen agreed with Palmerston in regarding France as "quite in the wrong",[7] but the first signs of disagreement appeared when he deliberately incurred the risk of war, rather than make concessions to French *amour-propre*. She considered that he minimised the danger of revolution in France, and urged upon him the need for not driving the French to extremities:[8] and she was evidently not impervious to Leopold's complaint that "Palmerston rex and autocrat is far too irritable and violent".[9]

But in this first period the young Queen sees everything through Whig spectacles. The Whigs are "the only safe and loyal people",[10] while the Tories "do everything to degrade their young sovereign in the eyes of the people". For Lord Melbourne she has the feelings which might be felt at one and the same time for a father and a guardian: he is indispensable, even for after-dinner conversation, and when, to her bitter sorrow, he falls, he is consulted daily, until the discreet Stockmar persuades Melbourne himself to represent such a correspondence as contrary to the spirit of the constitution. And as Palmerston is Melbourne's most indispensable helper, and his brother-in-law to boot, and the new Lady Palmerston's daughter is one of her ladies, Palmerston as yet shares the blind favour which she showers upon the Whigs.

But her marriage in 1840 worked a great change, which was bound up with the political transformation of the following year. In the first instance the Queen had not the slightest idea of having a master, and even refused her husband a seat in the House of Lords, in spite of King Leopold's plea. She selected his private secretary for him, and it taxed even Lord Melbourne's powers of persuasion to bring her to consent to the Prince's initiation into public affairs.

Prince Albert was regarded with suspicion when he first came to England: the Coburg family as a whole were viewed askance as time-servers. Leopold himself, whom the nation might have had as Prince Consort if his first wife had lived, had since then accepted first an Orthodox and then a Catholic throne, and other Coburgs had become Catholic in order to become King of Portugal and Duchess of Nemours. Even the lax Palmerston wrote hastily to enquire of Stockmar, "whether Prince Albert belonged to any sect of Protestants whose rules might prevent his taking the sacrament according to the ritual of the English Church":[11] and in stricter circles the Prince was suspected alternately of being a Catholic and an infidel!

But Prince Albert was nothing if not conscientious and persevering: and he slowly asserted himself both in home and in foreign politics and came to exercise decisive influence over the Queen. The first direction in which this found expression was in the altered attitude of the Crown to the two parties. The Queen parted from Lord Melbourne in an agony of mind, and was not sure how she could ever work with the shy, reserved Sir Robert Peel— "such an odd, cold man", she writes, whose "ignorance of character" is "striking and unaccountable".[12] She found some consolation for the loss of her beloved mentor in the praise which so shrewd a statesman conferred upon the Prince and in his advice to her to rely upon her husband's "judgment, temper and discretion".[13] Meanwhile Prince Albert soon found how many tastes and ideas he had in common with Peel and established intimate relations with him, with the result that in the end the Queen was almost as reluctant to part with him and the Tories as ever with Melbourne and the Whigs.

THE PEEL ERA

Peel took office in September 1841 and remained till June 1846: and this period is in many ways one of the most memorable in modern British history. It is a period of great decisions, culminating in the Repeal of the Corn Laws, a period of growing pains in the body politic, of grave unrest, yet

of a striking return of prosperity, of feverish development in every department of public life, of the expansion of the railway system and of our sea-
borne trade, of emigration and colonial experiment. The new industrial
class effects an entry into the old political fortresses, and Peel is its most
typical representative, enjoying *par excellence* the confidence of the mercantile class and of a Church which was still proud of its Protestantism, still
responsive to anti-Papal clamour, still ready to dogmatise and genuinely
shocked at doubts. To his administrative reforms we owe the splendid
development of the British civil service, to his organisation of the police the
disappearance of those riotous habits which had marked the previous fifty
years, to his great financial measures and to his achievement of free trade
the whole fabric of mid-Victorian prosperity. Above all, if we look below
the surface of his achievements, we see in Peel the great example of a Prime
Minister who could place country above party and risk the ruin, almost the
extinction, of his political influence for the sake of a fundamental reform.
We also see in him one of the foremost examples of that gift of political *flair*
and compromise, of forestalling real trouble and extracting the sting from
dangerous movements, that has hitherto been the political salvation of
Britain. To the reforms of the early 'forties, all the more impressive because
the work of a sane Conservative, is due the striking contrast between the
Chartist troubles of Britain and the desperate revolutionary outbursts of
practically every other country in Europe in 1848.

The main explanation lies in the fact that the tactics adopted by most
continental Governments were the very opposite of those employed in
England. During the 'forties, save for incidents here and there, the general
peace was not disturbed, but it was a period of profound unrest, in which
the breach between the peoples and their Governments steadily widened,
reform was frowned upon as the equivalent of revolution, private initiative
in social welfare was weak, while the twin ideas of liberty and nationality
exercised a corrosive force upon public opinion. In the three Eastern
monarchies varying degrees of repression prevailed. In Russia no political
criticism whatsoever was tolerated, and those malcontents who escaped
prison and the knout developed an intense and introspective creed directed
against all recognised authority, and established contacts with the exiles of
many other countries. In Austria the poor epileptic Ferdinand occupied
the throne of his father Francis, but power rested with a triumvirate divided
within itself, and the wheels of government almost ceased to go round. It
was at this period that Metternich said, " I have sometimes governed Europe,
but Austria never ". In the Austrian half of the Habsburg Monarchy the
police, the censorship and the Church were still all-powerful, and the
promising constitutional movement which had been gaining strength in

Hungary since 1825 was vitiated by the Chauvinistic and Magyarising tendencies of the ruling race, and inevitably rallied all the non-Magyar races round a reactionary throne. In Prussia too there was complete political stagnation, but this was counteracted by an efficient administration, strong military discipline, municipal self-government, and an unexampled spread of education, academic culture and research in history and all the sciences. Meanwhile, if Spain was still torn by savage civil warfare, Italy was honey-combed by secret societies, and the ideas promoted by Mazzini and " Young Italy" struck root all the more readily, because the petty rulers of the Peninsula—Naples, Parma, Modena and Lucca—offered so wide a target for scathing criticism, while the advent of a Liberal Pope, after the long repression of the mediocre Gregory XVI, only served to increase the fer-ment. In France alone—apart from Scandinavia and the Low Countries—was it possible to speak of stable government, yet even here there was a steady growth of agitation against the Bourgeois Monarchy, which, having rejected the old principles of divine right and authority, rested on a perilously narrow franchise and was felt by both Clericals and Democrats to be losing such *raison d'être* as it had ever had.

Such was the European background with which British foreign policy had to reckon in this period of Peel. Sir Richard Lodge has well said that Peel was "more definitely *Prime* Minister than most of his predecessors and probably than any of his successors":[14] he exercised a close control over all the great departments and dominated the whole Cabinet. But for that very reason he was absorbed mainly in home affairs, and had a somewhat insular and preoccupied outlook, with the result that his Foreign Secretary, Lord Aberdeen, had a much freer hand during these five years than in his first and somewhat inglorious tenure of office.

Lord Aberdeen as Foreign Secretary

It is certainly not too much to say that there was very wide relief abroad when Palmerston was replaced by Aberdeen. Metternich, who had been intimately associated with him twenty-five years before, wrote him a cordial letter welcoming the "revirement" which was "putting him face to face with old friends".[15] It is true that Metternich continued to distrust England, especially as the bourgeois element assumed growing prominence under Peel, and he had a poor opinion of Queen Victoria—though mainly, it appears, because she resented the recall of Prince Esterházy from the London Embassy.

But it was in France that the real difficulty lay. The French felt humiliated, and on both sides of the Channel there were very many who had again come to believe in the inalienable enmity of France and Britain, just as to-day there are many who still talk of peace among the nations as a dream and cling to the essentially pagan belief of the incurable depravity of human character and the utility of the "steel-bath" of war. In the teeth of this, Aberdeen devoted his whole energy to restoring the Entente Cordiale and removing the causes of distrust, yet without loosening friendly ties with other countries or falling into any kind of dependence upon Paris.

In this aim he was greatly helped by the fact that Guizot was now Premier. While still Ambassador in London, the latter had been on close terms with Aberdeen, many of whose interests were, like his own, those of a scholar: and now at a public meeting Guizot expressed the friendliest sentiments towards Britain and her new Government. Sir Robert Peel, in the opening Commons debate on the Address, hastened to grasp the proffered hand. Not merely did he speak of Guizot as "one so truly deserving the character of a great statesman", but he denounced as "a complete delusion" the idea that "the old feeling of hostility" against France still survived in Britain.[16]

Nor was Peel at all disposed to remain passive under Palmerston's criticism, and a year later he hit out fiercely. "For six years your constant boast was that you had formed and consolidated the alliance of Western Europe.... The influence of despotic power in the East was to be counterbalanced by the intimate union of states in the West, governed by liberal institutions." "What has become of the French Alliance?" he added, and drew the conclusion that France's "alienation and state of irritated feeling" were the direct consequence of Palmerston's policy.[17]

It is not uninstructive to quote Guizot's own epigram on the two Governments: "Peel and his colleagues", he said, "were Conservatives who had become Liberals: we were Liberals who had become Conservatives."[18] This very neatly sums up the truth. It may be added that Princess Lieven (who had come to exercise over Guizot an influence no less remarkable than that over Lord Grey in her London days) was now working hard for the Entente, which by now represented her last hope of political influence and achievement. Still more effective were the constant efforts of King Leopold to promote intimacy and mutual confidence between the courts of his niece and nephew and of his father-in-law. In this he was prompted by every motive of affection, dynastic ambition and political interest, and was materially aided by the wise Baron Stockmar, who had become, largely at Leopold's instance, the political mentor of the Prince.

In September 1843 the Queen and Prince Albert visited Louis Philippe, with the deliberate purpose of improving relations. The initiative lay with the Queen, who approved of the marriage ties between the Houses of Coburg and Orleans,* and was anxious not only to please the French by breaking down the ostracism in which the Orleans dynasty had been so long held by most of the ruling families of Europe, but also to show her sympathy for the tragic fate of Louis Philippe's heir.† Her motive is reflected in a letter which she received from Leopold immediately after her return to England. The visit, he writes, will show her that Louis Philippe, though vivacious, is not astute, and it "will do wonders in removing the silly irritation which had been got up since 1840, and which might in the end have occasioned serious mischief. The passions of the nations sometimes become very inconvenient for their Governors."[19] The effect of the visit upon public opinion on both sides of the Channel was excellent, and we have the contemporary assurance of Prince Albert that "little passed of a political nature, except the declaration of Louis Philippe to Aberdeen that he will not give his son to Spain, even if he were asked, and Aberdeen's answer, that excepting one of his sons, any aspirant whom Spain might choose would be acceptable to England".[20] During the following winter the Queen emphasised her desire to please the French Court, by refusing to receive the Duke of Bordeaux, the Legitimist claimant, when he visited London.‡ The two Speeches from the Throne, re-echoed by Peel, Aberdeen, Guizot and others, praised the Entente Cordiale and the restoration of hearty relations.

Fate, however, seemed bent on thwarting these well-meant plans of friendship, and during the early 'forties one unhappy incident followed another. The dispute over the right of search of ships suspected of carrying negro slaves—complicated by rival interpretations of the convention signed at Vienna in 1815—grew so heated that the French Parliament in 1842 refused ratification to a fresh convention which had been reached between the five Powers in London in December 1841. This caused very widespread indignation in England, where as usual humanitarian aims and national susceptibility became somewhat entangled. This question was one of the main causes which determined Guizot to dissolve the Chamber: but it was not till 1845 that the atmosphere had calmed sufficiently to make a new treaty possible.

---

* King Leopold's wife Louise was a daughter of Louis Philippe: another daughter, Clementine, married Leopold's nephew Augustus of Coburg and became mother of King Ferdinand of Bulgaria, while a niece of Leopold, Augustus's sister Victoria, married Louis Philippe's third son the Duke of Nemours.

† The Duke of Orleans was killed in a carriage accident in July 1842.

‡ On 1 December 1842 we find Guizot writing to Reeve to urge this refusal—a step which the latter's biographer describes as "either unnecessary or ineffective" (Laughton, *Memoirs of Reeve*, I, 160).

THE TAHITI INCIDENT

Much more serious friction was provoked by an incident in the Pacific, which though of very trifling importance in itself, was magnified by the tactlessness of local agents into a question of national prestige on both sides. The little island of Tahiti, ruled by a native dynasty, was the scene of rival effort between English Protestant and French Catholic missionaries. The chief of the former, Mr Pritchard, who was also British Consul, had won the ear of Queen Pomare and tried to check the proselytism of his competitors. But they on their side obtained the support of a French frigate, whose commander, Admiral Dupetit-Thouars, with the help of some of the chiefs, in September 1842 imposed a French protectorate. When the Queen, encouraged by Pritchard, tried to repudiate the convention, the French Admiral, without referring the matter to Paris, avenged what he regarded as an insult to his flag, by deposing Pomare and annexing the island. The British Government protested, and Guizot reversed the annexation, while upholding the protectorate. Even this concession to London aroused a gigantic outcry in France: a sword of honour was presented to the Admiral by public subscription, and no less an orator than Lamartine declared in the Chamber that while he understood the need for peace, "it must be a French peace, not an English". In Tahiti itself the rival parties continued the struggle, a skirmish occurred which cost the life of several French sailors, and their superior officer, holding Pritchard responsible, arrested and threw him into prison. He was only released on condition of leaving the island instantly, without even saying goodbye to his family.

The British press now began to clamour for "reparation", and Sir Robert Peel himself, in the heat of parliamentary debate, spoke of "a gross insult, accompanied with a gross indignity,...committed, so far as we can discover, by the direction of the French Government".* Guizot, on his side, had some difficulty in avoiding an excited debate in the Chamber, and appeased the House of Peers by promising to defend the honour of the French Navy. British public opinion, fanned by the agitation of Pritchard and the Protestant societies, was rendered still more restive by French policy in North Africa, where the suppression of Abd-el-Kader's Algerian rising was followed by hostilities on the Moroccan frontier. A minor complication had been added earlier in the summer by the publication of a pamphlet on French naval matters by the Prince of Joinville,† in which, with amazing

---

* House of Commons, 31 July 1844. It is noteworthy that Peel, in his last speech in the House, during the famous Pacifico debate (see *infra*, p. 283), made amends for this by referring to the expulsion of Pritchard as "the most stupid and frivolous cause of war that ever existed" (*Hansard*, CXII, 680).

† Third son of Louis Philippe.

tactlessness, he discussed the possibilities of damage which might be inflicted in war upon the coast towns of England.

All this was highly embarrassing, and it is hardly too much to suppose that if Palmerston and Thiers had occupied the places of Aberdeen and Guizot, there would have been war between the two countries. There is a private letter of Aberdeen himself to Princess Lieven, which declares it "impossible to deny that persons of all ranks had made up their minds to war".[21] But gradually calmer counsels prevailed. While in some quarters in England there was wild talk of reinstating Pritchard in Tahiti by the guns of the British navy, and while French opinion affected to regard Bugeaud's successful campaign in Morocco as a victory over England,[22] the King and Guizot refused to be stampeded and negotiated calmly with London. In the end the veto on Pritchard's return was upheld, but France expressed regret at the manner of his expulsion and indemnified him for his personal losses.* But the lengths to which mutual irritation had gone are most strikingly reflected in a private letter of the British Prime Minister to his Foreign Secretary, in which he declared "the conduct of France in the original occupation of Algiers" to have been "marked by a gross violation of her engagements towards Europe.... It is quite too late to call on France to fulfil them now: but the original wrong is now the cause that Morocco and Tunis are threatened: and unless we hold very decisive language to France and are prepared to act upon it with regard to Tunis and Morocco, they or so much of them as suits the purposes of France, will follow the fate of Algiers."[23]

Greek Affairs under King Otto

A third unfortunate incident arose over the Revolution which broke out in September 1843 at Athens against the arbitrary and incompetent rule of King Otto. This was a classic example of what was really the main trouble between France and Britain, namely that while the chiefs of the Governments were devotedly working for peace, their subordinate agents, in the consular and sometimes even in the diplomatic service, were frequently intriguing actively against each other in various parts of the world. Such was

---

* A highly instructive outside commentary on this affair is to be found in a letter of the Russian Foreign Minister Count Nesselrode, to his Ambassador in Vienna, Baron Meyendorff (10 September 1844—see Nesselrode, *Lettres et Papiers*, VIII, 254). He describes the whole affair as "trop absurde", but adds: "Malgré cela le coup est porté à l'entente cordiale, et il me paraît mortel, car j'ai trouvé ici [London on the occasion of the Tsar's visit] l'opinion publique plus montée contre la France qu'elle ne l'a jamais été en 1840. Ainsi la moindre étincelle peut allumer un grand incendie, et malheureusement les froissements et les causes d'irritation ne manqueront jamais entre les deux pays." Incidentally, this confidential letter indicates an entirely pacific attitude on the part of Russia.

unhappily the case with the British and French Ministers in Greece, who crowed shrilly upon rival dunghills.

Sir Edmund Lyons had been in command of the British warship which conveyed King Otto to Greece in 1833 and had been greeted so effusively two years later, when he came as British envoy to congratulate Otto on his majority, that Palmerston soon afterwards decided to appoint him as minister. But his first instructions were to "press on Armansperg and on the King the absolute necessity of establishing some form of representative government in Greece", and as time passed it became obvious that neither the King nor his Bavarian ministers had any such intentions. By 1840 Palmerston had lost patience with the Greeks and told Lyons that in 1830 he had favoured as large a Greece as possible, because Prince Leopold's character and pledges of a constitution were "a guarantee that under his rule Greece would have been politically independent and...the nation happy", but that under Otto Greece had been "a mere dependency of Russia" and the constitution withheld, and that he was therefore opposed to the union of Crete with the motherland.[24] On leaving office he wrote to him, "I certainly have made a great mistake when I persuaded France to give way to the wishes of Russia in favour of Otto." [25]

A lurid light is thrown upon Lyons's position at Athens by the first instructions which he received from Lord Aberdeen as Foreign Secretary. "I must begin by expressing a wish to see you on a better footing with our allies. Austria and Prussia have made a formal and official demand for your removal from Athens, and Russia and France have given me to understand that they would see it with pleasure. I shall not yield to this desire, but it cannot be right that the English Minister should be thus regarded by the Governments with whom we are acting in concert."[26] Lyons in his reply countered by complaining of "the united efforts of MM. Piscatory and Lagrene to hoodwink me".

On his side Piscatory—who had proved his friendship for Greece twenty years earlier as a volunteer with the insurgents—not altogether without reason suspected Sir Edmund Lyons of designs for the formation of a purely British party in Greece, and reported to this effect to M. Guizot in July 1844. The incident has its pleasant as well as its regrettable side: for it illustrates better than anything else the ideal personal relations that existed between the two Foreign Ministers. On 28 October Guizot wrote very frankly to Lord Aberdeen that the Greek Premier Kolettis "is full of prejudices and distrust against the policy of England towards Greece....He suspects you of wishing to keep his country in the state of a semi-English pashalik, as Wallachia and Moldavia are semi-Russian pashaliks. But one can extirpate from his mind these old *racunes*. *C'est un homme très* *perfectible, très éclairable*....I wish him to have confidence in you also and to believe that your policy towards Greece is what it really is, namely sincere, like ours. I am sure that he can be brought to this, and it would be a great step towards the solid restoration of our 'entente cordiale' at Athens. I beg you to ensure that my work in this sense is not criticised and destroyed by the sallies and obstacles of Sir Edmund Lyons, who seems to me much more exclusive and obstinate than Kolettis."[27] The good impression of this despatch is somewhat spoilt for us when we find that Guizot soon afterwards wrote to Piscatory that he had been "working very much on London" and hoped to "succeed in destroying all confidence in Lyons".[28] But after all the situation was sufficiently serious when the Greek Premier could inform the French Minister,[29] that Lyons was "a personal enemy. He behaves like a party chief: he heads the Opposition". The truth is that he was a bluff, not to say domineering, sailor, quite unfitted for a delicate diplomatic situation. He once told Piscatory, "There is only one good policy—for France and England to act together":[30] but he never acted on this principle himself and consistently treated the Greeks as inferior mortals. In the end Lord Aberdeen found it necessary to reprimand Sir Edmund Lyons for his attitude: but at the same time he very pertinently complained to Guizot that "notwithstanding our mutual confidence and the object which above all others we have in view, it is vain to think that our desires and endeavours will produce any good, unless our agents shall really act in the spirit of their instructions.* But Aberdeen found that even Peel himself was infected by the prevailing irritation. Early in 1845 we find Peel writing to him as follows: "What a pretty state the Entente Cordiale is in as regards Greece, if Louis Philippe, in conversation with the Austrian Ambassador at Paris, professes agreement with Austria and dissent from England, 'from the unfortunate tendency of the British Government at all times to support revolutions and thus disturb the peace of Europe'. Considering by whom this is said, and of whom it is said, the force of impudence cannot go much further."[31]

In a word, the personal relations of Guizot and Aberdeen more than once averted disaster in what were after all questions of secondary importance. But there remained a much more serious point of friction in the Spanish question, which simmered on through the early 'forties and speedily came to a head when Aberdeen was again replaced by Palmerston.

---

* Guizot's despatches to M. de Ste-Aulaire in London are even more convincing: "en vérité", he writes, "ne voulant en Grèce que ce que nous voulons, Lord Aberdeen et moi, si nous ne parvenions pas à obliger nos agents à le vouloir aussi et à l'accomplir, il y aurait du malheur" (8 October 1841—Guizot, *Mémoires*, vi, 265).

Louis Philippe and Nicholas I

Meanwhile, Tsar Nicholas, in whom the passage of time had in no way abated his vindictive hatred for Louis Philippe, and who wished to keep France in a state of permanent isolation, was naturally disturbed by the royal visit to Eu, the more so because at this time he was somewhat critical of his own special allies Prussia and Austria. Early in 1844, then, he indicated to Lord Bloomfield, our Ambassador at St Petersburg, his desire to visit London, and at the end of May he spent some time at Buckingham Palace and Windsor, sparing no effort to charm and conciliate the Queen, her husband, and her ministers. On the eve of his arrival the *Journal des Débats* had published some articles on Russian designs for a Central Asiatic confederation, and *The Times* had made fun of the whole idea, in a way which provided an admirable opening for Nicholas. With Aberdeen and Peel he raised the question of Turkey's future, affirming that he would do all in his power to maintain the *status quo*—in other words, to keep the sick man alive—but that he was bound to die sooner or later, and that it would be "wise to consider beforehand what might happen, and to attempt an honest and honourable understanding".* The reserve with which Lord Aberdeen received these overtures was unquestionably due to embarrassment at the Tsar's only too manifest hostility towards France. In view of subsequent events it is beyond all question regrettable that no more definite result was reached, and indeed if the personal contact established by the Tsar had been maintained, the whole Crimean tragedy might have been avoided. "Years ago", said Nicholas to Peel, "Lord Durham was sent to me, a man full of prejudices against me. By merely coming to close quarters with me, all his prejudices were driven clean out of him. This is what I hope, by coming here, to bring about with you and with England generally. By personal intercourse I trust to annihilate these prejudices. For I esteem England highly; but as to what the French say of me, I care not, I spit upon it."[32] In December 1840 Nicholas had already approached the Ambassador, Lord Clanricarde, in favour of an understanding between the four Powers and had insisted that "he did not require a treaty" and that the word of the Ambassador, if once authorised from London, would amply suffice.[33] This attitude—so flattering but so dangerously the reverse of constitutional—coincides entirely with his later attitude in 1853, when he urgently declared that ten minutes of personal conversation with Lord Aberdeen would probably suffice to clear up the growing misunderstandings between Russia

---

* To Aberdeen he roundly declared, "He [Louis Philippe] has attempted to undermine and ruin my position as Russian Emperor. That I will never forgive him" (cit. Th. Schiemann, *Gesch. Russlands*, IV, 50).

and Britain. But while the advantages of personal contact between statesmen can hardly be exaggerated, and in foreign policy may sometimes even avail to bridge over fundamental differences of political creed, it has to be admitted that British suspicions of the Tsar had been steadily augmented by his policy towards Poland and Hungary and indeed throughout Europe, and that the dispute over Turkish affairs was merely the culminating point of a series.

THE EU VISIT

The Tsar's English visit, if really intended to drive a wedge between London and Paris, was a failure: for no sooner had Sir Robert Peel announced the amicable settlement of the Tahiti dispute, than Louis Philippe and his Queen, accompanied by several of their family and by M. Guizot, paid a state visit to Windsor—the first such visit of a French sovereign—and were received with the greatest cordiality. The King wished Tahiti " at the bottom of the sea "[34] and assured his hosts that the French nation did not wish for war, "though they love cracking their whips like postilions". But though the visit unquestionably did much to smooth down susceptibilities on both sides of the Channel, there remained a latent possibility of friction, and the spirit in which the Queen received her guests is revealed in a letter to her uncle Leopold. "The good ending of our difficulties with France is an immense blessing, but it is really and truly necessary that you and those at Paris should know that the danger was *imminent*, and that poor Aberdeen stood *almost alone* in trying to keep matters peaceable."[35] It is not too much to say that the intimacy between Aberdeen and Guizot was the most valuable asset in maintaining the Entente Cordiale. We have the authority of Aberdeen's son, Lord Stanmore, for the statement that each showed the other not merely their official despatches, but even the confidential letters which accompanied them.[36] Things were not helped by Palmerston's critical attitude. Melbourne himself told the Queen in 1842 that Palmerston disliked Aberdeen, had a low opinion of him, and thought him weak and timid,[37] while Aberdeen, though he had endorsed Palmerston's Eastern policy, disapproved intensely of what he called Palmerston's "intermeddling".[38]

Aberdeen, we have seen, found himself almost alone, and the growing divergence of views between him and some of his colleagues was accentuated by the question of rival armaments. On 28 September 1845 he wrote a very gloomy letter to Peel, complaining that "a policy of friendship and confidence has been converted into a policy of hostility and distrust", and admitting that "in spite of all calculation it is possible that war may suddenly and when least expected take place". Though it was his "deliberate and firm conviction" that there was "less reason to distrust the French Government and to doubt the continuance of peace" than five years earlier, he none the less felt that "we are now acting under the influence of panic, both with respect to the intentions of France and our own real condition". He therefore asked to be allowed to resign, though explaining the step by reasons of health and revealing to no one the contents of this letter.[39] Peel in reply assured him that he was irreplaceable, and that his withdrawal might easily ruin the Government, and mobilised the Duke of Wellington in the same sense.

It is peculiarly instructive to read the Duke's comments on the situation. No one, he told the Prime Minister, was "more sensible" than he "of the absolute importance of connecting France with the councils of Europe, and above all, of a good understanding between this country and France". Moreover, he believed Louis Philippe and Guizot to be really pacific: "but look at the state of naval preparation in France", for which they were responsible, and which must be regarded as "symptoms", not of friendliness, but of "deadly hostility". Indeed, in his candid opinion "the prevailing sentiment in the minds of Frenchmen is implacable hostility. We cannot change their feelings."[40] Aberdeen allowed himself to be overruled, but wrote back to his chief, "We still talk of peace, having war in our hearts", and frankly regretted his own decision.[41] He went further and warned Peel that the principle of *Bellum para, pacem habebis*, on which both Governments were acting, was "entirely inapplicable to the condition of the Great Powers and to the political system of modern times and the present state of society".[42] From Peel's reply it may be inferred that Aberdeen had reached this philosophical conclusion by actual discussion with Guizot, but as the more sceptical Peel reminded him, it was rather late in the day, after so many French preparations, for Guizot to declare his abomination of *bellum para*.[43] On the other hand, Palmerston was an increasingly outspoken critic of the Government and expounded his own alternative attitude very clearly in the House. "Influence abroad is to be maintained only by the operation of one or other of two principles—hope and fear. We ought to teach the weaker Powers to hope that they will receive the support of this country in their time of danger. Powerful countries should be taught to fear that they will be resisted by England in any unjust acts either towards ourselves or towards those who are bound in ties of amity with us."[44] It was quite obvious that if Palmerston were to replace Aberdeen in the near future, British policy would follow markedly different lines. It was about this time that he gave to Greville the view that "we might hold any language we pleased to France and America", without risk of war, "as both knew how vulnerable they were".[45]

RUSSELL, GREY AND PALMERSTON

By the close of 1845 the growing anti-Corn Law agitation, accentuated by the Irish famine, forced the broadminded Peel to revise his views upon protection. A free trade manifesto, launched by the Liberal leader Lord John Russell in November, evoked a crisis, and the Government resigned. The Queen invited Russell to form an administration, but showed distinct alarm at the prospect of Palmerston returning to the Foreign Office. Fortunately for her, similar views were held by Lord Grey, without whose support in Whig circles Russell could not hope to stand, and who flatly refused to serve unless Palmerston were given some other post. "For Lord Palmerston", he wrote to the Liberal leader, "I have much regard, and I have always been on the most amicable terms with him.... But I could not be blind to the notorious fact that justly or unjustly both friends and opponents regarded with considerable apprehension the prospect of his return to the Foreign Office." In view of "the feelings of apparent alienation" between him and leading foreign statesmen, his appointment "might very materially increase the danger" of war.* Russell, whose mismanagement of the situation is further shown by his slightingly inadequate offer to Cobden, repudiated these "unjust aspersions", adhered to the view that Palmerston was "the person best fitted" for the post, and rather than yield to Grey, abandoned altogether the attempt to form a Government, or in the flamboyant phrase of Disraeli, "handed back with courtesy the poisoned chalice to Sir Robert".[46] As a result, the Queen recalled Peel, who dragged on for another six months of office. The incident, veiled in secrecy at the time, is of very great significance for the future; it shows that the Queen was not alone in her misgivings as to the effect of Palmerstonian methods upon our foreign relations, but it also prepares us for the growth of a situation in which no one in his own party is capable of setting bounds upon the masterful minister.

For the moment, at any rate, Palmerston had learned his lesson. In the spring of 1846 he paid a private visit to Paris, where he saw everyone from the King downwards, "met with nothing but smiles, *prévenance* and *empressement*",[47] and by his frankness did a good deal to tone down the prejudices against his person. In the previous winter Disraeli, who also cultivated relations with the Tuileries, had assured the King that Palmerston

* Letter of 19 December 1845, first printed in "Notes on the Greville Memoirs", *English Historical Review*, No. 1 (1886); cf. also Stanmore, *op. cit.* p. 186. For interesting new details, see chap. XVI of H. C. F. Bell, *Palmerston*, I, 354–64. Very active in the background were "Bear" Ellice, Henry Reeve (a close confidant of the Orleans Court) and Charles Greville, clerk to the Privy Council.

"was our first Foreign Minister who had taken the French intimacy as an avowed element of our national policy", and that from his frank character he "required frankness and decision" and "would never take a litigious view of the policy of France". This he duly communicated to Palmerston himself, who replied in these terms: "I have the strongest conviction that the great foundation of the foreign policy both of an English and of a French Government ought to be a cordial and sincere good understanding between England and France."[48] If we take a broad view of Palmerston's whole career, it becomes impossible to doubt that this was his genuine aim; though his actions were only too often of such a character as to confirm most people in London, and still more in Paris, in a contrary belief.

CHAPTER VII

PALMERSTON AND THE NEW SPIRIT

In June 1846 came the final crisis of Protection: the Tory Die-Hards under Lord George Bentinck and Disraeli revolted against Peel, and the latter split his party rather than renounce Free Trade. This time Lord John Russell was successful in forming what was to prove the last of the Whig Cabinets: and Lord Palmerston returned for the third time to the Foreign Office. The reasons against his appointment no longer seemed so strong. The last public announcement of Sir Robert Peel as Prime Minister had been the settlement of the thorny Oregon frontier dispute with the United States: while Anglo-French relations had for the moment again become normal. Hence Lord Grey, in accepting office for himself, consented to withdraw his former veto upon Palmerston, in return for the Prime Minister's express assurance that he would "exercise a control over the Foreign Office and secure the Cabinet against any imprudence of Palmerston".* Unhappily a situation was speedily to develop, in which Palmerston's methods again placed a dangerous strain upon the Entente Cordiale, and in which there was no one capable of holding him back.

Throughout his long career Metternich profoundly misjudged England, but he was very happy in one phrase that occurs in his diary for 1846: "At this moment there exists an alliance between France and England in name, though in reality it does not exist; just as the opposite is the case between France and Russia."[1] It was but too true that the Entente had been upheld mainly by the personal efforts of the two courts and their Foreign Ministers. No sooner was Aberdeen replaced by Palmerston, than it collapsed under the first strain to which it was subjected, though it must be admitted that the strain was very severe. But the difference of tone during the events now to be described can hardly be illustrated more effectively than by a quotation from a personal letter which Peel after his resignation addressed to Guizot. He expressed the hope that their "united labours...have established foundations of concord between England and France strong enough to bear the shock of all ordinary casualties". "We have succeeded in elevating the tone and spirit of the two nations, have taught them to regard

* Charles Greville, in his *Memoirs* (VI, 193, 3 June 1848) records these words as used to him by Lord Grey himself. Cf. also Maxwell, *Life of Clarendon*, I, 269.

something higher than paltry jealousies and hostile rivalries, and to estimate the full value of that moral and social influence which cordial relations between England and France give to each for every good and beneficent purpose. If it had not been for that confidence and esteem, how many miserable squabbles might have swollen into terrible national controversies!"[2] This tribute from so typical an Englishman, and from one who cannot always be acquitted of indiscretion in his pronouncements on foreign policy, illustrates the advantages of that personal contact of heads of government which is only now becoming one of the fundamental principles on which sound international relations must rest.

Guizot, for his part, has left on record a generous tribute to the great Englishman with whom fate had thrown him into contact. Peel, he considered, held "vague and undetermined notions" on foreign policy. While firmly bent on upholding the national dignity, he "had no mania for domination abroad", and above all, "he believed that morality and good sense are essential and practicable in foreign relations, as well as in the internal government of states".[3]

The Spanish Marriages

Palmerston had been but a very short time in office when the vexed question known as the Spanish Marriages assumed an acute phase and rapidly undid all the work of the previous five years in favour of Franco-British friendship. The origins of the dispute belong to Lord Aberdeen's term of office, but it is better treated as a consecutive whole. Viewed from the perspective of the twentieth century, it seems futile and petty, but it deserves to be studied as a thoroughly characteristic example of the part which matters of dynastic interest still played in the early Victorian era and the extent to which they were intertwined with national prestige.

After the horrors of the Carlist civil war Spain was slowly recovering her breath, and the question of the marriage of the young Queen Isabella and her sister dominated the internal situation. Louis Philippe and French public opinion were anxious that the succession to the Spanish throne should not pass outside one or other branch of the House of Bourbon, and for a time a younger brother of the King of Two Sicilies was regarded as a possible compromise candidate. The British view was opposed to any French prince marrying the Queen or her sister, on the ground that this would run counter to the provisions of the Peace of Utrecht (1713), by which the throne of Spain was secured to Philip V and his descendants, but its separation from that of France was definitely laid down. Lord Aberdeen, who never would admit Louis Philippe's point of view, was on the whole inclined to share Prince Albert's opinion that an entirely free choice should be left to the young Queen and her people. None the less the name of Prince Leopold of Coburg, a first cousin of Queen Victoria and her husband, was at one time put forward, thanks to that inveterate matchmaker the King of the Belgians. But it may be affirmed that Leopold's candidature was never pressed by London, though not of course absolutely frowned upon.

Louis Philippe had already refused an offer of Queen Isabella's hand for his son the Duke of Aumale, and when he met Queen Victoria at Eu in September 1845, Guizot and Aberdeen reached an agreement, by which both countries should approve Isabella's marriage with her cousin Henry Duke of Seville, and that "until the Queen was married and had children" there could be no question of her sister and presumptive heir marrying a French Prince. Louis Philippe told Aberdeen that he was not attracted by "the prospect of the Spanish throne", but thought of his son the Duke of Montpensier for the Infanta—not, however, "until it was no longer a political question, *which would be when the Queen is married and has children*".[4] In that case he would not engage to shut out his son from "the great inheritance which the Infanta would bring with her". In this the French subsequently claimed that Aberdeen had verbally concurred, though he himself could not remember having done so, and though there was no verbal record: in any case the French finally dropped the earlier candidature of the Count of Trapani, who was generally unpopular in Spain.

Early in 1846 the situation was complicated by the equivocal attitude of the Queen Mother Christina, and by the rivalry of the British and French representatives in Madrid, Sir Henry Bulwer and M. de Bresson. In May Christina reverted to the candidature of Prince Leopold and privately asked Bulwer to transmit the proposal by letter to Leopold's father the Duke of Coburg. Whether in the months that followed she was merely vacillating in temper or engaged in an elaborate intrigue, intended to compromise Britain through her Minister and thereby free Louis Philippe from his pledge regarding Montpensier,* remains an open question. Certain it is that Bulwer was captivated by the idea and wrote home to Aberdeen, "I could make the marriage, if you instructed me to do so and your instructions to me were kept secret." Aberdeen replied, "we have no English candidate", and forbade Bulwer to engage actively "in the support of another, be he who he may".[5] Meanwhile the Duke of Coburg visited England and finding that both Peel and Aberdeen disapproved of his son's candidature, formally declined Christina's offer.

---

* This explanation is put forward by Sir Theodore Martin in his *Life of the Prince Consort* (I, 347) and seems to have been accepted by the British Court at the time.

It was at this juncture that the change of Government took place in London, and there was at once an end to the mutual confidence between the two Foreign Ministers. In the previous year, when Palmerston seemed likely to return to office, Guizot, in a letter to Henry Reeve, had expressed "some uneasiness", but also "the conviction that Palmerston's policy towards France, the King and myself will be fair and friendly".[6] But the underlying nervousness which this phrase reveals now speedily became acute, owing to the impetus given to events by the rivalry of Bresson and Bulwer. The former was by now pressing strongly upon his Government the view that the action of English agents absolved it from the Eu agreement: and on 12 July, by taking Louis Philippe's name in vain, he obtained the consent of the Queen Mother and her Government to the simultaneous marriage of her two daughters to the Dukes of Cadiz and Montpensier.[7] Louis Philippe disapproved, and ordered Guizot to inform the Queen Mother that "Bresson was forbidden to say what he has said, and that the simultaneity is inadmissible....I will not rest under the imputation of causing an engagement to be contracted in my name, which I am neither free nor desirous to undertake."[8]

Unhappily before this order was executed, Lord Palmerston sent to the French Government a copy of his first despatch to Bulwer, instructing him not to give active support to any candidate whatsoever, but stating their number to be now reduced to three—namely, Prince Leopold and the two sons of Don Francisco (i.e. the Dukes of Seville and Cadiz). There is no reason to suppose that Palmerston meant mischief: it was merely his downright method. But by placing Leopold's name once more upon the list, and in the first place, and by omitting that of Montpensier altogether, he created upon Louis Philippe the impression of a definite abandonment of the Aberdeen policy. A memorandum which had been handed to Lord Aberdeen by the French Ambassador as long ago as February 1840 had summed up the French attitude in these words: "If the marriage either of the Queen or of the Infanta with Prince Leopold of Coburg or any other Prince, not a descendant of Philip V, became probable and imminent,...we should be set free from any engagement, and free to counterstroke at once by asking for the hand either of the Queen or the Infanta for the Duke of Montpensier."[9] This seemed to French eyes to be exactly the situation which had now arisen. It appears that the French Ambassador, M. de Jarnac, when Palmerston showed him the instructions for Bulwer, was stupefied,* and begged him to erase Prince Leopold's name from the first place, but that Palmerston declared this to be impossible, because it had already been approved by the Cabinet. This, when reported to Paris,

* The word is that used by Louis Philippe in his letter of apology for Queen Victoria.

aroused both resentment and suspicion, and the intended disavowal of Bresson was not sent to Madrid after all. That Louis Philippe genuinely believed himself duped is obvious from his letter of 25 July to Guizot, in which the phrase occurs: "Not that I expected better from Lord Palmerston; but I thought he would not have thrown off the mask so soon. My present impression is that we must return blow for blow."*

This was easy enough, with so much inflammatory material lying about in Madrid. A conciliatory tone on the part of the British Foreign Secretary would still have saved the situation. But Palmerston, instead of holding Bulwer back, encouraged him in his forward attitude. In August he was still "very loth to undertake the risk of advising Leopold to become a candidate",[10] but by September he was already telling Bulwer that he was coming round to his view, and that "we ought to have at once and boldly adopted Coburg and to have carried it in defiance of the French".[11] He went so far as to affirm that "the independence of Spain would be endangered, if not destroyed, by the marriage of a French Prince into the Royal family of Spain".[12]

Meanwhile Bresson and the Queen Mother came to terms, all the more readily because Don Enrique, the Duke of Seville, was regarded both by Christina and by Louis Philippe† as much too advanced in his political opinions. On 29 August the Spanish Government publicly announced the forthcoming marriage of Queen and Infanta to the Dukes of Cadiz and Montpensier. This in turn incensed London, and on 16 September Palmerston, writing to Bulwer, and identifying "the Queen, Russell, Clarendon, and all our colleagues" with himself, roundly declared, "We are all indignant at the bad faith and unscrupulous ambition and base intrigues of the French Government."[13] To Lord Normanby in Paris he called it "a scandalous breach of promise and good faith" on the part of the French Ministry "and of the King personally".[14]

Queen Victoria took a very active part in the whole affair—"sadly engrossed" are her words to her uncle.[15] "No quarrel", she wrote, "could be more disagreeable and to me more cruelly painful", and she could not understand how Louis Philippe could "wantonly throw away the friendship of one who has stood firm by him with sincere affection, for a doubtful object of personal and family aggrandisement".[16] The first announcement

---

* *Revue Rétrospective*, p. 185, cit. Martin, *op. cit.* II, 363. Palmerston on his side would seem to have intended to show himself conciliatory towards Guizot, but produced the very opposite effect. See H. C. F. Bell (*Palmerston*, p. 378) who remains in doubt as to Palmerston's real motives.

† In his letter, already quoted, to Queen Louise, he definitely charges "British agents" with favouring Don Enrique, "le chef ou plutôt l'agent de toutes les nuances des révolutionnaires" (cit. Martin, *op. cit.* II, 511).

had come to her from the Queen of the French, and her reply had expressed surprise and "a very lively regret":[17] and the lengthy explanation addressed to her by Louis Philippe himself through the medium of his daughter Queen Louise of the Belgians did not in any way alter her views. She expressed herself as "deeply pained", and emphatically denied that Leopold had ever been the British candidate.[18] It is but fair to add that the French professed themselves as equally aggrieved at the hostile comments of the British press. Guizot himself, who cannot escape his share of the blame, complained to Reeve[19] that for six years England had believed in his sincere attachment to the Entente, yet "all disappears like a puff of wind", and "I am no longer supposed to have any integrity, uprightness or sincerity". But neither he nor his master could now draw back, and the Spaniards were also in an unyielding mood. The double marriage was therefore celebrated at Madrid on 10 October 1846, and the second Entente Cordiale had received its deathblow.

It is unnecessary for the purposes of a general survey to go farther into the intricacies of this barren dispute. It may serve as a reminder of the strong influence still exercised by dynastic interests upon European history in the nineteenth century. But neither the fears nor the hopes which prompted London and Paris were realised. Queen Isabella bore a son, who after a stormy interlude eventually succeeded to the throne: and within less than two years of the marriage Montpensier shared his father's exile.

The real moral of the whole affair lies in the growing touchiness of national feeling, as voiced by a very vocal public opinion in Parliament and the press, and in the role of Palmerston as the typical mouthpiece of such opinion. It is difficult to avoid the conclusion that the marriage question was given an altogether excessive importance, that for this Lord Palmerston was in the main responsible, and that, if Lord Aberdeen had still been in power, a misunderstanding might have been avoided. This is not to exculpate Guizot, who undoubtedly took umbrage and embroiled the quarrel still farther, but this too was above all due to irritation produced by the change from Aberdeen, whom he knew intimately and trusted implicitly, to Palmerston, who kept him at arm's length. The calm verdict of history must undoubtedly be that the charges of gross perfidy and bad faith, levelled against Louis Philippe at the time and indeed long afterwards, rested in the main upon a misapprehension.

As Lord Aberdeen trenchantly pointed out in letters to Prince Albert, whom Palmerston had won over to his own view, "a good understanding with France is just as necessary now as it was at the moment when the Entente was most cordial and intimate. This marriage is not an adequate cause of national quarrel." And again, "The marriage of the Duke of Montpensier is really an affair of little importance to England, and it is an event with which in itself we have no right to quarrel."* This may fairly be regarded as the verdict of history. It does not conflict with Queen Victoria's view that it was "inexplicable" that Louis Philippe should risk a breach for such doubtful advantages: and it is certainly true that he and Guizot acted very shortsightedly in giving way to personal pique. Nor can it be denied that on purely political grounds they were still more shortsighted: for as Lord John told the Queen, there was "hardly a dissentient voice" in England as to France's behaviour.[20] The Queen seems to have had her doubts throughout the controversy, though at the moment she shared her Minister's view, and called the King's action "beyond *all* belief shameful and *so* shabbily dishonest".[21] She none the less retrospectively laid the chief blame on "the attempt of Lord Palmerston to reorganise the Progressista party and regain the so-called *English influence*", with the result that Louis Philippe and Queen Christina made up their old feud and rushed the marriages through.† In this connection it is worth quoting Charles Greville, who was behind the scenes of the dispute both in London and Paris and was shown most of the confidential documents by Jarnac and Normanby. Though convinced that Britain had been "jockeyed by France in a very shabby underhand way",[22] he inferred from a conversation with Lady Palmerston that her husband's "fixed idea is to humble France and make her feel her humiliation".[23] This aim, so thoroughly in keeping with Palmerston's policy in the earlier crisis of 1841, had been clearly divined by Guizot, who poured out to Greville his reasons for suspecting that Palmerston was "resolved to overturn French influence all over the world".[24]

Our survey may be fittingly closed by the verdict of Prince Metternich, to whom Louis Philippe and Palmerston were almost equally unsympathetic, but who in this instance severely condemned the tactical blunders of the former and his "Utopian" ideas. "He [Louis Philippe] knows that I do not think much of public opinion: it is not one of my instruments, but it has its effect. The English Government have done their best to establish Louis Philippe in public opinion. They can withdraw what they gave, and I have always said that the moment he loses that, he is on the very verge of a war, and his is not a dynasty that can stand a war." ‡ Here the veteran reactionary puts his finger upon one of the nerves of the European situation:

* Stanmore, *Life of Aberdeen*, p. 195. See also letter of Lord Aberdeen to Prince Albert, 9 October 1846—cit. Martin, *op. cit.* II, 375: "I care very little for the marriage, but I feel deeply the breach of the engagement."

† In letter of 6 July 1848, to Palmerston—see *Letters*, II, 183. This view was produced by the Queen's perusal of the *Revue Rétrospective*, a French collection of documents relative to the Spanish question. The Queen mars an otherwise measured judgement by speaking of the Spanish marriage as "the origin of all the present convulsions in Europe".

‡ *Nachg. Papiere*, VII, 342. In September 1847 we find him summing up the latent European crisis as caused by "the absolute feebleness" of the French Government, and "the profound hatred" of the English Government towards it (*ibid.* p. 335).

for the breakdown of the Entente Cordiale was undoubtedly much more injurious to France than to Britain, and the consequent isolation of France weakened the prestige of Louis Philippe and his ministers, at home no less than abroad, and contributed very materially to the Revolution of 1848. By the close of 1846 Metternich had no illusions left and regarded the Entente Cordiale as dead, and Louis Philippe as incapable of reviving it.[25]

THE NEW FERMENT IN EUROPE

Only eighteen months now separate us from that momentous event, and the state of Europe is increasingly insecure. All Italy was thrown into a ferment by the death of Gregory XVI, under whom reaction had reached the nadir of incompetence and immobility, and by the accession of Pius IX, hailed in the widest circles as "the Liberal Pope". The exaggerated hopes at first set upon him could not be realised, and Metternich was fully entitled to declare that "the liberalising Pope called forth monsters which he no longer had the strength to restrain".[26] Meanwhile, the King of Naples outdid even Pope Gregory in his reactionary methods, the small states balanced uneasily between Naples and Austria, and in Piedmont Charles Albert played the role of the doubter, hesitating between revolution and repression. In Austria Metternich, conscious of the urgency of reform, but powerless to restrain his two colleagues in the triumvirate, allowed the home situation to drift, partly from love of power, and partly from the genuine conviction that his hand was needed on the helm of policy, and indeed more than ever since Palmerston had returned to office. Every safety valve remained closed, stagnation was complete in the intellectual and political sphere, the censorship and the police system retained their all-pervading character: but the rising tide of nationality, hardly suspected by many of those in authority, was already transforming and complicating the situation. In Hungary especially the national renaissance, which had been in full swing since the 'twenties, had evoked an active movement for constitutional reform on lines unique in Europe, and in 1847 was already assuming semi-revolutionary forms, before the spark from the Paris Revolution kindled not merely Pest, but most of the other capitals of Central Europe, into flame.

Palmerston, when he resumed office in 1846, was 62. He saw clearly that Europe was moving towards the rapids, and his avowed aim was to promote constitutional and free government and thus avert revolution. The theory upon which he acted was quite unimpeachable. So far from being negative, he quite definitely put forward the view that a Government does better to grant "measures of improvement...with the grace of spontaneous concession, than to be compelled to adopt, on the sudden, changes perhaps insufficiently matured and which being wrung from them by the pressure of imperious circumstances, invert the natural order of things and being of the nature of a capitulation of the sovereign to the subject, may not always be a sure foundation for permanent harmony between the Crown and the people".[27]

In practice he had to apply these principles to three concrete cases in the years immediately preceding the Great Revolution—the Polish, the Swiss and the Italian questions. Few people in our own day will attempt to deny that in each case he was right: once more it is rather his method than his principles that are open to question.

THE REPUBLIC OF CRACOW

A new phase in the Polish question had been opened by the ruthless suppression of the rising of 1830–1 and by the failure of the Powers to press upon the Tsar the observance of the pledges of 1815, which he regarded as justly forfeited by the act of rebellion. Since then the only fragment of Polish soil where liberty survived was the tiny Republic of Cracow, which led an uneasy existence as a free city, subject to continual interference from her three great neighbours. Cracow enjoyed a certain privileged position for Polish culture, which otherwise found its chief home in Paris: it was thus peculiarly suspect to Russia and in a lesser degree to Prussia, but was recognised as lying more within the sphere of Austria, who even then adopted a milder attitude than her two Allies towards the Poles. The peasant rising of 1846 in Galicia and the equivocal part played by the Polish patriots inside Cracow, not unnaturally alarmed both the Tsar and the King of Prussia, who pressed Metternich to use it as a pretext for establishing Austrian control over the Republic. For some time Metternich hesitated, but the friction caused by the Spanish quarrel between London and Paris seemed to assure him of immunity, and on 11 November 1846 he proclaimed Cracow's annexation to Austria, without so much as a warning to the signatory Powers.

This was keenly resented by France and Britain as a violation of the Treaties of 1815, of which the Eastern Powers had made so much profession as against France: but though they both entered formal protests, they found it impossible to act together, and nothing happened beyond vigorous speeches. None the less, the incident had a very real significance: for by it the Legitimist Powers made a serious breach in their own principles and turned their theory of intervention against themselves. Palmerston was

embarrassingly right when he declared in the House of Commons that
"the Treaty of Vienna must be respected as a whole". "If it be not good
on the Vistula, it may be equally bad on the Rhine and on the Po." [28]
Metternich wanted the three Eastern Powers to make a public retort in
refutation of this view, and to reaffirm their loyalty to the treaties: but
neither Berlin nor St Petersburg was willing, and the Tsar took the line
that "action is our affair, words may be left to the others". [29] In London
Lord Palmerston was not alone in resenting the incident, and indeed Prince
Albert declared that he "would sooner have been burnt alive" than take
"such action as that of the Eastern Powers". [30] Even Palmerston was not
prepared to endorse the tirades of Joseph Hume and Monckton Milnes
against "the three despotic states" and their treatment of Poland: and
though referring to the Poles as "a great and noble people" who had
been "by injustice of the greatest magnitude, deprived of their national
existence," he argued that the British Parliament could not "in our considerations go farther back than the Treaty of Vienna. But to that we are
ready to go, and on that we have a right to take our stand." [31]

SWITZERLAND AND THE SONDERBUND

The Cracow affair was a shock to the principles of the Holy Alliance,
however disinclined it might be to admit this, and it was now easier for
Palmerston to obstruct their wishes in the Swiss question. At the very end
of 1845 the seven Catholic cantons of Switzerland, led by Luzern, had
formed the so-called "Sonderbund" (or separate League), and when in
July 1846 this was voted illegal by the Federal Diet, civil war followed.
France proposed intervention by the five Powers, but Palmerston refused.
While Guizot and Metternich both secretly encouraged the Sonderbund,
Palmerston persisted in treating, and most certainly rightly, the Jesuit
question, round which the quarrel centred, as more political than religious, [32]
and tried to get it settled by pressure upon the Pope. He regarded the
Franco-Austrian plan as "a paraphrase of the manifesto of the three Powers
last year about the extinction of Cracow", and wrote to Lord Minto that
"Guizot will have to choose between us and the three Powers". [33] He then
deliberately played for time, until General Dufour's military success ended
the war and averted all danger of intervention. Palmerston's delays helped
to save Swiss independence, and in this he acted quite consciously in the
interest of Liberalism on the Continent, and thereby of course greatly
increased Metternich's aversion for him. In many ways this was one of
his most successful enterprises, and events were soon to prove how

accurately he had judged the situation. To him the triumph of the Sonder-bund and the extension of Austrian influence to Switzerland would have been like closing yet another safety valve and hastening the catastrophe which he saw coming.

ITALY AND THE MINTO MISSION

Most characteristic of all, however, was Palmerston's attitude to Italy. In view of the general ferment throughout the Peninsula he sent Lord Minto there on a special mission of enquiry and instructed him to express to Charles Albert his surprise and regret at Austria's threat of invasion, and his pleasure at Charles Albert's offer to help the Pope. He was then to encourage the Grand Duke of Tuscany in further reforms, and to urge on the Pope himself "a system of progressive improvement", such as would remedy "the ancient institutions" of Italy. In short, "he had a roving commission to give any Italian Government which might ask for it, general advice on the best way of conducting a constitutional government and to assure such governments that England would protect them from inter-ference".[34] In general he declared British opposition to any external inter-ference with the reforms introduced by any Italian sovereign: he would not, he said, "see with indifference any aggression committed on Roman territory"—a plain hint to the Pope that Austrian policy would be opposed.[35] From Turin Minto reported that the danger of Austrian intervention was not imminent, and both here and at Florence he showed a discreet reserve: but in Rome his mere presence, prolonged as it was for three whole months, was felt as a provocation to the reactionaries and a stimulus to all reformist tendencies.

The mission was intensely resented in Vienna and long continued to be regarded as one of the prime sources of all the subsequent troubles, and indeed as one of Lord Palmerston's most unpardonable acts.* Yet again, it was not the underlying principle, but the manner of its ap-plication, that prompted moderate criticism against the British Foreign Secretary. No better statement of the sane middle position can be found than in the contemporary writings of Prince Albert. Writing to his faithful mentor Stockmar, he says: "I am strongly of opinion that England should declare betimes that it *will not endure* that independent states should be forcibly prevented from setting about such internal reforms as they shall think for their advantage (e.g. Germany, Switzerland, Italy)." On the other hand he realised that the British Government was "frequently inclined to

---

* See *infra*, p. 262. Mr Taylor (*Italian Problem in European Diplomacy*, p. 50) is fully justified in assuming that Palmerston deliberately encouraged Minto to stay on in Rome, in order to embarrass Metternich and Guizot.

plunge states into constitutional reforms towards which they have no inclination. This I hold to be quite wrong (Spain, Portugal, Greece), *though
it is Lord Palmerston's hobby*."[36] The root difficulty being that Austria was
definitely opposed to liberal and constitutional government in Italy, in
however mild a form, and that such a move as the Minto mission would be
regarded by her as "a most hostile step", the Prince suggested informing
Austria that we were not helping the Italians, but "consider every independent state has a perfect right to manage its own internal affairs" and
introduce the reforms it pleases. To Lord John Russell he developed his
theories still further: "Let England be careful (in her zeal for progress) not
to push any nation beyond its own march, and not to impose upon any
nation what that nation does not itself produce: but let her declare herself
the protector and friend of all states engaged in progress, and let them
acquire that confidence in England, that she will if necessary defend them
at her own risk and expense."[37] The Queen sanctioned the mission on
condition that its object was communicated to Vienna and Paris beforehand,[38]
but this does not appear to have been done: while the despatch of Admiral
Parker to the west Italian ports, as an encouragement to the Liberal
sovereigns, served to exasperate Austria still further. Indeed there seems
to have been some exchange of views between Paris, Berlin, Vienna and
St Petersburg early in 1848, as to the possibility of a league to hold in check
British encouragement to the constitutional movement.[39]

It may be very plausibly argued that as pure theory Prince Albert's
contention was excellent, but that in practice, during the period culminating
in the great year of revolution, there was an unbridgable gulf between the
views of the Eastern and the Western Powers, and that nothing could have
averted conflict. But it is impossible to escape the conclusion that Lord
Palmerston's alternating methods of hectoring interference, good advice
and downright menace made unnecessary enemies on all hands.

PALMERSTON'S POLICY IN PORTUGAL AND SPAIN

A good example of these methods is provided by events in Portugal, where
the rival factions of Queen Maria and Dom Miguel had produced a state
of chronic civil war, with its attendant excesses. Palmerston's attitude was
based on the perfectly sound view that the union of Spain and Portugal was
undesirable—especially if Spain should become a mere satellite of France,
as so many contemporaries of the Carlist troubles were prone to assume—
and indeed that Portugal as a separate state offered many counterbalancing
advantages, "commercial, political, military and naval". From this last
point of view in particular Palmerston held that the naval position of the

Tagus ought never to be in the hands of any possible enemy of England.[40] Preoccupations such as these, combined with a predisposition to favour all Liberal movements, led Palmerston and Russell to meddle actively in Portuguese affairs, and it was only the sound common sense of Queen Victoria that restrained them from committing themselves to the statement, at once exaggerated and offensive, that the Portuguese Government had 'shown a spirit of tyranny and cruelty...without a parallel in any part of Europe".[41] Our new Minister at Lisbon appealed to his chief "not to be obliged to begin his activities by administering a series of reproofs", such as would only confirm the Portuguese in the belief that Britain was backing the rebels. Here again the Queen took a hand and complained that "trifles about two horses and the beating of a gardener" were "made topics of serious complaint", and that a continuance of such tactics would deprive England of "all legitimate influence in Portugal".[42] Palmerston toned down the actual details complained of, but continued his policy of interference, with the result that in June 1847 the two opposing wings of the Opposition took the affairs of Portugal as the text for a sharp attack upon the Government in both Houses. Palmerston quite frankly admitted that "the object of our interference was a recall of the (Portuguese) Parliament", and that this was "the mainspring which directed our policy". He argued that the only real alternative to the line which he had taken would be war with Spain, "to prevent Spanish interference in Portugal", and he correctly assumed that the House of Commons would not sanction such an expedition, which would, he argued, present no analogy to that which Canning sent to Portugal in 1826, "in the exercise and fulfilment of treaties and engagement". He therefore thought best "to unite with the Governments of Spain and France, for the purpose, not of crushing the liberties of the people, nor of setting up an arbitrary and tyrannical despotism, but for the purpose of re-establishing the constitutional Government of Portugal, and of giving to the people the means of redressing their grievances in a legal and legitimate manner". His defence culminated in the following phrases. "Looking at Portugal as our natural ally, as a country which it was important for British interests to maintain as a material element in the balance of European power,...we thought we should best consult our duty in obtaining for the Portuguese nation those constitutional securities which by the bad advice of the counsellors of the Crown in that country had been suspended. And in bringing the war to a peaceful termination, in transferring the struggle from the field of battle to the arena of parliamentary debate, we have earned the thanks of political parties."[43] But if the House accepted the unrepentant minister's plea for interference to promote one set of political principles, it was above all because Sir Robert Peel, after calling the mission of Colonel Wylde to Lisbon "the most curious instance in parliamentary history", none the less gave his support to the Whig Government. Both now and during the critical years that followed, the confused state of British party politics forced him to the conclusion that Palmerston at the Foreign Office was a lesser evil than the advent of a ministry committed to protection, and that Russell must therefore be kept in office.

Palmerston's defence of his policy of interference in Portugal merits close attention, for he deliberately based it upon principles of world-wide application, such as are typical of the man and his outlook throughout life. "Our duty, our vocation, is not to enslave, but to set free: and I may say, without any vainglorious boast, or without great offence to anyone, that we stand at the head of moral, social and political civilisation. Our task is to lead the way and to direct the march of other nations. I do not think we ought to goad on the unwilling or force forward the reluctant: but when we see a people battling against difficulties and struggling against obstacles in the pursuit of their rights, we may be permitted to encourage them with our sympathy and cheer them with our approbation, and even if occasion require, to lend them a helping hand." This aim, he contended, had already been achieved in Greece, in Spain, in Belgium, and was being quite logically pursued in Portugal also.

The Queen had already complained more than once of the failure of these tactics of interference in Spain, where even the so-called Progressista party had become alienated from us. Striking confirmation was provided when Palmerston on 16 March 1848 advised the Spanish Government to adopt constitutional methods and call some of the Liberals to power, and when the Premier, the Duke of Sotomayor, treated this as "offensive to the dignity of a free and independent nation" and presented the British Minister with his passports.* This incident, which would doubtless have had a much graver sequel if attention had not been diverted to the general state of chaos in Europe, led Lord Aberdeen to declare in the House of Lords, that it was "the first time a British Minister ever suffered such an indignity".[44] Lord Stanley did not hesitate to affirm that Palmerston's administration of foreign affairs had "been marked by a spirit and animus which has often led him into measures detrimental to the interests of this country".[45] In the House of Commons Peel expressed objection, not to

* The Queen told Lord Palmerston (23 May 1848—*Letters*, II, 175) that she was not surprised, since Sir Henry Bulwer "has for the last three years almost been sporting with political intrigues", and suggested that "our diplomatists" should be "kept in better order". On 15 June she bluntly insisted that our relations with Spain must have been very much mismanaged, and told Lord Palmerston that she did not wish Bulwer to return to Madrid as Minister (II, 179). It is necessary to bear in mind that Bulwer, the first serious biographer of Palmerston, was himself deeply involved in Palmerstonian diplomacy, and in extolling his chief was defending his own escapades in Paris and in Madrid.

Palmerston "giving advice, but to his mode of giving it. There was an assumption of superiority in his despatch, calculated to give offence to a proud nation like that of Spain."[46]

CHARGES AND COUNTER-CHARGES

Apart from the motives of home policy which deterred Peel from pressing his attack, it may be supposed that another parliamentary debate, of recent occurrence, had by its very futility rallied considerable support in favour of the Foreign Secretary. On 8 February and 1 March 1848[47] Anstey, backed by the brilliant but erratic David Urquhart, actually invited the House of Commons to impeach Palmerston on a charge of high treason, arguing that he had always sacrificed British to Russian interests, and that thanks to his corrupt complaisance "our great and natural enemy the Tsar" was now on the point of realising his ambitious designs. He even quoted as an analogy the case of Lord Carmarthen, who had accepted a bribe from Peter the Great, and boldly declared that since that time "Russia has never been without an agent to represent her in some of the Cabinets of Europe". At this distance of time it is difficult to read without impatience the farrago of nonsense which Anstey's speeches contain, and it was easy enough for Palmerston to tear his fancied arguments to shreds and at the same time to deal resounding blows at Urquhart for the indiscretion and even "great breach of duty" involved in his conduct at the Constantinople Embassy.* It is not surprising that in view of such patent exaggerations—the full absurdity of which were to become apparent a few years later, when Palmerston steered his country into war with Russia—many who looked upon his methods with suspicion felt unable to co-operate with his most ardent assailants.

Moreover, while accepting the criticism of Aberdeen and Stanley, we must at the same time admit that the very essence of Palmerstonian policy was to forestall revolution by timely concession: and this indeed was also the foundation of our home policy in the 'forties, to which Britain owed her immunity in 1848, when every other continental country save Scandinavia and the Low Countries—and for a very different reason, Russia—was a prey to subversive movements.

URQUHART AND PALMERSTON

After the failure of the Polish insurrection of 1831 some of the Polish exiles entrusted to David Urquhart certain documents purloined from the private papers of the Grand Duke Constantine (as Viceroy in Warsaw), with a view to publication.

* See *Supra*, p. 187. His more general observations on British foreign policy are referred to *infra*, p. 459.

After a delay of several years—due, according to Urquhart, to Palmerston's pressure upon the Foreign Office, where they had originally been deposited—these documents appeared in Urquhart's review *The Portfolio* in 1835: and this was the beginning of his quarrel with Palmerston, which became irreparable owing to Urquhart's share in the affair of the *Vixen* and the smuggled arms for Circassia, and his consequent removal from the Constantinople Embassy (see *supra*, pp. 186–7). *The Portfolio* ceased publication after two years, but was revived in 1843, and in this second series (vol. II, no. 5, pp. 147–97) Urquhart published an article entitled "The Connection of the Foreign Office with 'The Portfolio'", in which he claimed proof of Palmerston's "Russian soul" in the original three years' veto on publication of the Polish documents. He went so far as to declare that publication, when at last it came, did not trouble the Russian Government, because it knew "all this time" that it "was secure of England". A deputation was sent from Glasgow to Peel and Aberdeen, to charge Palmerston with treason: but not unnaturally the two statesmen remained unconvinced.

Even the Crimean War did not convince Urquhart and his friends of Palmerston's Russophobia! In a signed pamphlet entitled *The Queen and the Premier: a Statement of their Struggle and its Results* (1857) Urquhart referred to "the history of that man's progress" as "written in crimes, perpetrated throughout the globe, and may to-day be listened to in the unconscious sighs of millions at home". He asserted that Napoleon III's *coup d'état* was due to the help of Russia, and that therefore Palmerston had to support it; that Russia was active in breaking up the Russell Cabinet and opening the way for a Coalition; and that Palmerston first ordered, then suppressed, the pamphlet against Prince Albert, in order to force himself upon the Queen.

Even after Palmerston's death Urquhart kept up the feud, and in 1866 published *Materials for the True History of Lord Palmerston* (reprinted from the *Free Press*). This is a summary of a report published on 20 September 1855 by a Newcastle Committee of eight, self-appointed "to examine a charge of bribery against Palmerston". These individuals took "evidence" from a certain Mr Porter, of the Board of Trade, who "as the result of his own observation and of facts within his own knowledge," alleged that Palmerston systematically sacrificed the interests of England to those of Russia, in matters relating to commercial treaties" (p. 7). Porter also charged him with receiving money in 1825, through a Jew called Jacob James Hart, who formerly kept a gambling house, and who was appointed British Consul at Leipzig—a man "universally shunned as a most disreputable character " and eventually dismissed at the instance of Gladstone. The sum of £20,000 is mentioned. Peel is accused of conniving by "a variety of terse and poisonous sophisms", and "the Ministers of England" in a general way, of carrying into execution the will of Peter the Great.*

It seems almost incredible that a man of Urquhart's high character, knowledge and experience should have believed such rubbish: it certainly helps to explain why he made no mark in politics, despite his remarkable achievement in rousing the interest of working-class clubs in foreign policy (see *David Urquhart*, by

---

* This famous mare's nest is dealt with in an article by Lawrence Lockhart, "The Political Testament of Peter the Great" in *Slavonic Review*, No. 41 (January 1936).

Gertrude Robinson). Henry Reeve, it is true, once called Urquhart "a mad political dervish".

It is but fair to add that Palmerston seems to have paid Urquhart back in his own coin. In a letter to his brother William Temple on 4 July 1852—which Evelyn Ashley publishes in his *Life of Palmerston* (1, p. 366), Palmerston alleged that Urquhart and Anstey owed their election to Parliament in 1847 to Louis Philippe's money, "in order that they might be set at me and demolish me if they could". They and Westmacott (editor of *The Portfolio*) "got from Louis Philippe for their attacks on me, something not short of £60,000 first and last. That same King was a mean fellow, true son of Égalité and true grandson of the Regent." This allegation seems to have been as groundless as the nonsense briefly summarised above: but it is curious that no legal action was taken against Ashley when his book appeared in 1874.

Some readers may think the incident unworthy of inclusion in a serious history: to me it seems of some value, as revealing the levity with which unproved charges could be bandied about in the Victorian era, despite our strict law of libel. After all, the incredible story about Prince Albert (see *infra*, p. 322) has its parallel in our own day, in the grotesque beliefs current in 1914 about Prince Louis, Lord Haldane, and the Russian troops in transit to the western front.

PALMERSTON IN THE YEAR OF REVOLUTION

The February Revolution of 1848 had the effect of a spark in a powder magazine. The overthrow of the July Monarchy, the flight of Louis Philippe to England and the proclamation of the Second Republic were swiftly followed by outbreaks in Berlin, Munich and other German cities, in Rome, Naples and Northern Italy, in Vienna, Prague, Pest and Zagreb.* The republican infection seemed about to sweep everything before it, and the conservative courts found it less possible than ever to draw the necessary distinction between the theories of red revolution and those of constitutional liberalism.

Whatever may have been his faults, Palmerston had far too clear a grasp of cause and effect not to foresee the dangers of the European situation, and the explosion did not cause him any surprise. Nor would he have been the man he was, if he had regretted the downfall of Louis Philippe and Guizot: as he wrote to Lord Minto, he had always thought of Louis Philippe as "one of the cunning who outwit themselves".† The exiled

---

* The reader should be reminded that revolution broke out a month earlier in Sicily than in Paris, and that even before the close of 1847 the parliamentary movement in Hungary was assuming a semi-revolutionary complexion. In a word, revolution was in the air almost everywhere.

† Ashley, *op. cit.* 1, 54. Lord John Russell, writing to the Queen, went still further and threw the whole blame for "a great calamity" on the King himself. "A moderate and constitutional government at home, coupled with an abstinence from ambitious projects for his family abroad, might have laid the foundation of permanent peace, order and freedom in Europe. Selfishness and cunning have destroyed that which honesty and wisdom might have maintained" (15 April 1848—*Letters*, 11, 169).

King always suspected Palmerston of having shared in, or at least connived at, the events of February 1848. But the suspicion was groundless and reveals a complete misapprehension as to the character of Palmerston, who was far too blunt and straightforward to indulge in conspiracy, and who, it may be added, never bore Louis Philippe any grudge for such imputations, but did his best to ease his position as an exile. To Guizot as a refugee he showed special courtesy and hospitality, though definitely regarding him as representative of opposite political principles both at home and abroad.[48] But he speedily reached the conclusion that Lamartine and the Second Republic were a great improvement upon the Orleanists from the point of view of Anglo-French relations, and that upon cultivating them further depended the best hope of peace in Europe.

If such was his attitude towards France, he was frankly delighted at the fall of his old enemy Metternich. "Happy would it have been for the Continent", he wrote to his confidant Minto, "if this had happened some years ago."[49] He had already felt constrained to warn Metternich that "if he takes upon himself the task of regulating by force of arms the internal affairs of the Italian states, there will infallibly be war". In urging upon Metternich up to the very last moment the need for "relaxing the severity of the system now established in Austrian Italy", he failed to realise that by now the veteran statesman saw less danger even in an European war than in constitutional concessions.[50] On the other hand, he very rightly assumed that France would soon become the champion of constitutional liberty in Italy, and was afraid that this might precipitate general war.

In a word, he was never so far-sighted and so statesmanlike as in this year of crisis, though once more his plain speaking caused trouble. His chief pre-occupations were with France and Austria. At first, like many people, he faced the possibility of the revolutionary French Government becoming aggressive and of other Powers wanting to interfere. He told his representatives abroad quite boldly: "We will engage to prevent the rest of Europe from settling with France";[51] but he accepted Lamartine's pacific professions, and he told Lord Ponsonby, now in Vienna, that "the only chance for tranquillity and order in France and for peace in Europe, is to give support to Lamartine". To Normanby he assumed a Republic to be less peaceful than a Monarchy, and "large republics to be essentially and inherently aggressive": but none the less he thought it wise "to acknowledge whatever rule may be established with apparent prospect of permanency, but none other".[52] His attitude undoubtedly had a steadying and moderating influence and proved his genuine desire to cultivate good relations with whatever Government ruled France, in spite of all that had transpired. At the same time it is highly amusing to find Frederick William IV blessing

Providence for placing Palmerston at the Foreign Office,[53] and the Tsar inviting the Queen to combine in the defence of social order, and even arguing that the "intimate union" of Russia and Britain, the only two Powers still standing upright in Europe, may be destined "to save the world".[54]

Palmerston was ready to respond within limits, and his instructions to St Petersburg contain the phrase: "We are at present the only two Powers in Europe (except Belgium) that remain standing upright,* and we ought to look with confidence to each other." He desired the settlement of Poland, but "we, the Government, will never do anything underhand or ungentlemanlike".[55] He therefore urged Russia to discourage Austria from holding on to northern Italy, which he rather too optimistically assumed to be finally lost.

PALMERSTON AND AUSTRIA

But in spite of the reputation which he was soon to acquire, Palmerston was not anti-Austrian. The motive of his message to Metternich on the eve of the Revolution is revealed in the phrase: "We set too great a value on the maintenance of Austria as the pivot of the balance of power in Europe."[56] To King Leopold he wrote, "As to poor Austria, every person who attaches value to the maintenance of a balance of power in Europe must lament her present helpless condition"—inevitably due, he argued, to Metternich's system of government—"to aim at being the only figure among ciphers." But, he added, dogmatically, "the Alps are Austria's natural barrier and her best defence".[57]

In the early months of 1848 his main concern was to prevent Austrian intervention in Italy, because he feared that its inevitable result would be "a war of principles", in which "the principal champions contending against each other would be Austria and France". Moreover, in such a war England and Austria would certainly not be on the same side—"a circumstance which would occasion to every Englishman the deepest regret". Indeed, he was genuinely concerned for the preservation of Austria as a Great Power, and told Ponsonby, "The Austrian Empire is a thing worth saving": "its maintenance is an object of genuine interest to all Europe and to no country more than England". But he held that "the cheapest, best and wisest thing which Austria can do is to give up her Italian possessions quietly and at once, and to direct her attention and energy to organising the remainder of her coast territories, to cement them to-

---

* It is curious to note that Palmerston, writing from London to Normanby on 31 March, and Nicholas, writing from St Petersburg on 3 April, should have used this identical phrase. Perhaps it seemed obvious at the moment.

gether and to develop their abundant resources". What wise advice, and
how different the course of European history might have been if it had been
followed! But how tactless and unpalateable, though doubtless not so much
so as his frankly avowed opinion that Ferdinand should abdicate, since it is
fatal "when the sovereign is an idiot".[58]

The sparks from Paris had kindled instantly into flame in Vienna and in
Italy, and Metternich's successor, Count Ficquelmont, was confronted
simultaneously by revolution at home, insurrection at Milan and invasion
by Sardinia, as the champion of North Italian unity. Sharing as he did the
veteran Chancellor's keen detestation of Palmerston as the villain of the
piece, he found himself in the uncomfortable position of having to turn to
London for help. In reality Palmerston at this period had no belief in, nor
desire for, an united Italian Kingdom, and indeed a whole year later told
the Austrian Ambassador, "I cannot conceive of liberty without two Houses
of Parliament and a free press".[59] His main aim was European peace, and
to that end Austria must be preserved, but this in its turn could only be
achieved, if her impossible government were reformed. At the same time
he was alarmed at the possibility of French intervention on the side of
Sardinia, and the complications which might easily ensue.

During April Stratford Canning came to Vienna on an informal mission
of enquiry, and various remarks let drop by him convinced the amiable, but
not very well informed Pillersdorff, head of the provisional Austrian
Government, that Britain had changed her policy, and that an appeal from
her ancient ally might not fall on deaf ears. Already on 4 May Ficquelmont
was forced to resign, and only two days later Hummelauer was sent to
London, with virtually a free hand to negotiate. On 23 May he saw
Palmerston and suggested that Lombardy-Venetia might be formed into
an autonomous Kingdom, under an Austrian Archduke as Viceroy, but
with its own national Parliament, Government and army. Palmerston in
reply suggested that it would be better to renounce Lombardy outright,
while reserving the concessions already indicated for Venetia. Hummelauer,
much impressed by his friendly reception, urged Vienna to accept, arguing
that British mediation on such lines "would drag our enemies before the
judgment-seat of Europe".[60] The Italophil group in the British Cabinet,
led by Russell and Minto, insisted that this was still inadequate, but
Palmerston got them to consent, if to Lombardy were added "such
portions of Venetian territory as may be agreed upon between the respective
parties". This, he told Russell, most disingenuously, gave away nothing to
Austria, because the Italians would agree to "nothing less than the whole:
but it saves the Austrian honour". To Hummelauer, however, he represented it as a substantial concession, while adding significantly that what

Austria needed was "a good victory" (*une bonne bataille de gagnée*).[61] On 10 June, then, the Pillersdorff Cabinet accepted in principle the independence of Lombardy and the main lines of the Hummelauer proposals to Palmerston. A week later, Baron Wessenberg, the one Austrian diplomat of whom Palmerston approved, became Foreign Minister: and Palmerston wrote to him in the most cordial terms: "So you are at last at the post which you should have held long ago, and where you would have spared your country and Europe much misfortune. But it is better late than never. Try, I beg you, to put an end to this Italian war as soon as possible, for the result of it, however delayed, cannot any longer be doubtful...."[62]

The Milan Provisional Government, however, in its blind elation, refused to negotiate with Austria, except on the basis of independence for Venetia and South Tirol as well as Lombardy: and hence Wessenberg, though still ready to cede Lombardy and resolved to keep upon good terms with Palmerston, decided perforce to continue the war, and gave Marshal Radetzky a free hand. On 25 July the latter's resounding victory at Custozza transformed the whole situation: for Sardinia had to purchase an armistice by the evacuation of all Lombardy. Yet Palmerston persisted in offering unpalateable advice, and as late as 31 August wrote to Ponsonby in Vienna: "We do not wish to threaten, but it is the part of a friend to tell the truth, and the truth is that Austria *cannot* and *must not* retain Lombardy.... North of the Alps we wish her all prosperity and success in the world." South of them, he contended, her attitude was bound to land her in disaster. Already Prince Windischgrätz, who had suppressed the Revolution in Prague and was now commanding against the Magyars, had made direct approaches to Queen Victoria, to counteract her Minister's attitude. But Palmerston, quite unabashed, told Ponsonby: "Pray make the Camarilla* understand that in a constitutional country like England these things cannot answer, and that a foreign Government which places its reliance on working against the Government of this country is sure to be disappointed."[63]

During the late summer the idea of Anglo-French mediation was much discussed, but in Palmerston's eyes it was above all a *pis-aller*, a means of preventing France from intervening alone. But even Wessenberg was no longer ready to negotiate on the Hummelauer basis, and after the revolutionary outburst of 6 October at Vienna his supersession was in any case imminent. Prince Felix Schwarzenberg, who now came rapidly to the front as the leader of Austrian reaction, declared on taking office that "We shall take our stand on the treaties, we shall not cede an inch of ground."[64] He hit upon the brilliant idea of dividing France and Britain, by convincing the former that London was interested in a North Italian Kingdom "entirely

---

* The inner clique at the Austrian Court.

as a barrier against France". As a matter of fact Palmerston himself had given an excuse for this idea by the language which he used to Baron Koller: "Lombardy united to Piedmont," he said, "would form a barrier between Austria and France". This barrier, which he described as a non-conducting body, "would be a guarantee of peace". Schwarzenberg's stray arrow found its mark, and France moved steadily towards a reconciliation with Austria.

Palmerston on his side completely lost his temper over Radetzky's wholesale measures of repression in Lombardy, and he sent a protest to Vienna against "a proceeding conceived in the spirit of the most odious oppression, and enunciated by doctrines which belong only to the disciples of Communism, and which are subversive of the very foundations of social order".[65] But this time he had met his master in vituperation: for Schwarzenberg issued a circular Note repudiating all interference in Austrian affairs. "Lord Palmerston regards himself too much as the arbiter of Europe. For our part we are not disposed to accord him the role of Providence. We never impose our advice on him in relation to Ireland: let him spare himself the trouble of advising us on the subject of Lombardy.... We are tired of his eternal insinuations, of his tone now protective and pedantic, now insulting, but always unbecoming. We are resolved to tolerate it no longer. Lord Palmerston said one day to Koller, that if we wanted war, we could have it: I say, if he wants war, he *shall* have it."[66] Here was a new note with which it would be necessary to reckon—a note of reviving despotism, conscious of its power. Palmerston for his part covered up his mortification by comparing Schwarzenberg to an enraged woman of the town when arrested by a policeman in the act of picking a pocket: but he was reduced to silence, while the text of the letter circulated in select London circles.[67]

Palmerston was for the moment unabashed, but fell back upon the task of maintaining good relations with France, and a little later he defended himself before the House of Commons, as having "prevented a war in Italy and joined France in a mediation which prevented an European war", and as having preserved a good understanding with the Republic of France and thereby essentially contributed to the maintenance of peace in Europe". There was not a word about the emancipation of Italy, for the simple reason that that was never his aim throughout the whole crisis of 1848–9. In the later stages, and especially during the second Italian war, which ended with the disastrous defeat of Charles Albert at Novara, he and Schwarzenberg, despite all their mutual antipathy, were equally anxious for a speedy termination of the war (and this, under the circumstances, inevitably meant the discomfiture of Sardinia), lest French intervention in

Italy should become a reality: and their anxiety was only increased by the interest displayed by France in the affairs of the Papal States.

The advent of Louis Napoleon to power in France had the effect of toning down the interventionist ardour of the Second Republic: and by the spring of 1849 France and Britain were almost equally eager to liquidate the whole Italian quarrel, if only Austria would moderate her terms and refrain from destroying Sardinian independence. Early in May, then, the British Ambassador in Paris, Lord Normanby, was instructed to approach Schwarzenberg's confidential agent in Paris, Alexander Hübner. "I know", he said, "that Prince Schwarzenberg has prejudices against Lord Palmerston, and that he opposes him: but he knows me, and I beg him to believe me. The Queen's Government wants Italy pacified as soon as possible. All our efforts are towards that end: Lord Palmerston desires it as much as you."[68] There was a last flare of trouble when de Tocqueville, newly appointed as French Foreign Minister, indicated that if Piedmont were again attacked, France would defend her, and suggested to London a joint protective expedition. But Palmerston at once told the French Ambassador that his Government, "whose interest in this affair is not equal to yours, will give the Piedmontese Government only diplomatic assistance and moral support".[69] A week later peace was signed at Milan, reimposing the territorial settlement of 1815 in North Italy.

PALMERSTON AND QUEEN VICTORIA

At a very early stage in the European crisis the Queen dissented strongly from her Foreign Secretary's attitude, and her letters of protest to both Russell and Palmerston show what was in the latter's mind. "The Queen must tell Lord John what she has repeatedly told Lord Palmerston, but without apparent effect, that the establishment of an *entente cordiale* with the French Republic, for the purpose of driving the Austrians out of their dominions in Italy, would be a disgrace to this country."[70]

The Queen was finding Palmerston incorrigible. In spite of what had happened in the Portuguese affair earlier in the year, he pursued his policy of hectoring interference. At the instance of the Queen and the Prime Minister he had instructed Sir Hamilton Seymour, our Minister in Lisbon, to refrain from mixing in Portuguese party intrigues. The draft of these instructions is so extremely characteristic that it deserves to be partially quoted. "As it is evident that the Queen and the Government of Portugal will listen to no advice except such that agrees with their own wishes, I have to instruct you to abstain in future from giving any longer advice to them on political matters, *taking care to explain both to the Queen and the*

Government your reasons for doing so. You will, however, at the same time positively declare to the Portuguese Government that if by the course of policy they are pursuing they should run into any difficulty, they must clearly understand that they will not have to expect any assistance from England."[71] Queen Victoria protested against the use of such menacing language, and Lord John insisted upon its deletion from the despatch; but at the same time he frankly admitted that "in the present critical state of Europe" he was afraid to raise a question "which might induce a belief" that Lord Palmerston "had not conducted foreign affairs to the satisfaction of his colleagues or of his sovereign".[72] Thus it is clear that Palmerston had the bit between his teeth, and that his political colleagues and opponents alike hesitated to proceed to extremities against him.

By the autumn of 1848 the Queen was in constant disagreement with Lord Palmerston, and protested to the Prime Minister against "the intemperate tone" of the Foreign Secretary's language[73] and against his writings, "always as bitter as gall". "I felt", she told Russell, "really I could hardly go on with him, that I had no confidence in him, and that it made me seriously anxious and uneasy for the welfare of the country and for the peace of Europe in general", that he was "distrusted everywhere abroad", and "often endangered the honour of England by taking a very prejudiced and one-sided view of a question." She therefore urged the substitution of Lord Clarendon as Foreign Secretary and suggested that Palmerston might be sent to Ireland as Viceroy. But Lord John confessed to a desire of avoiding "internal trouble", and above all to his fear "of making Palmerston an enemy by displacing him".[74] The Queen reluctantly gave way, but for the next three years her protests were almost chronic. Only three weeks after her talk with Russell she found that Palmerston's "partiality in this Italian question really surpasses all conception".[75] "Really it is quite immoral, with Ireland quivering in our grasp, and ready to throw off her allegiance at any moment, for us to force Austria to give up her lawful possessions."[76]

Her annoyance was increased when the young Francis Joseph and his advisers emphasised their resentment at British policy by refusing to send an Archduke to announce his accession, as was being done in the case of the Prussian and Russian Courts. Indeed, Schwarzenberg told Ponsonby that he would not place any Archduke "in contact with a person who had shown himself so great an enemy" of Austria:[77] and Koller, taking his cue from his new chief, actually went so far as to tell the Queen at a Drawing Room, that it was impossible for Austria to be on friendly terms with England "so long as the present Foreign Secretary has control of affairs".[78] But Palmerston merely treated this as "truly characteristic of the state policy of European China", and notified Ponsonby that he was "sincerely grateful to Austria for sparing me the trouble and inconvenience such a mission would have caused". If no Archduke came, the loss would not be England's, but his own, since "it must always be an advantage to a foreign Prince...to visit England and see with his own eyes how Liberty may be combined with Loyalty and Freedom with public order". Schwarzenberg, on his side, bluntly refused to accept a Note of Palmerston on behalf of Hungary, and told the Prime Minister that he regarded it as interference in Austrian home affairs, and that he in his turn intended to give London advice regarding its policy in Canada.[79]

That Palmerston had become little short of an obsession to Vienna may be concluded from a letter written by Schwarzenberg on 2 January 1849 to King Leopold of the Belgians: "The present condition of Italy is largely the work of English diplomacy and the fruit of the seed scattered by Lord Minto. Lord Palmerston in March broke the staff over Austria: he gave us up and erased us from the ranks of the Great Powers. A Kingdom of Italy under his protection was to be formed by revolution at home and treachery abroad, out of fragments of the Monarchy, in order to form a counterweight to France in the south."[80] This was of course a grotesque exaggeration, but Palmerston showed such complete disregard for the mental processes of Austrian statesmen, that if he could have seen this verdict, he would have had no right to complain at the failure to read his own mind.

THE HUNGARIAN REVOLUTION

In the meantime Kossuth and the revolutionary Hungarian Government made constant efforts to establish contact with the West, but their agent, the historian Szalay, was informed that Palmerston could only receive him through the medium of the Austrian Ambassador: for the Government, he argued, "has no knowledge of Hungary except as one of the component parts of the Austrian Empire".[81] In December 1848 Count Teleki came to London on Kossuth's behalf, but was rebuffed in identical terms, and his offer of special commercial concessions to British traders in Hungary was not taken seriously. Pulszky, who arrived in March 1849, at first found the situation rather more favourable, owing to Palmerston's alarm at the Russian occupation of Transylvania: he established many connections in society and with the press, and dined with one member of the Cabinet, Lord Lansdowne. But Kossuth's rash deposition of the Habsburgs and his designs of Danubian federation at the expense both of Austria and of Turkey were too much for Palmerston, who favoured a compromise between Hungary

and Austria, as the surest means of rendering Russian intervention unnecessary, and openly avowed this in the House of Commons on 22 July.
"Lord Palmerston and Lord Lansdowne", wrote Pulszky to Kossuth, "are
very kind to me, but they are afraid of war. They do not act against us, but
the most they are ready to demand in our interest is mediation on the
basis of the Laws of 1848."[82]

As a matter of fact, recent revelations from the Russian archives show
that Palmerston, whatever may have been his personal sympathies, was
even less disposed to help Hungary than has hitherto been assumed. That
Wellington, not once but repeatedly, pressed upon Brunnov the need for
Russian intervention in Hungary—saying every time they met, "Act, but
with enough forces"—need not surprise us unduly: and that Aberdeen also
favoured intervention, is mainly interesting as helping to explain the
friendly feelings of Nicholas towards him. But it appears that Palmerston
also encouraged Brunnov in favour of intervention, giving as his opinion
that Russia *must* act in aid of Austria, but must then "finish as quickly as
possible". From this the Ambassador drew the conclusion that Britain
wished Austria to be preserved, but did not wish the Russians to remain in
Hungary.[83]

This attitude, however, did not prevent Palmerston from sharing the
widespread indignation of public opinion at the drastic methods of repression
adopted by the Austrians in Hungary. In May 1849 the Russians crossed
the Carpathians in overwhelming numbers, and by August the main
resistance of Hungary had been overcome. After the capitulation of Világos,
while the Russian high command granted honourable terms to Arthur
Görgei, the Austrians executed thirteen generals of the revolutionary army
at Arad, including Count Charles Leiningen, a cousin of Queen Victoria,
and with even less reason shot the ex-Premier Count Batthyány and various
high administrative officials. On 9 September Palmerston vented his anger
to the unsympathetic Ponsonby: "The Austrians are really the greatest
brutes that ever called themselves by the undeserved name of civilised
men. Their atrocities in Italy, Galicia, Hungary, Transylvania are only
to be equalled by the proceedings of the negro race in Africa and
Haiti."[84] Austria, he declared, held various territories "at the goodwill
of three external Powers"—Italy as long as France chooses, Hungary
and Galicia as long as Russia chooses, Germany as long as Prussia
chooses. And he closed this half-prophetic phrase by asserting that "the
first quarrel between Austria and France will drive the Austrians out of
Lombardy and Venetia".[85]

If these and other remarks could have been read by the indignant
Radical sympathisers with Italy and Hungary who considered themselves

betrayed by Palmerston, public opinion would doubtless have been appeased. As it was, press and platform were very vocal against Austria during the summer of 1849, and became still more excited when Kossuth and other leading Hungarian rebels fled into Turkish territory and when Austria and Russia united at the Porte to press in the stiffest terms for their surrender.

Palmerston had never given such free rein to his sympathies for Hungary as for Italy, and even during the first half of 1849 he persisted in his negative attitude towards the internecine war that was being waged throughout the Danubian basin. Even the occupation of Wallachia and Moldavia by Russia, as a preliminary to action against the Hungarian rebels, did not affect this attitude. Sir Stratford Canning, who had entered upon his fifth mission to Constantinople in June 1848, had almost from the first set himself to stiffen the resistance of the Porte to Russian interference in the Principalities. The affairs of the two provinces were placed upon a new footing by the Russo-Turkish Convention concluded at Balta Liman on 1 May: and Canning not merely blocked it at every stage, but carried his dislike of its terms to the length of advocating a naval demonstration against Russia. This, however, was too drastic for Palmerston, who throughout the impending crisis was for once in a way admirably firm without being provocative. The capitulation of Világos was followed by the flight into Turkish territory of Louis Kossuth and other Hungarian leaders, accompanied by the Polish volunteer generals Bem and Dembinski. Austria and Russia promptly demanded their extradition, in accordance with certain treaties dating from the eighteenth century, and the Tsar even despatched Prince Radziwill with a fiery ultimatum to the Sultan. This was rejected by the Porte, thanks to the joint action of Canning and his French colleague General Aupick, but only when the former, on his own authority, held out the prospect of British and French assistance against Russia, and induced Admiral Parker to despatch a frigate to the Golden Horn, as a visible sign of British interest. He then appealed to Palmerston to "come to the rescue as fast as you can".[86]

On 2 October the British Cabinet decided in favour of "moral and material support" for Turkey, and Captain Townley, in a famous ride across the Balkans, brought detailed instructions to Canning. Palmerston secured the co-operation of France for "friendly and courteous representations at Vienna and St Petersburg, to induce the Imperial Governments to desist from their demands", and in the meanwhile, for the despatch of British and French squadrons to the Dardanelles, and to the Bosphorus if invited by the Sultan—"either to defend Constantinople from attack, or to give the moral support which their presence would afford".[87] In point of fact the fleets appeared off the Dardanelles in the first days of November, but it was not necessary to go farther, for Russia and Austria withdrew their demand for extradition, in deference, said the Russian representative, to the strength of public opinion in England. Palmerston, who already had a shrewd suspicion that the matter would be amicably settled, wrote to Canning: "In this affair we are trying to catch two great fish, and must wind the reel very gently and dexterously, not to break the line. The Government here have resolved to support the Sultan at all events: but we must be able to show to Parliament that we have used all civility and forbearance and that if hostilities ensue, they have not been brought on by any fault or mistake of ours. There never was such unanimity in England upon a question not directly affecting the immediate interests of England: but that unanimity would cease if we did not play our game with great discretion."[88] Stanley and Aberdeen, if they could have looked over his shoulder as he wrote, would have felt that their parliamentary action had not been altogether in vain. It may however at once be admitted that having once taken such action, he was absolutely right in declaring, "we ought either never to have sent our fleet, or to keep it there till matters are settled": Britain must not be represented "as a barking cur that runs off with its tail between its legs when faced and threatened".[89]

That British public opinion felt so keenly on this subject, was very largely due to disgust at the repressive measures adopted against Hungary, reviving as they did the worst memories of Italy. The Arad executions were ordered by the brutal Haynau, in total disregard of the wishes of the real victor, the Russian commander-in-chief. This, and the execution of Count Batthyány, the first Prime Minister of modern Hungary, was too much even for the suppressor of Polish liberties and prompted the Tsar to draw away a little from Austria. Moreover, when once the demand for actual surrender of the refugees had been abandoned, he was less interested in the minor question of their internment. It is true that he refused to receive Lord Bloomfield, on the ground that Britain's attitude had "dimmed the lustre" of Russia's successes in Hungary. Fortunately, however, Palmerston held that it "would be bad policy for us to accept a quarrel", unless absolutely forced upon us,[90] and kept his more flamboyant style for a private letter to Canning. "We have forced the haughty autocrat to go back from his arrogant pretensions; we have obliged Austria to forego another opportunity of quaffing her bowl of blood: and we have saved Turkey from being humbled down to absolute prostration. All this will be seen and felt by Europe."[91]

The Tsar's reserved attitude enabled Palmerston to concentrate his fire upon Austria, who demanded that the refugees should be kept under surveillance for twelve years. This he dismissed as "quite preposterous": indeed, "it is scarcely less derogatory to the Sultan to be jailor for Austria than to be purveyor to the Austrian executioners".[92] Encouraged by Canning, the Porte stood firm, and when in April 1850 Austria withdrew this claim also, Canning at once proceeded to work for the release of the exiles. It was not till September 1851 that Austria finally withdrew her veto, and that Kossuth was free to leave for America on a ship specially provided by the United States Government.

In all this, Palmerston does not seem to have regarded himself as really Austrophobe. "It is painful", he told Ponsonby,[93] "to see the Austrian Government led on in its blindness, folly and passionate violence into a course utterly at variance with the established policy of Austria." In his view, she obviously ought to have backed Turkey against Russia: yet "here is Schwarzenberg, in his fondness for bullying the weak", co-operating with the Tsar "to humble Turkey and lay her at the feet of Russia". "It is idle trash to say that we are hostile to Austria."[94] The downright and not very subtle Ponsonby may well be excused for not taking these assurances very seriously, and appears to have expressed his personal sympathy with the arch-reactionaries in power at Vienna. On this Palmerston wrote to him in the most outspoken terms: "I hear from many quarters that you oppose instead of furthering the policy of your government and that you declare that you disapprove of our course. No diplomat ought to hold such language as long as he holds his appointment."[95] This incident is thoroughly typical of Palmerston, who always hit straight from the shoulder, whether at a foreign Government or a political opponent or one of his own subordinates. Incidentally, it serves also to illustrate the boundless arrogance of Schwarzenberg, far exceeding even that of Tsar Nicholas. Moreover, it explains how Ponsonby came to say to Russell that "he had received from Palmerston letters which are not to be submitted to by any man".[96]

Palmerston, then, adhered to the view expressed to Stratford Canning: "We of course attach great importance to the maintenance of the Austrian Empire as an essential element, and a most valuable one, in the balance of power, and we should deeply regret anything which could cripple Austria or impair her future independence."[97] In the House of Commons, as late as 21 July 1849, when Hungary was on the very point of surrender, he denied "the imputation of unfriendly feelings" towards Austria, and declared her to be "a most important element in the balance of European power". He even went so far as to argue that "the political independence and liberties of Europe" were "bound up with the maintenance and integrity of Austria as a great European Power, and that anything which tends to weaken or cripple her, still more reduce her to the position of a secondary state, must be a great calamity to Europe".[98] After noting the many defects of the Austrian constitution and deeply regretting the failure to reach "some amicable arrangement" between Austria and Hungary, he closed by affirming that "to suppose that any Government of England can wish to excite revolutionary movements in any part of the world...shows really a degree of ignorance and folly which I never supposed any public man could have been guilty of".[99] But of course to the arch-reactionaries Prince Schwarzenberg, Alexander Bach and their young master Francis Joseph himself, as to Metternich before them, Palmerston remained the very incarnation of anti-Austrian feeling and of the subversive currents and views of western Liberalism. None the less he had had entirely his own way, he dominated the Prime Minister Lord John Russell, he held his own against all opponents in the House and he had more and more behind him the man in the street, who was now beginning to be a real political force.

At the same time he had against him more and more the influence of the Court, very largely owing to his incorrigible habit of taking vital decisions without even informing the Queen, who was after all, at least nominally, the highest constitutional factor in foreign affairs: and between 1848 and 1851 a whole series of incidents occurred which kindled the disapproval of the Queen and Prince Albert into acute resentment and constant protest. The mere catalogue of such incidents is sufficiently formidable—the status of Lord Normanby in Paris, the despatch of British rifles to Sicilian rebels, the question of co-operation with France in Italian affairs, the Kossuth agitation in England, the assault upon General Haynau in London, the prolonged controversy with Greece, culminating in the affair of Don Pacifico and the naval blockade, and finally Palmerston's attitude to the *coup d'état* of Louis Napoleon. On some of these it is unnecessary to dwell in any detail, but others deserve close attention, as illustrating not only the astonishing methods and mentality of one of our greatest Foreign Secretaries and the crude and fluid state of public opinion in the Victorian era, but also the complete transformation which has since been wrought in the outlook of every party and party grouping towards the fundamental facts of our foreign policy. In the decade following the Great War, by universal consent, an attitude of negation or neutrality has been adopted towards problems as acute and clamant as any that confronted Palmerston in 1848, problems in which not only he, but even the mildest of his contemporaries, would almost infallibly have intervened with the whole force of Britain behind them.

It must be added that there was very wide dissatisfaction in the country, and early in July 1849 the Opposition initiated a debate on "the state of the nation", in which of course the main stress was laid on home affairs. But t was highly significant that Disraeli, in the closing speech of the evening, turned at the last his weapons against those who "year after year have been murmuring opposition to a Government which they have not the courage manfully to oppose", and roundly declared that support of the Government was equivalent to "a vote of confidence in an empty and exhausted Exchequer...in an endangered colonial empire,...in Danish blockades and Sicilian insurrections,...in a prostrate and betrayed agriculture,...in Irish desolation".[100] The Russell administration was already being driven on to the defensive.

GREEK AFFAIRS

During Lord Palmerston's final tenure of the Foreign Office Greek affairs played an altogether disproportionate part in the public eye, but the course of events throws so much light not only upon Palmerston's policy and methods, but upon the general outlook upon foreign problems during the Victorian era, that it deserves fuller treatment than its own merits would suggest. Even under Aberdeen Athens had virtually been divided into rival factions, headed by the French and British Ministers: under Palmerston exaggerated importance was attached to the most trifling incident, and Lyons, on orders from London, bombarded the Greek Government with remonstrances about brigandage, frontier brawls and the minutiae of police administration. The claim of the historian Finlay for compensation for land expropriated for the King's garden, was at once unreservedly backed by Palmerston, though it afterwards transpired that Finlay was making an altogether exorbitant profit and had already received a far higher sum than any of the individuals concerned.* Early in 1847 a rupture occurred between Greece and Turkey, owing to words which had passed between King Otto and the Turkish Minister at a court ball: and Palmerston at once took advantage of the incident to read the Greeks a lesson. Declaring Greece to be clearly in the wrong, he warned her that the guarantee of the three Powers did not apply in the case of Greek provocation and persisted in treating as inadequate the King's letter of apology to the Sultan.[101] A series of stiff British Notes followed, complaining of financial maladministration, and demanding prompt payment of the interest due on the Greek Debt. At the same time Palmerston tried to convince Guizot as to the parlous state of Greece, but only obtained the reply, "Lord Palmerston thinks us badly informed, we think him badly informed. All English travellers in Greece agree with Lyons, all French travellers agree with

* Cobden stated in Parliament that Finlay was one of over 100 persons affected, and that all the others accepted the Greek Government's terms, including the Russian Consul-General and the agent of the Episcopal Society of America.

Piscatory." It is hardly necessary to add that Greece under King Otto was only too open to criticism, that the poison of prolonged Turkish rule was still working in the veins of her people, and that she was all too scantily supplied with leaders of integrity and efficient standards: but even at this early stage, and especially after the Revolution of 1843, there was a marked upward tendency, which was checked rather than promoted by the constant bullying and insult to which Palmerston subjected the little country.

The death of Kolettis in September 1847 removed the special bugbear of Palmerston and Lyons, and the general effervescence in Europe during 1848–9 provided a certain respite. On the eve of the February Revolution Piscatory had been replaced in Athens by M. Thouvenel as French Minister, and a year later Admiral Lyons was succeeded by Mr Wyse. But this, so far from ending the friction between London and Athens, was a signal for a series of fresh notes, advancing all manner of claims against the Greek Government. As Lord Stanley afterwards contended without exaggeration, Finlay alone of all the claimants could be described as "a person of character and responsibility", and he himself eventually accepted arbitration and a considerably lower sum of money than that demanded in his name. Among various claims of Ionian subjects the foremost was that of a certain Sumachi, who accused the police of having tortured him, but who turned out to be a burglar of notorious character, whose testimony was worthless. The incident of the British gunboats *Spitfire* and *Phantom* centred round a discreditable brawl during an attempted rising near Patras, in which through a misunderstanding the British Consul and a naval lieutenant became involved, and which with a very little good will on both sides could have been speedily settled up and dismissed to limbo. Again, the islets of Cervi and Sapienza were claimed for the Ionian Islands, on the basis of a doubtful reading of the Treaty of 1830 and without even consulting the other two Protecting Powers on a matter which concerned all.

The Pacifico Incident

But the main count of Palmerston's indictment against Greece was the notorious case of "Don Pacifico", a Portuguese Jew who claimed British citizenship as a former resident at Gibraltar, and who, as the result of usurious practices, had on 4 April 1847 had his house at Athens pillaged by the mob. Though according to his own story everything had been destroyed, Pacifico was able to present a strangely detailed inventory, including a couch and a "lit conjugal" valued respectively at £170 and £150 and totalling £8000 for furniture alone, while he estimated at £27,000 the value of Portuguese bonds, alleged to have been destroyed in the fire, but for which the arbiters to whom this detail was eventually submitted awarded about one-sixth of this figure. Palmerston endorsed every demand in its most exaggerated form, showed not the slightest readiness to listen to explanations, and when the Greeks took refuge in prevarication, ordered a British squadron of fourteen ships, under Admiral Parker, to proceed to Greek waters and concert with Wyse the best steps for enforcing payment. However gravely at fault the Greek Government might have been, this peremptory style was not the right remedy, and Palmerston's thoroughly unreasonable temper is shown by his correspondence with Wyse. For instance, referring to the suspended payments on the Greek Loan, he tells Wyse, "We can't go on requiring the people of this country to pay £50,000 a year to enable King Otto to corrupt his Parliament, bribe his electors, build palaces and lay up a stock purse for times which his bad policy may bring upon him": and he added a violent allusion to "the intrigues and cabals of French agents".[102]

On 17 January 1850 Wyse and Parker, having failed to obtain satisfaction, addressed an ultimatum to the Greek Government, and after the time limit of 24 hours had expired, proclaimed a general blockade of Greece. The Greek Foreign Minister, Landos, applied for the good offices of the other two Protecting Powers, and in a most dignified protest declared that "Greece is weak and did not expect that such blows would be aimed at her by a Government which she reckoned with equal pride and confidence among her benefactors." The French and Russian Ministers, Thouvenel and Persiany, protested at the seizure of Greek ships, and Palmerston's action may be said to have aroused general indignation on the Continent. On 5 February the French Government offered mediation, and Palmerston somewhat grudgingly accepted its "good offices". This was followed a fortnight later by Russian intervention. Nesselrode, on the Tsar's personal instructions, told Baron Brunnov to enter a complaint at Britain acting without taking the trouble to inform her two colleagues in the protectorate of Greece.* He was to enquire "whether Great Britain, abusing the advantages afforded by her immense maritime superiority, intends henceforth to pursue an isolated policy, without caring for those engagements which bind her to the other Cabinets, whether she intends to disengage herself from every obligation, as well as from all community of action, and to authorise all Great Powers on every fitting opportunity to recognise towards the weak no other rule but their own will, no other right but their own physical strength".[103] This scathing criticism, peculiarly unpalatable from

---

* That Nesselrode himself was already furious at Palmerston, is shown by one of his private letters to Baron Meyendorff in Vienna, dated 8 February, where he refers to "a new infamy" (*Lettres et Papiers*, x, 289).

such a quarter, and all the more so because it was so apposite, seems to have made but little impression on Palmerston, who wrote to Wyse, "They are furious at seeing that the spoilt child of Absolutism"—here he is identifying Otto and Greece—"whom they, encouraging for many years past to insult and defy England, should at last have received a chastisement from which they are unable to protect him."[104] With one of the principals in such a mood, even the most trifling incident was certain to be envenomed still further.

On 6 March Baron Gros, the French delegate, arrived in Athens on a special mission of investigation, and next day the blockade was temporarily raised. After a fortnight Gros proposed to Wyse the restoration of the detained ships, the payment of a lump sum as indemnity and the abandonment of the original six points: but Palmerston ordered Wyse to uphold the original claims, and at last Gros, on 23 April, declared his mission to have failed and refused to advise the Greeks to comply. But the very next day news reached him from home that direct negotiations had meanwhile been conducted between London and Paris and had resulted in a convention, by which Greece was to assign to Wyse the sum of £8500 for the satisfaction of individual claims, while the special claim affecting the lost Portuguese bonds was referred to three arbiters.* Incredible as it sounds, however, this agreement was at once notified by Paris to Gros, but not by London to Wyse, with the result that the latter, who had been growing restive at the delays, reverted to his still valid original instructions and reimposed the blockade. He took the pedantic and unconciliatory view that Gros had put an end to his own mission, and declined the latter's plea for postponement till the news from Paris could be confirmed from London. There was thus nothing left for the unfortunate Greeks but abject submission, after a secret session of the two Chambers: and on 27 April an immediate payment of 180,000 drachmae and 150,000 more on deposit, was made to the British Minister.

It is doubtful whether the exact workings of Palmerston's mind in this whole affair will ever be known. Certainly it is difficult to explain why he delayed for ten whole days sending fresh instructions to Wyse, why, if he wished to avert fresh complications on the spot, he did not send a special messenger to Athens as the French Government had done, and above all, why at the final stage he insisted on upholding Wyse's action, instead of treating it as superseded by his own convention with Paris. This last step had immediate repercussions. The Russian Ambassador Brunnov formally protested against the renewal of the blockade, and the French Ambassador, Drouyn de Lhuys, absented himself from the Queen's birthday celebra-

---

* It is highly significant, and deserves emphasis, that the final award at Lisbon gave to Pacifico not the 665,450 drachmae claimed, but only 4885. See Driault, *op. cit.* II, 360.

tions. In the French Chamber the Premier, General de Lahitte, charged the British Government with duplicity, and declared the Ambassador's "further residence in London" to be "no longer compatible with the dignity of the Republic". Palmerston was reduced to assuring Drouyn that "we never had intended any disrespect to the French Government", and urged "the many great and important interests, not merely English and French, but also European, which require a good understanding and close connection between England and France":[105] but this did not prevent Drouyn from leaving London, and Brunnov also expected to be recalled at any moment.

Rupture with France

That Palmerston's conduct of the Greek affair should thus have involved us in acute international friction, naturally aroused keen excitement, and Lord Stanley gave notice of a resolution criticising the whole policy of the Government. It seemed at last to give the Court their opportunity: and Prince Albert wrote sarcastically to the Prime Minister, "We are not surprised that Lord Palmerston's mode of doing business should not be borne by the susceptible French Government with the same good humour and forbearance as by his colleagues."* Three days later he returned to the charge and expressed in his own name and the Queen's, "the conviction... that Lord Palmerston is bringing the whole of the hatred which is borne to him—I don't mean here to investigate whether justly or unjustly—by all the Governments of Europe, upon England, and that the country runs serious danger of having to pay for the consequences".[106] This led Lord John to declare his "readiness not to remain in office any longer with Palmerston as Foreign Secretary",† and to admit that "Palmerston's personal quarrels with all Governments of foreign countries...were doing serious injury to the country". But though in secret confabulation he agreed with the Whig magnate Lord Lansdowne that a change at the Foreign Office was desirable, he was none the less reluctant to make Palmerston "the scapegoat", being long since unable either to control or to defy him and feeling doubtful whether the Government could survive his dismissal. The problem which Palmerston presented for the two great parties is best stated in the words of Peel to his friend and colleague Sir James Graham: "Either from choice or from necessity the present Govern-

---

* 15 May, Martin, *op. cit.* II. 275. As early as 2 April, however, Prince Albert had written to Russell: "at a moment in which England ought to stand highest in the esteem of the world, and to possess the confidence of all the Powers, she was generally detested, mistrusted and treated with indignity by even the smallest Powers" (*ibid.* p. 303).

† "I feel strongly that the Queen ought not to be exposed to the enmity of Austria and France and Russia, on account of her Minister" (18 May, to Prince Albert, *Letters*, II, 243).

ment is so identified with Palmerston, that his overthrow would be the fate of the administration....The case does not admit of faint attacks or of an idle war of words.... He must be endured until he destroy both himself and the administration *of which he is now the ruling member*; or active hostilities must be openly waged against the Government, on the avowed ground that his management of our foreign relations is inconsistent with the peace of Europe, with our national sentiments and with the reduction of our huge military and naval establishments." It was "a choice of dangers and evils", but Palmerston's foreign policy seemed to him "less to be dreaded than Stanley and a new Corn Law".[107]

There were, however, others on both sides of the House who, not realising Russell's virtual conversion to the Queen's views, favoured open war on Palmerston: and the Queen's fears lest the discussion should "place despotic and democratic principles in array against each other",[108] when it was above all a question of methods and tactics, were soon to be justified. Lord Stanley urged upon Disraeli "the great importance, on many accounts, of hitting hard and not sparing", and waging *guerre à outrance* against Palmerston.[109] He himself, on 17 June, in moving a vote of censure, dissected one by one the British claims against Greece, denounced Don Pacifico as "this petty usurer trading on a borrowed capital of £30", extolled "the dignified and touching" despatch of the Greek Foreign Minister, contrasted Palmerston's "humble rejoinder" to the Russian autocracy with his peremptory tone towards helpless little Greece, and ended by describing Palmerston's policy as "calculated to endanger the continuance of our friendly relations with other Powers".[110] Lord Aberdeen* condemned almost equally Palmerston's attitude towards Greece and towards the Powers. Greece was "a *corpus vile* on which you might try your experiments", and its submission had been enforced by "a fleet equal to that which won the battle of the Nile". "Four short years" earlier, Britain was "honoured, loved and respected by every state in Europe, with a cordial understanding with France": yet now "our relations with the Great Powers of Europe are unprecedented and cannot continue long without danger".[111]

On a division Lord Stanley's resolution was carried by 169 to 132, and this naturally roused Lord Palmerston's supporters to desperate efforts on his behalf. The debate which opened on 24 June in the House of Commons, on Mr Roebuck's motion, lasted for five nights and will always remain one of the most sensational incidents of its kind in parliamentary history. It is

---

* Of Aberdeen Graham writes to Peel (7 April 1850) that he "attaches primary importance to our foreign relations, and in his estimation our domestic policy is secondary. At home he is liberal, but not an enthusiast: abroad he is a zealot, in the sense most opposed to Palmerston" (Parker, *Life of Peel*, III, 540).

obviously impossible, within the limits set to this volume, to describe fully a debate in which Gladstone and Disraeli, Russell and Cockburn, Graham and Sidney Herbert all took an active part: yet certain features are far too illuminating to be passed over lightly.

As Palmerston himself intervened at an early stage—winning the admiration of the House by what Gladstone afterwards called "a gigantic intellectual and physical effort"—it is natural to take his speech first.[112] He opened on an aggressive note, arguing that the House of Lords by its resolution had limited British subjects to "that protection only which the law and tribunals of the land in which they happen to be may give them. Now I deny that proposition and I say it is a doctrine on which no British minister ever yet has acted, and on which the people of England never will suffer any minister to act." No claim can stand above the law, but "on a denial of justice or upon decisions manifestly unjust" the British Government "should be called upon to interfere". Turning to the Greek affair, he maintained that Britain stood alone in urging on Otto the fulfilment of constitutional pledges, and used very violent language about the abuses, brigandage and "revolting barbarity" practised by the Greek Government. The reflections passed upon Pacifico he brushed vigorously aside: "I know nothing", he said, "of the truth or falsehood of these stories...*but I don't care what his character is*", since his rights "depend on the merits of the particular case". Surely the smallness of a country could not justify the magnitude of its evil acts, while the sending of a large force actually diminished the humiliation inflicted. He failed to clear up the difference of opinion between Baron Gros and Mr Wyse, but admitted that it "turned on the claims of Mr Pacifico". The friction with France he not unnaturally slurred over, but insisted that all differences had since been removed.

When he turned from Greece to other fields, he at once became more effective, the more so as some of the criticisms directed against him were futile and off the point. When taunted with "my little experimental Belgian monarchy", he found it easy to retort that the experiment had proved a complete success. He was also on strong ground in defending the Quadruple Alliance and his policy in Portugal, both in 1834 and in 1847: and he denounced the attempt of his opponents "to bring down every question to a personal bearing" declaring this attitude to be "like shooting a policeman". In arguing that the Spanish embroglio and the consequent disagreement with Britain had led to the overthrow of the French Monarchy, he was less convincing, though he described it as "a calumny on the French nation to suppose that the personal hatred of any foreigner to their minister could have this effect". The French were "a brave, generous and nobleminded people", and "if they had thought that a knot of foreign conspirators were caballing against one of their ministers for no other reason than that he upheld, as he conceived, the dignity and interests of his own country...they would have clung the closer to, and supported the more the man against whom such a plot had been made". The inferences in this passage were so obviously intended to apply to his own case, that they provoked tumultuous cheering on his side of the House.

It was in the Italian question that Palmerston's defence was most effective. "It has always been the fate of advocates of temperate reform and of constitutional improvement to be run at as the fomenters of revolution. Now there are revolutionists of two kinds in this world.... There are those violent, hotheaded and unthinking men who fly to arms, overthrow established Governments and recklessly, without regard to consequences... deluge their country with blood and draw down the greatest calamities on their fellow-countrymen.... But there are revolutionists of another kind— blindminded men who, animated by antiquated prejudices and daunted by ignorant apprehensions, dam up the current of human improvement until the irresistible pressure of accumulated discontent breaks down the opposing barriers and overthrows and levels to the earth those very institutions which a timely application of renovating means would have rendered strong and lasting. Such revolutionists as these are the men who call us revolutionists." These phrases were an effective preface to his contention that Lord Minto had not been sent to Italy to make revolutions, but "in consequence of a wish on the part of the Pope", and that neither at Turin nor Florence nor Rome did he advise the immediate establishment of representative and constitutional government, while in Naples he was closeted for eight hours with the King and his ministers, and but for the spark of the February Revolution in Paris would probably have won back the Sicilians. It was therefore quite untrue to speak of a policy of "exciting revolutions and then abandoning the victims we had deluded".

Palmerston's brief peroration contains phrases as familiar as Canning's classic reference to the New World. "We have shown", he cried, "that liberty is compatible with order, that individual freedom is reconcilable with obedience to the law": and he "therefore fearlessly challenged the verdict" of the House, "as representing a political, a commercial, a constitutional country", on the question "whether the principles on which foreign policy...has been conducted and the sense of duty which has led us to think ourselves bound to afford protection to our fellow-subjects abroad are proper and fitting guides for those charged with the government of England; and whether as the Roman in days of old held himself free from indignity when he could say 'Civis Romanus sum', so also a British subject, in whatever land he may be, shall feel confident that the watchful eye and the strong arm of England will protect him against injustice and wrong."

Undoubtedly, however, the most striking feature of the debate was the long speech of Gladstone,[113] which despite a certain verbosity, ranks among his greatest utterances. Point by point he riddled the case made by Palmerston against Greece. An apology might easily have been obtained for the *Phantom* incident, without resorting to reprisals or force. The claims of Ionian subjects were mere "twenty pound cases", dismissed by the impartial Gros as "inadmissible", and here he stopped to rebuke those who questioned Gros's impartiality after having accepted and welcomed French mediation and recognised his selection as unexceptionable. Sumachi was "a man of no known character, under accusation of theft", and his allegation of torture had been blindly accepted by Lyons without "sifting, scrutiny, or resort to the tribunals", and then quietly dropped. Finlay's far more reputable case could have been solved in the Greek courts, and Finlay had himself in the end admitted the possibility, while Lyons had reported them to be "completely independent".

Concentrating on the Pacifico affair, he condemned "the execrable outrage", but contended that the question of the man's character was fundamental, since the claims rested "altogether on his personal credit", and Pacifico's "unsupported allegation has been the prime mover of the operations of the British fleet against Greece". Yet Pacifico had made no attempt to obtain civil redress or to refute a recent public allegation that he had forged a bill for £600, while his "celebrated inventory" was patently false, since a moneylender who had "not a single farthing" of capital except £30 advanced by the Bank of Athens on some plate, could hardly have been possessed of luxurious furniture, clothes and jewels worth £5000. The best proof that his claims were fraudulent was that when Palmerston had instructed Lyons to prosecute certain persons on Pacifico's behalf at the charge of the British Government, Pacifico himself had been afraid to proceed, while for the major claim of £26,000, which had been pending for some twenty-nine years against the Portuguese Government, he had never once invoked the help of our Minister at Lisbon, but only raised it as an after-thought now that the alleged bonds had been destroyed. To sum up, the British demands had been "urged in a tone and manner wholly unjustifiable" and "bore on the face of them abundant proofs of fraud, falsehood and absurdity", while the intervention infringed "the general principles of the law of nations". Palmerston had ordered the occupation of "the worthless islands" of Cervi and Sapienza, in defiance of the right of France and Russia to be consulted, and had only been saved from grave consequences because Wyse and Parker refrained from executing the order. He suggested that "while negotiating at home" with France, Palmerston had been "not very unwilling that the matter should again go to the issue of force abroad", and complained that it should have been left to "the Autocrat of All the Russias" to administer a well-merited rebuke through Nesselrode's Note of 19 February, which he quoted to the House.

It is, however, of quite minor importance that Gladstone's arguments on the merits of Pacifico's case have stood the test of time: what gives his speech a permanent value is his attempt, towards its conclusion, to define the foundations upon which British policy should rest. Palmerston's policy was "characterised by a spirit of interference", and this he regarded as "a fundamental fault", to which he opposed "the principle of non-intervention in the domestic affairs of other countries". No difference of opinion existed as to the desire to exercise British influence "in the spirit which we derive from our own free and stable form of government and in the sense of extending to such countries, as far as they are able and desirous to receive them, institutions akin to those of which we know from experience to be inestimable blessings". But "are we to go abroad and make occasions for the propagation even of the political opinions which we consider to be sound. I say we are not." Palmerston positively "boasted" of making such occasions, and his interest in Portuguese and Spanish affairs was measured by "the opportunities of propagating the political sentiments which we think sound". Gladstone, while admitting this to be "a most alluring doctrine", objected "to the propagandism even of moderate reform". "If in every country the name of England is to be the symbol and nucleus of a party, the name of France, of Russia or of Austria may and will be the same. And are you not then laying the foundations of a system hostile to the real interests of freedom and destructive of the peace of the world?...Interference in foreign countries should be rare, deliberate, decisive in character and effectual for its end."

Palmerston's seductive comparison of a British and a Roman citizen Gladstone met with a telling retort: "What was a Roman citizen? He was the member of a privileged caste: he belonged to a conquering race, to a nation that held all others bound down by the strong arm of power. For him there was to be an exceptional system of law: for him principles were to be asserted, and rights were to be enjoyed, that were denied to the rest of the world. Is such then the view of the noble Lord as to the relation that is to subsist between England and other countries?"*

This led him on to consider "what a Foreign Secretary ought to be".

* Earlier in the debate Sir William Molesworth had already protested against the analogy of "Civis Romanus", on the ground that "Rome was the master of the earth and could and did trample upon mankind", and again against the tendency to make of us "the political pedagogues of the world".

"Is he to be like some gallant knight at a tournament of old, pricking forth into the lists, confiding in his sinews and skill, challenging all comers for the sake of honour, and having no other duty than to lay as many as possible of his adversaries sprawling in the dust?" If so, Palmerston should hold office for life. But "I understand it to be his duty to conciliate peace with dignity. I think it to be the very first of all his duties studiously to observe and to exalt in honour among mankind that great code of principles which is termed the law of nations, which [Mr Roebuck] has found indeed to be very vague in their nature and greatly dependent on the discretion of each particular country: but in which I find on the contrary a great and noble monument of human wisdom, founded on the combined dictates of reason and experience—a precious inheritance bequeathed to us by the generations that have gone before us, and a firm foundation on which we must take care to build whatever it may be our part to add to their acquisition, if indeed we wish to maintain and to consolidate the brotherhood of nations and to promote the peace and welfare of the world."

"The English people are indeed a great and noble people: but it adds nothing to their greatness or their nobleness that when we assemble in this place we should trumpet forth our virtues in elaborate panegyrics and designate those who may not be wholly of our mind as a knot of foreign conspirators." "The only knot of foreign conspirators against the noble Lord, is the combined opinion of civilised Europe." "Indeed it seems as if there lay upon the noble Lord an absolute need for quarrelling."

"His policy tends to encourage and confirm in us that which is our besetting fault and weakness, both as a nation and as individuals. Let an Englishman travel where he will as a private person, he is found in general to be upright, high-minded, brave, liberal and true: but with all this foreigners are too often sensible of something that galls them in his presence, and I apprehend it is because he has too great a tendency to self-esteem—too little disposition to regard the feelings, the habits and the ideas of others. I find this characteristic too plainly legible in the policy of the noble Lord."

"There is an appeal from this House to the people of England, but lastly there is also an appeal from the people of England to the general sentiment of the civilised world: and I for my part am of opinion that England will stand shorn of a great part of her glory and her pride if she shall be found to have separated herself, through the policy she pursues abroad, from the moral supports which the general and mixed convictions of mankind afford —if the day shall come in which she may continue to excite the wonder and fear of other nations, but in which she shall have no part in their affections and regard." It is not too much to affirm that in all this there is a new note, leading quite logically to the attitude adopted by Gladstone at the height of his power towards arbitration and international relations and to his famous definition of policy during the Midlothian campaign.

Highly interesting also was Richard Cobden's contribution to the debate.[114] He was able to claim that no one could seriously accuse him of intervening as the ally of Russia or of Austria. His main contention was that "the wrong might have been readily settled by other means...than this immense array of force". Baron Gros, he affirmed, had discovered the whole case against Greece to be "a barefaced attempt at swindling": its only result was to "submit to rebuke from Russia, and next to humiliation before France", and Palmerston was "obliged to resort to my plan of arbitration, after all the display of force". Most striking of all and highly original was his plea for "non-intervention in the domestic affairs of other nations". "With what face", he asked, "could you get up and denounce the Tsar for invading Hungary after the doctrine advocated to-night? Do you want to benefit the Hungarians or Italians? Leave us to ourselves, they say. Establish the principle that we shall not be interfered with by foreigners." Kossuth was saved, not by any intervention of the Foreign Secretary, "but by an universal outburst of public opinion in western Europe". Cobden closed by repudiating Palmerston's championship of liberalism abroad. "I believe the progress of freedom depends more upon the maintenance of peace, the spread of commerce and the diffusion of education than upon the labours of cabinets and foreign offices." Whatever may be said of the efficacy of Cobden's doctrine in the final resort, there can be no question that it was far better calculated to avert friction and maintain good relations with other Powers, than that pursued by Palmerston.

Scarcely less paradoxical in other directions was the speech of Benjamin Disraeli,[115] who after brushing aside the claims of Finlay and Pacifico as "doubtful in their character and exaggerated in their amount" and after a contemptuous reference to the Spaniards and Jews of Gibraltar as "a teeming and scheming race, not distinguished by the highest morality", laid down the principle that "the maintenance of a good understanding with France is the cardinal point of the foreign policy of this country" and then went on to a total denial of the view that the Whig Government had stood for self-government and constitutionalism in Europe. On the contrary, it had maintained close relations during the revolution with Austria and Russia and before it with the unconstitutional governments in Italy, and deserved but little credit for its attitude towards the second French Republic, since it had taken four months to concede recognition. He then made the curious assertion that three main interests of England in Europe were that the north of Italy should belong to Austria, Sicily to the Kingdom of Naples and the Sound and the mouths of the Elbe to Denmark. Yet these three interests had "at once been given up" by the British Government, which indeed had simultaneously maintained relations with King Ferdinand of Naples and secretly entertained a proposal for depriving him of Sicily. Moreover, the "intelligence and energies" of the Government had been "concentrated on one object, the creation of a German Empire": yet where was it now? "The German Empire was a German romance, as wild and monstrous." He even went so far as to maintain that but for "the policy of Her Majesty's Ministers there would have been no war in Europe at all", and that they could perfectly well have prevented Sardinia's attack upon Austria and its indirect consequence, the insurrection of Hungary. He was on stronger ground when he argued that there was no other example of a Foreign Secretary having driven away from London within so short a space of time "four ministers of the highest class", and that the present policy of isolation could not be continued with impunity: though his comparison with Venice's position towards the Union of Cambrai was too remote to be impressive.

Towards the close of the debate Sir Robert Peel intervened in what proved to be his last public utterance,[116] for he was thrown from his horse after leaving the House the very next afternoon and died a few days later from his injuries. He took a characteristic middle line, condemning Palmerston's action as "not consistent with the dignity and honour of England", but refusing "to provoke any censure". He disclaimed all approval of the Greek Government, to whom he and Aberdeen had had to express their "deep dissatisfaction", but he contended that the whole dispute might have been quietly settled "without any compromise of dignity". "There never was a period", he declared, "in which it was more to the interest of England to conciliate the good feeling of Russia and France." "Diplomacy is a costly engine for maintaining peace", and is worse than useless "if your application of diplomacy be to fester every wound, to provoke instead of soothing resentments, to place a minister in every court of Europe for the purpose not of preventing or adjusting quarrels, but of continuing an angry correspondence and promoting what is supposed to be an English interest by keeping up conflicts with the representatives of other Powers."

"Which is the wisest policy," he asked, "to attempt to interfere with the institutions and measures of other countries not bordering on our own, out of an abstract love for constitutional government, or to hold that doctrine maintained by Fox, Pitt, Grenville, Canning and Castlereagh, that the true policy of this country is non-intervention in the affairs of others?"—to instruct Mr Bowring to read to the Chinese lectures on political economy and to insist upon self-government, or to live at peace with China and make allowance for those peculiar institutions under which the people live and with which we have no concern? He doubted whether "the institutions that take root under your patronage will be lasting. Constitutional liberty will be best worked out by those who aspire to freedom by their own efforts. You will only overload it by your help, by your principle of interference.... You are departing from the established policy of England, you are involving yourselves in difficulties the extent of which you can hardly conceive, you are bestowing no aid on the cause of constitutional freedom." He therefore protested against the resolution, which if carried, "will give a false impression with respect to the dignity and honour of this country and will establish a principle which you cannot carry into execution without imminent danger to the best interests of the country".

Lord John Russell's own contribution to the debate added but little and need not detain us. He advanced quite unreservedly the view that "it is our particular interest with regard to Europe, that freedom should be extended", but qualified this by adding that it was "a great advantage that we take part with neither of the extreme parties which divide it: that while we abhor the crimes which produced the assassinations of Rossi and Latour, we also disapprove of those acts which deprived nations of ancient rights and have given their best blood to be shed upon the scaffold".

The debate had lasted five days (24–9 June), and all the honours of argument and eloquence lay with Palmerston's opponents. But his own wonderful energy and his skilful alignment with the rather angular and aggressive views of Early Victorian England swept all before him, and Mr Roebuck's motion was carried by 310 to 264. Russell announced that so long as the Whigs retained office, Palmerston would "act not as the minister of Austria or of Russia or of France or any other country, but as the minister of England": and a large body of Whig M.P.'s presented Palmerston with his portrait and thanked him for "the independent policy by which he has maintained the honour and interests of this country".[117]

Yet on the very eve of the great debate *The Times* had written of the Foreign Secretary in the following almost unparalleled terms (22 June 1850): "There is no constituted authority in Europe with which Lord Palmerston has not quarrelled: there is no insurrection that he has not betrayed. The ardent partisans of Sicilian, Italian and Hungarian independence have certainly no especial cause for gratitude to a Minister who gave them abundance of verbal encouragement and then abandoned them to their fate.... On the other hand, when Lord Palmerston has made up his mind to court the goodwill of a foreign Power, no sacrifice of principle or interest is too great for him"...."Our foreign policy has degenerated into a tissue of caprices, machinations, petty contentions and everlasting disputes."

THE QUEEN AND FOREIGN POLICY

Lord John, finding his own position in the Government to be by this time considerably shakier than that of Palmerston, abandoned for the present all idea of dismissal. The Queen, who even while the Pacifico debate was at its height became involved in controversy with Palmerston on the subject of Holstein,[118] now saw herself forced to put up with the obnoxious minister for a further term of office. She did not, however, relinquish her efforts for a change at the Foreign Office and on 28 July flatly told the Prime Minister that "she can have no confidence" in Lord Palmerston, whose conduct has been "anything but straightforward and proper" and exposes "the country to the constant risk of alarming complications.... There is no chance of Lord Palmerston reforming himself in his sixty-seventh year, and after having considered his last escape as a triumph."[119] The fear which Palmerston inspired in his colleagues is reflected in the attitude of the Duke of Bedford, who admitted that his brother Lord John "can exercise no control over Palmerston" and was "frightened to turn him loose".[120] The utmost that could be obtained from Lord John was that he should lecture Palmerston on the "unfortunate manner" in which he had executed a policy approved by the Cabinet and the country at large: but Palmerston was entirely unrepentant, argued that he had been the victim of "a great conspiracy... urged on by foreigners", that his "acquittal had produced the greatest enthusiasm for him", and that for him to resign "would be loss of character to him, which he could not be expected to submit to".[121] The close of the interview, as reported by Prince Albert, is worth noting: "Lord John felt he could not press the matter further under these circumstances, but he seemed much provoked at the result of his conversation. We expressed our surprise that he had not made any offer of any kind. Lord John replied he had not been sure what he could have offered him."

The Queen was not unnaturally reluctant to leave matters in this unsatisfactory state and on 12 August 1850 drew up a memorandum for the Prime Minister, which "in order to prevent any mistakes for the future", set out "shortly to explain what it is she expects from her Foreign Secretary". The essential passage deserves quotation in full: "She requires: (1) That he will distinctly state what he proposes in a given case, in order that the Queen may know as distinctly to *what* she has given her Royal sanction; (2) Having *once given* her sanction to a measure, that it be not arbitrarily altered or modified by the Minister; such an act she must consider as failing in sincerity towards the Crown, and justly to be visited by the exercise of her Constitutional right of dismissing that Minister. She expects to be kept informed of what passes between him and the Foreign Ministers before important decisions are taken, based upon that intercourse; to receive the foreign despatches in good time, and to have the drafts for her approval sent to her in sufficient time to make herself acquainted with their contents before they must be sent off."[122]

This memorandum, which at the Queen's express request was handed on to Palmerston, was, strange to say, accepted by him without the slightest demur:* and it may therefore be presumed that two out of the three competent constitutional factors in foreign policy accepted it as a fair statement of what was due to the third. A few days later Prince Albert had a frank conversation with Palmerston and found him "low and agitated":[123] and Lord John in his turn expressed his opinion that "what had passed had done a great deal of good".

THE HAYNAU INCIDENT

The truce thus concluded, however, was of the shortest duration, for early in September an unfortunate incident occurred which brought into fresh relief those very habits of Palmerston which the Queen most resented. General Haynau—nicknamed in his native Austria "the hyaena of Brescia", and notorious for his brutal methods in Italy and Hungary, above all for the public flogging of women—paid a private visit to London, against the advice of Prince Metternich and Baron Neumann. While inspecting the brewery of Barclay and Perkins in the City, he was recognised and roughly handled by the draymen and other employees: and his own refusal either to prosecute or even identify his assailants rendered judicial action impossible. The Austrian Ambassador, Baron Koller, unfamiliar with *habeas corpus* and other safeguards of English law, treated this as a mere hypocrital evasion, and our already strained relations with Austria were strained still further. Prince Schwarzenberg demanded an apology for "the infamous ambush (*guet-apens*) laid for our illustrious general",[124] and Palmerston could not refuse: but the Note which he sent was handed to Koller without being submitted to the Queen, and was regarded by her and Lord John as "derogatory to the honour of the nation".[125] They therefore insisted on the drastic step of its withdrawal and the substitution of something less offensive, and to this Palmerston, after threatening resignation, eventually submitted—but only after a long letter to the Queen, in which he dwelt upon Haynau's "want of propriety" in visiting a country where he "was looked upon as a great moral criminal", not unlike Tawell and the Mannings,

* Palmerston to Russell, 13 August: "I have taken a copy of this memorandum of the Queen and will not fail to attend to the directions which it contains" (*Letters*, II, 264–5).

three notorious murderers of the day—"with this only difference", Lord
Palmerston's pen ran on, "that General Haynau's bad deeds were committed upon a far larger scale, and upon a far larger number of victims".[126]
The Queen stuck manfully to her guns, and denounced to Lord John his
colleague's "violent vituperations" against "public men in other countries":[127] and when Palmerston gave way, she gave the Prime Minister the
well-merited reminder that the incident proved him to possess "the power
of exercising that control over Lord Palmerston, the careful exercise of
which he owes to the Queen, his colleagues and the country—*if he will take
the necessary pains to remain firm*". Her attitude to Palmerston was now
frankly hostile:* and she kept a surprisingly firm hold upon diplomatic
appointments.[128]

Perhaps the most enlightening commentary on Palmerston's handling of
the Queen is to be found in his own wife's words of warning, written in the
year 1848. "I am sure the Queen is very angry with you. I am afraid you
contradict her notions too boldly. You fancy she will hear reason, when in
fact all you say only proves to her that you are determined to act on the line
she disapproves.... I am sure it would be better if you *said* less to her, even
if you *act* as you think best. You always think you can convince people by
Arguments, and she has not reflection or sense to feel the force of them.... I
should treat what she says more lightly and courteously and not enter into
argument with her, but lead her on gently, by letting her believe you have
both the same opinion in fact and the same wishes, but take sometimes
different ways of carrying them out."[129] This study in the art of managing
a sovereign instantly recalls to the mind a later situation between the Queen
and a still greater Minister: but if she resented Mr Gladstone's tendency
'to treat her as a public meeting", she no less resented Lord Palmerston's
treatment of her "as if she was a little girl".

On 22 February 1851 the Russell Cabinet, weakened by the futile controversy on Papal ecclesiastical titles and by the growing hostility of the
Radical wing, offered its resignation, and a prolonged deadlock ensued, in
which Lord Stanley declined, Lord John failed to win the Peelites in favour
of reconstruction, Lord Aberdeen refused to act alone, and Lord Stanley
again failed to form a ministry. After the Queen in her embarrassment had
sent for the Duke of Wellington, the crisis at last ended in her inviting
Lord John Russell to resume office. This decision was obviously a *pis-aller*,
and the Cabinet returned greatly weakened in power and prestige. The first
result of this was that despite the Queen's very definite "objections" to

* To her uncle King Leopold she lamented that "thanks to Palmerston we have contrived to quarrel *so happily*, separately with each" of the Powers (22 November 1850—
Letters, II, p. 277).

Palmerston and the Prime Minister's equally definite "promise" to respect them, the latter found himself too weak "either to expel Lord Palmerston or quarrel with him".[130] Once more the confused state of parties, consequent upon the protectionist quarrel, redounded to the advantage of Palmerston, who persisted in his refusal to be bribed out of the Foreign Office by the Irish Viceroyalty or other honours.

KOSSUTH IN ENGLAND

Meanwhile the Continental upheaval had slowly settled down into the stagnation of blackest reaction, and the Great Exhibition of the summer of 1851 afforded a further respite. But acute friction again arose in October 1851, in connection with the visit of Louis Kossuth to England. The great Hungarian patriot was no sooner released from his long internment in Turkey, than he accepted the offer of a steam frigate by the United States Government to convey him to America. He was refused entry into France, but in Britain at once became the object of enthusiastic demonstrations throughout the country. The Prime Minister, in writing to the Queen, did not hesitate to declare that Kossuth was "considered the representative of English institutions against despotism", and that such a view was "laudable".[131] As we saw, Palmerston's sympathies were by no means unreservedly on the side of Hungary, but compliments to Kossuth served the double purpose of annoying the Russian and Austrian reactionaries and increasing his own popularity with the Radicals. He therefore gave out his intention of receiving Kossuth and defied Lord John's "positive request" that he should not do so. "There are limits to all things", was his message to his chief, "I do not choose to be dictated to as to who I may or may not receive in my own house....I shall use my own discretion....You will of course use yours as to the composition of your Government."[132] The helpless Prime Minister, "as a last resource" advised the Queen to "command" Palmerston not to receive Kossuth.[133] Even this command, conveyed in the plainest terms, was not enough, and it was not until the Cabinet had unanimously endorsed the veto, that Palmerston most grudgingly abandoned his intention. But he more than spoilt the effect of this concession by accepting memorials from Radical deputations which referred to the Emperors Nicholas and Francis Joseph as "odious and detestable assassins", and by expressing himself as "extremely flattered and highly gratified".[134]

This was altogether too much for the Queen, who assured Russell that "her feelings have again been deeply wounded by the official conduct of er Foreign Secretary",* and reminded him that he had "invariably met er remonstrances with the plea" that to push Palmerston harder would nvolve the break-up of the Cabinet. "Under the present political circumstances" she chose "rather not to insist upon what is due to her", but wished the whole Cabinet to be informed that she did so "on their account, leaving it to them to reconcile the injuries done to her with that sound policy and conduct which the maintenance of peace and the welfare of the country require".[135] This time Russell attempted to defend his insubordinate colleague, urging that "every Minister must have a certain latitude allowed him, which he may use, perhaps with indiscretion, perhaps with bad taste, but with no consequence of sufficient importance to deserve notice". To this infelicitous phrase the Queen replied most convincingly, that to listen without protest to addresses in which allied sovereigns were called despots and assassins, seemed hardly to lie within that "latitude" which the Prime Minister claimed for every colleague.[136]

Whether as the effect of this plain speaking or because it was obvious to all his colleagues that Palmerston was utterly out of hand, the Cabinet blamed him for "want of caution", and Lord John urged upon him "the necessity of a guarded conduct, in the present very critical condition of Europe".

PALMERSTON AND THE FRENCH *COUP D'ÉTAT*

Yet this fresh exhortation had hardly been penned, when Palmerston provoked a new and still more serious incident. That very day news reached London of the French *Coup d'État*,† by which the Prince-President, Louis Napoleon, had overthrown the Second Republic. Both the Queen and the Prime Minister were at once agreed as to the need for an "entirely passive" attitude, and Lord Normanby, our Ambassador in Paris, was instructed accordingly. Next day, however, when he called upon the Foreign Minister, M. Turgot, and communicated this message, he was informed that already on the 4th Count Walewski, the French Ambassador in London, had reported home a conversation in which Palmerston expressed "entire approbation of the act of the President".[137] Lord Normanby not unnaturally addressed a formal complaint to his chief as to "the very awkward position" in which he had thus been placed, but he did not let the matter rest there.

---

* She did not even accept Palmerston's word and went so far as to assure Lord John that he had "every reason to believe" that he had seen Kossuth "after all" (21 November—*Letters*, II, p. 331).

† A footnote is surely here in place, to remind the reader of another and greater revolution that was in progress. The news reached London by "the wonderful Electric Telegraph", then still a novelty.

His wife wrote two long letters to his brother Colonel Charles Phipps, who was in the Royal Household and promptly showed them to the Queen. She in her turn remonstrated more strongly than ever to the Prime Minister

The fat was now in the fire, for a question of major policy was involved and with it the whole question of the relations of the Foreign Secretary with the Prime Minister and the sovereign. The actual *coup d'état* o 2 December had taken everyone by surprise, but it had long been obvious that the conflict between President and Assembly was drawing to a head and must end in an explosion. A fortnight earlier Palmerston, in a very outspoken private letter to Normanby, had passed in review the possible alternatives of government in France and reached the conclusion tha England had nothing to gain "by substituting Henry V or the Orleans family" for Louis Napoleon, and could have "no wish to see him fall".[138] Immediately after the event he wrote again in distinctly unmeasured language—language hardly suggestive of a veteran Whig leader—describing the Constitution which had just been abrogated as "tomfoolery" and "childish nonsense", invented by "the scatterbrain heads of Marrast and Tocqueville for the torment and perplexity of the French nation".[139] As Lady Normanby remarked, it was "a curious anomaly that he should quarrel" with her husband "in support of arbitrary and absolute govern- ment".[140]

Meanwhile it is certain that Normanby had shown his sympathies for the Orleans faction, and that Palmerston was genuinely convinced that the sons of Louis Philippe, from Claremont as their base, were preparing a rival *coup d'état*.* His old distrust of their father transferred itself to Joinville and Aumale and led him to throw all his weight in favour of Louis Napoleon. When taken to task by Lord John Russell, he wrote a lengthy defence of the new autocrat, as the saviour of France from otherwise in- evitable civil war: but he met with the rejoinder that the real question at issue was not the merits of the *Coup d'État*, but whether the Foreign Secretary was justified in taking sides in a situation of such delicacy, with- out previously consulting the Cabinet and the Queen. On 17 December Lord John expressed this view to Palmerston in most unequivocal terms and after affirming that "misunderstandings perpetually renewed, violations of prudence and decorum too frequently repeated, have marred the effects which ought to have followed from a sound policy and able administra- tion", he definitely asked him to resign the Foreign Office and accept the Irish Viceroyalty.

* Palmerston's memorandum, written in 1858, giving evidence for this belief, is published by Ashley (*op. cit.* I, 287–9). There does not appear to have been any truth in the stories that had reached him.

PALMERSTON'S DISMISSAL

There can be little doubt that the Queen's attitude turned the scale against Palmerston, but this time it was fortunately unnecessary for her to carry out her threat of dismissing him on her own responsibility: and Lord John was able to congratulate her "upon the change having been accomplished without her personal intervention, which might have exposed her to the animosity of Lord Palmerston's admirers, while she would have been pre-cluded from making any public defence".[141] That the Court this time observed a waiting attitude instead of rushing in to give the death-blow, was largely due to the advice of the sagacious Stockmar, who in his correspond-ence with the Prince that winter expressed his belief that Palmerston had been "for some time past partially insane".*

The fall of Palmerston produced a profound sensation throughout Europe, and was widely regarded as a triumph for the cause of reaction. Nesselrode told Meyendorff that it "offers to the Continental Powers the best reparation which the British Government could offer them"—better than any Aliens Bill.[142] The arrogant Schwarzenberg even went so far as to give a ball at Vienna in honour of the news. But though Radical circles both at home and abroad were correspondingly discouraged, and inclined to suspect foreign intrigue, the immediate issue involved was one which could not command their sympathy. Palmerston, by associating himself with their latest bugbear, the enemy of French liberties, had given Lord John a tactical advantage of which he readily availed himself. Sane Liberal opinion may probably be summed up in what Macaulay wrote in his diary at the time: "Palmerston is out. It was high time: but I cannot help being sorry. A daring, indefatigable, highspirited man, but too fond of conflict and too ready to sacrifice everything to victory when once he was in the ring."[143]

To use Charles Greville's words: "the case was cumulative",[144] and for

---

* *Denkwürdigkeiten*, p. 642. On 22 December he wrote, "In the last two months he has committed follies which confirm me in my former suspicion that he is no longer quite right in the head", and urged the Queen to wait until Palmerston destroyed himself. Greville, in his diary for 2 January 1852 (VI, 443) records Stockmar's restraining influence. It is interesting to compare the latter's verdict on Palmerston with that of Lady Normanby in writing to her brother-in-law on 8 December. Commenting on his recent letters to her husband, she says, "One would have supposed, from the whole tenor of his policy, from his Radical tendencies, and all that he has been doing lately, that Palmerston would have been the last person to approve of this *coup d'état*. Not a bit ...The curious thing is that it is a letter or rather letters that would completely ruin Palmerston with *his* Party. He treats all the wholesale cruelties of the troops as a joke—in short, it is the letter of a man half-mad, I think.... The more I think of Palmerston's letters, the less I can understand them: every sentence is in direct contradiction to his acts and words" (*Letters*, II, 338–9).

some time past it had been only a question of finding a suitable pretext for ejecting the insubordinate minister. It is quite clear that he himself had not realised his danger,* and therefore perhaps resented his downfall all the more keenly. In a long apologia written to his brother a month after the event he gave the following sensational explanation. "The real ground was a weak truckling to the hostile intrigues of the Orleans Family, Austria Russia, Saxony and Bavaria, and in some degree also of the present Prussian Government. All these parties found their respective views and systems of policy thwarted by the course pursued by the British Government and they thought that if they could remove the minister, they could change the policy. They had for a long time effectually poisoned the mind of the Queen and the Prince against me, and John Russell giving way, rather encouraged than discountenanced the desire of the Queen to remove me from the Foreign Office."† Lady Palmerston went even further and described the whole affair as "an intrigue of Normanby, Phipps and the Prince, worked up by the deep disappointment of the Orleans overthrow" and glibly repeated the phrase, "a Foreign Conspiracy", with two capital letters. She even appears to have believed that the aim was to secure "a pliant and subservient" Foreign Secretary who "would let Albert manage the Foreign Office". And at her highest note she declared that "John has behaved like a little Blackguard".[145]

The Queen was unreservedly delighted, but took an eminently sane view of the situation. To Russell she emphasised the dangers of the times, "in which military despotism and red republicanism will be for some time the only powers on the Continent, to both of which the constitutional monarchy of England will be equally hateful". England's "calm influence in assuaging the contest abroad...has been rendered null by Lord Palmerston's personal manner of conducting foreign affairs and by the universal hatred which he has excited on the Continent. That you could hope to control him has long been doubted by us, and its impossibility is clearly proved by the last proceedings."[146] There can be no doubt that she had grave grounds for complaint: for in the words of Palmerston's latest biographer, Professor Bell "At the Foreign Office he opened her private letters from continental royalties: he kept her in ignorance of essential facts. He frequently, and as his papers show deliberately, sent off despatches to which she had not

* Here again Greville's contemporary comment provides the key. "Upon this piece of indiscretion, to which it is probable that Palmerston attached no importance, being so used to act off his own bat, and never dreaming of any danger from it, Lord John determined to act." But the *causa causans*, he adds, was his speech to the Radical deputations in November (*Memoirs*, VI, 435).

† Here it is only possible to re-echo the comment of Sir Theodore Martin, in his *Life of the Prince Consort* (II, 411, note): "It is hard to believe that Palmerston himself would have wished this letter to appear as embodying his final convictions."

given her assent or altered those to which she had." And though she was certainly exacting, and often caused embarrassing delays in matters of urgent business, she had right on her side, and she was after all Queen of England!

THE QUEEN AND CONSTITUTIONAL DOCTRINE

Not content, however, with liquidating the past, she was naturally bent on preventing any recurrence of these troubles and told Lord John very plainly that "after the sad experience which she has just had of the difficulties, annoyances and dangers to which the Sovereign may be exposed by the personal character and qualities of the Secretary for Foreign Affairs, she must reserve to herself the unfettered right to approve or disapprove the choice of a minister for this office". "She cannot allow a servant of the Crown and her minister, to act contrary to her orders, and this without her knowledge."

This was raising a highly delicate issue, but it did not need to be pushed home, because the Queen and Lord John soon agreed upon Lord Granville as Palmerston's successor, as Lord Clarendon refused to put himself into the position of seeming to oust his former chief.[147] But she put on record a protest "against the Cabinet taking on itself the appointment of its own Members, which rested entirely with the Prime Minister and the Sovereign".[148]

She then suggested to the Prime Minister that the moment had arrived for reconsidering and *defining* the principles of British foreign policy. Her argument was that when revolution "had laid prostrate almost all the governments" of the Continent, and England alone was immune owing to "its stable, free and good government... the Queen, instead of earning the natural good results of such a glorious position,... had the grief to see her Government and herself treated with neglect, aversion, distrust and even contumely": and she refused to admit that this was due only to "the personal manner of Lord Palmerston", but to "a personal and arbitrary perversion" of the principles of policy laid down. She therefore asked for "a regular programme embracing these different relations" with other Powers.

Russell's reply is eminently British. He cautiously observed that the "traditionary policy of this country is not to bind the Crown and country by engagements, unless upon special cause shown arising out of the special circumstances of the day", and that "it is very difficult to lay down any principles from which deviations may not frequently be made".[149] But he asked Granville to draft a suitable memorandum for the Queen's consumption, and its main lines have been summarised by Lord Fitzmaurice in his biography of Granville.[150] It consisted mainly of discrete platitudes, describing "progress among the nations" as the natural aim of a country with such worldwide interests as Britain, but disclaiming any idea of enforcing her own ideas by hostile threats, and insisting that though anxious to promote Britain's foreign trade, we must not blindly support any undertaking which traders might have entered at their own risk. It reaffirmed the doctrine of non-intervention, but not as indicating a lack of interest in foreign countries, and it reiterated the impossibility of laying down any general rule. The Government would, however, try to cultivate specially intimate relations "with the countries which have adopted institutions similar in liberality to our own".

The whole question came up in the House of Commons on 3 February 1852, when the Prime Minister laid down "the general doctrine" that "a minister is bound to afford to the Crown the most frank and full detail of every measure taken, or leave to the Crown its full liberty...of saying that the minister no longer possesses its confidence". He then proceeded to quote the Queen's memorandum of August 1850, defining "what it is she expects from her Foreign Secretary",* and inferred, rather than stated in so many words, that Palmerston had not kept his promise to carry out the Queen's wishes. Palmerston defended at some length his attitude towards the *coup d'état*, incidentally contending that Lord John had expressed similar opinions to the French Ambassador on the very same day as himself, and denying any breach of duty either to his chief or to the Crown. But Russell's use of the memorandum had driven him on to the defensive, and he made a lame appearance before the House. It is but his due to add that he felt it to be inadmissible "to bring for decision at the bar of public opinion a personal quarrel" between himself and his sovereign.[151] His chivalrous conduct on this occasion prepared the way for his return to the Queen's good graces during the stress of the Crimean War.

GRANVILLE AT THE FOREIGN OFFICE

After this debate the question of the Crown's exact degree of control over foreign policy was wisely allowed to drop. The advent of Lord Granville appeased the Queen. He was full of tact and acted according to the well-known maxim that in diplomacy "c'est le ton qui fait la chanson". He was now only thirty-six, but had grown up in a diplomatic atmosphere as son of the first Lord Granville, one of our ablest Ambassadors in Paris. To his grandfather, Lord Gower, the younger Pitt had owed his entrenchment in office in the critical year of 1783, and his mother was a daughter of the beautiful

* See *supra*, p. 285.

Georgiana Spencer, Duchess of Devonshire. He was thus a highly typical product of the old Whig aristocracy, though himself holding relatively advanced views on many subjects such as Free Trade. He had been Under-Secretary in the Foreign Office from 1837 to 1840, but according to Prince Albert was "rather the sandwich between his principal and his clerks", to whom in three years Palmerston "had hardly once spoken on any of the subjects he had to treat".* His sudden advancement to the Foreign Office in 1851 came as "a sort of peace offering and concession to those who disapprove of Palmerston".[152] It was a public recognition of the fact that foreign affairs were still a monopoly of the aristocracy. A good example of the manner in which his appointment was received is provided by the strong approval of Lord Aberdeen, who wrote that "the real state of our relations with the whole world" was "perfectly unparalleled and pregnant with danger".[153]

The main concern of his very brief tenure of office was to tone down the annoyance caused to the new regime in Paris by press attacks in London and by the not unfounded belief that Palmerston's fall was due to his friendly attitude towards Napoleon. A rupture was even spoken of, and Lord Granville in appealing to Lord Lansdowne for his good offices with his kinsman M. de Flahault (an intimate of Louis Napoleon), used the phrase, "I should not like to begin with an European War": while Russell, not trusting Napoleon's assurances, wished Flahault to explain to the budding autocrat "the British interest in the independence of Belgium and Piedmont".[154] Lord Cowley, who was almost immediately sent to replace Lord Normanby at the Paris Embassy, ere long reported the President's pointed remark, "there is nothing which can prevent [peace between the two countries] except the proceedings of your [i.e. the British] press".[155] How Granville's role was interpreted by the Opposition may be gathered from a letter of Disraeli to Malmesbury which declares, "The fact is, the Government have entirely changed their foreign policy: under ordinary circumstances, instead of making a victim of the Secretary of State, they should have resigned."[156] But the real fact was that so far from modifying Palmerston's policy, as distinct from his tactics, they had immediately adopted the very same opportunism towards Napoleon, and no one was more anxious than the Queen that the Orleans Princes should remain quiescent, or more indignant at the suggestion that foreign influences had played their part in the change of minister.

Feeling was already calming down, when in February 1852 the Whig Ministry finally fell, and with it Granville, after only two months of office.

---

* Memorandum of Prince Albert, 27 December 1851—*Letters*, ii, 349. It is only fair to add that at the end of the period referred to Granville was still only twenty-five.

The fall was very largely due to Palmerston, who voted with his friends against the Government and wrote to his brother in wicked glee, "I have had my tit for tat with John Russell and turned him out on Friday last." [157] In a letter he wrote that he had lost all political confidence in Russell, because he "has shown on so many occasions such a want of sound judgment and discretion",[158] and he told Lord John's own brother, the Duke of Bedford, that "he is infirm of purpose, changeable in his views and perpetually swayed by influences which are known and felt only by their results".[159] He made but little concealment of his belief that but for the hostility of the Court, he himself had a much better prospect of forming a Cabinet than the acting chief of the party.

It is important to realise that Palmerston's uncertain, free-lance attitude contributed materially to the chaotic party conditions which mark the early 'fifties and which had so much to do with the nation's drift into war. It will be remembered that early in 1851 no less than four unsuccessful efforts had been made to form an alternative government, and that Russell had only returned to office because no immediate substitute could be found. This time, late in February 1852, Lord Derby succeeded in forming a weak Conservative Cabinet, but one which was even weaker and more lacking in prestige than its predecessor. An attempt was made to win the support of Palmerston, but it is not surprising that he preferred to bide his time, until his own party should find him to be indispensable.

DERBY AND MALMESBURY

The selection of a Foreign Secretary raised issues which were soon to react upon the international situation. On the previous occasion Lord Derby (then still Lord Stanley) had told the famous Ambassador, Sir Stratford Canning, that he wished to have him at the Foreign Office if he came into power, and this was regarded by Canning as a bargain.[160] But when the chance came in 1852, Canning was far away in Turkey, the post had to be filled rapidly, and it was also felt inadvisable, while relations with France were still doubtful, to appoint a Minister whom Russia would probably resent. And so Lord Malmesbury became Foreign Secretary instead. A grandson of one of our most eminent diplomatists—James Harris, first Earl of Malmesbury, whose papers he had studied and edited*—he had reached the age of forty-five without holding any kind of office, and having had no

---

* In his Memoirs he is perfectly frank about this (1, 41): "The experience which I gained by reading and collating the contents of above 2000 letters and despatches from and to my grandfather by all the important persons of the period from 1768 to 1800, stood me in good stead. Without this accidental education I should have been as great a novice in political business as were most of my colleagues."

practical experience whatever, was subject to the abuse of what Lord John called "a ribald press".[161] But then only two members of the entire Cabinet had ever held office before, and it may safely be regarded as the most inexperienced of the century. Malmesbury himself wrote to Derby: "Sir Stratford will never forgive me for being the innocent cause of this apparent slight. His talents are beyond dispute, but his temper is so despotic and irritable that he can only display them in a peculiar kind of diplomacy. He managed the Turks in their own way, and it was Sultan versus Sultan. With him at the Foreign Office there could have been no peace with Russia or in the Cabinet."[162] On this point the commonplace Malmesbury showed himself to possess better judgment than other more experienced statesmen, and Stratford Canning was passed over, though his great services in the Near East were recognised by the title of a Viscount. But the sting remained, especially as the Paris Embassy, a prize which alone could have consoled him for the loss of the Foreign Office, was given to his former junior, Henry Wellesley, now Lord Cowley: and Canning returned to the scene of his former triumphs, ready to vent his old rancour at a supreme moment of crisis.

MALMESBURY AND LOUIS NAPOLEON

What really turned the scale in favour of Malmesbury was the fact that he had long been on really intimate terms with Louis Napoleon—he had even visited him in his prison at Ham—and his selection gave the would-be Emperor very great satisfaction and smoothed over the latent friction. Men as different as Palmerston and Wellington urged on Malmesbury the need of "keeping well with France", but there was wide apprehension in England as to Napoleon's anti-British designs, shared even by Derby and Brougham, while Wellington pressed for military precautions, and King Leopold, influenced perhaps by his kinship with the Orleans family and still more by his fears for Belgian independence, added to the panic. Malmesbury was not brilliant, but possessed sound common sense. "I believe I stand alone", he said, "in disbelieving...the sinister feelings and intentions of Louis Napoleon", and he quoted the latter's remark, made to himself more than once in days when no ulterior motive was possible, that "his uncle's great mistake was not being friends with England".[163] Convinced that Napoleon's aim was to gain and secure the alliance with England and consolidate his position with Great Britain by a pacific policy", Malmesbury worked cordially with Paris and did his best to overcome the difficulties raised by the negotiations for a recognition of the Empire and of the title of "Napoleon III". He need not be blamed for regarding

Napoleon as peaceful, for it is now generally admitted that the famous catchword, "L'Empire, c'est la Paix", was quite genuinely meant, and that he, like our own country, was pushed on half unconsciously into the fatality of a war which really led nowhere.

Apart from this central aim of restoring and deepening "the amity between France and England" which he described as "necessary to the prosperity of both and to the general interests of civilisation",[164] Malmesbury also set himself to remove the very definite "animus" of Prince Schwarzenberg, the masterful Austrian Premier, against England, and let him know of his desire "to resume our old relations of cordial amity with Austria". Schwarzenberg responded, but already in April 1852 death removed the strong man of Austria at the height of his success, and relations in the years that followed were not improved by the fact that Count Buol—who as Ambassador in London had had violent scenes first with Granville and then with Malmesbury, and is described by the latter as "most coarse and insolent"—now became Austrian Foreign Minister and played a very feeble and obscure role throughout the critical years that followed. For the remainder of the absolutist period in Austria there was no Premier, and Alexander Bach, who was all powerful in home politics and has very fittingly given his name to the regime, was weakly represented and little known abroad.

It may be noted that in the winter of 1852 relations between London and Vienna again became strained owing to Francis Joseph's refusal to be represented at the funeral of the Duke of Wellington. This was keenly resented both by the Court and by the public, and was all the more marked because the French Ambassador, on special instructions from Napoleon, made a point of paying a last tribute to the victor of Waterloo. It at least showed how deep-seated was the aversion to England which Palmerston's behaviour had kindled at the Hofburg. "The Austrians," so ran Palmerston's not very accurate comment on the incident, "hate England, notwithstanding the civil compliments interchanged when Derby came into office.... Well, we can do without them, and I hope they can do without us,...for help from England they are not very likely to get."[165] This is a very characteristic attitude of his, towards friend and foe alike.

Palmerston's general attitude towards Malmesbury as Foreign Secretary was far from benevolent: and we find him writing in these terms to his brother: "Malmesbury has got into sad disgrace by his diplomatic mismanagement and his ungrammatical despatches: but every trade requires an apprenticeship and a man can't expect to start at once into being a good Foreign Secretary."[166] After what had happened at the time of his own dismissal Palmerston may perhaps be excused for noting with a certain trace of malice that the Conservative leader was not popular at Court, and did not know how to manage the Queen and the Prince. Derby, he notes, fought them "stoutly and successfully" over the Danish question.[167]

RUSSELL AND CLARENDON

There were elections in 1852, and neither Liberals nor Conservatives obtained a working majority. In December Derby fell, and as party conditions remained chaotic—Russell no longer commanding sufficient support, and Lansdowne declaring himself to be too old—the chief of the Peelites, Lord Aberdeen, became Prime Minister in a Coalition Cabinet. Palmerston was persuaded to accept the Home Office, and the momentary danger of his combining with Disraeli in opposition was averted. He justified his action by the jocular assertion that he had "for the last 12 months been acting the part of a very distinguished tightrope dancer, and much astonishing the public", and that therefore there was no other course to take but to join the Cabinet.[168] Meanwhile Gladstone went to the Treasury, and Russell was induced, in spite of professions that his health would not stand the strain, to take the Foreign Office, though the press was allowed to announce that this was only temporary.

Then in February 1853 Russell found that the leadership of the House was as much as he could cope with, and Lord Clarendon was the obvious compromise candidate for the Foreign Office. Clarendon, who was now fifty-three, had acquired a certain diplomatic reputation as British representative in Madrid during the Carlist war, and as Mr Algernon Cecil has said of him, he is "perhaps the only man with a right to be called a *diplomate de carrière*, who ever held the seals of the Foreign Office".[169] He belonged to the lesser Whig aristocracy. His chief characteristic was a certain suavity, and his biographer records "his inclination for drifting down-stream":[170] his tact was really compounded of indolence and courtesy. In 1839, after he declined the succession to Lord Durham as Governor-General of Canada, he became the Queen's candidate for the post of Palmerston. But though he strongly disapproved of the latter's policy, he felt "a sense of obligation" towards his former chief, and was determined not to get credited with the desire to oust him. In 1850 he was again the Queen's candidate for the Foreign Office, because "she knew his bad opinion of the mode in which foreign affairs had been conducted".[171] But this time Russell was opposed to the idea, and it was not till two years later that he was selected to succeed Russell himself in a Coalition Cabinet.

This Cabinet seemed at the time a very brilliant solution of an obscure situation: it may be said to have contained more men of the very front rank than any other British Cabinet save the famous Coalition of 1915. One peculiarity was that Clarendon as Foreign Secretary had as colleagues no less than four of his predecessors in office—Aberdeen, Palmerston, Russell and Granville. Apart from them, Sir James Graham and the Duke of Argyll were men of exceptional ability, while Mr Gladstone, by his first great budget, imparted added prestige. Yet it has left unhappy memories behind it, for it lacked the very elements of internal unity, and a question of foreign policy which was at first only a small cloud on the horizon, soon came to overshadow the whole sky and accentuated the latent divergence of outlook and temperament among its members, with the most fatal results to the country and to Europe.

CHAPTER VIII

THE ORIGINS OF THE CRIMEAN WAR

Any detailed study of the causes of the Crimean War would very quickly lead far beyond the limits deliberately set to this volume. But it is essential at the outset to stress certain features in the home and foreign situation, which provide a key to the policy pursued by the British Government. In the first place, it may be claimed that nothing contributed so much towards the impending disaster as the confused state of party politics at home. There was no clear line of division between the two great parties, the Peelites were in league with the Whigs, but the repeated attempts of Lord Derby to win over Lord Palmerston to his side is only one out of many indications that re-grouping was by no means impracticable. Moreover, though there were four or five active statesmen of the front rank, there was no longer any single commanding figure like Sir Robert Peel: and this, combined with the steady disintegration inside the various groups, added to the obscurity. And not least of all, we have reached the moment when public opinion has perhaps attained to its highest pitch of stridency and irresponsibility in the press. It is a time of many discordant voices, of unbalanced views and superficial information, of crude lampoons and broadsheets, and of such preposterous rumours as the treason of Prince Albert. The fact that a number of the most eminent public men did not see eye to eye on vital issues—even if not known in an altogether concrete form—was bruited about and served to increase the confusion in the public mind. And if there was one question upon which British public opinion, from Lord Palmerston downwards, was singularly misinformed and unbalanced, it was that very Eastern question which now gave rise to the Crimean War.

If the confused state of parties and of public opinion at home constituted a real danger, the uncertain situation on the Continent greatly increased it. This may be very briefly summarised as follows.

In France the Prince-President had steadily consolidated his position in the year following the *coup d'état* and the plebiscite, and in December 1852 the time seemed ripe for his proclamation as Emperor of the French. But while the Tsar had welcomed the first of these two steps, he resented the second, and the attitudes of Russia and Britain towards the new regime were speedily reversed. Our own country, which had objected to the overthrow of the French constitution and fallen into an absurd panic over Napoleon's alleged military designs against us, was appeased when he proclaimed the popular origin of his Empire, recognised the governments which had preceded him, and to use his own words, "assumed frankly before the face of Europe the position of *parvenu*—a glorious title when one acquires it by the free suffrages of a great people". But the Tsar could not pardon this intrusion and declined to address Napoleon as "M. Mon Frère", but only as "Mon Cher Ami"; and though this was explained as due to "the difference of principles which served as base to the two governments" (it being impossible for a Russian Emperor to recognise sovereigns who derived their rights from the principle of the national will[1]) the parvenu monarch was as hypersensitive as any other parvenu and bore Nicholas a lasting grudge. Other motives in the mind of Napoleon were interest in Italy, which to him always remained a second country, and reliance upon the Clericals in France, who were equally concerned with the fate of the Temporal Power in Rome and with the traditional interests of Catholicism in the Levant. Hence Napoleon from the first found it tactful to support the claim of the Latins in the humiliating dispute about the custody of the Holy Places in Palestine, round which the first stage of the Eastern Question centred in its new phase.

Turning from France, we find Central and Eastern Europe in the grip of extreme reaction. Austria in particular has recovered from her eclipse during 1848-9, the revolution has been suppressed first in Bohemia, then in Vienna, then in Lombardy and Venice, and finally, with the help of Russian armies, in Hungary; the new Emperor Francis Joseph has revoked the Austrian Constitution promulgated under stress of revolution, and has abolished Hungary's ancient constitutional liberties, on the plea that armed rebellion forfeits all rights: and the new bureaucratic absolutism of Schwarzenberg and Bach is far more efficient and constructive than the stagnant regime of Metternich. In foreign policy too it is efficient and aggressive: and Schwarzenberg not merely reimposes Austrian authority in Italy with a heavy hand, but dominates Germany and inflicts upon Prussia the grave public humiliation of Olmütz. Unfortunately for Austria, Schwarzenberg died prematurely in April 1852 and found no worthy successor in foreign policy, though the ex-revolutionary Alexander Bach established at home a system of bureaucratic absolutism which remained all-powerful till 1859. The young Emperor was surrounded in his youth by a group of very able men, but he already showed the qualities which throughout a long reign tended more and more to discourage and eliminate first-class talent from the control of affairs. While the autocratic Nicholas firmly believed that he had kept the pledges given to the Emperor Francis in 1833, by hastening o the aid of his grandnephew in distress in 1849, and was naïve enough to count upon Austria's gratitude and to assume identity of interests between Russia and Austria, Francis Joseph was resentful of his dependence upon he Tsar and was waiting to prove the axiom ascribed to Schwarzenberg, hat Austria would one day surprise the world by her ingratitude.

To complete the picture, we have Russia under Nicholas as the very embodiment of reaction enforced with a brutality and thoroughness which leaves the occasional outbursts of the Austrian military authorities and the easygoing Austrian police censorship far behind. The repression of culture in Russia was absolute: this was the period when Dostoyevsky was sent to Siberia, when Shevchenko was deprived of writing materials by express order of the Tsar, and when Alexander Herzen was a centre of all *émigrés* and conspirators in London. It was natural enough that in all Liberal and advanced circles of Europe there should be acute suspicion of the Russian autocracy. It was a fatality that that autocracy should have stood for progress and civilisation in the Balkans, and that its evil reputation should have betrayed the West into supporting a still more odious and decadent tyranny in Turkey.

The Eastern Question Re-opened

It was thus in a Europe radically transformed after the failure of 1848 that fresh signs of trouble began to appear in the perennial Eastern Question. It is humiliating to reflect that the rival claims of Greek and Latin monks for the custody of the Holy Places in Jerusalem and Bethlehem should have been magnified into a struggle for political influence, in which Napoleon III and Nicholas I became their respective champions and voiced the hostility of the Roman and Orthodox Churches. The Tsar had enjoyed certain specific rights of protection and interference in favour of the latter, ever since the treaty of Kainardji in 1774, and these had been reaffirmed at Bucarest in 1812, at Akerman in 1826, at Adrianople in 1829, at Unkiar Skelessi in 1833. Though Russia, in concluding the Five Power Convention of 1841, had freely renounced the fresh rights acquired at Unkiar Skelessi, she regarded this as in no way affecting those already in existence: she had, however, from the first been disinclined to limit them to the Orthodox Christians of the two Roumanian Principalities and Serbia, where her *raison d'être* could not be denied, but sought to interpret them as conferring a certain right of interference throughout the Turkish dominions. France, on the other hand, had always been interested in the Catholics of the Levant, especially of Syria: and Louis Napoleon had found in this question an admirable means of propitiating the French

Catholics, just as similar motives led him to prop up the Temporal Power of the Pope, despite all his sympathy for the Italian national movement. The Porte, on its part, vacillated between French and Russian claims, making petty concessions now to one, now to the other, and playing off the Powers against each other with varying degrees of skill and bad faith. The details of the rival firmans and the intrigues which dictated them are entirely barren and need not detain us. It is unnecessary to add that the dispute of the Holy Places was merely what the Defenestration, the Ems Telegram or the murder of the Archduke have been to other great wars—in a word, the spark and not the powder magazine.

Unquestionably what gave a fresh impetus to the whole question was the changed attitude of Tsar Nicholas and the changed outlook of the Powers towards him. It will be remembered that in 1829, when Turkey was at his mercy, he discussed with his military and political advisers the alternative policies of disruption or bolstering up, and reached the conclusion that it was more advantageous to let Turkey die of slow inanition and meanwhile to exercise the controlling influence over her, rather than destroy her at once and risk the dangers and embarrassments of partition and redistribution of power. Both the Treaty of Adrianople in 1829 and the Treaty of Unkiar Skelessi four years later, were based upon these calculations: and their logical sequel was the Tsar's secret agreement with Austria at Münchengrätz, pledging both Powers to maintain Turkish integrity as long as possible, but to agree promptly and act in concert if Turkey should collapse. Nicholas continued to act on these lines during the crisis of 1839–41, convincing Palmerston of his moderation by renouncing Unkiar Skelessi, and thereby promoting that isolation of France which he continued to desire, for reasons both of international policy and dynastic picque. Assuming that he could always carry Austria with him, his next aim was to win England finally for his designs. By 1844 the time seemed to him to be ripe. Turkey had not shown the recuperative powers which her friends had prophesied, the danger of a Turkish collapse was growing nearer, and it was therefore essential for the friendly Powers to be prepared with a programme for all eventualities. Nicholas talked in this sense to Aberdeen and Peel during his London visit in June 1844, and on his instructions Nesselrode carried the conversations further that autumn. The result was embodied in a memorandum, based on a mutual understanding to maintain the existence of Turkey as long as possible, but "if we foresee that it must crumble to pieces"—this phrase is a subsequent insertion by the Tsar himself, referred to and approved by Aberdeen—to consult together and ensure that the new order of things shall not injure the interests of individual states or the balance of power. Brunnov obtained from Aberdeen a confidential exchange of letters in the sense of the memorandum, and interpreted this as "an unprecedented event in the history of our political relations with England".[2] On his side Brunnov was perfectly explicit, announcing that the Tsar did not want Constantinople for himself, but could not allow either France or England to have it, or even a revival of the Byzantine Empire: while Aberdeen in a curiously clumsy phrase, expressed "much pleasure to find that no differences exist respecting the accuracy of your statement". The document was not deposited at the Foreign Office, and at each subsequent change of Government Brunnov tried to ensure that the secret should be confined to the Prime Minister and Foreign Secretary. In 1846 Palmerston gave this assurance, and though his successors do not seem to have done so, secrecy was duly preserved, but further commitments were avoided, first by Granville, and then by Malmesbury and Derby, the last of whom reminded the Ambassador in a thinly veiled phrase, that he was lucky not to have Lord Stratford to deal with at the Foreign Office.[*]

The Tsar and Sir Hamilton Seymour

The incident is a classic illustration of the difficulties inherent in agreements between an autocratic sovereign and a constitutional government: its danger lay in the fact that while Nicholas looked upon the document as a binding pledge, on this side of the Channel it remained, and could not legally be more than, a mere moral obligation on individual ministers. With the years the Tsar's belief in the impending collapse of Turkey deepened, and the troubles in Jerusalem and in Montenegro during 1852 seemed to him highly symptomatic. When, then, Lord Aberdeen, whom he regarded as a personal friend, became Premier in a strong and able Cabinet, he was correspondingly elated, and thought that the time had at last come when joint action might crown twenty-four years of moderation. He therefore tried to reopen the question on a wider basis, by his famous conversation with the British Ambassador, Sir Hamilton Seymour, on 9 January 1853, when he said, "we have a very sick man on our hands, and it would be a great misfortune if he should escape us, especially before all the necessary dispositions had been taken".[†] Five days later he returned to the charge

---

[*] Goriainov, *The Secret Agreement of 1844*, p. 114. On 31 March 1854 Lord Derby in the House of Lords treated the Memorandum of 1844 as binding upon Aberdeen, but not upon any subsequent Government, and as remaining with each Foreign Secretary, but not in the Foreign Office. This undoubtedly was the official British view, which the Tsar entirely failed to understand. See *Hansard*, cxxxii, p. 156.

[†] Prof. Temperley (*The Crimea*, p. 272) shows that the Tsar really spoke not of "the sick man", but of "the dying bear". "You may give him musk, but even musk will not long keep him alive."

and proposed a frank discussion with Great Britain as to the fate of Turkey, in order to avert chaos and "the certainty of an European war" if the catastrophe took them unawares. He wished to speak "as a friend and a gentleman", as one keenly interested in the fate of millions of Christians: and if once Russia and Britain were at one, "peu m'importe le reste". He could not allow Britain to take Constantinople, but he on his part "would undertake not to establish himself there as proprietor", though he did not rule out the possibility of going as "dépositaire" (tenant for a limited period).

Seymour's report home was answered by Lord John Russell, then at the Foreign Office. After throwing doubt upon the imminence of dissolution, Russell advanced the very cogent arguments that the proposed understanding was disloyal to the Sultan, and if once attained, would have to be notified to the Powers, and this might easily precipitate the very anarchy which it was desired to avert. He was, however, ready to disclaim all designs on Constantinople and to pledge Britain against making any agreement for disruption, without informing Russia beforehand. To this the Tsar promptly replied that he had not intended to propose to England a scheme of partition, but only to get a clear exchange of views as to what each Power would regard as contrary to its interests in the Near East. The break-up of Turkey, he felt, might still be remote or it might come at any moment, and if there should be a Christian rising, neither Russia nor Austria could tolerate such devastation as the Turks had attempted in Montenegro. Let England therefore not unite with France against Russia's legitimate requirements, but invite the Porte to treat its Christians well.[3]

Following on this came a report of Brunnov, to the effect that British opinion was increasingly indifferent as to the maintenance of the tottering Turkish fabric, and that Aberdeen had spoken to him of Turkey as the worst Government in the world. On this the Tsar comments: "the most remarkable despatch of all: it explains the unexpected success of our first steps". On 20 February, then, undeterred by Russell's cold water and the Ambassador's extreme reserve, he again insisted on Turkey's imminent demise and this time became sufficiently concrete, even while insisting that he asked for "neither treaty nor protocol", but merely "a general entente" between gentlemen. "Constantinople must not belong to any Great Power, nor must there be a new Byzantine Empire: still less could he allow Turkey to be partitioned into small Republics, as asylums for the Kossuths, Mazzinis and other revolutionaries of Europe." But he suggested that the Principalities, "which are in fact an independent state under my protection", could remain so further, and that both Serbia and Bulgaria

night be organised on similar lines, while he was ready that England should
ake Egypt and Crete in any partition.[4]

That this was only a very rough suggestion, is sufficiently proved by the
act that Nicholas omitted all reference to Austria's share, and yet that his
oot idea was an arrangement between Russia, Britain and Austria as
principals, with Prussia's approval and to the exclusion of France—in other
words, a virtual repetition of what happened in 1840. Besides, he told
Seymour, "When I speak of Russia, I also speak of Austria: our Turkish
nterests are identical". Almost at the same time (23 February) he bade
Count Francis Zichy assure Francis Joseph in his name, that he loved him
ike a son and counted on his help to end the dirty regime on the Bosphorus
nd stop the oppression of the Christians by the "Turkish dogs".[5]

There can be no doubt that the Tsar was entirely sincere in his professions of friendliness to England, and that he did not imagine himself to be
naugurating a new policy, but merely carrying to its logical issue one
already pursued for close on 25 years. The real trouble was the difference
n atmosphere between London and St Petersburg, or it may be said, the
difference in point of departure, the Tsar as a near neighbour and possible
heir of Turkey being imbued with the idea that nothing could save Turkey
rom speedy destruction, while the statesmen of London saw the Turks in
a halo and maintained a really pathetic belief in their reformability. But
apart from this, much had happened since the London visit of Nicholas to
make his overtures distasteful. Age had made him more arrogant and
rritable, and his role in 1849 in suppressing Hungarian liberties and thus
bolstering up reaction in Italy, Poland and Germany also, had not only left
an exaggerated impression of his power, but made him the bugbear of all
Liberal opinion. A final ingredient in the impending quarrel was his old
aversion to France. After eighteen years of implacable hostility to Louis
Philippe he had been inclined to welcome the Prince-President and looked
upon the *coup d'état* as a guarantee against subversive tendencies: but when
Louis Napoleon became Napoleon III and based his new empire upon a
popular plebiscite, the Tsar's anger flared up and he failed to reckon with
he forces which were drawing France and Britain together once more. He
expressed to Seymour his conviction that to reach an agreement, it would
suffice for him to have "ten minutes of conversation with Lord Aberdeen,
who knows me so well and has as complete confidence in me as I in him".
He failed to realise that the situation both in London and in Europe had
been completely transformed since 1844.

THE MENSHIKOV MISSION

It was amid such disastrous illusions that Tsar Nicholas decided upon direct negotiations with the Turks, and entrusted Prince Menshikov, who enjoyed his special confidence, with a mission to Constantinople. Menshikov was brilliantly characterised by the French Ambassador as "one of our *grands seigneurs* of the court of Louis XV, fond of women, play, horses, good and bad company", but also with probity and independence of character, "sparing none in his witty and caustic sallies".[6] In sending Menshikov, Nicholas was undoubtedly inspired by a very recent and successful precedent. The famous poet Prince of Montenegro, Peter II, had in 1851 been succeeded by his nephew Danilo, who resolved to separate the offices of Prince and Metropolitan and proclaimed himself as hereditary lay prince. The Porte treated this as a violation of Turkish suzerainty and sent an army against the Montenegrins: whereupon Francis Joseph despatched Count Leiningen to Constantinople with a virtual ultimatum which led the Turks to desist and greatly enhanced Austrian prestige in the western Balkans. The motive which prompted the mission was the fear lest some fresh incident "might be enough to light that which lies glowing beneath the cinders"[7] and cause a conflagration such as might react upon Austria's own Southern Slav subjects.

Menshikov's mission, which if wisely conducted, might have achieved similar results, was from the outset staged with an arrogance and tactlessness which defeated their own ends. He began by putting an open affront upon the Foreign Minister Fuad Pasha, whom the panic-stricken Sultan at once replaced by the much more mediocre Rifaat Pasha: and this caused such alarm to the French and British Chargés d'Affaires, that the latter Colonel Rose, at the request of the Porte, sent an urgent message to Admiral Dundas at Malta, asking him to send a British squadron to the Dardanelles. Dundas declined to move, and his decision was upheld by the British Government, but Paris was at this stage more excited than London, and on 23 March, despite the dissuasive efforts of Lord Cowley, a French fleet sailed from Toulon to the Aegean.

While the anxious Turks met Menshikov's insistence by their usual tactics of procrastination, Lord John Russell, during his brief tenure of the Foreign Office, took a decision which was to have the most momentous consequences. Lord Stratford de Redcliffe, who had been Ambassador to the Porte for the previous twelve years, had resigned in January, but was now induced to resume his post "for a special purpose and charged with special instructions", which he himself had been virtually allowed to draft.* He was to counsel prudence to the Porte and forbearance on the part of France and Russia, and was to stop in Paris in order to emphasise the common interests of France and Britain in the Near East: he was left a free hand in the question of the Holy Places, but was to warn the Porte roundly that its own misgovernment was largely responsible for its present troubles, that a general revolt of her Christian subjects might ensue and that only thorough reform could save the situation and win foreign sympathy. He was authorised, despite the Prime Minister's misgivings, "in the event of imminent danger to the existence of the Turkish Government", to summon the fleet from Malta.

Thus armed, Stratford reached Constantinople on 5 April: Kinglake, in one of his most purple passages has spoken of "the angry return of a King whose realm had been suffered to fall into a danger"—a phrase to which Professor Temperley moves an abrupt negative.[8] In any case, his presence had a magical effect in stiffening Turkish resistance, and the tension was increased by the overbearing attitude of Menshikov. Ostensibly bent merely upon securing equality of treatment for Greek and Latin Christians, he pressed the Porte for a new treaty, extending the rights conferred upon Russia in 1774 into what would amount to a Russian protectorate of all Orthodox Christians: and if Turkey would then conclude a defensive alliance on lines resembling those of 1833, the Russian fleet and an army of 400,000 men would be pledged to undertake her defence when required. This project, though intended to remain secret, was at once communicated to the British Ambassador, who placed on record his view that its effect "would infallibly be the surrender to Russian influence, management and authority, of the Greek churches and clergy throughout Turkey".[9] That Stratford had no illusions as to the Turkish situation, is shown by a letter which he wrote to his wife on his way eastwards: "As to any real change in the Porte's system of administration or the adoption of sound measures in a right spirit, I only don't despair because we live in miraculous times."[10] But he was not slow to respond, when the Turks appealed to him for help, and soon found himself virtual arbiter in the quarrel, much as Menshikov might resent his influence. His first advice, based strictly on instructions from home, was unquestionably sound—to separate the two questions of the Holy Places and of Russia's ulterior aims: a speedy settlement of the former would place the Turks in a stronger position to resist the latter. If, he added, they could also be induced "to confirm all the privileges hitherto conferred upon the rayas... with such precision and completeness as may

* See Lane-Poole, ii, 234, and Walpole, *Life of Russell*, ii, 179. Aberdeen, writing to Russell on 15 February, refers to the need "to be very careful in preparing instructions for Lord Stratford, if as I presume we must consider his memorandum as giving an outline of what he would desire".

throw any foreign influence into the shade", they would at once revive in their favour the sympathies of Europe, and especially of England.[11]

On this advice the Turks acted, and on 4 May the Russian and French Ambassadors signed a Protocol embodying a compromise with regard to the Holy Places. But it instantly became apparent that this had been merely the occasion, but not the underlying cause, of the crisis: for the very next day Menshikov, losing patience at the Porte's evasion of his other demands formulated them in a peremptory Note, to be answered within five days. Stratford made no concealment of his disapproval, but heightened the effect by waiting for three days and then informing the Sultan himself in solemn private audience, that "in case of danger he was instructed to request the commander of H.M.'s forces in the Mediterranean to hold his squadron in readiness".[12] This had a magical effect, and the Russian demands were rejected. Menshikov's last desperate effort to wring concessions from the weak Sultan in person, led to the resignation of the Grand Vizier and Foreign Minister, but was countered by the summons of a Crown Council and a meeting of diplomatic representatives at Stratford's house. The appointment of Reshid Pasha to the Foreign Office has usually been ascribed to Stratford's dominant influence: in reality, it appears to have been made without his knowledge, and as a concession to Menshikov, who fondly imagined him to be Russophil.[13] But the irritable and haughty Russian found out his mistake only too soon, and, after a final effort to bully the Porte into submission, sailed on 21 May for Odessa, without attaining his aim. Ten days later, the Russian Foreign Minister, Count Nesselrode endorsed his envoy's demands and threatened the Porte that unless they were accepted, Russian troops would occupy the Danubian Principalities as a pledge of fulfilment. On the very same day Stratford had reported home that there was "at least no threat of immediate war", and Clarendon drew the conclusion that the Ambassador did not "expect a resort to the *ultima ratio*".[14]

The Turks as usual played a cautious and dilatory game. On 4 June they issued a firman confirming all the privileges of their Christian subjects and of the Orthodox Church in particular—a decree intended rather to impress western opinion than to be put into practice: but their Note of 16 June evaded the question of "moral guarantees" demanded by Russia, and merely offered to send a special envoy to St Petersburg. At this the Tsar's anger flared up again: he issued a fiery manifesto summoning his subjects to "go forth to fight for the Orthodox faith" against "the obstinate and blinded" Ottoman Government,[15] and on 7 July his army crossed the Pruth into Moldavia.

This was unquestionably a false move: for though Russia possessed special treaty rights over the Principalities and had in actual fact taken possession of them on four or five previous occasions, it was none the less a high-handed act which at once placed him in the wrong both at Constantinople and in the west, and caused a swift revulsion of public opinion in favour of the Turks. It must, however, be made clear that the French and British fleets, already off Salamis, were ordered to the Dardanelles before the news of the invasion of Moldavia could arrive, and therefore that aggressive actions may be said to have come more or less simultaneously from both sides. Moreover, that Stratford was not one whit less overbearing and autocratic, but only more capable and more influential, than Menshikov, is abundantly proved by the incident that followed the first arrival of the news at Constantinople itself. Mustafa and Reshid Pashas were promptly dismissed from their posts, for their failure to avert invasion: whereupon Lord Stratford sought an audience with the Sultan and secured their reinstatement on the spot (7 July). In his own words, "I went bang down to the Padishah and put them in again".[16]

THE VIENNA NOTE

The summer of 1853 was filled by complicated negotiations between the Powers, directed towards a compromise between Russia and the Porte: and Stratford's biographer has enumerated and analysed no fewer than eleven such projects.[17] To treat these negotiations in any detail would far exceed the scope of the present volume, and belongs to that full-blooded history of the Crimean War which still remains to be written.* For our present purpose it will suffice to dwell briefly upon the Austrian initiative and the causes of its failure. Tsar Nicholas had invited Austria to join him in parallel action, by occupying Serbia and Bosnia: but Francis Joseph declined to move and sent Count Gyulai on a special mission to dissuade him from entering the Principalities. When this appeal was disregarded, the Austrian Foreign Minister, Count Buol, convoked the Ambassadors of the Powers and attempted to draft a compromise between the Russian and Turkish views. The result was the so-called "Vienna Note"—reaffirming the Sultan's resolve to respect the rights accorded at Kainardji and Adrianople—which was despatched to St Petersburg on 31 July, and almost immediately accepted by the Tsar. Meanwhile, however, quite independently similar negotiations had been initiated at Constantinople by Lord Stratford with his diplomatic colleagues and the Porte, and had resulted in another project known as the "Turkish Note", differing but little in substance from that of Vienna, but more satisfactory to Turkish *amour-*

* Prof. Temperley's second volume on *The Crimea* will soon fill the void.

propre. This Note reached Vienna two days after the other had left for St Petersburg and was therefore suppressed by Buol and Westmorland—a step which Clarendon duly endorsed. One motive appears to have been the fear that the Tsar was much less likely to accept a scheme that owed its acceptance by the Porte to the influence of Stratford, whom he quite rightly regarded as inspired by illwill towards him.[18] It is difficult to resist the conclusion that the Vienna Note contained the germ of a reasonable compromise, and that Lord Aberdeen was right when in later life he "so bitterly regretted" that no attempt was made to devise an alternative proposition.

TURKEY AND RUSSIA AT WAR

Fresh instructions were, it is true, sent by Clarendon to Stratford, in favour of the Vienna Note as superseding the Turkish, and Mr Lane-Poole, on the basis of the Ambassador's papers, is most emphatic in contending that he "scrupulously abstained from letting his personal opinions transpire".* But these instructions arrived by sea, after a delay of some days, and it is impossible to avoid the conclusion that long ere then Stratford had helped the Turkish ministers to make up their minds. In any case the Turks, who in Stratford's own phrase, were "altogether on their high horse",[19] declined to accept the Vienna Note without amendments (19 August), and these latter the Tsar in his turn rejected (7 September). The indiscreet publication of a Russian circular in Berlin showed that the Russians and Turks put radically different interpretations on the Note, and this made a compromise more difficult than ever. On 4 October Turkey summoned Russia to evacuate the Principalities, and even before the time limit of fourteen days had expired, the two countries found themselves at war upon the Danube.

Already at the end of August the French Ambassador, M. de Lacour, had lost his head and begged his Government to send the fleet through the Straits, in order to prevent a massacre of Christians at Constantinople! Paris, accepting these alarmist tales at their face value, invited London's co-operation: and Lord Clarendon, without waiting for Stratford's calmer and more sceptical reports, sent a summons to the fleet. No sooner had the Turks declared war than they plunged from war fever into panic and clamoured for the two fleets. Thus it came about that on 22 October the joint Franco-British squadron entered the Dardanelles and anchored off the Golden Horn. A dangerous lull followed in the situation, which was at the mercy of any incident.

* On 20 August he wrote to Clarendon: "I feel confident that you will give me credit for having done my official best in support of the Vienna Note. Reshid told me candidly that no personal influence would have induced the Porte to give way" (Lane-Poole, *op. cit.* p. 295).

The British Cabinet and Lord Stratford

It is now necessary to consider the peculiar position of the British Cabinet, which throughout the summer was paralysed by internal divisions. Lord Aberdeen with all his ability and tact was not strong enough to impose himself upon all his colleagues or to insist upon warning Turkey that Britain would be no party to a war, while Lord Palmerston and Lord John Russell were not strong enough to warn the Tsar that in the event of war Britain would place herself on the Turkish side. Either attitude might have led one or other of the disputants to pause before it was too late. As it was, Aberdeen allowed his riper judgement to be overruled on two vital points—the reappointment of Lord Stratford and the sending of the fleet. He realised the need of very carefully worded instructions: as he said, "the assurances of prompt and effective aid on the approach of danger, given by us to the Porte, would in all probability produce war. These barbarians hate us all and would be delighted to take their chance of some advantage by embroiling us with the other Powers of Christendom. It may be necessary to give them a moral support and to endeavour to prolong their existence: but we ought to regard as the greatest mischief any engagement which compelled us to take up arms for the Turks. Lord Stratford is not very consistent in his descriptions of the Turkish Government. He refers to their present course of rashness, vacillation and disorder, and speaks of their maladministration as hopeless. At the same time he looks to their power of carrying into effect a system of internal improvement."

He then draws the very sound conclusion that Britain ought to keep "perfectly independent and free to act as circumstances may require. Above all we ought not to trust the disposal of the Mediterranean fleet—which is peace or war—to the discretion of any man".[20] None the less, only a month later the Foreign Secretary is writing to the Prime Minister: "One good thing of Rose having sent for the fleet will be that Lord Stratford will wish to be without it",[21] and yet, though apparently agreed on this judgment, they resign themselves to leaving Stratford in control. This detached and negative attitude of London was soon to bear fatal fruit.

Another of Aberdeen's closest colleagues, Sir James Graham, the First Lord of the Admiralty, shared his doubts as to Stratford, and wrote on 9 May: "He (Stratford) is a Bashaw—too long accustomed to rule alone. Such temper and such manners are not the pledges or emblems of peace."[22] But both agreed with Clarendon that there was no obvious person to replace the "Great Elchi", except Lord Cowley, who was indispensable at Paris. Yet on 7 June the Prime Minister admitted that "we are drifting fast towards war", and towards the end of the month expressed the view that "any war...will speedily lead to the dissolution of Turkey as at present existing".[23]

Other Ministers, however, had no such fears. Russell, who as long ago as 1828 had published quite a good essay on "The Turks in Europe" and knew the hopelessness of the Turkish system, was now bellicose almost from the first, and as early as 20 March wrote to Clarendon: "The Emperor of Russia is clearly bent on accomplishing the destruction of Turkey, and *he must be resisted.*"[24] Both he and Palmerston, who remained a firm believer in Turkey's soundness of health, kept pressing for the despatch of the fleet to the Dardanelles or farther, and on 19 June Russell wrote a memorandum for the Cabinet, urging help for Turkey against Russia and an alliance with France and Austria. In Parliament periodical enquiries were made by the ex-ambassador Lord Clanricarde and the late Foreign Secretary Lord Malmesbury: but Clarendon appealed for discretion and declined to reveal his instructions to Stratford, and even the Radical Joseph Hume approved of this, though adding that "publicity is, on almost all occasions, of advantage".[25] On 8 August Clanricarde urged the Government to make "a categorical demand" upon Russia for the evacuation of the Principalities, arguing that the existing status was "either war or piracy":[26] and Clarendon replied that "the question has assumed a European character" and that Britain, France, Austria and Prussia were acting cordially together, to check designs which they considered inconsistent with the Balance of Power. A few days later Malmesbury insisted upon the immense importance of Turkish independence, without which "we could hardly maintain our hold of India", and declared it was an "absurd and ruinous theory" to treat Turkey as "in a state of decay" which led logically to partition.[27] Clarendon again made a cautious reply, emphasising the frequent assurances given by the Tsar: but he committed himself to the view that the occupation of the Principalities was a "violation of existing treaties", which might have been treated by the Sultan as a *casus belli.*[28]

COBDEN AND PALMERSTON

In the House of Commons about the same time there was a lively passage of arms between Cobden and Palmerston, which admirably illustrates the rising tide of public opinion. The apostle of Free Trade, who knew the Near East at first hand and had taken an open stand for Hungarian liberties against the Tsar, expressed the view that "Turkish independence" had become "a mere empty phrase", and that the Turks were intruders and could not exist much longer in Europe. "If I were a rayah", he said, "I

should prefer a Russian or any other Government rather than a Mohammedan one": and the real question to him was what were the wishes of the
Christian population. This speech deserves to be recorded, as the first
occasion on which a British statesman publicly took account of the rights
and interests of the subject races of Turkey, as opposed to their rulers. Nor
did his home truths stop at that: for he warned those members who sat for
manufacturing towns and talked "so glibly of war", that it was an illusion
to identify British interests with Turkish trade, that the very existence of
British commerce in the Black Sea was directly "owing to Russian invasion"
of Crimea, and that Russia, so far from being a military danger, "can't
move an army to her own frontiers except by the aid of foreign gold". On
this, Palmerston fell upon him for such detestable sentiments, and not
content with describing him as "greatly misinformed as to the state of
Turkey for the last thirty years", roundly denied that Turkey was in a state
of decay and declared that she not merely had "no Poland or Circassia to
distract her", but had made "greater progress and improvement than any
other country in the same period"—alike in her system of government, in
her army and navy, in justice and agriculture, in "such manufactures as
she has", in her commercial system and in religious toleration. After this
confession of faith it was not surprising that Palmerston should declare that
he did not "mean to go into a rearrangement of Turkey or to dictate to the
Bulgarians, Slavonians, Greeks or Mussulmans, who are to be their
governors or what form of government they are to have".[29] Palmerston
had the House behind him in a view based upon crass ignorance and falsified
by history, but Sir James Graham was prophetic enough to tell Clarendon
that "Cobden in the long run will have England with him".[30] Palmerston's
truculent attitude is clearly revealed in a letter to Sidney Herbert, in which
he bids the Tsar, if he wishes the Christians of Turkey to be safe from
"oppression and vexation", to relieve the Principalities of the miseries
inflicted by his own armies, and "beyond that, let him be satisfied, as we all
are, with the progressively liberal system of Turkey, and let him keep his
remonstrances till some case and occasion arises which calls for them".
But if he "wants to become acknowledged protector" of the Christians and
"to interfere between the Sultan and his subjects,... then let us manfully
assist Turkey in manfully resisting it and let the fortune of war decide
between the Emperor's wrong and the Sultan's rightful cause". And again,
"I am desirous that England should be well with Russia as long as the
Emperor allows us to be so, but if he is determined to break a lance with
us, why, then have at him, say I, and perhaps he may have enough of it
before we have done with him".[31] Russell, for his part, while confessing
that "this Eastern Question has got into as entangled a position as can well

be", declared himself "for the Turk against the Russian",[32] and ere very long was talking of "the English people fighting to the stumps for the honour of England".[33]

"THE REAL SULTAN"

To these explosives at London must be added the growing inclination of Napoleon III for war, the Tsar's irritation and growing lack of self-control, and above all the baneful influence of Lord Stratford upon the Turks. On this point there is abundant evidence from inside the British Cabinet. Graham, in giving Stratford control of the fleet, had written to him, "I am certain you will wield this power with discretion and in the spirit of peace. It will be a miserable end if Europe be convulsed in these latter days by a Holy War".[34] But by the middle of August he was alarmed at the "harsh and ominous tone" of Stratford's reports and told Clarendon that "notwithstanding the peremptory order to the contrary, he [Stratford] is quite capable of advising the Turks to be refractory. In this case you should be ready to supersede him without the loss of a day and send either Bulwer or Howden" to Constantinople.[35] Aberdeen fully agreed, but expressed the fear that "Stratford intends to give us some trouble", and told Clarendon that he had "prepared the Queen for the possibility of Stratford's resignation...which she will not at all regret".[36] "The conduct of the Porte", he wrote later,[37] "is suicidal, and some fatal influence must be at work. It can only be explained by a desire that the whole affair should end in war." About the same time Lord Cowley transmitted home the sense of M. de Lacour's reports to Paris on his British colleague's "strange conduct". Stratford, he stated, while nominally complying with his instructions and urging the Porte to accept the Vienna Note, "lets it be seen at the same time that his private opinion is at variance with his official language, and does not bring that personal influence to bear which would have been so useful at the present moment". Meanwhile he "uses to his *intimes* the most violent language", disapproves of the Vienna Note, declares war preferable to such a solution ...; "that they shall know that his name is Canning, that he will resign, that he knows the Government of England is not united on this question, and that a change must take place which will bring into power the friends and supporters of his policy in Turkey".*

In this passage we have the real clue to the weak attitude of the home Government: they were afraid to recall Stratford, because they knew that

---

* Cowley to Clarendon, 29 August—*ibid.* p. 19. This is confirmed by a memorandum of Prince Albert, of 16 October, summarising Aberdeen's positive assertions to the Queen as to Stratford's "insincerity" and his denunciation of the Government's conduct as "infamous" (*Letters*, II, 456).

in that case he and Palmerston would automatically coalesce—even though there might be no actual understanding between them (as has been alleged, and as firmly denied, and never proved)*—and stampede public opinion. "I hope you will not allow Europe to be embroiled in war," wrote Graham to Clarendon, "because Canning...is resolved to embroil matters at home and abroad, in the hope of obtaining a triumph for his own morbid vanity and implacable antipathies."[38] "Stratford," wrote Clarendon to his brother-in-law Lewis, "the real Sultan, though he ostensibly and officially obeys his instructions, lets his dissent from them be known, and upon that the Turks act."[39] To Russell the Foreign Secretary wrote, "If I had such a man as Cowley at Constantinople, I have little doubt that matters would long ago have been arranged: but I quite agreed with you at the time that Stratford's experience and influence rendered him the fittest man for the emergency: but then we were not prepared for such an amount of Russian deceit, and that called forth all his Russian antipathies and made him from the first look to war as the best thing for Turkey. In fact, no settlement would have been satisfactory to him that did not humiliate Russia. He has never entered sincerely into the views of the Government and has been making political capital for himself. However, there he is, and we must make the best of him."[40] And to Cowley he wrote even more flatfootedly. "It is a misfortune and complication that we cannot feel sure of Stratford acting with us for a peaceful solution. He pretends to do so and writes notes and gets promises and appears to carry out his instructions: but it is impossible to believe, if he put his heart into it and set about the work *as he knows how to do there*, that everything in our view should fail as it does. It is painful to arrive at such a conviction, but it is difficult to come to any other. He is *bent on war*, and on playing the first part in settling the great Eastern Question.... In short, he seems just as wild as the Turks themselves, and together they may and will defeat every combination coming from the west, however well devised it may be."[41] To Sidney Herbert he was equally explicit—"It is quite clear the Turks don't want a settlement. The titular Sultan is for peace, but the real Sultan thinks that now or never is the time for putting an end to Russia.... It is to Stratford's *amour-propre froissé* that the obstacles to peace must be attributed."[42]

---

* There would seem to be no grounds for Clarendon's contemporary suspicions that Stratford was in direct correspondence with Palmerston for the promotion of war (cf. Lane-Poole, II, 231, and Maxwell, II, 28): but on the other hand it has transpired that he was actively organising a Turcophil and Russophobe propaganda in the British press through the medium of his former secretary, Mr Layard, the explorer of Nineveh (Layard, *Autobiography*, II, 123–4; Kingsley Martin, *The Triumph of Lord Palmerston*, p. 109). Prof. Temperley (*The Crimea*, p. 337), on the basis of minute research, dismisses as "a foolish legend" the allegation that "Palmerston and Stratford were in league for war".

Stratford's letters to his wife show him to have feared at one moment the possibility of a revolution in Turkey,[43] and after the mischief was done, to have regretted his friend Reshid's "hotness upon war".[44] But his own animus is clearly revealed in his outburst against the Tsar—"the head and front of the offence is that man who has been humbugging Europe, and perhaps at times duping himself, for the last quarter of a century".[45]

About the same time Aberdeen expressed to Graham his alarm at the turn of events. "I thought that we should have been able to conquer Stratford, but I begin to fear that the reverse will be the case, and that he will succeed in defeating us all....Although at our wit's end, Clarendon and I are still labouring in the cause of peace: but really to contend at once with the pride of the Emperor, the fanaticism of the Turks and the dishonesty of Stratford, is an almost hopeless attempt."[*] Stratford's private letters drove the Queen to the same conclusion, and on 5 November she told the Prime Minister that "they exhibit clearly on his part a desire for war, and to drag us into it", and asked "whether we are justified in allowing Lord Stratford any longer to remain in a situation which gives him the means of frustrating all our efforts for peace".[46] As Prince Albert told Stockmar, "Lord Stratford fulfils his instructions to the letter, but he so contrives that we are constantly getting deeper into a war policy".[47] The evidence is overwhelming, and it says much for the uncritical character of historical writing on our foreign policy, that Lord Stratford should so long have been given the benefit of the doubt. This must be my excuse for dwelling upon this aspect of the crisis with such fullness.

In a word, the Prime Minister, the Foreign Secretary, the First Lord, the Queen, were all agreed upon the fatal results of leaving Stratford at Constantinople, and yet the Eastern helm was left in his hands, while the flagship, in Aberdeen's own phrase, "drifted" into action. It was in this frame of mind that Lord Clarendon announced to his wife, "The beastly Turks have actually declared war" on Russia: and it is the phrase of a man who has lost all control of the situation. Meanwhile public opinion grew irritable and unrestrained, the Queen and Prince Albert, who were still genuinely desirous of averting war, became increasingly anxious, and the Tsar's personal appeal to her not to allow "the English flag to float beside the Crescent, against the Cross of St Andrew"[48], was not well received and provoked an answer friendly in form, but distinctly argumentative.

---

* Stanmore, *Life of Aberdeen*, p. 271. Lord Morley, in his *Life of Gladstone* (I, 487), records that Gladstone demurred to the word "dishonesty", when this letter was shown to him by Sir Arthur Gordon (Lord Stanmore) as the biographer of Aberdeen: but Morley himself, while calling it a hard saying, adds, "Why not call things by their right names?"

DRIFTING TOWARDS WAR

Hostilities opened on the Danube in the second half of October, and to the Tsar's mortification the Turks were able to take the offensive and drive back his troops in two engagements near Isaccea and Oltenița. For the moment, however, Western Europe maintained a watching attitude and after conciliatory discussions between Nicholas, Francis Joseph and Frederick William at Warsaw in October, negotiations were resumed at Vienna, and on 5 December a Protocol of the two Western and two Central Powers declared against any curtailment of Turkish sovereignty or territory, but invited the Porte to reopen the discussions.

Meanwhile Aberdeen at home fought week by week a losing game for peace. Public opinion, in Clarendon's words, seemed to think "there is nothing to do but to declare war against Russia, just when she is yielding the point in dispute, and back the Turk just when he acts contrary to our advice....I believe the Turks expect to take Petersburg before Christmas".[49] The Cabinet was riddled with dissension and there was constant leakage of secrets.[50] At one moment Aberdeen, with the approval of Gladstone and other colleagues, was prepared to send a clear warning from the four Powers to Turkey, that "they would not permit themselves...to be drawn into a policy inconsistent with the peace of Europe".[51] But he found both Palmerston and Russell "determined to resist this to the utmost extremity", and rather than risk a split, abandoned his project. All this time Russell behind the scenes was pressing the Prime Minister to resign in his favour, as had originally been planned: but while he appears to have genuinely thought that a stronger line against Russia would avert rather than precipitate war, Aberdeen, not without excuse, feared the triumph of the Jingo wing in the Cabinet and felt bound in honour to stay on and "prevent any rash decision". As he wrote to the Queen, "no doubt it may be very agreeable to humiliate the Emperor of Russia: but Lord Aberdeen thinks it is paying a little too dear for this pleasure, to check the progress and prosperity of this happy country and to cover Europe with confusion, misery and blood".[52]

As if the situation were not bad enough already, Lord John complicated it still further by raising the question of the franchise and pressing for a new Reform Bill. To this Palmerston objected, both on its merits and because it was so obviously ill-timed. Some of their colleagues believed that Palmerston hoped "by raising the war-cry to drown the demand for an extension of the suffrage".[53] In any case on 15 December Palmerston resigned office, thereby dealing a grave blow to the Government. He had consistently pressed upon Aberdeen the view that Turkey must be defended against Russia—"by negotiation if possible, and if negotiation fails, by force of arms", that all stories of Turkish fanaticism were "fables", that neither the Greeks nor the Slavs provided a sufficient nucleus for creating independent states, and that therefore "the reconstruction of Turkey means neither more nor less than its subjection to Russia",[54] and that the Conference in Vienna was dead.* His resignation may be ascribed in almost equal proportions to disapproval of Lord John's project and of Lord Aberdeen's definite refusal "to adopt the mode which you think most likely to restore peace".[55] But his decisive reason was the news of the battle off Sinope, which had just reached London, and the intense public excitement which it evoked both in England and France.

Towards the end of November the Porte, disregarding even the warnings of Lord Stratford, sent the Turkish fleet to reconnoitre in the Black Sea, following tactics highly reminiscent of coat-trailing at Kilkenny Fair: and then, instead of re-entering the Bosphorus, its incompetent commander anchored in the open roadstead of Sinope. On 30 November a Russian squadron surprised it there, and in the engagement that followed the Turks lost all their ships and 4000 men. The two countries had been at war for over a month, and if the Turks were justified in attacking and defeating the Russians by land on the Danube, the Russians were equally justified in retaliating by sea. Nor can there be much doubt that the Turks, though of course not prepared for such condign punishment, had deliberately aimed at provoking a conflict between Russia and the Allies. Prince Albert at the time showed his perspicacity when he argued that to allow Turkish ships to "pass before Sebastopol...can only be meant to insult the Russian fleet and to entice it to come out, in order to bring our fleet into collision with that of Russia and so make an European war certain".† Lord Stratford, when he heard the news of Sinope, hailed it as good, "for that means war. The Emperor of Russia chose to make it a personal quarrel with me: and now I am avenged."[56] "Thank God, that's war", he said to the Embassy physician, Dr Sandwith, who afterwards repeated it to Lord Stanmore.[57]

In a word, the very situation had arisen which the Queen, anxious but clear-sighted, had foreseen some weeks earlier, when she told Lord Clarendon

---

* "A Vienna Conference means Buol, and Buol means Meyendorff, and Meyendorff means Nicholas, and the Turks know this, and so does all Europe" (24 October, to Russell —Ashley, *op. cit.* p. 54). Meyendorff was Buol's brother-in-law.

† Sir James Graham, speaking officially in the House of Commons, on 27 February 1854, gave it as his opinion that Sinope was due to "the culpable negligence of the Turkish commander" (*Hansard*, cxxx, 1360).

"My belief is we shall have to go into the Black Sea. I wish devoutly that it were otherwise, and I also wish that we had other friends than those of Islamism to support" (Stratford de Redcliffe to Clarendon, 5 December—Lane-Poole, *op. cit.* II, 330).

that we had "taken on ourselves, in conjunction with France, all the risks of an European war, without having bound Turkey to any conditions with respect to provoking it".[58] Moreover, Nesselrode was on unassailable ground when he claimed that war was war and asked whether Turkey had an exclusive right to take the offensive.[59]

PUBLIC OPINION AND WAR

None the less, British public opinion, calmly oblivious of the treatment meted out to the Turkish fleet at Navarino in 1827, and under far more questionable circumstances to the Danish fleet off Copenhagen in 1807, clamoured against the "massacre" of Sinope.* At this crisis we are faced by the growth of a factor which had never before dominated British politics to the same extent, namely irresponsible public opinion expressed through the press. The older tradition of broadsheets and tracts had not yet died out, while the deluge of pamphlet literature was now in full swing: both catered for the masses and for the lower fringes of the new half-baked middle class which Early Victorian prosperity had rendered active and vocal. It was this opinion to which Palmerston gave a lead by his resignation, and when he was induced to withdraw it ten days later, his place was already assured as the leader of the nation in its warlike mood. The French at once proposed joint measures to protect Turkey, as otherwise the Black Sea would become a Russian lake: and before the end of the year Drouyn de Lhuys was able to announce the decision of the two Governments to send their squadrons into that sea.

THE CAMPAIGN AGAINST PRINCE ALBERT

In England meanwhile public opinion fell into a positive frenzy of nationalist suspicion and jingoism, of which nothing was more characteristic, more undignified or more humiliating than the attacks directed against Prince Albert, and so indirectly against the Queen, as being German or Russian or both—many people seemed incapable of distinguishing between the two —and therefore pacific and even guilty of actual treason. He was roundly denounced as the chief agent of "the Austro-Belgian-Coburg-Orleans clique, the avowed enemies of England and the subservient tools of Russian ambition".[60] His unpopularity, due to his "un-English" habits and outlook, made him an easy butt, and for some weeks he was attacked with persistent scurrility by large sections of the press—notably the *Morning*

* Even Mr Lane-Poole, writing in cold blood in 1888, uses such phrases as "massacre" "barbarity" and "wantonness" (II, 329).

Advertiser, then at its height, the *Morning Herald* and the *Daily News*, but also the *Standard* and *Morning Post*. The most concrete charge was that he had had illegal access to the Queen's correspondence with her ministers, had himself corresponded with British diplomats abroad, and had used his influence and special information to the detriment of British interests. A great deal of nonsense was talked about his "unconstitutional position", and for a time it was very widely believed that the Prince had been committed to the Tower and was about to be impeached. This may seem too fantastic to be recorded, yet can the general public be blamed for running amok, when a leading Radical journal could seriously write in one of a series of leading articles—"Better that a few drops of guilty blood should be shed on a scaffold on Tower Hill than that the country should be baulked of its desire for war?"*

So widespread was the mischief, that the Queen seriously considered whether she could open Parliament in her husband's presence, without being publicly insulted: and ministers found it necessary to grasp the nettle firmly and rob it of its sting. In the House of Lords it came to recriminations between the Prime Minister and Lord Derby as leader of the Opposition, each accusing the other's press organs of the initiative in launching these "despicable" and "disgraceful" imputations. Aberdeen, after reminding the House that he himself was accused of having "received a hogshead of gold from Russia" and of being "Austrian as well as Russian"—though Britain was "acting in direct concert with Austria" against Russia—clearly affirmed the Prince's constitutional right to be the Queen's adviser, and quoted abundant proof that Melbourne, Peel and Wellington alike had the highest opinion of his "judgment, temper and discretion", the former advising her "to rely upon him with confidence" and the latter desiring to have the Prince to succeed him as commander-in-chief. Derby "entirely concurred" in the Prime Minister's praise of the Prince, but denied his right "to insinuate that countenance has been given to the slanders by members of the Conservative party". The origin, he said, of "the absurd charges...which led crowds to attend at the doors of the Tower to see His Royal Highness go in, and which led individuals to say he was sure to have been sent there if the Queen had not announced her intention to go with him", was to be found in the *Morning Advertiser*, "a favourite paper of the licensed victuallers", which he himself did not read, but which, he suggested, was in touch with the Duke of Newcastle and other Liberals.

* *Morning Advertiser*, cf. Simpson, *Louis Napoleon and the Recovery of France*, p. 241. A very graphic account of the popular agitation of these years is to be found in Mr B. Kingsley Martin's book *The Triumph of Lord Palmerston*, which throws a great deal of fresh light, not only on the recesses of the Crimean War, but on mass psychology and press psychology in general, and therefore deserves to be widely known.

The myth was laid, and public opinion soon sought other scapegoats. But the Court had to show great reserve and discretion, in face of divergent outlooks inside the Cabinet itself. By the next summer Prince Albert was confiding to his brother, "We have much trouble with the Ministry. Aberdeen still lives in 1814, Lord John in 1830 and Palmerston in 1848. Parliament and the Press have suddenly become born generals." [61]

THE RUPTURE

Meanwhile the Vienna Collective Note had been forestalled by another Note of the four Ambassadors in Constantinople, to which Stratford induced the Porte to accede: and this was duly despatched on board a British frigate to Sebastopol, for transmission to the Tsar. This was in itself well calculated to wound the pride and kindle the national sentiment of Nicholas, who resented what he described as a summons before an "European council of war".[62] What aroused him still further was the news that a joint Franco-British squadron had entered the Black Sea (3 January 1854). A personal letter from Napoleon III only made matters worse: for Nicholas was still highly incensed at the upstart Emperor and could not resist replying that Russia in case of need would be the same in 1854 as in 1812. His nervous state was heightened by the failure of his envoy Count Orlov to win over Austria, and by what he fairly regarded as the equivocal attitude of Francis Joseph and his Foreign Minister Count Buol. But his chief anger was directed against England: he chafed at Aberdeen's weakness, saw in Stratford a personal enemy and in Palmerston "revolutionary propaganda incarnate".[63] Foreign observers thought that he had aged ten years under the strain of this crisis, and his half-mystical mood was reflected in a manifesto rousing his people against the enemies of Christianity. This was in one sense the counterpart of the agitation in the Turkish capital for a Holy War.

The Tsar's mental processes during this period are reflected in his eloquent appeals to Francis Joseph for co-operation against Turkey—reminding him of the agreements of Münchengrätz for just such a contingency, and assuring him of his resolve to do nothing except in consultation. "Could you really want", he wrote, "to espouse the cause of the Turks, toi, Empereur apostolique? Could your conscience permit you? Well, in that case Russia will march alone, under the Holy Cross, to her sacred predestination."[64]

On 6 February it came to the rupture of diplomatic relations between Russia and the Western Powers. In England the majority of the Aberdeen Cabinet found itself slowly driven towards war, against its better judgment, by the strong pressure of public opinion. Long afterwards Gladstone denied that they had "drifted" into war, but the phrase is Lord Aberdeen's own and is overwhelmingly proved by the course of events. The unhappy Minister assured John Bright that "his grief was such that at times he felt as if every drop of blood that would be shed would rest upon his head".[65] But the public frenzy held him as in a vice, and Palmerston by his "dexterous move"* of resignation and his discreet manipulation of the press, especially after Sinope, soon became the mouthpiece of aggression. Even the Radical Molesworth admitted Palmerston to be indispensable to the Government, and Lord John, no doubt in a state of passing huff, declared that the tactics employed "would ruin anybody but Palmerston".[66]

Nothing illustrates better Palmerston's relations to public opinion than the speech which he delivered as chairman of a banquet at the Reform Club, in honour of Sir Charles Napier, on the eve of his departure as commander of the Baltic fleet. The frivolous and vulgar tone of this speech —punctuated in the newspaper reports by cheers and roars of laughter— led John Bright to enter a protest in the House of Commons against what seemed to him "reckless levity...discreditable in the last degree to the great and responsible statesmen of a civilised and Christian nation". But Palmerston was entirely unrepentant, began his speech by a reference to "the honourable and reverend gentleman", and though called up sharply by Cobden, went on to treat Bright's opinion as "to me a matter of the most perfect indifference", since "he stands almost singly" in the opinion that the country should "submit to any degradation rather than have recourse to war". He would gladly listen to Bright at the next Reform Club dinner, "whatever state he may be in", but "it might not add to the conviviality of the evening".[67] This was too much for Macaulay, who noted in his diary that "Palmerston's want of temper, judgment and good breeding was almost incredible":[68] while Disraeli denounced Palmerston's "invective" against the Tsar as "most undignified and indiscreet".[69]

Palmerston, however, undoubtedly had the nation behind him and quite rightly claimed that he could "not reckon Cobden, Bright and Co. for anything". It was the time when Tennyson wrote of "this broadbrimmed hawker of holy things" and declared that

The cannons are God's preachers when the time is ripe for war.

And again,   So I wake to the higher aims
Of a land that has lost for a little her lust of gold,
And love of a peace that was full of wrongs and shames,
Horrible, hateful, monstrous, not to be told....

* Aberdeen's own phrase to Graham, who replied, "We have a crafty foe to deal with" (Martin, *op. cit.* II, 178).

> For the Peace, that I deem'd no peace, is over and done,
> And now by the side of the Black and the Baltic deep,
> And deathful-grinning mouths of the fortress, flames
> The bloodred blossom of war with a heart of fire....
> It is better to fight for the good than to rail at the ill:
> I have felt with my native land, I am one with my kind,
> I embrace the purpose of God, and the doom assigned.

If ever a war was made by an ill-informed but ardent public opinion, against the better judgment of a divided Government, it was the Crimean War. It is the classic disproof of the view that peoples are always pacific and only the statesmen or financiers warlike.*

During the winter and spring events inexorably drove France and Britain together: for the great adventure on which public, press and Parliament were more and more resolved, an ally was essential, and while France had more troops available, we had the ships and the means of transport. It was a fatality that neither country could very well have risked action alone, because each had one eye questioningly directed across the Channel: but a common adventure provided exactly the vent desired, when the one could safely indulge its ambitions and the other its sentiments. There was a fatal madness in the very atmosphere, for even to the last Castelbajac, the French Ambassador in St Petersburg, himself an opponent of war, strongly upheld the view that the Tsar was really pacific,[70] while Drouyn de Lhuys realised well enough that the Vienna Note, accepted by the Tsar, met all just demands, and even Thouvenel, who attached considerable importance to the question of the Holy Places, complained from time to time of the mischievous role of Stratford de Redcliffe, who had fallen foul of three successive French Ambassadors to the Porte. Stratford himself hesitated at times: on 5 December he told Clarendon that he wished devoutly that the fleet could be kept out of the Black Sea, and also "that we had other friends than those of Islamism to support",[71] and in the following April he told his wife, "no pen can write the crimes the Bashibezuks have committed".[72] But these passing qualms did not affect the main issue. The lists were now set—disappointment, wounded pride and mysticism working upon the autocratic nature of the Tsar, a divided Cabinet and irresponsible press in London, an all-powerful ambassador making a policy of his own in Constantinople, and a monarch bent on cementing his newly established power by the glamour of foreign alliances and a victorious war. All these factors completely outweighed the not very impressive efforts of the two

---

* Mr Reddaway, in his apologia for Palmerston (C.H.F.P. II, 381), is perfectly right in saying that "it was the nation, not Palmerston or any other man who really made the war".

German Powers at mediation.[73] On 27 February France and Britain addressed an ultimatum to the Tsar, giving him two months to evacuate the Principalities: debates in the House of Commons and the French Legislative Assembly poured oil upon the fire, and the publication of Sir Hamilton Seymour's report of his conversations with the Tsar and of the Nesselrode Memorandum of 1844 both infuriated Nicholas and brought British public opinion to the boiling point. As Nicholas disdained to answer the ultimatum and sent his troops across the Danube on 20 March, hostilities against Russia were officially declared in London and Paris eight days later. A national day of prayer was ordained, but the Queen made good her protest against its being one of "humiliation" also: it would not do, she argued, to ascribe war to "the great sinfulness of the nation,...when it is the selfishness and ambition of *one* man and his servants who have brought this about".[74] It was on this characteristically Victorian note that the Crimean War opened, those true and logical pacifists Bright and Cobden being treated everywhere with ignominy, and those later Prussian arguments of the steel bath for effeminate mankind being put forward in every variety of form by the poets and imaginative writers of the day.

Palmerston was the soul of the war party and the hero of its unbalanced enthusiasm. To Lord John he confided his "beau ideal" of the terms on which peace should be concluded: "Aland and Finland restored to Sweden. Some of the German provinces of Russia on the Baltic ceded to Prussia. A substantive Kingdom of Poland re-established as a barrier between Germany and Russia. Wallachia and Moldavia and the mouths of the Danube given to Austria. Lombardy and Venetia set free from Austrian rule and either made independent states or incorporated with Piedmont. The Crimea, Circassia and Georgia wrested from Russia, Crimea and Georgia given to Turkey and Circassia either independent or connected with the Sultan as suzerain."[75] In other words, his mind was full of vast and impracticable schemes for remodelling the whole east of Europe to Russia's disadvantage, and bolstering up the crumbling rule of Turkey.

In order to stiffen public opinion still further, the Government took the then somewhat unusual step of publishing Seymour's confidential despatches, recounting the overtures of the Tsar, and Lord Clarendon justified the step in a speech to the House of Lords. While suggesting that Nicholas's attitude was no worse in 1853 than in 1844 or in 1829,* he claimed that if England had admitted the dissolution of Turkey to be at hand, then his prophecy might have come true: but we denied the impending dissolution and rejected the territorial bribe. To yield would have placed "the affairs of all Eastern Christians" at the mercy of Russia, and the maintenance of

* See *supra*, pp. 134, 236.

the Turkish Empire would have been "a vague and unmeaning term". Britain's aims were unselfish; "we want nothing for our trade, and we fear nothing for our Indian possessions.... It is to maintain our honour and self-respect." Her main object was "to check and repel the unjust aggression of Russia": it was a "battle of civilisation against barbarism", to maintain the independence of Europe.[76]

CHAPTER IX

THE DIPLOMACY OF THE CRIMEAN WAR

The Search for Contact

The Aberdeen Cabinet survived the outbreak of war for eleven months, but though it contained more men of high ability than almost any ministry of last century, it was rent by internal dissensions and continually dogged by misfortune. Indeed, it was not until the scandals and disaster of the ensuing winter raised an outcry at home and brought the popular hero Palmerston to power upon the shoulders of the mob, that real energy and efficiency began to be shown.

Of few other wars in history can it be said that six months elapsed before the two sides could get to grips with one another. The history of the war has as a rule been written in entirely false perspective: a few deeds of extreme heroism have received such exuberant publicity that the plain man is still unaware of two capital facts—that the brunt of the war was borne by the French forces, which always greatly outnumbered the British,* and above all, that the actual field of operations was really determined by circumstances altogether outside the control of the western allies. Throughout 1854 and even 1855 the key to the whole situation lay in Vienna. That Austria under Francis Joseph and Buol pitiably mismanaged her foreign policy, and ended by finding herself dangerously isolated in Europe, in no way affects the truth of this contention.

The Tsar never even deigned to answer the Franco-British ultimatum, and long before it had expired, sent his troops across the Danube. The Western Alliance was proclaimed on 10 April 1854, and its terms included an invitation to other Powers to assist a campaign in which all conquest and aggrandisement was expressly disclaimed and Russia's inordinate power and ambition were treated as full justification. Only ten days later, however, the two Powers to which this appeal was mainly directed— Austria and Prussia—concluded an alliance of their own for the period of the war now opening, by which they gave a mutual guarantee of territory,

---

* According to Pélissier the French losses up to December were 72,000, as against 22,500 British. Raglan on 18 January 1855 officially estimated the strength of the French army to be at least four times that of the British (Martineau, *Duke of Newcastle*, p. 233).

forswore separate alliances with other states, and made it clear that they would only go to war with Russia if she should decide to annex the Principalities or to cross the Balkan range and thus threaten Constantinople.

There can be little doubt that this was a disastrous step and that Bismarck and his friends were right in the disapproval which they expressed at the time. An agreement between the two Central and the two Western Powers could almost certainly still have been achieved on terms halfway between the British and Russian extremes, and the Tsar would then have yielded to the inevitable, instead of allowing his illusions as to Austrian support to stiffen his resistance to the West.* In actual fact, the camarilla which now controlled Austria was deeply divided between a Russophil and a Russophobe current, the hesitant Francis Joseph leaning on the whole slightly towards the latter, under the influence of his mother and of his cousin Archduke Albrecht. Despite the financial stress and a growing deficit, the Austrian army was put on a partial war footing, and the concentration in Galicia became a serious threat to Russia's right flank. On 3 June Vienna addressed to St Petersburg a demand for the evacuation of Moldavia and Wallachia, and, furious as he was at such a proof of ingratitude towards him, Tsar Nicholas found the strategic arguments against him overwhelming, and complied, though with a very bad grace. Neither he nor his generals could shut their eyes to the patent military fact that Austria, in the event of war, would threaten his land communications with the Danube and perhaps even cut off his armies' retreat to Odessa. His annoyance was increased by the knowledge that evacuation also meant the abandonment of his Danubian campaign, which had been held up by Turkey's successful defence of Silistria.†

RUSSIA, AUSTRIA AND THE PRINCIPALITIES

No sooner, however, had the Russians withdrawn from the two Principalities, than the Austrians themselves filled the vacuum, on the basis of a secret convention concluded on 14 June with the Porte. Bucarest was left in Turkish hands and the rest of Wallachia jointly occupied, but Moldavia was held exclusively by Austria. The result was to insert a wide neutral wedge between the Turks and Russians on the lower Danube, and as Francis Joseph, on the attainment of his immediate objective, resumed his old policy of hesitation between the two groups, all idea of a joint advance

* On 29 January 1856 the Queen told her uncle King Leopold: "I repeat now what we have said from the beginning...if Prussia and Austria had held strong and decided language to Russia in 1853, we should never have had this war" (*Letters of Queen Victoria*, III, 170). In this she was unquestionably right.

† With the help of a group of able British officers, Butler, Nasmyth and Ballard.

of the Western Allies and the Turks, from the delta in the direction of Odessa, had to be abandoned. The Austrian Foreign Minister, Count Buol, it is true, favoured alliance with the West, very largely because he feared lest Napoleon, if Austria refused his overtures, should actively espouse the cause of Italian liberty: and he had the support of the clerical party, whose concern for the Temporal Power led them to favour the Power which garrisoned Rome for the Pope. On the other hand the high aristocracy, and most of the high command, leaned to the side of Russia.

It was Austria's insistence upon the Russian evacuation of the Principalities and then her adoption of a passive role that really decided the Crimean expedition. But for that, the struggle would inevitably have taken place on the Danube. As it was, the Allies had positively to search for a point of contact with their enemy. An invasion through Poland was impossible without the active intervention of Prussia, an attack in the Baltic involved the support of Sweden: and there thus remained, by a process of exclusion, the Russian coasts of the Black Sea. The Allies, possessing an absolute naval superiority, set themselves to destroy the strategic centre from which Russia might hope to dominate that sea and achieve her designs on Constantinople. The first point of concentration for the French and British forces had been Gallipoli, but in June headquarters were transferred to Varna, where, however, cholera decimated their ranks and a mysterious fire destroyed a vast accumulation of stores. Everything seemed to conspire in favour of making the capture of Sebastopol the prime objective of the war.

CRIMEA AS THE OBJECTIVE

As early as March 1854 Graham, as First Lord, spoke to Clarendon of the Crimean fortress as "the eyetooth of the Bear": and in April the Duke of Newcastle (soon to become the first Secretary for War, on the separation of the Colonial and War Offices) instructed Lord Raglan to make "careful but secret inquiry into the present amount and the condition of the Russian force in the Crimea and the strength of the fortress of Sebastopol. Your first duty will be to prevent by every means in your power the advance of the Russian army on Constantinople. . . . No blow which could be struck at the southern extremities of the Russian Empire would be so effective for this purpose as the taking of Sebastopol."* After discussions with Paris, in which Napoleon was more constrained than constraining, definite in-

---

* 10 April—James Martineau, *Duke of Newcastle*, p. 143. Gladstone congratulated *Palmerston* on being the first man in England to suggest the Crimea as the main point of attack (Guedalla, *Gladstone and Palmerston*, p. 100).

structions were sent to Raglan on 29 June, "to concert measures for the
siege", in the belief that without such action and the capture of the Russian
fleet, it would be "impossible to conclude an honourable and safe peace".[1]
It should be unnecessary to emphasise the immense difficulties presented
in the 'fifties by the transport and supply of such large armies at such a
distance. Indeed to-day, with the perspective of 80 years, and only too
ample revelations at our disposal, the lamentable breakdown of commis-
sariat, road transport and medical services should cause no surprise. But
it requires a greater effort to admit—what is none the less an undoubted
fact—that not all the valour of the British and French troops could have
saved them from disaster, but for the double handicap which circumstances
imposed upon the Russians in their turn. These were on the one hand the
lack of proper communications between the Crimea and the interior of
Russia, and on the other the doubtful and at times menacing attitude of
Austria, which rendered necessary the concentration of a large Russian
army along the Galician frontier and thus prevented the Tsar from throwing his whole weight against the invaders from the sea. Whether, if that
had been possible, Russia's overwhelming numbers would have made up
for defects of transport even more faulty than those of the Allies, is a question
for military historians to decide. Certain it is in any case that the responsibility for the Crimean adventure rests rather upon the political than upon
the military chiefs. Raglan and St Arnaud, Dundas and Hamelin alike disliked the idea and acted more in deference to the known views of London
and the acquiescence of Napoleon III, "than to any information in possession of the naval and military authorities".* The decisive factor was the
combined optimism and aggressive nationalism of Palmerston, who was
convinced that "60,000 English and French troops with the fleet would
accomplish the object in 6 weeks after landing", and that parallel operations
might be conducted in Georgia and Circassia, and that this would be the
surest way of winning over Austria, who "has as usual been playing a
shabby game".[2] His ideas of territorial change were so vast as to wrest
from Lord Aberdeen the plaintive phrase, "We have the plan sketched out
for a thirty years' war."[3]

The Court, and in particular Prince Albert, took what was then a sane
middle course: his main desire was to avert an European war, but he felt
that "we cannot look on and see the Porte destroyed by Russia".[4] But after
the outburst of popular fantasy against the foreign consort, it was necessary

---

* Raglan's official despatch in Kinglake, *Invasion of Crimea*, ɪɪ, 277–9, and Martineau,
op. cit. p. 149. Newcastle replied to Raglan: " I cannot help seeing through the calm and
noble tone of your announcement of the decision to attack Sebastopol, that it has been taken
in order to meet the views and desires of the Government and not in entire accordance
with your own opinions" (*ibid.* p. 150).

to walk circumspectly and play a somewhat effaced role: and though Palmerston was now more and more in favour, there was the recent memory of how he could defy and even browbeat or ignore the Crown.

AUSTRIA AND THE FOUR POINTS

It is not too much to affirm that throughout the war Austria remained the key to the diplomatic situation: and this explains the negotiations which led on 8 August 1854 to the adoption of the so-called "Four Points" of Vienna as the joint programme of the Western Powers and of Austria. They may be summarised as follows:

(1) The renunciation of Russia's special treaty rights in Wallachia, Moldavia and Serbia and the substitution of a general guarantee by the Powers.

(2) The freedom of Danubian navigation.

(3) The Revision of the Straits Convention of 1841.

(4) The renunciation of Russia's Protectorate over the Christians of Turkey.

Though they really contained the germ of the future settlement, they were in the first instance rejected with great indignation by Tsar Nicholas and Nesselrode, and this rendered the Crimean expedition inevitable. During the middle of September 58,000 Allied troops were landed and within the first week won the battle of Alma: but the first assault upon the fortress was unsuccessful, the genius of Todleben organised a most formidable defence, and after the heroic but not decisive actions of Balaklava and Inkerman (25 October and 5 November), it became obvious that a long and strenuous winter siege was inevitable. None the less, extravagant hopes were still entertained in both London and Paris, and Napoleon planned—it may be only as a *ballon d'essai*—an elaborate revision of the map of Europe which would give the Danubian Principalities and Bessarabia to Austria, Lombardy to Sardinia, Caucasus and Crimea to Turkey, and either restore Poland's independence or assign it in its entirety to Prussian rule.

Meanwhile every effort was being made to induce Austria to throw in her lot with the Western Allies, while the irresolute Frederick William IV did his utmost to prevent Vienna and St Petersburg from quarrelling (or, if Bismarck's rude interpretation be allowed, "ran after Austria like a masterless poodle"). His attitude was at least partly responsible for Russia giving her assent to the Four Points on 28 November. But the Tsar had waited too long, and on 2 December Austria, yielding to strong diplomatic pressure, signed an alliance with the Western Powers, couched, it is true, in somewhat vague and elastic terms, but including a pledge of joint defence of the Principalities against Russia and, if peace were not attained by the end of the year, a joint discussion of the best "means for securing the aims of the alliance". If Napoleon was unduly elated, Palmerston remained somewhat sceptical, while the Tsar fulminated against the ingratitude of Francis Joseph and ordered the young Emperor's bust to be removed from his room. He had already coined the characteristic phrase, "The two most foolish Kings of Poland were Sobieski and I, who helped Austria."[5] But Francis Joseph seemed bent upon alienating friend and foe alike: for, finding it impossible to carry Frederick William with him, he drew back and stood irresolute between the two groups, thus leaving Sardinia free to step into the vacant place in the alliance. The consummate diplomacy of Cavour thus prepared the way for French advocacy of Italian liberation and acceptance of a free Italy as an equal among the Great Powers. Buol meanwhile fondly imagined that he had pegged out Austria's claim to the two Principalities, and that in the end it would prove possible to annex them without war: and the Roumanian question bulked largely in his calculations, since the union of Wallachia and Moldavia under a foreign Prince was likely to react upon Austria's numerous Roumanian subjects, and it therefore seemed advisable to bring them once for all within the political orbit of the Habsburg Monarchy.

THE FALL OF LORD ABERDEEN

During the winter of 1854 the Aberdeen Government was growing steadily weaker, and suffered a series of annoying parliamentary reverses. The unexpected resistance of Sebastopol, the hardships and obstacles due to an unusually rigorous winter, and above all the harrowing accounts of incompetence, neglect and disease taking their toll upon a gallant but wellnigh helpless army and slowly trickling through to a public entirely unprepared for anything save a speedy and overwhelming victory—all this provoked intense excitement and impatience. Public opinion turned against the Government and began to search for scapegoats.

The crisis was rendered still more acute by dissensions inside the Cabinet. Lord John Russell in particular showed great restiveness, not merely pressing the cause of franchise reform with a zeal that was all the more ill-timed because of the indispensable Palmerston's active opposition to any such idea, but at the same time arguing that Aberdeen's very love of peace and his good relations with the Tsar increased the danger of actual war, and thus reaching the naïve conclusion that the time was now ripe for his assumption of the Premiership.* Clarendon, who had long chafed at Russell's strange mentality, now wrote of him that he "was wrong in his facts, insolent in his assertions, and most ill-tempered in his replies. No spoilt child could be more perverse or inaccessible either to kind or firm words."[6] Prince Albert found in the Cabinet an "universal feeling of indignation...at Lord John's conduct": but he also found that it seriously weakened the Prime Minister's moderating influence. Indeed Lord Aberdeen confided to the Prince that his "great difficulty was not only the long antecedent and mutual opposition between him and Lord Palmerston, but also the fact that Lord Palmerston loved war for war's sake, and he peace for peace's sake".[7]

It was only with difficulty that Russell could be dissuaded from resigning at the turn of the year, and he continued, very rightly, to press for more energetic measures of co-operation with the French. He also demanded that the Duke of Newcastle should be removed from the War Office and replaced by Palmerston; but we now know that the Duke by no means deserved the unstinted abuse levelled against him by contemporaries and was already earnestly engaged upon remedial measures in the War Office.†

Matters came swiftly to a head on 23 January 1855, when Roebuck gave notice of a motion in the House of Commons, to enquire into the conduct of the war, and when Russell demonstratively resigned and left the sinking ship. After much plain speaking the motion was adopted, a week later, by 305 votes to 148: and Lord Aberdeen at once resigned. The Queen sent successively for the Conservative leader Lord Derby—who recognised that he could not hope to stand without Palmerston's alliance, but refused the latter's condition of an equal coalition; for Lord Lansdowne, whose age and feeble health prevented him from accepting, and for Lord John Russell, who imagined himself to be the natural heir to the Premiership, but soon found that at the moment only one of his colleagues would hear of accepting office under him, and that, by a supreme irony of fate, this was no other than Palmerston.[8] A fourth combination, of Clarendon as Prime Minister, Russell as Foreign Secretary and Palmerston as leader of the House, was wisely rejected by the Queen and her husband, on the ground that it would "spoil two efficient men"—one who lacked courage for the chief office in the state, the other whose conduct of foreign affairs had been a decided failure.[9]

* Already on 10 May 1854 he had written to Clarendon: "The great want of all is a head of the English Cabinet. If a head could be found, all might be well." But Clarendon did not respond (Walpole, *Life of Russell*, II, 218).

† On 19 October 1864 *The Times* expressed the view that the Duke "had been made the scapegoat of a powerful but ineffectual Ministry", and this is probably not far from the verdict of history.

PALMERSTON AS PRIME MINISTER

Thus, by a process of elimination, Palmerston became Prime Minister on 6 February 1855, and was able without arrogance to call himself the *inevitable* Prime Minister.* He had made the retention of Clarendon at the Foreign Office an absolute condition, and Clarendon himself was not prepared to serve under Russell. Meanwhile it is entirely characteristic of the chivalrous Aberdeen that he should have used all his influence to induce the Peelites to enter the Government of his successor. Thus for the moment the new Cabinet was identical with the old, save for the elimination of Aberdeen, Russell and Newcastle, who was succeeded by Lord Panmure. But within a very few weeks Palmerston found it advisable to accept an unrestricted enquiry on the Roebuck lines, and the three Peelite Ministers —Gladstone, Graham and Herbert—taking the view that such an enquiry was a most dangerous constitutional innovation, announced their final withdrawal. Palmerston, however, held the tiller firmly; the ship, whose gunwales had been awash in the squall, swiftly righted itself and made increasing way. The Queen recorded, with evident approval, Lord Derby's conviction "that the whole country cried out for Lord Palmerston as the only man fit for carrying on the war with success".[10] The country was unquestionably behind him, ready to endorse more vigorous measures and a less conciliatory peace programme: and one of his first steps was to assure Napoleon III how much the alliance owed to His Majesty's "loyalty, frankness and sagacity", and how firmly resolved he himself was "to restore order to our camp before Sebastopol and to imitate the fine example of the French camp".[11] This seems for the moment to have revived the old anxieties of the Queen and the Prince, who asked each other what control the Cabinet could hope to exercise on foreign affairs, if the Prime Minister acted in direct concert with the Emperor of the French.

By an irony of fate, at the very moment when Britain's warlike attitude was strengthened by Palmerston's advent to power, an event occurred which led to the growth of less aggressive sentiments in France. This was the death of the intransigeant Tsar Nicholas, to whom victory had become a matter not merely of prestige but of personal honour, and whose autocratic outlook rendered compromise wellnigh impossible (2 March). With the accession of the milder Alexander II, Napoleon, whose attitude towards the war had from the first been determined rather by calculation than by

* Ashley, *op. cit.* p. 77. "Wherever I go", said Lord Dudley Stuart, "in the House [of Commons] I have heard but one opinion...and that has been pronounced in a single word or a single name—Palmerston." Cf. Mr Kingsley Martin's admirable survey in *The Triumph of Lord Palmerston*, pp. 224–44.

principle, addressed himself to the task of re-establishing Franco-Russian relations. It is true that shortly before the Tsar died, Napoleon had sent reinforcements to the Crimea under Pélissier and Niel, and was even contemplating a personal visit to the seat of war. But this was conceived rather as the final act in the great drama, timed to coincide with the fall of Sebastopol: the army could then return crowned with laurels, and the stability and virtues of his regime would be apparent to all the world at the very moment when the Universal Exhibition was to open in Paris. In striking contrast to the 'thirties or 'forties, French opinion in 1855–6 was far less bellicose, far less liable to panic, than opinion across the Channel, which, as the war dragged on, grew steadily more aggressive and exacting.

With some difficulty the Emperor was induced by Persigny, Morny, Drouyn, Clarendon and others to renounce his journey: on the one side there was fear lest some evil might befall him, such as would react upon the home situation, on the other there was the suspicion that in presence of the Emperor "the British army would become a mere brigade".[12] But it was impossible to disregard his pacific wishes and those of the new Tsar, as expressed in Nesselrode's Circular Note: and a Conference was therefore convened at Vienna on 15 March, to explore the possibilities of peace on the basis of the Four Points. While Napoleon stressed the value which he attached to the negotiations by sending his Foreign Minister, Drouyn de Lhuys, to Vienna, Palmerston invited Russell to become the British representative, thus ridding himself of an irksome colleague at a time of crisis and yet seeming to win future support by entrusting him with so important a mission and pleasing the French by the selection of an ex-Premier.[*]

The Conference of Vienna

Into the complicated discussions that followed it would be an error to enter in any general history: for the reader would then be in danger of not seeing the wood for the trees. On the first two Points—the collective guarantee of the Principalities, and the free navigation of the Danube—agreement seemed within easy reach: and the main controversy centred round the third Point, which dealt with the status of the Straits. Discussion ranged between the two alternatives of restricting the naval forces of Russia or of authorising the Allies to maintain equivalent forces of their own in the

[*] "The reasons against," wrote Palmerston to Clarendon, "are his habit of acting upon sudden impulse, his rather dry and stiff habits, his aptitude to be swayed by others, and the circumstance that if he came back with success, he would be more inconvenient to the Government than he would otherwise be" (10 February 1855, Maxwell, *op. cit.* II, 63). This throws a somewhat harsh light upon the friendship of the two veteran Whig chiefs.

Black Sea. The difficulty of agreement was increased by Buol's shifty and arrogant attitude and still more by the absence, and when he at last arrived, by the extreme reserve, of the Turkish delegate. This was largely due to Stratford de Redcliffe, who discouraged the Porte from sending an envoy. 'It is just like him," wrote Clarendon to Russell, "He never will help anybody else and will always thwart any business which is not carried on at Constantinople, where he can have the principal finger in the pie."[13] But it is altogether characteristic of Clarendon that though he keenly resented Stratford's behaviour, and told him so with a frankness that would have been brutal towards almost any other man,* he declined to consider Russell's suggestion that the Ambassador should be recalled, in the belief that he would be an even greater obstacle to peace if he returned to England. Yet he confided to Cowley that Stratford "hopes the negotiations will fail: which of course means that he won't allow the Porte to accept any terms of peace. He appears to think that John Bull has not yet bled either in purse or in person as he ought to have done...."

Once more, as in 1853, Clarendon's weak attitude must be condemned as altogether inexcusable: for he was fully aware that quite apart from Stratford's fatal influence upon the Turks, he had been engaged in constant quarrels with Admirals Dundas and Lyons, had greatly complicated the problem of assistance to Fenwick Williams in beleaguered Kars, and above all maintained a vendetta with his colleagues at the French Embassy, thus introducing an awkward element of friction in the relations of Paris and London. Lacour had already found it impossible to work with Lord Stratford: his successor General Baraguay d'Hilliers (whom Stratford himself regarded as "the very quintessence of French vanity and recklessness", and who was certainly little suited to delicate diplomatic tasks)† was soon recalled to Paris: and no other than Napoleon informed Clarendon that he was deliberately sending a Chargé d'Affaires instead of an Ambassador, in order to avoid further friction. That Chargé, Benedetti, has left on record his own views and those of a former Chargé, Sabatier, as to the impossible temper of "The Great Eltchi". The one said of him, "His colleagues were his enemies: he never allowed one of them to join him on the height where

---

* "I have deferred in all things to your eminent position and great local experience. I have marked but not noticed your general disregard of whatever had the appearance of instructions....Last, though by no means least, hardly a week passes without my fighting some battle somewhere for you. The Emperor has told me that he has no Ambassador at Constantinople now, because he thought his Chargé d'Affaires would be beneath your notice: but that things were not improved and the message I received two days ago was: 'qu'ici et à Londres nous sommes les meilleurs amis du monde: à Constantinople nous sommes en guerre'." (12 February 1855—Clarendon to Stratford, Maxwell, op. cit. II, 66).

† Hübner, on learning of the appointment, refers to him as "brise-raison et mauvais coucheur qui se brouillera avec tout le monde, à commencer par Lord Stratford" (Neuf Ans de Souvenirs, I, 162).

he had placed himself": while the other wrote, "Systematically hostile to France, he has always been our adversary in all questions where we would not let ourselves be dragged in his wake or submit to his jealous and haughty patronage." [14] Even the Porte itself, "in great confidence", conveyed through Musurus to Clarendon "the earnest entreaties of the Sultan and Government to be relieved from an oppressor who prevents their doing what is right, because he will have all the merit of it exclusively, and thereby lowers them in the eyes of their people".*

The Vienna discussions continued throughout April. Austria being opposed to the complete neutralisation of the Black Sea, the Western Powers advocated a limitation of the naval forces of the riverine states. Prince Gorchakov, in rejecting this, suggested that the Straits Convention of 1841 should be abolished and free passage assured to the ships of all nations at peace with the Porte: but as the effect of this was to accord to Russia free access to the Mediterranean, France and Britain in their turn refused. Buol made a final effort to avert a failure of the Conference, and his proposals are worth summarising—an European guarantee of Turkish independence and integrity; closure of the Straits, but maintenance of allied ships in the Black Sea; limitation of the Russian fleet and in the event of any infringement an automatic increase by the Allies: and finally the right reserved by the Powers to keep the Straits open to the entire naval forces of the Allies, if the Porte should be in danger. In the belief that these terms would at last secure the active support of Austria, both Russell and Drouyn assented, the latter admitting that the motive of his visit to Vienna was "not so much peace with Russia as an alliance with Austria".[15] The fact is that Drouyn never really trusted England and hoped for an agreement between the Second Empire and Catholic Austria: but his direct secret overtures to Francis Joseph were met by evasion and led to nothing. Meanwhile, however, Napoleon and Eugenie had paid their state visit to England, and the British statesmen had held a joint council of war with Marshal Vaillant. The result was that Napoleon was induced to repudiate his own Minister, while Clarendon raised objections to what he regarded as tantamount to the "permanent policing" of the Black Sea, and Palmerston denounced the Austrian scheme to the Queen as "really a mockery", "alike dangerous and dishonourable".[16] It has always remained somewhat of a mystery why Russell failed to realise that he was committing himself far beyond what not merely Palmerston, but even Clarendon, was ready to accept. Clarendon was on tenterhooks as to what he called "the devilries at Vienna",[17] and the only two explanations of what happened—and neither entirely fits the

---

* This Clarendon repeated confidentially to Cowley, adding, "Of course I could not listen to this, but I believe it and sympathise with the sufferers" (Maxwell, *op. cit.* II, 68).

acts—would seem to be that the envoy went beyond his instructions, or that the Foreign Secretary gave him a free rein in the hope that he would fall at a fence.

Early in May Drouyn was succeeded by the pliant Walewski as Premier, and Russell also resigned, but yielding to the earnest entreaties of both Clarendon and Palmerston, consented to remain in office and remain silent. What finally decided him was the view put forward with equal insistence from London and Paris, that acceptance of the Austrian terms might have led to "the instant acquiescence of Russia and the consequent evacuation of the Crimea", that a withdrawal before Sebastopol had fallen would be intensely resented by the French army, and that both the Alliance and even the Emperor's throne would be endangered.

LORD JOHN RUSSELL RESIGNS

Lord John, who had acted from motives of loyalty to the Government and the Alliance, soon found himself in an utterly false position. For on 24 May Disraeli brought forward a motion condemning "the ambiguous language and uncertain conduct" of the Government, and pledging the House to active prosecution of the war; and he concentrated much of his criticism upon Russell's conduct of the negotiations in Vienna. Lord John's defence was unexceptionable in its warlike tone and its denunciation of Russia; and there is some piquancy in the fact that in passing he eagerly disclaimed the idea ascribed to him of wishing "to make this a war of nationalities", and committed himself to the view that the cause of Poland was "hopeless". For the moment he was able to regain the confidence of the House on the eve of the Whitsun Recess. But, naturally enough, under the peculiar circumstances, he passed over many essential facts, as seen by Vienna or by Paris: and Count Buol, never an easy or too tactful colleague, felt constrained to issue his own version of what had happened and disclosed for the first time the exact nature of his proposals and the fact that both Russell and Drouyn had endorsed and recommended them. The result of this revelation was a storm of obloquy against Lord John in the entire London press: he was pressed for an explanation in the House of Commons from two such different quarters as Milner Gibson and Bulwer Lytton, and his defence on 12 July left so much unsaid (in particular, his fears for the Emperor and his dynasty obviously had to be suppressed, and yet they had really turned the scale of his decision), that few on either side accepted them as adequate. Indeed Cobden went so far as to say that he had never heard a speech in the House of Commons which struck him "with such astonishment and grief", while Disraeli held that Lord John's explanations "would not greatly reassure the daunted spirit of the nation", and were "utterly inconsistent with the facts of the case". Russell's resignation followed almost inevitably next day: and for a time there was a complete breach between him and Palmerston. How acute was the feeling is shown by Clarendon's manifestly unfair remark that Russell "filled up the measure of mischief, and with malice prepense did all the harm in his power to every English interest".[18]

More important than the temporary eclipse of a single statesman was the definite failure of the Vienna Conference, which did not meet after 4 June, and the general tendency to treat Austria as the European scapegoat and her alliance with the West, in Palmerston's unconciliatory phrase, as "a stillborn child". Even less complimentary was Napoleon's passing reference to her at the opening of the French Legislative Assembly—"We still await Austria's fulfilment of her obligations."[19] Francis Joseph, deeply offended, withdrew into his shell, the number of Austrian troops under arms was reduced, and the outbreak of cholera in Galicia still further diminished the likelihood of her armed intervention.

The Final Struggle for Sebastopol

During the summer of 1855 feeling in England was more bellicose than ever. The Peelite speeches of 4 June in favour of coming to terms with Russia seemed even to the moderate Prince Albert to be mere "Russian speeches";[20] and Palmerston's strident tones were obviously directed to preventing further overtures between the belligerents. In the main debate he roundly affirmed that "the intention of Russia to partition Turkey is manifest as the sun at noonday, and it is to prevent that that we are contending. That is the object of the war.... If Russia were to stride like a Colossus from the Baltic to the Mediterranean, British interests and commerce would be in peril." On 30 July he attacked Gladstone for his advocacy of the Austrian proposals and flatly accused Russia of "aiming at the normal and physical subjugation of the Continent of Europe and the extinction of those principles of political and commercial liberty upon which the independent existence of the Kingdoms of Europe must mainly depend". Granville was certainly right when he and Gladstone agreed in thinking that the French could easily have been won for the terms offered at Vienna, "if Palmerston and Co. had not refused their consent".[21]

There can be no doubt that Napoleon III's policy underwent an abrupt change at the beginning of May 1855 and that this was above all due to strong pressure from London and the personal impressions gathered during his visit to the Queen. Just as Drouyn was above all concerned to win

Austria, whom he regarded as a useful corrective to British influence on the Continent, so his master, now as ever, attached more weight to the friendship and alliance of Britain and the satisfaction of national *amour-propre*. The Allies now had no choice but to prosecute the war more vigorously than before, and had to abandon all hope of immediate assistance from Austria or her Prussian ally. Early in June the two fleets under Admiral Lyons made a somewhat ineffective naval onslaught upon Azov, and this was followed by a series of determined attacks upon Malakov and Redan, the two main defences of Sebastopol (7–18 June). The Russians were still able to repulse the Allies, but their fast failing strength proved unequal to the counter-offensive on the Chernaya (16 August). Lord Raglan had in the meantime died and had been succeeded by the plodding and ineffectual General Simpson: but Pélissier had strict orders from Paris to force on a final issue, and the end came soon after Queen Victoria's memorable return visit to Paris (during which the Third Napoleon led her as his ally to his uncle's tomb at the Invalides).

On 9 September the Malakov redoubt was captured by Marshal Pélissier and gave its name to the victor's dukedom: the Russians found it necessary to evacuate the fortress and withdraw to defensive lines in the centre of the Crimean peninsula. But the immense joy with which this was greeted in the West could not long conceal the divergent outlooks of Paris and London. For months past there had been marked sympathy, and periodic exchanges of courtesy, between the French and Russian lines: and so notable a victory was felt alike by military and civilian opinion in France to offer a fitting occasion for compromise and peace. British opinion, on the other hand, was mortified by the contrast between Pélissier's success and the serious British rebuff before the Redan. The Queen, in congratulating General Simpson, urged him to "lose no time in following up the great victory and driving the Russians from the Crimea".[22] The fall of the great fortress was thus treated as merely incidental—as possessing in itself no intrinsic value for the Allies, but simply serving as a pledge in hand for future bargaining. It still remained to weaken Russian power in the Baltic, and the London press soon wrote of Cronstadt as the next objective.

THE ALLIES DISAGREE

In the Crimea itself, meanwhile, such was the exhaustion and war-weariness of all the combatants without exception, that a long pause automatically followed the surrender, the only further active step being Bazaine's seizure of Kinburn on 14 October without meeting any determined resistance. The Emperor for a time favoured the design of driving the Russians from the whole Crimea and even pushing farther north: but Pélissier did not conceal his scepticism and made it quite clear that he would only attack on the receipt of explicit orders—in other words, that he would not accept responsibility for the possible consequences. Napoleon hesitated, and nothing was done. The winter was already upon them, and the more closely the Allies came to consider alternative plans, the greater was the divergence of views between them. The Emperor was of the opinion that the only sound basis for a further extension of the war was to appeal to all the subject nationalities of Eastern Europe, to free Poland, Finland and the Caucasus and to restore Crimea to Turkey. In particular he would have liked to see the resuscitation of the Polish state, either in complete independence or at least on the lines laid down at the Congress of Vienna. "I could comprehend a policy", so he wrote to Queen Victoria, "which would have a certain grandeur and would put the results aimed at on a level with the sacrifices to be made." But to such a cause the British Cabinet was indifferent, if not definitely hostile: it had every justification for feeling that its capricous taskmaster, public opinion, would utterly fail to comprehend. The Queen reminded her ally that she had "no uncontrolled power of decision, but must defer to Ministers and Parliament"; and she reverted to the hope that Austria could now at least be won for active participation in the alliance.[23]

These disagreements were reflected in the British and French Embassies at Constantinople. Stratford accused Benedetti of trying to counter his influence with the Turkish Ministers, and on this occasion his complaints were only too well grounded. For during a temporary visit of the Ambassador to the Crimea, the weak Sultan was persuaded to appoint as Capudan Pasha his own brother-in-law Mohammed Ali, who was not merely the open enemy of Stratford's close friend Reshid Pasha, but was a man of infamous character, guilty of corruption and even murder! The irrepressible Stratford, on his return, demanded an audience with Abdul Medjid and read aloud to him a formal protest, which described the appointment as "an open contradiction to Your Majesty's laws against venality, to Your Majesty's previous commands, to the efficiency of the administration, to the hopes of Your Majesty's subjects, and to the just expectations of Your Majesty's allies".[24] Small wonder if Paris—all the more resentful because this particular French protégé was not easy to defend—saw in this incident the comble of a long series of insults and pressed the London Cabinet, though in vain, to recall Stratford. Small wonder if Stratford's relations with the new French Ambassador, Thouvenel, were bad from the very outset.

During the autumn and winter Palmerston was more powerful, and more uncompromising, than ever: and it is not surprising that the Queen and the Prince should have reverted to their old misgivings. A letter on this subject from the all too negative Clarendon to his future successor Granville deserves quotation as the verdict of a constant and experienced observer from the *coulisses* of every act. The Queen and the Prince, he notes, "are always ready to let their old rancour against him (Palmerston) boil up and boil over, though he has done nothing to justify this since he has been in office....Like everybody else, he requires to be dealt with after his own fashion, and he won't bear to be *brusqué* or put down by *authority*. They don't bear in mind the total change in Palmerston's position. He has no colleagues to fear or to upset: he has attained the object of his ambition: he can't act upon his impulses at the Foreign Office: he is more immediately responsible to Parliament than he ever was before: and he is proud of having, as he thinks, overcome the repugnance of the Court. The Queen therefore must not persist in thinking him the Palmerston of old. He has put off the old man and has become a babe of grace with his altered position. He cannot wish to get into trouble: but he requires to be delicately handled."[25]

This extract serves also to illustrate the extent to which Clarendon had at this time fallen under the spell of his more masterful chief, even though he endorsed Sidney Herbert's *mot*, that Palmerston "always wishes to play double or quits".[26] In foreign policy the Prime Minister naturally had the last word, but he also had most of the initiative, and the Foreign Secretary's main function was to water down Palmerston's impulsive utterances and to keep Windsor calm. Mr Guedalla deprecates a certain tendency to represent him as flippant and truculent, but he quotes the comments of Disraeli in this very period upon his adversary's "rollicking air" and love of poking fun. He also quotes a series of summary verdicts upon men with whom Palmerston had to deal. Walewski, for a time the French Ambassador in London and afterwards Foreign Minister and Premier, Palmerston denounced as "a tricky rogue": Thouvenel—Drouyn's successor at the Quai d'Orsay—was "an accomplished follower of Loyola", with an intense hatred of England: Prokesch-Osten—Austria's brilliant representative in Constantinople—was "a low-minded strolling player": King Otto of Greece—this with perhaps more pardonable exaggeration—was "the curse of the Greek people".[27] But Palmerston's recklessness of statement could easily be multiplied tenfold.

As early as 25 August Palmerston had warned his brother in Naples that after the impending fall of Sebastopol "our danger will then begin—a danger of peace, not a danger of war".[28] The other side of the medal is reflected in Cobden's melancholy comments to his friend Henry Richard, of the Peace Society, on "the deluge of fierce passions which everywhere covers the land.... I am actually so amazed and disgusted and excited at the frenzy to which all classes—and especially those called middle and respectable—have abandoned themselves, and am so horrified at the impudent impiety with which they make God a witness and partaker of their devilish paroxysm, that I would rather say nothing about it. My only hope is in Louis Napoleon, his interests and necessities." [29] And indeed French feeling, official and popular, henceforth grew week by week more pacific, in contrast to the bellicose lucubrations of the London press.

Clarendon was at this time completely under the ban of the Prime Minister. Realising to the full the difference between the two allied capitals, he told his wife that "a termination to the war would be as popular in France as it would be unpopular here, that Louis Napoleon would be applauded for it, and we stoned with stones that we died".[30] Thus the British Cabinet followed meekly in the wake of the Jingo opposition, of which Palmerston had constituted himself the mouthpiece, and resented the fact that France had long since shaken off her illusions. Clarendon's private annoyance found expression in the strange phrase, "Those French are mad with fear and roguery":[31] but even to Persigny, the new French Ambassador in London, he was outspoken enough. "Your public opinion", he told him, "favours peace, ours war." [32]

Napoleon's Peace Feelers

Realising only too well the intransigeance of British statesmen and the growing impatience of his own subjects, Napoleon had no course open to him save to put out fresh feelers for Austrian mediation, despite the latent friction between the courts of Paris and Vienna. But quite apart from this channel, there was a keen desire for peace on the part of the lesser German states, and the Premiers of Saxony, Bavaria and Württemberg—Beust, von der Pfordten and Hügel—each contributed in a small way towards establishing direct contact between Napoleon and the Russian Government. There were soon parallel negotiations on foot, though of a secret and informal character—the one set between Napoleon's half-brother and confidant, Count Morny, and the Russian Ambassador in Vienna, Prince Gorchakov (Morny using his financial connections with Baron Eskeles and Baron Sina, two prominent Viennese bankers), the other between Napoleon's other kinsman, the French Premier Count Walewski, and the Saxon diplomat, Baron Seebach, who was a brother-in-law of the veteran Russian Chancellor, Count Nesselrode. There were hesitations and reluctance on both sides, for the Tsar's *amour-propre* had to be considered, while the Emperor, with all his eagerness for peace, was not ready to sacrifice to it the alliance with Britain. But these talks, though they had no concrete results, created an atmosphere in which others could work: and already on 14 November a Protocol was signed at Vienna by France and Austria, defining the terms of peace which the latter was prepared to submit to Russia in the form of an ultimatum. These terms were in effect a stiffening of the original Four Points, the third of which, now as ever the most contentious, provided for the neutralisation of the Black Sea and the abolition of all arsenals and even of all naval forces save a few light vessels for the control of commerce. Austria insisted on the addition of a demand for the restoration of southern Bessarabia to Moldavia (which latter she herself secretly hoped to retain), while a further clause, added at the instance of London, entitled any belligerent to put forward special conditions at a later date. Austria at last bound herself to enter the war in the event of Russia's refusal of the ultimatum. There was some further delay while the final terms were communicated to Paris and London, but in the last week of the year Count Valentin Esterházy was sent with them to St Petersburg, and Austria could no longer draw back.

While Napoleon was full of eager hope that they would be accepted, London was far from enthusiastic and held out for the neutralisation of the Sea of Azov as well as the Black Sea, and for a direct Russo-Turkish agreement as to the number of warships on both sides. The fall of Kars on 28 November, which of course increased Russia's powers of bargaining, caused great excitement in England, and the state visit of Victor Emanuel and Cavour was made the occasion for fresh warlike demonstrations. The Emperor wrote to Queen Victoria, disclaiming all idea of "peace at any price", but there was no longer any doubt that he regarded the negotiations now proceeding with Austria, Prussia, Sweden and even Spain, not as aids to a more vigorous prosecution of the war in the coming spring, but simply as a means of isolating Russia in Europe and thus inducing her to accept the inevitable. "I would give four fingers of my hand", he had said early in November, "to sign peace at this moment." [33]

AUSTRIA AND THE PEACE PRELIMINARIES

At first Tsar Alexander made reservations, but after a Crown Council in St Petersburg on 15 January 1856 he yielded to the inevitable, under the joint pressure of the military situation, disordered finances, the urgent appeals of his uncle Frederick William IV, and a consciousness that it would be little short of insanity to add Austria to his other enemies at this stage. The ultimatum was therefore unreservedly accepted as the basis of peace preliminaries, though it was made clear to Buol that Austria was risking the permanent alienation of Russia.[34] Moreover, the Tsar had by now every reason to regard Francis Joseph and Buol as shifty and unreliable, and threw his whole weight in favour of Paris rather than Vienna as the seat of the future Peace Congress. This met with the approval of Clarendon for a somewhat similar reason: it would be easier there to pursue what he already regarded as his chief task, "to keep the Emperor straight".[35] The British Government was indeed disconcerted by the prospect of peace, and public opinion remained bellicose. The Queen could not bear the thought that "the failure on the Redan should be our last *fait d'armes*", and told the Emperor that in her view "our position towards Russia will be better after rupture" with Austria.[36] Palmerston could still write to the Queen, "The cabal of stock-jobbing politicians by whom Napoleon is surrounded, must give way to him if he is firm": and he adhered to his old view that it would be better "to continue the war without any allies save Turkey".[37] But the Duke of Cambridge, then on a visit to Paris, was in no way exaggerating when he warned the Queen that "France wishes for peace more than anything else on earth, and this feeling does not confine itself to Walewski or the Ministers—it extends itself to all classes".[38]

Palmerston remained adamant against all suggestion of concessions in the Black Sea question, saying, "I can fancy how I should be hooted in the House, if I were to say we had agreed to an imperfect arrangement about one of the most important points, as a personal favour to Count Buol or to save the *amour-propre* of Russia."[39] Writing to Clarendon a little earlier, he had already defined his aim as follows: "We went to war not so much to keep the Sultan and his Mussulmans in Turkey, as to keep the Russians out of Turkey."[40] He even went so far as to inform Seymour in Vienna that he regarded Buol's proposals as "impertinent"— adding that it would be well for Buol to "keep his *threats* for elsewhere and not send them over here".[41] But in the words of Clarendon, "France was determined on peace, and whatever Palmerston in his jaunty mood may say, we could not have made war alone, for we should have had all Europe against us at once, and the United States would soon have followed in the train." The Emperor "to this day has not got over Palmerston's letter to Persigny, saying we were quite able to carry on the war alone, with the aid of Sardinia and Turkey".* Cowley, whose ear detected every echo from

* 12 March 1856—to Granville, Maxwell, *op. cit.* II, 119; Palmerston to Persigny, 21 November 1855—Ashley, *op. cit.* II, 103. On 21 January he had written to Stratford de Redcliffe: "France—Government, people and army—are bent on peace at any price. We have no such feeling and are determined not to have peace unless it be a safe and honourable one. The Emperor inclines towards us, but his position is becoming daily more embarrassing, and in one way or another the Alliance is being sorely tried" (Lane-Poole, *op. cit.* II, 434).

the Tuileries, had reached the unhesitating verdict that "the Emperor could not, if he would, continue the war".[42]

The interval which elapsed between Russia's acceptance and the actual opening of the Congress was filled by a long controversy as to the admission of Prussia. Britain, angry at Prussian neutrality and anxious lest Frederick William should throw his weight in favour of his nephew the Tsar, strongly opposed Prussia's admission, arguing that she had throughout the war sheltered herself behind her status as a German Federal State, and could not therefore now suddenly pose as a Great Power. The Emperor, though distinctly embarrassed, followed England's lead in this, if only to be more able to restrain her in other directions: but in the end it became abundantly obvious that Prussia, if excluded, would refuse all international obligations such as the Congress might lay down, and that this would create a most awkward gap in the European system. As Hübner very plausibly argued to the Emperor, "one can't chastise a great state as if it were a small boy, and it would be wrong to humiliate Prussia without diminishing its material power...To exasperate it would only drive it into the arms of the enemy".[43]

Meanwhile the British Cabinet made little attempt to conceal its preoccupation as to the possibility of a Franco-Russian rapprochement. The Tsar was represented by his father's intimate friend, the veteran Count Orlov, a soldier of gigantic stature whose manners and dress recalled the Paris of 1815, but who possessed diplomatic gifts second to none at the Congress and won the goodwill of the Emperor in his first audience. He was ably seconded by the astute Baron Brunnov, who worked in the coulisses while Orlov's fame filled the salons, the press and the print-shops of Paris. While Brunnov took the line that war could have been avoided altogether but for the West's excessive and unjustified suspicion of Tsar Nicholas, Orlov freely admitted his late master's rash diplomacy in sending Menshikov to Constantinople and occupying the Principalities, and he even affected regret for Sinope and the refusal to accept the Turkish amendments to the Vienna Note. Austria was represented by Buol himself, arrogant and bad-tempered, and now about to reap in isolation the fruit of his policy of vacillation and greed: and by Hübner, the very able *parvenu* Ambassador, whose memoirs are so useful a source for the diplomatic history of the Second Empire. Ali Pasha, though Grand Vizier and a declared friend of France, played a somewhat effaced part: and Cavour, the greatest of all, represented a Power which was as yet only on probation in the Concert of Europe. The presidency of the Congress naturally fell to Count Walewski, who was but a pliant instrument of his Imperial cousin, weak and singularly ill-informed, and all too attentive to the fluctuations of the Bourse. Clarendon, who knew him from London, did not hesitate to speak of him to Napoleon himself as "insignificant, inept and of bad faith":[44] while Hübner in his diary describes him as "more Russian than Orlov". In reality the keynote to his actions was supplied by an intense conservatism and a genuine devotion to the Napoleonic idea and dynasty. *

The British representatives were Lord Clarendon himself and Lord Cowley, the Ambassador who enjoyed Napoleon's confidence, but did not return it. Granville records that "Clarendon is dying to be forced into going", and that "Palmerston does not like his going".[45] but it seems more probable that in the end Clarendon went without misgivings and, above all, lest worst might befall. He was certainly right in opposing Palmerston's strange idea that Admiral Lyons, with his doubtful record, would be a suitable representative. There can be equally little doubt that the sending of Palmerston himself would have had most disastrous consequences. The more pliant Clarendon was from the first leagued with Buol in opposition to all idea of leniency towards Russia: but he maintained close and cordial relations with the Emperor and possessed the tact which knew how far it was possible to go and when it was necessary to yield.

THE CONGRESS OF PARIS

The Congress of Paris opened on 25 February 1856 and lasted just over a month. Its history still remains to be written: for our present purpose it must suffice to summarise the main problems—Turkish integrity, Turkish reform, naval power in the Black Sea and the Straits, and the status of the vassal Principalities—and to indicate the manner of their solution.

The opening discussions turned round the evacuation of occupied territory: the Russians naturally enough wished to use Kars as an object of barter, and if possible as a means of saving southern Bessarabia, while the British and Austrians held that Kars must be evacuated forthwith, and without compensation.

After an obstinate resistance during the first two sittings, Orlov and Brunnov realised that refusal would almost certainly have involved a fresh rupture, and that Napoleon, on whom their chief hopes rested, would have

---

* See a discerning study of Walewski and other contemporary French statesmen in Beyens, Le Second Empire, I, chap. XII. Clarendon once wrote of Walewski as "a man whose moral sense is misty...and whose duties are subordinate to his vanity or interests". This was probably too severe (22 December 1855, to Lady Clarendon—Maxwell, op. cit. II, p. 108). On another occasion Clarendon summed up Walewski in one of his drastic phrases, as "with an empty head and an abundant abdomen" (Wellesley, The Paris Embassy, p. 170).

had no choice but to fall into line with his allies. They therefore yielded gracefully and took advantage of an evening reception at the Tuileries in order to address a personal appeal to the Emperor for his mediation with the British Government. The result of his ensuing conversations with Clarendon was that "the special examination of the territories situated to the east of the Black Sea"—an ominous and elastic phrase on which the British delegates had hitherto insisted—was reduced to the establishment of a mixed commission to delimit afresh the Turco-Russian frontier in Asia: while the British no longer raised the question of the fortresses on the east coast of the Black Sea and contented themselves with the engagement not to restore the fortifications of the Åland Islands. The discussion continued as to the neutralisation of the Black Sea, Britain endeavouring to extend it to the Sea of Azov also: but in the end the Congress rested content with the formal assurances of Orlov that construction at the arsenals of Nikolayev and Kherson would be restricted to ships expressly sanctioned under the Treaty.

The navigation of the Danube was easily disposed of in a single sitting, but the question of the future frontier between Russia and the Principalities was long and keenly contested, Austria now taking the place of Britain as the party mainly interested and most intransigeant. The Russians eventually yielded ground and consented in principle to the cession of the southern districts of Bessarabia, but made reserves with regard to certain Russian and Bulgarian colonies there: the exact details were therefore left to a special commission, which was to find extreme difficulty in making a settlement. The main object of this change was to cut off Russia from the mouths of the Danube and thus debar her from all claim to figure as a riparian state.

Austria, however, soon found that while the Congress did not wish Russia to remain on the Danube, it was not prepared to lift one finger to preserve Austrian rule in the Principalities. Buol's whole calculation had centred upon their eventual annexation without a war: what, then, was his dismay and fury when at the sitting of 27 March Count Walewski, as President, pointedly enquired as to the date at which evacuation might be expected! Buol "grew red with anger and went off like a rocket":[46] but he found himself completely isolated and had no choice but to comply. Over a year was to pass before the last Austrian troops departed, but already the final issue was wellnigh irrevocable. Palmerston had no sympathy for Buol, whom he described as "fond of *Buollying*", and prophetically foretold that "in the next war between Austria and Sardinia, if it is brought about, as it will be, by the fault of Austria, Sardinia will not be left alone as she was last time".[47]

From the first days of the Congress the fate of the Roumanians threatened to embroil the relations of the Powers: for the line of division cut across existing alliances. Napoleon III's devotion to the cause of Italian independence needs no emphasis, for it was constantly in evidence and provided one of the keys to his action at most points of his career. But his sympathies for Roumania were scarcely less pronounced, though far less attention has been devoted to them. In his mind this neglected and half-submerged people figured as an emblem of reviving nationality in the Near East, as a Latin sentinel set between Turk and Slav and Magyar, as a possible barrier to Russian expansion southwards, as a medium of French culture and political influence. "The great fault of the Congress of Vienna", he one day told Lord Clarendon, "is to have only admitted the interests of sovereigns, not those of the peoples": and thus by implication this strange autocrat, with his mystical leanings, espoused the cause of democracy against Turkish rule, while his British Liberal allies unreservedly supported the Sultan against his oppressed subjects, and denied in the Balkans the principles which they upheld in Italy.

Napoleon's solution was the union of the Principalities under a foreign Prince, and this he urged upon London, and more indirectly upon Vienna.* In a personal conversation Clarendon raised every possible objection and even affected to regard the union as "an act of spoliation towards Turkey": but this did not deter Walewski, on the Emperor's orders, from formally proposing it to the Congress, as conforming with the wishes and interests of the Roumanian people. Clarendon did not at first oppose, but grew steadily more lukewarm as both Austria and Turkey reacted violently against union. Queen Victoria wisely argued that "nothing will oppose a barrier to Russia and her intrigues but the arrangement which will satisfy the people themselves, viz.: an *hereditary* monarchy", and that "the example of Egypt might perfectly well be followed in Wallachia and Moldavia".[48] But Palmerston remained obstinately of the opposite opinion. Russia on her side could not be expected to show enthusiasm for a barrier state: but she saw a means of widening the rift between Paris and London, and therefore sided with the French. Napoleon naturally was not prepared to risk a real quarrel with his ally over a question that was secondary despite all its implications: and the union might have been indefinitely delayed but for the unwise tactics of Austria and Turkey, in strenuously denying all desire for union on the part of the Roumanians themselves. The

---

* Duke Ernest of Saxe-Coburg transmitted to Francis Joseph Napoleon's suggestion that Austria should relinquish Lombardy in return for the Principalities and a free hand in Serbia, but Francis Joseph declined all discussion (Ernest II, *Memoirs*, III, 66, 105).

ogical outcome of this was that the Congress appointed a commission to investigate conditions on the spot and to report back to Paris, after specially elected Assemblies in each Principality had had time to express their opinion. This was an honourable compromise between the French and British standpoints, ensured a thorough airing of the question, and had the supreme advantage of eliminating from discussion the chief remaining subject of discord. In a word, the Roumanian question was put into cold storage for the time being: and the Treaty of Paris could be concluded on 30 March 1856.

THE TREATY OF PARIS

The main provisions of the Treaty may be briefly summarised:

All conquered territory was restored on both sides: but the Tsar consented to a "rectification" of frontier in Bessarabia, to be traced out by special delegates, and the restored districts were to form an integral part of Moldavia.

Turkey was included in the Concert of Europe, the Five Great Powers and Sardinia guaranteeing its independence and territorial integrity and promising to refer to the others any dispute which one of them might have with the Porte. A special clause mentioned the newly issued firman of the Sultan in favour of his Christian subjects, took note of its spontaneous character and high value, and disclaimed all idea on the part of the Powers of interference in Turkey's internal affairs.

The Straits Convention of 1841 was revised, the Sultan promising in future "to maintain the principle invariably established as ancient rule of the Empire", prohibiting the entry of war vessels into the Dardanelles and Bosphorus, and the Powers pledging themselves to observe this. The Sultan was entitled to give a special permit for the passage of light vessels. The Black Sea was then neutralised and all arsenals on its shores prohibited, and freedom of trade was established in its waters.

Danubian navigation was placed under the control of two Commissions—one of the Five Great Powers, Turkey and Sardinia, for two years, and one permanent, consisting of delegates from all the riverine states.

The ancient protectorate of Russia over Wallachia, Moldavia and Serbia—dating from Kutchuk Kainardji and extended by subsequent treaties—was expressly abolished, and in its place there was to be a collective guarantee of the three vassal states by the Great Powers, no one of whom might intervene without consulting the others previously. In other respects all existing privileges and immunities were upheld, and the terms of investigation into the Roumanian situation were more closely defined. In particular, the two new assemblies were to be based on "the most exact representation of the interests of all classes of society", in order that the wishes of the population might find expression. Other clauses aimed at still further reducing the possibility of armed intervention from the outside.

The net result of the Treaty was to check Russia in her advance towards Constantinople and to secure for Turkey a further respite of twenty years within which to re-establish herself by internal reforms. It was an attempt, and a successful attempt, to substitute collective action for the separate action of a single Power. But unhappily it proved impossible to make collective action an organised reality: and the Turks, by playing off the rival jealousies and interests, were able to evade serious control and rest content with improvements upon paper only. British policy at the Congress was based upon the assumption that Turkey was capable of reform: and even to-day historians can still be found who plead that at that date Turkey was "not clearly moribund".[49] To the Jingo press and the war party, blinded by hysteria and ignorant of Eastern institutions, Turkish decadence was naturally not clear: but it would be easy to quote many eminent contemporaries who knew the Turk to be incorrigible as a ruler of subject races, and who were not deceived by Palmerston's shallow optimism. Few more damning admissions are to be found than those of Lord Stratford himself, at the very period when he was labouring to bolster up the Ottoman regime. It may suffice here to quote the verdict of the Duke of Cambridge, who wrote home to the Queen his impressions of the Sultan Abdul Medjid, then highly popular in the British press. "He is, to say the truth, a wretched creature, prematurely aged and having nothing whatever to say for himself....As to his Ministers and in fact the whole population and country, with the exception of Reshid Pasha, they are all a most wretched and miserable set of people, and far, far worse than anything I could possibly have imagined or supposed. In fact the Sick Man is excessively sick, indeed dying as fast as possible: and the sooner diplomacy disposes of him the better, for no earthly power can save him....This is the opinion of every person out here, of both armies, French and English."[50] But Palmerston clung stubbornly to the opposite view, and supplemented it by the no less erroneous theory that "the Sclavonians [the name then often used for Slavs] do not possess the conditions necessary for becoming the bones and sinews of a new state".

The Turkish reforms (known as Hatti-Humayun) issued on 21 February 1856 and referred to in the text of the Treaty itself, were the supreme effort of Lord Stratford, who had negotiated untiringly with the Porte throughout 1855 and secured the Sultan's signature only four days before the Congress opened. The great Ambassador's attitude was logical throughout: he recognised the immense difficulty of applying reforms, and put it to Lord Clarendon that "three levers are requisite—1st, the provincial authorities to act in a right spirit; 2nd, the power of the Government duly exerted for their appointment and direction: 3rd, a force *from without* to keep up a steady animating pressure on the Government. The last, I am persuaded, can alone constitute—if even *that* can—a durable and efficient *principe moteur*." This pressure could come from "England alone, the Alliance, or Europe", and the order in which he named the three indicated his preference.[51] Near the end of the negotiations he warned Clarendon that "if the integrity of the Sultan's dominions be formally secured, there is but too much reason to fear the Porte will give way to its natural indolence, and leave the firman of reform, now almost completed, a lifeless paper, valuable only as a record of sound principles".* It was for this reason that his first reaction to a treaty which expressly disclaimed all idea of pressure upon the Porte, was voiced in the words, "I would rather have cut off my right hand than have signed that treaty."[52] His fears were only too well-grounded, and though numerous important changes were effected in the structure of the Turkish state, the dry-rot of corruption and misrule, so far from being arrested by the reforms, spread further with every year.

If, however, Palmerston and other mid-Victorian statesmen were radically wrong in their hopes of Turkish regeneration, the respite accorded to the Porte had one important effect which Napoleon III was probably alone in foreseeing. For the next twenty years served as a respite not merely to the Turks, but also to the young Greek, Roumanian and Serb national states, which under the collective guarantee of Europe steadily grew and consolidated, and were soon to become centres of national aspiration for their still unemancipated kinsmen in Bulgaria, Bosnia, Macedonia and Albania. The foundations of the Near East were in process of slow reconstruction, but in a manner as yet incomprehensible to Liberal opinion. While, however, to Palmerston and Russell national movements meant but little outside Italy, Gladstone's far-sighted and prophetic vision made him the champion of Roumanian, Serb and Bulgar no less than of Greek or Italian, and vindicated the honour of Britain in the Near East.

The British Government was far from enthusiastic as to the terms of peace, and its view was shared by public opinion. The decisive factor was the knowledge that nothing more could be wrung from Russia save by a prolonged and bloody war, which France was no longer ready to contemplate. Palmerston made it clear to the Queen that "additional security"

---

* Lane-Poole, *op. cit.* ii, 437. His full programme was drastic, if logical—a barrier of neutral or independent states between Russia and Turkey: the Dniester as a frontier: Crimea disarmed, and the restoration of the Grand Duchy of Warsaw.

against Russian aggression could only be attained by detaching Finland, Poland and Georgia,[53] while Clarendon pointed out that "a continuation of the war would hardly have been possible either with or without France". To drag her on reluctantly would have kindled her ill-will, and "on the first favourable occasion she would have left us in the lurch", whereas, "if we had continued the war single-handed, France would feel that she had behaved shabbily to us, and would therefore have hated us all the more, and become our enemy sooner than under any other circumstances". Clarendon even hinted at the possible "coalition of Europe", aided by America, against Britain.[54] To Granville he used the same arguments: "whatever Palmerston in his jaunty mood may say, we could not have made war alone, for we should have all Europe against us at once, and the United States would soon have followed":[55] and he had already warned Palmerston that "the alliance, such as it has hitherto existed, is *en jeu*". The Queen found these arguments convincing, made Palmerston a knight of the Garter, and offered marquisates to Clarendon and Cowley. But the terms of peace were hissed by the crowd at Temple Bar, and Palmerston gave them a half-hearted reception. Lord Malmesbury in the name of the Opposition moved that the phrases "joy and satisfaction" and "honourable conditions which fully accomplish", in the Address to the Crown, should be toned down to "satisfaction", and "conditions which have appeared adequately to effect!"[56] Lord Derby accepted the Treaty, "as I believe the country will accept it, with some degree of reluctance", and not as completely attaining all the objects for which Britain had gone to war.[57] Lord Aberdeen found nothing better to say than that "upon the whole" it was "all we could expect—honourable to Her Majesty's arms and creditable to the noble earl", and contrasted the "triumphant character" of another treaty signed at Paris forty years earlier. Another speaker drew a singular comparison with the Peace of Amiens, "at which all men rejoiced, but of which all men were ashamed".[58] In the Commons Layard doubted whether "all the great objects of the war" had been accomplished; Lord John Russell expressed "neither joy nor satisfaction": while Disraeli held that "peace is a great blessing when war has been carried on so inefficiently". Gladstone, in a notable speech, regretted that nothing more "substantial" had been done for the Principalities, had his doubts about the efficacy of Christian rights under the Treaty, and saw in the neutralisation of the Black Sea "nothing more than a series of pitfalls"; but he spoke of the proposal to submit international differences to arbitration as "a great triumph".[59] Moreover, all these lukewarm utterances followed several nights of acrid debate upon the Government's "want of foresight and energy" in permitting the fall of Kars. James Whiteside, the mover in the debate, claimed that Kars could have been saved by a credit of £30,000 and quoted, a little irrelevantly, the lines

> The age of virtuous politics is past
> And we are deep in that of cold pretence:
> Patriots are grown too shrewd to be sincere,
> And we too wise to trust them.

Palmerston on his side made an effective, though not altogether con-clusive rejoinder, insisting that neither Bessarabia nor Moldavia nor Asia Minor was a sound line of attack, and that the Government had throughout concentrated upon dealing "a blow at the heart", which they could effect at Sebastopol. In parenthesis he admitted that a campaign in Georgia after the fall of the fortress had "formed part of our intentions".[60] He claimed that the object of the war had been to free Turkey from "eternal dictation" and to raise a firm "barrier against future aggressions", but not to secure territory or indemnities for Britain herself. The importance of the Sultan's firman of reform could not in his opinion be overrated: and he also defended the Triple Treaty of Guarantee as "not the offspring of a day, but the result of full deliberation". He closed with a few conciliatory phrases addressed to the Tsar and to Russia. In the end he won by a majority of 127 (176–303). Clarendon in the Lords defended his own secret bugbear Stratford and contrasted the position of Russia two years earlier, astride over the Continent, and her position after the war, with her Black Sea fortresses dismantled and her Baltic designs against Norway and Sweden equally thwarted.[61] Palmerston, in the months that followed, took an increasingly opportunist line, arguing that "when people ask one... for what is called a policy, the only answer is that we mean to do what may seem to be best upon each occasion as it arises, making the interests of one's country one's guiding principle".[62]

Before the Congress separated, one further decision was taken, on the initiative of France, to which brief reference must be made. The exist-ing sea-law was revised by the so-called "Declaration of Paris", consist-ing of the four following rules:

1. "Privateering is, and remains, abolished.

2. The neutral flag covers enemy's goods, with the exception of contraband of war.

3. Neutral goods, with the exception of contraband of war, are not liable to capture under enemy's flags.

4. Blockades, in order to be binding, must be effective: that is to say, maintained by a force sufficient really to prevent access to the coast of the enemy."

By this decision the old principle of unrestricted search and seizure of shipping in time of war was abandoned, in response to the humaner sentiments of the age. How little even the ablest minds could, either then or later, foresee subsequent developments is shown by the emphatic contention of Sir Robert Morier in the 'seventies that the Paris Declaration "*must* lead to the *total* enfranchisement of private property at sea". Since then the hard and fast line between combatant and non-combatant has tended to disappear, and with it and with the vast requirements of raw materials for armament industries the word "contraband" has received a new definition.

In the long period between 1856 and 1914 Britain's power rested in the first instance upon her Sea Power, and as in many respects the British Navy performed the functions of an international police force and as a general war was avoided, the issues raised by the Declaration of Paris remained discreetly in the background. In 1908, as a result of the Second Hague Conference, an attempt was made to codify the principles of sea-law and the very widely divergent interpretations of "blockade" which had survived from earlier times. But the Declaration of London never achieved its purpose of defining the respective rights of belligerents and neutrals, never obtained the general sanction of the nations and of their respective public opinion, and proved unworkable in the Great War, in face of the new problems which it raised. The issue is fundamental, and had to be stated here: but it hardly belongs to a general survey of our foreign policy such as the present volume, since it requires detailed and perhaps even technical treatment, in order to be fully understood.

THE TRIPLE TREATY OF GUARANTEE

The actual Treaty was supplemented by a separate and secret treaty between France, Britain and Austria (14 April), the text of which was not made public: its main purpose was to ensure beyond all doubt the integrity of Turkey, any attack upon her by Russia constituting a clear *casus belli*. In signing this new instrument Napoleon yielded reluctantly to British insistence and revealed its existence to the Russians: and it is not too much to say that it was almost from the first day a dead letter. The rapprochement between France and Russia which was already so marked during the closing weeks of the Conference, was now apparent to all the world, and Orlov actually attended a big military review held by the Emperor in honour of Pélissier's troops. No sooner was peace definitive, than Morny was sent to St Petersburg on a special diplomatic mission and at once entered into most cordial relations with Tsar Alexander and Prince Gorchakov, who had just succeeded Nesselrode as Chancellor. Napoleon again sacrificed his very genuine sympathies with Poland for the sake of Russian friendship. He already foresaw that the Italian question would soon dominate the European situation, and that Russian benevolence might be decisive for the success of his plans. The Russians fell in all the more readily with his views, because their main resentment was directed against Austria.

In striking contrast to the dissatisfaction so widely expressed in England was the general approval bestowed in France upon the Emperor's diplomacy and its concrete results. Never did his prestige stand higher: victory seemed to wipe out the humiliation of the treaties of 1815, and the new settlement signed in the capital of the restored Empire atoned for the abandonment of any concrete "revision". This was the moment at which Victor Cousin hailed Napoleon as "Emperor of Europe" and arbiter among nations.

OPINIONS ON WAR AND PEACE

The closing period of the Crimean War saw the British nation in one of its most touchy, exacting and unreasoning moods, and of that mood Palmerston was the supreme expression. The urbane Clarendon once lamented that "if in the remotest corner of the earth any Englishman gets a well-deserved but uncompensated black eye, the newspapers and Palmerston immediately demand an enquiry into the conduct of the bloated sinecurist in Downing Street, who has no sense of British honour".[63] This hits off very exactly the prevalent temper. The logical outcome was that the principle of intervention in continental affairs, habitually practised by Palmerston, was now carried farther than ever before. It doubtless had an underlying psychological explanation in what may be called the "cock-sureness", the moral certainty of the mid-Victorian era, when infallibility was quite as much a political as a religious dogma, when it was assumed by so many excellent people that British liberal and constitutional doctrines were a sure panacea for every ill and justified almost any interference, and when at the same time it was assumed even more confidently by the Radical interventionists of the Manchester school, that Free Trade was the perfect economic remedy and was destined to triumph everywhere.

During the autumn of 1856, Lord Granville, who headed a British mission to the Tsar's Coronation, put it on record that "Palmerston and Clarendon have been too scolding lately. They are at everybody. They have tried by bullying to get out of difficulties caused by carelessness in the negotiations. They have almost broken up the French alliance, which now only depends on what is its best security—the importance to his own interests which Louis Napoleon may attach to it." [64] That Granville in no way exaggerated Palmerston's reckless mood, is shown by a letter which the latter addressed to Clarendon only two months later. "Our marriage with France", he writes, "will soon end in a separation on account of '*incompatibilité de mœurs*'. After all, when we consider the different private interests of England and France, the different characters and habits of the two nations, we ought rather to be thankful at having got so much out of the alliance and at having maintained it so long, than to be surprised or disappointed at its approaching end." [65] To this we can only oppose the saner phrase of a famous French writer of that day, Prosper Merimée, who enjoyed the Emperor's confidence. "England and France", he declared, "often quarrel, but at bottom they resemble those married couples who, though they nag at each other, cannot separate." [66]

It would not be proper to pass on from the Paris settlement without alluding to one important factor in the situation at that time, namely the peace agitation of Cobden and Bright. It is a striking proof of the extent to which war fever had seized upon the country, that these two men, within so short a time of their unexampled triumph in the Free Trade controversy, should have failed to move even their most ardent supporters in the business world or in nonconformist circles, and should have been treated, not merely with rudeness, but to use Morley's phrase, with "bullying and contempt" by Palmerston himself in the House.[67] Presumably the reason was that while they were far better informed on the merits of the case than their supporters, they overreached themselves by their exaggerated "peace at any price" attitude, and by their assumption of complete indifference to the quarrels of others. And indeed the man in the street saw a curious inconsistence in those who had been in specially close contact with Kossuth or Mazzini, trying to hold back a public opinion which had been justly incensed at the Tsar's treatment of Hungary or Poland.

They—unlike Palmerston, who complained in 1853 that the Tsar should "be satisfied, as we all are, with the progressively liberal system of Turkey"[68] —knew the real facts about Turkey and knew that no such "liberal" system had ever existed.[69] Hence to Cobden "the Integrity of the Turkish Empire" and the "Balance of Power" were "words without meaning, the mere echoes of the past, and so, admirably suited for the mouths of senile Whiggery".[70] To them diplomacy consisted in the prevention of strife— not as, with Palmerston and Russell, in "veiled menace or tart lecturing".[71] To take but a single example, they would never have sanctioned the despatch to Constantinople of an Ambassador who was the bitter personal enemy of the Tsar. After opposing war from the very outset in the teeth of much obloquy, they came by the autumn of 1855 to set their "only hope in Louis Napoleon, his interests and necessities".[72] Cobden had gauged the situation very accurately when he wrote on 18 September, "How can *our* Government make out a case to their deluded followers, to justify a peace which must certainly involve the abandonment of the Crimea? The danger is that Louis Napoleon, whose one dominant idea is the alliance with England, may yield to Palmerston and the warlike spirit of our people, and go on with the war." And a little later (5 October) he passed this remarkable verdict upon Palmerston. "It is only because the Parliamentary chiefs shrink from the responsibility of continuing the war that he has been enabled to seize the reins. All men of the age of 72, with unsatisfied ambitions, are desperadoes: and Lord Palmerston, in addition to this qualification, having had the experience of nearly half a century of parliamentary life, having continued to persuade the democracy that he was a revolutionist, while the aristocracy knew him to be *their* safe friend, became the fittest incarnation of the delusion, bewilderment and deception into which the public mind had been plunged: and he and his colleagues hold office to carry on a war for the continuance of which no other statesman chose to be responsible."[73] There is an echo of this in Lord Granville's remark that Palmerston, even in his old age, was "always dying to connect his name with something".[74]

The Crimean War has come to be regarded by most historians as the most unnecessary in the history of modern Europe: and even if this be too sweeping a verdict, it will remain beyond all question as the classical proof that in foreign policy the voice of the people is not necessarily the voice of God, and that an ill-informed and excitable public opinion can plunge a country into war no less effectually than a dictator or a crowned autocrat. The war cost France close upon 100,000 lives, Britain 22,737, Turkey 30,000 and Russia 110,000 (if the Russian figures are reliable): British expenditure reached the sum of £76,000,000. The chief gains of the war lay with Napoleon III, whose regime it stabilised, and who could now aspire to be arbiter in Europe, and with the Porte, which proved entirely incapable of profiting either by the enhanced international status assured to it or by the respite of time within which to set its home affairs in order. As a result, Palmerston's whole calculation, which had rested on the assumption of Turkish regeneration, went awry, and Russia, though checked in her advance upon Constantinople, only had to await patiently the moment when she would be able to shake off the restraints imposed upon her in the Black Sea, and when inexorable events would restore to her the right to champion and to liberate the Christians of the Near East. With the perspective of eighty years we may fairly argue that the ultimate beneficiaries of the war were those very Christians to whose interests little more than lip-service was paid at Paris, but who, thanks to the delay in a real settlement, were at last enabled to achieve real national independence. Yet if that be so, it follows that Gladstone and Cobden, not Palmerston and Clarendon, were the true prophets in the Crimean period.

CHAPTER X

THE AFTERMATH: ROUMANIA AND ITALY

FRONTIER DISPUTES

The Congress of Paris separated after five weeks in session: but several years were to elapse before all the outstanding questions could be liquidated. In the first place, London protested vigorously at the slowness with which the Russians evacuated Kars, and then still more against their destruction of the citadel before finally withdrawing. A second dispute arose over the Island of Serpents, an islet in the delta of the Danube, to which no reference had been made in the peace treaty and on which a detachment of marines were sent to hoist the Russian flag. On this point Napoleon opposed Russia with the unanswerable argument that a treaty which was designed to exclude Russia from the whole course of the Danube could not be interpreted as assigning to her an island commanding one of its two main exits to the sea.

Even more troublesome was the dispute about the Bessarabian frontier, which was to pass "to the south of Bolgrad". It now transpired that there were two places of that name—one situated north of Lake Yalpuk, the other considerably to the south of it and with access by water to the river. The Tsar claimed to be concerned with Bolgrad as "the centre of the Bulgarian colonies", and this description could only apply to the more southerly of the two. Napoleon cared as little about "the hamlet" as he had cared about "the rock", but he found himself between two utterly intransigeant Powers —Britain, who in her disillusioned mood refused even the most infinitesimal concession, and Russia, who held her ground not merely from motives of prestige, but in the hope of splitting the Franco-British Alliance. The British Government went so far as to send four ships to the Black Sea and to suggest that they should transport the Russian marines to Odessa. Gorchakov appealed to the French; Count Morny tried to hold back his British colleague Lord Wodehouse; Clarendon accused Russia of deliberately creating a misunderstanding: and when Walewski, despite all the friction with London, wished to yield for the sake of the alliance, St Petersburg treated the issue as "the touchstone of French loyalty and firmness of character".[1] How unconciliatory London was may be gathered from

Palmerston's comment to Clarendon: "The Russian Government is acting in all things like the most incorrigible ticket-of-leave man, who begins robbing and cheating in every direction the moment he is let out."[2] After long and acrid discussions between London and Paris, the Tsar consented to abandon Bolgrad in return for compensation, and endeavoured to push Napoleon into the position of arbitrator. In the end Bolgrad was left to Moldavia, while the territory to be ceded by Russia was diminished at another less contentious point: and this was linked up with the withdrawal of British ships from the Black Sea and Austria's final evacuation of the Principalities. Morny, however, failed in his hope of substituting a Franco-Russian for a Franco-British alliance, and though the rift within the latter was at times painfully apparent, the tender plant of Tsar Alexander's new enthusiasm for Paris suffered from a series of minor incidents. The joint Franco-British occupation of Greece—originally established to prevent a Greek rising in Turkey—was in the nature of things distasteful to Russia as the third protecting Power, and was prolonged till February 1857—far beyond all reason or necessity. The joint naval demonstration against King "Bomba" of the Two Sicilies caused even greater qualms to the Tsar, who condemned it as "an act of interference in the internal government of a free King", and instructed Gorchakov to protest to Morny. The fact that Palmerston's own brother was Minister at Naples certainly did not diminish Russian nervousness.

The background to these negotiations is supplied by Count Morny's mission to Russia and by his master Napoleon's very definite desire to add Britain as third party to a new Franco-Russian entente. London was altogether obdurate, but Napoleon persisted, and put it very frankly to the Russian Ambassador Count Orlov. "Could we not agree à trois? We shall dominate Europe." Kiselev duly reported this to the Tsar, whose comment was, "An alliance à trois with England telle quelle, is impossible." Morny, however, was extremely active in St Petersburg, and argued that Russia must choose between a French alliance or a return to "les affinités anciennes" with the German Powers. His only motive was obviously enough the encirclement of Germany. He found his ideas and projects strongly opposed by Persigny, who, from the vantage ground of the French Embassy in London, complained that Napoleon was in danger of repeating the old blunder of Louis Philippe in trying to come to terms with Russia behind the back of England. Morny remained in Russia till 1857, but meeting with only partial success in the political sphere, concentrated his efforts on financial and commercial operations, backing a French railway group, the "Grande Société", against a rival group of Paxton, and writing home to Paris, "Je vois dans la Russie une mine à exploiter pour la France".[3]

The Problem of Roumanian Unity

Much more serious than any of these secondary questions was the conflict over the Roumanian Question, which ere long threatened to divide Europe once more into two rival camps. Napoleon III—not uninfluenced by the very active group of Roumanian liberal exiles in Paris (notably the Bratianus, Rosetti and Kogalniceanu), and true to that idea of nationality which dominated him throughout life—showed scarcely less interest in the fate of the Roumanians than in that of Italy. He remained inflexibly of opinion that 'no peace would be solid and durable which does not provide for the union and independence of the Principalities'[4] and pressed this upon the wavering Clarendon. Queen Victoria inclined towards union under a foreign Prince, and Walewski told his Ambassador at the Porte, Thouvenel, that "union is especially in the odour of sanctity at Windsor"[5]. But Palmerston was hostile, and Stratford de Redcliffe made this clear to the Porte, and argued in his despatches home that "where Moldo-Wallachian interests conflict with European interests, the former must be sacrificed". Thouvenel, like all his predecessors at the French Embassy, found it impossible to work with his domineering colleague, whose *protégé*, Reshid Pasha, led the opposition against the Francophil Ministers Ali and Fuad. Thouvenel wrote of Stratford as "my special cross", and reported that so long as Stratford's "artillery was dumb", there was no hope of the Turks yielding.[6] Even the Austrian representative Prokesch-Osten, who was Stratford's principal ally in the fight against union, complained that he behaved not as an Ambassador, but as a sovereign![7] Once more Clarendon was fully aware of the Ambassador's insubordination, but was incapable of checking it. At a later stage he wrote as follows: "He [Stratford] has consistently and unremittingly hated the French and done his utmost to thwart them: and having for a number of years occupied the Eastern dunghill without competitors, he could not find an inch of room upon it for the French Ambassador, who, having been backed by 150,000 men, thought he might have a *locus standi* there."[8]

The struggle centred round the elections to the two Roumanian Assemblies, which the Congress prescribed as the principal means of ascertaining the true wishes of the population. The Unionist party in each province had the active backing of France, whom Russia supported not from enthusiasm but for tactical reasons, while Britain and Austria no less openly worked against union. In Moldavia in particular, where the Turkish Kaimakam or Regent—Theodore Balş, and after his death in March 1857, Nicholas Vogorides—employed wholesale corruption and intimidation against the popular party, the contending factions were led and encouraged by the

Austrian and French Consuls, Baron Gödel and Victor Place respectively. In Bucarest there was a similar though less violent rivalry between the British and French Consuls, Colquhoun and Béclard. On the international Commission to which the Congress had delegated the study of local conditions, Baron Talleyrand-Périgord openly favoured union, and was greeted by torchlight processions and demonstrations in favour of Napoleon III. Fortunately the British member, Sir Henry Bulwer, though necessarily on the Turkish side, adopted a much more reserved attitude; but for that very reason he fell foul of Lord Stratford, who quarrelled with him at a full sitting of the Commission, the facts being then recounted with much gusto in the European press.

Meanwhile Thouvenel, though himself no enthusiast for the Roumanian cause, had strict orders from the Emperor to "spare no effort" to promote union: and he was of course strengthened in this when the *Moniteur*, again by order of Napoleon, reaffirmed belief in union. Stratford on his side strained every nerve to stiffen Turkish resistance: the unprecedented offer of the Garter to the wretched Abdul Medjid stood the Ambassador in good stead and may have turned the scale in favour of the overthrow of Ali and Fuad and the return of his own creature Reshid as Grand Vizier. Some faint idea of his hectoring treatment of the Turks may be gathered from a despatch in which he assures Clarendon that "it is only by acting like a bully that I can at all keep Reshid up to the mark".[9] Thouvenel on his side reported home to Paris that "Stratford has made of the separation of the Principalities and the maintenance of Vogorides a personal question", and "has become, by his defects more than his merits, the sixth Great Power of Europe".[10]

Throughout the first half of 1857 the struggle of the Powers for influence at the Porte and in the Principalities continued, and culminated in the Moldavian elections of 19 July, at which, as a protest against the manipulation of the voting rolls, the greater part of the electors—including the Metropolitan and most of the leading boiars and clergy—kept altogether away from the polls and made a complete farce of the results. Victor Place and Thouvenel greatly increased the scandal by making public intercepted letters which proved that the Regent Vogorides was acting on definite instructions from the Grand Vizier, backed by Stratford and Prokesch: and Alison, the counsellor of the British Embassy, whom Stratford had unwisely sent to Jassy, was freely accused of being in the conspiracy. As if all this were not enough, Stratford saw fit to give a big dinner and reception on the anniversary of Waterloo!

The news of these events caused keen indignation in Paris, and Napoleon gave personal instructions to Thouvenel to demand the immediate annul-nent of the Moldavian elections. There was now an open trial of strength at Constantinople, in which the first blow was the fall of Reshid and the return of Ali and Fuad to office under the colourless but Francophil Mustafa (31 July). Thouvenel, however, persisted in his full demands, and on 5 August asked for his passports and embarked on a French warship, while the Russian, Prussian and Sardinian Ministers, acting in conjunction with him, also broke off diplomatic relations with the Porte. The British Cabinet had meanwhile, at Palmerston's instance, advised the Porte to "decline compliance with this arrogant demand"[11]: and Palmerston, with his customary intransigeance, actually wrote to the French Ambassador, "we are ready for any eventualities, however painful".[12] Well might Napoleon complain of Palmerston's "violence", when a question of altogether secondary importance was pushed to the verge of a rupture with France, on the basis of highly indefensible procedure.*

What alone saved the situation was the fortunate accident that the Emperor Napoleon III and Empress Eugénie arrived on 6 August, in fulfilment of a long-standing engagement, at Osborne, as the guests of Queen Victoria and Prince Albert.† As a result there were lengthy discussions between the four and their Ministers, Walewski and Persigny, Palmerston and Clarendon: and agreement was certainly rendered easier by the extent to which the British Ministers and British opinion were absorbed in the first full news of the Indian Mutiny. A compromise was reached in the Roumanian Question, Napoleon no longer insisting on complete union under a foreign prince, while Britain associated herself with the demand for new elections in Moldavia on a revised voting register. As both agreed that the Roumanians should receive "a common system in all things civil and military", there was henceforward the certainty that the national movement would soon find expression in one form or another.

Even now the *détente* was delayed and endangered by Stratford's stubborn resistance. Disregarding his instructions not once but thrice, he protested to Clarendon against annulment, as being "in public opinion a complete surrender": and when the instructions were repeated, he waited for eleven days before acting upon them. The fact that when at last he acted the Porte

* Napoleon told Prince Albert that he had found it necessary to forbid Persigny to show him Palmerston's missives, owing to their violent nature. See memorandum of 6 August in Martin, *Life of the Prince Consort*, IV, 105. Cowley learned of this in time and put Palmerston on his guard, and so at Osborne the latter "was as civil and friendly as possible" (*The Paris Embassy*, p. 127).

† At the last moment Napoleon very nearly postponed the visit, owing to Persigny reporting to Paris a tactless outburst of Palmerston—"pourquoi donc vient-il à Osborne?" The no less tactful Cowley had time to smooth down Walewski, who then saw the Emperor and explained away the phrase (Cowley Papers in *The Paris Embassy*, p. 125). On the preparation of the visit see Clarendon's letter of 20 May 1857 to Prince Albert, *Letters of Queen Victoria*, III, 232.

instantly gave way and ordered fresh elections, is conclusive proof that it had counted to the last upon Stratford carrying his Government with him, and that his obstruction had greatly prolonged the crisis. As the indignant Clarendon wrote to Cowley, "half the difficulties which now exist at Constantinople are owing to the *rix* (sic) between him and Thouvenel, and his doing the right thing always in the wrong way. He has behaved very ill to Bulwer throughout." And again, "I believe he would think his own personal triumph in the struggle *cheaply* purchased by dividing Europe into two hostile camps, and cementing an alliance between France and Russia, founded on the extinction of Turkey." [13] This time indeed Clarendon was thoroughly roused, and roundly told the Ambassador that the reasons which he gave for delay were "inadequate", and added, "You seem to be creating for us as much embarrassment as the nature of the case admits, as of course the Porte does exactly what you advise. It is an unenviable responsibility you are taking upon yourself." [14]

These incidents have been treated in some detail for more than one reason. Firstly, they illustrate once more the somewhat negative character of Clarendon's diplomacy, and the extent to which he could allow his policy to be overborne by a masterful subordinate, on a matter which even if it made no appeal to him on its merits—namely the Roumanian problem—none the less reacted upon the fundamental question of Anglo-French relations. Secondly, Stratford's whole attitude must be branded as a flagrant and perhaps unique example of ambassadorial mischief-making, which throws back a harsh light upon his earlier methods in envenoming the quarrel with Russia in 1853. Thirdly, the course of the crisis reveals the very different measure meted out by the London Cabinet to questions of nationality in the West and in the East, to the oppressed races of Turkey and the Near East in contrast to Italy or Poland. Palmerston himself argued very frankly in the House of Commons on 4 May 1858, that if the Principalities had been independent states, Europe would not have taken up arms to save them from Russia, but that the War had been fought "because they were outposts of the Turkish Empire, and because their invasion was a menace to its integrity and independence, which we deemed to be essential to the interests of Europe". He opposed their independence on the ground that this was bound to lead to vassalage or even partition, and would be the first step towards the dismemberment of Turkey. He committed himself to the preposterous view that their oppression came not from Turkish rule, but solely from foreign invasion. Fortunately in the same debate British foresight and sanity were vindicated by Gladstone, who unsuccessfully urged the House to give "just weight" to the wishes of the Roumanians themselves and rightly assumed them to be overwhelmingly in favour of union.

The new elections were held in Moldavia in September and resulted in an Unionist victory. Stratford continued to the very last his conflict with Thouvenel, and scored a final point in October by securing the re-appointment of Reshid as Grand Vizier. To the very last he expressed the "firm conviction that we ought to join stoutly with Austria and the Porte in resisting the scheme or the fancy—call it what you will—of France in seeking to unite the two Provinces".[15] But in December he went home on leave, and when Palmerston fell in February 1858 unwarily offered his resignation, which was accepted by the new Conservative Government. Bulwer took his place at the Embassy and lived on correct if uncordial terms with Thouvenel, whose position was still further strengthened by the sudden death of Reshid. The fate of Roumania came up for consideration in May 1858 before the Paris Conference, and this time the details of a new constitution were gradually evolved, the initiative of Napoleon triumphing over the obstruction of Turkey and Austria and the feeble indifference or suspicions of Lord Malmesbury. The two Principalities were still held apart, but their institutions were framed on exactly parallel lines, Turkish suzerainty became purely nominal and the new regime was placed under the collective guarantee of Europe. The Convention was signed at Paris on 19 August 1858, and towards the turn of the year the Assemblies met to fill the vacant thrones. Early in 1859 the Roumanians, encouraged by a revolution in Serbia, and by the grave tension due to the impending struggle in Italy, cleverly broke through the artificial restraints imposed by the Great Powers, by the double election of Alexander Cuza in Moldavia and Wallachia. With Austria paralysed by the military situation, Britain essentially negative, Russia ready to comply with France's wishes and France more than ever bent upon union, Europe's acceptance of the accomplished fact was only a matter of time, and was facilitated by the new Prince's tactful management of the Porte.

The main credit for Roumanian Unity, so far as European diplomacy is concerned, unquestionably rests with Napoleon III, and the acclamation with which his agents were greeted showed that the Roumanians themselves were not slow to recognise the fact. The attitude of Britain in obstructing a movement which it had radically misjudged was short-sighted and discreditable. At the same time it was doubtless natural enough that London should view with suspicion Napoleon's eager overtures to the Russian arch-enemy and his frank indifference to "such a sorry set as the Turks", to quote his own phrase to Prince Albert at Osborne. "The maladministration of the Turks was such", he told Cowley about the same time, "that it was impossible that Christian Powers should not sympathise with those Christian subjects of the Sultan who asked for a better government":[16] and when he met the Tsar at Stuttgart, he went even farther on the same lines, admitting that "the late war had opened his eyes with regard to Turkey", and arguing that in face of such misgovernment, Turkey's "dissolution should be provided for by all prudent and far-seeing Governments".[17] We can see now that he was right, but at the time the London Cabinet asked why, in that case, he had fought the war, or what were the ulterior motives of such a swift change of views: and a whole generation was to pass before such an opinion could find official acceptance in England.

The extraordinary perversity of Palmerston's attitude towards Roumania may be studied in his speech to the House of Commons on 4 May 1858. In it he argued that the connection of the Principalities had not been "marked by oppression"; that their sufferings had been owing to "foreign aggression and military occupation"; that "the appointment of a foreign Prince would be the first step towards separation": and that Roumania could not avoid "either becoming the conquest of Russia", or being partitioned between Russia and Austria, like Poland before them. This was said on a motion in favour of the Union of the Principalities, in which his plea for consulting the wishes of the Roumanian people itself was eloquently pleaded by Gladstone and supported by his future rival Lord Robert Cecil, who contended that union would "erect a barrier against Russia greater than by annexing them either to Austria or Turkey".[18]

This is perhaps a suitable connection in which to quote the considered view of the Duke of Argyll, one of the most consistent Liberals of the Victorian Era, and a member of both the Aberdeen and the first Palmerston Cabinet. "There were none in the Cabinet", he says, "who sympathised with Turkey, except perhaps Palmerston, whose habit of mind did not lead him to dwell upon, hardly even to glance at, those deeper-seated moral causes which affect the strength and prepare the fall of states."[19] This verdict from within the magic ring is perhaps in some ways the most damning of all.

THE CHINESE WAR AND DISSOLUTION

In the period immediately following peace Palmerston's position was probably stronger than ever before, and even that section of public opinion which had wished the imposition of more severe terms was well aware that he shared its views, and therefore laid the blame elsewhere. While, however, opinion was still in this irritable and exalted mood, an incident occurred in the Far East which ran a course only too reminiscent of Palmerstonian methods in the Pacifico affair and many others. Sir John Bowring, a man of wide culture and attainments (who in politics was a Benthamite Radical, an active member of the Peace Society, and had played a great part in the foundation of the University of London), had been appointed Governor of Hong Kong, and in that position became involved in a dispute with the Chinese authorities at Canton over a vessel built and owned by Chinese merchants and wrongly flying the British flag as a screen for piratical acts. Bowring demanded an apology from the Governor of Canton for his seizure of the delinquents on board the *Arrow*, and when this was declined he requested Admiral Seymour to bombard first the forts and then the city (23–25 October 1856). A state of war with China resulted. Bowring's attitude was in the highest degree tactless and arrogant: Lord Elgin, who was afterwards sent out officially by the British Government to take charge of the whole Chinese situation, refers in his diary to "that question of the *Arrow*, which is a scandal to us and is so considered, I have reason to know, by all except the few who are personally responsible".[20]

It must none the less in common fairness be remembered that at that period even official communications took seven weeks each way to pass between China and London, that this inevitably imposed upon those on the spot infinitely greater responsibilities of initiative and decision, and that it became correspondingly difficult for the home Government to reverse or repudiate any such decision or to recede from a situation created without its knowledge or control. To-day, however, no one will attempt to deny that Sir John Bowring acted in defiance of the plain sense of the situation and of his own Liberal principles, and that the essence of the dispute lay in the fact that the *Arrow* was a Chinese ship, illegally flying the British flag, and therefore that its lowering could not be construed as an insult to Britain.

The details of a Chinese quarrel lie beyond the scope of this survey of policy in Europe, but the incident had a very direct bearing upon the whole political situation at home. On 24 February 1857 Lord Derby brought forward a motion in the House of Lords strongly condemning the Government's Chinese policy and contrasting the Chinese Governor, "forbearing, courteous and gentlemanlike", with the "menacing, disrespectful and arrogant" Bowring, whom he charged with picking a quarrel with the Cantonese;* and he had the backing of that formidable old lawyer Lord Lyndhurst, who described Bowring as "one of the most mischievous men I know".[21] The Lords rejected the motion by the small majority of 146 to 110: but in the House of Commons the subject was debated for four nights at even greater length and with much greater acrimony, on the motion of Richard Cobden for a select committee of enquiry into our relations with China. Cobden's exhaustive yet calm indictment was all the more impressive

---

* *Hansard*, CXLIV, 1185. "We went on", he added, "from one act of cruelty to another, until we committed an amount of barbarity which would have been wholly unjustifiable under any circumstances whatever" (*ibid.* p. 1191).

because he had for years been on terms of friendship and political agreement with Bowring; and he had the powerful support of Gladstone and Disraeli, of Russell and Bulwer Lytton, of the future Lords Salisbury and Selborne. Cobden challenged the tendency to abuse the Chinese as barbarians,* and defended China as a state "which had its system of logic before Aristotle and its code of morals before Socrates", and as "the very soul of commerce in the East". Lord John Russell complained that too much had been heard of the "prestige" of England, whereas "we used to hear of the character, of the reputation, of the honour of England". He was indeed fully entitled to paraphrase the official argument in these words: "it is true we have a bad case, it is true we were in the wrong, it is true we have committed injustice, but we must persevere in the wrong, we must continue to act unjustly, or the Chinese will think we are afraid". Gladstone in one of his most famous orations condemned the recklessness with which we had plunged into war. "You have turned a consul into a diplomatist, and that metamorphosed consul is forsooth to be at liberty to direct the whole might of England against the lives of a defenceless people." On the last night of the debate Disraeli denounced the Government's "weak and shambling case", and was unwise enough to challenge Palmerston as "the worthy leader of the cause of progress and civilisation" to appeal to the country on a programme of "No Reform! New Taxes! Canton Blazing! Persia Invaded!" But Palmerston remained entirely truculent and impenitent, treated the Opposition speeches as mere "parodies of Chatham and Burke", taunted Cobden for his "un-English spirit", and harking back to the watchword of "Civis Romanus sum", declared him to be equally unfit to be a citizen of England or of Rome. Cobden had described that famous phrase as "not a very attractive motto to put over the doors of our counting-houses abroad", and Palmerston rejoined, "If he write up instead 'I am a British subject', that inscription would be held by those who knew him to be untrue in spirit and at heart".

When the debate ended in the defeat of the Government by 16 votes, Palmerston took Disraeli at his word and ordered a dissolution. The general election fully justified his *flair*, for many of his strongest critics—and notably Cobden, Bright, Milner Gibson and Layard—were unseated, and the man whom Disraeli had attacked as "the Tory chief of a Radical Cabinet", pursuing a "turbulent and aggressive" policy abroad "that his rule at home may be tranquil and unassailed", now returned triumphantly to power with a majority of 70. He had opened the address to his own electors at Tiverton by a volley of violent phrases: "An insolent barbarian, wielding authority at

---

* Palmerston described the Governor of Canton as "one of the most savage barbarians that ever disgraced a nation", and asserted that 70,000 heads had been struck off by his orders in the course of one year! (*Hansard*, CXLIV, 1410, 1822).

Canton, violated the British flag, broke the engagements of treaties, offered rewards for the heads of British subjects in that part of China, and planned their destruction by murder, assassination and poison." Lord John Russell might denounce this address as unworthy of a gentleman, but it unquestionably suited the taste of the electors of that day: and the victor flatly refused to change his policy by one iota or to recall Bowring. The disgraceful Chinese war continued, and our Commissioner in the East, Lord Elgin, on the eve of a fresh bombardment, entered in his journal, "I never felt so ashamed of myself in my life. I thought bitterly of those who for the most selfish objects are trampling underfoot this ancient civilisation."[22]

It seems difficult to believe that the country could have tolerated so inequitable a policy, had it not been for the outbreak of the Indian Mutiny. Its horrors revolted and stiffened public opinion, rendered it uncompromising in its attitude towards all Asiatics, and convinced it that British prestige on the Continent was at stake and could only be recovered by drastic measures alike in India and in China. This attitude may help to explain the Prime Minister's boastful Guildhall speech of 9 November 1857, declaring that "there is no nation on the face of the globe which can surpass—I might without too much national vanity say no nation which can equal—the people of the British Islands". It is true that a series of Chinese outrages against the lives and properties of Europeans seemed for the time to justify Palmerston's stiff attitude and actually led to the co-operation of a French squadron in disciplinary measures against the Chinese Government: but to-day it is possible to endorse the view of Lord Derby, that "these horrors have been the consequence, and not, as Lord Palmerston would fain make them appear, the provocation to our acts".[23] At the same time the Guildhall speech gave great offence to the French by its pointed warning that it would not be "a safe game" for any nation "to take advantage of that which was erroneously imagined to be the moment of our weakness", even though "the Englishman is not so fond as the people of some other countries are of uniforms, of steel scabbards, and of iron heels". That these phrases were deliberate is shown by the terse note found in Palmerston's own pocketbook—"Gave much offence at Compiègne—can't be helped—il n'y a que la vérité qui blesse". His attitude towards Napoleon was to say the least ungracious, in view of the Emperor's unexampled offer of a passage across France to Marseilles for British reinforcements destined for India.[24] Cowley in no way exaggerated when he stressed the absurdity of offering a gratuitous insult to "the country with which his whole policy is identified".* Palmerston, with characteristic

* Greville's contemporary comment is very pertinent, "...a swaggering speech...very ill-timed and in very bad taste". "He might have observed on the remarkable good taste and forbearance which had been conspicuous in all foreign nations towards us" (*Memoirs*, VII, 131).

recklessness, told his colleague Clarendon that the speech had been "pointed, not at the French particularly, but at the whole Continent, where for the last six months we have been talked of, and written of, and printed of, as a second-rate power".[25]

It is clear that at seventy Palmerston remained as unregenerate as in his sparring matches with Guizot, Metternich, Schwarzenberg and Nicholas. It is singular that no one should have attempted to draw a comparison, or rather a contrast, between the Chinese policy of Palmerston and that adopted by Sir Austen Chamberlain in 1927 in dealing with a curiously similar situation at Canton. There can be no doubt that anything approaching similar tactics would have involved Britain in warlike complications of which no one could foresee the end. A comparative study of the two incidents is highly instructive, as enabling us to measure the progress in diplomatic urbanity and pacific tendencies since the 'fifties. Palmerston will always remain typical of a certain phase of British policy and British psychology—in a mood of self-assertive nationalism which we ourselves have since outgrown, but which we find somewhat irksome when adopted by younger nations.

THE ORSINI AFFAIR

The elections of 1857, by virtually labelling pacifism as defeatism, seemed to have made Palmerston irresistible and irreplaceable, and his popularity was increased by the energy with which he set himself to quell the Mutiny. It was however most fortunate that a Governor-General held office whom posterity will always know as "Clemency Canning", and that Disraeli had the courage to protest publicly against the bloodthirsty and unchristian sentiments so freely expressed, or, in his own words, "against taking Nana Sahib as a model for the conduct of the British soldier".[26] Palmerston thought that he could act almost as he pleased, and hurried through his bill for the Government of India, with but small consideration for other views. Yet within a fortnight of its adoption by 318 votes to 173, he was suddenly overthrown by an entirely unforeseen incident of foreign policy, which was compounded of many tragic and ironic elements. Close observers, it is true, had of late noticed a marked diminution of Palmerston's "power and energy", a recrudescence of his old hectoring manner, and a consequent decline in his general popularity: and his appointment of Lord Clanricarde as Privy Seal was widely resented in his own party. On the other hand, the Queen, whose main interest lay in foreign policy, was by now entirely reconciled to Palmerston, made no secret of her delight at having "a really strong Minister", and enquired about his health in "almost affectionate terms".[27]

The fall of the Government was as totally unexpected even to its opponents in the lobbies of the House, as the bolt from the blue to which it was actually due. This was of course the famous attempt upon the life of Napoleon III at the Paris Opera, by the Italian terrorist Felice Orsini (14 January 1858). It was speedily proved beyond all possibility of doubt that the plot had been laid in London and the bombs manufactured in Birmingham: and it was but natural that the French should regard what had happened as an abuse of the right of asylum, and should expect from free England the same stiffening of the law as was immediately taken in hand by the subservient French legislature. It had to be admitted that a law which treated conspiracy to murder as a mere misdemeanour and not as a felony, and which lacked the power to expel a foreigner from English soil, was obsolete and stood in real need of amendment. On the other hand, any suggestion that the hospitality so long extended to political refugees should be infringed or curtailed, at once kindled mid-Victorian resentment. London was the principal refuge of continental liberals and revolutionaries, and the right of asylum was closely associated with such names as Mazzini, Ledru-Rollin, Kossuth and Herzen, of whom the two former had long been regarded by the Emperor himself as plotting his assassination.* Moreover, Napoleon, though so recently our ally, was widely distrusted as an enemy to French liberties—and more than ever so since he had begun to coquette so openly with Tsarist Russia. Thus to the plain Englishman two bogies seemed to join forces.

Suspicion was followed by intense irritation when the official *Moniteur* began to publish congratulatory addresses on the Emperor's escape— notably from a group of colonels who spoke of England as a "lair of assassins" which it might be necessary one day to "clear out".† Morny too was tactless enough to complain of "regular laboratories of murder", and even Walewski, while conveying the Emperor's very frank apology for the publication in the *Moniteur*, caused still greater offence by the manner in which he complained of the hospitality accorded to assassins. "Ought the English legislature", so ran Walewski's despatch, "to contribute to the designs of men who were not mere fugitives, but assassins, and continue to shelter persons who place themselves beyond the pale of common right and under the ban of humanity?": and he went on to demand "a guarantee of security which no state can refuse to a neighbouring state, and which we are authorised to expect from an ally". At this distance of time the sense of the demand will appear altogether unexceptionable: but the tone was resented,

---

* Napoleon made this allegation to Lord Cowley on 18 June 1857. See *The Paris Embassy* (Cowley Papers), p. 117.

† Palmerston was able to point out that military addresses to the sovereign were nothing new in France, but had been in vogue for at least sixty years (8 February 1858, *Hansard*, CXLVIII, 935).

following, as it did, so soon upon the lucubrations of the Colonels, and followed as it was by the French Ambassador's perhaps somewhat querulous reply to the official regrets of the Lord Mayor.* Moreover, it was obviously impossible to treat such men as Ledru-Rollin and Victor Hugo as murderers upon the "simple declaration" of Walewski, and this was pointed out very firmly by Cowley at the very moment when he was urging Clarendon not to allow Mazzini's return to England. Incidentally, nothing illustrates better the curious contrast between Clarendon's drastic views in private and his reluctance to put them into practice publicly, than his comment on the Orsini dispute in a letter to our Ambassador in Paris. "We are a nuisance to Europe, we have our laws and our systems and our policy and our extreme difficulties in making the slightest change; but these are internal affairs, and their external result is terror and danger to others, and people are therefore justified in voting us a pest."[28]

For almost the first time in his career Palmerston showed extreme moderation, urged the House of Commons to ignore the idle vapourings of the Colonels, and consented to introduce a Bill to make conspiracy a felony punishable with penal servitude for life. He flatly denied that Walewski's despatch was an insult to Britain, or that it called upon us to give up the right of asylum: and it is only necessary to read the original text to see that he was absolutely right. But public opinion was by now extremely touchy and unreasonable, and in Parliament a number of quite heterogeneous elements combined in the assault upon Palmerston—the Radical Milner Gibson,† the pacifist John Bright, the doctrinaire Lord John Russell and Kinglake the historian, whose hatred for Napoleon III was strangely compounded of public and personal motives. A popular note was struck by Roebuck, who spoke of Britain as "an oasis in the desert": "despotism", he declaimed, "has been daily narrowing the speech of liberty in Europe, and we are in the proud position of being the sole depositaries of liberty in Europe". It would therefore be a "degradation and a humiliation" for Parliament "to alter our law upon threat".[29] After lively debates the Government was defeated on 19 February by a majority of 19, no fewer than 84 Liberals voting against their chief.

This defeat of Palmerston within a few months of his great triumph at the

---

* It is impossible to read the text of this speech of a declared Anglophil (J. Delaroa, *Persigny, et les doctrines de l'Empire*, pp. 82–5) without feeling that the offence which it unwittingly caused was above all due to the peculiarly irritable susceptibility of Victorian public opinion, to which allusion has already been made (*supra*, pp. 301, 357).

† The Milner Gibsons had a sort of salon frequented by French, Italian, Hungarian and other continental exiles. In the Cowley Papers (see *The Paris Embassy*, p. 169), there is a mysterious reference to the purchase of a revolver in Paris (about the time of the Orsini outrage) which was traced to a maid of Mrs Milner Gibson, who then hurriedly returned to London.

polls is one of the most curious incidents in British Parliamentary history. It is all the more curious when looked at in perspective; for he was defeated just because he showed unusual restraint and moderation. In short, nothing more clearly reflects the jumpiness, the insularity, the aggressive tendencies of public opinion in the mid-Victorian era. In Lord Morley's words, "Palmerston suited the temper of the times, while old maxims of government and policy were tardily expiring, and the forces of a new era were in their season gathering to a head."* We are entitled to conclude that it was the dictatorial and hectoring side of Palmerston which most appealed to his countrymen.

Equally piquant and instructive is the contemporary comment of his old rival Guizot, by this time of course living in strict retirement. "After having committed absurdities for twenty years with impunity", he told Nassau Senior, "Palmerston is upset for having behaved for once in his life with prudence and temper. A man ought to be consistent. If bullying and chicane are his natural role, he should keep to them. If he deviates into moderation and good sense, he is lost." † There is a note of personal resentment to be discounted, but there is none the less an uncomfortable spice of truth in the argument. And indeed about the same time a former close colleague confided to Lord John his opinion of Palmerston as first Minister. "I think him dangerous", he wrote, "and I have always understood that Melbourne, who knew him best, dreaded him most." [30]

Derby and Malmesbury

A highly paradoxical situation now arose. An all-powerful Minister, who had swept the country at the recent elections, had suffered a passing eclipse of popularity and resigned office, but Lord Derby, whom the Queen summoned as the only possible alternative Premier, could not hope to rob him of his majority in the House of Commons. John Bright was therefore fully entitled to argue that "a Derby Government can only exist on forbearance, and will only last till it is convenient for us and the Whigs to overthrow it".‡

---

* *Life of Gladstone*, I, 543. There was, however, a personal incident which contributed to Palmerston's fall—the widespread resentment against the appointment of Lord Clanricarde, which in Prince Albert's view would have sufficed to overthrow him (Martin, IV, 195).

† W. Nassau Senior, *Conversations with Thiers, Guizot, etc.*, II, 178. Another phrase of Guizot on the same occasion deserves to be recorded: "No despotic sovereign would have dismissed Lord Palmerston. No constitutional sovereign could retain Walewski or Morny. The balance is in favour of constitutionalism."

‡ Morley, *Life of Gladstone*, I. 587–8: Buckle, *Life of Disraeli*, IV, chap. v. The moderation of Disraeli's views on foreign policy in all this period deserves some emphasis. In 1857, during the debate on the Address, he had favoured "salutary economy" and had voiced the opinion that "it is not advisable that England should become what is called 'a great military nation'"—cf. Walpole, *Twenty-five Years*, I. 74.

The attitude of the Liberal fronde encouraged Lord Derby to invite the
co-operation of the Peelites, and in particular to offer Gladstone a seat
in the new Cabinet: and this offer, renewed in May after a first refusal, was
backed up by a strong personal appeal from Disraeli.[31] It forms a dramatic
incident, and in some sense marks the parting of the ways between the two
men for whom fate had reserved the most titanic political rivalry in Victorian history: but Gladstone's refusal was a foregone conclusion.

Without the adherence of him and his colleagues the new Cabinet was
mediocre and undistinguished, though Disraeli at the Treasury imparted a
certain unconventionality. In the absence of any stronger or more obvious
candidate, Lord Malmesbury returned to the Foreign Office and, as in 1852,
owed much to his personal relations with Napoleon III: indeed he soon
found, as Clarendon ironically assured him on handing over, "that the chief
employment of the Foreign Secretary was to make bridges for the Emperor
of the French".[32] One of Lord Malmesbury's first tasks was to convince
the Queen, on the basis of his own youthful intimacy with Louis Napoleon
30 years earlier, that the story of his having taken "the oath of the Assassin's
Society" was an entire fable, and that his association with "the higher class
of the Carbonari" had been due to "those romantic feelings which the
former history and present degradation of Italy may naturally inspire even
at a more advanced time of life".[33] He next had to overcome the irritation
caused to the Emperor by the news that the British Cabinet found it quite
impossible to pass into law its predecessor's Conspiracy Bill and must for
the moment postpone legal reform. But his urgent private assurances, and
the weighty and tactful support of Cowley, had a calming effect upon
Napoleon, who, to the Ambassador's dismay, actually consulted him as to
the possibility of commuting the death sentence on the assassin Orsini, for
whom "he felt the greatest sympathy". This attitude made it easier for
Malmesbury to remind him and Walewski that they had taken an exactly
opposite attitude in 1852, when Austria and Russia demanded the surrender
of their refugees. On 8 March, then, Walewski was instructed to offer
explanations of his original Note, and to express the readiness of the French
Government to leave it "to the English nation alone to determine in what
manner, and in what measure, a remedy could be applied". A few days
later Disraeli was able to announce to the House that the "painful misconceptions" between the two Governments had "entirely terminated".

All danger of a relapse was not yet over. Shortly before Palmerston's fall
a certain Simon Bernard, secretary of "La Commune Française" in London, had been arrested on a charge of conspiracy, and the Conservative law
officers now raised this charge to one of wilful murder and ordered his trial
before a special commission. Though his complicity in the Orsini plot was

beyond dispute, he was on 18 April acquitted by the jury, thanks mainly to an eloquent but impudent tirade of his defending counsel against the crimes of Louis Napoleon, a former refugee in England and a conspirator against Louis Philippe. Napoleon can hardly be blamed for showing intense irritation at this and losing that "habitual calm" of which he once boasted to Queen Victoria :[34] and the Empress Eugenie wrote a long private letter to Lord Cowley to express her "indescribable stupefaction".[35] But fortunately Napoleon kept his head and even reaped the full advantage of his recent decision to recall Persigny from the London Embassy. It was high time, for Persigny, though an old personal friend of Malmesbury, "literally raved" during his first visit to the new Foreign Secretary—shouting "C'est la guerre"—and talked wildly against the Conservative Government in London drawing-rooms.* His successor, who arrived providentially on the very day of Bernard's acquittal, was no other than Marshal Pélissier, Duke of Malakoff, a bluff, outspoken and unconventional soldier whom all his old comrades of the Crimea held in high honour. Pélissier received a civic welcome at Dover, was cheered in the streets of London and fêted by Society and Clubland: and Cowley only voiced the instinct of the man in the street when he privately assured the Queen that "there could not be a greater reparation for the offence given by the military addresses than in sending the greatest man in the Army to maintain friendly relations".†

The agitation on both sides slowly died down, but in England there remained a profound suspicion of Napoleon's motives. We know enough to-day to be certain that Napoleon was in his own way profoundly attached to the cause of Franco-British friendship, and that his mind was already moving towards an objective whose attainment would have been gravely compromised by any rupture. But his contemporaries were misled by a curious "time-lag" between his far-reaching yet slowly evolved ambitions and the marked vacillation of his attitude before any irremediable decision was reached. In the words of an acute observer, "His temper is procrastinating. He resolves, and what he has resolved he executes: but the interval between the resolution and the execution is often long. We know that he had decided on the *coup d'état* in January 1849: he did not execute it till December 1851."[36] And again, "The English alliance is his settled policy. If he attempted an invasion and failed, his ruin would be immediate." This fits in curiously with a statement made about the same time to Vitzthum—doubtless intended for Malmesbury's ears: "*L'alliance, c'est moi!* If they don't under-

---

* Malmesbury, ii, 106. But as lately as 12 November 1859 the Queen had written to Clarendon of Persigny as "a good honest warmhearted man" (*Letters*, iii, 253).

† *The Paris Embassy*, p. 161. Malmesbury told Cowley that "the diplomatists particularly looked glum, but I think more at what they knew was a compliment and earnest of the Emperor's goodwill, than because they thought it hostile" (i, 110).

stand this, so much the worse for them and for us. The two peoples don't know each other and have little love for each other."[37]

British opinion was at this moment diverted from the French situation by an acute controversy over the future Government of India. The vindictive folly of Lord Ellensborough and his tactless criticism of the clement Viceroy Lord Canning encouraged the Opposition to attempt the overthrow of a minority Government: but the issue of the debate in Parliament—one of the great debates of the Victorian era—was, on the contrary, to give Lord Derby a new lease of life. Disraeli reached a fresh stage of notoriety through his famous mockery of the unsuccessful "Cabal". "It was like a convulsion of nature rather than any ordinary transaction of human life", he told his delighted constituents, "I can only liken it to one of those earthquakes which take place in Calabria or Peru. There was a rumbling murmur, a groan, a shriek, a sound of distant thunder.... There was a rent, a fissure in the ground; and then a village disappeared; then a tall town toppled down; and then the whole of the Opposition benches became one great dissolving view of anarchy."[38] The result was a very definite strengthening of the Conservatives.

It might at first sight be supposed that Napoleon would have welcomed the return of his old friend Malmesbury to office: but in reality it was a true instinct which led him to fear the probable reactions of the High Tory Ministers to his fast maturing Italian designs, and to realise that the sympathies of the Liberals for Italy were an asset far outweighing the drawbacks of Palmerston's explosive temper. The visit of the Queen and the Prince Consort to Cherbourg was the occasion for a renewed exchange of cordial greetings between the two courts, but the French naval display and the evidence of extensive fortification aroused no little concern, especially among the parliamentary delegates who accompanied the Queen, and stimulated the feeling which was to vent itself in the great Volunteer Panic of 1859–60. Prince Albert, moreover, was "conscious of a change in the Emperor", and saw signs of "a hot friend cooling", to which the Italian adventure of the coming year was to provide the clue. On the other hand it is not surprising that Napoleon grew increasingly reserved when his suggestions for an Anglo-French understanding "on the revision of the map of Europe" met with no response whatsoever from Prince Albert.[39] Napoleon was already full of secret plans, which had assumed a concrete form at Plombières a month before Cherbourg (see *infra*, p. 381): and it was unquestionably in pursuance of these that he took the strange step of inviting Palmerston and Clarendon to Compiègne in November. Their acceptance, though freely criticised on both sides of politics in England, was probably wise: their warnings as to Austrian obstinacy may have served as a momentary deterrent upon the Emperor, and they learned from his own lips his intense eagerness to "clean up Italy", and the embarrassment which the Roman occupation caused him. But far from revealing his whole mind on the subject, he suppressed all reference not merely to his talks with Cavour, but even to the projected marriage of his reprobate cousin "Plon-Plon" to the daughter of Victor Emanuel.

Malmesbury took a generous and statesmanlike view of this incident, and when warned by Cowley of the extent to which Napoleon listened to Palmerston's opinions, at once authorised the Ambassador to get into touch with Palmerston, and tactfully to urge on him the dangers which any incautious utterances in the House of Commons might so easily evoke.* To Malmesbury himself Cowley expressed himself with almost equal tact, arguing that it was possible to tell France almost anything without giving offence, "provided we go gingerly to work. Your object must be to have sufficient influence to guide France and prevent her from getting herself and others into scrapes, but this will never be obtained without the application of *a little soft solder*." Cowley knew his Paris as few Englishmen, and could give advice by which more than one British statesman might have profited.

THE ITALIAN QUESTION

The change in Napoleon was a spiritual process that defies the psychologist: it originated in the mental crisis that followed the Orsini outrage and the published appeal of the assassin upon the scaffold: "I adjure Your Majesty to restore to Italy the independence her children lost in 1849 through the fault of France.... Deliver my country, and the blessings of 25,000,000 citizens will follow you down the ages." †

The Congress of Paris had altogether evaded the Italian question and left its solution to some other occasion. Cavour's secret aim in joining the Allies and sending Piedmontese troops to the Crimea had been, not merely to secure for his little country an equal place among the Great Powers, but to extend the scope of the war in such a way that the Italian cause might profit. But though he was admitted to the Concert and the Congress while Prussia's position at the latter was challenged, he soon found that all the Powers without exception shrank from making Nationality the foundation of

* Contrast the petty attitude of Russell who, as Foreign Secretary, objected to Cowley continuing his private correspondence with Clarendon, but lacking the courage to say so in so many words, circularised to all embassies and legations a kind of general veto on private letters (see Maxwell, II, 188).

† He also won many sympathies by declaring that despite "a fatal mental error" (the plot!) "murder is no part of my principles", and by begging free Italy of the future to compensate his victims!

their policy, realising that this must almost infallibly lead to fresh hostilities
Even Napoleon, despite his very genuine Italian sympathies, was held back
by considerations for the Pope, whose Temporal Power rested on French
bayonets, maintained in Rome at the instance of the powerful French
Ultramontanes. Clarendon had given Cavour the advice that Danton's old
recipe of "audacity" was his best policy: but though he himself stupefied
his colleagues at the Congress by a frontal attack upon Papal and Neapolitan
rule, he not merely withheld his support from any idea of territorial gains
for Piedmont, but as it were barred the door to such ambitions by the conclusion of the Triple Guarantee Treaty of 9 April 1856 with Austria and
France. All that Cavour could do for the moment was to memorialise the
French and British Governments, and to depict Austria's arrogant domination of the whole Italian situation as a permanent danger to peace.

For the next two years Cavour's position was one of extreme difficulty
he had to humour the federalist current, to hold in check Mazzini and the
wilder revolutionaries, to overcome Garibaldi's impatience and separate
him from the republicans, and above all, to make preparations for a war
which he regarded as not merely inevitable, but actually desirable. This
meant that there must be constant incitement against Austria, yet never to
the point of provoking an open rupture, but that Austria must be manœuvred
into the position of the aggressor, while Piedmont must secure strong allies,
capable of redressing her military inferiority. It was typical of such tactics
that in February 1857, on the very day when Francis Joseph installed his
brother Maximilian as Viceroy in Milan, to inaugurate a milder regime,
Cavour delivered a speech culminating in the phrase, "Italy is marching
by great strides towards independence and liberty." This led to a passing
diplomatic rupture with Austria, but peace was not broken: and Cavour
continued to fan the national movement throughout the Peninsula, while at
the same time doing all in his power to make of the House of Savoy the
focussing point of the future. Above all, he cultivated close relations with
Napoleon III, and the extent to which he avoided giving offence to Paris is
reflected in his cautious attitude towards the designs of the mediocre Lucien
Murat, the Emperor's cousin, upon the Neapolitan throne. But he dealt
very firmly with Mazzini's ill-advised plot at Genoa, and thereby laid
himself open to much misapprehension and misrepresentation from the
Left.

The Orsini outrage seemed at first to be fatal to Cavour's designs, by
identifying in many minds the Italian national cause with assassination, and
the French were as insistent in Turin as in London, that exceptional
measures should be taken against the terrorists. But after a month Napoleon's mood began to change; to Victor Emanuel's special envoy he hinted

he possibility of active help for Piedmont. He even showed sympathy for Orsini, thought seriously of pardoning him, ordered his letters to be published in the official *Moniteur*, and took to heart that strangest of appeals which the assassin had addressed in the name of Italy to his would-be victim. It has often been affirmed that fear for his own life from other revolutionaries was a prime motive with Napoleon: but though contemporary enemies of that most enigmatic and romantic of autocrats may be excused for believing this of him, they were almost certainly misled by hate and passion. Far truer is it to recognise that his imagination was fired, and that a fatalist belief in destiny and in his own guiding star led him on logically to assume that the opportune moment for action was at last drawing near.

In July 1858, then, he invited Cavour to a secret meeting at Plombières, and there the two conspirators reached agreement upon a joint campaign against Austria. Cavour reported to Victor Emanuel the Emperor's insistence on the need for justifying war before the diplomacy and public opinion of Europe, and described with a curious blend of cynicism and naïveté "the search for this cause of war so difficult to find". Napoleon made it clear that he could not take too strong a line against the Pope or the King of Naples without on the one hand alienating French Catholic opinion and on the other jeopardising his new-found friendship with the Tsar: but also that he was ready to drive the Austrians beyond the Isonzo. It was agreed that the future Italy should consist of four states instead of seven— a Kingdom of Upper Italy or Piedmont, augmented by Lombardy-Venetia; Parma and Modena; a revived Kingdom of Etruria, consisting of Tuscany and most of the Papal States, and perhaps assigned to the evicted Duchess of Parma; Papal Rome, reduced to the original Patrimony of St Peter; and a Kingdom of Naples, from which Murat might oust the hated Bourbons. The four would form a federation under the presidency of the Pope. Napoleon's price was Savoy and Nice; Cavour did not finally commit himself, but argued unanswerably that on a basis of nationality it was almost equally impossible to withhold the former and to concede the latter. Finally Victor Emanuel was to give his daughter Clotilde in marriage to Prince Napoleon.*

The net result was to lay the main stress upon independence and to place Italian unity altogether in the background: and indeed to some it savoured far more of a dynastic "deal" between the Houses of Savoy and Bonaparte than of a true national programme—in the words of M. Bourgeois, it was "a partition of the Peninsula, dictated and controlled by 'raison d'état', and

---

* Cavour's report to Victor Emanuel on the conversations is to be found in *Lettere di Cavour*, III, Nos. 1–14. The reasoning by which he sought to win his master for the marriage is truly amazing and has more than once been pilloried.

destined to produce prolonged misunderstandings between the two peoples associated in the enterprise ".[40]

During the summer, while Cavour secretly continued his preparations, Napoleon sent his cousin to Warsaw, to win the Tsar for benevolent neutrality in the event of a Franco-Austrian conflict. In the crude form submitted to Gorchakov, the French proposal virtually amounted to the destruction of Austria as a Great Power: for not merely was she to lose all her Italian possessions, but Hungary was to become independent, while Galicia was to be Russia's share in a war of Coalition.[41] It is doubtful whether Alexander II would ever have taken the scheme seriously, but in any case he refused to consider it unless the Treaty of 1856 were revised—a concession which Napoleon could not make without alienating Britain. None the less, Prince Jerome left with a reasonable hope that Russia would not merely be neutral, but by a concentration of troops on her western frontier would create a diversion against Austria and deter Prussia from possible activity on the Rhine. Less successful was the Berlin mission of Marquis Pepoli, a grandson of Joachim Murat and therefore a kinsman both of Napoleon and of the Prussian Premier Prince Antony of Hohenzollern. The Prince Regent—the future William I—showed great reserve at the time, and then by his confidential enquiries in London helped to augment the growing alarm of the British Court and Cabinet, which in its turn increased the secretiveness and hesitations of the Emperor. It was, however, a significant fact that the French press, though as completely at the mercy of the Imperial authorities as the corresponding press under our modern dictatorships, was left free to indulge in violent tirades against Austria and her henchmen in Italy: and while the *Moniteur* itself published Edmond About's criticisms of Papal misgovernment, *La Presse*, the organ of Prince Napoleon, insulted Francis Joseph and the Archduchess Sophy and even went so far as to declare that while "we do not love war, and hope that it will some day disappear from the surface of Europe, we should none the less like to see one war, and that one directed against Austria ".[42] On 24 December Cavour transmitted to Paris a draft convention confirming the main decisions of Plombières: the new Northern Italian Kingdom was to take Lombardy and Venice from Austria and the Romagna from the Pope, while Savoy was to be ceded to France (this time no mention was made of Nice). Everything, then, pointed to war when in the last week of 1858, while the movement for Roumanian union was reaching its height, a sudden revolution in Serbia overthrew Prince Alexander Karagjorgjević and restored the exiled Miloš Obrenović. Count Buol, arrogant as ever, notified Paris that he might send troops to assist the Pasha of Belgrade against the insurgent Serbs: even the lukewarm Walewski was highly inlignant, and the Austrian Ambassador Hübner was gravely embarrassed ind wrote of a tile falling upon his head.[43] This was the background of the famous scene at the New Year reception in the Tuileries, when the Emperor expressed to Hübner his regret that Franco-Austrian relations were not as good as he could wish. The phrase resounded through Europe, and there was consternation in Paris, reflected in movements on the Bourse; but there are grounds for doubting whether Napoleon had intended anything more than a momentary snub to a diplomat whom he detested.* Much more serious was the speech of Victor Emanuel in opening Parliament ten days later: for on that occasion he referred to "the cry of anguish" (*grido di dolore*) which came to him from many parts of Italy, and the reaction from Vienna was immediate.

BRITISH EFFORTS FOR PEACE

Now that most of the diplomatic secrets of those days have been laid bare, it would be absurd to deny that the policy pursued by Piedmont, under the guidance of Cavour and his King, was one of calculated aggression, planned to manœuvre the enemy into an aggressive pose before Europe. But if we look deeper, we must endorse as fundamental Hudson's view that "the mere existence of a system of government as free as that of Sardinia is excitement enough to people in the condition of the Lombards, Venetians and the Pope's subjects".[44] In a word, Piedmont's crime was that she was there at all.

Malmesbury entirely shared the apprehensions of the Queen, and already on 12 January recorded in his diary that his whole mind was occupied by the object of preventing a war "which would cost 100,000 lives and desolate the fairest parts of Europe". At the same time his well-meant warning to Vienna that war "would soon assume the character of a revolutionary contest", and that while Britain would remain neutral, her public opinion "had a natural tendency to sympathise with Italian nationalists", provoked a haughty reply from Buol, who, in the Foreign Secretary's considered view, behaved "with a folly which is perfectly inconceivable".[45] "Buol", he told Cowley a week later, "has received our counsels of prudence with nearly equal sulkiness, and I think the best attitude for us now is to fold our arms like men who have advised madmen in vain to refrain from mutual follies...and leave them with sorrow to their fate." And indeed the unfortunate Malmesbury soon found himself between two, or even three, stools. He suspected Napoleon,

---

* The press recalled the energetic language used by Napoleon I to Lord Whitworth in 1803, when he had resolved upon tearing up the Treaty of Amiens. But there is probably a much truer parallel in the open encounter between Napoleon III and Lord Cowley at another Tuileries reception in the year 1860. (See *infra*, p. 416.)

not without justice, of being "very hostile to our administration and anxious to upset it"; a chance phrase of his to the effect that Austria had the same right to Lombardy as England to Ireland and India, had been repeated to the Emperor and been much resented by him.[46] Moreover, Malmesbury had grounds for suspecting an alliance between Napoleon and Algernon Borthwick, of the *Morning Post*, and behind this he seemed to see a plot of Palmerston for the overthrow of the Conservative Cabinet. Meanwhile, Malmesbury instructed his Minister in Turin, Sir James Hudson,* to warn Cavour: but the effect of this was marred by the fact that Hudson was more Italian than the Italians and virtually conspiring with the Turin Government. This explains the flat-footed answer that Piedmont was "following the path marked out by England, and Europe was to blame for rousing the hopes of the Italians". Malmesbury vented his wrath on "that little conceited mischievous state now called Sardinia.... That Europe should be deluged with blood for the personal ambition of an Italian attorney and a tambour-major, like Cavour and his master, is intolerable."† But like Prince Albert, he gravely misjudged and under-estimated Cavour when he spoke of him as "bankrupt and desperate". Lord Clarendon may perhaps be excused for thinking Malmesbury "unfit for the oncoming European crisis":[47] and indeed there was more than an undercurrent of this same feeling in Malmesbury's own colleague Disraeli, who had already in December taken the unusual step of sending his secretary Ralph Earle to urge moderation upon Napoleon, and who early in January wrote a very critical letter to the Prime Minister on the subject of our foreign policy.[48]

At the opening of Parliament on 3 February the Queen's speech laid very special stress on Britain's resolve "to maintain inviolate the faith of public treaties": and this attitude, which found universal acceptance from public opinion, was voiced by no one more explicitly than Palmerston himself, who argued quite openly that "no Power could violate" the settlement of 1815 "by attempting, without reason or cause, to dispossess Austria of what that treaty gave her". He even went so far as to allude to a possible Austro-French war over the possession of Lombardy; but this, he concluded, "would be to involve Europe in calamities...for a cause which, however in the abstract desirable, would by no means justify such a war". Of special interest was the speech of Disraeli on the same occasion: for after allusions

---

* Malmesbury himself in his diary for 11 April says of Hudson that "he is more Italian than the Italians, and he lives almost entirely with the ultras of that cause" (*Memoirs*, II, 169).

† *The Paris Embassy*, p. 175. Palmerston's comment to Granville was that Malmesbury was "really unfit for his office", if he had told France that she would not be permitted to go to war; for that "is to insult her without being strong enough to make good the affront" (Fitzmaurice, I, 326).

to "the great jealousy and distrust" between France and Austria and an appeal for patience addressed to "that interesting state", Sardinia, he placed his main emphasis upon "the high policy of an alliance with France", such as all the greatest statesmen of England had advocated. He claimed that there were deeply rooted reasons for calling it "a natural alliance,...an alliance independent of dynasties, individuals or forms of government": and he expressed his confidence in the character of Napoleon, as "a faithful ally and...a sagacious Prince". At the close of the debate Lord John Russell endorsed Disraeli's belief in the value of a French alliance, and advanced his favourite theory that the people of Central Italy should be allowed to settle their own affairs without foreign interference, and that this was the surest way of averting war in Europe.[49]

These utterances had a momentary influence on the Emperor, who four days later, in opening the French legislature, repeated the watchword "L'Empire, c'est la paix": yet the general tone of his speech was anything but reassuring, and its effect was counteracted by the very different language of the inspired pamphlet *L'Empire et l'Italie*, in which Austria's stranglehold upon the minor states of the Peninsula was mercilessly denounced. He admitted to the Queen that "the treaties could only be altered by common agreement, but respect for them does not conflict with my duty, which is to follow the policy which best conforms to the honour and interests of my country". As Prince Albert told Stockmar, "it is not on words like these that the funds will rise".

During the second half of February London, realising that nothing save some form of friendly mediation from the outside could avert the slow but steady drift towards war, sent Lord Cowley on a mission to Vienna. His four proposals were the joint withdrawal of Austrian and French troops from the Papal States, an agreement for reform of the Papal Government, permanent guarantees for Austro-Sardinian friendship and revision of the treaties binding Parma and Modena to Austria. Friendly letters passed between the Queen and Francis Joseph, and Cowley was well received by Buol and found his position eased by the sudden dismissal of Prince Napoleon from his position as Colonial Minister, which was interpreted as a sign of pacific views on Napoleon's part. But Cowley's suggestion that a disarmed Piedmont should be guaranteed by the Great Powers as a kind of Switzerland, never had any prospect of success:[50] and in any case, before it could be discussed, the situation was transformed by a Russian proposal that the Italian question should be submitted to an European Congress, and by its ready acceptance by France. This proposal in its turn remained stillborn: for on the one hand Britain, though also accepting it, suspected the motives that prompted Russia. Prince Albert told his uncle that the Russian aim was "to increase the difficulties of an arrangement", and thought that Gorchakov "looked to Congress to regain for Russia the position she had lost since 1855".[51] On the other hand, Austria insisted on the exclusion of Sardinia—an impossible humiliation after her role at Paris three years earlier—while Malmesbury and even Cowley entertained for a time the preposterous alternative of excluding all six Italian states. It is possible to sympathise with the Foreign Secretary's view that to admit all six to the Congress "would make it a Babel"; but it was surely obvious that to exclude all Italians from a Congress convoked to settle the Italian Question,* was a *tour de force* worthy of the Holy Alliance, and certain to be rejected by Western opinion. It was, however, left to Austria to make a proposal which Malmesbury at once called "perfectly inadmissible"[52]—namely that Sardinia should be excluded and the other five admitted.

At this critical juncture, when foreign Governments were closely watching London, and when so much depended upon the Derby Cabinet taking a clear and firm line in favour of peace, its prestige was diminished by a precarious situation at home. The electoral reform to which Lord Derby stood pledged, and which he laid before Parliament on 28 February, proved too conservative for the Liberals and too liberal for the Tories: John Bright held up its "fancy franchises" to ridicule, and Lord John Russell, denounced by Disraeli† for the "restlessness which will not brook that delay and patience needed in our constitutional Government", rallied all the hostile groups against the Government. On 31 March it was defeated by 39 votes, and a dissolution followed: nor did the gain of about 30 seats at the general elections suffice to give the Government a clear majority. Thus, in Mr Buckle's words, "Malmesbury's advice necessarily lost half its weight abroad",[53] and such chance as he still had of damming back the torrent was reduced almost to zero. Napoleon, it is true, was full of hesitations, concealed his designs from his Ministers, whose clerical outlook rendered them hostile to Turin, and, as the event was to prove, made altogether inadequate military preparations. British disapproval, Russian dislike of anything savouring of revolution, doubts as to Prussian intervention—all these served to increase his irresolution. In a word, Napoleon sat at the Tuileries, "brooding over Italy", and faced, in the view of Prince William of Prussia, and of many other good judges, by a choice of "la guerre ou le poignard".[54]

No wonder that Cavour was intensely alarmed; for though anxious "not

---

* To quote Malmesbury's own words in the House of Lords, on 28 March, "intimately connected with the political and social happiness of the Italian people" (*Hansard*, CLIII, 908).

† *Ibid.* p. 1253. He accused Russell of sneering at the Foreign Secretary and embarrassing the Government before Europe at "a moment the most critical...for many years past".

to triumph solely by means of the French", he fully realised that without their aid he was helpless. At the end of March he paid a visit of despair to Napoleon and spared no effort to brace him for the plunge: for the next few weeks he seriously thought of resigning, withdrawing to America and publishing an account of the Plombières talks and Napoleon's written pledges.* He was resolved to resist any attempt, even on the part of a Congress, to impose disarmament upon his country, and was reduced to pinning his last hope upon Austria placing herself in the wrong by an aggression which he himself was of course only too ready to forestall.

London's alarm was heightened by a conversation between Cowley and Napoleon on 9 April. Asked to say frankly whether he desired peace or war, the Emperor replied that though he should be glad of peace, he was not afraid of war, and feared it to be unavoidable. England, he added, had always disliked Austria's presence in Italy: why should she not come to terms with France on this matter, and he would give guarantees that he had no ambitious projects. Cowley, feeling this to be "the cloven foot", gave the Emperor a piece of his mind: he roundly declared that "if he attempted without reason any scheme so iniquitous, he would have both the moral and material efforts of England arrayed against him" and concluded with an impassioned appeal "to help Italy by pacific means", rather than by drawing the sword.[55] This was reported to the Cabinet, who "all agreed", Malmesbury told Cowley, "that you did not say a word too much to the man who broke his word to you, and who, it is evident to me, had from the first meant an Italian War".[56] But he was also only too conscious that "England cannot go running from one to the other like an old aunt trying to make up family squabbles", and yet this was in effect what British policy was rapidly coming to. Malmesbury's final effort on 19 April took the form of proposals for simultaneous disarmament on the part of Austria, France and Sardinia, to be followed by a Congress to which Sardinia and all the other five Italian states should be invited, but only *en titre consultatif*, according to the Laibach precedent of 1821. It was on this very day that Clarendon, speaking in the House of Lords, summed up the situation somewhat cynically as follows: "that one despotic Power has proposed to another despotic Power that by means of a Congress a third despotic Power should pave the way for liberal institutions in Italy".[57] He was followed by the Prime Minister himself, who openly blamed Victor Emanuel for "stepping out of his legitimate course" by the famous speech from the Throne in which the words "a cry of anguish" occur.

The attitude of Malmesbury on this occasion was far from effective, and

* Cf. Martin, IV, 416. Ollivier (*L'Empire Libéral*, III, 562) rejects the possibility of such action, but it is to be found in *Lettere di Cavour*, III, 96.

really led in neither of the two obvious directions. He spoke of sympathies for "the Austrian people", because "we are of the same Teutonic origin", but added that we were "to a certain extent alienated from them by the signal difference which exists between the two Governments. Theirs is an essentially despotic Government and ours an essentially free one." On the other hand, Britain was not of the same race or descent as Sardinia, "but there is such a resemblance between our Governments, they are so identical in character, that the greatest desire for the prosperity of Sardinia has always existed in this country.... We accept the revolutions which they bring about by their own hands and judgments. We recognise their *de facto* Governments." Such utterances, from such a quarter, could only incense Vienna and encourage Turin, this producing an effect quite at variance with Malmesbury's intentions and a clear impression abroad of hesitancy and weakness.

It is quite obvious that Malmesbury under-estimated the strength of Italian national feeling: but after the event he strenuously denied ever having objected on principle to the idea of Unity. Nor would he admit that hostility towards Napoleon of which the latter came to suspect him: and in 1861 he pressed for, and succeeded in obtaining, an audience with the Emperor, in order to convince him that Conservative hostility to his person, and still more the suggestion that Malmesbury was "getting up a German coalition against him", was a myth, and probably originated with Palmerston.[58]

Parliament was dissolved on 19 April 1859, and thus the European crisis came to a head while the British Government was absorbed in a losing electoral campaign. On the very eve of dissolution Disraeli had spoken on the Italian Question, and argued that "the waters of the Adriatic cannot be disturbed without agitating the waters of the Rhine". Palmerston intervened, in order to "express his opinion in favour of a much more liberal policy than H.M.G. seemed inclined to pursue towards the unhappy people of Italy".[59]

The Italian War

Cavour feared the ruin of all his plans and was on the point of resignation, perhaps even of suicide, when he was saved by the impatient folly of Austria. To the Cabinet of Vienna a Congress offered no satisfactory solution: for it opened the door to general European interference in matters which Austria regarded as her own concern, and in the meantime gave her enemies a breathing-space for further military preparations. Buol refused even to enter the Congress unless Sardinia disarmed, and told Lord

Augustus Loftus that he had no illusions and expected France to offer him not an olive branch, but the sword's point.[60] Unduly encouraged by anti-Italian manifestations in the south of Germany, Francis Joseph and Buol sent the Archduke Albrecht on a special mission to Berlin, urging a joint Austro-Prussian campaign upon the Rhine. The Prince Regent William was not attracted by a scheme which not merely involved a great war, but perhaps also Austrian predominance in Germany: and he may well have been influenced by Prince Albert's pressing advice in favour of a waiting attitude as the true Prussian policy.[61] But in any case before he had even left Berlin, the war party in Vienna gained the upper hand and induced Francis Joseph to launch an ultimatum against Sardinia, giving her only three days in which to accept the principle of radical disarmament.* After the disaster Count Buol wished it to be believed that he had opposed such precipitate action and that this was the cause of his dismissal, which took place on 4 May. In reality there seems no doubt that at the decisive Crown Council he had not opposed the ultimatum, and that he was dismissed because Austria's isolation in Europe instantly became apparent and the main blame was, not without reason, laid upon his arrogant and inept conduct of foreign policy. Two of his many outbursts in these critical weeks were to the effect that "we want allies, not mediators", and that "I would sooner go to the gallows than to this conference".[62]

The ultimatum put Austria in the wrong and tied the hands of London, the more so as Cavour, with despair in his soul, had a day earlier accepted the programme of disarmament. Austrophil though he was, Lord Derby told the Queen that "Austria deprives herself of all claim to the support or countenance of England":[63] and at a dinner of the Lord Mayor he went so far as to declare that "there was nothing in his judgment to justify the hasty, precipitate, and, because involving the horrors of war, the criminal step which had been taken by Austria". The Queen, already "dreadfully disgusted with politics and Europe", wrote to King Leopold, bewailing "the madness and blindness of Austria", and also "the most vehement sympathy for Sardinia" which Austria's action was evoking in England.[64] Malmesbury made a last unavailing effort at mediation and urged Buol at least to delay the attack upon Piedmont. But his appeal was disregarded, and Loftus's warning that Austria would be isolated met with Buol's answer, "Perhaps, but we are fighting against Revolution and for European order."[65]

Austria and Sardinia were at war by 26 April, and manifestos in the name of Francis Joseph, Victor Emanuel and Napoleon served as the flourish of trumpets that ushered in a tournament. But one phrase of the Emperor

---

* This offers a highly interesting analogy to the Austrian ultimatum of 23 July 1914, when a respite of only 48, instead of 72, hours was given.

drowned all the rest and echoed thunderously throughout the Peninsula—his assumption that either Austria must rule up to the Alps or "Italy must be free from the Alps to the Adriatic". Cavour's despair was turned to exultation by the unfriendly Walewski's telegram promising full military support: and soon French troops began to pour over the Mont Cenis pass and to land at Genoa. Fortunately for the Italian cause, the Austrian commander Count Gyulay showed marked incompetence and by his inaction wasted the ten days during which he might well have overwhelmed Piedmont's resistance before her ally's numbers began to tell. It was not till 20 May that the first serious engagement took place at Montebello: on 4 June the battle of Magenta was won by Macmahon after confused and almost haphazard fighting, and four days later Napoleon and Victor Emanuel made a joint entry into Milan. Meanwhile a sudden revolutionary outburst, from embers long secretly fanned by Cavour, drove the Grand Duke of Tuscany and the Dukes of Parma and Modena from their dominions and struck terror into the hearts of the Pope and the King of Naples.

Austria, Prussia and the Rhine

Thanks to the arrogant infatuation of Buol, Austria found herself in complete diplomatic isolation on the outbreak of war. To the last moment he had calculated that Napoleon would compel Sardinia to submit, and that Prussia and Britain would give Austria their backing.[66] But the Bund refused to move, and though Moltke as a soldier favoured action, and though Albert of Saxony and Frederick of Baden appealed to the Prince Regent against "the disturber of the peace", and bade him answer "the call of Germany", he preferred to follow the advice of Bismarck, who held that Prussia would only be helping Austria to establish her hegemony over Germany. South German sentiment was on the Austrian side, in spite of the obvious drawbacks of the Bach regime; but Schleinitz, Prussia's Liberal Foreign Minister, felt both national and political affinities with the cause of Piedmont, and knew that Francis Joseph dreamt of a reversion to Austria's full territorial status in the eighteenth century. Moreover, he was fully alive to the dangers of action in the West before Russia's intentions could be clearly ascertained.* Russia, for her part, was definitely pleased to see Austria endangered and defeated: to the Tsar and Gorchakov it meant an easy vengeance for Austrian ingratitude in the Crimean War, and Francis Joseph's arguments

---

* Schleinitz at first only wanted to mobilise three, in order "not to give umbrage" (see Prince Regent's memorandum of 12 June 1859, No. 440 in *Auswartige Politik Preussens*, I, 654).

as to the essentially revolutionary character of the Italian war fell upon deaf ears. Napoleon was not slow to invite the Tsar to declare himself. "We understand", he wrote, "the *ménagements* which it is wise to show towards the Confederation, and above all Prussia. But without adopting a menacing attitude, it is essential that the neutrality of Russia should inspire in Germany a salutary fear—the sole possible brake upon the passions which agitate her."[67] Alexander in his reply expressed his desire to fulfil his engagements and to effect in France's favour "the strongest possible diversion", and promised to use his influence upon all his German relations. He then informed Schleinitz that Russia would remain neutral so long as the war was localised, but that "her attitude would change if without the territory of the Confederation being attacked, Prussia and Germany were to range themselves on the side of Austria".[68] In the following autumn Gorchakov informed the French Ambassador that a Russian warning had been addressed to Berlin, but that he had concealed it from France, "so as not to encourage the extension of a war which it was our interest to circumscribe".[69] Whether this was literally accurate or not, it is certain that Russian policy aimed at restraining Russia from aggression, yet without entirely freeing France from the fear of it.

The news of Magenta revived the patriotic agitation in South Germany, and voices were heard demanding action against France and even the conquest of Alsace. Alarm spread through Europe, the Danes and Swiss placed part of their forces under arms, and Russia gathered four army corps on the Galician and Moldavian frontiers. Prussia, though anxious not to offend Russia, accepted the proposals put forward at the Diet of Frankfurt and mobilised six army corps, while inviting Russia and Britain to join her in mediation. After Solferino the tension increased still further, and Prussia proposed that a federal observation corps should be placed on the upper Rhine, in contact with her own forces. If at this stage Russian pressure was the decisive deterrent in Berlin, it must not be overlooked that the British Conservative Cabinet, already at its last gasp, sent a circular to all the German courts, strongly discouraging any action on the Rhine, and warning them that if they should be "so ill-advised as to provoke a war with France, and should without any sufficient cause make general a war which on every account ought if possible to be localised, Her Majesty's Government...can give to Germany no assistance nor contribute...to protect her coast from hostile attack".[70]

It was in circumstances such as these, and amid a growing German clamour for a "Front against the West", that Napoleon took the fateful decision of direct overtures to Francis Joseph, and thus by the compromise of Villafranca averted the danger of an attack on the Rhine. The further details need

not concern us here, but the respective attitudes of Prussia and Russia form
the essential background to Napoleon's Italian policy, while it was being
converted from theory into practice.

THE BRITISH ELECTIONS

Events in Italy undoubtedly diminished the chances of the Tories at the
elections, and their hold upon the new Parliament, which met early in
June, was distinctly precarious. Feeling in the country was strongly in
favour of "a strict and impartial neutrality", and in including so pointed a
phrase in the Queen's speech, Derby was going farther than Gladstone
himself felt to be expedient:[71] but there was also widespread sympathy for
the Italian cause, and the suspicion that the Government was siding with
Austria lost it many votes.

A curious episode deserves passing mention. On 5 May Napoleon III
received in audience Louis Kossuth, the exiled Governor of Hungary, with
a view to rousing against Austria her disaffected populations. The conversation turning upon the need for France's flanks being secured against
attack while she was winning freedom for Italy, Kossuth argued that British
neutrality was the key, and offered to contribute towards the overthrow of
Derby's Government by using his personal influence with Cobden and the
Radicals. He did actually go straight to England and with the help of
Charles Gilpin, Member for Northampton, organised four big meetings in
favour of neutrality, in London, Manchester, Bradford and Glasgow, the
Lord Mayor presiding at the first of the four.[72] This was neither the first
nor the last occasion on which Hungarian patriots meddled in British party
politics for their own ends.

Already during the debate on the Address the Government was in a
minority of 13, and this time definitely resigned. Lord Malmesbury afterwards recorded his view that if the Blue Book on his conduct of affairs
during the Italian dispute had appeared before the debate, instead of being
held back by Derby and Disraeli, the voting would have been the other way.
But it seems obvious that even in that event the fall of the Government could
not have been averted for more than a few weeks. Its failure to check the
Austro-French quarrel was certainly a prime cause of its defeat, but that
failure was above all due to Napoleon's calculation that Derby was tottering,
and that his Liberal successors would favour a forward policy in Italy.
Malmesbury at least saw this clearly enough: for on 25 March he noted,
"None of the Great Powers (excepting Russia, who agrees to everything),
would move an inch till it is decided whether Lord Derby's Government
can hold on or not. If we were secure, Austria might make the concession

we require, which she would not if Palmerston and Lord John were in office: and Louis Napoleon, seeing a chance of his friends being in power and following a policy in accordance with his wishes, throws of course every kind of delay in the way of settling the case by negotiation." [73] In other words, the weakness of the Conservatives formed an essential factor in French calculations, and therefore in the ultimate Italian issue.

There followed a brief political interlude: the Queen, in her embarrassment between "those two dreadful old men" Lord Palmerston and Lord John Russell, hit upon the idea of inviting Lord Granville (whom Russell in 1852 had described as one of the best Foreign Secretaries the country ever had) to become Prime Minister and hold the balance between them. Greville very acutely interpreted this as "a significant notice to them of her great reluctance to have either of them at the head of affairs". There were several days of astute manœuvring, Palmerston consenting to serve under Granville, if he could remain leader of the Commons, while Russell also claimed this for himself and expected Palmerston to be Foreign Secretary, but to go to the Lords. In the end, to use Lord Fitzmaurice's witty phrase, "neither of the two elder statesmen would consent to be the third person in the political trinity, though each was ready to consent to be the second". "With Palmerston", Lord John bluntly told Lord Granville, "I could only have to consider who is to have the first, and who the second office in the State. With you I could only occupy the third, and should not feel that I had sufficient security either on foreign affairs or on reform." [74] Granville's biographer is fully entitled to interpret this as meaning that while there were at that moment two main aims of British Policy—the maintenance of peace and the better government of Italy—"Lord John and Lord Palmerston thought most of the second, Lord Granville most of the first, of these objects. Lord John was prepared to risk war to secure Italian liberation: Lord Granville was not prepared to do so". Already in May Lord John's mind had been moving on the lines of "a division of power on fair and equal terms" between himself and Palmerston, [76] and this became the only possible solution as soon as Granville handed back his mandate to the Queen.*

To complete the picture, it must be added that inside the Conservative ranks Disraeli was urging upon his chief Lord Derby the regrettable necessity for dropping Lord Malmesbury, in the hope that Lord Clarendon might consent to take his place. He also expressed the view that there was only

---

* The secret of these negotiations was revealed in *The Times* of 14 June, owing to the deliberate indiscretion of its great Editor Delane, and the innocent Granville was placed in a very awkward situation towards the Queen (*Letters*, III, 347). Disraeli's idea of reconstruction under Lord Stanley, with Clarendon in place of Malmesbury, was never taken seriously and belongs to the curiosities of politics (Buckle, *op. cit.* p. 1659).

one man who could rally all Conservatives and win them allies outside, and that was Lord Stanley. "My friendship for him is so complete, and his confidence in me so perfect that if I sat below the gangway, he would know I was only there for his interests." [76] Nothing came of this combination, but the friendship of Disraeli and Stanley was to remain one of the decisive factors in British party politics for close upon two decades to come.

CHAPTER XI

INTERFERENCE AS A POLICY

RUSSELL AT THE FOREIGN OFFICE

Palmerston again became Prime Minister, with Granville as President of the Council, Gladstone as Chancellor of the Exchequer, Newcastle, Sidney Herbert and Wood as Secretaries for the Colonies, War and India. But Russell, who in his own estimation was no less fitted for the supreme post, made it an absolute condition of his co-operation that he should himself be Foreign Secretary. Clarendon, who could not be induced to accept any alternative post, and again showed, as on other occasions, a singular indifference to political office or advancement, now dropped out altogether, to the great regret of the Queen and of Palmerston himself.*
But to-day it is impossible to regret this, in view of the utterly erroneous views which he held on the vital issues of his time: and it will suffice to quote his publicly avowed opinion that "the bubble of Italian Unity has at length burst",[1] and his private appeal to Cowley to use his influence on Napoleon "to put some check on the brigandage of the King of Sardinia".[2]

After some years of friction and divergent views the two Liberal veterans re-established an intimate personal alliance, in which it was observed that Russell's eagerness for office was far greater than Palmerston's. Palmerston's attitude on foreign policy had not really changed since 1848. "The Austrians have no business in Italy, and they are a public nuisance there", he had told Lord Granville: but on the other hand he held it to be "greatly for the interests of Europe that Austria should continue to be a Great Power in the centre of the Continent",[3] and war on too drastic a scale might, he feared, end in her dismemberment. In April he openly defended Sardinia's right to take part in any Conference, but privately he looked upon Austria as the aggressor. He recognised that Napoleon had "for many years past had a fixed desire to improve the internal condition of Italy by freeing as much of that country as possible from the crushing weight of Austrian domination", and that if war ensued, "we shall have Italy freed from the Austrians,

---

* In November 1857 he had already told the Queen that he could never succeed Palmerston and that Lord John was the right successor (Greville, VIII, 136).

and that would be another good thing".[4] The Queen's entourage doubtles: shared Aberdeen's view that Austria was "still fighting the battle o Europe":[5] but public opinion with every week rallied more decisively to the Italian side.

Even more pronounced was Russell's attitude towards the Italian Ques- tion: and indeed his keen sympathy with the Italian cause was a prime factor in his insistence upon the Foreign Office. Professor Trevelyan make: the strong, but by no means excessive, assertion that Lord John's part in the making of Italy, "next to his part in the great Reform Bill, stands as the principal achievement of his life".[6] For years Russell had been in close contact with leading Italian patriots, and even with French official agents who late in 1858 sounded him as to the attitude of the Liberal press in the event of Napoleon crossing the Alps and asking only Savoy as the reward of his assistance to Sardinia. This he confided to his father-in-law Lord Minto, whose famous mission of 1847 had identified him with the Italian cause: but he refrained from telling Palmerston and Clarendon, "as I suspect their advice would be quite against Italy".[7] This was written before his recon- ciliation with Palmerston, and while his relations with Clarendon were definitely strained: but it shows quite clearly that long before taking office he was prepared to go very far in the Italian Question. None the less, his somewhat doctrinaire outlook stood revealed during the debate on the Queen's speech: for, starting from a criticism of the Conservatives as un- duly Austrophil and perhaps even as ready to take the Austrian side, he argued "that the honour of Britain demands that she should not assist in rivetting the chains of Italy, and her interest requires peace with all the Powers of Europe". It was soon to be brought home to him that only war could destroy the chains of Italy. When the Italian War was already at its height, he summed up his real sentiments to the no less ardent Italophil Hudson, in the phrase, "I don't wish to see either the Tedeschi or the Galli drinking the waters of the Po. Let the Italians govern their own affairs; that is my motto."[8] To the Queen he wrote: "The Emperor must either give independence to Italy, or be stigmatised as the betrayer of the Italian people."[9]

Russell took over the Foreign Office on 1 July, at a highly critical moment. The battle of Solferino, fought a week earlier, had ended in an Austrian retreat, and the fearful bloodshed and lack of doctors had a harrowing effect upon the nerves of Napoleon III, who was no soldier and had not inherited the brutal callousness of his uncle. More important still, it could not be regarded as a decisive victory, and the unconquered Quadrilateral still con- fronted the French Army with a truly formidable task and caused lively dis- sensions inside the French High Command. It was clear that Austria, in

pite of financial difficulties and the discontent so rife in Hungary, was by
no means at the end of her resources. Meanwhile the revolutionary movement in Italy itself was going too fast and too far for Napoleon: to free the
north from foreign rule was one thing, to unite the whole Peninsula was
quite another. The effect upon the Papal States was highly embarrassing,
and alarmed that French Catholic and Conservative opinion upon which
Napoleon so much relied. Above all, France's eastern frontier was by now
seriously denuded of troops, while the Prince Regent of Prussia mobilised
his whole army and began to sound London and St Petersburg as to possible
mediation. The Tsar and his Chancellor Prince Gorchakov viewed with
almost equal disquiet the ferment in Italy and the attitude adopted by
Prussia, and urged Paris to lose no time in making peace.

All this lay behind the proposals laid before the new British Foreign
Secretary by Persigny, who was now back at the French Embassy in London.
The rebirth of Italy was to be achieved through the cession of Lombardy
and Parma to Sardinia, the creation of an independent Venetia (with
Modena) under an Austrian Archduke, the restoration of the Grand Duchy
of Tuscany, and the placing of Romagna under a Piedmontese Governor:
the superstructure was to be provided by an Italian Confederation under
the presidency of the Pope. But Palmerston refused to be a party to any
such scheme, arguing that it would embroil Britain with both parties and
merely perpetuate existing quarrels: the Emperor might favour it out of
'jealousy of Sardinia and tenderness for the Pope: but we feel neither of these
mental affections and are not bound to adopt them".[10] To Persigny he was
no less frank: such a confederation would deliver Italy to Austria "bound
hand and foot": Piedmont alone would be "for a liberal system", the rest
would always favour absolutism, and there could be no agreement.[11] Russell
gave it as his opinion to the Russian Ambassador that such a confederation
would involve "either the total supremacy of Austria in Italy or a renewal of
the war".[12] None the less, both Palmerston and Russell were ready to give
to the Emperor "the moral support" which he asked, but the Queen strongly
objected and clung to a policy of strict neutrality.

THE PEACE OF VILLAFRANCA

It was in these circumstances, and again urged on by the Tsar, that
Napoleon decided upon a sudden overture to Francis Joseph, on whom the
horrors of the battlefield had made a scarcely less overwhelming impression.
On 11 July the two Emperors met at Villafranca, and Europe was suddenly
confronted with a treaty of peace which left the Italian question only partially
solved. Instead of handing over Lombardy to Victor Emanuel direct,

Francis Joseph ceded it to Napoleon and left him to complete the transfer
No reference was made to Parma, which thus remained in the hands of
Piedmont. Tuscany and Modena were to be restored, the Pope was to
head a new Italian Confederation, but the two Emperors were to urge upon
him immediate constitutional reform. Venetia remained in Austrian hands

The motives for concluding peace were almost equally strong on both
sides. Napoleon was swayed by fear of Prussia, doubts as to Italian unity
Russian and Ultramontane pressure, and failure to win British support; but
Francis Joseph was scarcely less eager to avert Prussian intervention, which
he felt might easily lead to Prussian predominance in Germany, and he also
had good grounds for fearing serious trouble in Hungary. The keenest
reaction was of course in Turin, and Hudson summed up the universal
opinion of the Italians in the phrase "We are betrayed." Napoleon, it is true,
in his proclamation to the army, declared that the aim of the war had been
attained: "Italy will for the first time become a nation....Henceforth
mistress of her own destinies, Italy can only blame herself if she does not
advance steadily in order and in liberty." He was probably quite sincere
when he declared, "To serve Italian independence I made war, against the
wish of Europe: as soon as the fate of my country seemed imperilled, I made
peace." Privately he explained to Cavour that he should have needed
300,000 men to continue the campaign, and he simply had not got them.[13]
But this was entirely unconvincing to the Italians, who only remembered
the catchword of "Alps to Adriatic". Victor Emanuel protested, and perforce submitted, but Cavour, after violent scenes, resigned office in a fury,
declaring "This treaty will never be executed: I will turn conspirator." At
one stroke Napoleon had extinguished all feeling of gratitude on the part of
the Italians towards France, and the events of the next twelve months were
to render this attitude permanent.

In London also the settlement was badly received by Cabinet, press and
public opinion. Granville describes Palmerston as "deeply mortified and
annoyed".[14] The Queen was thankful that the British Government had not
"fallen into the trap to ask from Austria, as friends and neutrals, concessions
which he (the Emperor) was ready to waive".[15] But Lord John made no
concealment of his desire that Italian soil should be freed "as soon as
possible from the presence of foreign troops, whether French or Austrian";[16]
he warned both Paris and Vienna against any foreign attempt to restore the
sovereigns of Tuscany and Modena: and he insisted on an Assembly in
Tuscany, "so that the wishes of the people in favour of autonomy may be
fully expressed".[17] He made no concealment of his disapproval of the
form which the new Confederation was to take, arguing that the Emperor of
Austria would "infallibly exercise a preponderating influence", under which

"the light of Italian independence will be quenched".[18] Thus "Italy for the Italians" was his openly proclaimed watchword. His steady encouragement to the Italians became more and more a prime factor in the European situation.

The Movement for Italian Unity

Nothing could now arrest the national movement. During the second half of August the Tuscan Assembly rejected the Grand Duke and voted for union with Piedmont, and its example was followed not only by Modena and Parma, but also on 7 September by the Romagna. To these events the London Cabinet gave its unequivocal backing, holding the annexation of the Duchies to be "unmixed good for Italy, for France, and for Europe". "Restoration", Lord John held, "was to return to that system of foreign interference which for upwards of forty years had been the misfortune of Italy and the danger of Europe." Victor Emanuel, despite such encouragement, hesitated as yet to follow Mazzini's behest and "place himself at the head of the national revolution"; but he ignored the protests of Pius IX, there was an open rupture between Turin and Rome, and Garibaldi was given a military command in Piedmont. Meanwhile Napoleon sought an escape from his embarrassments by referring the Italian question to an European Congress. Torn hither and thither by rival interests at home and abroad—the clerical campaign in favour of the Temporal Power, the fear of revolutionary infection, the fear of complications on the Rhine, the misgivings inspired by the emergence of a new Italian Kingdom—and feeling that he could not let England supplant him in the affections of the Italians, he did not challenge the view that French troops should be withdrawn, and he refused to share in any forcible restoration of the dispossessed sovereigns. Walewski had told Cowley in August that a Sardinian annexation of Tuscany was "an impossibility",[19] and in October, while disclaiming all idea of forcible restoration, hinted that "if a state of anarchy should arise" in Italy, France could not remain indifferent.[20] How fluid the Italian situation remained, and how little the British Government saw into the future, is shown by the fact that in September Palmerston accepted in principle a scheme for ending the Temporal Power and dividing the Papal States between Sardinia and Naples.[21] No wonder that there was acute friction between Queen and Premier: she was of course fully aware that Palmerston rather than Russell was the real driving force in foreign policy.

But the various projects of dynastic rearrangement discussed in Paris during the autumn were doomed to failure, above all by the resolute attitude of Lord John. When notified of them by Lord Cowley, he declined to give any answer at all, "for I should use terms of abhorrence and indignation too strong for eyes and ears diplomatic. The disposal of the Tuscans and Modenese as if they were so many firkins of butter, is somewhat too profligate."[22] He only gave his sanction to the Congress after long pressure from Paris, and sought to allay the Queen's anxiety by explaining that to refuse and "to leave France to settle with Austria the future condition of Italy would be to withdraw voluntarily from the first rank among the Powers of Europe".[23] The Queen on her side, by steady insistence, succeeded in deterring Russell from any commitments to Napoleon, who for a time played for an English alliance in the event of a fresh campaign against Austria. Doubtless in the hope of keeping him in this mood, Russell offered to accept a compromise by which only Parma and Carrara should go to Sardinia, while Tuscany and Modena would elect a new sovereign of their own, preferably from the House of Savoy. He assumed that in that case French troops would leave Rome and reforms would be made a reality by the Pope and the King of Naples. "In the independence of Italy," he added, "placed on solid and durable bases, Her Majesty's Government will recognise the germs of her future welfare and the sources of her permanent freedom."[24]

Late in November invitations to a Congress in Paris were issued, the three Italian Powers—Rome, Turin and Naples—being included, but the prospects of its success were not promoted by the selection of Cavour as Piedmontese delegate. That the Congress never met was above all due to the action of its chief promoter, Napoleon III, who late in December launched an anonymous but notoriously inspired pamphlet under the title of "Le Pape et le Congrès". Its main contentions—with which the Emperor did not conceal his agreement—were that the Pope's territorial power was a handicap to the exercise of his spiritual authority, that the States of the Church should therefore be restricted to the Eternal City and the Patrimony of St Peter, that the loss of the Romagna must be accepted as final, and that the Catholic Great Powers and the future Italian Confederation should share the responsibility for the Pope's defence. Such sentiments were generally approved in Britain, but raised a storm of indignation among the French Clericals, who accused the Emperor of having "burnt the Pope on the altar of the English alliance". Pius IX, instead of listening to Napoleon's appeal to "the inexorable logic of events" and to "the interests of European peace", unwisely engaged in polemics against the hypocrisy and contradictions of the anonymous writer. Austria demanded a disavowal of such views before she could attend the Congress, and thus extinguished its last spark of life. To the world at large Napoleon seemed, after some hesitation, to be reverting to his revolutionary past. Meanwhile Russell was the last man to show much sympathy for the Pope, whom he was ready to leave undisturbed in Rome itself, but frankly regarded as "an anachronism" which Italy had "outgrown ".[25] Colourless though he was, the French Premier, Count Walewski, could not stomach such a policy, and in January 1860 surrendered Foreign Affairs to the still more pliant and somewhat cynical Thouvenel. These changes and the active encouragement of Russell led Victor Emanuel to recall to favour the great Cavour, whose collaboration with Sir James Hudson was henceforth more intimate than ever. To the no small alarm of the Queen, Lord John now laid before Paris and Vienna "Four Points" for an Italian settlement.[26] France and Austria were to pledge themselves not to interfere in Italian affairs unless invited by all the Powers: Napoleon was to withdraw French troops from Rome by arrangement with the Pope: and the internal government of Venetia was not to be discussed by the Powers. Above all, France and Britain were to request Victor Emanuel not to send troops to Central Italy until each of the states affected could hold elections and vote upon their future destiny: if their decision was in favour of union with Sardinia, the Western Powers were not to oppose it. The Queen's speech on 24 January laid down as a foremost principle of British policy, that there should be "freedom from foreign interference by force of arms in the internal concerns" of "the People of Italy".

The Austrian Foreign Minister did not conceal his annoyance at the British attitude, but was not prepared to interfere in Italy by force of arms and made this quite clear to the French. Palmerston favoured an understanding with France and Sardinia for "common and united action", even at the risk of war with Austria: but for this neither Queen nor Cabinet was prepared, and Britain avoided binding commitments, while continuing to fan the flames of Italian popular feeling. Cavour, a stern realist for all his embitterment, consented, on his return to power, to enter upon negotiations for the cession of Savoy and Nice to France: for the Emperor, none too tactfully, explained to Victor Emanuel himself that Sardinia's expansion, not merely to the Adriatic but across the Apennines and to the very borders of Rome, lay quite outside the original programme, and that a revision of France's strategic frontiers was a necessary "measure of security". Cavour resigned himself to the inevitable, but with consummate skill made the decision dependent upon a plebiscite, and thus made it finally impossible for Napoleon or anyone else to oppose a similar method of decision in Central Italy. No time was wasted in entrenching still further the already accomplished facts: in March overwhelming plebiscites swept Tuscany and Emilia into the Sardinian fold, and already on 2 April Victor Emanuel opened the first "National Parliament" of modern Italy.

SAVOY AND NICE: BRITISH SUSPICIONS OF NAPOLEON

Napoleon on his side also had to act quickly if the booty was not to slip from his grasp. In his speech from the Throne on 1 March he announced to all Europe his claim to Savoy and Nice, and before the end of the month the treaty of cession was signed by Cavour. His alleged remark to the French Minister at Turin, "and now you are our accomplices!" was long believed, but is now abandoned as a picturesque myth.[27] Minor complications were caused by Garibaldi's rage at the abandonment of his birthplace and by Swiss protests regarding Northern Savoy: but in the case of both provinces the plebiscite on which Cavour had insisted went overwhelmingly in favour of France, and it only remained for Victor Emanuel to divert attention so far as possible from the sacrifice of the cradle of his race, by solemn state entries into Florence and Bologna.

Russell and Palmerston viewed the course of events with very mixed feelings. The former, while regretting that his views on Italy were not shared by Queen Victoria, went on to assure her that "whatever may be the consequence, the liberation of the Italian people from a foreign yoke is in the eyes of Lord Palmerston and Lord John Russell an increase of freedom and happiness at which, as well-wishers to mankind, they cannot but rejoice".[28] It is hardly surprising that the Queen should have resented this tone and complained to the Prime Minister.

On the question of Savoy, however, and its bearing upon Franco-British relations, there was much more agreement. "If Victor Emanuel sells his inheritance of Savoy to obtain Tuscany", so Russell wrote to Hudson as early as 31 January 1860, "he will be disgraced in the eyes of Europe",[29] and even after Cavour had signed the Treaty of Turin Russell maintained his attitude of protest. But he also argued before the Cabinet that "the reasons which are given for the frontier of the Alps apply more strongly to the frontier of the Rhine, inasmuch as the German armies will at all times be much more formidable than the Piedmontese, Lombards and Tuscans". While Cavour himself yielded, while Austria refused to see any distinction between the cession of Tuscany to Piedmont and of Savoy to France, while Russia saw no danger to the general balance of power, Russell openly declared in the House of Commons that "it will produce a great deal of distrust all over Europe", and created a sensation by hinting at the possibility of "other acts of aggression" on the part of "a nation as warlike as the French" (26 March). Worse even than these tactless and doctrinaire opinions was the attitude of Palmerston himself, who told Count Flahaut to "repeat to your Emperor Lord John's speech and tell him it expresses my own opinions". "Mais c'est la guerre", replied Flahaut, all aghast. "Eh bien," said Palmerston, "si c'est la guerre, c'est la guerre. Que voulez-vous? Nous sommes préparés et nous l'attendons de pied ferme." In these remarks all the old recklessness reappears, but beyond all doubt in a calculated form: for he had no desire for war with France and to the end of his life retained a certain partiality for Louis Napoleon. In a note to Cowley only a few days later he admitted that "we had no ground for war and no sufficient reason for war about Nice and Savoy".

Palmerston, it is clear, only reflected the suspicious mentality of Victorian England towards her nearest neighbours, and the volume of feeling which had been growing throughout the winter of 1859–60. In the previous November he confided to Russell his growing distrust of Napoleon, and only a little later he told the Duke of Somerset: "I have watched the French Emperor narrowly, and have studied his character and conduct. You may rely upon it that at the bottom of his heart there rankles a deep and inextinguishable desire to humble and punish England, and to avenge if he can the many humiliations, political, naval and military, which since the beginning of the century England has, by herself and by her allies, inflicted upon France."[30] By the autumn of 1860 he had reverted to a more moderate view, which clearly reflects his riper judgment. "The Emperor and those about him", he wrote to Cowley, "fancy we are making a coalition to attack France. We should be insane to do so. What would be the object of such an attack, and what possible hopes would anyone have of success? France is an essential element in the Balance of Power in Europe, and I may say, in the world. All we want is that France should be content with what she is, and should not take up the schemes and policy of the first Napoleon."[31] Cowley on his side, though far from edified at many of the Emperor's actions, had not hesitated to report home: "I defy anyone to listen to the Emperor when speaking of the English alliance, without the conviction that the preservation of it is that which he has most at heart....His *amour-propre* is wounded by our suspicions of his intentions."[32] The accuracy of this view is abundantly confirmed by Napoleon's attitude to the Indian Mutiny, by his eager cooperation in Syria and China and above all by his welcome to Cobden and his personal interest in the Commercial Treaty (see *infra*, p. 414).

It would not, indeed, be difficult to show that while Napoleon's views on Britain scarcely fluctuated, Palmerston's views on France were in perpetual flux. In September 1859 Russell, presumably not without consulting Palmerston, had told the Queen that "there never was a time when it was less expedient to fetter this country by prospective engagements".[33] Yet by December they were already contemplating a French alliance, in the idea that fear of it would "prevent Austria from disturbing the peace of Europe":[34] and in the first days of 1860 Palmerston himself presented to the

Cabinet a memorandum advocating such an alliance, with special regard to the Italian Question.* But his colleagues were divided and Parliament showed itself so unmistakably hostile to any such entanglement that within a month the Prime Minister was assuring it, with all the emphasis of a guilty conscience, that the Government was "totally free from any engagement whatever with any foreign Power upon the affairs of Italy".[35]

Throughout this period, as a decade earlier, the Queen had grown increasingly restive at the attitude of her Ministers, and this time in particular of Lord John. Her rigid interpretation of "non-intervention" would have ruled out even the offering of friendly advice, to say nothing of mediation: and this, Palmerston very plausibly argued, would have reduced Britain "to the rank of a third-class European state".[36] Doctrinaire as ever, Russell must needs seek to convince the Queen that his attitude to the Italian Duchies was based on "the doctrines of the Revolution of 1688", by which "all power held by Sovereigns may be forfeited by misconduct, and every nation is the judge of its own internal government".[37] The Queen refused to admit any connection between the two things and appealed to the Prime Minister to restrain his Foreign Secretary from "covert insinuation" and a lack of due respect.[38] But Lord John remained incorrigible, and after the Sicilian revolt he assured her that "the best writers on international law consider it a merit to overthrow a tyrannical government", and received the feminine but pertinent answer that "if William III had made England a province of Holland, he would not have received the applause Lord John quotes".[39]

In England the French claim to Savoy and Nice, Thouvenel's unwise reference to the theory of "natural frontiers", and above all the tortuous methods employed by Napoleon to achieve this aim, and the no less tortuous tactics of Cavour in denying everything to London and in the same breath bargaining with Paris—all this caused intense, and doubtless exaggerated, annoyance and alarm. Lord Grey in the House of Lords voiced a very widespread opinion when he refused to believe in a Franco-Sardinian compact, because "it would be difficult to find in the annals of the world a case of more flagrant iniquity", and because "if such a principle were to be established, no Government in Europe is safe for a day".[40] Napoleon on his side was cut to the quick by British criticism and lost his temper to Lord Cowley, in front of other diplomats, though he afterwards made a handsome apology. What really saved the situation in the face of an aggressive press and a jumpy

* Printed *in extenso* by Ashley, II, 174–80. It contains the phrase, "There is no ground for imputing to him [Napoleon] bad faith in his conduct towards us as allies." Clarendon's estimate of Palmerston's alliance policy is to be found in a very frank letter to the Duchess of Manchester: "he would place England in the honourable position of canister to the Imperial tail" (Maxwell, *op. cit.* II, 206).

public opinion, were the parallel negotiations of Cobden in Paris (see *infra*, p. 414), fortified by Gladstone's memorable Budget reforms and their introduction to Parliament by a speech of truly European calibre. John Bright also contributed to the *détente*, by insisting that Savoy was no direct British interest and insignificant compared with Franco-British friendship, and by warning the Government against making itself "the common scold of Europe": but as so often, his pacifism overshot the mark and caused offence in many quarters.* Behind all the sound and fury of British protest there was also the highly practical fact, freely admitted by Lord John himself in debate, that Austria regarded the annexation of Savoy to France as "at all events not worse" than that of Tuscany to Sardinia, while the Tsar had declared that Victor Emanuel was "free to give away his own province" and Napoleon free to receive it.⁴¹ In other words, Britain would have had no allies in an attempt to make France desist.

GARIBALDI AND THE REVOLUTION

The excitement engendered in England by the plebiscite was ere long diverted into fresh channels. Already in April the smouldering discontent in Sicily burst into open insurrection, and on 7 May Garibaldi and his immortal "Thousand", after preparations to which the Government of Turin discreetly closed its eyes, landed at Marsala, and by his daring tactics speedily freed the whole of Sicily from Bourbon rule and drove the incompetent Francis II on to the defensive. The French and British Governments were equally outdistanced by events. On more than one occasion Russell had sent to the young King outspoken and urgent advice "to adopt a liberal system of internal policy, as the only chance of averting a political convulsion and of maintaining himself and his dynasty on the throne". "If he supports [his evil counsellors] and places himself under their guidance, it requires not much foresight to predict that the Bourbon dynasty will cease to reign at Naples, by whatever combination, regal or republican, it may be replaced."⁴² Russell's brother-in-law Henry Elliott, since May 1859 British Minister at Naples,† had not failed to press this advice upon

---

* "I say, 'Perish Savoy'—though Savoy, I believe, will not perish and will not suffer—rather than that we...should involve the government of this country with the people and government of France...." Lord John Manners reminded Bright in the House that this line of argument would justify French annexation of Belgium or the Rhine provinces (2 March 1860—*Hansard*, CLVI, 2170; *ibid.* 26 March, CLVII, 1265). It is perhaps worth recording that Monckton Milnes defended annexation, on the ground that the people of Savoy had always represented the opinions of the Government of France, "and had very little sympathy with the struggles in which the people of Italy were engaged".

† He succeeded William Temple, who was Palmerston's brother; Minto was Russell's father-in-law. Britain was represented in Rome by Lord John's brilliant nephew Odo Russell, afterwards famous as Ambassador in Berlin.

Francis, though of course without the slightest effect. When, however, misrule ended, as he had predicted, in revolution, Russell was far from regarding the union of Northern and Southern Italy as either desirable or feasible: and his nervousness was increased by a persistent rumour that France was preparing to extract Liguria and Sardinia from Victor Emanuel as the price of annexation in the south. Even the ardent Hudson was at first doubtful,[43] and favoured the transference of the Crown of the Two Sicilies to a cadet of the House of Savoy. But Garibaldi's capture of Palermo led Hudson to write of "the tidal wave of unity" and to regard Victor Emanuel as the only man who could save Naples from "anarchy and civil war, plunder and massacre, a licentious foreign soldiery and a degraded mob". Moreover, he argued, annexation was certainly "less prejudicial to British interests than the anarchy of Sicily and Naples", which might easily end in France placing "a creature of her own" on the Neapolitan throne. Palmerston and Russell seem to have been agreed in theory that the independence of the Two Sicilies coincided with the interests of Britain as a naval Mediterranean Power, but they rightly regarded the Bourbon dynasty as impossible and gradually came to regard a united Italy as "the best arrangement, with a view to the general balance of power in Europe".[44] Francis II, it should be added, had stubbornly declined the suggestion of Cavour that he should ally himself with Piedmont and introduce constitutional government at home: and he even appears to have contemplated the occupation of Umbria and the Marches, in order to prevent the spread of subversive ideas from the north.

At an early date public subscriptions were raised in England to assist the Sicilian insurgents, and indignant protests were lodged in the House of Commons, the Irish members Henessy and Maguire demanding intervention by the Attorney-General, to prevent any active assistance being rendered by British subjects to "the filibustering expedition of Garibaldi". Lord John, however, was entirely unabashed, referred to his early association with a committee formed to assist the Greek insurrection, and reminded the House that "we had once a great filibuster who landed in the month of November 1688", round whom "all the people of England flocked". "Our sympathies and the judgment of history will distinguish between the cases of the filibuster and felon, and that of the hero and patriot."[45] He flatly declined to prosecute on such an issue.

If however Russell had made up his mind, Palmerston would seem to have been in a fresh mood of opportunism, for he told Russell that he had "no strong objection to the union of all Italy and Sicily into one monarchy": and yet he was ready to assure King Francis that "our desire is to maintain his dynasty and the integrity of his dominions, but that we cannot be of any active assistance to him unless he will at once alter his system of government". In that case Britain should give him naval assistance and "political support".[46] This, it is true, was too much for Russell, who could not "stomach defending Bombino": but the whole incident shows how unstable and improvised Britain's Italian policy was.

Napoleon on his side felt gravely embarrassed by the Sicilian enterprise, and his Foreign Minister, Thouvenel, put forward in all seriousness the suggestion that the French and British Fleets should combine to police the Straits of Messina and warn Garibaldi against transferring his operations to the mainland. Russell was on the point of accepting the proposal laid before him by Persigny, but was held back at the very last moment by a dramatic appeal of Sir James Lacaita, acting in the name of Cavour, and based his refusal upon the principle of non-intervention.[47] This is one of the classic examples of amateur and improvised methods in diplomacy. Napoleon, who was becoming involved in the Syrian Question, and henceforth sought more and more to restrict his active share in the Italian problem to his unhappy Roman commitment, speedily gave up any idea of acting alone. Already on 28 July Garibaldi had reached Messina; on 20 August he successfully crossed the Straits; on 7 September he entered Naples in triumph; and the King, betrayed by his nearest kinsmen and incapable of organising the defence of his capital, was soon a fugitive in the strong fortress of Gaeta. Meanwhile Cavour had been playing a perfidious double game, determined by speculations as to what course France and Austria might adopt. He himself defined the problem before him as that of "helping the revolution, but in such a way that it may appear in the eyes of Europe to have been a spontaneous act".[48] To D'Azeglio he was brutally frank and admitted that "if we did for ourselves what we are doing for Italy, we should be great knaves".[49] "If once the Italian flag flies at Taranto, it means the end of the Temporal Power and the liberation of Venice", he wrote to Ricasoli as early as 27 June:[50] in other words, Palermo was to him a mere stepping-stone to the richer prizes of Rome and Venice. And so the Redshirts had the cryptic support of the Turin Government; Admiral Persano was held in readiness to help them in case of need; Victor Emanuel's emissary to Garibaldi carried with him an open veto, for the press of the world, and a secret encouragement to disregard it, for the hero's own guidance. But Cavour took alarm at Garibaldi's dictatorial methods, feared that the revolutionary movement might easily take an anti-monarchical turn, and convinced himself that the only sure remedy was to occupy Umbria and the Marches before Garibaldi could get there, and that Napoleon would not intervene so long as Rome itself and its French garrison were not attacked.

We shall be grumbled at, he said, but not too much: and the calculation proved correct.

Cavour and Victor Emanuel, then, decided upon speedy and drastic action. A quarrel was picked with the Pope, on the ground of the very inadequate force of mercenaries which Lamoricière had been enlisting for his service. Only 24 hours were allowed for a reply, and then the Sardinian forces swiftly overran Papal territory: Urbino, Perugia, Spoleto, and by the end of the month Ancona, fell before them. Cavour summoned Parliament to ratify the new annexations: and this was followed by the King's triumphal progress to Naples, which took the wind out of Garibaldi's sails and checkmated the designs of Mazzini and the extremists. Preparations for a plebiscite in Papal and Neapolitan territory were rapidly pushed forward and ended in an overwhelming vote for union.

Meanwhile the attitude of the Powers caused some anxiety. Prussia entered a protest against Victor Emanuel's breach of international law, Russia and Spain recalled their Ministers from Turin, Austria began to move troops in Venetia and was only held back from further actions by the advice which Tsar Alexander and Prince Regent William administered to Francis Joseph at their meeting in Warsaw on 22 October. Much more decisive was the inaction of Napoleon III, who expressed anger, "but in a very loving manner",[51] and who under no circumstances could have taken action such as might have undone his recent work for Italy.

Russell's Despatch of 27 October

If Napoleon's restraining influence upon the Tsar did much to avert further complications in Europe, it is hardly too much to assert that the scales were turned by the decisive intervention of Lord John Russell, in the name of the British Government.[52] On 27 October, entirely on his own initiative,[53] he wrote a despatch to Sir James Hudson which was immediately published and deserved the sensation which it aroused. After alluding to Russian and Prussian indignation at Piedmont's action, he laid it down that for the British Government the essential question was; were the people of Italy justified in asking assistance of the King of Sardinia to relieve them from Governments with which they were dissatisfied, and was he justified in helping the Roman and Neapolitan peoples? In his view, the misgovernment was so great that the overthrow of their rulers was felt to be "the necessary preliminary to all improvements", and united government for Italy was the sole means of securing "independence of foreign control". "The people in question", he added, "are the best judges of their own affairs", and reinforced his arguments by quoting the great jurist Vattel's approval of Dutch support to William of Orange's invasion of England. It was not true that the peoples were attached to the King of Naples or to the Pope; there was "universal disaffection". This led to a peroration eminently characteristic both of its author and of his whole school of political thought:

The Italian Revolution has been conducted with singular temper and for-bearance. The subversion of existing power has not been followed, as is too often the case, by an outburst of popular vengeance. The extreme views of the demo-crats have nowhere prevailed. Public opinion has checked the excesses of the public triumph. The venerated forms of constitutional monarchy have been associated with the name of a Prince who represents an ancient and glorious dynasty....Her Majesty's Government can see no sufficient ground for the severe censure of Austria, France, Prussia and Russia. Her Majesty's Govern-ment will turn their eyes rather to the gratifying prospect of a people building up the edifice of their liberties and consolidating the work of this independence, amid the sympathy and good wishes of Europe.

This was no longer a diplomatic document, but a political pronunciamento of explosive force. Vitzthum, the Saxon Minister in London, one of the best informed of contemporary observers, was entitled to regard it as unique in the annals of diplomacy: and it is interesting to find him also treating it as a complete reversal of all previous oral and written assurances, prompted by exigencies of party politics. Meanwhile Brunnov, the Russian Ambassador, roundly denounced it as "polissonnerie" rather than "diplomacy".[54] Certain it is that Britain's alignment saved the situation for Cavour and gave the Italian cause that moral backing before Europe which his none too scrupulous policy had obscured. Feeling had grown steadily more intense since the beginning of the struggle. There were many in England who shared the opinion expressed by Malmesbury to Cowley:* "That Europe should be deluged with blood for the personal ambition of an Italian attorney and a tambourmajor, like Cavour and his master, is intolerable." But with the appearance of Garibaldi on the stage, and especially after his attack on the Papal States, feeling was still more keenly divided: to some he was a lawless and godless brigand, yet to the vast majority he stood forth as a true hero of romance. It would be ridiculous to deny that indignation against gross Papal misgovernment was coloured by Protestant prejudices (and Lord John was a particularly ardent opponent of Romanist claims), or that fear of French designs in the Mediterranean supplied an added incentive to Lord John's action. But with the perspective of 70 years we can unhesitatingly

* February 1859—*The Paris Embassy*, p. 175. It is worth noting that Russell had warned Cavour on 31 August that "Great Britain has interests in the Adriatic which Her Majesty's Government must watch with careful attention" (cf. Martin, v, 228).

affirm that Russell had most of the British nation enthusiastically behind him as he wrote, and that zeal for United Italy was one of the consuming passions of mid-Victorian liberalism. It was compounded of many qualities —on the one hand a somewhat naïve satisfaction at Italian imitation of constitutional and parliamentary principles, on the other a personal love of Italy, her artistic and literary traditions. Doubtless at times this was a mere superficial fashion, stimulated by the growing habit of travel among the wealthier classes: yet it needs but little reflection to realise the extent to which Italian traditions permeated every aspect of English intellectual life in the middle of last century. The accumulation of Italian art treasures, the vogue of pre-Raphaelite painting, the pontifical exposition, but also the seductive eloquence, of Ruskin; the immense popularity of Italian opera, from Donizetti to Verdi, maintained by a long succession of virtuosi—all this was as nothing compared with the fact that all the great English poets from the days of Keats, Shelley and Byron onwards (with the one signal exception of Wordsworth) were deeply imbued with Italian influences and sympathised in varying degrees with the national cause. The Brownings, Tennyson, Clough, Landor, all repaid in a living present their debt to Italy's past: Swinburne went farther than any in his *Songs before Sunrise* and in his homage to the revolution: and a special niche must be reserved for Meredith's *Vittoria* and Addington Symonds' *Renaissance* at a slightly later date.

It is highly characteristic of Russell and Palmerston, that they should have sent off this memorable despatch without consulting the Cabinet. The Queen and Prince Albert, already profoundly alarmed at the Government's Italian policy, and reduced to the same state of nervous resentment into which Palmerston had driven them in the years 1848–51, now protested very vigorously when Russell proposed to send another despatch—this time addressed to all the Powers—expressing "the hope that Rome and Venetia, from their Italian nationality, will soon share in the freedom and good government of the rest of Italy". There was unanswerable logic in the Queen's comment, that this "can only be understood as a declaration on our part that we wish to see them share the annexation to Sardinia, after that of the Two Sicilies shall have been completed".[55] Russell actually desired to add that "if any other Power should attempt forcible interference, Her Majesty's Government will hold themselves free to act in such a manner as the rights of nations, the independence of Italy and the interests of Europe may seem to require". Despite his genuine desire for peace, he apparently failed to see that this was provocative in two directions, and indeed meaningless unless he was ready to risk war with Austria, and moreover, that such language was a direct incentive to adventure on the part of

Cavour. It may fairly be doubted whether Russell himself foresaw the explosive character of his own eloquence.

The despatch of 27 October, however, was amply sufficient. In the words of Mr Trevelyan, it was "greeted with ecstasies of joy by the Italian people": and Hudson reported that when Cavour first read it, "he shouted, rubbed his hands, jumped up, sat down again, then began to think, and when he looked up, tears were standing in his eyes. Behind your despatch he saw the Italy of his dreams, the Italy of his hopes, the Italy of his policy." The most realist of modern statesmen expressed overwhelming gratitude to the most sentimental of Liberals, and his trusted agent Villamarina said that the despatch was "worth more than 100,000 men".[56] Lord John's nephew Odo, already making his mark as a diplomatist in the tense atmosphere of Papal Rome, wrote home as follows: "Ever since your famous despatch...you are blessed night and morning by twenty millions of Italians.... Thousands copied it from each other, to carry it to their homes and weep over it for joy and gratitude in the bosom of their families, away from brutal mercenaries and greasy priests."[57]

Europe having renounced the idea of intervention, the Italians were not slow to push their advantage. The Papal mercenaries were speedily scattered to the winds, and Lamoricière, when he surrendered Ancona, was already a general without an army. The King of Naples announced his intention of "holding out alone against all the forces of the European revolution":[58] but when his last fortress of Gaeta fell in February 1861, the Bourbon dynasty faded into the obscurity of well-merited exile. Russell's active share in the Italian Revolution may be said to have ended in the same month, when he wrote to Garibaldi, begging him to refrain from further war: the Queen objected to his writing at all, but Palmerston gave his sanction, and action from such a quarter undoubtedly had a deterrent effect.[59] A French garrison continued to hold Rome for the Pope, but towards this policy— dictated to Napoleon by his ultramontane commitments at home—Palmerston was something less than unsympathetic, testily asking Russell why a portion of the Italian people should be doomed to misery on the theory that the Pope "would not open the gates of paradise if he had not the power to make some little hell upon earth".[60]

That even Russell only advanced very haltingly and without any perception of the Italian problem as a whole, is sufficiently proved by the fact that as late as 5 February 1861 he disclaimed, in the name of the Government, any wish to prevent the return of the Grand Duke of Tuscany or the Duke of Modena, and added that "in our opinion the happiness of Italy would be better secured by the establishment of two Kingdoms of Italy than of one". That this was not a mere momentary aberration, is shown by his letter of 25 August 1859 to Corbett, the Minister to Tuscany: "I dare say the dreamers wish to unite Naples and Sicily, and make a kingdom of the whole of Italy. But that is wild and foolish. It would make a despotism instead of a free government, an unwieldy power instead of a compact one, and it would increase tenfold the European difficulties."[61] To Russell the grant of a constitution to Naples might still have saved the situation, and he flatly condemned any idea of a Sardinian attack upon Venice. His main theme, as ever, was the right of the Italians to decide their own form of government. On the same day in the House of Lords, Lord Derby, as leader of the Conservatives, expressed "very serious doubts" about the "dream of Italian unity" and spoke of Victor Emanuel's "flagrant violation of International law". He also doubted "the good faith and discretion of the Emperor of the French", but added that there could be no greater calamity "than the rupture or dissolution of the friendly alliance of Britain and France".[62] It was left for Gladstone to sum up the Italian controversy in the closing debate of 7 March, when he spoke of Russell's Italian policy as "stamped with approval throughout the body of the people of England, from the greatest to the least": but even he might have been at a loss to define that policy. He was certainly to the point in claiming that "it is the Powers hostile to Italy who, in the mysterious counsels of Providence, have been the means of compelling the people to forget those local feelings with which they were strongly imbued", and to merge "every jealousy, every petty tradition...in one desire" for Unity. "The miseries of Italy have been the danger of Europe. The consolidation of Italy, her restoration to national life, will...add to the general peace and welfare of the civilised world a new and solid guarantee."*

None the less, though Russell saw the issue of unity much less clearly than that of liberty, he certainly believed himself to be "directed by a consistent principle", and in a revealing despatch to Lord Cowley maintained that British policy had always followed the same line since the days of Castlereagh, instancing Spanish America, Greece and Belgium. "Britain", he argued, had "uniformly withheld her consent to acts of intervention by force to alter the internal government of other nations", but no less "uniformly gave her countenance, and if necessary her aid, to consolidate the *de facto* governments which arose in Europe or America." The reasons which prompted Canning or Palmerston now applied no less strongly to Central Italy.[63] It may seem a left-handed compliment if the apologist of a leading British statesman can describe his share in the achievement of

---

* *Hansard*, CLXI, 1565–79. It was in this debate that the Irish M.P., Maguire, spoke of Victor Emanuel as "one of the stolidest stupids in Europe", who had "combined with this stupidity the morality of a moss-trooper and the temperament of a he-goat" (*ibid.* p. 1599).

Italian Unity as "his one resplendent triumph".[64] But from the wider European angle his contribution may fairly be regarded as decisive. The problems of Rome and Venice still remained unsolved, but the consolidation of Italy henceforth depended above all upon the Italians themselves. Mazzini and Garibaldi had achieved their tasks as forerunners, and the development of constitutional liberties now lay in the hands of a statesman of rare genius, and of a sovereign who appreciated and used him to the full. The premature death of Cavour in June 1861 was a disaster whose full effects have only become apparent in our own day, but not all the disillusionment and misery of the south, not all the obstacles to Cavour's ideal of "a free Church in a free State" could arrest that process of "growing together" from which United Italy was to emerge within a decade.

In the House of Commons Palmerston paid an eloquent tribute to the greatest of all Italian liberals and democrats. "We have seen under his guidance a people who was supposed to have become torpid in the enjoyment of luxury...rising from the slumber of ages with the power of a giant refreshed, breaking that spell by which they had so long been bound, and displaying on great occasions the courage of heroes, the sagacity of statesmen, the wisdom of philosophers, and obtaining for themselves that unity of political existence which for centuries had been denied them."[65]

COBDEN, NAPOLEON AND THE TREATY OF COMMERCE

It is perhaps not surprising that the tortuous policy pursued by Napoleon in the Italian question, and above all in the affair of Nice and Savoy and towards the Roman See, should have aroused keen contemporary suspicion on the other side of the Channel: and yet nothing is more certain to-day than that friendship with Britain was a cardinal aim of the Emperor throughout his reign. The classic proof of this is to be found in the Commercial Treaty of 1860.

French opinion had been wedded to extreme protectionist views ever since the days of Colbert and the First Napoleon, and though under Louis Philippe French industry had rapidly expanded and was now less dependent upon artificial support, the bulk of the industrialists, and especially in such towns as Lille and Rouen, were hostile to any idea of change. Napoleon himself, however, had Free Trade leanings, and was inspired with the ambition to improve the conditions of the working class by cheapening the cost of the more necessary articles. His views were known to a few enlightened theorists on both sides of the Channel, and when John Bright appealed to the Government to extend trade intercourse with France instead of piling up armaments against her, Michel Chevalier, a Professor at the Collège de

France, and the doyen of French Free Traders, wrote to Cobden to urge practical action in this sense. They met soon afterwards at a congress in Bradford, and it was decided that Cobden, during the winter which he was about to spend in Paris, should carry the discussions a stage further. Cobden had recently declined office under Palmerston, but was of course on not uncordial terms with both him and Russell, and consulted them before leaving London. But the decisive factor was his meeting with Gladstone, who as Chancellor of the Exchequer was preparing the most famous of his great Budgets: and the two men found themselves in enthusiastic agreement as to the possibility of combining a further extension of free trade at home and concessions to France such as would promote friendship between the two countries.

Cobden obtained an audience with Napoleon, found him an apt pupil in economic theory, and was sent by him to continue the discussions with Fould and other Ministers, whom Cobden found timorous and none too well informed. But the real decision lay with the Emperor himself, as Rouher did not hesitate to confess to him: and when once Cobden received official powers from London and found Lord Cowley magnanimously ready to co-operate,* and as sane and tactful in this as in the more beaten tracks of diplomacy, the negotiations advanced rapidly, and all the agitation of the French cotton-spinners and other manufacturers proved of no avail. Cobden showed great wisdom in resisting Napoleon's passing idea of combining a commercial agreement with that treaty of alliance for settling Italian affairs which for a brief moment caught the fancy of Palmerston.

The Treaty of Commerce, which was signed on 23 January 1860, has quite rightly been described as "one of the landmarks in the fiscal history of Europe in the nineteenth century".[66] Its main provisions were, on the British side, the abolition of duties on French silk, articles of fashion and many other manufactured goods and a reduction of the duty on wine and spirits: on the French side, the fixing of an *ad valorem* duty of 30 per cent on British textiles, iron and steel—to be reduced after three years to 25 per cent—and the reduction of duty on British coal to 3 fr. 60 per ton. Napoleon, in a letter published in the official *Moniteur*, had stressed the need for removing undue restrictions on trade and agriculture, denounced prohibition as a worn-out system, and placed the welfare of the working class in the forefront of his argument: and he was able to override the hostility of the Corps Législatif. For six months longer Cobden laboured in Paris as chief

---

* Cobden's own word, see Morley, pp. 290, 311. Cowley's broad and generous outlook is reflected in his letter of 23 January 1860 to Gladstone, hoping that the treaty "may prove the keystone to uninterrupted peace between the British and French nations.... It will be to you and Cobden on the one side and to a few brave and enlightened spirits on the other, that the gratitude of posterity will be due" (*The Paris Embassy*, p. 195).

ommissioner for working out supplementary conventions, which were at ast signed in the winter of 1860. In the meantime the Treaty was keenly lebated in Parliament, and opposed by men as different as Disraeli and Graham: but all objections were triumphantly borne down by the arguments of Gladstone, who proved that "at a small loss of revenue we had gained a great extension of trade".[67] His advocacy of the Treaty in the Budget speech of 1860 was one of his greatest oratorical efforts, of which Lord George Bentinck said, "I believe that fellow could persuade me to eat dead dog every day of the week."[68] To quote Gladstone's words on another occasion: "A treaty with France is even in itself a measure of no small consequence: but that which gives to a measure of that kind its highest value is its tendency to produce beneficial imitation in other quarters. It is the fact that, in concluding the Treaty, we did not give to one a privilege which we withheld from another, but that our Treaty with France was in fact a treaty with the world, and wide are the consequences which engagements of that kind carry in their train."[69] In other words, while trade between France and Britain was more than trebled during the next two decades, it was far more important that the Treaty served as a landmark for the abandonment of protection by Britain and the adoption of a new system of moderate duties by France. If it may be admitted that the theories of free trade which underlay the action of Cobden or of Gladstone were unduly dogmatic, it is but just to add that they were also swayed by farsighted and statesmanlike views of general policy, in strong contrast to the pettiness and suspicions of Palmerston and Russell. Gladstone realised that for the unreasoning panic into which the Government had whipped the country, "the Treaty of Commerce was the only sedative. It was in fact a counter-irritant, and it aroused the sense of commercial interest to counteract the war passion. It was and is my opinion, that the choice lay between the Cobden Treaty and not the certainty, but the high probability, of war with France."[70]

THE VOLUNTEER MOVEMENT

There is an extraordinary contrast between these negotiations, ardently approved and furthered by Napoleon himself, and the almost pathological distrust of his motives entertained by ministers, re-echoed in the press, and periodically sweeping over the House of Commons. These attacks both incensed and wounded the Emperor, and perhaps more particularly the crude language of Mr Roebuck, who accused "this man" of "a disgraceful and dishonourable act", begged the House not to be "base enough to truckle to an Emperor", but to "maintain the character, dignity and honour of

England ".* Next day, at a social function, Napoleon's annoyance vented itself upon Lord Cowley, in presence of the Russian Ambassador,[71] and for a moment there were highly disagreeable possibilities. But only a few days later Napoleon wrote the frankest possible apology to Lord Cowley, ascribing his outburst " to the pain I feel at seeing the animosities and prejudices of another age springing up afresh in England ". At the same time he promised that he would " always continue to do everything in my power to cement more and more closely the alliance of the two nations, for it is my profound conviction that their harmonious action is indispensable for the good of civilisation, and that their antagonism would be a calamity to all ".[72] In the previous summer Cowley, who knew his psychology better than most people, had already reported home: " I defy anyone to listen to the Emperor speaking of the English alliance, without the conviction that the preservation of it is that which he has most at heart.... His *amour-propre* is wounded by our suspicions of his intentions."[73] Even more illuminating is a passage in a later memorandum of Cowley: " I do not believe the Emperor to have any fixed policy at all. He has certain ideas and desires floating in his mind, which turn up as circumstances seem favourable, but a man of less decision of character, of more indolent disposition, or more inclined to wait upon events, instead of creating them, I never came across."[74]

The Treaty negotiations served to allay the acerbities of the moment, but the press fanned public alarm, and the new Volunteer Movement kindled the enthusiasm of the Victorian middle class. By midsummer 1860, when the Queen held great reviews in Hyde Park and at Holyrood, their numbers had already swollen to 130,000, and Wimbledon rose to fame as the centre of the National Riflemen. Behind the scenes the Queen and the Prince Consort were consumed with anxiety, complaining that Cowley was "not alive to the enormous crimes" which Napoleon was "meditating against Europe". Clarendon confided to the Ambassador his impression that the Prince "seems demented", having written "a diatribe against patching up the alliance with France":† and there is no doubt that the Royal couple had since Villafranca radically changed their views upon Napoleon. Meanwhile, more publicly, there was a trial of strength between Palmerston, who encouraged the armament campaign of *The Times*, and was always somewhat indifferent to ideas of economy, and Gladstone, who shared the views of Bright and Cobden on France, and resented the havoc which his chief's projects would play with budget plans. In the middle distance Disraeli, as

* *Hansard*, CLVI, 2248–50. In the Italian debate of 7 March 1861 Roebuck reaffirmed his lack of faith in Napoleon III and at the same time his scepticism as to a United Italy (*ibid.* CXLI, 1607).

† *The Paris Embassy*, pp. 207–10. Cowley "found extreme bitterness at Windsor: the Prince called the Emperor a 'walking lie'" (Maxwell, *op. cit.* II, 207).

Leader of the Opposition, for all his friendship for France and even Napoleon, felt that events might occur such as would render "war a necessity for Louis Napoleon",[75] and therefore accepted rearmament. Sir Charles Napier, now in the House of Commons, made himself the mouthpiece of popular alarm and the galloper of Palmerston.

On 23 July, then, Palmerston brought in a bill for voting what was then the enormous sum of £11,000,000 on the fortifications of Portsmouth, Plymouth, Chatham and Cork. With his habitual preference for a frontal attack, he spoke at the outset of "a horizon charged with clouds which betoken the possibility of a tempest....In the main I am speaking of our immediate neighbours across the Channel, and there is no disguising it." He went on to extol the "great value" of the Commercial Treaty, and claimed to be speaking "in no unfriendly spirit": but the mischief was already done, and he gave added offence some weeks later by a futile reference to the "most painful impression" produced in England by the Savoy affair, as infringing the rights of Switzerland under the Treaty of Vienna.[76] Futile, because he had long since abandoned, if he had ever entertained, any idea of resisting the *fait accompli* of Savoy, and was therefore, as *Punch* clearly saw, merely brandishing an ineffectual birch at someone long since outside his jurisdiction. Well might Rouher express his indignation to Cobden, and Cobden protest to Cowley.

Napoleon sought to allay British suspicions by a letter to his Ambassador in London, intended for Palmerston; but he despatched it without consulting his own Ministers, and he also took the unconventional step of publishing it in the press, thereby underlining the difference between British and French institutions in the 'sixties. Its main tenor, to be conveyed "in terms the most unqualified", was "that since the Peace of Villafranca I have had but one thought, one object—to inaugurate a new era of peace and to live on the best of terms with all my neighbours and especially with England". He begged British statesmen to "lay aside pitiful jealousies and unfounded distrust. Let us deal frankly and loyally with one another like honest men, as we are, and not like rogues, each bent on cheating the other."[77] He pursued the same line in his New Year letter to the Queen and this time obtained a gracious assent to his view that "l'Europe est bien agitée, mais tant que l'Angleterre et la France s'entendent, le mal pourra se localiser".[78]

None the less, panic continued in England, and Gladstone became doubly suspect in many circles for his dislike of armaments and for the democratic tendencies of his Budget. John Bright's overture to Disraeli, to combine for the overthrow of Palmerston and Russell, belongs to the curiosities of party government, and on the former's side is to be explained very largely by his anger at armaments and panic-mongering. But the very opposite resulted, and Derby offered to Palmerston the support of the Conservative Party against any *fronde* from inside his own party. None the less, "there was far less difference of opinion between Bright and Disraeli on this question than might have been supposed. The Quaker statesman held that "there has *never before in any time* been a Government in France more willing to act honourably and amicably with England", and that "at least 15 millions a year might be saved to the two countries at once", by an agreement for the limitation of armaments.[79] A few months later Disraeli, from his very different standpoint, deprecated "undignified panic and readiness for reckless expenditure", and referred to an "insane race of competition for naval power". It might be inferred from the speeches of the Prime Minister and Foreign Secretary that "the good understanding between England and France was in great peril": but he reminded the House that "for many years past" there had been "a perfect willingness" on the part of France to agree on "relative proportions of naval powers", and to recognise England's great superiority on the sea.[80]

None the less, what Disraeli called "this irritating discussion" as to iron-plated ships was continued between London and Paris. New inventions had been rapidly rendering obsolete the old wooden fleets, and much replacement was inevitable. But it is now known that as early as 1849 Napoleon, as Prince President, had been ready for a limitation of naval armaments, virtually at Britain's discretion, and that it was Palmerston who then declined the offer and maintained a similar attitude a decade later.

In May 1862 Disraeli returned to the charge in one of his most notable speeches, reminding the House that "your armaments lead to rival armaments", and pleading for a French alliance as "the great object of policy", resting on identical interests. "The French Alliance is not the boast or the glory of any party." It "must be founded on mutual forbearance, carried on in a spirit of conciliation": but instead of this, under the existing Government we found "constant jealousies, constant distrusts, frequent misunderstandings, occasional insults—and this to a high-spirited ally". And to make a reality of the alliance, it was above all necessary "to put an end to those bloated armaments"—a phrase that instantly caught the public fancy and is still remembered.[81] Nowhere was Disraeli more consistently sane than in his attitude to France: and here at least is a theme on which he never really clashed with his great rival Gladstone. Cobden, too, was eminently sane on this subject, and when Russell met his criticisms on fortifications by the phrase, "But I cannot consent to place my country at the mercy of France", Cobden retorted that he "would, if necessary, spend £100,000,000 sterling to maintain an irresistible superiority over France at sea".[82] "Palmerston", he confided to Chevalier, "likes to drive the wheel close to the edge and show how dexterously he can avoid falling over the precipice."[83]

The Syrian Massacres and the Chinese War

If British public opinion had not been brought to a high pitch of nervous excitement by the deliberate encouragement of the Government, it ought to have been realised that quite apart from the Commercial Treaty, Napoleon was only too eager to co-operate with Britain in at least three directions, in Syria, in China, and in Mexico.

In May 1860 the trouble which had long been brewing in the district of the Lebanon came suddenly to a head. The population was fairly equally divided between the Druses, a strange and warlike Moslem sect tinged with ancient pagan traditions, and the Maronites, descended from a Christian community founded by a monk of the fifth century, and linked with the Latin Church since the days of the Fourth Crusade. They had lived for generations under their own feudal chiefs, but after the expulsion of Mehemet Ali from Syria in 1840, the Turks divided the Mountain into two provinces, each under a Kaimakam belonging to the dominant persuasion: but both were placed directly under the Pasha of Damascus, and the new-fangled Turkish efforts at centralisation led to the crudest possible forms of bribery and corruption, and nowhere more so than in Syria. The situation was aggravated by the rivalry of the Powers, and especially of France and Britain, the former having passed for centuries as protector of the Latin Christians* and having given her full political support to the Jesuit and Lazarist missions in Syria, while for that very reason the Druses had looked to the more consistently Turcophil Britain. A lesser part was played by British and American missionaries, who found that opening for proselytism among these Moslem heretics which they sought in vain amid the fanatical Mohammedan masses, and who were not sorry to counter Catholic activities in the Middle East. The Turks, on their side, keenly resented the Reform Charter of 1856, and were not in the least inclined to make a reality of the paper pledge of equality between Moslem and Christian: and this attitude was very marked among the incompetent and corrupt higher officials of Syria.

During May 1860 there was sporadic rioting in the Lebanon, in which the blame must be divided between the Maronites and Druses, but in which the Turkish authorities put their whole weight in favour of the latter. By the end of the month it was already described by Consul Moore as "civil war";

* The Maronites had by a charter of St Louis been made part of the French nation.

but by 1 June it had swelled to wholesale massacre, first by the Druses, then by the Turkish troops. Then, after an ominous pause, the Moslem population in Damascus itself rose against its Christian neighbours, and killed at least 5000 of them by fire and sword: the massacre lasted for three days (9–11 July). The Turkish Government took no steps to stop it, and eventually the Turkish troops took an active part. The Consuls had meanwhile intervened at Beirout, and a sort of truce had been arranged: but French opinion instantly reacted to the news, and Napoleon instructed his Foreign Minister, Thouvenel—himself so recently Ambassador to the Porte—to propose to Lord Cowley a Commission of the Great Powers, to investigate the situation on the spot, and the despatch of troops and warships to maintain order. The British Government at first adopted a niggardly and negative view, being at the height of its suspicions with regard to Napoleon's Italian policy: but the events of Damascus made action imperative, since the epidemic of massacre might at any moment spread to the coast towns, and then France and Russia were certain to intervene alone. On 3 August, therefore, Palmerston reluctantly signed a Convention for the despatch of French troops to Syria, and in due course they occupied Beyrout and prepared to carry out the repatriation of the fugitives. Meanwhile the Sultan, whose main concern it was to play off France and Britain against each other, appointed one of the foremost Turkish statesmen of the day, Fuad Pasha, as special commissioner in Syria: and he, with the manifest object of saving the high officials implicated, proceeded to hang and shoot 168 of the rioters in Damascus. But though the wretched Governor Ahmed Pasha was too deeply involved and was therefore handed over for secret execution, Fuad, only too evidently, set himself to screen the Turkish officers and to let the Commission slake its thirst for vengeance on the Druse chiefs. In the end Fuad found it expedient to sacrifice the Pasha of Beirout and some of his subordinate officers, but this time they were not executed, but merely transferred in temporary disgrace to the capital.

The concluding stages of the incident do not throw a pleasing light upon British policy: indeed, it was only redeemed by the high-minded and tactful attitude of its Commissioner Lord Dufferin, who however preferred to acquit Fuad of connivance and to blame the stupidity of the latter's agents. Long before there could be any real talk of pacification, Russell kept pressing Paris for a recall of the expeditionary force, and on 21 February 1861 he openly declared, "We do not want to create a new Papal State in the East and to give France a new pretext for indefinite occupation." In June a fairly reasonable compromise was reached. The French troops were withdrawn, while a special Statute for Lebanon autonomy was drawn up by the Powers and accepted by the Sultan. Lord Dufferin had recommended autonomy for the whole of Syria, but the close resemblance of the scheme to that which had finally entrenched Mehemet Ali in Egypt led both the Sultan and the French, and even British, Governments to oppose it, though each for quite different reasons. Under the scheme first signed on 9 June 1861 and modified in 1864, the Lebanon was placed under a Christian Governor, nominated by the Sultan and entirely independent of the neighbouring Pashas. It was divided into six districts, each with an administrative council in which the various communities were proportionately represented: and mixed tribunals were also set up. Under its first Governor, Daoud Pasha, an energetic and astute Catholic Armenian, the Statute speedily justified itself, and the Lebanon, recovering from the horrors of 1860, remained till the Great War a welcome oasis amid the arid waste of Turkish misrule. While, however, Dufferin, for all his tenderness for the Druses, left golden opinions even among French observers, Russell's whole attitude was grudging and unjust, and it is again Napoléon III who, despite his obvious motive in placating outraged Catholic opinion, emerges with most credit from the affair. In the words of Dr Rachel Reid, "it must be admitted that our foreign policy has seldom shown itself less circumspect".[84]

The Chinese and Mexican episodes lie outside our province, and their bearings upon Europe may be dismissed quite briefly. France and Britain had already collaborated in the more than questionable dispute with China which originated in the misdeeds of Chinese pirates masquerading under the British flag (see p. 369): and the Treaty of Tientsin (26 June 1858), by which the Celestial Empire was for the first time forced to accept foreign diplomatists at the Court of Peking, was the joint work of the two Powers, following upon joint military action. A year later, however, when the first French and British Ministers presented themselves, the Chinese refused to receive them, and a British gunboat was fired upon. In November 1859, then, the British and French agreed upon another joint expedition, which in July 1860 stormed the Taku Forts: and when their envoys, on the way to Peking, were assaulted and seized as hostages, the Franco-British forces advanced on the capital and routed the Tatar army at Palikao. The British civil commissioner Lord Elgin, ordinarily the mildest of men, was roused into giving orders for the burning of the Summer Palace—much to the disgust of his French colleague Baron Gros, who none the less ere long had to confess that this was the only language which the Chinese seemed capable of understanding. Only six days later (24 October 1860) peace had been signed by a brother of the Emperor, and while a virtual French protectorate over the Catholic missions in China was assured, Britain obtained a cession of territory at Hongkong which was to prove invaluable for the development of her trade in the Far East. The part played soon after by "Chinese Gordon" in the high command and by Robert Hart in the organisation of the Chinese Customs, testified to the enhanced prestige of Britain, following upon her abrupt enough action in forcing China to abandon the mysterious seclusion of centuries. Incidentally the war and the peace showed Franco-British collaboration to be perfectly practicable, and to be genuinely desired by Napoleon III and his advisers.

That similar co-operation in Mexico was only of a temporary character, has an altogether valid explanation, for here we touch upon the adventure that was to exercise so long and fatal an influence upon the Second Empire. The chronic civil war in that rich and undeveloped country had by 1860 reached a phase of acute anarchy, in which the foreign residents appealed to their respective Governments for support: and the fact that the United States were becoming absorbed in their own disastrous quarrel, both increased the anarchy and seemed to render intervention safer. Napoleon III had long dreamt American dreams, and as a prisoner at Ham had actually concocted a plan for a Pacific Canal and a new Constantinople at Nicaragua. He now saw fresh visions of a Latin Confederation holding the Anglo-Saxon states of the North in check, and already hoped to regain the friendship of Austria by the offer of a Mexican throne to the Habsburgs.

At first his lead was followed by Britain and Spain, and a triple convention was signed in London on 31 October 1861, recognising "the right of the Mexican nation to choose and set up its own form of government", but also authorising the seizure of Mexican ports and fortresses. Troops of all three Powers were duly landed at Vera Cruz in January 1862, but the British corps, which was much the smallest, was opposed to any advance, while France wished to advance inland to the capital. There was also acute disagreement as to the compensation to be demanded from the Mexican Government: and ere long the British Government withdrew altogether from the expedition, leaving France to become more and more involved in the slough of Mexican politics and military adventure. This is not the place to tell the tragic story of the Emperor Maximilian, or to estimate the deterrent effect of Mexican commitments upon Napoleon's policy in Europe during the critical years that followed. But it is safe to affirm that a continuance of British intervention in Mexico in these years might have turned the wavering scales in favour of an Anglo-American conflict, for the Union, though momentarily paralysed by civil war, keenly resented the whole Mexican adventure and would undoubtedly, after peace returned, have taken action if the Mexicans themselves had not been able unaided to overwhelm the unhappy Maximilian and his foreign abettors.

As a passing indication of the dangers in which we might so easily have become involved, it is admissible to quote the half cynical remark of Clarendon to Cornwall Lewis: "It would have been very wrong if war against Mexico had been declared without the knowledge of the Cabinet: but it would have been Palmerstonian."[85] This verdict, passed at a moment when Palmerston favoured a blockade of Vera Cruz, is equally characteristic of the reckless, fire-eating Palmerston and of the nonchalantly negative Clarendon.

The Death of the Prince Consort

In June 1861 Lord John Russell, whose health had always been fragile, was made an Earl, and for the next four years directed his foreign policy from the Upper Chamber. Amid all his interest in the Italian problem, he had in the previous year devoted much of his time to yet another project of franchise reform, and meeting with firm opposition from about half of his colleagues inside the Cabinet, had dropped it with a precipitancy and an apparent indifference which deeply angered John Bright. It had long since become clear that he could not simultaneously bear the brunt of two such questions as Reform and Italy.

The close of 1861 brought with it a real disaster to the nation in the premature death of the Prince Consort, at the age of 42. His health had long been failing and was further impaired by overwork; and strangely enough, despite his wide interests, his affectionate nature and keen sense of duty, he lacked the vitality that makes recovery possible. He had slowly lived down the insular prejudice with which he had so long been regarded, and the full maturity of his judgment had latterly been revealed by his attitude to German and American affairs. Indeed his last public act may be said to have had a decisive and permanent effect upon the relations of the two chief English-speaking communities.

The long-threatened American civil war had broken out in January 1861, and the blockade proclaimed by President Lincoln against the secessionist States of the South had speedily produced a cotton famine in Lancashire and thereby caused an acute division of British opinion. The Federal defeats of the following summer encouraged many in England to treat Secession almost as a foregone conclusion: even Gladstone was guilty of this miscalculation. All the greater was the indignation aroused in November 1861 by the so-called *Trent* affair, when a British mail steamer was held up on the high seas and two of her passengers, the Confederate envoys to France and England, were forcibly carried off prisoners to a northern port, and when the officer responsible for this outrage received the thanks of the American Congress. Such a situation demanded the exercise of peculiar tact, and this was a quality in which both the Prime Minister and Foreign Secretary were conspicuously lacking. But at the critical stage Prince Albert, already racked by illness, received the two draft notes which the Cabinet proposed to send to Washington—emphasising in somewhat abrupt language the violation of international law involved, and demanding "reparation and redress". Next morning he submitted to the Queen a memorandum—the last he ever wrote —urging that the draft was "somewhat meagre" in its original form and ought to include a distinct assumption that the American captain did not act under instructions, and that the United States Government had no intention of "wanton insult", and would "upon full consideration...spontaneously offer redress" by restoring the two prisoners and apologising.[86] These amendments were adopted by the Cabinet, and thus the request addressed to Washington acquired a moderate and conciliatory tone. The support given to Lord Lyons by the French, Austrian and Russian Ministers contributed to the final result. By Christmas President Lincoln had consented to comply with the demand, and the danger of war was averted. It is strange that no attempt has ever been made to contrast the action of the Prince Consort in "toning down" the Cabinet draft of 1861 with that of Bismarck and his colleagues in "toning up" the Ems telegram of 1870.

Prince Albert's death on 17 December 1861—in no small degree the result of medical incompetence—was a memorable incident in the history of British foreign policy, both in respect of what it took away and what it left behind. The Prince had had many prejudices to overcome, but had at last lived down the most of them and had come to occupy a unique position in the country, not merely as a paragon of the domestic virtues, but as a man of taste and judgment in many fields—music and literature, science and commercial enterprise—and an expert in many continental problems. High character, industry, experience and imagination already far outweighed, both with the governing class and with the masses, that touch of priggishness or of "foreignness" of which they had at first accused him. Disraeli won the Queen's heart by comparing the Prince with Sir Philip Sidney, and the comparison was not unmerited. Palmerston, with whom he had so many disagreements, was far more deeply moved than was his wont,* while Clarendon, remembering the Prince's "sagacity and foresight", felt his loss to be "a national calamity of far greater importance than the public dreamt of".[87] In the words of Mr Paul,[88] "Palmerston and Russell were antipathetic to him, because they represented the spirit of the Whig Revolution and in their hearts considered the Queen an appendage of the Crown. Within the

---

* I cannot resist quoting Mr Bolitho (*Albert the Good*, p. 285): "Palmerston came, an old crafty man who had sneered at her and who had been rude to the Prince. He was ushered into the room, and when he saw her, sitting upon the sofa, fighting her agony, he wept bitterly." This may rest partly on the diary of Count Vitzthum (*St Petersburg und London*, 1852–64, II, 162).

limits of law and custom, which he had too much sense to infringe, he never failed to push the prerogative as far as he decently could, and it is possible that if he had lived he might have done something to revive the personal power of the Sovereign." Guided by duty rather than ambition, his prestige would have been enormous, if he had survived the elder statesmen who were now nearing the end of their careers. It has sometimes been argued that if he had lived as long as the Queen, he might have aspired to give England "the blessing of absolute government". It is quite true that his first mentor Baron Stockmar looked at the British Constitution through the eyes of a German, but it betrays a complete misapprehension both of him and of his two apt pupils Leopold and Albert, to suppose that they would ever have risked flouting those traditions of constitutional and parliamentary government which they recognised as deeply entrenched in their adopted country and genuinely believed to be best suited to the Europe of their day.

The essential fact is that his place remained unfilled. The Queen maintained to the end of her reign a keen interest in foreign policy and a vast knowledge of continental affairs, maintained and extended by voluminous correspondence with many of her fellow sovereigns. But none the less her influence was henceforth less decisive and more fitful, while she jealously opposed the initiation of her son in foreign affairs. It is only too excusable if the main aim of Queen and Prince alike was to make their son "as unlike as possible to any of his great-uncles",[89] but the exaggerated regime by which they sought to promote this end often had the opposite effect upon its victim. Meanwhile, the shock to her nervous system was so overwhelming, that for a time her ministers seriously feared for her reason: and it may be noted that already in June 1861 Prince Albert himself had written to his brother Ernest of the "horrid vile rumours" about the Queen's "mental state".[90] For some years, then, she withdrew into a seclusion so rigid and so irksome to the nation, that Russell and Palmerston found themselves more powerful than ever and were only too ready to take a free hand in affairs. The full pathos of her attitude is revealed in her words to Lord Clarendon: "I depended on him for everything. I had absolutely no will of my own. He told me when to go to bed and when to get up. He ordered all my actions, all my thoughts."[91] It was really not till the advent of Disraeli, with his unlimited powers of soothing flattery, that the Queen plunged with her old zest into foreign affairs, but no longer with that restraint and balance which had characterised the joint regime.

GREECE AND THE IONIAN ISLANDS

The great upheaval in Italy was not without its reactions upon the various Balkan nationalities, and Britain found herself directly involved in Greek affairs, thanks not merely to her position as one of the three Guarantor Powers of the Greek Kingdom, but also thanks to the protectorate which she had exercised over "the United States of the Ionian Islands" since the Convention of 5 November 1815. Under a series of able Governors—notably "King Tom" Maitland, Sir Frederick Adam and Lord Seaton—the islands had prospered and enjoyed just, if sometimes arbitrary, government; but the hearts of the population were set upon union with Greece, and after the ferment of 1848 no occasion was allowed to pass without an open demonstration of this sentiment. In 1857 there were specially loud protests against a reference in the British Parliament to the islands as a British colony; and the publication in the *Daily News* of a confidential report of the Governor in favour of colonial status for the protectorate was water on the agitator's mill. The Colonial Secretary, Bulwer Lytton, described this indiscretion as "an inconceivable misfortune": it revived the demand for union and aroused the suspicions of the other two Protecting Powers. Towards the end of 1858, then, it was decided to send Gladstone, then out of office, as special High Commissioner, to investigate Ionian conditions. He was not slow to recommend the recall of his old schoolfellow Young, and taking over the latter's post until the arrival of a successor, made a progress through the islands and soon found that nowhere were his well-meant proposals for a more liberal constitution accepted as an adequate alternative to union. The Archbishop of Cephalonia publicly appealed to him for union, and the Assembly two days after its first meeting with him as the Queen's representative, voted unanimously in the same sense. Gladstone's report was compounded of a firm rejection of Union, a criticism of the existing Charter of 1817, a plea for a responsible ministry, but also an admission that "not Cherubim and Seraphim could work" the system as it stood. The result of his Ionian mission was a complete deadlock, from which his successor, Sir Henry Storks, was equally unable to extricate himself.

The changes of regime which were almost simultaneously taking place in Serbia and Roumania kept Greek opinion in a ferment, which was rendered still more acute by the great events in Italy. Lord John Russell's famous despatch of 27 October 1860, bestowing Britain's blessings upon the cause of Italian independence and declaring with such emphasis that the Italians were "the best judges of their own interests", served as a watchword for the Ionian unionists, who invited him to apply the same principles in the protectorate of the seven islands. In 1861 a motion was brought forward in favour of a plebiscite on the Italian analogy, and Storks thought it was wiser to prorogue the Assembly. The whole question came up for debate in the House of Commons on 7 May 1861: and the Irish member Maguire pertinently accused the Foreign Secretary of using "one set of weights and measures for Italy and another for the Ionian Isles". The principal speech was that of Gladstone, who took the perverse line of denying the existence of "evidence of any great wish on the part of the Kingdom of Greece for such a union". He believed that it would be nothing less than "a crime against the safety of Europe" to surrender the protectorate, in view of the probable effect upon Candia, Thessaly and Albania. He even went so far as to justify the rejection of the Union by the claim that "we are stewards and guardians of the general peace of Europe".[92] The debate is a drastic illustration of the rapidity with which statesmen are sometimes forced to eat their own words: for within 18 months the Gladstonian policy in Greece had been blown sky-high.

Palmerston had in 1859 denounced the idea of surrendering Corfu, which he was not alone in regarding as under certain circumstances the key to the Adriatic: and in 1851 he argued in favour of retaining Corfu, even if the other six islands should be handed over. In November 1862, however, he informed the Greek Minister Tricoupis that the Ionian Islands were "of no use to England...except the fortress of Corfu", and he and Russell soon afterwards admitted the seven to be indivisible.[93] They were both by now rapidly coming to the view that the islands represented a liability, and they hoped by their cession to ease the precarious situation of King Otto and his Government, which was barely able to cope with a determined insurrection at Nauplia in February 1862. In the following October the revolution broke out in earnest, King Otto and Queen Amalia took refuge on a British ship, and the provisional Government declared the Greek throne to be vacant. This decided the British Government to take action, the other three signatory Powers were privately sounded, and in December the Greeks were informed that subject to their approval of the King whom they elected to the vacant throne, the Islands would be united with the Kingdom. It was no doubt partly under the impression of favours to come that at a plebiscite of Greeks, at home and abroad, an overwhelming number of votes were cast for Queen Victoria's second son, Alfred Duke of Edinburgh, and that this was duly ratified by the Greek Parliament. London had already made it abundantly clear that it felt itself tied by the self-denying ordinance of 1830 in respect of the reigning families of the three Protecting Powers—an attitude which ruled out any Russian or French candidate: and the Queen formally declined the Crown on behalf of all her sons. After the ex-King Consort of Portugal,

Duke Ernest of Coburg and Archduke Maximilian had all been considered, the name of Lord Stanley was for a moment put forward: but in the words of his close friend and colleague Disraeli, "they are not an imaginative race, and I fancy they will prefer Knowsley to the Parthenon".[94] In the end the three Protecting Powers agreed to recommend Prince William of Denmark, who was duly elected as King George I, on 30 March 1863; and the way thus lay open for the consummation of the Union under a triple guarantee.

The final stage was unfortunately marred by various incidents. In the British Parliament the Conservatives vigorously opposed the cession, though they did not press the matter to a division in either House. Lord Derby's main criticism was directed towards the conditions attached to the cession—Greece's abandonment of "*grandes idées*", her non-extension of territory, her acceptance of dynastic and constitutional government. This, he argued, was to ask the impossible and to postpone a settlement till the Greek Kalends. Both he and Malmesbury stressed the very serious naval considerations which told against the surrender of Corfu, "an important harbour and fortress, the key of the Adriatic":[95] while Disraeli reminded the House that we had held the islands for years before the treaties of 1815 "by right of conquest", and with unanswerable logic pointed out that the cession was a direct encouragement to the Greeks "to aspire to the possession of Albania, Thessaly and other provinces". Russell was on strong ground when he retorted that it was quite impossible for Britain to say that she did not care for the wishes of the islanders and that "what we do care about is a harbour for Great Britain". It was, however, left for Palmerston to state the official case most forcibly, pointing out that the Ionian Islands were "no part of the dominions of the British Crown", but "a separate and independent state", of which "the Queen is not sovereign"—placed under her protection, not "given as a possession". Hence it followed that "the Crown may by its prerogative make a treaty, alienating such possessions without the consent of the House of Commons", and precedents were to be found in the case of Senegal, Minorca, Florida and Banea. On the other hand it was necessary to obtain the consent of the other parties to the Treaty of Vienna, and of the population itself: and this was being duly considered.

Meanwhile the conditions attached by the British Government to its consent to Union aroused lively, and not always very reasonable, protest among the Ionians themselves. Some financial arrears were to be written off, the British cemeteries were to be maintained, and a special contribution was to be made to the new King's civil list. But much more important was the provision—included out of deference to Austria and Turkey—that all fortifications were to be destroyed and the islands of Corfu and Paxo to remain neutral territory. This and the somewhat irksome conditions attached to the cession at first marred the effect among the islanders: but Europe took note of the fact that after two generations of possession a British Government was still ready to admit the higher obligations incumbent upon it under an international trust.

SERBIA, TURKEY AND BRITAIN

Meanwhile, the illogical nature of British policy towards the various national problems was strikingly exemplified by the course of the Serbian crisis. The Serbs, who had been the first Balkan race to rise against the Turks and owed far less to foreign assistance than any of their neighbours, had even by the middle of the nineteenth century established only the scantiest relations with England. It was not till 1837 that the British Government sent its first diplomatic agent to Belgrade, in the person of Colonel Hodges, and even then the real motive of this step was not interest in the growing movement in favour of Serbian self-government, but merely the desire of Palmerston to counteract the spread of Russian influence in the Balkan Peninsula. There soon developed a highly paradoxical situation, in which the Government of Tsar Nicholas encouraged the so-called "Defenders of the Constitution" against the arbitrary rule of Prince Miloš, and pressed for the erection of a Senate, while the representative of Liberal England threw his whole weight in favour of the autocratic Miloš and encouraged him in subservience to the Porte and in opposition to free institutions. Ere long Hodges evolved a plan for inducing the Porte to hand over the citadel of Belgrade to the Serbs, but warned Palmerston that unless the Prince were supported against the Chiefs, Russia would be able to lay her hands upon Serbia, and would then control Bosnia and Bulgaria also and would be in a position to organise a general Christian rising. During the summer of 1838 Hodges went to Constantinople, in the hope of stirring up the Porte to action: but even with the help of Lord Ponsonby he effected nothing, and the only result of his whole mission was to strengthen Russian influence still further. Unlike Metternich, Palmerston had not realised that Miloš had nothing behind him, and that it was mere folly to drive the leaders of the Serbian nation into the Russian camp. When Hodges was transferred to Egypt, he left behind him in Serbia the general impression that Britain was opposed to popular liberties, and even to a national assembly.[96]

Miloš and his dynasty were eventually expelled from Serbia, and the somewhat ineffective Alexander Karagjorgjević, who was Prince from 1842 till the very end of 1858, leant mainly upon Austria and carefully avoided all adventure, even in 1848, while his kinsmen were engaged in a fierce racial conflict with the Magyar Revolution. So far as Serbia was concerned, the Treaty of Paris weakened still further for a time the influence of Russia and placed her, like her two Roumanian neighbours, Wallachia and Moldavia, under an inadequately defined dual control—the suzerainty of the Sultan and the guarantee of the Concert of the Powers. In Serbia's case, however, Turkish rule found practical and irksome expression in the garrisons maintained in the fortress of Belgrade and at five other strategic points in the Principality. The weak Alexander was overthrown in 1858, and Miloš, returning at the age of eighty, hastened to secure the sanction of the Porte and thereby averted all excuse for either Austrian or Russian intervention. Austria, moreover, was absorbed by Italian affairs and the approaching conflict with France; and before she could again take an active interest in the Balkans, Miloš had died, and the stabilisation of Serbia made rapid and steady progress under his son Michael, the ablest of all her modern rulers. Michael, with the help of a French staff officer, trained up a standing army of 50,000 men, secured a revision of the constitution on lines such as would increase his own princely power, and as time passed, aimed definitely at a loose Balkan federation under Serbian leadership. Speaking broadly, his motto was first union, and only then freedom. It was inevitable that there should be chronic friction between him and the Porte, and not surprising that the latter, who always played for time, should have refused Michael's periodical appeals to end the unsatisfactory dual jurisdiction in the towns, and that the Consuls should on the whole have taken an unsympathetic attitude towards the ambitious Prince. Longworth in particular misjudged the Serbs and wrote home contemptuously of "a nation of shepherds and swineherds", who "have no desire apparently to be anything else".[97]

In June 1862 the long latent trouble came to a head: after a series of petty scuffles between the Turkish police and the Serbian mob, the Pasha suddenly bombarded the open town of Belgrade for four hours, until the Consuls intervened, and to prevent fresh firing, pitched their tents on the glacis between town and fortress. Michael at once appealed to Napoleon III, Tsar Alexander and Lord John Russell, and after some delay the Austrian Foreign Minister, Count Rechberg, proposed that the question should be referred to a conference of ambassadors at Constantinople. In the end a compromise was reached, by which the Moslem residents of Belgrade were to be evacuated, the garrisons were reduced from 6 to 3, and "guarantees" against bombardment were laid down. That a mere stopgap solution was reached, such as could not last and satisfied no one, was mainly due to the attitude of Lord John Russell, who instantly and without investigation attributed the original trouble to "the violations by the Serbs of the relations established by treaties with the Porte". He actually proposed "to leave in the hands of Austria the pacification of Belgrade", his motive being fear that Russia might encourage the Serbs "to start for the cup of independence".[98] Fortunately Austria herself was not inclined to send troops, and it was left to Russell to be "more Papal than the Pope".

Michael, despite his natural anger, had perforce to submit to this distasteful compromise, but he began to buy arms abroad for his young army, and was soon on very bad terms with Longworth, whom he had every reason to distrust, and who on his side accused the Prince of lying. On one occasion Michael reduced Longworth to silence by enquiring why the British Liberal Government supported the cause of nationality on the west side of the Adriatic, but opposed it no less firmly on the east. There could be no answer, for he had detected the fundamental inconsistency of Russell and Palmerston. Michael none the less made a series of efforts to overcome the unfriendly attitude of the British Government towards Serbia: and the Conservative statesmen Marinović and Philip Hristić, and finally Princess Julia herself—née Countess Hunyady, a woman of great charm and ability —were entrusted with missions to London, but without any success beyond the asking of a few questions in the House and the publication of a few friendly articles in the press.

The sequel may be summed up here very briefly. With the advent of the Conservatives to power, a new and fresher wind blew at the Foreign Office: and Lord Stanley readily co-operated with Count Beust, to whom Francis Joseph entrusted foreign affairs in Austria after his defeat at the hands of Prussia. Stanley realised that conditions in Turkey rendered concessions to the Christians indispensable, and instructed Lord Lyons, now Ambassador at Constantinople, to associate himself with the French initiative for a settlement of the garrison dispute. Troubles in Crete rendered the Porte more amenable, all attempts to divide the Powers into two opposing groups proved unavailing, and in February 1867 the Sultan consented to yield the fortresses to Serbia. The Grand Vizier was deceiving no one when he grandiloquently announced, "We have not yielded Belgrade to the Serbs, but have designated them as guardians of the Empire, demanding that the Turkish and Serbian flags should wave together over the ramparts." The last serious restraint upon Serbian freedom had thus been removed, but the British Liberal statesman whose services to the Italian cause are so often quoted as his chief title to Fame, had adopted the same obstructive and unfriendly attitude towards Serbia's just grievances, as an earlier Liberal Cabinet had shown towards Roumanian unity.

THE SECOND POLISH RISING

The hold which the new spirit of Nationality exercised upon Napoleon III is sufficiently exemplified in his attitude to Italy and Roumania. But he also showed a steady interest in the fate of Poland, and not all his desire for close accord with Tsar Alexander could deter him from dabbling in the Polish problem. The outbreak of a serious insurrection in Warsaw at the beginning of 1863 was in one sense the result of a competition between an extremist and a moderate group of patriots, and had received persistent encouragement from the numerous emigrants who made Paris their head-quarters. The more conciliatory measures adopted by Tsar Alexander II, which in his mind were intended to lead to a gradual, if inadequate, restoration of autonomy, were unfortunately counteracted by the blunders of the local authorities, and the appointment of the Grand Duke Constantine as Governor-General, though also intended as a concession, had in no way mollified Polish opinion. Our Ambassador described the new order of conscription in Poland as "a simple plan, by a clean sweep of the revolutionary youth of Poland, to kidnap the opposition and to carry it off to Siberia or the Caucasus".

During the previous two years the Tsar had given Napoleon more than one warning of his "noli me tangere" attitude, though couched in the most cordial terms.[99] But Napoleon himself could not conceal the fact that he still felt towards Poland as in 1831, while French public opinion—Conservative, Catholic and revolutionary alike—flared into almost unanimous enthusiasm for the Poles. In England contacts with Poland were rarer, but there was considerable sympathy, and a National League was formed by Edmund Beales and others to promote the Polish cause. On 20 February Lord Ellenborough raised the Polish Question in the House of Lords, amid cheers from both sides of the House,[100] and invited the Government to admit that the insurrection was "provoked by the conduct of Russia", who could not be "considered any longer as in Europe". In his reply Lord Russell, while quite polite towards the Tsar and his intentions of reform, criticised the conscription ordered in Poland as "a measure which no British Minister could venture to justify", and announced that he had informed the Russian Government of his opinion that it was "the most imprudent and unjust step it could take".[101] A week later Palmerston, after a debate in which many private members had intervened,* bluntly informed the House of Commons that the Government had "always held that the conduct of Russia towards Poland had been a violation of the stipulations of the Treaty of Vienna".[102]

* Including Lord Robert Cecil, the future Lord Salisbury.

Disraeli followed in a speech mainly devoted to praise of Castlereagh's Polish policy, but ended with the words: "It is a natural movement: it possesses all the elements of a sound cause—the love of country, the memory of a glorious past, and, as I hope and will believe, the inspiration of a triumphant future."[103]

The insurrection had the immediate effect of drawing the three Eastern Powers together: community of interest in upholding the joint crime of partition outweighed for the moment many points of rivalry between them. Austria was alarmed at possible reactions in Galicia, and Bismarck had no difficulty in inducing William I to propose a Prusso-Russian convention for mutual help in the event of the revolt spreading. This step angered Napoleon, who made the *Moniteur* print a warning against arousing hopes which could not be fulfilled, but meanwhile tried to persuade London and Vienna to join Paris in expressing to Berlin their regret at the convention.[104] Palmerston suspected a trap, and refused his co-operation, but he wrote a letter, amazing even for him, to the Russian Ambassador, treating the insurrection as "a just punishment of Heaven" for the arms and secret encouragement which, according to his information, Russia had been supplying to Roumania, Serbia and Bosnia.[105]

On 2 March the British Government took action for the first time, claiming "as a party to the Treaty of 1815, and as a Power deeply interested in the tranquillity of Europe", to be entitled to express its opinion upon the events now taking place, "in the most friendly spirit towards Russia and with a sincere desire to promote the interests of all parties concerned".[106] Lord Russell went on to suggest "an immediate and unconditional amnesty" by the Tsar "to his revolted Polish subjects", and a restoration of the political and civil privileges granted in 1815, as likely to "content the Poles and satisfy European opinion". He then informed Paris that in his view "the next step to be taken is to invite all the chief Powers who signed the Treaty of Vienna to concur in advising Russia to recur to the stipulations and to revert to the policy of the Treaty of Vienna in regard to Poland".[107] Such proposals, unless backed by force, were entirely divorced from reality, and he speedily found a growing reserve on the part of Austria and a disposition on the part of Russia to invoke "the right of the conqueror".[108]

Moreover, it was with some reluctance that Napoleon followed the British lead, for he was notoriously more than cold towards the Treaties of 1815: and indeed he had only reluctantly abandoned the strange illusion that the Tsar might be disposed to create an independent Poland under the Duke of Leuchtenberg, a Russified kinsman of the Bonapartes. There followed a slightly less fantastic day-dream, strongly favoured by Eugénie, of a re-united Poland under an Austrian Archduke. Prince Richard Metternich was sent to Vienna to suggest not only this, but a thorough rearrangement of European territory—Venice to Italy, Silesia and Serbia to Austria, the Rhineland to France, Saxony and Hanover as compensation for Prussia, and a partition of Turkey between the Balkan states.[109] Napoleon was ready to "bind himself with body and soul" to Francis Joseph, and in talking of new alliance projects with his Foreign Minister Drouyn, used the questionable simile that hitherto he had only had mistresses, but now wanted a wife! But Metternich warned him against mixing the Polish and Venetian questions, and Francis Joseph politely declined any alliance, being quite well pleased to see friction between Paris and Petersburg. And this was increased by Prince Napoleon's outburst in the Senate in favour of the Poles and against Russia—an outburst so unmeasured as to necessitate official disavowal.

On 10–12 April three parallel notes were addressed to Russia by the Western Powers and Austria: but their effect was curiously guarded, for while Austria stressed the reactions of Polish unrest on the three Eastern Powers, and France invoked the general interest of Europe, Russell, in his most didactic style, harked back to Russia's engagements under the Treaty of 1815, and referring to Gorchakov's argument of conquest, declared that "Her Majesty's Government cannot acquiesce in a doctrine which they deem so contrary to good faith, so destructive of the obligations of treaties, and so fatal to all the international ties which bind together the community of European States and Powers". Moreover, he reminded Russia that "besides the obligations of treaties, she has, as a member of the community of European states, duties of comity towards other nations to fulfil", and that the Polish question was "a source of danger, not to Russia alone, but also to the general peace of Europe".[110] While the Tsar issued a manifesto promising pardon and autonomy if the insurgents surrendered within a month, Prince Gorchakov gave a sharp answer to Lord Napier, virtually repeating the arguments employed by Nesselrode in a similar situation after the rising of 1831. The Polish Constitution of 1815, he argued, had been a free act of grace on the Tsar's part, Russia had no obligations whatsoever towards foreign Powers, and the main trouble was due to revolutionary propaganda, culpably furthered in the West. The British, Gorchakov ironically added, "would not claim that there was only one form of government possible for all peoples, whatever their history and development".[111]

The action of the Powers only served to encourage the insurgent Government, who proclaimed that "Poland will crush the hordes of Russia" and rejected the proferred amnesty. Lord Napier sent an earnest warning to London: "If the Government does not mean to fight, let them say so and stop the loss of life and suffering attendant on a rising which unaided cannot succeed."[112] But Russell does not seem to have realised the dire effects of

...is attitude. The month's respite ended, the brutal Muravyev was sent to 'oland as Governor-General to drown all resistance in blood, and the Tsar, nowing that Napoleon was still playing with the idea of Franco-Austrian ction in favour of the Poles, countered by offering his uncle King William n alliance and "comradeship in arms" against Austria. It is true that ismarck did not allow him to accept anything so concrete, but the Polish uestion had become a very definite bond of union between Prussia and Russia.

The diplomatic struggle reached its height in June, when the three 'owers presented their advice to Russia under Six Points—a general am-esty, a Polish National Assembly, an autonomous administration, freedom or the Catholic Church, the use of Polish in public life and education, and a egal recruiting system—and went on to suggest that Russia should suspend ostilities and allow a Conference of the eight Powers, signatories of Vienna, o be convoked.[113] Gorchakov kept them waiting for nearly a month, and hen his reply, received on 18 July, consisted in a flat refusal to submit to a onference a matter of such purely internal concern, or to grant an amnesty o the rebels.[114] Lord Malmesbury caused no small sensation in the House f Lords by regretting that our Ambassador had not been recalled from t Petersburg and drawing an analogy between the Tsar and the King of Vaples.* But by now British zeal for action was rapidly cooling: Russell in speech at Edinburgh declared that Poland "could count on our sym-athies, but not on our material aid": and it was from Paris that the stiffest ejoinder came. Indeed if the Tsar had not shown studied moderation and een aided by the French Ambassador, Montebello, a rupture between 'rance and Russia might easily have resulted.[115] But the hesitancy of both Britain and Austria and the obvious intimacy of Russia and Prussia brought ome to Napoleon the danger of isolation, and he too began to hesitate. The urther Notes of 3–12 August sought to lay upon Russia the responsibility or the rejected advice. "The principal obstacle to the re-establishment of rder in Poland is not the assistance obtained by the insurgents from abroad, ut the conduct of the Russian Government itself": and again, "If Russia .. does not enter upon the path which is open to her by friendly counsels, he makes herself responsible for the serious consequences which the rolongation of the troubles of Poland may produce."[116] This was bad nough, for Russell was pressing claims which Russia would obviously never dmit except at the point of the bayonet: but he sent yet another despatch, f which the sense was that Russia had forfeited her treaty rights towards

* 24 July, *Hansard*, CLXXII, 1353—thus showing "that you would no longer have any elations with a Power so uncivilised, so uncertain in its faith, and whose acts are so revolting o the feelings of the people of this country".

Poland. Providentially Lord Napier thought it wise to sound the Russian Chancellor privately, and so the culminating phrase was never communicated officially, but returned to the Foreign Office for revision.[117] Thoroughly typical of Lord Russell's final methods was a speech delivered at Blairgowrie on 26 September. In the first place he put it on record that "neither the obligations, the honour nor the interests of England require that we should go to war for Poland...and I think it would be unbecoming to rail at Russia when we are not prepared forcibly to resist her assertions" Yet almost in the same breath he argued that Russia had not complied with the conditions of the Treaty of 1815, and "without the conditions of the tenure, the title itself can hardly be upheld".[118] Small wonder that Russia persisted in refusing all idea of intervention, though graciously consenting to refer the issue to the three Partitioning Powers!

Finally, while the despairing Poles already felt the knife at their throats Napoleon on 4 November launched proposals for a European Congress "which would not only regulate the fate of Poland, but would substitute for the treaties of 1815, now in decay, new stipulations apt to assure the peace of the world". "It is on the Treaty of Vienna", so he addressed his fellow sovereigns, "that now reposes the political edifice of Europe, and yet it is crumbling away on all sides." But this was the last thing which the British Cabinet desired: and Palmerston wrote very frankly, and very tellingly, on the subject to King Leopold: "In 1815 a Congress was a necessity", whereas "nothing of the kind exists in the present state of Europe. Such territorial changes as have since been effected, had all been legalised and confirmed by treaty. To range over the wide and almost endless extent of proposed and possible changes, would give rise to endless animosities between the Powers."[119] In plain words, he and Russell feared that a Congress would enable Russia to reopen the Eastern Question, and in particular that of Black Sea neutrality, and to use it as a means of bargaining in other parts of Europe. They therefore declined the proposal, in terms bordering upon discourtesy: declaring that in their view the main provisions of the Treaty of 1815 were in full force and formed the basis of the European balance, and then adding that they "would feel more apprehension than confidence at the meeting of a congress of sovereigns and ministers without fixed objects, ranging over the map of Europe, and exciting hopes and aspirations which they might find themselves unable either to gratify or to quiet". Instead of writing thus, they need only have waited for an almost certain refusal of the Tsar, who was quite resolved not to admit all Europe to a discussion of the Polish problem. They thus gratuitously offended Napoleon and advertised their retreat before Europe. After all his high-sounding phrases, Russell had already informed Napier on 20 October, that "H.M.G. have no wish to

rolong the correspondence for the mere sake of controversy".* And so the
ery event which Napier had feared occurred: the Poles, already foolishly
nfatuated, had been led on to utter destruction by their western well-
wishers. The crown was set upon our attitude when on 26 May 1864 Lord
Palmerston assured the House of Commons that to wage war on Russia for
he sake of Poland would have been "an act of insanity" which "we did not
t any moment contemplate, that Poland was not accessible to England and
France as Greece was, and that the Poles had been "very short-sighted".[120]
This was adding insult to injury.

France once more found herself alone; Prussia, while careful not to
offend Russia, took a somewhat negative line:[121] the idea of a Congress
collapsed, and Russia was left undisturbed to complete the pacification of
Poland. Queen Sophia of Holland may have overstated her case, but was
near the heart of things when she told Clarendon that Russell's answer was
deplorable. "It is the death-blow of an alliance which ought to have dominated the world, managed the affairs of the Continent, assured us an era of
peace."[122]

The Polish incident was of far more than local importance: it fore-
shadowed a redistribution of forces in Europe. In the first place it loosened
still further the ties between London and Paris, Napoleon treating Russell's
behaviour as a personal affront, and being driven to suspect that the British
Government had merely been leading on the French, with a view to spoiling
the new cordiality between France and Russia. Moreover, it made it clear to
Europe that British statesmen were ready enough to bombard a Greek or
Japanese fortress, a South American or Chinese port, on account of some
dispute capable of peaceful adjustment, but found it prudent to eat their
words when confronted by the resolute attitude of a Great Power such as
Russia. Lord Derby was in no way guilty of overstatement when he described Lord Russell's handling of the Polish question as "meddle and
muddle", and Disraeli agreed that it was "very priggish and pedantic".
'The Polish question', he wrote to his friend Mrs Brydges Williams, "is
a diplomatic Frankenstein, created, out of cadaverous remnants, by the
mystic blundering of Lord Russell."[123] Napoleon had sought to cover his
diplomatic reverse in the Polish question by a gesture which in effect drew
him away from Britain and from Austria, and once more nearer to Russia.[124]
The real profit of the whole affair was reaped by Bismarck, who by his
astute tactics rapidly extricated Prussia from her isolation, won the Tsar's

* In France Jules Favre took the same fatuous line: "Ni paix ni guerre, affirmation de
droit. La Russie est déchue de toute espèce d'autorité légitime sur la Pologne, car elle a
violé les traités: les traités sont le droit, et quand nous aurons affirmé le droit, nous nous
retirerons de celui qui l'a violé" (Charles Roux, op. cit. p. 363). But Favre was a mere
deputy, Russell spoke for the British Government.

sympathies to her side, and was thus able to alter the balance of force
in Central Europe to his own advantage, with decisive results during th
following three years.

DENMARK AND THE DUCHIES

While the Polish rising, and with it Russell's ill-judged project of mediation
were in their death throes, another question rapidly came to absorb th
anxious attention of foreign statesmen, and its solution was in no sma'
degree affected by the fiasco of the Western Powers in Poland. The German
Danish dispute regarding the Duchies, which had been slowly festerin,
throughout 1863, was still further intensified by the death of Frederick VI
of Denmark on 15 November.

The question of Schleswig-Holstein was one of great complexity: of i
Lord Palmerston, with characteristic levity, had once said that only thre
men in Europe had ever understood it, and of these the Prince Consort wa
dead, a Danish statesman (unnamed) was in an asylum, and he himself ha
forgotten it. The two Duchies had lived together ever since the fifteentl
century under a Personal Union with the Danish Crown, and their positio
had been guaranteed by Britain and France under a Treaty of 1720. I
1806 Christian VII had incorporated them with Denmark, amid the stress o
the Napoleonic upheaval, but in 1815 he became a member of the new Ger
man Confederation, in respect of Holstein. In 1839 his son Frederic V
was succeeded by his cousin Christian VIII, and as it was by then alread
clear that the main royal line would die out on the death of the new king'
only son and heir, the question of the succession became a live issue
since unless it could be regulated anew, the Duchies, following the Sali
law, would fall to the Duke of Augustenburg, while Denmark itself woul
pass through the female line to a still more distant cousin, Christian o
Glücksburg. The revolution which followed the accession of Frederic VI
in 1848 led to the dissolution of the Union between Schleswig and Holstein
the former being incorporated in Denmark, while the latter was left to th
German Confederation. Holstein appealed to the Federal Diet, whicl
declared Schleswig a part of Germany, and entrusted Prussia with the tas
of mediation. This led to war between Denmark and the Confederation, ir
which the latter, crippled at home by a dangerous revolution, was defeatec
at the battle of Fredericia (6 July 1849), and again, when after an armistice
hostilities were resumed, at Idsted (25 July 1850). Thanks to the paralle
mediation of Palmerston and Tsar Nicholas peace was signed on term;
entirely favourable to Denmark, and the so-called London Protoco
(August 1850) established a uniform law of succession for the Kingdom an

the Duchies, Palmerston having convinced Copenhagen that the succession was "the key to the whole questions pending between Germany and Denmark". The humiliating settlement imposed by Austria upon Prussia at Olmütz in November 1850 rendered the latter's resistance in the Danish question impossible, and Palmerston informed Berlin in September 1851 that "it is for the general interests of Europe that Denmark, Schleswig and Holstein should remain united under the same sovereign". Prussia, then, gave her assent to the integrity of the Danish Monarchy and to the succession of Christian of Glücksburg.* Finally a Conference of Ambassadors was convoked, and on 8 May 1852 signed the Treaty of London, by which the succession was unified in favour of Prince Christian, but the rights of the Confederation were reserved. The fatal weakness of the Treaty lay in the fact that it was a diplomatic patchwork of the Great Powers and that no attempt whatsoever was made to ascertain or consider the wishes of the inhabitants of the Duchies. A specially active part was played by the Tsar, who wished to strengthen his Danish kinsman's throne and looked askance upon turbulent Prussia. As Prince Albert wrote to his brother Ernest, "The poor Schleswigers have to pay for everything—even for the sins of our Angel of Foreign Affairs."[125] Meanwhile internationally, in Sybel's words, the Treaty was "equally distasteful to the Danes and to the Germans".†

One result of Denmark's successful war was to seal the fate of the royal absolutism and to introduce a really democratic constitution: but it also roused Danish national feeling, and the so-called Eider Dane party‡ upheld a chauvinist racial policy against the Germans. For the next ten years the grievances of the Duchies gathered and festered, opinion in Germany, and perhaps especially among the liberal intellectuals, remained extremely restive, and the new Danish Constitution of 1855, under which Holstein was to enjoy autonomy, but Schleswig to be incorporated in Denmark, was keenly criticised. It was of course in the nature of things that the two leading German Powers could not hold aloof from the dispute, but that so long as their mutual relations remained as strained as they were during the Italian War, little initiative could be expected from the German side, and Denmark could disregard with impunity the reactions of the Federal Diet. British opinion, ill-informed and from the first prone to regard the dispute as one between Prussia and Denmark, a Great Power and a small one, and to neglect the standpoint of the populations most concerned, leant definitely to the Danish side. Malmesbury while in office took the view that Schleswig

---

* Two of whose children were in 1863 to become King of Greece and Princess of Wales.
† *Begründung des Deutschen Reiches*, III, 61. "A treaty made only to be broken", is the considered opinion of Sir Adolphus Ward, *History of Germany*, II, 123.
‡ The river Eider, as the southern frontier of Schleswig, was claimed as being also the frontier of Denmark as a whole.

was "under full and complete exercise of sovereignty by the King of Denmark", and that "any attempt to acknowledge a union between Schleswig and Holstein would lead to complications".[126] Lord John, when he went to the Foreign Office, was conscious of a certain moral obligation under the Treaty of 1852, and urged the Danish Government to "go almost any length in the way of conciliation". At this stage he was much influenced by Robert Morier, who as a pupil of Stockmar, an intimate friend of the Prussian Crown Prince and Princess and an ardent believer in friendship between Britain and a Liberal Germany, warned him most earnestly that "running amuck" against German national sentiment was "the most suicidal act which England can be capable of".[127]

It is quite impossible within the framework set by this volume to lead the reader through the maze of this long dispute, to which a fresh complication was added by the constitutional struggle inside Prussia. The new King William I and his new minister, Otto von Bismarck, were for a time regarded as traitors to the national cause, and it was only very gradually that the latter's true aims emerged to view. He was determined at all costs to avoid the isolation in which Prussia had found herself in 1849, to retain Russian friendship, to keep Napoleon inactive, to play for time with Great Britain, above all to secure the co-operation of Austria through the fear of being outbid at the Federal Diet as the champion of Germanism. The relation of two to three, he argued, was better than that of one to four (which had prevailed at Olmütz):[128] and he was quick to perceive that the three Powers which remained, if once Austria could be won over to the Prussian side, were quite incapable of united action in such a cause as the Duchies. Within two months of his accession to power he regarded it as "certain that the whole Danish question can only be solved by war in a sense satisfactory to us",[129] but he rightly calculated that the divergent views of the Powers and the obstinacy of the Danes were working for him, and that everything would come to him who knew how to wait, so long as the watcher was served by such a friend as Roon, who could supply an army of 60,000 men against Denmark at a moment's notice. Meanwhile the triangular struggle seemed to be narrowing down to the alternatives of incorporating Schleswig in Denmark, or separating it altogether from the Kingdom. The Danes on their side hoped for a Swedish alliance and support from the Western Powers, and calculated that at the worst, by disgorging the purely German Holstein, they would secure the complete absorption of Schleswig: while throughout Germany there grew up the idea of Federal Execution—in other words, that German troops should occupy Holstein and hold it till the Danes consented to the administrative changes which German opinion considered just. When Count Bernstorff threw out the idea of partitioning Schleswig on racial lines, Palmerston assured the Queen that this was not practicable. Russell, to whom the Treaty of 1852 had hitherto seemed to be the beginning and end of all wisdom, was now in search of a compromise, and on 24 September 1862, while in attendance upon the Queen during a visit to her Coburg relatives, penned the famous "Gotha Despatch", which Lord Derby found so "extraordinarily offensive". It proposed to Denmark that "Holstein should have all that Germany demands for her", that Schleswig should have complete self-government, and that Denmark, Schleswig, Holstein and Lauenburg should have four independent assemblies of equal authority, even in matters of finance. Robert Morier claims to have been "the moral author" of this strange project: he had already assured himself of Prussia's acceptance, and thus was acting upon the deliberate calculation that Prussia "would obtain *gratis* the creditable position of having done her best to solve the question", and that Britain could then withdraw quite honourably from the obligations of the Treaty of 1852.[130]

In actual fact both Austria and Prussia accepted the despatch as a basis of negotiations, but Denmark refused. Her rigid attitude was very largely determined by an over-confident belief in European support: in particular she failed to realise that Russia was drawing near to Prussia, while France and Britain could not agree and the latter preferred big talk to action. Her illusions were increased by the marriage of the Prince of Wales to Prince Christian's daughter Alexandra (10 March), which seemed to Danish opinion a sure gauge of British sympathy.

The so-called Patent, issued by King Frederick on 30 March 1863, recognised Holstein to belong to the German Confederation, while at the same time demanding from it a contribution to joint affairs, but it insisted on Schleswig being an integral part of the Danish state. Austria and Prussia entered vigorous protests against what was unquestionably a breach of the Treaty; public opinion in Germany began to clamour for a declaration that as the Danes had torn it up, it was no longer binding, and should be denounced: and on 9 July the Federal Diet gave Denmark six weeks to withdraw the Patent. A prime factor in deciding Denmark's refusal was the provocative speech of Palmerston in the House of Commons (23 July). It was, he declared, "an important matter of British policy to maintain the independence and integrity of the Danish Monarchy": and while Holstein was a German state, the Confederation had "no rights" in Schleswig, which was "a matter of international law and of European concern". There was no use in disguising the fact that "what is at the bottom of the German design" (to connect Schleswig with Holstein) "is the dream of a German fleet and the wish to get Kiel as a German seaport". He was convinced that "if any violent attempt were made to overthrow those rights,...it would not be Denmark alone with which they would have to contend".[131] Morier in no way exaggerated when he wrote that the speech "has produced all the effect which the most determined wellwisher to Europe's disquiet could desire".[132] Nor was Russell less aggressive than his chief: for on 31 July he sent a message to Count Rechberg as Austrian Foreign Minister, that "if Germany persists in confounding Schleswig with Holstein, other Powers of Europe may confound Holstein with Schleswig and deny the right of Germany to interfere with the one any more than she has with the other, except as a European Power"[133]—a phrase which it is difficult to reconcile with a clear grasp of the national issues involved. A month later he warned Rechberg that if the two Powers persisted in advising Federal execution, they would do so against British advice and "must be responsible for the consequences", and "will be entering upon a grave European question".[134] Yet another month, and Russell warned the Federal Diet that "H.M.G. could not see with indifference a military occupation of Holstein", or "be indifferent to the bearing of such an act upon Denmark and upon European interests", and he entreated it to pause and to submit to mediation.[135] "The constitution of the Danish Monarchy", he told Malet, was "pre-eminently a Danish and not a German affair", and "it is precisely the attempt to involve Denmark in the sphere of German affairs ...which H.M.G. feel bound to resist".[136]

In the meantime, however, the prospects of effective mediation had steadily declined. On the one hand the Danes were confident of foreign support; on 26 August they rejected the Diet's demands and denounced execution as a warlike act: and on 28 September Frederick VII announced to a specially convoked Parliament a new constitution for Denmark and Schleswig—"our kingdom". On the other hand, the competition between Prussia and Austria for the leadership of German opinion grew apace: specially symptomatic was the Congress of German Princes (Fürstentag) which Francis Joseph had convoked at Frankfurt in August and which King William had politely declined to attend. The small German states were virtually unanimous in favour of Duke Frederick of Augustenburg, as sovereign of the united Duchies: but Bismarck had quite other designs and meanwhile held back, kept his eye on the French, and concentrated upon winning Russia to his side by services rendered in the Polish question. Moreover, in September Russell had sounded the French Government as to the possibility of joint action, but received from Drouyn de Lhuys the chilling reminder that any such démarche "would be analogous to the course pursued by British and French in the Polish question", and that the Emperor "desires to preserve entire liberty of action for France".[137]

Events took their course. On October 1 the Federal Diet answered King

Frederick's gesture of 28 September by demanding the withdrawal of the March Patent by the end of the month, under threat of federal execution in Holstein—in other words, German military occupation. Russell now appealed to Prussia to stay execution, and Bismarck was prepared to propose this, if only Denmark would first accept British mediation. But the infatuated Danish Government held on its course of incorporating Schleswig, and even Sir Augustus Paget, our very Danophil Minister at Copenhagen, regarded the proposed constitution as little less than a declaration of war. On 13 November the new constitution was voted at Copenhagen, and two days later Frederick VII, the last of the direct male line of Danish Kings, died, leaving to his distant cousin of Glücksburg, now Christian IX, the task of extricating Denmark from the deadlock. No more unfortunate moment could have been chosen for "this wretched King" to die:[138] for while a wave of Danish nationalism threatened Christian with expulsion if he refused to ratify, German opinion also flamed up when the nearest heir-male of the House of Oldenburg put forward his claim to the Duchies under the title of Duke Frederick VIII, and, with the enthusiastic backing of the smaller German courts and the whole Liberal German movement, appealed to Berlin for help. Bismarck showed a fresh mastery of tactics when he set himself to relegate this dynastic dispute to the background, without allowing anyone to suspect that he wanted the Duchies for Prussia, not for Frederick, and concentrated his efforts upon the constitutional issue. He cleverly professed himself ready for concessions, being virtually assured that the Danes in their blindness would save him from the necessity of ever implementing them. Christian IX's dilemma was a cruel one: by refusing his sanction to the November Constitution he would have risked his throne, by granting it he gave the German Courts a *casus belli* independent of the dynastic question, and indirectly promoted the Austro-Prussian accord.

Meanwhile a not unimportant role in the background was being played by Queen Victoria, who constantly urged moderation upon her Ministers, and reminded them that she and Albert had "always deprecated as unjust the arrangements of 1852".[139] Already in August Lord Granville, her special confidant in the Cabinet, told Lord Clarendon that "the Queen is up in her stirrups, very German".[140] She kept repeating "her determination not to consent to any measures which may involve her in the threatened rupture between Denmark and Germany";[141] she was "averse to our taking part in an attempt to coerce the people of Holstein":[142] and she showed an understanding of the German situation to which her Ministers (despite the sane reports of Malet and Ward) never attained, when she insisted that the "two German Powers will be supported by the whole of Germany", and that German public opinion would not allow the Governments to act according to "the luckless Protocol of 1852".[143] Incidentally, Malet reminded London that the Treaty of 1852 had never been submitted to the Federal Diet,[144] which therefore felt itself less than ever bound. In this connection it is instructive to note a conversation between the Saxon Minister, Count Vitzthum and Lord Palmerston, who complained of the attitude of Austria and Prussia, "who had signed the Treaty of 1852 as mandatories of the Confederation": it was necessary to remind him that that was exactly what they had not done. This is not the only incident which suggests that Palmerston's *bon mot* was quite true and that he had really forgotten the essential facts of the dispute.*

Russell found himself in an extremely awkward position, recognising grave faults on both sides, aware of the shortcomings of the Treaty of 1852, and unable to carry France with him, after his retreat in the Polish question and his abrupt rejection of Napoleon's proposals for a Congress. In this plight he sent Lord Wodehouse on a special mission to Copenhagen, whose declared aim was "to reconcile Denmark with Austria and Prussia, and if possible prevent a war"[145]—in other words, to square the circle. He urged repeal of the constitution, as the only way of staying execution, but the Danes refused to listen, the new Premier, Bishop Monrad, took an even stiffer line than his predecessor, and Russell exclaimed in despair, "We cannot give active support to a Government which puts itself so manifestly in the wrong." On the other hand, he feared that Germany was "mixing federal right in Holstein, international promises in Schleswig, a common constitution and the succession to the Crown, all in one hash".[146] Palmerston wrote to Russell with his usual frankness: "Schleswig is no part of Germany, and its invasion by German troops would be an act of war versus Denmark, which would in my clear opinion entitle Denmark to our active military and naval support. But you and I could not announce such a determination without the concurrence of the Cabinet and the consent of the Queen."[147] On 24 December Holstein was occupied, the enthusiasm for Frederick VIII was at its height, and the Federal Diet was quite obviously bent upon "rushing" Prussia. In the first days of the year Bismarck told Sir Andrew Buchanan very plainly that Denmark, by bringing the new Constitution into force at the New Year, had infringed the *status quo*, and that unless she revoked this action, the occupation of Schleswig must

---

* Vitzthum, *St Petersburg und London*, II, 253. Bernhardi records the wide indignation caused by Palmerston's public denial of having had any share in fixing the Danish succession and treats it as "an impudent lie" (*Der Streit um die Elbherzogtümer*, p. 389). The Danish Premier Hall issued a pamphlet containing the documentary proofs, but Palmerston is alleged to have bought up the edition, whereupon Trübner brought out an *English* edition and distributed it to members of Parliament and others. But may it not simply have been that Palmerston's memory was failing?

follow. Prussia could not simultaneously adhere to the Treaty of 1852 and tolerate its violation by Denmark. If, then, England interfered, Prussia would denounce the Treaty, there would be a new Cabinet, and it would be certain to adopt the Prussian Parliament's demand for the recognition of Duke Frederick.[148]

THE DANISH WAR OF 1864

By January it was clear to everyone on the Continent that Britain stood alone and was likely to be left talking. "It is not the Polish torch that frightens me," said the witty Clarendon, "but the Holstein match."[149] "At no period in the history of this question", writes Sir Adolphus Ward, "had British diplomacy been more active, and at no time had it had less effect."[150] On 16 January, then, Austria and Prussia addressed a joint ultimatum to Denmark, demanding the withdrawal of the constitution within two days. In vain was it pointed out that this was physically impossible, because Parliament was not in session: in vain did Denmark at last, on 30 January, accept a British proposal that the signatory Powers of 1852 should again meet in Conference at London. In the words of Roon, not of course advertised to the outer world, "The question is not one of right, but of force, and we have the force."[151] Already two years earlier Bismarck had said: "Only by war can the Danish question be solved in a manner favourable to us: the occasion for war can be found at any moment, when our relation to the Great Powers is one favourable for the conduct of a war."[152] On 1 February, then, Austro-Prussian forces invaded Schleswig, and the Danewerk was taken after five days. Palmerston used violent language to Bernstorff, but Bismarck, now that he was sure of Austrian co-operation, was not in the least disturbed.

Russell had hitherto been torn in two directions: he now turned his whole indignation against Germany. He again proposed joint action to the French: mediation should be offered on the basis of 1852, and if Austria and Prussia refused, a British squadron should be sent to Copenhagen, and a strong French corps to the Rhine. In conversation with the Prussian Minister he hinted at the possibility of the fleet going to the Baltic to protect Denmark.[153] But at this point Palmerston himself hesitated: a few weeks earlier he had told the Queen that "England could not consistently with her honour allow Denmark to perish without aiding in her defence".[154] But now he wrote to Russell that he fully shared his indignation, yet doubted "whether the Cabinet or the country are as yet prepared for active interference. The truth is that to enter into a military conflict with all Germany on continental ground would be a serious undertaking." They were at last up against the reality that Britain could at best place 20,000 troops in the field against a minimum of 200,000–300,000! Napoleon, on 28 January, warned London that he was not prepared to risk a war against the two German Powers, which for him would be a very serious matter upon land, and not merely a naval blockade, as in the case of England.

Palmerston, again, feared that French intervention might mean French conquest on the Rhine, which "would be an evil for us and would seriously affect the position of Holland and Belgium".[155] And so on 19 February Russell informed the Danes that Her Majesty's Government "will take no steps to arrest the conflict till after full consultations with France and Russia". Bernhardi, sent on a mission to study the English situation, has left on record the scornful comment, "They don't want to pay more than 7d. in the £ income tax, and know very well that it will rise to 10d. if there is war."[156] It soon became clear to him that Palmerston could not carry a war policy, despite all the bitterness and big talk so much in evidence, and that the real decision lay in Berlin.[157]

None the less, criticism grew steadily more vocal, and on 4 February 1864, in his speech on the Address, Lord Derby delivered a frontal attack upon Lord John Russell, such as has rarely been addressed by any Leader of the Opposition to a Foreign Secretary—summing up his policy "in two short, homely, but expressive words, 'meddle and muddle'. During the whole course of his diplomatic correspondence, wherever he has interfered—and he has interfered everywhere—he has been lecturing, scolding, blustering and retreating", and making it clear that for all his roaring he was "no lion at all, but only Snug the joiner." And he proceeded in still more mordant tones to declare that "as an Englishman I am lowered and humiliated in my own estimation by the result of the noble Earl's administration of foreign affairs. Thanks to the present Government we have at this moment not one single friend in Europe, but this England—this great country whose failing, if it was a failing, was that it went too direct and straightforward at what it aimed, which never gave a promise without the intention of performing, which never threatened without a full determination of striking, which never made a demand without being prepared to enforce it—this country is now in such a position that its menaces are disregarded, its magniloquent language is ridiculed, and its remonstrances are treated with contemptuous indifference by the small as well as by the Great Powers of the Continent."[158]

During March and April, then, the war continued, and all the time Queen Victoria was tireless in her efforts to restrain "those two dreadful old men", as she called them privately to dear Uncle Leopold. She fully shared the latter's view that it was as impossible to keep the Duchies with Denmark as it had been to keep Belgium with Holland.[159] To Granville especially she appealed. "She would feel it her duty, in the interests of this country and of the peace of Europe, to resist any proposal for war": she would ever be ready "to make a stand upon it", even if Russell were to resign.[160] She more than once forced Russell to withdraw or redraft some of his more pugnacious despatches.

Meanwhile, any real hope of French co-operation was diminished by two unfortunate incidents. A fresh plot was discovered against Napoleon's life, and it was alleged that Mazzini, the famous exile of Soho, was implicated in it, and that he enjoyed the special protection of Stansfeld, then one of the Civil Lords of the Admiralty. The Government refused to take action against Mazzini, and the House of Commons refused a vote of no confidence against Stansfeld:* and this was noted at the Tuileries as a double act of unfriendliness. Almost immediately afterwards this impression was heightened when in April Garibaldi visited England, and for a brief space became the darling alike of the populace and of the great world, receiving ovations such as probably no foreign visitor to these shores had ever received before. Nothing was ever more spontaneous, yet in Paris it was inevitably interpreted as something suspiciously near to an anti-French demonstration. Even the Prince of Wales took a part, and indeed Disraeli was alone among politicians of the front rank in holding aloof. The incident had the additional disadvantage of offending the Austrian no less than the French Emperor.

Russell does not seem to have realised the implications of these incidents, for almost at the same time he persuaded Clarendon to go over to Paris and sound the French once more. The envoy's conversation with Napoleon III dispelled the last hope of joint action. "We had received a *gros soufflet* with respect to Poland from Russia", Clarendon reported him as saying, "and to get another from Germany without resenting it was more than he could stand. He could not therefore join us in strong language to the German Powers, not being prepared to go to war with them." "He must be all the more cautious owing to the widespread belief in his designs for compensation on the Rhine: and he was not ready to pursue one policy on the Eider and a totally different one on the Po."[161]

Irritated by such incidents, and still hankering after a Prussian alliance against Austria, Napoleon made a secret overture to Berlin, offering his support to Prussia if she should decide to annex the Duchies as far as the Canal. His only condition was a popular plebiscite, and he asked for no compensation, though it was an obvious case of "favours to come": he even promised of his own accord to be very reserved towards Clarendon. Bismarck replied on 14 April that Prussia might consent to acknowledge

* When it afterwards transpired that he had allowed Mazzini to have letters addressed to his London house under an assumed name, Stansfeld insisted on resigning.

Duke Frederick, but was not prepared to wage war on his behalf: he approved the idea of consulting the population, but only on condition that it was quite clear to them that the partition of Schleswig was inevitable. When a few days later the news of the Danish defeat at Düppel reached Paris, Napoleon congratulated King William, adding later that for him the question of nationality and the wishes of the population were the main thing.[162] He also advised the King of Sweden to abandon all idea of armed intervention on behalf of Denmark.[163]

British public opinion was by now ardently on the Danish side, the press was full of warlike incitements, and there was much romantic sympathy with the Princess of Wales—Christian "the sea-king's daughter from over the sea"—the first non-German consort to reach these shores for a century and a half.* Lord Shaftesbury told the House of Lords that he "had never known the people of this country more profoundly stirred", and the egregious Lord Ellenborough urged the Government to take "any measures necessary to maintain the independence of Denmark".[164] But while the Lords made speeches, the German Powers made war. The British proposal for a conference was accepted without enthusiasm by the French, and on the German side was referred to the Federal Diet, which involved fresh delay: and even after it had accepted, the lines of Düppel were stormed on 17 April. At the end of the month Napoleon warned the Danish Minister that Britain would do nothing, and that Denmark would be wise to accept the frontier line offered by Prussia, as otherwise she risked losing everything.[165]

One further factor militated strongly in favour of peace. The patriotic press might preach support of Denmark, but the effects of the cotton famine upon Lancashire and upon industry generally, and our delicate relations with America, were a constant stimulus to caution.

THE LONDON CONFERENCE

The opening of the London Conference on 25 April seemed to offer some hopes of a settlement. But still the war went on, and that very week Fredericia fell before the Germans: over a fortnight elapsed before an armistice of four weeks could be negotiated, and all the time the Danish position was

---

* Married at Windsor just a year earlier, 10 March 1863. As King Leopold wrote to the Queen, now that the Prince Consort was no longer there, "Bertie and Alix...are constantly before the public in every imaginable shape and character, and fill entirely the public mind" (*Letters*, p. 218, 15 June 1864). A letter of Prince Albert to his brother Ernest, dated 21 July 1861, shows that the Queen and the Prince were fully conscious of "the political difficulties" of the Danish marriage and were only responsible for it in the sense that they did not oppose their son and could not find any alternative Princess. "But", he adds, "we must now see that this marriage is not looked upon as a triumph of Denmark over us and Prussia" (Bolitho, *Prince Consort and his Brother*, p. 215).

growing weaker. Palmerston again grew bellicose, and, this time without consulting the Cabinet, asked the Austrian Ambassador to call upon him (1 May) and warned him that if the Austrian fleet, then passing up the Channel, were to enter the Baltic or threaten Copenhagen, "I should look upon it as an affront and an insult to England: I could not and would not stand such a thing". Fortunately Apponyi gave a tactful assurance that the naval attack would not be made: but Palmerston found the Cabinet divided, and Granville, at the Queen's instance, complained of the way in which it had been ignored and advocated for it "perfect liberty of action".[166]

Palmerston had declared in Parliament that the only possible basis for the Conference was the Treaty of 1852, and Russell, that Austria and Prussia were "conscious that Schleswig and Holstein cannot be transferred to any other Power without a general concert and consideration of the whole question among the European Powers".[167] But Disraeli in a devastating speech, expressed great distrust of any Conference "*pendente lite*" and cruelly compared the experiment with that other "disastrous and fruitless" effort of Russell, the mission to Vienna in 1855. Then, coming to the kernel of the whole matter, he asked, "Is armed Europe to interfere and by force of arms render Holstein and Schleswig loyal and contented subjects of the King of Denmark?" Such a policy was "not consistent with the principles of British policy nor in harmony with the spirit of the age in which we live....The drivers have lost the road, the reins have fallen from their hands: the horses are wild."[168] Here Disraeli clearly grasped what the Liberal Foreign Secretary, for all his advocacy of Italian liberty, had almost wholly overlooked, that the Duchies had their own point of view, which was neither Danish nor Prussian.

Russell reached the height of ineffectiveness in his speech of 11 April before the House of Lords. A plan had been conceived, he said, for the dismemberment of Denmark, and "to prevent its execution we sought the co-operation of France, Russia and Sweden, in order to give material assistance to Denmark in resisting....Were we to intervene *alone*? Our object was to maintain the balance of power and the peace of Europe", but it was not the business of England alone. "I remember hearing Canning say, 'I am told that we must have war sooner or later. If that be the case, I say later.' *I say with Canning, 'later'.*" The Premier had declared "that this is an iniquitous aggression on the part of Austria and Prussia, and the resistance of the Danes is justified". But "if we are to interfere, the Powers of Europe ought to go together....While fully conscious of the power of England, yet we do not wish to hurry into war without necessity. And for my own part I think a pacific policy is our true policy." This lame conclusion gave Lord Derby an opening of which he was not slow to take advantage: and he proceeded to argue that Russell "by the strength of his remonstrances and the feebleness of his acts has confirmed the impression so prevalent throughout Europe that we have ceased to be a Great Power, that our military and naval position has been made subordinate to our trading and commercial interests, and that however England may bluster...there is not the slightest danger of her interfering materially to exercise the slightest influence or control in the affairs of Europe".[169]

On 12 May the armistice—proposed by Britain with the backing of France, Sweden and Russia—was at last concluded, but at the Conference agreement seemed as far off as ever. This was the moment which Lord Ellenborough chose in order to make a venomous attack upon the Queen in the House of Lords. There was, he affirmed, "a strong impression on the Continent, that in all public questions relating to Germany Her Majesty's Ministers have as much difficulty in carrying out a purely English policy, as was experienced...in the reigns of the two first sovereigns of the House of Hanover", before George III "gloried in the name of Briton". He hoped that the Government would now "so act as to show the whole world that the policy and feelings of George III shall animate the Government, and will succeed...in restoring to our diplomacy the authority and influence which it has now lost". Lord Russell was at his best, and more than usually tactful, in pointedly claiming for the Government the entire responsibility for policy: and if he made the inevitable reference to William III as "the great founder of the foreign policy of England in modern times", he had more than the usual excuse for doing so. In passing he took the line that "of all the wild, imprudent and extravagant wars...a war to establish Poland would have been the most wild, imprudent and extravagant."[170]

THE QUEEN PROTESTS

It is not surprising that the Queen, still nerve-wracked from the loss of her husband, should have reacted very strongly and hoped "everyone will know how she resents Lord Ellenborough's conduct and how she despises him".[171] She complained of his "malignant and unmanly insinuations" to Lord Derby as his party chief, and received in reply a long and embarrassed letter, admitting that the "impulsive and unguarded" Ellenborough was defiant of all party discipline, but soothing her by a warm recognition of "how fully Your Majesty understands and appreciates the duty of a constitutional Sovereign".[172] To-day we can form a fairer estimate of the cruel wrong done to the Queen: for though she felt very keenly on the German question and may sometimes have unduly betrayed her feelings, history has in the main confirmed her reading of events. Her main desire was to avert war, not only on general principles, but because it meant a conflict with the Germany which she loved, and because she knew Britain's utter lack of military resources for a continental war. But it ought never to have been necessary for her to assure Palmerston, as she did in January, that "no feeling for Germany could ever make her view an international question otherwise than as it might affect the interests of the people of England".[173] "My heart and sympathies are all German", she told the Crown Princess:[174] she had always condemned the futile treaty of 1852. But on the Prussian side she saw "a want of forbearance" towards the amiable King Christian, while she recognised that in Denmark government was "in the hands of a most violent party who are utterly regardless of consequences". British interests did not seem to be sufficiently involved, so long as Denmark proper was not in danger of conquest: she deplored the resentment kindled in Germany by British interference and advice, and objected to her own Government's "imputations on the motives of the German Powers". "Lord Russell", she told Lord Granville, "is very fair, but Lord Palmerston alarms and overrules him."[175] Above all, throughout the crisis, she never ceased to stress "the absolute necessity of settling nothing contrary to the feelings and wishes of the Duchies": and here it was that British opinion was most astray. It was too much inclined to regard the issue as one between a gallant little Power and two big bullies, and to ignore the fact that all Holstein and a large section of Schleswig looked to Germany for aid against Danish chauvinism, and that the small states and all the Liberal Princes and intellectuals were enthusiastically on the side of the Duchies, and long critical of the Prussian Cabinet's reserve and seeming indifference. To sum up, the Queen's three main points were eminently sane: "(1) not to let this country be dragged into a useless war; (2) not to agree to a settlement which could not be durable; (3) not to let a sovereign be imposed upon the Duchies against their will".[176]

For two months (25 April–25 June) the Conference sat in London, but little profit is to be gleaned from its barren records. Criticism of the Government welled up in the country, but the Opposition showed great restraint so long as there was the faintest hope of agreement. Disraeli, it is true, on the very eve of the Conference, pointed to "the total want of system" noticeable in foreign affairs, to the "climax of mismanagement reached in the Polish affair, and to our recent folly in leaving France in the lurch before Europe": but he refrained as yet from moving any vote of censure and listened in silence to Palmerston's denial that "we lured France into a position of humiliation". Behind the scenes, however, Russell once more sounded Paris, but Cowley was informed by Rouher that while France would on no account be against England in the Danish question, the Emperor was only disposed to act "*if England sends troops and disembarks them*", and that his main preoccupations were Venetia and "perhaps the Rhine", the Danish question seeming to him quite secondary.[177] From this Russell drew the doubtless accurate conclusion, that if Britain entered the war, France would in all probability join in, but that this would give an entirely new and far more dangerous turn to the war. Even Palmerston came to the conclusion that "the absorption of Schleswig-Holstein in Germany was a lesser evil than the incorporation of the Rhenish provinces in France", and that the attempt to realise this latter would mean a general European war. In actual fact, Napoleon III at this stage made the highly sensible proposal of a plebiscite, and the Danes refused, thus wrecking the last hope of a peaceful agreement.

Meanwhile the excitement had steadily grown in Germany, heightened by news of the successful seafight off Heligoland on the very eve of the armistice. This time it suited Bismarck to fan the flames: "we'll let the whole pack give tongue", he said: and the cessation of hostilities was balanced by a declaration from the two German Powers that they no longer regarded the Treaty of 1852 as binding. On 17 May they went farther and rejected the idea of Personal Union between Denmark and the Duchies. By this time Bismarck had got the whiphand of Austria: when Rechberg showed dislike of the Augustenburg candidature, he mentioned for the first time the possible alternative of Prussian annexation, half veiling his design in perfectly plausible reluctance that the erection of yet another petty state should be the sole reward for Prussia's great exertions in the wider German cause.[178] He had told Duke Frederick's mother that he knew nothing of her son's right of inheritance, but only Prussian power: and so utterly was he possessed by this outlook, that King William, in his simple way, once asked him in astonishment whether he was not a German![179] And all the time he was slowly but surely supplanting German liberalism in its leadership of the cause of German unity.

RUSSELL'S UNSUCCESSFUL MEDIATION

The last stage of the Conference centred round Russell's proposal for partition, both sides accepting in principle, but any agreement on the actual line proving quite unattainable. When during the negotiations Bernstorff declared that Germany could not trust a single German subject to the King of Denmark, Russell, with tears in his eyes, declined to communicate so insulting a message to the Danes. Bernstorff and Beust retorted by suggesting that the people should be consulted: but to this Apponyi, the Austrian delegate, demurred.[180] On 18 June the Prussian proposal was definitely put forward and rejected. Russell's final effort at a compromise was that the disputed frontier line should be submitted for arbitration to a neutral sovereign, and that Britain should promise material assistance to Denmark "if the German Powers refused their consent". At this the Queen protested most vigorously, realising the position in which Britain would be placed— "standing alone in support of Denmark against all Europe". She realised too that, in her uncle's words, "the game of the Danes is to resist and to draw England into the struggle in its favour". "Only imagine", she wrote to King Leopold, "that Johnny had again stated to me what he proposed most dangerously, without the slightest authorisation from the Cabinet! And this for the third time!"[181] This was too much for Granville, Charles Wood, Gladstone and other members of the Cabinet, and in face of such internal dissensions the plan was stillborn. Even then Russell was rash enough to tell Parliament that the fleet was "ready for any service which it may be called upon to render", and three days later Palmerston had to explain the phrase away.[182]

The last straw was Prussia's refusal to renew the expiring armistice, except for a period of six months. The candid Clarendon told Bernstorff, "You have won: you entered as masters of the situation, and as masters you have left it."[183] The Conference finally broke down on 25 June: next day hostilities were resumed, and the Prussians effected a landing in Alsen and threatened to overrun the little country. On 28 June Bishop Monrad made a last despairing appeal to the London Cabinet, reminding it that Denmark had "step by step followed the advice of the neutral Powers, and especially that of the English Cabinet", but that "Denmark was still without allies". To this Lord Russell replied on 6 July that Her Majesty's Government sympathised "with King and people in the severe trial which they have been obliged to undergo", but that they "have never engaged themselves, nor can they now, to support the Danish cause by force of arms, or to impose upon Germany the conditions suggested in the Conference".[184] The background of this humiliating Note, which brought down the Eider-Dane Cabinet and left Denmark with no choice save to sue for peace, was a week of acute dissensions inside the British Government, increased by the emphatic and well-reasoned protests of the Queen.[185] Yet on 9 July Russell was still sufficiently complaisant to write to Cowley, "I trust the Danes and Germans will now make peace, leaving the Danes free from German interference and giving the Germans over to German rule....I am very glad we have not given in to the temptation of a war between France and Germany. The French, if they get an inch, will certainly take an ell."[186] Who can to this day read such words without a glow of shame for a Foreign Secretary to whom fear of French action on the Rhine outweighed all considerations of honour towards the little nation whose very mistakes and obstinacy were above all due to British encouragement?

On 18 July the armistice was renewed, and by the peace preliminaries of 1 August Denmark ceded to Prussia and Austria jointly Lauenburg and the whole of Schleswig-Holstein. The ardent Danish minority of the north had to pay for the intransigeance of Copenhagen, which might, even at a late date, have saved for Denmark most of what the world-conjuncture of 1918 restored to her. The settlement was rendered definitive by the Peace of Vienna (30 October). Bismarck had only to bide his time: the *condominium* he knew to be in the long run untenable, but before Austria could be edged out, her assistance was needed to keep Duke Frederick from his inheritance. "Prussia", wrote the Queen to her daughter the Crown Princess, "must only NEVER take it for herself, but let good and much tried Fritz Holstein have it."* At the final *dénouement* in 1866 her disappointment was correspondingly great. But Bismarck had taken his measure of Britain's inertia, of France's blindness, of their essential inability to cooperate, while Western statesmen utterly failed to realise how formidable a force Prussia was becoming under his bold guidance.†

RUSSELL ON THE DEFENSIVE

Meanwhile, on 27 June Russell had had to face a sceptical and angry House of Commons. He began by quoting the precedent of Canning's attitude towards the French invasion of Spain in 1823: on that occasion there had been a "protest against invasion, as contrary to all the principles of English policy, opposed not only to the sentiments of the country, but to the settlement of Europe", and yet had "kept peace and declared neutrality". The main part of the speech was a lengthy historical discursus, into which it would be impossible to follow him. Britain, he argued, had been unable to look upon federal execution as a matter of indifference, because her aim was "the integrity and independence of Denmark": yet when the two German Powers persisted in demanding the separation of the Duchies and refused to acknowledge King Christian as their sovereign, it was useless to insist, unless all the neutral Powers were "prepared to carry on a great war". The later proposal, that Holstein and south Schleswig should be

* The Duke's younger brother Christian married Queen Victoria's daughter Helena in 1865.

† It is worth recording Sir Spencer Walpole's verdict: "He [Palmerston] liked to play a game of brag on the card-table of Europe, and habitual success had convinced him that he was master of the game. He was fated, before his life closed, to meet a player far stronger than himself, whom it was his misfortune to misunderstand and despise. He met Herr von Bismarck with the same easy confidence with which he had met other antagonists, and he retired from the contest a broken and a beaten man" (*Twenty-Five Years*, 1, 528).

surrendered by Denmark, but a general guarantee laid down for the rest of the Danish possessions, had been met by the insistence of Prussia and Austria on their right of conquest. Denmark had assumed that Britain was "bound to maintain at all hazards" this proposal, but, said Lord Russell, this had never been stated by Britain. The French project of a plebiscite on a basis of racial division had been rejected by the Danes, and it now became "the duty of England to show a greater attachment to peace than Austria and Prussia have shown". Her policy was neutrality, and he refused to answer what he would do if joint Austro-Prussian forces went to Copenhagen. Lord Derby spoke of the peace of Europe as "in fearful peril": there was danger of war with Germany—"that Power...which is the great conservative counterpoise to the ambitions of East and West".[187]

On the same day in the Commons Palmerston voiced "great sympathy" for Denmark, which "had been ill-used". "We should have been glad if we had found it possible to advise our Sovereign to take part with Denmark in the approaching struggle." But Denmark had at first been very wrong, her independence was not involved, France and Russia declined to take a hand, and "the whole brunt of the effort requisite for dislodging the German troops would fall upon this country alone". If, however, the existence of Denmark as an independent state should be at stake, if Copenhagen were stormed and the King captured, "we might then think it our duty to adopt another course". This, coming from the venerable fire-eater, was too much for the House of Commons, which broke into angry and ironical cheers. Disraeli was quick to declare that he heard with astonishment "a continuation of those senseless and spiritless menaces which have impaired the just influence of this country in the councils of Europe". He would sooner see affairs entrusted to men like Cobden and Bright; they at least would threaten nobody, would not exasperate Germany, and would not "lure on Denmark by delusive counsels and fallacious hopes".[188]

The final stage of this humiliating controversy was reached in the full-dress debate on a Vote of Censure moved by Disraeli, and expressing "regret that while the course pursued by Her Majesty's Government had failed to maintain their avowed policy of upholding the integrity and independence of Denmark, it has lowered the just influence of this country in the capitals of Europe, and thereby diminished the securities of peace". Disraeli opened all his batteries upon Palmerston and Russell, starting from the former's fatal encouragement of the Danes in his speech of 23 July 1863 (*supra* p. 441), and then turning to the latter's Polish policy and "that curt, and as I conceive, most offensive, reply" to the Emperor's suggestion of a Congress. If, however, the intervention urged by Russell had been accepted by Napoleon, it "must inevitably have produced a great European War". As it was, the

Government's policy was one of "menaces never accomplished and promises never fulfilled". The London Conference just completed was "a barren failure"; and the British Government's contribution to it had been proposals for "the dismemberment of Denmark—so much for integrity", and for a "joint guarantee of the Powers—so much for independence". It had shown "equal lack of capacity, prudence, dexterity...and knowledge of human nature". Seldom has a leader of the Opposition offered such an indictment of a Premier, as his concluding phrases. "The position of England in the counsels of Europe is essentially that of a moderating and mediatorial Power. Within twelve months we have been twice repulsed at St Petersburg. Twice have we supplicated in vain at Paris. We have menaced Austria, and Austria has allowed our menaces to pass her like the idle wind. We have threatened Prussia, and Prussia has defied us.... They have alienated Russia, they have estranged France, and then they call Parliament together to declare war against Germany....I find Europe impotent to vindicate public law, because all the great alliances are broken down." [189]

Palmerston replied in what was probably the least effective speech of his whole career. He could not help alluding to his speech of the previous July, so universally accepted as a pledge of armed support to Denmark: but all he had to say was, "What I was pointing to was an European war, not a war between this country and the German Powers." The Government had "tried to persuade France and Russia to concur with us in every step we took", but the French (who, he most misleadingly contended, were *not* offended by the Polish affair) were entitled to object that for Britain it would be "a naval war, but that they had all Germany on their frontier". None the less, he argued, the doctrine of the Balance of Power was not exploded, but was "founded on the nature of man". "It means that it is to the interest of the community of nations that no one nation should acquire such a preponderance as to endanger the security of the rest: and it is for the advantage of all, that the smaller Powers should be respected in their independence and not swallowed up by their more powerful neighbours." [190] For the rest, he was reduced, in his denial that British influence had been lowered, to reciting all the financial achievements and economies of the last four years, which, it was only too notorious, had been effected by Gladstone as Chancellor of the Exchequer, in the teeth of an indifferent, if not positively hostile, Prime Minister. Outstanding features of the long debate were the speeches of Cobden, who denounced Russell's "diplomatic anarchy", and "diplomatic meddling", and of Lord Robert Cecil, who agreed with Cobden that if we did not mean to fight, we ought not to interfere. "If Mr Cobden had been Foreign Secretary instead of Lord Russell", said the future holder of the same office, "I fully believe this country would occupy a position proud and noble compared to that which she occupies at this moment. She would at least have been entitled to the credit of holding out in the name of England no hopes which she did not intend to fulfil, of entering into no engagements from which she was ready to recede."[191]

In the end the Government was defeated in the Lords by 9 votes (177 to 168), but was saved in the Commons by an amendment suggested by Cobden and moved by Kinglake, yet only by the narrow margin of 313 to 295. Palmerston, in addition to eclipse on the Continent, had the added mortification of owing his safety to Cobden, his special bugbear in the House, and to Gladstone, the least congenial of his own colleagues. After the debate was over Gladstone made a brief entry in his diary—"This debate ought to be an epoch in foreign policy. We all have much to learn."[192]

Very forcible was the attack made by Lord Carnarvon upon the language "now used for several years" by Lord Russell. "The Prime Minister", he said, "was, I think it will be admitted, the first during the many years that he was Foreign Secretary, to import this new system of strong expressions into the diplomacy of the Foreign Office: but there is this at least to be said, that he generally backed up his language by strong action, and at all events his strong expressions were for the most part regulated by the conventions of diplomatic intercourse. But the noble Earl opposite (Russell)... has gone far beyond his model. We have heard from him during the last two years denunciations against every one of the Great Powers in Europe—France, Russia, Austria, Prussia—and I am bound to say that the strength of his action has been exactly in inverse proportion to the strength of his expressions. The language which he has used would in a former generation have been tantamount to a declaration of war....His speeches...are in fact electioneering speeches addressed from the platform of the Foreign Office to the free and independent Governments of Europe."[193]

Russell's activities as Foreign Secretary may be summed up in the words of Walter Bagehot: "He hardly conducted a foreign controversy in which the extreme intelligibility of his words did not leave a sting behind them."[194] In short, the exact opposite of that other conception of the ideal diplomatist, as one who uses words to conceal his thoughts: and surely we may stop for an instant to admit that, as so often, the true ideal lies halfway between the two extremes. As Mr Cecil has neatly put it, Russell's "diplomacy was not unlike himself—slight and thin and shrill".[195] Even Lord Morley accepts as the judgment of history Disraeli's contemptuous criticism of the Russell-Palmerston era, "that whether we looked to Russia, to Greece, to France, there had been exhibited by ministers a confusion, an inconsistency, a contrariety of courses and a total want of planning in their diplomacy".[196]

THE DEATH OF PALMERSTON

Leaving aside the long tragi-comedy of Anglo-American relations during the Civil War, which was sadly bungled by Lord Russell, and which left behind it the aftermath of the "Alabama Case", we may treat the Danish controversy as the last big incident of foreign policy in the Palmerstonian Era. Though England was only too conscious of failure and diminished prestige abroad, the storms of 1863–4 were followed by a curious lull in 1865, due perhaps to absorption in the manifold changes of the industrial age, of railway and shipping development and of overseas expansion. To the end of his life, however, Palmerston continued to enjoy wide popularity, and even his party rivals were by no means eager to overthrow him—partly doubtless owing to the personal problem still presented by "Dizzy". But the Prime Minister was noticed to be ageing rapidly, though his physical powers were even now remarkable. Then, on 18 October, somewhat suddenly, he died at the age of eighty, and Russell, recognised by the Queen as the inevitable substitute, reigned in his stead. "Lord Russell again Prime Minister is strange," commented King Leopold to his royal niece, "but these politicians never refuse."[197] But as Clarendon very astutely observed, Palmerston had "held a great bundle of sticks together: they are now unwound, and there is nobody to tie them up again".[198]

GENERAL ESTIMATE OF PALMERSTON'S POLICY

It is the natural moment for considering Palmerston's foreign policy in its broader aspects. Thus regarded, on a basis of pure theory, it is likely to commend itself to the vast majority of his countrymen since that day, for its implications at home were eminently sound. He sought, as we saw, to promote constitutional and free government and so to avert revolution by timely concession: and his attitude undoubtedly contributed to the consolidation of the internal situation in Great Britain, and the remarkable contrast which it offered in 1848 to almost every continental country.

In defending himself against the attacks of Anstey and Urquhart in 1848,* Palmerston laid down as the basis of his policy "the principle of maintaining peace and friendly understanding with all nations, as long as it was possible to do so consistently with a due regard to the interests, honour and dignity of this country". England, he said, is "a Power sufficiently strong to steer her own course and not tie herself as an unnecessary ap-

---

* See *supra*, p. 255.

pendage to the policy of any other Government". "Her real policy is to be the champion of justice and right, pursuing that course with moderation and prudence, not becoming the Quixote of the world, but giving the weight of her moral sanction and support wherever she thinks that justice is, and that wrong has been done. As long as she sympathises with right and justice, she will never find herself altogether alone....I say it is a narrow policy to suppose that this country or that is to be marked out as the eternal ally or the perpetual enemy of England. We have no eternal allies and we have no perpetual enemies. Our interests are eternal and perpetual, and those interests it is our duty to follow. It is our duty not to pass too harsh a judgment on others because they do not exactly see things in the same light as we see: and it is our duty not to lightly engage this country in the frightful responsibilities of war, because from time to time we may find this or that Power disinclined to concur with us." And he ended by quoting Canning's famous phrase, that "with every British Minister the interests of England ought to be the shibboleth of his policy".[199]

Again, in the Pacifico debate, before his famous comparison of a British and a Roman citizen, he coined the phrase: "We have shown that liberty is compatible with order: that individual freedom is reconcilable with obedience to the law."[200]

These were views unexceptionable in themselves, and thoroughly in keeping with the sentiments of Victorian England, and with the new spirit of nationalism which was so characteristic of the age. In our day there is in many quarters a tendency to depreciate the idea of nationality and to forget that if indeed it be a disease, we ourselves suffered from it last century in quite as aggressive and virulent a form as any of the Continental nations. Of that form Palmerston and the public opinion which made the Crimean War are the most typical expression.

It is not the theory so much as the practice of Palmerston which is open to criticism. That he was from the first alive to the significance of the new national currents in Europe, redounds entirely to his credit: and he certainly helped on the process which linked together the national and liberal movements towards the middle of the century. This deserves special emphasis, for it is still too little realised that even in Italy—perhaps the classical instance—the two currents were by no means always or necessarily blended in one.

But if he was open to the idea of Nationality in its new nineteenth-century form, he had still enough of the eighteenth century about him to retain a belief in the Balance of Power in Europe as the basis of our continental policy. As the true successor of Canning, he distrusted the attempt to govern Europe by Conference, but mainly because he realised so clearly the essential conflict of opinion and outlook between the Western and Eastern groups of Powers. Even Castlereagh, as we saw earlier, had been conscious of the intermediate position of Britain between the purely absolutist and the purely revolutionary theory of the State, and never overlooked the fact that though in his view she was an essentially Conservative Power, her constitution had passed through more than one revolutionary phase. Palmerston found a situation that had ripened further, and though obviously differing greatly in his outlook from the Tory Castlereagh, he still held in its essentials the intermediate British view that while Absolutism only made ultimate revolution certain, a constitutional regime was everywhere the best antidote to revolution. This theory, however, though sound in itself, led him to regard constitutional government as a panacea, and with a view to attaining this, to support democratic currents everywhere. The wise Stockmar, in noting this, ascribes it, as in the case of Pitt, to "insufficient knowledge of Continental Europe"[201] and it is indeed true that Palmerston, though an admirable French scholar, remained entirely insular.

Where his eighteenth- and nineteenth-century outlooks mingled and produced a curiously hybrid result, was in his attitude to the Eastern Question and to Turkey: for like many other British statesmen, he was not prepared to apply the new national principles to South Eastern Europe, and yet rejected the assumption of the eighteenth century that Turkey was doomed to partition. The only practicable alternative was to proclaim its reformability, and to urge reforms upon the Porte with varying degrees of insistence.

This, the worst of Palmerston's miscalculations, was due to his suspicion of Russia, both on account of its autocratic principles and its alleged designs upon India: and till a very much later date we find the dogma that the road to India must be defended at Constantinople, not at Suez.

One other point in Palmerston's creed was his belief in Austria as a Great Power and almost as the keystone of the vault: and the fact that his contemporaries, both in Austria and outside it, failed to credit him with such sentiments and indeed imagined him to be Austria's deadliest enemy, illustrates in a somewhat drastic way the difference between his theories and his methods.

Undoubtedly the soundest point in his whole policy was his desire for a French alliance, both as a guarantee of European peace and as a natural development of Liberal as against autocratic principles. Hence his cooperation with Louis Philippe in the first years after the July Revolution, and especially in the Belgian question. Hence also the speed and readiness with which he accepted the new French regime in 1848 and again in 1851. Even in the crisis of 1839–41, when, as we saw, he was mainly responsible for alienating France, or again in 1846 during the quarrel over the Spanish marriages, he undoubtedly regarded friendship with France as the aim, even though his methods were ill calculated to promote it.

Palmerston was daring, consistent, far-sighted, very clear in the definition of foreign problems, ready to take risks, anxious to avoid dubious inter-pretations, true to his word when given, and jealous of the honour of his country: but he also possessed the defects of these qualities. For he was not merely provocative, but provocative with a veneer of flippancy and raciness such as foreigners could neither understand nor appreciate, and despite his very considerable acquaintance with the Continent, he was yet lacking in the sympathies which create a diplomatic atmosphere. In short, Palmerston always acted *fortiter in re*, but rarely *suaviter in modo*. Indeed, it is no injustice to his memory to quote the verdict passed upon him by Prince Metternich in 1840—in other words, at a time when the two were working together—"Lord Palmerston has a kink in the mind (*un travers dans l'esprit*) which always prevents him from being entirely right in any affair. Where his mind goes straight in principle, he forgets to scrutinise the means of execution, whereas where his attitude is wrong in fundamentals, he is fertile in expedients."[202] After 1848 we have the grotesque irony of the exiled Metternich describing Palmerston as "a tyrant, and we are no longer in the century of tyranny".*

Professor Hearnshaw, in his admirably clear estimate of Palmerston, says as much as can be said for him, but certainly does not exaggerate when he credits him with "the instincts of an autocrat", and has to admit that "few indeed except Lord John Russell would have tolerated so long" the utter insubordination towards his chief and colleagues and sovereign alike, with which he directed the Foreign Office, while exacting complete obedience from his subordinates.[203]

This is the place to quote Queen Victoria's comment on the dead minister. Writing to King Leopold, to whom she could safely unburden herself, she said: "Palmerston had many valuable qualities, though many bad ones, and we had, God knows, terrible trouble with him about foreign affairs....I *never* liked him or could ever the least respect him....He was very vindic-tive, and personal feelings influenced his political acts very much."[204] This criticism from one who had unequalled opportunities for judging and who herself showed marvellous personal restraint in dealing with him, must be placed in the forefront of any estimate, even if not fully accepted. It

---

* "C'est un tyran et nous ne sommes plus au siècle de la tyrannie" (Duchesse de Dino, I, 294–6). Another hostile French verdict was that of M. de Jarnac, once Ambassador in London, who in his memoirs wrote of Palmerston: "It was the influence of a storm upon nature, a simple disturbance without profit....In politics restraint and opportunity are everything, and the best causes may be cruelly served when reprehensible means are persistently employed" (article on "Lord Palmerston" in *Revue des deux Mondes*, CIV, 587).

coincides exactly with Metternich's considered opinion. "Lord Palmerston is an awkward bedfellow (*un très mauvais coucheur*). He wants to take his revenge on whatever does not move in his direction—whether straight or crooked, matters little to him."[205] And again, referring to the Greek affair, he wrote that Palmerston, "*ne connaissant point de ménagements*", had "given free rein to his personal hates".[206] On the other hand it would be unjust not to insist upon his capacity for hard work,* and for mastering a subject in all its details, with the result that he was often enough able to overbear sound criticism by a serried array of facts.

His autocratic temper was combined with a recklessness and vehemence of language such as has rarely been equalled in a responsible statesman. This is abundantly proved by the numerous extracts already quoted from his correspondence: but as a crowning instance it may perhaps be permissible to adduce an incident from the year 1848. King Ludwig of Bavaria, presumably at the instance of his son King Otto of Greece, had hinted to the British Minister in Munich, Sir John Milbanke, that relations between Athens and London might be improved, if a certain member of the British Legation could be transferred to another post. Milbanke duly reported this to London and at once received instructions from Palmerston to inform the Bavarian Premier that if he wished "to be on good terms" with London, he would do well "to abstain from any attempt to interfere with our diplomatic arrangements, as such attempts are as offensive as they will be fruitless". "Pray make him clearly comprehend that I will never sacrifice any British diplomatic officer, high or low, to the whims or caprices of any foreign Prince or potentate, and that even if I were disposed to do so...King Otho is the last sovereign on earth whose wishes would have the slightest influence on my mind. Otho has behaved too ill in every respect to deserve the slightest consideration from the British Government, and he must greatly alter his conduct, both to England and Greece, before we can feel the smallest desire to consult his feelings in the most trifling matter."[207] This outburst, it is true, was addressed to a Government too weak to express its resentment in the natural way: but we have already seen that the tone adopted towards France or Austria was equally unwarrantable.

It may seem to some readers that more than enough has been said in criticism of Palmerston, and it is the barest justice to close this estimate by stressing his uprightness of character and high sense of patriotism. There is a passage in one of his earlier speeches as Foreign Secretary, which is more revealing than many volumes, and has therefore been reserved for quota-

---

* M. de Jarnac quotes, with evident approval, a remark once made to himself by Palmerston at the Foreign Office: "I think I am to-day the politician in Europe who has worked the most."

tion at this later stage. On 2 August 1832 he dealt in the following terms with a motion of Henry Bulwer on what the latter regarded as the precarious situation of the German Federal constitution. "I am prepared to admit that the independence of constitutional states, whether they are powerful like France and the United States, or of less relative political importance, such as the minor states of Germany, never can be a matter of indifference to the British Parliament, or, I should hope, to the British public. Constitutional states I consider to be the natural allies of this country.... Let persons recommend as much as they will the propriety of England withdrawing itself from all political connection with the rest of the world, my opinion is that as long as our commerce is of importance to us, as long as continental armies are in existence, as long as it is possible that a power in one quarter may become dangerous to a power in another—so long must England look with interest on the transactions of the Continent, and so long is it proper for this country, in the maintenance of its own independence, not to shut its eyes to anything that threatens the independence of Germany."[208]

It may be that Palmerston was all too prone to regard British institutions as a panacea for all political evils in the world: this was, we know, an illusion which most people in Victorian England shared, and which even our own generation has not altogether shaken off. But the case which he then presented to the House is one of general application, and rests upon principles which are just as true in our own day as in his.

Palmerston's vindication of British interests has endeared him to many and certainly entitles him to rank as one of Britain's greatest Foreign Ministers: his genuine devotion to the principles of free, progressive and representative government was a very vital factor in the evolution of the whole Continent towards that democratic ideal which even now is so far from realisation, but which is the sole alternative to desperate political adventure. But of his methods and tactics no real defence can be offered, and to-day they deserve the close study of all statesmen and diplomatists, as the very model of what should be avoided. It is not to Palmerston, but to Castlereagh and Canning before him, to Salisbury and Grey after him, that we must turn, if we wish to see true statesmanship tempered by character and restraint.

THE TWO PARTNERS

No estimate of Palmerston would be complete which ignored the unique relationship in which, for the last six years of his life, he stood to Russell. Clarendon, some months after he had gracefully relinquished his own claim to the Foreign Office, expressed the view that "John Russell has neither policy nor principles of his own, and is in the hands of Palmerston, who is an

artful old dodger".[209] This verdict of the two men's closest colleague is not
to be dismissed lightly, but it hardly does justice to the ardent and restless
character of Russell, who had his own views on every point of detail and
could never let well alone. It is certainly remarkable that two men who
were almost at the opposite poles in temperament and outlook, and had
quarrelled so incessantly, should in the evening of life become the closest of
partners and work together better than ever before.*

The return of the Liberals to power in 1859, and the definite absorption
of the Peelites, was a landmark in our parliamentary history, marking as it
did the revival of the two-party system at its best. In foreign policy also
there was a change during these six years of dual control. The policy of non-
intervention enforced by Castlereagh had been reinterpreted and transformed by Canning and then actually inverted by Palmerston, till, after the
sober interlude of Aberdeen, intervention in its extreme form in almost every
part of the world had been the chief feature of Palmerston's last term at the
Foreign Office. The culminating point had been reached in the Crimean
War, but there was a long aftermath of arrogance and panic. At last, however, the current set once more in favour of non-intervention: and there was
a double incentive from the Tory wing under Derby, and from the extreme
Radicals, led by Cobden and Bright. The Palmerston-Russell regime represents the last flicker of the old mentality. There is still Palmerston's incorrigible love of downright expression and peremptory interference, but it
is now blended with the didactic and meddlesome tones of Russell, all the
more irritating because so insularly earnest. For Palmerston was always
frank and courageous to the point of recklessness, but thought out beforehand the implications of his action, whereas Russell only too often launched
forth into verbose theories without a notion of whither they would lead him.
On one occasion we find him proposing, in deference to the Queen, "to omit
everything which might be construed as a threat and to confine himself to
pure reasoning": here is the true mid-Victorian doctrinaire, who if his sex
had been different, would have been the supreme blue-stocking of his age.
In one of Palmerston's instructions to Stratford Canning there occurs the
phrase, "we must not give Russia a chance of representing Britain as urging
Turkey on to resistance, but backing out ourselves".[210] But here lies the
difference between Palmerston, who sometimes trailed his coat, and Russell,
who beat more than one undignified retreat and gravely injured British
prestige. And so it could be asserted, not without reason, from the Conservative side, that our foreign policy in these years produced "a rich harvest
of autumnal indiscretions".

* There were many who regretted the reconciliation and echoed Charles Greville's
sigh, "How much was sacrificed for that object!"

It would, however, be most unfair to take leave of Lord Russell on such a note. There was a flash of pure enthusiasm about the man which won all hearts and atoned for his frail and unimpressive appearance—when in the phrase of Lytton "languid Johnny glowed to glorious John". After his final retirement he confessed, in a disarming preface to his collected speeches, that he had "committed many errors, some of them very gross blunders". "But the generous people of England are always forbearing and forgiving to those statesmen who have the good of their country at heart." There is another saying of his by which he deserves to be remembered and which won the especial praise of Gladstone—"When I am asked if such or such a nation is fit to be free, I ask in return, is any man fit to be a despot?"*

There can, however, be no question that the net result of the Danish crisis was to injure British prestige on the Continent, to make other Powers doubt our reliability as possible allies, and to accentuate our general isolation. It also had the effect of stimulating a desire for isolation, systematically pursued. The strict non-interventionist view was strongly advocated from two quite opposite directions, by the Manchester School of Cobden and Bright—as a certain counterpart to the general principle of *laisser faire*, and by the Conservatives, who disliked continental complications and looked more and more overseas. Neither school would have relished the view of Moltke, uttered in 1865 while he was perfecting the Prussian war machine: "England is as powerless on the Continent as she is presuming."[211]

---

* Queen Victoria's considered verdict, when he died in 1878: "A man of much talent, who leaves a name behind him, kind and good, with a great knowledge of the constitution, who behaved well on many trying occasions: but he was impulsive, very selfish (as shown on many occasions...), vain and often reckless and imprudent" (*Letters*, 2nd series, II, 625).

CHAPTER XII

NON-INTERVENTION AND ISOLATION

RUSSELL WITHOUT PALMERSTON

Lord Russell, when he succeeded Lord Palmerston as Prime Minister, was seventy-two and not in robust health, though even two years later Lord Granville could write of him that "Johnny remains very cocky, restless and physically strong".[1] It was obvious that he must now relinquish the Foreign Office, quite apart from his growing absorption in the question of franchise reform. His successor was Lord Clarendon, whose claims outweighed not only his own personal reluctance—he had to be pressed strongly by his only serious rival, Lord Granville—but also the hesitations of the Queen. "I can't say I rejoice to have Clarendon", she wrote to King Leopold.[2] "I don't quite trust him: still he is conciliatory to other Powers and *is* attached to me." That this attitude was not overcome, is shown by a later letter to Lord Russell himself,[3] in which she complains of Clarendon's "petulant, irritated tone, frequently of a reproachful and *defensive* character, which at once put a stop to all discussion, and indeed was so unpleasant as to make the Queen shrink from seeing him".* The view of his colleagues was very different, and we find Granville assuring Gladstone that Clarendon during this period "communicated more freely with the Cabinet and carried out their policy more faithfully than any Foreign Secretary I have known".[4]

Russell without Palmerston was something very different from the old dual alliance. In many ways Palmerston had in later life become a real Conservative in home politics, and it had for a time suited the Conservatives well enough to leave him in office. Now the Liberal Government was on its last legs, and its enemies were eager for power. It was further handicapped by the fact that the Prime Minister, the Secretaries for Foreign Affairs and War and the First Lord of the Admiralty were all in the Lords. The question of parliamentary reform, in which Russell had taken a keen interest ever since his share in the movement of 1832, now began to

---

* It is not without interest to compare this with the comments of Sarah, Lady Lyttelton in October 1840: "Clarendon is a very clever man, but his manner is consummately disagreeable to me—so very biting, sarcastic and sharp." And again, "the most brilliant conversationalist of all one meets nowadays, but faulty in manner". See her *Correspondence*, ed. Mrs Hugh Wyndham, p. 307.

absorb the country. His new Reform Bill was widely regarded as a mere halfway house, and was opposed both by the Conservatives and by the so-called "Cave of Adullam" under Robert Lowe. By May 1866 the Government majority had sunk to five, and on 19 June it was defeated on the Redistribution Bill.

This situation inevitably reacted upon foreign policy. The natural reserve of Clarendon was strengthened by his knowledge of the Cabinet's internal weakness, while the rebuffs which British policy had suffered over the Polish and Danish questions, coupled with an almost exaggerated distrust of Drouyn de Lhuys, were an incitement to increased caution. As Robert Morier wrote a little later, "I don't credit the Whigs with much wisdom in foreign politics, but the tremendous scalding they got in 1864 has at least taught them to keep as much as possible in the background." [5]

By a strange fatality the interaction of home and foreign affairs was very similar in 1866 to that in 1859. For while the Russell administration was tottering to its fall, the long-drawn trial of strength between Prussia and Austria, ostensibly over the fate of the Elbe Duchies, but in reality over the hegemony in Germany, which was definitely too small to hold them both, reached its climax in the winter and spring of 1865-6, the final breach taking place only a day before Russell resigned. It is not quite fair to allege, as has sometimes been done, that those in office entirely failed to grasp the issues involved in Central Europe. Both the Queen and Lord Clarendon were perfectly aware of what was brewing: indeed the latter told the Prussian Minister to his face on 4 April, that Bismarck's policy was territorial aggrandisement, and that "war with Austria had become necessary for his position and his designs". [6] This plain speaking followed upon the failure of Clarendon's attempt in March to obtain a reference of the Austro-Prussian dispute to some friendly Power, under the Arbitration Protocol included in 1856 in the Treaty of Paris. So alarmed was the Queen—mainly as a result of her correspondence with her daughter the Prussian Crown Princess and with the Duchess of Coburg*—that she urged upon Russell "the absolute necessity of our attempting to do something, in conjunction with France, to arrest the misfortunes a war would entail". [7]

But this time both Russell and Clarendon were opposed to active intervention, and sceptical as to co-operation with France. They believed Napoleon to be not averse to war in Germany, since it might "divert public attention from the unsatisfactory state of things in France", and they considered it quite clear that "the good offices of England single-handed would not be accepted by Prussia" and would be met with "an insolent refusal".

* The latter assured her that no one in Berlin wished for war, except "singly and solely Count Bismarck" (28 March 1866—*Letters*, 2nd series, I, 312).

But they went further than this, and while treating Bismarck as "the sole author of all these impending troubles", and his case for war as "utterly groundless", they also held that "neither English honour nor English interests are involved", and that the country would not tolerate any direct interference.[8] This was doubtless a just estimate of public opinion, but it showed how rapidly that opinion was turning away from the tactics pursued till so recently by those in control of our policy. The Queen was thus virtually left to her own resources, and on 10 April wrote an earnest appeal to the King of Prussia, against the possibility of a war "begun for mere objects of ambition, for imaginary affronts and wrongs".[9]

AUSTRIA AND PRUSSIA

During the critical month of May 1866 British influence had become entirely negative. The Prime Minister was absorbed in the problem of parliamentary reform, and remained deaf to the Queen's urgent appeal that a Cabinet crisis at such a moment would have "a most injurious influence" on peace.[10] Meanwhile Napoleon pressed forward his old panacea of an European Congress, and Britain and Russia having given their consent, invitations were actually sent out on 24 May, the subjects of discussion being somewhat vaguely defined as "the question of the Elbe Duchies, the Italian dispute and the reforms to be introduced into the Federal Pact, so far as they may affect the Balance of Power in Europe". But the stars in their courses were fighting for Bismarck, for after Prussia and her still secret ally Italy had given their consent, Austria made hers conditional upon no Power obtaining at the Congress any fresh accession of territory. The two main issues, the fate of the Duchies and of Venetia, were thus ruled out *a limine*, and the onus of a rupture fell upon Austria. Her attitude also exploded the maximum concession which Russell was willing to make to the Queen's insistence, namely that we should assure Austria of our backing in Germany, if she on her side would surrender Venetia to Italy. This Francis Joseph, who throughout life never consented to a cession of territory till it was too late, was utterly unwilling to consider, and London was again reduced to negation. Russell's excuse may perhaps be sought in his own crisp phrase, that "Austria is wrong in Italy, right in Germany".[11] But the Cabinet's outlook is best revealed in the Queen's own notes of a conversation with Clarendon on 4 May, when he admitted that "Europe was in a most combustible state and there was great danger of our being isolated, he thought, and God knows how long we should be able to keep out of it: Belgium we were bound to defend".[12] At the same time he was quite definite that nothing could be done to prevent war, either by threats or remonstrances, by joint action with France or by a naval demonstration.

On 7 June Prussian troops entered Holstein, on the 14th diplomatic relations were broken off between Berlin and Vienna, and Prussia declared the contract upon which the German Confederation rested to have been violated and therefore to have lapsed. Within two days Saxony and Hesse had been overrun, and Hanover was in grave danger. On the 18th and 19th the successive war manifestos of Austria and Prussia completed the rupture between the two principal rivals, and on the 20th Italy also declared war upon Austria. It was under circumstances such as these that the Russell Cabinet was defeated on 18 June in the House of Commons, and though the Queen argued it to be " the bounden duty of her Government, in the present state of the Continent, to set aside all personal considerations and to continue at their posts ", she could not induce Russell to withhold his resignation.

Derby again in Power

The new Government was formed by Lord Derby, who thus became Prime Minister for the third time without a majority. His right-hand man in a Cabinet consisting mainly of novices in office was Mr Disraeli. Lord Malmesbury's health not permitting him to resume the Foreign Office, it was by no means obvious who should fill that post. It is characteristic of the loose state of party allegiance and of the anxiety shared by the new Prime Minister and the Queen, that an attempt should have been made to induce Lord Clarendon to remain as Foreign Secretary under the Conservatives. We have already seen that the Queen was not without personal feelings against Clarendon, while it was notorious that the latter regarded Derby with special antipathy, despite the marriage which had united their children: yet both of them sank these personal considerations in their eagerness " that the thread of our foreign diplomacy should not be broken ".[13] But Clarendon declined, on the characteristic and unanswerable ground that " allegiance to party is the only strong political feeling I have ".[14]

Thereupon Lord Derby appointed his own son, Lord Stanley, as Foreign Secretary, as being in his opinion, failing Malmesbury, " the only person at all fit for it ".[15] The Queen, it is true, expressed herself to her private secretary, General Grey, as " greatly alarmed at Lord Stanley's inability for that office ", despite his " great abilities " in other directions, and begged that this very frank opinion should be transmitted in a slightly more palatable form to the Prime Minister himself. But Lord Derby boldly paid his royal mistress back in her own coin, thanked her for her " gracious communication ", and " speaking with the entire frankness which Your Majesty encourages him to use", declared "he does *not* think that the Foreign Office is the one best suited to Lord Stanley: but on the other hand he is satisfied that Lord Stanley is better suited to the Foreign Office than any person whose services he can command". He clinched the matter by adding that "it is unfortunate that so few of our public men give much of their attention to foreign affairs", and that there was no one else on the Conservative side whose name "he could honestly submit".[16] His choice was endorsed by one of the ablest diplomatists in the British service, Robert Morier, who at this time expressed the opinion that "Lord Stanley is the only statesman we have got, who can treat foreign politics objectively".[17]

It may be of interest at this point to note Palmerston's comment upon Derby at an earlier period—obviously uttered with the usual solicitude of the pot for the kettle. "All royal persons", he said, "like acquiescence and subserviency of demeanour. Peel and Aberdeen spoilt them"—meaning Queen Victoria and Prince Albert—"but Derby has an off-hand and sarcastic way about him, which is not the manner of a courtier."[18] By this time Derby was much more acceptable to the Queen, and it is hardly necessary to point out that his immediate successor in the party leadership, Mr Disraeli, understood how to humour her and win her confidence and support, to a degree almost unique in the relations between sovereigns and ministers.

The policy of the new Government, as defined by Lord Derby to the Queen, was "to keep this country as far as possible from any entanglement in continental politics", though "not shrinking from using the moral influence of England, and especially if in conjunction with France,...to restore to Europe the blessings of peace".[19] This was a vague and unimpressive programme. And though Mr Disraeli made an eloquent speech asserting that "the abstention of England from any unnecessary interference in the affairs of Europe is the consequence, not of her decline in power, but of her increased strength",[20] yet the cynic might be tempted to ascribe it to the success of "that horrible needle-gun" of Prussia, of which the Duke of Cambridge wrote so urgently to Lord Clarendon as he was quitting office.[21]

Not for the first or last time the advent of a new chief to the Foreign Office coincided more or less closely with events of a decisive and far-reaching character upon the Continent. It will therefore be necessary to consider the effect of Prussian victory upon the Balance of Power and the general diplomatic situation, in order that we may understand the exaggerated policy of *désintéressement* pursued by both the great parties in the State during the eight years following.

The whole situation in Central Europe was transformed with almost lightning rapidity. As we saw, the Prussian armies overran Saxony, Hesse and Hanover within the first week, and pressed on across the Bohemian frontier. The Austrians defeated the Italians on 24 June at Custozza, but Benedek, who to his extreme reluctance and against his better judgment had been given the supreme command of the Austrian armies in the north, soon found himself outgeneralled and outmanœuvred. A whole series of minor engagements culminated as early as 3 July in the battle of Königgrätz (or Sadowa), at which larger numbers were engaged than in any battle since the Napoleonic Wars, and which resulted in a crushing defeat of Austria. Benedek was promptly made the scapegoat of the Habsburgs, but his successors warned Francis Joseph that Austria had lost all powers of offensive. Her only hope lay in foreign complications.

Bismarck on his side was surrounded by dangers, but played a masterly diplomatic game, realising that not a moment was to be lost in concluding peace with Austria, consolidating Prussian gains in Germany, and not arousing a spirit of insatiable revenge in Austria by unwise annexations of territory. The key of the situation lay in Paris. Napoleon III, who was regarded as a sphinx not merely by foreign opinion, but by one so closely initiated as the Austrian Ambassador, Prince Richard Metternich,* had in the last days of May got the length of considering the draft of an alliance with Prussia, brought to him by the Hungarian emigrant Colonel Kiss.[22] Yet on 12 June he concluded a secret convention with Austria,[23] which, being based on the assumption of an Austro-Prussian war, might easily have developed into an alliance if the Austrian arms had been victorious. When the tide began to turn against Austria, desperate efforts were made through Metternich to win Napoleon for active intervention, and on the very day of Königgrätz he at least promised his mediation. Under the immediate impression of defeat Francis Joseph wired to Paris offering Venetia to the Emperor Napoleon, and the news was at once published, in the hope of convincing the Italians that further hostilities were superfluous. Drouyn de Lhuys, the French Foreign Minister, now favoured war on the Austrian side, and had the backing of the Empress: but he was counterbalanced by Rouher, Lavalette and Prince Napoleon. Napoleon III was at this moment a very ill man, and his health made him more irresolute and vacillating than ever: and so, to the anger of Metternich, and in spite of a special mission of the Saxon statesman Beust to Paris, he refused an alliance with what his more liberal cousin called "the Austrian corpse", and took towards Austria the line of "ultra posse nemo obligatur". It has only recently become known that the Empress Eugénie was in a panic at her husband's "physical and moral decay

* Metternich to Mensdorff, 16 May 1866: "L'Empereur continue a s'envelopper envers chacun dans les nuages de son rôle de sphinx"—Oncken, *Rheinpolitik Napoleons III*, i, 201 (No. 108).

(*défaillance*)", to use the phrase reported by Metternich to Vienna,[24] and on 23 July actually pressed him to abdicate and entrust her with the Regency.

During this critical month of July Bismarck fought a desperate game to convert his master King William from designs of annexation, and meanwhile played for time in his negotiations with Paris, instructing his Ambassador Count Goltz to test the appetite of the French and the extent to which he might safely indulge his own without their actually moving. Even at the last moment a fresh danger presented itself in a Russian proposal for an European Congress. Fortunately for Bismarck, it was launched too late (27 July), for peace preliminaries had been signed the day before at Nikolsburg by Prussia and Austria. The Tsar was not unnaturally alarmed at Bismarck's revolutionary attitude towards the minor German dynasties and was also inclined to insist that the overthrow of the German Confederation was an illegal act such as required formal sanction from all the Powers which had guaranteed its creation in 1815. Indeed he only abandoned this attitude when he found that Lord Stanley was not disposed to endorse it.

The military genius of Moltke, the dilatory tactics of Bismarck, the in-decision of Napoleon, the negative policy of Russia and Britain combined to secure the complete triumph of Prussia and a radical change in the conti-nental Balance of Power. Austria was definitely excluded from Germany, the old Confederation was dissolved, and Prussia, having annexed the minor states which had hitherto divided her territories into two separate halves, and having added four millions to her population, founded a new North German Confederation, absolutely controlled from Berlin, and at the same time concluded treaties with the defeated South German states. Germany north of the Main was thus strongly consolidated, and an extension of economic and military ties, to include all the non-Habsburg states, was only a matter of time. Meanwhile Austria by the surrender of Venetia lost her last foothold in Italy. The new Kingdom was soon to rank as a Great Power, its capital was transferred to Florence, and Rome was obviously the next and final stage. Despite the great services already rendered by Napoleon III to the Italian cause in 1859 and his role of intermediary in the transfer of Venetia, his fatal support of the Temporal Power of the Pope was undermining the gratitude of the Italians towards France and driving them into the German sphere of influence.

In the early days of the Seven Weeks' War a German progressive leader, in conversation with Bismarck, compared the situation with that at the outbreak of the Seven Years' War, "but", he added, "with all respect for the King—" "Without Frederick the Great", interrupted Bismarck: "yes, and yet it must be put through."[25] Bismarck's achievement in the summer of

1866, in the face of a hostile parliament and nation, a King who understood neither events abroad nor events at home, and a suspicious and disapproving Europe, is the most remarkable even in his career, and showed what transformations a giant could effect when confronted by a race of pygmies. Contemporaries realised how essentially mediocre King William was—it must suffice to quote Devaux, the Belgian Minister in Berlin, who writes home that "Bismarck only moves 'son vieux sot de roi' by continually saying, 'If you yield, it is the revolution'".[26] But even the best of them scarcely realised the dynamic force represented by Bismarck, with his allies Moltke and Roon, and the revolutionary character of his work. It was not till long after the Great War that the systematic glorification of "William the Great" by those who fawned upon his grandson, was seen to be ridiculous, and that a German historian of the period with which we are concerned could write freely of "the revolution from above" which Bismarck brought about.

In this connection, however, it is worth quoting one contemporary opinion which may fairly be claimed as having forestalled the verdict of history. It is that of Robert Morier, that able British diplomat who had devoted twenty years to the study of German politics and was one day to earn the nickname of "l'homme qui roulait Bismarck". It is worth comparing with the view expressed by Professor Ziekursch in his highly original *History of the New German Empire*. "The heartbreaking part of this war", writes Morier, "is that its aims, as regards the anti-Prussian portion of it, are so thoroughly legitimate, while the means used are so thoroughly damnable. The presence of Austria in Germany and Italy is the fatal bar in the way of progress, first for Austria, second for Germany, third for Italy. I am myself convinced this might have been effected by peaceful means and by the mere natural course of liberal development. Bismarck has determined it otherwise. He has had recourse to a brutal surgical operation to effect what, I am convinced, might have been done by diet and steady training. [The patient will very likely die under the operation.] But heartily as I hate the operation, I must wish for its success. A signal victory on the part of Austria in the present struggle would throw Europe back three generations."[27] And again, "Bismarck has by the impress of his own detestable individuality on the political canvas so utterly disfigured the true outline of the picture, that not only public opinion, but the judgment of wise and thoughtful men, is almost sure to go wrong." Prussia, he argued, was so strong that she could have asserted her predominance "*with* instead of *against* the liberal and national forces of Germany".[28]

Morier's views had been formed in the school of Prince Albert, the veteran Baron Stockmar and the South German Liberals: he was on close terms with the Crown Prince and Princess and was for that very reason regarded with suspicion by Bismarck. Queen Victoria shared many of his political views, and starting from a firm belief in German unity, went on to argue that "a strong united liberal Germany would be a most useful ally to England".[29] But she too keenly resented Bismarck's methods, and after having strained every nerve in 1864 to prevent Britain from being involved in war upon what she regarded as a false issue, now urged with equal insistence how "highly important" it was "that England should not appear utterly indifferent to what passes in Germany".

REACTION FROM PALMERSTON'S METHODS

But the wheel of British policy had gone almost full circle since the Danish crisis, and she now found the Conservatives if possible even more anxious than the Liberals to avoid continental complications. The natural reaction against the excessive habits of interference practised by Palmerston the bully and Russell the busybody, made of Non-intervention the fundamental creed of both parties, and was greatly increased by the knowledge that we had no army capable of making its weight felt amid the gigantic conscript forces of the Continent, armed with new and deadly weapons. The humiliation of Saxony, and still more the annexation of Hanover and the ejection of the Queen's first cousin, the blind King George, was a very bitter pill to swallow: but the Conservative Government was not prepared to do more than mildly urge Berlin to be lenient, and when its advice was ignored, submitted to the inevitable. As early as 20 July Lord Stanley in the House of Commons declared his inability to see how the establishment of a strong and compact Power in North Germany could be a menace to Great Britain.

There were two further considerations which increased their reserve. The first was the fact that Prussia had secured the alliance of Italy, and that the victory of Austria would have left her free to defeat and probably destroy the new Kingdom—an event which London could not desire for its own sake, even apart from all popular sentiments in favour of the Italian cause, and which it was also bound to fear as almost inevitably involving France, and so probably all Europe, in war. Bismarck, by winning Italian co-operation, had taken the main step towards neutralising Britain and restraining France, for a long enough period to enable him to achieve a military success. "You can't believe", said Bismarck at a later date, "how hard it was for me to win the King for an alliance with Victor Emanuel. *When I had that, I had everything.* But", he added, in a self-revealing phrase, "I had to go so far as to control the King's reading."[30]

The second ground for British caution was the increasingly tortuous policy of France. If Palmerston had been unreasoningly suspicious after Villafranca, it was by this time indeed difficult to be sure of the real motives and policy of Napoleon III and his ministers. His fatal irresolution during the crisis of the war had enabled Bismarck "to get away with it" in time, and now instead of rapidly deciding either to accept Prussia's new position with a good grace or to challenge it by coming to the help of Austria and her South German allies before it was too late, he embarked upon the fatal policy of bargaining for compensation, or as it was slightingly nicknamed at the time, "la politique des pourboires". Already on 23 July the French Ambassador in Berlin, Count Benedetti, was instructed to discuss the possibility of a restoration of the French frontiers of 1814, with the possible addition of Luxemburg.[31] Four days later Napoleon himself asked Count Goltz what prospect there was of Prussia consenting to the cession of Landau and Luxemburg, in order that France might have the necessary defensive lines:[32] and the draft of a convention embodying these ideas was on 5 August submitted by Benedetti to Bismarck, but not at all well received. On 8 August Drouyn de Lhuys drew up a memorandum suggesting the formation of a neutral buffer state, comprising the provinces west of the Rhine and thus separating France and Prussia. Finally, on 16 August Rouher, in Napoleon's name, instructed Benedetti to propose in Berlin the public cession of Landau, Saarbrücken and Luxemburg, and further a secret offensive and defensive alliance, entitling France to annex Belgium later, leaving Antwerp as a free city, in order to meet British objections.[33] Goltz, in discussing this plan with Rouher, insisted on the impossibility of ceding German territory and expressed the conviction that "sooner or later France would want to expand towards Belgium, and that it would then be important for her if Prussia did not oppose this step".[34] To this period also apparently belongs an undated memorandum, afterwards found among Napoleon's papers in the Tuileries:[35] in it occurs the sinister phrase, "If France boldly places herself on the basis of Nationalities, it is important to establish right away now, that a Belgian nationality does not exist, and to fix this essential point with Prussia."

Bismarck's reception of Benedetti's proposals was not encouraging, though not abrupt. He declined to consider the frontier of 1814, so long as the inhabitants of the districts affected did not express their desire for a change. As regards Luxemburg, he did not claim it for the North German Confederation, but must leave to France the initiative of obtaining Dutch consent and could not compensate Holland with German territory. As regards Belgium, he promised to recommend the proposed secret convention to King William, but pointed out the great difficulties likely to be raised by London.

It is interesting to note that Count Goltz, in an able despatch of 20 August to Bismarck, advocated a Franco-Prussian alliance as a means of securing a free hand in south Germany and for the event of complications in Austria or Turkey:[36] and the draft of such a treaty actually exists, in the handwriting of Benedetti, embodying the designs upon Luxemburg and Belgium, but abandoning the frontier of 1814.[37] This draft appears to have originated during a conversation between the Ambassador and Bismarck, the latter asking the former to give a concrete form to his proposals, with a view to their submission to the King. Bismarck, having thus possessed himself of a written document which suggested designs infinitely more concrete than the fluctuating fancies of Napoleon really justified, proceeded to play for time and to make himself as inaccessible as possible. Four years later he was to give to the document a sensational publicity, under circumstances such as decisively influenced public opinion in Europe, and especially in England, at the crisis of the Franco-German War.[38] (See *infra*, p. 497.)

Meanwhile there were floating rumours as to French designs, and there can be little doubt that these were fed by Bismarck, in order to arouse the suspicions of London, St Petersburg, Vienna and Florence. Queen Victoria, greatly alarmed by a telegram from Lord Cowley—hinting that the frontier of 1814 was in question—wrote to the Prime Minister that "England cannot remain a passive spectator of such proceedings, and the Queen relies on Lord Derby and his Cabinet giving this his immediate and serious consideration".[39] As a result, Lord Cowley was instructed to ask for an audience with the Emperor and to demand assurances that he had no designs upon Belgian territory, or "contemplated a step which would cause a very painful impression in this country, and which it would be impossible to justify in the eyes of Europe". How grave a view of the situation was taken by the British Cabinet, may be judged from Lord Derby's report of this decision to the Queen, for it contains the phrase, "It is therefore to be feared that war is imminent between France and Prussia: for the Emperor can hardly recede from a demand formally made."[40] But as a matter of fact Napoleon at once drew back and through Drouyn de Lhuys assured Cowley that England need have no alarm about Belgium, that he did not regard the possession of Philippeville and Marienburg by a neutral state like Belgium as dangerous, and above all that he "did not desire to obtain cessions of territory by force or intimidation, but only from the good will of the Powers concerned".[41] The fact is that Napoleon, doubtless affected by his precarious state of health, was wavering between nervousness at the internal condition of France, desire for her territorial aggrandisement, coupled with his fixed idea of the injustice of the Treaties of 1815, and on the other side a very genuine enthusiasm for the principle of Nationality and the feeling that he could not logically oppose in Germany a process exactly parallel to that which he had so actively promoted in Italy or Roumania. It would be quite unfair to assume that at this time he was plotting war or was even hostile to Prussia—it would indeed be easy to make out a case for pacific and Prusso-phil leanings. But the fact remains that his restless unstable temperament, the unhealthy basis upon which the Second Empire rested, and the ambitions of his immediate entourage, made up a situation from which war might easily eventuate, which amply justified the reserve of London and which played into the hands of the unscrupulous Bismarck.

In September 1866, at any rate, Napoleon tried to demonstrate his good will by dismissing his Foreign Minister, Drouyn de Lhuys; and in the interval before his successor Moustier could come from Constantinople to take up his post, Rouher and Lavalette, the two chief members of the Cabinet, assured the Prussian Minister that the dismissal was due to the Emperor's desire for a Prussian alliance, and Napoleon himself dwelt with great insistence on the same theme.[42] When they found it quite impossible to extract any definite decision from Bismarck and his master, a circular was published in the name of Lavalette, the Minister *ad interim* (16 September), which roused considerable dust at the time by its ingenuous attempt to demonstrate the splendid situation of France in a Europe "governed by the principle of liberty of alliances",[43] and enjoying an equilibrium due to satisfied nationality. Its main achievement was to cover up in grandiloquent platitudes the fact that the policy of compensation had failed. As M. de La Gorce sarcastically comments, "England was surprised at not being even mentioned and Austria at the persistence in pushing her towards the East."

FRANCHISE REFORM OVERSHADOWS FOREIGN POLICY

For the moment the circular seemed to have added the word "Finis" to the newly written chapter of European history: and England was all the more ready to assume this because it was absorbed in the excitements of a second Reform agitation. When Russell fell, there was a demonstration outside Gladstone's house, and on 23 July occurred the famous Hyde Park riot, which was the signal for monster meetings and processions in many parts of the country. Long before Parliament met in February 1867, the question of parliamentary reform had become the main preoccupation of the Government, and it was clear that a solution must be attempted by the Conservatives. The resolutions put forward by Disraeli, with the avowed object of "lifting the question above the level of party discussion",[44] were very badly received on both sides of the House and had to be withdrawn. The Government was in danger of breaking up, and its internal dissensions led to the resignation of three ministers, including Lord Cranborne (the future Lord Salisbury). Disraeli was now free to reframe his proposals on a basis of household franchise, tempered by dual voting (18 March): and in the end he steered his ship successfully between Scylla and Charybdis, Gladstone on the one hand denouncing it as "a gigantic instrument of fraud", likely to cause a class war, and Cranborne protesting against "a political betrayal which has no parallel in our annals". Its final adoption—the third reading in the House of Commons was on 15 July—was due to two main factors besides his own adroitness—(1) the attitude of Lord Derby, who was far less concerned to uphold Conservative theory than to "dish the Whigs", to use his own famous phrase; and (2) the split inside the Liberal party, which destroyed all hope of overthrowing the Government, aroused "the disgust and deep mortification" of Gladstone,[45] and first led him to contemplate withdrawal from the party leadership. The decisive "Leap in the Dark" was thus taken in the interests of what was soon to be spoken of as "Tory Democracy". But it must be confessed that no parliamentary measure of the front rank during the past century owed its adoption so little to principle and so much to tactics. The political situation still remained unusually fluid.

THE LUXEMBURG CRISIS

These brief allusions to home politics were needed to explain the atmosphere of detachment in which our statesmen were living when a new crisis in Franco-Prussian relations seemed for a short time likely to result in a general European war. Their general attitude cannot be better summarised than in the words of Disraeli, delivered to his constituents on the very day of Königgrätz, and foreshadowing later and more famous utterances. England, he argued, had outgrown the European Continent. "Her position is no longer that of a mere European Power....She is as ready, and as willing, to interfere as in old days, when the necessity of her position required it. There is no Power indeed that interferes more than England. She interferes in Asia because she is really more an Asiatic Power than a European."[46] The result is that she has "a greater sphere of action than any European Power, and she has duties devolving upon her on a much larger scale. Not that we can ever look with indifference upon what takes place on the Continent. We are interested in the peace and prosperity of Europe, and I do not say that there may not be occasions in which it may be the duty of England to interfere in European Wars." Meanwhile, if there was one point upon the Continent with regard to which British opinion, alike official and unofficial, was inclined to be sensitive, it was the status of Belgium and the somewhat kindred subject of Luxemburg: and this was the very point towards which Napoleon's thoughts kept returning, like a moth flitting round a lamp. Oblivious of the fact that the principle of Nationality had been proclaimed as the very foundation of his Empire, he was constantly considering schemes of aggrandisement in which the peoples most directly concerned were to have no say.

The motive of Napoleon in not letting the Luxemburg question rest was twofold. First, he realised the irritation and nervousness of French public opinion at the consolidation of North Germany and the fear that prevailed —to use a common contemporary phrase—lest the Main frontier might be overstepped by Prussia. In other words, it is useless to deny that France was in the main hostile to German unity and that paradoxical as it may sound, Napoleon himself was probably less hostile than anyone in all France. Secondly, he hoped not only to appease public opinion and rehabilitate the regime, but actually to strengthen the defences of France on her eastern frontier and to drive a breach, this time by peaceful means, in the treaties of 1815, which throughout his career he had regarded as galling and objection-able. It seemed to him that the psychological moment had arrived, for Luxemburg was quite genuinely "in the air" since the dissolution of the German Confederation. It is to be remembered that at the Congress of Vienna in 1815 the little Grand Duchy had been attached by a Personal Union to the Kingdom of Holland, but had remained a member of the German *Bund* and since 1842 of the Zollverein, while a Prussian garrison was left in the capital, Luxemburg itself. When Belgium broke away from Holland after the Revolution of 1830, a portion of Luxemburg was definitely incorporated in the new Kingdom, and the status of what remained as Grand Duchy was regulated by the Treaties of 1839—that is, the Treaty which restored peace between Belgium and Holland, and that of London, by which the Great Powers endorsed the new settlement and guaranteed Belgian independence and neutrality. The changes produced in Germany by the war of 1866 rendered some readjustment of Luxemburg's position inevitable, and there can be no doubt that its inhabitants were then opposed to entering the new *North* German Confederation under Prussia's leadership, while Napoleon actually received overtures from the Dutch themselves, to the effect that the retention of the Grand Duchy was more of an embarrassment than an advantage. At the turn of the year all seemed to favour the annexation.

Early in January 1867, then, Benedetti, acting upon urgent instructions, succeeded in coming to grips with Bismarck on the whole question, after long months of evasion: and on this occasion it was made clear to him that there could be no question of an *offensive* alliance, and that if the Prussian garrison were to be withdrawn from Luxemburg (to which Bismarck was careful not to commit himself) this must in any case be followed by the dismantlement of the fortress. This meant, in other words, (1) that Napoleon must pull the chestnuts out of the fire for himself and could at the very best count upon Prussian passivity in the whole affair; (2) that the Franco-Prussian alliance which Napoleon had proposed could not, even if concluded, be utilised for any ulterior motive; and (3) that Luxemburg could not be turned by France into a fortified position against Germany.

The King of Holland and his Government were now ready to cede Luxemburg to France, if only Prussia could be induced to renounce her rights upon Limburg:* and in February the Grand Ducal Minister Baron Tornaco definitely began to negotiate with France. But they still had qualms as to the possibility of Prussian aggression, and when Moustier declared his readiness to guarantee Holland and Limburg against Prussia, in return for the cession of Luxemburg (28 February), the King of Holland talked of a discussion *à trois*, and showed that he was afraid to take the final step without the sanction of the Great Powers which had signed the Treaties of 1815 and 1839, and of course above all of Prussia. His doubts were not diminished by the language of the Dutch Minister in Paris, who after a talk with Moustier reported that "everyone here agrees that Luxemburg is the black spot on the horizon, and that without a solution of this question war cannot be avoided".[47] The situation was rendered still more delicate by debates during March in the French Assembly, where Thiers attacked the foreign policy of the Government and declared, "*Il n'y a plus une faute à commettre*," and in the new North German Parliament, where Bismarck hedged, denying any idea of renouncing Luxemburg and Limburg, but admitting that Luxemburg did not wish to join the Confederation. There was a growing effervescence of public opinion both in France and in Germany, and it seems probable that Bismarck was secretly encouraging the press to protest against French designs. Moreover, he chose this moment to publish the offensive and defensive alliances concluded with Bavaria and Baden (Württemberg and Hesse were soon to follow): in other words, he openly avowed his resolve to efface the Main frontier and his disregard for the terms of the Treaty of Prague, of the previous year, in which Austria's exclusion from Germany was counterbalanced to some degree by the north and the south remaining separate.

The King of Holland was now more alarmed than ever, and on 26 March informed Napoleon that he could only consent to cession if Prussia's endorsement could be obtained. At the same time he notified Bismarck as to what was going on, thereby putting an end to the tactics to which the latter had hitherto adhered, of urging the French to keep Prussia out of the

---

* The projecting piece of territory running southwards between Belgium and Germany, which at an early stage of the Great War seemed likely to involve Holland.

negotiations and to prevent the King of Holland from intimating their progress to Berlin. The Treaties had actually been drafted, and the Prince of Orange had left for Paris to sign them on behalf of his father, when the situation was definitely transformed by an incident in the North German Parliament. On 1 April the National Liberal leader Bennigsen, speaking in the name of seventy deputies, pronounced a violent harangue against the proposed abandonment of German territory to France. Amid the excitement that ensued, Bismarck's reply was one of studied moderation: but while disclaiming any desire to draw Luxemburg into the Confederation and admitting that Prussia's right of garrison had expired, he made it clear that Luxemburg was not a subject of negotiation between Prussia and France, that he was unaware of any treaty having been concluded, and that in his view the signatory Powers ought to be consulted before any decision. This was amply sufficient to make the King of Holland draw back, and the Treaties remained unsigned. Paris was very angry, and Napoleon regarded himself as having been cheated by Bismarck. It still remains a moot point, whether, as Benedetti always believed, Bismarck was genuinely disposed to let France annex Luxemburg (and there is some evidence for thinking that he looked upon this as a harmless way of satisfying Napoleon's appetite and giving Prussia at least some years of respite) or whether he only held out Luxemburg as a bait which he never intended the French to swallow. This is what Bennigsen believed, and some colour is lent to it by the knowledge that his interpellation was specially arranged between himself and Bismarck.[48]

During April the situation remained tense, but Napoleon had been forced on to the defensive by Bismarck's appeal to the signatory Powers, and was at pains to affirm his readiness to co-operate with them. The Circular Note of Moustier on 15 April prepared the French retreat from an untenable position, by disclaiming all idea of conquest. Only if Luxemburg freely gave herself to France, but not otherwise. On the other hand Prussia could not continue to garrison Luxemburg in the name of a Confederation that had already been dissolved. In a word, he suggested that there should be renunciation on both sides—France should abandon the union and Prussia should withdraw her troops.

QUEEN VICTORIA, PRUSSIA AND RUSSIA

In this apparent deadlock the alarm began to spread to other capitals. Queen Victoria urged upon Lord Stanley "the danger to Belgian independence", if France took Luxemburg.[49] She defined his policy hitherto as a refusal " to allow England to be made a party to the personal (for such they are) differences between France and Prussia", and she was insistent that no new step must be taken without consulting the Cabinet. A week later she had reached a still higher note. If Napoleon, she wrote, this time to the Prime Minister, were to adopt a "politique de brigand", Belgium would be exposed to ruin and "England placed in a most painful and humiliating position". "England must not stand aloof. She is bound by *every* tie that *can bind a nation* to *assist another*, to stand by Belgium in her hour of need. . . . She *must* show the world that she is not prepared to abdicate her position as a Great Power and is determined to fulfil her obligations and (*even singlehanded* if need be) to defend the independence of Belgium with the whole strength of the British Empire."[50] But, she argued in conclusion, the necessity would not arise if the language used towards both Napoleon and Bismarck were sufficiently "firm and unequivocal". With Derby's strong approval the Queen then wrote to King William of Prussia, stressing the responsibility which he would incur if war came over the Luxemburg question (22 April): and this appears genuinely to have done good. But Lord Stanley, while agreeing with her views, felt bound to urge that "there never was a time when English public opinion was more thoroughly bent on incurring no fresh responsibilities for Continental objects".[51]

Meanwhile Austria and Russia were scarcely less nervous. Beust, now Austrian Foreign Minister and actively engaged in reframing the Habsburg Monarchy on a Dualist basis, refrained from any protest against the Treaties between Prussia and the South German states, though they violated the whole spirit of the Austro-Prussian peace Treaty. But when he received through a Bavarian intermediary, Tauffkirchen, the offer of an Austro-Prussian alliance, he declined to discuss it at all, and leant more and more towards Paris. If Austria's attitude had been reduced to a negation, Russia under Tsar Alexander and Prince Gorchakov was definitely disposed to criticise France for raising the question at so awkward a moment: and when on 1 April Moustier telegraphed to St Petersburg that he could no longer yield, and that it was for Prussia to make the concessions necessary in order to escape from the impasse, Gorchakov was seriously alarmed, but spoke to Talleyrand quite frankly of the "terrible extremity" in which Bismarck was thus likely to be placed, between the loss of popularity and influence and a great war.[52] He went even further, and after expressing his regret that Napoleon had not joined the Tsar at the decisive moment in defending the interests of the dispossessed German dynasties, he added, "The circular of M. de La Valette admitted M. de Bismarck to be right, and now six months later you go back upon the approval which you had accorded him." This cold attitude undoubtedly contributed towards Napoleon beating a retreat. But as soon as Moustier's public renunciation was known, the Tsar and his

Chancellor set themselves eagerly to press moderation upon Berlin. On 26 April they were able to propose a Conference of the Powers at London, in the knowledge that Bismarck would consent.[53]

"SEVERAL" AND "COLLECTIVE" GUARANTEES

The result was a general sigh of relief in all the capitals, and though there were still one or two dangerous moments, the Conference, at which Lord Stanley presided from 7 to 11 May 1867, succeeded in liquidating the dispute. Luxemburg remained under the sovereignty of King William of Holland, but also a member of the German Zollverein, while Prussia withdrew her garrison and the fortress was dismantled. Limburg became an integral part of Holland, while the Grand Duchy of Luxemburg was neutralised under the collective guarantee of the Great Powers. It is true that the general effect was seriously diminished by the public interpretation placed upon this guarantee by Lord Derby in the Commons. On this occasion the most instructive commentaries are to be found in the discussions in the House of Lords. Lord Russell expressed a natural satisfaction that war had been averted, but put to his hearers the double question, was European peace so great a British interest as to excuse "diplomatic offices" by Britain, and "might we have to pay a higher price than the product was worth?" While praising the Foreign Secretary, he was glad that the Government had not listened to theories, under the name of a new foreign policy, and that "however great our interest might be, we were not to interfere in the affairs of foreign countries". Lord Derby in his reply "felt it incumbent not to shrink from any responsibility which might attach to an additional guarantee on our part", since "we knew that if we had refused, nothing could have prevented war". A collective guarantee of neutral Powers was made a *sine qua non*. The guarantee of the possession of Luxemburg to the King of Holland was "a joint and several guarantee similar to" that respecting Belgium. "Now a guarantee of neutrality is very different from a guarantee of possession. . . . The guarantee is only collective, that is, binding only upon all the Powers in their collective capacity, . . . but not one of those Powers is bound to fulfil the obligation alone." If, then, either of the only two likely to infringe should violate neutrality, "the obligation on all the others would not accrue". Later in the debate Lord Clarendon insisted that the Belgian guarantee was an "individual guarantee", whereas this new one was a collective one—"a moral obligation, a point of honour": whereupon Lord Granville, not perhaps without a trace of sarcasm, pointed out that after all the explanations given, the guarantee seemed "so utterly free from danger, that it is difficult to understand the importance which Prussia attaches to it".

Some weeks later the question was again raised by Lord Houghton, who argued that "in the eyes of Prussia the neutrality of Luxemburg means the integrity of Belgium, while in the eyes of France it means the integrity of Holland": and he quoted Lord Stanley as having assented "with more doubt and anxiety than he had ever felt on any public question". Lord Derby in reply drew a clear distinction "between a collective and a separate and several guarantee", the former being binding on all collectively, but "no one of them can be called on to take upon itself the task of vindication by force of arms". He added an interesting historical summary, pointing out that in 1831, and again in 1839, the five Powers had bound themselves *severally* to uphold the Belgian Treaty, but that in 1832 Austria, Russia and Prussia had declined to act. In 1856 there was a collective guarantee of Turkey by seven Powers, yet a fortnight later a tripartite treaty of guarantee was concluded between Britain, France and Austria, "jointly and severally" —its very existence thus "admitting the insufficiency of its predecessor". The Luxemburg Treaty, he added, "rests on the collective voice and on the honour of all the Powers signatory". If, then, one Power violated the territory of Luxemburg, would all the signatories, he asked, be bound to go to war against it? and his answer was a clear negative—"such a construction was contrary to all the rules of interpretation". Britain was not bound to take upon itself "the quixotic duty of interfering to prevent violation": neutrality "must rest on the honour of all the guaranteeing Powers".

For the Opposition Lord Russell and the Duke of Argyll tried to dot the i's of the Prime Minister, by concluding that there would remain "a moral obligation" to act against any Power violating that neutrality, "if necessary by resorting to arms". But all these attempts at definition only served to leave the position still more indefinite. "A several guarantee", Lord Derby declared—and this would seem to be the crucial phrase—"binds each of the parties to do its utmost individually to enforce the observance of guarantee. A collective guarantee is one which is binding on all the parties collectively, but which, if any difference of opinion should arise, none of them can be called upon to take upon itself the task of vindicating by force of arms."[54] It is hard to avoid the conclusion that this was intended to leave loopholes of escape in both directions, and that the Opposition hesitated to press the matter too far, since it might well be they who would have to deal with the problem in its next stage. In passing, there is a certain picquancy in the fact that the only serious hitch in the London Conference was due to Bismarck's insistence that the guarantee undertaken for Luxemburg should be identical with that for Belgium.

This equivocal attitude on the part of the Prime Minister and Foreign Secretary must not of course be charged against one British party rather than another: it unquestionably represented the opinions of an overwhelming majority in both parties at that time. Against this may be set the fact that King William of Prussia, answering the letter of Queen Victoria, treated "the timely intervention of England by proposing the Conference" as having averted war, and that the Empress Eugénie on her side expressed the firm conviction that the Queen's letter had saved the situation.[55]

EUROPE ON THE EDGE OF WAR

Peace was thus assured, and the festivities of the Paris Exhibition, which almost every European sovereign visited during the summer of 1867, gave a semblance of calm to the situation. But in reality the delicate balance of continental politics had been rudely disturbed, and peace was at the mercy of any incident. Moltke in Prussia, and Napoleon's new War Minister Niel, were concentrating more than ever upon military preparations: while the Second Empire, whose prestige had already been shaken by Sadowa and the Luxemburg affair, received a deadly blow in June 1867, when Napoleon's unhappy dupe Maximilian of Mexico was executed at Queretaro by the revolutionary Government. Still more embarrassing was the attempt of Garibaldi upon Rome, which led Napoleon after Mentana to re-establish a French garrison (6 November 1867) for the defence of the Temporal Power, and thus created a latent conflict between him and those aspirations towards Italian unity which he himself had done so much to foster. This conflict was almost paraded before the world, when a few days after Her Majesty's Government had expressed the hope that the French troops could be withdrawn at an early date, M. Rouher flatly declared that "Italy shall never possess herself of Rome", since that would be an outrage alike to French honour and to Catholicism. To the uncertainties of foreign policy was added the conflict between the regime at home and those liberal principles to which this strangest of all modern despots paid theoretical homage: and chronic ill-health made him wellnigh incapable of dealing resolutely with the problems confronting him.

The events of 1866 and 1867 have been dealt with in perhaps disproportionate detail, because they were in many ways a turning point for all Europe. They represent the high-water mark of British non-intervention: for from this point of view 1870–1 was a mere sequel, as our attitude then had virtually been predetermined by our attitude in 1866. In a word, our non-intervention was most marked at the very moment when effective intervention would have had the most decisive results. It is now necessary to revert to British home politics and to show how they threw foreign policy into the shade for some years to come.

The inconsistency between the Cabinet's attitude during the Luxemburg crisis and the negative policy put forward in Parliament led the Queen during the following summer to press her ministers for a clearer definition. Through her trusted private secretary General Grey she addressed herself to Mr Disraeli, who already occupied an almost dominant position in the Conservative party. Alluding to "the rival armaments and recrimination" on the Continent, she felt bound to "ask herself seriously whether England, adhering to a cold policy of non-interference, or rather to one of total abstention from all concern in the affairs of the Continent, is to continue her passive attitude, nor make any attempt to avert such a calamity". She again insisted on the need for making quite clear the British policy towards Luxemburg and Belgium. She quoted the view of Lord Stanley "that we are equally bound by ties of alliance and friendship both to France and Prussia and should hold the balance between the two", but argued that the danger from France was much more direct. For Prussia was not likely to violate pledges, "unless she sees reason to believe that England means her guarantee to remain a dead letter, in which case she might think it her interest to come to an agreement with France, fatal to the independence of the rest of Europe". The Queen, General Grey concluded, obviously quoting her more or less verbatim, "is confirmed in her conviction of the expediency of our acting firmly on a well-defined and understood system of foreign policy, by the advantageous result of our intervention on the Luxemburg question".[56] In reply, Disraeli assured Grey that Lord Stanley "has entirely dropped the phrase, and I hope the abstract policy, of non-intervention". Stanley, he added, leans towards Prussia, and he, Disraeli, has encouraged him in this.[57] The Queen was still not entirely reassured and dwelt upon the dangers of passivity. As she very acutely observed, the real problem was how to prevent a quarrel between France and Prussia, if both countries were bent upon it.[58] She still favoured an assurance to both sides that Britain would not tolerate the violation of either Belgium or Luxemburg.

Lord Stanley for his part, in replying to General Grey, spoke of "a growing expectation of war both in France and Prussia. We have helped them out of one quarrel at some risk of burning our own fingers, but can't go on doing this every six months." Hence the only course for Britain in the event of a war, was "that of a rigidly impartial neutrality".[59]

This whole incident deserves special emphasis, for it once more reveals Queen Victoria at her very best, placing her already remarkable knowledge of continental politics at the disposal of her ministers, and laying her finger upon certain points which a future age was to recognise as of fundamental importance.

Soon afterwards a difference of opinion arose between the Queen and the Foreign Secretary, which apart from its sidelights upon their respective attitude towards Germany, illustrates her saneness of outlook in the matter of diplomatic appointments, as against the hidebound views of the Foreign Office, but also her inability to enforce her wishes when even so relatively sluggish a Minister as Lord Stanley disagreed. She urged very strongly that Robert Morier should be sent to Berlin, and that the fittest, not merely the senior, candidate should be selected for such a post. Moreover, she argued, "Bismarck's objections to him are no disadvantage, because Count Bismarck dislikes England and does not wish for any intimate relations between the countries"[60] (probably an overstatement of the undoubted fact that Bismarck throughout his career was alternately attracted and repelled by Great Britain). Stanley's reason for not appointing Morier was that the latter "feels in fact as though he were himself a German politician.... We have nothing to do with the internal politics of German states, and by meddling in them only destroy our proper and legitimate influence."[61] The incident raises a question of some delicacy which is as alive to-day as it ever was in the past. It is instructive to note that though Stanley had encouraged Morier to hope that he might one day become Permanent Under-Secretary at the Foreign Office, he was in actual fact passed over in 1873 when the post became vacant on Hammond's retirement. On that occasion Stanley, now Lord Derby, expressed the view that Morier had "one defect for that particular position—he was too much in *earnest*, and earnest men with ideas and great abilities are sometimes unsafe men".[62] This is a standpoint which raises very far-reaching issues in public life, and may perhaps be more fittingly left to the unassisted verdict of the reader.

Stanley was emphatically a follower of the *via media*, alike in foreign and domestic politics. It was doubtless this fact which inspired the two-edged comment of that uncompromising observer *Vanity Fair*—"The most pleasing conclusion is that Lord Stanley is a phenomenon considerately framed by a merciful Providence to meet the modern necessities of conservatism, that he thinks with one party and acts with the other—a course which enables him to think as he likes and to act as he is told."

DISRAELI AS PRIME MINISTER

On 24 February 1868 Lord Derby's health obliged him to resign the Premiership, and thanks above all to the Queen's eager approval he was succeeded by Mr Disraeli. From the first there is a new note of flattery, so fulsome as to render competition difficult. In his first letter after taking office, he already writes, "He can only offer devotion.... It will be his delight and duty to render the transaction of affairs as easy to Your Majesty as possible".[63] He even thought it useful to define his idea of perfect relations between a sovereign and a minister—"on her part perfect confidence, on his, perfect devotion":[64] and even before this we find that the Queen had already noted in her diary, "Disraeli shows more consideration for my comfort than any of the preceding Prime Ministers since Peel and Aberdeen".[65]

During 1868 the Conservative Government was in steady decline and underwent a series of defeats. In the end it concluded an agreement to dissolve in November, and a special Registration Bill was passed, enabling those who only qualified in January 1869 as voters under the new franchise, as it were to antedate their qualifications. In this brief provisional period of the first Disraeli Cabinet nothing occurred upon the Continent that seemed directly to affect British interests. But Lord Stanley took one step which, though it does not fall within the scope of the present volume, deserves special passing mention, for the happy precedent which it created in the vital sphere of Anglo-American relations and for the impetus which it gave to the idea of the peaceful settlement of international disputes. He definitely committed this country to arbitration on the vexed dispute of the Alabama claims and laid a basis upon which Clarendon, Granville and Gladstone were to work. On the other hand he refused the exaggerated pretension of President Johnson and Mr Seward to include among the grounds for compensation Britain's ill-judged recognition of the Confederate States during the early stages of the Civil War.

GLADSTONE, CLARENDON AND THE QUEEN

The elections of 1868 gave the Liberals a majority of 121: and the next six years were to prove the heyday of Liberal supremacy. It at once became obvious that Mr Gladstone must be Prime Minister—obvious to all save the veteran Lord Russell, of whom Lord Granville wrote on 11 November, "Johnny's power of self-assertion is one of the strong points of his nature, which, as someone said, is a compound of a giant and a little child".[66] Of Russell Gladstone himself appears to have said at this very time to the Queen, that "he had for the last few years done nothing but injure a brilliant reputation".[67]

In forming his new Cabinet Mr Gladstone found the Queen for the second time opposed to the selection of Lord Clarendon as Foreign Secretary. Some gossip which had reached her ears appears to have caused offence, and in one of her memoranda she speaks of "his temper, his manner, his want of discretion".[68] But apart from the fact that he had already invited Clarendon's co-operation, Gladstone found it possible to describe him to the Queen as "the only living British statesman whose name carried any influence in the councils of Europe"[69]—a high testimonial to the individual, but a lamentable proof of that neglect of foreign problems of which we found Lord Derby complaining in 1866 when he appointed his own son for lack of a better candidate. It is painful to find Gladstone trying to humour the Queen by promising that Clarendon should be "brought as little in personal contact with her as possible".[70]

The country was soon fully absorbed by numerous contentious problems of home policy, such as Irish Disestablishment and the Irish Land Bill, soon to be followed by educational and military reform and a determined attempt to reduce expenditure. The seclusion into which the Queen had withdrawn herself and the apparent eclipse of the Crown's influence led to a good deal of criticism in the public press, and helped to increase that latent friction between sovereign and Prime Minister which was to become so marked in the 'seventies and early 'eighties. In the words of Lord Morley, "her loyalty to the constitution and to ministers in office was unquestioned, but she was not well placed, nor was she perhaps by character well fitted, to gauge the fluctuating movements of an age of change". Gladstone was nervous when he found his advice resented, and she, we are told, disliked being treated as though she were a public meeting. Lord Morley affirms that neither was devoid of humour, and that it was therefore "at once a wonder and a pity" that they could not do justice to each other. With all due respect it may be suggested that while "devoid of humour" would be an exaggeration, "deficient in humour" may fairly be alleged of both of them, and that this was the main cause of friction which left its mark alike on home and foreign policy for many critical years.

On the very eve of taking office, Lord Clarendon had paid a visit to the Continent, during which he discussed the general situation with Napoleon III on the one hand and with the King, Queen and Crown Prince of Prussia and Moltke on the other: and it is a curious fact that he really enjoyed the confidence of both the French and Prussian sovereigns to a higher degree than that of his own. His main impression, as reported to London by Lord Lyons (since 1867 our Ambassador in Paris) was that Napoleon "has nothing to fear from Prussia if he does not give her just provocation, but on the other hand that Prussia does not fear a war if she can show Germany and the world that she is really forced into it".[71]

BELGIAN NEUTRALITY

During 1869 apprehensions revived in many quarters as to possible French designs upon Belgium—this time owing to the proposed amalgamation of two Belgian railways with the Eastern Railway of France. Leopold II succeeded in alarming his cousin Queen Victoria, who reiterated to Clarendon her views upon Belgian independence and neutrality, arguing that "the best security for these essential objects would be found in the knowledge that any proceedings which seemed to threaten their violation would bring England at once into the field".[72] Lord Newton is fully justified in speaking of the "ineptitude" with which Napoleon III managed this whole affair, frightening and offending the Belgians and deepening the suspicions of all Europe as to his dark designs. All this time Napoleon was simply playing into the hands of Bismarck, who merely had to "bide his time quietly". The extent to which the Emperor was spoiling his own case may be judged from the acid comments of Clarendon in his correspondence with Lyons. "If the Emperor attaches value to the English alliance, he ought not to sacrifice it by a sneaking attempt to incorporate Belgium by means of a railway company and its employees."[73] And again (19 April), "I have never felt any confidence in the soft sayings and assurances of the French Government, but I did not think they could have exposed the cloven foot so soon and completely as they have done".[74]

The Queen's insistence on the Belgian question drew from Mr Gladstone the opinion that Belgian independence was "an object of the first interest to the mind of the British people", and the Ambassador was instructed to inform the French Government that "the suspicion even of an intention on the part of France" not to respect it, would at once be fatal to "the good understanding and harmonious co-operation of the two Governments".[75] Meanwhile Gladstone was led to face the more abstract principles involved, and in a letter to the Queen's secretary in April 1869 referred to "the fear abroad that England has for ever abjured a resort to force other than moral". "Is England", he went on to ask, "so uplifted in strength above every other nation that she can with prudence advertise herself as ready to undertake the general redress of wrongs?...Of course the answer is No. But do not allow it to be believed that England will never interfere." But prudence at once forced him to qualify once more, and he expressed agreement with Clarendon's view that it was "dangerous for England to assume alone an advanced and therefore isolated position in regard to European controversies, and that it was better to promise too little than too much".[76] His only concrete suggestion was that we "should seek to develop the action of a common European opinion ". But he was left still confronted with the old dilemma, how to determine the stage at which British interests were affected by changes on the Continent and at which we must therefore intervene, and again, how to make any such intervention effective against conscript armies with the diminutive forces at our own disposal. It was contended by Morier at the time, and has often been repeated since, that this country could by energetic intervention have prevented war in 1870 between France and Germany. But it has never yet been made clear how we could permanently, in such a world as that of the 'seventies, have prevented the clash which hidden forces on both sides had deliberately willed and prepared, and which was no mere outcome of blind chance.

This exchange of views between the Queen and her two ministers led nowhere. But her concluding words are again worth quoting. She claimed to have noted a disposition on the Continent to believe that England is not to be moved, either by interest or the obligation of treaties, into giving more than *moral* support in any complications that may arise, and that the aggressive Power may dismiss all fears of finding "England across its path ". She therefore urged on him, as on Lord Stanley earlier, the need for making clear "beyond the possibility of mistake ", that England will "maintain the obligation of treaties ".[77]

CLARENDON AND DISARMAMENT

A practical light is thrown upon this abstract problem by the last diplomatic action in which Lord Clarendon was engaged. In the summer of 1869 the Emperor Napoleon with much hesitation had launched his project of a so-called "Liberal Empire ", and the leaders of the new regime were fully aware that many reforms were required to calm down the general *malaise* of French opinion, and that for their execution the first essential requirement was peace. Early in 1870, therefore, secret overtures were made to Lord Clarendon by M. de Lavalette, now Ambassador in London, on behalf of the new French Foreign Minister Count Daru, in favour of disarmament, and similar ideas were expounded to Lord Lyons by the Premier, M. Emile Ollivier. It was suggested that Clarendon might in his turn raise the question with the King of Prussia, whose confidence he enjoyed, and that Britain might thus serve as intermediary in a general scheme of disarmament. The atmosphere in which the new Liberal Ministers had to work is clearly revealed in one of Ollivier's phrases. A public rebuff from Prussia, he argued, would be fatal—*un échec, c'est la guerre*—for a parliamentary government in France was less able than the former regime to risk "any wound to the national pride ".[78]

Clarendon skilfully used an opportunity that presented itself and conveyed to Bismarck a tentative proposal for partial and parallel disarmament by France and Prussia, without giving any hint that the idea had emanated from Paris. As might have been expected, Bismarck was quite as indisposed as his master King William to adopt any such plan, and drew the usual contrast between our "happy island" and his own country, surrounded by three great Empires. He thought it worth while to set forth his views at some length for Clarendon's benefit:[79] but though Clarendon returned to the charge in March and there was a further amicable exchange of opinion, there was not the slightest prospect of the proposals being acted upon, and Daru, though he took the failure very calmly, had not the courage to act upon Clarendon's closing suggestion that the best way of converting Prussia to disarmament was for France to begin by reducing her own army. That peace was the main object of Daru's policy is clearly revealed by the memorandum found among his papers and quoted by M. de La Gorce.[80] Unhappily the ministerial crisis which broke out in Paris during April 1870 led to Daru's fall, and he was replaced as Foreign Minister by the Duc de Gramont, who was not merely less restrained and conciliatory, but had as French Ambassador in Vienna been actively working for the creation of a triple alliance against Prussia.

GRANVILLE SUCCEEDS CLARENDON

Lord Clarendon died on 27 June 1870. The Queen's journal places on record that he was "very clever, had great experience and knowledge of foreign affairs and countries and very conciliatory. He was very satirical and could be irritable and hasty, but was much attached to me."[81] He was much more of an old Whig than of a young Liberal, as is revealed in his assurance to the Queen, in August 1869, that the chief danger in Germany is "the democratic spirit", which, he adds, in Germany (of other countries he is careful not to speak) "means Socialism".[82] He was certainly one of the most versatile and attractive of the Victorian Foreign Secretaries, but he seemed to lack the vitality that mastered and shaped a difficult situation. And yet there is on record the famous story of Bismarck's encounter with Clarendon's daughter in 1871. "Never in my life was I so glad to hear of anything as of your father's death", and then apologetically, "Ach, dear lady, do not take it like that. What I mean is that if your father had lived, he would have prevented the war."[83]

In the usual dearth of suitable candidates for the Foreign Office, Gladstone's choice fell upon Lord Granville, who had much of his predecessor's charm, and a good deal more tact, was *persona grata* with the Queen, but lacked the necessary prestige on the Continent and was scarcely in the saddle when one of the supreme crises in European affairs was upon him. When Lord Granville took over on 3 July, Mr Hammond, who had been Under-Secretary for close on twenty years (1854–73), committed himself to the statement that he had never known "so great a lull in foreign affairs": yet only two hours later came the telegram of Lord Lyons, announcing the first protest of France against the Hohenzollern candidature for the Spanish Crown.

THE FRANCO-GERMAN WAR

This is not the place to describe in detail the quarrel between France and Prussia or even to apportion the responsibility for war. We are concerned with the difficult dilemmas with which the war confronted British statesmen. Since the well-merited expulsion of Queen Isabella in 1868 the Spanish throne had gone begging through Europe, and after more than one unsuccessful attempt Marshal Prim, the chief of the Provisional Government, had definitely offered it to Prince Leopold of Hohenzollern, of the South German and Catholic branch of that family. The repercussions of this incident were out of all proportion to its real importance and illustrate the state of nerves into which Europe, and above all, France, had fallen. Only four years before Napoleon had given his approval to Leopold's brother Charles in accepting the Roumanian throne, and had actually backed him against Austria, despite the *rapprochement* which had taken place between Paris and Vienna. Moreover, Leopold, like Charles, though acknowledging the King of Prussia as head of their family, was closely related to the Murats and the Beauharnais, and so in a sense to the Bonapartes themselves. We know now that Bismarck, while evading the very concrete enquiries of the French Ambassador, had in secret[84] strongly encouraged Prince Leopold's candidature for definitely political reasons and even took into his reckoning its possible value in a war with France.[85] Indeed Prince Charles Anthony, the candidate's father, was definitely of opinion that Bismarck "started or exploited the candidature solely in the interest of thus obtaining the *casus belli* against France".[86] But all this was unknown and indeed barely suspected at the time, whereas it was notorious that King William was most reluctant to give his consent (he actually used the phrases "with a very heavy heart" and "the daring decision"[87]). Nor is it too much to say that the French Government, notably Ollivier, Gramont and Lebœuf, committed every possible error of judgment and tactics, played upon the ill-health and vacillating moods of the Emperor, encouraged instead of restraining the Chauvinist press and public opinion, and contrived to create in

Europe an impression of unreason which Bismarck was eagerly waiting to exploit. Among many acts of folly the precipitancy with which they pushed matters to an issue without waiting for the conclusion of an Austrian alliance, was perhaps the greatest. The failure to secure the alliance with Italy falls into another category, for it was due to Napoleon's loyalty to the Pope and his refusal to sanction an Italian occupation of Rome: but it has rightly been diagnosed as the crowning blunder of his foreign policy and the main cause of France's isolation at her hour of need. In a word, it is still possible to endorse Mr Gladstone's statement that French diplomacy in 1870 was "a chapter which for fault and folly taken together is almost without a parallel in the history of nations".[88]

Already on 5 July Napoleon had appealed to Gladstone to use his good offices for a withdrawal of the Hohenzollern candidature, and three days later Gramont, in suggesting to Lyons Prince Leopold's voluntary renunciation, spoke of this as "a most fortunate solution". A little later he assured Lyons that "if the Prince should now withdraw *on the advice of the King of Prussia*, the whole affair would be at an end".[89] Lord Granville lost no time in urging Madrid to abandon the candidature, and Berlin to encourage the Spanish Government in this sense. He enlisted Queen Victoria in favour of voluntary renunciation and encouraged her to advocate it to the Count of Flanders, Prince Leopold's brother-in-law, while the King of the Belgians did the same. And in actual fact, during the night of 11–12 July, Prince Charles Anthony of Hohenzollern, in his anxiety to avert war, announced his son's renunciation of the Spanish throne. King William, on hearing the news, wrote to the Queen that a stone had fallen from his heart.[90]

But this did not satisfy Paris. On the 12th Gramont informed Lyons that his Government, if it was to avert its own fall, required a more direct satisfaction, in the form of some endorsement by the King of Prussia himself.[91] On learning of Gramont's attitude, Gladstone and Granville promptly ordered Lyons to represent to France "the immense responsibility which will rest" on her, "if she does not at once accept as satisfactory and conclusive" the withdrawal of Leopold: and this message was delivered at St Cloud while the Council of Ministers was actually sitting. On this Gramont appealed for British good offices to obtain a guarantee against any future Hohenzollern candidature, and promised in writing that this would end the incident. But the British Cabinet meeting on the 14th decided that it would not be justified in taking such a step, and meanwhile Granville had wired back to Lyons that such a request "gave us the right to point out the grave responsibility of not accepting the renunciation *and constituting themselves the aggressors in this war*". This was the considered view of London on the very eve of the famous Ems incident. The most that the Cabinet was prepared to sanction was a suggestion to Bismarck that as King William had consented in the first instance to the candidature, he might now without any loss of dignity tell the French that he now consented to its withdrawal.[92] Nothing however came of this formula: for when it reached Berlin on the 15th, Bismarck declined to lay it before the King.

Meanwhile Benedetti had called upon King William at Ems on the 13th, and the King had telegraphed to Bismarck his account of their perfectly friendly interview. That evening Bismarck dined with Moltke and Roon, who were both sunk in depression at the thought that war might still be averted: and the telegram was then and there edited for publication, without the alteration of a single word, but with such judicious omissions that, to quote the words of Moltke, what had "sounded before like a parley, was now like a flourish in answer to a challenge".[93] When the document in this form reached Paris, the excitement was intense, and at the Council of Ministers, held under the Emperor's presidency, general mobilisation was ordered.

One last effort was made by London to avert the catastrophe. Lord Granville proposed that if France should waive her demand for a future guarantee, King William might inform the French that he approved of Prince Leopold's withdrawal. This was refused by both Bismarck and Gramont. Secondly Granville invited both parties to accept the friendly offices of a third Power, in terms of the Arbitration Protocol drafted at the Congress of Paris in 1856. But this was equally unsuccessful, for on 18 July Bismarck threw the onus of acceptance upon France, and next day France not merely declined, but declared war upon Prussia.

The precipitancy of the French Government played direct into Bismarck's hands and gave no time for the other Powers to mediate effectively. It seems abundantly clear that Britain in particular could not have prevented war except by declaring her own readiness to take the field herself on one side or the other, and this public opinion most certainly would not have tolerated. Granville reported to the Queen that "everyone seems to have been in the wrong", and added that it was "evident that the sentiment of the House on both sides generally condemns the conduct of France".[94] Once more we may fairly quote Gladstone's own criticism of the French Government, not merely as representing sane and well-informed inside opinion in London at the time, but as an estimate which history has in the main endorsed: "As the advisers of the Emperor knew nothing of public rights and of the sense of Europe, so they knew nothing about Austria and the mind of the German states, and less than nothing about not only the Prussian army, but even their own."[95]

There was, however, very grave concern in London, and daily consultations took place: but that the Government, while aware of the possible dangers of the situation, was really impotent to cope with them in time if they had arisen, is shown by Mr Gladstone's discussions with Mr Cardwell, then Secretary for War. For the idea of sending troops to protect Antwerp is seriously considered, but the number mentioned is only 10,000 to 20,000 men! The Queen, as ever, was urging the need for being prepared, but how could the British Army of those days have hoped to affect a decision upon land between the two great adversaries? It is but fair to recall in passing the fact that the British Navy had between the years 1866 and 1870 almost doubled in tonnage.

M. de La Gorce has very well summed up the fatal aberrations and miscalculations of the French Government in 1870. There were three very definite policies which could have been followed—that of "territorial ambitions" and that of "satisfied effacement", or the intermediate tactics of a "concentration of forces" (*recueillement*). Unhappily the first two were inextricably mingled and confused, and when "a violent access of exasperated *amour propre*" provoked the final crisis, "war fell upon the country, as fruit falls upon the ground when it is ripe".[96]

New Light on the Ems Telegram

I am greatly indebted to Dr Winifred Taffs (author of a forthcoming *Life* of Lord Odo Russell) for drawing my attention to a hitherto unpublished, and seemingly unnoticed, piece of evidence as to the role played by the Ems Telegram. On 24 May 1883 Colonel Swaine, British Military Attaché in Berlin, reported a conversation with Emperor William I after a dinner in honour of Queen Victoria's birthday. The conversation turning to the deciphering of telegrams, the Emperor remarked that "it was possible to get more than enough of such work. 'When I left Ems', so said the Emperor, 'to return here just before the war, it took about eleven hours to run over the distance, and wherever we halted on the road, cypher telegrams were handed into the carriage. Answers to these had also to be sent. The consequence was that Dr Busch and another gentleman were kept employed for the whole of those 11 hours unremittingly cyphering and decyphering.

"On arrival at Berlin, I was met at the Station by my son, by Minister Bismarck and many other Ministers and gentlemen of my Government and Household. On alighting, a long telegram was placed in my hands, coming from Paris and reporting the debate of that day in the Chamber of Deputies.

It had evidently been very warlike, and the Ambassador commenting on it seemed to think that the French were in earnest, and that the moment was a very serious one. While I was still greeting my numerous friends on the platform, a second telegram, longer than the first, was given to me. As there was a considerable crowd surrounding us, I suggested that we should adjourn into the waitingroom specially improvised for me. It was a very small room, and lighted only by a small dimly burning gas lamp.

"Minister Bismarck was unable by so little light to read the telegram. My son therefore took it up and amid a dead silence read it out. It gave in greater detail the speeches of the same debate in the French Chambers and was so decidedly warlike, that when my son had finished, and after a second's pause, I turned to the assembled gentlemen and said, 'Can you suggest to me a better answer to this telegram than the order for the mobilisation of the entire German Army?' A unanimous 'No' was given to this question. I then said that I would be ready in half an hour to sign the order...." [97]

It is quite clear from this document that the decisive influence upon the Emperor himself was not the doctored telegram, but the detailed news of the French official attitude.

BRITISH NEUTRALITY

If the French played their cards in such a way as to reduce to a minimum the sympathy of public opinion in Great Britain, Bismarck increased the impression by a masterstroke of unofficial diplomacy. On 25 July there appeared in *The Times* the text of the Franco-Prussian draft treaty of 1866, to which reference has already been made, and which Benedetti had been unwise enough to leave in Bismarck's possession at the time. The net effect was to make British public opinion more negative and suspicious than ever, and bent upon avoiding all complications. Lord Granville's own comment to the Queen's private secretary (Colonel Ponsonby, the successor of General Grey) was highly characteristic: "I believe the Emperor and Bismarck to be what it is better not to put on paper." [98] In one direction, however, this revelation acted as a stimulant. On the initiative of the Queen [99] the Cabinet decided to invite both belligerents to sign a treaty for the protection of Belgium, by the terms of which Great Britain bound herself at any period during the war or the twelve months following its conclusion, to go to war upon whichever Power violated Belgian neutrality. This treaty, which was signed on 9 August, Gladstone justified on the ground that it was impossible to stand aside and "see actions done which would amount to a total extinction of public right in Europe".[100] In reaching this view he was doubtless influenced by the official opinion of the Law Officers, that "refusal or incapacity of one or more of the guaranteeing Powers to act" in defence of Belgian neutrality "does not in our opinion liberate the remaining Powers from the obligation to do so".* At the same time Parliament voted an increase of the naval and military estimates, and though the addition of 20,000 men to the army was of little or no use for the contingency of war, it at least showed that public interest had been aroused in the cause of Belgium.

As the war went on, the position of Britain became extremely delicate. As early as 9 August Morier overstated it most unfairly in the following terms: "We sit by like a bloated Quaker, too holy to fight, but rubbing our hands at the roaring trade we are driving in cartridges and ammunition."[101] But it is perfectly true that our refusal to impose restrictions upon the export of munitions was keenly resented in Germany: and at the same time the legend of Granville's personal sympathies for the French Court was widely circulated, partly by no other than Bismarck himself.† Indeed, it is hardly too much to assert that Great Britain was soon equally unpopular in both the belligerent countries, and that each of them had a sufficient number of ardent adherents on this side of the Channel for the other to be able to assume our hostility to *it*.

That our role was extremely ineffective and left traces that can be followed to the very eve of the Great War, can hardly be seriously denied: but it is by no means so easy to show what effective alternative could have been adopted, short of *armed mediation*, which no one on either side of politics advocated. Even if it had been desirable, no coalition could have been formed, as Europe was then constituted. For Russia, partly from dynastic reasons and partly in view of favours to come, stood behind Prussia, while Austria, which had got the length of discussing a draft treaty of alliance with France,[102] and had early in 1870 sent the Archduke Albrecht to Paris to clinch the matter, drew back after the first German victories, mainly under pressure from Hungary. Italy, who might have joined France if Napoleon had yielded on the Roman question, was by September no less devoutly thankful than Austria that she had not committed herself, and was absorbed in the acquisition of Rome as her capital. Under such circum-

---

* 6 August 1870—*B.D.* VIII, No. 311. To this may be added here the considered opinion of Sir Eyre Crowe and the Foreign Office, drawn up on 15 November 1908 and approved by Sir Edward Grey: "Britain is liable for the maintenance of Belgian neutrality whenever either Belgium or any of the guaranteeing Powers are in need of, and demand assistance in opposing its violation"—*ibid.* p. 377.

† This was alleged to Morier both by the Duke of Coburg and by the Crown Prince of Prussia.

stances Granville was on strong ground in admitting the French complaint that we had circumscribed the war, but claiming that "this was no injury to France: for if Austria had joined her, Russia would have joined Germany, and the conflagration would have been general".[103]

When the Second Empire fell after Sedan, opinion in England veered more towards France, and when it became evident that Prussia was bent on annexation, opinion hardened still further and resented the drastic treatment of the *franctireurs*. None the less, Gladstone, in his desire to organise a protest of the neutral Powers against the seizure of Alsace-Lorraine, found himself without the support of any of his colleagues in the Cabinet, including Granville, and had to abandon the idea. But whatever we, wise after the event, may think of his views on the origins of the war, we must regard him as a true prophet of its consequences, when he wrote: "While I more and more feel the deep culpability of France, I have an apprehension that this violent laceration and transfer is to lead us from bad to worse, and to be the beginning of a new series of European complications."[104] He had already protested to Queen Victoria against the tendency to decide this question "without any reference whatever to the attachments of the people", and had gone on to argue that it involved "considerations of legitimate interest to all the Powers of Europe", bore upon "the Belgian question in particular", and was "likely to be of great consequence in the eventual settlement of the Eastern Question".[105]

RUSSIA REPUDIATES THE BLACK SEA SETTLEMENT

Quite apart, however, from the fact that any such protest or attempted mediation was likely to meet with a severe snub and might in the end even involve us in the war, the Cabinet found itself faced by a fresh complication in the early winter of 1870. On 31 October the Russian Chancellor, Prince Gorchakov, issued a Circular Note to the Powers, declaring that Russia no longer considered herself bound by the Black Sea clauses of the Treaty of Berlin. It soon became apparent that Prussia's compliance was part of the price which she had paid for the Tsar's benevolent neutrality: and indeed Granville had to admit to his chief the awkward fact that all the Powers, "with the exception of ourselves and the Turks",[106] had already reached the conclusion that the clauses to which Russia took exception had long been in need of revision. There was much indignation in London and even a certain recrudescence of the old Russophobe feelings of the Crimean War. But the Queen was once more at her best in warning against "precipitate action, so that we may not be drawn into war for so unsatisfactory a cause as in fact the upholding of a Mohammedan state with so little intrinsic power must in the abstract be called ".[107] For once in a way we played a successful game of bluff, by sending Mr Odo Russell (as he then was) on a special mission to German headquarters, where he convinced Bismarck that Britain might go to war with Russia, even without allies, unless the latter withdrew the obnoxious circular and consented to negotiate with the other signatory powers. Bismarck could not take even the risk of a fresh war which might so easily involve Austria-Hungary also, and was in any case certain to upset all his calculations on the eve of victory: he therefore undertook to propose an European Conference for the regulation of the Black Sea question, and to secure Russia's consent. Granville declined to accept St Petersburg as its place of meeting, and in the end the Conference sat in London, from 17 December 1870 till 13 March 1871. It was already characteristic of the altered situation in Europe, that France was only represented at the final sitting. The Protocol had to be redrafted no less than fourteen times before agreement could be reached, but due emphasis was laid on "the essential principle of the law of nations, that no Power can liberate itself from the engagements of a treaty, nor modify the stipulations thereof, unless with the consent of the contracting parties, by means of an amicable agreement ".[108] The final Protocol abrogated Articles 11, 13 and 14 of the Treaty of Paris, by which the Black Sea had been neutralised and the naval forces of Russia in that sea restricted. The Straits remained closed, subject to the Sultan's right in time of peace to permit the passage of specific ships of war. They of course remained free to merchant vessels of all nations.

GLADSTONE AND FOREIGN POLICY

The Black Sea incident had led to a temporary breakdown of the Concert of Europe, and had shown that it was not strong enough to resist the strain of war between two of its foremost members. Britain, finding herself incapable of either preventing or arresting the war or even of dissuading the victors from a vindictive peace, had at least been able to save the principles of international law from the wreckage: and it was not till 1908 that the precedent created by Russia in 1870 for the one-sided and arbitrary revision of general treaty obligations was followed up by any of the Great Powers.

In another respect Britain under the second Gladstone administration proved herself to be in advance of the age, and indeed of public opinion at home. The acceptance of the principle of arbitration in our long dispute with the United States over the Alabama Case, and the patience, good temper and courtesy which Lord Granville showed in the face of considerable abuse and unpopularity, and of the extravagant private claims sometimes put forward from the American side, may be regarded to-day without fear of challenge as the chief claim to the gratitude of posterity on the part of a Foreign Secretary who carried much less weight in the counsels of Europe than his very real abilities might have warranted. And that Granville persisted was largely due to the fact that Gladstone, despite many obvious defects, regulated his conduct, to a greater degree than most statesmen of his day, by very definite principles: and nowhere more than in the sphere of foreign policy have they been so thoroughly vindicated by time. This will become still more apparent towards the close of the period under review.

Despite this signal service rendered to the cause of Anglo-American relations, the position of Great Britain abroad after 1870 was one of considerable embarrassment. A necessity which even the most partisan critics could hardly deny, had driven her into an attitude of negation and actually strengthened the desire for non-intervention, while making her almost equally unpopular on both sides of the continental struggle. But this attitude, which was, as we saw, a rebound from the incessant and not always dignified meddling of the 'fifties and early 'sixties, was already preparing the way for a fresh swing of the pendulum. Morier was grossly unfair when he spoke of "the strange mania for eating dirt", under Gladstone and Granville, but he was merely guilty of undue emphasis when he accused the latter of "absolute inertia".[109] His plea for "a policy of self-assertion" rested on the belief that England might be "the rallying point for the immense peace forces distributed over Europe", but that nothing could be done unless "the Imperial sense" sprang up in one of the great British parties. A few years later Disraeli was to become the interpreter of such ideas, but to give them a somewhat different form from that which Morier had hoped.

It is hardly necessary to point out that the eclipse of France in 1870 completely altered the distribution of forces in Europe, and ushered in the period of "Armed Peace". The achievement of German unity under the auspices of Prussia, sealed by the annexation of Alsace-Lorraine, left Germany predominant on the Continent; France, exhausted by her defeats and by sanguinary civil dissensions, found herself completely isolated abroad, and the legend of her decadence was widely disseminated and believed. In Austria-Hungary the French defeats determined the failure of the federalist experiment, and the fall of the Francophil Beust, who was succeeded as Foreign Minister by Count Julius Andrássy, meant not merely the triumph of the Dual System and a virtual Hungarian predominance inside that system, but in foreign policy the beginnings of a rapprochement with Germany which was eventually to develop into the Triple Alliance. Meanwhile Spain had long since ceased to be a Great Power, while Italy was still consolidating her new position. Thus Britain's attitude in the war of 1870 had resulted both in her own isolation and in the temporary eclipse of the Western and Liberal Powers as a serious factor in the European Balance. But parallel with this there was a revival, in the years following the war, of the old alliance of the three Eastern Courts—the Three Emperors' League, as it was now called—a combination wellnigh irresistible so long as it held together. In its essence, it stood for the same ideals of conservatism and authoritative government as the earlier Holy Alliance—toned down, it is true, in Germany and Austria-Hungary to meet the requirements of the time, but none the less effectually resting upon dynastic control of military and foreign affairs—opposed to popular control wherever possible, and united by a further bond in the common necessity of preventing the resurrection of Poland.

The Liberal Decline

It was this combination which confronted Britain at every turn when Disraeli returned to power in 1874, and his main efforts in foreign policy were devoted to creating a breach between the three Conservative Powers. What gave him his opportunity was the undoubted *malaise* produced by the dislocation of the old European system. It was one of those cases where everyone felt that something energetic required to be done, yet objected to the only practical form of energy. England's isolation was resented, and it was felt that we had not merely failed to impose peace by some unspecified miracle, but had been weak towards Russia on the one hand and towards America on the other. While these sentiments gained ground in the country, the outburst of Liberal legislation gradually spent itself, and the new franchise brought grist to the Tory mill, showing that Disraeli's calculations of party advantage to be derived from the Bill of 1867 were not so far wrong after all. And so it was possible for him, in one of his most audacious speeches, on 3 April 1872, to compare the Liberal Front Bench to "a range of exhausted volcanoes. Not a flame flickers upon a single pallid crest. But the situation is still dangerous. There are still occasional earthquakes, and anon the dark rumbling of the sea." In the same speech, while especially condemning the Government's foreign policy towards Russia and America, he disclaimed all desire for a "turbulent and aggressive diplomacy", but argued that Britain's relations to Europe had "undergone a vast change during the century that has just elapsed", that the New World was "throwing lengthening shades over the Atlantic", and creating "vast and novel elements in the distribution of power". He endorsed a policy of "proud reserve" towards Europe, but added his belief that "there never was a moment in our history, when the power of England was so great and her resources so vast and inexhaustible. And yet it is not merely our fleets and armies, our accumulated capital and our unlimited credit on which so much depends, as upon that unbroken spirit of her people, which I believe was never prouder of the Imperial country to which they belong."[110] This was a new note, all the more significant in that it was struck at Manchester, in the very citadel of Free Trade.

Later in the same year Disraeli assumed the offensive in another memorable speech at the Crystal Palace, pleading for better housing and improved standards of living for the working man, and at the same time challenging the narrow outlook of the Liberal party upon Colonial and Imperial problems and roundly accusing it of promoting the disintegration of the Empire. If this was a partisan overstatement of the facts, no one to-day will attempt to deny that it was Disraeli who first assigned to the colonies their due place in the political world, first responded to their passionate loyalty, and first voiced their desire for fuller self-government, though on the other hand it was reserved for an extreme Radical, Sir Charles Dilke, to coin the phrase of "Greater Britain" and to give it full literary expression in a once famous book.

During 1872 and 1873, then, there was a slow but very marked trend of opinion in favour of the Conservatives, due no doubt in part to Tory suspicion towards those who had disestablished the Irish Church and had laid themselves open—so far at least as a tiny but active group on the extreme left was concerned—to the charge of inadequate respect for the Crown. This feeling was intensified by the steady revival of Queen Victoria's popularity: the turning point may be said to have been her abandonment of extreme seclusion after the Prince of Wales's recovery from a dangerous illness in 1871. The nation's mood was at this moment essentially insular and introspective, and Disraeli voiced a widespread opinion when he declared, "It would have been better for us all if there had been a little more energy in our foreign policy, and a little less in our domestic legislation."[111]

It was on an eminently domestic issue that the first real clash came: on 12 March 1873 the Government was defeated by three votes, on the Irish University Bill. After some hesitation Gladstone decided to resign, and the Queen sent for Disraeli, but the latter, with the full approval of Derby, Cairns and other leading Conservatives, "declined altogether to accept office" in the existing Parliament, and also deliberately refrained from asking for a dissolution. After thinking it over for some days, he even sent the Queen a full memorandum, representing his rival as in effect telling the

House of Commons, "unless you are prepared to put someone in my place, your duty is to do whatever I bid you".[112] He took the line that his party had not defeated the Government, but only thrown out "a stupid blundering Bill", and that Gladstone could "now resume office with perfect freedom".[113] Gladstone affected considerable indignation at this attitude and only consented to retain office after the Queen had brought home the absolute character of Disraeli's refusal. But he was quite right in treating the political situation as "seriously unhinged by the shock": and for the next nineteen months the Liberals were steadily losing ground, and the inclusion of John Bright in the Cabinet in no way revived their popularity. In January 1874, then, Gladstone made a sudden decision to dissolve Parliament, hoping to win the country by a programme of economy and reduced taxation such as was always dear to his heart. But he was happy neither in his choice of moment nor in his prolix presentment of the Liberal case: the caustic Harcourt was quite right in thinking that there had been "a great deal too much want of common sense in the conduct of the party. We must learn not to bark when we cannot bite."[114] The country turned away from what Disraeli had most unfairly called a policy of "plundering and blundering": and the Conservatives emerged from the election with a clear majority of 50 over the Liberals and the new Home Rule Party combined. Montagu Corry wrote to his victorious chief of "the panic at Brooks's" and described Gladstone as "prostrate and confounded". "The strongest Government since Pitt", was Disraeli's confident comment to Lady Bradford: but on reflection, racked as he was by gout and asthma, he complained rather sadly, "Power has come to me too late."[115] The Queen was relieved at the prospect of quieter times at home, and an infusion of new energy into foreign policy, after the all too nerveless regime of Granville. Gladstone admitted very frankly to the Queen, that his defeat was "the greatest expression of public disapprobation of a Government that he ever remembered, though he did not think it was quite just". He drew the logical conclusion and resigned the Liberal leadership, his place being taken by Hartington in the Commons and by Granville in the Lords. "The Liberal Party", he told the Queen, "must learn how through their divisions and self-seeking they had brought the present disruption about".[116] On the other hand he described the new House as "the most reactionary, the most apathetic and the least independent", in which he had ever sat.[117] Disraeli's main indictment against Gladstone had related to internal policy, but there can be small doubt that the Liberal Government's increasingly "negative and lethargic" attitude towards foreign affairs had largely contributed to its loss of prestige.

CHAPTER XIII

DISRAELI AND THE EASTERN QUESTION*

The new Cabinet, still limited to 12 members, was admitted by friend and foe alike to be one of the strongest of the century. Lord Cairns as Lord Chancellor, Lord Carnarvon as Colonial Secretary, Lord Salisbury (reconciled to Disraeli after a long period of estrangement, through the influence of his stepmother Lady Derby) as Indian Secretary, Gathorne Hardy as Secretary for War, Sir Stafford Northcote as Chancellor of the Exchequer, were all men of known ability, and the only real newcomer, Assheton Cross, soon proved a very competent Home Secretary. The appointment of Lord Derby to the Foreign Office was a foregone conclusion, after the sober judgment which he had shown during his first term of office. His old intimacy with Disraeli, which despite great disparity of character had survived unbroken for many years, was now at its height, and at first their co-operation and mutual trust was very close, offering a marked contrast to the reserve with which Salisbury and Carnarvon regarded their chief. Derby had the further advantage of great territorial influence in the north, and was looked up to in the party as eminently sound and cautious. He had "that plain common sense, love of peace and moderation of political faith which appealed to the middle classes".[1] No other than Robert Morier expressed the opinion that Derby "thoroughly knows foreign politics, and...England's position abroad would be steadied" by his selection. "To take an unknown man just now, in the very dangerous and inflammable state of Europe...would be madness, especially with the perfectly demoralised and disorganised state into which our diplomacy had been thrown by Lord Granville's absolute inertia during the last three years."[2] It must, however, be confessed that Derby, as he grew older, was already developing a certain apathy, or reluctance to take strong action, which had the effect of goading his chief into assuming an initiative that was on occasion reckless. Curiously enough, he did not find it easy to get on with the Queen, and was once exhorted by his chief "to step out of his icy panoply", and do himself justice. She on her side wrote of "that very peculiar person Lord Derby", who was "very difficult to manage".[3]

* For a detailed account of the whole Eastern crisis of 1875–80 and its bearings upon British policy, see my *Disraeli, Gladstone and the Eastern Question* (1935).

THE RETURN FROM ISOLATION

On his return to office at the age of 70, Disraeli found an entirely different Europe from that of 1868. The Second Empire, with which he had maintained such close relations, was gone, the Third Republic, though fortunate in finding men of such different qualities as Thiers, Macmahon and Gambetta, was still under eclipse and seemed much weaker than it really was, even though it had paid off the war indemnity and begun to reorganise the army. Italy, newly united and admitted to the ranks of the Great Powers, was in the throes of financial crisis and gravely handicapped by the Roman question. Spain, reduced to misery by a generation of civil war and feeble governments, was almost negligible in Europe. Britain, entirely isolated, though enjoying the safe shelter of her powerful fleet, was almost irresistible overseas, but on the Continent was faced by the powerful combination of the three Imperial Powers of Eastern Europe, of whom two, Russia and Austria, watched each other with suspicion, but none the less maintained their traditional policy of co-operation in the Eastern Question, dating as far back as Peter the Great, while the third, Germany, was above all concerned to avert a quarrel between her two allies, in which she would almost inevitably be forced to take sides.

"There is no balance", such was the conclusion drawn by Disraeli,[4] "and unless we go out of our way to act with the three Northern Powers, they can act without us, which is not agreeable for a state like England." It followed, in his view, that if Britain was to adopt the more forward continental policy at which he already aimed, an attempt must be made to drive a wedge between the three allies: and the history of the three years of Eastern Crisis from 1875 to 1878 is punctuated by a series of opportunist, and invariably unsuccessful, efforts in this sense. Even after the crisis had died down Disraeli, on the eve of retirement, hugged the illusion that he had split the alliance: but the reconstruction of the Three Emperors' League in 1881 showed how he had misjudged the situation.

BRITAIN AND RUSSIA IN CENTRAL ASIA

From the very first Disraeli showed keen interest in the problems of the Near and Middle East, and particularly in Russia's activities in Central Asia. The appointment of General Kauffmann as Governor of Turkestan in 1867 inaugurated an era of steady advance against the decadent, but turbulent, native states which lay between the Caspian, the Pamirs and the Tian Shan. The reduction of Samarkand and Bokhara in 1868 made Russia the neighbour of Afghanistan on the south-east: in 1873 Khiva also fell, and in 1875 Khokand, the last of these petty states, made its submission. Many acute observers, even if hostile to Russia, recognised that the Turkoman states were centres of slavery and hideous tyranny, and that the policy pursued by Kauffmann closely resembled that of Napier in Scinde in the 'forties, and was probably even more inevitable. The great Lord Lawrence, as Viceroy of India, refused to take an alarmist view, arguing that the establishment of order and culture by a Great Power was preferable to a continuance of chronic anarchy and misrule: and his two successors, Mayo and Northbrook, upheld the same tradition. In 1869 and again in 1873 conversations took place between the British and Russian Governments, with a view to defining their respective spheres of influence and if possible establishing a neutral zone between the two Empires. How fluid the whole situation still remained, is best shown by the fact that on the latter occasion the Tsar accepted the Oxus as the northern boundary line and denied all idea of taking Khiva, but that within a year events forced him into an occupation from which he could not, with the best will in the world, ever again recede. But though even that stalwart Russophobe, Sir Henry Rawlinson, admitted the step to be inevitable, it caused no little alarm in India, and while in Russia itself there was a constant struggle of opinion between the "forward" school of Kauffmann himself and the officials of the Tsar's Court, so also Russophobia grew steadily stronger in the Viceroy's Council at Simla and found fresh grounds for vigilant suspicion in the troubles which now broke out in Afghanistan, and which were unquestionably encouraged from the side of Russia. Northbrook's successor, the gifted but all too impressionable Lytton, went out to India without any preconceived hostility towards Russia, but soon surrendered to the military extremists, and drifted gradually towards an Afghan policy which saw in expansion from the south the only means of countering a Russian advance from the north. Lord Salisbury, as Secretary for India, took a middle view, and, while regarding a Russian invasion of India as a "chimaera", did seriously reckon with the possibility of Russia inciting the Afghans.

The Prime Minister, on his side, so far from showing any marked suspicion of Russia at this stage, was in full accord with the policy of friendship between the two Courts which he found on taking office, and whose outward expression was the marriage of the Queen's second son, the Duke of Edinburgh, to the only daughter of Alexander II on 7 March 1874. This was followed in May by a state visit of the Tsar to Windsor, during which he had cordial conversations with the new Prime Minister, and obtained the Queen's approval for a direct correspondence if difficulties should arise between the two countries. Disraeli confided to Salisbury a certain scepti-

cism as to "a real understanding",[5] but definitely favoured close co-operation, and the renewed tension between Germany and France during the
next eighteen months increased the friendly outlook of London towards
Russia.

THE WAR SCARE OF 1875

The disastrous eclipse which had befallen France in 1870–1 had been
followed by a recovery which filled both friend and foe with admiration and
surprise. Not merely had Thiers's efforts to pay the indemnity and assure
evacuation been completely successful, but the French army was steadily
re-organised and material prosperity was again apparent. The French
Chargé in Berlin after the war, in reporting his first conversation with
Bismarck, used the afterwards famous phrase, "La France se relève trop
vite à ses yeux: he thought he was done with her for twenty years". The disappointment was rendered more acute by the conservative, and even
monarchist, trend of opposition in the French Chamber in the early
'seventies, and by the natural resentment voiced on the Right, and in corresponding circles in Belgium, at the fierce "Cultural" conflict which had
broken out between Bismarck and the Roman Church. The French
Embassy in Berlin was in the hands of Gontaut-Biron, who leaned strongly
to the Right and was known to be playing upon the Empress's personal
detestation of the Chancellor: and Bismarck's antipathies were increased
when the Broglie Cabinet fell, and the more pessimistic and nervous Duke
Decazes became Foreign Minister. Already in February 1874 Morier, from
his point of vantage in Munich, detected the sharper note in the inspired
German Press and in his reports speculated as to "this unexpected blast
upon the war trumpet".[6] Decazes's worst fears seemed confirmed when
Moltke, in introducing the new army bill before the Reichstag, spoke of "a
savage cry of revenge from beyond the Vosges". The Tsar refused to believe
in Germany's warlike designs: but Queen Victoria wrote to the Emperor
William a letter in which, after stressing her friendship for him, her attachment to Germany and the cause of unity, and her Protestant sympathies,
she also alluded to the persistent rumours as to Germany's "disposition to
crush and annihilate a beaten foe", and urged upon him a policy of "magnanimity" and "generosity". In reply William I, who was himself undoubtedly pacific, insisted upon the Ultramontane danger, but strenuously
denied all desire for another war.[7] Bismarck drew back, and in May spoke to
Lord Odo Russell of the importance to Europe of "a strong France".

These and other incidents had already aroused the suspicions of both
Disraeli and Derby towards Bismarck, and at the Guildhall Banquet in

November 1874 the Prime Minister went somewhat out of his way to compliment the new French Ambassador upon "the elasticity, nerve and resource" by which France had extricated herself from her troubles. Later in the winter there were fresh incidents of a disquieting kind, Bismarck complaining of the Belgian attitude towards the *Kulturkampf*, and his press spreading a story of large purchases of horses for the French army. But Derby did not conceal from the French that non-intervention was to him the beginning and the end of political wisdom, while Disraeli told the German Ambassador that he had never believed in France as a sincere ally of England, and that "the only people who could go hand in hand were Germany and England".[8]

Public opinion was already in a jumpy mood when early in April 1875 one of Bismarck's organs, the Berlin *Post*, published an alarmist article on the increase of French armaments, ending with the question, "Is War in Sight?" The stir caused in diplomatic circles was increased by a conversation between Gontaut-Biron and Radowitz, one of Bismarck's most valued assistants at the German Foreign Office, who used abstract and reflective, but none the less ominous, phrases about *revanche* and a preventive war. We now know that Bismarck himself used similar language to the Austrian Ambassador, and that both Odo Russell and his Military Attaché were disturbed by the views expressed by Moltke. Morier showed his alarm to the full, and urged most strongly upon his friends the Crown Prince and Princess the need for countering Bismarck's warlike designs.

The scare reached its height on 6 May, with the publication in *The Times* of a resounding article by that strange prince of journalist-adventurers, "M. de Blowitz"—a Moravian Jew named Fritz Oppert, who had calmly invented both surname and particle, and combined flair, fantasy and assurance to an unrivalled degree. But if this provided the necessary publicity in Europe, the really decisive action was taken by the Tsar, who already on 15 April had assured the French Ambassador that he regarded French and Russian interests as identical, and that if the former should be threatened, "you will know it very quickly—*through me*".[9] Early in May he and his Chancellor, Prince Gorchakov, were in Berlin, on the way to an annual cure at Ems, and they threw their whole influence with the Emperor in favour of peace, while Russell received timely instructions to intervene with Bismarck on similar lines. The Queen too appealed to the Tsar to use his "great influence to maintain peace and dissipate the profound alarm aroused throughout Europe by the language of Berlin".[10] There was thus a concentric effort from all quarters to restrain Bismarck, and the vain Gorchakov was credited with placing a public slight upon the German Chancellor in his own capital by announcing that "now" (after his and the

Tsar's visit) "peace is assured".* Bismarck, putting a bold face upon it, expressed his gratitude for Derby's good offices, while utterly failing to understand why London should ever have credited him with warlike designs: to the Crown Prince he made a scapegoat of Moltke as being "destitute of political ideas"[11] and incapable of holding his peace, and he even had the effrontery to suggest that not only Blowitz, but *The Times* itself, had been bribed by Decazes, who was engaged in large speculations on the Bourse. To Russell Bismarck was "as civil, confidential and amiable as ever", but as the Ambassador warned Morier, "Behind our backs he raves like a maniac, and swears he will take his revenge."[12]

In the meantime the Emperor and Crown Prince sent to the Queen the most explicit assurances of their pacific aims, while at the same time regretting that *The Times* should have "so lamentably overstepped all bounds". But the net result of the Scare was to inspire London with extreme suspicion and reserve towards Berlin, and this applied equally to the Court, to Disraeli, Derby and Salisbury, to Gladstone and Granville, to Morier and Russell, though the latter maintained good relations with Bismarck and indeed was often the only member of the diplomatic corps in Berlin who could penetrate the Chancellor's reserve. The Queen wrote to her daughter, "No one wishes more than I do for England and Germany to go together: but Bismarck is so overbearing, violent and unprincipled, that *no one* can stand it, and *all* agreed that he was becoming like the First Napoleon, whom Europe had to join in putting down."[13] Derby told her private secretary, General Ponsonby, "it is really imposing on our supposed credulity, to tell us now that our ears have deceived us, and that nothing was said or meant against France".[14]

Another no less definite, but more ephemeral, result was to bring Britain and Russia closer together. On 6 May the Queen recorded in her journal that Disraeli favoured "an alliance with Russia, as we know the Emperor's pacific feeling":[15] and she herself would have liked to see the addition of Austria-Hungary, presumably in the hope of encircling her bugbear in Berlin. A year later she expressed to Derby the view that "the interests of Russia and England are not antagonistic".[16] Eastern complications were only too soon to arrest the process of Anglo-Russian understanding, but it was not until the close of the long crisis that Bismarck really lived down London's suspicion that he was bent on war.

* From *Grosse Politik*, i, No. 182, it would appear that the correct version took the quite unexceptionable form, "L'Empereur quitte Berlin parfaitement convaincu des dispositions conciliantes qui y règnent et qui assurent le maintien de la paix", and that Bismarck communicated the version quoted above to Blowitz, who then gave it publicity in *The Times*.

The Empress of India

As Disraeli's biographer is careful to remind us, it was of no small importance that at this juncture Britain should have had "a Prime Minister of Oriental extraction and imagination, whose outlook had been coloured at the most impressionable period of his life by his travels in the Levant, and who had played a large and decisive part in the affairs of India in the troubled 'fifties".[17] Needless to say it was from the Indian angle that he was interested in the Suez Canal, and no sooner in power, was alert to the possibility of purchase and entirely untrammelled by the mistaken Palmerstonian tradition. He was anxious in every way to promote India's internal consolidation, and he at once gave his eager backing to the idea that the Prince of Wales should visit the great dependency and establish personal relations between the Crown, the Princes and the peoples. Encouraged by the very marked success of this experiment, he proposed to the Queen that she should assume the title of Empress of India. Unfortunately he omitted to consult the Opposition leaders, and when the bill came before Parliament, there was much acrimonious and sometimes petty criticism, compounded in part of fear lest the older title of "Queen of England" should be submerged, and distrust towards a title which had of late suffered two resounding blows in France and in Mexico, and for the rest conveyed an unduly despotic flavour. The Liberals took a distinctly narrow view, and Disraeli accused Gladstone of "vituperative casuistry":[18] but both in society and in the press there was a widespread disapproval of the measure, and the Radical wing insisted upon opposing it at every stage, though in the end Disraeli's big battalions forced it through. The Queen took a very personal view of the dispute, writing to the Viceroy that the Opposition attitude was "factious" and "unpatriotic":[19] and there can be little doubt that the very different attitudes adopted in the question by the two great rivals, Disraeli and Gladstone, contributed to that estrangement from the latter, that growing infatuation for the former, which was to become so marked a feature of British politics during the next five eventful years.

It was not till 1 January 1877 that the Empress of India was solemnly proclaimed at a great Durbar in Delhi. But by that time the Eastern Question had assumed menacing proportions, a heavy cloud hung over Anglo-Russian relations, and it was felt in some quarters that the new title, and the pageantry which accompanied it, would impress the Oriental mind and counteract any temptation to look towards that other Imperial Power which seemed to be steadily advancing southwards from the steppes of Asia.

The Bosnian Rising

The widespread alarm occasioned by the famous War Scare had scarcely died down when the perennial Eastern Question was re-opened by a dangerous insurrection in Hercegovina, which soon spread to Bosnia and had its repercussions in all the neighbouring lands. Since 1856 Turkey had enjoyed a period of unusual calm, and indeed much more than those "ten years of peace under the joint protection of the Powers" which Palmerston in 1839 had declared necessary for her re-organisation. Unhappily the Charter of 1856, like its predecessor of 1839, had remained to a very large extent on paper, and though it would not be true to say that there had been no reform (for the army had been modernised, and the central machinery of government reconstituted), the cancer of corruption and inefficiency had only eaten deeper into the body politic. Abdul Aziz was a vicious and grossly incompetent tyrant; the statesmen of real calibre whom Turkey had possessed in the 'fifties, such men as Reshid, Fuad and Ali—had been replaced by mediocrities; Turkish finances had gone from bad to worse, and after a series of nine foreign loans between 1854 and 1875, bankruptcy was imminent.

For four centuries Bosnia-Hercegovina had formed a little world of its own, isolated from the main Balkan trade routes, ruled by a small group of moslemised feudal begs, deeply divided in religion between Moslem, Orthodox and Catholic, and in the nineteenth century racked by periodical revolts. During the 'sixties unrest had become chronic, owing to a combination of misrule and grinding taxation: and the despairing peasantry looked increasingly for help to their kinsmen in Serbia, which under Prince Michael was preparing itself for the leadership of the Southern Slavs; in Montenegro, which in 1858 and again in 1862 had held at bay large Turkish armies, and in Croatia and Dalmatia, where the movement for Jugoslav unity under the Habsburgs was steadily gaining ground. The declared aim of the insurgents was union with Serbia and Montenegro: and it was therefore only natural that these two vassal states of Turkey should be roused to intense sympathy and excitement. Benjamin Kállay, Austria-Hungary's able diplomatic agent in Belgrade, had for some years past been reporting to Vienna that the Serbs "see in Bosnia the natural complement of their territory", and "count one day upon possessing it".[20] A further factor of great importance was the latent rivalry between the two rival native dynasties—the Obrenović under Prince Milan of Serbia, the Petrović-Njegoš under Prince Nicholas of Montenegro—for leadership in the national movement: and ere long this was intensified when the heir to the third exiled dynasty, Peter Karagjorgjević, himself joined one of the insurgent bands in the mountains of Bosnia. Henceforth it became increasingly difficult for the unpopular Milan to hold back his people, without risking his own throne and perhaps his life.

At first the Powers showed but little interest in the rising. The first to react was Austria-Hungary, partly because of the numerous refugees who fled from Bosnia into her territory, partly because of the consequent agitation among the Croats: and there was a section of military opinion in Vienna which looked upon the occupation of Bosnia as a logical strategic consequence of Austria's possession of the Dalmatian coast, and as the surest means of securing the direction of the Jugoslav movement. In Russia public opinion, as on earlier occasions, was stirred by the sufferings of the Orthodox Slavs of Turkey, and the reactionary Slav societies of Moscow began to agitate in their favour. But there was a very definite line of division between Moscow, with its Orthodox mysticism and its contempt for "the rotten West", and official St Petersburg, which frowned upon the Serbs as revolutionaries, and had no desire to be dragged into war at a time when Russian finances were disordered and when the army was still being recast. The Russian Foreign Office of course belonged to the latter school, but in the diplomatic service there were individuals who far outstripped instructions, and among them were the consuls at Belgrade and Ragusa. Above all, General Ignatyev, since 1864 Russian Ambassador at the Porte, a man of great energy, resource and assurance, was credited with a "forward" policy and came to occupy an altogether special position as the natural champion of the oppressed Christians of Turkey. The diplomatic game at Constantinople centred more and more round the rivalry between Ignatyev and his British colleague Sir Henry Elliot, who headed the Turcophil school. Meanwhile the British Government remained indifferent to the point of cynicism, and in August Disraeli wrote to Lady Chesterfield of "this dreadful Herzegovinian affair", which "might have been settled in a week,...had there been common energy, or perhaps pocket-money even, among the Turks". Even in October Derby still spoke to the Russian Ambassador, Count Shuvalov, of the agitation in Serbia and Montenegro—"petit peuple à demi barbare"—as a mere manœuvre. He and his chief strongly opposed autonomy for Bosnia—apparently from the fear lest the insurgents' demand for land reform might create a precedent in Ireland.[21]

In August 1876 the consuls of the Powers were instructed to negotiate with the insurgent chiefs, but this resulted in a complete fiasco, firstly because the Turkish authorities in Bosnia, taking advantage of the occasion, made a treacherous attempt to waylay and massacre the chiefs, but above all because the Bosnians put forward demands which there was no chance of the

Porte conceding, and so far from reducing them in order to promote a
settlement, saw their interest in keeping Europe in a ferment, and eagerly
desired complications between the Powers. There is a curious analogy with
1914, when once more the real initiative lay, not with the statesmen of
Europe, but with an obscure group of Bosnian nationalists, operating this
time by terrorism rather than by insurrection.

The Suez Canal Coup

For the remainder of the year there was a pause, in which the rebels held
their own, while the attention of the Powers was diverted by the sudden and
unexpected default of Turkey, who announced the reduction by half of the
interest on all foreign loans contracted since the Crimean War, but had the
effrontery to make an arbitrary exception in favour of the Sultan's large
personal holding. The City was naturally furious, and there was a noticeable
cooling off of Turcophil feeling. It was at this moment that Disraeli learned,
from several quite different quarters, that the Khedive of Egypt, Ismail
Pasha, an even more dissolute and extravagant ruler than his suzerain Abdul
Aziz, was in no less dire financial straits, and was therefore in negotiation
with a French syndicate for the sale of his personal holding of 177,000 shares
in the Suez Canal. He had about a fortnight in which to meet the coupons
on the Egyptian public debt, or to follow the Sultan into bankruptcy. Mortgage or sale were his only alternatives, and the conditions laid down for the
former by the French seemed exorbitant. Already in the spring of 1874 he
had made discreet overtures to de Lesseps, the builder of the Canal, through
the medium of his Rothschild friends in London and Paris, and it was therefore known to the French that the British Government was interested.

While Derby took a distinctly narrow and unsympathetic line towards the
British bondholders in Turkey, Disraeli instantly realised the possibilities
of the Egyptian situation, and won over the Cabinet and Queen for his
ideas, arguing that "it is vital for Your Majesty's authority and power at
this critical moment, that the Canal should belong to England". Not a day
was to be lost, since it was "doubtful whether a financial catastrophe can
be avoided" in Egypt. "Scarcely breathing-time", he added, "but the
thing must be done."[22] An offer to purchase was accordingly telegraphed
to the British agent in Cairo: but the Khedive wavered between London and
Paris, and for a time reverted to the idea of a mortgage. Fortunately, however, the syndicate again held out for exorbitant terms, and did not receive
any active backing from Duke Decazes, to whom the British Government
made it clear that they would disapprove of the Khedive's interest falling
into the hands of a new French company, similar to that which de Lesseps

had originally founded. Derby quite reasonably pointed out that the Canal was our highway to India, and that no other country was so much interested in its management as Britain. As a result, the negotiations between the Khedive and Paris broke down, and on 25 November the contract was signed in Cairo at a price of £4,000,000 and the shares handed over to the British Consulate.

No sooner was the bargain concluded than the Prime Minister was confronted by a Chancellor of the Exchequer who denied all possibility of obtaining Parliament's consent within the necessary period, or of raising the money without that consent. In this quandary he turned to his friends the Rothschilds, who advanced the £4,000,000 almost at a moment's notice. "After a fortnight of the most unceasing labour and anxiety", Disraeli's *coup* was completely successful, and "the Fairy" was "in ecstasies" and "in the tenth heaven" at what Leopold II, who understood "big business" as few kings ever have, described as "the greatest event of modern politics".[23] Disraeli wrote to Lady Bradford, "we have had all the gamblers, capitalists, financiers of the world, organised and platooned in bands of plunderers, arrayed against us, and secret emissaries in every corner, and have baffled them all, and have never been suspected. The day before yesterday de Lesseps, whose company has the remaining shares, backed by the French Government, whose agent he was, made a great offer. Had it succeeded, the whole of the Suez Canal would have belonged to France, and they might have shut it up."[24] This was doubtless a somewhat highly coloured version, and critics were not lacking in Parliament who argued that the Rothschilds, so far from running any great risk, had made a very good bargain—the equivalent of 15 per cent on their money. But the grudging attitude of the Opposition only served to bring into higher relief the initiative and vision of Disraeli: and posterity is unanimous in endorsing his claim to have achieved a feat of high policy. His suggestion that, if Gladstone had been in power, the shares would have gone to France, was almost certainly justified.

The effect throughout Europe was profound; it was assumed, and with justice, that Britain was abandoning her passivity and embarking upon "a very spirited foreign policy". No one was more pleased, from their different angles, than the German Crown Princess and the German Chancellor, who regarded the *coup* as a first step towards British intervention in Egypt. For this Disraeli was definitely not prepared, and he resisted more than one such proposal, because in his last term of office, as throughout his career, he attached a capital value to good relations between France and Britain, and rightly suspected Bismarck of wishing to drive a wedge between them. None the less the mission of Stephen Cave to investigate Egyptian finances, though undertaken at the Khedive's request, created in many quarters the impression that Britain had definite designs in Egypt and was preparing at last to act upon the advice which Tsar Nicholas had given to Sir Hamilton Seymour, and treat Egypt as her share in the Turkish spoils.

THE ANDRÁSSY NOTE AND THE BERLIN MEMORANDUM

By the end of December Count Andrássy, now at the very height of his prestige as Austro-Hungarian Foreign Minister, but gravely underestimated by Disraeli,[25] feeling that a situation so near his southern borders could not safely be allowed to drift, and also that a passive attitude on his part would redound to the advantage of Russia, took the initiative, with Bismarck's full approval, in pressing for collective action at the Porte. The Andrássy Note of 30 December 1876 outlined a minimum of reforms which might be expected to pacify the two disturbed provinces—equality of religions, abolition of tax-farming, restriction of taxes to the use of the province in which they were raised, land reform and an European commission of revision. The Continental Powers at once endorsed these proposals, but Britain held back for some weeks, until the Porte itself, under pressure from Vienna, requested London to adhere. Even then Disraeli remained hostile and described Austria's action as "an act of imbecility or treachery":[26] some of the details, "so far as they are intelligible, would appear to be erroneous in principle and pernicious in practice". Here again, in denouncing the right of the peasantry to the soil, he was evidently thinking of Ireland and afraid of committing himself to "principles which may soon be matter of controversy in our own country". The lukewarm attitude of the British Government towards the Andrássy Note encouraged the Porte in its obstructive attitude and contributed very largely towards its failure, while the insurgents in their mountains had good reason to hope for fresh international complications. For the first four months of 1876, then, the deadlock was complete: but while the Turks were quite unable to suppress the rising, popular excitement steadily grew in Serbia and throughout the Southern Slav lands.

In the hope of finding an escape from this deadlock, Tsar Alexander, who was due for his annual cure at Ems, suggested that the Foreign Ministers of the three Eastern Powers—Bismarck, Andrássy and Gorchakov—should meet him in Berlin and concert a joint policy. Before, however, the meeting could take place, events were hastened by a sinister incident at Salonica, the French and German consuls being murdered by a disorderly Moslem mob. This was followed by riots in the capital and the overthrow of the Grand Vizier. On 12 May, then, the two Emperors and the three statesmen met according to programme, and feeling that they could no longer fall in with

Britain's policy of masterly inactivity, drew up the famous Berlin Memorandum, which proposed an armistice of two months, both sides retaining their arms pending negotiations, but added the warning that if no agreement could be reached during that period, it would be necessary for the Powers to take "efficacious measures in the interests of peace".

The proposal was at once accepted by France and Italy, but met with a hostile reception in London. Disraeli told the Russian Ambassador very flatly at a levee, that Britain was being treated "as if we were Montenegro or Bosnia", and Derby, in a later conversation with Shuvalov, submitted the memorandum to more urbane but detailed criticism, without indicating any constructive alternative. They both disregarded the advice of their Ambassador in Berlin, Lord Odo Russell, and also the wise warning of the Queen that Britain's refusal would encourage the Turks and "thus precipitate, rather than prevent, the catastrophe".[27] It is important to note that Lord Granville, as leader of the Opposition, endorsed the Government's attitude, and that no note of criticism was heard from that side till the Commons debate of 31 July.

Britain's abstention killed the project at its birth, and the Emperor William I was fully justified in expressing to Queen Victoria his regret at the absence of any "counter-proposal".[28] Disraeli indeed was worse than merely negative, for on 24 May he ordered the British Fleet to Besika Bay— a step which the Porte greeted "as a harbinger of a British Alliance such as twenty years ago led to the Crimean War".[29] When the Queen objected, the unrepentant Premier rejoined that the fleet had "not been ordered to the Mediterranean to protect Christians or Turks (the excuse before public opinion), but to uphold Your Majesty's Empire. Had Your Majesty sanctioned the Berlin Memorandum, Constantinople would at this moment have been garrisoned by Russia, and the Turkish fleet placed under Russian protection."[30]

Within a week the situation was further complicated by a revolution in Turkey. Abdul Aziz was overthrown and found dead under mysterious and still unexplained circumstances (30 May), and his brother Murad V was soon found to be weakminded and incapable of governing. Government passed into the hands of the Liberal statesman Midhat Pasha, but before he could consolidate the situation his two colleagues, the Ministers of War and Foreign Affairs, were murdered at the Council table by an officer of the Imperial Guard. Turkey seemed on the very point of dissolution.

This news, coupled with the apparent failure of Europe to impose a settlement, the growing restiveness of home opinion, the ferment among the Slavophils of Russia and the first reports of atrocities in neighbouring Bulgaria, combined to precipitate events in Serbia and Montenegro, who declared war upon Turkey on the last day of June, in defiance of all the exhortations of Russia and Austria. Their action proved to be a gambler's throw, prompted by anger and impatience at the prolonged tragedy among their Bosnian kinsmen. Disraeli, in his anger at what he called Serbia's "infamous invasion", went so far as to argue that one of the "legitimate consequences" of Turkish victory would be "the restoration of Belgrade" to the Turks—in other words, the destruction of Serbian autonomy! Meanwhile he soothed the Queen's nervousness by assuring her that his "policy of determination" was already "restoring Your Majesty's influence in the general councils, which for some years had not been so marked as could be desired....Mr Disraeli looks upon the Tripartite understanding between the three Imperial Powers as virtually extinct." "It was an unnatural alliance", he told Lord John Manners, "and never would have occurred, had England maintained of late years her just position in public affairs."[31] Apart, however, from this entirely mistaken assumption, there was nothing very definite in Disraeli's policy: and he presumably is not as yet to be regarded as Russophobe, for on 9 June he suddenly made a private overture to Shuvalov, denying any suspicion of Russia or of her policy either in Asia or in Turkey, treating Turkey's disappearance from the map of Europe as "sooner or later inevitable", cynically assuming that "blood letting" was necessary in the Balkans, since "the insurgents are not fighting for reforms, and nothing will satisfy them, since they aim at independence",[32] but urging direct conversations between London and St Petersburg, without any intermediaries. Shuvalov was suspicious, but puzzled, and sought to explain British policy as "hesitating, tortuous, but not warlike. England feels isolated and dares not admit her solidarity with Turkey....The British Government wishes an agreement with someone, and cannot find anyone."[33] Nothing came of the overture, which is only interesting as a proof of Disraeli's opportunist tendency to wait upon events.

Meanwhile the three Imperial Powers decided to make their own plans. On 8 July, on their way home from Ems, Alexander II and Gorchakov met Francis Joseph and Andrássy at Reichstadt, in Bohemia, and concluded a secret convention based upon the two alternatives of a Serbian defeat, in which case the Powers were to force the Porte to accept the *status quo*, or a Turkish defeat, in which case both Serbia and Montenegro were to extend their territory, most of Bosnia-Hercegovina was to fall to Austria, and Russia was to re-annex southern Bessarabia and round off her Asiatic frontier, while Bulgaria, Roumelia and Albania might become autonomous, Constantinople a free city, and Thessaly and Crete part of the Greek Kingdom. It was only after some months that Andrássy revealed these details even to his German ally: in London he intimated that "there were no written agreements whatsoever ", and only " a verbal exchange of opinion " : and he did not even initiate his own Ambassador, Count Beust—a fact which served to mislead the British Government still further at a later stage of the crisis.

Bulgarian Atrocities

For a brief moment in June it seemed as though Britain's abstention had been justified by events, and as though the most essential thing was to secure a respite for the Turkish reformers after their first accession to power. But the situation was once again radically transformed by the news of horrible massacres in Bulgaria, perpetrated early in May by Turkish Bashi-bazouks, but also in certain cases by Turkish regulars, with the direct connivance of the authorities. The news slowly trickled through to London in mid-June, and first acquired concrete form in the *Spectator* and in the *Daily News*, whose correspondent in Turkey, Edwin Pears, and the Irish-American journalist MacGahan, owed most of their information to the American missionaries of Robert College, on the Bosphorus. Disraeli, when questioned in the House of Commons, denied the accuracy of the stories and assumed an impatient and flippant tone towards what he described as " coffee-house babble ". He appears to have been kept inadequately informed by the Foreign Office and thus committed himself to an attitude from which it was difficult to recede : and he privately admitted to Derby that the debate had been " very damaging for the Government ", and that if he had seen a certain despatch of Consul Reade, he " would never have made those answers ". In the end Walter Baring was sent from the Constantinople Embassy to investigate on the spot, and his conclusions, as embodied in an official report, did not materially differ from those of the American Consul-General Eugene Schuyler, or of the more ardent MacGahan who accompanied him. That at least 12,000 unarmed Bulgarians of both sexes were " slaughtered like sheep " under circumstances of peculiar horror, such as the burning of the crowded church of Batak, and that the Turkish officers and soldiers responsible for this were not punished, but promoted and even decorated, was proved beyond all possible doubt.

British opinion was thoroughly roused by the revelations, and during August meetings of protest were held throughout the country, but especially in the North of England, where W. T. Stead and his paper the *Northern Echo* of Darlington was the main focus of agitation. It was not till early September that Gladstone—then living in retirement at Hawarden and indeed confined to his bed by acute lumbago—first intervened in the great controversy : but his pamphlet *Bulgarian Horrors*, of which over 200,000 copies were sold, served as a clarion call against the Turks. There is a certain irony in the fact that it was dedicated to Lord Stratford de Redcliffe, now in his extreme old age a cordial supporter of Gladstone, and that the one winged phrase which it contains—"bag and baggage"—had first been coined as long ago as 1821 in a letter of that same Stratford to his cousin George Canning.

The lists were soon to be set in the Eastern Question between the two protagonists. At Blackheath Gladstone came forward "as one of the authors of the Crimean War", bound in honour to secure the fulfilment of the obligations contracted at the peace of 1856 in favour of Turkey's subject races. Disraeli, on his side, in a farewell speech to his constituents at Aylesbury (he now went to the House of Lords as Earl of Beaconsfield), laid all the blame upon Serbia and identified her with "the secret societies of Europe...societies which have regular agents everywhere, which countenance assassination and which, if necessary, could produce a massacre". He thus revealed his inability to distinguish between such different forces as Russian Nihilism, Russian Slavophils, Serb nationalists and Bulgarian or Bosnian insurgents.

RUSSIA IMPOSES AN ARMISTICE

From the very first the fortunes of war had gone against Serbia, whose army was ill-led and badly equipped: the Russian volunteers who flocked to her assistance under General Cherniayev did not help matters, and their ill-judged offer of a royal crown to Prince Milan had to be declined by him under pressure from Austria and the Tsar, who already looked askance upon the Serbs as revolutionaries, wrongly assumed them to be bad soldiers also, and made slighting references to them in a public speech at Moscow. The victorious Turks pressed on into the heart of Serbia, and after the battle of Aleksinac (1876) were only deterred from occupying Belgrade by a Russian ultimatum insisting upon their acceptance of an armistice before the end of the month. In private Beaconsfield spoke of the Russian proposals as "a real Bulgarian atrocity", and put forward the untenable view that "Constantinople is the key of India, and not Egypt and the Suez Canal".[34] But by now British opinion was hopelessly divided, the Queen nervous, Liberal agitation reviving, Derby pacific, and two such important members of the Cabinet as Salisbury and Carnarvon convinced that Turkey's "friendship is a reproach to us", and wishing that "the Turks were out of Europe". That the Tsar on his side was by no means bellicose, as British Turcophils assumed, is shown by the proposals which he transmitted to Francis Joseph, and at the same time communicated to London, as a proof of his goodwill. Assuming that only joint intervention could avert a crisis, he favoured a simultaneous occupation of Bosnia by Austria-Hungary and of Bulgaria by Russia, while the fleets of all the Powers entered the Straits and brought the Porte to reason. Unfortunately this scheme, which should have reassured, and indeed was intended to reassure London, was rejected by Vienna and fell to the ground.

On 2 November a happy compromise was reached in Derby's proposal for a European Conference: and Salisbury's selection as the principal British delegate won the almost unanimous approval of the country, as at once a conservative and a churchman capable of sympathising with the Christians of the Near East. It is significant that Salisbury, in sending his consent to the Prime Minister, wrote: "But it is essential that your policy should be settled first", and that on the very same day Disraeli was urging on Derby "the importance, if we wish to secure a long peace, of coming to some understanding *with some European Power*"—if not Germany, then Austria and perhaps France.[35] It is a fair inference from these two remarks that the Prime Minister was at this stage entirely opportunist, without any definite line of policy. In his Guildhall speech of 9 November he criticised both the Andrássy Note and the Berlin Memorandum, and reaffirmed existing treaties, by which he meant the Treaty of Paris and the triple treaty of guarantee of April 1856, which both France and Austria had almost from the first day treated as inoperative, but to which British statesmen continued to appeal throughout the long crisis. In his peroration he stressed peace as "especially an English policy", but warned Europe that despite this there was "no country so well prepared for war as our own. If she enters into conflict in a righteous cause...her resources are, I feel, inexhaustible. She is not a country that, when she enters into a campaign, has to ask herself whether she can support a second or third campaign." Only a day later, but before the words of this speech could reach Moscow, the Tsar publicly announced his earnest desire for the success of the Conference, but also his determination to act independently, if the necessary guarantees could not be obtained from the Porte.

SALISBURY AT CONSTANTINOPLE

The prospects of success were vitiated by two blunders. Constantinople was chosen as the place of meeting, and the encouragement which this gave to the Turks was increased by the strongly Turcophil attitude of the British Ambassador: indeed Salisbury and Elliot neutralised each other, and various causes—the presence of the British fleet at Besika and of British engineer officers to inspect the defences of the Turkish capital, and the activities of Butler-Johnston, who was regarded as a private emissary of Disraeli—led the new Sultan and his pseudo-Liberal advisers to conclude that it was Elliot, and not Salisbury, who represented the true policy of the London Cabinet. Thus Salisbury's mission was foredoomed to failure, even though he had important meetings with Bismarck and Andrássy on his way eastwards, though he speedily reached a working arrangement with General Ignatyev, and though he found that not one of his fellow-ambassadors agreed with Elliot's views. On the very day on which the Conference opened, Midhat proclaimed a most elaborate paper constitution for the whole Empire, intended not so much to be the herald of real reform, as a broad hint to the Powers that their proposed assistance was unnecessary. Elliot had complete confidence in Midhat, but Salisbury judged more accurately in regarding him as even falser than the plausible Ignatyev, who, we now know, had explicit instructions from the Tsar and Gorchakov to work for peace "without any *arrière pensée* whatever".* The Conference ended, after nine formal sessions, in complete failure (20 January 1877), the Porte having resolutely declined to give the required guarantees, and having obtained endorsement of this refusal by a subservient Council of Notables nominated for the purpose by the Sultan. Salisbury had gone the length of urging the Cabinet to recall Elliot and thus publicly disavow his Turcophil attitude: but Beaconsfield and Derby refused, fearing that such a step would be put down to Russian influence, and that the Government would "be turned out the first day of the session by our own men". Beaconsfield at this moment regarded Salisbury as "much duped by Ignatyev", and complained to Derby: "He seems most prejudiced, and not to be aware that his principal object in being sent to Constantinople is to keep the Russians out of Turkey, not to create an ideal existence for the Turkish Christians."[36]

Salisbury returned home convinced that Turkey was doomed and that Russo-British co-operation was at once a practicable, and the safest, solution. He urged the Cabinet to abandon the old Palmerstonian policy and to substitute "a bold initiative in partition":[37] but he failed to carry his colleagues with him and appears to have regarded its abandonment as a lesser evil than the risk of splitting the Conservative party at so critical a juncture. It must not, however, be concluded that Beaconsfield had even now a clear-cut policy: indeed he assured Salisbury that he felt "stronger than ever, that all that is occurring portends, and that not remotely, parti-

---

* He continues: "We have nothing to conceal. His Majesty prefers above all a pacific solution and would rejoice exceedingly if military demonstration is not imposed upon us by our dignity"—*R.B.D.* IV, No. 127. 17 November, Gorchakov to Ignatyev, cit. *D.G.* pp. 124, 126. "The military campaign...would be risky both politically and materially, and would above all bear heavily on our financial position"—*ibid.* No. 125. In a later despatch Gorchakov speaks of "the main aim of maintaining agreement between the Christian Powers"—*ibid.* No. 143, 11 December.

tion", and to Derby also he used the fateful word "partition".[38] "English policy", Salisbury told his friend Lytton the Indian Viceroy, "is to float lazily downstream, occasionally putting out a diplomatic boathook to avoid collisions": "the system of never making a plan beyond the next move is bearing its natural fruits".[39]

The Secret Austro-Russian Agreement

With the failure of the Conference a deadlock had been reached in the European situation, and war became wellnigh inevitable. This had long since been reluctantly recognised by the Tsar and his immediate advisers, who also saw clearly that the key to action on Russia's part lay in a previous agreement with Austria-Hungary. Experience during the Crimean War had shown that the latter Power could threaten Russian land communications and render it dangerous for her to engage in operations in Roumania or on the Danube: and these considerations were now more vital than ever, since the Crimean War had destroyed Russian naval power in the Black Sea and exposed its waters to attack by a British fleet allied with Turkey. Serbia's defeat had rendered the Convention of Reichstadt virtually inoperative; Vienna had in September rejected the Tsar's overtures for parallel occupation of Bosnia and Bulgaria: and the further negotiations opened through Novikov, the Russian Ambassador in Vienna, had revealed certain divergences of interpretation between the two Courts. At last, on 15 January 1877, a secret Austro-Russian Convention was concluded at Budapest, expressly framed to avert a "collision of interests" in the event of a Russo-Turkish rupture. By it Austria-Hungary, in return for benevolent neutrality and for a promise to oppose all collective mediation and not to act upon Article VIII of the Treaty of Paris or the triple guarantee treaty of April 1856, obtained the right to occupy Bosnia-Hercegovina at the moment convenient to her. An additional convention of 18 March reaffirmed the arrangement of Reichstadt as the basis of future Austro-Russian joint policy.

The Ignatyev Mission and the March Protocol

With the conclusion of this double instrument Russia was ready for all eventualities, though in any case anxious to defer hostilities till the Balkan snows had melted. Late in February, while she was still playing for time, Beaconsfield again revealed his essential opportunism in the Eastern Question by a second private overture to Shuvalov. Once more he spoke of Turkey's days as numbered, claimed that in sending Salisbury to the Conference he had selected him "as the man most favourable to the entente with Russia",[40] and spoke of his desire to build not merely a golden bridge, but "a bridge of diamonds and rubies", between Britain and Russia. It seems to have been this incident which encouraged the Tsar and Gorchakov to send Ignatyev on a mission to London. The choice was not a wise one, as the General had long been the chief bugbear of the London Russophobe press: and Salisbury, in no little alarm, urged postponement, though he eventually entertained Ignatyev at Hatfield. In the end a Protocol was signed in London, on 31 March, by Derby and the five Ambassadors, which after reaffirming their "common interest in the amelioration of the lot of the Christians of Turkey", advised the Porte to put its armies on a peace footing and introduce prompt reforms, failing which they would discuss common action in the interest of the Christians. Shuvalov, to prove Russia's concilia-tory attitude, suggested that a Turkish envoy should be sent to St Peters-burg, to discuss parallel demobilisation. That Derby, not Beaconsfield, framed the policy of the Protocol, is seen from the Prime Minister's letter to Salisbury next day: "So the Protocol is signed, and everybody writes to me about our triumph and the humiliation of Russia. I can't yet quite make head or tail of it."[41]

THE RUSSO-TURKISH WAR AND "BRITISH INTERESTS"

The Turks proved their intransigeance by rejecting the Protocol (7 April), and this led inevitably to a Russian declaration of war (24 April). Shuvalov warned his Government that England would not be slow to join in if she could find an ally, and that it would be wise for them to notify London, without a moment's delay, the substance of what they intended to impose upon Turkey, as only this could keep Britain neutral, and prevent some *coup de tête* of Beaconsfield, perhaps even the seizure of the Dardanelles.[42] In actual fact Beaconsfield, on 21 April, proposed to the Cabinet the occupa-tion of the Dardanelles, "as material guarantee against Russia seizing Constantinople"; but though backed by the Queen, who even talked of abdicating rather than "kiss Russia's feet", he could not carry his design in face of the opposition of "the three Lords", as they came to be called— Derby, Salisbury and Carnarvon. Derby on his side drew up the Note of 6 May to Russia, which summed up very succinctly Britain's interests in the Near East. There must be no interference with the Suez Canal and the trade route to India: Constantinople must not be allowed to pass into other hands, and "the existing arrangements" as to the Straits should be upheld: and changes on the Persian Gulf were also deprecated. This Note cleared the situation and gave a respite to Shuvalov, which he wisely used in order to visit St Petersburg and explain to the Tsar the true inwardness of the British situation. He returned to London with the assurance that Russia had "neither the interest, the desire, nor the means" to touch Egypt and Suez, and had no idea of "troubling England in her Indian possessions nor in her communications", unless forced to do so as a measure of war. The Tsar reiterated his pledge against the annexation of Constantinople, but persisted in the very reasonable view that a pledge against even temporary occupation would simply encourage the Turks to resist longer. He also indicated the main terms on which he would conclude peace if the Porte consented to treat before Russian troops had crossed the Balkans—a vassal Bulgarian state, administrative guarantees for the Bulgarians south of the Balkans and for the other European provinces, Bosnian autonomy, territorial concessions for Serbia and Montenegro, and for Russia herself Bessarabia and Batum, Roumania receiving compensation in the Dobrogea. The full text of Gorchakov's confidential instructions to Shuvalov is a proof of Russian sincerity such as could not have failed to convince contemporaries, if it had been available to them.[43] Shuvalov was able to convince the cautious Derby of the sincerity of his pacific aims, and for the next nine months an intimate working alliance between the Ambassador and the Foreign Secretary, in which Lady Derby also plays an active part, is one of the decisive factors in saving the situation. The Note of 6 May, as a minimum definition of much-quoted "British interests", rallied moderate opinion and came to be described as "the charter of England's policy": it shows that Derby, negative and sluggish though he may have been, was at times capable of active and constructive statesmanship.

GLADSTONE AND THE OPPOSITION

Meanwhile the Opposition campaign against Disraeli had reached its height. Rarely did any cause unite so many men of real distinction in every rank of life as that of Bulgarian freedom: and the "National Convention", which met at St James's Hall in December 1876 to hear one of Gladstone's most formidable philippics,* had a strongly deterrent effect upon the Government, though the Queen regretted that the Attorney-General could not "be set at these men"! It was the Eastern Question more than anything else, and his innate distrust of Disraeli's attitude towards it, that brought Gladstone back into active politics, with the almost inevitable result that he overshadowed his two successors in the party leadership, Lords Granville

---

* Its two chairmen were the Duke of Westminster and Lord Shaftesbury, and it had the support of Bryce, Freeman, Trollope, Trevelyan, Carlyle, William Morris, J. R. Green, Lecky, Ruskin, Burne-Jones, Darwin, Herbert Spencer, Browning and many others.

and Hartington—the more so as the latter at least regarded the whole question as an embarrassment. If the Cabinet was divided on the issue, so was the Opposition, Harcourt sharing Gladstone's views but condemning his tactics, Dilke torn between detestation of Turkey and acute distrust of Russia, Chamberlain looking upon Gladstone as "the best card" of the Radical wing, while Bright opposed the return of the old chief. A series of discussions in Parliament culminated in the debate of 7–12 May, which centred round five resolutions drafted by Gladstone, in favour of "local liberty and self-government" and against any material or moral support to Turkey, on lines similar to those followed by George Canning in an earlier stage of the Eastern Question. Gladstone's strategy was confused and faulty, and the resolutions were lost by 223 to 354, despite a speech which Arthur Balfour a generation later was to describe as "unequalled as a feat of parliamentary courage, skill, endurance and eloquence", and which culminated in the cry that if Russia succeeded in her efforts of liberation, "as an Englishman I shall hide my head, but as a man I shall rejoice".

The British Overture to Austria-Hungary

This check to the Turcophobe agitation served as an encouragement to Beaconsfield and the extreme Tories: and there can be little doubt that if the Russian advance south of the Danube had not been held up throughout the summer by the stubborn genius of Osman Pasha, Britain would have entered the war on the Turkish side. The Queen in particular fulminated against Russia, repeatedly threatened abdication,[44] complained to the Prime Minister of Derby's inertia, and snubbed the latter severely when he pointed out that feeling was much divided and that war would be thoroughly unpopular.[45] "Such a Foreign Minister", she told his chief, "the Queen never remembers", and she suggested that he should be replaced by Lord Lyons. It was against Derby's better judgment, but with the Queen's strong approval, that Beaconsfield decided upon overtures for an alliance with Austria-Hungary and gave Count Andrássy the highly questionable assurance that he controlled the British Cabinet and could win it for a joint policy of action. But Andrássy was not only suspicious of England and very well aware that Austria-Hungary and not Britain would have to bear the brunt of the war: he was also bound to Russia by the secret Convention and bent on concealing its existence from Beust, but thereby misleading London all the more effectually. He distrusted his Russian ally just enough to make it desirable for him to maintain cordial relations with London, but he had no motive, or even excuse, for allying with Britain, unless or until it became obvious that Russia was playing him false. In a word, the secret Convention was a fundamental factor in the general situation, and London's ignorance of its existence drew Beaconsfield into a path that led nowhere.

THE WELLESLEY MISSION AND CABINET DISSENSIONS

At this period Beaconsfield was full of extravagant aims, encouraged by his private correspondence with Henry Layard, whom he had sent to Constantinople in April as Elliot's successor, and who was now more Turcophil than any Ambassador before or after him, showing a pathetic belief in the virtues of Abdul Hamid. At the end of June the Queen was urging Beaconsfield to "be bold" and bid the Government "rally round their sovereign and country", and he replied that all their difficulties "would be removed if we declared war against Russia: but there are not three men in the Cabinet who are prepared to advise that step".[46] On 21 July he took advantage of Russia's renewed refusal to pledge herself against a temporary occupation of Constantinople, and won the Cabinet's consent in principle to a declaration of war if such an event should occur. Encouraged by this, he wrote next day to the Queen that in the event of war, "Russia must be attacked from Asia, troops should be sent to the Persian Gulf, and the Empress of India should order her armies to clear Central Asia of the Muscovites, and drive them into the Caspian".[47] On more than one occasion during the summer he was considering the seizure of Batum by a British army and a march upon Tiflis:[48] and he discussed with Layard the idea of seizing Gallipoli "as a material guarantee". The extent to which he was drifting apart from his old friend Derby is shown by the mission with which he and the Queen, behind the Foreign Secretary's back and in a clearly unconstitutional manner, entrusted Colonel Wellesley, the British Military Attaché at Russian headquarters. Wellesley was to assure the Tsar that in the event of a second campaign England would not be able to maintain neutrality and "would take her part as a belligerent", and he added in the Queen's name a strong denial of "dissensions in the Cabinet which would prevent active intervention", and a crude attack on Bismarck as being responsible for driving Russia into war. The Tsar, who was being closely informed by Shuvalov as to the acute quarrels inside the British Government, knew the second statement to be false, and knew the inner mind of William I and Bismarck too well to believe the third: and the main effect of the incident was to bring home to him the urgency of finishing the war at all costs, without going into winter quarters. London had unwittingly forewarned the enemy.

During the summer, then, repeated efforts were made to reduce Plevna, and it was found necessary to apply for the help of Prince Charles of Roumania, whose young army had its baptism of fire on Bulgarian soil and contributed materially to the final victory. The Tsar showed his marked bias against Serbia by a categorical warning to Prince Milan that he did not wish her renewed intervention. The Russians were again repulsed in September, but by the end of October Turkish resistance began to weaken: on 11 November the fall of Kars left the Russians triumphant on the Asiatic front, and at last on 10 December Osman Pasha was forced to capitulate at Plevna, and the last serious obstacle to an advance across the Balkans had been removed.

On 5 October Beaconsfield, still bent on preventing a second campaign, laid before the Cabinet a concrete proposal of intervention[49] but met with resistance from the three Lords and from Sir Stafford Northcote, now Leader in the Commons. But though very ill and even contemplating retirement, he still discussed with Layard a plan for "an outline of terms" to be drafted by Turkey, but proposed by England to Russia: if then she refused, "it would be very difficult for us to adhere to our present neutrality".[50] There was, however, nothing for it but to adopt a waiting attitude, for, as he confided to the Queen on 3 November, "in a Cabinet of twelve members there are seven parties or policies".[51] The seventh, that of himself and the Queen, was "that in the first place the Cabinet shall decide upon something", and shall inform Russia that "British neutrality cannot be depended upon for another campaign", except in return for a secret promise not to occupy Constantinople or the Dardanelles. At the Guildhall banquet, in the marked absence of the Ambassadors of the five Great Powers, he paid high compliments to Turkey, her army and even her constitution, spoke of "a conditional neutrality" and sneered at "men who are the friends of every country but their own". His inner mind was revealed to Lady Bradford a few days earlier, when he wrote, "Plevna is our only chance".[52]

PLEVNA AND ITS REACTIONS

On 4 December Beaconsfield invited the Cabinet to make "the occupation, or rather the *menaced* occupation, of Constantinople a *casus belli*",[53] but Derby definitely demurred, and would not go beyond a Note to Russia, expressing the hope that in the interests of good relations neither Constantinople nor the Dardanelles would be occupied. During December the Cabinet was more acutely divided than ever, and the alarmed Northcote told Salisbury, "We cannot go on without a policy, with nothing but a *non possumus*, and a break-up...may lead to chaos and war."[54] On the 17th a compromise was at last reached, by which Parliament was to be summoned for 17 January and to be asked for "a large increase of force", while the principle of mediation was accepted, even by Derby. Meanwhile the Turkish Ambassador appealed direct to the Prime Minister for a loan to finance a second campaign, and in return the possibility of "some territorial concession" was hinted at. In Beaconsfield's correspondence with Layard at this period, Batum, Crete and the Persian Gulf are passed in review. "The Sultan", Layard reported, "was greatly delighted with Lord Beaconsfield's language (to Musurus) and at once counted upon armed support from England at no very distant period." [55] Beaconsfield's closing message for the year was that he "adopts Your Majesty's motto, BE FIRM". [56]

There can be no doubt that it was these frankly bellicose sentiments on the part of the Prime Minister which completed the alienation of his oldest political friend, Lord Derby. Derby's main aim in retaining office was to ensure "that nothing shall be done without the Cabinet being consulted" and to "keep military preparations within bounds": while Lady Derby expressed to Lord Carnarvon her belief that her husband "holds the key of the position and can save the country from war by remaining". [57] This explains, if it does not justify, their close co-operation with the Russian Ambassador, of whose earnest desire to avert war there can be no possible doubt. Nothing shows better the gravity of the situation than the fact that Shuvalov, who, relying on this valuable connection for much of his innermost information, had hitherto thought it wiser to hold aloof from the Opposition leaders, now decided to establish daily relations with them. A chance meeting with Harcourt in the street was followed by conversations which the latter reported in great detail to Granville, and so of course to Gladstone, who on his side had steadily avoided all intercourse with the Russian Embassy, though Malcolm MacColl appears to have carried occasional verbal messages to and fro. [58] Meanwhile, between the fall of Plevna and the assembly of Parliament the Opposition revived, on a large scale, its agitation in the country, which now found itself deeply and passionately divided on the Eastern Question, the home counties, London and especially "Clubland" being Turcophil and responding to the famous music-hall cry, "we don't want to fight, but by Jingo if we do", while the north and Scotland were overwhelmingly Turcophobe and turned out in tens of thousands to do honour to Gladstone at a time when London roughs amused themselves on Sunday afternoons by breaking the windows of his Harley Street house.

DERBY RESIGNS AND IS REINSTATED

On the eve of Parliament meeting fresh dissensions rent the Government: Beaconsfield reported to the Queen that he was "nearly alone in the Cabinet";[59] and the Queen replied that she was "utterly ashamed of the Cabinet" and could not "remain the sovereign of a country that is letting itself down to kiss the feet of the great barbarians". "It is something to serve such a sovereign", was the Prime Minister's rejoinder.[60] One source of friction was a speech of Lord Carnarvon, in which he affirmed that "there is nobody insane enough to desire a repetition" of the Crimean War: this brought upon him a severe rebuke from the Queen and a reference to him by Beaconsfield as "his disloyal colleague".[61] "The Cabinet", such was Shuvalov's comment on 14 January 1878, "is in extremities (aux abois) and caught in the net of its own policy." The very next day, while Derby was ill in bed, Beaconsfield obtained the Cabinet's authority to order the fleet to the Dardanelles and to make fresh overtures to Vienna, but as Derby and Carnarvon protested, the order was again suspended.

Parliament met on 17 January, while the Russians were still steadily advancing southwards. On the 9th the Shipka Pass had fallen, and ten days later direct negotiations with the Turks were opened at Kazanlik by the Grand Duke Nicholas. On the 29th even Adrianople fell, and two days later in that city an armistice was signed. The Russian army occupied Rodosto and San Stefano on the Sea of Marmora, and the heights above the Bosphorus, but did not enter the capital or seize the lines of Gallipoli.

Amid the excitements and uncertainties of this fluid period Beaconsfield began to prepare the Queen for "the disruption of the Cabinet and inevitable war with Russia", to which she responded by an embarrassing offer of the Garter. On 23 January he won a majority of the Cabinet for a Vote of Credit and the prompt despatch of the fleet through the Dardanelles. Derby and Carnarvon at once resigned, to the "immense satisfaction and relief" of the Queen.[62] Shuvalov feared an immediate rupture. But before Admiral Hornby had time to execute his orders, an urgent appeal was sent by the Sultan, insisting that to send the fleet might be regarded by Russia as a threat and would give her an excuse for seizing Constantinople, and that if England was bent on action, she must let the world know that she was acting against the express wishes of the Porte. This was obviously impossible in the teeth of an excited public opinion: and the Admiral was instructed not to enter the Straits after all, but to wait at Besika Bay.

Meanwhile panic had spread among the Conservative ranks, and the Prime Minister warned the Queen that the retirement of Derby, whose influence was so strong in Lancashire and the North, was having a "disintegrating" effect upon the party. While, then, Carnarvon was allowed to go, Northcote was given the task of winning Derby back to the fold: and to the Queen's lively regret he resumed the Foreign Office, having won from his colleagues a reaffirmation of the conditions of neutrality laid down by him in the Note of 6 May 1877. But the estrangement between him and his chief was henceforth irremediable: and during February and March the real control of foreign affairs was in the hands of a secret unofficial committee of three—Beaconsfield, Salisbury and the Lord Chancellor, Lord Cairns—often acting behind the back of the Foreign Secretary and sometimes even of his office. In Parliament, meanwhile, tension reached its height between the two parties: and in a fighting speech at Oxford on 30 January, Gladstone denounced the sending of the fleet as "an act of war, a breach of European law", accused the Government of rousing "false hopes" in Turkey, and went so far as to declare that for eighteen months past his purpose had been, "day and night, week by week, month by month, to counterwork what I believe to be the purpose of Lord Beaconsfield". "Dizzy's" comment was, "The mask has fallen, instead of a pious Christian we find a vindictive fiend".

Gladstone had information which led him to suspect Beaconsfield of a scheme for the purchase of Egypt, thereby enabling the exhausted Turks to prolong their resistance: but we now know that though both Bismarck and Crown Princess Frederick were advocating a British protectorate in Egypt—the former with the double aim of embroiling France and Britain and finding a bone to occupy the British mastiff while Russia reduced Turkey to complete submission—Beaconsfield was far too wedded to good relations with Paris to discuss the idea seriously.[63]

THE ARMISTICE AND SAN STEFANO

The news that the Russians had reached Rodosto and the Tchataldja lines caused a virtual panic in London, and fresh orders were sent to the fleet. Hartington, leading the Opposition, did not dare to vote against it, for the Liberal party was in real danger of breaking up, and the Government had a three to one majority on a division. The Queen wrote three letters to the Prime Minister on a single day, denouncing Russia's "monstrous treachery" and demanding "strong measures". The very contingency had now arisen, so she argued, which in the previous July and November he had treated as justifying war with Russia. In reply he had to explain that alliance with Turkey was impossible, but that she had "the clear constitutional right to dismiss the Government"—a very questionable doctrine, which was obvious bluff on his part.

This time orders to the fleet to enter the Straits were countered by the Grand Duke Nicholas's warning that Russian troops would at once occupy Constantinople. Once more the Sultan, this time strongly backed by Layard, appealed to London to cancel the orders: but Salisbury turned the scale against any fresh concession by arguing that we should make ourselves "utterly ridiculous" and "lose all weight in Europe".[64] On 13 February the fleet passed up the Straits unresisted, but anchored, not off the city itself, but 40 miles away, on the south side of the Sea of Marmora: and the Grand Duke fortunately did not carry out his threat. No severer comment can be found than that of Layard himself, who wrote to the Viceroy: "Our ships were sent up here to protect the lives and property of British subjects which required no protection. But we gave the Russians a pretext for entering the capital and causing the very danger apprehended."[65] What really saved the situation was the pacific attitude of the Grand Duke and his staff, who realised the exhaustion of the Russian troops and were eager to see the war ended: and there was a providential breakdown of telegraphic communications with the Tsar which caused delays at the most critical moment.[66] Fortunately also, Shuvalov extracted from the Tsar an explicit pledge not to occupy Gallipoli, on condition that no British troops were landed.

At this critical juncture the close co-operation of Derby and Shuvalov probably just turned the scale in favour of peace.[67] The Court and Clubs fulminated against Russia, and Beaconsfield authorised Layard "to purchase, if possible, the chief ships of the Turkish fleet": Derby's denial of this to Shuvalov is only credible on the theory that it was done behind his back.[68] Beaconsfield made yet another overture to Austria-Hungary, who was scarcely less alarmed at the Russian advance, despite the very explicit pledges which she held from the Tsar: but Andrássy remained sceptical as to the value of Britain as an ally and continued to pursue that hedging policy which was in the end to secure two new provinces without a war. Derby gave great offence to the Queen by a speech in the House of Commons on 24 February, which treated neutrality as the only feasible policy, since the great majority of the nation disapproved action which might lead to another Crimea: nor did he flinch before the insulting answer of Lord Campbell, who quoted against him the lines of Coriolanus, "He's a disease which must be cut away".

On 5 March peace was concluded at San Stefano between Russia and Turkey, without Britain being in any way able to affect the decision. By this treaty Montenegro, Serbia and Roumania obtained their independence, the first doubling her territory, the second receiving Niš, but not Pirot, the third having to restore South Bessarabia to Russia, though obtaining Dobrogea as compensation. A large part of Turkish Armenia, with Kars and Batum, was also assigned to Russia. The Greeks obtained nothing, but Epirus, Thessaly and the remaining European provinces of Turkey were to receive constitutions similar to that of Crete. There was no clause implementing Russia's pledge of Bosnia to Austria-Hungary. But the most sensational part of the Treaty was that which made of Bulgaria an autonomous Principality under an elected Christian Prince and assigned to her frontiers which extended on the south to the Aegean, and westwards to include most of Macedonia and portions of what is now Albania. In one word, it drew its frontier in defiance of geography and ignored the claims of five out of the six chief Balkan races.

The Russian Government committed the further blunder of keeping secret the terms of the Treaty until the Tsar's own signature had been obtained: and as a result London was kept waiting for over a fortnight, in a state of nerves and fury. When at last they became known, there were violent outbursts in the Jingo press, and Gladstone himself at once made it quite clear that he could not justify the robbing of the Roumanians or "the immense extension westwards which has been given to Bulgaria". Layard on his side was straining every nerve to retain his influence over the Sultan and made violent attacks upon Gladstone, even going so far as to hold him primarily responsible for the Russo-Turkish War.[69]

CHAPTER XIV

THE BERLIN SETTLEMENT

SALISBURY SUCCEEDS DERBY

Beaconsfield was not slow to act. On 27 March he proposed to the Cabinet that the reserves should be called out, and Indian troops brought through the Canal, "to occupy two important posts in the Levant", commanding the Persian Gulf. Derby at once resigned, and this time his decision was final: indeed public opinion had veered so much that the Tories thought it quite safe to let him go. For the moment his departure seemed a blow to the cause of peace, and Shuvalov, whom his German colleague Münster recognised as "tirelessly working to preserve peace between England and Russia", was correspondingly depressed. The Sultan's reaction was a secret message to Beaconsfield himself, asking to be informed "as soon as possible" if war between England and Russia were imminent, and declaring that he could still mass 100,000 troops within a fortnight for the defence of the Bosphorus.

The worst danger was, however, by now over. Beaconsfield's choice for the Foreign Office fell almost inevitably upon Lord Salisbury, as alone combining the necessary energy, prestige and knowledge. After prolonged hesitations during 1876-7, Salisbury seems at last to have realised that he must either take Derby's place or face one of two alternatives—combine forces with Gladstone and a disunited Opposition, or split his own party and go into the wilderness with Carnarvon and Derby: and he cannot be blamed for dismissing both as equally impossible. But during March he had already made it quite clear to his chief that he did not believe in "setting the Turkish Government on its legs again", and that the aims which he favoured were to prevent a Slav state south of the Balkans, to help the Greeks, and to concentrate on the freedom of the Straits and the acquisition of "two naval stations for England, say Lemnos and Cyprus".[1] Thus Beaconsfield appointed him with his eyes open, and thereby tacitly abandoned his own policy of "Turkish integrity". It is true that on 8 April in Parliament he made a bellicose speech, denouncing San Stefano as "completely abrogating what is known as Turkey in Europe" and making "the Black Sea as much a Russian lake as the Caspian". But this was countered by a vigorous speech from Derby, declaring the restoration of Turkey to be hope-less, denying the existence of a *casus belli*, and claiming that the war into which we were "not drifting, but rushing", would be "a war without necessity, without a clear and definite object, with a divided country and in all probability without an ally". Coming from the late Foreign Secretary, this reinforced the arguments of the Opposition, who conducted a fresh campaign throughout the country during April. Public excitement again became intense, when it was revealed during the Easter Recess that 7000 Indian troops had been brought to Malta.

None the less, from the first moment of Salisbury's accession to power, a new note is perceptible in our foreign policy: the Committee of three ceased to exist, the Prime Minister discontinued his secret correspondence with Layard, and it was much remarked that the Home Secretary, Assheton Cross, presumably not without previous consultation, announced that "the object of Her Majesty's Government is not the independence and integrity of the Ottoman Empire, as has been stated, but the good government and assured peace of those populations of Turkey". It is characteristic of Salisbury that on first taking office he worked till three in the morning at a statement of policy, which was then approved by the Cabinet and published as the Circular of 1 April 1878. Its essential features were an insistence that the validity of the Treaty must depend on the assent of the Powers, a criticism of the excessive cessions made to Bulgaria, as "a strong Slav state,...under the auspices and control of Russia", an advocacy of Greek rights against the Slavs, opposition to "the compulsory alienation of Bessarabia" and to Russia's acquisition of Batum and Armenia, and anxiety as to "the political independence of the Government of Constantinople". Britain, it declared, would not enter a Congress unless all changes in the Treaties of 1856 could be freely discussed there.

THE PROTOCOL OF 30 MAY AND THE CYPRUS CONVENTION

Shuvalov's statesmanship was now put to a remarkable test, and by the end of April he had already convinced the more than suspicious Salisbury that Derby's belief in his pacific aims had not been mistaken. Early in May Shuvalov carried to St Petersburg a Note of British objections to San Stefano, and after ten days of discussion with the Tsar and his Ministers, and visits to Bismarck on the way, he returned with authority to reach a final accord. Salisbury meanwhile had reached the conclusion that "the Turkish breakwater" in Europe was "shattered beyond repair", that the main effort must be directed towards keeping Turkey's Asiatic Empire together, and that by leaving Kars and Batum to Russia, a *quid pro quo* might be extracted for Britain—in Beaconsfield's phrase to the Queen, "Some island or station on the coast of Asia Minor, which will neutralise the presence of Russia in Armenia."[2]

A week's hard bargaining, after Shuvalov's return to London, ended in the Protocol of 30 May, which provided a basis of agreement for the proposed Congress, and which indeed contains the embryo of the final settlement. Russia consented to the division of Bulgaria into two provinces—one north of the Balkans under its own Prince, and a southern, with "wide administrative autonomy", under a Christian Governor: it was to lose its access to the Aegean and was restricted to a line east of the Vardar river. The Powers were to be consulted as to the organisation of Epirus, Thessaly "and the other Christian provinces left under the Porte". Bessarabia was reluctantly conceded to Russia, on the ground that the other signatory Powers were indifferent and Britain herself was "not so immediately interested". Britain also consented to Russia retaining Batum and most of Armenia, "despite the grave dangers menacing the peace of the populations of Turkey in Asia" which might result. "But Her Majesty's Government", it was added, "are of the opinion that the duty of protecting the Ottoman Empire from this danger, which henceforth will rest in a special measure upon England, can be effected without exposing England to the calamities of a fresh war." There was no longer any pretence at upholding the old policy of "independence and integrity". By an awkward indiscretion a summary of these terms was published in the *Globe* only twenty-four hours later: and the Government made a not very creditable attempt to treat as "wholly unauthentic" what eventually proved to be accurate in all save a few details. The Duke of Argyll was entitled to argue that the Protocol abandoned four of the main positions upheld in the Circular of 1 April—respecting Bessarabia, Batum, Armenia and Bulgarian access to the Black Sea—and also the old military frontier of Turkey on the Danube, which Layard held to be essential to her survival in Europe. Thus "the British plenipotentiaries went into Congress with their hands bound and their tongues only untied for the purpose of keeping up an appearance of freedom".[3]

Meanwhile the Cabinet had been searching for the long coveted "place of arms", and during May secret negotiations were pursued with the Porte. The Prime Minister, whose fancy had ranged from Varna to Batum, from Mitylene to Crete and Basrah, now assured the Queen that "Cyprus is the key to Western Asia" and proposed, in return for its cession, a defensive alliance with the Porte, "guaranteeing Asiatic Turkey from Russian invasion".[4] By 10 May the Cabinet had decided that Russia could not be expelled from Kars, and that "the only remedy" was "a direct alliance" for the protection of Turkey's Asiatic Empire. A definite proposal in this sense was sent to the Sultan through Layard on 24 May, but as this coincided with an abortive conspiracy against his life which led to a series of ministerial changes, it was not until 4 June, and then only after a severe struggle, that the Ambassador could obtain the Sultan's signature. He had got the length of considering whether it might not be necessary to put aside Abdul Hamid "if the safety of the state and our paramount interests require it".[5]

THE CONGRESS OF BERLIN

The signature of the Protocol removed the last obstacles to a European Congress, which had been originally proposed by Andrássy in the last days of January. The assembly, which opened at Berlin on 13 June and sat for exactly a month, remains one of the great milestones of nineteenth-century diplomacy, and for good or for bad prescribed the fate of Europe for a generation to come. It was presided over with consummate skill and energy by Bismarck, who some months earlier had offered himself as "honest broker", and who in the winter of 1876 had roundly declared his inability to see in the whole Eastern Question any "interest for Germany which would be worth the healthy bones of a single Pomeranian musketeer". Although the Congress was not attended by foreign sovereigns like that of Vienna, and though the ceremonies were shorn of some of their pomp by the absence of William I (who had narrowly escaped from an attempt on his life), there had never been, even at Vienna, such a gathering of statesmen of the first rank— Bismarck himself, Andrássy, Beaconsfield and Salisbury, Gorchakov and Shuvalov, outshining the more mediocre Waddington, Corti and Caratheodory. It was the first time that Britain sent both her Premier and Foreign Secretary on such a mission: and certainly Beaconsfield himself was one of the main centres of interest, courted on all sides, though much hampered by ill-health and wisely reserving himself for major occasions. In Salisbury's own words, "What with deafness, ignorance of French and Bismarck's extraordinary mode of speech, Beaconsfield has the dimmest idea of what is going on, understands everything crossways and imagines a perpetual conspiracy."[6] But the alliance of the two men was an ideal combination, which served at the time to conceal the fact that British policy had abandoned the full Palmerstonian doctrine so long upheld by Disraeli himself, and that Salisbury stood almost exactly halfway between the two extremes of Disraeli and Gladstone.

This is not the place to tell the story of the Congress, and indeed one of its main features consisted in face-saving manoeuvres to conceal the extent to which each of the two protagonists, by accepting the Protocol of 30 May, had modified his original position. The main struggle centred round Bulgaria, Beaconsfield threatening to return to London, but allowing himself to be talked round by Bismarck during a prolonged evening *tête-à-tête*. But if the abandonment of the "Big Bulgaria" of San Stefano was a very real concession on Russia's part, the readiness with which Salisbury consented to include Sofia on the one hand, and the port and coast line of Varna on the other, within the bounds of the new Principality, came as a thunderbolt upon the Turkish delegates. To us, who know Bulgaria's development in the sixty years that followed, it seems wellnigh incredible that serious statesmen should have attempted to deny to her both her future capital and her outlet to the sea.*

The second crisis opened on 28 June, when Salisbury proposed that Austria-Hungary should be entrusted with a mandate for the occupation of Bosnia-Hercegovina, to which he himself had given Britain's consent by a secret convention directly concluded with Andrássy on 6 June. Russia was of course bound by the secret engagements of Reichstadt and Budapest, Bismarck at once gave his full backing, the French seem to have regarded their consent as an equivalent for the veto of any discussion of Egypt and Syria, while the Italians were hostile, but completely isolated. The Turks, though browbeaten by Bismarck from the chair, held out obstinately, but in the end had no course save to agree direct with Austria-Hungary. Andrássy could certainly have obtained the approval of the Powers if he had desired to annex outright, and Balkan history might have taken a very different turn: but reasons of internal Austrian and Hungarian politics led him to prefer at that juncture a provisional arrangement.

The final crisis of the Congress came over Russia's Asiatic frontier: and there was an incident between Beaconsfield and Gorchakov in which it seems almost certain that the two veterans inadvertently exchanged their most secret maps,[7] and in which Salisbury pleaded the cause of the Lazes outside Batum, but most unfortunately forgot the name of "cette intéressante tribu", as Bismarck sarcastically described them. In the end Salisbury, who confided to Layard that "on both sides Batum is little more than a flag", consented that Russia should receive it as a free port, but restore Bayazid to Turkey, in the interest of an almost imaginary trade route to Persia.

Towards the end of the Congress it began to leak out that Britain had made her own arrangements with Turkey behind the back of the Powers and had obtained in Cyprus what Bismarck, drastically, but not inaccurately, described as "Disraeli's *pot de vin*".[8] Salisbury only just had time to re-

---

* It is some measure of Layard's blindness that in his *Memoirs* he placed on record that "he could not understand why Sofia should have been given to Bulgaria, or if so, why Varna was not retained as compensation for Turkey". *Layard Papers*, cit. *D.G.E.Q.* p. 525.

assure the alarmed Waddington as to Egypt, and to silence him by advising a French occupation of Tunis. At the last moment the Porte made difficulties as to the surrender of the island, and these were only overcome by a peremptory telegram, denouncing the "Porte's refusal of firman as a flagrant breach of faith and act of ingratitude" and threatening, unless it was issued at once, to support Bismarck's proposal that Thessaly, Epirus and Crete should be given to Greece. This had the desired effect, but it savours unpleasantly of blackmail. In the blunt words of Harcourt, "It was necessary to bring back something, and that something was Cyprus." To this day there is no justification for its retention, unless to keep out the Italians: and Sir Samuel Baker's dictum still holds good—"If we are supreme at sea, Cyprus is not wanted, and if not, it is an encumbrance."⁹

If the Turks were treated with scant courtesy at the Congress—Bismarck showing special *animus* against their second delegate Mehemet Ali Pasha, a renegade Prussian officer—the lesser Balkan nations were refused admittance, except for a brief moment to state their case or learn the decisions of Europe as to their fate. Greece, it is true, enjoyed the competing favour of Britain and France, but in the end nothing was done for her beyond stiffening up the Cretan constitution, and three years of disorder followed before even a partial solution of the Thessalian problem could be achieved by methods of armed defiance. Towards Serbia the British official attitude had throughout this period been frankly hostile, and now at Berlin the Russians also withheld their full backing, and advised Prince Milan "to come to terms with Austria-Hungary on all points". Bosnia was snatched away before their eyes, and they were fortunate in obtaining even Niš and Pirot. Montenegro received more attention from Russia and not merely doubled her territory, but acquired her first access to the sea, although she was not allowed to have warships of her own. In the case of Roumania much even public indignation was expressed at Russia's insistence upon depriving her little ally of Southern Bessarabia—due apparently to a personal whim of Alexander II; but not a single Power was prepared to break with Russia on this point, and indeed Bessarabia had quite obviously become the small change which facilitates large monetary transactions. Roumanian protests were therefore overborne, and while the relatively barren Dobrogea, with its mainly non-Roumanian population, was assigned to them in exchange, Silistria was withheld and the frontier inadequately drawn.

Berlin corrected the worst flaws in San Stefano, but the most essential features of the latter remained. The independence of the three former vassal states, Roumania, Serbia and Montenegro, was recognised as an accomplished fact, and each of the three received partial aggrandisement, pending a final settlement after the Great War. Bessarabia was restored to Russia, while

Austria-Hungary occupied Bosnia-Hercegovina, with the right to garrison the Sandjak of Novipazar and thus separate Serbia from Montenegro. The *status quo* in the Straits and on the Danube was upheld, and the powers of the Danubian Commission improved and extended. Bulgaria was denied complete independence and was divided into three fragments—a vassal state, an autonomous province and a residue which was only to enjoy the same self-government as other integral parts of European Turkey. In the first there was to be a freely elected Christian Prince, a national militia and a constitution drafted by an assembly of notables; in the second—to be arbitrarily known as "Eastern Roumelia"—a Christian Governor-General, "under the direct political and military authority of the Sultan", with a native gendarmerie and militia and an internal statute drawn up by a special European commission; for the third—what Shuvalov meant by "Western Roumelia", or such Bulgarian districts as were left an integral part of Turkey—a scheme of local self-government was to be drawn up by another special commission, as in the case of Thrace, Macedonia, Albania, Thessaly and Epirus. Unhappily both Article XXIII of the Treaty, which prescribed these local autonomies, and Article LXI, which pledged the Porte to grant reforms to the Armenians, under the supervision of the Powers, and to guarantee them against the Circassians and Kurds, remained from the very first a dead letter: the Porte, so far from fulfilling its pledges, never even appointed the original commissions, and the conditions in all these provinces went from bad to worse during the next thirty years. In criticising the Berlin settlement it is vital to remember that if these two Articles had been carried out as effectively as the others, the whole situation in Turkey might have been transformed. Unfortunately their non-fulfilment was an essential feature of the baneful Hamidian tyranny which hung like a nightmare over the Near East from 1878 to 1908: and when it was at last removed, the situation was beyond repair.

"Peace with Honour"

Beaconsfield and Salisbury had a triumphant reception on their return to England, and won the great debate in Parliament by a majority of 143 (being about 90 in excess of the normal). But the country remained much divided on the Eastern Question, the extremer Tories—men like Lord Elcho, Henry Chaplin and Lord John Manners—suspecting a betrayal of Turkey, while Gladstone, admitting that the Treaty had brought "some great results for humanity", none the less denounced the secret Cyprus agreement as "an insane convention" and the manner of its conclusion as "an act of duplicity not surpassed, and rarely equalled, in the history of nations ". It was these charges that stung Beaconsfield into a famous, if wholly unedifying, denunciation of his great rival as "a sophistical rhetorician, inebriated with the exuberance of his own verbosity" and other phrases of a no less verbose "tu quoque".* The main argument of the Prime Minister's defence was that "a country may have lost provinces, but that is not partition"; that "Turkey-in-Europe once more exists" and had saved its richest province; that Varna was "not a place of importance" and Batum more comparable to Cowes than to Portsmouth; that "in taking Cyprus the movement is not Mediterranean, it is Indian": and that "the Eastern nations" had confidence in Britain and her Empire. It was reserved to Derby to make the most damaging criticism of official policy—ridiculing the finality of the Bulgarian arrangement and the usefulness of Cyprus whether as a naval station or as a means for the defence of India, and challenging our dangerous commitments against Russia. It was in this debate that Derby revealed the fact that it was the decision in favour of seizing Cyprus and Alexandretta, with or without the Sultan's consent, which prompted his final resignation:[10] and Salisbury in his anger went the length of comparing Derby to Titus Oates! The Queen and many high Tories at the time were indignant at his revelations; but he was able to produce the Queen's own express sanction for explaining his motives "at such a time as he in his discretion might think fit",[11] and in private he told the Liberal chief Lord Granville, to whom he was already gravitating, "a more complete surrender of all that the Cabinet professed to stand for could not be".[12] It is only in our own day that the full facts have become available.

THE AFTERMATH OF BERLIN (1878–81)

The Congress of Paris, dealing with a less complex, because less highly developed, situation, left the unsolved Roumanian problem to simmer on for three years: but though at times it threatened rupture between the Powers, in the end bloodshed was avoided. The Congress of Berlin, sitting for almost exactly the same length of time, left far more "ragged edges" to be trimmed, and three years of unrest in the Near East were to elapse before this process was complete. The election of Alexander of Battenberg as Prince of Bulgaria was followed by the gradual withdrawal of Russian troops, but friction between the new state and its liberators soon became endemic, and by 1885 was so acute that the very Powers which seven years earlier had frowned upon Bulgaria as a prospective instrument of Russian aggression

* *Punch* on 10 August 1878 summed up the verdict of middle opinion by its cartoon of "the two head boys of the school" caught mud-flinging by an indignant headmaster.

against Turkey, now sought to strengthen it as a barrier against Russia. During the Congress Beaconsfield himself had admitted to the German Crown Princess that "without Eastern Roumelia the affair would not hold for more than seven years"; and it was Salisbury who in 1886 threw his whole weight into the scale in favour of the union of "the Two Bulgarias". But even during the interval Turkish power had remained a mere shadow in the southern province, and little more was heard of Turkish garrisons and of that "line of the Balkans" on which Beaconsfield and Layard had laid such stress.

Meanwhile the occupation of Bosnia by Austria-Hungary met with determined resistance from the native population, and guerilla warfare was not suppressed till October 1878. In April 1879 Turkey concluded a detailed convention with Vienna, reserving the Sultan's suzerainty and full sovereign rights, and in the following summer a small Austrian garrison was allowed to occupy the Sandjak of Novipazar. Andrássy had made it quite clear to Prince Milan that he would not tolerate either union of the two Serb states or their interference in Bosnia, but that they might eventually hope for some extension of territory towards Macedonia. Milan's assumption of the royal Crown in 1881 would not have been possible without Vienna's help, and for the remainder of his reign he remained in an ignominious vassalage of which the amazing details were concealed from his own people. Britain continued to show but little interest or confidence in Serbia, was only too glad to see it within the sphere of Austria-Hungary, and approved Vienna's restraining influence upon Belgrade and Sofia, when Milan's incompetent folly and greed involved the two Slav neighbours in unjustifiable war in 1888.

By the Treaty the two overwhelmingly Albanian districts of Gusinje and Plava had been wrongly assigned to Montenegro, and this was firmly resisted by the local population. Throughout 1879 the new "Albanian League", strongly entrenched in Skutari and encouraged from Constantinople, was able to defy Europe: and the final compromise was only reached after protracted negotiations between the Porte and the Powers, a joint naval demonstration off the Albanian coast, and a threat on the part of the new Gladstone Government to occupy Smyrna as a pledge of submission. Gladstone's marked sympathy for Montenegro played its part in the settlement, but in the end Gusinje and Plava remained Turkish, and at last, in November 1880, the so-called "port" of Dulcigno was handed over to Montenegro. In April 1881 the Albanian League was rudely suppressed by the Turks, and the Albanian movement slumbered till the Young Turkish Revolution of 1908.

The Greek problem also caused acute difficulties, and the French and

British Governments continued to hesitate between their desire to favour Greek claims and the danger of international complications. If the Greeks had been content to renounce their claims, they could have obtained Crete without the delay of another generation: but it was just upon Thessaly and Epirus that their aspirations were fixed, and here the Turks met them with a point-blank refusal. Interminable negotiations, in which now France, now Britain, played the most active part, were still in full swing when the Liberals came into power in England. Eventually, by the Convention of May 1881, Greece obtained most of Thessaly, but only a fragment of Southern Epirus. The British plea for the strategic frontier of Mount Olympus was not upheld, and Crete remained under a revised version of the Organic Law of 1868.

It was, however, the Asiatic aspect of the Turkish problem in which the British Government was most interested. After the Congress Beaconsfield was quite content to rest upon his laurels and showed a marked indifference to Turkish reform. But Salisbury was in earnest and soon submitted to the Porte through Layard a scheme for the appointment of Governors in five Asiatic vilayets, and European control of the police, the courts, and the collection of taxes. In the teeth of obstruction and prevarication from Abdul Hamid—whose high character and qualities, as preached by Layard, he had long since realised to be a myth—and handicapped by the Treasury's refusal to provide the necessary financial groundwork, Salisbury appointed Sir Charles Wilson as Consul-General for Anatolia, with four other British officers under him, and obtained for Baker Pasha the post of Inspector-General of Reforms. But it soon became painfully evident that the whole idea of administrative reform for Asia Minor was foredoomed to failure, unless Britain was prepared to undertake a large experiment on an Indian scale, enforce it upon the Porte and expend large sums upon it. What proved finally fatal to the idea was on the one hand the extension of the odious Hamidian police regime, which stifled all political life in Turkey for a generation, and on the other the emergence of a similar, but still more pressing, problem in Egypt, as the result of Khedive Ismail's financial misrule and the discords of the Anglo-French *condominium*. The Gladstone Government withdrew Layard from Constantinople, and subsequently the military consuls, to the very pardonable disgust of Salisbury: but it is difficult to see how the Asia Minor scheme could ever have come to fruition under the circumstances of the 'eighties.

DISRAELI'S SWAN SONG

The acute controversy regarding the Eastern Question had seriously shaken the position of the Conservative Government in the country, and during 1879 foreign problems continued to occupy the forefront of public controversy. Indeed Lord Granville's biographer in no way exaggerates when he affirms that "the general election of 1880 was fought almost entirely on issues of foreign and colonial policy".[13] By then the unsatisfactory position in South Africa and Afghanistan had provided the Liberals with fresh incentives to agitation: and Sir William Harcourt in particular attacked the Treaty of Berlin and the Government's whole policy in unmeasured terms. He pointed out the unanswerable fact that, on the one side, the impregnable Balkan frontier demanded by Beaconsfield for Turkey was non-existent, and on the other, "no progress had been made with the regeneration of Asia Minor" and that "the populations are not pacified and reforms are not begun". Lord Salisbury, never seen to advantage on a public platform, found himself on the defensive at Manchester, and his curious attempt to subordinate the question of Turkish reform to that of Russian aggression was widely denounced by Hartington, Argyll and other Liberal leaders. Lord Cranbrook, perhaps the boldest and most trenchant of the Conservative leaders, spoke quite frankly of "our ineffectual attempts to save Turkey from her own idiotic follies during and since her war". The Hamidian regime was already proving a fatal handicap to co-operation or constructive policy.

It was in this situation that Beaconsfield delivered his "swan-song" at the Guildhall, culminating in the famous phrase: "One of the greatest of Romans, when asked what were his politics, replied, 'Imperium et Libertas'. That would not make a bad programme for a British Ministry." There is another passage which for dignity and foresight is on a level with his greatest utterances, and which deserves the special attention of our own age. "If...one of the most extensive and wealthiest empires in the world,...from a perverse interpretation of its insular geographical position, turns an indifferent ear to the feelings and fortunes of continental Europe, such a course would, I believe, only end in its becoming an object of general plunder. *So long as the power and advice of England are felt in the councils of Europe, peace, I believe, will be maintained, and for a long period.* Without their presence war...seems to me inevitable." Here in a few phrases Beaconsfield summed up the very essence of British policy, reminding us that despite our favoured insular position and our vast interests overseas, we can never neglect Europe save at our mortal peril, and that a neglect of our commitments and our international responsibilities, so far from achieving the ideal of "splendid isolation", would almost infallibly confront us with a hostile continental coalition. These wise words are the corollary of the great Chatham's teaching that we owe our success overseas to a skilfully conducted continental policy. They form a fitting conclusion to Disraeli's active share in foreign policy, and help to redeem his blunders in the Near East. It is well to remember that the greatest exponent of Imperialism, in what proved to be his farewell message on foreign policy, recognised and insisted upon our fundamental and decisive role as an European Power. Nor should the blunders and miscalculations of his Eastern policy blind us to the clearsighted and steadfast loyalty with which, throughout his long political career, he pursued the aim of friendship with France, avoiding, and sometimes making good, the petulant outbursts of Palmerston, and yet on the other hand avoiding the tendency of Liberal statesmen to underestimate the forces that were preparing a Prussian hegemony in Central Europe. As his oriental blood has so often been cited as explaining his interest in Eastern affairs, it is necessary to insist that it was in the affairs of *Western* Europe that his vision was clearest and most consistent.

CHAPTER XV

THE RETURN TO ISOLATION

MIDLOTHIAN AND THE LIBERAL TRIUMPH

In many ways the Eastern Crisis of the 'seventies was to prove a turning point in the history of our foreign policy, just as its sequel, the return of the Liberals to power, marked an epoch in home affairs. That wider electorate, which had seemingly not taken advantage of the reform of 1867, now responded with enthusiasm to a new kind of popular appeal such as a large section of the old governing class resented as mere hypocrisy. In thunderous moral tones Gladstone denounced the Tory Government for mismanaging the nation's interests and tarnishing its honour, and appealed for a moral verdict on "a grander and more august" scale than "the forms of a judicial trial" could offer. And the result of the elections of 1880 was to convert a House of 351 Conservatives and 250 Liberals into a House of 349 Liberals and 243 Conservatives (the Irish Party increasing its seats from 51 to 60).

This victory had been ushered in by the two amazing "Midlothian Campaigns" of the septuagenarian Gladstone: one of the most singular features was his own slowness to face the fact that these truly volcanic outbursts and the wide popular endorsement of his views were making his resumption of the Liberal leadership quite inevitable. On this point Hartington and Granville were in no manner of doubt, and in December 1879 had already agreed that Gladstone was "the only possible Prime Minister". Their main anxiety was that he should be once more assuming the lead without the responsibilities of leadership being "brought home to him".[1] A further complication was caused by the Queen's attitude. She expressed herself as "greatly distressed" by the election and was unable to give Gladstone her confidence.[2] But her attempts to induce Hartington or Granville to form a Government were foredoomed to failure, in view of the growing popular demand for "The People's William": and on 28 April 1880 Gladstone formed his second administration.

In Midlothian, and especially at West Calder, Gladstone had attempted to define the fundamental principles on which British foreign policy should rest: and whatever may be thought of them from the point of view of practical application, it may reasonably be argued that their public enunciation by a statesman who, during his first administration, had notably advanced the cause of international arbitration by his handling of the *Alabama* Case, was in itself an act of constructive statesmanship. Moreover, a summary of Gladstone's famous six heads is just as essential an introduction to any study of late Victorian policy, as is a knowledge of Wilson's Fourteen Points and later qualifying speeches, to any study of the Peace Settlement of 1919 and of post-war European policy. They are as follows:

I. "To foster the strength of the Empire... and to reserve it for great and worthy occasions." The means of attainment are characteristically defined as "just legislation and economy at home, thereby producing two great elements of national power—namely wealth, which is a physical element, and union and contentment, which are moral elements".

II. "To preserve to the nations... the blessings of peace"—and here occurs the no less characteristic parenthesis, "especially were it but for shame, when we recollect the sacred name we bear as Christians, for the Christian nations".

III. "To cultivate to the utmost the Concert of Europe", because you thus "neutralise and fetter the selfish aims of each", and because common action alone can unite the Great Powers for the common good.

IV. "To avoid needless and entangling engagements", which only reduce the power of the Empire.

V. "To acknowledge the rights of all nations." "You may, you must, sympathise with one nation more than another, and as a rule with those most closely linked by language, blood, religion or other circumstance of the time." "But in point of right all are equal, and you have no right to set up a system under which one is to be placed under moral suspicion or espionage, or made the subject of constant invective. If you do that, and especially if you claim for yourself a pharisaical superiority,... you may talk about your patriotism as you please, but you are a misjudging friend of your country and are undermining the basis of esteem and respect of others for it."

VI. Finally, foreign policy "should always be inspired by love of freedom"—"a desire to give it scope, founded not on visionary ideas but upon the long experience of many generations within the shores of this happy isle. In freedom you lay the firmest foundation both of loyalty and of order, for the development of individual character and the best protection for the happiness of the nation at large. In the foreign policy of this country the names of Canning, of Russell and of Palmerston, will ever be honoured by those who recollect the erection of the Kingdom of Belgium and the union of the disjointed provinces of Italy. It is that sympathy—not with disorder, but on the contrary founded on the deepest and most profound love of order—which ought in my opinion to be the very atmosphere in which the Foreign Secretary of England ought to live and move."

Though framed on abstract lines, this definition of policy still corresponds with modern requirements: so far from conflicting with Disraeli's Guildhall views (*supra*, p. 544) or with Canning's demand that intervention should be as rare as possible, but then with our whole force, it may be said to supplement them both, and to form quite logically the half-way house between Castlereagh's first efforts at international co-operation and that fuller and more august doctrine of a League of Nations, which is to-day on trial at Geneva.

*　*　*　*　*　*　*　*

Among the members of the new administration no one possessed such obvious claims to the Foreign Office as Lord Granville, and to him Mr Gladstone unhesitatingly offered it. None the less it may be doubted whether the appointment was a happy one: for though a man of character, charm and sanity, punctiliously loyal to colleagues and to party, his conduct of affairs was to lack the energy and drive which the times demanded. From the very outset he and his chief were gravely embarrassed by their own recent denunciations of the Tory Government. In his electoral manifesto Gladstone had accused his opponents of weakening the Empire "by needless wars, unprofitable extension and unwise engagements", and of dishonouring it in the eyes of Europe by filching the island of Cyprus from the Porte under a treaty clause distinctly concluded in violation of the Treaty of Paris, which formed "part of the international law of Christendom". It was widely assumed in the country that "a complete reversion in foreign affairs" would follow the Liberal victory. Yet in the Speech from the Throne the new Government proclaimed as one of its foremost aims "the early and complete fulfilment of the Treaty of Berlin", and when the Queen told Granville that she would never "sanction a reversal of the policy of the last few years", he assured her that "instead of destroying the Berlin Treaty, the Government were determined to do their best to carry out its provisions".[3] Even as regards Cyprus, Granville put forward the view that it could not be made "a place of arms" without impossible expenditure, and that the guarantee to defend Asia Minor was in Salisbury's words "a very onerous obligation".[4] But he followed this up by the highly disingenuous proposal to keep the island—not merely because the inhabitants did not wish to return to Turkey, but also because Turkey did not wish to have it back—and yet to ask the Porte to uphold the Treaty, minus the guarantee—in other words, minus its sole *raison d'être* in Turkish eyes. Small wonder if the Sultan, who saw us simultaneously supporting Greek demands, grew more hostile than ever.

Amid the dust of Midlothian Gladstone had accused Francis Joseph of publicly wishing the victory of Beaconsfield at the polls, and carried away by his indignation at this, he had denounced Austria as "the unflinching foe of freedom in every country of Europe", adding, "there is not a spot upon the whole map where you can lay your finger and say, 'There Austria did good'".[5] Granville's persuasive tact, combined with Vienna's official repudiation of the story about the Emperor, induced Gladstone to write a frank letter to the Austro-Hungarian Ambassador, Count Károlyi, admitting his criticism to have rested on "secondary evidence", and regretting the use of words "of a painful and wounding character".[6] This apology was accepted by Francis Joseph as the letter of an English gentleman and served to allay the alarm of Bismarck, lest the new British Cabinet should throw itself into the arms of Russia.

Our relations to the leading continental Powers under the Gladstone Government may be briefly summarised. They were in the first instance determined by the fact that for some time after the Congress Russian Chauvinist opinion, and the Tsar himself as its dupe, were disposed to make of Bismarck and Shuvalov twin scapegoats for Russia's failure to achieve the full San Stefano programme, and that Bismarck, harking back to his lifelong "nightmare of coalitions", sought desperately for "re-insurance". He found it in October 1879 in the Dual Alliance with Austria-Hungary— an arrangement which was to prove the first step towards a fateful new constellation in Europe. Meanwhile, during the summer recess, he had made tentative overtures to Britain, and Count Münster was instructed to sound both Beaconsfield at Hughenden and Salisbury at Hatfield. At first Beaconsfield was well disposed to the idea of joining a Triple Alliance against Russia, "as the Power that will ultimately strike at the root of our Empire", and Salisbury publicly referred to the report of an Austro-German accord as "good tidings of great joy". But Bismarck cooled off in proportion as Berlin's relations with St Petersburg again improved, and he had no desire to be used as the tool of British Russophobia. Some months after his fall Beaconsfield confided to his friend Drummond Wolff that "next to making a tolerable settlement for the Porte, our great object was to break up, and permanently prevent, the alliance of the three Empires", and he was naïve enough to imagine that this had actually been effected.[7] In reality it had always been Bismarck's aim to reconstitute the Three Emperors' League, and no sooner had he come to terms with Vienna than he began to negotiate discreetly with Saburov, a Russian diplomat of the school of Shuvalov.

Without entering upon an analysis of the Bismarckian policy, it is possible to reduce its essentials to three fundamental axioms—at all costs to prevent a Franco-Russian alliance such as might force Germany to fight on two fronts, and at all costs to avert any situation in which it might be necessary for Germany to choose between Russia and Austria-Hungary, since a contest between these two Powers might result in a war *à outrance* and in such a dislocation of forces in Eastern Europe as would be excessively dangerous to Germany. General dynastic and conservative principles, as well as common interests in the Polish question, increased still further his desire for a triple accord. "All politics", he told Shuvalov, "reduce themselves to this formula: Try to be *à trois* in a world governed by five Powers. I have made an *entente à deux*, in order to return thereafter to an *entente à trois* if you really wish it." The assassination of Alexander II in March 1881 hastened a *rapprochement* which was already imminent: the new Tsar, in thanking Francis Joseph for his condolences, wrote: "My Father fell on the breach, but it is Christian society which was struck in him. It is lost unless all the social forces unite to defend and save it."[8] Already in June 1881 the League was again in being, and was renewed for three years in 1884. Its main point was a mutual undertaking, on lines reminiscent of Münchengrätz and Reichstadt, not to permit any territorial change in the Balkans without an agreement between them.

Bismarck did not, however, rest content with the Dual Alliance and the reconstituted League. True to his desire to isolate France and to divert her main attention from the Vosges and the Rhine, he did not rest until she had occupied Tunis and thereby fatally alienated Italy who, fearing to stand completely alone, attached herself in May 1882 to Berlin and Vienna, thereby uniting the whole centre of the Continent as a Triple Alliance. This did not, however, invalidate the direct Austro-German Treaty of 1879, of which Italy had no knowledge: and though the Italian parties accepted the new alliance with their reason, Italian opinion rejected it with their voices, and the Irredentists demonstrated in favour of Oberdank, the Italianised Triestine German who had tried to assassinate Francis Joseph. Meanwhile, to this constellation were also attached the lesser planets of Serbia and Roumania, the first by a secret treaty of June 1881, which was renewed in 1889, but eventually lapsed in 1895, the second by a similar treaty of October 1883, which was four times renewed and guarded with such extreme secrecy that at the supreme crisis of 1914 the country was still in ignorance of its existence, and refused to accept liability for its fulfilment.

In face of all this diplomatic activity Granville was passive enough, his main efforts being expended in quite other directions. Their liquidation of the forward policy pursued by Lytton on the Indian frontier was not unsuccessfully accomplished: the Liberals were definitely opposed to the partition of Afghanistan, and after General Roberts's brilliantly successful

march to Kandahar, it proved possible to evacuate without any loss of
prestige and to establish close and durable relations with Abdur Rahman,
the ablest Amir whom Afghanistan had known for many generations. Much
less satisfactory was the situation in South Africa, which, though bungled
by the late Government, had been rendered still worse by the Liberal
Opposition's unwise tactics towards Sir Bartle Frere. Shepstone's annexation of the Transvaal in 1877 had proved an obstacle rather than an aid to
federation: and the Zulu War, though it probably saved the Boers from
extermination, roused public opinion both in England and in Africa, even
without the added tragedy of the Prince Imperial's death. The new
Government recalled Frere, but decided to uphold the annexation of the
Transvaal: when, however, the Boers rose in rebellion and inflicted an
ignominious defeat on a handful of British regulars at Majuba, no attempt
was made to redeem the military position, and a convention was ratified,
assuring to the Boers a sort of conditional independence, under the
suzerainty of the British Crown, so framed as to convince the Boer leaders
of their innate superiority and only too open to rival legal interpretations.
Not merely did this settlement bear within itself the seeds of future trouble
in South Africa, but it was keenly resented by a large section of home
opinion, which was henceforth predisposed to suspect the Liberal Government of a proneness to craven surrender of Imperial interests. Events in
Egypt and the Sudan were to strengthen these suspicions and give them an
acrid tone which dominated a public already poisoned by the Irish dispute.

Egyptian affairs were a legacy of which the late Government could be
much more proud. The financial exhaustion, to which the Khedive Ismail's
extravagance had reduced his country, had given Disraeli the opportunity
for his famous Suez Canal coup, and was followed in 1876 by the Cave
commission of enquiry and the establishment of the so-called "Dual
Control", in the interests of British and French bondholders. At the time
Salisbury neatly summed up the three alternatives which offered themselves.
"You may renounce, or monopolise, or share. Renouncing would have
been to place France across our road to India. Monopolising would have
been very near the risk of war. So we resolved to share."[9] The first real
crisis of the Condominium was forestalled by the action of Abdul Hamid in
deposing the impossible Ismail (June 1879). But the growth of Egyptian
national feeling under Arabi, and French eagerness to intervene, led to a
marked divergence of view between London and Paris, despite the fact that
Gambetta, who dominated the so-called "Grand Ministère" of November
1881, was ready for co-operation, and for almost Cobdenite agreements
with Britain. The instability of French Governments and the skill with
which Bismarck and his son Count Herbert played upon Granville's

preference for an international rather than a dual solution, confused the issue still further: and the Conference of the Powers which met at Constantinople in the spring of 1882 only made confusion worse confounded, since no one had thought out a clear programme beforehand. This notorious divergence of views was obviously a contributory cause of Arabi's rebellion in June of that year. Gambetta, who had in the meantime been succeeded by Freycinet, appealed fervently to the French Chamber in favour of Anglo-French co-operation: "never, even at the risk of the greatest sacrifices, break off the alliance with England". But French opinion was overwhelmingly adverse to any such step, and overthrew yet another Government; Italy, who in Granville's opinion, had been "at the bottom of much of the Egyptian mischief",[10] also held back: and Britain, screwed up to the necessity of prompt action, had perforce to act alone. The bombardment of Alexandria and the defeat inflicted by Wolseley on Arabi at Tel-el-Kebir created a new situation in which Egypt gradually became, in all save name, a British Protectorate. The Circular addressed to the Powers by Britain on 3 January 1883 took account of the new situation and long remained, in the apt words of Lord Fitzmaurice, "the original charter of British policy in Egypt". The Dual Control was abolished, and Lord Dufferin, who had spent the previous winter at Cairo on a special mission, was replaced by Sir Evelyn Baring as Diplomatic Agent, thus ushering in the memorable Cromer regime.

There can be no doubt that at this stage the main desire of Gladstone and Granville was to take advantage of Britain's heightened prestige in order to withdraw our garrisons from Egypt with as little delay as possible. But unforeseen events intervened and soon weighed the scales heavily against them. The rise of the Mahdi, as the extreme exponent of Moslem fanaticism, and ere long as a direct menace to the Khedive's already enfeebled regime, compelled the London Cabinet to retain British forces, however inadequate, in Cairo: but from the very first it betrayed a half-hearted attitude, and eventually fell between two stools. Late in 1883 an ill-disciplined Egyptian army under Hicks Pasha was cut to pieces by the Mahdi, and in the following February a further force of Egyptians under Baker Pasha was driven into headlong flight. The whole Sudan was speedily overrun, and soon found itself under a grinding tyranny, to which the very elements of constructive government were a sealed book. The evacuation of all the territory south of Assuan became a military necessity of the moment, and was recommended by Sir Evelyn Baring as such. But Gladstone, clinging vainly to any excuse for limiting our North African commitments, coined the ominous phrase of "Rescue and retire", thereby provoking a vote of censure in Parliament which was only rejected by a narrow margin. His well-meant efforts to place the Egyptian question on a broader European basis were quite unsuccessful, and the Conference convoked in London for its discussion in the summer of 1884 had been insufficiently prepared, and broke up on 2 August without reaching any decision. Indeed, it merely stimulated that growth of "mutual suspicion and irritation" between London and Paris, which so perturbed the unemotional Lord Lyons.

BRITAIN AND GERMAN COLONIAL AIMS

Thus during 1884, while the Government at home was absorbed by franchise reform and Irish unrest, the foreign situation was complicated by the carping attitude of France, which saw in the patent weakness of London a possible means of "regaining a political foothold"[11] in Egypt, by the sullen hostility of the Sultan to Britain's whole Egyptian policy, and by Bismarck's obvious efforts to encourage French colonial expansion under Jules Ferry—as a diversion from Alsace and the Rhine—and incidentally to extract colonial concessions for Germany in Africa and Asia. Bismarck had been favourably impressed by London's energy after the Arabi revolt, and made this clear to Odo Russell, now Lord Ampthill. He genuinely believed that Egypt, owing to the Suez Canal, was "of the utmost importance to England", being indeed "like the spinal cord which connects the backbone with the brain":[12] and he felt that events were justifying his policy of the "gradual dismemberment of Turkey"—Bosnia to Austria-Hungary, Tunis to France, and Egypt to Britain. Unhappily, however, he also regarded it as a practical contribution towards the further embroilment of France with Britain on the one hand and with Italy on the other. Moreover, as Ampthill reminded his chief, Bismarck "disapproves of parliamentary government, Liberal principles and free trade for Germany, and deplores their effects on England".[13] He never shook off this view, and in a Memorandum of 1882 wrote of "the absolute impossibility of confidential intercourse, in consequence of the indiscretions of English statesmen in their communications to Parliament, and the absence of security in alliances for which the Crown is not answerable in England, but only the fleeting Cabinets of the day".[14] This expression of opinion came as the result of somewhat tentative British overtures for an alliance with Germany and Austria-Hungary, made through the Prince of Wales and Crown Prince Frederick.

At the same time Germany's appetite for colonies grew steadily, and Bismarck, though personally indifferent to extra-European or naval problems, found that he could not safely ignore the insistence of public opinion, and in his contempt for the Liberals tried somewhat heavy-handed tactics of threat and of negotiation. Thus from 1883 onwards there was quite a series of colonial incidents between Britain and Germany, centring round Angra Pequeña, Cameroon, Congo, Zanzibar, New Guinea and Samoa. In 1883 the Germans annexed a large, if arid and utterly undeveloped, territory between Cape Colony and the southern border of Angola, to the intense annoyance of the South Africans: in 1884 they arrived in Togo a few days earlier than the British, while their attempt to install themselves in Zululand was only forestalled at the very last moment by the hoisting of the Union Jack. More important still were the activities of Carl Peters and his friends on the East African mainland opposite Zanzibar, and the occupation of part of New Guinea by a German company, in bland defiance of Australian protests. Bismarck found it necessary to humour what even Ampthill called "the colonial mania", and he owed his success to a skilful exploitation of the "Weltkonjunktur". On the one hand he fanned the reviving nationalistic susceptibilities of the French and Jules Ferry's projects of a Colonial Empire, and in the process Paris and London drifted dangerously apart. On the other hand, having captured Italy for the Triple Alliance, he was able to reassure her by a promise that it could never involve her in war with Britain, which would at that time have far outweighed the advantages of her association with Berlin.[15] In October 1884, however, Germany and France found a common interest in convoking an international Conference at Berlin, which secured freedom of trade in the Congo and Niger basins, and measures for the suppression of the slave trade, while at the same time confirming the German annexation of Cameroon and Togoland, and temporally making Leopold II absolute master of vast tracts of "Darkest Africa". It would be useless to deny that in all this the policy of Granville and of Derby, now his colleague as Colonial Secretary, had been hesitant, ill-thought-out, and sometimes niggling towards Powers which shared our own healthy colonial appetite. On the other hand the German attitude is best revealed in a London report of Count Herbert Bismarck to his father: he had told Lord Granville, he wrote, that "if he attached more value to the consent of the Colonies and to the French press than to Germany's friendship, let him at least say so, and we would then try and prove to him how unpleasant we could make ourselves, and put him into the position of judging what Germany's friendship or enmity was worth".*

* 7 March 1885—*G.P.* IV, 101. This document has to be read *in extenso* in order to be believed. Some flavour of its arrogance and presumption may be gained from another passing phrase: "To let oneself in with Mr Gladstone to discussing the essence of foreign policy of a great country, is pointless, since he simply lacks all understanding for this!" (*ibid.* p. 104). Further insight is afforded by the diary of Sir Charles Dilke, with whom Count Herbert also talked. "If at his former visit he had only tried to get us to dismiss Lord Derby, on this occasion he wanted us to dismiss Lord Granville and Lord Derby" (Fitzmaurice, *op. cit.* II, 430).

A few weeks later in Parliament Gladstone declared that "if Germany is to become a colonising Power, all I say is, God speed her! She becomes our ally and partner in the execution of the great purposes of Providence for the advantage of mankind." Such phrases came three years too late, and Berlin was merely confirmed in the belief that bullying methods were needed to bring London to reason. The New Guinea dispute was now amicably settled, but cynics ascribed London's more accommodating attitude to British isolation from France, to entanglements in Egypt, and to the reviving danger of war with Russia on the Afghan border.

THE DEATH OF GORDON

Simultaneously with its decision that the Sudan must be evacuated, the British Government, in deference to a highly nervous public opinion, and without regard for Baring's twice repeated disapproval, selected General Gordon—an heroic survival from the age of faith and chivalry—as the man best fitted to liquidate the desperate situation on the Upper Nile. No incident has ever stirred British sentiment more deeply than the story of "Chinese Gordon" in Khartum, and few have caused such deep divisions of opinion: but if there is one point on which posterity would seem to be agreed, it is that the choice of Gordon for such a mission was, as Gladstone himself came to recognise very frankly, "a grave error". For he was sent out by a Cabinet which, for good or for bad, was pledged up to the hilt before Britain and before Europe to a policy of withdrawal from Egypt and therefore *a fortiori* from the Sudan: and yet within a few weeks of his arrival he had "either forgotten or deliberately put aside his instructions"[16] —which were doubtless lacking in precision—and was not merely proclaiming that "if Egypt is to be kept quiet" Britain must adopt the policy of "smashing up the Mahdi", but was actually urging the appointment, as Governor-General of the Sudan, of his old adversary Zobeir the slave-trader. By March he was shut up in Khartoum, and virtually isolated from the outer world: and the question of a relief expedition at once began to be mooted. But precious months were wasted in discussion, and even when the decision had at last been reached, both the civil and military authorities disagreed as to the rival prospects of advance from the Red Sea coast or up the Nile. The pledge was given to Parliament in July, but Wolseley was not ready to move forward until October, and when at last Wilson's advance guard reached Khartoum on 28 January 1885, Gordon and his little band had been done to death two days earlier.

With the long and tragic controversy we are not concerned, except in so far as it is germane to the major issues of foreign policy. But it is essential to insist that while nothing—not even the Home Rule dispute—did so much to discredit the Liberal Government with the nation at large and to kindle those bitter feelings which were so soon to split the Liberal party, the tendency to saddle Gladstone with almost exclusive responsibility is not justified by the facts. That the head of a Government can never escape responsibility for a national disaster is the merest of platitudes: but that in this case it was shared by four others—Granville, Hartington, Northbrook, Dilke, none of whom ever attempted to evade it[17]—is a necessary corrective to the fierce verdicts still passed by historical writers. If we are to understand Gladstone's own mind, we must turn to a letter which he addressed to Granville after the Mahdi's first victories, and in which he gives as the three motives of his Egyptian policy, (1) respect for European law and peace, (2) the just claims of the Khedive, (3) "an indisposition to extend the responsibilities of this country".[18] Unquestionably this last point weighed too strongly with him, and exposed him to merciless criticism, which he accepted with singular meekness. Thus, for good or for ill, the Queen's emphatic affirmation—"Mr Gladstone and the Government *have* Gordon's innocent, noble, heroic blood on their consciences",[19] coincided with a large section of contemporary opinion. On the vote of censure the Government's majority fell to fourteen, and Granville was probably right in thinking that it would have been wiser to resign at once. Khartoum may be said to have given the *coup de grâce* to the second Gladstone administration, and to have prepared the way for twenty years of almost uninterrupted Tory predominance.

BRITAIN AND RUSSIA

Meanwhile, in the sphere of Russo-British relations, the stricken Liberal Government acquitted itself more successfully, perhaps because it felt its back against the wall and its last credit abroad at stake. A first step towards the diminution of tension towards St Petersburg had already been taken by Lord Salisbury when he appointed Lord Dufferin as Ambassador to the Tsar. But the advent of Gladstone to power and the departure of Lytton from India eased the situation still further. Count Shuvalov, it is true, had in the meantime fallen a victim to an intrigue of his enemies at the Russian Court, and had to the general regret been recalled from the London Embassy. But his successor Prince Lobanov at once established cordial relations with Lord Granville, and was able to convey the Tsar's assurances that "he had nothing more at heart than to see re-established between Russia and England those good relations which only misunderstandings or evil passions could have troubled". Lobanov followed this up by a personal letter, urging "a general entente on Asiatic affairs".[20] Nothing concrete came of this, and a lull followed after the pacification of Afghanistan under Abdur Rahman. But Russia was slowly extending her influence in Southern Turkestan, and early in 1884 occupied Merv, a strategic point which she had more than once disclaimed any desire to possess. There was a certain irony in the parallel advance of Russia in Asia and Britain in Africa, under pressure of events and with a reluctance whose exact proportions no man can measure.

The policy urged upon the British Government by Lord Ripon as Viceroy of India had been directed towards an Anglo-Russian convention defining the frontiers of the Afghan "buffer-state": and Lord Dufferin, who succeeded him at Delhi in the following December, was peculiarly fitted to deal with the situation, having so recently been Ambassador both at St Petersburg and at Constantinople. But unfortunately the boundary commission set up by Russia and Britain was very slow in getting to work, and meanwhile a Russian column under Komarov was allowed to advance towards the disputed territory. The British Cabinet took alarm, and on 4 March the Queen, following the precedent of 1875, sent a direct telegraphic appeal to the Tsar, in the cause of peace. As this produced no effect, the Cabinet on 25 March warned the Russian Ambassador of "the necessary consequences of any design upon Herat, in bringing about a case of war between the two countries":[21] and as Komarov only five days later occupied the oasis of Penjdeh, after an armed skirmish with the Afghans, a conflict seemed imminent. On 27 April Gladstone asked Parliament for a credit of £11,000,000, and in one of the most eloquent and persuasive speeches of his career contrived to accuse Russia of aggression and yet to remain conciliatory and pacific. In the end the dispute was referred to the arbitration of King Christian of Denmark, and only the Jingo press on both sides was left lamenting.

Government policy during this crisis was materially influenced by the menacing attitude of Bismarck. Granville, while defending before the House of Lords an almost indefensible position, had indiscreetly enough alluded to the encouragement given by Bismarck both to Salisbury and to himself to take Egypt. Thus confirmed in his convictions as to the impossible character of British parliamentarism, and embarrassed in his new plans for influencing the Sultan, Bismarck made an angry retort in the Reichstag and categorically denied ever having given such advice.* His true attitude is revealed in an instruction to Count Münster, in which he declares that "all Egyptian matters are only of indirect interest for us, but the Colonial question, for reasons of internal policy, is for us a question of

---

* The denial was repeated more fully in a despatch to Radowitz, his Ambassador to the Porte, who must have been well aware of its falsity. See *Grosse Politik*, IV, No. 761.

life and death".[22] The timorous Münster, in first broaching the Heligoland question a year earlier, had argued to Granville that it was "as good as impossible that Germany and England should ever be at war":[23] and as recently as January 1885 Bismarck himself had publicly challenged "the possibility of once standing in arms against England".[24] But this did not prevent him from sowing trouble between Britain and France, a policy easy enough in view of the reviving chauvinism of French opinion and the vast ambitions and testy temper of the Ferry Cabinet. A serious reverse in Cochin-China led to Ferry's overthrow within a few days of the Penjdeh incident, and for the moment France was absorbed in her own affairs.

Gladstone and Granville regained some of their lost prestige by their firm and skilful handling of the Russian crisis, but nothing could dispel the popular disapproval of their Egyptian policy, and no one was more critical than the Queen herself. Hartington was able to silence her keen protest against the "total reversal of the policy declared two months ago", by showing that Wolseley and Baring, on whom she relied, both held a further expedition to be impossible before the autumn, and did not fear an invasion of Egypt. But henceforth the Government was fighting a losing game, and was itself fully conscious of the fact. On 8 June 1885 it was defeated on the Budget by a passing Tory-Irish alliance, and Lord Salisbury returned to power. A malignant fate seemed to have pursued the Gladstone Cabinet, but it had itself signally failed to rise to the occasion or to translate into practice the admirable theories propounded to the Midlothian electors, or even to remedy those deficiencies in the Near East settlement by denouncing which it had climbed to power five years earlier.

SALISBURY'S SEVEN MONTHS AT THE FOREIGN OFFICE

On returning to office, Salisbury kept the Foreign Office in his own hands. He was extremely critical of his predecessors, whom he accused of achieving the Concert of Europe by "uniting the Continent—against England".[25] Indeed to one of his Ambassadors he expressed the view that "for some time to come England will remain comparatively isolated, and her word will weigh less in Europe than it did 20 years ago".[26] It is interesting therefore to note that one of his first acts was to write privately to Bismarck, regretting the recent cloud upon "the good understanding between the two countries, which we value as of supreme importance".[27] His brilliant but reckless Chancellor of the Exchequer, Lord Randolph Churchill, also looked towards Germany and told Bismarck's son William, "À nous deux, nous pourrions gouverner le monde; mais vous n'avez pas voulu". But the Chancellor heatedly challenged both halves of the statement and treated the incident as confirming his doubts as to any close relations with an unstable parliamentary Government such as the British. "If England had clear and strong aims, and above all the courage to avow them publicly, she could find any alliances she needed: but if to her parliamentary weaknesses she adds indecision and dishonesty, and a disposition to use her Allies with a certain egotistical card-sharping, then every one is on the watch."[28]

Salisbury's position was distinctly precarious: he had to face a permanent minority of nearly 100 in the House of Commons, and the wits spoke mockingly of a "Government of caretakers". On the other hand dissolution was impossible until the new franchise came into operation in the following winter. This was an additional incentive for the Premier to concentrate his attention on the foreign situation. Within two months events occurred in the Near East which might very easily have led to an European war. A bloodless revolution proclaimed the union of "the two Bulgarias" in a single state, without any reference either to the Turkish suzerain or to the signatories of Berlin: and the masterful Bulgarian statesman Stambulov gave Prince Alexander the blunt choice of entering Philippopolis or withdrawing to Darmstadt. The Sultan remained unexpectedly passive, but the Tsar, who had always detested his young cousin of Bulgaria, showed open hostility. Salisbury's first reaction had been "to uphold the treaty". As he wrote to the Queen, "If England now takes the lead in tearing up the arrangement which she forced on Europe seven years ago, her position will not be honourable, and her influence will be much diminished": and he added significantly, "The wish of the Bulgarians *for union* was as wellknown then as it is now".[29] The Queen on her side believed in "defending the cause of liberty as well as that of Europe, against Russian aggression and tyranny".[30] In the Conference of Ambassadors held at Constantinople to consider a solution, Sir William White, acting upon instructions, opposed any too strict adherence to the letter of the Treaty of Berlin, and laid stress on the wishes of the inhabitants as a no less vital element. His attitude rendered unanimity impossible, and the Conference broke down. Meanwhile the incompetent King Milan of Serbia, his mind fixed upon a Balkan Balance of Power, and finding little sympathy among the Powers for his demand of territorial compensation, determined to seek it sword in hand, calculating that the Tsar's sudden withdrawal of his officers from the Bulgarian army would leave it at Serbia's mercy. But the short Serbo-Bulgarian War upset all expectations: and after the Bulgarian victory at Slivnica Milan was only saved from the occupation of Belgrade and the overthrow of his dynasty by the diplomatic intervention of Austria-Hungary. Thanks on the one hand to Kálnoky's defence of Serbia and on the other to Salisbury's clear refusal to sanction "a Turkish campaign of repression",[31] peace was signed at Bucarest on the basis of the *status quo*, and the Sultan consented to recognise Prince Alexander in Eastern Roumelia for a preliminary period of five years. One of Salisbury's last instructions to White ran, "Make it very clearly understood that Turkey must not count on our support unless she agrees with Bulgaria".[32] Meanwhile he was ready to join the other Powers in preventing a parallel demand of Greece for compensation, by a naval blockade of the Piraeus. His own Philhellene feelings, and his recognition that Epirus had as much right to join Greece as Eastern Roumelia to join Bulgaria, were overborne by the knowledge that the Sultan could not give way a second time, and that war between Turkey and Greece would lead to grave international complications.

Meanwhile the Irish crisis pursued its devastating course, and the new elections left the 86 members of the Irish party in control of the balance between 335 Liberals and 249 Conservatives. Salisbury was decisively defeated, and on 1 February 1886 Gladstone resumed office as Premier, resolved to force the issue of Home Rule, even at the risk of splitting his own party and driving it into the wilderness. The Queen was in acute distress, and her appeal for "a coalition of all moderate and intelligent people" fell upon deaf ears. A Coalition being as yet impossible, she was of course bound to accept Gladstone, but she strongly resisted the return of Lord Granville to the Foreign Office or the idea of Lord Kimberley as a possible substitute. "She thinks most of the country and of our Foreign Relations", so she told Salisbury[33] "and of the absolute necessity of having strong and able and safe men to conduct the Government of the Empire": and in saying goodbye she spoke of "the triumphant success of his conduct of foreign affairs, by which he had in seven months raised Great Britain to the position which she ought to hold in the world".[34] She was soon to agree with the verdict of Lord Lytton that Salisbury was "Out and away the greatest foreign Minister we have had in my time".[35]

ROSEBERY AND IDDESLEIGH

Gladstone was "greatly distressed, though not unprepared", and submitted to the elimination of Granville: but there was very general satisfaction at the choice of Lord Rosebery as a compromise and stop-gap candidate. He showed a most tactful deference to the Queen's vast European experience, and assured Salisbury of his intention of "maintaining the continuity of British policy".[36] This was all the easier because both he and Gladstone disapproved of Greece's headstrong action and accepted the joint naval blockade as inevitable. Meanwhile Rosebery shared to the full the Queen's indignation when Russia, following the example which she herself had set in 1870 by repudiating the Black Sea clauses of the Treaty of Paris, now repudiated the clause of the Treaty of Berlin which made of Batum a purely commercial port. "As an act of insolent perfidy it stands almost alone", so he assured the Queen. But he was not in a position to translate words into action, for the Irish crisis had now reached its height: on 8 June the Government was defeated over Gladstone's revised Home Rule proposals, the breach with Hartington, Chamberlain, Goschen and others became irreparable, and early in August 1886 Salisbury was again Prime Minister, after in vain urging Hartington to accept precedence. The long years of "Resolute Government" were at hand.

This time Lord Salisbury assigned the Foreign Office to Stafford Northcote, who had been made Earl of Iddesleigh when it was clear that his health was no longer equal to the strain of leadership in the Commons. The Queen was distinctly nervous, for though she admired Iddesleigh's lovable and conciliatory character, she doubted whether he possessed either the firmness or the knowledge to cope with the constantly recurring squalls through which the ship of Europe was passing, and more of which were already visible on the horizon. On 21 August Prince Alexander of Bulgaria was suddenly kidnapped in his palace by malcontent officers inspired by Russia, and conveyed across the frontier. He was brought back in triumph by Stambulov, but was unwise enough to telegraph to the Tsar, offering to surrender the crown which Russia had given him: and to the general consternation the vindictive Alexander III took him at his word. Bismarck, to whom it was a matter of complete indifference who occupied a Balkan throne, took the side of Russia and would even have accepted a Russian protectorate over Turkey. But Austria-Hungary and Britain strongly espoused the Bulgarian cause. The British Cabinet, it is true, was somewhat divided on the question, Lord Randolph Churchill urging complete *désintéressement* in the Balkans: and no one went so far as the Queen (who wrote to poor "Sandro" of Bulgaria about his "barbaric, Asiatic, tyrannical cousin" the Tsar).[37] But Salisbury admitted the Prince to be "the guardian of European peace",[38] and in his Guildhall speech in November made very outspoken reference to "traitors debauched by foreign gold". When the Russian Ambassador protested, Iddesleigh feebly argued that the effects of foreign gold in Ireland had often enough been denounced, without causing offence to the United States Government![39] Meanwhile the vacant Bulgarian throne was hawked round Europe and repeatedly declined: but the Regents stood firm in their defiance of Russia.

SALISBURY, BISMARCK AND THE MEDITERRANEAN AGREEMENTS

While Europe was full of rumours of war, Iddesleigh died suddenly of heart failure at No. 10 Downing Street (12 January 1887), and Salisbury decided to retain Foreign Affairs in his own hands. Thus the next six years may be said to represent his diplomatic zenith. His daughter, in her brilliant and discerning biography, does well to contradict the still widely current theory that he believed in "splendid isolation", or put it into practice. It is not too much to say that his whole natural bent and sympathies lay with France rather than with any other country: it was there that he made his second home and found his main relaxations. But blended with this and with a deep, almost physical, reserve which he threw to the winds on certain rare occasions, there was a cautious realism which accepted facts, however unpleasant, and never allowed policy to follow inclination. Hence on his return to the Foreign Office, he found it necessary to reckon with France in one of her most petulant and incalculable moods, striving to make good a consciousness of failure in Europe by the rapid development of a new colonial empire, and yet suddenly turning longing backward looks towards the Rhine, and strangely attracted by the theatrical figure of General Boulanger, and of the more reputable but scarcely less unbalanced Déroulède or Barrès. He had to reckon with the possibility of a Franco-German war at a moment when he suspected Russia of planning a most dangerous aggression in the Near East:* and he did not conceal from the Queen his view that Britain "torn in two by a controversy which almost threatens her existence, cannot in the present state of public opinion interfere with any decisive action abroad. . . We have absolutely no power to restrain either France or Germany, while all the power we have will be needed to defend our influence in the South East of Europe"[40] He was, moreover, only too well aware that "when war has once broken out" in Europe, "we cannot be secure from the danger of being involved in it": and his realism led him to the further point of recognising the possibility of continental rivals—"if England was left out in isolation"—"treating the English Empire as divisible booty, by which their differences might be adjusted", in which case, "though England could defend herself, it would be at fearful risk and cost".[41] If, then, the former friendship with France could not be re-established, it seemed necessary to come to some terms with Germany, the Power whose attitude and armed resources at that

* His attitude is revealed in a letter of 20 July 1887 to Lord Lyons, where, after a list of six points on which the French were making difficulties, he added the phrase, "Can you wonder that there is, to my eyes, a silver lining even to the great black cloud of the Franco-German war?" (Newton, *Lord Lyons*, p. 549.)

moment exercised the chief restraining influence upon the Chauvinists of Paris: and the motives for such an understanding were multiplied by the circumstances of Germany's alliance with Austria-Hungary, Italy, and the Balkan satellites.

The astute Bismark was fully aware of Salisbury's dilemma, and spared no pains to draw Britain into the orbit of the Central Powers, thereby killing two birds with one stone, since he was raising the value of a renewal of the Triple Alliance in the eyes of both Vienna and Rome. Already on 12 February a secret Convention was concluded between Britain and Italy, by which the two Powers undertook to uphold the *status quo* in the Mediterranean, Adriatic, Aegean and Black Seas, while Italy accepted the British position in Egypt and Britain bound herself to the support of Italy in the event of "encroachments" in North Africa by another Power which, though not named, could only be France.[42] In signing such a document the British Government gave to Italy "the widest guarantee which any parliamentary state could give, namely, that in the event of a Franco-German War England would actively join that group of states which forms the peace police in the East. No English Government can give an absolute guarantee for military or naval co-operation in a future conflict, simply because it is not certain whether Parliament will fulfil those promises. But so far as Lord Salisbury can judge he is convinced that England, jointly with Austria and Italy, will make front against Russia, if Turkey and especially Constantinople should be threatened. He thinks he can assume the same, but less certainly, if Austria is attacked by Russia, without touching Turkey. In this case it would be hard for England to give effective support."[43] This document should finally dispel the legend of Salisbury's belief in isolation, and it is confirmed by his private correspondence with the Queen, from which it transpires that he had made it quite clear to Count Corti that "England never promised material assistance in view of an uncertain war, of which the object and cause were unknown", and again, that there never could be any question of Britain taking part in an agressive war against France.[44]

Austria-Hungary speedily announced her adherence to the Mediterranean Agreement, and later in the year it was rendered still more precise by a triangular agreement between London, Vienna and Rome, for the maintenance of the *status quo* in the Near East, and for joint action to prevent any cession of territory by Turkey, even to the point of provisional occupation of Turkish territory.[45] Meanwhile Spain had entered into a special agreement with Italy to maintain the Mediterranean *status quo*, and not to lend herself to any action aimed against Italy, Germany and Austria-Hungary.[46]

At this stage Bismarck, who from the background had never ceased to encourage the three Mediterranean participants, addressed himself directly to Salisbury, and after laying great stress upon the defensive character of German armed power and on the impossibility of any change upon the Imperial throne deflecting the fundamental lines of German policy, reached the conclusion that France and Russia were the two unstable elements in Europe, and that Germany would always be obliged to take action, "either if the independence of Austria-Hungary were threatened by Russian aggression, or if England or Italy were in danger of being set upon by French armies".[47] Salisbury in his reply went boldly to the root of the matter by considering the contingency of a Franco-German war. In that event he credited Russia with a seizure of the Straits, a step from which Britain and Italy alone "would not be sufficient to deter her", and "all would depend, therefore, on the attitude of Austria", who without German help could hardly risk war with Russia. His closing phrase ran, "The grouping of states which has been the work of the last year will be an effective barrier against any possible aggression of Russia, and the construction of it will not be among the least services which Your Highness has rendered to the cause of European peace."[48]

Salisbury was clearly reassured by this correspondence, following as it did upon Bismarck's revelation of the secret clause of the first Austro-German Treaty of 1879: for he had drawn from it the conclusion that "Germany *must* take the side of Austria in any war between Austria and Russia".[49] Needless to say, however, he—and with him all the world, including the Government of Vienna—was kept in ignorance of the secret "Reinsurance Treaty" which Bismarck on 18 June 1887 had signed with Russia. Bismarck, it is true, never admitted the charge of perfidy afterwards levelled against him, and definitely wished that the Tsar should reveal the Treaty to Francis Joseph. But it remains the crowning example of Bismarck's uncanny skill in juggling with four or five conflicting forces, and could not permanently have been kept up by any successor of lesser calibre. It would at any rate seem probable that Bismarck had finally disabused himself of his former suspicions towards Salisbury, whom he had described to St Vallier at the Congress of Berlin as "ce clergyman laïque obstiné et maladroit".[50]

It is thoroughly characteristic of Bismarck that no sooner had he secured the renewal of the Triple Alliance and reinforced it by the Mediterranean Agreements, than he once more proceeded to woo Russia, as he had done after concluding the Austrian Alliance in 1879. As ever, the key to his policy was his "permanent dread" of an Austro-Russian war, in which he would have to choose between his two allies and to risk the actual collapse of one of them.[51] In the words of Dr Gooch, "from the crisis which broke up the Dreikaiserbund and brought Austria and Russia to the brink of war, the Chancellor's genius extracted securities for the Empire he had founded, purchasing the assurance of Russian neutrality in a war provoked by France, by a promise of German neutrality in a war provoked by Austria".[52] The long-drawn Bulgarian crisis enabled him to court Russia more openly than ever before. While all Bulgaria rallied behind the Regents in their resistance to Russian dictation, and after no less than eighteen unsuccessful offers of the Crown at last secured the acceptance of Prince Ferdinand of Coburg (a young cousin of Queen Victoria* and a grandson of Louis Philippe), Bismarck pressed his Russophil orientation to the length of imposing a veto on the marriage of ex-Prince Alexander with the German Crown Prince and Princess's favourite daughter Victoria, lest this should trouble Russo-German relations. In his Reichstag speech of 11 January 1887 he quoted, "'What's Hecuba to him?' What's Bulgaria to us?" The friendship of Russia was of far greater value, and above all else peace must be kept between Russia and Austria-Hungary. A year later, in the same place (6 February 1888), he balanced his absolute trust in the Tsar's word against the danger of coalitions, and declared, "Think of Austria off the map, and we are isolated, with Italy, between Russia and France. We cannot think Austria away." It was on this occasion that he closed with the memorable words, "We Germans fear God and nothing else in the world." To Frederick III on his deathbed he insisted that the "focussing point" of German policy lay in Russia and in preserving the personal friendship of Alexander III.[53]

WILLIAM II AND BRITAIN

The deaths of William I, and three months later of his chivalrous son Frederick (March–June 1888), created a new situation, political no less than dynastic. From the very first there was a latent conflict between the veteran Chancellor and the impulsive and headstrong young sovereign William II, who demonstratively paid his first state visit to St Petersburg, and yet was always turning to the magnetic influence that called him from his mother's country. His grandfather's legacy was a whispered appeal to remain always friendly with Russia, but the Germanophobe Alexander III disliked his cousin William alike for his nationality and his temperament, and William in the first decade of his reign showed a marked preference for Britain. From this time, then, dates Bismarck's final overture to London, in a more concrete form than ever before. In January 1889 Hatzfeldt was

* For her opinion on the relative value of Alexander and Ferdinand, see *Letters*, 3rd Series, I, 259, 348, 351.

instructed to convey to Lord Salisbury the Chancellor's belief that peace could best be secured by an Anglo-German defensive alliance against France, and its public adoption in the two Parliaments.[54] Salisbury received the proposal most cordially, but after due reflection hinted that "we unfortunately no longer live in Pitt's times, when the aristocracy ruled and we could conduct an active policy....Now the democracy rules, and with it has come personal and party government, which has made every English Government absolutely dependent on the *aura popularis*. This generation can only be taught by events." His conclusion was that the plan could only be "left on the table, without saying yes or no".[55] There is no direct evidence as to Salisbury's views, but it certainly seems probable that the democratic difficulties which he raised were merely a polite device for evading an embarrassing offer. He disliked, and would fain have avoided, the constant petty disputes with France in both hemispheres—in Newfoundland, Somaliland and the South Seas: he was not ready to quarrel with France over Egypt, and saw that this would not in any way have distressed Bismarck. He even confided to Drummond Wolff, whom he sent on a special mission to Cairo, his "hearty wish we had never gone into Egypt". But once more his sense of realism drove him to recognise that "for the present the enemy is France",[56] and that popular feeling was much roused against that country. On the other hand he had no belief whatsoever in "that spirit of haughty and sullen isolation which has been dignified by the name of 'non-intervention'". On the contrary, he recognised that "we are part of the community of Europe, and we must do our duty as such".[57] And so he continued upon the line which seemed to him least perilous, that of co-operation with Germany.

From the very first day the change on the German throne cast its shadow on the future. The tragic controversy about the accession of a dying Emperor and the divergent opinions of English and German specialists had already created an electric atmosphere in Berlin. Following on this and on the dispute about "Sandro's" marriage, the more than unchivalrous treatment of the Empress Frederick by her son and by the two Bismarcks, while her husband still lay unburied in Potsdam, was keenly resented by the Prince of Wales: and William II soon took his revenge by compelling the embarrassed Francis Joseph to exclude the Prince from the official reception offered in Vienna to the new German Emperor. Reasons of state, urged by Salisbury and by Queen Victoria, who alone could exercise some authority over her wayward grandson, led the Prince to waive his right to any apology: and from 1889 onwards the visits of William II to Osborne and Cowes were constant, and seemed to suggest a real attachment to England, or what his own subjects called Anglomania. Certainly he was delighted at being made a British Admiral and honorary Colonel of "The Royals", and more than once urged London to convert the Mediterranean Agreement into a regular Quadruple Alliance. For this neither Salisbury nor his Germanophil successor Rosebery could be won: and the fall of Bismarck in March 1890[58] only increased Salisbury's reserve. For though he had always felt the Iron Chancellor to be ruthless and unscrupulous, he had also known him to be worthy of his foeman's steel, immensely experienced and resourceful, and in his own peculiar way very sincerely desirous both of European peace and good relations with Britain. On the other hand, with all the cautious reticence then necessary towards so close a relative of Queen Victoria, Salisbury never trusted William II, knowing him to be both false and unstable, and, despite his great lineage, in essence a cad and a bully. "He has no doubts," Bismarck had truly said of him, "he thinks he can do all things, and he wishes to have the entire credit all to himself."[59] His advisers were from the first men of lesser calibre—the straightforward but uninformed Caprivi, the honourable but somewhat effaced Hohenlohe, and already in the background the sinister Holstein, and Bülow, specious but ever perfidious. A phrase uttered by the Premier to Chamberlain in 1891 speaks volumes for his state of mind. Alluding to the impending departure of the Emperor from one of his visits to Cowes, Salisbury told the Colonial Secretary that he would gladly discuss colonial questions with him, "when this tyranny is overpast".[60]

HELIGOLAND AND ZANZIBAR

There was, however, one direction in which Salisbury saw his way to concessions in favour of Germany, namely in the colonial field. A proposal vaguely aired by Bismarck to Granville in 1884, and taken up again in 1889 in a more concrete form by Joseph Chamberlain,* now rapidly ripened into an Anglo-German Convention, by which Uganda and Zanzibar were transferred to the British sphere of influence, in return for Germany's access to the Zambesi river by the so-called "Caprivi Tail" (or *Zipfel*), and above all for the little North Sea island of Heligoland, which had been in British hands since 1814. This transaction is a classic instance of the inability, even on the part of the most farsighted and experienced statesmen, to read the political or strategic secrets of a none too distant future. The increased value of Heligoland to Germany after the completion of the Kiel

* In conversation with Herbert Bismarck on 27 March 1887 he appears to have used the phrase *sine Germania nulla salus*, and to have offered Heligoland, "which is useless for England and perhaps worth having for you, were it but for the prestige" (*G.P.* IV, No. 946).

Canal (already begun in 1887) seems to have been less apparent than the possibility of a French naval attack upon it after it had passed into German hands! Indeed the explorer Stanley, with his eyes fixed upon equatorial Africa, seems to have voiced the general opinion when he spoke of exchanging a trouser button for a suit of clothes.

The main objection of the Queen lay in another direction. She regretted that the people of the island had been handed over "to an unscrupulous despotic Government like the German" without first being consulted. But she was above all anxious that no precedent should be created for this cession of territory: "the next thing will be to propose to give up Gibraltar, and soon nothing will be secure".[61] Salisbury defended his decision to the Queen by arguing that "any indefinite postponement of a settlement in Africa would render it very difficult to maintain terms of amity with Germany, and would force us to change our system of alliances in Europe", and this, he added, would "necessarily involve the early evacuation of Egypt".[62] This seems to have satisfied the Queen, but she was far from pleased at another notable precedent created by Salisbury's insistence upon making the cession of Heligoland dependent upon the approval of Parliament. There can be no doubt that this was a restriction of the constitutional rights of the Crown, which had in the eighteenth century been assumed to be competent to cede Minorca, Florida and even the American colonies, without statutory sanction. By a strange irony it was Gladstone, as leader of the Opposition, who constituted himself advocate of the earlier tradition, and spoke of "our long, uniform and unbroken course of practice". There was, he argued, no kind of territory—whether colonies acquired by conquest or by settlement, with or without representative institutions—for which "you cannot show cases of cession by the Crown without the authority of Parliament".[63] In the end, however, the common sense of Salisbury had its way, and the precedent thus created was followed in the case of the Anglo-French Convention of 1904, and since the Great War has become the invariable practice in questions of treaty-making. Meanwhile the Emperor was full of enthusiasm that "without a battle, without the shedding of a tear, this beautiful island has passed into my possession": and soon after Caprivi, in the Reichstag, endorsed his master's dictum that Heligoland, "was the last piece of German soil that we coveted. We have got it, and we covet nothing more."

Almost simultaneously with the German Convention a similar settlement was reached with France, who recognised Britain's position in Zanzibar and in Nigeria, in return for a recognition of her own position in Madagascar. The partition of Africa between the European Powers had thus reached an advanced stage, and there now remained a bare decade in which the efforts of rival imperialisms seemed to be converging upon the upper reaches of the Nile, where the Khalifa's tyranny had succeeded that of the Mahdi, and where it was obvious that all frontiers were in an entirely fluid state.

THE "FRANCO-RUSSE"

The fall of Bismarck was followed by William II's momentous decision to allow the lapse of the "Reinsurance Treaty" with Russia, then due for renewal. Caprivi denied that "the wire to St Petersburg had been cut: on the contrary, every care had been taken to preserve it". None the less a new phase had opened in Russo-German relations, deplored by William's veteran Ambassador Schweinitz, and still regarded to-day by many high German authorities as the root and origin of all Germany's subsequent misfortunes.* Whatever may be thought of this view, it is clear that the abandonment of the Treaty, coupled with William's exuberant enthusiasm at the agreement with Britain, with his evasive attitude at the meeting with the Tsar and Giers, and with his open overtures to Vienna, served to underline Russia's growing isolation in Europe, and positively encouraged the uneasy Tsar to look for a new ally. This tendency was confirmed by Staal's reports from London, attaching undue importance to the Anglo-German *rapprochement*. This situation was naturally enough exploited by the French, who felt their reviving strength, but also the impossibility of resisting a combination of the Triple Alliance with Britain. A badly staged visit of the Empress Frederick to Paris early in 1891, intended by her son to improve Franco-German relations, had the opposite effect, and led to demonstrations and fierce press polemics. Russian statesmen saw in this their opportunity, the Tsar was induced to send a high order to President Carnot, and the French Government at once put an indiscreet question as to Russia's attitude in a Franco-German war.[64] Giers was not prepared to go beyond the private assurance that "while the Triple Alliance ruins itself in armaments, the intimate accord of our two countries is needed to maintain in Europe a just equilibrium of forces".† But the British naval visit to the Adriatic, the state visit of William II to London, and his Guildhall speech, and above all the renewal of the Triple Alliance, seemed to confirm the worst fears of France and Russia. A visit of the French Fleet to Cronstadt was therefore

* The theory that Germany should at all costs have upheld the Russian alliance and never tied herself to Austria-Hungary is worked out by Prince Lichnowsky (Ambassador in London in 1914) in his essay "Die Wurzeln der Katastrophe" (*Auf dem Wege zum Abgrund*, I, 166–209).

† Professor Langer, in treating "the ill-fated *flirt anglo-triplicien*" as giving the impetus to the Franco-Russian Entente, relies very much upon the Diaries of Count Lamsdorff, first published in 1934 (in Russian). He makes out a convincing case.

arranged, and festivities of the most demonstrative kind were prolonged for a whole fortnight. In the words of a recent historian, the figure of Alexander III standing bareheaded to the salute, while the battle-hymn of the "infidel Republic" was played, has a historical symbolism comparable with Henry IV's admission that "Paris is worth a mass".[65] The document signed between France and Russia on 27 August 1891 was still of a very vague character, merely pledging them to "concert measures" if peace should be in danger: but the name of "Entente Cordiale" was already accepted, and henceforth events moved inexorably in the direction of diplomatic co-operation and French financial support for Russia. Despite the combined logic and impatience of the French, which was increased by the renewed friction between Paris and London, nearly eighteen months passed before the Tsar and his ailing Foreign Minister could be induced to take a further step in the direction of alliance. At last in October 1893 a Russian squadron met with a delirious welcome at Toulon, and on 4 January 1894 a Franco-Russian military convention came into force, pledging the two countries to immediate mutual support in the event of an attack by Germany or Italy on France, or by Germany or Austria-Hungary on Russia. "The forces to be employed against Germany" were to be 1,300,000 French and 7–800,000 Russians: the two staffs were to co-operate, and the agreement was to have the same duration as the Triple Alliance. While these terms remained a closely guarded secret till after the downfall of Tsardom, the fact that an alliance had been concluded was openly proclaimed in January 1895, by Ribot as French Premier. William II, in his correspondence with the new Tsar, Nicholas II, affected to be in no way disturbed by what had happened, but urged him to "keep those damned rascals [the French] in order", and to beware of the revolutionary infection exhaled by all Republics.[66] But there can be little or no doubt that the determining factor which set official Russia in motion was not reviving sympathy for France, but simply and solely distrust of Germany under her theatrical and incalculable ruler. For France, on the other hand, it was a welcome sign that she was again capable of throwing her full weight into the European scales and was no longer alone in case of a German attack. For the world at large it was the writing on the wall, which none would read, a warning that Europe was gradually falling into two armed camps, more or less equally balanced. In such a situation the attitude of Britain became one of capital importance, for her definite adherence to one side or the other was certain to deflect the balance. For the next decade she was to remain full of hesitation as to how she should use what Mr Spender has called her casting vote.

THE ROSEBERY INTERLUDE

The dissolution of 1892 brought the Liberals back to power, but without the strong majority needed to convert a Home Rule measure into law. Gladstone, now eighty-two and rapidly failing, was dependent upon the Irish vote, and it soon became evident that the mass of opinion in *England*, as opposed to the so-called "Celtic fringe", was still unconverted and unrepentant. "You have attached yourself to a corpse", Gladstone told an ardent supporter.[67]

As in 1885, the Queen pressed for continuity of foreign policy, and this time the Prince of Wales addressed a personal appeal to Lord Rosebery to accept the Foreign Office.[68] Though the Government to which he belonged was by no means a strong one, he certainly upheld British prestige in every part of the world. The post was none of his ardent seeking, and indeed when less than two years later Gladstone found it necessary to resign the Premiership, Rosebery made it clear that he did not want the succession, though if he became Prime Minister he "must be a real one".[69] The Queen for her part hoped that he would "act as a check and a drag upon his Cabinet", and he found himself in the uncomfortable position of damping down policy on matters to which he had pledged himself under his late chief, and indeed virtually waiting for the defeat that always follows inaction. Abroad he leant towards Germany rather than France: and though he became involved in certain difficulties with Berlin over the agreement with the Congo Free State, he on the whole took the line that "planting a flag here and there or demarcating regions with a red line on a map are vain diversions".[70]

His relations with France were determined by the necessities of the Egyptian situation. While a section of the Cabinet was against "a strong Egyptian policy", he himself feared an eruption there, but held that "while we hold Egypt, both Constantinople and India are safe".[71] The main trouble was due to the Anglophobia of the new Khedive, to the undoubted desire of the Sultan to recover his lost hold upon Cairo, and to the persistence with which the French hinted at evacuation. Yet throughout the 'nineties it was patently impossible to withdraw from Egypt without exposing it to instant attack from the fanatic who held the Sudan in his grip: and this was so obvious that London was forced to impute to Paris the desire to take its place in Egypt. But it was not till well after the return of Salisbury to power that London really faced the necessity of a Sudan expedition: and what finally turned the scale in its favour was probably the disastrous defeat suffered by the Italians in Abyssinia early in 1896.

Meanwhile Franco-British rivalry had spread to South-Eastern Asia. During the 'eighties the French, undeterred by occasional military reverses, were pushing steadily forward in Indo-China, while the British annexed

Upper Burma and tried, in the words of Lord Salisbury, "to obtain access to the markets of China from behind".[72] The conception of Siam as an independent buffer state between the British and French possessions was soon in danger, and early in 1893 the frontier disputes between France and Siam led to open hostilities. Rosebery, fearing that Siam might share the fate of Annam, took a strong line diplomatically and kept British troops in readiness for action. In the end the quarrel was patched up, thanks in part to the outbreak of the Sino-Japanese War and the necessity in which China found herself of making concessions to the French on the other side of Indo-China. But the relations between Paris and London had suffered a further strain, and the Anglophobes who controlled the Quai d'Orsay in the 'nineties were all the less disposed to a policy of moderation in Central Africa. Fashoda was in a sense bred on the Mekong river.

It should be noted in passing that the mistaken estimates drawn by Germany from this incident contributed materially to the Emperor's attitude in the decisive years that were approaching. William was at Cowes when the Siamese question became acute, at the end of July 1893. He and Hatzfeldt were entitled to reckon with the possibility of a Franco-British war, and Caprivi's comment was, "For us the most desirable opening of the next big war is if the first shot should come from an English ship. We are then certain of being able to enlarge the Triple into a Quadruple Alliance."[73] Hatzfeldt calculated that in case of need Rosebery would invite Italian help against France and so come closer to the Dreibund, and that he could convince Gladstone of the "political necessity" of such action.[74] He assured Sir Philip Currie that internal political sympathies played no part with the German Government, and that its reserve would vanish if it had "the certainty that Lord Rosebery had a decisive influence on foreign policy and was not always subject to the intervention of his colleagues at the decisive moment".[75] Baron Marschall, then German Foreign Minister, was not disposed to give a "*de but en blanc* promise that Germany would not allow a French attack upon England"—to formulate the question in this way is in itself a revelation of mentality—and held that Rosebery had not proved "either the power or the will to go his own way".[76] He might have thought otherwise if he had seen Rosebery's letter of 14 June 1894 to the Queen, asking her to convey to her grandson a discreet warning that "Germany is playing an extremely dangerous game". He had told the Austrian Ambassador—in the hope that it would reach Berlin via Vienna—that "if Germany were going to side with France in African questions, we must reconsider our position as regards our general attitude in Europe, most particularly in the Mediterranean and in the East".[77]

During his brief tenure of the Premiership Lord Rosebery relinquished the Foreign Office to Lord Kimberley, and between them two decisions were taken which were destined to have important consequences. On the one hand the Anglo-Congolese Treaty of May 1894 evoked the open opposition of the French Chamber and of the Anglophobe Foreign Minister Hanotaux, but also a protest from the German Government against the lease to Britain of a strip of Tanganyika Territory. London consented to cancel the Treaty, but while not surprised at the captious attitude of France, took note of Germany's increasing hostility towards British policy in Africa, which was so soon to flare up in connection with the Boer Republics. Just as the Russophil Gladstone had failed to achieve real friendship with Russia in the 'eighties, so the Germanophil Rosebery witnessed a slow deterioration of Anglo-German relations during his term of office.

On the other hand in 1895, when Japan had imposed upon a beaten China the Treaty of Shimonoseki, Lord Kimberley definitely declined to associate Britain with Russia, France and Germany in their action to rob the new Asiatic Great Power of "the fruit of her victories". Here again it was Germany, under the shortsighted and braggart leadership of William II,* who took a specially strong line against Japan and the alleged "Yellow Peril", while Britain had already been the first Great Power to admit Japan to recognition as an equal, and to sign a treaty abrogating her extra-territorial rights and making economic concessions. These events were to bear memorable fruit both for Britain and for Germany—for the one in the Japanese alliance, for the other in a declaration of war couched nineteen years later in the very words of 1895.

SALISBURY AND THE WRONG HORSE

During Rosebery's last year of office relations with Turkey, already strained owing to the situation in Egypt,† grew still worse, when the news of an Armenian rising in Asia Minor, followed by wholesale massacres on a more than Bulgarian scale, reached England, and public opinion pressed for intervention. Lord Kimberley ordered Sir Philip Currie to protest at the Porte, and the consular enquiry that followed revealed, in Rosebery's own words, "not merely massacres, but horrors unutterable, unspeakable, unimaginable by the mind of man".[78] Turkey evaded all real reform, and neither France nor Russia showed any disposition for joint action.

Such was the situation which Salisbury found on his return to power. He

---

* In July 1895 William gave as one of his motives, "One must try to nail Russia to East Asia, so that she can concern herself less with Europe and the European East" (cit. Brandenburg, *Von Bismarck bis zum Weltkrieg*, p. 87).

† On 16 June 1893 Rosebery had written to the Queen of "the Sultan, if possible more unfriendly than before" (*Letters*, II, 260).

had never had many illusions as to Turkish methods, and now he lost no time in warning the Turkish Ambassador that Turkey was losing ground in British opinion, and that "a settled conviction was growing" that there was no hope of reform, "and that all that could be done was to finish with it".[79] Within a month, in conversations with Count Hatzfeldt, he was speaking of Turkey as "trop pourrie" to survive. He did not desire her break-up, but he could not shut his eyes to approaching events: and he volunteered the remark that Britain had been wrong in refusing the famous partition over-ture of Nicholas to Sir Hamilton Seymour (see *supra*, p. 305). The ever distrustful Holstein assumed that Salisbury's aim was "to ease England's uncomfortable position in Egypt towards France and Russia, by creating complications in Asia Minor and the Balkans": but Hatzfeldt disproved this by quoting Salisbury's readiness to give Tripoli, Tunis and most of Morocco to Italy, Salonica to Austria, and "most ample satisfaction" to Russia—perhaps even "Constantinople, avec tout ce qui s'ensuit", and access to the Mediterranean.[80] A few days later Salisbury aired these same views at Cowes to the Emperor, who made little of the Armenian massacres, insisted on the improvement in Turkey and would not hear of its dis-memberment. The incident was much less sensational, and also less clear-cut, than has often been alleged:[81] but there can be no doubt that it in-creased the growing distrust on both sides.* Ten days later Salisbury publicly warned the Sultan that Europe's patience was failing, and that "no treaties and no sympathy" would save his Empire from ruin if he con-tinued to disregard the advice of the Powers. But so far from this helping, it was followed late in September by fresh massacres throughout Armenia. Russia, encouraged by Germany, gave her backing to the Sultan, Count Goluchowski's proposal for joint naval action off the Golden Horn was in its turn rejected by his German ally, and despite the fulminations of Gladstone, William Watson and the Nonconformist leaders against "Abdul the Damned", Salisbury and Rosebery were in agreement that "isolated action means a European War". The crowning infamy came in August 1896, when for two days the Armenians of Constantinople itself were massacred wholesale under the eyes of the police. Salisbury was brought to the tardy acknowledgment that in backing Turkey, Britain "had put her money on the wrong horse": but this only served to em-phasise our impotence in the Near East, or at least our unwillingness to risk war. And once more it was the fickle William II who extracted the main profit: his condonation of the massacres was followed in 1897 by strong

---

* On 31 October 1891 Holstein, in conversation with Valentine Chirol, reverted to this incident, and stated that the view of the Emperor and his Government at that moment had been that Turkish partition would have meant an European war (*G.P.*, XVII, No. 5026).

support of Turkey in her war with Greece and in her resistance to Cretan autonomy, and in 1898 by his pilgrimage to Jerusalem, his theatrical appeal at Damascus to the Moslem world, and his state visit to the pariah Sultan at Yildiz Kiosk. By the turn of the century British influence at the Porte was negligible, while German predominance, already entrenched by the military mission under Kolmar von der Goltz Pasha, found its economic expression in railway concessions in Asia Minor, the germ of "Berlin-Bagdad".

The interconnection between the Near East, Far East and South Africa is not obvious at first sight, but becomes very clear on reflection. Germany had at first been alarmed at the Dual Alliance, which her abandonment of Bismarckian tactics had rendered possible: but then, seeing the anti-British trend of French and Russian policy, set herself to accentuate this still further. After Shimonoseki Britain found herself in a position of isolation which, thanks to her new friendship with Japan, was less dangerous in the Far East than her rivals fancied, but which in Europe and Africa was distinctly disquieting. The Emperor's double aim, first in the Far East, then in the Near East, had been by isolating Britain to force her finally into the orbit of the Triple Alliance: and having achieved the first, but failed in the second, he now turned to a new field of action in South Africa.

GERMANY AND THE JAMESON RAID

During 1895 the long-drawn conflict of interest between Britain and the two Boer Republics came rapidly to a head. Our account of it must of course be strictly confined to its reactions upon European policy.

It was in many ways a tragedy that the two farmer republics could not be spared the inroad of industrialism and high finance, but once the situation had been transformed by the discovery and development of the gold mines round Johannesburg,* there was in the end no real alternative between excluding or expelling the Uitlanders from whom the main revenues of the state were derived, and granting them some approach, however modest, to representative government. Yet President Krüger was resolutely opposed to both alternatives, and in his efforts to stem the in-rushing tide, turned for help to any foreign Power that would afford it. The first public sign of German activities in the Transvaal was Krüger's speech in honour of the Emperor's birthday on 27 January 1895. Rhodes, who was in London at the time, was alarmed for his dream of South African federation, and viewed with suspicion the introduction of a new foreign element into South African affairs. In June German ships were sent to Delagoa Bay, whence the newly opened railway ran to Pretoria. When Sir Edward Malet left the Berlin

---

* "Montecarlo superimposed upon Sodom and Gomorrah," said a Cape politician to Sir W. Butler (Butler, *Autobiography*, p. 415).

Embassy, he spoke to the Foreign Minister, Baron Marschall, of the Transvaal as "the black spot" in Anglo-German relations, which might lead to "serious complications". William II took great offence at this and rated our Military Attaché, Colonel Swaine, ending with the threat that if England continued to "insult and fool" the Dreibund as she had for the past seven years, he would be "simply forced to make common cause with France and Russia". Britain, he concluded, could only escape from her isolation by "coming out unreservedly and openly on the side of the Triple Alliance or against it", and the former meant giving "sealed and signed guarantees".[82] This was indeed letting the cat out of the bag. Britain was to be browbeaten into the central alliance, and meanwhile, in one of his revealing *marginalia*, the Kaiser noted, "we must make great capital out of this story, also for possible naval demands to protect our growing trade".[83]

Salisbury at once disavowed Malet, but was otherwise evasive. His caution was doubtless partly due to the difficult situation which he saw arising in connection with the Venezuelan frontier dispute and President Cleveland's unmeasured application of the Monroe doctrine. There can be little doubt that the excitement and friction following on the President's message to Congress on 17 December was an incentive to German action in South Africa and elsewhere: for if Britain should be involved in war with America, her isolation would indeed be alarming.

The long expected explosion in South Africa took the form of the discreditable Jameson Raid, which was launched on 29 December 1895 with the full collusion of Cecil Rhodes, but ended in complete fiasco on 2 January 1896. While the issue was still pending, Baron Marschall laid it down that Germany could not accept the annexation of the Transvaal, and told the new Ambassador Lascelles that Berlin had warned London "repeatedly for two years past" of the danger, but without any clear response.[84] Though Salisbury at once repudiated the Raid on behalf of himself and of Chamberlain, and notified this to Berlin both through Hatzfeldt and through Lascelles, a German Note of protest was sent to Hatzfeldt for formal presentation. The news of Jameson's failure, however, led to a change of tactics: and Hatzfeldt, acting on telegraphic orders, had still time to recover the Note unopened from the Foreign Office, thereby doubtless averting grave diplomatic trouble. But none the less on 3 January the German Government officially suggested to President Krüger the idea of a Conference to regulate the international status of the Transvaal, though of course perfectly aware that the London Cabinet would regard this as an infringement of its suzerain rights. Not content with this, it sent in the Emperor's name a telegram of congratulation to President Krüger on his successful vindication of independence "without appealing to the aid of friendly

Powers".* Some idea of the extent of William II's perfidy may be gathered from the fact that almost simultaneously he informed the Tsar that he had used "very severe language" in London, and had "opened communications with Paris for common defence of our endangered interests".[85] He also saw Dr Leyds, Krüger's Secretary of State, spoke of German military help and added that "if Lorenzo Marquez ever changed owner, it could only come into German or Boer hands".[86] At a conference with his civil, military and naval advisers he was prepared to contemplate war with England, and was only gradually restrained,[87] on being assured that a land war in Africa would involve a naval war in Europe also. He seems to have been influenced by his animus against "Uncle Bertie", whom he accused of being implicated in the Raid, with his friends Beit and Cassel.

The intense, and indeed excessive, anger of the British press was probably compounded of several quite different sentiments—disappointment at the attitude of a sovereign who had hitherto passed, largely owing to his own public utterances, as pronouncedly Anglophil: annoyance at the sudden burst of Anglophobia in the German press and Parliament, and not least, resentment at Germany taking advantage of a moment when Britain's hands were tied by the dispute with America. Behind all this of course was keen sympathy for the Uitlanders, based partly on tendencious exaggerations, and also the consciousness that in the words of Chamberlain, "the Raid has placed Britain in a false position"[88] before the whole world, and made it almost equally impossible to protest against Boer armaments or to champion the helots of Johannesburg. "The Transvaal situation was a sore spot, and the meddling of outsiders was resented on principle."[89] Rhodes had made himself impossible for the time being, and fell from power; co-operation with the Afrikander party at the Cape was rendered more difficult, and Chamberlain was not believed when he denied complicity. It is characteristic of the man that in his defence before the House of Commons he boldly declared that "but for Englishmen like Rhodes our English history would be much poorer, and our British dominions would be much smaller", but at the same time broke a lance for his former chief by insisting that Gladstone's magnanimity to the Boers after Majuba "had never met the response it merited".[90] A complete deadlock ensued in South

---

* *G.P.* xi, Nos. 2609, 2610. The exact proportion of responsibility for the telegram and its wording has even now not been established: but it can safely be divided between the Emperor, his Chancellor Prince Hohenlohe, the Foreign Minister Baron Marschall, and the permanent officials. Next day Marschall told Valentine Chirol, then *Times* Correspondent, that "it was a state action and that it was necessary to give England a lesson" (G. P. Gooch, *History of Modern Europe*, p. 219). William II maintains that the original text was stiffened against his wishes, while the evidence of Marschall, Holstein and Bülow tends in the opposite direction (cf. *Grosse Politik*, xi, note on No. 2610; Bülow, *Denkwürdigkeiten*, i, 473–4; Hammann, *Der neue Kurs*, p. 180).

Africa. Krüger evaded the invitation to England, challenged the claim of suzerainty, demanded a modification of the Convention of 1884 in respect of foreign affairs, continued to treat the Uitlanders as before, and spent the revenue derived from their industry upon huge armaments which could only have one purpose.

Meanwhile the Emperor was simultaneously writing fulsome excuses to his grandmother, inciting the Tsar against England, and sounding Paris and St Petersburg as to the possibility of a triple intervention in favour of the Transvaal. Fortunately the French Cabinet saw through the manœuvre and remained passive,[91] while the Italian Foreign Minister Baron Blanc, whom Bülow sounded in a similar sense, warned his ally that a "permanent estrangement of Germany and England must force Italy on to the side of France and Russia".[92] Holstein doubted whether even "the Transvaal experience will suffice to convince England of the necessity of a continental attachment (*Anlehnung*)"; Marschall frankly regarded co-operation of the three continental Powers as "the best means of settling disputes between England and the Continent"; and even that sober veteran Prince Hohenlohe reckoned that Britain would find it necessary to join that group of Powers which could help her to defend the route to India.[93] In Berlin's attitude bluff and blackmail were strangely blended: as Salisbury told Eckardstein in 1899, the telegram was a blunder even more foolish than the Raid itself, and the cloud which it cast upon Anglo-German relations was to grow year by year more menacing. The press on both sides was in a Jingo mood, and foolish attempts were made to injure German trade in Britain: but the Queen and the Premier set themselves to calm public opinion, and the tumult gradually subsided. But Salisbury was more than ever disposed to act on the lines expounded to Chamberlain in their previous term of office— "to keep absolutely clear of engagements and to leave the country free to take any action which it might think fit in the event of a war".[94] Moreover, Professor Brandenburg is doubtless right in concluding that it was the growth of tension with Germany that led Salisbury, in February 1896, to refuse the renewal of the Mediterranean Agreement with Austria-Hungary and Italy.[95]

During 1897 Britain found herself definitely isolated, alike in face of the Greco-Turkish conflict and the collusive seizure of Kiaochau and Port Arthur by Germany and Russia. Moreover, while a colonial conference and a naval review formed the most striking features of Queen Victoria's Diamond Jubilee, William II set himself the goal of world-power, based upon a Navy "raised to the same standard as that of my army". "The trident", he declared, "belongs in our hands", and with the help of his new adviser Admiral von Tirpitz he introduced the first of a series of Navy

Bills which were soon to upset all the calculations on which Britain naval strategy rested. On 23 September 1898 he proclaimed to all the world, "Our future lies on the water".

FASHODA

French suspicions of Berlin prevented any serious response to overtures for a Continental League against Britain, and meanwhile the agreement signed between France and Britain in that very month of January on the Siamese boundaries removed a dangerous cause of misunderstanding. But in other parts of the world, and particularly in Central Africa, friction continued, and peace between France and Britain was increasingly at the mercy of rival zealots, bent on pegging out priority claims. There is some obscurity as to the exact moment at which London's resolve hardened: but looking backward, we can see that what was at stake on Britain's side was the "through connection" between Cairo and the Cape, whereas on the side of France it was already too late to expand from west to east of the African continent, and it therefore became in effect a mere question of extending her Saharan possessions as far east as possible and securing foothold on the Nile, with a view to causing subsequent embarrassment to Britain and regaining the lost position in Egypt. Hanotaux, as French Foreign Minister, quite apart from his distinctly Anglophobe outlook, held as late as 1897 the view that the Nile was the "key point (*le nœud*)" to all questions then pending, and might therefore become the key to a general agreement.[96] From 1894 onwards, then, several able and energetic officers—such as Monteil, Liotard, Marchand—were employed by the French Government in an expansive sense. Alarmed by speeches in the French Chamber, hinting that these activities were set on foot in order to compel the evacuation of Egypt, *The Times* demanded that the Liberal Cabinet should make clear its intentions: and thus it came, soon after Gladstone's retirement, to a statement of the new Foreign Under-Secretary Sir Edward Grey (28 March 1895). While denying any knowledge of a French expedition to the Nile Valley, he declared quite bluntly that in view of existing British claims any such action would be "not merely an inconsistent and unexpected act", but would be viewed by Great Britain as "an unfriendly act".

This clear warning did not, however, serve as a deterrent, and French activities continued. In the background Leopold II of Belgium tried unsuccessfully to mediate between Paris and London, and even made the extraordinary suggestion that the Khedive should be allowed to lease to him, as sovereign of the Congo, the whole valley from Khartoum to Lake

Nyanza (October 1895). Moreover, after Italy's disastrous defeat in Abyssinia and its repercussions in Italian home politics, William II, apparently alarmed for the credit of the Triple Alliance, made somewhat hysterical[97] advances to Sir Frank Lascelles, whom he tried to convince that Russia would instal herself on the Red Sea in Italy's place, and that France would buy the Canaries from Spain. Britain, he hoped, would either join the Dreibund or at least help Italy, or she might find both her routes to India endangered.[98]

The combined pressure of all these events, and the warnings of such men as Lugard and Samuel Baker, at last decided the British Government in favour of a military advance in the Sudan, and to overcome the financial obstruction of the Powers by itself providing the sinews of war. In April 1896 Kitchener started southwards, and on 23 September successfully occupied Dongola, the first stage towards Khartoum. The result was to heighten the friction between London and Paris: and though a really satisfactory and final agreement was reached by the Niger Commission, and the British somewhat grudgingly recognised the French annexation of Madagascar, France persisted in her ambitions on the Upper Nile, and as early as February 1896 authorised Captain Marchand's expedition eastwards. His instructions contained the eloquent phrase, "If we are to anticipate the English, we must arrive there first." Hanotaux denied that the Marchand mission was "a military enterprise", aiming at conquest: but in that case it became still more obviously an attempt to peg out a claim for purposes of bargaining, and indeed in his African book Hanotaux treats the mission as a direct reply to Kitchener's expedition.

Kitchener devoted 1897 to railway construction and military preparations at his new base, and by March 1898 was ready for a fresh advance. In April he defeated the Khalifa and his Dervish army at the Atbara, and on 8 September completed their destruction at the decisive battle of Omdurman. But meanwhile Marchand, leaving the Congo in March 1897, had reached Fashoda on 10 July 1898, and hoisted the French flag: it was not till 18 September that Kitchener arrived there with his Nile flotilla. He was instructed to act upon Grey's warning of 1895, and upon its explicit endorsement by Salisbury to Hanotaux on 10 December 1897—to the effect that no other Power "has any claim to occupy any part of the Valley of the Nile":[99] as soldiers the two men met and parted on cordial terms, but not unnaturally neither would yield without further orders from home. Fortunately there was a new Government in France since 18 July, and Delcassé had replaced Hanotaux as Foreign Minister. Delcassé found himself between two fires—on the one hand Salisbury's unequivocal claim that "all the territories which were subject to the Khalifa passed to the

British and Egyptian Governments by right of conquest",* and on the other the rising tide of French susceptibilities. As he was genuinely desirous of a comprehensive settlement with England, and was so obviously handicapped by the unwisdom of his predecessors, it is difficult to avoid the conclusion that the London Cabinet did nothing to make his position easier: and indeed the speeches of Rosebery and Hicks-Beach—the latter hinting that there are "worse evils than war"—were on their side sops to the rabid jingoism of the British press. On 30 September Delcassé refused Monson's request for the recall of Marchand: but he had to admit that Marchand was completely "in the air"[100] and could not hope to be relieved from any quarter, and at last on 3 November the order for recall was sent. For some months still France was, according to Monson, "staggered and humiliated",[101] and war was very near: it is hard to say whether the dissensions already caused by the Dreyfus Case served most as a deterrent or as an irritant.

A fortnight after the recall, Chamberlain, as though bent upon lashing a bruised back, denounced the French "policy of pinpricks", and pointed out that "Fashoda is only a symbol: the great issue is the control of the whole valley of the Nile". This led to fresh press polemics and much bad blood: but at last on 21 March 1899 a convention was signed between France and Britain, which made the watershed of the Nile and the Congo the dividing line between the two spheres of influence. The Egyptian situation remained unaffected. When at last the dust of controversy had cleared away, it became obvious that a sound solution had been reached. Egypt was freed from the Dervish menace and from the danger of interference with the waters of the Nile: Britain secured land access from the Sudan to Uganda and South Africa, while France found ample scope for expansion in the Sahara from the Atlantic to Lake Chad. There were French extremists who, finding Russia too absorbed in Asia to give them much help, favoured reconciliation with Germany, but Alsace proved a fatal obstacle, and Berlin was still ready to be bought off by London. Meanwhile the old loyalties were being dislocated, Asia and Europe were interlocked, existing alliances were at the mercy of new and unforeseeable events. Five hectic years were still required before Delcassé could place relations with London on a new basis.

* 9 September, Salisbury to Monson—*British Documents*, I, No. 189. In Parliament he reaffirmed the right of conquest as "the most useful, most simple and soundest of the two", the other being that the Sudan had "formed part of the possessions of Egypt".

LAST HOPES OF A GERMAN ALLIANCE

In the closing years of the century, Joseph Chamberlain occupied an almost unique position in the Cabinet, and as his chief grew older and harder to move, foreign and colonial policy became interlocked and forced the initiative upon the younger man. Moved by the conviction that isolation was increasingly dangerous, and that for Britain the ideal combination was one with the "Anglo-Saxon" rather than the Latin or Slav world, he was inclined in the first instance to explore the possibilities of understanding with Berlin. In March 1898 he met the German Ambassador Count Hatzfeldt, and admitting that British policy had for years been one of "isolation, or at least of non-entanglement in alliances", raised the question of a defensive alliance.[102] Bülow's reply was distinctly non-committal: he argued that "time was against England", and insisted that any treaty must be ratified by the British Parliament,[103] but doubting this to be practicable, held that they must wait till a later date for its fulfilment. In a further conversation early in April Chamberlain, though careful to speak in a private capacity, suggested an agreement "equivalent to entering the Triple Alliance" (the Emperor's comment is, "The dead ride fast"), and challenged the view that England would ever abandon such a treaty if it were once adopted. Hatzfeldt warned his chief that Chamberlain was not to be regarded as a real friend of Germany, and in any case was "a naïve beginner in foreign policy".[104] Bülow and Holstein were full of doubts, and were not influenced by Chamberlain's very broad hint that if "the natural alliance" had to be abandoned, there was "no impossibility in reaching an understanding with Russia or France".[105] Bülow's view was that "France could not be led by any price which England would pay, to enter an alliance, however platonic and defensive, against Russia"[106] in other words he started from the assumption that such alliances would be necessarily directed *against* other Powers, whereas Britain's chief aim was to win over or detach Powers who might otherwise join a hostile combination against her. Salisbury's own phrase to Hatzfeldt, "You ask too much for your friendship", was hardly tenable, since the Germans had declined to name any terms, but it reveals the Premier's deep suspicion of Germany. The Ambassador had to report that Chamberlain was keenly disappointed, but still ready to make colonial concessions, yet *only in the event of a political accord*:[107] his own tactics would be to keep the door open for a possible agreement in the future.

Chamberlain, as Hatzfeldt had feared, proceeded on his own way: and his speech of 13 May was a landmark, the more so as it closely followed

Salisbury's public reference to "the jargon of isolation". Starting from the axiom that ever since the Crimean War Britain had followed "a policy of strict isolation"—with no allies and, he feared, no friends—he reached the conclusion that he who sups with the devil must have a very long spoon, and "must not reject the idea of an alliance with those Powers whose interests are most nearly approximate to our own". It was above all Russian aggression in China that prompted his speech: little did he know that William II, while listening to British overtures, was trying to make capital for himself by revealing the secret to Tsar Nicholas, and by asking "What you can offer me and will do if I refuse." The Tsar, however, was cautious and sent a polite refusal, coupled with a hint that Britain had already addressed herself to Russia, though without success. Meanwhile the speech was badly received in the press of both countries, and for a time nothing more happened. In August, it is true, the Emperor asked his mother to approach the Queen, and when Salisbury failed to respond, complained of "his overtures being received with something between a joke and a snub".[108] By the end of the year, however, the Emperor had recovered both his temper and the desire for a deal, for Lascelles reported a very frank conversation with the Emperor, who agreed that there was "no necessity for a formal alliance", since the arrangements for common action could be made within 24 hours![109]

This more genial attitude on the part of William II was due to two things. On the one hand the British attitude towards the United States in its quarrel with Spain, and in particular the naval incident at Manila, had speedily destroyed all trace of the stupid Venezuelan quarrel, and made possible a *rapprochement* between what it was still the fashion to call the two "Anglo-Saxon" peoples. On the other the Colonial Secretary, arguing that "it is worth while to pay blackmail sometimes", had secretly negotiated a treaty with Germany dividing the Portuguese colonies into two spheres of influence, which would become a reality in the event of Portugal wishing to sell, but not otherwise (30 August 1898). Portugal was not informed of the result, and in the same way, a year later, London negotiated with Portugal direct the Treaty of Windsor (14 October 1899) and did not inform Germany. The later did not, it is true, infringe the earlier Treaty, since it merely renewed "the old mutual guarantee against attack": but at this distance of time the net impression is dictinctly unsavoury—but in all directions, not as regards Britain in particular.* The whole series of manœuvres turned mainly round Delagoa Bay, admittedly the key to the

---

* Sir Arthur Nicolson described the Convention as "the most cynical business that I have come across in my whole experience of diplomacy". (Harold Nicolson, *Lord Carnock*, p. 393: and this view is endorsed by Langer, *op. cit.* p. 625.)

Transvaal—"the key of peace in South Africa". Britain would have liked to lease it from Portugal, while Germany blocked the plan.

During 1899 Chamberlain was more than ever convinced of the need for allies, even if the name were withheld and the exact aims ill-defined: and it was this feeling that lay behind his occasional speeches on "Anglo-Saxon liberty and Anglo-Saxon interests" and on the belief that blood will be found to be thicker than water.[110] But despite the ardour with which Cecil Rhodes, after a visit to Berlin, also advocated a German alliance, Chamberlain's original hopes were already changing rapidly, and he kept hinting to Hatzfeldt that "last year we offered you everything and you would not have it: now it is too late".[111]

There was fresh friction over the Samoan question, which was in itself entirely insignificant, but became an object of rival susceptibilities and a fruitful source of misunderstanding. While Chamberlain complained that German policy "since Bismarck has always been one of undisguised black-mail", the Emperor William on his side told Colonel Grierson that the British Government "appears to have two heads" working against each other. "You make any concession asked for by France or Russia, you cede half continents to them, but when Germany asks for an island...she is met by a refusal."[112] And it must be freely admitted that the Salisbury Cabinet might have continued to haggle indefinitely over Samoa, had not the outbreak of the Boer War rendered a settlement with Germany imperative.

Distrust was deepened still further owing to the attitude of Germany to the Peace Conference which met at the Hague in May 1899 on the initiative of the Tsar, to consider "the maintenance of universal peace and a possible reduction of excessive armaments". William II's attitude from the outset was: "I'll share in the comedy, but when waltzing I'll keep my sword at my side."[113] He took it for granted that the real motives were shortness of money in Russia and the hope of countering Germany's superior speed in mobilising. But while the German military expert, Colonel Schwarzhoff, almost at the outset knocked the bottom out of the whole programme of the Conference by rejecting the reduction or even restriction of armaments, the British naval expert, Sir John Fisher, took an even more extreme view of the relations of might and right. The real difference was that with Germany political questions were completely dwarfed by questions of strategy and power, whereas the British case lay with that able diplomatist Sir Julian Pauncefote, who was mainly instrumental in securing the creation of a permanent Court of Arbitration at the Hague.

EUROPEAN REACTIONS OF THE BOER WAR

The Jameson Raid had produced an unhappy deadlock in the South African situation, tying the hands of the British Government and giving President Krüger a perfect excuse for increasing his armaments, and acting as though the Treaty of 1884 did not exist. On both sides, and among the Afrikanders of the Cape, distrust and resentment had deepened, and the farmers of the Veldt were inclined to look with contempt upon the British as a military power and to rely on Krüger's rigidly patriarchal standards. In 1897 Sir Alfred Milner, who had already made his name as an administrator in Egypt, became High Commissioner at the Cape, and conscious of the Uitlander problem as a running sore on the body politic, gradually reached the conclusion that there was "no way out of the political troubles of South Africa except reform in theTransvaal, or war". "I am fighting all the time", he wrote home, in October 1897.[114] But the policy of the home Government was quite definitely "to keep the peace with Krüger unless he were very outrageous".[115] "Transvaal must be clearly in the wrong before we can interfere", Chamberlain told Milner, adding the warning that Britain had "difficulties of the most serious character with France, Russia and Germany", and that the Government's "principal object in South Africa at present is peace".[116] He refused Milner's suggestion of provoking a crisis, and even in April 1899 his response to Milner's "Helot despatch", treating "the case for intervention" as "overwhelming", was to propose a Conference at Bloemfontein between the High Commissioner and the Boer President. After its failure he would still have accepted a compromise, but it could not be one by which "one of the two white races was deliberately placed in a position of political inferiority to the other".[117]

The deadlock remained absolute, and in the end the Cabinet authorised an ultimatum to Pretoria, but it was never actually despatched, for the Boers forestalled it by an ultimatum of their own, and when it was declined, by the prompt invasion of Natal. Neither side seems to have fully foreseen the magnitude of the struggle, or the certainty that it would be fought to a finish. The Continent, which had turned a strangely deaf ear to the appeals of the Armenians, now espoused the Boer cause with enthusiasm and plunged into blatant Anglophobia: while British opinion, cured of its over-confidence by a series of military reverses, settled down to a long and difficult campaign and consoled itself by the splendid rally of Colonial loyalism. The relief of Ladysmith and Kimberley in February 1900 marked the first turn of the tide; during the summer Roberts and Kitchener steadily overran the two Republics, till annexation could be proclaimed on

25 October: but the period of guerilla warfare was prolonged for nearly two years, and peace was not proclaimed till 31 May 1902.

This time the Emperor, in defiance of an Anglophobe opinion at home, threw himself strongly on to the side of Britain, and in November 1899 paid a state visit to Windsor, bringing Bülow with him. Following upon "Black Week", this visit unquestionably had a great moral effect upon the Continent. In their talks with Chamberlain and Balfour the idea of an Anglo-German understanding, and of its possible extension to the United States also, constantly recurred: but the German attitude, though now cordial, was distinctly reserved, and remained unmoved when Chamberlain spoke of Morocco and even suggested that if Britain took Tangier, Germany might console herself with a coaling station on the Atlantic coast.[118] Bülow was frank enough to admit that opinion in England was far less anti-German than opinion in Germany was anti-British, and that consequently men like Chirol and Saunders, of *The Times*, who knew the intensity of the feeling, were "most dangerous for us".[119]

Chamberlain apparently thought that he was acting in the spirit of his visitors when, on the very day after their departure, he made a big speech at Leicester, first welcoming the newfound friendship with America, both on its own account and as a guarantee of world-peace, and then going on to declare that "the natural alliance is between us and the great German Empire", to attack the French press for its abuse of Queen Victoria, and to advocate "a new Triple Alliance between the Teutonic race and the two great branches of the Anglo-Saxon race"—an alliance which might either be "committed to paper" or "merely exist in the minds of the statesmen of the respective countries". "Every farseeing English statesman", he claimed, "had long desired that we should not remain permanently isolated on the Continent" (30 November 1899). But the speech had an almost equally bad reception in the British and in the German press: and Bülow, so far from grasping the proffered hand, spoke in the Reichstag of Germany's growing power and prestige amid a world of political and economic envy, and declared that "in the coming century the German people would be hammer or anvil". Above all, he used the bad feeling engendered by the searching of a German ship for contraband, in order to push a second Navy Bill through the Reichstag, and thereby curry favour simultaneously with the sailors, the Emperor, and with the Pan-German and Nationalist sections of the German public. On the other hand, William definitely refused to respond when the Russian Foreign Minister, Count Muravyev, suggested joint "amicable pressure" upon London by Russia, Germany and France, to save the Boer Republics: and Bülow's insistence on their mutual guarantee of territory as a preliminary condition almost automatically ruled out French co-operation. When Salisbury made it clear that Britain would not consider mediation from any quarter, the project died a natural death. But the Queen and the Prince of Wales thanked the Emperor warmly for his friendly attitude,[120] and as the tide turned against the Boers, he was careful to withhold any real assistance and refused to receive the exiled President in Berlin.* On two occasions he sent his uncle "aphorisms" amounting to suggestions for the proper conduct of the military campaign in South Africa—perhaps a sign of sympathy, but certainly not of confidence in Roberts and Kitchener.

In the summer of 1900 the Boxer troubles in China and the despatch of an international expedition to Peking led to further co-operation, and the Emperor compared his contingent with that which the Great Elector had sent to William of Orange on his famous invasion of England. Unfortunately he also told them to give no quarter, and to make the name of Germany as terrible in China as that which the Huns of Attila had made for themselves in Europe. Waldersee, for whom the Kaiser secured the supreme command, was strongly Anglophobe: but the expedition, after scandalous looting, attained its main objective, and Anglo-German co-operation was extended by the Yangtse Agreement of October 1900, based on the double principle of the open door and Chinese integrity. But Salisbury continued to have his doubts about William II, who flared up suddenly to his uncle and described British ministers as "unmitigated noodles".[121]

THE END OF ISOLATION

Germany's attitude was decisive in preventing a continental bloc against Britain during the Boer War, but at last the dangerous possibilities resulting from such a bloc were brought home to British public opinion more clearly than ever before, and the need for some sort of alliance, or at least understanding, was widely felt. For the last time Chamberlain turned to Germany, though no longer with his old enthusiasm. In March 1900 he had a very frank talk with Count Paul Metternich (then replacing Hatzfeldt), to whom he insisted that he was no diplomat, but would continue all his life to believe in a "general agreement" with Germany, if "alliance" were the wrong word. Metternich quoted Bülow's phrase on Chamberlain: "he is like all big men, ahead of his time", but Chamberlain remained highly sensitive and nervous.[122]

* There was however a curious incident in January 1900, when he assured the Russian Ambassador that if ever the Tsar sent armies against India, he (William) "would guarantee that none should stir in Europe" (quoted from the despatch of Osten-Sacken to Muravyev, cited by Low, *Edward VII*, I, p. 763). On 10 April Salisbury, writing to the Queen, still had a lingering doubt "whether a proposal for a combination against England was ever really made by France and Russia to Germany" (*Letters*, III, 527).

In the following winter there were two vital changes. Lord Salisbury, now in failing health, found it necessary to relinquish the Foreign Office, and in November 1900 Lord Lansdowne took his place: and less than three months later Queen Victoria died (21 January 1901). The influence of the Crown upon policy had been in steady decline ever since the death of the Prince Consort, but this does not of course mean that it was ever negligible. On the contrary the Queen's personal prestige as matriarch of European royalty grew steadily, and was strengthened by her intimate knowledge of continental affairs, her untiring correspondence with hordes of relations, her *flair* and *savoir faire*, her simple faith and high patriotism, her power to inspire devotion and to command respect. The awe which she inspired in two such different men as the Prince of Wales and the German Emperor very well illustrates the unique position to which she had attained. Under Edward VII the influence of the Crown upon foreign policy was no longer due so much to the office as to the personality of its holder, who, side by side with petty punctilio and a mania for form, also possessed remarkable gifts for acquiring information, sensing a political situation and subtly transforming a hostile atmosphere. Balfour in his farewell tribute in the House claimed that "the importance of the Crown in our Constitution is not a diminishing, but an increasing factor. It increases and must increase with the development of those free selfgoverning communities beyond the seas, who are constitutionally linked to us through the person of the Sovereign, the living symbol of Imperial Unity." In 1901 this was still a new note: to-day we are all conscious of its truth. But it must be added that this "importance" rightly ascribed to the Crown has suffered a sea-change. It will never again be what it was under the Great Queen, but it has indeed become "something rich and strange"—something unique in history.

Meanwhile the appointment of Lansdowne, whom the Queen and the Premier had agreed in regarding as "the only person fit to take the Foreign Seals",[123] meant also from the first, however little it was intended, a steady evolution away from the circumspection and the silences of his great predecessor. Lansdowne was one of the last of the great Whig politicians, though events had placed him among the Tories: he had in his veins such different strains as those of Flahault, Talleyrand and Lady Nairne, and in Mr Cecil's phrase "had the best qualifications in the world for merging the foreign policy of a Conservative in that of a Liberal Government, and bridging the gulf that separates the temperament of the French from that of the English".[124] Arthur Balfour, a good psychologist—and Lansdowne's fag at Eton!—once spoke of "a sort of continental quality of mind in Lansdowne".[125]

In these changing circumstances the idea of an Anglo-German alliance was relaunched during a conversation at Chatsworth between Chamberlain and the Duke of Devonshire on the one hand and Baron Eckardstein on the other. But it seems quite certain that the latter, who knew England well and had many connections through his wife,* went far beyond his instructions, presumably spurred on by ambition at a moment when his chief, Count Hatzfeldt, was incapacitated by illness. Eckardstein even spoke to Lansdowne of a possible "defensive alliance",[126] but the new Foreign Secretary was cautiously sceptical and inclined to accept such talk *cum copia salis*.[127] None the less, Hatzfeldt himself, when at last able to see Lansdowne, also spoke of Britain joining the Triple Alliance, and suggested that in view of the dangers of continued isolation "it was our interest to join one of the two great groups", that agreement with Russia would cost too much, and that "Germany, if nothing should come of these overtures, might find herself obliged to look elsewhere for alliances".[128] This corresponds entirely with the views of Bülow, who held that "England's threatened agreement with the Dual Alliance is only a bogey invented to sober us", and would be "far too expensive",[129] and with those of the Emperor himself, who in his first official talk with Lansdowne not merely tried to poison his mind against Russia and America for coming to an agreement, but took the arrogantly comic line that the old balance of power was "exploded", and that he (William II) was "now the Balance of Power in Europe".[130] Holstein for his part put on the official brake, arguing that a formal suggestion of alliance from the German side was "exactly what we wish to avoid".[131] In short, Berlin fatally misjudged the possibility of Britain coming to terms with the Dual Alliance, and assumed that it was only necessary to wait until she accepted the German terms.[132]

An attempt was now actually made to draft a Convention, but in Sir Thomas Sanderson's view, "however it may be worded,...it will practically amount to a guarantee to Germany of the provinces conquered by France", and he failed to see "exactly what Germany will guarantee to us".[133] The decisive rejection came from Lord Salisbury, whose memorandum of 29 May 1901[134]—his last considered pronouncement on foreign policy—remains as a classic plea for caution and the avoidance of general commitments. He doubted "whether the bargain would be for our advantage", since "the liability of having to defend the German and Austrian frontiers against Russia is heavier than that of having to defend the British Isles against France". He also threw doubts on the danger of isolation, arguing that even in the war against revolutionary France, "our fall would not have been due to our isolation", but to "failure to command the Channel". But his main objection was "the fatal circumstance that neither we nor the

* Daughter of the wealthy furniture manufacturer Blundell-Maple.

Germans are competent to make the suggested promises. The British Government cannot undertake to declare war for any purpose not approved of by the electors": otherwise "the promise would be repudiated, and the Government would be turned out". The only way round this difficulty would be to lay the agreement before Parliament, but to this there were "very grave objections". "The impropriety of a secret contract ...would apply to German policy as much as to English", and a public promise "would excite bitter murmurs in every rank of German society." No British Minister, he concluded, could venture to forecast "Britain's probable conduct if Germany or Italy were involved in war with France". Their course "in such a case must depend on the view taken by public opinion in this country, and public opinion would be largely, if not exclusively, governed by the nature of the *casus belli*".

The project again languished during the summer, and Bülow refused any idea of co-operation with Britain in Morocco, arguing that that question was not important enough for Germany to risk international complications.[135] But in August the Emperor, when he met King Edward at the funeral of the Empress Frederick, urged "the conclusion of a definite and binding treaty",[136] thereby throwing to the winds Holstein's ideas on initiative. According to his own memorandum, William wished to bring England, and especially Salisbury, away from their "passive policy", and to open their eyes to "the slow but unceasing decline of England's prestige and world-position".[137] By this time it was Germany who was wooing and Britain who was holding back. But the long series of discussions may be said to have ended in the winter of 1901, when Lansdowne drew up a formidable catalogue of "the difficulties in the way of a full-blown defensive alliance with Germany"—the impossibility of a clear definition of the *casus foederis*, the certainty of alienating France and Russia, complications with the Colonies, the risk of anti-American entanglements, and "the difficulty of carrying Parliament with us".[138] There followed a talk between Lansdowne and the new Ambassador, Count Paul Metternich, who found "our preference for isolation unintelligible", and made it clear that no "minor proposal" would satisfy Berlin: "it was a case of the whole or none".[139] If Salisbury continued averse to any such agreement, Chamberlain's enthusiasm was still more effectually* cooled by the reception given to his Edinburgh speech (25 October): for his justification of British military methods in South Africa, as milder than those of other nations in Poland, Algeria, Bosnia and the Franco-German War, roused a storm of denuncia-

---

* Already in June he said to Alfred Rothschild:—"If the people in Berlin are so short-sighted as not to see that a whole new world-constellation depends on it, nothing can be done with them"—Eckardstein, *op. cit.* II, 301.

tion in Germany. Even Bülow, now speaking as Chancellor in the Reichstag, treated Chamberlain's words as a disparagement of the glorious German army, quoted Frederick the Great's contemptuous phrase, "Let the man alone, he is biting on granite", and left uncondemned the gross insults of a Pan-German deputy against the British army. Chamberlain publicly refused to withdraw or qualify, and refused also to accept lessons from a foreign minister. For a time the relations between uncle and nephew were again cordial, but the idea of an alliance was henceforth abandoned by both sides as impracticable, and by most of the press as undesirable. The year 1901—which ends the Victorian Era, the longest and greatest reign in British history—was also the parting of the ways between Britain and Germany. The propitious moment had been lost, and the two sides moved steadily apart.

EPILOGUE

The Japanese Alliance

While Salisbury himself was in failing health and increasingly negative in outlook, his colleagues were more conscious of the dangers than of the splendours of isolation. British opinion during 1901 began to favour an agreement with Russia, to which Salisbury had long inclined in theory, though without taking any very active steps. But not only was there no response from St Petersburg, but the signs of Russia's forward policy in Asia multiplied, and early in 1901 the elder statesmen of Japan authorised their Ambassador in London, Baron Hayashi, to sound the British Cabinet. It had been Germany who first suggested that Japan should be included in any arrangement reached between her and Britain: but in proportion as Berlin insisted on a strict neutrality in the Russo-Japanese dispute as to Manchuria, London and Tokio felt encouraged to go on alone. A last desperate effort was made by Marquis Ito to achieve a Russian alliance on a basis of virtual partition—Korea for Japan and Manchuria for Russia: but his negotiations came to nothing, and the Japanese Cabinet on 7 December 1901 unanimously decided in favour of an alliance with Britain. On 30 January 1902 Lansdowne and Hayashi signed the momentous Anglo-Japanese Agreement, which was to transform the whole structure of Far Eastern politics: and the text was at once published and laid before Parliament—the German Emperor and Chancellor having been previously informed, at King Edward's suggestion.* This, the first modern alliance concluded between an European Great Power and an Asiatic state, rested on the perception that in the Far East isolation was almost equally dangerous for Britain and for Japan, but that their co-operation would completely checkmate any other possible combination of Powers, either for the purpose of squeezing British traders out of China or of repeating the methods which robbed Japan of the fruits of victory after Shimoneseki. In form the Treaty was defensive, based on mutual recognition of the independence of China and Korea, and it was laid down that Britain's special interests lay in the former country, Japan's ("politically as well as commercially and industrially") in the latter. But while the express disclaimer of "aggressive tendencies in either country" was at the time genuine enough, or at least

---

* But Bülow, while affecting satisfaction to London, transmitted to Count Lamsdorff William II's opinion that the agreement was "the hard but not undeserved punishment for Russia's flirting with England, her passivity during the Boer War, and her unresponsive attitude to His Majesty's wellmeant hints" (*Grosse Politik*, xvii, No. 5048).

limited to the desire to "prevent the absorption of Korea by any foreign power" (a phrase to be found in Lansdowne's first draft), it must be admitted that Japan's ulterior aim was to conquer Korea for herself, and that the alliance greatly increased her prospect of success, in the event of an armed conflict with her chief rival, Russia. Each Power was pledged to neutrality if the other became involved in war, to use his efforts to prevent others from joining in, and to come to his ally's aid in the event of a third state joining in. In effect, this left Russia without hope of an ally in war with Japan. Lansdowne himself did not publicly marshal all the arguments in favour of a revised policy—if only out of consideration for his chief, who felt its necessity, but also felt that a younger man must carry it into effect. In the House of Lords Lansdowne urged that the increase of armaments, and the suddenness with which wars broke out, had transformed the arguments in favour of isolation, that judgment must no longer "be swayed by any musty formulas or old-fashioned superstitions", and that a country with allies was to be envied, so long as its ally was "desirable", its objects "commendable", and the price paid not too great.[1] The implication that the Japanese alliance fulfilled these and other conditions was allowed to remain unchallenged.

It was no accident that Britain inaugurated her new policy at that point of the earth's surface where, in view of Russia's forward policy, the possibilities of war seemed greatest. "The real origin of this Treaty", said Lord Cranborne in the House, "was our anxiety to maintain the *status quo* in China": and he made it clear that Manchuria was not excluded from the agreement. But it is safe to assume that the British Government was by no means abandoning the hope, entertained by Salisbury in particular for years past, of still reaching a direct agreement with Russia: and indeed the Japanese also continued to negotiate with Russia for a peaceful settlement of the Korean question. If then war eventually came, it was above all due to the criminal folly of the military and naval *camarilla* which surrounded Nicholas II and carried him whither he knew not.

In the first instance, however, the agreement roused the anger of Russia, who of course realised that France would now, less than ever before, be disposed to risk her fleet for the sake of some Russian adventure in the Far East. German policy meanwhile followed the line indicated by William II's personal predilections against "the Yellow Peril": "Peoples of Europe, preserve your holiest possessions", he had written as the motto of an allegorical picture.* The Emperor saw a chance of playing *tertius gaudens*,

---

* Very different was the attitude of King Edward, who at Kiel in June 1904 challenged the theory of the Yellow Peril, and said, "The Japs are intelligent, brave and knightly, as civilised as Europeans" (*Grosse Politik*, XIX, No. 6038).

by putting spokes in the wheel of any Anglo-Russian understanding and encouraging Russia in her Far Eastern designs and, as friction grew, by inciting Tsar Nicholas as "Admiral of the Pacific" against Japan. On the very eve of the Russo-Japanese War William II, in conversation with Bülow, referred to his last epistle to "Nicky", whose warmth, "he had hoped, would induce the Tsar to turn all his forces against Japan". It looked as though the Tsar would end by surrendering Manchuria without fighting, and "such a turn of events must be prevented under all circumstances".[2] For the future it was of vital importance that while William II was bent on embroiling Nicholas II with Japan, Edward VII and Lansdowne, in a quiet way behind the scenes, were warning the Tsar and his advisers of the impending danger—warning them that Japan was indeed in deadly earnest. They were not believed at the time, but after the disaster their words were remembered as a proof of good faith and sound judgment, and contrasting as they did with the advice from Berlin, eventually smoothed the path to the reconciliation of 1907.

The Japanese alliance was the last great achievement of Salisbury's Premiership: on 10 July he resigned, and was replaced by his nephew and trusted friend Arthur Balfour. Salisbury had spent longer at the Foreign Office than any other Foreign Secretary save Palmerston: and he will always rank among the greatest of them, in the same class as his great ancestor Burghley. As continuity was upheld under Rosebery, it may be said that in foreign policy at any rate Salisbury achieved the aim of "20 years of resolute government". There are, however, still many misconceptions about his policy, which it may be hoped the final volume of his daughter's brilliant and searching biography will at last dispel. It is too often assumed that "splendid isolation" was a supreme and satisfying aim: it would be far more correct to regard it as in his mind an uncomfortable necessity imposed by the fluid state of continental politics. There can be little doubt that his preferences were in favour of the old friendship with France which he had known in his youth, and that to a lesser degree he would have viewed a *rapprochement* with Russia with much relief, owing to our Indian and other Asiatic commitments.[3] But his innate caution and realism convinced him that so long as that interpenetration of alliances of which Professor Salvemini has written subsisted, and was further accentuated by "the scramble for Africa" and by the economic and military evolution of the Far East, it would be a fatal blunder to commit Britain irrevocably to a place in one of the rival fronts.

But that he had no doctrinaire leaning towards isolation, and was fully alive to the danger of hostile coalition, is abundantly shown by his Mediterranean Agreements, his temporary alignment with the Triple Alliance, his overtures to Germany on the Turkish issue, his definite toleration of Chamberlain's experiments in foreign policy, his periodic efforts to agree with Russia. Above all, his relations with Bismarck in the last three years before the latter's fall dispose of the idea that he was unduly identified with the Balance of Power, for he then attached himself to what was already far the strongest combination, instead of trying to redress the balance in Europe. There is only one motive which will explain the permutations of his policy in the 'eighties and 'nineties, namely his conviction that peace in Europe was Britain's greatest interest, and that he must give his backing only to those Powers whose policy was essentially pacific. He had his suspicions of Bismarck, but he knew enough of him to be sure that he was working for peace, and it was because he was afraid that the "Epigoni" of German policy, under the masterful but erratic hand of William II, were being driven slowly but surely in a less pacific direction, that his reserve towards Germany was so marked a feature of his later years. For the same reason the France of Boulanger or of the Dreyfus agitation, the Russia of Skobelev and the Pan-Slavs, enjoined great caution upon him; and it is safe to assume that his attitude would have been quite different if he had had to deal with such sane and balanced French and Russian statesmen as confronted his successors in office. It is of course true that towards the end he had lost his old vigour and initiative; but the Machiavellian designs sometimes attributed to him—for instance that of holding aloof until the two main groups of Powers had been incited into conflict, and then profiting by their ruin—were quite accurately dismissed by his chief confidential secretary as "grotesque".[4] The most that can be said is that Salisbury possessed a detached and introspective quality which lent itself to misunderstanding on the part of foreigners, and led them to infer that absentmindedness in the home meant isolation in the nation's policy.

THE THIRD ENTENTE CORDIALE

Twelve yet more crowded years still separate us from the great catastrophe: and it is not possible, without exceeding the purposes and proportions of this volume, to treat them in other than the barest outline. The abandonment of isolation is the "Great Divide": it remains above all to consider the negotiations with foreign Powers which resulted in the final groupings of 1914. But it is at least necessary to place on record that other new factors contributed to render that isolation impossible: rapid improvements in world communications—by rail, road, steamer and telephone—the expansion of rival imperialisms in the waste places of earth, were only the outward and visible signs of a process by which European and world policy were more and more interlocked. The Spanish-American and Boer Wars were soon followed by the Russo-Japanese War, and the next great European conflict at once assumed world-wide proportions. The "diplomatic revolution", as it has aptly been called, began outside Europe.

British public opinion, which is almost always outstripped by events, was not yet alive to the menace of the German naval programme, as embodied in the two Navy Laws of 1898 and 1900: but those responsible for our defences and for the maintenance of a "Two-Power Standard" on the sea, could be under no illusions as to the ultimate purpose of the German armaments. To-day we have the evidence of Admiral von Tirpitz's memoirs and of the Emperor's *marginalia*. The latter, on the eve of his visit to England in November 1899, had told the French Ambassador that Germany had to be neutral in the South African War, because she had no fleet, "but in 20 years, if this is ready, I'll use another language".[5] And a little later he consoled the Queen of Holland for German inaction by quoting "Vengeance is mine, saith the Lord" and urging "silence and work" until a powerful fleet could arise "under the joint banners of Orange and Brandenburg".[6] Moreover, behind this sound and fury was the cold flame of Tirpitz's resolve, and the famous "risk theory" which sought to make the German fleet so strong that even a victorious rival would be crippled and "could no longer meet a coalition of other naval Powers". As Mr Woodward points out, the Admiral's reasoned memorandum for the Reichstag never mentioned Britain, but it was only to Britain that the theory could apply.[7] Those who ascribe the alienation of the two peoples to trade jealousy are talking the crudest of nonsense; for their mutual trade was immensely and increasingly profitable, and only fools fail to regret that it has not been resumed.* The root cause, apart from nerves and prestige, was always the question of Sea Power, which was vital for these islands and only secondary to the owner of the greatest army in the world.

British susceptibilities had to be lulled to sleep by Bülow and his master while Germany passed through the "danger zone" of the fleet-building period. But the British Admiralty was not asleep, and these were the years when a new naval base was established on the Firth of Forth, the Channel Fleet strengthened and naval redistribution carried out throughout the world, until, under that daring and wayward genius "Jacky Fisher", the laying down of the first Dreadnought opened up a new era in the policy of the capital ship and in building competition between the sea Powers *in esse* and *in posse*. This policy, and the fact that it necessitated the widening

---

* On 9 July 1908 Herr von Stumm, in a report from the London Embassy, pointed out that economic rivalry only applied in the case of a few particular interests which were affected by German competition (*Grosse Politik*, XXIV, No. 8213).

of the new Kiel Canal, should have enabled us to outdistance the German fleet: but unfortunately between 1906 and 1908 the Campbell-Bannerman Government threw away the lead, and fatally encouraged the Tirpitz school to sustain competition.[8] If the Fisher-Cawdor programme stands to the credit of Balfour, the subsequent course of events has also strikingly vindicated one of the first acts of his administration, namely the creation of the Committee of Imperial Defence, which has never fallen into mere party grooves and has a bearing on foreign policy too obvious to require elucidation. Rarely has any British statesman of modern times shown so clear a perception of the inter-relations of policy and military and naval power and mobility.

The Peace of Vereeniging (1 June 1902) was followed by a pacification of South Africa more rapid than any contemporary observer had dared to hope. From the first Chamberlain had resolved that victory should be followed by conciliation, had refused Milner's proposals for the suspension of the Cape Constitution, had proclaimed "a reign of justice and equality" as "the only cure for racial antagonism" (1 May 1900), and now combined with Kitchener to expedite a settlement by generous terms of peace. This result, combined with the Japanese Agreement, brought immediate relief to an embarrassed Foreign Office; but relations with Germany steadily deteriorated, and the Emperor had a bad press when he paid a family visit to Sandringham in November 1902. Balfour, in his first Guildhall speech, attempted to atone for this by a reference to the press's "fantastic imaginings": but relations still did not improve, despite fairly amicable negotiations over the Bagdad Railway, and despite parallel action during a recrudescence of the Venezuelan dispute. In this latter case the British press, with sure instinct, feared that German statesmen might succeed in embroiling us with the United States and then playing the *tertius gaudens*. The danger was well illustrated by the intolerable attitude of President Roosevelt in the Alaskan dispute less than a year later.[9]

The moment was obviously propitious for discussions between France and Britain, which would not, however, have been possible without "long and patient work"[10] on the part of the Ambassador Paul Cambon and such unofficial envoys as Sir Thomas Barclay, Lord Avebury and others. By 1902 Delcassé had recovered from his soreness over Fashoda, hinted to Salisbury the possibility of a *rapprochement* resting on the *status quo*, and having meanwhile concluded a secret agreement with Italy (on the basis of mutual *désintéressement* in Morocco and Tripoli, even sounded Lansdowne as to a Moroccan agreement.* But the ship remained motion-

* King Edward told Eckardstein in February 1902 that we were "being urged more strongly than ever by France to come to an agreement in all Colonial disputes" (Eckardstein, *Lebenserinnerungen*, II, 379).

less on the slips, and to set it in motion the daring experiment of a visit of King Edward to Paris was required. The story has often been told, how his initiative added Paris to Lisbon, Malta and Rome, and how his genial tact and the personal note which he gave to every utterance turned Parisian coldness into reserve, and reserve into half-incredulous enthusiasm. "The friendship of the two countries is my constant preoccupation", he said, and three months later, at a state banquet to President Loubet in London, the King could speak, without fear of challenge, of the "true friendship, indeed I will say the affection, which my country feels for France". Preceded by Étienne, the leader of the French Colonial group in the Chamber, Delcassé had decisive and extremely frank conversations with Lansdowne at the Foreign Office (7 July 1903). The negotiations were continued through the autumn and winter between Lansdowne and Cambon, and in the former's phrase to Cromer, "after sticking in all sorts of ignoble ruts, suddenly began to travel at the rate of an express train".[11] At last, on 8 April 1904, the Anglo-French Convention was signed and given to the world.

The essence of the agreement can be summarised very briefly, for it consisted above all in the elimination of points of friction. The Newfoundland fishery dispute, which was nearly two centuries old, was finally wiped out, in return for a series of frontier rectifications in West Africa, which substituted stable for fluid conditions in all the territory stretching from Lake Chad and the Niger basin to the Atlantic coast. Minor disputes relating to Siam, the New Hebrides and Madagascar were cleared up in a special Protocol. But all else was subordinate to the "tit for tat" laid down with regard to Morocco and Egypt. Each Power disclaimed any intention of altering the political status of either country; and this can only be described as disingenuous. For Britain, though only too anxious at that moment to let sleeping dogs lie in Egypt, certainly wished to be free to act as circumstances might dictate, without any longer being dependent upon French consent: while it is equally certain that France on her side had long since made up her mind to absorb Morocco, and realised that the first preliminary was British consent. This was very clearly understood and stated by Lord Cromer, who from the first had a preponderant influence upon Lord Lansdowne's decisions. "Everything", he wrote home, "depends on our attitude as regards Morocco." And then, "Have we any objection to Morocco becoming a French province?"—a question which he at once answered in the negative, "provided always (1) that we get an adequate *quid pro quo* in Egypt and elsewhere", and (2) that the French observed Lansdowne's three conditions, the neutralisation of the coast, due regard for "Spanish interests and susceptibilities", and a guarantee for British trade.*

There were also five secret articles which were not revealed to the world till the crisis of Agadir in 1911. By the first each Power declared itself bound by the agreement as published, in the event of circumstances forcing them to change their policy in Egypt or Morocco, while the third defined Spain's share of Morocco in the event of its break-up:† and it is obvious that in signing them the British Government knew that it was paving the way for French absorption of Morocco. That it also insisted upon due consideration for Spain is certainly an extenuating circumstance. That there were to be no fortifications on the coast facing Gibraltar could only redound to the peace of Europe. That commercial liberty was to be upheld for at least thirty years both in Egypt and in Morocco was as clearly to the general advantage as the provisions for the "Open Door" in China. That secrecy was enjoined is objectionable to post-war standards, but was no crime in an Europe where the two main alliances rested on secret clauses, and where secret treaties were a common feature. But that the Convention was expansive in aim and tendency cannot be denied, as also that it tried to solve the Moroccan question by a bilateral arrangement—squaring Spain by a contingent share in the spoils—and that it ignored the internal status of Morocco and the equal rights of other Powers, and especially of Germany, under the Madrid Treaty of 1880.

On the other hand, the picture sometimes painted of two traditional enemies patching up their quarrel out of jealousy towards the rising power of Germany will not hold water for a moment. In the first place, it ignores the fact that the two countries, though often disagreeing and sometimes acutely suspicious of each other, had not been at war since 1815, had fought on the same side in 1827, had stood together in the 'thirties, had formed two ententes in the 'forties and conducted a joint war in the 'fifties. Colonial issues had driven them apart again in the 'eighties, but there was at last a dawning perception of the futility of most of these disputes. The Convention was in no sense an alliance, like that between London and Tokio: its aim was, in the considered words of Lord Grey,[12] to "smooth away and remove possible causes of conflict", such as had so continually disturbed relations and placed them at the mercy of some loudmouthed agitator.

---

* 17 July 1903, Cromer to Lansdowne—*British Documents*, II, No. 359. On 1 November Cromer wrote, "we *must* manage to come to terms," and again, "*We must not fail*"—his point being that "one of our main objects" was to get a free hand for dealing with the finances of Egypt and the Sudan" (Newton, *Life of Lansdowne*, p. 284). "The immediate origin of the Entente", Cromer wrote on another occasion "is to be found mainly in the local situation in Egypt" (*Cambridge History of British Foreign Policy*, III, 309).

† It was laid down that Spain must undertake not to alienate any of the territory thus assigned to her—secret Article III (*B.D.* II, 394).

This was especially the view of King Edward, who had for years past deplored what he regarded as quite avoidable friction with France. That in the eyes of London the new Entente was in no way directed against Germany, was clearly perceived by Count Metternich, who wrote home, "The English Government has the satisfying feeling of having one opponent fewer, without this having cost her heavily. It increases her credit at home and to some extent her prestige abroad. But reconciliation with one opponent does not necessarily mean enmity with a third. On the contrary, I know it does not wish to destroy, but to maintain, the wire to Berlin. It would be strange if it were otherwise...."* Moreover, at the time none of the Treaty's critics foresaw its possible effects on Anglo-German relations: Rosebery in particular denounced it as a one-sided surrender, and was afraid for Gibraltar.[13] Lansdowne himself thought he was concluding an essentially Colonial agreement, and long after Grey in his Memoirs recorded the view that the Japanese and French Conventions "were apparently not parts of one settled policy. Each was like a first step in a different policy."†

One interesting feature is still to be recorded. When Balfour submitted the Convention to Parliament for ratification, Edward VII protested on the ground that "power to cede territory rests with the Crown". But the Premier stood firm, making clear that he was acting on the advice of the Foreign Office and the Law Officers: and, undeterred by criticism from *The Times*, he told the House that the clauses relating to cession of territory "require the assent of Parliament". The King considered that he had been "treated with scant courtesy", but found it necessary to give way:[14] and so one of the main surviving prerogatives of the Crown was taken from it—on the basis of the very precedent against which Queen Victoria fourteen years earlier had striven to guard herself, in connection with Heligoland.

The weak spot in the Treaty was undoubtedly its tendency to ignore the international aspects of the Moroccan question. The French were entitled to argue that German interests in Morocco were almost negligible compared with their own, and that they themselves, with a common frontier of 700 miles, could not be indifferent to the growing anxiety at their very doors. None the less, Germany possessed rights under the Treaty of 1880, and these had been ignored at a moment when the German people was in a more than usually susceptible mood, eager to secure "a place in the sun", and

---

* He goes on, less convincingly, to argue that even Delcassé will not be able to achieve an Anglo-Russian alliance (2 June 1903—*Grosse Politik*, XVII, No. 5376). On 10 May Eckardstein had warned Bülow to expect a *rapprochement* of Britain with the Dual Alliance, but Bülow continued to treat this as impossible (*ibid.* Nos. 5369, 5370).

† Grey, *Twenty-five Years*, I, 48. Sir Eyre Crowe's brilliant apology for the motives underlying the Treaty (*British Documents*, III, Appendix A, 397–420) deserves very close study, but is not entirely convincing. Cf. also J. A. Spender, *Fifty Years of Europe*, pp. 218–20.

genuinely alarmed at the possible loss of a market. Germany, however, at first raised no objections; and Bülow in the Reichstag referred to the Treaty as "an attempt to remove a number of difficulties by peaceful methods. We have nothing, from the standpoint of German interests, to object to in that."[15] Nor was this attitude affected by the Moroccan agreement between Paris and Madrid in the following October. Bülow himself in his Memoirs tells us that the change was due to Delcassé's adoption, after that agreement, of a forward policy of "pénétration pacifique" and "Tunisification". There was, however, another reason for the change: just as the imminence of war in the Far East had stimulated the anxiety of French statesmen to reach the accord so nearly within their grasp and thus to diminish the risk of conflict with the ally of Japan, so now the military and naval successes of Japan, the diversion of Russia's whole efforts to distant Manchuria, the impetus which disaster gave to revolutionary currents in Russia itself, resulted in the increasing military isolation of France in face of a Germany who treated the Panama and Dreyfus Affairs and the ever recurring parliamentary crises as sure signs of French decadence.

JAPAN, RUSSIA AND THE ENTENTE

War broke out between Russia and Japan on 6 February 1904. Japan at once secured command of the sea, landed in Korea and advanced steadily into Manchuria, winning the great battles of Liao Yang in August, and of the Sha-ho river in October. It was not, however, till 1 January 1905 that Port Arthur surrendered: the forces thus released were victorious at Mukden in the last week of February, and the naval victory of Tsushima in May put an end to all hope of Russian recovery. Thenceforward Russia was completely paralysed for any action in Europe and absorbed in the negotiations which opened with President Roosevelt's mediation on 10 June and culminated in the Treaty of Portsmouth on 29 August.

It is with these dates in our minds that we must consider three curious incidents in German policy. The Russian fleet's panic-stricken onslaught upon Hull trawlers off the Dogger Bank in August 1904 brought Britain and Russia to the verge of war, but the two Governments kept their heads, and the incident was referred to arbitration. In this connection, however, there was a sinister exchange of telegrams and letters between "Willy" and "Nicky", in which the former, after trying to fan the latter's anger against "Anglo-Japanese arrogance" and England's "brutal assurance", suggested a defensive Russo-German alliance, to localise the war, but also to remind France of her obligations.[16] When the Tsar consented, subject to France being consulted, the Kaiser treated this as "absolutely dangerous", and for the moment dropped the project. Two further overtures failed—the first in connection with the coaling necessities of the Russian fleet on its way eastwards (December 1904), the second on the basis of a Russo-German self-denying ordinance in respect of Austrian territory (February 1905). But on 23 July William met Nicholas on a yachting cruise in Finnish waters and, in the absence of their ministers, induced him to sign the so-called "Treaty of Björkö", for mutual aid "in Europe" against any attack by an European Power. "In fact Germany enters the Dual Alliance as third party", he wired triumphantly to Bülow. The full perfidy of the Kaiser[17] emerges from the phrases which assured the almost weeping Tsar that all friction with France was over, and that "we should become great friends of the Gauls": while his lightheaded folly is shown by his failure to realise that his own voluntary insertion of the words "in Europe" destroyed much of the Treaty's value for Germany. Björkö ended in a complete fiasco, for Bülow threatened to resign the Chancellorship if the Treaty were not abandoned, while Lamsdorff and even the Germanophil Witte made it clear to the Tsar that its adoption would mean the end of the "Franco-Russe". But the incident serves as a flare to illuminate the secret places of German policy: for Bülow's threat to resign was due not so much to the Treaty's contents as to the Emperor's action without consultation.[18] It ended with a definite cooling of relations between St Petersburg and Berlin, from which the main profit eventually accrued to London. Moreover, the main facts of Björkö were almost immediately given by Lamsdorff to Dr E. J. Dillon and communicated to the Foreign Office, where they increased the tendency to follow up the Entente with France by clearing away current misunderstandings with Russia.

The Testing of the Entente

Meanwhile Russia's paralysis seemed to offer Germany a good occasion for breaking up the Anglo-French Entente before it had had time to solidify. Bülow and Holstein, in assuming the offensive, were encouraged by the belief of Count Schlieffen, Chief of Staff and author of the famous plan for the invasion of Belgium, that no more favourable moment could be found for "a clearing up with France at arms", while Britain was from the military standpoint simply negligible. In March 1905, then, it was decided that the Kaiser should begin his Mediterranean cruise by a demonstrative visit to Tangier. For once, his own instincts were against action, but he was over-persuaded by Bülow, and his speech in praise of the Sultan of Morocco as an independent sovereign was a direct answer to the French mission to Fez, and caused a sensation throughout Europe. Delcassé expressed his readiness to clear up the misunderstanding, but the German Ambassador replied that he had no instructions, and German diplomacy veiled itself in silence, except for hints that Delcassé was to be overthrown, and attempts to drive a wedge between him and the timorous Premier Rouvier. Delcassé continued to believe that the growing pressure from Berlin was mere bluff: and he interpreted the cordial messages which he received from Lansdowne as proof that Britain was ready to conclude an immediate alliance against Germany.* But Rouvier claimed to have sure information to the contrary on both points, and when an official from the German Embassy indicated to him quite bluntly that the best way to improve the situation was to change his Foreign Minister,† he took fright, and invited the Cabinet to choose between him and Delcassé. The latter, who in Bertie's view "had got to

* There has been much controversy as to how far Lord Lansdowne committed himself to Cambon and Delcassé. M. Halévy (*Histoire du Peuple Anglais, Épilogue,* II, 407-8) summarises the references in Grey, Loreburn, Asquith, as well as Gooch and Bourgeois. But the publication of *British Documents* has made it clear that the explicit offer of an alliance, still more the promise to blockade the Elbe, or to send 100,000 British troops to Slesvig, was a complete myth. On 22 April Lansdowne had informed Delcassé of Britain's opposition to a German port in Morocco and treated the German attitude as "most unreasonable" (*B.D.* III, No. 90): and on 17 May he urged upon Cambon that the two Governments "should continue to treat one another with the most absolute confidence" and "discuss in advance any contingencies by which they might in the course of events find themselves confronted" (*ibid.* No. 94). The undated minute of Lansdowne attached to this despatch—"I suppose this was the origin of the offensive and defensive alliance—L." (*B.D.* No. 94)—makes it quite clear that Lansdowne himself (evidently at a later period in the year, when the matter was under discussion at the Foreign Office) did not imagine himself to have offered such an alliance. On Lascelles' despatch of 15 June referring to German suspicions of such an alliance, King Edward wrote a marginal note, "Nearly as absurd as it is false" (*ibid.* No. 98). On 16 June Lansdowne wrote to Lascelles a formal statement of his assurances to Metternich that no such alliance was offered to France (*ibid.* No. 99): and we also have Metternich's account of this talk, with the words, "I regard Lord Lansdowne as incapable of deceiving me with this" (*G.P.* xx, No. 6858). *British Documents* (III, No. 805) contains an explicit denial from Lord Sanderson, dated 1922, and endorsed by Lord Lansdowne in 1927.

On the other hand the King seems to have wired to Delcassé in June, urging him not to resign (Newton, *Life of Lansdowne,* p. 341), and in the previous April had shown him very marked attention and may perhaps have used some incautious phrase to which Delcassé attached undue weight. Certainly Delcassé after the war upheld his belief in such a pledge (see *Figaro* of 24 March 1922 and *Correspondance d'Orient* of 31 December 1922). Some of the Emperor's *marginalia* show that he suspected the promise to have come from the King, and not from his Government. Cf. also Eckardstein, *op. cit.* III, 105, who is not, however, a very reliable source. The Emperor in December 1905 continued to believe that Lansdowne had lied to Metternich (see his own account, to Bülow, of a talk with Alfred Beit—*G.P.* xx, No. 6887).

Meanwhile on 9 June A. J. Balfour had assured Metternich "that no sane person in England wishes to have a quarrel or war with Germany", which would be "an act of perfect lunacy" (*G.P.* xx, No. 6855).

† 30 May, Bülow to Radolin—*Grosse Politik,* xx, No. 6669. Here Rouvier is told that Bülow trusts his honesty, but not Delcassé's, and has ordered a press truce "in expectation of his dismissal"! (Memorandum of Herr v. Miquel, 30 and 31 May—*G.P.* Nos. 6674, 6675). Rouvier said, "Je ne puis faire tomber M. Delcassé sur un froncement de sourcils de l'Allemagne, on me le reprocherait toujours": but this is exactly what he did.

consider himself indispensable",[19] now found himself completely alone and resigned on 1 June 1905.[20] But this did not end the matter. The German Government insisted on a Conference, and warned Rouvier that "we are behind Morocco": it disregarded his plea that "a Conference might be dangerous if not preceded by an entente, and useless if it follows one". In the end Berlin induced the United States to intervene in favour of a Conference,[21] and Rouvier, finding it inexpedient to offend Roosevelt, gave his consent on 1 July. But at the end of the month both Emperor and Chancellor were considering the possibility of Britain being at war with Germany, and agreed that in that case France and Belgium must be given six hours to take sides, and that the latter must be invaded at once, whichever side she takes.[22]

The "testing of the Entente", to use Mr Spender's phrase, proved in the end to be its welding. The whole Moroccan affair caused intense annoyance in England, in the Foreign Office no less than in the press: and it was generally understood that the German motive was, in Sir Francis Bertie's words, "to show to the French people that an understanding with England is of little value to them, and that they had much better come to an agreement with Germany. To this end the Emperor 'fait la guerre à l'Angleterre sur le dos de la France'."[23] "The French", says Grey in his Memoirs, "were humiliated because of an agreement that we had made with them": and it was a lively sense of this on the part of Edward VII which now led to fresh friction with his nephew William. The Emperor on his side, touchy and perfidious as ever, imputed to the King those habits of mining and countermining which he himself practised, and thus there gradually arose the legend of "encirclement" which represented the King as always blocking his path, in whatever direction he might turn.

In September a preliminary agreement was reached between Paris and Berlin, resting on the assumption "that Germany will not pursue any aim which would compromise the legitimate interests of France or her rights resulting from her treaties": and a phrase coined by the German Ambassador in Paris, Prince Radolin—ni vainqueur ni vaincu—obtained a wide publicity. On this basis it was not clear what Bülow had gained, save to arouse intense distrust and resentment in France, even among Delcassé's critics, and almost automatically to force Britain closer to the French, since the alternative course of leaving a newly won friend to her fate, while pocketing her own gains in Egypt, would have wrecked the very foundations of the Entente. On the other hand, Germany had a strong legal and even moral case, so long as she upheld the validity of the Treaty of 1880 and insisted upon an international rather than a mere French settlement of the Moroccan question. It was because her prime motive of breaking the

Entente grew more and more obvious as time passed, that France and Britain found themselves steadily driven closer together. But once more nothing could equal the bad psychology of the Germans: for if, in Dr Gooch's words, Delcassé had committed a fatal error in omitting "to purchase Germany's assent in advance", so the policy of Tangier and Algeciras was "a no less colossal blunder, for its inevitable result was to turn a limited obligation into a general defensive undertaking".[24]

THE LIBERAL VICTORY AND STAFF TALKS

Still more unwise was it to seek advantage from the new situation which had arisen in England, thanks to the general election which followed Balfour's ill-calculated dissolution, and which brought the Liberals back to power with a hitherto unequalled majority (eighty-four over all the other parties combined). Though the new Cabinet soon proved to be one of the ablest and most stable of modern times, and though what is rather foolishly called the "Imperialistic" wing of the party secured the Foreign Office for its member, Sir Edward Grey, it was supposed at that moment in Berlin that the radicalism of the new Prime Minister, Sir Henry Campbell-Bannerman, and the known devotion to pacifism and social reform of himself and his colleagues, would strengthen that fresh wave of British "insularity" of which the Chinese labour incident was a hysterical symptom. Certain it is that the height of the British crisis coincided with a more menacing note on the part of Berlin, and Metternich's renewed efforts to interpret British psychology to his chiefs were outweighed in the Kaiser's eyes by the promptings of Tirpitz and a succession of Naval Attachés at the London Embassy. Campbell-Bannerman in his first official statement of policy spoke of his "real friendship" for France and "emphatically reaffirmed" his "adhesion to the policy of the Entente Cordiale", but at the same time expressed "nothing but good feeling for Russia" and declined to see "in the case of Germany also" any "cause whatsoever of estrangement". That little word "also" may stand as a straw in the wind that was blowing across Europe and forcing the Liberals, almost with their first breath, to proclaim the continuity of foreign policy. But French alarm was not allayed, and when Cambon urged upon Grey the necessity for discussing "the eventuality of war", the Foreign Secretary gave it as his "personal opinion" that in the event of a German attack on France in consequence of an agreement with Britain", "public opinion in England would be strongly moved in favour of France". Moreover, while declaring himself unable "at present to pledge the country to more than neutrality", he consented to "unofficial communications between the French and British War Offices and Admiralties", it being made clear that "they did not pledge either Government".[25] Of necessity, the Cabinet could not be consulted, since most ministers were absent fighting elections: but Grey's action was known to, and endorsed by, Campbell-Bannerman, Haldane, Asquith and Ripon, in the belief that it left the hands of the Government free for the event of war. The essence of Liberal policy, to which Grey remained consistently true to the end, is to be found in this passage in a private letter to Bertie.[26] "Diplomatic support we are pledged to give and are giving. A promise in advance committing this country to take part in a continental war is another matter, and a very serious one: it is difficult for any British Government to give an engagement of that kind. It changes the Entente into an alliance, and alliances, especially continental alliances, are not in accordance with our traditions. My opinion is that if France is let in for a war with Germany arising out of our agreement with her about Morocco, we cannot stand aside, but must take part with France. But a deliberate engagement pledging this course in advance before the actual cause of war is known or apparent, given in cold blood, goes far beyond anything that the late Government said or, as far as I know, contemplated."[27]

The Conversations between the two Staffs[28] have formed the subject of prolonged and acrid controversy: but if we consider the facts in cold blood after the interval of a quarter of a century, it is difficult to see how Grey could possibly have refused without risking the return to an isolation still more precarious than that of the 'nineties, or how any German with a knowledge of his own General Staff and its relations with Austria-Hungary and Italy throughout the period of the Triple Alliance, can possibly take exception to Grey's action.

ALGECIRAS

The Algeciras Conference, lasting from 16 January to 7 April 1906, was a long trial of strength between the French contention that the Sultan was incapable of carrying out reform and the German attempt, under cover of internationalisation, to divide Morocco into zones of influence. Germany, realising that if it came to a vote she and her Austrian ally might find themselves alone, tried, but in vain, to make terms direct with France. The fall of the Rouvier Cabinet encouraged Bülow to address a circular note to the Powers, denouncing French intransigeance. But Grey made it quite clear to Germany that he would support the French proposals with regard to the Moroccan police;[29] Francis Joseph warned Bülow of the danger of a regrouping of the Powers if the clash in the Conference assumed too open forms; and above all President Roosevelt warned his friend the German Ambassador at Washington, that if Berlin took the responsibility of disrupting the Conference, he would publish his private* correspondence with the Emperor since the beginning of the crisis. William II took alarm, Bülow dismissed the "mystery man" Holstein, whom he rightly recognised as working for war, and a settlement was reached at Algeciras which can only be described as a drawn battle. But though drawn, it was far from enhancing German prestige in Europe, and nothing could conceal the fact that while France's allies had given their support and rallied the smaller Powers round them, Italy had almost demonstratively separated herself from Germany, while Austria-Hungary had shown surprising detachment and impartiality. Nothing better illustrates the ineptitude of the Kaiser and his advisers than his famous telegram of thanks to Count Goluchowski, as Germany's "brilliant second on the duelling ground". Many contemporaries assumed it to be sarcastic and prompted by ulterior motives, so little had it been deserved: but it was almost certainly William II's idea of a supreme compliment. Incidentally, Goluchowski was politically dead from that moment, and fell soon afterwards. Professor Brandenburg—far the ablest German authority on pre-war German policy—rightly contends that from the juristic standpoint Germany's insistence on the Act of Madrid was unassailable, but doubts whether it was "politically wise" and admits that Berlin knew the Moroccan situation to be quite untenable. He is thus driven to conclude that Berlin's motive was either prestige or a desire for compensation, whether in Fernando Po, Cameroon or the Bagdad Railway. Emperor and Chancellor alike seem not to have seen, or to have underestimated, the dangers of a policy which simultaneously baited and wooed France. "German policy in Morocco is only seen in true proportion if we bear in mind the contemporary events of Tsushima and Björkö."[30] It is well to stress this sage verdict, for it serves as a reminder that European peace was at the mercy of brilliant but unstable impresarios.

Algeciras resulted in a temporary *détente*: and Metternich drew the conclusion that the "Entente Cordiale has stood its diplomatic baptism of fire and emerged strengthened".[31] During the summer he reported that beyond all doubt the main aim of Grey's policy was to preserve the Entente, and "in addition (*daneben*), and so long as it did not injure the Entente, to cultivate good relations with Germany", but that he regarded reconciliation with Russia as more urgent.[32] In other words, German policy had caused general disquietude and served as an incentive for the removal of outstanding points of difference between the Powers, lest otherwise William II should exploit them.

* P. Renouvin, *op. cit.* (ed. Hauser) II, 51. Bülow assured Washington that "Germany thinks neither of special advantages nor of war" (*G.P.* XXI, No. 7118).

EDWARD VII AND WILLIAM II

The years 1905–6 represent the height of the friction between King and Emperor. We have the authority of Lord Esher and other qualified observers, that on coming to the throne Edward VII desired nothing so much as to be on good terms with Germany. At the Kiel meeting in 1904 he most earnestly denied all idea of isolating Germany by the French Entente, and gave the frankest possible notice that he desired a similar reconciliation with Russia. But he saw that his nephew was incapable of responding, and full of secret ambitions and resentments. He described the Tangier incident to Lansdowne as "most mischievous and uncalled-for": the Emperor was to him "no more nor less than a political *enfant terrible*". That August he objected to visiting at Homburg, told Lascelles "he doubts whether the Emperor retains any affection for him", and resented "the tone of peevish complaint" with which William vetoed the Crown Prince's proposed visit to England—a true incident which the Emperor described to the Tsar as "the finest lie I ever came across". By the end of the year Lansdowne told Lascelles that the King "talks and writes" about the Emperor "in terms which make one's flesh creep":[33] while the Emperor flared out to Lascelles and to Bülow, insisting to the latter that before all else "H.M. Ed. 7 *has to make a personal approach to me*". When the Danish minister Count Frijs was sent to the King to discuss the dangers confronting Europe, the Emperor wrote to the Tsar about "the arch-mischiefmaker of Europe": while the King himself, though insisting on "a distinct will-to-peace tendency in Europe", had to admit that "with a man of so impulsive temperament as the German Emperor at the head of the greatest military Power in Europe, anything may happen". In this phrase may be said to lie the key to our policy in these fateful years. William II was like an irresponsible child armed to the teeth, and it seemed advisable, as speedily as might be, to reduce the amount of explosives or gunpowder lying within his reach.

NAVAL RIVALRY

Such feelings were only strengthened by the experience of the second Hague Peace Conference, which took place in July 1907. Campbell-Bannerman himself, an ardent believer in peace and disarmament, had tried to prepare the way for limitation by a famous article in the first number of the new Radical weekly *The Nation* (7 March 1907): but his open appeal to Europe—for this in effect it was—was shattered against the rigid and resentful *non possumus* of the German Emperor. Not merely did the discussions advocated at the Hague come to nothing, but in Mr Spender's words "Germany now manœuvred the British into a position in which they seemed all but single-handed to be holding out for the largest belligerent rights, for the greatest fleet, against the humane opinion of the rest of the world".[36] Never was the clash of civilian pacifism and military or naval "expertism" more mockingly exemplified: and the good work devoted to the reform of naval law and the erection of an international Prize Court could not conceal the fact that the capital issue had again been shelved *sine die*.

Henceforth Anglo-German naval rivalry becomes the dominant factor in the European situation—overstressed or minimised in each country according to the fluctuations of public opinion or the strategic requirements of rival propagandists, but an ever present spectre in the minds of statesmen. There was never any idea of a preventive war, save on the part of "Jacky Fisher", who was severely snubbed for his plan of "Copenhagening" the German fleet, and sadly recorded in his diary that "even the very whisper of it excited exasperation". There was equally no challenge of Germany's perfect right to build what ships she pleased. But for once a deep-laid instinct forced the British to be strictly logical: and in such a mood it became obvious that indefinite building, coupled with absolute and irascible refusal to discuss limitation, could only have one end, namely war. "The real cause of political tension", Metternich warned Berlin, "is not commercial rivalry, but the growing importance of our navy." But the Emperor made it clear that he "did not wish good relations at the expense of the fleet":[37] and he openly warned Sir Charles Hardinge that he would rather go to war than accept such dictation "as naval limitation".[38] The crux of the whole matter is summed up in a memorandum prepared by Sir Edward Grey for the King's guidance during a visit to the Kaiser: "If the German Navy ever became superior to ours, the German Army can conquer this country. There is no corresponding risk of this kind to Germany: for however superior our fleet was, no naval victory would bring us nearer to Berlin".[39] Or, as he said on another occasion: "There is no halfway house in naval affairs...between complete safety and absolute ruin." Those who refused to see this were past all argument, and foremost among them were William II and his advisers.*

* An entirely convincing, detailed and scholarly treatment of the whole naval problem in these years is to be found in E. L. Woodward, *Great Britain and the German Navy*. See especially the sinister story of Tirpitz's accelerations of programme and the long-drawn attempt to delude the British Cabinet.

EPILOGUE

THE ANGLO-RUSSIAN CONVENTION

In proportion as the hopes centred upon the Hague seemed likely to be disappointed, the wisdom of a speedy understanding with Russia became all the more obvious. The advantages of peace in Asia overcame even the doubts of Lord Curzon, whose viceregal visit to the Persian Gulf in 1903* had been a ceremonious "Hands off" addressed to Russia, and who in 1904 had countered Russian intrigues in Tibet by the famous Younghusband Mission. Tentative overtures had more than once come from both sides, and France naturally sought to promote an accord. The Japanese War caused a postponement, but the Dogger Bank and Björkö incidents were "the prelude to a new orientation of Russian policy".[40] In England the growth of a Russophil party was facilitated by the faint beginnings of constitutional life in Russia, and Campbell-Bannerman caused a sensation by his cry, "La Douma est morte, Vive la Douma!" Meanwhile the appointment as Foreign Minister of Alexander Izvolsky, who came from the Danish Court with a strongly Anglophil reputation, the selection of Hardinge as Ambassador at St Petersburg, the clouding over of the traditional Austro-Russian entente and the precarious state of affairs in Turkey since 1903, all served to stimulate negotiation. Finally the urgent good offices of the French Government, backed by a gigantic loan in Paris, outweighed the advice of the Kaiser and completed the weak Tsar's conversion.

The Anglo-Russian Convention, concluded on 31 August 1907, and due almost equally to the initiative of Grey and Izvolsky, fell under three heads. I. Both Powers were to respect the territorial integrity and aloofness of Tibet: in effect, Russia was assured that the expedition to Lhasa was an incident, not a prelude, and on her side renounced any advance from the north into Tibet or Chinese Turkestan. II. Afghanistan was recognised as outside the Russian sphere of influence, while Britain was pledged not to touch Afghan independence or interfere within her borders, in return for a certain control of Afghan foreign relations. III. Persia's independence and territorial integrity were jointly guaranteed, but in effect Persia, which then seemed to be slowly degenerating into an eastern Morocco, was divided into three zones—a large Russian, a smaller British, and a neutral zone in the centre of the country, where the two reconciled rivals might compete. The Persian Gulf was left outside the Convention, on the plea that it was confined to the border regions between Russia and Britain; while the question of the Straits was also passed over, probably in the

* What Lansdowne had called "George Curzon's prancings in the Persian puddle".

calculation that the supreme crisis in Turkish and Balkan affairs was at last imminent, and that by eliminating causes of friction in the Far and Middle East a new atmosphere would be created in which to discuss the Near East also.

The Convention contained nothing to which Germany could reasonably take exception—nothing which even remotely affected her interests or her rights in the sense that they were involved in Morocco or Egypt. Yet though it was confined to purely Asiatic questions, it may be said to have altered the whole focus of Europe, by ridding Britain of all reasonable anxiety on the Indian frontier, and in effect creating a series of neutral zones all round India from Tibet to the Gulf, while at the same time it reduced almost to zero the danger of any combination by the Continent against Britain on such lines as Shimonoseki or Björkö. For Russia, meanwhile, it was the prelude to an active return to European, and in particular to Balkan, politics after the tremendous diversion of the Japanese War: and this was revealed by the marked attention which she now began to pay to Italy.

The weakest point in the Convention was the sinister treatment of Persia: for though no other than Count Witte objected to it as making a Russian annexation impossible, it can hardly be denied that such designs did exist and that Britain connived at them, despite a certain encouragement to the cause of Persian reform. That Persia maintained her independence despite the Convention of 1907 was due above all to the diversion of the Great War, to the temporary eclipse of Russia and to the emergence of a strong native ruler. Of paramount importance was the diplomatic change, which blended the Dual Alliance and the Entente Cordiale in a new Triple Entente; the lists were now set in Europe between the two rival groups of Powers. Britain still preserved a relative freedom of action and would fain have played the mediator in the interests of peace: indeed in the years which still remained before the great catastrophe she showed an increasing readiness to apply to her relations with Germany the same methods of investigation and discussion which had produced successive *détentes* with Japan, France and Russia. But once again, and indeed increasingly with every year, the problem of naval rivalry proved a fatal obstacle. For the second time in two decades increased naval estimates were presented to the German Reichstag, this time as an answer to Admiral Fisher's rearrangement of British naval forces. It was at this time that the Admiral's talk of "Copenhagening" the German fleet evoked such a severe snub from King Edward. But meanwhile the extraordinary course adopted by the Kaiser, of writing a private letter to Lord Tweedmouth, then First Lord—intended, by an array of inaccurate facts, to deter him from augmenting the British building programme—not merely caused annoyance to the King, but grave suspicions at the Admiralty. It was typical of the atmosphere thus engendered that when criticisms began to appear in the British press, the Kaiser at once jumped to the conclusion that "*The Times*' move comes from the King".[41]

REVAL AND THE MYTH OF ENCIRCLEMENT

Meanwhile the Russian Convention was followed quite logically by a desire for closer relations between the two countries; and after a certain delay caused by Labour attacks against the Tsar (whom Mr Ramsay Macdonald described as "a common murderer"),[42] Edward VII followed up his Scandinavian tour by a visit to Nicholas II at Reval. To this meeting an altogether legendary importance has been attached—by the Germans, who came to regard it as one of the landmarks in the new policy of "encirclement", and by the Young Turks, who suspected the two sovereigns of planning the pacification of Turkey in Europe, and therefore resolved to forestall them by revolutionary action from within. The fact that Sir Charles Hardinge accompanied the King seems to have given shape to the theory: but Hardinge's memorandum[43] shows that while he and Izvolsky discussed the whole Near Eastern problem and the Tsar spoke of "a new era" in Anglo-Russian relations, no new binding arrangements of any kind were concluded. It is quite clear that one of their main preoccupations was to avoid exasperating Germany and her incalculable ruler: but he on his side was furious at the thought that henceforth the weak Tsar would no longer be dependent on the exclusive wire to "Cousin Willy", but would listen to "Uncle Bertie" also. The Russian disclaimer of "encirclement" he treated as "a mere blind for an anti-German grouping, like before the Seven Years' War".* Henceforth "Reval" was to play a prominent part in convincing the gullible Germans of their "encirclement" and of the consequent need for ever growing naval armaments.

Only a month later the King visited the Emperor at Cronberg, primed with a memorandum of Grey on the possibilities of a naval agreement: but a wise instinct warned him not to touch more than the fringe of the subject, and the snub administered by William to Hardinge when he suggested that Germany should stop ship-building, was deliberately allowed to percolate through official circles in Berlin, and confirmed them in the view that "that is how one must always deal with Englishmen".[44]

* 12 June 1908—*Grosse Politik*, xxv, No. 8807. On a report of Count Metternich in the same connection, which treats King Edward's "personal policy" as one of peace, the Kaiser comments, "False! He wants war. Only another is to wage it, and I am to begin it, so that he doesn't get the odium" (*ibid.* No. 8821).

The King then went on to his annual cure at Marienbad, and paid the usual visit to the Emperor Francis Joseph at Ischl. The main subject of discussion between the two sovereigns and also between Hardinge and Aehrenthal was the new situation created by the Young Turkish Revolution: and both sides emphasised the desire for close Anglo-Austrian co-operation in the Near East. But when Aehrenthal declared that Anglo-German rivalry did not concern Vienna, and asked whether it had been discussed at Cronberg, Hardinge "pointed out that Austria, the ally of Germany, could contribute effectually to the cause of Peace by acting as a drag on any ambitious naval policy which the German Government might be tempted to pursue".[45] Aehrenthal replied that the negative character "of the Cronberg talks did not surprise him, since King Edward's successful Entente policy" made it very difficult for the Emperor William to modify his naval plans.[46] Edward VII on his side seems to have asked Francis Joseph to use his good offices to convince William II of the dangers of unrestricted naval rivalry.[47] At Ischl, then, the suspicious Aehrenthal already had in his hands a circular of Bülow, stating that "Germany will not consent to any proposals aimed at a reduction of armaments by land or sea. Should England's efforts take concrete form, Germany would resort to arms. Meanwhile the German fleet is to be developed further."[48] Aehrenthal, already annoyed at the Anglo-Russian Convention, the Reval meeting and Grey's divergent attitude towards the Porte, treated the Ischl visit as nothing less than an attempt to detach Austria-Hungary from Germany, and reported in this sense to Berlin.[49] As Aehrenthal for his part was already planning his *coup* for a unilateral settlement of the Bosnian and Bulgarian questions, and prevented his master from breathing a word about it to his visitors, the impression of falsity and distrust was all the more profound, when the crisis came in October. The "traditional" Austro-British relations were never wholly resumed:* and it is not too much to affirm that Ischl, following on Cronberg, was an even more fruitful source of misunderstanding and misrepresentation than "Reval". The constant journeys of Edward VII were beginning to get on the nerves of the German people, and it suited both Emperor and Chancellor to prevent them from calming down. But Bülow in particular admits in his Memoirs that he knew at the time that no new decisions had been taken at Reval, and the circular which he issued to his ambassadors on 21 July is a valuable confirmation.[50]

* Mr Steed warned King Edward at Marienbad on 14 August that the annexation was imminent, but not being able to produce proofs, was naturally enough not believed. But we now know the Austro-Hungarian Crown Council which took the Bosnian decision was held just a week later, on 19 August (*A.H.D.* 1, No. 40).

MACEDONIA AND BOSNIA[51]

While the main weight of British policy during the first eight years of the century was directed towards eliminating causes of dispute with her two chief rivals in the two preceding decades, events in the Near East had once more taken a threatening turn, and indeed acted with corrosive force upon the Concert of the Powers.

While William II played with the Pan-Islamic movement, trained the Turkish army and planned the Bagdad Railway, British protests against the Armenian massacres had destroyed the last vestige of our influence at the Porte and left the German Ambassador, Baron Marschall, in a position comparable with that of Stratford de Redcliffe a generation earlier. But Turkish peace now rested above all on the Austro-Russian Agreement of 1897, which pledged the two Powers in favour of the *status quo* and against territorial conquests. Nothing, however, could arrest internal decay, and in 1903 the Macedonian insurrection on the one hand and the Serbian revolution on the other, ushered in a new era in the Balkan Peninsula. Once more Austria-Hungary and Russia went hand in hand and aimed at a joint European mandate as a substitute for the cumbrous methods of the Concert. Lord Lansdowne, though recognising that these two Powers were "specially interested" and that the situation had "become almost intolerable",[52] none the less favoured general action: but the scheme of reform which he put forward was forestalled—literally by a few hours—by a fresh agreement concluded at Mürzsteg on 29 September 1903. For the next three years the initiative lay with the two Imperial Powers, but the appointment of Hilmi Pasha as Inspector-General of finances in Macedonia, and of a *gendarmerie* to which all the Powers save Germany contributed officers, only served at best to postpone, not to avert, the final disintegration. The stiff attitude adopted by the British Government, and especially King Edward, in refusing for three whole years to recognise the new Serbian regime, until the regicide officers had been dismissed, contrasted strikingly with the immediate recognition accorded by the Austrian and Russian Emperors.

With the substitution of Izvolsky and Aehrenthal for Lamsdorff and Goluchowski as Foreign Ministers of Russia and Austria-Hungary in 1906, co-operation was soon replaced by acrimonious personal rivalry:* and not the least of Aehrenthal's motives was distrust of the Anglo-Russian Entente, as a step towards a constitutional regime in Russia, and perhaps away from the reactionary Three Emperors' League which was his ideal. He even tried to win Russia for separate action in the Near East by four of the six

* They used to refer to each other as "ce crapaud" and "ce sale Juif"—see G. P. Gooch, *op. cit.* I, p. 423.

Powers, to the exclusion of Britain and Italy: but when Russia, in order not to offend London, declined the proposal, he told Count Mensdorff to deny this to Grey.[53] It is instructive to note that while Grey used his newly acquired influence upon the Russian Government to urge restraint in all Turkish questions and so to promote the cause of Turkish reform, Aehrenthal sought to isolate Britain in the Macedonian question, told Baron Marschall that the Balkan peoples should be left "to cook in their own juice", and purchased his betrayal of the Concert by a special railway concession from the Sultan in the Sandjak of Novipazar, early in 1908.

In the kaleidoscopic situation with which Europe was confronted as a result of the Young Turk Revolution of July 1908, Grey's policy was as straightforward as that of Aehrenthal was tortuous. He had good grounds for fearing "that the habit of vicious and corrupt government will be too strong for reform":[54] but he told his Ambassador at the Porte that he was "ready to help the better elements in Turkey", and even after the second Revolution of April 1909 and the final overthrow of Abdul Hamid, he argued that "whether the chance of really permanent reform is great or small, we must back the chance as long as it exists".[55]

It was above all from this angle that Grey condemned Austria-Hungary's annexation of Bosnia on 6 October 1908, as likely to compromise the reforming party in Turkey, bring other claimants into the field against her, and so precipitate partition and perhaps a general war. He was also indignant at Aehrenthal's unilateral action in tearing up an international treaty, all the more since on the last occasion which offered a precedent (the repudiation of the Black Sea clauses of the Treaty of Paris in 1871) it was Austria-Hungary who had protested most vigorously. His indignation was heightened by the discovery that Aehrenthal had lied to Sir Edward Goschen, pretending "on his solemn word of honour" to be taken by surprise at Bulgaria's declaration of independence, when all the time he was acting in collusion with Sofia.[56] Grey of course did not know that while he was complaining of "being treated with such bad faith"[57] William II, whom Aehrenthal had not informed in advance, was denouncing the latter's "frightful stupidity" and even "felony" and declaring himself "deeply hurt in my feelings as ally".* Bülow also was angry, but none the less decided

---

* One specially enlightening detail is the fact that the Kaiser, on first learning that something was in the wind in Bulgaria (on 24 September, and still in ignorance of Austrian plans), at once took it for granted that "the whole Bulgarian action is a coup of King Edward, arranged at Marienbad" (*Grosse Politik*, xxvi, No. 8952). In reality Edward VII knew nothing of what either Ferdinand or Francis Joseph was planning, and was terribly upset and affronted. This illustrates the extent to which suspicion can create myths.

In exactly the same way his anger at Aehrenthal, smashing "my Turkish policy, built up laboriously for twenty years", is at once swallowed up in his obsession, "a great triumph of Edward VII over us" (*ibid.* xxvi, No. 8892).

that unless Germany backed Austria-Hungary to the uttermost, the alliance itself might be endangered: and in the end he talked the Kaiser round.

We are not here concerned with the long-drawn details of the Bosnian crisis, but only with its bearing upon British policy. Grey's position was delicate in two directions. Some obscurity still surrounds the famous interview of Izvolsky and Aehrenthal at Buchlau on the eve of annexation: but it is fairly certain that the Russian statesman learned of Austria's decision, but was misled as to its imminence; that he was counting upon a *quid pro quo* in the Straits question, and then was suddenly confronted with an accomplished fact, before even his French and British colleagues had been won over. Grey made it clear to Izvolsky that he was ready for concessions to Russia, but argued almost unanswerably that to raise this question on the top of the Bosnian and Bulgarian would fatally compromise the new Turkish regime. On 29 October he informed Russia that she would have his "*diplomatic support, but not to the point of provoking a conflict*": and at the same time he warned Serbia against provocative action.[58] Meanwhile he instructed Lowther to put no obstacles in the way of a direct Austro-Turkish arrangement and assured Count Metternich that he "did not wish the discussion of Near Eastern affairs to lead to the formation of two opposing camps".[59] He treated as "nonsense" "all this talk about 'ringing in' Germany"—and this, characteristically, not to the German, but to the *Russian* Ambassador.[60] And to the Austrian, Count Mensdorff, he spoke of "the absurdity of trying to make mischief between Germany and Austria-Hungary" and disclaimed all desire "to disturb the existing balance of power".[61]

It is instructive to contrast Grey's difference of method in 1908–9 and in 1914. In the first case he made quite clear in advance the limitations of British liability, and as a result war was averted, because Russia, and *a fortiori* Serbia, could not risk fighting without allies and therefore had to give way, while Austria-Hungary, being certain of the unreserved support of Germany, knew that Britain certainly (and *perhaps* France also) would not go to war. In the second case he left both sides in doubt till the very last minute as to whether Britain would intervene, and only took the decision when it was already scarcely possible for either side to draw back. We are tempted to wonder whether his previous experience of the collapse of an ally and the intransigeance of an adversary made him reluctant to commit himself so long as even a glimmering of hope remained. If in each case we leave entirely aside the obvious obstacles to an alternative policy, we may at least regard 1908 and 1914 as two classic instances of rival diplomatic methods.

In the end the relentless and intractable Aehrenthal imposed his will upon Serbia, did nothing to ease Izvolsky's position and showed marked indifference towards London's efforts at mediation. The final *dénouement* was, however, the work of Germany, who addressed to Russia an enquiry, to be answered by an immediate "yes" or "no", and amounting, in Izvolsky's own phrase, to "a diplomatic ultimatum".[62] Both Hardinge at the Foreign Office and Nicolson at the Embassy in St Petersburg felt Izvolsky's surrender to be "really too deplorable", and suspected a design to "break the ring and dissipate the Triple Entente".[63] But Russia could not risk war when she was only convalescent from the wounds inflicted by Japan: "the Austro-German plan", Izvolsky told Nicolson, "was skilfully conceived, since they knew that in three or four years Russia could speak differently".[64] Meanwhile Aehrenthal's triumph was short-lived: he had envenomed, almost beyond remedy, the relations of the Dual Monarchy with the whole Southern Slav race, and this was a decade later to prove its final undoing. It remains to add that the German "ultimatum", though quite unequivocal, was not humiliating in form, and Bülow's Reichstag boast of "Nibelung loyalty" was not regarded as offensive at the time. It was left for William II himself, during a demonstrative visit to Francis Joseph at Vienna a year later, to remind the world that if peace had been preserved, it was because he had stood shoulder to shoulder with Austria-Hungary "in shining armour". The phrase stuck, and was not forgotten or forgiven by Russia.

The subdued attitude of France during the whole crisis facilitated a further agreement with Germany on the Moroccan question, and it was hoped that Edward VII's visit to Berlin in February 1909 might restore a certain calm to Anglo-German relations. This was all the more necessary because public controversy in both countries had been rekindled, during the winter of the crisis, by a fresh incident analogous to that of the Tweedmouth letter. This was the Kaiser's notorious *Daily Telegraph* interview, of which Mr Spender has aptly said that "if some ingenious person had set himself to pack into a few thousand words all the things most calculated to set Germans and English by the ears, he could hardly have done better".[65] In Germany it was resented for its revelations of what had been the Kaiser's attitude while all Germany was on the Boer side, and it evoked the first and last constitutional crisis of the Second German Empire, which Bülow exploited to strengthen his position as Chancellor as against the Crown, while the Kaiser for a moment talked of abdication. In England, where some of its many misstatements of fact leapt to the eye, it had a profoundly disturbing effect: and Grey confided to Bertie that "never since I have been in office has opinion here been so thoroughly wide awake with regard to Germany, and on its guard, as it is now". The agitation was no longer confined to the yellow press or to men of such extreme opinions as Maxse or Arthur Lee, but roused an echo with men as different as Lord Cromer, Lord Roberts, Sir Ernest Cassel and Mr J. A. Spender.

The plan of an Anglo-German entente drafted by Kiderlen-Wächter early in 1909 was condemned by Sir Charles Hardinge and Sir Eyre Crowe as "a trap" and regarded by Grey himself as likely "to establish German hegemony in Europe".[66] Already in the previous summer Bülow himself had reached the point of challenging his master's view that "the English could not risk a war with us": "I now regard war as definitely conceivable, if the English are quite certain that naval armaments will go on like this *ad infinitum*".[67] But he, and above all the Emperor, were annoyed by Metternich's ever recurring refrain, that "it is not Germany's economic development that is year by year injuring our relations with England, but the rapid growth of the German fleet",[68] and that "for England security is only possible on the basis of a naval agreement".* We now know that on 3 June 1909 Metternich had to defend his views before Bülow, Tirpitz and Moltke, and that the discussion centred round the old question, how Germany was to get out of the "danger zone", which of course meant how she was to catch up the British building programme.[69] A month earlier Herr von Stumm, during a special mission to London, had been told very frankly by Hardinge that "British feeling towards Germany was due exclusively to German naval policy", but had assured Grey himself that Germany had no *reservatio mentalis* in this question, and that "it was a matter of complete indifference to us whether England built 100 Dreadnoughts and 50 more hypothetical Dreadnoughts or not". The obtuse Stumm actually records that Grey twice fell into "a longish meditative trance" and finally expressed the opinion that "for the present nothing was to be done, and the two Governments must limit themselves to being as open as possible in their intercourse".[70]

During the summer discussions continued, but without result, for Britain pressed for a naval before a political agreement, whereas Germany wished a political first. This involved the enunciation of general principles such as had not been necessary in the three previous Ententes, which were limited to clearing points of disagreement out of the way: and Grey naturally held out for a formula which would not "look as if we were intending to change friends. I want a good understanding with Germany, but it must be one

---

* Metternich to Bülow, 27 November 1908, and to Bethmann, 5 November 1909—*Grosse Politik*, XXVIII, Nos. 10234 and 10360. Cf. also his letter of 2 June 1909—"our relation to England is mainly poisoned by the Fleet Question", and "*I would falsify history if I reported otherwise, and I cannot sell my conviction even for the favour of my sovereign*". Even Sir Frank Lascelles (who generally found it wise to agree with the Kaiser) while speaking of his compatriots as "stark staring mad", added "It is the navy"—11 August 1908, William to Bülow (*G.P.* XXIV, No. 8223).

which will not imperil those which we have with France and Russia."[71] But in actual fact an absolute pledge of neutrality was the only price which Germany would accept in return for a naval holiday. "We ask from England a new orientation of her general policy, in the sense that she should give up her existing ententes and that we should take the place of France": so Tirpitz, behind the scenes, defined the German attitude.[72] And so, though the general situation was calmer for the next two years, the deadlock continued, and however much men of goodwill might seek to cover up the fact, the challenge to British naval superiority had become the axis of the whole European situation.

Against the grim background of future war let us set an anecdote which reveals the reckless outlook of the Emperor. Sir Edward Goschen, in one of his conversations with him, ventured to hint that in England the man in the street wanted to know why he was building the German fleet. "Because I want to make myself safe", the Emperor replied—safe against France and Russia and England too. "And there is another reason. I am all for the white man against the black, whether they be Chinese, Japanese, niggers, or Slavs." For he foresaw the time "when white men will have to stand shoulder to shoulder, . . . and then you will come crawling on your knees to me, not to beg me to diminish my naval strength, but to increase it to the utmost of my power".[73] It is necessary to remember that the Emperor was not as all-powerful as he fancied himself: but it is not less necessary to remember that without his constant, active and imperious backing the naval party could never have achieved its aims.

KING EDWARD

Ill-health had forced Campbell-Bannerman to resign in February 1908, in favour of Herbert Asquith who, as leader of what has been called the "Imperialist" wing of the Liberal party, was in specially close touch with Grey and Haldane, but on the whole concerned himself less with foreign policy than his predecessors as Prime Minister. In any case, his attention during 1908 was increasingly absorbed by the constitutional conflict with the House of Lords and by the general election which their challenge to the Finance Bill involved. Despite a renewed Liberal victory, a deadlock seemed to have been reached when on 7 May 1910 Edward VII died rather suddenly. The crisis over the Parliament Bill necessitated a second general election in the following December, and was prolonged until August 1911, when the much debated Parliament Act finally became law. The long controversy undoubtedly diverted public opinion from the foreign situation during what we now know to have been the final lull before the storm.

No modern sovereign has been more keenly discussed and more profoundly misjudged than Edward VII: the dramatic contrast between uncle and nephew, and the rivalry which it engendered interested public opinion at home and abroad and soon created a legend which still lingers both in Germany and in France. It was very largely due to William II's inability to understand that the King, alike owing to his constitutional position and his own character, was not invariably the pivot round which everything turned, but that it was his ministers who shaped and controlled policy. On the one side the versatile, restless, unstable Emperor, overweeningly self-confident, suspicious, dogmatic, self-centred and convinced of his divine mission, on the other a tolerant, experienced, slightly cynical, self-indulgent man of the world, who though lacking in intellectual tastes or original ideas, combined to an amazing degree social and political *flair*, tact and personal charm, and a gift for extracting knowledge from other men—showing himself at once jovial, familiar and yet ruthless towards any undue familiarity in others. He had a natural taste for politics, and an interest in the men and affairs of the Continent, which was stimulated by close ties of blood with almost every court in Europe:* and in choosing friends he drew his net much wider than most contemporary sovereigns. In the 'seventies, while still jealously excluded from affairs by his mother, he confided to his friend Lord Carrington that when he came to the throne, he intended to be his own Foreign Minister: and when at long last he became King, he insisted on knowing every detail and claimed a say in all appointments and honours. That he was far from being a cipher is shown by his attitude towards the Norwegian Crown, the Serbian regicides, the Congo administration of his cousin Leopold, the promise of a Garter to the Shah. But that he ever held the thread of a consistent world-wide policy in his own hands is a myth far less convincing than the at least plausible theory of "Encirclement". In Lord Grey's words, "A legend arose in his lifetime, that British foreign policy was due to his initiative, instigation and control. This was not so in my experience. He did not care for long and sustained discussion about large aspects of policy, though he brought strong common sense and good judgment to bear on any concrete matter of the moment."†

* Prussia, Russia, Denmark, Greece, Norway, Spain, Portugal, Belgium, Bulgaria and Roumania.

† *Twenty-five Years*, I, 204. Lord Newton in his *Life of Lansdowne*, p. 293, prints a letter from Balfour to Lansdowne, written in 1915 *à propos* of a war book of Professor Holland Rose, exalting the King's role. In this there occurs the passage, "So far as I remember during the years when you and I were his ministers, he never made an important suggestion of any sort on large questions of policy. I wish you would cudgel your own memory and tell me whether in this opinion I am right." No answer is recorded, but the two Conservative leaders clearly took for granted the King's subordination to the Cabinet in matters of foreign policy, as a simple historical fact. Unhappily Mrs Dugdale, in her brilliant biography of Arthur Balfour, passes over this aspect in silence.

This, however, is not the whole truth. There remains the immense prestige which he enjoyed upon the Continent, and which is a signal example of the miracles that can be wrought by sheer personality. While the statesmen of his reign never took their hands off the helm of state, Edward VII contributed the all-important *imponderabilia* of many a situation, smoothed obstacles, added momentum, established contacts, created or dissipated atmosphere and often made possible what his ministers could never have achieved alone. M. Maurois rightly argues that to deny Edward VII's influence on European policy would be to create an equally false legend in the opposite direction. "Son action, pour être humaine et plus simple, n'en avait pas moins été réelle. Par sa bienveillance et son tact, il avait inspiré confiance." The simple truth is that King Edward had the happy instinct of identifying himself, in every fibre of his being, with his people and the policy which geography and tradition had imposed upon them.

Edward VII was succeeded by George V, at home the model of a constitutional sovereign, and known to be more closely acquainted with Imperial and overseas than with continental politics, and for that reason as well as his downright and unaffected character never accused, even by the most distrustful, of political intrigue or personal *rancunes*. If then anything were still needed to dispel the absurd legend of encirclement, it is that during the four years following the removal of the "arch-villain"—the chief mischief-maker in Europe, as William II had told Nicholas II in 1904—events pursued their inexorable course without the slightest divergence of policy on the part of Britain and her ministers. Once again, the explanation is to be found in the unsolved problem of naval armament. When Bethmann Hollweg succeeded Bülow as Chancellor in July 1909, the prospects of an accord slightly brightened, and in proportion as British statesmen convinced themselves of his integrity and goodwill, they too indulged new hopes and engaged in wellnigh interminable negotiations. But the combination of the Emperor and Admiral Tirpitz remained too strong for Bethmann, and Germany steadily refused to modify her naval programme save in return for a promise of British neutrality such as would have ended the Triple Entente. That Grey foresaw disaster, that his mind was already tuned to the memorable phrases of August 1914, but that he dared not publish the full facts without risking a dangerous rupture, is shown by his speech of 13 March 1911 in the House of Commons. Speaking of the intolerable burden of armaments, he expressed the view that it "will be dissipated by internal revolution, not by nations fighting against each other, but by the revolt of masses of men against taxation. . . . When you begin to make hunger by taxation, as sooner or later every country will come to make it if naval and military expenditure goes on increasing, then you will be within measurable distance of that revolt which will put an end to it." He lived to see the alternative of an European War: he did not live to see the defeated nation rearmed and openly invited by its rulers to choose between "guns or butter".*

AGADIR

The Moroccan agreement of February 1909 brought about a temporary *détente* between France and Germany, but even if French ambitions had been less persistent, the chronic anarchy and misgovernment in Morocco would ere long have rendered some kind of intervention inevitable. Early in 1911 there was a rising in Fez, against which the Sultan found himself powerless, and French troops were sent to suppress it. Pan-German feeling at once reacted, and Bethmann Hollweg was not unreasonable in warning the French Ambassador that "if you go to Fez you will stay there, and then the Moroccan question will be raised in its entirety, which I wish at all costs to avoid". His Foreign Secretary Kiderlen-Wächter, however, was less moderate, and took the line (while fully recognising the hopeless incapacity of Mulay Hafid and his advisers)[74] that France was tearing up the Algeciras settlement and that Germany might resume her liberty and insist upon compensations. On 21 June he had a talk with Jules Cambon at Kissingen, in which the idea of recognising a French protectorate in Morocco, in return for colonial concessions elsewhere, was pretty broadly hinted: but to his mind the best way of achieving this was to take and hold a pledge or *Faustpfand* in advance. The first idea had been to send four cruisers to occupy the ports of Mogador and Agadir:[75] in actual fact a single gunboat, the *Panther*, was despatched to Agadir on 1 July. This sudden step caused a profound sensation in Europe: and the French Foreign Minister, de Selves, told the German Ambassador very frankly that "negotiations had been rendered more difficult by Germany creating an accomplished fact, without first trying to reach a friendly entente with the French Government". Privately Jules Cambon discussed with Kiderlen-Wächter the possibility of an exchange of territory, and the words "Congo" and "Togo" were mentioned: but nothing seemed to happen, and the Emperor, who this time had not been in favour of the action taken, grew impatient and declared that "this kind of diplomacy is for my brain too subtle and too high".[76] French and Germans were now playing for time, and Grey's attempts to obtain information as to German aims were unsuccessful. As early as

* For an eminently sane (as opposed to a sloppy sentimental) *pacifist* treatment of the whole problem of naval and military rivalry, the reader should consult the late Mr G. Lowes Dickinson's *The International Anarchy*, especially Chapter xv, entitled "Armaments".

3 July he took things so seriously as to ask that the Cabinet should be summoned, and warned Metternich that "we could not remain passive spectators of a new settlement made between Germany, France and Spain, to take the place of the Act of Algeciras".[77] At the same time he told Paul Cambon that "we had both commercial and strategic interests to consider":[78] but while opposed to any such thing as a German naval base in Morocco, he would not rule out "an open commercial port".[79]

By 12 July Sir Arthur Nicolson and Sir Eyre Crowe were both definitely of opinion that Germany was embarked on "her well-tried policy of blackmailing", and that the French would have to pay up, but that nothing would stop "further extortions of exactly the same nature, . . . except a firm resolve, and the strength to refuse, and if necessary to fight over it".[80] Four days later Kiderlen-Wächter suggested the cession of the whole of French Congo in return for Togoland, and told the indignant Ambassador, "You bought your liberty in Morocco from Spain, England and even Italy, and you have left us out: you should have negotiated with us before you went to Fez." The deadlock continued, and Grey, who was kept informed by Paris and left for over a fortnight without any answer to his representations to Berlin, definitely took alarm on 19 July and asked Asquith for authority "to impress on Germany that if her negotiations with France come to nothing, we must become a party to the discussion", and send ships to Morocco.[81] As a result it was arranged (but without consulting the Cabinet as a whole), that the Chancellor of the Exchequer, Mr Lloyd George, should include in his Mansion House speech of 21 July words which were "no sudden inspiration, but carefully thought out".[82] The essential phrase was that "Britain should at all hazards maintain her place and prestige among the Great Powers", and that "if a situation were to be forced upon us in which peace could only be preserved by the surrender of the great and beneficent position which Britain has won by centuries of heroism and achievements, . . . then I say emphatically that peace at that price would be a humiliation intolerable for a great country like ours to endure". *The Times* took an even stronger line, and there was general approval in the press. The speech had all the more effect, because it came from a pronouncedly pacifist Minister who passed as Germanophil. Grey himself has given it as his considered opinion that the speech, coming from such a quarter, "had much to do with preserving the peace in 1911".*

Even now, however, Grey assured Metternich that he was by no means opposed to an extension of German colonial possessions in Africa,[83] and

---

* Words of Nicolson to Cartwright, 24 July—*B.D.* VII, No. 418. Mr Lloyd George himself claims initiative even for "the wording": but it was submitted to both Grey and Asquith and approved by them (*War Memoirs*, I, 43).

wrote to Bertie that the best solution would be a Franco-German deal in the French Congo, or, failing that, "a tripartite partition of Morocco between France, Spain and Germany, in which France got the lion's share".[84] He was, however, careful to treat French consent as essential, and France would not look at any such suggestion. On the other hand, Kiderlen-Wächter's reaction to Lloyd George's speech was not violent, and he instructed Metternich to assure Grey that Germany "had never dreamt of a war-port in Morocco", and that the very idea was a "hallucination".[85] There can be no doubt that Britain's attitude led Germany to draw back, and for that very reason confirmed large sections of German opinion in the belief in British malignance. For a time there was real danger of war on their North Sea. Metternich was instructed to protest, and he reported his conversation with Grey as having been "very strong, but within the bounds of diplomatic etiquette".[86] Grey's own impression must have been still stronger, for he warned Mr McKenna and Mr Churchill, and precautionary orders were sent to the fleet.[87] The Agadir incident thus proved to be a sort of naval rehearsal for the events of August 1914.

From the first week of August more moderate counsels prevailed, and a series of interminable negotiations, or rather hole-and-corner bargainings, began between Berlin and Paris, with various strange intermediaries carrying messages from Kiderlen-Wächter to Caillaux. The essence of the situation, so far as Germany was concerned, lay in the knowledge that if pressed beyond a certain point, de Selves would resign and almost infallibly involve Caillaux in his fall, and that the prospects of a more complaisant Government coming to power were almost negligible. On second thoughts the German Government resisted the clamour of the Pan-Germans and decided that Morocco was not worth a war with France and Britain from which Russia, however reluctant, could not have held aloof: while the French resigned themselves to compensation in the colonial field. Nor can it be denied that Germany had her grievances in Morocco and was entitled to some equivalent for her consenting to French penetration: it was her extraordinarily clumsy and aggressive tactics that roused opinion against her and administered a serious check to the more friendly sentiments which had undoubtedly been growing up in both countries since 1909.[88] By the Franco-German agreement of 4 November 1911 a large section of French Congo was ceded to Germany, there was an exchange of territory in Cameroon, and France withdrew her counterclaim to Togo.* But on the other hand France obtained a free hand in Morocco, and within four

* On 15 August the Emperor assured Sir E. Goschen that in May 1911 France "had offered Germany the Congo, Madagascar, and he did not know what in return for a free hand in Morocco" (*B.D.* VII, No. 476). This is not recorded in the Emperor's own version (*G.P.* XXIX, No. 10639). It seems to have been evolved out of his own imagination.

months of the Treaty was able to impose a French protectorate upon the incompetent Sultan (March 1912). Hanotaux and a few colonial experts might scream, but France had rounded off her growing empire and signally increased her prestige and her prospects in Black Africa. Germany, on the other hand, had but little to show for the long crisis. She had pointed her guns, and "a damp squib"[89] was the only result. So far from breaking the Entente, she had made it stronger than ever. In the words of Professor Brandenburg, "where extreme caution was indicated, there was a crazy hussar escapade, which cost Germany far more in reputation than it brought in".* On the other hand the nearness of the danger shocked the moderates in both countries into a last effort to make such incidents impossible.

It will always be permissible to suppose that what turned the scale in favour of peace was that Admiral Tirpitz, when faced by the prospect of Britain being drawn into a Franco-German conflict, warned the Emperor and his Ministers that the German fleet would not be ready until 1915, when the widening of the Kiel Canal would have been completed. Another point which requires emphasis is ruthlessly analysed in Sir Eyre Crowe's memorandum of 14 January 1912:[90] the secrecy in which certain Franco-German transactions were veiled both before and after the Agadir crisis, especially by Caillaux and his friends, affords the strongest presumption that a German understanding with France "was an alternative to the understanding with England, and not a step towards it". The fall of Caillaux in February 1912 showed that French opinion emphatically repudiated such an aim: it remained to be seen whether any attempt at a triangular understanding, cutting across the two main political divisions of the Powers, and thereby diminishing the risks of armed conflict, would command sufficient support in France, Britain and Germany. It was to this aim that Sir Edward Grey addressed himself between November 1911 and July 1914.

THE TRIPOLITAN WAR

The precarious nature of the European situation and the extent to which all international problems reacted upon each other was shown by Italy's action in declaring war upon Turkey and seizing Tripoli, thereby setting in motion an avalanche which was soon to transform the Near Eastern landscape. She took skilful advantage of a moment when the other Powers were too preoccupied with the Moroccan crisis to raise any objection: and she could point to the fact that she already possessed the consent of France and

---

* *Op. cit.* p. 330. In Grey's words, "France was left with her prestige intact, and free of the Morocco thumbscrew" (*Twenty-five Years*, I, 241).

Britain, who had long since pocketed their share of the bargain in Tunis and Egypt. She knew enough of Russian and Balkan plans (especially since the Tsar's visit to King Victor at Racconigi in October 1909) to be convinced that grave trouble was brewing in Turkey, and to realise the wisdom of settling the Tripolitan question in her own favour beforehand, in order to have a free hand later on in the Adriatic against her nominal Austrian ally. Grey was quick to see the awkward implications of the affair, and fearing a possible appeal of the Turks to London, told Nicolson that "we must refer them to Germany and Austria as being Italy's allies".[91] At the same time he was resolved to be "on our guard against becoming tools of Aehrenthal to convey unpleasant warnings to Italy".[92] Despite his unsavoury experience of Aehrenthal during the Bosnian crisis, he thought it desirable that he should remain in power,[93] because he regarded him as now in favour of peace. Here his instinct was right, for we now know that Conrad, Chief of the Austro-Hungarian Staff, was urging that the psychological moment had come for a preventive war against Italy, but that Aehrenthal, though in rapidly failing health, was still able to secure a decisive rejection of such an idea both by Francis Joseph and Francis Ferdinand. Conrad resigned in November 1911, and, though Aehrenthal died in the following February, his policy was continued by his successor, the nonchalant Count Berchtold, who like Aehrenthal himself in 1906 owed his selection to his supposed Russophilism, but almost from the first became the exponent of Russophobe policy.

Grey meanwhile was under no illusions as to "the risk of complication in the Balkans in the spring",[94] and was distinctly embarrassed by Russia's desire to reopen the Straits Question. He shared Germany's disapproval of the annexation of enemy territory by Italy while the war was still in progress,[95] and he regretted the double loss of prestige by the Sultan-Caliph, and not least of all, keenly disliked, but was not prepared to oppose by force, Italy's occupation of the Dodecanese. None the less, it is not easy to see what other course he could have taken, quite irrespective of the Triple Entente's desire to humour, and perhaps even detach, Italy. For if Italy had embarked upon a policy of naked conquest, she had as much, or as little, excuse as France farther to the west, and indeed she was not, like France in Morocco, tied by any international contracts, but on the contrary had the signatures of each of the three Entente Powers in her favour,[96] and might reasonably expect at least equal support from her two allies. If, however, the war did not lead to immediate complications, it was only because Italian command of the sea kept the Turks out of Africa: and it gave the first impetus to a movement which was very soon to involve the whole of Europe.

THE HALDANE MISSION

In 1911 war had been imminent and had been averted: but the British Cabinet now found itself on the horns of a dilemma. A return to isolation would have speedily led to a hostile coalition against Britain: an attempt to reconstruct the British Army on a continental scale would not have been tolerated by public opinion at home and would in Germany have been exploited as a proof of aggression, and would almost certainly have "provoked a preventive war" on her part,* long before we could have been ready. The desire of the British Liberal Government to explore the only remaining alternative course and attempt to reach an understanding with Germany, similar to those successively concluded with Japan, France and Russia, has often been treated with incredulity, especially by German writers. That it was none the less deep and genuine is abundantly apparent in the *British Diplomatic Documents* of these years. But perhaps the most conclusive evidence as to their intentions is to be found in the confidential statement made by Sir Edward Grey in May 1911, with the approval of the Prime Minister and the Cabinet, to the Committee of Imperial Defence and the Dominion Premiers. After insisting upon the need for "absolute secrecy", he declared that "it is the naval question which underlies the whole of our European foreign policy", explained how the agreements of 1904 and 1907 "had transformed for the better our relations with France and Russia", and laid down as "a cardinal condition in all our relations with Germany", that any similar agreement with her "must not put us back into the old bad relations with France and Russia", and must "take with us our existing friends in Europe". Britain's hands were free, but she could not, in his opinion, view with equanimity the risk of any Power or Powers dominating the Continent: for if we stood aside, "we should be left without a friend", and in order to keep command of the sea, should have to reckon with "a combination against us of not two, but five, Powers". Public anxiety "arises entirely from the question of German naval expenditure", and hence it was on this point that the Government most desired an agreement with Germany. It could give her guarantees of non-aggression, because "we could not build a fleet with any aggressive purpose so long as we keep our army within its present small dimensions", whereas Germany, if she had a bigger fleet, "obviously could not only defeat us at sea, but could be in London in a very short time with her army".[97]

It was with such views as these, stimulated by the Agadir crisis, that the

* This was Lord Haldane's view (*Before the War*, p. 6), and was shared by General Lord Nicholson.

Cabinet learned through Albert Ballin, director of the Hamburg-Amerika line, and a personal friend of the Emperor, and the banker Sir Ernest Cassel, a former intimate of King Edward, that Berlin would welcome an exchange of views with London. At the end of January 1912 Cassel was authorised to see the Emperor and Chancellor and brought with him a note declaring Britain's readiness, in return for a suspension of Germany's supplementary naval programme, to discuss German colonial aspirations and what we now call a pact of non-aggression. Bethmann Hollweg replied that the Bill before the Reichstag could not be abandoned, but suggested that Grey himself, and perhaps Churchill, should visit Berlin.* The Cabinet very wisely compromised by sending its most Germanophil member, the Secretary for War, Lord Haldane, who, though coming officially, was "merely to talk over the ground, and not to commit either himself (i.e. the Chancellor) or my own Government at this stage to definite propositions".[98] Grey, no less wisely, took care to keep Paris and St Petersburg informed of what was on foot.† Haldane came to a Berlin where the struggle between Tirpitz and Bethmann Hollweg had reached its height, and formed a definitely favourable opinion of the latter. The atmosphere was not exactly improved by the Glasgow speech of Mr Churchill, the new First Lord, who treated a big navy as a necessity for Britain, but for Germany a luxury (9 February).

Haldane began by recognising that armament was of course "within the unfettered rights of the German people", but that "the policy had an inevitable consequence in the drawing together of other nations in the interests of their own security". Britain had "no secret military treaties", but "if France were attacked,...our neutrality must not be reckoned on by Germany". Britain's security would be affected by Germany's possession of the Channel ports: she was "under treaty obligation" to help Belgium if invaded, "just as we were bound to defend Portugal and Japan in certain eventualities": and "our dependence on freedom of sea communications for food and raw material" would force us "to lay down two keels to each one of the new German additions". Moreover, in reply to the Chancellor's insistence upon the creation of a third German squadron, Haldane hinted

* Even to-day there is some obscurity as to the original initiative. Grey in *Twenty-five Years*, I, 250, says that he was never quite sure which side it came from. The Emperor denies that it came from the German side. Bethmann Hollweg and Stumm expressed to Goschen their surprise at the choice of Cassel as the British intermediary (*British Documents*, VI, No. 502). It is quite probable (and this is the view of the Editors of *Grosse Politik*—see note on No. 11347 in vol. XXXI), that Ballin may have acted on his own: but it is quite impossible that he should not first have assured himself of the approval of the Wilhelmstrasse.

† *B.D.* VI, Nos. 498, 499. Haldane told Jules Cambon that "our object was simply to improve the state of feeling between London and Berlin, but on the basis, and only on the basis, of complete loyalty to our Entente with France" (*Before the War*, p. 63).

that it might be necessary to transfer ships from the Mediterranean to the North Sea. To the Kaiser he took the same line, but added that "the initiative in slackening competition was really not with us, but with Germany", and that a political agreement "would be bones without flesh if Germany began new shipbuilding immediately", and indeed the world would laugh at it.[99] In a further conversation with the Chancellor they discussed the possibility of concessions to Germany in Zanzibar, Angola and other parts of Africa, as well as the status of the Bagdad Railway: and Bethmann Hollweg drafted a "formula of neutrality" which Haldane duly took back to London with him, together with a copy of the naval supplements handed to him by the Kaiser himself.

Grey expressed himself to Metternich as "immensely impressed", and hoped that means would now be found for dispelling the "warcloud".[100] But when the Cabinet came to examine the formula, it soon became obvious that it was incompatible with the Entente as it then existed, and above all that a cessation of the German naval programme was an essential preliminary to any bargain. On 15 February, then, Haldane reiterated to Metternich in the most friendly way what he had said to the Chancellor about two keels to one: and a week later he and Grey, speaking in the name of the Cabinet, assured him that the German Navy Bill (or "Novelle") was the only obstacle, but that its maintenance would make agreement impossible.[101]

This was treated by the Emperor as a "disavowal" of Haldane and as "an impudent interference in the selfdetermination right of a great nation": "every discussion of my 'Novelle' I reject a limine".[102] It was left to Haldane to warn Metternich of the consequences of such an attitude: the Cabinet was definitely resolved, if the Novelle were upheld, to introduce supplementary naval estimates in Parliament, and to transfer part of the Mediterranean fleet to home waters.[103] This made William II more furious than ever: London must be told that such a transfer of naval forces was "a threat of war" and would be answered by a return to the Novelle in its old form, and by mobilisation.[104]

This, however, was too much for the Chancellor, who offered his resignation, and thus forced his master to moderate his tone and demands, but only at the expense of a rival offer of resignation on the part of Tirpitz, who had not concealed from Haldane his pride in the role of "bogeyman of Old England". This trial of strength between the two protagonists lasted for some time, and meanwhile Ballin was sent to London, to discuss the naval deadlock informally with the First Lord. On 14 March Grey proposed a new formula in the following terms: "England will make no unprovoked attack upon Germany and pursue no aggressive policy towards her.

Aggression upon Germany is not the subject and forms no part of any treaty understanding or combination to which England is now a party, nor will she become a party to anything that has such an object."[105] But even Metternich felt this to be inadequate, because no mention was made of neutrality, and hinted at the possibility of "a change of personnel in Berlin":[106] he wanted some such addition as "England will therefore adopt at least a benevolent attitude, should war be forced upon Germany". Grey on his side feared that "this might give an impression...that under no circumstances, if there was war on the Continent, could anything be expected from us".[107] But he gave the Ambassador assurances that he, and the whole Cabinet, had absolute confidence in the Chancellor and could undertake, even if the Novelle were upheld and no agreement were reached, to "conduct British policy in the sense of the proposed formula, so long as he was responsible for German policy".[108] He added that the aim of his own policy was that "*Europe should no longer be divided into groups*".

On this William II exploded altogether: the decision depended on himself, not on Bethmann Hollweg: Grey did not understand "who is master here", and was trying to dictate who should be minister in Germany. If then Britain would not accept neutrality, let her be offered "a defensive and offensive alliance, including France": her refusal of this would put her flagrantly in the wrong before the whole world.[109] He actually appears to have written to King George in this sense.[110] Nothing of course came of the outburst, but Metternich, acting on previous instructions, intimated to Grey the German view that "only an agreement of a far-reaching character guaranteeing absolute neutrality", would satisfy Berlin.[111] Grey reminded him that Germany "was asking for something which went much farther than anything we had with France or Russia". On 22 March the German Government published its naval proposals (on 14 April they were laid before the Reichstag, and on 14 May adopted): and though Grey expressed the hope that negotiations respecting the colonial field would still continue, the prospect of agreement on the major issue was now at an end.

It only remained to find a scapegoat, and Count Metternich was soon afterwards recalled from the London Embassy. It is the duty of the historian to pay a tribute to his sanity and breadth of view, his conscientious interpretation of public opinion, his singleminded efforts towards an understanding and his courageous refusal to suppress facts which he knew to be true, but also to be unpalatable to his chiefs. His influence had been persistently undermined by successive Naval Attachés in his own Embassy: but nothing is more remarkable in the whole history of Anglo-German relations than the uniform testimony of the last four Ambassadors before the war—Hatzfeldt, Metternich, Marschall and Lichnowsky—confirmed by such able understudies as Eckardstein, Stumm and Kühlmann—and above all the rapidity with which Metternich's successor, Baron Marschall, who came from Constantinople after nearly two decades of Anglophobe activities, found himself converted to similar views.

Few statesmen have been more ungenerously maligned in their lifetime than Lord Haldane, and few have been so speedily and completely vindicated by history. To-day we know that but for his long and untiring work of organisation there would in August 1914 have been no British Expeditionary Force fit for the tremendous task that confronted it: and since the publication of the *British Documents* we also know that during his Berlin Mission, so far from giving away any essential position, he gave the German Government an urbane, but unmistakeable warning as to British policy, while observing perfect good faith towards France and Russia. The Mission was not wasted, for it stands in history as convincing evidence of intention: and it at least established cordial relations with Bethmann Hollweg and thus opened up a new line of advance. So long as this line remained open, Haldane's silence before British public opinion had its justification: where he laid himself open to criticism was by outwardly assuming a false optimism which misled that public opinion and was also misinterpreted in Berlin.

The essence of the whole incident was summed up by Sir Eyre Crowe in a memorandum on German policy. " She wants to have an absolutely free hand in dealing with any problem of foreign policy, without fear of meeting with the opposition of third parties. She wants to make herself so strong that she can dictate terms to every Power."[112]

The failure of the Haldane Mission had two logical results. British naval estimates were laid by Mr Churchill before Parliament, on the basis of a 60 per cent. superiority in vessels of the Dreadnought class over the German navy, and it was hinted that the time might come when the Admiralty might demand two keels to one against Germany.[113] The idea of "a naval holiday" was also hinted, but not unduly pressed. The Opposition's view was voiced in a contemporary article of A. J. Balfour, which contained the effective phrase, "Without a superior fleet Britain would no longer count as a Power. Without any fleet at all Germany would remain the greatest Power in Europe."[114]

Meanwhile the French Government, doubtless somewhat relieved at the failure, suggested a further definition of the relations between Paris and London: and the necessities of naval policy led to fresh consultations between the British and French experts. By the autumn of 1912 it was agreed that the main strength of the French fleet should be concentrated in the Mediterranean—where it would be a match for Austria-Hungary and Italy—while Britain transferred part of her Mediterranean squadron to the

North Sea. The Notes exchanged between Grey and Paul Cambon on 23 November, whose tenour was not published or submitted to Parliament, expressly laid down that these consultations were "not an engagement that commits either Government", and that the new disposition of the two fleets "is not based upon an engagement to co-operate in war".[115] None the less, Britain was in a certain sense bound in honour to the full implications of an arrangement that could not easily be undone. Mr Churchill warned the Prime Minister of "the tremendous weapon which France would possess to compel our intervention, if she could say, 'On the advice of and by arrangements with your naval authorities we have left our northern coasts defenceless. We cannot possibly come back in time.'"[116] Mr Lloyd George tells us that the Cabinet was now for the first time informed of the negotiations of 1906, and that most of its members felt not merely "hostility", but actual "consternation":[117] but they accepted the situation, doubtless because they felt the grip of inexorable facts. The Entente Cordiale was in process of moral evolution.

THE BALKAN WARS

To-day it is abundantly clear that the central problem in Europe was Germany's bid for naval superiority, ending either in the splitting of the Triple Entente by the enforced detachment of Britain or in Britain's confrontation by a continental combination. Thanks, however, very largely to the genuine efforts of Grey in these closing years to cut across the two alliances and re-establish a real European concert, a certain *détente* was achieved, but the catastrophe was eventually precipitated by a recrudescence of trouble in the Near East.

The fraternisation between Turk and Christian, which had followed the first Young Turk Revolution, all too soon yielded to an internecine conflict among all the races of Turkey in Europe and a combined policy of forcible Turkification and extreme centralism on the part of her new rulers. The ruthless repression of the Albanians in 1910-18 was a foretaste of what awaited Slavs, Greeks and Vlachs also: and the idea of a Balkan League including Turkey—as first put forward by Charikov, the Russian Ambassador at the Porte, and welcomed both by Milovanović and Venizelos on behalf of Serbia and Greece—soon proved impracticable. Spurred on by the combined fanaticism and incompetence of the Committee of Union and Progress, the Balkan states began to get together and plan both military and political co-operation. The Tripolitan War confirmed their belief in Turkey's impending collapse and in the need for speedy action, and secret negotiations began between Athens and Sofia, sometimes with J. D. Bourchier, *The Times* Balkan correspondent, as intermediary. Still more serious were the overtures made by Milovanović to the Russophil Bulgarian Premier Geshov, this time with the active knowledge of the Russian Minister in Belgrade, Hartwig, a notorious exponent of the Russian "forward" school. On 13 March and 29 May 1912 secret treaties of alliance were concluded between Serbia and Bulgaria, and between Bulgaria and Greece, in each case supplemented by military conventions which committed them to mutual support against Turkey, and in certain contingencies, against Austria-Hungary. Provision was made for possible conquests, Serbia recognising Bulgaria's rights east of the Rhodope Mountains and the Struma river, and Bulgaria Serbia's rights north and west of the Šar. The districts lying between these limits, the Aegean and the Lake of Ohrid were to be autonomous, and if partition should prove inevitable, any territorial dispute was to be referred to the arbitration of the Russian Tsar. In the case of the Greek Treaty the division of the spoils was not defined, but left to chance, the plain fact being that none of the Allies anticipated the overwhelming victory which awaited them.

The Italian War had a disintegrating effect upon Turkey in Europe: the komitadjis resumed their internecine quarrels, and the Albanians in particular proved more than a match for the repressive measures of the Young Turks, who by the summer of 1912 were reduced to offering them a certain inadequate autonomy and then to extending their pledge to the whole Empire. This was received on all sides as a sure sign of impending collapse, and merely convinced the Balkan states that the moment for action had at last come. The well-meaning efforts, first of Count Berchtold, then of the French Premier, Poincaré, to bring pressure from the Concert upon the Porte and meanwhile to restrain the Balkan states by the warning that no change in the *status quo* would be tolerated, merely had the opposite effect of hastening mobilisation on both sides. At the last moment the Porte announced its intention of putting into force the provisions of the Treaty of Berlin and the Vilayet Law of 1880—after they had remained a dead letter for over thirty years! This, and the belated collective action of the five Powers, were resented by the Balkan League, as likely to result in a new set of worthless paper reforms, and to rob them of a golden opportunity for settling the whole problem. King Nicholas of Montenegro was therefore hurriedly put up to declare war upon Turkey on 8 October 1912, and within a few days hostilities had become general. The Powers remained passive, having been assured by their Military Attachés that the Turks would be victorious and that Europe could then dictate a settlement. But in actual fact the Balkan League swept all before it—the Bulgars at Lüle Burgas, the Serbs at Kumanovo and Monastir, the Greeks on their march to Salonica: and by the end of November Turkish rule in Europe was restricted to the Tchataldja and Gallipoli lines, and to the three fortresses of Adrianople, Janina and Skutari. The Balkan *status quo* was as dead as a doornail, and Serbia's victories in particular, coinciding with Magyar repression in Croatia, gave an astonishing impetus to the movement for Southern Slav Unity throughout the southern provinces of the Habsburg Monarchy.

Throughout these complications Sir Edward Grey's efforts were consistently directed towards appeasement. In January 1913 he told Bertie that he desired a working understanding between Russia and Austria-Hungary. "War would be very inconvenient: I do not think we could take part in it and intervene on the Russian side, and yet our abstention would prove a danger to the maintenance of the present grouping of the European Powers."[118] While Cartwright in Vienna disbelieved in a Balkan alliance or in support for it from Russia,[119] our extremely well-informed Minister in Sofia, Bax-Ironside, learned the contents of the secret Serbo-Bulgarian Treaty on the very day of its conclusion, long before either France or Austria-Hungary.* If those in control of British policy had been engaged in the machinations with which they are sometimes credited, they would of course have been delighted at the news and used it to strengthen their ties with Russia. But instead of this Nicolson wrote privately to Cartwright, "it is most unfortunate that such a convention has been concluded, especially under Russian auspices".[120] When in May Sazonov revealed the facts to O'Beirne, Buchanan's deputy at St Petersburg, the latter showed no enthusiasm and was afraid lest Vienna "might get wind and resent" such action: and Nicolson, replying to this, feared that Sazonov was "embarking on an adventurous policy. But don't indicate our apprehensions, as it is exceedingly necessary to keep on the best possible terms with Russia".[121] This may have been weakness, but it was not encouragement or collusion.

There is ample evidence in the *British Documents* that Sazonov, after encouraging Balkan union, took fright at its effects[122] and tried first to hold back the Allies and then to separate them:[123] Izvolsky in Paris may have been more aggressive, but Sazonov was jealous of him, and Poincaré distrusted him.† Grey had told Mensdorff in July that he desired the Balkan *status quo*,[124] and Buchanan reported to Sazonov his chief's "anxiety to do nothing that might divide Europe into two hostile camps on the Balkan question". Fortunately Sazonov was visiting Western Europe when the

---

* 14 March 1912, Bax-Ironside to Nicolson—*B.D.* Nos. 558–9. Bax-Ironside enjoyed the close confidence of the Anglophil Premier Geshov. Poincaré only heard of its existence when he visited St Petersburg in August—see *Les Balkans en Feu*, p. 49.

† A common accusation against Poincaré is that he and Izvolsky worked for war: and the former's strictures on Izvolsky (*Les Balkans en Feu*, pp. 128, 294, 314, 340–1, 351, 417) have sometimes been treated, though unconvincingly, as a mere attempt to construct an alibi. The mischievous role of Izvolsky is, however, not open to dispute, and can be studied in detail in *Briefwechsel Izvolskis*, 4 vols, ed. F. Stieve.

trouble came to a head, and his conversations with Grey and King George at Balmoral are on record.* To the Russian statesman's enquiry as to the British attitude in war Grey gave in substance the same reply as to Cambon and Delcassé in similar circumstances. "The question of whether we went to war would depend upon how the war came about. No British Government could go to war unless backed by public opinion. Public opinion would not support any aggressive war for a *revanche* or to hem Germany in, and we desired to see differences between Germany and other Powers, particularly France, smoothed over when they arose. If, however, Germany was led by her great, I might say unprecedented, strength to attempt to crush France, I did not think we should stand by and look on, but should do all we could to prevent France from being crushed."[125] It was clear to Sazonov that none of the Powers, and his two allies as little as the others, desired to see the question of the Straits reopened: but his nervousness was justified by Bulgarian and Greek designs upon Constantinople. France stood committed to helping Russia in a war of Balkan origin, but was extremely anxious to avoid it, for financial as well as higher reasons. With both France and Russia, doubts as to Britain's armed support and memories of the precedent of 1909 served as a strong deterrent: but indeed none of the Great Powers at this moment wanted war, and the hesitations which this engendered were actually an incentive to the Balkan Allies, who cared little for the admonitions of Russia or even Europe as a whole, and only saw a heaven-sent opportunity that might never recur.[126]

The completeness of the League's victory speedily dissolved any idea of upholding the *status quo*. As early as 28 October Grey told Kühlmann that British public opinion "would not be a party to ejecting the Balkan states by force from their conquests", but that Constantinople was an European question: while Asquith spoke in favour of recognising the accomplished fact and re-making the Balkan map. Russia notified London on 1 November that she could no longer support the *status quo*, and Grey answered that he saw no reason for making reservations.[127] Meanwhile the Emperor William had from the first treated the Powers' efforts at mediation as "a *testimonium paupertatis* for Europe" and assumed that if the Allies won, "no one could prevent them from taking their share". He was opposed to any action which might "cramp the League in its victorious career", and suggested to Kiderlen-Wächter that Germany's aim should be to make of the four

---

* Sazonov's long report to the Tsar (R. Marchand, *Un Livre Noir*, II, 345–59) contains the often quoted remark of King George, that in case of war "we shall sink every German merchant ship we get hold of".

† 4, 6, 8, 16, 25 October—*G.P.* XXXIII, *marginalia on Nos.* 12225, 12235, 12246, 12277, 12297. "The Eastern Question must be solved with blood and iron. But in a period favourable *for us*! That is *now*."

Balkan Allies "a seventh Great Power, leaning upon Austria and the Triple Alliance".[128] This, however, proved quite impracticable owing to the very dangerous quarrel which developed between Vienna and Belgrade, Austria-Hungary being bent at all costs upon excluding Serbia from direct access to the Adriatic, and insisting, with Italy's support, upon the creation of an independent Albanian state. William II saw "no danger to Austria's existence or prestige in an Adriatic port for Serbia",[129] and Kiderlen-Wächter was afraid that Austria-Hungary had "great territorial plans which would make peaceful agreement with the Balkan states impossible".[130] Conscious that Russia would support Serbia if attacked by Austria-Hungary, and feeling that it was monstrous that Germany should be involved in "a life and death struggle with three Great Powers because of Albania or Durazzo",[131] Bethmann Hollweg, Kiderlen-Wächter and the Emperor agreed to exercise a restraining influence upon Vienna, while making it clear that they "would not for a moment evade their treaty obligations".[132] Grey on his side was naturally far more concerned to maintain European peace than to secure full satisfaction for the Balkan Allies: and Nicolson went so far as to describe the Serb attitude as "hopelessly idiotic and dangerous".*

There was thus an obvious basis for that co-operation between Germany and Britain for which Grey had so earnestly appealed to Herr von Kühlmann in October, assuring him "that he was heartily tired of the long dispute and offered the olive-branch of peace, for a cordial and lasting reconciliation", and adding that British and German interests in the present crisis seemed to him "entirely identical".† In reply Bethmann and Kiderlen-Wächter declared their readiness for discussions, but insisted on "absolute secrecy". Some weeks later Lord Haldane visited the new Ambassador, Prince Lichnowsky, and while warning him that in case of war Britain could hardly hold aloof, pleaded for every effort to prevent "a hardening of the groups".[133] The Kaiser wrote scornful comments on this, but events were meanwhile imposing upon Germany and Britain alike the most strenuous efforts to hold back their Austrian and Russian allies, who had both ordered partial mobilisation. In the background, it is true, the German and

---

* 26 November 1912—B.D. IX (ii), No. 286. Sir Ralph Paget called the Serbs "utterly obstinate and unreasonable"—30 November, ibid. No. 313.

† The message was sent through Mr (now Lord) Tyrrell, then Grey's principal private secretary. Kühlmann to Bethmann Hollweg, 15 October—G.P. XXXIII, No. 12284, and Bethmann Hollweg's answer of 20 October—ibid. No. 12287. If they could once agree in the Balkans, Grey considered "co-operation in China, Persia, Turkey and Africa as hopeful" (ibid. No. 12295).

Professor Brandenburg (op. cit. p. 377) regards the incident with suspicion, in view of the exchange of letters between Grey and Paul Cambon on 23 November—already referred to, supra, p. 632.

Austro-Hungarian Chiefs of Staff held fresh conversations, and the Triple Alliance was renewed: but Francis Ferdinand, though as Inspector-General of the army he took the precaution of reinstating the bellicose General Conrad, none the less spoke openly of war with Russia as a "monstrosity", and was known to favour a renewal of the Three Emperors' League. It thus proved possible to win the assent of all the Powers for a Conference of Ambassadors* to discuss outstanding disputes, and there was prompt agreement that it should be held in London, under the chairmanship of Sir Edward Grey. Austria-Hungary had already withdrawn her objections to Serbia remaining in the Sandjak of Novipazar and thus acquiring a common frontier with Montenegro: but she remained adamant against a Serbian port, whether at Medua or elsewhere. The Ambassadors therefore accepted in principle Albanian autonomy under the guarantee of the six Powers, and promised the Serbs commercial access to the sea through a free neutral Albanian port, connected with the interior by an international railway.[134]

In the meantime an armistice had been concluded between Turkey and Bulgaria, and the five belligerents were invited to conduct their negotiations for a Balkan peace in London, in close proximity to the Conference of Ambassadors. But there was complete intransigeance on both sides, complicated still farther by a Roumanian demand for compensation from Bulgaria. After long resistance the Turkish Government was on the point of yielding to the pressure of the Powers and ceding the coveted fortress of Adrianople, when Enver Bey engineered a revolution at the Porte, shot down his own Commander-in-Chief, and set up a Government pledged to further resistance (23 January 1913). On 3 February the Balkan War resumed its course. The task of Greece was completed with the fall of Janina (6 March): Adrianople surrendered on 26 March to the combined efforts of Bulgars and Serbs, and with the surrender of Skutari on 23 April to the Montenegrins and Serbs, Turkish rule disappeared from Europe, save for the Capital and the land connections of the two Straits.

Once more, there can be no question of even a brief survey of events, but at the most an attempt to relate them to British policy.[135] The sudden death of Kiderlen-Wächter on 30 December deprived Germany of an able statesman who, despite his record in the Agadir crisis, was undoubtedly working for peace and for Anglo-German friendship. Ten days later Bethmann Hollweg said to the British Ambassador, Sir William Goschen, "I can assure you that if it had not been for England and Germany, Europe would be in a state of war at this moment":[136] and both he and his under-

---

* They were M. Paul Cambon, Prince Lichnowsky, Count Mensdorff, Count Benckendorff, and Marquis Imperiali.

study Zimmermann stressed "the value of co-operation,...both as a useful factor in the crisis, and as a foundation for more cordial relations in future".[137] The worst danger was over when Russia ceased to insist upon an Adriatic port for Serbia, and when Francis Ferdinand put a veto upon Conrad's plan for the conquest and partition of "the Southern Slav Piedmont". Germany refused to join in a naval demonstration against the Turks, but supported a collective step at the Porte, and accepted as reasonable Grey's view that Russia could not be expected to give way on every point, Skutari and Djakovo as well as the Adriatic port. There followed endless haggling about contested points along the Albanian frontier: and this led the Montenegrins, supported by Serbian troops, to concentrate upon the siege of Skutari and finally on 23 April to compel its surrender. This time even the existence of the Ambassadors' Conference would not have averted war, if Grey had not propounded a scheme for a joint naval blockade off the Montenegrin coast, and finally the occupation of Skutari by bluejackets from all the fleets, under command of Admiral Burney. King Nicholas yielded with a very bad grace, Serbia had to withdraw her troops, and the largest Albanian town was saved for the new Albania.

Meanwhile a collective Note to the Porte led to a second armistice, and during May the Balkan diplomats again found themselves in London, though in an even more uncompromising mood than before. Haggling continued throughout the month, until Grey, losing patience, saw the various delegates separately and gave them to understand that "the only thing to be done" was to sign the treaty "as it stood" or to leave London, and that "our support would be given to those who signed". This had the desired effect, and the Treaty of London was signed on 30 May. It was a settlement imposed by the personal prestige of Grey, speaking in the name of a country standing half-way between the two camps, upon small, reluctant men, consumed by passion, fear and greed. They assumed, all too rashly, that its terms would have the full backing of the country which had secured its adoption.

It was called peace, but it was no peace: for the four Allies found themselves quite unable to reach agreement as to a division of the spoils. No line had ever been drawn between the Bulgars and Greeks, and now both claimed Salonica and the north Aegean coast: while the Serbs, excluded from the Adriatic by Austria's veto, insisted upon retaining the Vardar valley as their only alternative outlet to the sea, and this meant Monastir, Ohrid, and the great bulk of Slav Macedonia, as well as the "contested zone". Austria-Hungary pursued the parallel aims of preventing Serbian expansion westwards, checking her growing influence among the Jugoslavs of the Monarchy, and embroiling her with Bulgaria: and to her encouragement it was very largely due that Bulgaria remained adamant, and disregarded Russia's successive proposals for parallel demobilisation, for acceptance of the Tsar as arbiter (as provided by the secret treaty) and for a conference of the four Balkan Premiers at St Petersburg (a suggestion which Grey actively favoured, in preference to mediation by the Triple Entente).[138] At last, on 29 June, the Bulgars, hopelessly underestimating the strength of their late allies, made a treacherous midnight attack upon the Serb and Greek positions on the Bregalnitsa, and after several days of desperate fighting were slowly driven back. As late as 4 July the Bulgarian Premier wished the British Minister to believe that his country was "not at war",[139] and the generals, who thought they could cut through the Serbs "like a knife through rotten cheese" and separate them from the Greeks, now wished to treat the incident as a regrettable blunder—though King Ferdinand admitted that in ordering the night attack he had counted on Vienna's help.[140] But Serbia and Greece, united by a defensive treaty of 1 June, were resolved to complete their victory; Roumania, who had given Bulgaria fair warning that she would not sit still and let Serbia be crushed, now declared war and threatened Sofia from the north, while the Turks reoccupied an undefended Adrianople. During July Austria-Hungary was on the point of attacking Serbia from the rear: Berchtold warned Berlin that she could not tolerate an aggrandised Serbia, "against whom the Southern Slav provinces of Austria-Hungary would not be tenable".[141] She was with difficulty held back by Germany, who argued that it would be a grave blunder to put the same veto on Monastir as formerly on Durazzo, that to divert Serbia to Salonica had certain advantages[142], and above all that it was a vital interest of the whole Dreibund not to alienate Roumania by undue favours towards Bulgaria. Zimmermann treated "Great Serbia" as a "cauchemar", while Italy warned Berlin that she on her side could not allow Austria-Hungary to overpower Serbia.[143] Berchtold's isolation was completed by Berlin's growing interest in the cause of Greece, whose new Queen was the Kaiser's sister. Grey's attitude during this second war was more negative: he seems to have been absorbed in ambassadorial discussions as to the frontiers and internal structure of the new Albania, and this undoubtedly helped on the final peace by meeting Austria-Hungary's Adriatic requirements. Meanwhile the visit paid by Nicholas II and George V to Berlin for the wedding of the Kaiser's only daughter had also helped to create a calmer atmosphere and cut across the main groupings of the Powers.

There was thus no choice for Bulgaria but to consent to a Balkan Peace Conference: and the Treaty of Bucarest, concluded on 6 August 1913, stereotyped the territorial gains of Serbia and Greece. This time the real decision lay with Berlin, though Rome's determination to extract compensation for any Austrian gain undoubtedly helped to hold back Vienna. William II virtually forced the hands of Count Berchtold by exchanging cordial telegrams with King Charles of Roumania: "thanks to you", ran the latter's flattering reply, "peace remains definitive". At the same time the Emperor demonstratively made his brother-in-law King Constantine a German Fieldmarshal, and turned the scale in favour of assigning Kavala to Greece and thus again shutting off Bulgaria from the Aegean. On 12 August Tschirschky was instructed to inform Berchtold of Germany's opposition to any modification of the Treaty, and showed comparative indifference to Austrian misgivings about the Southern Slavs.[144] "We are sitting on the ground between all the stools", wrote General Conrad to a military colleague.[145]

It still remained to appease the Turks: and here Grey again allowed himself to follow in the wake of events. He told Berlin that he had not changed his views regarding Adrianople, for whose cession he had pressed in the previous January:[146] but he evaded a question in the House of Commons which justified Turkish recovery of Thrace on a basis of nationality. Sazonov at first took a stiff line,[147] but he found neither France nor Britain disposed to adopt financial pressure against Turkey; Grey's suggestion that Germany and Russia should take joint action in the question was misunderstood by the Kaiser as an attempt to shift upon them the trouble and odium of compulsion: if the Triple Entente disagreed about Adrianople and fell to pieces, so much the better.[148] Grey, however, had publicly laid down "that British policy should never be one of intolerance or wanton or unprovoked aggression against a Mussulman Power...but we cannot undertake the duty of protecting Mussulman Powers outside the British Dominions from the consequences of their own inaction" (12 April 1913). And now many voices were raised in favour of inaction, lest by forcing the Caliph of Islam to respect the Treaty of London, we should cause trouble for ourselves among the Indian Moslems. This argument, which is known to have weighed with the British Cabinet, had momentous results in the Great War, for Britain's attitude was felt by Bulgaria as a betrayal and ere long drove her into alliance with Turkey and Germany. Its complete futility was shown when India calmly accepted our four years of war with the Sultan-Caliph, and when in due course the Caliphate and Islam itself were dethroned by an infidel Turkish dictator. On 29 September helpless Bulgaria was left to sign the Treaty of Constantinople, relinquishing Adrianople and most of Thrace. On the other hand, Grey had in 1913 rejected the renewed overtures of the Porte for a defensive alliance with Britain,[149] and had also declined its proposals for the appointment of

British civil servants to reorganise Asia Minor and Armenia. He was probably right in thinking that Russia would take offence, and accepted Sir Lewis Malet's view that such an alliance "would in the present circumstances unite Europe against us". None the less, the result was to reinforce more strongly than ever the military ties between the Young Turks and Germany.

The Balkan Wars opened a new era in the Near East. Slav co-operation gave place to hate, and the two sister-nations were flung into opposing camps: Greece was torn in two by equally balanced tendencies, Roumania's ties with the Dreibund were loosened under the stress of Magyar oppression in Transylvania, while Serbia, enlarged by one-third and now bordering with her Montenegrin kinsfolk, was hailed as the Piedmont of the Southern Slavs. The Magyar quarrel with Croatia and her Magyarising designs in Hungary proper, counteracted the "Trialist" designs of Francis Ferdinand and envenomed the whole Balkan policy of the Habsburg Monarchy. In every Balkan country Austria-Hungary and Russia manœuvred for influence and position.

THE TWO CAMPS

During the Balkan Wars Anglo-German co-operation had, not once but repeatedly, taken the sting out of a dangerous crisis: and Grey was fully entitled to claim in his post-war Memoirs that the Conference of Ambassadors over which he presided might, if revived in 1914, have averted the great catastrophe.[150] His aim was undoubtedly to prevent the Powers from falling irrevocably into two camps: "separate groups of Powers need not necessarily mean opposing diplomatic camps", he had told Mensdorff.[151] But Bethmann Hollweg's outlook was different: while thankful that "England to-day forms a mediating element, through which we have repeatedly been able to exercise a calming and retarding influence upon Russia", he hopes, if the crisis can be surmounted, "that the Entente policy will have passed its height, and that it will come to a *new orientation of English policy*".[152]

Meanwhile the naval question remained unsolved. In March 1913 new naval estimates were presented to Parliament, and Churchill "explicitly repudiated the suggestion that Great Britain can ever allow another Naval Power to approach her so nearly as to deflect or restrict her political action by purely naval pressure. Such a situation would unquestionably lead to war."[153] His renewed suggestion of a "Naval holiday" was not listened to, and indeed was not very practical: and the Kaiser and his Naval Attachés in London were as intransigeant as ever. But for the first time there was a note of anxiety on the side of Tirpitz, who felt that after fourteen years of effort the "danger zone" was not yet passed, and that "the bow is overstrung here as much as in England".* Grey, in one of his last pre-war speeches,[154] again sounded a warning note, protesting against the misleading idea that armament competition was "a race with some prize to be won at the end of it", but admitting that "to reduce naval expenditure when there was no certainty that it was going to have a corresponding influence on the rest of Europe, would be staking too much on a gambling chance". Armaments "must lead to catastrophe, and may even sink the ship of European prosperity and civilisation": and yet he had no remedy. "I think in foreign affairs we must modify the maxim of doing unto others as you would be done by." He, and with him the other Foreign Ministers of Europe, were bankrupt and standing on the brink of disaster while the nations chased prosperity: they at least had not yet learned the dire lessons of universal war, which we, their successors, having learned, are deliberately disregarding.

There was, however, one direction in which real progress could still be made. While Germany increased her army by 170,000 men and France replied by adopting the three years' service: while Russia cautiously explored the possibility of a change in the status of the Straits; while international suspicions were revived by the appointment of a Prussian general, Liman von Sanders, to a high post in the Turkish army: while France urged on the reluctant and distinctly sceptical Grey to authorise Anglo-Russian naval discussions; while William II set himself to remove the temporary coolness between Berlin and Vienna which had followed the Treaty of Bucarest, and made to Berchtold the most far-reaching promises of support;[155] while Pašić escorted Prince Alexander of Serbia to St Petersburg to thank the Tsar for his support, and received the answer that he had only done "his Slav duty"; while King Albert was entertained at Potsdam and came away in grave alarm—amid all these cross-currents two distinct sets of secret negotiations continued between the British and German Governments, one on the Bagdad Railway and the Middle East, the other on the whole question of African colonies.

Into the long and complicated story of the Bagdad Railway it is quite impossible to enter here;[156] special agreements between Turkey and France and between Turkey and Britain inevitably preceded, and prepared the way for, the final Anglo-German accord of June 1914. Its salient feature was a compromise by which Britain withdrew her objections to German control over the Railway, but was to exercise a joint control over the final section to Basra, while special provisions were added with regard to navigation on the

---

* See the last two chapters of Mr Woodward's indispensable study, *Britain and the German Navy.*

Tigris and Mesopotamian oil. Meanwhile, however, something perilously like a partition of Asiatic Turkey into spheres of interest was in process of execution. Britain was to assume a protectorate of Koweit, at the head of the Persian Gulf, while Russia and France were to establish control of Turkish Armenia and Syria respectively. Italy too had pegged out her claim, and in spite of the most explicit assurances of speedy evacuation, kept her hand on the Dodecanese Islands, and never had the slightest intention of withdrawing. She could point to a series of precedents provided by Britain in Cyprus and in Egypt. Germany was thinking of Alexandretta, and even Austria-Hungary told her German ally that if it should come to Turkish partition, she too would expect a share, in Adalia.

The idea of Anglo-German colonial discussions had slumbered since the Portuguese Treaties of 1898 and 1900, but revived after a speech of Grey's in the House on 28 November 1911, deprecating any further extension of the British possessions in Africa, and disclaiming all idea of hindering German colonial expansion. Bethmann sounded Metternich on the British attitude, and the latter evidently hoped that the moment had come when Portugal, discredited by the regicide, an atheist republic, and shattered finances, might be forced to sell her colonies, and that Germany might secure Angola and part of the Congo by bribing South Africa with Delagoa Bay.[157] Kühlmann reported from London that to increase the fleet would be "to destroy the hope of a colonial agreement, and to increase the probability of an armed conflict with the Triple Entente".[*] After the failure of the Haldane mission Grey, to show his good will, offered further colonial discussions,[158] and these ranged over a very wide field—Angola, S. Thomé, Zanzibar, Pemba, Timur. Grey was naturally reluctant to take any step which Portugal could represent as a betrayal of the alliance, though on the other hand conditions in her colonies were so bad as to be almost untenable: and Baron Marschall was inclined to think that it might come to "self-help" in the sense of "helping oneself", in which case it might prove possible to apply the motto, *Si duo faciunt idem, non est idem*.[159] Talks went on throughout 1913, till at last on 20 October an Anglo-German Treaty was initialled, on a basis of mutual renunciation of claim, by Britain as regards Angola and S. Thomé, by Germany as regards Mozambique and Timur. Somewhat tortuous provisions were made for the hypothetical case of

* 8 January 1912—*ibid*. No. 11345. "Clear and sharp", wrote Kühlmann, "lie the two paths before German policy. On the one side the possibility of honourable peace, colonial expansion, successful cultural work with growing riches, on the other renewal of the old quarrel, strengthening of every hostile policy and the conjuring up of grave dangers." "On the contrary," commented William II, "Kühlmann is a ready pupil of Metternich and brings up all the twaddle (*Quatsch*) which has been put to me since I have been building my fleet....I want no colonial presents from England, as they are always made at the expense of others...." Cf. his further comment in No. 11346.

Portugal being forced by financial troubles to cede or mortgage her colonies, and in the event of one or other colony breaking loose from the motherland, it was implied that Britain's guarantee of 1899 would no longer hold good. Grey refused to give his final signature to the Treaty, unless it could be published, together with the earlier Treaties of 1898 and 1899. For not quite obvious reasons,[160] the German Government still clung to secrecy, and it was not till early in July 1914 that Lichnowsky, when returning for the last time to his London post, was able to convey their consent to publication in the autumn.[161]

With the outbreak of war the two agreements were of course stillborn, and during its course the British Government strained every nerve to preserve that very secrecy against which it had formerly protested. There is no little irony in this evident fear of condemnation by an inflamed public opinion. For now that the "war psychosis" has passed and they can be judged with sanity, the Anglo-German agreements of 1914 deserve special emphasis as in some sense an alibi for Sir Edward Grey and his colleagues. They are the crowning proof that Britain, ever since it abandoned "splendid isolation" at the beginning of the century, aimed at removing one by one the obstacles to cordial relations with other Powers, and desired nothing more earnestly than a further arrangement with Germany, such as would help to bridge the gulf between the two main camps in Europe, instead of widening it. Even in the light of all that followed we must not dismiss this aim as either Utopian or insincere, simply because we know that strong currents in both these camps were driving him in a very different direction. On the one hand the Emperor William and his Ministers, while ready enough to deal with anyone who came their way, and not deliberately working for war, really aimed at detaching Britain from her existing allies, and even hoped to achieve naval equality with her—which would have had the effect of establishing a political hegemony over her and all other Powers. Russia, on her side, though also willing for an occasional bargain with the other side—as in Persia, Armenia or the Balkans—was above all concerned with twisting the separate strands of the Triple Entente into a single rope that would resist even the greatest strain. But Grey held to a middle course, in the belief that British mediation could alone avert a conflict. "To bring the two groups nearer"—so Lichnowsky summed up Grey's programme.[162]

In this connection it is necessary to allude to one final incident of importance. In April 1914 King George V paid a state visit to Paris, taking Sir Edward Grey with him: and, incredible as it may seem, this was the Foreign Secretary's first and last foreign visit during eleven consecutive years of office. Some weeks earlier, letters passed between Izvolsky, at the height of his activity as Russian Ambassador in Paris, and the Russian Foreign Minister Sazonov, as to the possibility of setting up a permanent organ of the Triple Entente, on lines which had been tested at the ambassadorial conference. It is highly significant that Izvolsky explicitly warned his chief that the Anglo-French political and naval conventions had "no binding force", that the decision of war would be made by Parliament "in accordance with circumstances", and that it was probably impossible to go further in view of the British and French constitutions.[163] Conversations followed during the royal visit, and Doumergue suggested that existing agreements between the three Powers, instead of remaining parallel, should be embodied in a single document. Grey showed himself ready to put his relations with Russia on to more or less the same footing as with France, with the qualification that no Anglo-Russian *military* agreement was possible: but he also made it clear that part of the British Cabinet was averse to taking any further commitments towards Russia.[164] As a result, conversations opened a month later between Grey, Paul Cambon and Benckendorff, who on 28 May was able to notify Sazonov that Grey, though naturally treating an alliance as quite out of the question, was ready to negotiate a convention on French lines.*[165]

On 11 June in the House of Commons Grey denied the existence of any unpublished agreements which would restrict "freedom of decision" as to war: and as late as the 29th he told Lichnowsky that "though we were not bound by engagement as Allies, we did from time to time talk as intimately as Allies, but this intimacy was not used for aggression against Germany".[166] Meanwhile Colonel House visited Europe on a peace mission prompted by President Wilson. He was appalled at the situation—"militarism run mad"—in which only someone acting from outside Europe could avert "an awful cataclysm".[167] He met with a cordial response from the Emperor and still more from Grey, but he only got to grips with the latter on 26 June 1914, two days before the Sarajevo murder. It was already too late.

Berlin was aware of what was on foot, and asked itself suspiciously whether it was with Germany or with Russia that Grey was playing false. In reality he was taking big risks of offending both sides, and some will say that in the end he fell between two stools: but now that we have access to his official correspondence, his Memoirs and a biography that is worthy of

---

* 12 May, Benckendorff to Sazonov—B. v. Siebert, *Diplomatische Aktenstücke*, p. 810 (1921). It is of considerable importance to note that Siebert, an official of the Russian Embassy in London, was from 1909 to 1914 regularly betraying to the German Embassy Benckendorff's whole secret correspondence with his Government; that the documents were transcribed in Berlin by the historian Professor Schiemann (wellknown for his weekly chronicles in the *Kreuz-Zeitung*) and supplied to the Chancellor and the Wilhelmsstrasse (see Schiemann's article in the *Tägliche Rundschau*, 15 March 1919); and Siebert's book, quoted above, contains a big selection of these documents. They are authentic.

him[168] it is surely impossible to deny that he was wholeheartedly pursuing a higher European aim. His failure to grasp the full significance of Balkan problems bore bitter fruit in 1913, but must remain a mere detail in any general estimate of his policy. Colonel House thought he lacked imagination, but long before the war came, he had been obsessed by the dangers of "complete collapse" in Europe, quite "irrespective of who were victors": and in his final appeal to Lichnowsky on 30 July he proclaimed his readiness, if the crisis could be peacefully surmounted, to seek a further arrangement with Germany such as would assure her and her allies against any "aggressive hostile policy".[169] He had failed in his main purpose, but he had most emphatically failed with honour. The dilemma which confronted him in 1914 still confronts his successors in 1937.

The Main Lines of British Policy

It was almost a century since Britain had been engaged in a general war of the first magnitude, and the effort required of her peoples proved altogether unprecedented. Yet if we consider the broad lines of British policy at the close of the Victorian era (and of the brief period of transition that followed it, from 1901 to 1914), we find that there has been surprisingly little change since the days of Napoleon. Britain's hybrid position as part of Europe, and yet in some respects outside it, served as a natural stimulus to overseas commercial and political development—trade following the flag—and to reliance upon a strong navy, which could not only defend these islands but also impose a handicap upon the ambitions of rival Powers. She had never possessed a large conscript army and for that reason was all the more dependent upon naval superiority, against any continental Power: and this crystallised into the principle of the Two-Power Standard. As a logical consequence of this outlook she tended to favour a balance of power and to look askance at any Power which seemed to be aiming at hegemony in Europe. For her the real test was whether that Power sought to add naval to military superiority. To possess an infinitely stronger army than the British did not necessarily constitute a danger or prevent friendship: to supplement this by decisive naval power meant to endanger, in the most literal sense, the very existence of the Empire and the independence of these islands. It is of course true that Britain presumed upon her possession of sea power in order to extend her rule in all parts of the world, and often played the dog-in-the-manger. It is also true that she used her European alignments to secure a free hand overseas, profiting from the big battalions of her allies and even on occasion recruiting foreign mercenaries for colonial wars, and again that she sometimes used her colonial acquisitions as small change in hard European bargainings.

Nothing is more inexact than to suppose that her interventions on the Continent cramped her colonial style: on the contrary, the elder Pitt's design for "conquering America in Germany" does not stand alone. Selfish isolation was always the surest way of endangering British overseas interests: and alliances might serve not merely to achieve a specific purpose, but to frustrate a hostile combination. The years that separate Fashoda from Algeciras suggest that if Britain had held aloof much longer from both groups, she would have been risking their uniting against her. On the other hand, Salisbury's attitude to the Mediterranean Agreements of the late 'eighties shows that British statesmen did not necessarily take a doctrinaire view of the Balance of Power, but were quite prepared under certain circumstances to throw their weight into the heavier of the two scales. But there was always one condition attached—the certainty that those to whom our support would secure political predominance were genuinely devoted to peace and not aiming at territorial conquest. For if there is one fact which emerges from the speeches and actions of all successive Foreign Secretaries from Pitt to Grey, it is the paramount importance which they attached to Peace as the foremost British interest. In modern parlance this may be dismissed as the hypocrisy of the "Haves" towards the "Have-Nots": and it would be idle to deny that those who have most to lose have a greater temptation to shrink from the arbitrament of war. But there is also the much more legitimate and fundamental fact that for Britain territorial ambitions on the Continent have become as inconceivable as a return to villeinage or to legislation in Norman-French, and that she regards designs of racial conquest or assimilation both as contrary to the spirit of the age, and as the surest source of continental unrest. One of the most hopeful features of the nineteenth century was the steady growth in importance of the small and medium states in Europe, and this was favoured by Britain not merely from natural sympathy, but also because it was felt to make on the whole for peace in Europe. The settlement of 1919 and the institution of the League were to render their role still more important, and to create an identity of interest between them and Britain.

Naval strength has always been identified in British eyes with the safety of the Narrow Seas, and of the route of our merchantmen to London and the North Sea. It followed that Britain could never view with indifference the fate of the Low Countries and the Channel Ports. This was the focusing point of our struggle with Louis XIV: it explains successive Barrier Treaties. It was French designs upon Belgium, and then upon the mouths of the Rhine, that first roused British suspicions against the French Revolution.

The reversal of the settlement imposed upon Belgium and Holland remained a cardinal aim during the long wars with Napoleon, and the desire to prevent any repetition lay at the root of the ill-starred Netherlands Union of 1815–30. After 1830 these preoccupations took the form of treaty guarantees of Belgian neutrality. In the 'sixties and during the war of 1870 Stanley and Disraeli, Clarendon, Granville and Gladstone alike adhered to the principles laid down by Palmerston in the Belgian question, though in the Luxemburg crisis of 1867 there had been a certain reluctance to define them anew. And if the question receded into the background for over a generation—thanks not least of all to its keen reactions upon British opinion in 1870—it at once resumed its importance in 1914 and became a touchstone of the British attitude towards continental engagements with all those whose political thought extended beyond these islands. The suddenness with which the strong movement for neutrality collapsed on the news of the German invasion of Belgium is one of the most remarkable instances of *unconscious* political instinct in our history.

There is another direction in which a long political tradition has remained almost unaltered. Britain's resolve to maintain her special position in the Mediterranean, both as a guarantee of her Levantine trade, and as a vital stage upon the route to India, has not varied for over two centuries, though circumstances have altered the stress laid upon this or that strategic base. At different times and for different reasons Minorca and Corfu have been relinquished, Malta and Cyprus acquired: but Britain has adhered to her essential aim of preventing any single Power from dominating the Mediterranean and threatening the main sea routes. She has on occasion been highhanded towards lesser Powers (Palmerston's bullying of Greece in 1843 and 1850 was even more scandalous than Mussolini's action at Corfu in 1924). But in the main British Mediterranean policy has been to live and let live, and rests upon a clear aspiration towards peace, coupled no doubt with a selfish preference for the *status quo*.

The problem of Mediterranean strategy was closely linked up with the Eastern Question, which in its later phase may be defined as the problem how to fill the vacuum created by the shrinkage and decay of the once conquering Ottoman Empire. To those who consider that undue space has been accorded to the Eastern Question in this history, or to those who hesitate to include it among the catalogue of British interests, it should be sufficient to rejoin that no less than eleven times in the last hundred years were we involved in major international crises owing to complications in the Near East. Neither the Iberian nor the Italian Peninsula, neither Germany nor the Habsburg Monarchy, have proved to be so persistently and inextricably interwoven with every imaginable issue of foreign policy, as have the issues involved in the fate of Turkey and her former vassals. If Britain played an active part in all these crises, this was not due to the stupidity of her statesmen (though their ignorance more than once complicated and delayed the solution), but to the world-wide character of her commitments, to the interaction of commercial and strategic interests, and to her close concern with anything that might endanger the Suez Canal, or even the possible alternative land routes to India through Syria and Persia. If at times Palmerston or Disraeli exaggerated the dangers of a conflict between Britain and Russia in Asia, this does not of course alter the fact that preoccupations about the safety of India were a legitimate and necessary consequence of British initiative in the East.

There is one other important direction in which British policy has been much more fluctuating—that which is summed up in the seemingly crystal-clear, but really most equivocal, words "intervention" and "non-intervention". The one extreme has rested on the assumption that every state, being sovereign, is entitled to govern or misgovern itself without any interference from without: the weak point in this theory is that a certain degree of misgovernment makes a state so easy a prey to ambitious or interested neighbours, as to render interference wellnigh inevitable. The opposite extreme is that any assault upon established order in one country is a menace to all other Governments, and that intervention on each other's behalf is not only a right but a positive moral duty. This theory in its turn obviously breaks down over the impossibility of inducing autocratic governments to support even lawfully constituted democratic governments, or, vice versa, in such a way as to perpetuate political systems distasteful to them. Halfway between these two extremes lies the double-barrelled theory of Palmerston, that British liberal institutions are an article of exportation and that governments who adopt them should enjoy Britain's active support against their rivals, and again that the only sure way of preventing revolutionary and subversive movements is to cut them at the root by the maintenance of good, and so far as possible free, government, or where necessary by the introduction of political reforms. The second half of this theory was abundantly justified by the experience of 1848, when several of the Governments which had disregarded Palmerston's sound, if unpalatable, advice were swept away by the hurricane. But the first half was far more questionable, savouring as it did of the cocksure and blissful belief in progress and permanency for which the Victorian era is memorable.

We thus have the strange paradox that in the days of Castlereagh and Canning the doctrine of non-intervention was interpreted by the legitimist Powers in an interventionist sense—notably in the Spanish and Italian affairs—while at a later period Palmerston and Russell made out of their very opposition to intervention by others a weapon of at least moral intervention—as in the latter's resounding diplomatic support of Sardinia against Austria, or, by way of contrast, in his attitude to the Polish question. This country has never insisted upon identity of political outlook as a basis of alliance and friendship, as our relations with the Second Empire, with Turkey or with Tsarist Russia abundantly show. But in this respect the wheel is again coming full circle, and it is quite clear that political affinities render co-operation easier. There must of course sometimes be cases where geography or economic or military necessity render an alliance between a free and a despotic country possible and even effective: the "Franco-Russe" in its original form, and in its latest permutation, the Franco-Soviet Pact, offer notable examples. Moreover it is useless to deny that in the sphere of foreign policy a country where the last word lies with a Parliament dependent upon public opinion and liable to party fluctuations, is in some measure handicapped, both in decision and in continuity, as against a country where the decision rests in the hands of the Crown. If such considerations acted as deterrents upon Metternich, Bismarck or successive Tsars, there are many no less obvious reasons which lead parliamentary countries to hesitate before they enter into too close alliance with autocracies. In the modern world experience goes more and more to show that while war forces the citizen to a temporary surrender of certain liberties, it is only states resting upon consent of the governed and their willing participation in all measures of defence and decisions of policy, which can survive the appalling strain of scientific warfare. On the eve of the Great War, and still more amid the conflict of ideologies to which it has given birth, Britain occupies a middle path, in which social and political progress are to be slowly and steadily built up by men of practical experience upon old and well-tested foundations, imposed neither by the whim of an autocrat nor by the decree of some inhuman doctrinaire. Her interests are more worldwide than ever before, and her need for peace is correspondingly greater: this explains the eagerness with which men spoke of "the war to end war". Adversity has on the whole taught even those of us who genuinely believe in Democracy to admit that it is a phrase capable of much misinterpretation, and that Britain stands above all for representative institutions—infinitely adaptable to each individual case—and freedom of thought, speech and action, alike in the religious, the intellectual, the political, the social and the economic field. The lesson of the 19th century is her readiness to collaborate with any country irrespective of political creed or system, but not at the expense of her own free institutions, and only on a basis of international peace and co-operation.

NOTES

PROLOGUE

[1] See Sir Richard Lodge's brief, but admirably clear survey, "The continental policy of Great Britain 1740–60", in *History* for January 1932.
[2] Lecky, *History of England*, III, 44. [3] G. M. Trevelyan, *History of England*, p. 534.
[4] *Cambridge History of British Foreign Policy*, I, 137.
[5] *War Speeches of William Pitt*, ed. R. Coupland, p. xvii; Rose, *Pitt and National Revival*, p. 551. [6] *C.H.F.P.* I, 213. [7] *C.H.F.P.* I, 220, 230.
[8] *C.H.F.P.* I, 266. [9] J. H. Rose, *Pitt and the Great War*, p. 275.
[10] *History of England*, p. 576. [11] Rose, *Pitt and the Great War*, p. 281.
[12] 10 November 1797—*War Speeches*, p. 227. [13] 5 December 1797—*ibid.* p. 231.
[14] Rose, *Pitt and the Great War*, p. 321; *War Speeches*, p. 237.
[15] Rose, *op. cit.* p. 384. [16] *War Speeches*, pp. 246–84.
[17] 17 February 1800—*ibid.* p. 285.
[18] Grenville to Minto, 13 May 1800—cit. Fyffe, *Modern Europe*, p. 126.
[19] Rose, *op. cit.* p. 450. [20] *C.H.F.P.* I, 304.
[21] Rose, *op. cit.* p. 468; Fyffe, *Modern Europe*, p. 157.
[22] 3 November 1801—*War Speeches*, p. 303. [23] C. D. Yonge, *Life of Liverpool*, I, 68.
[24] Malmesbury, *Diaries and Correspondence*, IV.
[25] Yonge, *op. cit.* pp. 94, 129. [26] 23 May 1803—*War Speeches*, pp. 306–7.
[27] 18 July 1803—*ibid.* p. 315. [28] Rose, *op. cit.* p. 533.
[29] Edward Lascelles, *Life of Charles James Fox*, p. 323—an admirably clear and compact biography (1933). [30] G. Brodrick, *History of England*, p. 48.
[31] Cit. H. W. V. Temperley, *George Canning*, p. 69.
[32] For a very detailed and penetrating study of Anglo-Austrain relations during the next four years, see C. S. B. Buckland, *Metternich and the British Government* (1932).
[33] Yonge, *Life of Liverpool*, I, 158.
[34] Webster, *The Foreign Policy of Castlereagh*, I, 26. [35] *Ibid.* I, 25.
[36] 27 October and 22 December 1812—*Wellington's Despatches*, VII, 503; Yonge, *Life of Liverpool*, I, 442. [37] July 1813—cit. Webster, *Castlereagh*, I, 146.
[38] *Ibid.* I, 160, 163. [39] Cit. *ibid.* I, 224.
[40] Cit. *ibid.* I, 269. [41] Cit. *ibid.* I, 370, 372, 379.

CHAPTER I

[1] *Histoire du Peuple Anglais*, I, 558.
[2] Published for the first time in an unexpurgated form in Appendix A of *C.H.F.P.* II, 629. [3] Text in Alison Phillips, *The Confederation of Europe*, pp. 301–2.
[4] *The Foreign Policy of Castlereagh*, II, 59. [5] Cit. *C.H.F.P.* I, 508.
[6] *Nachgelassene Papiere*, I, 315–21. [7] Webster, *op. cit.* II, 101.
[8] Full and authoritative surveys will be found in *The Confederation of Europe*, by W. Alison Phillips, in *The Foreign Policy of Castlereagh*, vol. II, by C. K. Webster, and in the three chapters by them in vols. I and II of *C.H.F.P.* See also the relative chapters in vols. I and II of Alfred Stern, *Geschichte Europas*.
[9] Cit. Stern, *Gesch. Europas*, I, 460. [10] Cit. Fyffe, *Modern Europe*, p. 454.
[11] *Cast. Corresp.* XII, 62: cf. also Fyffe, p. 455; Webster, *Castlereagh*, II, 154.
[12] *Ibid.* II, 148. [13] *Ibid.* II, 151; Alison Phillips, p. 182.

[14] Webster, *Castlereagh*, II, 157.

[15] 4 October 1818, to Bathurst—cit. Webster, *op. cit.* II, 144.

[16] Webster, *op. cit.* II, 147. [17] *Nachg. Papiere*, III, 171–81.

[18] *Ibid.* III, 288, 217; cf. Stern, *op. cit.* I, 580.

[19] Cit. Webster, *op. cit.* II, 192, 198; *Cast. Corresp.* XII, 259. [20] *Cast. Corresp.* X, 18.

[21] *Nachg. Papiere*, III, 319. [22] Memo. of 16 April 1820—*W.N.D.* I, 116.

[23] Cit. Webster, *op. cit.* II, 279, 284. [24] Webster, *op. cit.* II, 301–2; *C.H.F.P.* II, 38.

[25] Cit. Stern, *op. cit.* II, 135. [26] Alison Phillips, *The Confederation of Europe*, p. 203.

[27] Cit. Stern, II, *op. cit.* 171. [28] Webster, *op. cit.* II, 321–3.

[29] 21 June 1821, *Hansard.* [30] 6 May 1821—*Nachg. Papiere*, III, 438.

[31] Cit. Driault, *Hist. diplom. de la Grèce*, I, 159.

[32] Castlereagh to Tsar, 16 July 1821—cit. Webster, *op. cit.* II, 360.

[33] Esterházy to Metternich, 3 January 1822—cit. Webster, *op. cit.* II, 371.

[34] *Nachg. Papiere*, III, 490–3. [35] Cit. Srbik, *Metternich*, p. 610.

[36] C. K. Webster, in *C.H.F.P.* II, 43. [37] 28 June 1822—cit. Webster, *op. cit.* II, 433.

[38] *Croker Papers*, I, 219.

[39] A useful general survey entitled *Castlereagh* has just been published by Sir John Marriott (1936).

[40] Reported by Neumann to Esterházy, 21 September 1822, cit. Webster, *op. cit.* II, 489.

CHAPTER II

[1] Brougham to Creevey—*Creevey Papers*, I, 178.

[2] 17 July 1818, to Creevey—*ibid.* I, 277.

[3] Cf. also *The R——l Lover*, published in the same year.

[4] *The Irish Avatar* (1821). [5] H. W. V. Temperley, *Life of Canning*, p. 36.

[6] Temperley, *Foreign Policy of Canning*, p. 32. [7] *Ibid.* p. 46.

[8] It was first published in full in an Appendix to vol. II of *C.H.F.P.*, exactly a hundred years later. [9] *Op. cit.* II, 627.

[10] 22 August 1822—Metternich, *Nachg. Papiere*, III, 522.

[11] 18 July 1823—*ibid.* IV, 12.

[12] 20 March 1821—*Hansard*, IV, 1365–76: cf. Temperley, *Foreign Policy*, p. 46.

[13] 14 April 1823—*Hansard*, VI.

[14] 15 November 1822—*Canning Correspondence*, I, 57.

[15] *Wellington Despatches*, I, 304. [16] Temperley, *Foreign Policy*, p. 67.

[17] Cit. Stern, *Gesch. Europas*, II, 313. [18] Cit. Temperley, *Foreign Policy*, p. 77.

[19] 2 January 1823—Marcellus, *Souvenirs Diplomatiques*, p. 111.

[20] *Hansard*, VIII, 885–9, 894–6. [21] 30 April 1823—*ibid.* p. 1514.

[22] Memorandum to Cabinet, February 1823—*Canning Corresp.* I, 84–8.

[23] 10 February 1823, Wellington to Canning—*Wellington Desp.* II, 33.

[24] 30 January 1823—Marcellus, *op. cit.* p. 129.

[25] 11 and 18 February—*ibid.* pp. 143, 145.

[26] 3 and 13 March, Chateaubriand to Marcellus—*ibid.* p. 155.

[27] Cit. by H. W. V. Temperley, in *Diary of Princess Lieven*, p. 63.

[28] *Foreign Policy*, p. 241. [29] Marcellus, *Souvenirs Diplomatiques*, pp. 15–16.

[30] 11 March 1825—Stapleton, *Canning Corresp.* I, 258. [31] *Nachg. Papiere*, IV, 161.

[32] 11 March 1823, to Frederick Lamb—*Wellington Desp.* II, 164.

[33] 8 November 1823, cit. Temperley, *Foreign Policy*, p. 112. [34] 25 August 1823.

[35] 22 January 1824, *Wellington Desp.* I, 511. [36] *Canning Corresp.* II, 37.

[37] 22 January 1824—J. Bagot, *Canning and his Friends*, II, 221–2.

[38] Yonge, *Life of Lord Liverpool*, III, 297–304.

[39] 27 January 1824—*Wellington Desp.* II, 402.

[40] 8 December 1824, Liverpool to Wellington—Yonge, *op. cit.* III, 305.

[41] 17 October 1824—*Wellington Desp.* II, 325.

[42] 23 November 1824—*Canning Corresp.* I, 205. [43] Cit. Temperley, *For. Pol.* p. 153.

[44] 9 February 1823, Canning to A'Court—cit. Temperley, p. 81.

[45] *Manuel de la Politique Étrangère*, II, 698.

[46] See Webster, *Foreign Policy of Castlereagh*, pp. 247-56.

[47] J. Bagot, *Canning and his Friends*, II, 183.

[48] 19 July 1824—cit. Temperley, *Foreign Policy*, p. 204.

[49] 21 February 1825—*ibid.* p. 208.   [50] 3 February 1826—*Canning Corresp.* II, 1-11.

[51] 2 July 1826, Canning to Granville—*Canning Corresp.* II, 118.

[52] 6 March 1826, Canning to Granville—*Ibid.* II, 18.

[53] *Hansard*, XVI, 352-69, 12 December 1826.   [54] *Ibid.* p. 398.

[55] 8 January 1827, to Bombelles—cit. Stern, *Gesch. Europas*, III, 108.

[56] *C.H.F.P.* II, 83.   [57] 3-6 February 1827—Yonge, *Life of Liverpool*, III, 447-9.

[58] 23 August 1826, to Gentz—*Nachg. Papiere*, IV, 310.

[59] 29 January 1825, to Ottenfels in Constantinople—*ibid.* p. 209.

[60] 28 May 1823, to Vincent in Paris—*ibid.* p. 56.

[61] 16 August 1825, to Gentz—*ibid.* p. 189.

[62] 7 August 1825, to Esterházy—*ibid.* pp. 212-18.

[63] 8 August 1824, *Nachg. Papiere*, IV, 90.   [64] 24 May 1826, to Neumann—*ibid.* IV, 275.

[65] 22 June 1826, to Neumann—*ibid.* IV, 280-1.

[66] 25 October 1825—*Canning Corresp.* I, 317.

[67] 23 July 1823, to Marcellus—Marcellus, *Souvenirs Diplomatiques*, p. 361.

[68] *Diary of Princess Lieven*, p. 92.

[69] Cit. Webster, *Foreign Policy of Castlereagh*, II, p. 360.

[70] 23 July 1821—cit. Webster, *op. cit.* II, 356.

[71] 27 July 1822—cit. Driault, *Histoire Diplomatique de la Grèce*, I, 180.

[72] 27 August 1822—cit. ibid. I, 183.   [73] *Dépêches inédites de Gentz*, II, 157.

[74] Cit. Temperley, *Foreign Policy of Canning*, p. 326.

[75] Virginia Penn, Philhellenism in England (*Slavonic Review*, No. 42, p. 656).

[76] Cit. Lane-Poole, *Life of Stratford de Redcliffe*, I, 307.

[77] *Ibid.* I, 343.   [78] *Ibid.* I, 349, 352.   [79] *Wellington Desp.* II, 327.

[80] 2 November, Liverpool to Canning—*ibid.* II, 329.

[81] 5 November, Canning to Liverpool—*ibid.* II, 330.

[82] 16 December 1824—*ibid.* II, 367.   [83] Lane-Poole, *op. cit.* I, 372.

[84] *Wellington Desp.* III, 86, quoted by Canning in his instructions to Wellington, 10 February 1826.   [85] *Lieven Diary*, p. 96.   [86] Villèle, *Mémoires*, III, 172.

[87] See Mrs Penn's article in *Slavonic Review*, No. 42 (April 1936), p. 658; W. A. Phillips, *The Greek War of Independence*, p. 213, and the romantic book entitled *Sir Richard in Italy and Greece*. See also *Reminiscences of the Greek War of Independence* (from Church's Papers) by F. H. Marshall, in *Slavonic Review*, No. 15, pp. 552-64.

[88] Canning to Sir Henry Wellesley, 27 September—*Wellington Desp.* II, 511.

[89] *Wellington Desp.* II, 535.   [90] 2 January 1826—*Nachg. Papiere*, IV, 261.

[91] *Canning and his Friends*, II, 337.

[92] Baron Damas' views, as expressed to Lord Granville and reported by him to Canning, 2 January 1826 (*Wellington Desp.* III, 58).

[93] 29 January 1826, memorandum of Wellington—*ibid.* III, 79.

[94] 10 February 1826—*Wellington Desp.* III, 86-93.

[95] 17 February—*ibid.* III, 115.   [96] 26 January—*ibid.* p. 61.

[97] *Canning and his Times*, p. 471, and Crawley, *The Question of Greek Independence*, p. 52.

[98] 10 February, 1826—*Wellington Desp.* III, 94.   [99] Driault, *op. cit.* I, 310.

[100] Lane-Poole, *op. cit.* I, 402.

[101] 9 January 1826 to Stratford Canning—Lane-Poole, *op. cit.* I, 395.

[102] 6 March 1826—cit. Schiemann, II, 131.

[103] Canning to Wellington, 11 April—*Wellington Desp.* III, 288.

[104] 7 March 1826—J. Bagot, *Canning and his Friends*, II, 335.

[105] Nesselrode to Wellington—23 March, *Wellington Desp.* III.

[106] 5 September 1826—cit. Lane-Poole, *op. cit.* I, 431.

[107] To Neumann, 24 May 1826—*Nachg. Papiere*, IV, 275.

[108] To Lebzeltern, 16 May—cit. Stern, III, 88.

[109] To Neumann, 12 June—*Nachg. Papiere*, IV, 279.

[110] To Esterházy, 8 June—*ibid.* IV, 307.   [111] To Neumann, 12 May—*ibid.* IV, 274.
[112] 27 July 1826—cit. Driault, *op. cit.* I, 334.
[113] See La Gorce, *Charles X*, p. 168; Stern, *op. cit.* III, 91.
[114] Cf. Damas to La Ferronays, 22 December 1826—cit. Schiemann, II, 189.
[115] 23 September 1826—cit. Driault, *op. cit.* I, 335.
[116] Canning to Liverpool, 22 December 1826—in Stapleton, *Canning and his Times*, p. 486.   [117] 27 January 1827, to Apponyi—*Nachg. Papiere*, IV, 342.
[118] 19 November 1826—cit. Driault, *op. cit.* I, 340.   [119] Parker, *Life of Peel*, I, 457.
[120] Wellington to Canning, 11 April—*Wellington Desp.* III, 629.
[121] Wellington to the King, 12 April—*ibid.*
[122] 4 December 1826—*Canning Corresp.* II, 170.
[123] *Ibid.* II, 279.   [124] 17 June 1827—*ibid.* II, 325.
[125] Sir R. W. Wilson, *Canning's Administration*, p. 21. For the friction between Wellington and Canning see also the Duke's remarks to Lord Colchester, as recorded by the latter in his *Diary*, III, 500–2 (15 May 1828).
[126] Lord Redesdale to Lord Colchester, 19 January 1828—Colchester, *Diary and Correspondence*, III, 538.
[127] 24 August 1827, to his brother—Bulwer, *Life of Palmerston*, I, 199.
[128] *Diary* (ed. Temperley), p. 126.
[129] 14 February and 26 March, to Esterházy—*Nachg. Papiere*, IV, 343–4.
[130] 20 February 1827—cit. Driault, *op. cit.* I, 359.
[131] 18 April—cit. *ibid.* I, 363; Schiemann, II, 191.
[132] 24 October 1827—Nesselrode, *Lettres et Papiers*, VI, 259.
[133] 19 August 1827—*Nachg. Papiere*, IV, 372–3.
[134] 14 August—cit. Stern, *Gesch. Europas*, III, 117.
[135] 10 August—*Letters to her Brother*, p. 104.
[136] Mackintosh, *Miscellaneous Works*, II, 455.

CHAPTER III

[1] *D.N.B.*, article on Lord Goderich.
[2] H. Dodwell, *The Founder of Modern Egypt*, p. 88.
[3] Driault, *op. cit.* I, 373–7.   [4] Dodwell, *op. cit.* pp. 82, 90.
[5] *Wellington Desp.* IV, 205.   [6] Lane-Poole, *op. cit.* I, 449.
[7] Cf. Bourgeois, *Manuel Politique*, III, 757.
[8] Douin, *Navarino*, p. 245; Dodwell, *op. cit.*, p. 89.
[9] Stratford Canning to Foreign Office, 20 Nov. 1827—published as Appendix III in Stern, *op. cit.* III, 392.   [10] *Wellington Desp.* IV, 303.
[11] 1 January 1828—*Nachg. Papiere*, IV, 410.
[12] Quoted with approval by Sir Charles Oman in *Prime Ministers of the Nineteenth Century*, ed. Hearnshaw, p. 19.   [13] Crawley, *Greek Independence*, p. 108.
[14] 10 September 1821—*Letters of Earl of Dudley to Bishop of Llandaff* (1841), p. 288.
[15] Lord Stanmore, *Life of Lord Aberdeen*, p. 75.
[16] The Treaty of Constantinople, 5 January 1799.
[17] *Parliam. Hist.* XXIX, 76.   [18] 29 January 1828—*Hansard*, XVIII, 1–25, 75–7.
[19] Quoted with approval a year later (12 August 1829) by Wellington in a memorandum for Aberdeen—*Wellington Desp.* VI, 80.   [20] Yonge, *op. cit.* II, 141.
[21] *Wellington Desp.* IV, 274.   [22] Metternich to Ottenfels—*Nachg. Papiere*, IV, 425–6.
[23] In a confidential memorandum sent to Esterházy on 15 March—*ibid.* IV, 445–53.
[24] Quoted by Bourgeois, *op. cit.* II, 761.
[25] Memorandum to Cabinet, 26 February—*Wellington Desp.* IV, 287.
[26] Zichy to Metternich, 24 April 1828—*Nachg. Papiere*, IV, 467.
[27] Report of Schwebel, 11 May 1828—cit. Stern, *op. cit.* III, 151.
[28] 30 April—text in Appendix V of Stern, *op. cit.* p. 396.
[29] 5 March, Wellington to Dudley—*Wellington Desp.* IV, 297.

[30] Memorandum of 16 March—*Wellington Desp.* IV, 312.
[31] 17 March, Aberdeen to Wellington—*ibid.* IV, 315.
[32] Spencer Walpole, *History of England*, II, 559.
[33] See letter of Frederick Lamb (Lord Beauvale) to Wellington, 14 December 1827—*Wellington Desp.* IV, 22.　　　　[34] Stanmore, *Life of Lord Aberdeen*, p. 71.
[35] La Gorce, *Charles X*, p. 183.　　　[36] Cit. Stern, *op. cit.* III, 155.
[37] 6 August—*Wellington Desp.* IV, 576–7.
[38] Cit. Driault, *Hist. Diplom. de la Grèce*, I, 421.
[39] Lane-Poole, *Life of Stratford de Redcliffe*, I, 479.
[40] *Ibid.* p. 482.　　　　　　[41] *Ibid.* p. 484.
[42] Cit. Stern, *op. cit.* III, p. 169.　　　[43] 28 March 1829—*Wellington Desp.* VI, 11.
[44] 14 July, Wellington to Stratford Canning—*Wellington Desp.* VI, 14.
[45] 8 September, to Heytesbury—*ibid.* VI, 145.
[46] 22 December 1829—*ibid.* VI, 376.　　[47] 10 November—*ibid.* VI, 294.
[48] Müffling to Wellington, 30 September 1829—*Wellington Desp.* VI, 187.
[49] 22 September—Martens, *Recueil*, XI, 410–13, cit. Stern, III, 87.
[50] Aberdeen to Wellington, 19 July—*Wellington Desp.* VI, 29.
[51] 24 and 25 August—*Wellington Desp.* VI, 103, 108.
[52] 26 August—*ibid.* p. 110.　　　[53] 30 August—*ibid.* p. 119.
[54] 11 September, to Aberdeen—*ibid.* p. 152.　　[55] 4 October, to Aberdeen—*ibid.* p. 192.
[56] Memorandum of 10 October—*ibid.* p. 218.　　[57] Stanmore, *op. cit.* p. 79.
[58] 21 September 1829—*Nachg. Papiere*, IV, 592.
[59] Stanmore, *op. cit.* p. 83.　　　[60] *Ibid.* p. 82.
[61] 14 October 1829, Wellington's draft letter for Lord Heytesbury in St Petersburg—*Wellington Desp.* VI, 229.　　　[62] Stanmore, *op. cit.* p. 86.
[63] 12 February 1830—*Hansard*, XXII, 408, 415.
[64] 28 October 1829—*Early Correspondence of Lord John Russell*, I, 296.
[65] Villamil to Russell—*ibid.* I, 317.
[66] See Stockmar, *Denkwürdigkeiten*, pp. 152–4; Stern, III, *op. cit.* p. 188; Driault, *op. cit.* I, 449; La Gorce, *Charles X*, p. 220.　　　[67] Bulwer, *Life of Palmerston*, I, 322.
[68] 24 September, to Wellington—*Wellington Desp.* VI, 176.
[69] 14 and 16 October—Wellington to Aberdeen, *ibid.* VI, 226, 234.
[70] 1 and 2 January 1830—*ibid.* VI, 372.
[71] Maxwell, *Life of Clarendon*, I, 179.
[72] Stanmore, *Life of Aberdeen*, p. 91; Stern, *op. cit.* III, 285.
[73] 7 July—*Wellington Desp.* IV, 497.　　[74] 19 September—*ibid.* V, 63.
[75] Stanmore, *op. cit.* p. 92.　　　[76] 4 February 1830—*Hansard*, XXII, 42.
[77] Memorandum of 7 May—*Wellington Desp.* VII, 23–4.
[78] La Gorce, *Charles X*, p. 253.　　　[79] *Ibid.* p. 260.
[80] 19 July—cit. Stanmore, *op. cit.* p. 98.　　[81] *The Times*, 16 July 1830.
[82] *Histoire du Peuple Anglais*, II, 283.　　[83] *Memoirs*, II, 151.
[84] 12 August, Wellington to Aberdeen—*Wellington Desp.* VII, 157.
[85] Memorandum of 14 August—*ibid.* p. 158.
[86] Molé to Wellington, 18 August—*Wellington Desp.* VII, 183.
[87] Wellington to Aberdeen, 16 September—*Wellington Desp.* VII, 267.
[88] 23 July 1830, *Hansard*, XXV, 1315. Cf. Mr Hammond's rash prophecy in July 1870 (see *supra*, p. 493).　　　[89] Bulwer, *Life of Palmerston*, I, 362.

CHAPTER IV

[1] Cit. by Sir Charles Oman in *Prime Ministers of the Nineteenth Century*, p. 31.
[2] *Nachg. Papiere*, V, 25.
[3] *Correspondence of Princess Lieven and second Earl Grey*, ed. Guy le Strange, 3 vols.
[4] 11 October 1831—*op. cit.* II, 289.
[5] *Princess Lieven's Diary*, ed. H. W. V. Temperley, pp. 165–8.
[6] 17 November 1830—*ibid.* p. 12.

[7] Cit. Halévy, *Histoire du Peuple Anglais*, III, 56.

[8] 1 August 1830—Lady Airlie, *Lady Palmerston and her Times*, I, 173.

[9] For a full account of the events leading to this Union, see G. J. Renier, *Great Britain and the Establishment of the Kingdom of the Netherlands* (1930).

[10] 8 September—*Wellington Desp.* VII, 247.

[11] *Hansard*, I, 9.   [12] Cit. Bourgeois, *Manuel*, III, 9.

[13] 16 November—Pallain, *Ambassade de Talleyrand à Londres*, p. 90.

[14] Webster, *Palmerston, Metternich and the European System*, p. 131.

[15] 7 January 1831—Bulwer, *Life of Palmerston*, II, 29.

[16] 7 October 1830—*Grey-Lieven Corresp.* II, 104.

[17] Talleyrand to Sebastiani, 28 December 1830—Pallain, *op. cit.* p. 147.

[18] The future King of Greece.   [19] Son of Eugène Beauharnais.

[20] Report of Bülow to Berlin—cit. Stern, *Gesch. Europas*, IV, 237.

[21] 1 February 1831—Bulwer, *op. cit.* II, 36.

[22] 3 and 5 January—*Mémoires de Talleyrand*, ed. Broglie, IV, 6.

[23] 25 January—Pallain, *op. cit.* p. 188.   [24] 8 February—Bulwer, *op. cit.* II, 39.

[25] *Ibid.* p. 41.   [26] 17 February—*ibid.* p. 43.

[27] 9 March—Bulwer, *op. cit.* II, 49.   [28] 15 March—*ibid.* p. 51.

[29] 25 March—*ibid.* p. 58.   [30] *Mémoires* (ed. Broglie), IV, 41.

[31] Cf. Talleyrand to Sebastiani, 25 and 31 May—Pallain, *op. cit.* pp. 363, 379.

[32] 22 June, to Sebastiani—Pallain, *op. cit.* p. 420.

[33] William IV to Grey, 10 April and 5 August 1831—*Corresp. of Grey and William IV*, I, 212, 317.   [34] 25 March—Bulwer, *op. cit.* II, 60.   [35] 17 August—*ibid.* pp. 109–110.

[36] 26 August—*ibid.* p. 122.   [37] 23 August—*ibid.* p. 115.

[38] 17 August—*ibid.* p. 107.   [39] *Mémoires de Talleyrand*, ed. Broglie, IV, 271.

[40] *Hansard*, IV, 317.   [41] 28 August 1831, *Wellington Desp.* VII, 515.

[42] 26 July—*Hansard*, V, 312.   [43] 8 August—*ibid.* V, 931.

[44] 22 August—*ibid.* VI, 409.   [45] 12 August—Bulwer, *op. cit.* II, 102.

[46] Stockmar, *Denkwürdigkeiten*, p. 190.

[47] Théodore Juste, *Léopold I et Léopold II*, p. 492.   [48] Arneth, *Wessenberg*, II, 141.

[49] *Ibid.* II, 154: cf. Stern, *op. cit.* IV, 254, and Srbik, *Metternich*, I, 658.

[50] Metternich to Wessenberg, 16 April 1832—*Nachg. Papiere*, V, 325.

[51] Stockmar, *op. cit.* p. 246.   [52] Arneth, *op. cit.* II, p. 150.

[53] 1 April 1831—Bulwer, *op. cit.* II, 62.   [54] 24 June 1831, *Hansard*, 3rd Series, IV, 310.

[55] 25 July 1832—cit. Corti, *Leopold von Belgien*, p. 50. Cf. Le Hon to Lebeau, cit. Juste, *op. cit.* p. 77. "Leopold offers the best guarantee for a really *Belgian* Prince."

[56] Bulwer, *op. cit.* I, 126.   [57] *Hansard*, XI, 877–82.

[58] *Hansard*, XXI, 1643–70.   [59] H. C. F. Bell, *Palmerston*, I, 142–3.

[60] This in conversation with the Prussian Minister—see Stern, *op. cit.* IV, 426.

[61] *Hansard*, XVIII, 440.

[62] 21 March 1833, Palmerston to Wm Temple—Bulwer, *op. cit.* II, 146.

[63] 8 October 1833, Palmerston to Wm Temple—*ibid.* I, 169.

[64] Metternich to Apponyi, 16 March—*Nachg. Papiere*, V, 124.

[65] Austrian Archives, cit. Silva, *La Monarchia di Luglio*, p. 80.

[66] H. Dodwell, *The Founder of Modern Egypt*, p. 55.   [67] *Ibid.* p. 105.

[68] Mandeville to Palmerston, 15 February 1833—cit. Hall, *England and the Orleans Monarchy*, p. 157.

[69] Ficquelmont's report of 25 February 1833, in Vienna Archives, cit. H. W. V. Temperley, *The Crimea*, p. 67.   [70] 16 October 1833.

[71] For full details, see G. H. Bolsover, "Lord Ponsonby", *Slavonic Review* (July 1934), p. 103.   [72] 15 February 1833—*Nachg. Papiere*, V. 476.

[73] 4 February and 17 March 1834, *Hansard*, XXI, p. 104; XXII, pp. 319–29.

[74] Bulwer, *op. cit.* II, 145.   [75] 4 February 1833—Dodwell, *op. cit.* p. 117.

[76] 8 October—Bulwer, *op. cit.* p. 169.   [77] 3 December—*ibid.* p. 175.

[78] 3 March 1834—*ibid.* p. 179.   [79] 21 April 1834—*ibid.* p. 182.

[80] 18 April 1831—Bulwer, *op. cit.* II, 73, 79; Bell, *Palmerston* I, 166.

[81] Czartoryski, *Memoirs*, II, 329; cf. Bell, *Palmerston*, I, 169.

[82] *Hansard*, VI, 1217.   [83] *Ibid.* p. 1218.

[84] Stuart J. Reid, *Life of first Earl of Durham*, I, 303.
[85] Lane-Poole, *Stratford de Redcliffe*, II, 20.
[86] Castlereagh's successor in the Marquisate. [87] 13 March 1835—*Hansard*, XXVI, 954.
[88] Stuart Reid, *op. cit.* II, 53. [89] 12 May 1934—Bulwer, *Life of Palmerston*, II, 186.
[90] 3 March 1834—*ibid.* II, 180. [91] Srbik, *Metternich*, I, 693.
[92] Bulwer, II, 186; Bell, I, 149. [93] Bulwer, *op. cit.* II, 205
[94] 10 July 1834—*Grey-Lieven Corresp.* II, 506. Cf. Wellington's remark, quoted *supra*,
p. 133. [95] Stuart J. Reid, *op. cit.* II, 129.
[96] 10 March 1835—Bulwer, III, 5. [97] Guedalla, *Life of Palmerston*, p. 193.
[98] Stuart J. Reid, *Life of Durham*, II, 41.
[99] Howick MSS.—cit. Bell, *Palmerston*, I, 198. [100] Guedalla, *op. cit.* p. 198.
[101] The phrase used by Mr Guedalla, *op. cit.* p. 221.
[102] January 1833, to Apponyi—*Nachg. Papiere*, V, 443.
[103] *Ibid.* VI, 51. [104] *Melbourne Papers*, p. 337.
[105] *Ibid.* p. 348. [106] *Melbourne Papers*, p. 339.
[107] Note on despatch of Ponsonby, 21 November 1837—cit. H. W. V. Temperley, *The Crimea*, p. 75.
[108] 12 and 16 August and 15 September 1834, Ponsonby to Palmerston—quoted by G. H. Bolsover, "Lord Ponsonby", *Slavonic Review*, No. 37, p. 105.
[109] Notably *The Spirit of the East* (1838) and *Turkey and her Resources* (1833).
[110] Bolsover, *op. cit.* pp. 106-7. [111] 3 February 1837—Bulwer, *op. cit.* II, 249.
[112] *Hansard*, XCVII, 87. [113] *Lord John Russell*, ed. Rollo Russell, II, 238.
[114] A phrase used by Villiers, Maxwell, *Life of Clarendon*, I, 94.
[115] Guedalla, *op. cit.* p. 181. [116] 13 December 1835—Maxwell, *op. cit.* I, 103.
[117] 29 July 1837—*ibid.* I, 132. [118] Bulwer, *op. cit.* II, 240.
[119] *Melbourne Papers*, p. 350. [120] Guizot, *Mémoires*, V, 9.

CHAPTER V

[1] Cit. Rodkey, *Lord Palmerston and the Rejuvenation of Turkey*, p. 573.
[2] Stern, *Gesch. Europas*, V, 380.
[3] Palmerston to Granville, 8 June 1838—Bulwer, *op. cit.* II, 267.
[4] 10 June 1839—cit. Temperley, *The Crimea*, p. 89.
[5] 27 May 1839, to Granville—cit. *ibid.* p. 90.
[6] 20 July 1838, to Ponsonby—cit. *ibid.* p. 92.
[7] On 31 October 1838. See interesting details in F. S. Rodkey's essay, cit. *supra*, pp. 592-3.
[8] Nesselrode's phrase to Ficquelmont—cit. Guichen, *La Crise d'Orient et l'Europe*, p. 13.
[9] 5 June 1838—Bulwer, *op. cit.* II, 266.
[10] To Bulwer, 13 September 1838—*ibid.* p. 285.
[11] To Bulwer, 22 September 1838—*ibid.* p. 287.
[12] To Bulwer, 1 September 1839—*ibid.* p. 299. [13] *Ibid.* p. 252.
[14] Ponsonby to Palmerston, 22 April 1839—*Levant Corresp.* I, 13; cf. Rodkey, *op. cit.* p. 77. [15] But against the advice of Moltke.
[16] Ponsonby to Palmerston, 20 May—cit. Guichen, *op. cit.* p. 57.
[17] Dodwell, *The Founder of Modern Egypt*, pp. 129-30.
[18] *Ibid.* p. 180. [19] Rodkey, *op. cit.* p. 77.
[20] Cf. his talk with Bourqueney on 31 July—Appendix 18 to Guizot, *Mémoires*, IV, 525.
[21] 8 December 1837—Dodwell, *op. cit.* p. 139.
[22] 10 June—cit. Stern, *Gesch. Europas*, V, 385.
[23] To Granville, 27 May—cit. Bell, *Palmerston*, I, 295.
[24] 18 June—cit. Guichen, *op. cit.* p. 62.
[25] 19 July, to Granville—Bulwer, *op. cit.* II, 295. [26] 26 July—Rodkey, *op. cit.* p. 106.
[27] 11 July—cit. Hasenclever, *Die orientalische Frage* 1839-41, p. 70.

S-W

42

[28] Rodkey, *op. cit.* p. 89.   [29] 17 July—Guichen, *op. cit.* p. 101.

[30] 1 September, to Bulwer in Paris—Bulwer, *Life of Palmerston*, II, 297.

[31] 7 and 28 August—cit. Stern, *op. cit.* V, 391.

[32] Cit. Guichen, *op. cit.* p. 119. But in the words of Thureau-Dangin (*Hist. de la Monarchie de Juillet*, IV, 6), "leurs avertissements se perdaient dans l'engouement général".

[33] 6 August—Guizot, *Mémoires*, IV, 532.

[34] Metternich to Esterházy, 3 July—cit. Hasenclever, *op. cit.* p. 69.

[35] Treitschke, *Deutsche Geschichte*, V, 70.

[36] Cf. Greville, *Memoirs*, 23 September 1839, IV, 251.

[37] Guichen, *op. cit.* p. 123.   [38] 24 September, to Bulwer—Bulwer, *op. cit.* II, 502.

[39] 23 September, to Bulwer—Guichen, *op. cit.* p. 144.

[40] 29 October 1839, to Granville—Guichen, *op. cit.* p. 159.

[41] 14 October—Guizot, *Mémoires*, IV, 365; see also Rodkey, *op. cit.* p. 127.

[42] Palmerston to Ponsonby, 2 December—Guichen, *op. cit.* p. 174.

[43] Reshid's memorandum on reform, of 12 August 1839, has been printed by Mr F. Rodkey in the *Journal of Modern History* (Chicago), No. 2.

[44] Neumann to Metternich, 30 December 1839—cit. Hasenclever, *op. cit.* p. 110.

[45] Palmerston to Granville, 11 March 1840—Bulwer, *op. cit.* II, 30.

[46] Guizot, *Mémoires*, IV, 370.   [47] 1 February 1840—cit. Stern, *op. cit.* V, 396.

[48] As recently as 13 January 1840 in the Chamber.   [49] Cit. Guichen, *op. cit.* p. 198.

[50] *Ibid.* p. 241.   [51] Cit. Hasenclever, *op. cit.* p. 133.

[52] 16 and 13 April—Bulwer, *op. cit.* II, 310–11.   [53] Guizot, *op. cit.* V, 41.

[54] 21 March—*ibid.* V, 63–5.   [55] 11 June—Guizot, *op. cit.* V, 200.

[56] 15 and 30 June—*ibid.* V, 203.

[57] This is stated in a letter to his brother William Temple, then Minister at Naples, cit. Hasenclever, p. 163.   [58] Rodkey, *op. cit.* p. 144.

[59] 18 July 1840—Dodwell, *op. cit.* p. 185.

[60] Usedom, *Polit. Briefe*, p. 270; cit. Treitschke, *Deutsche Geschichte*, V, 76–7.

[61] 5 and 6 July—Bulwer, *op. cit.* pp. 356–63.   [62] *Life of Gladstone*, I, 368.

[63] 9 July 1840, cit. Temperley, *The Crimea*, p. 114, and Hasenclever, *op. cit.* p. 161.

[64] 21 July—Bulwer, *op. cit.* II, 316–17.   [65] *Ibid.* p. 319.

[66] 20 July—cit. Guichen, p. 217.   [67] 21 July—Guizot, *op. cit.* V, 229.

[68] 17 July—Guichen, p. 335; Hobhouse, *Recollections*, V, 290; Hasenclever, p. 190.

[69] 23 August—Bulwer, II, 320.

[70] *Accounts and Papers*, 1841–2; 23 April and 29 June, Ponsonby to Palmerston; 22 July, Wood to Palmerston; 12 December, Palmerston to Ponsonby. Cf. comments of Haussonville, *Histoire de la politique extérieure*, I, 301–8.

[71] Hall, *England and the July Monarchy*, p. 289.   [72] Guizot, *op. cit.* V, 308.

[73] Walewski to Thiers, 29 August—cit. Guichen, p. 367.

[74] 28 September—Greville, *op. cit.* p. 328.   [75] *Melbourne Papers*, p. 481.

[76] 26 September—Greville, *Memoirs*, IV, 320.

[77] Greville here reports Russell's and Holland's own phrases to himself, *ibid.* IV, 331.

[78] Walpole, *Life of Russell*, I, 352, 360.

[79] Walpole, *op. cit.* I, 354.   [80] Greville, IV, 342.

[81] Cit. Hall, *England and the Orleans Monarchy*, p. 298.

[82] 26 July—*Letters*, I, 227.   [83] 22 September—*ibid.* p. 229.

[84] 19 August 1840—*Melbourne Papers*, p. 455.   [85] *Letters*, I, 234.

[86] 7 November—cit. Treitschke, V, 111.   [87] 22 September—Bulwer, *op. cit.* II, 328.

[88] Full text in appendix to Guizot, *Mémoires*, V, 470–6.   [89] Guizot, *op. cit.* pp. 506–7.

[90] To Duke of Broglie, 23 September—*ibid.* p. 369.   [91] *Ibid.* p. 378.

[92] 3 October—Bulwer, II, 332.   [93] 5 October—*ibid.* p. 334.

[94] 8 October—*ibid.* p. 339; cf. Hasenclever, p. 223.   [95] 7 October—*ibid.* p. 338.

[96] 11 October—*Letters*, I, 238.   [97] 16 October—*ibid.* p. 242.

[98] Melbourne to the Queen, 12 October—*ibid.* p. 240.

[99] 19 September—*Melbourne Papers*, p. 478.   [100] 11 November—*Letters*, pp. 246–9.

[101] 26 November, Leopold to Albert—*Letters*, pp. 249–50.

[102] Report of Count Apponyi, 3 October, in Austrian Archives, cit. Stern, *Gesch. Europas*, V, 416.   [103] Guizot, *op. cit.* VI, 14.

[104] H. Noel Williams, *Life and Letters of Sir Charles Napier*, p. 200.
[105] *Ibid.* p. 205.   [106] Hasenclever, *op. cit.* pp. 247-50.
[107] Bulwer, II, 333.   [108] 7 October—*ibid.* p. 337.
[109] 23 October—*ibid.* p. 345.   [110] Cit. Temperley, *Crimea*, p. 138.
[111] 25 November 1840—Laughton, *Memoirs of Reeve*, I, 141.
[112] 29 October—Bulwer, II, 347-9.   [113] 30 November—*ibid.* p. 365.
[114] Bell, *Palmerston*, I, 311.   [115] *Melbourne Papers*, p. 488.
[116] Cf. his criticisms in May 1840—*Nachg. Papiere*, VI, 404-6.
[117] In January 1841; see Hasenclever, p. 279.
[118] For details see Prof. Newton's chapter in vol. II of *C.H.F.P.*
[119] 30 June 1841—*Berlin Archives*, vol. XXII, cit. Hasenclever, p. 303.
[120] 17 August 1841—Guizot, *Mémoires*, VI, Appendix 3, pp. 414-17.

CHAPTER VI

[1] Emily Crawford, *Victoria Queen and Ruler*, p. 156; Strachey, *Queen Victoria*, p. 53.
[2] *Letters of Queen Victoria* (Pop. Ed.), I, 82.
[3] *Ibid.* p. 72.   [4] *Ibid.* pp. 66, 82.   [5] *Ibid.* p. 105.
[6] *Ibid.* p. 242.   [7] *Ibid.* p. 231.   [8] *Ibid.* p. 249.
[9] *Ibid.* p. 250.   [10] 21 January 1840—*ibid.* p. 213.
[11] Stockmar, *Denkwürdigkeiten*, p. 341; Martin, *Life of the Prince Consort*, I, 58.
[12] *Letters*, I, 337.
[13] Lord Melbourne to King Leopold, August 1841—cit. Martin, *op. cit.* I, 117.
[14] *Prime Ministers of the Nineteenth Century*, p. 75.   [15] *Nachg. Papiere*, VI, 530.
[16] 27 August 1841—*Hansard*, LIX, 402-3.   [17] 10 August 1842—*Hansard*, LXV.
[18] Cit. Alfred Stern, *Gesch. Europas*, VI, 58.
[19] 8 September—*Letters of Queen Victoria*, I, 491.
[20] 10 September 1844, Prince Albert to Baron Stockmar—Martin, *op. cit.* I, 183.
[21] Stanmore, *Life of Aberdeen*, p. 158.   [22] H. Martin, *Histoire de France*, V, 207.
[23] Peel to Aberdeen, 12 August 1844—C. S. Parker, *Life of Peel*, III, 395.
[24] 10 March 1840, Palmerston to Lyons—S. E. Wilmot, *Life of Admiral Lyons*, p. 88.
[25] September 1841—*ibid.* p. 91.   [26] *Ibid.* p. 93.
[27] Cit. Driault, *Histoire Diplomatique de la Grèce*, II, 269.
[28] March 1845, Piscatory to Guizot—*ibid.* p. 281.   [29] *Ibid.* p. 271.
[30] This Piscatory reports to Guizot after Kolettis' arrival in Athens in 1843. Cit. Guizot, *Mémoires*, VII, 297.   [31] 31 January 1845—Parker, *Life of Peel*, III, 399.
[32] Stockmar, *Denkwürdigkeiten*, p. 399.
[33] For details see Temperley, *The Crimea*, p. 252.
[34] Queen's journal, 9 October 1844—cit. Martin, *op. cit.* I, 237.
[35] 15 September 1844—*Letters*, II, 21.   [36] Stanmore, *op. cit.* p. 173.
[37] 17 January 1842—*Letters of Queen Victoria*.   [38] Stanmore, *op. cit.* p. 113.
[39] Parker, *Life of Peel*, III, 402.   [40] *Ibid.* p. 407.
[41] Stanmore, *op. cit.* p. 177.   [42] 11 October 1845—Parker, *op. cit.* III, 409.
[43] *Ibid.* p. 411.   [44] 17 August 1844—*Hansard*, LXXVI, 1870.
[45] "Notes on the Greville Memoirs", in *E.H.R.*, No. 1 (1886), p. 122.
[46] Monypenny and Buckle, *Disraeli*, II, 345.
[47] Greville, *Memoirs*, V, 392.   [48] Monypenny, II, 343.

CHAPTER VII

[1] Metternich, *Nachg. Papiere*, VII, 291.   [2] C. S. Parker, *Life of Peel*, III, 411.
[3] Guizot, *Peel*—cit. A. Ramsay, *Peel*, p. 257.
[4] Martin, *Life of the Prince Consort*, I, 305, 349.
[5] Aberdeen to Peel, "in the spring of 1846"—Stanmore, *Life of Aberdeen*, p. 165.
[6] 15 February 1845—Laughton, *Memoirs of Reeve*, I, 172.   [7] Martin, *op. cit.* II, 357.
[8] *Revue Rétrospective*, p. 182; cit. Martin, *op. cit.* p. 358.
[9] Aberdeen to Peel—cit. Stanmore, *op. cit.* p. 164.
[10] Bulwer, *Life of Palmerston*, III, 268.
[11] *Ibid.* p. 291.   [12] *Ibid.* p. 273.   [13] *Ibid.* p. 294.
[14] *Ibid.* p. 299.   [15] *Letters*, II, 102.   [16] *Ibid.* p. 106.
[17] 10 September—Martin, *op. cit.* I, 502.   [18] 27 September—*ibid.* p. 371.
[19] 19 November—*Memoirs of Reeve*, I, 182.   [20] Cit. Bell, *Palmerston*, I, 382.
[21] 6 October 1846, to King Leopold—*Letters*, II, 108.
[22] Greville, *Memoirs*, VI, 25 December 1846.   [23] *Ibid.* 30 December 1846.
[24] *Ibid.* 7 December 1847.   [25] *Nachg. Papiere*, VII, 319.
[26] H. v. Srbik, *Metternich*, II, 130.   [27] Ashley, *Life of Palmerston*, I, 4.
[28] 17 August 1846—*Hansard*, LXXXVIII, 830; Alfred Stern, *Gesch. Europas*, VI, 374.
[29] *Ibid.* p. 375.
[30] Letter to Dowager Duchess of Coburg, 26 November—cit. Martin, *op. cit.* I, 381.
[31] *Hansard*, LXXXVIII, p. 826.   [32] Ashley, *Life of Palmerston*, I, 8.   [33] *Ibid.* p. 10.
[34] A. J. P. Taylor, *The Italian Problem in European Diplomacy* 1847–9, p. 45, which
contains a very detailed and able survey of these two years.
[35] Ashley, *op. cit.* I, 35.   [36] 2 September 1847—Martin, *op. cit.* p. 426.
[37] 5 September—*ibid.* p. 433.   [38] 3 September—*Letters*, II, 128.
[39] Haussonville, *Histoire de la politique extérieure*, II, 381.
[40] Ashley, *Life of Palmerston*, I, 19.
[41] Queen Victoria to Lord John Russell, 14 February 1847—*Letters*, II, 119.
[42] Queen Victoria to Lord John Russell, 14 March 1847—*ibid.* p. 120.
[43] 5 July 1847—*Hansard*, XCIII, 1202–14.   [44] Martin, *op. cit.* II, 66.
[45] 5 May 1848—*Hansard*, XCVIII, 672.   [46] Martin, *op. cit.* II, 67.
[47] *Hansard*, XCVII.
[48] 4 April 1848, to Normanby—Ashley, *op. cit.* I, 89.   [49] 28 March 1848—*ibid.* p. 55.
[50] Palmerston to Ponsonby, 13 March 1848—cit. Taylor, *The Italian Problem*, p. 78.
[51] Palmerston to Normanby, 26 February 1848—Ashley, *op. cit.* I, 77.
[52] 26 February 1848—cit. Ashley, *op. cit.* I, 77, 83.
[53] *Letters of Queen Victoria*, II, 151.   [54] *Ibid.* p. 165.
[55] 31 March—Ashley, *op. cit.* I, 92.
[56] 11 February 1848, to Ponsonby—*ibid.* I, 65.   [57] 15 June 1848—*ibid.* p. 87.
[58] 21 April, to Ponsonby—*ibid.* p. 105.
[59] 4 June 1849, to Koller—cit. A. J. P. Taylor, *The Italian Problem*, p. 90.
[60] 28 May 1848—*ibid.* pp. 105–6. For this mission see Metternich, *Nachg. Papiere*, VIII,
432–9, and Arneth, *Wessenberg*, II, 94–136.
[61] See Taylor, *op. cit.* p. 110. His whole narrative throws much new light on the Italian
problem before and during the year of Revolution.
[62] 20 June 1848—Arneth, *Wessenberg*, II, 230.   [63] Ashley, I, 112.
[64] 4 December, to Werner—cit. Taylor, p. 207.   [65] 20 November—cit. Taylor, p. 189.
[66] Schwarzenberg to Werner, 4 December—cit. Taylor, p. 191. Cf. also Bell, *Palmerston*,
(I, 442), who has used a copy in the Windsor Archives, sent to the Queen, and translated a
little differently.   [67] Bell, *op. cit.* I, 442.
[68] Hübner to Schwarzenberg, 3 May 1849—cit. Taylor, p. 230.
[69] Drouyn to Tocqueville, 26 July 1849—Tocqueville, *Souvenirs*, p. 392.
[70] Queen Victoria, *Letters*, II, 186.   [71] Cit. *Letters*, II, 179, note.
[72] 18 June 1848—*Letters*, II, 180.   [73] 13 September—*ibid.* p. 194.
[74] 19 September 1848—*ibid.* p. 195.   [75] 7 October, to Lord John—*ibid.* p. 197.

[76] 10 October, to King Leopold—*ibid.* p. 199.   [77] Ashley, *Life of Palmerston*, I, 113.
[78] December 1848 to Schwarzenberg—cit. Taylor, p. 193.
[79] Friedjung, *Oesterreich von 1848 bis 1860*, II, 137.   [80] Corti, *König Leopold*, p. 186.
[81] Sproxton, *Palmerston and the Hungarian Revolution*, p. 46.
[82] For full details see Eugene Horváth, "Kossuth and Palmerston" (*Slavonic Review*, No. 27, March 1931).
[83] See despatches of Brunnov, of 23 and 29 April (5 and 11 May, N.S.) 1849, printed in R. A. Averbukh, *Tsarskaya Interventsiya v Borbe s Venyerskoy Revolutsiey* (1935), pp. 287–91. For this reference I am indebted to my colleague Dr Serge Jakobson.
[84] Ashley, *op. cit.* I, 139.   [85] *Ibid.* p. 141.
[86] 17 September 1849—cit. Lane-Poole, *Life of Stratford de Redcliffe*, II, 188.
[87] *Ibid.* p. 198.   [88] 6 October, Palmerston to Canning—*ibid.* p. 199.
[89] 14 November 1849—Ashley, *op. cit.* I, 163.
[90] 30 November, to Ponsonby—Ashley, *op. cit.* I, 173.
[91] 28 October—Lane-Poole, *op. cit.* II, 202.   [92] 30 November—*ibid.* p. 204.
[93] 6 October 1849—Ashley, *op. cit.* I, 153.   [94] 27 November—*ibid.* p. 169.
[95] *Ibid.* p. 169.   [96] *C.H.B.F.P.* II, 327.
[97] 7 May 1849—Lane-Poole, *op. cit.* II, 188.   [98] *Hansard*, CVII, 808–9.
[99] *Ibid.* p. 815.   [100] 6 July 1849—*ibid.* CVII, 1486–97.
[101] Instructions of 19 March 1847—cit. Driault, *Histoire Diplomatique de la Grèce*, II, 309.
[102] 3 December 1849—Ashley, *op. cit.* I, 184.
[103] Cit. Driault, *op. cit.* II, 347.
[104] 27 March 1850, to Bloomfield—Ashley, *op. cit.* I, 196.
[105] Palmerston to Normanby, 19 May—Ashley, *op. cit.* p. 203.
[106] 18 May—*Letters*, II, 243.
[107] 3 April 1850—C. S. Parker, *Life of Peel*, III, 536, and *Life of Sir J. Graham*, II, 102.
[108] 21 June, Queen to Lord J. Russell—*Letters*, II, 248.
[109] Buckle, *Disraeli*, III, 261.   [110] *Hansard*, CXI, 1332.
[111] *Ibid.* p. 1361.   [112] *Ibid.* CXII, 380–444.
[113] *Ibid.* pp. 543–90.   [114] *Ibid.* pp. 670–93.
[115] *Ibid.* pp. 720–39.   [116] *Ibid.* pp. 674–93.
[117] Guedalla, *Palmerston*, p. 306.   [118] *Letters*, II, 249–51.
[119] *Ibid.* p. 257.   [120] 5 August—*ibid.* p. 260.
[121] Memorandum of Prince Albert, 8 August 1850—*Letters*, II, 261–4.
[122] *Letters*, II, 264.
[123] See the Prince's memorandum of 17 August—Martin, *op. cit.* II, 310.
[124] For details see Correspondence in *State Papers*, XLII (1852–3).
[125] Martin, *op. cit.* II, 325.   [126] 8 October, Palmerston to Queen—*Letters*, p. 267.
[127] 12 and 19 October, Queen to Russell—*ibid.* pp. 270, 272.
[128] See 31 January and 15 February 1850—*ibid.* pp. 284–6.
[129] Lady Airlie, *Lady Palmerston and her Times*, II, 122.
[130] Memoranda of Prince Albert of 2 and 3 March 1851—*Letters*, II, 310–12.
[131] 31 October—*Letters*, II, 325.   [132] Walpole, *Life of Russell*, II, 133.
[133] 31 October 1851—*Letters*, p. 325.   [134] Martin, *op. cit.* I, 409.
[135] 20 November 1851—*Letters*, p. 329.   [136] 21 November—*ibid.* p. 331.
[137] Martin, *op. cit.* II, 412.   [138] Letter of 20 November 1851—Ashley, *op. cit.* I, 270.
[139] Palmerston to Normanby, 3 December—Ashley, *op. cit.* I, 291. This was written on the same day as Palmerston's conversation with Walewski.
[140] Lady Normanby to Col. Phipps, 7 December—*Letters*, II, 337.
[141] Memorandum of the Prince, 23 December—*Letters*, II, 346.
[142] 5 January 1852—Nesselrode, *Correspondance*, x, 120.
[143] 24 December 1851—Sir G. Trevelyan, *Life and Letters of Lord Macaulay* (new ed.), p. 555.   [144] Written at Brocket on Christmas Day 1851—*Memoirs*, VI, 439.
[145] Lady Palmerston to Lord Beauvale, 7 and 8 January 1852, and to Mrs Huskisson—cit. Guedalla, *Life of Palmerston*, pp. 323–6.
[146] Queen to Russell, 20 December 1851—Martin, *op. cit.* II, 419.
[147] Maxwell, *Life of Clarendon*, I, 336.   [148] 23 December 1851—*Letters*, II, 345.
[149] 29 December—*Letters*, II, 353.   [150] *Life of Granville*, I, 49.

[151] See letter to Lord Lansdowne, October 1852—Ashley, *op. cit.* I, 330.
[152] Words of Lord Canning—cit. Fitzmaurice, *Life of Granville*, I, 44.
[153] 26 December 1851—*ibid.* I, 46.   [154] *Ibid.* p. 65.
[155] 20 February 1852—*ibid.* p. 67.   [156] Malmesbury, *Memoirs*, I, 297.
[157] Palmerston to Sir W. Temple, 24 February—Ashley, *op. cit.* I, 334.
[158] Palmerston to Sir W. Temple, 30 April—*ibid.* p. 339.
[159] Palmerston to Lansdowne, October 1852—*ibid.* p. 374.
[160] Lane-Poole, *Life of Stratford de Redcliffe*, II, 219-27.
[161] Malmesbury, *Memoirs of an Ex-Minister*, I, 377.
[162] *Ibid.* p. 307.   [163] *Ibid.* p. 356.
[164] *Ibid.* p. 309.   [165] Ashley, *op. cit.* I, 379.
[166] 20 June 1852—cit. Ashley, I, 347.   [167] *Ibid.* I, 349.
[168] 31 December 1852, to his brother-in-law Sulivan—Lady Airlie, *Lady Palmerston*, II, 152.
[169] *C.H.F.P.* III, 584.
[170] Maxwell, *op. cit.* I, 159.
[171] Memorandum of Prince Albert, 3 March 1850—*Letters*, II, 236.

CHAPTER VIII

[1] Harcourt, *Les Quatre Ministères de Drouyn de Lhuys*, p. 65. The best account of the new regime is to be found in R. H. Simpson, *Louis Napoleon and the Recovery of France*—apart of course from the much fuller narrative of M. de La Gorce, *Histoire du Second Empire*.
[2] S. Goriainov, *The Secret Agreement of* 1844 (*Russian Review*, Nos. 3 and 4), pp. 106, 114.
[3] Goriainov, *loc. cit.* No. 4, pp. 79-83.
[4] *Eastern Papers*.   [5] Friedjung, *Der Krimkrieg*, p. 3.
[6] Castelbajac to Thouvenel, 15 April 1853—*Nicolas I et Napoléon III*, p. 118.
[7] Phrase used by Count Colloredo to Lord J. Russell, 10 February 1853—cit. Temperley, *The Crimea*, p. 302.   [8] *The Crimea*, p. 317.
[9] Memorandum in Lane-Poole, *op. cit.* II, 255-7.   [10] March 1853—*ibid.* p. 236.
[11] 23 April—*ibid.* p. 259.   [12] Lane-Poole, *op. cit.* II, 269.
[13] Stratford, reports the Dutch Minister, was "as surprised as the rest of us"—cit. Temperley, *The Crimea*, p. 324. Cf. also p. 331.   [14] Cit. Temperley, *op. cit.* p. 336.
[15] This was first quoted by Lord Fitzwilliam in the House of Lords, on 7 July 1853—*Hansard*, CXXVIII, 1356.
[16] Lane-Poole, *op. cit.* II, 282.   [17] *Ibid.* pp. 278-80.
[18] Cf. the reference in the Tsar's letter to Francis Joseph, July 1853—Redlich, *Francis Joseph*, p. 131.   [19] 21 August, to his wife—Lane-Poole, II, 298.
[20] 15 February 1853, to Lord John—Walpole, *Life of Russell*, II, 178.
[21] Clarendon to Aberdeen, 18 March—*ibid.* p. 179.
[22] Maxwell, *Life of Clarendon*, II, 12.   [23] *Ibid.* p. 15.
[24] Walpole, *op. cit.* II, 181.   [25] 8 July—*Hansard*, CXXVIII, 1427.
[26] *Ibid.* p. 1419.   [27] 12 August—*ibid.* p. 1617.
[28] *Ibid.* p. 1631.   [29] 16 August—*ibid.* pp. 1800-10.
[30] Maxwell, *op. cit.* II, 16.   [31] 21 September—Ashley, *Life of Palmerston*, I, 37-40.
[32] 29 August, to Clarendon—Walpole, *op. cit.* II, 186.
[33] 27 September—Maxwell, *op. cit.* II, 21.   [34] 8 July—Parker, *Life of Graham*, II, 222.
[35] 18 August—*ibid.* p. 223; Maxwell, *op. cit.* p. 16.
[36] 19 and 20 August—Maxwell, *op. cit.* II, 17.
[37] 26 August—*ibid.* p. 18.   [38] 3 September—*ibid.* p. 19.
[39] 12 September—*ibid.* p. 20.   [40] 1 October—*ibid.* p. 25.
[41] 10 November—*ibid.* p. 29.   [42] 11 September—Stanmore, *Life of Herbert*, I, 197.
[43] 1 October—Lane-Poole, II, 302.   [44] 19 November—*ibid.* p. 320.

[45] 9 October—*ibid.* p. 303.   [46] *Letters of Queen Victoria*, II, 460.

[47] 27 November—Martin, *Life of Prince Consort*, II, 532.

[48] 30 October 1853—*Letters*, II, 459.

[49] 5 October—Stanmore, *Life of Sidney Herbert*, I, 203.

[50] Duke of Argyll, *Autobiography*, I, 460.

[51] Stanmore, *Life of Aberdeen*, p. 234.   [52] 6 October—*Letters*, II, 453.

[53] Graham to Russell, 11 December—Parker, *op. cit.* p. 198. Cf. Palmerston's own explanation to his brother-in-law (Ashley, *op. cit.* II, 19–20) and Prince Albert's letter of 19 December to Aberdeen (*Letters*, II, 466).

[54] 1 November, to Aberdeen—Ashley, *op. cit.* II, pp. 45–9.

[55] 13 December, Aberdeen to Palmerston—Ashley, *op. cit.* II, 54.

[56] Simpson, *Louis Napoleon and the Recovery of France*, p. 239.

[57] Stanmore, *Life of Aberdeen*, p. 254, note.   [58] 11 October—Martin, *op. cit.* II, 521.

[59] La Gorce, *Second Empire*, I, 204.   [60] Martin, *op. cit.* II, 538.

[61] H. Bolitho, *Prince Consort and his Brother*, p. 147.

[62] Cit. Alfred Stern, *Gesch. Europas*, VIII, 53.

[63] Phrase used by Castelbajac to Thouvenel, 11 February 1854—L. Thouvenel, *Nicolas I et Napoléon III*, p. 332.   [64] H. Schlitter, *Aus der Regierungszeit Franz Josephs*, p. 99.

[65] Bright's Diary, 22 March 1854—Trevelyan, *Life of Bright*, p. 232.

[66] Memorandum of Prince Albert, 25 December 1853—*Letters*, II, 471.

[67] 13 March—*Hansard*, CXXXI, 676–81.   [68] Trevelyan, *Life of Bright*, p. 234.

[69] *Hansard*, CXXXI, 685.   [70] Thouvenel, *Nicolas I et Napoléon III*, p. 282, etc.

[71] Lane-Poole, *op. cit.* II, 330.   [72] *Ibid.* p. 345.

[73] The details are given by Alfred Stern, *op. cit.* VIII, 61–73.

[74] Queen to Aberdeen, 1 April 1854—*Letters*, III, 20.

[75] Guedalla, *Life of Palmerston*, pp. 360–1.

[76] 31 March 1854—*Hansard*, CXXXII, 141–56.

CHAPTER IX

[1] Guedalla, *Gladstone and Palmerston*, pp. 145–6.

[2] 16 July, Palmerston to Newcastle—*ibid.* p. 147.

[3] Walpole, *Life of Russell*, II, 214.   [4] Martin, *Life of Prince Consort*, III, 519.

[5] For the Austro-Russian and Austro-Prussian aspects of the war, see especially Friedjung, *Der Krimkrieg*, pp. 102–6, 126, but also *cursim*.

[6] 12 December 1854—Maxwell, *Life of Clarendon*, II, 54.

[7] Memorandum of Prince Albert, 9 December—*Letters*, III, 60.

[8] Ashley, *Life of Palmerston*, II, 76.

[9] Memorandum of Prince Albert, 2 February 1855—*Letters*, III, 86.

[10] 31 January—*Letters*, III, 81.   [11] 10 and 11 February—*ibid.* pp. 105–6.

[12] Devaux to Beyens, 21 February 1855—cit. Beyens, *Le Second Empire*, I, 105.

[13] 28 March—Maxwell, II, 76; Walpole, *Life of Russell*, II, 257.

[14] Benedetti, *Essais Diplomatiques*, pp. 229–30, 273–6.

[15] Stern, *Gesch. Europas*, VIII, 112.   [16] 26 April—*Letters*, III, 120–1.

[17] Fitzmaurice, *Life of Granville*, I, 101.   [18] To Cowley, 7 August—Maxwell, p. 87.

[19] Stern, *op. cit.* p. 115.   [20] Martin, *op. cit.* III, 272.

[21] 2 June—Parker, *Life of Graham*, II, 283.   [22] 14 September—*Letters*, III, 143.

[23] Napoleon to the Queen and the Queen to Napoleon, 22 and 25 November—Martin, III, 395–7.   [24] Lane-Poole, *Life of Stratford de Redcliffe*, II, 421.

[25] 16 September—*ibid.* p. 93.

[26] 25 April 1855, Clarendon to Granville—Fitzmaurice, *op. cit.* I, 105.

[27] Guedalla, *Palmerston*, pp. 389, 489.   [28] Ashley, *Life of Palmerston*, II, 100.

[29] J. A. Hobson, *Cobden: the International Man*, p. 128.

[30] 16 November—Maxwell, II, 103.

[31] 16 and 24 November—Maxwell, II, 103-4.

[32] Paris Archives, 19 November—cit. Stern, *Gesch. Europas*, VIII, 126.

[33] Charles-Roux, *Alexandre II, Gortchakoff et Napoléon III*, p. 59.

[34] Friedjung, *Der Krimkrieg*, p. 176.   [35] Martin, *Life of the Prince Consort*, III, 432.

[36] 15 January to Lord Clarendon and to Napoleon III—*Letters*, III, 163-4.

[37] 17 January—*ibid*, p. 166; Ashley, *Life of Palmerston*, II, 104.

[38] 20 January—*Letters*, III, 167.

[39] Palmerston to Clarendon, 26 November—Ashley, *op. cit.* II, 105.

[40] 25 September 1855—cit. Bell, *Palmerston*, II, 138.

[41] Palmerston to Seymour, 24 January 1856—*ibid*. p. 107.

[42] 18 January to Clarendon—cit. Reddaway in the *C.H.B.F.P.* II, 386.

[43] Hübner, *Neuf Ans de Souvenirs*, I, 389.   [44] Charles-Roux, *op. cit.* p. 97.

[45] Fitzmaurice, *Life of Granville*, I, 174.   [46] Hübner, *op. cit.* p. 409.

[47] 27 May—Clarendon MSS., cit. Bell, *op. cit.* II, 152.

[48] 6 March, 1856—*Letters*, III, 180.   [49] W. F. Reddaway in *C.H.B.F.P.* II, 392 *seq*.

[50] 13 May 1854—*Letters of Queen Victoria*, III, 27.

[51] Lane-Poole, *op. cit.* II, 439.   [52] Lane-Poole, *ibid*. p. 436.

[53] 30 March—*Letters*, III, 183.   [54] *Ibid*. p. 184.

[55] 12 March—Maxwell, *op. cit.* II, 119.   [56] 5 May 1856—*Hansard*, CXLI, 1988.

[57] *Ibid*. p. 2002.   [58] *Ibid*. p. 2012.

[59] 6 May—*Hansard*, CXLII, 99.   [60] *Ibid*. p. 1902.

[61] *Ibid*. p. 1992.   [62] 20 July to Clarendon—cit. Bell, II, 161.

[63] 26 December 1856 to Normanby—Maxwell, *op. cit.* II, 13.

[64] Fitzmaurice, *Life of Granville*, I, 216.

[65] 10 December 1856—Guedalla, *Palmerston*, pp. 385, 489.

[66] Cit. La Gorce, *Le Second Empire*, II, 247.   [67] Morley, *Life of Cobden*, II, 127.

[68] Ashley, *Palmerston*, II, 37.   [69] Morley, *op. cit.* II, 126.

[70] *Ibid*. p. 123.   [71] Morley's own phrase, *ibid*. p. 124.

[72] *Ibid*. p. 151.   [73] *Ibid*. p. 154.

[74] 23 August—Fitzmaurice, *Life of Granville*, I, 355.

CHAPTER X

[1] Charles-Roux, *Alexandre II, Gortchakoff et Napoléon III*, p. 144.

[2] Guedalla, *Palmerston*, p. 386.

[3] See much new material in E. Schüle, *Russland und Frankreich*, pp. 35-43 (*Osteuropäische Forschungen*, vol. XIX, 1935).

[4] Napoleon to Walewski, quoted by Clarendon to Palmerston 7 March 1856—cit. W. G. East, *Union of Moldavia and Wallachia*, p. 47.

[5] Thouvenel, *Trois Années de la Question d'Orient*, pp. 7, 8.

[6] Roux, *op. cit.* p. 147.   [7] 11 February 1856 to Buol—cit. East.

[8] Lord Clarendon to Lord Howard de Walden, 12 January 1858—Maxwell, *Life of Clarendon*, II, 159.   [9] 25 May—cit. Riker, *The Making of Roumania*, p. 105.

[10] Thouvenel, *op. cit.* p. 125.   [11] 30 July—cit. East, p. 123.

[12] 3 August—Riker, *op. cit.* p. 130.

[13] 29 July, 20 August 1857—Maxwell, *op. cit.* II, 146-7.   [14] *Hansard*, CL, 90.

[15] 10 April 1857 to Cowley—E. F. Malcolm Smith, *Life of Stratford Canning*, p. 311. For a fuller account of events in Roumania see my *History of the Roumanians*, pp. 246-68.

[16] Cit. Simpson, *Louis Napoleon and the Recovery of France*, p. 364.

[17] *The Paris Embassy*, p. 135.   [18] *Hansard*, CL, 83-91.

[19] Duke of Argyll, *Autobiography*, I, 446.   [20] Elgin, *Letters and Journals*, p. 209.

[21] *Hansard*, CLXIV, 1220.

[22] Elgin, *Letters and Journals*, pp. 212–13.
[23] Malmesbury, *Memoirs*, II, 70.
[24] *The Paris Embassy*, p. 136.
[25] 16 November—Ashley, *op. cit.* II, 140.
[26] Buckle, *Life of Disraeli*, IV, 101.
[27] Greville, *Memoirs*, VIII, 57, 113, 136.
[28] *The Paris Embassy*, pp. 148–9.
[29] *Hansard*, CXLVIII, 963.
[30] 17 January 1858—C. S. Parker, *Life of Graham*, II, 331.
[31] 21 February 1858, John Bright to Gladstone—Morley, *Gladstone*, I, 579.
[32] Clarendon to Prince Albert, 22 March 1859—Martin, IV, 406.
[33] *Letters of Queen Victoria*, III, 274.
[34] Martin, *op. cit.* IV, 155.
[35] *The Paris Embassy*, p. 163.
[36] Grimblot to Senior, 27 April 1858—Nassau Senior, *Conversations*, II, 200–1.
[37] Count Vitzthum was Saxon Minister in London—see his *St Petersburg and London*, I, 238.
[38] At Slough, 26 May.
[39] Vitzthum, *St Petersburg and London*, I, 297.
[40] *Manuel Historique*, III, 447.
[41] E. Schüle, *Russland und Frankreich*, pp. 114–6.
[42] 22 November 1858—La Gorce, *op. cit.* II, 374.
[43] *Ibid.* II, 242.
[44] *Affairs of Italy*, No. 4—3 January 1859.
[45] Malmesbury, II, 148; *Correspondence*, Nos. 7, 9, 22–5.
[46] Malmesbury, pp. 150–2; Buckle, IV, 226.
[47] Maxwell, *Life of Clarendon*, II, 176.
[48] Buckle, IV, 226.
[49] 3 February 1859—*Hansard*, CLII, 89–90, 99.
[50] Thayer, *Cavour*, I, 578.
[51] Martin, IV, 415, 417.
[52] 25 March—Malmesbury, II, 166.
[53] Buckle, I, 1604.
[54] To Prince Albert—Martin, IV, p. 380.
[55] Martin, IV, 422–3; *The Paris Embassy*, p. 180.
[56] Malmesbury, II, 167.
[57] *Hansard*, CLIII, 1843.
[58] *Memoirs*, II, 202–4.
[59] *Hansard*, CLIII, 1872, 1881.
[60] *Correspondence re Affairs of Italy*, 6 April.
[61] Martin, IV, 396.
[62] Sybel, *Begründung des Deutschen Reiches*, II, 233.
[63] 21 April—*Letters*, III, 327.
[64] Martin, IV, 427–8; *Letters*, III, 328.
[65] *Correspondence*, p. 321.
[66] See Srbik, *Deutsche Einheit*, II, 352.
[67] Charles-Roux, *Alexandre II et Napoléon III*, p. 257.
[68] *Ibid.* p. 255.
[69] *Ibid.* p. 265.
[70] *Memories of an Ex-Minister*, II, 205.
[71] *Letters*, III, 335–9.
[72] Kossuth, *Schriften aus der Emigration*, I, 252–60; see also Ollivier, *L'Empire Libéral*.
[73] *Memories of an Ex-Minister*, II, 164.
[74] 12 June—Fitzmaurice, *Life of Granville*, p. 337.
[75] 17 May to Graham—Walpole, II, 305.
[76] Buckle, *Disraeli*, IV, 263.

CHAPTER XI

[1] 18 April, House of Lords.
[2] *Cowley Papers*, p. 182.
[3] 30 January 1859—Fitzmaurice, *Life of Granville*, I, 325.
[4] 24 April, to Clarendon—Maxwell, *Life of Clarendon*, II, 182–4.
[5] 18 July, to Prince Albert—Windsor MSS., cit. Bell, *Palmerston*, II, 221.
[6] *Garibaldi and the Thousand*, p. 117.
[7] Walpole, *Life of Russell*, II, 301.
[8] Gooch, *Later Correspondence*, II, 234.
[9] 7 July—Martin, *Life of Prince Consort*, IV, 462.
[10] 6 July—Ashley, *Life of Palmerston*, II, 160.
[11] 13 July—*ibid.* p. 162.
[12] State Papers, No. 92, 17 August, Russell to Crampton.
[13] La Gorce, *Second Empire*, III, 118.
[14] 13 July, Granville to Prince Albert—Fitzmaurice, *op. cit.* I, 351.
[15] 13 July, Queen to Russell—Martin, *op. cit.* IV, 465.
[16] Walpole, *Life of Russell*, II, 312.

[17] Walpole, *Life of Russell*, II, 311. In his despatch of 25 July to Cowley, he speaks of "the free votes of Tuscany" (*State Papers*, XLIX, 111).

[18] 25 July—*State Papers*, XLIX, 111, No. 30.

[19] *State Papers*, No. 95, Cowley to Russell, 18 August.

[20] *Ibid.* No. 154, Cowley to Russell, 14 October.

[21] Windsor MSS., cit. Bell, *Palmerston*, II, 229.   [22] Walpole, *op. cit.* II, 313.

[23] Gooch, *Later Correspondence*, II, 238.

[24] *State Papers*, 26 November 1851, Russell to Cowley.

[25] 12 December 1859, to Odo Russell—Gooch, *op. cit.* II, 250.

[26] Cf. Martin, *Life of the Prince Consort*, V, 25.

[27] Cf. Ollivier, *L'Empire Libéral*, IV, 594; Stern, *Gesch. Europas*, VIII, 387 n.

[28] 9 February 1860—*Letters*, III, 387.   [29] Walpole, *Life of Russell*, II, 319.

[30] Undated letter—cit. by Ashley, II, 190.   [31] 2 November to Cowley—*ibid.* p. 198.

[32] *Cowley Papers*, p. 187; cf. Martin, IV, 472.   [33] 7 September—*Letters*, III, 370.

[34] 1 December—*ibid.* p. 374.   [35] 24 January 1860—*Hansard*, CLVI, 111.

[36] August–September 1859—*Letters*, III, 361–9.   [37] 11 January 1860—*Letters*, III, 383.

[38] 10 February—*ibid.* p. 388.   [39] 30 April—*ibid.* pp. 397–8.

[40] 7 February 1860—*Hansard*, CLVI, 587, 594.   [41] 26 March—*ibid.* CLVII, 1255.

[42] 9 July 1859—See *Affairs of Naples* (1860), vol. LXVIII.

[43] G. M. Trevelyan, *Garibaldi and the Making of Italy*, Appendix A, pp. 306–8.

[44] Palmerston to the Queen, 10 January 1861—*Letters*, III, 428.

[45] 17 May 1860—*Hansard*, CLVIII, 1406.

[46] Palmerston to Russell, 12 April, 17 May—cit. Bell, *Palmerston*, II, 265.

[47] G. M. Trevelyan, *Garibaldi and the Making of Italy*, pp. 104–8.

[48] Sir H. Elliot, *Some Revolutions*, p. 21.

[49] Bolton King, *History of Italian Unity*, II, 153.

[50] Cavour, *Lettere*, III, 266–74; VI, 565.

[51] "Molto amorevolmente", Cavour to Pepoli—*Lettere di Cavour*, IV, 18, 37. Cf. La Gorce, *op. cit.* III, 436.

[52] It is barely mentioned in Stern's very detailed narrative, *Gesch. Europas*, IX, 79.

[53] Walpole, *Life of Russell*, II, 325; Trevelyan, *op. cit.* p. 282.

[54] Vitzthum, *St Petersburg and London*, II, 120.

[55] 3 November 1860—*Letters*, II, 411.

[56] *Garibaldi and Making*, pp. 283, 314.   [57] Walpole, *Life of Russell*, II, 328.

[58] Letter of 6 October 1860 to Francis Joseph—cit. Stern, *Gesch. Europas*, IX, 83.

[59] *Letters*, III, 431–4.   [60] 17 September 1861—cit. Bell, *Palmerston*, II, 278.

[61] Gooch, *Later Correspondence*, II, 239.   [62] *Hansard*, CLXI, 30, 84, 91.

[63] *State Papers*, XLIX, Nos. 188, 201—15 and 26 November 1859.

[64] W. F. Reddaway in *Prime Ministers of the Nineteenth Century*, p. 173.

[65] 7 June 1861—*Hansard*, CLXIII, 777–8.   [66] E. H. Benians in *C.H.F.P.* II, 486.

[67] Morley, *Cobden*, II, 276; *Hansard*, CLVII.   [68] *The Paris Embassy*, p. 197.

[69] Cit. Morley, *Cobden*, II, 337.   [70] Morley, *Gladstone*, II, 23, 638.

[71] *Letters*, III, 340–4.   [72] Martin, V, 38–41.

[73] *The Paris Embassy*, p. 189.   [74] *Ibid.* p. 237—10 January 1862.

[75] Letter of 23 August 1860 to King Leopold—Buckle, *Life of Disraeli*, IV, 17.

[76] 24 August 1860—*Hansard*, CLX, 1808.   [77] 25 July 1860—text in Martin, V, 154–6.

[78] Letters of 31 December and 1 January—*Letters*, III, 423, 427.

[79] January 1861 to Gladstone—G. M. Trevelyan, *Bright*, p. 293.

[80] 26 July 1861—*Hansard*, CLXIV, 1680–2.   [81] 8 May 1862—*Hansard*, CLXVII, 1412–26.

[82] 31 July, 2 August 1860—Morley, *Cobden*, II, 302–3.   [83] *Ibid.* p. 385.

[84] *C.H.F.P.* II, 456.   [85] 1 October 1861—Maxwell, *op. cit.* II, 240.

[86] Martin, V, 422–3 (with facsimile); *Letters*, III, 469.

[87] Maxwell, II, 251.   [88] *History of England*, II, 313.

[89] Bolitho, *Albert the Good*, p. 176.   [90] Bolitho, *Prince Consort and his Brother*, p. 213.

[91] *The Paris Embassy*, p. 232.   [92] *Hansard*, CLX, 1687–90.

[93] Driault and Lhéritier, *Histoire Diplomatique de la Grèce*, III, 97.

[94] 9 December 1862—Buckle, IV, 65.

[95] 5 February 1863—*Hansard*, CLXIX, 35, 49, 55, 89, 127; and 10 February, pp. 230–1.

[96] For full details see three articles of Dr Milan Gavrilović on "The Early Relations of Great Britain and Serbia" in Nos. 1-3 of *Slavonic Review*.

[97] 10 Ap. 1860—cit. T. W. Riker, "Michael of Serbia and the Turkish Occupation"— three articles in *Slavonic Review*, Nos. 34, 35 and 38, which give a full account of the whole diplomatic conflict.

[98] 18 June 1862, the day after the bombardment, and 25 June, to Bloomfield in Vienna— Riker, I, p. 147.   [99] Charles-Roux, *Alexandre II, Gortchakoff et Napoléon III*, p. 31.

[100] Queen Victoria, *Letters*, 2nd Series, I, 67.   [101] *Hansard*, CLXIX, 560-8.

[102] *Hansard*, 27 February, p. 934.   [103] *Ibid.* p. 943.

[104] Lutostanski, *Les Partages de la Pologne*, Nos. 325, 326.

[105] 4 February—Ashley, *Life of Palmerston*, II, 230.

[106] *State Papers*, LIII, *Affairs of Poland*, No. 60—Russell to Napier, 2 March.

[107] *Ibid.* No. 68—Russell to Cowley, 5 March.

[108] *Ibid.* No. 96, Russell to Bloomfield, 17 March; No. 101, Napier to Russell, 9 March.

[109] *State Papers*, No. 138—Russell to Napier, 10 April.

[110] *Ibid.* No. 171—Gorchakov to Brunnov.

[111] F. O. Russia, 631, No. 335; quoted by Dr R. Reid, *C.H.F.P.* II, 462.

[112] *State Papers*, No. 173—Russell to Napier, 17 June.

[113] H. Oncken, *Die Rheinpolitik Napoleons III*, I, 1-15; Stern, *Gesch. Europas*, IX, 165; Charles-Roux, *op. cit.* p. 345. Oncken goes too far in assuming that the Rhenish ambitions of Napoleon were the focusing point of the whole incident; but undoubtedly they played their part and were constantly at the back of his mind.

[114] *State Papers*, Nos. 174, 175.   [115] Cf. Roux, *op. cit.* p. 355-6.

[116] *State Papers*, No. 177—Russell to Napier, 11 August.

[117] Cf. A. A. Ramsay, *Idealism and Foreign Policy*, p. 98.

[118] *The Times*, 28 September 1863.   [119] November 1863—Ashley, *op. cit.* III, 236-42.

[120] *Hansard*, CLXXV, 652-4.   [121] See *Auswärtige Politik Preussens*, IV, Nos. 65, 66, 72, 90.

[122] 13 January 1864—Maxwell, *op. cit.* II, 286.

[123] 30 October 1863—Buckle, *op. cit.* IV. 73.

[124] Cf. Sybel, *Begründung des deutschen Reiches*, III, 107.

[125] Ernest of Coburg, *Denkwürdigkeiten*, I, 460; cf. Mrs Rosslyn Wemyss, *Life of Morier*, I, 364.   [126] February 1859—*Memoirs*, II, 544.

[127] Wemyss, *Life of Morier*, I, 371.   [128] Sybel, *op. cit.* p. 117.

[129] 22 December 1862—Sybel, *op. cit.* III, 89.   [130] Wemyss, *op. cit.* I, 389.

[131] *Hansard*, CXXII, 1252.   [132] Wemyss, *op. cit.* I, 391.

[133] Cf. *Denmark and Germany*, I, No. 99—31 July, Russell to Bloomfield.

[134] *Ibid.* No. 117—31 August, Russell to Lowther.

[135] *Ibid.* No. 137—29 September, Russell to Malet.

[136] *Ibid.*; cf. Walpole, *Life of Russell*, II, 379.

[137] *Ibid.* No. 125, 16 September, Russell to Grey; No. 126, 18 September, Grey to Russell.

[138] The phrase of Queen Victoria when she heard the news—*Letters*, 2nd series, I, 117.

[139] 1 January 1864, to Russell—*Letters*, I, 139.

[140] 3 August 1863—Fitzmaurice, *op. cit.* I, 453.

[141] 4 October 1863 to Russell—*Letters*, I, 111.

[142] *Letters*, I, 119, 121.   [143] *Ibid.* I, pp. 126, 130.

[144] *Denmark and Germany*, II, No. 266, 21 November.

[145] For the Wodehouse mission, see *Denmark and Germany*, IV, No. 451 and *cursim*.

[146] 29 December to Wodehouse—*ibid.*; cf. Walpole, *Life of Russell*, II, 388.

[147] 26 December—*ibid.* p. 388.   [148] Sybel, *op. cit.* p. 153.

[149] *Origines Diplom. de la Guerre de* 1870, I, No. 4.   [150] *C.H.F.P.* II, 570.

[151] La Gorce, *Second Empire*, IV, p. 49.   [152] 22 December 1862—cit. Sybel, III, 126.

[153] Sybel, *op. cit.* p. 161.   [154] 8 January to Queen—*Letters*, I, 146.

[155] 13 February 1864—Ashley, *op. cit.* II, 247-8.

[156] Cit. Zwiedineck-Südenhorst, *Deutsche Geschichte*, III, 282.

[157] Theodor von Bernhardi, *Der Streit um die Elbherzogthümer*, pp. 367, 376; *Aus den letzten Tagen des deutschen Bundes*, p. 37.

[158] *Hansard*, CLXXIII, 28-9.   [159] Sybel, *op. cit.* 210.

[160] 12 and 14 February—Fitzmaurice, *Granville*, I, 457–60.
[161] La Gorce, *op. cit.* IV, 502; Walpole, *Life of Russell*, II, 390–1.
[162] Sybel, III, 225; cf. *Auswärt. Pol. Preussens*, IV, No. 599.
[163] *Origines Diplom. de la Guerre*, II, No. 439.
[164] *Hansard*, CLXXIII, 1627–30.   [165] La Gorce, *op. cit.* IV, 511.
[166] Granville to Russell, 5 May—*Letters*, p. 182.
[167] *Hansard*, CLXXIII—26 February, p. 1190–1 and 15 February, p. 560.
[168] *Ibid.*—29 February 1864, pp. 1261–70.   [169] *Hansard*, CLXXIV, 758–65, 777.
[170] 26 May 1864—*Hansard*, CLXXV, 609 and 613; cf. Granville's report to the Queen—*Letters*, I, 197.   [171] Queen to Russell, 27 May—*Letters*, I, 198.
[172] 29 May, Derby to Queen—*ibid.* p. 201.
[173] 5 January 1864, to Palmerston—*ibid.* p. 142.
[174] 27 January—*ibid.* p. 150.   [175] Fitzmaurice, *Life of Granville*, I, 456.
[176] 5 June—*ibid.* I, 468.   [177] La Gorce, *op. cit.* IV, 512.
[178] Sybel, *op. cit.* III, 246.   [179] See Ziekursch, *Politische Geschichte*, I, 130.
[180] Sybel, *op. cit.* p. 349.   [181] 16 June—*Letters*, I, 220.
[182] *Hansard*, CLXXV, 1924, 2033.   [183] Sybel, *op. cit.* III, p. 260.
[184] *Denmark and Germany*, VII (1864), Nos. 1, 2.
[185] Queen to Palmerston, 23 June, to Russell, 23 and 25 June, to Clarendon, 25 June—*Letters*, I, 225–32.   [186] Walpole, *Life of Russell*, II, 396.
[187] 27 June—*Hansard*, CLXXVI, 305–22, 328.   [188] *Ibid.* pp. 350–4.
[189] 4 July—*Hansard*, CLXXVI, 725–50.   [190] 8 July—*ibid.* pp. 1274–82.
[191] 5 July—*ibid.* pp. 835, 853.   [192] Morley, *Life of Gladstone*, II, 120.
[193] 8 July 1864—Hardinge, *Life of Lord Carnarvon*, I, 252.
[194] In *Biographical Studies: Earl of Clarendon*.   [195] *C.H.F.P.* III, 582.
[196] *Life of Gladstone*, II, 120.   [197] 28 October—*Letters*, I, 281.
[198] 21 October, to Granville—Fitzmaurice, *Granville*, I, 487.
[199] *Hansard*, XCVII (1 March 1848), 87 *sqq.*; cf. also Ashley, *Life of Palmerston*, I, 63.
[200] *Hansard*, CXII, 444.   [201] *Denkwürdigkeiten*, p. 577.
[202] 6 May 1840, Metternich to Apponyi—*Nachg. Papiere*, VI, 406.
[203] *C.H.F.P.* II, 328.
[204] 20 October 1865—*Letters*, 2nd series, I, 279. "Vindictive" causes surprise and is less convincing.
[205] 25 February 1847, to Apponyi—Metternich, *Nachg. Papiere*, VII, 321.
[206] *Ibid.* p. 385.
[207] 31 January 1848, Palmerston to Milbanke—Lady Airlie, *Lady Palmerston and her Times*, II, 133.   [208] *Hansard*, XIV, 1045–9.
[209] 7 January 1860, to Duchess of Manchester—Maxwell, *Life of Clarendon*, II, 206.
[210] 16 November 1849—Ashley, I, 163.
[211] 24 January 1865, to his brother—Moltke, *Letters to his Family*, II, 125. See A. A. Ramsay, *Idealism and Foreign Policy*, p. 143.

CHAPTER XII

[1] Fitzmaurice, *Life of Granville*, I, 517.   [2] 25 October 1865—*Letters*, 2nd series, I, 280.
[3] 29 March 1866—*ibid.* p. 313.   [4] Morley, *Life of Gladstone*, II, 417.
[5] Mrs Rosslyn Wemyss, *Life of Morier*, II, 84.   [6] Cit. *C.H.F.P.* III, 5.
[7] Queen's journal—*Letters*, 2nd Series, I, 314.
[8] Clarendon to the Queen—*ibid.* p. 314.   [9] *Ibid.* p. 317.
[10] Queen to Russell, 31 May—*ibid.* p. 332.   [11] Maxwell, *op. cit.* II, 318.
[12] *Letters*, 2nd series, I, 325–6.   [13] Maxwell, *op. cit.* II, 318.
[14] Queen Victoria, *Letters*, 2nd Series, I, 346.
[15] Memorandum of Queen, 28 June 1866—*ibid.* p. 345.

[16] 1 July 1866—*ibid.* II, 353.
[17] Wemyss, *Life of Morier*, II, 85.
[18] Ashley, *Life of Palmerston*, I, 349.
[19] *Letters*, I, 354.
[20] *Hansard*, CLX (1866), 1271–3, 1290.
[21] Maxwell, *op. cit.* II, 323.
[22] For text see Oncken, *Rheinpolitik Napoleons* III, I, 243 (No. 127 C).
[23] For text see *ibid.* p. 265 (No. 147).
[24] Metternich to Mensdorff, 26 July 1866—*ibid.* p. 379 (No. 233).
[25] Cit. Ziekursch, *Politische Gesch.* I, 158.
[26] Baron Beyens, *Le Second Empire*, II, 88.
[27] Wemyss, *op. cit.* II, 68.
[28] *Ibid.* p. 72.
[29] *Letters*, 2nd Series, I, 364.
[30] Ziekursch, *op. cit.* I, 157.
[31] Oncken, *op. cit.* II, 3 (No. 237).
[32] *Ibid.* p. 9 (No. 239).
[33] *Ibid.* p. 83 (No. 288).
[34] *Ibid.* p. 84 (No. 289).
[35] It was published in the new Republic's *Journal Officiel* in 1870; see *ibid.* II, 81 (No. 287).
[36] *Ibid.* p. 93 (No. 296).
[37] *Ibid.* p. 94 (No. 297); La Gorce, *Histoire du Second Empire*, v, 67–9.
[38] *Letters*, II, 53.
[39] 8 August 1866—*Letters*, I, 364–5.
[40] 10 August—*ibid.* p. 365.
[41] See report of Count Goltz (15 August 1866), to whom Cowley had shown the answer, Oncken, *op. cit.* II, 81 (No. 286).
[42] *Ibid.* p. 101 (No. 302, report of Goltz to William I).
[43] La Gorce, *op. cit.* v, 74.
[44] Low and Sanders, *History of England* (1837–1901), p. 203.
[45] Cit. from Sir R. Phillimore's diary, 12 April 1867—Morley, *Life of Gladstone*, II, 232.
[46] Buckle, *Life of Disraeli*, IV, 201.
[47] Alfred Stern, *Gesch. Europas*, x. 90–1.
[48] *Ibid.* p. 98.
[49] 11 April 1867—*Letters*, 2nd Series, I, 417.
[50] 19 April—*ibid.* p. 420.
[51] 26 April—*ibid.* p. 423.
[52] Charles-Roux, *Alexandre II, Gorchakoff et Napoléon III*, p. 424.
[53] *Ibid.* p. 430.
[54] 20 June and 4 July 1867—*Hansard*, CLXXXVIII, pp. 146–53, 967–77.
[55] King William to Queen Victoria, 26 June—*Letters*, I, 439.
[56] Grey to Disraeli, 29 July 1867—*Letters*, 2nd Series, I, 454.
[57] Disraeli to Grey, 31 July—*ibid.* p. 455.
[58] Grey to Disraeli, 5 August—*ibid.* p. 457.
[59] Stanley to Grey, 9 August—*ibid.* p. 458.
[60] Queen to Derby, 29 September 1867—*Letters*, 2nd Series, I, 463.
[61] Stanley to Derby, 3 October—*ibid.* p. 465.
[62] Wemyss, *Life of Morier*, II, 287.
[63] 26 February 1868—Queen Victoria, *Letters*, I, 505.
[64] 4 November—*ibid.* p. 551.
[65] 28 September 1868—*ibid.* p. 539.
[66] Fitzmaurice, *Life of Lord Granville*, I, 531.
[67] Queen's memorandum of 3 December 1868—*Letters*, I, 565.
[68] *Ibid.* p. 564.
[69] Morley, *Life of Gladstone*, II, 255.
[70] *Letters*, I, 564.
[71] Lyons to Stanley, 13 October 1868—Lord Newton, *Lord Lyons* (cheap edition), p. 141.
[72] General Grey to Clarendon, 14 January 1869—*ibid.* p. 148.
[73] *Ibid.* p. 151; cf. Baron Beyens, *Le Second Empire*.
[74] Newton, *op. cit.* p. 152.
[75] *Ibid.* p. 149.
[76] Morley, *op. cit.* II, 317–18.
[77] *Letters*, I, 592.
[78] Newton, *op. cit.* p. 172.
[79] Bismarck to Bernsdorff, 9 February—cit. Newton, *op. cit.* p. 182.
[80] La Gorce, *op. cit.* VI, 175.
[81] *Letters*, II, 21.
[82] *Ibid.* I, 624.
[83] Maxwell, *op. cit.* II, 366.
[84] E.g. 11 May 1869—see La Gorce, *op. cit.* VI, 196.
[85] See Stern, *op. cit.* x, 312.
[86] June 1871—cit. Ziekursch, *op. cit.* I, 273.
[87] See Stern, *op. cit.* x, 315.
[88] Cit. Morley, *op. cit.* II, 327.
[89] Lyons to Granville, 16 July—Newton, *op. cit.* p. 211.
[90] Stern, *op. cit.* x, 333.
[91] Morley, *op. cit.* II, 328.
[92] *Letters*, II, 32.
[93] Bismarck, *Reflections*, II, 95–101.
[94] *Letters*, II, 34.
[95] W. E. Gladstone, *Gleanings*, IV. 222.
[96] La Gorce, *op. cit.* VI, 125.
[97] F.O. 64: 1026—26 May 1883, enclosure to No. 187 of Sir John Walsham, 2 June 1883.
[98] *Letters*, II, 53.
[99] 30 July—*ibid.* p. 54.
[100] Morley, *op. cit.* II, 341.
[101] Wemyss, *Life of Morier*, II, 165.

[102] See Oncken, *Rheinpolitik Napoleons III*, III, Nos. 671 (French Note of 1 March 1839), 685 (draft sent by Metternich to Beust, 18 April 1869), 691 (new draft submitted by Beust to Francis Joseph, 25 April), 693 and 698 (final draft approved by Napoleon, 20 May 1869).

[103] Fitzmaurice, *Life of Granville*, I, 70.

[104] Morley, *op. cit.* II, 348; Fitzmaurice, *op. cit.* I, 71.

[105] 5 October 1870—*Letters*, II, 74–5.

[106] Morley, *op. cit.* II, 350.

[107] 20 November 1870—*Letters*, II, 85.

[108] Fitzmaurice, *op. cit.* I, 76.

[109] Wemyss, *Life of Morier*, II, 296.

[110] Buckle, *Life of Disraeli*, V, 198.

[111] Address to his electors in 1874.

[112] Buckle, *op. cit.* V, 217.

[113] Paul, *History of England*, III, 327.

[114] Buckle, *op. cit.* V, 283.

[115] 17 and 20 February 1874—*Letters*, II, 318, 323.

[116] 12 March, to Granville—Fitzmaurice, *op. cit.* I, 134.

CHAPTER XIII

Note—The full references for this and the following chapter will be found in my *Disraeli, Gladstone and the Eastern Question* (1935).

[1] Buckle, *Life of Disraeli*, V, 178.

[2] Wemyss, *Life of Morier*, II, 299.

[3] Buckle, V, 424.

[4] To Lady Bradford—Buckle, VI, 23.

[5] Buckle, V, 416; *Letters of Queen Victoria*, II, 338.

[6] Wemyss, *op. cit.* II, 323.

[7] 10 and 26 February 1874—*Letters*, II, 314, 325.

[8] Taffs, "The War Scare" (*Slavonic Review*, No. 26, p. 342), one of the best summaries available.

[9] *Documents Diplomatiques Français*, I, No. 388.

[10] Queen Victoria, *Letters*, 2nd series, II, 396.

[11] Wemyss, *Life of Morier*, II, 343.

[12] Newton, *Lord Lyons*, p. 338; Wemyss, *op. cit.* II, 355.

[13] *Letters*, II, 400–8.

[14] *Ibid.* p. 407.

[15] *Ibid.* p. 391.

[16] 18 June 1876—*ibid.* p. 465.

[17] Buckle, V, 415.

[18] *Ibid.* p. 473.

[19] *Letters*, II, 464.

[20] See my *Role of Bosnia in International Politics* (Raleigh Lecture), p. 13, original reports of 17 December 1868, cit. in my "Les Relations de l'Autriche-Hongrie et de la Serbie" in *Le Monde Slave*.

[21] 12 January 1876, Shuvalov to Gorchakov—*Russo-British Documents*, II (*Slavonic Review*, No. 9).

[22] 18 November—Buckle, *op. cit.* V, 443.

[23] *Ibid.* p. 456.

[24] *Ibid.* p. 455.

[25] See Buckle, VI, 13, 15, 18, 49.

[26] Disraeli to Derby 9 January 1876—*ibid.* pp. 18–19.

[27] *Letters*, II, 453.

[28] 3 June—*ibid.* p. 459.

[29] A Gallenga, from Constantinople to *The Times*, 8 June 1876.

[30] *Letters*, II, 455.

[31] Buckle, *op. cit.* VI, 31.

[32] Shuvalov to Gorchakov—"Russo-British Documents", No. 38 (*Slavonic Review*).

[33] *Ibid.* No. 57.

[34] 23 October—Buckle, *op. cit.* VI, 84.

[35] 3 November—*ibid.* p. 87; Cecil, *Life of Salisbury*, II, 91.

[36] Buckle, VI, 109.

[37] *Life of Salisbury*, II, 134.

[38] Buckle, VI, 114.

[39] 9 March, 4 May—*Life of Salisbury*, II, 130, 135.

[40] 20 February 1877—*R.B.D.* V, No. 179.

[41] Buckle, VI, 131.

[42] *R.B.D.* No. 214.

[43] First published by me in *R.B.D.* VI, No. 228, and in extract in *D.G.E.Q.* pp. 193–5.

[44] See Buckle, VI, 148, 217, 245.

[45] *Letters*, II, pp. 541–3.

[46] Buckle, VI, 149.

[47] *Ibid.* pp. 155, 172, 178, 199.

[48] *Ibid.* p. 172.

[49] *Ibid.* p. 182.

[50] *Layard Papers*, cit. *D.G.E.Q.* p. 234.

[51] Buckle, *op. cit.* VI, 194–5.

[52] *Ibid.* p. 192.

[53] *Ibid.* p. 199.

[54] *Life of Salisbury*, II, 163.

[55] *Layard Memoirs*, V, 308, cit. *D.G.E.Q.* p. 245.

[56] *Letters*, II, 582.   [57] Harding, *Life of Carnarvon*, II, 365.
[58] See extracts from the Granville, Gladstone and Harcourt Papers in my *D.G.E.Q.*
pp. 253–62.   [59] Buckle, *op. cit.* VI, 217.
[60] *Ibid.* p. 218.   [61] *Letters*, II, 587–9.
[62] Buckle, *op. cit.* VI, 229.   [63] *D.G.E.Q.* p. 310.
[64] *Life of Salisbury*, II, 197–8.   [65] *Layard Papers*, cit. *D.G.E.Q.* p. 317.
[66] For details, see *D.G.E.Q.* pp. 263–6, 329–32.
[67] For details, see *D.G.E.Q.* pp. 315–20.
[68] *Layard Papers*, and unpublished Russian documents, cit. *D.G.E.Q.* pp. 321–2.
[69] *Layard Papers*, cit. *D.G.E.Q.* pp. 207, 213, 243, 355–60.

CHAPTER XIV

[1] Lady G. Cecil, *Life of Salisbury*, II, 214.
[2] *Ibid.* II, pp. 264–7; Buckle, VI, 290.   [3] Argyll, *The Eastern Question*, II, 130–5.
[4] Buckle, VI, 221, 294; *Life*, II, 265. See full extracts from the *Layard Papers* in *D.G.E.Q.*
pp. 432–30, and a still fuller account in Mr Dwight Lee's admirable monograph, *The Cyprus Convention*.
[5] *Layard Papers*, cit. *D.G.E.Q.* p. 428.   [6] *Life*, II, 287.
[7] Colonel Wellesley, *With the Russians in Peace and War*, p. 297; Buckle, VI, 339.
[8] Radowitz, *Denkwürdigkeiten*, II, 60.   [9] *Cyprus as I saw it in* 1879, p. 441.
[10] For details based on the Granville and Gladstone papers see *D.G.E.Q.* pp. 512–17.
[11] Buckle, VI, 268.
[12] *Granville Papers*, cit. *D.G.E.Q.* p. 514.   [13] Fitzmaurice, *op. cit.* II, 198.

CHAPTER XV

[1] Fitzmaurice, *Life of Granville*, II, 185.
[2] 2 April to Sir Henry Ponsonby, and Diary of 22 April—*Letters*, 3rd Series, I, 73, 80.
[3] 18 and 19 September 1880—*Letters*, 3rd Series, I, 141.
[4] 9 June 1880—*ibid.* p. 111.
[5] Edinburgh Music Hall, 17 March 1880: cf. Fitzmaurice, II, 201.
[6] Fitzmaurice, *op. cit.* II, 206.   [7] 4 November 1880—Buckle, VI, 367.
[8] 22 March/3 April 1881—Austrian State Archives (unpublished).
[9] Cecil, *Life of Salisbury*, II, 331.   [10] 11 August 1882—Fitzmaurice, *op. cit.* II, 271.
[11] Phrase of Lyons to Granville, 3 June 1884—Newton, *Life of Lyons*, p. 494.
[12] Busch, *Memoirs*, III, 52.   [13] 24 October 1881—Fitzmaurice, *op. cit.* II, 233.
[14] *Ibid.* p. 276.   [15] *Grosse Politik*, III, 237.
[16] Morley's words, in *Life of Gladstone*, II, 385.
[17] Fitzmaurice, *op. cit.* II, 383, 400.   [18] 22 March 1884—Morley, *op. cit.* III, 119.
[19] 17 February 1885 to Sir H. Ponsonby—*Letters*, 2nd Series, III, 608.
[20] 30 April and 7 May 1880—"Mr Gladstone, Lord Granville and Russia", ed.
R.W.S.W. (*Slavonic Review*, No. 25, pp. 209–12).
[21] Gladstone to the Queen—*Letters*, 2nd Series, III, 630.
[22] 25 January 1885—*G.P.* IV, No. 758.   [23] Fitzmaurice, *op. cit.* II, 351.
[24] 10 January 1885 in Reichstag.   [25] Cecil, *op. cit.* III, 136.
[26] *Ibid.* p. 226.   [27] 2 July 1885—*G.P.* IV, No. 782.
[28] 9 December 1885, to Münster—*ibid.* No. 789.
[29] 24 September 1885—*Letters*, 2nd Series, III, 691–2.
[30] 22 October—*ibid.* p. 705.

[31] His words to Lord Lyons, 16 October 1885—Cecil, *op. cit.* III, 245.

[32] 25 January 1886—*ibid.* p. 255.   [33] *Ibid.* p. 273.

[34] 29 January 1886—*Letters*, 3rd Series, I, 31.   [35] Cecil, *op. cit.* IV, 104.

[36] 8 February 1886, Salisbury to Queen—*Letters*, 3rd Series, I, 49.

[37] E. C. Corti, *Alexander von Bulgarien*, p. 266. As a corrective to this, see her violent, but eminently sane, letter to Lord Salisbury on 20 January 1887—*Letters*, 3rd Series, I, 259.

[38] 23 August, to the Queen—*Letters*, 3rd Series, I, 182.

[39] Staal to Giers, 22 and 25 November—*Correspondence Diplomatique du Baron de Staal*, I, 322.   [40] 24 January 1887, to the Queen—Cecil, *op. cit.* IV, 15.

[41] 10 February 1887, to the Queen—*ibid.* p. 24.

[42] Pribram, *Secret Treaties of Austria-Hungary*, p. 95. French draft in *G.P.* IV, No. 890.

[43] Memorandum, presumably of Lord Salisbury, addressed to Queen Victoria, and communicated by the German Crown Prince to the German Foreign Office 23 February 1887—*G.P.* IV, No. 918.   [44] Cecil, *op. cit.* IV, 21, 22.

[45] Pribram, *op. cit.* p. 125; *G.P.* IV, No. 918.   [46] Pribram, *op. cit.* p. 117.

[47] 22 November 1887—*G.P.* IV, No. 930.   [48] 30 November—*ibid.* No. 936.

[49] To the Queen—Cecil, *op. cit.* IV, 72.   [50] *D.D.F.* 1st Series, II, 414.

[51] Cf. his conversation with Sir Philip Currie, in September 1885—Cecil, *op. cit.* III, 256; cf. *supra*, p. 550.   [52] *History of Modern Europe*, p. 140.

[53] 3 April 1888—*G.P.* VI, No. 1331.   [54] *G.P.* IV, No. 943.

[55] 22 March 1889, Herbert Bismarck to his father—*ibid.* No. 945.

[56] 10 August 1887 to Sir W. White—Cecil, *op. cit.* IV, 50.

[57] 11 April 1888—*ibid.* p. 90.

[58] The Emperor sent a long and detailed Memorandum on his quarrel with Bismarck to Queen Victoria and the Emperor Francis Joseph (first published in K. F. Nowak, *Das dritte deutsche Kaiserreich*, pp. 266–76).

[59] Sir E. Malet to Salisbury, 12 February 1890—*Letters*, 3rd Series, I, 566.

[60] Garvin, *Life of Chamberlain*, II, 460.   [61] 9 June 1890, to Salisbury—*Letters*, I, 612.

[62] 10 June 1890—Cecil, *op. cit.* IV, 298.

[63] *Hansard*, CCCXLVII, 764. See Anson, *Law and Custom of the Constitution*, III, 106.

[64] For details see W. L. Langer, *Diplomacy of Imperialism*, I, 16.

[65] Baron Boris Nolde, *L'alliance Franco-Russe*, p. 625.

[66] *Willy-Nicky Letters.*

[67] Diaries of Sir Algernon West—cit. Garvin, *Life of Chamberlain*, II, 549.

[68] 14 August 1892—*Letters*, II, 144.   [69] *Ibid.* p. 376.

[70] *Miscellanies*, II, 260—cit. Algernon Cecil, *British Foreign Secretaries*, p. 274.

[71] August 1892, January 1893—*Letters*, II, 152, 211.

[72] Speech of 30 June 1896—see Langer, *Diplomacy of Imperialism*, I, 378.

[73] Note on despatch of Hatzfeldt, 31 July—*G.P.* VIII, No. 1753.

[74] *Ibid.* No. 1759.   [75] 27 September—*ibid.* No. 1761.

[76] 24 October—*ibid.* No. 1762.   [77] Lord Crewe, *Lord Rosebery*, II, 449.

[78] 15 May 1896—cit. *Cambridge History of Foreign Policy*, III, 234.

[79] 10 July 1895—*ibid.* p. 236.

[80] 31 July, 31 August—*G.P.* X, Nos. 2372, 2375, 2377, 2381, 2392.

[81] See Eckardstein, *Lebenserinnerungen*, I, 211–13 (unreliable); E. Brandenburg, *op. cit.* pp. 62–5.   [82] 25 October 1895, William II to Marschall—*G.P.* XI, No. 2579.

[83] *Ibid.* note to No. 2580.   [84] 1 January 1896—*ibid.* No. 2594.

[85] *Briefe Wilhelms II an den Zaren*, p. 300.   [86] 6 January—*G.P.* XI, No. 2617.

[87] Details in Sir Sidney Lee, *Edward VII*, I, 721.

[88] 16 March 1898 to Milner—Garvin, *op. cit.* III, 366.

[89] Langer, *op. cit.* I, 243.   [90] Garvin, *op. cit.* III, 133.

[91] Cf. Halévy, *Histoire du Peuple Anglais, Épilogue*, I, 32.

[92] *G.P.* XI, No. 2649.

[93] *Ibid.* 8 January (No. 2621), 19 January (No. 2651) and 1 January (No. 2641). A very full and fair account of the whole Raid crisis will be found in Langer, *op. cit.* Chapter VIII.

[94] Memorandum of July 1891—Garvin, *op. cit.* II, 461.

[95] *Von Bismarck zum Weltkriege*, p. 75.

[96] *Le Partage de l'Afrique*, p. 89; Algernon Cecil, *British Foreign Secretaries*, p. 306.

[97] The word is Professor Langer's (*op. cit.* p. 283).

[98] 4 March 1896, Hohenlohe to Hatzfeldt, and notes of Marschall—*G.P.* xi, Nos. 2770, 2771.   [99] 2 August 1898, Salisbury to Cromer—*British Documents*, i, No. 185.

[100] 16 October—*B.D.* No. 212.   [101] 12 November—*B.D.* No. 233.

[102] *G.P.* xiv, No. 3782. See the five Memoranda of Chamberlain in Garvin's *Life of Chamberlain*, iii, pp. 259, 263, 271, 273, 276.   [103] *G.P.* xiv, No. 3783.

[104] 7 April, Hatzfeldt to Hohenlohe—*ibid.* No. 3789.

[105] 26 April—*ibid.* No. 3793.   [106] 30 April, Bülow to Hatzfeldt—*ibid.* No. 3794.

[107] 3 June, Hatzfeldt to Hohenlohe—*ibid.* No. 3801.

[108] 4 August, Salisbury to the Queen—*Letters*, 3rd Series, iii, 263; Low, *Edward VII*, i, 737.   [109] 26 December, Lascelles to Salisbury—*B.D.* i, No. 124.

[110] E.g. 13 May, 10 June, 15 November—Garvin, *op. cit.* iii, 302-4.

[111] 22 April 1899, Hatzfeldt to Holstein—*G.P.* xiv, No. 4071.

[112] 18 September 1899—Garvin, *op. cit.* iii, 334; 5 November, Grierson to Gough—*B.D.* i, No. 154.   [113] 14 May 1899—*G.P.* xv, No. 4257.

[114] *Milner Papers*, i, 220-4; Garvin, *op. cit.* iii, 365-8. See also commentary of Langer, *op. cit.* ii, 607-8.

[115] Salisbury's view, as quoted by Chamberlain, 30 November 1898—*ibid.* p. 380.

[116] 16 and 19 March 1898—*ibid.* pp. 366-8.   [117] *Ibid.* p. 423.

[118] Garvin, *op. cit.* pp. 501-6; Asquith, *Genesis of the War*, p. 23.

[119] *G.P.* xv, No. 4398, which at the end contains Bülow's personal estimates of British statesmen.   [120] 7 March 1900—*G.P.* xv, No. 4480; 11 March—*Letters*, iii, 508.

[121] 10 April 1901—Eckardstein, *op. cit.* i, 298; Lee, *op. cit.* ii, 119; *G.P.* xvii, 52.

[122] 19 March, Metternich to Bülow—*G.P.* xv, No. 4456; Garvin, *op. cit.* iii, 524; Bülow, *Denkwürdigkeiten*, i, 422.

[123] 23 October 1900, the Queen's memorandum—*Letters*, iii, 611.

[124] *British Foreign Secretaries*, p. 311.   [125] Mrs Dugdale, *A. J. Balfour*, i, 336.

[126] 18 and 29 March and 13 April 1901—*B.D.* Nos. 77, 79, 81.

[127] Count Metternich's phrase—cf. Langer, *op. cit.* ii, 727.

[128] 24 May, Memorandum of Lansdowne—*B.D.* No. 82.

[129] 21 January 1901—*G.P.* xvii, No. 4983.

[130] 29 January—*ibid.* No. 4987. "There is no Balance of Power in Europe except *me*—me and my 25 corps"—is Asquith's version in *Genesis of the War*, p. 22.

[131] 29 May—*G.P.* No. 5015.

[132] On German calculations see Brandenburg, *Von Bismarck zum Weltkriege*, pp. 148-55.

[133] Memorandum of 27 May—*B.D.* No. 85.   [134] *Ibid.* No. 86.

[135] 9 June—*G.P.* xvii, No. 5177. Langer (*op. cit.* p. 740) seems to regard this refusal as the turning point.

[136] 30 August, Lascelles to Lansdowne—*B.D.* No. 90. Lansdowne's memorandum for King Edward was given by him to the Emperor, and is printed as No. 5033 in *G.P.* xvii.

[137] 23 August—*G.P.* No. 5023.   [138] Memorandum of 11 November—*B.D.* No. 92.

[139] 19 December, Lansdowne to Lascelles—*ibid.* No. 94.

EPILOGUE

[1] 13 February 1902—*Hansard*, 4th Series, cii, 1174.

[2] 14 February 1904—*Grosse Politik*, xix, No. 5961.

[3] On this see the interesting passage in Langer, *Diplomacy of Imperialism*, i, 380.

[4] *British Documents*, ii, No. 98.   [5] 29 October 1899—*G.P.* xv, No. 4394.

[6] 27 March 1900—*ibid.* xv, No. 4494.

[7] E. L. Woodward, *Great Britain and the German Navy*, p. 33.

[8] R. C. K. Ensor, *England*, 1870-1914, pp. 401, 413.

[9] For details see Newton, *Lord Lansdowne*, pp. 261-6.

[10] Phrase used by Lord Grey in *Twenty-five Years*, i, 50.

S-W

[11] 14 March 1904—Zetland, *Lord Cromer*, p. 281.
[12] Grey, *Twenty-five Years*, I, 48.   [13] Woodward, *op. cit.* pp. 70–1.
[14] Lee, *Edward VII*, II, 253.   [15] *Denkwürdigkeiten*, II, 107.
[16] October–November 1904—*G.P.* Nos. 6118–33.
[17] The full text of his own report to Bülow should be read in *G.P.* XIX, No. 6220, and compared with Bülow's post-war comments in *Denkwürdigkeiten*, II, 137–51.
[18] Brandenburg, *op. cit.* p. 202.   [19] Newton, *Lord Lansdowne*, p. 342.
[20] The two most up-to-date accounts of this conflict are to be found in Renouvin, *Histoire Diplomatique de l'Europe*, Chapter II (ed. Hauser), and in Gooch, *Before the War*, pp. 163–83.   [21] *G.P.* XX, Nos. 6707, 6731, 6738.   [22] *Ibid.* XIX, No. 6229.
[23] 25 April 1905, to Lansdowne—*B.D.* III, No. 95.
[24] *History of Modern Europe*, p. 354.
[25] 19 January, Grey to Bertie—*B.D.* III, No. 210. Grey, *op. cit.* p. 72.
[26] Grey's despatch of 31 January to Bertie, recording his talk with Cambon (*B.D.* III, No. 219), should be read in conjunction with his despatch of 9 January to Lascelles (recording his talk with Metternich) (Grey, *op. cit.* I, 82–5) and with Metternich's own account of the talk in *G.P.* XXI, Nos. 6923 and 6924, and also with the Memoranda of Cambon and of Sanderson (*B.D.* No. 220).   [27] 15 January 1906—*B.D.* III, No. 216.
[28] For the full correspondence between General Grierson and Colonel Barnardiston see *B.D.* III, 187–281. "Provisional and non-committal" is the phrase applied to the conversations with the Belgian Staff.   [29] See Grey, *op. cit.* pp. 105–12; *B.D.* III, No. 361.
[30] *Von Bismarck zum Weltkriege*, pp. 197–8.
[31] May 1906, Metternich to Bülow—*G.P.* XXI, No. 7180.
[32] 31 July—*ibid.* No. 7191.   [33] Lee, *op. cit.* II, 340.
[34] Willy-Nicky Correspondence, 22 August 1905.
[35] Newton, *op. cit.* p. 335; *G.P.* Nos. 6882, 6885–3 December 1905.
[36] *Fifty Years of Europe*, p. 269.   [37] 16 July 1908—*G.P.* XXIV, note on No. 8217.
[38] Hardinge's Memorandum of 16 August 1908—*B.D.* VI, No. 117: cf. the Emperor's Memoranda of 12 and 13 August—*G.P.* XXIV, Nos. 8225, 8226. See also Bülow's account of William's talk with Hardinge, and of William's letter to Lord Tweedmouth which, as it contained false statements, enormously increased the suspicion of England towards German naval policy (*Denkwürdigkeiten*, II, 322–6).
[39] 31 July 1908—*B.D.* VI, No. 779. Cf. Grey's speech of 29 March 1909 in the House of Commons.   [40] G. P. Gooch, *Modern Europe*, p. 388.
[41] 6 March 1908—*G.P.* XXIV, No. 8187.
[42] *Labour Leader*, May 1908—cit. Lee, *op. cit.* II, p. 587.
[43] 12 June 1908—*B.D.* V, No. 195.
[44] "Mit Engländern muss man immer so verkehren": 13 August 1908, William to Bülow—*G.P.* XXIV, No. 8226.
[45] Hardinge's memo of 16 August—*B.D.* V, Appendix IV, 827–30.
[46] Aehrenthal to Berlin, 15 August—*Austro-Hungarian Documents* (*Oesterreich-Ungarns Aussenpolitik*) I, No. 36.   [47] Lee, *op. cit.* II, 626.
[48] Circular of 1 July 1908, sent by Chancellor to the Prussian Ministers in Munich, Dresden and Stuttgart, communicated by Tschirschky to Aehrenthal and by him to Conrad. See Conrad, *Aus meiner Dienstzeit*, I, 95.
[49] E.g. Aehrenthal's "spontaneous assurances" to Schoen, see latter's report of 5 September 1908—*G.P.* XXIV, No. 8242. Cf. also report of Brockdorff-Rantzau to Bülow, and William's marginalia, 19 August 1908—*ibid.* No. 8230: cf. also Conrad, *op. cit.* I, 55.
[50] *Denkwürdigkeiten*, II, 326–30.
[51] I may perhaps be excused for referring the reader to three detailed studies of my own—"William II's Balkan Policy" (*Slavonic Review*, June 1928), "British Policy in the Near East" (*Contemporary Review*, June 1929) and "La Politique du Comte Aehrenthal" (*Le Monde Slave*, June 1933).
[52] *B.D.* V, Nos. 1, 2.   [53] 31 May, 4 June, 1907—*B.D.* V, Nos. 159, 161.
[54] 23 August—*B.D.* V, No. 208.   [55] 30 April—*ibid.* No. 219.
[56] *Ibid.* Nos. 289, 299; cf. also King Edward's sarcastic comments on Aehrenthal, *ibid.* Nos. 381, 484.   [57] *Ibid.* Nos. 299, 487.   [58] *Ibid.* Nos. 416, 419.
[59] *Ibid.* Nos. 402, 408.   [60] *Ibid.* No. 441.

[61] *Ibid.* No. 505. [62] *Ibid.* No. 753.

[63] 24 and 26 March, Nicolson to Grey—*ibid.* Nos. 764, 775; 30 March, Hardinge to Nicolson—*ibid.* No. 807. [64] 24 March 1909, Nicolson to Grey—*ibid.* No. 761.

[65] *Fifty Years of Europe*, p. 316. For full details see *B.D.* VI, Nos. 125–42; *G.P.* XXIV, Nos. 8249–74; Bülow, *Denkwürdigkeiten*; Gooch, *op. cit.* p. 266 seq.; Brandenburg, *op. cit.* pp. 249–56. [66] Cf. Woodward, *op. cit.* p. 262; *B.D.* V, Appendix III.

[67] 26 August 1908, Bülow to William—*G.P.* XXIV, No. 8239.

[68] Cf. three letters of Metternich, 27 November 1908—*G.P.* XXVIII, No. 10234; 2 June 1909, No. 10305; 5 November 1909, No. 10360. [69] *G.P.* XXVIII, No. 10306.

[70] Memorandum of 7 May 1909—*ibid.* No. 10304.

[71] 1 September 1909, Grey to Goschen—*B.D.* VI, No. 195.

[72] Tirpitz, *Aufbau der deutschen Weltmacht*, I, 299; Woodward, *op. cit.* p. 341.

[73] 16 October 1910—*B.D.* VI, No. 403.

[74] Memorandum of 3 May—*G.P.* XXIX, No. 10549.

[75] Memorandum of Zimmermann, 12 June—*ibid.* No. 10572.

[76] 9 and 10 July—*ibid.* Nos. 10598, 10601.

[77] *B.D.* VII, No. 347. [78] *Ibid.* No. 351.

[79] 6 July—*ibid.* No. 363. [80] *Twenty-five Years*, I, 226.

[81] Minutes on Bertie's telegram to Grey—*G.P.* VII, No. 369.

[82] Grey to Asquith—*ibid.* No. 399.

[83] 21 July, Metternich to Bethmann Hollweg—*G.P.* XXIX, No. 10617.

[84] 20 July—*B.P.* No. 405. [85] 23 and 24 July—*G.P.* Nos. 10618, 10623.

[86] 25 July—*ibid.* No. 10626. [87] *The World Crisis*, I, 48: Spender, *op. cit.* p. 335.

[88] Cf. Metternich's estimate in the report of 19 August—*G.P.* XXIX, No. 10641.

[89] Bülow's malicious phrase, in *Denkwürdigkeiten*, III, 86.

[90] *B.D.* VII, Appendix III. One of the clearest modern statements of British policy.

[91] 19 September 1911—*B.D.*, IX, No. 231. [92] 2 October—*ibid.* No. 263.

[93] *Ibid.* No. 212. [94] 29 December 1911, to Buchanan—*ibid.* No. 352.

[95] 26 June 1912—*ibid.* No. 428.

[96] France in 1882 and 1904, Britain in 1887, Russia in 1909.

[97] Quotations in Asquith, *The Genesis of the War*, pp. 121–7: full text in Appendix V of *B.D.* VII, 781–90. [98] *Before the War*, p. 105; *B.D.* VI, No. 506, p. 676.

[99] Haldane's Diary, *B.D.* VI, No. 506, p. 650. Cf. Tirpitz's version in *Memoirs*, I, 218–24.

[100] 12 February—*G.P.* XXXI, No. 11365. [101] *Ibid.* Nos. 11369, 11370, 11371.

[102] 24 February—*ibid.* No. 11374. [103] 1 March—*ibid.* No. 11380.

[104] *Ibid.* Nos. 11380, 11385. [105] *B.D.* Nos. 537, 538.

[106] *Ibid.* No. 538. [107] *Ibid.* No. 539.

[108] 17 March—*G.P.* No. 11403.

[109] *Marginalia* on Nos. 11403, 11405—*ibid.*; cf. Brandenburg, *op. cit.* pp. 352–3.

[110] Quoted by E. L. Woodward, *op. cit.* p. 351, but not referred to either in *B.D.* or *G.P.*

[111] 19 March—*G.P.* No. 11410; *B.D.* No. 545; Brandenburg, *op. cit.* p. 353.

[112] Minute of 6 April 1912—*B.D.* VII, No. 564. [113] Woodward, *op. cit.* pp. 368–71.

[114] In *Nord und Süd* for July 1912—cit. Woodward, p. 375.

[115] *D.D.F.* 3rd Series, IV, No. 534.

[116] W. Churchill, *World Crisis*, I, 112: Woodward, *op. cit.* 380–4: P. Renouvin in Chapter VI of *Histoire Diplomatique de l'Europe* (ed. Hauser), II, 270–86.

[117] *War Memoirs*, I, 50. [118] 9 January—*B.D.* IX, No. 537.

[119] *Ibid.* Nos. 539, 557. [120] 18 March—*ibid.* No. 560.

[121] 21 March—*ibid.* No. 570.

[122] 30 August, Buchanan to Grey; 31 August, Bertie to Grey—*B.D.* Nos. 679, 684.

[123] 18 and 23 September—*ibid.* Nos. 732, 737. [124] 23 July—*B.D.* No. 598.

[125] Memo. of 24 September 1912—*B.D.* IX, No. 805.

[126] 9 September, Colville Barclay to Grey—*B.D.* IX, No. 711.

[127] *B.D.* IX (ii), No. 91. [128] 3 November—*ibid.* Nos. 12319, 12320, 12321.

[129] 7 November—*G.P.* XXXIII, No. 12339. [130] 3 November—*ibid.* No. 12315.

[131] 11 November—Notes of William II, *ibid.* No. 12349.

[132] 19 November, Kiderlen to Tschirschky—*ibid.* No. 12397; 21 November, William to Kiderlen, No. 12405. [133] 3 December—*G.P.* XXXIX, No. 15612.

[134] 20 December—*B.D.* IX (ii), No. 404.

[135] For a fairly detailed account of the diplomatic course of events during the two wars, see my three works, *The Rise of Nationality in the Balkans*, pp. 143–283; *A History of the Roumanians*, pp. 442–63, and *Serbia* in the *Encyclopedia Britannica*, XXXII (1922), 399–404.

[136] 10 January 1913—*B.D.* IX (ii), No. 484.　　　　[137] 24 January—*ibid.* No. 556.

[138] 2 June, Grey to Bertie—*ibid.* No. 1024.　　　　[139] *Ibid.* No. 1109.

[140] 18 July—*Austro-Hungarian Documents*, VI, No. 7838.

[141] Message of Berchtold to Tschirschky, 4 July—*G.P.* XXXV, No. 13483.

[142] William II's message, 5 July—*ibid.* No. 13486; Tschirschky to Bethmann Hollweg, 11 July—*ibid.* No. 13508.　　　　[143] 6 and 7 July—*ibid.* Nos. 13490, 13493.

[144] 9 and 12 August 1913—*G.P.* XXXV, Nos. 13741, 13749.

[145] Conrad, *Aus meiner Dienstzeit*, III, 404.

[146] 5 August—*B.D.* No. 1203.　　　　[147] 8 August—*G.P.* No. 13766.

[148] *Marginalia* to Lichnowsky's report of 13 August—*G.P.* No. 13778.

[149] See Documents in *B.D.* X, Appendix, pp. 901–2. Nos. 475–505 relate to Armenian Reforms.　　　　[150] Grey, *Twenty-five Years*, I, 272–7.

[151] 23 July 1912, Grey to Cartwright—*B.D.* IX (i), No. 598.

[152] 10 February 1913, Bethmann Hollweg to Berchtold—*G.P.* XXXIV, No. 12818.

[153] *Hansard*, 5th Series, I, 1749–91.　　　　[154] Manchester, 3 February 1914.

[155] See Berchtold's memo of conversation with William II, 26 October 1913—*A.H.D.* VII, No. 8934—first published by me as Appendix to "William II's Balkan Policy" (*Slavonic Review*, No. 19, June 1928).

[156] See E. M. Earle, *Turkey, the Great Powers and the Bagdad Railway* (1923), and M. N. Howard, *The Partition of Turkey*, pp. 19–79.

[157] 6 and 9 December 1911—*G.P.* XXXI, Nos. 11338–9.

[158] 11 March—*ibid.* No. 11437.　　　　[159] 5 June, 19 July 1912—*ibid.* Nos. 11450, 11456.

[160] See criticisms of Lichnowsky in *Meine Londoner Mission*, p. 113.

[161] 14 July 1914—*G.P.* XXXVII, No. 14714. The full text of the treaty is printed in No. 14682.　　　　[162] In *Meine Londoner Mission* (*Auf dem Wege*, I, 97).

[163] 18 March 1914, Izvolsky to Sazonov—*Un Livre Noir*, II, p. 249.

[164] 29 April—*ibid.* pp. 259–62.

[165] The full correspondence of Izvolsky and Benckendorff, from the Russian Archives, has been published in four and two volumes in a German translation. See the narrative of G. P. Gooch in *Cambridge History of Foreign Policy*, III, 476–86.

[166] Grey, *op. cit.* p. 304.

[167] 29 May 1914—*Papers of Colonel House*, I, 255, 268.

[168] By Professor George Trevelyan, *Grey of Fallodon* (published March 1937).

[169] *White Paper* (1914), Nos. 3 and 101, 23 and 24 July.

SELECTED BIBLIOGRAPHY OF PRINTED SOURCES

The following list is intended neither for the historian nor for the general reader, but for an intermediate set of readers, who desire to pursue their studies further, on serious lines. It makes no claim whatsoever to be complete, nor on the other hand is inclusion in it intended to guarantee the value of a book. But it will be found that so far as possible nothing has been included which does not contain some specific contribution to the period under review. In most cases the title or the author's name provides the clue.

It seemed to me unnecessary to include long lists of Blue Books and Official Papers, for which any student will have to find his own clue. In the same way a reference to Hansard should be superfluous.

PART I. 1815–1878

GENERAL HISTORIES

C.H.F.P. Cambridge History of British Foreign Policy (1783–1919). Ed. Sir A. Ward and G. P. Gooch. 3 v. Cambridge 1923.
C.M.H. Cambridge Modern History. Ed. A. W. Ward, G. W. Prothero, S. Leathes. 12 v. Cambridge 1903.
LAVISSE, E. et RAMBAUD, A. *Histoire Générale*, vols. X–XII. P. 1899.

BOURGEOIS, ÉMILE. *Manuel Historique de la Politique Étrangère*, vols. II and III (1789–1878). P. 1916.
DEBIDOUR, A. *Histoire Diplomatique de l'Europe* (1815–78). 2 v. P. 1891.
FISHER, H. A. L. *History of Europe.* 3 v. L. 1935.
FYFFE, C. A. *History of Modern Europe.* L. 1880; new ed. 1928.
SEIGNOBOS, CHARLES. *Histoire politique de l'Europe Contemporaine.* P. 1896; new ed. 1923.
SOREL, ALBERT. *L'Europe et la Révolution Française.* 8th. ed. 8 v. P. 1908.
STERN, ALFRED. *Geschichte Europas von 1815 bis 1871.* 10 v. Stuttgart 1894–1925.

(Among numerous text-books special mention may be made of A. J. Grant and H. W. V. Temperley, *Modern Europe*, L. 1928; W. Alison Phillips, *Modern Europe*, L. 1900; R. B. Mowat, *History of European Diplomacy*, L. 1930.)

SPECIAL HISTORIES

ARNAUD, RENÉ. *La Révolution de 1848 et le Second Empire.* P. 1927.
BEYENS, Baron. *Le Second Empire.* 2 v. P. 1924.
DRIAULT et LHÉRITIER. *Histoire Diplomatique de la Grèce.* 5 v. P. 1925.
FINLAY, GEORGE. *History of Greece*, vol. VII. Oxford 1877.
HALÉVY, ÉLIE. *Histoire du Peuple Anglais*, vols. I–III (1815–46). P. 1923.
HANOTAUX, GABRIEL. *Histoire de la France Contemporaine.* 4 v. P. 1907.
HILLEBRAND, K. *Geschichte Frankreichs* (1830–70). 2 v. Gotha.
Histoire de France Contemporaine (1789–1919). Ed. E. Lavisse. 8 v. P. 1921.
KING, BOLTON. *History of Italian Unity.* 2 v. L. 1899.

LA GORCE, PIERRE DE. *Histoire de la Seconde République.* 2 v. P. 1904.
—— *Histoire du Second Empire.* 7 v. P. 1894–1904.
PAUL, HERBERT. *History of Modern England.* 5 v. L. 1904–6.
PIRENNE, HENRI. *Histoire de Belgique,* vols. VI and VII. Brussels 1932.
SCHIEMANN, THEODOR. *Geschichte Russlands unter Kaiser Nikolaus I.* 4 v. Berlin 1904–19.
SYBEL, HEINRICH VON. *Die Begründung des deutschen Reiches.* 7 v. (Volksausgabe). Munich 1901.
THUREAU-DANGIN, PAUL. *Histoire de la Monarchie de Juillet.* 7 v. P. 1911–14.
TREITSCHKE, HEINRICH VON. *Deutsche Geschichte im XIX Jahrhundert.* 5 v. (7th ed.). Leipzig 1904.
WALPOLE, Sir SPENCER. *History of England* (1815–58). 5 v. L. 1879.
—— *History of Twenty-five Years.* 4 v. L. 1904.
WARD, Sir ADOLPHUS. *History of Germany* (1815–71). 3 v. Cambridge 1918–19.
ZIEKURSCH, JOHANNES. *Politische Geschichte des neuen deutschen Kaiserreiches,* vol. I. Frankfurt 1925.

DOCUMENTS, COLLECTIONS, ETC.

Auswärtige Politik Preussens (1858–71). Ed. Brandenburg, Hoetzsch and H. Oncken. Vols. 1, 3–5, 8–9. Oldenburg 1933–6.
BIANCHI, L. *Storia documentata della diplomazia europea in Italia* (1814–61). Turin 1865–72.
BISMARCK, Prince. *Politische Reden.* Ed. Horst Kohl. Stuttgart 1892, etc.
Étude Diplomatique sur la Guerre de Crimée. Par un ancien Diplomate [Baron Jomini]. 1878.
HALT, ROBERT. *Papiers sauvés des Tuileries.* P. 1871.
HERTSLET, E. *The Map of Europe by Treaty.* 4 v. L. 1875–91.
HOLLAND, T. E. *The European Concert in the Eastern Question.* L. 1885.
JASMUND, J. VON. *Aktenstücke zur orientalischen Frage.* 3 v. Berlin 1855–9.
LUTOSTANSKI, KAREL. *Les Partages de la Pologne.* P. 1918.
MARTENS, F. *Recueil des Traités et Conventions entre la Russie et les Puissances Étrangères.*
MOWAT, R. B. *Select Treaties and Documents* (1815–1916). Oxford 1932.
OAKES, Sir A. and MOWAT, R. B. *Great European Treaties of the Nineteenth Century.* L. 1920.
ONCKEN, HERMANN (Ed.). *Die Rheinpolitik Napoleons III von 1863 bis 1870 und der Ursprung des Krieges von 1870–1.* 3 v. Stuttgart 1926.
Origines Diplomatiques de la Guerre de 1870–71. 14 v. P. 1910, etc.
Portfolio, The. Ed. David Urquhart. 4 v. L. 1836.
Revue Rétrospective. Ed. Taschereau. P. (N.D.).
SATOW, Sir E. *A Guide to Diplomatic Practice.* 2 v. L. 1917.
WEBSTER, C. K. (Ed.). *British Diplomacy* (1813–15). L. 1921.

MEMOIRS AND LETTERS

ADAIR, Sir ROBERT. *A Mission to the Court of Vienna.* L. 1844.
ARGYLL, 8th Duke of. *Autobiography and Memoirs.* 2 v. L. 1906.
BARANTE, Baron P. DE. *Souvenirs.* 6 v. P. 1882–9.
BENEDETTI, Comte. *Ma Mission en Prusse.* P. 1871.
—— *Essais Diplomatiques,* II. P. 1897.

BEUST, Count F. F. *Memoirs*. Ed. Baron H. de Worms. 2 v. L. 1887.

BISMARCK. *Gedanken und Erinnerungen*. 2 v. 1899.

—— *The Man and the Statesman*. L. 1899.

BOLITHO, HECTOR. *The Prince Consort and his Brother*. L. 1933.

BROGLIE, A. L., Duc de. *Souvenirs*. 4 v. P. 1886.

CANNING, GEORGE. *Some Official Correspondence*. Ed. E. J. Stapleton. 2 v. L. 1887.

CASTLEREAGH, Viscount. *Memoirs and Correspondence*. 12 v. L. 1848–53.

CAVOUR, Count CAMILLO. *Lettere Inedite*. Ed. L. Chiala. 6 v. Turin 1887.

—— *Nuove Lettere*. Turin 1895.

CHATEAUBRIAND. *Correspondance*. Ed. Comte Marcellus. 2 v. P. 1858.

—— et HYDE DE NEUVILLE. *Correspondance Inédite*. Ed. Marie Durry. P. 1929.

COLCHESTER, Lord. *Diary and Correspondence*. 3 v. L. 1861.

COWLEY, 1st Earl. *The Paris Embassy*. Ed. F. Wellesley. L. 1929.

COWLEY, 1st Lord. *Diary and Correspondence*. L. 1930.

CROKER, J. WILSON. *Correspondence and Diaries*. Ed. L. J. Jennings. 2 v. L. 1884.

D' AZEGLIO, Count MASSIMO. *Lettere*. Ed. N. Bianchi. Turin 1883–4.

ELGIN, 8th Earl of. *Letters and Journals*. L. 1872.

ELLIOT, Sir HENRY. *Some Recollections and Diplomatic Experiences*. L. 1922.

ERNEST, Duke of COBURG. *Denkwürdigkeiten*. 3 v.

FREDERICK, Empress. *Letters*. Ed. Sir F. Ponsonby. L. 1928.

GAVARD, C. *Un Diplomate à Londres*. P. 1895.

GENTZ, FRIEDRICH VON. *Dépêches inédites aux Hospodars de Valachie*. 3 v. P. 1877.

Gladstone and Palmerston. Ed. P. Guedalla. L. 1928.

GONTAUT-BIRON, Vicomte. *Mon Ambassade en Allemagne* (1872–3). P. 1906.

GREVILLE, CHARLES. *Memoirs*. Ed. Henry Reeve. 8 v. L. 1874–87.

GREVILLE, CHARLES, and REEVE, HENRY. *Memoirs*. Ed. A. H. Johnson. L. 1924.

GUIZOT, FRANÇOIS. *Mémoires pour servir à l'Histoire de son Temps*. 8 v. P. 1858–67.

HÜBNER, Comte A. *Neuf Ans de Souvenirs*. 2 v. P. 1908.

—— *Ein Jahr meines Lebens*. Leipzig 1891.

HYDE DE NEUVILLE, Baron. *Mémoires*. P. 1890.

KOSSUTH, LUDWIG. *Meine Schriften aus der Emigration*. 3 v. Pressburg 1880.

LIEVEN, Princess. *Correspondence with 2nd Earl Grey*. Ed. G. Le Strange. 3 v. L. 1890.

—— *Letters*. Ed. L. G. Robinson. L. 1902.

—— *Diary*. Ed. H. W. V. Temperley. L. 1921.

LOFTUS, Lord AUGUSTUS. *Diplomatic Reminiscences*. 4 v. L. 1892–4.

MALMESBURY, 1st Earl of. *Diaries and Correspondence*. 4 v. L. 1844.

—— 3rd Earl of. *Memoirs of an Ex-Minister*. 2 v. L. 1884.

MARCELLUS, Comte. *Souvenirs Diplomatiques*. P. 1858.

MARMONT, Marshal (Duc de Raguse). *Mémoires*. 9 v. P. 1857.

MELBOURNE, Viscount. *Papers*. Ed. L. C. Sanders. L. 1889.

Metternich in neuer Beleuchtung. Ed. Viktor Bibl. Vienna 1928.

MEYENDORFF, Baron PETER. *Briefwechsel* 1826–63. Ed. O. Hoetzsch. 3 v. Berlin 1923.

NESSELRODE, Comte CHARLES DE. *Lettres et Papiers*. 11 v. P. 1904–12.

NORMANBY, Marquess of. *A Year of Revolution*. L. 1857.

OLLIVIER, ÉMILE. *L'Empire Libéral*. 15 v. P. 1895 etc.

PALLAIN, G. *Correspondance Inédite du Prince de Talleyrand*. P. 1881.

—— *Ambassade de Talleyrand à Londres* (1830–4). 3 v. P. 1891.

POSCHINGER, C. H. VON. *Erinnerungen an Bismarck*. Berlin 1905.

RADOWITZ, G. M. VON. *Aufzeichnungen und Erinnerungen.* Ed. Hajo Holborn. 2 v. Berlin 1925.
RAIKES, T. *Journal.* 4 v. L. 1856.
REEVE, HENRY. *Memoirs.* 2 v. L. 1898.
RUMBOLD, Sir H. *Notes from a Diary.* L. 1898.
RUSSELL, Lord JOHN. *Recollections and Suggestions.* L. 1875.
—— *Early Correspondence.* Ed. Rollo Russell. 2 v. L. 1913.
—— *Later Correspondence.* Ed. G. P. Gooch. 2 v. L. 1925.
SAINTE-AULAIRE, Comte de. *Souvenirs (Vienne).* P. 1927.
SCHWEINITZ, General VON. *Denkwürdigkeiten.* 2 v. Berlin 1927.
SENIOR, W. NASSAU. *Conversations with Thiers, Guizot, etc.* 2 v. L. 1878.
STOCKMAR, Baron. *Memoirs.* 2 v. L. 1873.
TALLEYRAND, Prince de. *Mémoires.* Ed. Duc. de Broglie.
THOUVENEL, L. *Le Secret de l'Empereur.* 2 v. P. 1889.
—— *Nicolas I et Napoléon III.* P. 1891.
—— *Trois Années de la Question d'Orient.* P. 1896.
VICTORIA, Queen. *Letters.* 1st Series, ed. A. C. Benson and Visc. Esher, 3 v. L. 1907; 2nd Series, ed. G. E. Buckle, 2 v. L. 1926–8; 3rd Series, ed. G. E. Buckle, 3 v. L. 1930.
VILLÈLE, Comte. *Mémoires.* 5 v. P. 1880–90.
VITZTHUM VON ECKSTÄDT, Graf. *Berlin und Wien.* Stuttgart 1886.
—— *St Petersburg und London.* 2 v. Stuttgart 1886.
—— *Gastein und Sadowa.* Stuttgart 1889.
WELLINGTON, ARTHUR, Duke of. *Despatches and Correspondence.* 8 v. L. 1867–80.
—— *Supplementary Despatches and Memoranda.* 15 v. L. 1858–72.

BIOGRAPHIES

AIRLIE, MABELL, Countess of. *Lady Palmerston and her Times.* 2 v. L. 1922.
ASHLEY, EVELYN. *Life of Viscount Palmerston.* 2 v. L. 1879.
BALFOUR, Lady FRANCES. *Life of 4th Earl of Aberdeen.* 2 v. L. 1922.
BELL, H. C. F. *Lord Palmerston.* 2 v. L. 1936.
BOLITHO, HECTOR. *Albert the Good.* L. 1932.
BUCKLE, GEORGE and MONYPENNY, W. F. *Life of Disraeli.* 6 v. L. 1910–20.
BULWER, Sir HENRY (Lord DALLING). *Life of Viscount Palmerston.* 3 v. L. 1870–76.
—— *Historical Characters.* L. 1876.
CECIL, Lady GWENDOLEN. *Life of Robert Marquis of Salisbury.* 4 v. 1921–32.
CORTI, EGON C. *Leopold I von Belgien.* Vienna 1922.
—— *Maximilian und Charlotte von Mexiko.* 2 v. Leipzig 1924.
—— *Alexander von Battenberg.* Vienna 1920.
DASENT, A. I. *John Delane of 'The Times'.* 2 v. L. 1908.
DODWELL, H. *The Founder of Modern Egypt.* Cambridge 1930.
FITZMAURICE, Lord (EDMOND). *Life of 2nd Earl Granville.* 2 v. L. 1905.
GARDINER, A. G. *Life of Sir William Harcourt.* 2 v. L. 1923.
GUEDALLA, PHILIP. *Palmerston.* L. 1926.
GUIZOT, FRANÇOIS. *Peel.* P. (N.D.).
HARCOURT, Comte BERNARD D'. *Les Quatre Ministères de M. Drouyn de Lhuys.* P. 1882.
HARDINGE, Sir ARTHUR. *The 4th Earl of Carnarvon.* 3 v. L. 1935.
HOBSON, J. A. *Cobden: the International Man.* L. 1918.
HOLLAND, BERNARD. *The 8th Duke of Devonshire.* 2 v. L. 1913.

LANE-POOLE, STANLEY. *Life of Stratford Canning.* 2 v. L. 1888.
LANG, ANDREW. *Life of Sir Stafford Northcote, Earl of Iddesleigh.* 2 v. L. 1890.
LYALL, Sir ALFRED. *Life of Lord Dufferin and Ava.* 2 v. L. 1905.
LYTTELTON, SARAH, Lady. *Correspondence.* Ed. Mrs Hugh Wyndham. L. 1912.
MALCOLM SMITH, E. F. *Life of Stratford Canning.* L. 1933.
MARTIN, Sir THEODORE, *Life of the Prince Consort.* 5 v. L. 1880–91.
MARTINEAU, JOHN. *Life of 5th Duke of Newcastle.* L. 1908.
MATTER, P. *Bismarck et son Temps.* 3 v. P. 1908.
MAXWELL, Sir HERBERT. *Life of 4th Earl of Clarendon.* 2 v. L. 1913.
MORLEY, JOHN. *Life of W. E. Gladstone.* 3 v. L. 1903.
—— *Richard Cobden.* 2 v. L. 1908.
NEWTON, Lord. *Lord Lyons.* 2 v. L. 1913.
PARKER, C. S. *Life of Sir James Graham.* 2 v. L. 1907.
—— *Sir Robert Peel.* 3 v. L. 1899.
RAMSAY, ALICIA A. W. *Sir Robert Peel.* L. 1928.
REDLICH, JOSEPH. *Francis Joseph.* L. 1929.
ROBERTSON, C. GRANT. *Bismarck.* L. 1918.
ROBINSON, GERTRUDE. *David Urquhart.* Oxford 1920.
RUSSELL, G. W. E. *Malcolm MacColl.* L. 1914.
SRBIK, H. VON. *Metternich.* 2 v. Munich 1925.
STANMORE, Lord. *Lord Aberdeen.* L. 1893.
—— *Sidney Herbert.* 2 v. L. 1906.
STAPLETON, A. G. *Life of Canning.* L. 1831.
STAPLETON, A. J. *George Canning and his Times.* L. 1859.
STRACHEY, LYTTON. *Queen Victoria.* L. 1921.
TEMPERLEY, H. W. V. *Life of Canning.* L. 1905.
—— *The Foreign Policy of Canning.* L. 1925.
THAYER, W. R. *Life and Times of Cavour.* 2 v. N.Y. 1911.
TORRENS, W. M. *Life of Sir James Graham.* 2 v. L. 1873.
TREVELYAN, G. M. *Life of John Bright.* L. 1913.
—— *Life of Lord Grey.* L. 1920.
TREVELYAN, Sir GEORGE. *Life and Letters of Lord Macaulay.* 2 v. L. 1876.
WALISZEWSKI, P. *Tsar Alexandre I.* 3 v. P. 1923–5.
WALPOLE, Sir SPENCER. *Lord John Russell.* 2 v. L. 1889.
WEBSTER, C. K. *The Foreign Policy of Castlereagh* (1812–15). L. 1931.
—— *The Foreign Policy of Castlereagh* (1815–22). L. 1925.
WEMYSS, Mrs ROSSLYN. *Life of Sir Robert Morier.* 2 v. L. 1911.
WERTHEIMER, EDUARD VON. *Graf Andrássy.* 3 v. Stuttgart 1910–13.
YONGE, C. D. *Life of Lord Liverpool.* 3 v. L.

MISCELLANEOUS

ACTON, Lord. *Historical Essays and Studies.* L. 1907.
ANTIOCHE, Comte F. M. A. D' *Chateaubriand, Ambassadeur à Londres.* P. 1912.
ASPINALL, A. *Lord Brougham and the Whig Party.* Manchester 1927.
BAMBERG, L. *Gesch. der orientalischen Angelegenheit.* Leipzig 1892.
BAPST, EDMOND. *Origines de la Guerre de Crimée.* P. 1912.
BECKER, OTTO. *Bismarcks Bündnispolitik.* Berlin 1923.
BEER, ADOLF. *Die orientalische Politik Oesterreichs seit 1774.* Prague 1883.
BEYENS, Baron. *Le Second Empire.* 2 v. P. 1924–6.
BINGHAM, CLIVE. *The Prime Ministers of Britain.* L. 1922.

BLANC, LOUIS. *Histoire de Dix Ans* (1830–40). 5 v. P. 1841–4.

BUCKLAND, C. S. B. *Metternich and the British Government.* L. 1932.

CAPEFIGUE, J. B. H. R. *Histoire de la Restauration.* P. 1845.

CECIL, ALGERNON. *British Foreign Secretaries* (1807–1916). L. 1927.

CHARLES-ROUX, FRANÇOIS. *Alexandre II, Gortchakoff et Napoléon III.* P. 1913.

CHIALA, LUIGI. *Politica segreta di Napoleone III e Cavour in Italia ed Ungheria* (1858–61). Turin 1895.

CLAPHAM, J. H. *An Economic History of Modern Britain.* 2 v. Cambridge 1926–32.

CLARK, CHESTER W. *Franz Joseph and Bismarck before* 1866. Cambridge (U.S.) 1934.

CRAWLEY, C. W. *The Question of Greek Independence.* Cambridge 1930.

DAVIS, H. W. C. *The Age of Grey and Peel.* L. 1929.

DAVID, HEINRICH. *Englands Europäische Politik im XIX Jahrhundert.* Bern 1924.

DUPUIS, CHARLES. *Le Principe d'Équilibre et le Concert Européen.* P. 1909.

EAST, W. G. *The Union of Moldavia and Wallachia,* 1859. Cambridge 1929.

EGERTON, H. E. *British Foreign Policy in Europe.* L. 1917.

FISHER, H. A. L. *The Republican Tradition in Europe.* L. 1911.

—— *Bonapartism.* Oxford 1908.

FRIEDJUNG, H. *Der Krimkrieg und die österreichische Politik.* Stuttgart 1907.

GORIAINOV, SERGE. *Le Bosphore et les Dardanelles.* P. 1910.

—— "The Secret Agreement of 1844" (*Russian Review,* Nos. 3 and 4).

GOSCH, C. A. *Denmark and Germany since* 1815. L. 1862.

GRANDMAISON, GEOFFROY DE. *L'Expédition Française en* 1823. P. 1928.

GUICHEN, Vicomte de. *La Crise d'Orient de* 1839 *à* 1841 *et l'Europe.* P. 1921.

HALL, JOHN. *England and the Orleans Monarchy.* L. 1912.

HASENCLEVER, ADOLF. *Die orientalische Frage in den Jahren* 1838–41. Leipzig 1914.

—— *Gesch. Ägyptens* (1798–1914). Halle 1917.

HARCOURT, Marquis B. *Les Quatre Ministères de Drouyn de Lhuys.* P. 1882.

HAUSSONVILLE, CLÉRON. *Histoire de la Politique extérieure de la Monarchie de Juillet.* 2 v. P. 1850.

HEADLAM-MORLEY, J. W. *Studies in Diplomatic History.* L. 1930.

KING, BOLTON. *Life of Mazzini.* L. 1912.

KINGLAKE, A. W. *The Invasion of the Crimea.* 8 v. 1863–87.

LA FARINA. *Storia d' Italia.* 5 v. Turin 1851.

LA GORCE, PIERRE DE. *Louis XVIII.* P. 1926.

—— *Charles X.* P. 1928.

LA MARMORA, General. *Un po' piu di Luce.* Rome 1872.

LASCARIS, S. TH. *La politique extérieure de la Grèce* (1875–81). P. 1924.

LAVALEYE, ÉMILE DE. *The Balkan Peninsula.* L. 1886.

LEE, DWIGHT E. *Great Britain and the Cyprus Convention Policy of* 1878. Cambridge (U.S.) 1934.

MARRIOTT, Sir JOHN. *The Eastern Question.* L. 1917.

MARTENS, T. T. *Russia and England in Central Asia.* L. 1879.

MARTIN, B. KINGSLEY. *The Triumph of Lord Palmerston.* L. 1924.

MARX, KARL. *The Eastern Question.* L. 1897.

MAURICE, C. E. *The Revolutionary Movement of* 1848–9. L. 1887.

MOLDEN, E. *Metternichs Orientpolitik.* Vienna 1913.

NOTHOMB, Baron. *Essai historique et politique sur la Révolution Belge.* Brussels 1876.

PHILLIPS, W. ALISON. *The Greek Revolution.* L. 1903.

PLEHN, HANS. *Bismarcks auswärtige Politik.* Munich 1920.

RACHFAHL, FELIX. *Deutschland und die Weltpolitik.* Stuttgart 1923.

RAMSAY, ALICIA A. W. *Idealism and Foreign Policy*. L. 1925.
RAWLINSON, Sir HENRY. *England and Russia in the East*. L. 1875.
REDDAWAY, W. F. *The Monroe Doctrine*. Cambridge 1898.
RENIER, G. J. *Great Britain and the Establishment of the Kingdom of the Netherlands*. L. 1930.
RIKER, T. W. *The Making of Roumania*. Oxford 1931.
RODKEY, F. S. *The Turco-Egyptian Question*. Urbana 1923.
ROTHAN, GUSTAVE. *L'Europe et l'Avènement du Second Empire*. P. 1892.
—— *La Politique française en 1866*. P. 1883.
—— *La France et sa politique extérieure en 1867*. 2 v. P. 1893.
ROTHFELS, HANS. *Bismarcks englische Bündnispolitik*. Stuttgart 1924.
RUSSELL, Earl. *The Foreign Policy of England*. L. 1871.
SALOMON, FELIX. *Die Grundzüge der auswärtigen Politik Englands*.
SAX, CARL RITTER VON. *Geschichte des Machtverfalls der Türkei*. Vienna 1913.
SIMPSON, F. A. *The Rise of Louis Napoleon*. L. 1921.
—— *Louis Napoleon and the Recovery of France*. L. 1923.
SOREL, ALBERT. *Histoire diplomatique de la Guerre franco-allemande*. 2 v. P. 1875.
SPROXTON, CHARLES. *Palmerston and the Hungarian Revolution*. Cambridge 1919.
SRBIK, H. VON. *Deutsche Einheit*. 2 v. Munich 1935.
STEEFEL, LAWRENCE D. *The Schleswig-Holstein Question*. Oxford 1932.
TAUBE, ALEX. V. *Fürst Bismarck zwischen England und Russland*. Stuttgart 1923.
TAYLOR, A. J. P. *The Italian Problem in European Diplomacy (1847–9)*. Manchester 1934.
URQUHART, DAVID. *Recent Events*. L. 1854.
VALENTIN, VEIT. *Geschichte der deutschen Revolution von 1848–9*. 2 v. Berlin 1931.
WEBSTER, C. K. *The Congress of Vienna*. L. 1919.
WILSON, SIR ROBERT. *Sketch of the Military Power of Russia*. L. 1817.

PART II. 1878–1914

GENERAL HISTORIES

C.H.F.P. Cambridge History of British Foreign Policy. Ed. Sir A. Ward and G. P. Gooch. 3 v. Cambridge 1923.

ANCEL, JACQUES. *Manuel Géographique de Politique Européenne*, P. 1936.
BOURGEOIS, ÉMILE. *Manuel Historique de Politique Étrangère*, vol. IV (1878–1919). P. 1926.
DEBIDOUR, A. *Histoire Diplomatique de l'Europe* (1878–1916). 2 v. P. 1916.
DICKINSON, G. LOWES. *The International Anarchy*. L. 1926.
FAY, S. B. *The Origins of the World War*, vol. I. N.Y. 1928.
GOOCH, G. P. *History of Modern Europe* (1878–1919). L. 1923.
Histoire Diplomatique de l'Europe (1871–1914). Ed. H. Hauser. 2 v. P. 1929.
LANGER, W. L. *European Alliances and Alignments* (1871–90). N.Y. 1930.
—— *The Diplomacy of Imperialism* (1890–1902). 2 v. N.Y. 1935.
ONCKEN, HERMANN. *Das deutsche Reich und die Vorgeschichte des Weltkrieges*. Leipzig 1933.
PINON, RENÉ. *Histoire Diplomatique*. P. 1932.
RENOUVIN, PIERRE. *La Crise Européenne et la Grande Guerre* (1904–18). P. 1934.
SLESSON, P. W. *Europe since 1870*. L. 1935.
SPENDER, J. A. *Fifty Years of Europe*. L. 1933.

SPECIAL HISTORIES

DAWSON, W. H. *The German Empire* (1867–1914). 2 v. L. 1919.
ENSOR, R. C. K. *England* (1870–1914). Oxford 1936.
HALÉVY, ÉLIE. *Histoire du Peuple Anglais: Épilogue* (1895–1914). 2 v. P. 1926–7.
IORGA, NICOLAS. *Histoire des États balcaniques.* Bucarest 1914.
PAUL, HERBERT. *History of Modern England* (1846–95). 5 v. L. 1904–6.
MOMMSEN, WILHELM. *Politische Geschichte von Bismarck bis zur Gegenwart* (1850–1933). Frankfurt 1935.
RECOULY, RAYMOND. *La Troisième République.* P. 1928.
SEIGNOBOS, CHARLES. *L'Évolution de la Troisième République.* (Vol. VIII of Lavisse, *Histoire de France Contemporaine.*) P. 1921.
WAHL, ADALBERT. *Deutsche Geschichte* (1871–1914). 4 v. Stuttgart 1936.
ZIEKURSCH, JOHANNES. *Politische Geschichte des neuen deutschen Kaiserreiches,* vols. II, III. Frankfurt 1930.

DOCUMENTS, COLLECTIONS, ETC.

A.H.D. = *Oesterreich-Ungarns Aussenpolitik* (1908–14). Ed. Bittner, Uebersberger, Pribram, Srbik. 8 v. Vienna 1830.
B.D. = *British Documents on the Origins of the War* (1898–1914). Ed. Gooch, Temperley, Penson. 11 vols. in 13. L. 1926–36.
D.D.F. = *Documents Diplomatiques Français* (1871–1914). 3 series (in course). P. 1929–37.
G.P. = *Die Grosse Politik der Europäischen Kabinette* (1871–1914). Ed. Lipsius, Mendelssohn-Bartholdy, Thimme. 53 v. Berlin 1921–7.

BOURGEOIS, É. et PAGÈS, G. *Les Origines et les Responsabilités de la Grande Guerre.* (Text and Documents.) P. 1922.
GREY, Sir EDWARD. *Speeches on Foreign Affairs* (1904–14). Ed. P. KNAPLUND. L. 1931.
MARCHAND, RENÉ (Ed.). *Un Livre Noir.* 3 v. P. 1922–4.
PRIBRAM, A. F. *Die politischen Geheimverträge Oesterreich-Ungarns.* Vienna 1920.
SIEBERT, B. VON. *Diplomatische Aktenstücke zur Geschichte der Ententepolitik der Vorkriegsjahre.* Berlin 1921.

MEMOIRS AND CORRESPONDENCE

ASQUITH, H. H. *The Genesis of the War.* L. 1923.
BARCLAY, Sir THOMAS. *Thirty Years of Anglo-French Reminiscences.* L. 1914.
BARDOUX, JACQUES. *Essai d'une psychologie de l'Angleterre contemporaine.* P. 1906.
BETHMANN HOLLWEG, THEODOR VON. *Betrachtungen zum Weltkriege,* vol. I. Berlin 1919.
BISMARCK, Prince. *New Chapters of Bismarck's Autobiography.* L. 1920.
BÜLOW, Fürst BERNHARD. *Denkwürdigkeiten.* 4 v. Berlin 1933.
—— *Deutsche Politik.* Berlin 1913.
CHÉRADAME, ANDRÉ. *L'Europe et la Question d'Autriche.* P. 1901.
—— *Le Chemin de Fer de Bagdad.* P. 1913.
CHIROL, Sir VALENTINE. *Fifty Years in a Changing World.* L. 1927.
CONRAD, Feldmarschall. *Aus meiner Dienstzeit,* vols. I–III. Vienna 1921.
CRISPI, FRANCESCO. *I Mille.* Milano 1912.
—— *Politica Estera.* Milano 1912.

CROMER, Earl of. *Modern Egypt*. 2 v. L. 1908.
—— *Abbas II*. L. 1915.
CZERNIN, Count OTTOKAR. *In the World War*. L. 1919.
ECKARDSTEIN, Baron H. *Lebenserinnerungen und politische Denkwürdigkeiten*. 3 v. Leipzig 1919–20.
FREYCINET, C. DE. *Souvenirs*. 2 v. P. 1914.
GREY, Viscount. *Twenty-five Years*. 2 v. L. 1925.
GUEDALLA, P. ed. *The Queen and Mr Gladstone*. 2 v. L. 1933.
GUESHOFF, IVAN. *The Balkan League*. L. 1915.
HALDANE, Viscount. *Before the War*. L. 1920.
—— *Autobiography*. L. 1929.
HAYASHI, Count, *The Secret Memoirs of*. Ed. A. M. Pooley. L. 1915.
HOHENLOHE, Fürst CHLODWIG. *Denkwürdigkeiten*. 2 v. Stuttgart 1906.
—— *Aus der Reichskanzlerzeit*. Stuttgart 1931.
IZVOLSKY, ALEXANDRE. *Mémoires*. P. 1923.
LICHNOWSKY, Fürst. *Auf dem Wege zum Abgrund*. Dresden 1927.
LLOYD-GEORGE, DAVID. *War Memoirs*, vol. I. L. 1933.
Milner Papers, The. Ed. Cecil Headlam. 2 v. L. 1931–3.
MOUY, Comte DE. *Souvenirs d'un Diplomate*. P. 1909.
POINCARÉ, RAYMOND. *Au Service de la France*, vols. I–III. P. 1926.
ROSEN, Baron. *Forty Years of Diplomacy*. 2 v. L. 1922.
STAAL, Baron DE. *Correspondance Diplomatique*. 2 v. P. 1929.
TIRPITZ, ALFRED VON. *Erinnerungen*. 2 v. Leipzig 1920.
VICTORIA, Queen. *Letters*. 3rd series. 3 v. L. 1931.
Willy-Nicky Correspondence. Ed. H. BERNSTEIN. N.Y. 1918.
WITTE, Comte. *Mémoires*. P. 1921.

BIOGRAPHIES

CECIL, Lady GWENDOLEN. *Life of Robert Marquis of Salisbury*, vols. III, IV. L. 1931.
CHURCHILL, WINSTON J. *Lord Randolph Churchill*. 2 v. L. 1906.
COLVIN, IAN. *Life of Jameson*. 2 v. L. 1922.
CREWE, Marquess of. *Lord Rosebery*. 2 v. L. 1931.
DESCHANEL, PAUL. *Gambetta*. P. 1919.
DUGDALE, Mrs EDGAR. *Arthur James Balfour*. 2 v. L. 1936.
EDWARDS, H. SUTHERLAND. *Sir William White*. L. 1902.
ELLIOT, A. D. *Life of Lord Goschen*. 2 v. L. 1911.
ESHER, Viscount. *The Influence of Edward VII*. L. 1914.
GARDINER, A. G. *Sir William Harcourt*. 2 v. L. 1923.
GARVIN, J. L. *Joseph Chamberlain*. 3 v. L. 1932–4.
GATHORNE-HARDY, A. E. *Gathorne-Hardy*. 2 v. L. 1910.
GLADSTONE, Viscount. *After Thirty Years*. L. 1928.
GWYNN, STEPHEN and TUCKWELL, GERTRUDE. *Sir Charles Dilke*. 2 v. L. 1917.
HARDIE, FRANK. *The Political Influence of Queen Victoria*. L. 1935.
HULDERMANN, B. *Albert Ballin*. Berlin 1922.
JÄCKH, E. *Kiderlen-Wächter; der Mann und der Staatsmann*. 2 v.
LEE, Sir SIDNEY. *Edward VII*. 2 v. L. 1925–7.
LICHTERVELDE, Comte LOUIS DE. *Léopold II*. Brussels 1926.
LUDWIG, EMIL. *Bismarck*. Berlin 1927.
—— *Kaiser Wilhelm II*. L. 1926.
LYALL, Sir ALFRED. *Lord Dufferin*. 2 v. L. 1905.

MATTER, P. *Bismarck et son Temps.* 3 v. P. 1905–8.
MILLIN, SARAH G. *Rhodes.* L. 1933.
MOLDEN, B. *Graf Aehrenthal.* Stuttgart 1917.
NEWTON, Lord. *Lord Lansdowne.* L. 1929.
NICOLSON, HAROLD. *Lord Carnock.* L. 1930.
RAMBAUD, ALFRED. *Jules Ferry.* P. 1903.
RUSSELL, G. W. E. *Malcolm MacColl.* L. 1914.
SPENDER, J. A. *Sir Henry Campbell-Bannerman.* 2 v. L. 1923.
—— and ASQUITH, CYRIL. *H. H. Asquith.* 2 v. L. 1932.
TREVELYAN, G. M. *Grey of Fallodon.* L. 1937.
WILLIAMS, BASIL. *Cecil Rhodes.* L. 1921.
ZETLAND, Marquess of. *Lord Cromer.* L. 1932.
—— *Lord Curzon.* 3 v. L. 1928.

MISCELLANEOUS

ALBIN, P. *Le Coup d'Agadir.* P. 1912.
—— *D'Agadir à Sarajevo.* P. 1915.
ALLEN, BERNARD M. *Gordon and the Sudan.* L. 1931.
ANDERSON, EUGENE N. *The First Morocco Crisis.* Chicago 1930.
ANDLER, CHARLES. *Les Origines du Pangermanisme.* P. 1915.
—— *Le Pangermanisme continental sous Guillaume II.* P. 1915.
—— *Le Pangermanisme colonial.* P. 1915.
ANDRÁSSY, Count JULIUS, jun. *Bismarck, Andrássy and their Successors.* L. 1927.
AUERBACH, BERTRAND. *Les races et les nationalités de l'Autriche-Hongrie.* 2nd ed. P. 1914.
BAERNREITHER, J. M. *Fragments of a Political Diary.* L. 1930.
BALCANICUS (Stojan Protić). *The Aspirations of Bulgaria.* L. 1916.
BECKER, WILLY. *Fürst Bülow und England.* Greifswald 1929.
BIGHAM, CLIVE. *The Prime Ministers of Britain.* L. 1923.
BODLEY, J. E. C. *France.* L. 1902.
BRAILSFORD, H. N. *Macedonia.* L. 1906.
BRANDENBURG, ERICH. *Die Reichsgründung.* 2 v. Leipzig 1916.
—— *Von Bismarck zum Weltkriege.* Berlin 1924.
CAILLAUX, JOSEPH. *Agadir.* P. 1919.
CARROLL, E. M. *French Public Opinion and Foreign Affairs* (1871–1914). N.Y. 1931.
CECIL, ALGERNON. *British Foreign Secretaries.* L. 1927.
CHURCHILL, WINSTON S. *The World Crisis,* vol. 1. L. 1926.
COCHERIS, JULES. *La Situation internationale de l'Égypte et du Soudan.* P. 1903.
CYON, ÉLIE DE. *Histoire de l'Entente Franco-Russe.* P. 1895.
DENNETT, TYLER. *Roosevelt and the Russo-Japanese War.* N.Y. 1925.
EARLE, E. M. *Turkey, the Great Powers and the Bagdad Railway.* N.Y. 1924.
EISENMANN, LOUIS. *Le Compromis austro-hongrois.* P. 1904.
ELIOT, Sir CHARLES (Odysseus). *Turkey-in-Europe.* L. 1900.
FOURNIER, AUGUST. *Wie wir zu Bosnien Kamen.* Vienna 1908.
FREYCINET, C. DE. *La Question d'Égypte.* P. 1914.
FULLER, JOSEPH V. *Bismarck's Diplomacy at its Zenith.* Cambridge (N.S.) 1922.
GOOCH, G. P. *Studies in Modern History.* L. 1932.
—— *Before the War,* vol. 1. 1936.
HALLER, JOHANNES. *England und Deutschland um die Jahrhundertwende.* Leipzig 1929.

HALLER, JOHANNES. *Die Aera Bülow.* Stuttgart 1922.
HAMMANN, OTTO. *Der neue Kurs.* Berlin 1918.
—— *Zur Vorgeschichte des Weltkrieges.* Berlin 1919.
—— *Um den Kaiser.* Berlin 1919.
—— *Deutsche Weltpolitik* (1890–1912). Berlin 1925.
HANOTAUX, G. *Fachoda.* P. 1909.
—— *L'Affaire de Madagascar.* P. 1896.
HANSEN, JULES. *L'Ambassade à Paris du Baron de Mohrenheim.* P. 1907.
HIGGINS, A. P. *The Hague Peace Conferences.* L. 1909.
HOETZSCH, OTTO. *Russland.* Berlin 1913.
HOSKINS, H. L. *British Routes to India.* Philadelphia 1928.
JOHNSTON, Sir H. H. *The Colonisation of Africa.* Cambridge 1899.
KANTOROWICZ, HERMANN. *The Spirit of British Policy and the Myth of Encirclement.* L. 1932.
KEHR, ECKART. *Schlachtflottenbau und Parteipolitik* (1894–1901). Berlin 1932.
KENNEDY, A. L. *Old Diplomacy and New.* L. 1922.
KORFF, Baron S. A. *Russia's Foreign Relations during the last Half Century.* L. 1922.
LANGER, W. L. *The Franco-Russian Alliance.* Cambridge (U.S.) 1929.
LÉMONON, E. *L'Europe et la politique britannique.* P. 1910.
MADARIAGA, S. DE. *Spain.* L. 1930.
MASARYK, THOMAS G. *The Spirit of Russia.* 2 v. L. 1919.
MEINECKE, FRIEDRICH. *Geschichte des deutsch-englischen Bündnisproblems.* Munich 1927.
MICHON, P. *L'Alliance Franco-Russe.* P. 1927.
MILNER, Viscount. *England in Egypt.* L. 1892.
MOREL, E. D. *Morocco in Diplomacy.* L. 1912.
MOYSSET, HENRI. *L'Esprit public en Allemagne.* P. 1911.
MURRAY, GILBERT. *The Foreign Policy of Sir Edward Grey.* L. 1915.
NINČIĆ, MOMČILO. *La Crise Bosniaque et les Puissances Européennes.* 2 v. Paris 1937.
NOLDE, Baron BORIS. *L'Alliance Franco-Russe.* P. 1936.
PINGAUD, ALBERT. *L'Italie depuis* 1870. P. 1915.
PINON, RENÉ. *L'Europe et la Jeune Turquie.* P. 1911.
—— *L'Europe et l'Empire Ottoman.* P. 1909.
REVENTLOW, Count E. *Deutschlands auswärtige Politik.* Berlin 1913.
—— *Der Vampir des Festlandes.* Berlin 1916.
—— *Politische Vorgeschichte des grossen Krieges.* Berlin 1919.
ROHRBACH, PAUL. *Der deutsche Gedanke in der Welt.* Leipzig 1912.
SALOMON, FELIX. *Der britische Imperialismus.* Leipzig 1916.
SCHMITT, BERNADOTTE E. *England and Germany* (1740–1914). Princeton 1918.
—— *The Annexation of Bosnia* 1908–9. Cambridge 1937.
SETON-WATSON, R. W. *Racial Problems in Hungary.* L. 1908.
—— *The Southern Slav Question.* L. 1911.
—— *The Rise of Nationality in the Balkans.* L. 1917.
—— *History of the Roumanians.* Cambridge 1934.
SOSNOSKY, THEODOR VON. *Die Balkanpolitik Oesterreich-Ungarns.* 2 v. Stuttgart 1913–14.
STEED, H. W. *The Hapsburg Monarchy.* L. 1913.
STEEVENS, G. W. *Naval Policy.* L. 1896.
TARDIEU, ANDRÉ. *La France et les Alliances.* P. 1908.
—— *La Conférence d'Algeciras.* P. 1909.

TARDIEU, ANDRÉ. *Le Mystère d'Agadir.* P. 1912.

THEAL, G. M. *History of South Africa,* vols. X, XI.

TREITSCHKE, H. VON. *Politik.* 2 v. (3rd ed.). Leipzig 1911.

—— *Historische und politische Aufsätze.* 4 v. Leipzig 1903.

TREND, J. B. *The Origins of Modern Spain.* L. 1934.

TRUBETZKOI, Prince GREGORY. *Russland als Grossmacht.* Stuttgart 1913.

VALENTIN, VEIT. *Deutschlands Aussenpolitik* (1890–1918). Berlin 1921.

WALLACE, Sir DONALD MACKENZIE. *Russia.* New ed. L. 1912.

WEDEL, OSWALD. *Austro-German Diplomatic Relations* (1908–14). Stanford 1932.

WHITE, ANDREW D. *The First Hague Conference.* Boston 1912.

WOODWARD, E. L. *Great Britain and the German Navy.* Oxford 1935.

INDEX

44-2

s-w

CAMBRIDGE: PRINTED BY W. LEWIS, M.A., AT THE UNIVERSITY PRESS